Aphrodite's Killers

Map of Cyprus

APHRODITE'S KILLERS

Cyprus, the EOKA conflict
and the
road to partition

David Carter

**Downlow
Productions**

First published in the United Kingdom in 2010 by
Downlow Productions

ISBN 978-0-9537170-1-9

Contents

David gave so much of his life and love to the Island of Cyprus and to all her people both Greek and Turkish. He tried very hard to be fair to everyone. I hope you the reader will feel he was. My husband was one of the most generous and caring people I have had the privilege of knowing. He was as giving in death as he was in life leaving his body to the Norfolk and Norwich University Hospital, for whose staff he had the greatest regard. David died on Friday 18th December, 2009.

Wendy Carter, May 2010

Foreword

ON A FINE, hot afternoon in early September 1955 various members of 40 Commando Royal Marines were involved in an inter-service cricket match at the Marsa Club. Tea was being taken at this delightful cricket ground in Malta and nothing had seemed likely to disturb this quintessentially English scene. Then the message was received to return to barracks as soon as possible; the Unit was under 'sailing orders'.

We had been aware that the situation in Cyprus had been deteriorating since the bombings on 1 April but had no inkling that 40 Commando would be a very early rein-forcement. One might have expected a move by air but being Royal Marines – and assumed to be well accustomed to 'a life on the ocean wave' – the answer was to cram 400 of us into the cruiser HMS *Birmingham* for a 48-hour dash across the Eastern Mediterranean. Almost immediately, we were on the streets of Limassol endeavouring to maintain law and order in the face of serious rioting – with precious little time to appreciate Aphrodite's Isle of Love!

As a 20-year-old, my personal perspective over the eight months that I was on operations in Cyprus was very much from the coalface – and that surely applies to the vast majority of the Armed Forces, UK Police and civilians involved in their own singular spheres of responsibility.

Thus, *Aphrodite's Killers* is an excellent and valuable addition to the bibliography of what has become generally known as the EOKA Campaign, with the author skilfully weaving the convoluted politics with eyewitness accounts of virtually all the major incidents. He has put an incredible amount of research and work into the book and I have found it to be an enjoyable and fascinating read.

Sadly, of those involved in the Campaign, 371 British servicemen, 19 UK and Colonial Police officers and 35 British civilians linked to the British Forces lost their lives; and it should be remembered that 39 Greek, Turkish and Maronite Cypriot Police officers were also killed in the line of duty. Tragically, it should never be forgotten that, over the last 50 years, literally thousands of Greek and Turkish Cypriots have been the victims of the blood-shed.

In 2009 – the 50th anniversary year of the end of the EOKA campaign – the British Cyprus Memorial Trust dedicated a Memorial to the British Servicemen who gave their lives. Most of them are buried in Wayne's Keep Military Cemetery, which today lies in the UN Buffer Zone that separates the two sides of the Island, and it is not easy for relatives and friends to visit these graves. Thus, the Memorial is located in the old British cemetery at Kyrenia. The hope is that, one day, the Greek and Turkish communities will come together and the Memorial can be moved to Wayne's Keep.

Therein, of course, lies the very nub of the problem – and one that has defeated international leaders, diplomats, politicians and representatives of both communities for over half a century. In 1955 it may have looked to the Greek Cypriot community as if the rundown of the Empire in the face of world opinion would work in its favour. However, the British withdrawal from the Suez Canal Zone and the move of significant elements to Cyprus was clear evidence that Britain saw this 'colonial backwater' as critical to its Middle and Far Eastern strategies; a straightforward transition to independence was not to be. Perhaps not surprisingly – although it clearly wrong-footed the British – this was what triggered the insurgency.

How will international history judge Archbishop Makarios and General Grivas? Readers can make up their own minds, as the author covers them and their (and often conflicting) roles in great detail but, from today's perspective, the indomitable Turks were never going to accept *enosis* – union with Greece – and what might conceivably – with less strident nationalistic aims – have been peaceable independence has ended in *de facto* partition, and ongoing friction 50 years later.

From the military point of view, the campaign posed the British very significant problems, with an almost equal emphasis on urban and rural operations. The Security Forces lacked the intelligence required to counter the murders and coercion of the urban terrorists, which EOKA used to generate the publicity that is the lifeblood of any terrorist organization. They were abhorrently cowardly tactics, which we despised then, but what is the terrorist norm today – and what will it be tomorrow?

In the rural areas, the Security Forces (40,000 by late 1957) gained a decent measure of control, forcing EOKA on the defensive. However, ambushes in the significantly mountainous terrain resulted in frequent British casualties, and remotely detonated mines were a deadly danger: not as technologically advanced as today's Improvised Explosive Devices (IEDs) so beloved of terrorists worldwide, but nor were the counter-measures of the sophistication later developed in response to the IRA bombers. Despite coordinating command through committees of military, police and civilian administration on lines that proved so successful in the Malayan Campaign, the nationalist organization proved extremely durable and the Security Forces were unable to counter widespread public support for the insurgents. The Security Forces were faced with a population that could never be reconciled to British rule and, not least from ruthless intimidation, could never be persuaded to inform.

Testament to that is that Grivas, despite one very close shave in the Troodos Mountains, was never captured, despite living in urban Limassol for some three years. Nor were attempts to win 'hearts and minds' ever going to gain real traction, and a Malayan-style 'Briggs Plan' (the forcible resettlement of about 25 per cent of Malaya's Chinese population in an attempt to isolate the Communist terrorists from their supplies) could never have been a starter in the glare of the world's media. The reality was that any attempt to find a purely military solution in Cyprus was doomed from the start and gave impetus to a series of negotiations, which finally came to fruition with the Zurich and London Agreements.

It was against that unpromising background that the very high percentage of British National Servicemen undergoing their mandatory two-year period of military service excelled with their spirit and dedication to the demanding task in hand. They may have been 'civilians in uniform' but they proved themselves first-class soldiers, both tough and skilful, good humoured, fair and humane despite often sore provocation and very trying conditions – both on and off duty. Those conditions contributed to the significant number of deaths from road accidents and 'friendly fire' tragedies: young men, often tired and anxious, grappled with hazardous terrain and the edginess prompted by the constant threat of unexpected action. In many ways, this book serves as a tribute to them – as well as to all who died as victims of the violence.

The author also served his period of National Service and, in *Aphrodite's Killers*, has contributed mightily to our knowledge of the Cyprus Campaign. Also, through the splendid website, *Britain's Small Wars*, with its sections on every campaign since 1945, he and his colleagues have made available information of great interest to the widest readership.

Lieutenant General Sir Henry Beverley,
KCB, OBE

Preface

THE EOKA conflict in Cyprus lasted four years between 1955 and 1959. For the majority Greek Cypriot population it was a freedom struggle for independence from Britain's colonial rule and a desire for self-determination – *enosis* – union with Greece, something that the Island's Turkish Cypriots refused to accept under any circumstances. If the British were to leave, they demanded either partition – *taksim* – or union with Turkey, 40 miles to the north.

Contrary to what many Cypriots might argue today, 'Britain, had no "imperialistic" reason for clinging to a small island in the Mediterranean,' as Sir Anthony Parsons, the veteran British diplomat, has pointed out. 'We were concerned with safeguarding our residual strategic interests, but our principal preoccupation was to avoid civil war in Cyprus and an armed conflict between NATO allies, Greece and Turkey.'

At the height of the Cold War, there had to be stability in the region and no splits in NATO for Moscow to exploit. For Cyprus to have peace, it was clear that Turkey and Greece would have to participate in any decision-taking process about the Island's future independence, and for its own global interests America demanded to play a part as well. The US was desperate to ensure Britain did not relinquish its bases in any independence package. They had to remain in an absolutely 'dependable pair of hands'.

From Britain's point of view, Cyprus was a vital strategic location. With Gibraltar in the west, Malta in the centre and Cyprus at the eastern end, the Mediterranean was under its control. In the event of trouble with the Soviet Union or the oil-rich states of the Middle East, the Island would be the springboard of military and air action. It was an unsinkable aircraft carrier anchored off the shores of the Levant.

When, at last, Britain realized that its days of Empire were drawing to a close and it could no longer exercise its military muscle without the permission of the United States (proved by its failed intervention in Egypt to reclaim the Suez Canal), and unable to control events in Cyprus, it decided the Island must go, but to whom and how?

The late Sir Anthony Nutting, as Minister of State for Foreign Affairs, gave his answer to the question concisely: 'In geography and tactical considerations, the Turks have the stronger claim; in race and language, the Greeks; in strategy, the British, so long as their industrial life depends on oil from the Persian Gulf. Progress in self-government could not be made until these claims were reconciled, and one of two methods had to be chosen. Greeks and Turks could be associated with the British in control of the Island, or the Island could be partitioned. The first course we proposed on two occasions. Partition also had its advocates, especially in Turkey, and we agreed that it must be included among the eventual options before the Cypriot people ... but I regarded it as the last refuge of baffled states-manship.'

In this book I attempt to tell the story of Britain's 82-year occupation, the conflict that ensued between the British military (consisting of mainly young conscripts) and EOKA, the Greek Cypriot underground organization that fought for *enosis* and the end of the Island's colonial status, and how events more than half a century ago caused today's partition of Cyprus.

As far as possible, I have used the eyewit-ness accounts of those who were directly involved, gathered during interviews with more than 500 former service personnel and people from both sides of the Cyprus divide. I have drawn also on a wide range of source material and the knowledge I gained from my countless visits to Cyprus – north, south, the UN Buffer Zone and the British Sovereign Bases – to compile this account.

To the authors, historians and researchers, whose works I have 'plundered', I express my gratitude and hope they will not be offended. Their contributions are acknowledged with appreciation. The images that illustrate many of the book's pages have been drawn from a variety of sources, making it nigh on impossi-ble to credit their original copyright holders for which I hope they will forgive me.

I also wish to thank the people who have encouraged me to complete this project, which began more than 10 years ago. They are too many to mention all by name, but include my colleagues, Martin Spirit and James Paul, at *Britain's Small Wars*, a website that publishes articles about all the conflicts since 1945 in which the British Armed Forces have played a significant role; Sir Henry Beverley who has read every line of the text; Dave Cranston, who served in Cyprus as a young man and introduced me to his comrades for their memories; my Cypriot and Greek friends, Michael and Alexander Hajilyra of Nicosia; Alkan Chaglar, editor of the English language

pages of *Toplum Postasi*; and Dr Panagiotis Dimitrakis in Athens, all of whom have contributed in various ways.

On a more personal front, my gratitude goes to my daughter, Sheryl, whose opinions of the 'Cyprus problem' are as dogmatic as those held by any citizen of the Island; my son, Matthew, who gave me his computer and took away my trusty battle-scarred portable type-writer built in the dark ages; and Wendy, my wife and dearest friend, who read every page, suggested improvements and refused to let me give up when the going was tough.

Some readers, I know, will be deeply offended by my use of certain terminology. Greek Cypriots honour the memory of EOKA and see its members as heroes, liberators and soldiers of freedom and erect monuments to their memory; Turkish Cypriots and the British have always considered them terror-ists, pointing to the large numbers of innocent civilians they killed and condemning the methods they used.

Any book about Cyprus, therefore, leads to accusations from one side or the other that the author is not impartial. To describe, for example, the landings of the Turkish Army in Cyprus in July 1974 as an 'invasion', pleases Greeks, but upsets Turks who want the words 'intervention' or 'peace operation' to be used instead. Greeks expect writers to refer to north Cyprus as the 'occupied' area and their part as 'free'. They object to the Turkish side being called the 'TRNC' – the Turkish Republic of Northern Cyprus – the name applied by the Turks. And so it goes. Cypriots are masters of semantics.

Another difficulty for any author is the spelling of names – people and places. There are many variations in the English language that can cause confusion. For simplification, I have taken the most commonly used nomen-clature and attempted to be consistent. For towns and villages administered today by Turkish Cypriots and 'Turkified', I refer to them by names the British used during the Island's colonial period.

I recognize that there may be omissions and inaccuracies in the content, but where the reader spots them and notifies the publisher, they will be corrected in future editions, as will any credits that may have been accidentally omitted due to my fallibility.

Finally, I am reminded of what George Mikes, the Hungarian humorist, wrote years ago. His comments, I believe, are equally valid in the present:

'Cypriots know that they cannot become a World Power; but they have succeeded in becoming a World Nuisance, which is almost as good.'

David Carter
December 2009

CHAPTER ONE

The conflict begins on the Day of Fools

If we like them, they're freedom fighters . . . If we don't like them, they're terrorists. In the unlikely case we can't make up our minds, they're temporarily only guerrillas.

Carl Sagan

LIEUTENANT COLONEL W. Byford-Jones, a former intelligence officer, was enjoying a stroll with another military friend down a quiet street in Nicosia as midnight approached. Spring was in the air and a light breeze carried the scent of lemon blossom. The rain had stopped and lights glistened in puddles on the pavements. Suddenly there was the distant rumble of an explosion, followed by another and another. 'What was that?' he asked his companion. 'A quarry blast?'

'No,' replied his friend. 'That's EOKA. The campaign for Cyprus has begun.'

It was 15 minutes after midnight on 1 April 1955.

EOKA, the National Organization of Cypriot Combatants, was a group rumoured to exist, but otherwise unknown except for its name appearing in crude paint on the walls of buildings from time to time. There were whispers, but only whispers, that its purpose was to fight to force the British to surrender the Island as a colony and allow *enosis* – union with Greece – for which Greek Cypriots had overwhelmingly voted in a referendum conducted by the Greek Cypriot Church and His Beatitude Archbishop Makarios III in 1950. The British dismissed the results as meaningless, arguing that the Church had threatened voters with ex-communication and other sanctions if they opposed the motion laid down by their religious leaders.

In the Archbishopric in the heart of the old city, Makarios had been flicking through the pages of T. S. Elliot's *Murder in the Cathedral*, waiting patiently in his study to hear the first blasts. His was a modest rectangular room with a large desk, a remarkable piece of carving in the Byzantine tradition. On the wall behind his chair, he had placed a striking, exotic and unexpected symbol of modernity – a small copy of a Salvador Dali crucifix. The *New York Times* correspondent in Cyprus, much taken by him, rhapsodized that he was 'handsome, slender, with glistening black eyes and trimmed black beard (a must for Orthodox priests), with a soft, musical voice, which he uses without oratorical tricks. He is quiet-spoken, impassive, with no trace of emotion except, occasionally, a quick, bland smile that crinkles his face like that of a boy who knows where the pot of jam is hidden.'

Stubbing out a cigarette, His Beatitude lit another and chain-smoked his way to the balcony, listening as more explosions followed. Eighteen would take place across the Island before morning. The operation he had ordered was under way. Satisfied, he smiled and decided it was time for bed, but not before he smoked one more cigarette. His ashtray was overflowing with dog-ends: one more or less would not matter.

His Beatitude Makarios III, Archbishop and Ethnarch of the
Orthodox Church of Cyprus.

his community at the Sultan's court – and been responsible for collecting taxes on behalf of the Sublime Porte. The British administration had continued the tradition – except it took charge of the raising of taxes and their collection, something that priests did not welcome as their personal incomes were suddenly considerably reduced.

AT A SMALL inconspicuous house in Strovolos, not far from Nicosia airport, a retired Greek Colonel of Cypriot origin, George Grivas, waited for news from his bombers. Throughout his life, he saw his duty as rebuilding a 'greater Greece', which was why he decided to mastermind the EOKA campaign. It would be conducted in three stages. The bombs were part of the first – and only a warning to the British of what was to follow. Greek Cypriots would be targeted in

Born Michael Christodoulou Mouskos on 13 January 1913 in Ano Panayia, a village in the Troodos Mountains, 20 miles from the birthplace of the goddess Aphrodite, Makarios was the son of a shepherd, who sent him, at the age of 13, to Kykko Monastery for his early education. The monastery would become the mountain headquarters of the EOKA movement.

After spending the Second World War in Athens, studying religion and law, he was ordained in 1946 and became deacon of the fashionable Ayia Irini church. Soon afterwards he attended Boston University College in the United States. From being Mouskos, a clever, quietly spoken young priest, he streaked up the religious hierarchy. By the age of 37, he had reached the top and stamped his personality on the Church's supreme post of Primate of the Autocephalous Greek Orthodox Church of Cyprus. Since Ottoman Turkey had seized Cyprus in 1570, the holder had represented

Colonel George Grivas in his Greek Army uniform.

Sir Robert Armitage, KCMG, CBE.

the second: those who did not wholeheartedly support EOKA or 'collaborated' with the British were to be assassinated. Guerrilla war would be the final act.

In the more luxurious surrounds of the Ledra Palace Hotel, Sir Robert Armitage, the Governor, who had returned to Cyprus from London only the week before, was having dinner with friends, perhaps to celebrate becoming a KCMG, which his civil servants joked meant 'Kindly Call Me God'. Barely had they finished their coffee when the building shook and windows shattered, glass fragments flying in all directions to injure his guests.

EOKA had placed a bomb near the hotel's entrance. The culprit, Euripides Charalambous, a carpenter, was later caught and pleaded guilty to a charge of 'preparing to procure the alteration of the Cyprus Government by armed force'. The prosecutor in the case was Rauf

Denktas, who was to become a forceful defender of Turkish interests in Cyprus.

Sir Robert's Fool's Day had started badly and could only become worse.

Appointed Governor in 1953, after serving in the Gold Coast (later Ghana) as the finance minister of the colonial administration, Armitage's mission was to create some form of self-government for the Island. Under no circumstances, however, was he to hint at, let alone negotiate, *enosis*. Although Archbishop Makarios and his aides had refused to discuss any aspect of constitutional change with Armitage unless he put *enosis* on the agenda, he was optimistic he could persuade the prosperous classes to come round to his way of thinking. Not until late 1954, when the first street riots began, did his security advisers hint that serious trouble was brewing.

Field Marshal Sir John Harding, later to become Governor of Cyprus, recalled: 'When the terrorists launched their opening offensive little or nothing was known of the pattern on which EOKA was organized or of the names and personalities of the leaders. The reaction of the Greek Cypriots seems to have been largely one of surprise and admiration.

'The Turkish Cypriots, the British and the other communities were definitely alarmed and critical of the Government. Immediately steps were taken to mobilize and put into action the forces of law and order, but they were unprepared to deal with such a widespread outbreak, too weak in numbers to meet the many demands put upon them and their plans were uncoordinated.'

John Newsinger, Senior Lecturer in History, Bath Spa University College, supported Harding's view. In his study, *British Counterinsurgency: From Palestine to Northern Ireland*, he observed: 'The outbreak of the EOKA rebellion came as a complete shock to the British. They had convinced themselves over the years that the Greek Cypriot population was not capable of armed resistance ... As one Conservative MP commented only six months earlier: "It seems inconceivable that the Cypriots should become vicious like the Egyptians".'

WHEN THE first explosions occurred, Lawrence Durrell, later to author *Bitter Lemons*, was sitting in his Nicosia home with his brother Gerald, who was due to leave for Britain the next day. 'A string of dull bumps now – from many different quarters at once. We ran down the steps and along the unlit gravel road to where the main road joined it. A few bewildered-looking civilians stood dazed in the shadows of the trees. "Over there," said a man. He pointed in the direction of the Secretariat building, which was about 200 yards down the road,' Durrell wrote. For him, Cyprus was 'a rather lovely, spare, bland sexy island, totally unlike Greece, with a weird charm of its own'. But he was disillusioned by having been misled by Kranidiotis, Makarios's mouthpiece, although, by his own admission he had never been enamoured with Greek Cypriots and called them 'l'parrots of the Greeks'.

The explosions surprised Durrell. Only six weeks earlier, on 22 February, he and Nikos Kranidiotis, the Secretary to the Ethnarchy Council, had met privately. Kranidiotis had told him that Makarios feared 'the drift towards local violence as a possible next step'. According to the detailed history of *Britain and the Revolt in Cyprus 1954–1959* by Robert Holland, Governor Armitage was anxious for the same reason: 'The intermediaries sketched out a plan for a secret meeting at night in the remote monastery of Kykko between the two leaders, after which they could issue an agreed communiqué' about keeping the peace, but the Governor 'could not make a move of such importance without the permission of Her Majesty's Government. Perhaps left to himself, and with the weight of responsibility on him, Lennox-Boyd [Secretary of State for the Colonies] might have authorized the Governor

to go ahead. But the real power lay elsewhere.

'Eden [the British Prime Minister] gave short shrift to what he and his officials saw as the proposition that the Governor should go "cap in hand" into Makarios' territory, effectively suing for help in governing his own colony. Reluctantly explaining to Armitage why this was not possible, Lennox-Boyd told him on 25 February that it would "suggest a readiness and even anxiety on your part to seek an accommodation on self-determination".

'When he made a second attempt, pointedly arguing that any such meeting would be a triumph in breaking down the "boycott imposed by the Church [on the administration] for the last 20 years", he was refused again.'

The Archbishop continued to preach: 'We demand self-determination and nothing less,' he pronounced in a sermon. 'How shall we get this? By persistent and firm continuation of our struggle in all directions. By the weapon of our right. The wind of freedom is blowing everywhere, tearing down the colonial regimes.'

Durrell, who spoke fluent Greek, was the Colony's civilian Head of Public Information, a job he had accepted reluctantly when he could not meet his bills as an author and sometime teacher. He never denied that those who loaned him money would have a long wait before they were repaid. To his credit, he did not forget his debtors and accepted work, whatever it was, short of, as he put it, 'selling my bottom to a clergyman'. He had washed up on the Island on 26 January 1953 with his two-year-old daughter Sappho to start a new life and complete his novel *Justine*. The Greek Cypriot literati welcomed his arrival. One of those who befriended him was a fellow writer: Rodis Roufos, who was the Greek Consul from 1954 to 1956 and acted as a conduit for communication between his government and the leaders of the enosis movement. When Durrell authored *Bitter Lemons*, the two men fell out, with Roufos describing the book as a work of fiction, passed off as fact, and called him 'a pocket Machiavelli'. While Durrell saw no harm in revealing the weaknesses and misdemeanours of others, he was never completely open about his own private life, especially his relationship with his daughter, Sappho, who later committed suicide.

In the early hours of that April's Fool morning, the two Durrell brothers walked quickly to the Secretariat through 'a fog of cordite fumes' and saw 'a tidy rent in the wall of the building out of which smoke poured as if from a steam engine'. Because Laurence was a government employee, he did not wait to admire the view, but rushed to the Police HQ located at the Paphos Gate.

'It had a forlorn deserted air, and was, apart from one sleepy unarmed duty sergeant, unguarded as far as I could judge,' Lawrence Durrell said. 'In the operations room on the top floor the Colonial Secretary sat at a desk tapping a pencil against his teeth; he was wearing a college blazer and trousers over his pyjamas, and a silk scarf. Behind him the two clerks crouched in an alcove beside the receiving set, which scratched out a string of crackling messages ...'

The Colonial Secretary was slow to react to what was happening. It took until 02.00 before 30 police constables had been raised from their beds to report for duty and start investigating the damage caused in Nicosia.

Richard Taylor, a junior British Army officer, watched as events unravelled. 'I had been having one of those very deep conversations we all have at times and which were generally fuelled by brandy, when Durrell arrived, dressed only in a sleeveless shirt and shorts, which, in retrospect, I find a little odd. He left at dawn to find a bar,' he recollected.

THE LIGHTS stayed out in the *Times of Cyprus* offices. Located in a nondescript concrete building behind the Archbishop's Palace, it was hidden in a network of streets that during the day were alive with peddlers, beggars, men beating things out of sheet copper, motor cars, cycles, priests and furtive-looking young Hellenes – but Charles Foley, the founding editor, was yet to produce the first copy of his newspaper that would become a thorn in the flesh of the British establishment. When the explosions began, he was fast asleep after a busy day trying to recruit full-time staff locally and abroad.

Jobless after his sudden resignation from his highly paid post as the Foreign News Editor of the London *Daily Express*, Foley had been open to new challenges, one of which came his way from a fellow journalist, Michael Davidson, who had set up shop on the Island. 'Davidson said that I might consider striking out in a new direction, which would make me my own boss and give me a chance to do something, which nobody else was attempting,' the Anglo-Irish Foley wrote later. 'There were good prospects for a newspaper on the Island and new readers: the troops coming from Egypt.' Throughout the period of its existence, Foley never revealed who financed the publication.

A mile from Metaxas Square, Robert Egby had just made the closing announcement and played the *Evening Hymn* and *Last Post* at the end of another day's programmes from the new studios of the Forces Broadcasting Station in Severis Street. Now he was heading home when he heard the exploding bombs. Egby had worked for FBS in the Canal Zone in Egypt and knew the dangers of terrorism – one of the reasons why British Forces were moving to Cyprus to establish new bases for use in defending UK interests in the Middle East and why ministers in London were determined to never give up their Island.

The official line from Whitehall, put plainly and concisely, stated: 'In short, we are here to ensure control of a British military strongpoint, the maintenance of which is essential to the defence of the free world. Cyprus holds the Middle East Joint H.Q. of British Land and Air Forces, and is the nerve centre of our Middle East strategy. It is being equipped with important airfields and staging facilities, and is thus the springboard of any military and air action we may have to take in the Middle East. The airfields of Cyprus, part of a wide network of Western airfields in the Middle East, make the Island into what might almost be described as an unsinkable aircraft carrier anchored off the shores of the Levant. All our Western allies including Greece have recognized the necessity for a British base in Cyprus.'

RALPH SWIFT, an RAF officer, told the author: 'We used to go to Cyprus on detachments from the Canal Zone in 1953–4 and based ourselves at Nicosia for Armament Practice camp and did air-to-air firing on towed banners over the sea, north of Kyrenia. Even then the words "enosis" and EOKA were appearing in the least expected places, yet Cyprus was a real oasis in those days and what an enormous shame it was to see the whole place descend into strife. It had so much going for it until Greek nationalism reared its ugly head.'

In the years since 1950, only the blind would have been able to ignore the angry appeals, protests and demonstrations by Cypriots calling for self-determination. They had intensified after Minister of State for Colonial Affairs Henry Hopkinson told the House of Commons in 1954 that Cyprus would 'never' be granted either self-determination or independence. Yet the local police consisted of only 1,386 officers, quite insufficient to deal with any insurrection. David Burke, a press agency correspondent, described them as 'a band of rural-type constables recruited in a peaceful backwater. The signs are all there: the placid smiling, the head scratching and the comfortable paunches. Watch them

in action, as I have, controlling demonstrators and breaking up riots: they have a "let the others go first" attitude, which is striking.' It was 'a Cinderella service in a Cinderella colony,' a senior British police adviser told the Colonial Office.

Such was the state of the police that in the previous December the 2nd Battalion the Green Howards and 2nd Battalion the Royal Inniskilling Fusiliers, recently arrived in Cyprus, had to be called out to stop riots in Nicosia and Limassol, because the police were overwhelmed. In Nicosia, the authorities had only 20 constables available to face 2,000 marching youths who began to run out of control.

The 2nd Battalion the Green Howards had arrived in Cyprus in dramatic fashion. After training as amphibious troops, they landed at Morphou Bay on 2 September 1954 at 03.00, in an 'opposed' operation, code-named *Floodtide*. After coming ashore successfully, they were commended by GOC MELF (General Officer Commanding, Middle East Land Forces) for their professionalism as a seaborne force. From Morphou, they were transferred to their new 'home' – Nine Mile Camp outside Larnaca, 80 miles south, today the site of Larnaca International Airport. Because the camp was still being built, the battalion lived in Second World War tents, while tasked to build 60 iron frame storage buildings, which were clad with corrugated iron sheets. At first, the local people welcomed them with great warmth and hospitality.

The 2nd Battalion the Royal Inniskilling Fusiliers from 2 Brigade in Suez joined the Green Howards a few weeks later, on 22 September, as part of Britain's plan to establish its Middle East Land Forces Headquarters in Aphrodite's Island. For a short period the Irish regiment was based at Wayne's Keep, when the troops made a ceremonial flag march round the walls of the old city, which they reported as 'very popular'. The Inniskillings were then given responsibility for Famagusta and 140 square miles of the surrounding countryside. The Turkish Cypriots lived in the old walled city and the Greeks in the new town of Varosha, the scene of most of the early disturbances.

'Initially the local situation on the surface did not seem serious,' Lieutenant Colonel Filmer-Bennett, the regiment's official historian, recorded. 'Although there was some hooliganism, which was well within the control of the British forces, there was the underground beginning of a troubled period of Cyprus history.'

Although infantry battalions had begun to spread out across the Island, the largest numbers of troops belonged to the Royal Engineers, whose job was to build the new bases. In November 1954, Main GHQ MELF including the Chief Engineer, Major General W. G. Fryer, had moved to Cyprus and set up in the capital. The Cyprus garrison in 1954 consisted of a Brigadier's HQ at Nicosia and four major units: infantry battalions at Larnaca, Famagusta and Nicosia with the 35 Army Engineer Regiment based at Polemidia, where it became increasingly involved in internal security duties. In December 1954 it was decided to dust off internal security plans. In Limassol, 35 Regiment, Royal Engineers, worked alongside the Assistant District Commissioner, a Turkish Cypriot who had been at Eton and Oxford. On the 17th of the month, all normal duties and exercises were cancelled because of school children's riots in other parts of the island. The following day adults joined in.

The Royal Engineers now put their training into practice 'in a copybook episode of riot control in aid of the civil power', according to its official historian. Following the withdrawal of a police cordon, the Assistant Commissioner formally requested the Army to take over. 'After appropriate visual and oral warnings to the crowd to disperse, a ringleader was shot and nearly killed. Tension

eased and sporadic outbursts in Limassol finally ended in a heavy downpour of rain.'

Lieutenant Colonel J. R. G. Finch, the military commander of the area, ordered his men to keep the initiative by active patrolling and to avoid a 'fortress mentality' behind barbed wire. At least one attack was pre-empted at a crucial moment, and on another occasion the 'ready troop' stopped an impending riot by deploying quickly and charging with fixed bayonets.

AT THE Colonial Office in London, however, officials still saw no reason to strengthen the security forces. On 25 January 1955, a member of staff blithely noted: 'Sir Robert Armitage is satisfied that the police and military available in the Island are sufficient to quell any riots on a scale that can at present be considered even remotely possible. He would, I am sure, let us know at once if he had any doubt on that score.'

British officials privately thought Greek Cypriots were an ungrateful lot, misled by their priests. As far as they could see, Cyprus had only benefited by being a colony. Britain had built roads where there were none, and provided 714 elementary schools for 627 outlying villages, leading to the Island's 95 per cent literacy rate. Medical facilities and a malaria-control programme had brought an average life expectancy of 66 years, one of the highest in the world. In addition, Cypriots were British subjects, without having to pay the high taxes applied in the UK, and they had the right to settle in Britain. In fact, some 30,000 were happily settled there.

Lord Winster summed up the situation when he addressed the House of Lords: 'I feel that Cyprus offers a perfect example of a modern phenomenon – an easy-going, happy, moderately prosperous people, living happily in the sun in neighbourly peace and friendliness. And what happens? They are freed one day from the curse of malaria, only to become infected by the modern bug of what is known as "political consciousness".

'Greeks, Turks, Armenians, Maronites, were living side by side without any racial animosities, under an efficient, tolerant and thoroughly well disposed Administration. Then, like the demon king in the pantomime, up comes the demon of political unrest, encouraged by political agitators of what is, unfortunately, a well-known type.

'The people are told that they are oppressed and down trodden and exploited, and that under another form of Administration, they would be free, richer and happier. Men and women under the agitator's manipulation, cease to be Cypriots living as one race: they become Greeks and Turks encouraged to hate each other. They become divided into Democrats and Communists and, again, are taught to hate each other. To divide the people and teach them to hate is the agitator's technique.'

Old Colonial stalwarts, too, were awfully perplexed by the unrest in Cyprus. Aside from advances in the Island's infrastructure, education and health, there were further benefits. According to Sir David Hunt, the author of *Footprints in Cyprus,* 'One of the most remarkable successes of the British administration was the reforestation of the mountainous regions and the creation of a Forestry Service that was a model for and a teacher of the other services in the Empire.'

Add to all these benefits the peasantry's freedom from the grip of money-lenders, the creation of cooperative businesses, preferential markets, a stable currency, freedom from enemy occupation in two world conflicts and being spared the Civil War which their mother country suffered – what could make the Greek Cypriots take the road to wanton destruction? Time and time again, British expatriates posed the question between their brandy sours.

IN JANUARY Archbishop Makarios had returned to Cyprus after attending the UN General assembly in New York where he had failed to drum up support for Greek Cypriots to be allowed 'self-determination' and union with Greece. Now he was determined to change his battle of words to a war of violence. On the 11th he met Grivas secretly in the Larnaca Bishopric and gave him the green light to launch his 'freedom campaign'. Perhaps the ambitious cleric felt slighted that the only backing he had secured at the UN came from Thailand and he wanted to place his homeland on the front pages of the world's newspapers. To aid reporters, he asked Grivas to suggest a name for the new militant organization. 'EOKA,' replied the diminutive Colonel, an acronym for *Ethniki Organosis Kyprion Agoniston* (National Organization of Cypriot Fighters).

D-day was set for 25 March, Greek Independence Day. 'In Makarios's view, some acts of sabotage might prove sufficient to impress foreign opinion, particularly in the United States, that the prolongation of British rule in Cyprus was fast leading to a new crisis in the Middle East,' wrote Greek scholar Ioannis Stefanidis. 'Makarios now tried to galvanized the faithful with ever more combative rhetoric. He braced his flock for sacrifices, arguing that Britain never set any people free unless forced to do so by violent means.' Only in the final stage would terror tactics be used against British forces.

The two men had met for the first time in 1946. Makarios – or Michael Mouskos, as he was then – was a young priest serving the Athenian Church of St Irene, a place where only influential Greeks prayed on Sundays. One of them was Grivas, well known for his extreme politics and dubious activities during the Second World War, when he and his followers refused to battle alongside the Greek underground against the nation's Nazi German occupiers. Many people thought of him a collaborator.

'While Communist and Royalist bands

were raiding German installations from the Greek mountains,' Stefanidis continues, 'Grivas was creating his first terrorist group in occupied Athens. He called it X, and its members were mostly young cadets whom he had trained in Salonika, with a sprinkling of older unemployed army officers. X had twin objectives: externally, the wild irredentist dream of "greater Greece", stretching, on specially printed maps, over southern Albania, European Turkey and Cyprus; internally, the restoration of the Greek monarchy as an acceptable facade for a fascist-type regime of the extreme right ...

'Because X played no part in the resistance, it did not qualify for allied assistance. The allied mission to the Greek guerrillas, under Colonel C. M. ("Monty") Woodhouse, supplied arms to the major resistance groups, including the left-wing *Elas*, but not to X – a further source of anti-British grievance to the fanatical Colonel from Cyprus.'

In *Apple of Discord*, Colonel Woodhouse said of X: 'This body, later known as the direct-action instrument of the Royalist Right Wing under the leadership of Colonel Grivas, has claimed to have been a resistance movement during the occupation. If that claim were true, it would be classifiable as the only resistance organization of the Right then active in Athens; but in fact its name was unknown until shortly before the Germans left; and even then the name signified nothing connected with resistance.'

But the priest and army colonel found they had much in common, especially when Mouskos attacked Communism from 'a Christian viewpoint'. So they kept in touch.

Once Mouskos was elected Archbishop Makarios III, he re-visited Athens several times to gather support for his *enosis* campaign. Always received well, his plans began to take shape on 13 March 1951 after he met the Cypriot brothers Savvas and Socrates Loizides, and George Stratos, the former Minister of War, a personal friend of King George of Greece. To rid Cyprus of the British would require more than patriotic sermons from the pulpits, the trio agreed: there would have to be 'military operations' led by a person with a 'military mind'.

According to Charles Foley, the journalist who 'ghosted' Grivas's *Memoirs*, the Archbishop suggested Grivas for the job and asked the brothers to meet him and others. In April, they met in the Tsitas Café – 'one of those spacious Athenian establishments dedicated to the discussion of politics over innumerable small cups of strong black coffee. It stands among the series of neo-classical buildings that line University Street, under the eye of a marble statue of Gladstone, British liberator of the Ionian Isles.'

Socrates Loizides had been exiled from Cyprus as a dangerous agitator and was eager for fresh adventure, but it was left to Savvas to explain to Grivas the reason for their meeting. Would the Colonel be willing to lead war for *enosis* under Makarios? Socrates added that he was sure the Island's youth would follow him without question. 'Grivas had long entertained thoughts of leading a revolt in Cyprus. He had revealed them to a few intimate friends, such as his old colonel from the 30th Infantry, General G. Kosmas – now chief of the general staff, who had the ear of the Prime Minister, Field Marshal Papagos; but without result,' wrote Charles Foley.

'Now he accepted the offer with a reply that was as long as it was passionate, carrying the others away on the flood of rhetoric. An hour later the meeting broke up in a glow of patriotic sentiment. It was agreed that Grivas should make a personal tour of Cyprus to refresh his mind on possibilities for sabotage and guerrilla warfare.'

Perhaps his ready acceptance was due more to his need to be accepted by the Greek elite, because most of his other endeavours had failed. Brian Crozier, the author of *The*

Rebels, explained that Grivas was less of a military expert than he thought himself. 'His first experience of active service was on the defeated side in the ill-starred Greek invasion of Asia Minor in 1922 – a bitter rebuff to those who, like him, believed wholeheartedly in "greater Greece."' Stephen Barber of London's *News Chronicle* put it bluntly: 'In the eyes of Greek sophisticates, he was a vulgar fellow – a "Cypriot donkey".' In his bitterness, Grivas had his own description of Athenian politicians, including the formidable General Papagos: 'Faint-hearted traitors,' he labeiled them.

The signatures of the members of the Cyprus Struggle Committee established in Athens in 1953.

In 1953 Makarios joined the so-called Cyprus Struggle Committee in Athens by taking an oath to support *enosis* unto death, in the fashion of nineteenth-century secret societies. At that point, Grivas was appointed military chief, with the Archbishop reserving the last word for himself. As time passed he disagreed many times with the Colonel and his associates over the scale of the operations, which he wanted limited to acts of sabotage. They were both short men, barely inches more than five feet in height, and still did not see eye-to-eye.

Nevertheless in August 1954, Makarios asked Grivas to step up preparations for a terrorist campaign. The Archbishop had decided that this was the only course open to realize *enosis* after Britain's abandonment of its base in Egypt and Prime Minister Anthony Eden's declaration that Cyprus was vital to protecting the United Kingdom's Middle East oil supplies. 'No Cyprus,' he explained, 'no certain facilities to protect our oil. No oil, unemployment and hunger in Britain.'

But what form of action should the terrorists take and when? As historian Ioannis Stefanidis observed, 'the dilemma arose whether to sanction the use of force pending the discussion of the Greek/Cyprus debate at the General Assembly or to await its outcome'. Grivas and Makarios agreed to meet again in Athens in six weeks to present their considered opinions. When they did, a Greek diplomat told them he was hopeful that he could persuade the US to bring pressure on Britain to give up Cyprus and so there might not be a need to resort to violence. 'Thus, it was decided to postpone action until after the Assembly.'

Always a militant, Grivas was not convinced. He sailed for Cyprus secretly, landing on 10 November, with forged papers. On the way he was violently seasick. Without waiting for any go-ahead from Makarios, he methodically set about organizing small guer-

The forged identification card used by George Grivas in 1954.

rilla groups, personally training them in the use of arms and explosives and setting in place an effective network of couriers in towns and villages to communicate between his groups. He drew his activists from former members of the right-wing Pancyprian National Youth Organization, PEON, believing that the younger they were, the easier they would be to indoctrinate. Each recruit took a secret oath, presided over by a priest, pledging allegiance to *enosis*, swearing never to reveal the organization's secrets – even if tortured – and promising to sacrifice their lives if the need arose.

'When we set off,' he disclosed, 'we started with nothing. Young men who had responded to my call had never laid hand on firearms. They were so clumsy with the guns we gave them that when they loaded them the barrels pointed towards their chests. But they learned.'

WORTH MORE than £65 million, just in the properties it owned in 1955, the Orthodox Church delved into its coffers and paid agents in Greece to have Grivas's arms delivered to Cyprus by boat. Under Makarios, the Church had increased its wealth spectacularly. As a Greek lawyer told an American reporter: 'He is a very cute financier. When he became Archbishop, he was smart enough to unload most of the farm property and put the money into urban real estate.' He realized that renting land to villagers was not a secure proposition. Besides, you can't evict farmers without becoming unpopular.'

The Bishop of Kition arranged the arms deals, paying in gold sovereigns. His latest order was placed aboard a caique called the *Aghios Georghios* on 13 January. It sailed with silenced engines, its crew planning to land the weapons and explosives on a lonely beach at Khlorakas, near Paphos, where the cargo would be collected. Unknown to Grivas's men, however, Christopher Phillpotts, the MI6 station chief in Cyprus, had got wind of the plan. A former Royal Navy officer, he had served in the 9th MTB Flotilla during the Second World War and easily calculated the caique's course and speed. When it sailed, it was followed at a distance by HMS *Charity*.

As a consequence, long before all the explosives could be landed, the vessel was intercepted by HMS *Comet*, caught by its searchlight like a rabbit in the beam of an approaching car. A few shots were fired, while some of the munitions were dumped in the sea, but the smugglers soon surrendered after Lieutenant Michael Clapp, RN, and a party of sailors boarded. The captured crew included Anargyros Melos (the ship's owner) and Evangelos Louca (the captain). Unknown to Clapp, a loaded dinghy had left the *Aghios Georghios* minutes earlier. Its rowers were trying to reach the shore under the cliff at Khlorakas, where police under the command of Superintendent Alexis Ioannou awaited their arrival. 'Hands up!' he shouted. 'Wait where you are or we'll fire!' He had already rounded up the others on the beach who had been signalling where to land. 'We're not armed. You needn't shoot!' replied the men in the dinghy, raising their arms aloft.

The beach party had been waiting several days for the arms to arrive, but due to poor communication between Makarios and Grivas they were unaware that the security services were watching too. Earlier, Constable Pavlos Stokkos of the Special Branch, whose father was involved in the 1931 insurgency, had told the Archbishop that he had seen secret documents about how the *Aghios Georghios* was being followed. For inexplicable reasons, Makarios, nevertheless, sent Socrates Loizides to supervise the landing of the weapons. Meanwhile, Andreas Azinas, who was in Paphos and in contact with the caique, alerted Grivas that there was a lot of unusual activity by local police. He told Grivas: 'Five Special Branch men have arrived this afternoon from Nicosia. The Army's radar is in constant operation, sweeping over a 15-mile radius.' Still the caique was not warned to stay in international waters.

When the authorities counted their catch, they found 30 boxes labeled DANGER – EXPLOSIVES, containing 10,000 sticks of dynamite. 'Trampled into the sand police found a receipt for money signed by Azinas, which Loizides had tried and failed to destroy by swallowing,' reported Charles Foley. 'Now Azinas, Grivas's top aide, was a wanted man –

his offices in Nicosia were searched and records of his numerous trips to Athens discovered.'

For his part, Socrates Loizides was found carrying an extremely incriminating document, which later sealed his fate in court. It was addressed to several prominent Greek Cypriots, telling them that a secret revolutionary organization had been formed. It was called EMAK – the name used before EOKA was adopted. 'The people must not be led away by patriotic zeal as a result of EMAK's successful struggle, nor must they rise in open revolt against the occupying power. This will lead only to heavy sacrifices and there must be no unlawful revolutionary acts even by hot-blooded patriots who are not organized,' it advised. 'Only the organized fighters of EMAK will take action ...' In his book, *Cyprus in the Struggle for Freedom*, Nikos Kranidiotis said: 'The Communists were told even more bluntly that their help was not wanted. In other words, this was to be a private Right-wing "army" directed by – the Church ...'

In his nightly diary, Grivas, 'The Leader', believing there was a spy in his midst, showed his bitterness: 'There will always be traitors, but I had not imagined that there could be in this particular instance Greeks whose love for money overrides all else.'

In the years ahead, Grivas, a teetotaller, non-smoker and devout Christian, who portrayed himself as a typical village Cypriot by frequently dressing in peasant clothes, would lead his terrorists to kill, blast and intimidate any one who stood in the way of his ambitions, applying a two-fold programme: setting up guerrilla bands in the mountains for raids and ambushes; and organizing cold-blooded murders in the towns. At the moment, only his closest associates knew his real identity. By the morning, all would know him as 'Dighenis', the name he had taken from a legendary figure in Byzantine times. For an extreme nationalist, who promoted the purity of Greekness, it was a curious *nom de plume* to choose, because the word means 'born of two races' – Byzantine and Arab – which is never mentioned in Greek historiography.

'DIGHENIS' PUT away his stamp collection, checked his watch and told his bodyguard Gregoris Louka to stand down. He then began writing his diary. There was never a day when he failed to record in detail what he had done and his *Memoirs* provide a fascinating first-hand account of his activities. In an old-fashioned style of the Greek language, he penned: 'At 00.30 I noticed a short interruption of the current but without any other result. What has happened? Has the attempt to cut off the current failed? Some minutes after 00.30 the first explosions are heard. They are followed by others and finally the last one, which is also the biggest. We went to bed at 03.00. We shall know the results tomorrow.'

The day before, Grivas had considered moving out of Nicosia in case the authorities tracked him down as soon as the campaign began. 'I examined the question of my HQs. I thought that I was not safe in the house where I am staying and so I would not be able to lead the struggle,' he wrote. 'I was thinking of moving to Kyrenia, but finally decided to stay in Nicosia in order to communicate more easily with the various centres and intervene more actively in Nicosia where the centres did not seem to be active. I made this decision against the exhortations of Evagoras ... I have definitely decided to stay in Nicosia.'

Lawrence Durrell already knew more than 'Dighenis'. In *Bitter Lemons of Cyprus* he wrote: 'By now the press had begun to block the meager lines and I diverted them to an outer office where I dealt with them as faithfully as I could, but police reports were very slow in coming in and in many cases the Agencies were hours ahead of us.' Who the culprits were behind the explosions, no one knew.

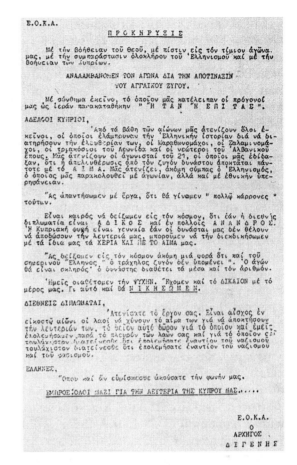

The first EOKA leaflet scattered in Nicosia on 1 April 1955.

'We drove up in an old Morris that broke down when we were a few hundred yards away. Someone got out to look under the bonnet and a grenade fell out of his satchel and bounced in the road,' said Yanakis Droushiotis, one of the seven-man EOKA group led by Makarios's cousin, Haralambos Mouskos. Talking about their first amateurish attempt to terrorize, he continued: 'Quite a few bombs didn't go off, and the ones that did caused more smoke than fire. We drove away without seeing a soul. Afterwards, one of our group, Haralambos Xenofontos, picked up the EOKA leaflets from Markos Drakos's house and distributed them in the street from his bicycle.'

Code-named *Averof*, Droushiotis became Grivas's chief aide in Nicosia. He was a major financial donor to 'the cause'. When he was eventually arrested, he told his interrogators that his leader was no longer in Cyprus, having sailed away in a submarine of the Royal Hellenic Navy!

In Nicosia the other targets had been the public broadcasting station, the Department of Education and Wolseley Barracks. The attack on the latter by Christakis Eleftheriou caused the military no bother at all, as his Molotov cocktails thrown over the boundary fence fizzled with no more effect than a child's firework.

At the studios of the Cyprus Broadcasting Station, two night watchmen had been overpowered, bound and gagged. The intruders then dynamited the studios, including a fully soundproofed concert studio, the generator room and the transmitters. The place was ablaze. 'When you are in the radio business, it's demoralizing to see a radio station being destroyed,' said Robert Egby. Markos Drakos, whose reputation as an EOKA 'hero' would soar in the months ahead, led the attack. His gang of four used Molotov cocktails too – *Spey Royal* whisky bottles filled with petrol – to set fire to the building and leave it ablaze.

'The radio station was indeed badly blitzed,' said Durrell, 'but it was lucky to have the possession of an engineering staff which had been eating its heart out for a chance like this; by two o'clock the engineers had crawled into the wreckage and produced a fairly detailed report on the damage and the welcome information that one of the transmitters had escaped, which would allow some sort of programme going out next day, on reduced power.'

AFTER a mere three hours' sleep Grivas was up at 06.00 and sent his bodyguard Gregoris Louka to buy the morning newspapers to find out how the start of his campaign had been reported. Louka returned and told 'The Leader' that Cypriots were slightly bewildered by the events of the previous night, but were enjoying their favourite pastime: spreading rumours, discussing conspiracies and exaggerating the truth. Durrell, meanwhile, noted 'walking about the calm streets of the town, watching the shopkeepers taking down their shutters and sipping their morning coffee, [nobody] could have told that some decisive and irrevocable action had taken place in the night'.

The newspapers' coverage was disappointing. There was little to suggest that much had happened. Grivas saw the English-language *Cyprus Mail* and fumed at its editorial, which said: 'Views on what should be done by Government differ only on the severity of the measures to be expected ... all are agreed that acts of terrorism will never drive the British out of Cyprus – and that there is evidently a great deal of truth in Dr. Johnson's dictum that patriotism is the last refuge of a scoundrel.'

Grivas twiddled with the dial of his radio and tuned it to Radio Athens – 'the Voice of the Fatherland' – and complained bitterly. 'It has said nothing at all about the events,' he seethed and then found the official government station was back on the air, broadcasting music, as if all was well with the world. The Colonel's mood blackened. His carefully waxed mustache twitched. Why was there so little enthusiasm for his revolutionary exploits? Had nobody read his proclamation that was so carefully crafted that it had brought tears to his eyes?

Grivas's mimeographed pamphlets had been scattered by his young helpers around the streets of the sites of the EOKA attacks, but without much thought about who might pick them up and read the content. Those that did were left puzzled, not least of all the Security Forces. Some were labelled as coming from EOKA, others from EMAK. Who and what were these? They were signed 'Dighenis', who called himself 'The Leader'. But leader of what exactly? While his proclamation sounded patriotic, its language was heavy with passion and light on real substance. It raised more questions than answers.

'Brother Cypriots, from the depths of past centuries all those who glorified Greek history to preserve their freedom are watching us: the warriors of Marathon, the warriors of Salamis, the 300 of Leonidas ... Let us be worthy of them,' the pamphlets urged the ordinary man in the street, as he carried his harvested fruit and vegetables to market. 'It is time to show the world that if national diplomacy is unjust and cowardly, the soul of a Cypriot is brave ... Greeks, wherever you may be, hear our call: FORWARD ALL TOGETHER FOR THE FREEDOM OF OUR CYPRUS.'

In his cause, 'Dighenis' invoked help from the Almighty, called on Cypriots to overthrow their Colonial masters, because 'right and justice are on our side', and promised 'We shall emerge victorious'. A different leaflet was dropped in the Turkish quarter of the city, advising the inhabitants that EOKA had no quarrel with them, unless they aligned themselves with the British 'oppressors'.

In the press and street cafés, Robert Holland claimed 'there was no ready approval of the saboteurs, but neither was there much criticism'. The late Nancy Crawshaw, a former Manchester *Guardian* correspondent, elaborated on Greek reaction in her book, *The Cyprus Revolt*. 'The first explosions were followed by a general revulsion against violence. However strongly some sectors of the Greek Cypriot community might desire *enosis*, few of them when it came to the point welcomed the prospects of prolonged rebellion, the disruption of normal life and trade,' she wrote.

Only Leftist Cypriots spoke out. Greek Cypriot historian Doros Alastos described their reaction: 'They condemned the violent methods of EOKA, ridiculed its activities, characterizing them as childish and described its bomb-throwing as displays of fire-works!' He also alleged that the Communists were convinced EOKA was the creation of a British intelligence agency determined to destroy those whom they considered were puppets of the Soviets in the ongoing Cold War.

The Pan-Cyprian Labour Federation, representing 14,000 workers, passed a resolution deprecating the terrorist activities. The resolution claimed that the outrages were inspired by people who wanted to make 'Government measures against the working class appear justified'. These were also acts calculated to stir up and intensify hostility between Greeks and Turks in Cyprus, it added. The Communists were to persistently call EOKA a group of 'hooligans' and 'pop gun wielders'. Later, the Greek Communist Party's leader, sitting in exile in Moscow, revealed Dighenis's identity. But, according to Grivas, 'the British did not take this piece of information seriously. The idea of an elderly retired officer as the Leader of EOKA was too strange for them to accept.'

For their part, the Turks believed that EOKA 'was an organ of the Greek General Staff officered by Greeks; and some, the traditional Americano-phobes, ... saw in it the influence of the State Department to eject Britain and use Cyprus as an American base'.

DURING THE morning of 1 April, Governor Armitage interrupted a sequence of tango music on the state radio to assure listeners that all measures would be taken to trace and apprehend the wrongdoers. Shy and inexperienced in using a microphone, he said awkwardly that the 'outrages committed by dynamiters must be viewed with the deepest concern not only for the maintenance of law and order but also for the safeguarding of vital military installations in Cyprus'. He was certain the people of Cyprus shared the dismay and regret of the authorities at such 'terrorist attacks', and appealed to the local press to condemn them. An official statement followed to announce the detention of 'a number of people' in connection with the incidents.

Later, Sir Robert reported to London that the government radio station had gone back on air by 'borrowing' a small transmitter to re-establish a broadcasting service around Nicosia and Larnaca. Programmes, he said, would 'consist of mainly gramophone records and talks'.

At this stage, none knew how deeply Archbishop Makarios was involved in EOKA, nor about his relationship with Colonel Grivas, still unidentified by the authorities. Governor Armitage chose nevertheless to mobilize and put into action the forces of law and order, but, argued Field Marshal Sir John Harding, 'they were unprepared to deal with such a widespread outbreak, too weak in numbers to meet the many demands put upon them and their plans were uncoordinated'.

It was not until 18 October 1955 that a Cyprus Intelligence Committee, which included the Colonial Secretary and fluent Greek speaker John Reddaway from Government House, produced a report that concluded:

(a) EOKA is a clandestine nationalist terrorist organization which aims at leading the struggle for Enosis. It has recruited its active membership largely from middle class youth and has drawn on the former nationalist youth movement PEON.

(b) EOKA is anti-Communist, but is careful not to antagonize Turkish Cypriots. It has received material support from the Ethnarchy, from a complementary organization in Greece and sufficient popular support in Cyprus to make it impolitic for the Greek Orthodox hierarchy to condemn it openly.

(c) EOKA is believed to be led by a Greek subject of Cypriot birth. Its activities and its direction are based on experience in the Greek armed forces and the Khi organization in Greece.

(d) The virile direction exhibited by EOKA suggests other than local Cypriot influence and some additional persons of Greek nationality and Cypriots with Greek army experience have been tentatively identified in leading positions.

THAT EVENING – the first day of the EOKA conflict – Yannakis Droushiotis, Grivas's chief aide in Nicosia, gave 'The Leader' a full briefing of what had taken place, but Grivas was at a loss to understand the incompetence of his recruits. Because he had spent the greater part of his life on the mainland, it is possible that he had forgotten, in Nancy Crawshaw's words, 'certain aspects of the Cypriot national character'. He may have been dedicated to the pursuit of Hellenism and prepared to fight and give his life in the cause, but Greek Cypriots were not of that ilk. They talked about *enosis*, but were less eager to shed their blood to achieve it. At heart, they were not soldiers or disciplined by nature. Furthermore, as he would discover, they had highly developed trading instincts, which did not sit easily with Grivas.

In Larnaca, the attacks were a complete failure. The gang and its leader Poskottis were caught in the deed. Elenitsa Seraphim, who became one of EOKA's few female group leaders, heard the first Larnaca explosions. They had slightly damaged the homes of the police commissioner and the district commissioner.

She remembered: 'I awoke with a start, sat up and made the sign of the cross. The campaign had started: God help us. I jumped out of bed, threw on my dressing gown and went out on to the balcony. Everything was pitch black; the town had sunk into darkness owing to a sabotage done by EOKA to the electricity supply. Startled from their sleep, people rushed to their verandas and balconies to find out what was going on. I was a member of the National Organization of Cypriot Fighters, known by its Greek acronym of EOKA, but at that time I was in the reserves, so although I knew what was going on I did not know exactly where the bombs had been planted.'

For EOKA, the Limassol group fared little better. The attack started late, at 02.00, although Grivas had ordered Notis Petropouleas to explode his bombs at precisely 00.30. By the time Petropouleas, a former Greek soldier, got started, the police were on their guard. A section leader and several others were arrested after detonating three sticks of dynamite outside the harbour police station. They led the police to an EOKA 'safe' house that contained the group's entire arsenal, consisting of hundreds of pounds of dynamite, old mines, shells, detonators, ammunition for a light machine gun and 24 smoke grenades. A second group caused some damage to an electric generator at Episkopi, the British cantonment near Limassol, where the new British Middle East Air and Land Headquarters was under construction.

Grivas was furious on hearing how Petropouleas, code-named *Evagoras*, had failed. When the police released him soon after his arrest, 'The Leader' was convinced he had been bribed to become an informer and would lead the security forces to him. 'I am in danger in the house where I am staying. Evagoras is walking around Nicosia and is staying in a pension with his mistress. I am afraid that he is a coward,' he penned. 'I strongly suspect Evagoras is betraying us. He is a man who can do anything. He is a thief and rake and he can do everything; he can even betray his fatherland.'

Grivas immediately moved house and considered having Petropouleas killed for treachery. In the end, he was given money, false identity papers counterfeited by a village headman and policeman, for a fee of five pounds, and a one-way ticket to Beirut.

The failure of the Famagusta group was even greater. None of its planned attacks on army depots and petrol dumps had succeeded, except for a minor blast near 9 Signal Regiment's secret radio monitoring station at Ayios Nikolaos. Intending to disable the electricity generating station near Dhekelia, Modestos Panteli electrocuted himself by throwing a damp rope across the high-tension cables – which was why the lights had flickered in Nicosia at 00.30. His brother, Christofis, another EOKA man, was caught and sentenced to seven years' imprisonment.

Worse, a car loaded with bombs and EOKA leaflets had been captured and traced to Gregoris Afxentiou, Grivas's right-hand man, who was hiding near Lysi, his home village. Police had searched his house and found orders from 'Dighenis', even if they did not yet know his true identity. It was clear, however, that they were dealing with someone with a military mind – or perhaps a committee of skilled planners. Afxentiou, a former Greek Army officer, was now a wanted man with a price on his head. He would lead British troops a merry dance in the months ahead.

Although the EOKA plotters were convinced that the Island's Greek Cypriot population would throw its full weight behind the organization's violent campaign for self-determination and *enosis*, they would quickly discover that not everybody shared their aims. Overall, life in Cyprus had never been better. It was enjoying unprecedented economic prosperity and businessmen saw no reason to become a minor part of Greece, still dependent on American economic aid, where the national standard of living was barely above the poverty line.

Many other Cypriots were full members of AKEL (The Cypriot Progressive Workers' Party) which saw itself as the Communist alternative to the Church. It was deeply opposed to Western 'imperialism' and the right-wing monarchy of the mainland. Some AKEL members knew very well, too, that the EOKA leadership was virulently anti-Communist.

Hard as Droushiotis tried to play down the first night's failures, the more irritated Grivas became. According to Nancy Crawshaw, the peppery colonel wanted to find scapegoats to blame for the shortcomings and distance himself from any recriminations – 'a regular feature of EOKA operations'. He told Droushiotis that the campaign would have to become more dramatic to convince Cypriots that he was not playing games and they were either wholeheartedly on his side or ready to experience his wrath. The Communists would have to be taught a lesson for criticizing the bomb attacks. He went on to say that he had heard they were forming a militia of their own and imagined they could seize Lefka from the Turks and the British.

More than that, lied Droushiotis, they were buying arms and paying higher prices for them than EOKA. Grivas grew incandescent with rage. 'Patriots must be satisfied with moral rewards,' he shouted. In the weeks ahead, he would personally train his cadres, teach them how to use weapons, make them disciplined, instil loyalty to 'the cause' and drain them of any mercenary qualities. He was true to his word, but first the compulsive diarist had to put down his thoughts for posterity.

When eventually Grivas put pen to paper to write his memoirs after the end of the conflict, the truth about 1 April 1955 was put in the shade by the new light he threw on events. 'The attacks took the world by surprise,' he boasted, 'but none were more shocked than the British officials who ran Cyprus. Both they and their military advisers appeared stunned and panic-stricken … pathetic bleats of protest and condemnation were broadcast.'

Grivas was correct in one respect: reporters from Britain and America were arriving, after studying an atlas to find Cyprus, and filing articles to make their readers at home aware of the Island – and its location, if nothing else. Typical of these was the introduction to a piece syndicated by the Associated Press of America: 'Cyprus, a tiny Mediterranean Island famed in many a story and myth, is Greek by nature and British by flag. It is also a rich prize in the war between democracy and communism. This is the story of how the currents of nationalism and the complexities of the Cold War have turned a vital Western defense base into a potential powder keg.'

The AP's Foreign News Analyst, William L. Ryan, continued: 'An elegantly tailored gentleman with a bristling British-type mustache waved his cane and shouted a cheery greeting. '"Who was that?" I asked the British officer with whom I was riding. "That chap is a Cypriot," he replied, "but he's more British than the British. He speaks like a Briton, talks like one, dresses like and acts like one. He loves the British. And he is also one of the leaders of the campaign to throw the British out of Cyprus".'

Ryan concluded: 'This was a good demonstration of the split personality of the sunny island of Cyprus, a dot half the size of New Hampshire in the eastern Mediterranean. The Island, now a British Crown Colony, is not only caught up in the currents of nationalism, but the British withdrawal from Suez is making it a strategic nerve center in the Western defense line. And with the pushing and pulling of many forces, the shadow of terrorism is moving slowly over the Island.'

CHAPTER TWO

The mapping of Cyprus by the 'insufferable' British

| *'Everything will come to him who waits.'* |
| Eastern proverb |

CRAFTSMAN DUDLEY MARTIN from Kent flicked through a travel brochure when he heard his National Service would take him to Aphrodite's Island. How his friends would envy his posting: 'Cyprus: Blue sea, hot sun, vineyards, olive groves and orange, lemon and grapefruit plantations. Honeydew and gigantic watermelons everywhere. Donkeys walking slowly circuiting wells and, of course, elsewhere the monotonous chuff-chuff of the one-lung Lister engines drawing up water.'

After battling terrorism in service in Malaya, Major William Clare Harrison was unsure about Cyprus. He had arrived in January 1955 without preconceptions. His superiors had told him he was long overdue a rest. Fair enough, he thought, he would accept the boredom of office routine for a while and master hula hooping, which he was told was all the rage among those who wanted to keep their weight down. There were those who politely referred to him as 'eccentric'. Others, less flattering, said he was 'reckless and unpredictable', a 'loose canon' in fact.

Three months before the start of the EOKA conflict, neither Harrison or Martin would find the Island matched their expectations any more than those of the first British soldiers sent to occupy Cyprus 77 years earlier: they had found Cyprus a mess when they took over. They found a population of 180,000 Greeks and 46,000 Turks, all living in the Middle Ages and, with few exceptions, extremely poor. The judicial system was corrupt. There was only one half-good road – it connected Nicosia and Larnaca – practically no bridges, no postal system, few schools, ravaged forests, and harbours in poor condition. Agriculture was old-fashioned and there was a lack of knowledge about hygiene. To remedy the situation would be no easy task.

'The possession of Cyprus, combined with that of Malta and Gibraltar, makes the Mediterranean as completely a British lake as the Black Sea was a Russian one. An unbroken

Major William 'Bomber' Harrison, MBE, GM, of the Royal Army Ordnance Corps.

communication with India, a powerful hold upon Western Asia, Turkey protected, Egypt secured, Russia virtually checkmated, the command of the Levant, the supremacy of the Mediterranean – all hang upon the possession of one little nook of earth,' suggested the *New York Times*, adding a qualification that would prove truer than the writer probably ever imagined. 'Should England succeed in holding it, she will attain a position which even the annexation of Egypt could never have given her; *but it is more than doubtful that she will be suffered to do so unchallenged.*'

On 12 July 1878 Vice Admiral John Hay rode his stallion imperiously ahead of a column of 53 dust-covered, sweating Royal Marines, armed only with Martini Henry rifles. They had covered mile after mile by foot, carts and donkeys to reach Nicosia on the only track which connected the capital to the southern port of Larnaca, the birthplace of Zenon, the Stoic philosopher who taught in Athens in the fourth century BCE. Noah's grandson Khittium founded the oldest city in Cyprus, after whom it was originally called.

Hay and his Marines were accompanied by two mules, each 'laden with sacks of new sixpences' to pay the salaries of the Turkish civil servants, who would now work for new masters. The Admiral carried a *firman* (an edict in Turkish) or directive from the British Prime Minister Benjamin Disraeli and Sultan Abdul 'The Damned' of the Sublime Porte in Istanbul by which the Island passed from Ottoman control to the British.

Twelve days earlier, he, as commander of a Royal Navy squadron at Suda Bay in Crete, had received a telegram from the Admiralty in London, ordering him to Cyprus. He immediately set out for the Island on board HMS *Minotaur*, accompanied by HMS *Raleigh*. The British had long eyed Cyprus for its strategic value. As far back as 1814, the East Indian Company representative John Kinneir had advised London: 'The possession of Cyprus would give to England a preponderating influence in the Mediterranean, and a place at her disposal the future destinies of the Levant. Egypt and Syria would soon become her tributaries, and she would acquire an overawing position in respect to Asia Minor, by which the Porte might at all times be kept in check, and the encroachments of Russia, in the quarter, retarded, if not prevented ... It is of easy defence. Under a liberal government, it would, in a very short space of time, amply repay the charge of its own establishment, and afford the most abundant supplies to our fleets at a trifling expense.'

On 8 July Reuter's news agency told London: 'Her Majesty's ships *Invincible* and *Raleigh* are cruising off Cyprus, and Lord John Hay's squadron has been sighted near Larnaca. There is no confirmation, however, of the rumour that it has entered the port.' Rear-Admiral Commerell, while in one of the boats of his flagship near Gallipoli, was caught in a sudden storm. Three of the boat's crew drowned, and the Admiral himself narrowly escaped. The next day orders were received in Malta for the 42nd, 71st, and 101st Regiments to embark for Cyprus immediately. The first ship to leave was the transport *Canara,* which carried Indian sappers and miners to prepare for the reception of British troops. The 25th Madras Regiment was also under orders to join them.

The Times editorialized: 'Cyprus has gone through the usual vicissitudes of places over which conquest after conquest has rolled. The Greek, the Roman, the Saracen, the Crusader, the Genoese, the Venetian, and the Turk have all in turn been its masters and woven its name into the literature of Europe. They have all used it for purposes of conquest, and for little else. The idea that the masters of a dependency should look to the welfare of its people is a modern addition to political morality, and the light of it has never shone on Cyprus.

'The Crusaders employed it as a resting-place, the Italian Republics as a source of wealth, and the Turks as a place for the production of revenue. As the Ottoman Empire has made little change in its fiscal practices, Cyprus lives under a system admirably fitted for stifling human energy, and the Island is in much the same state as it was generations ago. But now everything will be changed. The strength, the quietude, and the security of British public will provide capital to the place and offer a rich field for commercial enterprise ... In fact, the best news, which Cyprus has ever heard in the course of its long history, is that it has now passed under the rule of England.

'The Mussulman as well as the Christian part of the population cannot fail to rejoice over the arrival of an English Governor as nations do when delivered from foreign occupation. Cyprus will now be able to profit by some of the prosperity that has come to Western lands, which were peopled by wandering tribes when it had already a considerable place in history.'

Even as Hay and his men were about to enter Nicosia's walled city, the United States was eyeing the Island as a place to develop its interests. Americans had already established friendly relations with the Porte in Istanbul, were teaching Turks at the Robert College and establishing businesses. *The Globe*, a minor American newspaper, was now so excited by Britain's acquisition that it hollered: 'The policy which is to emerge from the Eastern chaos is one that will make the name of England from Constantinople to Calcutta.' In treating the subject of Cyprus, it added a compliment to the genius and enterprise of America by saying: 'It is not without truth that America lays claim to a greater daring in conception than the inhabitants of the Old World' and went on to discuss the possibilities for US expansion to rival that of the Island's new rulers.

Adding weight to the argument that Cyprus was ripe for the picking, the *New York Times*

correspondent in London reported: 'Already I hear of English engineers, prospectors and "merchant venturers" starting for Cyprus and the next few weeks will find America duly represented among the crowd who will migrate thither to have dealings under the guarantee of a British protectorate. Cyprus will wake up to find itself busy with new works. Englishmen will work her minerals. Americans will possibly look up its cotton growing plains. The Island has capacities for agricultural work and a fund of other underdeveloped resources.

'The security of the British administration will encourage new commercial relationships ... The influence of England, from a "shopkeeping" point of view cannot fail to be highly beneficial to the miscellaneous people who will now gradually come under a civilizing and just rule, which must have a good effect upon Turkey in Europe.'

Maria Roussou-Sinclair, a Greek Cypriot researcher, who studied the Island's development of the tourist industry, pointed out: 'Even Thomas Cook sent a special commissioner to the island after the British take-over, in order to discover Cyprus' touristic potential, due to the fact that "the enquiries we have received respecting Cyprus are so numerous".'

British author R. Hamilton Lang in his work *Cyprus: Its History, Its Present Resources and Future Prospects*, enthused: 'A field is open at once for solicitors, builders, surveyors, architects, engineers, farmers, stable keepers, dealers, merchants etc., who will be quickly followed by tram, railway, harbour and other contractors, manufacturers, and professional men of every description, who ought to take some competent workmen, employees and assistants with them, as the natives will not be of much service to the colonists until taught.'

For W. Hepworth Dixon, in his book, *British Cyprus*, the Island opened the way 'for British energy and enterprise to develop its many resources, and work its mines of gold and silver and its caves of jasper and agate'. Hardly a thought was given to the interests of Cypriots or any understanding of the two main communities' differences, especially on the matter of religion, which previous visitors had noted and sometimes condemned.

After his visit to Nicosia in 1873, the Austrian Archduke Louis Salva wrote: 'Great is the contrast between the town and its surroundings, and greater still between the objects within the city. There are Venetian fortifications by the side of Gothic edifices surmounted by the Crescent, on antique Classic soil. Turks, Greeks and Armenians, dwell intermingled, bitter enemies at heart, and united solely by their love for the land of their birth.'

In 1815, William Turner, a British diplomat had observed: 'These Greek priests, every-where the vilest miscreants in human nature, are worse than usual in Cyprus from the power they possess. They strip the poor ignorant, superstitious peasant of his last para [Ottoman currency], and when he is on his deathbed, make him leave his all to their convent, promising that Masses shall be said for his soul.'

Turner's view was supported by Domingo Badia y Leyblich, a Catalan traveller. He wrote: 'These [the bishops] parade in their houses and followers a princely luxury. They never go out without a crowd of attendants, and to ascend a flight of stairs they must needs be carried by their servants.' He also said: 'The Greeks are extremely submissive and respectful towards their bishops. In saluting them, they bow low, take off their cap, and hold it before them upside down. They scarcely dare speak in their presence.'

Sir Harry Luke explained the power of the Orthodox Church over the Greek-speaking Christian populace, when he wrote: 'During the Ottoman regime, the Archbishop repre-sented to his own flock on a smaller scale that which the Patriarch of Constantinople repre-sented to the generality of the Orthodox in Turkey. That is to say, he was not only the spiritual chief of the Cypriots; he became the ethnarch, the political and national represen-tative of his people in its relations with the Ottoman Government. By an astonishing reversal of fortune the Archbishop of Cyprus, whose office had been created by the Turks after lying dormant for 300 years, secured in the course of the 17th and 18th centuries the supreme power and authority over the Island, and at one period wielded influence greater than that of the Turkish Pasha himself.'

Hepworth Dixon added: 'The Turks also tolerated their tardiness in paying their local taxes. Although the native Turks paid regu-larly and punctually, the Orthodox Greeks were very often in arrears. The Turks never forced the Greeks to settle their arrears on time; instead, they tried to obtain the money by making terms with the Archbishop of Cyprus ... The Church in Cyprus was a free democracy under Turkish rule.'

Only when Greece began its war of libera-tion from the Turks in 1821 and the Orthodox Church began to stir up trouble against them in Cyprus, did the Ottomans decide the priests had over-stepped their mark and they would not be tolerated any longer. Kutchuk Mehmet, the Turkish Governor, with the approval of the Sublime Porte, closed the gates of Nicosia on 9 July, rounded up Archbishop Kyprianos and the Bishops of Paphos, Kition and Kyrenia, together with several other clerics, and used his Janissaries (mercenaries) to execute them in public. Sir Harry Luke later wrote: 'The hierarch paid a terrible penalty for its abuse of power.' Reverend Jacob Berggren, a Swede, on his way to the Holy Land, witnessed this dispro-portionate Turkish vengeance as hundreds of Christians were encouraged to rise up in support of the rebellious mainland Greeks. 'The Panayia was everywhere covered in black, many houses lay empty and splashed in blood,' he recorded. 'Almost every day was marked with executions and murders and wherever I went I saw executioners with hands covered in blood.'

AS HAY'S Marines in their deep blue uniforms reached Nicosia, a junior officer gave the order for them to march, backs straight, chests out, holding their heads high. Followed by his column, Hay purposefully clip-clopped towards the Kyrenia Gate, one of the capital's three entrances. During their occupation, the Venetians had called them Paphos, Famagusta and Kyrenia, each gate's size determined by the importance of their city namesakes.

Horoz Ali was there, waiting to open it for the latest rulers. He was renowned for his reliability and had been warned to expect the British, and here they were. Nicknamed 'The Cock' for always rising early, Ali glanced at Sultan Mahmoud's monogram above the Gate and quietly read the Arabic script: 'O Mohammad, give these tidings to the Faithful; Victory is from God and triumph is very near. O opener of the doors, open for us the best of doors.' Had he looked closer, Ali would have noticed the Venetians had left their mark, too: *Porta de la Proveditore*. The British entered peacefully and unopposed.

At the Ottoman Seraglio, not far from the Paphos Gate, Bessim Pasa, the Island's last Turkish Governor, surrendered the city to Admiral Hay. Harry Rawson, the Captain of HMS *Minotaur*, had been sent ahead to check whether force would be needed to take over the capital. Not that the Turkish garrison in Cyprus could have, even it had wanted, fought off the British: it consisted of a mere 100 artillerymen and 300 *nizamis* (regular infantrymen). To guard Nicosia, there were less than 100 locally recruited soldiers, none of whom were ever expected to fight at home or abroad. *The Times* reported: 'Cyprus can be counted as one of the luckiest provinces of the

Captain Harry Rawson, RN, of HMS *Minotaur*, raises the Union Flag in Nicosia, on 12 July 1878, watched by Vice Admiral John Hay.

Turkish Empire in never having suffered the calamities of any war.'

Now, exactly at 17.00, friendly Cypriots witnessed the small Marine contingent present arms as Rawson lowered the Turkish Ottoman flag and raised in its place the Union flag, on behalf of Queen Victoria, watched by Hay. The flag would flutter over the capital for the next 82 years, sometimes limply, a visible symbol to Cypriots, like Horoz Ali, that they had been absorbed into the British Empire and 'the government administered on behalf of Her Majesty'.

A few days later, Captain Rawson wrote in his diary: 'Here I am, installed as the first English Commandant of Nicosia, and a fine lot of work I have had getting things in order and settled down. Such a baking hot 22 miles between Larnaka and Nicosia I never came across. We have been having the thermometer at 97°, 98°, and twice 108° inside a thick-walled house. Tomorrow (22 July) I go down to Larnaka with the Admiral, and the new Governor (Sir Garnet Wolseley) is expected to arrive.

'I had the honor of hoisting the flag, and have since worked very hard. I sent in my report, which pleased the Admiral very much, and surprised the Secretary of the Government out here by the amount of information it contained, procured in such a short time. My trips backwards and forwards between Nicosia and Larnaka surprise them most. They cannot understand how I go on without sleep for so long without being knocked up. In 10 days I have had 40 hours sleep. Every night at 11 o'clock I go around the whole city by myself.'

Because Britain had sided with Turkey against Czarist Russia at the Congress of Berlin, Sultan Abdul-ul-Hamid had agreed to lease the Island to the British in return for an annual rent of £92,799 11s. 3d. A future governor of Cyprus wrote that the haggling to settle this figure had 'all that scrupulous exactitude characteristic of faked accounts'. The Sultan's government was bankrupt, disorganized and the country was full of starving refugees from the Balkans. The situation in Istanbul was not much better than in the interior. The Sultan had already concentrated the administration of the government in the palace and begun 'to gather around him the sort of adventurers who have since been the great curse of the empire', an American visitor reported.

To 'persuade' the Sultan not to prevaricate about signing the agreement, which was clearly in his interest, HMS *Minotaur* dropped anchor off Istanbul and trained its cannon on the city. The British, not fully aware of conditions in Cyprus, only wanted the Island as a fortress to safeguard their interests in the East, whatever they declared in public. The agreement's terms were set out clearly and, at first,

contained two articles to which an annex was added and signed by the both sides elaborating the conditions relating to the British administration of Cyprus.

According to the first article, signed on 4 June, Great Britain was guaranteeing to 'join His imperial Majesty the Sultan in defending by force of arms if Russia at any future time attempts to take possession of any further Turkish territories in Asia and in return, in order to enable England to make necessary provision for executing Her engagement, the Sultan further consents, to assign the island of Cyprus to be occupied and administered by England'.

The annex was approved on 1 July. Its most important part was Article 6 which would be used by the Turks during the EOKA conflict to argue its case for the return of the Island. The article said: '... if Russia restores to Turkey Kars and other conquests in Armenia during the last war, the Island of Cyprus will be evacuated by England and the convention of the 4th of June, 1878, will be at an end'. The provinces to which the article referred were returned to Turkey by Russia in 1917, but Britain did not evacuate and hand back Cyprus.

After signing the Cyprus Convention of Defensive Alliance with the Turkish Government, the Prime Minister, Lord Beaconsfield (formerly Benjamin Disraeli), declared in the House of Lords on 18 July 1878: 'I only hope that the House will not misunderstand – and I think the country will not misunderstand – our motives in occupying Cyprus, and in encouraging those intimate relations with the Government and population of Turkey. They are not motives of war: they are operations of peace and of civilization ... In taking Cyprus, the movement is not Mediterranean, it is Indian. If that be our first consideration, our next is the development of the country. We have taken a step there, which we think necessary for the maintenance of our Empire, and for its preservation in peace.' Long before Disraeli entered politics, he had visited the Island and in 1847 penned *Tancred*, a novel in which his intentions are voiced by one of his fictional characters: 'The British want Cyprus and will get it.'

And get it the British did – at a cost to the Cypriots. Between 1878 and 1914, local taxes were collected less to pay for improvements and more to cover the costs of the Island's lease from the Ottomans. The young Winston Churchill was one of the few British politicians who argued against the local people's financial burden. He declared: 'We have no right whatever, except by *force majeure*, to take a penny of the Cyprus tribute to relieve us from our own just obligations, however contracted. There is scarcely any spectacle more detestable than the oppression of a small community by a Great Power for the purpose of pecuniary profit.'

ON 22 JULY 1878, Lieutenant General Sir Garnet Wolseley KCB, GCMG, who had been appointed the first Lord High Commissioner, reached Larnaca on HMS *Himalaya*. With him came an expeditionary force sent to occupy the Island. It comprised the 42nd Royal Highland Regiment, the Black Watch, including 31 Field Company Royal Engineers, led by Major J. R. M. Chard, VC, a survey detachment commanded by a young Lieutenant (later Lord) Horatio Herbert Kitchener, and several troops from an Indian regiment. The force totalled more than 1,100 men. They had been transported from Malta and were brought ashore in a convoy of long boats by Hay's advance party of Royal Marines, supervised by HRH the Duke of Edinburgh, who officiated as Beachmaster. Officially they were the first Imperial troops to land in Cyprus since Richard The Lionheart.

For the General, a soldier with a distinguished military career, and his troops, all battle-scarred veterans who had fought wars in far-flung outposts of Empire and the Russians in the Crimea, it was an unusual experience to take over a foreign country without having to fire a shot in anger.

Wolseley soon afterwards toured the port city, liked what he saw and wanted to lease a house there, but could not settle terms with the owner, Ricardo Matthei, in all appearance a Greek Cypriot, but with Italian roots that made him a member of the Latin Church. Had agreement been reached between the two men, it is likely that Larnaca, not Nicosia, would have been the Island capital during British rule as it was home for most foreign consulates.

Wolseley immediately proclaimed how Queen Victoria intended to rule: 'It is Her Majesty's gracious pleasure that the Government of Cyprus shall be administered without favour to any race or creed, that equal justice shall be done to all, that all shall enjoy alike the equal and imperial protection of the law, and that no measures shall be neglected which may tend to advance the moral and material welfare of the people.

'And it is the express desire of the Queen that in the administration of public affairs regard shall be paid to the reasonable wishes of the inhabitants with respect to the maintenance of their ancient institutions, usages and customs provided that they be consistent with just and good Government and with those principles of civilization and liberty which must always and everywhere be upheld by those who govern in Her Majesty's name.'

Bishop Kyprianos of Kitium responded with an address of welcome and served notice of Greek Cypriot intentions: 'We accept the change of Government in as much as we trust that Great Britain will help Cyprus, as it did the Ionian Islands, to be united with mother Greece, with which it is naturally connected.' His remarks appear to have gone unnoticed by the new occupiers. They did not see the Island as having anything to do with the mainland.

Sir George Hill in his *History of Cyprus* emphasized: 'At no time has the Island of Cyprus been a constituent part of Hellenic Greece. It was absorbed along with but as an integral part of Greece by the Byzantine Empire.' Looking further back, Sir Harry Luke observed: 'As early history comes gradually into focus we see the Island's cosmopolitan character taking shape, influenced by Crete and Mycenae on the west, Cilicia and Phoenicia on the north and east, Egypt in the south. It received something of the cultures, arts and languages of three continents. But there was little fusion. Politically, until there came the artificial unity imposed by collective allegiance either to Persia or to Alexander the Great and his successors and finally Rome, ancient Cyprus was parcelled out among the rulers of small independent kingdoms, some Greek in civilization and language, others Phoenician ...'

The zenith of Greek influence had been in the fifth century BCE, when the Island contained 11 Greek city kingdoms, which eventually came under Rome. When Rome broke apart, Cyprus became a minor province in the Byzantine Empire, the seat of which was Constantinople. To suggest Byzantium was Greek was comparable to saying an orange was a pear because both were fruit.

Before the troops spread out, the Army established a camp at Pasa Ciftligi, near Larnaca's Salt Lake. Indian *sepoys* were left to carry out much of the construction, while the rest of the force began its long, hot march to the capital, accompanied by William Palmer, a correspondent for *The Times*. On the way several British soldiers experienced fits and collapsed, and one died of heat exhaustion, unused to the high temperatures of Cyprus in mid-summer. Sergeant McGaw, VC, was one of those who died of heat apoplexy. (There will be more about him later.)

Many soldiers still wore the heavy red coats of the British Army, which were completely unsuitable. It would be seven years before they would be issued with lightweight khaki uniforms made from cotton. A month after they came ashore, more than half were dead, victims of a malaria epidemic that swept through their ranks. Even the Indians found conditions in Cyprus too much and they were eventually sent back to the south of their own country. By the time the Black Watch left Cyprus, the highland regiment was reduced to an establishment of 693 of all ranks.

High Commissioner Garnet Wolseley arrived in Nicosia on 23 July and again raised the Union flag after it had been consecrated at a local convent and paraded the Regiment as an unnecessary show of strength at a public ceremony. It was the very day Sergeant McGaw, VC, one of the regiment's legendary heroes, died.

Captain Rawson, the Military Commandant of Nicosia, wrote: 'I do not suppose I shall remain much longer in Cyprus, as our

Lieutenant General Sir Garnet Wolseley KCB, GCMG, rides into Nicosia, accompanied by the Black Watch and Indian *sepoys*.

On 17 August 1878, with the British visibly in control of Nicosia, the Black Watch marched Turkish criminal prisoners to Kyrenia Castle, for holding before being transported to jails in Turkey.

[the Marines'] work is nearly done.' He set sail from the Island two weeks later on HMS *Minotaur*, leaving behind a large fleet off Larnaca. It consisted of *Monarch*, *Invincible*, *Black Prince*, *Raleigh*, *Salamis*, *Foxhound*, the troopships *Himalaya*, *Tamar* and *Orontes*, and 20 hired transports. With British rule visibly established, the Black Watch marched out on 17 August, with a line of chained Turkish criminals from the Central Prison for incarceration in Kyrenia Castle, while two companies moved to Paphos.

THE AMBITIOUS Wolseley hated his role as an administrator and made no secret of the fact. 'I feel like an eagle that has had his wings clipped,' he said. It was not until the war in Egypt in 1882 that he was able to put what he believed were his true talents to the full test again and able to soar back into full flight. He had lived through the Indian Mutiny with the 90th Light Infantry in Cawnpore and Lucknow and, during the Burma War, led a desperate charge while wounded. His cavalier attitude to danger was in evidence again at the siege of Sevastapol in 1855, where, attached to the Royal Engineers 'in the post of greatest danger', he was wounded by a bursting shell, losing the sight of his right eye. Posted to Canada in 1861, with the rank of Colonel, he was given his first independent command at the Red River Campaign of 1869-70. It was here that he managed to crush Louis Riel's rebellion with a minimum of bloodshed. It showed him to be a master of careful planning and preparation, giving rise to the Cockney expression 'All Sir Garnet'.

For every critic, there were twice as many who lavished him with praise. Charles Rathuone-Low, a contemporary author, glowed with pride when he penned: 'Critics who cannot gainsay Sir Garnet Wolseley's capacity, and rivals who view his success with an unworthy feeling of jealousy, speak of him as "a very lucky man". But truth should compel them, to own that he has forced his way to the forefront of his profession by sheer hard work and good service, without adventitious aid, or the exercise on his behalf of interest or favouritism, and that he has chained Fortune to his chariot-wheels by seizing every opportunity to win her favours. It was no "luck" that induced him, when all appeared lost, to volunteer to lead two storming-parties in one day, in Burma, or that led him, after storming the Mess-house, according to Lord Clyde's orders, to break through the Motee Mahul, and be the first to make an entrance into the Lucknow Residency. These deeds were the result of courage and enterprise. Again, it was no "luck" that induced him, when suffering from wounds and ill-health, to remain throughout that dreary winter in the trenches at Sebastopol, where, as an officer writes to us, "he showed the highest capacity as a military engineer in the siege operations".'

Embittered by being brushed over to fight in the Afghan campaign and disgruntled by his appointment in Cyprus, Wolseley was nevertheless determined to brand the Island with what he saw as British discipline and law and order. Not a person gifted with great imagination and understanding, there was only one correct form of behaviour and that was the British way. The British knew what was right and what was wrong. Cypriots must learn to behave like them under the Union flag. A statement of his in 1882 provided an insight to his character. During a debate in the House of Lords about whether or not there should be a Channel tunnel, he said the very notion was anathema. He fumed: 'Surely John Bull will not endanger his birthright, his liberty, his property, simply in order that men and women may cross between England and France without running the risk of sea sickness.'

John Bull was Wolseley's role model, and he had harsh words for both Turk and Greek alike. 'I had always heard the Turk was a clever diplomatist but of all the good bargains he has ever made this one about Cyprus is much the best,' he blustered. 'He takes all the plums out of the island, throws upon us the responsibility of governing well, which means large expenditures, while he reserves to himself the power to sell three fourth of the area of the island and insists on our paying him a large sum annually as a rent for the estate he has ruined.'

He continued: 'There is an air of decay about the place that tells one that it is an apanage of Turkey's Sultan. Wherever one goes here is the same. The face of the Island is stamped with relics of a past prosperity that has been destroyed by the Muslims. It is said that wherever the horse of the Turk treads nothing will ever grow afterwards.'

Wolseley showed no more respect for the people committed to his charge than the previous rulers whom he readily despised. Looking down from his high office, he

Sir Garnet Wolseley receives a delegation of Cypriot Turks 'of influence' to celebrate the Muslim festival of *Bayram* in August 1878.

observed that the locals were 'a wretched lot as far as I can learn, but what can be expected of a people bred under such a form of slavery and ground down as they have been by masters who did not even care to conceal the contempt in which they held them'.

If the Island's Muslim Turks did not match up to his high standards nor did the Greeks and their religious ceremonies. The Greek Orthodox Mass, he declared, was 'a mockery of everything sacred', involving 'dirty greasy priests attempting to intone some dreary dirges that were utterly devoid of music or melody'. He felt the service was far too long and criticized the congregation, whom he said, 'advanced to the screen which hides the altar and kissed the pictures of the Virgin and of some ugly-looking saints'.

With the arrival of the British, life changed visibly in Cyprus. Even the cocks crowed at unaccustomed hours, according to a writer of the period.

AFTER TAKING control of Larnaca and raising the Union flag in Nicosia, Royal Navy warships sailed for Kyrenia. When the first naval officers went ashore, large crowds came out to greet them at the quayside of the harbour. The Greek Cypriot historian Georgios Georgiou records: 'Waves of people

Kyrenia harbour photographed in 1878 by John Thompson, FRGS. Taken from his book, *Through Cyprus with a Camera*.

The Selimiye Mosque, originally the Roman Catholic Ayia Sofia Church of Nicosia, another of John Thompson's 1878 photographs.

inundated the area in front of the Castle, wondering at the events and applauding the smart English officers in their gold-trimmed uniforms and glittering swords. Smiling complacently, the officers scattered silver coins, which reflected in the July sun as they fell among the groups of shouting children, who were delighted by the happenings, dancing and cheering ... The Turkish people, so masterful and proud, accepted the momentous change fatalistically and in a twinkling of an eye became a quiet and orderly element.' He added, however, that some cried, aware that their complete domination of the Island was no more.

Another Greek Cypriot writer, Rita Catselli, declared: 'The Greeks celebrated the change because they expected from the British not occupation, but union with Greece. Most people recalled that this same great power only 14 years previously had ceded the whole of the Ionian Islands to Greece.'

To promote *enosis*, the Greeks grabbed the opportunity to launch Kyrenia's first newspaper, *O Raylas*, modelled on Athens' *O Romios*. It was virulently anti-British and anti-Turk. George Stavrides, the editor, claimed his people were 'doubly enslaved' and deserved to be freed to rejoin 'the Motherland'. He certainly raised the standard of nationalism in the community, leading to many Greek Kyrenians joining the mainland army in Crete in 1896 and fighting in the war against the Turks in 1897. They were hailed as 'worthy descendants of the ancient Greeks' and deserved 'wreaths of violets from the glorious fields of the Valley of Ferrrae', where one of them died in battle.

Captain F. W. H. Hobeach, the first District Commissioner, arrived on 1 August 1878. He brought with him 900 soldiers of the 42nd Highlanders. Among them were Gurkhas from Nepal. Some soldiers never returned home, dying from heatstroke and malaria. They included James McDonald, George Marr, James Barrye and Stephen Truebridge. All rest in the local English cemetery. Their commander was Colonel Andrew Scott Stevenson, whose wife, Esme, became the first British lady to take up residence in the town. She recorded her memoirs and these were published in 1880 under the simple title of *Our Home In Cyprus*.

She told the amusing story of a Greek called Ttooulis. For some alleged sin, the local Orthodox bishop had ordered the man to go naked everywhere and eat only raw food as a penance. He did as he was bid, but Esme's husband thought the man's nudity was an affront to female sensibilities. He had him detained in the Castle. While there, the British officer tried to encourage the said Ttooulis to lead a 'normal life', providing him with fresh clothing and prepared meals.

'No, no, I cannot accept,' replied Ttooulis, fearing the wrath of his Church more than the might of Queen Victoria's representative. He stripped off his shirt and trousers again, refused the food and fled. There followed many sightings of the naked man throughout the Island for several months. What happened to him eventually is not recorded, but Greek Cypriots have kept his memory alive to this day. 'You're a real *Ttooulis*,' they say of anyone they think stupid.

Like Wolseley, Colonel Scott Stevenson was a stickler for discipline. He did not hesitate to use the whip he carried to strike any official of whom he disapproved. The Turkish Mayor of Kyrenia was among those who felt the sting of the lash for not immediately and rigidly applying the new British rules. Eventually, the British officer became a victim of those same rules. A Cypriot, after having his bottom whipped, took him to court, where the local magistrate found him guilty of an unprovoked attack and he was fined.

Mrs Scott Stevenson appears to have been slightly more intelligent than her husband for she noticed some of the incompetence of their masters in London towards their new acquisition. Looking out from the 'small but cool house in a shady garden, occupied by the Duke of Edinburgh for a few weeks' from which he watched the landing of stores and troops on their arrival in Kyrenia, she noted, 'there are still large quantities of unused stores. On the beach I saw, I should think, over one thousand large iron coal-boxes piled up in one corner, where they had lain for eleven months. They were not made to fit one within the other, and so had filled the entire hold of HMS *Humber*, the vessel dispatched from England with this *most useful* cargo. Were it not true, as I have heard, that in spite of example, the *same thing has since been repeated in the Zulu War*, one could not

conceive that a person could exist so entirely ignorant as to advise Government to send out such utterly useless articles to an Island where not only it is impossible to use coal (there are no fireplaces), but without any means of transport for such unwieldy objects. It requires four men to carry a single box a few yards. But this is not all. I have it on the highest authority that several hundred *warming-pans* were also sent out for the use of the troops. Can any one imagine the folly of such a thing, with the thermometer at one hundred and twenty degrees?'

Unfortunately the Scott Stevensons left the Island uniformly disliked by the local people, but to their credit, they remembered the death of the first British soldier in Cyprus, Sergeant McGaw, VC. He had been buried in a hurry, close to where he died, and a wooden cross

Sergeant Sam McGaw, VC, of the Black Watch, the first British soldier to be buried in Cyprus.

Today Sergeant McGaw's tomb rests in the old British Cemetery in Kyrenia.

was erected to mark the spot. Colonel Wauchope conducted the burial, as the Regimental Chaplain was unavailable.

Three years later, on hearing that a Greek farmer had removed the marker and ploughed the land over the soldier's grave, Colonel Scott Stevenson, formerly of the Black Watch, traced the site, exhumed McGaw's remains, placed them in a coffin and brought them to Kyrenia. There, covered with a Union Flag and carried by six Turkish *Zaptiehs* (policemen) the VC holder was reburied in the English Cemetery. According to the records of the regiment, his sarcophagus in Kyrenia was one 'of Byzantine splendour'. Mrs Scott Stevenson decorated the grave with wreaths of passion flowers and jasmine.

His men wrote the following doggerel in his memory:

The rain may rain and the snaw may snaw
The wind may blaw and the cock may craw
But ye canna frichten Jock M'Gaw
He's the stoutest man in the Forty-Twa.
The Ashantees,
When they saw the shanks of Jock McGaw
They turned about and fled awa'

No. 141 Sergeant Samuel McGaw of the 42nd Royal Highlanders had won his VC for bravery in the African Ashanti War and received it from Queen Victoria at Osborne Castle in the Isle of Wight on 18 April 1874.

While stationed in Kyrenia, the Black Watch guarded the Turkish convicts confined in the Castle, where prison cells were always full and the gallows kept busy. Some convicts were put to work cutting stones for the harbour's new mole. The Regiment left Cyprus for Gibraltar on 9 November 1878.

Kyrenia Castle was also the place where the new administration began training its reformed police force, a combination of Greek and Cypriot Turks, supposedly an incorruptible body of men, to maintain civil law and order. Under the Ottomans, the 275 policemen were exclusively Turks commanded by a Turkish Army Major, whom the British replaced with General Sir H. Brackenbury, PC, GCB, as Chief Commandant of Police and Inspector of Prisons, with a British Officer as local Commandant in each district. Police were no longer to collect taxes and were told they were responsible only for stopping crime and arresting suspects. They were to be known as 'The Cyprus Military Police'. By the end of 1879. The force had been expanded to 17 officers, 390 rank and file policeman and 220 troopers, distributed in the six districts of the Island.

Despite Britain's efforts to develop Kyrenia, the local population failed to respond. In 1910, it was still no more than a village by the sea. There were only 1,336 inhabitants, according to the official census: 830 Greeks, 487 Turks and 19 British. 'Now Kyrenia harbour, or the Shipbreaker, as our sailors call it, not only fails to provide a refuge for ships in distress, but more often than not is itself responsible for great financial losses,' wrote Georgios Stavrides in 1911. 'And all this because the malice and disagreements among the parties prevent us from working together for all ... No one cares the slightest about the promotion of trade, industry, agriculture or the improvement of communications ...' In due course, the British community of Kyrenia would become the largest in Cyprus, but rather than seeing the latest arrivals as contributors to the local economy, young Greek Cypriot nationalists considered them 'insufferable', complaining that 'they brought an atmosphere of their own country with them and were unable to understand the local people.

Nevertheless, by early 1879, The Lord High Commissioner Sir Garnet Wolseley was proclaiming 'Cyprus is going to be a great success ... Laugh at any one who tells you Cyprus is not going to be a complete success.'

By then he headed the local Executive Council that consisted of the Chief Secretary, the Queen's Advocate, the Senior Officer in charge of the troops and the Receiver-General, with, as 'additional members', two Greeks, Mr Glykys and Mr Riccardo Matthei (the same Larnaca landlord from whom the Wolseleys had wanted to rent a house) and one Turk, Mustapha Faid Effendi. There was also a Legislative Council of six non-elected members and 12 elected members, three from the Turkish community and nine Christian inhabitants, who could be British subjects, foreigners who had resided five years or more in Cyprus, or Ottoman subjects.

The work of the councils involved conversion of tithes, a customs tariff, the reorganization of the judicial system, including the appointment of a Chief Justice and Puisne Judge, questions connected with the stamp duties, game licences, and other matters of administration and social order. They were always divided by argument, and usually left the last word to Kitchener who was also Commander-in-Chief of the Army. However much he may have wanted to progress needed reforms, because Cyprus was only leased from Turkey, he was hampered by having to work within the boundaries of existing Ottoman Laws and Penal Code. In addition, Parliament was not keen to use British taxes to subsidize Cypriots. Despite his efforts to be unbiased, Greek Cypriots protested most British actions, while Turks cooperated fully and so were often advantaged.

Charles Rathuone-Low observed: 'Of course, where abuses and intrigue had flourished from time immemorial, there were complaints, but these were due either to disappointed adventurers who, at the time of the British occupation, descended upon the island like a cloud of its indigenous locusts; or to those inhabitants having Hellenic aspirations, who thought that by vilifying British administration they would promote the annexation of the island to Greece, as was done in the case of the Ionian Islands. But the people could not be brought to abet these intriguers, and the obvious reply to those who wished to substitute the rule of the King of the Hellenes for that of the Queen of England was to point to the reforms carried into effect with such striking results for their well being. Such were the reductions in the taxation, and the abolition of all export duties; the removal of the onerous restrictions on the wine trade, and the equalization and reduction of the tax for military exemption.'

In Limassol, Colonel Warren, the first district commissioner, fared better than Wolseley in his relations with the Greek community in his area. From the moment he took charge, the town showed visible improvements. Work began to pave the road to Nicosia at a cost of £350 per mile and a daily rate of 1 shilling for labourers. Even today, Greek Cypriots praise his efforts to have roads cleaned and repaired, wandering animals removed, trees planted and, most importantly, the docks developed to allow ships to be loaded and unloaded without having to anchor offshore. During the first years of British occupation, a post office, a telegraph office and a hospital began to operate, followed by hotels for tourists. The place began to prosper commercially, unlike Kyrenia. By 1912, Limassol was alight with electricity.

FOR THE British administration in 1878, one of the first priorities was to have Cyprus properly mapped. On his arrival, Wolseley had been astonished that the maps left behind by the Ottomans were not worth the paper on which they were scrawled. Captain Horatio

Kitchener, the 28-year-old Royal Engineers officer, who had come ashore with the High Commissioner, was given the job of putting matters right. The two officers were soon at loggerheads.

Wolseley wanted Kitchener to hurry, so that the correct taxes could be levied in every district. Kitchener demanded to be left alone to do the job properly. The High Commissioner took umbrage and had the young upstart removed from the Island for a posting in Asia Minor, arguing that his decision had been taken on economic grounds. In less than a year, however, Kitchener was back mapping under his replacement. Seven years later, the first one-inch to the mile maps of the Island were running off printing presses.

During his mapping expeditions, Kitchener kept copious notes about the people he met and the places he passed through. He wrote that members of the two main Island communities belonged to 'very distinct types', with the Turks taller and more independent than their Greek counterparts, who were timid by comparison. 'They hide in villages as a government official passes through, without any real cause. They are very religious, generally go to church every evening and keep a great number of saints' days,' he jotted,

Horatio Kitchener as a young Royal Engineers' lieutenant (centre of picture) photographed in 1883 with his mapping survey team.

adding that village priests were admired by their flock as they could usually read and write. 'The Turks are not at all fanatical about their religion,' he observed, 'and, although good Moslems, do not share the sterner precepts of the law of Mohammed.'

Kitchener found there many rich landlords of 'a superior class' who had great influence in the villages, but unlike the Turks preferred to live in towns, while letting their properties to farmers at high rents. He summed up his mapping experience with the words: 'We have had our eyes on Cyprus as a desirable position for some time ... as early as 1876 it appears something had been decided, for the innumerable and very bad maps of the Island issued from the War Office are all stamped with that date. Now we know the advantages of a sea-girt shore. No complications of holy sites and sentimental interests.'

For much of his stay, Kitchener lived with his pet bear in a modest house in Lefkosa's Haydar Pasa street, which today stands close to the so-called 'Green Line' which separates the Greek and Turkish sides of the capital. In many ways, he was an odd, often solitary man, with a facial demeanour that did not endear him to people. Because one of his blue eyes had a squint and the other was short-sighted, he looked evasive. Despite his poor eyesight, he enjoyed shooting and hunting, although he was good at neither. In India, his fellow officers had nicknamed him 'Bang damn'.

Although he surveyed and mapped the Island with dedication and efficiency, he always found time to pursue his hobbies. He thought local dogs were not up to scratch and so he imported British hunting hounds – and the foxes for them to chase, but was heard to say, 'man-shooting is the finest sport of all; there is a certain amount of infatuation about it, the more you kill the more you wish to kill'.

Fluent in French, Arabic and Turkish, he thoroughly enjoyed donning Arab robes and galloping around the countryside on a white stallion. His sudden arrival in Cypriot villages often caused consternation. 'He is either very stupid or very clever,' a contemporary of his declared.

A deeply religious man, he was a dedicated Christian and member of the Guild of Holy Standards. As such he was not very tolerant of other faiths or those individuals whom he considered as not living up to his high ideals. Yet he thought nothing of breaking 400-year-old Turkish laws, which prohibited the removal of artefacts from burial sites. Wherever they were, he burrowed and burrowed archaeological sites throughout Cyprus until he filled his army knapsacks with his finds. In 1881, he packed them in 17 cases and shipped them to London, addressed to the Victoria and Albert Museum. Because he had no formal training in archaeology, he neglected to keep proper records of what he found and where. Nor did he write notes to describe the surroundings of the tombs he raided, which meant that experts were unable to place them in a correct historical order or determine their original ownership.

The Irish-born British officer's actions may have been wrong, but it has to be said that they were conducted only out of curiosity, not personal gain. By contrast, Luigi Palma di Cesnola, the Italian American who was the US Consul in Cyprus, by his own admission, plundered more than 10,000 tombs during his stay on the Island, using diplomatic immunity to send his discoveries abroad and making a lot of money in the process.

The first serious archaeological research began in 1896, launched by an expedition from the British Museum, its appetite whetted by the bits and pieces which had arrived in London, sent by British military officers and civil servants who had found them on their weekend 'digs', all within a single square mile of the ruins at Salamis, near Famagusta.

By then, the port city's reputation as the

Famagusta port in 1905. The British modernized the dockside with the introduction of a railway.

malaria capital of the Island was no more. In 1878, photographer John Thomson nearly died from the disease as he recounted: 'Famagosta [*sic*] is considered the unhealthiest place in Cyprus, and it was here that I fell victim to the malarious fever, as I was at a point of quitting the Island. The attack was a sharp one, and lasted about a week, but it yielded in the end to the prompt and friendly treatment of Dr Craig of the 71st Regiment. Its effects were prostrating but not long continued. There can be no doubt that this malady prevails chiefly during the summer months, and in the neighbourhood of marshes, such as are to be found not far from Famagosta.'

Slowly conditions in Cyprus began to be seen to improve, but, at the same time, Greek Cypriot demands for *enosis* became stronger. When Gladstone became Britain's Prime Minister, the Greeks thought they would receive his sympathy, but in 1881, he replied: 'While HM Government leniently desires the happiness of Cyprus they must remind the inhabitants that the island is held by England under the convention with the Porte, as a part of the Ottoman Empire, and that proposals [*enosis*], which would be a violation of that convention, cannot be discussed.'

Now began a battle of wills that would continue until open conflict between the British and the Greek Cypriots exploded in 1955. Six weeks after Gladstone's statement, the Cypriot Archbishop and Greek representatives from six Island districts wrote to Lord Kimberley to say they 'considered it a sacred duty to report the wishes of the people of Cyprus, who declared recently that their only desire is union with mother country Greece' and asked him to intercede on their behalf.

In reply, the British instead offered proportional representation in an expanded Legislative Assembly, only to find the Turkish Cypriots objected. Their leaders visited the High Commissioner and reminded him that under Ottoman rule, the two communities were always equally represented on councils, even in those Turkish provinces where Christians were a minority. Their opinion was heard politely, but the British Government changed the arrangements to suit the Greeks, allowing proportional representation, based on the 1881 census. 'By this arrangement our ancient and present privileges shall be trodden under foot,' The Mufti of Cyprus, Esseid Ahmet Asim Efendi cabled to Lord Kimberley. 'We reject most positively the proposed system.'

Speaking in the House of Lords, Lord Carnarvon justified the Turkish claim for

Crowds celebrate the opening in 1905 of the railway line between Nicosia and Famagusta, where it crosses the Pedios River.

continued equal representation and warned that any change would create deep differences between two communities. His words fell on deaf ears. Once the Greek Cypriots achieved proportional representation, their next step was to press more vigorously to unite with Greece. Again, the Turks registered their protest with the High Commissioner, now Sir Walter Sendall. The Mufti told him that his community would resist any cessation of the Island and was content with the existing administration as long as Cyprus stayed part of the Ottoman Empire.

Alongside the cries of *enosis*, the Greek Cypriots launched an anti-Turkish campaign. They were encouraged by settlers from the mainland and the resident Greek Consul Philemon, who prompted them to raise his national flag at every opportunity. The agitation reached fever pitch when Philemon used a festival of sport in Limassol in 1899 to address the crowds and spread Hellenic ideals. The District Commissioner took him aside and stressed that Cyprus was still a province of Turkey, even it were ruled by HMG, and those the Consul addressed remained subjects of the Ottoman Empire.

Official warnings did not stop the pro-*enosis* demonstrations in the months ahead, prompting Sir W. F. Haynes Smith, the latest High Commissioner, to notify London on 20 February 1901 that 'the agitators are mostly Athens-trained professional people such as doctors, advocates and teachers. They return to the Island imbued with Hellenic propaganda ... they have been bred up in the history of the success of agitation applied to the "Ionian Islands" and may have seen the success of organized agitation and violence in Crete.'

Representatives of Turkish Cypriots of Paphos district added their weight by sending a telegram to the Colonial Office, which said: 'Should the island be handed over to an uncivilized and unjust government the evil methods of the Cypriot Greek, which are known to you, will increase and the catastrophe of the Muslim-Turks, is ensued certain ... should you deem it necessary to hand over Cyprus to another nation we pray it may be returned to Turkey whose right is indisputable.'

By 1911, the Turks were at war with Italy: a war which they were to lose in the following year to the great pleasure of the Greek-

Field Marshal Horatio Herbert Kitchener, 1st Earl Kitchener, KG, KP, GCB, OM, GCSI, GCMG, GCIE, ADC, PC.

A year later, on 25 April, British, Australian and New Zealand forces, with the French and other Commonwealth troops, attacked Turkey at Gallipoli, hoping to win easily and clear the way to the capture of Istanbul. The campaign ended with disastrous results for the Allies. Their combined loss of soldiers was 336,048 against a death toll of Turkish troops estimated at 98,750.

In London, there were bitter recriminations over the conduct of allied operations, but Turks were jubilant and heaped praise on their young Army commander, a Lieutenant Colonel Mustafa Kemal. He would later become the founder and first president of the Turkish Republic after the fall of the Ottomans. He become known as Ataturk – 'father of the nation'. Later he would raise a memorial to all those who were killed. Inscribed on it are the lines he wrote:

> *Those heroes that shed their blood and lost their*
> *lives …*
> *You are now lying in the soil of a friendly*
> *country.*
> *Therefore, rest in peace.*

speaking world. For Europe another, greater war was heading its way. It would involve the world. Turkey would join Germany to fight the Allies.

Almost immediately the British published an Order in Council on 5 November 1914 declaring the annexation of Cyprus, thus unilaterally abrogating the terms of the Convention of 1878. With a garrison of 502 officers, the Crown felt confident the Island could be defended.

ON THE battlegrounds of Europe, Lord Kitchener, who had mapped the Island as a young man and risen to become a Field Marshal, deployed the British Army. As his country's Minister of War, he tried to be Commander-in-Chief at the same time. He warned that the conflict would plumb the depths of the country's manpower 'to the last million'.

Lieutenant Colonel Mustafa Kemal, who would become the founder of modern Turkey, views the positions of ANZAC forces at the Battle of Gallipoli in 1915.

There is no difference between
The Johnnies and the Mehemets to us,
Where they lie side by side, here in this country
of ours.
You, the mothers, who sent their sons from far
away countries
Wipe away your tears, your sons are now lying
in our bosom
And are at peace.
After having lost their lives on this land, they
have become our sons as well.

When the Allies faced defeat at the height of the Gallipoli campaign, Britain urged Greece to throw in its lot on the Allies' side and open another front, which the Turks would have to face. In return for Greek support, Sir Edward Gray, the Foreign Secretary, told an emergency Cabinet meeting held on 16 October 1915, the Greeks could have Cyprus. Athens replied that pro-German King Constantine did not wish to renounce the country's neutrality. The British offer of Cyprus, therefore, lapsed and Parliament was informed of the Greek decision on the 27th. A year later Constantine was forced to abdicate and Greece, under Prime Minister Venizelos, joined the War.

BEYOND GALLIPOLI, Britain was beating Turkish forces and capturing great numbers as Prisoners of War. Cyprus was considered the ideal place to hold them. A camp was built quickly at Karaolos to hold 2,000 Turks and a Mr E. A. Howe was appointed commandant. In a letter dated 11 October 1916 and marked 'secret', he requested the Famagusta District Commissioner to provide him with 'a sufficient supply of civil police' when the prisoners are 'disembarked at the port in a week's time', because, 'there will be a shortage of troops'. In addition, he wanted help to keep the quay at Famagusta clear of civilians and was concerned that road traffic could interfere with the prisoners' 'progress to the camp'.

The same day he wrote another letter. It showed his concern about 'the large Turkish population in the Island, more especially in the Famagusta district' and how they might react if they heard the British were imprisoning Turks. 'I think it well to ask your cooperation in the matter of restricting the curious civilians, and of pointing out to them that the camp is placed out-of-bounds, and that the natives and civilians found loitering in the neighbourhood of the camp will be arrested by the military authorities,' Howe suggested. He asked the 'proper authorities' to make sure 'no boats are allowed to moor or land on that part of the beach fronting the camp'.

With the Turkish prisoners due on 15 October Howe requested that these measures to be authorized by Sir John Eugene Clauson, the British High Commissioner, before that date. He told the BHC that 'the lighthouse near the PoW camp is inhabited by Turks' and he felt that they should be removed, 'substituting in their place either British-born subjects or British subjects other than Turkish'. He concluded: 'I feel sure, you will see the necessity for this step, without my entering into further explanations, and I trust you will see that the exchange is effected not later than the date mentioned.'

As so often happens in Cyprus, the best laid plans were delayed. The first Turkish PoWs did not arrive until 26 November and, it seems, the lighthouse keeper and his staff stayed at their posts, although they were viewed with suspicion throughout the war's duration. When some prisoners escaped, Howe immediately accused the lighthouse keeper of complicity and demanded his arrest. The keeper was questioned, but not arrested or charged with any offence. He told his interrogators that the commandant was 'a very foolish ignorant bastard'. His words are still filed in the UK's Public Records Office in Kew.

Throughout the camp's seven-year existence, the British authorities were worried that there could be a mass breakout by the soldiers who would then link up with the Cypriot Turkish community and seize the Island for themselves. The authorities had some justification for thinking this way. Three Turkish Cypriots – Dr Esat, Dr Behic and a Hasan Karabardak – were drawing up such a plan. They intended to tie down British troops and civilian police by starting riots every evening at dusk during the 1916 Christmas period. Simultaneously, the military prisoners would seize the camp. Prison guards, however, discovered the plan in the nick of time for the British. A matchbox containing a letter from the outside plotters was found before it reached any of the prisoners. The letter instructed them to go to their beds dressed and to wait for a signal to trigger their uprising.

Dr Esat and Hasan Karabardak were arrested immediately and imprisoned in Kyrenia Castle. In due course Esat was expelled to Istanbul. Karabardak's release was conducted in secrecy. There are no records to explain why. He left for Turkey, where he involved himself in the Turkish war for independence. His supporters in Cyprus contributed funds and some Cypriot Turks joined him as volunteers in Mustafa Kemal's forces.

What happened to Dr Behic has all the elements of dark tragedy so typical of Cypriot history. With insufficient evidence to prosecute him for involvement in the escape plot, British intelligence officers decided to use other means to punish him. They devised a scheme which would destroy him and his family. Agents went to see his wife privately and told her that her husband was unfaithful and regularly visited a nearby brothel. This was completely contrary to the truth. A more devoted husband would have been hard to find.

Mrs Behic disbelieved what she was hearing. Nevertheless, the agents pressed on, claiming she could see for herself. They would accompany her to the brothel on a specific day when her husband would be there.

Reluctantly, she agreed, although she was convinced the security agents were lying. Meanwhile, other agents told Dr Behic that his wife was a prostitute. If he went to the brothel in question, he would see for himself that she solicited for custom from the brothel's lounge, sitting alongside the other women.

On the appointed day and time, one agent took Mrs Behic and her maid to the brothel to await her husband. Another agent accompanied Dr Behic to the same place, but half an hour later. He entered the lounge and saw his wife and her maid there, just as he had been told. Mrs Behic, stunned at the sight of her husband, exactly as the British had predicted, thought immediately their accusations were true and began screaming. Shocked, his brain in turmoil, he could not make sense of his wife's hysterical outburst, but found himself suddenly accepting the lies he had been told. In a moment of madness, he pulled a pistol from his jacket pocket, aimed and fired several shots. Both his wife and the maid fell to the ground, dying, as the prostitutes cried and dashed for safety. The British agents immediately arrested Dr Behic, who was then charged with murder, tried, convicted and eventually executed by hanging.

At the prison camp, illness was rife. Death was commonplace. Those caught escaping were executed. Stonemasons among the prisoners carved the tombstones for the dead. Of the 33 graves that have survived and been identified, the earliest is dated 24 November 1916, two days before the first large batch of prisoners arrived. It seems the incumbent must have died on his way to the camp. The last date that can be deciphered reads 20 February 1920. It is assumed that the last stonemason died soon afterwards and that nobody was left who was capable of carving his name or those of the soldiers who followed him.

AFTER THE war officially ended, the Turkish PoWs in Cyprus posed a dilemma for the

British. As the Allies were still occupying some Turkish territories and Greece was being allowed to capture the rest, nobody was quite sure if the prisoners should be released. Furthermore, the authorities in London were ambiguous about their intentions for the Island's future. They had allowed 3,000 Greek soldiers to base themselves in Cyprus. Officially their stay was temporary, but some officials hinted that plans were ready to hand the Island to Greece. Cypriot Turks added two and two together – their four suggested the soldiers were part of an advance party preparing to take over and they became nervous.

Sir Malcolm Stevenson, the new High Commissioner, bit his fingernails. On 6 May 1919, he sent a letter to the Colonial Office in London, in which he requested help to dampen down the rising tension between Greeks and Turks. He explained: 'In this connection I would mention that persistent rumours as to the imminence of cession of Cyprus to Greece have much perturbed the Moslems and all classes of the Island and should a cession be ultimately decided upon, I consider highly desirable that before any announcement to this effect is made, the present small garrison in the island should be temporarily strengthened by the addition of two or three companies of infantry as a precautionary measure against disturbances.'

London replied that no extra troops were available, but in an effort to calm the situation, the Greek soldiers were sent home and the PoWs kept incarcerated. Only after Turkey declared itself an independent republic and the Allies recognized its borders did the British deem it suitable to release the remaining prisoners held at the Karaolos Concentration Camp. They had been in captivity longer than any other Great War prisoners.

Much later Jeff Ertugrul, a Turkish Cypriot researcher based in London, told the author about part of a letter, dated 1927, that he had found. It talked about a Turkish war cemetery in Famagusta and 271 Turkish soldiers who were buried there. The writer, a British officer, listed the dead by name, rank and serial number and requested that the government hire a man to look after their graves for an annual salary of three pounds. In 2009, only 33 graves had been found. Where were the others?

At the conclusion of the First World War,

On 1 May 1925, the British declared Cyprus a colony.

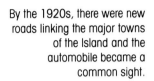

By the 1920s, there were new roads linking the major towns of the Island and the automobile became a common sight.

Turkish Cypriots were at first more anti-British than anti-Greek, because they were deeply offended by the way the Island's administration saw them as the enemy, taking control of their Islamic institutions, including the Evkaf Pious Foundation, schools and courts. Forty miles away from the Island's north coast, they saw Ataturk's new Turkey modernizing, while they suffered as an underclass under their British rulers who were clamping down on them. With the Treaty of Lausanne, signed on 24 July 1923, all outstanding issues had been settled between the Allies, Greeks and Turks over the Republic's new boundaries, which excluded Cyprus.

ON 1 MAY 1925, Britain formally declared the Island a colony of the Empire. Ottoman laws were swept away and the two communities tried to adjust to the new situation, but without much enthusiasm. They saw many material improvements taking place, but in their hearts and heads they longed for independence and self-determination and dreamed they would find it in their lifetimes, even as the divide between Greeks and Turks widened. The motorcar took over from donkey-powered carts and camel-trains. The people began to travel between villages and towns for work and pleasure. Not all done in the name of progress was to Horoz Ali's liking.

Modernity paid scant regard to traditional virtues. In 1931, Ali watched in sadness as the British cut a broad road through the city wall after one of Nicosia's first buses proved too high to go through the original gate, and to accommodate the increasing traffic from the suburbs. That which he guarded so diligently was no more worth protecting. He died in 1946, aged 121 years, still a British subject. During his long lifetime, he saw Cyprus change beyond recognition.

'Prior to 1878 Cyprus experienced a partial and incompetent administration of justice. The venality of the ill-paid Ottoman judges, who professed to administer an admirable code founded on the Code Napoleon, was equalled only by their ignorance of the law. The first administrative step of the British Government was to establish Courts under the presidency of Englishmen, in which both Turkish and Greek Christian interests are represented on the bench. These Courts, admittedly impartial and incorruptible, have gained the confidence of all classes and creeds,' boasted the 1920 edition of the Government's *Cyprus Handbook*.

The *Handbook* continued: 'The general health of the inhabitants of the island has been greatly improved under the care and supervision of English medical officers … Improvements in sanitation and a dissemination of a knowledge of the first principles of hygiene have rendered Cyprus more and more healthy, with the result that, instead of being a pestilential spot, as it was stated to be in former days and, as it was reported at the occupation, it is now as healthy and as a pleasant a place as may be found in the Mediterranean. Hospitals, of which there were none in 1878, are now to be found in every district, under the supervision of government medical officers and are in receipt of government grants and free drugs. In Nicosia, there is a large central hospital, entirely maintained by the Government.'

The British also took great pride in the introduction of the Government Railway and the Post Office. By 1918, they had established 65 post offices and 196 rural mail stations, and dealt with three million pieces of mail. Every district was connected to the telegraph.

But the British, despite these advances, had not stifled the demand for *enosis* or the nationalism of the Greek Cypriots. As far back as 1902 Canon F. D. Newham, the Inspector of Schools reported that Hellenic ideals remained the daily diet at Greek schools delivered by teachers from the mainland, which had fought and gained independence from its Ottoman rulers and was flushed with pride. 'A song book consists of material intended to inflame Greek patriotism and songs against the Turks. In practice, whenever I ask to hear children sing, it is a war song – *FORWARD, FOLLOW THE DRUM THAT LEADS US AGAINST THE TURKS.*'

Horoz Ali's treasured Kyrenia Gate still stands, but only as an island surrounded by a sea of traffic that ebbs and flows along the main road into Nicosia, an architectural oddity of no great importance, but given respect because, on one side, there is a statue of Kemal Ataturk, the founder of modern Turkey, while on the other, there is another of Dr Fazil Kutchuk, a nationalist who devoted his life to the cause of Turkish Cypriot independence. Guarding both are two huge cannon, not Turkish but British, built in 1790 at London's Woolwich Arsenal. They were delivered to Cyprus after their action against Napoleon's forces in Egypt.

CHAPTER THREE

The 1931 Rebellion:
a week that shook Cyprus

'Whatever you do, do cautiously, and look to the end.'
Gesta Romanorum No. 103

TWENTY-FOUR years before the start of the EOKA conflict, Greek Cypriots rebelled against British colonial rule of Cyprus and demanded *enosis*. If it had not been for British military forces rushed by land, sea and air to bring an end to the Island-wide riots, the government would have collapsed, Greeks and Turks would have fought each other and anarchy would have prevailed. The bomb blasts of 1 April 1955 were no more than Christmas crackers compared to what took place in 1931.

For a week in October of that year, the Colonial administration shook as Greek Cypriots went on the rampage in towns and villages. But before the rebellion collapsed, Government House would be destroyed, civil servants would flee for their lives, Greek Cypriot priests, politicians and trade unionists would be sent into exile, 2,952 would receive prison sentences and harsh punishments would be applied to Greek and Turk alike irrespective of their involvement or otherwise.

For the British, the night of Wednesday 21 October 1931 was to be the worst in the 82-year-long rule of Cyprus. The Island had been leased from the Turks in 1878 by the Sultanate of the Ottoman Empire and taken as a colony in 1925. From the outset of British rule, the Greek Cypriot population, led by the priests and bishops of the Orthodox Church, prayed to become part of a greater Greece, while the minority Turkish Cypriot community looked to the British to prevent that happening.

As far as the British were concerned in 1931, Cyprus was a comfortable and not very important part of the Empire with a people that had no desire or means to overthrow their administrators. They thought themselves extremely benevolent rulers by allowing the Island's inhabitants to go about their day-to-day business without undue interference. What went unnoticed were the inequalities between the two main communities, with the British simply accepting the Greeks as belonging to the merchant class, with Levantine skills in doing business, and the Turks as happy-go-lucky farmers. Because the Turks were Muslims and the Greeks Christian, the colonial masters felt they had more in common with the latter.

'Though worthy, reliable and highly respected,' wrote Nancy Crawshaw, the author of *The Cyprus Revolt*, 'the Turkish Cypriot leaders were out of touch with the processes of modernization which had taken place in Turkey since the revolution. As a result, Ataturk's religious, social and legal reforms were slow to reach Cyprus and the general progress of the Turkish Cypriot community was held back.' Perhaps the British administrators saw, but did not

Sir Ronald Storrs, KCMG, CBE, Governor of Cyprus in 1931.

register: to quote William Lunn's speech in the British House of Commons, 'in Cyprus there is fearful poverty at the moment and such a condition of affairs will ferment disturbances in any community'.

In 1931, the Governor of Cyprus was Sir Ronald Storrs, a classically trained administrator with a love for all things Ancient Greek. Straight-backed, crisp and granite-hard, he had been in Egypt with Kitchener and Arabia with Lawrence, who described Storrs as 'the most brilliant Englishman in the Near East, and subtly efficient, despite his diversion of energy in love of music and letters, of sculpture, painting, of whatever was beautiful in the world's fruit ... Storrs was always first, and the great man among us'.

When he arrived in Cyprus to become Governor in 1926 his popularity soon soared as he convinced the British Government to abolish the detested 'tribute', the annual payments the Island made to pay off a share of the Turkish debt. His appreciation of Greek culture also endeared him to the majority of Cypriots. However, he ran into bitter opposition on several fronts: trade unionists objected to his crackdown on leftist agitation and Church leaders were infuriated by his Elementary Education Bill of 1929, which sought to keep schools from being used to spread Greek or Turkish nationalist propaganda. Many saw him by then as an archetypical autocrat who ran the Island as his personal fiefdom.

Although Storrs' personal library and valuable art collection would be destroyed by fire in the uprising, he regarded these as lesser losses than his shattered and mistaken belief in the goodwill of the Greek Cypriots towards himself as an individual and the British as a whole.

But the truth is that by leading their comfortable life, the British had lost touch with their subjects and, as Nancy Crawshaw wrote, 'failed to notice the ground swell of dissatisfaction that was growing in the Greek Cypriot community, stirred by the Orthodox Church.' Another historian wrote: 'By allowing the Greek flag to fly in public, except on Government House, the Commissioners' residences and the Governor's car, the nationalists mistook this freedom for weakness.'

The British had allowed Greek schools to teach Greek history and geography. They had ignored anti-British articles in Greek Cypriot newspapers and the rabble-rousing at political meetings. The young nationalists also believed Britain was on the point of financial collapse because the value of the pound had fallen dramatically after the Wall Street crash of 1929, which had led to increased taxes for the local population, which, by and large, had subsidence living. The new budget caused the Greek members of the Legislative Council to resign in protest. They set up the National

Radicalist Union, whose aim was a 'fanatical pursuit of the union of Cyprus with the Greek political whole'. Meanwhile Nicodemos Mylonas, the Bishop of Kition, was calling for the violent overthrow of the administration. 'For the benefit of this country we must not obey their laws,' he told his supporters in Larnaca. 'Do not be afraid because England has a fleet. We must all try for union and if necessary let our blood flow.'

British administrators, as was their custom, had spent the summer of 1931 in the Troodos Mountains to escape the oven-heat of the capital Nicosia. It was only when they returned in mid-September that they discovered for the first time just how active and successful in their absence the Greek Orthodox Church and local Greek Cypriot politicians had been in generating hostility towards their rulers. Cyprus had become a powder keg of discontent. Only a spark was needed for it to explode. That spark was provided on 21 October. Spontaneous riots erupted in several towns almost simultaneously. Priests told the crowds that the Orthodox Patriarch had proclaimed the end of British rule and the union of Cyprus with Greece 'because the people will it!' Six members of the Cyprus Legislative Council vocally supported them. They denounced Storrs for enforcing an Order-in-Council, which overturned their earlier rejection of the new tariffs. 'Citizens! Greeks!' cried the disgruntled leaders, 'ΚΑΤΩ ΟΙ ΤΥΡΑΝΝΟΙ!' ('Down with the Tyrants!'), 'ΚΑΤΩ ΟΙ ΞΕΝΟΙ!' ('Out with the Foreigners!').

The day before, 20 October, Bishop Nicodemus Mylonas had arrived in Limassol at the request of Mr N. K. Lanitis, a leading nationalist. Church bells were rung to summon the people and a cortege, headed by a slowly moving motorcar draped with a large Greek flag, went out between 16.00 and 17.00 to meet him. He was thus escorted to the Stadium, where a crowd of about 3,000

Bishop Nicodemos Mylonas.

people, including schoolboys, had assembled. After several speeches, the crowd moved off singing and cheering to a club in the town where, from a balcony, the Bishop again addressed them briefly in inflammatory terms.

Storrs wrote later: 'Invective against British rule became more bitter and more direct in the political speeches, and vague incitement to unspecified deeds was more frequently included, with occasional references to the revolutionary example of other dependent countries. Among the peasantry the campaign of misrepresentation and abuse of Government had been favoured by the deterioration of economic conditions and by rustic ignorance.

'In the towns, generations of youth sedulously indoctrinated with disloyalty that had been launched by the secondary schools [permeated] all the professions. Every branch of public life in the Orthodox community was in some way allied to the cause of union.'

Wednesday 21 October 1931

In the afternoon Mr Lanitis telegraphed his supporters in Nicosia about the Limassol address by the Bishop. 'Never before has there been a more panegyric approval by town and district,' he exaggerated. The telegram was duplicated and distributed to supporters. At the Phaneromemi Church in the capital, Dionysios Kykkotis, the chief priest, read the telegram with glee and immediately rang the church bells, a signal for Greek Cypriots to gather. Within minutes, a large crowd arrived and unfurled a Greek flag, which the priest kissed. Now tempers were running high and the crowd of 3,000 decided to march on Government House, a wooden building a mile and a half away. It was 18.45.

'I proclaim the revolution,' shouted Kykkotis. 'I declare *enosis*.' The procession moved slowly in dense formation. Passing the Government timber yard, the Greek Cypriots helped themselves to sticks of various sizes. A breakaway crowd now moved off the main road and walked in a parallel procession through the suburban village of Ayii Omoloyitades. A patrol of five policemen watched the procession and reported its movements by telephone to Government House.

Phaneromeni Church in Nicosia, where Bishop Nicodemos roused Greek Cypriots to march on Government House.

At 19.45 advance elements of the crowd, carrying wooden staves, bicycle chains and lanterns, reached the first gate of Government House. Eight mounted police and a baton party of 12 police, with instructions to prevent the crowd from entering the grounds, met them. The police tried to push the crowd back, but were unsuccessful. The horses stampeded and the crowd poured in. Greatly outnumbered by the advancing crowd, the police were pushed back to the front doors of the house. Now the 5,000 demonstrators stopped and sang the Greek National anthem (the English translation is by Rudyard Kipling):

We knew thee of old Oh divinely restored
By the light of thine eyes
And the light of thy sword.

From the graves of our slain
Shall thy valour prevail
As we greet thee again
Hail, Liberty! Hail!

At 20.20, Mr Hart Davis, Commissioner of Nicosia, and Major A. B. Wright, Chief Assistant Secretary to the Government, tried to address the crowd. They both agreed to meet three of the crowd's representatives to discuss grievances. Theofanis Theodotou, George Hajipavlou, Pheidias Kyriakides of Limassol and Kykkotis, the priest, struggled to the front of the mass, which enveloped the whole terrace and surrounding garden. A man carrying a trumpet and a large Greek standard accompanied them.

At 20.45, a further 22 armed policemen began arriving in cars. Inspector Yianni commanded them. The inspector, using a devious route, avoided the crowd and brought his men into Government House from the rear without opposition. He reported to the Commissioner at the porch. The Commissioner and leaders were then attempting to parley with the crowd, but their words were drowned in a cacophony of noise. 'A few stones were thrown and some windows broken and, as I learnt afterwards, a Greek flag was hoisted on the roof of the house,' Storrs reported to London. 'It became increasingly clear that words would not move the crowd to disperse and that its enthusiasm and determination would not easily be exhausted.'

The crowd drove both Hart Davis and Major Wright from the porch into the house, where Police Inspector Faiz, a Turk, and 40 policemen had taken up positions. Further police reinforcements and a copy of the Riot Act were sent for. The bombardment of stones increased and soon all the windows in the front of the building had been smashed, a number of police were injured, many electric lights were broken and the telephone room, near the porch, had been wrecked and rendered untenable.

At about 21.30, the leaders, 'realizing that they had lost control, and fearing the consequences, sent messages of apology to me and decamped,' Storrs claimed. Minutes later Lieutenant Colonel Gallagher, the Police Commandant, warned he would fire on the crowd if it did not disperse and read the Riot Act. His words were translated into Greek. The crowd stood its ground and stepped up its stone-throwing. 'Many of the stones or rocks thrown were larger than coconuts and some, propelled with slings, arrived with sufficient force to shatter the masonry of the porch and to break in the front door. The door was propped up with heavy furniture but was again smashed in by timber used as a battering ram,' said Storrs. 'To the occupants of the house the only clearly visible targets were the parties of youths in front. The roughs behind made occasional sallies to support them in destructive acts.' Others poured gasoline on six Government cars and burnt them with yells of triumph as the stench of burning rubber and paint spread.

Unknown to the defenders, a very drunk Greek Cypriot – a Karakoushis from Ayios Dhometios – had entered the building from the rear. No one noticed him as he ripped paintings from the walls and fouled several rooms before heading for the Governor's State Room. Here he sat down in Storrs' chair and shouted: 'Mother come and see your son who is now the governor.'

Police reinforcements, so far held in reserve, arrived in four cars at the front of the house at 22.15. They entered through the broken windows, taking a battering from the stone-throwers. Their cars were set ablaze. Burning brands were lobbed through the broken windows of the house and fires began to take hold.

Commissioner Gallagher immediately told his 12 officers to prepare to shoot at the crowd. Each was told that only one round per man was to be fired, and that they should aim at legs, not the body. He took his men out from the back of Government House to the east side.

'Open fire,' he shouted. The volley of shots followed immediately. The time was 22.35. The crowd scattered, pursued by the police. Two injured rioters were left on the ground. Seven others were wounded, one of whom, Onoufrios Clerides, aged 18, died.

At 23.00, the police reported that the grounds were clear, but flames from the curtains at the west corner of the frontage of the house spread to the roof and took hold of the whole building. Within five minutes, fire raged out of control through Government House. The British civil servants fled. The Governor and Major Wright escaped through a tunnel at the side of the building, led by Inspector Faiz and several of his men. They reached a dry riverbed, found a car and headed for the safety of the Secretary's Lodge. For his gallantry, Faiz was awarded the King's Police Medal.

Inspector Faiz, who had studied law in London, came from a prominent Turkish Cypriot family who lived in Nicosia. His father, Mehmet Ziya ed Din Efendi, had been an Islamic scholar with a detailed knowledge of the Holy Qur'an and the Arabic language. With his background, Faiz was a natural choice for the role of Mufti of Cyprus and later an elected Turkish representative on the British Governor's Legislative Council in the early days of colonial rule. His wife could trace her lineage to Ahmet Beligh Pasa, who received his education in France, encouraged by Empress Eugenie, Napoleon III's consort, who had been impressed by his dissertation during her visit to Egypt for the opening of the Suez Canal. After Faiz and his family moved to London to live out the Second World War in Kensington, their son, Suha, was sent to some Christian middle-class boarding schools and later to Worcester College, Oxford, where he became a Classics scholar proficient in Latin, before becoming a member of the British establishment in 1947 by enrolling in the Colonial Service.

Next morning all that remained of Government House was a gutted, smoking ruin. A Mr Z. Williamson, from a well-known

Police search the debris of Government House, set ablaze the night before by Greek Cypriot rioters.

contracting family, had built it. Williamson became better known as the armaments' salesman Sir Basil Zaharoff.

'On arrival at Secretary's Lodge I sent immediately for the troops from Troodos and decided that further military reinforcements would be required,' said Storrs. 'The police were trained and employed almost exclusively in the prevention and detection of crime and were in no sense of the term a military force. The siege of Government House had shown that they could not be expected to cope with serious disorder adequately except by rifle fire.

'If similar situations were to arise in the other towns and spread to villages, or if there was to be any concerted outbreak, widespread anarchy was likely to follow. The swiftest precautions were necessary to ensure that any such consequence could be forestalled.

'I therefore telegraphed the General Officer Commanding British Troops in Egypt for additional troops to be sent by air as soon as possible and the Commander-in-Chief of the Mediterranean Fleet for an aircraft carrier or cruiser from Crete. I also cabled an account of the situation to London and cancelled the leave granted me. In addition I advised all Commissioners by wire to take precautions in their districts and to report the situation by wire twice daily until further notice. They were informed that grave disturbances had occurred at Nicosia.'

Had Sir Ronald acted decisively and called

The charred remains of Government House on the morning after the Greek Cypriot riots.

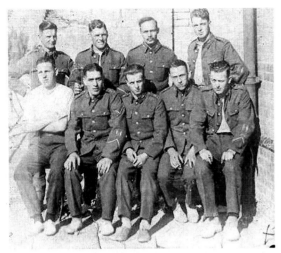

Members of The Royal Welch Fusiliers, the resident garrison in Cyprus, 1931.

The rough road in the Troodos Mountains that Captain H. A. Freeman, OBE, MC, TP, travelled to reach Nicosia.

for reinforcements as soon as the 'fiery cross' had been raised two days earlier in Limassol, the probability is that he could have stopped the insurgents before their rage brought them to Government House and the rebellion spread.

The military garrison in Cyprus consisted of 'C' Company, 1st Battalion the Royal Welch Fusiliers and members of the 1st King's, with a few RAMC and RASC troops. Because of a shortage of accommodation the company strength was a mere 125. Captain H. A. Freeman, OBE, MC, TP, was their commander. His role was to liaise directly with the Civil Government and with Headquarters, British Troops in Egypt. In October, the garrison was alone at Troodos, as the Government had moved back to the capital in September. Ordinary routine work was being carried out with special attention to the physical fitness of the men in preparation for a march down to Polemidia at the end of the month.

Thursday 22 October 1931

In the *Army Quarterly* of January 1933, Captain Freeman described how his garrison

reacted to the events in Nicosia: 'On the night of the 21–22 October, a few minutes after midnight, I was awakened by the telephone ringing in my house. On answering it, I was told by an assistant secretary to the Colonial Secretary Mr Henniker-Heaton that there was a disturbance in Nicosia and that the company was wanted down there at once. I pointed out that the only available transport was one wood lorry and a car. I was told that if I marched the company to Evrykhou, a special train would meet me there.

'As it is 18 miles to Evrykhou and I had to move my Lewis guns, ammunition, rations, etc., I decided to commandeer all available motor transport within reach. By this means I hoped to get the troops to the capital by dawn, while by marching and train I could not get to Nicosia until midday. I sent a sergeant in the one available car, therefore, to the villages about five miles down the hill, with orders to collect all the cars and lorries that he could, and at the same time I rang up other towns for cars. In this way I procured 10 cars, and, as soon as I heard that they were on the way up to Troodos, I started off with one platoon in the wood lorry and the car.

'The remainder of the company was to follow as soon as the other cars arrived. Being a bitterly cold night, we moved with great coats on, 100 rounds SAA per man, Lewis gun magazines loaded, and two days' rations. The drive down was not without excitement. The lights of my car failed after a mile, and, in spite of new bulbs being put in, they went again almost at once. I learned afterwards that the driver – a Cypriot – had blown them on purpose to avoid taking any of the troops to Nicosia. On a mountain road, with a precipice on one side, this was in itself unpleasant, and valuable time was wasted in trying to find out what the trouble was. Finally, I transferred to the lorry, and with one oil light we made a slow descent to the plains, arriving in Nicosia at 07.30, where the Chief Commandant of Police informed me of the situation.'

Captain Freeman had to decide quickly how best to deploy his few soldiers in aid of the police of whom there were only 800, distributed over the six districts of the Island. By now most of the rioters had disappeared within the walled city, which was shaped as an octagon with a large moat surrounding it. 'I decided to keep the crowd inside the town and to leave the initiative for the next move to the Greek Cypriots. The town lends itself to such a course of action. The exits and entrances are well defined. These are named from the roads coming into them. The chief are the Paphos Gate, Kyrenia Gate, Famagusta Gate, and the New Entrance where the Larnaca and Limassol roads come in. I reinforced the police pickets on these gates and also at the telegraph office. We did not know what the next move would be, or how soon the other districts would join in the rebellion.'

The rest of Freeman's company arrived about 08.30. Even then, Freeman had only one officer and 91 men. The others were left at Troodos to guard the barracks, the married families and a supply depot. From two platoons, he created pickets. They were composed half of police and half of troops. One half-platoon was placed at the Secretary's Lodge and the Government Offices, another half was detailed to guard at the aircraft landing-ground, and one platoon was held in reserve, divided between the Police Depot near the Paphos Gate and the Police Barracks between the Kyrenia Gate and the Telegraph Office. The picket was issued with a written warning order, which stated that any assembly of five or more people was illegal, and if such a body did not disperse by order, it was to be 'dispersed by force'.

At 10.00 Freeman attended a conference at the Secretary's Lodge: The Governor, the acting Colonial Secretary, the Attorney General, the Commissioner for Nicosia and the Chief Commandant of Police were present. 'I was then asked for my opinion from a military point of view,' he recalled. 'I pointed out that my first duty appeared to be to protect the Government Offices and the British population at Nicosia, and that with the small force at my disposal I was unable to send troops to the other districts until I saw what line the crowd inside the town of Nicosia intended to take. While I was talking, a cable arrived from HQ, BTE, asking if I agreed to the Governor's request for reinforcements. I replied that I wanted one company, and later I heard that it was being sent by air and would arrive that evening – hence the guard on the landing-ground. The Governor asked whether I wanted martial law declared. I had to think about this, and decided that with one officer I was quite unable to enforce it, even if it were declared.'

As officials in Limassol, Larnaca and Famagusta reviewed their local situations, they called Nicosia for reinforcements. Freeman told them they must do their best with the available police and civilian British residents. At 11.00, he saw Nicosia was quiet and as no effort was being made by the crowd to break out, he reduced the strength of his pickets by a half and sent Captain Hardie – his only officer – with two platoons in trucks to Larnaca. One remained there and the other went to Famagusta.

At noon, the British women and children of Famagusta were taken aboard a Khedivial steamship in the harbour for their safety. The General Manager of the Cyprus Railway had also raised an armed volunteer force of 20 British officials and others to support the local police. At 17.00 the military platoon arrived, established a protected area and closed all licensed premises.

During the day, Turkish Cypriot leaders told their community not to get involved, but sided emotionally with the rioters 'because our Greek brethren are only demanding what is their right'.

In Nicosia, Freeman, left with only half a platoon in reserve, expected the first company from Egypt to arrive by air in the afternoon. Then he heard it would not reach Cyprus until the next day. Greek Cypriots must have realized the weakness in the British position, because, by 17.00, a crowd had gathered in Ledra Street and began working its way towards the New Entrance picket. Here there was a causeway across the moat, 80 yards long and 30 yards wide. 'I found this causeway a seething mass of people passing each way. I had a sergeant with five men and five police there and a Lewis gun in reserve,' Captain Freeman noted. 'We tried to make the people who lived outside the town return to their homes, and the people who lived in the town keep inside the moat. As a curfew had been ordered for 18.00, I considered it was time to clear the causeway, more especially as stone-throwing was becoming heavy and I was afraid my small party might be overwhelmed by sheer weight of numbers unless I could get some space for manoeuvre.'

He ordered his troops and police to withdraw to the southern end of the causeway, fix bayonets and advance from there on the crowd. Some soldiers took up defensive positions at the rear. Now the front ranks of the crowd of 6,000 strong came almost chest-to-chest with the British troops. The leaders claimed the crowd was a funeral procession for Onoufrios Clerides, the 18-year-old who had died the night before outside Government House.

Captain Freeman said: 'The situation was very tense. We were being heavily stoned and the men wanted to fire. If we had fired, it would have given the agitators a handle against us afterwards. Finally, by withdrawing, in close contact with the mob, to the cross-roads some 100 yards in the rear, we were able to let the procession proceed on its way.'

That evening he arranged a rest for his men, who had gone without sleep for over 48 hours. Members of 1st King's took over the pickets for the night.

The insurgents now switched their attention to Limassol.

The city had remained comparatively quiet until 18.30, but when two military trucks arrived with a few soldiers from Nicosia to buy provisions denied them in the capital, a crowd hemmed them in. As they began loading their supplies from the market, their trucks were rushed and their purchases thrown on the ground. Church bells rang out and the people were urged to assemble at the Bishopric, where the Bishop addressed them. 'Since the Nicosia people refused to supply rations to the troops it is a shame for the Limassol people to give them. We must prevent by every means the taking out of rations from Limassol,' he boomed.

At 20.15 the Commissioner in Limassol went to the post office and telegrammed a report on the situation to the Governor in Nicosia. He then straddled his bicycle and rode towards his house, a mile and a half away. Not far from his destination, he overtook a growing mob, heading in the same direction. He was pushed off his bicycle, ran to the rear of his house and entered ahead of the crowd, which had begun to stone the windows. One of the rebels cut the power lines, while another lit a fire. A car arrived and the passengers carried cans of gasoline that they poured around the house and set alight.

Inside the house the Commissioner, alone with his wife, 12–year-old daughter and two servants, was powerless, and they barely escaped with their lives through the front door. Outside, two friendly Turkish Cypriots saw their distress and escorted them to the sea, where they found a small boat and rowed to the safety of the customs' shed. Here they contacted the police. By the time the constables arrived at the Commissioner's house, it was completely destroyed, as were several nearby cars.

'I received the Commissioner's telegram reporting his house had been burnt and that the police were unable to cope with the situation at 22.45,' said the Governor. Captain Freeman immediately agreed to transfer his platoon from Larnaca to Limassol, which it reached at 03.00. Earlier there had been demonstrations in Paphos, but the situation in the town was unclear, as the rioters had cut the telegraph lines.

That same day, 22 October, the Governor had heard that two cruisers and two destroyers were on their way to Cyprus. He recommended that one cruiser should sail to Limassol and the other to Larnaca. The destroyers should head for Paphos and Famagusta. 'The fortunate decision of the Commander-in-Chief to send four vessels when one only had been asked for enabled the troops to take the initiative in suppressing the insurrection much earlier than would otherwise have been possible and it ensured in the meanwhile the prevention of further extensive destruction of property in the towns,' said Storrs.

Friday 23 October 1931

The first Royal Navy ships arrived in Cypriot waters early in the morning.

In Larnaca, as soon as HMS *London* dropped anchor, the Commissioner went on board and described the situation to Rear-Admiral J. C. W. Henley. The Admiral decided to discuss 'rules of engagement' with the Governor to end the rebellion and, under escort, motored to Nicosia, arriving at noon.

The Governor asked, and Henley agreed, to land a total of 200 Royal Marines and RN personnel, divided between Limassol and Larnaca from HMS *London* and HMS *Shropshire* and 50 each in Famagusta and Paphos from his destroyers, HMS *Achates* and HMS *Acasta*. The situation in Paphos was critical. Intelligence indicated that Nicodemos, the Bishop of Kitium, planned to stir up trouble there on 24 October. The only British

Soldiers of the 1st King's Regiment board a Victoria troop carrier to fly them from Egypt to Cyprus to put down the insurgency.

Seven Victoria troops were used to ferry 150 soldiers from Moascar to Nicosia. It was the first time British forces had been transported by air.

residents were the Commissioner and his wife. To defend them, there were less than 40 policemen in the whole district.

But the Admiral made it clear to the Governor that only to meet a grave emergency would he send naval parties inland. In the event of necessity for armed intervention by His Majesty's Forces, he insisted the senior naval officer on the spot was to take command at the ports, while Captain Freeman would carry responsibility for any army actions ashore. Cooperation between the police, navy and army elements was established and worked smoothly.

An hour earlier, at 11.00, a Company of 150 soldiers of the 1st King's Regiment had landed safely on the makeshift airfield, five miles west of Nicosia. They had been carried in a flight of seven Victoria troop carriers from Moascar in the Suez Canal Zone. They had reached Cyprus and touched down successfully.

With the arrival of the Navy and Army reinforcements, plans were drawn up to arrest the rebellion's ringleaders. After consultation between the Governor, the acting Colonial Secretary and Captain Freeman, a telegram was sent to the Commissioner in Limassol, asking him if he thought the arrest of the Bishop was feasible. He replied that he did not think so as it might lead to bloodshed and

'have a bad effect throughout the island'.

But Captain Freeman insisted and the Governor shared his view. He asked the Admiral if he could reinforce the naval parties ashore at Limassol and be prepared to meet 'maximum opposition'. The Admiral said he was ready for all eventualities. He added that he would take all prisoners on board HMS *London* in Larnaca.

Because Alexander Kyrou, the Cyprus-born Greek Consul General, continued to stir up anti-British emotions, Storrs declared him *persona non grata*. Kyrou had strong links to the Greek Cypriot agitators, whether political or ecclesiastical. The next day he was ordered to pack his bags and leave. As soon as the riots started, he had been ordered home, but remained. For this alone, he was unlikely to have been greeted in Athens with an enthusiastic slap on the back. His behaviour had embarrassed Greek Prime Minister Eleutherios Venizelos, who had stated several times that there was no Cypriot question between the British and Greek Governments; it only existed between the British Government and the Cyprians.

'I cannot but express my sorrow,' said the foxy old statesman, 'and if only the Greek Press would listen to me I would recommend it to rebuke these excesses. No serious person could imagine that such revolts against Great Britain could accomplish the national desires of the Greek Cyprians.' He stressed that the maintenance of friendly relations with Great Britain had been the stable policy of Greece since her independence, and 'those who jeopardized them were insane'.

News of these events was slow to reach London, but by Friday *The Times* was able to editorialize: 'The Cypriot agitators for union with Greece have at last led their followers down the steps of riot and arson. On Wednesday night a procession led by three elected members of the Legislative Council of the island appeared unexpectedly at

Government House, which lies a short distance outside Nicosia. It is said that the leaders proposed to offer their resignations to the Governor and at the same time to demand union with Greece ...

'The causes of this serious outbreak are tolerably familiar. For many years a section of the Greek majority of the Cypriots has demanded union with Greece. The movement has varied in its intensity at different periods. It has been chiefly promoted by the Greek lawyers, money-lenders, school teachers, and latterly by the Greek Orthodox clergy; it has been assisted in the past by the tolerance or indifference of British officials, and by the admitted neglect of the Island before the outbreak of the Great War, when Cyprus from an Ottoman province under British occupation definitely passed under British title.

'In this connexion it must be admitted that the attitude of the Greek Government towards the Cypriot agitation has been scrupulously correct, both before and since M. Venizelos stated publicly that he did not consider the union of the Island and of the Dodacannesse with Greece to be a political issue. From the international standpoint, therefore, there are no grounds for the agitation; from the British point of view its promoters are demanding the surrender of Cyprus to a country, which has not asked for it and could not defend the embarrassing gift – in return for nothing at all.

'That the majority of the islanders call themselves Greeks, speak Greek, and have Greek sympathies is perfectly well known; but they have never been prevented from manifesting their racial and literary sympathies, any more than the important Turkish minority in the island, of which the agitators take no account ...

'The efforts of a Governor of imagination and energy to improve the condition of the Island have been neutralized by a group of office-seekers and by the fanaticism of ecclesiastical politicians. Their blind disregard of Lord Passfield's declaration of 28 November 1929, that the question of the cession of Cyprus to Greece was definitely closed, and of his defence of British administration in Cyprus, and their fear that recent administrative reforms would weaken their hold over the peasantry, have now led them to excite passions which they cannot control and to incur the consequences of their folly.'

The same day the Paphos Commissioner told the Governor that it was essential that the Bishop of Kition not be allowed to address the people there. Meanwhile a large crowd stood guard outside his Limassol house as his arrest was anticipated. 'To consider the situation I summoned a conference at which among others were present the acting Colonial Secretary, Officer commanding the troops, Chief Commandant of Police, and Commissioner, Nicosia. All were agreed that the Bishop should be arrested that night, and that if possible the most prominent ringleaders in Nicosia should be arrested simultaneously,' said Storrs. 'Their detention within reach of the populace would be likely to provoke the crowds to further excesses in the hope of securing their liberation. I viewed with apprehension the prospect of an assault on the prisons such as was actually threatened in Nicosia. The avoidance of situations which would lead to bloodshed was my constant duty. In my belief and that of all competent observers at the time it was mainly due to the power of deportation that I was able to take the initiative decisively at this critical stage.

'I proposed that the arrested leaders should be deported under the powers I had by then acquired under the Defence Order in Council and regulations, and that they should be removed forthwith to the warships until arrangements could be made to deport them finally. I was advised this proposal was preferable to any alternative both from the legal aspect and that of public security. No adequate alternative, indeed, was seen. There could be no serious question of the criminal guilt of the responsible ringleaders.'

It was decided to arrest and deport five Nicosia ringleaders: George Hajipavlou, Dionysios Kykkotis, Theofanis Tsangarides, Theofanis Theodotou and Theodoros Kolokassides.

Saturday 24 October 1931

The arrests in Limassol and Nicosia were timed to start at 03.00. Two cars were detailed for each arrest. The lead vehicle carried a police guide who knew where the wanted man lived, a police officer to make the arrest and two soldiers to help him. The second had five soldiers to guard the outside of the house while the arresting party was inside.

At precisely 03.15 all 10 cars left the Police Barracks and by 03.45 four prisoners – Dionysios Kykkotis, Theofanis Tsangarides, Theofanis Theodotou and Theodoros Kolokassides – were in a waiting lorry at the New Entrance picket, waiting to be taken to Larnaca. George Hajipavlou, the fifth, arrived about 10 minutes later, as he had refused to open his door and it had to be broken down. He had then tried to escape by a back door and ran straight into the arms of the guard outside. All the prisoners were delivered on board HMS *London* at Larnaca before dawn.

The arrest in Limassol of Nicodemos Mylonas, the Bishop of Kition was just as successful. A naval party found no difficulty in entering his house and removing him to HMS *Shropshire*. A man up a tree let off a rocket, which was probably intended as a signal for a crowd to gather and support the Bishop, but no one noticed at that hour in the morning, and it was not for about another hour that the people realized that he had been arrested. Half an hour later the church bells rang and a crowd collected and approached the building, while police and sailors were still inside. An

officer sent for reinforcements and 11 police arrived to stop the crowd. His men were stoned and driven back to a position guarded by an RN party facing the house. The crowd increased and began to force the door of the house and the police opened fire. Twenty-one rounds were fired, six casualties were inflicted and the crowd dispersed; one of the wounded subsequently died.

No further rioting occurred in Limassol. The Commissioner rigorously suppressed irregular bell ringing and the flying of Greek flags. The police were soon able to turn their attention to troublesome outlying villages.

On board *Shropshire*, Bishop Nicodemos 'removed his priestly hat, around the inside of which he had taken the precaution of fastening the Episcopal jewels, and called for a stiff whisky and soda,' Storrs recorded.

In Paphos, two RN officers and a naval party landed at 10.00 from their destroyer and went straight to the police barracks. The Commissioner's wife was taken on board ship for her safety. Demonstrations had started early in the morning, the telegraph wires were again cut and attempts made to block the road to the harbour. Meanwhile the Navy had relieved The Royal Welch Fusiliers' platoon in Limassol. At 18.00 the Marines turned back a procession which was moving in the direction of the Commissioner's house intent on destruction. Guards were posted on Government property. Earlier, a deputation from Morphou had arrived at the entrance to Nicosia by motorcar. The car was stopped and its occupants severely warned and sent back.

As news of the arrests spread throughout the capital, crowds attempted to storm the Law Courts, but withdrew when troops opened fire. One Greek Cypriot – Kyriacos Papadopoulos – was hit and died the next day.

During these troubles British women and children living outside the guarded zone were concentrated in a hotel within it. At midday 1st King's took responsibility for the northern

A Handley Page Hinaidi bomber of the type that Sir Ronald Storrs ordered to demonstrate its capabilities above Greek Cypriot villages as a show of Imperial force.

half of Nicosia and the Royal Welch Fusiliers the southern half.

The Governor now asked the commanding officer of the Victoria troop carriers and a flight of Handley Page Hinaidi day-bombers from Headquarters, Middle East, Royal Air Force, to demonstrate their capabilities in the sky above Cyprus. The aircraft took off, swooped and circled the main towns, dropping pamphlets that warned rebels to stop or else face the consequences. To underline the point, small bombs were released on vacant land, where their explosions were clearly visible.

Shortly afterwards Archbishop Vasiliou Kyrillos (nicknamed *Kyrilloudin*), a man with an incendiary personality, sent his chaplain to seek an interview with the Governor. Storrs replied that he was willing to see the Archbishop but that Captain Freeman would prescribe his route to and from the Secretary's Lodge. Kyrillos, a former member of the Government's Executive Council, had a reputation of being sympathetic towards the colonial rulers and was often criticized by the nationalists.

At the meeting the Archbishop read the Governor a long statement demanding the release of the rebel leaders. 'In my capacity as Ethnarch of Cyprus and on the insistence of the people who have of their own accord assembled outside the Archbishopric I came here in order to bring to Your Excellency's knowledge that on account of the arrest of certain citizens of Cyprus the situation created is such as to be pregnant of imminent dangers in general,' he stated in solemn tones. 'I have felt it my duty to inform Your Excellency of the situation and to recommend, for averting any untoward events, that all those arrested should be released. This measure will ward off any danger. I divest myself, Your Excellency, of any responsibility in case you will not be willing to enforce this measure, so imperatively called for in the present circumstances and highly beneficial for the interests of the Government and the country.

'This is what I had to state, Your Excellency, with the certainty that His Majesty's Government will not delay any longer the fulfilment of the sacred and just national aspirations of Cyprus which is unanimously demanded by the entire Greek population of the Island.'

Storrs replied calmly, 'The Government and not Vasiliou Kyrillos is responsible for law and order and the armed forces will not hesitate to take extreme measures to repress any further disturbance. The Archbishop's proper sphere of responsibility is to urge your flock to obey the civil power and to warn them, as I warn you, of the consequences of disobedience.' The Governor's chaplain took notes of what was said. The meeting over, His Beatitude was shown the door.

Later *The Times* published an intriguing report from its correspondent in Cairo. He said: 'It is understood here that the "Enosis" movement in Cyprus has been strengthened by the economic unrest, which has arisen owing to the present high taxation. It is also suggested that there is an influential minority in the island, which suffers commercially from the rigorous nature of British justice, inasmuch as its members are connected with the illicit narcotic trade. It is understood that the extremists started the trouble at this particular moment because special attempts at conciliation were being made by the British Government the success of which would not have suited the professional agitators.'

Throughout the day, there were further skirmishes between the forces of law and order and the rebels, resulting in the death of Michael Ioannou – on 27 October – from a bullet injury. In Larnaca disturbances were renewed at 17.00. A crowd gathered and marched towards the Commissioner's house, which lay a mile away from the centre of the town. The local Police Commandant ordered his 12 troopers to ride through the rear of the crowd and disperse them, using their whips if necessary. The Commissioner followed with an armed party of 14 police in two motorcars.

The troopers, six of whom were injured, drove the crowd to the sides of the road, and the police cars rushed through, heavily assailed with stones. An armed party took up a position blocking the way. A platoon of Royal Marines arrived at the rear of the crowd. The Commissioner ordered the crowd to disperse or face fire. The crowd broke up into small groups and fled in all directions. One group fired two revolver shots at the Marines. Their officer replied with a volley of six rounds. No casualties resulted. No further demonstrations were reported from Larnaca.

At 17.50, HMS *Colombo* reached Famagusta, the ship's marines ready to subdue any rebels they encountered. The marines later relieved the army units in Famagusta and Paphos. Now Captain Freeman was able to concentrate his force in Nicosia and strike out quickly into the districts, if required.

There had been a mass meeting of 8,000 in Famagusta. Their Greek Cypriot leaders, after warnings from the authorities, tried to discourage violence and called on the crowd to disperse quietly, but their appeals were very much half-hearted. 'We have called you here to demand our rights and in order to approve the measures taken by our representatives. My position does not allow me to go farther,' said

Despite the efforts of the Greek Cypriot rioters, the Union flag continued to fly over Kyrenia Castle.

the Mayor. The Archimandrite followed, telling the crowd that freedom could not be realized without sacrifice and bloodshed, but adding that freedom should be fought for lawfully. The police clerk who reported the speeches records that he heard much 'grievance' expressed. 'While the British soldiers and *zaptiehs* are killing our brethren and innocent schoolboys who are unarmed in other towns, must we leave them here untouched?' a priest from Paralimni asked. 'How can we go back to our village after we have kissed our wives and children and bade them good-bye?'

The situation in Kyrenia town and district had so far been quiet. Nevertheless, the Commissioner had suggested that as there were 54 Europeans in the town, naval or military protection should be sent to the area. Storrs, however, told him that he could not expect any forces unless he reported 'a serious emergency'. He was advised to organize the male British residents and visitors as a defence corps.

During the evening intelligence was received that Makarios II, the Bishop of Kyrenia, intended to visit Nicosia next day and the Commissioner confirmed the information by wire.

That night all district headquarters were supplied with copies of the Defence Order in

Council and large printed posters containing translations of the Defence Regulations were posted for the population to read.

Sunday 25 October 1931

At 05.00 Makarios II arrived at the outskirts of Nicosia, where he was stopped by a picket, and, after a scene of violent protest, obeyed the order to return to the small north coast port. He arrived there just as morning church service was ending. White with rage and suppressed emotion, he stormed into the church and addressed the congregation from the pulpit. 'I went to Nicosia,' he declaimed, 'and was stopped by bayonets.' His voice rose and words and phrases flowed in a tumult. 'This is a Greek place and must be given to Greece. Englishmen are tyrants and malefactors ... I shall hoist the Greek flag where it should be.' With that he led the people – about 300 – straight to the Government offices. On his orders, the crowd hauled down the Union flag and tore it to pieces.

The Bishop's personal servant then hoisted the Greek flag in its place. Warned of the event the Commissioner came running to the scene, mounted the stairs to the balcony and called on the crowd to disperse immediately. 'Speak to us in Greek,' the Bishop shouted, and, after further warnings, led the procession back to the town, where they cut the telegraph wires. Commission staff, meanwhile, pulled down the Greek flag and hoisted a new Union flag. Recognizing the increasing danger in Kyrenia, the Commissioner sent an immediate report on the situation by car to Nicosia.

Storrs immediately asked his Admiral on HMS *London* whether he could send one of the seaplanes attached to the cruisers or release his destroyer, HMS *Colombo*, from Famagusta to reinforce Kyrenia. Naval support was not, however, practical owing to the distance. Thirty Royal Marines from *Colombo* had already been in action in Famagusta, where they had successfully dispersed rebels. The substantive Commissioner had returned from leave in England and took over.

Although there were signs of a return to normality in the town, around 17.00 a mob forced the proprietors of licensed premises to reopen and moved on to attack the Varosha police station. Windows and doors were smashed and police property and records thrown into the street or destroyed. Now the captain of the *Colombo* chose to intervene personally. With two officers, two ratings, and a party of police, he went to Varosha and established a guard there. Returning through Famagusta town, he and his men were insulted and stoned. Bottles and earthenware pots were dropped on their heads from balconies.

Threatened by the crowd on two flanks and assailed with various missiles, including iron shovels, the party opened fire. One rioter – Haralambos Fili, aged 18, from Lefkoniko – was killed and two wounded. The Marines sustained minor injuries and an officer's steel helmet was heavily dented. Additional forces were landed from *Colombo*, and guards posted. There was no further rioting in Famagusta after that night. Slowly the Island was being pacified.

Captain Freeman had reported to Storrs earlier that he could deploy two sections of his soldiers in Kyrenia, once Nicosia, his prime objective, was reasonably under control. He added that his men had arrested Communist Party leader Haralambos Vatiliotis while he was addressing another crowd. Major Wright advised that the Bishop of Kyrenia be taken into custody and that this action should occur after dark.

During his morning conference with his advisers, the Governor had asked Freeman if he required further reinforcements from

Egypt. He replied in the negative, but said he would request a section of armoured cars to suppress village disorders. In addition, he wanted another flight of day-bombers from HQ BTE. (They arrived the next day, but the Captain used them only for carrying messages and reconnoitring landing grounds for the troop carriers.)

Freeman also suggested the RAF establish a radio communications centre in Nicosia because of the constant cutting of telegraph lines. At this time, the Royal Navy was handling wireless messages between all district headquarters, except for Kyrenia.

At 12.30 two sections of Freeman's soldiers reached Kyrenia under the command of a sergeant and began patrolling and setting up pickets, supported by a handful of local police. Throughout the day the crowd at the Bishopric grew in number as people from surrounding villagers poured in. Some came in buses, which disgorged their passengers outside the town.

By 20.00, 1,000 people had assembled there, most of them armed with heavy sticks and pieces of iron. About 21.30 it was reported from Karmi, a hill village five miles from Kyrenia, that most of its inhabitants were on their way too. A party of troops and police were sent to stop them, but found they had already reached the Bishopric. Soon the yelling mob advanced on the armed soldiers. A police inspector ordered the rebels to back off. They did not. The British soldiers now advanced with fixed bayonets, but were heavily stoned and forced to retreat, with their injured sergeant. After a further warning, the soldiers fired 12 rounds in the air. The crowd recoiled and then came forward again. A second volley was fired. The mob withdrew for a time and then reassembled at the Bishopric. During the encounter three rioters were wounded and taken immediately to hospital, where Michael Ioannou from Karavas died two days later.

Savvas Loizides, a Greek Cypriot lawyer, who was exiled from Cyprus with several other organizers of the Rebellion.

Monday, 26 October 1931

At 01.00, Captain Freeman's snatch-platoon arrived in Kyrenia in two trucks and went straight to the Bishopric in search of its prey. The soldiers found 50 men armed with sticks inside, but they offered no resistance. The Bishop attempted to resist arrest, but was overpowered, placed in a lorry and brought straight to the central prison at Nicosia. Placed in a British cell the bishop loudly said Orthodox prayers for hour after hour to irritate his guards.

The search was now on to capture the elusive Savvas Loizides – who was seen everywhere and nowhere – and his colleague Costas Skeleas. Loizides, the radical union leader, was eventually run to ground in Nicosia, while Skeleas was seized later in the day at Limassol, where he had arrived with pamphlets announcing the Communist Party's decision to join the nationalists.

On orders from the Air Ministry, another flight of 45 Bombing Squadron put on a further demonstration – without bombs – diving and wheeling like hungry vultures above outlying villages, using loudspeakers to broadcast news that the rebellion was over.

Despite this, 300 people attempted to stop army lorries and stoned soldiers in Kato Zodhia. They paid no attention to warnings that were shouted by the police and, taking cover behind a wall at the side of the road, continued to throw stones. Once more, the order to fire was given by Captain Hardie. One man was killed, another wounded. A ricochet bullet hit a girl – Helen Polycarpos – inside a house. In Akacha, a ration lorry was held up by a crowd in the morning and the warrant officer in charge, who had an escort of only two soldiers, was forced to open fire. Two men were wounded, one of whom died later. In a village in Paphos district, the police opened fire in defence of a police station and one man was slightly wounded. No other casualties were inflicted by rifle fire in the villages.

Small patrols of the Royal Welch Fusiliers, with British officials as guides and interpreters, were also sent by car to villages in remote areas, including Kambos, in the Paphos Forest, where there had been disorder since 22 October. Here Mr G. W. Chapman, Assistant Conservator of Forests, had been held up by the villagers on his way to Nicosia and forced to return to his station. To warn Captain Hardie and his troops if the villagers were setting an ambush for them, an RAF aircraft flew overhead. On their arrival the patrol soon dispersed the agitators and imposed obedience with the threat of force, supported where necessary by the butts of rifles. The villagers were rounded up and taken to the local coffee house to be addressed by Chapman. He said they had to return stolen telephones, yield their arms, help repair the telephone line, and 'must refrain from hostile demonstrations or other action against the interests of the Government'.

After some parleying, the telephones were produced and troops searched the houses for arms, recovering six shotguns and one barrel of a broken gun. A Greek flag found in the coffee shop was seized and, together with the arms, taken to Nicosia and lodged at the Police Depot. The Fusiliers were back in Nicosia by 16.15.

Tuesday 27 October 1931

The new Defence Regulations had been posted throughout Cyprus and there was no more rioting either in the capital or the villages. The sight of military patrols, the scope of the Defence restrictions, the knowledge that ringleaders had been arrested and the increasing consciousness that crime would be punished and damage paid for by those responsible sobered the turbulent and encouraged the law-abiding to exert their influence.

Only minor disturbances and sabotage continued in outlying villages where there were no military patrols. In Paphos district the Navy cooperated with the police in village patrols. During the day a rifle was stolen when a small detachment of police was ambushed and forcibly disarmed on its way to Limassol. An army platoon then visited the area in troop carriers. The rifle was returned to the police soon afterwards.

Wednesday 28 October 1931

Normality began to return to the once peaceful Island. In Mandria, the inhabitants set about rebuilding the bridge they had destroyed on the main road from Troodos to Limassol. One of the repair workers – Saloumis – stumbled, had a heart attack and died within minutes. Investigations and arrests continued of the culprits who had set alight police stations, looted and otherwise made a nuisance of themselves. District policemen took up their customary duties again at their normal stations. An army platoon arrived at Famagusta by air from Nicosia and patrolled villages in the immediate neighbourhood to capture those who had cut the telegraph and phone lines and damaged the railway line to the capital. The troops returned to Nicosia the same day in their Victoria aircraft.

The rebellion was over, but the cry for *enosis* would be heard again. Next time the Greek Cypriots' insurrection would be meticulously planned and executed under Colonel George Grivas. To end it would require a British force in excess of 35,000 military personnel.

Every nerve of government had been strained during the rebellion and many lessons learned, but the authorities were also cheered by the fact that the majority of villages had not participated in the uprising. A few *mukhtars* (village leaders) even supported the police. In Stroumbi, Savas Papanicolaou wrapped himself in a Union flag and marched through the village. 'I am for the British,' he proclaimed.

In *The Times*, a Josiah Wedgwood of Moddersall pointed out: 'The Orthodox Church in Cyprus is wealthy by comparison with the rest of the inhabitants' and suggested 'it would seem only just that the rebuilding of the ruined property and such money compensation as would meet the financial side of Sir Ronald Storrs's personal loss should be more properly charged against the revenues of the Church than of the island.'

He continued: 'Moreover relations between the Church of England and the Orthodox Church are known to be friendly and intimate. Might it not be possible, therefore, to persuade the authorities of the latter Church to effect an exchange of Bishops between Cyprus and Rhodes? The Cypriot Bishops would acquire in Rhodes and the Dodecanese a valuable sense of discipline and a knowledge of other Governments, while the Rhodian Bishops in Cyprus would give helpful expression to that friendship for England and the English, which is indisputably the prevailing temper both in Great Greece and in the islands.'

On 3 November, six of the deported ringleaders sailed for England and Gibraltar. The same day the Governor declared the cost of reparation of destroyed Government property would fall on the Greek Orthodox communities. It amounted to £34,315 sterling. 'There were in all some 200 villages in which excitement prevailed and demonstrations were made, but without breach of the law. Less than 70 villages were guilty of destruction of property,' an official report stated. 'Many outrages were the work of small gangs of malefactors or individuals, but no satisfactory distinction can be drawn between communal and individual responsibility for incitement.

'The nature of the occurrences in disturbed villages is, as will be appreciated, difficult to define. The news that the towns had defied authority appears to have been brought to many villages by special emissaries from the towns who assured the villagers that the Government was overthrown and the millennium was approaching. Meetings were held at which the shout was raised, "There is no Government – this is the end of the English period – this is the day of revolution and hurrah for union." Drunkards and bad characters generally made the most of the occasion. Law-abiding villagers who continued to pay their taxes were derided. Police and tax collectors were avoided or ignored. If they obtruded themselves and persisted in unpopular duties they were told that they were no longer required. No tax collectors and only a few police were assaulted in the villages. Thus situated, some of the police went out discreetly on patrol until conditions should improve, and others displayed very considerable courage and resource remaining at their posts to reason with the people and resisting, sometimes single-handed, illegal acts and acts of violence on the part of the crowd.

'There are 598 Greek Orthodox villages

and mixed Orthodox and Turkish villages in the island. Three hundred and eighty-nine of these took no part at all in the disturbances.'

Among those who were deported was Savvas Loizides who took his passport with him. With other exiles he was provided accommodation in a boarding house in London's Bayswater with the Bishop of Kyrenia. Later, when the police had stopped watching him, he slipped away to Calais and on to Athens. Throughout the Second World War, he practised as a lawyer in the Greek capital. In 1947, he began agitating for *enosis* once more and was to become a leading instigator of the EOKA conflict.

Meanwhile Sir Ronald Storrs told London: 'The goodwill of the large Moslem population and the other minorities towards the Government never wavered throughout the disturbances, though they suffered the hardships of the curfew orders and other restrictions in common with their fellow townsmen. Their loyalty was fully shared by their Greek-Orthodox compatriots, who form the majority of the civil service and the police. A greatly increased burden of work and responsibility was cast upon almost all branches of the administration: it was borne cheerfully. The police responded to every call made upon them without hesitation.'

But the Governor warned with foresight: 'Until the shadow of union is finally removed from the political horizon, the leading inhabitants are not likely to come forward in large numbers to support the Government and cooperate openly in the progress of their country under British rule.'

On 6 November the remaining four ringleaders of the 1931 Rebellion left Cyprus. Their departure and deportation for life was announced through the local press.

The Governor promulgated new laws. These prohibited the unauthorized flying or exhibition of Greek flags, restricted the ringing of church and other bells as a call to the people to assemble and introduced rigid media censorship. Storrs granted himself sole power to appointment village authorities.

On 5 November an additional company of infantry arrived from Egypt and relieved the naval landing parties at Famagusta, Larnaca, Limassol and Paphos. Lieutenant Colonel King, who would also act as the liaison officer between the military and civilian authorities, commanded the infantry. A section of armoured cars from the 12th Lancers also arrived. They toured the Island and then, unnecessary for practical purposes, were returned later.

Next day the RN ships sailed for Malta. One infantry company was stationed at headquarters in Nicosia, the second company was divided equally between Famagusta and Larnaca, and the third was stationed at Limassol with two sections at Paphos.

By now all the bridges that were destroyed had been repaired by those who damaged them during the riots. Telegraphic and telephone communications were also back in working order. 'Everywhere things are now quiet, but the people, having done just as they liked for the last 53 years, are unaccustomed to discipline and appear sullen and surprised at the strictness of the measures now being enforced to prevent further disturbances,' *The Times* reported. 'Business is still almost at a standstill, but is gradually improving. Many villagers are now cursing the political agitators from the towns who incited them to that destruction of public property for which they are now being held liable. The absence of reprisals or harshness on the part of the Government is favourably noticed.'

The Turkish Cypriot community had reconsidered its position after the rebellion and, through Mehmet Munir Bey, Chairman of the Governing Body of the Turkish Elementary Schools and a member of the Board of Education, articulated its conclusions. The recent serious disturbances were the outcome of 50 years' tolerance and leniency on the part of the Government, said Munir Bey. Now was the opportunity to stamp out the trouble once and for all. He raised the spectre that would haunt the British in years to come: Turkish inhabitants were bitterly opposed to union with Greece and would never agree to it.

'It is often alleged that Turkish Cypriots were roused to oppose *enosis* by the British colonialists, but there was a core of opposition in the Turkish Cypriot community from an early stage,' wrote George Georghalides in his book, *Cyprus and the Governorship of Sir Ronald Storrs*. He quoted a Mr Zekia, who was a member of the Legislative Council: 'We vehemently protest against this [pro-*enosis*] representation as we have always done in the past. We believe that if Cyprus were annexed to Greece there would be no chance of life for the Moslems in Cyprus. We know that the Greeks are in the majority in Cyprus, but there are many other countries in the world similar to Cyprus, which are being administered by foreigners in spite of the fact that the majority of the people belong to another race.

'As is known, there is no principle in international law providing for the annexation of every country to the country which is homogeneous to it. The divergent national feelings and sentiments prevailing in the Island would make impossible the administration of justice in the island.'

On Christmas Eve 1931 the curfew was lifted.

By 31 December the reinforcements from Egypt were no longer needed as the original Cyprus garrison had been brought to a full strength of four officers and 175 men. The rebellion had cost six Greek Cypriot lives and another 30 suffered serious injuries, according to official figures. There were no British fatalities. Nine individuals had been deported and 2,952 were tried in court on various charges. All were found guilty.

'The Turkish Cypriots played no part in the 1931 riots,' Nancy Crawshaw noted, but 'the suspension of the Constitution and the rights that went with it, aimed at containing the seditious activities of the Greeks, equally left the Turkish community without a voice in the Island's affairs through elected representatives. The Turkish Cypriots tended to remain silent rather than risk alienating the British administration, their sole protector against the demands of the Greek majority.'

On the other end of the scale, prior to the rebellion, there had been no radio communication facilities between district offices, the capital and military headquarters in Egypt. Now there were. The police had become slightly better organized and received training from the military in more effective use of their weapons. A special constabulary had been formed too, which all British residents were asked to join. Though only small in numbers, these 'specials' – several of whom had been in the army – would provide solid support to the police in times of trouble, until the arrival of military assistance.

Tri-service operations had been proven to work, as had the cooperation between the Civil Government and the Services. 'No action was decided upon until the Governor had consulted the military commander,' Captain Freeman pointed out in his final report. But, most important of all, flying troop carriers had been invaluable for moving platoons to and from the main Cyprus towns, speedily and at short notice. 'The aircraft did not need a guard while on the ground,' reported Captain Freeman. 'At the first sign of any attack they took to the air at once.' This method of deployment had never been used before by the British Army and established a precedent that would become common practice in the years ahead.

From Athens, the Greek Cypriots had received no support from the mainland government.

'A great change has taken place in the

demeanour of the Greek inhabitants, who were previously inclined to parade their disrespect of British rule in every possible manner, but are now markedly respectful to British people whom they may meet in the streets or roads,' a *Times* correspondent commented from the Island.

LESS THAN a month after the destruction of Government House, Storrs commissioned the renowned architect Austen Harrison to design a replacement that was representative of the grandeur of the British Empire and would impress those entering. Its foundation stone was formally laid on 3 June 1932, but progress was slow and costly. Sir Ronald Storrs left Cyprus before the building was completed, utterly disappointed with the 'ungrateful' people of the Island. He was transferred to Northern Rhodesia where his unhappiness grew as he found himself far from the Near East that he loved. Sir Reginald Stubbs, the new High Commissioner, fired Harrison and replaced him with Maurice Webb to complete the project swiftly and more economically.

Three years before the start of the Second World War, the new Government House was ready for business. Visitors would now be greeted under a monumental British Coat of Arms above its central porch. Carved by Costas Kasmiris, a stonemason from Kaimakli, it included eight sculptured gargoyles that represented the works' foreman, the head mason, head carpenter and the builders. A camel, donkey, ox and goat – Cypriot animals that played a part in the construction – stand in a row above.

From the American *Time* magazine correspondent came a health warning to the occupants: 'The formerly ubiquitous Greek flag has vanished as if it were non-existent. Undoubtedly a great deal of sullen resentment, however, is smoldering under the surface. This is shown by the fact that no unofficial Greek has yet dared publicly to denounce the dastardly burning of the old Government House. Traces of resentment against agitators are apparent among the village population, which, having been discouraged from looting Government stores and burning police stations by British troops, finds that the leaders from the towns who encouraged it in heroic language to raise the standard of revolt are skulking unscathed at home. It may be guessed that disloyal propaganda is ready to break out again in the Island as soon as the opportunity offers. The Governor's strong policy prevents this at present.'

A quarter of a century later, EOKA decided it was time to try again to oust the British, ignore the Turks and fight a terrorist campaign for *enosis*, lasting not a week, but for four years. Many of the original agitators came out the shadows and lent their support. The foremost two of the 'old guard' were the brothers Loizides, Savvas and Socrates. They had settled in Greece, where in 1951 they attended a secret meeting in Athens between George Stratos, a former Greek war minister, and George Grivas. Together they proposed Grivas 'should undertake the leadership of an armed struggle to throw the British out of Cyprus'.

All sides had learned lessons from the failed rebellion and put them to use to achieve their ends, but there would be no winners. The Island of Love would be lashed by storms of violence and hatred.

Sir Ronald Storrs died on 1 November 1955, before the EOKA conflict reached its zenith.

A monument to commemorate the rebellion stands today in south Nicosia. The work of sculptor Panayiotis Pasantas, it consists of a larger than life bronze statue of a man wielding his clenched fist to 'demonstrate the will of the people'. A marble scroll lists the names of 17 people who died in the 1931 uprising.

CHAPTER FOUR

Forbidden Cargo and farewell Sir Robert

'A jewel is still precious, though trampled in the earth.'
Namik Kemal, Turkish poet

EMPIRE DAY had started badly. Everywhere secondary school children were making a nuisance of themselves, carrying Greek flags, shouting nationalist slogans and demonstrating outside Government buildings. In Nicosia, 1,300 pupils poured out of the Pancyprian Gymnasium, whose alma mater included Dighenis and Makarios. They were joined in the streets by another 1,000 from the Samuel School. Both academic establishments were considered the Island's equivalent of Britain's Eton and Harrow, but not for the behaviour of their young students, although they were very polite to their teachers. 'Sir, we've decided to abstain from school today,' a spokesman would declare and the entire class laid down their books and walked out. 'There was no holding them back,' said an assistant headmaster. Another declared: 'The youth, in its generous impulse, threw itself wholeheartedly into the fight. As far as they were concerned, the national struggle came first, lessons second.'

To put an end to these disturbances, Victor Bodker, the editor of the pro-British *Cyprus Mail* proposed the authorities remember how miscreants in India had been sprayed with coloured dye, tossed into police vans, driven 20 or so miles from where they lived and dumped, without their shoes, and then ordered to walk home. Later some soldiers adopted this practice.

At Government House, Sir Robert Armitage sighed and reluctantly accepted the advice of his inner circle and ordered the

In Nicosia, 1,300 pupils pour out of the Pancyprian Gymnasium.

Police and troops set out to disperse the student demonstrators.

police to take whatever action was necessary to disperse the demonstrators. And so, on 25 May 1955, began running battles between baton-wielding officers and youngsters adept at throwing stones and firing catapults. As they were cleared from one area, they reassembled at another to challenge the authority of the colonial administration. For the police it was a thankless task, no more enjoyed than by Sir Robert. Only the youngsters, some with sore heads, took pleasure from expressing their ideals.

Once the streets were calm again, Sir Robert took a bath and dressed to attend a special evening screening of a new British motion picture at the Pallas Cinema. It was planned as a fund-raising event for the Cyprus branch of the British Legion and would be attended by the capital's elite, including the Greek Consul who had booked two seats. The Governor thought it would be a good opportunity to exchange a few words informally with the man from Athens. Perhaps he could use his good offices to persuade Greek Cypriot youth not to misbehave as they had throughout the day. But first he would have to sit through 90 minutes of celluloid featuring acting stalwarts of the British cinema Jack Warner, Nigel Patrick and Elizabeth Sellers in a story about contraband called *Forbidden Cargo*, an apt title considering the trial of the *Aghios Georghios* smugglers had recently ended.

Whether the Governor and the audience enjoyed this humourless movie is hard to tell, but they were grateful it lasted five minutes less than its scheduled running time, because barely had they left the cinema when a Coca-Cola bottle packed with explosive and a time pencil fuse went off. It had been placed not far from where Sir Robert and Lady Armitage were sitting, sending shards of metal and wood in all directions. The blast shattered the cinema's gallery and destroyed seven rows of seats. Had the assassination succeeded, not

Haralambos Xenofontos planted a bomb in the Pallas cinema to kill Sir Robert Armitage.

only would the Governor have died, but so too would the colonial secretary and chief justice, together with their wives, who were sitting with him.

Curiously the Greek Consul had failed to attend the premier.

The bomb had been planted under a seat during the film's afternoon screening by Haralambos Xenofontos, a member of the gang run by Markos Drakos, one of EOKA's earliest recruits. The assassination attempt had been sanctioned by 'The Leader' himself, contrary to the wishes of Archbishop Makarios, who still only wanted attacks against property, not Government officials. Although the Governor came away unharmed, Xenofontos was promoted from scattering EOKA leaflets through Nicosia from his bicycle to a full-blooded member and allowed to join those who later guarded Grivas in the Kyrenia Mountains.

IN PAPHOS, sentences were passed on the smugglers caught in January when they tried to land arms and munitions for use by EOKA.

The smuggling ship *Aghios Georghios*.

Police deliver boxes of evidence to the Paphos Court
where the captured *Aghios Georghios* smugglers
stand trial.

Amongst them was Evangelos Louca, the master of the *Aghios Georghios*, who argued: 'As a Greek citizen I have done my duty. I have a sacred obligation to help my Cypriot brethren.' Socrates Loizides boasted: 'I am a Greek Cypriot with Greek nationality. I believe in the principles of freedom, democ-

racy, justice, and self-determination and therefore have done what I did.' Anargyros Karadimas said very little. In a plea of mitigation their lawyer produced a document, signed by Field Marshal Lord Alexander, expressing gratitude to Louca for helping British servicemen to evade capture during the Second World War, when he was employed as skipper of a caique which made many dangerous trips in enemy waters, he said. He had also fought on the British side and was wounded and taken prisoner. He continued that Savvas Loizides had fought the Nazis as well – and the Communists in Greece.

The Chief Justice, Sir Eric Hallinan, passing sentence, said it was useless for the accused to say they were not criminally responsible for what they had done. They were responsible both criminally and morally. He told Loizides that no doubt his fanatical ideas were sincere 'but you were prepared through a well planned organization, and by importing weapons and dynamite into the island, to introduce armed force and violence into the political affairs of Cyprus'.

With Sir Eric's words ringing in their ears, the guilty were marched off to prison to start their sentences of varying duration.

ON 30 MAY, the *Times of Cyprus* appeared for the first time, with Charles Foley at the editorial helm, to compete against the long-established *Cyprus Mail*. From the outset he intended to challenge the colonial administration. His staff consisted of a motley collection of writers and budding journalists who had washed up on the Island's shores. Greek historian Doros Alastos said: 'His conscience made him the ally of a people of whose history and language he knew little, but he had made his choice and did not deviate from it.'

Foley's news editor, Michael Davidson, had left Britain because homosexuality was against the law and he was a self-professed pederast with a long record of convictions. It was

Davidson who had suggested the creation of the newspaper and found a Mr Manglis, a multimillionaire who owned the only Rolls Royce in Cyprus, to guarantee its advertising revenue. Jill Russell, a freelance, joined the reporting team and continued to feed 'stories' to the international press from Foley's point of view. She was 'a slim young thing, who had trained as a teacher'.

Other contributors included Warrant Officer Knox who reviewed films and a WRAC sergeant who earned a few bob on the side as a cartoonist. They were joined by Wing Commander Walker-Brash as a gossip columnist. For a short period Richard Lumley, the son of the Lord Chamberlain and heir to the earldom of Scarborough, acted as the paper's proofreader. He had been introduced by Lawrence Durrell with whom he was sharing a house. Davidson described him in his autobiography as 'a delightful companion: languidly amusing and charmingly intelligent; but the suave quietude of his discerning mind seemed to be founded on an ingrained unhappiness, as lichen charmingly colours the hardness of stone'. Lumley, a product of Eton and a graduate of Magdalen College, Oxford, later moved on to join the news desk at the Government's Public Information Office, until the arrival of Field Marshal Sir John Harding who enlisted him as an extra ADC, where his experience as a National Service officer with the Hussars served him well.

Another member of Foley's editorial team was Barbara Cornwall, an ambitious American, who stopped off in Cyprus on her way to India, and stayed. When Davidson left the Island, she replaced him as news editor and also became *Time* magazine's stringer on the Island. She later married Dr Lyssarides, whose EOKA code-name was *Spartacus*.

The newspaper never denounced EOKA's violence and the expatriate community began to look upon it as a megaphone for *enosis* and a daily delivery of anti-British propaganda, acting just within the limits of the law.

'In the centre of Nicosia, we on the *Times of Cyprus* were safer than most British: we were known by sight, I suppose, to the local "killer squad" and probably excused death because we were anti-Government,' Davidson explained, overlooking the fact that the leader of the 'killer squad' was Nicos Sampson, once employed by him as his Famagusta correspondent. They had met when Sampson was 'a charming, but plainly unstable, Greek youth bursting with keenness and brash conceit' to quote his mentor. 'A Government clerk, who, aware of his vocation, was plying journalism in his spare time.'

In his autobiography, Davidson, clearly charmed by Sampson's 'boyish way', enthused about his qualities as he saw them. 'We hired a car and spent the day in the bleak, dried-up villages of this savage zone where nobody ever went and which drove like a roughened tongue into the sea (the heart of EOKA land, I called it in my story): villages with gleaming Hellenic names like Xylophagou, Paralimni, Liopetri, Sotira,' he wrote.

'On this trip Nicos' companionship was delightful; a perfect interpreter, asking the questions, as I wanted them put, enticing with his charm the frankest answers possible in the circumstances; he was the impersonal reporter, never the partisan. Indeed, in all my early acquaintance with him, he seemed to me detached from politics. But that day he was interested only in himself: he talked naively of his own abilities and ambitions, volubly vain.'

Although Foley and colleagues denied any connection to Archbishop Makarios, the paper's offices and print shop were owned by the Church and stood in the precincts of the Archbishopric. Among the employees were several individuals who would later figure prominently in EOKA terrorist acts.

Davidson found the situation amusing: 'It was useful to me, doing most of the political writing, to have the Archbishop living at the bottom of the garden. I could see him any day

I wanted to or, if he were away, his brilliant and delightful principal secretary, Nicos Kranidiotis.' For the next four years, the Security Forces perceived the *Times of Cyprus* as the enemy.

London journalist Dennis Pitts on a visit to Cyprus reported: 'A British Colonel, red-faced after breaking up an ugly Turkish riot, turned to me and said: "I don't know who the biggest danger is here – the Greeks, the Turks or the *Times of Cyprus*".' Sergeant Eric Bradley of the RAF probably expressed the sentiment of most British troops, when he told the author: 'There was a general feeling that most of the *Times* people were EOKA sympathizers. One of the female reporters actually published the full addresses of servicemen who had been involved in "incidents". Some families had to be relocated because of her reports. But her ardour for EOKA cooled when she was hit on the head by a brick thrown during an anti-British student demonstration.'

ARCHBISHOP MAKARIOS, meanwhile, was on his travels again, trying to drum up support for his cause among the non-aligned nations. At the African-Asian Bandung Conference, he accused the British of provoking the 'precarious' situation in Cyprus, a subject he pursued in Athens in an address to the Foreign Press Association. He declaimed: 'I accuse the British Government that by its international machinations it undermines and endangers the peace and security of the eastern Mediterranean. This policy was being pursued with unusual stubbornness and offensive arrogance.' With a straight face, he insisted that as a religious man he had expressly urged Greek Cypriots to avoid violence, but they were driven to it by Britain's 'imperialistic policy'. He then categorically denied any association with EOKA.

Asked about rumoured tripartite negotiations between Britain, Greece, and Turkey on the Cyprus problem, he replied these could only make matters worse. 'Turkey,' he said, 'has no right over Cyprus except when the time comes to discuss the safeguarding of Turkish minority rights.'

Makarios focused only on union with Greece. For him there was no bigger picture to see. For Alan Lennox-Boyd, Secretary of State for the Colonies, Cyprus was a mere corner of the canvas, although important. He told the House of Commons that Her Majesty's Government had a number of duties on the Island, which it intended to fulfil. Britain had a strategic responsibility 'on which our survival, the survival of Greece, the survival of Turkey, and of the NATO nations, and, indeed, of the free world, depend'. It was essential that a power vacuum should not be allowed to build up on the Turkish flank, he argued, and the defence of this area was vital. To promote stability and cohesion in the Middle East and defend it in war, 'we must be able to station sufficient forces in Cyprus and have a secure base from which they can operate'. Cyprus had many advantages, he pointed out. It was the only place where Britain had freedom from externally imposed restrictions on its military requirements. Geographically it was well placed, and its airfield facilities would be of the first importance.

IN CYPRUS, 30 Field Squadron 35 Army Engineer Regiment had arrived from the Canal Zone and was settled in Polemidia Camp. To the troops' surprise, they found 30 wooden huts there, which had been erected by Captain H. H. Kitchener, RE, in 1882. Former Sapper Eric Reed smiles wryly: 'We had all the mod cons – showers and a hole in the ground, which was our latrine!'

The unit's main task was to prepare the ground for Britain's Middle East Land Forces HQ at Episkopi, near Limassol. One of its first tasks was to ensure that there was a secure water supply for the new cantonment. In the small village of Kissousa, 1,800 feet above sea level in the Troodos Mountains, the Engineers found an ideal source. 19 Topographic Squadron chose the site. To carry the water to the new base, they built a gravity feed system and 18 miles of pipe brought from the Canal Zone in Egypt. During this major building project, they also worked to improve and modernize living conditions for local people. Typical of their many chores was a large civil aid project carried out by 40 Field Squadron and the Plant Troop of 18 Field Park Squadron to connect the villages of Trozina and Yerovasa in the Troodos foothills with a one-and-a-half mile road and a 130-foot Bailey Bridge.

'As time went on, we were always on edge, never knowing the kind of welcome we would receive during our surveying missions,' Reed remembers. 'Take, for example, the case of our trip to Amiandos, one of the remoter villages in the Troodos. It consisted of two small rows of tiny houses divided by a donkey track. This particular day there was an eerie silence as we approached. There was not a soul in sight. Even the dogs and stray cats had disappeared. We knew something was up. Then, without warning, a shower of stones descended on us. We jumped out of our vehicle and took up firing positions.

'Seeing that we were fully armed the villagers slowly began to emerge from their homes, some holding opened Pepsi Cola bottles, which they offered us as a gesture of friendship, telling us *Dighenis poly gala*, which we discovered meant "Grivas is very good". This was the type of thing we dealt with daily.'

During early summer, the security forces in Cyprus investigated bomb explosions and attacks on police stations, chased leaflet throwers and monitored curfews, while the courts were kept busy with trials of those arrested after April's start of the conflict. And still the authorities had little knowledge about

A British soldier stands guard outside the Law Courts in Nicosia.

EOKA's structure, membership and leadership. In London, the Cabinet debated the best way to prevent the troubles escalating and prevent the 'local issues' from dragging Turkey and Greece into the squabble in any significant way, although Radio Athens was keeping up its virulently anti-British broadcasts to its listeners on the Island.

The Turkish Cypriot community began to feel threatened. Dr Fazil Kutchuk, as its leader, was particularly incensed by injuries inflicted on members of his constituency when a bomb exploded outside Police Headquarters. He wrote to the Governor: 'As a result of the Government's tolerance and negligence, extremist Greek elements have tonight attacked our right of existence and the blood of 14 innocent Turks has been shed.' So far not one Briton had been killed.

Dr Fazil Kutchuk, the leader of the Turkish Cypriots.

At the end of June, the Government of Cyprus, including the Governor, gave up their summer stay in the cool of the Troodos Mountains for the first time since the British had arrived and remained in the hot oven that was Nicosia, such was their concern to keep the temperature of the populace down. Theirs was an impossible task as EOKA honed its methods.

In early July, unlike Armitage, Grivas decided he would spend his time in the less stifling atmosphere of the Troodos area, where he launched a vigorous training programme for his latest EOKA recruits. He showed them how to ambush troop convoys as they trundled through the winding mountain roads and instilled fire in the bellies of his post-pubescent teenagers, something he thought was severely lacking among his ill-disciplined motley collection of budding terrorists. He

was pleased that his terror tactics against the police were starting to pay dividends. Anyone who served the British was to be crushed for their disloyalty to his cause, he declared. By the end of the summer Grivas was ready for all-out conflict: he had created an effective command and control system of his gangs, both in town and country, and developed secure supply lines for food and munitions. 'Safe houses' had been arranged and well-equipped hides in the mountains were complete.

When a gang of his killed a police officer in Amiandos, close to the asbestos mines, the authorities reacted by offering a reward of one thousand pounds to the person or persons who would lead the authorities to the capture of the killers. Further, if anyone pointed a finger at those participating in any terrorist activity, he or she would be given five hundred pounds. These were the highest rewards ever offered in Cyprus, but wise heads doubted they would be collected in view of the public's fear of reprisals by Dighenis's followers.

Raymond Courtney, the US Consul in Cyprus, was all the while keeping his Washington masters fully informed of the situation. He presented a gloomy picture. 'Step by step the enosists have tested the Cyprus Government and proved that they can get away with open and even violent defiance,' he reported.

MONEY – more precisely the lack of it – was also an issue for many of the increasing numbers of troops arriving in Cyprus. A National Service private was paid only one pound, eleven shillings and sixpence a week, out of which he was compelled to purchase certain essential items, which was why George Jeger, the Labour MP for Goole, asked the Secretary of State for War in the House of Commons whether he would make a statement on the new webbing equipment cleaner that had replaced Blanco.

Mr Anthony Head replied that as a result of research by the Ministry of Supply, a formula for a new cleaner had been developed and tested. It proved highly satisfactory and so it had been introduced into the Army, but the soldiery neither liked it nor found it efficient. Further research had shown that its manufacture was not entirely in accordance with specification and a new version was now being distributed.

Mrs Lena Jeger, another Labour MP, responded with a question. 'Will the new cleaner be as inflammable as the other stuff, which was recognized as a great danger in tents and wooden huts, and will it be cheaper?' she asked. 'One of the complaints I have received is that it costs four shillings and four pence a week to keep equipment clean, as against one shilling and three pence for the old Blanco.'

Replied the Secretary of State: 'The question of cost depends on how long one dressing lasts. I hope it will last a long time. So far as I know, it's not inflammable.'

And that was the end of the matter.

Shortly afterwards Sir Anthony Eden, the Prime Minister, stood up in the Commons and confirmed rumours that a tripartite conference was being mooted in British circles, as Makarios had heard during his last visit to Athens.

On 30 June, the House suddenly fell silent as Sir Anthony stood up to announce some unheralded news. He said: 'I wish to inform the House that the Government has this morning made the following communication to the Greek and Turkish Governments through her Majesty's representatives: "Her Majesty's Government have been giving further consideration to the strategic and other problems affecting alike the United Kingdom, Greece, and Turkey in the eastern Mediterranean. They consider that the association of the three countries in that area, based on mutual confidence, is essential to their

common interest. Her Majesty's Government accordingly invite the Greek and Turkish Governments to send representatives to confer with them in London at an early date on political and defence questions which affect the eastern Mediterranean, including Cyprus".'

He continued: 'The Government very much hopes that the Greek and Turkish Governments will accept this invitation. The House will note that the terms of the invitation are not restricted and it is our intention that there should be no fixed agenda, and that these discussions should range widely over all the questions involved. The discussions will be without prior commitment by any party.'

The Prime Minister's Tory supporters cheered. Mr Clement Atlee for Labour welcomed the announcement. 'I am sure this meeting will be very welcome, in view of the disturbed conditions in Cyprus at present,' he said. For the Liberals, Mr Clement Davies congratulated the Government for taking this step, 'because the situation in Cyprus is causing anxiety not only here but also in the Middle East. Assuming, as we all hope, that this invitation will be accepted.'

Later Eden wrote in his memoirs that the conference was intended to bring the difficulties of the Cyprus question to the attention of countries critical of British polices. 'We knew how wide the difference of opinion was between the Greeks and Turks, but the world did not. Too many thought our troubles were due to old-fashioned British colonialism,' he said. 'By securing a precise definition of those differences we hoped to show the true nature of the problem. The exact terms of our proposals for the future could then be presented.'

In Athens, the Papagos Government met the invitation with reserve. 'It is prompted, *The Times* explained, 'by the fear that the round-table conference may be a "British trap" to deprive Greece of what has been achieved so far through her appeal to the

United Nations and the "fighting spirit" of the Cypriot people. In responsible Greek political circles it was stated that the Cyprus issue was now entering "a most crucial" period.

'It was obvious that in a survey of defence problems in the eastern Mediterranean, Turkey had its word to say, but when the Cyprus issue comes to be considered the talks should be conducted on a bilateral level between the Greeks and the British.'

While the Papagos Government demanded more details about the planned conference, Turkey accepted, but Prime Minister Menderes, referring to the invitation said: 'The fact that the most parts of the Turkish shores are surrounded by the threatening observation posts of foreign states should be acknowledged by everyone. Today only the shore facing Cyprus seems to be safe. Therefore Cyprus is a continuation of Turkey and forms one of its essential security points. Thus, if any doubt is raised about its present status, this has to be resolved not on technical merits but on the basis of other more important and more substantial realities. Our delegation in London will defend the preserving of the status quo as a minimum condition.'

The Turkish press expressed satisfaction, which was interpreted as recognition of Turkish rights in Cyprus, the complete opposite of opinion in Greece, which wanted no place at the table for the Turks.

America watched the situation carefully. The US Ambassador to Greece said: 'The British offer is interesting and of good intention. Greece and Turkey should not miss it.' That afternoon the Greek newspaper *Ethnos*, in a leading article, said that the Americans, 'who proclaim their anti-colonialist spirit, are nevertheless paving the way for the British' and are 'prepared to exert pressure so that we may tolerate the definite strangling of Cypriots' freedom'. It stressed that Greece had no interest in participating in the 'miserable comedy, which will be staged in London'.

Radio Ankara, meanwhile, commented that the Turkish Government was determined to defend to the utmost Turkish rights and to prevent the safety of the Turkish minority on the Island being jeopardized by local agitators.

Archbishop Makarios surprised no one when he preached that any discussion about Cyprus was inconceivable without representation by Cypriots. 'Our case clearly remains one of self-determination, and only on this basis can it be properly dealt with and settled,' he said. Vias Markides, a member of the Ethnarchy office and editor of *Ethnos*, represented Makarios's view in a leading article. He quoted 'a close confidant of the Archbishop' as saying that if the scope of the London talks did not include the goal of immediate self-determination the talks either would not start or would break down.

Mufti Dana was the first to express Turkish Cypriot reaction. He said his community would abide by any decisions taken in London by the Ankara Government. Dr Kutchuk, editor of *Halkin Sesi*, the Turkish newspaper in Nicosia, published his opinion, printed in English. He described the demand for *enosis* as a call for imperialism by 'little but arrogant' Greece and warned 'Turkey will never tolerate *enosis*. The Turks of Cyprus will never submit to Greek rule.'

IN THE House of Commons, it was business as usual. At Question Time, Mr Simmons, the Labour Member of Parliament for Brierley Hill, asked the Secretary of State for War what proficiency regimental barbers were required to attain, and if they were allowed to give National Servicemen any choice of hair style 'when operating upon them'. Mr Head replied: 'Paragraph 1003 of Queen's Regulations states that hair will be kept short. A soldier may please himself what style he wears provided this rule is observed. There is no establishment for regimental barbers and, although units usually provide civilian or soldier barbers, any man may choose his own civilian hairdresser.'

Mr Simmons remained dissatisfied by the answer. He claimed that 'many people who practised their arts as hairdressers upon National Servicemen are more fitted to practise as carpenters or metal shearers'. Would the Minister, he asked, look at a photograph, which he had of a National Serviceman, who 'looked a perfect fright after the operation of the regimental barber'? He continued: 'It is an important question. If National Servicemen are to be encouraged to continue in the Services, they must be treated as human beings.'

The Secretary of State agreed that he favoured people having decent haircuts, and he promised to look at the photograph Mr Simmons had in his possession.

Then came the news that Greece had agreed to attend the London conference, even if Turkey were present. Earlier, British diplomats had told the Greek Foreign Minister Stephanopoulos quietly that if his government made its acceptance conditional on Turkey being excluded, it would get short shift from Foreign Minister Harold Macmillan. Now Stephanopoulos only drew attention to the fact that the conference would have no agenda – it would be 'simply a free discussion' – though he emphasized that self-determination would be the central issue. Formal acceptance was delivered by letter a few days later. It said: 'The Royal Government of Greece have taken cognizance with satisfaction of the decision reached by her Britannic Majesty's Government to discuss with them political and defence questions which affect the eastern Mediterranean, including Cyprus.

'The Royal Government of Greece quite agree that their association with the United Kingdom and Turkey, based upon mutual confidence, is essential to their common interests in the eastern Mediterranean, and are therefore prepared to send their representatives to London at as early a date as possible.'

DIPLOMACY AND politics stepped up a gear when Alan Lennox-Boyd flew to Nicosia for consultations with Governor Armitage and Greek and Turkish Cypriot leaders. It was the first visit to Cyprus of a Secretary of State for the Colonies since Britain occupied the Island in 1878. It was also the first occasion for an Archbishop and Governor of Cyprus to talk directly since the 1931 Rebellion. The two-hour Saturday meeting was held in the Ledra Palace Hotel. Security was so tight that the public was completely unaware it was taking place.

Ethnos, the Archbishop's mouthpiece, commented: 'It is significant that for two hours the Cyprus question was discussed, for the Cyprus question is self-determination. Thus the meeting constitutes a milestone in the history of the Cyprus struggle. Progress has been achieved, thanks to our reaction to British designs and our insistence on self-determination. We shall reach our goal more quickly if we steadfastly adhere to the line we follow. We have no doubt that the Ethnarch made this clear to Mr. Lennox-Boyd and that Mr. Lennox-Boyd is convinced that the Ethnarch speaks for all Greeks, free or not free.'

Privately Governor Armitage had growing doubts about the conference as it would give no voice to Cypriots to express themselves. He put his feelings to Lennox-Boyd during his visit. Armitage suggested the British Government was manipulating events and the conference would be seen as a ploy 'to prevent the possibility of the emergence of a Cypriot nation and a Cypriot government'. He could not understand why a Colonial Office problem was being exploited by the Foreign Office. More trouble and violence was sure to follow, he said. Whatever Sir Robert's virtues, they did not include an understanding of internecine politics.

Immediately after the Ledra Palace meeting Makarios caught a plane to Athens to report to the Greek Government. The Turkish Government, he reminded Ministers in the capital, must have no say in the future of the Island, four-fifths of the population of which was Greek.

Earlier Lennox-Boyd had met a delegation of 21 prominent Cypriot Turks, including the Mufti, who told him of their fierce opposition to the mere idea of the union of the island with Greece, and warned him of the danger of civil war in such an eventuality. He also discussed the Cyprus situation with the Communist mayors of Limassol, Famagusta and Larnaca, and heard their views and grievances.

At a press conference on Sunday, the Secretary of State asked the journalists to remember that two mainland countries had to be considered when governing Cyprus. He insisted that Greek and Turkish cultures on the Island were respected and understood, and there was no desire by Britain to disturb them. He also expressed complete support for the Governor, which turned out to be in an inexactitude of the truth.

The Minister's visit was marred by only two bomb incidents. One occurred at 14.30 in a store near Wolseley Barracks, Nicosia, probably caused by a hand-grenade. The other took place at the same time in the Income Tax Commissioner's office, part of the Government administrative buildings. As it was Sunday, nobody was working there and so nobody was hurt, but considerable damage was done to the roof and walls. Michael Karaolis had planted the bomb. He would become the first terrorist to be hanged, found guilty of the murder of a Greek Cypriot policeman. His case became a cause célèbre. Today he is considered a martyr by Greek Cypriots.

Then, with masterful political mis-timing, Governor Armitage published a special issue of the *Cyprus Gazette*, which contained the text of a Detention of Persons Law. It was similar to Defence Regulation 18b issued in Britain during the Second World War. Essentially it stated that if the Governor was satisfied that a person was a terrorist, he could order their detention without trial. Conditions of confinement were to be as little oppressive as possible. If anyone protested, they had the right to lodge an appeal with an advisory committee – consisting of members chosen by Armitage. He said the law initially would be on the statute books for three months and was part of his strategy to crush EOKA.

To explain his reasons, Armitage released the following statement: 'Terrorists have shown by their recent actions their intention to murder police officers, and have also made threats against the Governor, leaders of the Turkish community, and Army personnel. This state of affairs cannot be tolerated, and the Government is confident that in taking the present step it will have the support of all those who have the true interests of Cyprus at heart.

'A special law is necessary because people are reluctant to come forward with evidence or information for fear of reprisals. It is emphasized that this law is directed only against active terrorists. The Government is determined to bring to an end the acts of terrorism, which have been committed against persons and property during recent weeks. Since 20 June attacks have been made resulting in two deaths and injuries to 22 persons.'

Another law followed swiftly, banning persons under 21 from possessing firearms. It also provided for the registration with the police of all firearms in the Colony, and for the imposition of penalties of six months' imprisonment and a fine of £25 for illegal possession.

Of course, the new laws did nothing to improve the Government's popularity. Instead EOKA supporters and the Communists of the Island united for the first time in opposition. Calls went out to hold general strikes and demonstrations in protest, just as Whitehall planned to start the Tripartite Conference on 29 August.

DURING THE first 24-hour strike, towns were placed out of bounds to soldiers and their wives, while police watched potential trouble spots. Before the day was over, they and the demonstrators clashed. To prevent protesters from setting alight the British Council building in Nicosia, tear gas and baton charges were used. The strike did not stop Armitage from applying the new law, indiscriminately many believed.

EOKA responded by distributing another leaflet – signed by 'The Leader' – that sent a stern message to Greek Cypriot policemen, who might do their duty on the Governor's behalf. 'I have warned you: you have taken this warning as a mere threat, and my forbearance has weakened. What I have threatened I will carry out to the letter. Do not try to block our path or you will stain it with your blood. But you will not stop us. I have given instructions: Anyone who tries to stop the Cypriot patriots will be EXECUTED.

'YOU HAVE NOTHING TO FEAR SO LONG AS YOU DO NOT GET IN OUR WAY.'

And 'execute' EOKA did. Ignoring his popularity as a local football star, Special Constable Nikki Stavros was murdered on 13 August. His brave brother sent a letter to the press condemning terrorism and blamed Dighenis for the 'hell' and loss of freedom he had brought to the Island. All this achieved was to add him to the organization's hit list. Police officers began to resign in droves or offered their services secretly to EOKA.

Then, on 18 August, Armitage demonstrated his authority by approving a roundup of 31 individuals from Nicosia and its surrounds. They included clerks, students, shepherds, grocers and a deacon of the Orthodox Church. In Agros, 55 miles from the capital, the entire village committee was taken into custody. One of the men was the operator of the local power generating station, leaving inhabitants without electricity and farmers without power to irrigate their fields.

The total number of detainees mounted to 57. All were confined in the capital's central prison.

On the very eve of the conference in London's Lancaster House, Grivas showed his displeasure immediately after the Island's Communist Party leader Ezekial Papaioannou finished addressing a rally of 1,500 supporters outside the Alhambra Hall in Nicosia. They had gathered to approve civil disobedience if Britain, Greece and Turkey did not agree immediate self-determination for the Island's people. Papaioannou had also lunged a verbal lance at the Orthodox Church and EOKA. 'We do not know and do not wish to learn the cowardly tactics of political murder,' he shouted. He was seconds away from watching another killing.

Just as the gathering was breaking up at noon, a man stepped out of the crowd and fired three shots into the chest of Special Branch Constable Herodotus Poullis, 40, who fell dead in front of hundreds of onlookers. Dighenis explained: 'We struck the fatal blow against police morale by the public execution of Poullis, who had been spying on the Nicosia groups and interfering with their work: two attempts had already been made on his life but he chose to ignore our warnings.'

In the panic that ensued, the killer escaped on a bicycle.

That night, the administration's acting Colonial Secretary, Mr J. Sykes, went on the radio to appeal for witnesses to come forward. 'A fortnight ago Miki Zavros, a special constable, was shot down from behind by a pair of callous murderers. Before that Sergeant

Demosthenous was brutally assassinated. Sergeant Costopolos died of wounds received in a cowardly ambush. Tonight it is the home, wife and family of Constable Poullis, which is grieving for a good and honest man murdered by the evil agents of political terrorism ... I pray your political leaders may be forgiven for condoning and even praising terrorism,' he said. 'Let them know that you ordinary people can distinguish right from wrong in the methods by which political ends can be pursued; that you are not to be driven by conscienceless political hysteria into approving what you know to be wrong, and that you detest vicious brutality which threatens to leave the island a legend of vicious hatred and violence for which many more families will grieve in years to come.'

By contrast Athens Radio greeted the police murders with great approval in its broadcasts to Cyprus.

THE TRIPARTITE Conference began in London with delegates sounding as if a needle had stuck in a long-playing record, repeating their well-known national policies. Foreign Secretary Macmillan spoke again of Britain's responsibility for Cyprus and of its position as 'the hinge of the North Atlantic and Middle Eastern defence systems' and stressed self-government would be granted once terrorism ceased.

For the Greek Government, Mr Stefanopoulos said, 'Greece recognized the need for Britain's presence for defensive purposes in Cyprus' and offered any guarantee desired by Britain for military bases in the Island, or by Turkey concerning the Turkish minority. He emphasized that the military and defensive value of the British bases in Cyprus would be enhanced when the Cypriot population was granted self-determination and people changed from a mood of hostility into one of 'spontaneous and unqualified cooperation'.

Turkey's Foreign Minister Fatin Rustu Zorlu gave delegates a lesson in history – as he saw it. He recalled first that administration of Cyprus had been transferred to Britain in 1878 in return for a military commitment to aid his country in case of aggression by Russia. Later, when Cyprus became a British colony under the Treaty of Lausanne, the treaty was made on condition that the inhabitants became British, if they did not opt for Turkish nationality. Hence Cyprus had been exclusively a 'matter of concern' for Turkey and Britain, as all the signatories, including Greece, had recognized. A change in the status of Cyprus would be a modification of the Lausanne Treaty and of 'the whole political settlement in the area based upon the abandonment of an expansionist policy by Greece ... and would create a number of grave questions, which would also enable Turkey to put forward certain demands'.

Only Macmillan hinted at anything new. He offered Cyprus a form of limited self-government and a constitution, which could be monitored and improved by a standing committee composed of members from Britain, Greece and Turkey. Once peace in the Island was shown to last and the administrative machine ran smoothly, another conference would be called, this time with Cypriots participating. Until then, said the wily Foreign Minister, matters of sovereignty and independence should be shelved, but he emphasized 'we do not accept the principle of self-determination as one of universal application'.

The record stopped playing on 7 September. The delegates went home. The gap between Turkish and Greek Governments, rather than narrowing, had widened. Greek Cypriots believed the British were plotting a divide-and-rule policy, pitting Turk against Greek by bringing mainland Turkey into the debate, a view held to this day.

Robert Stephens, an expert on Anglo-

Cypriot relations, did not agree. He said: 'Senior Turkish officials with whom I have discussed this period of history insist that Turkey's interest in Cyprus was not created by Britain nor was it only a result of British stimulation. Britain, they say, stressed the Turkish interest for her own purposes, but this interest already existed independently of Britain. From 1950 onwards the Turkish Foreign Ministry had seen the way the wind was blowing over Cyprus, but the Turkish government made no move because it trusted Britain to stay in control of the island: a situation which was acceptable to Turkey and to the Turkish Cypriots.'

Another expert, William Mallinson, suggested it was Turkey that took the lead in making relations with Greece explosive. He talks of Foreign Minister Zorlu telephoning Ankara in the middle of the conference and requesting some 'little' trouble-making that 'would be useful'. Almost immediately, on 5 September, a bomb exploded outside the Turkish consulate in Salonica and damaged the adjacent house in which the founder of

modern Turkey, Mustafa Kemal Ataturk, was born. For the Turkish public, it was tantamount to burning the national flag and they demanded retribution, believing Greeks were responsible for the outrage. In fact, an agent of Turkey's secret service had perpetrated the incident.

In retaliation, crowds took to the streets of Izmir and Istanbul. Such was the hostility that during the night of 7–8 September mobs rampaged through Istanbul seeking out Greeks and destroying hundreds of their properties and several churches. An outside observer would have been forgiven if they thought they were watching a replay of *Kristallnact* – the 'Night of Broken Glass' – when German Nazis vented their anger against the Jews.

IN CYPRUS platoons of the Royal Inniskilling Fusiliers went about their routine business, patrolling and setting up roadblocks to search vehicles, their drivers and passengers in the hopes of catching a terrorist. 'On patrol they wore baseball boots,' said Charles Pepper.

Turkish mobs in Istanbul attack Greek properties on the night of 7–8 September 1955.

'Naively I asked why and the answer came: "These boots are made for bopping." Being a simple REME [Royal Electrical and Mechanical Engineers] soul, I thought of bee-bop, the dance craze. Then my question was explained by a "Skin" with a downward movement of the arm, accompanied with the curt sound of BOP!'

The regiment was not known for kid-glove treatment. 'There was a village in the Kyrenia Mountains that was particularly troublesome. The locals always gave us a hard time. They were a real pain in the arse,' said a former rifleman. 'A sergeant of ours and 10 men were ordered to restore discipline there. On arrival, the sergeant summoned the *muhktar* to meet him for a friendly chat in the local coffee shop. While the village elders seated at various backgammon boards eavesdropped, the sergeant read the headman the riot act. He ended his short lecture with the words: "Mr. Muhktar, you have 24 fuckin' hours to stop trying to shaft us. If you don't, I'll personally, fuckin' shoot your head off."

'We never again had any more difficulties there. Instead, we'd be greeted with smiles and offers of cold drinks. When the time came for us to leave the area, the *muhktar* went to see the sergeant and told him how much we would be missed and invited us to return any time we wanted.

'Many years later, while on holiday in Cyprus, the hotel tour representative asked a group of us if we'd like to see the tomb of the first president Archbishop Makarios, "who led our struggle for freedom, with General Grivas whom we honour with another monument".

'"Grivas?" came a chorus of sneers, "not bloody likely. We chased that bloodstained bastard through the mountains for four years ..."'

Then, on 8 September, one lucky platoon received a message that Archbishop Makarios was in its area. The soldiers immediately set up additional checkpoints at 100-yard intervals, smartened themselves up and waited for His Beatitude. When he arrived, he was stopped, questioned and searched at every one. For the Inniskillings' Corporal at the first roadblock, the incident had brightened his otherwise boring day. 'I thought he was the spitting image of Rasputin,' he quipped. 'Black Mak's eyes were evil and his smile was a smirk. Even that was wiped off his face by the time he and his entourage cleared the final roadblock, to our amusement.'

'It is the fate of slaves to suffer humiliation,' Makarios moaned later. 'I declare in future I will not submit ...' He continued defiantly: 'What irony to strangle freedom in the name of freedom! Britons are mistaken if they think they can bend our national resistance. What can they do? Send us to prison? Let them do it. Exile us? Let them do it. Put us to death? Let them do it. Freedom does not die.'

Stopping and searching the Archbishop and his entourage soon became a popular sport as they moved around the Island on their priestly duties. The next time Makarios's limousine arrived at a checkpoint, the newly arrived troops in charge did not recognize him, not even when he waved his golden staff. Historian Robert Holland wrote: 'There was a commotion until a Greek Police Sergeant came along and identified the Primate. By then there was a crowd of over 2,000 people milling angrily about. After hurried requests for instructions to Police Headquarters, Makarios was allowed to proceed – although his companions were frisked.'

In London Conservative MPs asked Lennox-Boyd why the Archbishop had been left alone. The minister promptly complained to Armitage that Makarios should either not have been stopped at all, or, if he were stopped, the search operation should have been 'rigorously carried through, including the person of His Beatitude'.

'Now every Greek Cypriot might expect at

any moment to be bodily searched as he walked the streets or drove about,' Charles Foley of the *Times of Cyprus* belly-ached. 'Not even the person of the Archbishop was sacrosanct. One Saturday evening, on his way to dedicate a church at Lefkonico, his caravan of cars was halted by an army patrol. Makarios was ordered to descend from his car while suitcases containing his ceremonial vestments were searched and the following carloads of priests and ethnarchy officials minutely examined.'

Robin Neillands, a Royal Marine, backed the searches as necessary: 'Priests were frequent supporters of the terrorists, but their clerical garb did not always ensure them undisturbed passage, as when a carload of monks arrived at a 45 Commando Royal Marines' roadblock set up by Sgt Tom Powell of 'B' Troop. "Out!" said Tom, "and quick about it."

'"His Beatitude does not like this," protested the driver.

'"I don't like his B-attitude either," said Tom. "Now hop out quick, the lot of you, and let me search this car."'

AS EACH September day passed, more problems piled on Sir Robert Armitage's desk in Government House. While his in-tray grew larger, his out-tray stayed empty. The Turks had warned of their dislike of EOKA, but now they appeared to have set up a counter organization of their own. It was called *Volkan* – or volcano. It was the successor of another underground group known as *Kara Yilan* – Black Snake – which was so underground that even the majority of Turks knew nothing of it! Until then, there had only been the *Kibris Turktur*, or 'Cyprus is Turkish' party, established in 1954 with Hikmet Bil at its head. He boasted a membership of 100,000 in Cyprus, Turkey and Britain. To say the least, this was bending the truth, although the party's objectives may have been supported by many more.

Bil became famous for holding enthusiastic demonstrations and writing letters to *The Times* in London.

Just as EOKA made its announcements in leaflets scattered in Nicosia's maze of narrow streets, so did the new setup. Volkan would 'not hesitate to react in the same way' if EOKA directed any terrorist acts at the Turkish community, its leadership declared. It claimed possession of an EOKA 'terror list' of prominent Turkish Cypriots to be assassinated. In unambiguous terms Volkan warned: 'We shall do our utmost to prevent bloody clashes between Greeks and Turks in Cyprus, but if EOKA attacks Turkish Cyprus Government officials, policemen, or civilians we shall reciprocate instantly.' For every Turk killed, five Greeks would die, Volkan threatened.

Cyprus had been described as 'a place of arms', but as more British troops exited the Canal Zone in Egypt and arrived, cynics wondered how long it would be before Aphrodite's Isle sank with their weight. The 1st Battalion of the Royal Scots, accompanied by RASC, RAOC, and REME detachments, with a field ambulance unit, were the latest to land to help with internal security. Then there were the 500 men of 40 Royal Marine Commando from Malta and the 1st Battalion of the South Staffordshire Regiment sailing to Famagusta on board the troopship *Asturia*. Soldiers aplenty there were, but the increasing numbers of anti-British Greek Cypriot rioters that plagued the main towns matched them.

The worst riot of the year began in the late evening of Battle of Britain Day, Saturday, 17 September, when a police patrol car drove into Metaxas Square (known today as Eleftheria Square) in central Nicosia, where some youths were pasting EOKA posters on the walls of buildings. Barely had police boots landed on the pavement to chase the junior lawbreakers, when their wearers were pelted with rocks and bottles and had to retreat in a hurry, carrying one of their own, who had been injured.

At that moment, a Royal Military Police Land Rover of GHQ Provost Section screeched to a halt, bringing three military policemen to the scene. One of them, Lance Corporal Tom Glenister, 23, told the author, 'We immediately came under attack too, but managed to protect the civil policemen by firing two pistol shots in the air. The little bastards ignored us, upturned our vehicle and set it alight.'

The handful of youngsters had suddenly grown like Topsy and become a crowd of several hundred, many of whom were school-boys in uniform, all determined to turn a minor incident into a major confrontation with the powers of law and order. 'I can tell you, me and the others breathed a sigh of relief when two more RMP Land Rovers pulled up with six of our provost mates,' Glenister remembered with a smile. 'There wasn't much we could do to stop the trouble, but we were out of danger. We could only sit back and watch the ruffians tear down a Union flag, cheering and whooping as they went. I collected the flag and sent it back home to my mum in Holloway.'

Adult hooligans, hearing the noise, swelled the crowd. Together they marched on the British Institute, housed in an old wooden two-storey building on the corner of the square. The mob smashed its way inside, tossed furniture and books onto the road and set them ablaze in an orgy of pyromania, using petrol to spread the flames. Just before the Institute became an inferno, the British Council librarian, Reid Smith, barely escaped with his life by jumping over a fence at the back.

Still there were no police or troops to push the rioters away, only a solitary fire brigade vehicle that had rushed to the scene and had been driven off three times by more bottles and stones. When the firemen eventually managed to roll out their hoses, rioters cut them.

'It was two hours before any fully armed troops arrived,' Glenister said. 'We heard they had been standing-by at the police station just a mile away, waiting to be called out to support the civil coppers. They couldn't act alone because there was no martial law or State of Emergency. Eventually the guys from the South Staffordshire Regiment ignored the rules and acted on their own initiative by rushing to the scene.'

First the troops unwound a large linen

British troops and police in Metaxas Square watch the British Institute go up in flames.

banner with a message in Greek and Turkish that said: 'Disperse or we fire'. The rioters ignored the threat. The soldiers, in parade ground fashion, loaded blank rounds into their rifles and on command fired into the air. From their rear, a party of policemen arrived and lobbed tear gas grenades into the crowd. Eyes smarting and throats burning, the crowd began to move away as firemen struggled to put out the flames. By midnight, except for the troops, police and firemen, the square was empty, three hours after the start of the demonstration.

Gradually curious onlookers and journalists gathered to see what had happened. British officers and their wives, who had been celebrating Battle of Britain day at Nicosia Airport and were slightly worse for wear, joined them. 'High heels and patent leather shoes now picked their way through the pools of water and piles of broken glass and stones,' reported Charles Foley.

An officer of the South Staffordshires commented later: 'Demonstrations are comparatively easy to break up; but a demonstration can gather momentum, if not checked immediately, and become a riot. This was one of those instances. And a riot is a different matter altogether, requiring harsher measures and considerable determination. One thing was clear: however provocative their action, there was never the smallest pretext for us opening fire. More in keeping with this situation, we preferred the police baton and shield, with which we were equipped.'

Next day sneering and sniggering Greek Cypriots walked by the still smouldering British Institute, obviously pleased at the destruction of one of the Island's most distinguished establishments, which for 15 years had provided local students with free tuition in the English language and literature, access to more than 16,000 books and 600 volumes on British contributions to Hellenic studies. All were ashes blowing in the gentle morning breeze.

British residents were furious. How could Cypriot students destroy an irreplaceable academic resource open to all? They condemned the police for laxity and failure to nip violence in the bud and demanded the Governor allow the Army in future to take control of civil order. Volkan, the secret Turkish organization, shared their opinion in leaflets it distributed. It accused the administration of a 'lack of adequate security measures' to deal with the Metaxas Square riot.

Colonel 'Tiger' White, the Army's Senior Information Officer, called a press conference and placed the blame full square on the shoulders of the civil police for failing in their duty. He alleged that four times between 22.20 and 23.20 the army had volunteered to intervene, but four times the police had turned them down. Lawrence Durrell, the civilian Public Relations Officer, was not present to field questions from the assembled hacks.

His absence allowed John Walters, the *Daily Mirror* man, to dip his pen in venom and scribe a poisonous attack on the author's personal life. 'I had no prejudice against Durrell as a superb writer, but as Press Officer he was hopeless in his general indifference to daily happenings. He loved his home and young Greek companions.' With his fangs firmly fixed he criticized the 'pro-independence attitude of the British Press Relations Officer who lived with male friends in a lovely villa outside town and never talked to the Press until late in the day'.

Foley reported the police account of the matter in kinder words. 'Their explanation was still more wretched: the two constables on duty had given the warning an hour after the trouble began,' he said. 'At 10 p.m. a "stand-to" had been called. This turned out to mean that a policeman on a bicycle went round other policemen's homes to get them out of bed, or from their favorite coffee shop. The total in reserve was 12.'

Colonel White, the Police Commissioner, kept his head low, but released information for the journalists, who were swarming like hungry flies over the rotting carcass of a sheep, that police and army conversations had, unfortunately, taken place 'at a junior level in absence of anyone more exalted'. His spokesman suggested that the police had felt initially that if the crowds were not provoked, the troubles would 'fizzle out on their own'.

Foley's newspaper the *Times of Cyprus* condemned the Governor's administration for bringing 'humiliation on itself, on its hard-pressed and loyal police force, on the British Army and on the name of Britain'. The *Daily Mail* in London demanded Sir Robert Armitage's head. It was reacting to Ralph Izzard, its correspondent in the capital, who described the riot in graphic detail: 'For three hours I witnessed one of the most shaming scenes in the history of British rule in Cyprus.' His report appeared under the screaming headline: '*Daily Mail* man sees handful of boys take control of the heart of Cyprus.'

Izzard pressed on: 'I'd sack the Governor for this ... Nobody acted for three hours ... not the slightest organized attempt was made to stop this act of vandalism ... Three hours of this hooliganism passed before riot squads of the South Staffordshire Regiment were introduced ... It took them less than one minute to clear the entire Metaxas Square ... This lamentable and deplorable incident need never have occurred ... the lack of coordination at top level is ridiculous ... But unless consider-able changes in personnel are made, there is no guarantee that it will not occur again.'

Governor Armitage politely called for a public enquiry to 'clear the air'.

Historian Robert Holland said: 'Washing its Cypriot laundry in public was something Her Majesty's Government could do without, and this provided the immediate background to the decision, taken by the Cabinet at its resumed discussion on 24 September, to dismiss the hapless Governor.'

At GHQ Provost section, the OC, Captain I. H. Ellis, commended Lance Corporal Glenister and his team for saving the Greek Cypriot police officers. 'Your actions were in the best tradition of the Corps,' he said.

BY NOW there were 83 men and youths held on suspicion of being terrorists. They had been transferred to the Crusader castle in Kyrenia after rowdy scenes in Nicosia Central Prison when they shouted for *enosis*, sang the Greek National Anthem and banged the tables in protest against their detention without trial. Guarding them were members of the 1st Battalion the Wiltshire Regiment, who claimed the detainees' living conditions were better than theirs.

Hastily converted into a detention centre, the castle, once a popular tourist attraction with good reason, overlooked the harbour and the exclusive Kyrenia Club beach – better described as 'The Slab' – and nearby Harbour Club, run by Judy and Roy Findlay, MC. Their club was a haven of peace for the officer elite, with delicious food and a beautiful balcony from which to watch the world sail by. Throughout the conflict, EOKA never attacked it once. Some wondered if Findlay had done Grivas a good turn during the Second World War when he had served in Greece with the partisans.

Several of EOKA's key figures were held in Kyrenia Castle. They included Markos Drakos, who had planned Governor Armitage's assassination, and Grigoris Afxentiou, the organization's second-in-command, who had recently married his child-hood sweetheart Vasilou in a secret ceremony while on the run.

The EOKA suspects, confined in the north tower of the castle, complained daily, to the annoyance of the Wiltshires, about shortages of water, inappropriate lavatories, the noise their guards made at night and anything else that came into their minds. The authorities conceded that they should have sheets for their beds and provided them. On 15 September, several of the inmates began knotting their new sheets together and put the final touches to a plan for a mass breakout. Others sang nationalist songs loudly on the floor below to hide the sound of cannon balls being hammered against the tower's sturdy walls above them. Here several prisoners were slowly and painstakingly removing centuries-old bricks to widen arrow slits. When one was large enough for a man to slip through, they stopped and looked down at 'The Slab' and the mountains of southern Turkey, 40 miles away. If the prisoners' 12 Greek Cypriot warders, responsible for checking the cells, had seen or heard any of this activity, they did not report it to the British soldiers, who patrolled the parapets day and night.

Some days later the father of one of the inmates, Michael Rossides of Larnaca, smuggled out a draft of the escape plan and it was passed to Dighenis for approval – which he gave readily, with the date on which it was to be implemented, so that arrangements could be made to meet the escapees and smuggle them away quickly to 'safe houses'. The date 'The Leader' gave was 24 September. Instead, Drakos decided to act the day before because another inmate, Petros Papaionnou, said an informer had revealed the details of the planned escape to the authorities and they would be waiting to catch them. It would be best to leave earlier and thwart the guards. He said that he would prefer to stay behind, as it would help his defence in the event that he was charged later for being a member of an EOKA execution squad.

The rope of eight knotted sheets was slung out of the improvised window as darkness fell on the evening of the 23rd. Drakos had timed how long it took the parapet guard to patrol a complete circuit of the castle. As soon as he

was out of sight he ordered the first escapee to slither down to a flat rock below, often used by sunbathers. One after the other, 15 inmates wobbled down and hid in any shadow they could find. Drakos was the last to land. Later EOKA claimed a guard had spotted him and so he wished him good night, which the soldier shouted back.

Charles Foley, the editor of the *Times of Cyprus*, gave another version: 'From his post on the parapet a young officer had seen something move and telephoned for orders. "People on the Country Club beach?" came the reply over the muffled din of yet another party. "You'd better ask them if they're members, old chap!"'

'The Slab' or 'beach' was made of concrete at the base of the castle wall and was known to all that mattered. Peter Paris, an Irish doctor of the main Nicosia hospital wrote disparagingly of the place: 'There was no beach there, no sand, no flowers, and no shade. Middle-aged English figures, singly or in pairs, would parade on the area until they found a vacant square of knobbly concrete on which to deposit the bath towel, the suntan lotion, the goggles, flippers, bathing cap and cigarettes, then to lie, self conscious, in the sun. Behind "The Slab" were changing huts, for the sake of modesty, numbered 1 to 12, 12a, 14 to 20. Bathing hut 13 did not exist. On the cement British upper-class infants were reared, and the retired found serenity beneath a foreign sun.' Fortunately for the runaways, there was none there to bother them.

Among the escapees were Markos Drakos, Christos Eleftheriou, Lambros Kafkallides, Mikis Firylas and Evangelos Evangelakis of Nicosia; Lefkios Rhodosthenous of Limassol; Antonis Georgiades, Michael Rossides and Archimandrite Stamatopoulos, all committed terrorists.

What none of them knew was that Petros Papaionnou had been the informer in their ranks. He had told the authorities about the escape plan and they had wanted his comrades to get away on the earlier day, hoping the escapees would lead them to Dighenis.

That same evening, Royal Marine Robin Neillands had been ordered, without knowing exactly why, to take his platoon to a position near St Hilarion Castle in the mountains, about 10 miles from Kyrenia. The Marines were to keep their eyes peeled for any unusual activity. 'We trailed up there and it was quite uneventful for a while,' Neillands remembers. 'Then an Army Kinema Corporation van arrived in our camp below in Aghirda and began entertaining the lads with a screening of *Seven Brides for Seven Brothers*. We could hear the music clearly and fought each other for the use of my binoculars to see the screen. Halfway through the show the unit had to rush off after some terrorists who had escaped from Kyrenia Castle. It was over 20 years before I finally saw that Howard Keel movie.' So much for 'unusual activity'.

Within 24 hours six of the runaways were captured, but nine remained at large and went on to become EOKA group leaders. Several of them would die within two years, while 'The Leader' remained elusive.

Next morning EOKA heard about the breakout, but feared the men would run into difficulties. Father Photios, a priest-collaborator in Larnaca, explained why to the local area commander: 'Sixteen fighters have escaped from Kyrenia Castle. For some reason they got away yesterday instead of today and, of course, there was no one there to meet them in the places we'd arranged. We don't know where they've gone or how many have been caught. We desperately want news of their whereabouts.'

IN LONDON, Ministers finally agreed that a tougher regime was required on the Island. Not a single terrorist had been caught in the act and EOKA continued to taunt the administration. Perhaps it was time for a military man to take charge at Government House and for the current incumbent to be posted somewhere more comfortable for a civilian administrator, like, for instance, Nyasaland, where there was a vacancy for a governor. On 25 September, Sir Robert received a hard order from Whitehall to pack his bags. Colonial Secretary Mr J. Fletcher Cooke was to go with him.

Sir Robert, a kindly man, had been out of his depth from almost the first moment he arrived in Cyprus. Colonel Byford Jones, who came to know him well, remembered a conversation he had with the hapless governor:

'"Can you explain," I had asked Sir Robert, "why the Cypriots are so pleasant to us in spite of what one reads daily in the newspapers about their desire to unite with Greece?"

'"The *enosis* disagreement has never disrupted relations between the British and the Greeks in Cyprus," he replied. "Indeed official Ethnarchy policy has always emphasized the peaceful and orderly nature of the struggle."

'"Greek Cypriots who feel a psychological need for *enosis*," went on Sir Robert blandly, "are not blind to the material consequences. Many dread union with Greece for this alone. Despite attempts to create bad blood in the Press, the British still enjoy considerable affection and respect in Cyprus. This is immediately apparent to visitors who come in from abroad. The Cypriot leaders have repeatedly emphasized, as indeed, the metropolitan Greeks have too, that there is nothing anti-British about the *enosis* movement."'

'One should not ignore,' he added a little later, 'that a pre-disposition towards *enosis* is created by the ties of language and religion not less than by the methods of teaching history in the schools. That is to say the psychological problem of *enosis* would always exist as obstinately as the perverse attachment of the Welsh to their language, however useless and obsolete in their case it may be. Its political aspect would not, however, have assumed serious proportions without the active campaigning of the Press and the Church.'

Had Cyprus been an island of peace in other times, Armitage might have fared better, but, as Robert Holland explains: 'He was emotional and also prone to a crippling uncertainty which led him to hedge every judgement about with qualifications. His capacity to alter his advice from day to day was indeed frustrating … Her Majesty's Government was at least equally prone to evasion and indecision …'

On 29 September, the Armitages' bags were packed and loaded in the black limousine to be taken to Larnaca, where a ship awaited to sail them away. The couple took a last look at the carefully tended grounds. With their domestic staff, grouped on the veranda, they exchanged farewells. They were sorry to leave them, but had mixed feelings about their 19-month stay on the Island.

'It was a very touching moment. All of us were sorry because they were leaving, and the girls were crying,' said Neophytos Sophocleous, their 20-year-old personal servant, who cared for the Armitages' cats – Benji and Poo. 'Then the couple shook hands and said a few words to each of us. Sir Robert said to me, "Goodbye, my son, and thank you for everything." I said, "Goodbye Your Excellency and God bless you." Lady Armitage said to me, "Goodbye, Neophytos, and do continue to look after the cats, please." I replied, "I will do, my Lady, I like the cats, you should know that." Then she said, "Yes, I know that and thank you, Neophytos."

'Finally, I said: "Goodbye, my Lady, and I shall think of you often." We were ready to go back to work, when we saw them returning.

They went up to the telephone operators' room to say goodbye to the blind boys. It was a very touching moment, which I will never forget. And I shall remember forever that both of them treated us, not only as servants, but as human beings too.'

Government House looked a very different place from the one Sir Robert and his wife Lyona had taken over when they arrived in Cyprus. This time their official car glided past barbed wire, floodlights and guards at the gate and down deserted streets (another 24-hour protest strike was taking place) as they started their journey into history.

Crowds waited near the Customs House in Larnaca to see off the Governor. Police pushed them back to a chorus of jeers and boos, while Sir Robert inspected a Guard of Honour provided by the Green Howards and shook hands with officials. Young Greek Cypriots began chanting 'enosis, enosis'. They should have known better as he had supported their wishes. Late in the afternoon, looking 'sad and tired', observers said, Sir Robert turned to an aide and murmured, 'I do hope George remembered my umbrella.' With those last memorable words on Cypriot soil, he and his party boarded a launch to carry them to their ship, accompanied by a meaningless 21–gun salute to a man who had failed. He still believed the only solution to the Cyprus problem was to grant the people full independence and self-determination. The catcalling was his only thanks as he sailed away.

Now people's fate would be in the hands of the new Governor – and military Commander-in-Chief – of Cyprus, Field Marshal Sir John Harding. Cypriots waited his arrival with curiosity, hope and fear.

CHAPTER FIVE

Hearts and minds to be won: welcome Fighting John

'Guerrillas never win wars but their adversaries often lose them.'
Anon

'LET'S CUT the cocktails and go straight to town,' snapped Field Marshal Sir John Harding at the assembled dignitaries present to greet him. From the moment his feet touched the tarmac of Nicosia Airport he stamped his authority on Cyprus. For the new Governor, there was much to be done and time was short. A sleek black limousine drew up in the shade of the four-engined RAF Hermes transport that had brought him and his wife Mary to Nicosia Airport. His hand-picked civilian deputy, Mr G. E. Sinclair, had accompanied them. The polished car's doors opened, in they

stepped and off they went to Government House, flags flying, escorted by police outriders and followed by two Land Rovers filled with armed Royal Military Police. En route His Excellency could not have failed to notice the blue and white words in foot-high letters on walls that bluntly stated: 'Death to Harding'.

Striding up the stairs of Government House, Sir John entered the building and was led to where the Chief Judge was waiting with a Bible and a scroll. With one hand on the Bible and his other raised, he took the oath of

Field Marshal Sir John Harding, the new Governor, arrives at Nicosia Airport.

Sir John Harding takes the oath of office at
Government House.

Governor Harding visits a 'mixed' village of Greeks and
Turks to hear their views and get to know the people.

office, after which the official proclamation of
his appointment was solemnly read aloud.
'This way, your Excellency,' said a young
officer, taking the Governor out to the garden
to inspect a Guard of Honour from the 1st
Battalion the Staffordshire Regiment.

Formalities over, Harding ordered his aides
to telephone Archbishop Makarios and
arrange a meeting as a matter of urgency.
Within the hour the details were fixed for
them to gather on 'neutral' ground the next
day – in the card room of the Ledra Palace
Hotel. Then, before evening, Harding
conferred with 35 officials, called in news
correspondents and said he looked forward to
'man-to-man' talks with the Ethnarch and
would 'lay all my cards on the table'.

For the pencil-poised journalists, he had
plenty to fill their lined notebooks. He said his
task was three-fold: to restore law and order
so that everybody could go about without fear
of threats, intimidation or terrorism; to
improve the social and economic conditions
of the people of Cyprus; and to prepare the
way for constitutional reforms on the basis of
the three-power talks in London. He proposed
to go all over the island and to hear the views
of everybody who represented the people and
talked responsibly.

Did Harding know that on the eve of his

arrival Makarios had preached unflatteringly
about him? He declined to comment. In a
passionate speech from the altar of the Holy
Virgin in Trakhoni village church, the
Archbishop had told his congregation: 'If
Harding uses his Kenya and Malaya tactics
against the Cypriot people he will undoubtedly fail. Cypriots are not afraid of any steps
the foreign ruler may take. They will continuously defy military measures and force until
the day when freedom reigns under Cypriot
skies.'

Eager not be overshadowed in the *enosis*
stakes, Grivas or 'Dighenis' churned out his
latest leaflets in which he boasted: 'You
cannot exterminate EOKA, as it now numbers
half a million. For each one of us, 10 British
shall die ... EOKA will ignore our beloved
Archbishop's call to passive resistance, and
will answer force with force.' Another typed
sheet followed almost immediately. It alleged
to come from 'the voice of justice' and said:
'Beware of David's sling, you well armed
Goliath. A bomb, a bullet, a dagger, or even a
stone is enough to end your life. To freedom or
death we march.'

Harding had been reluctant to accept the
post of Governor as he marched towards
retirement, peace and life with his wife on
their farm after a long and illustrious career in

the Army, which was ending now with him as Chief of the Imperial General Staff. There was no higher post to which he could aspire, even if he wanted to. In September, however, Prime Minister Anthony Eden had appealed to his patriotic nature and offered him Governorship of the Crown Colony. Harding was leaving with his reputation standing high, but the new offer carried more chance of failure than most other challenges he had faced. Was the risk worthwhile? Could he, in all honour, reject his prime minister? Despite his apprehension, he accepted.

Eden replied on 25 September: 'I quite understand how little attraction such a post can have for you at this time. After a brilliant military career there is nothing to be gained, and may be something to be lost, in undertaking such responsibilities, but equally know how little you allow matters of that kind to weigh in the scale when national interest is concerned.

'I have been profoundly unhappy about Cyprus for some time past. I do not think we could have avoided this situation. Papagos was headed for it and attempts to stop him only created resentment. On the other hand, for the Turks, Cyprus is the last of the offshore islands. What we must now hope to do is to show the Cypriots steadily and firmly rather than harshly that we mean to carry out our responsibility and that the offers we have made still stand. The sooner these last can be discussed again the better it will be for all concerned.'

On the long flight to Cyprus, the Field Marshal took several naps and thought about his past career and what could be in store. In August 1915, a young Lieutenant John Harding had led a platoon against the Turks at Gallipoli, where British forces, too little and too late, were defeated. Now was he returning to the eastern Mediterranean – to offer too little too late to the irate Greeks? 'Fighting John' as he was known, had served alongside

Montgomery in the desert of North Africa against Rommel's forces, marched alongside Alexander to push the Nazis out of Italy and, post-war, presided over Britain's crackdown on the Communists in Malaya and the Mau Mau terrorists in Kenya. He held an MC and DSO. Would Cyprus be an easier nut to crack? From what he would see in the weeks ahead, the answer had to be 'No' – not unless he could change the entire method of the Island's administration. It was a mess. Colonial rule was in a crisis. Nevertheless he hoped for a political solution to the Cyprus problem.

In the morning Charles Foley of the *Times of Cyprus* told his English language readers that he was sure a military man was the right choice to restore calm and editorialized: 'If this is a job for a soldier, no better soldier could be found.' The newspaper would later change its tone.

The first discussion between Harding and Makarios opened. Both short men had done their homework. Both smiled for the cameras. Harding stood clean-shaven, dark hair brushed flat and shining like his polished lace-up shoes, wearing a grey pin-striped Saville Row suit, not a crease out of place, eager to get down to business. Makarios, with bright, darting eyes and glistening beard, gave the illusion of height in his familiar Eastern Church stove-pipe hat, his *kalliimafchi*. He was a black-robed ascetic

Sir John Harding and Archbishop Makarios meet. John Reddaway (centre), the Governor's adviser, watches.

with the guile of a peasant expressed in quiet, measured tones. Above his beard, his face was pallid and waxen. His hands were almost feminine, delicate with long fingers, nails carefully manicured. Neither man revealed their thoughts as each smiled and studied the other for any vulnerability, while the cameras flashed. Harding always spoke plainly. The Archbishop wrapped his words in sophistry. The two could not be more different, one rooted in the present, ambitions fulfilled, the other from some past age still wanting a greater place in history.

Of course, Harding knew that Archbishop Makarios was up to his neck in the EOKA movement. Of this he was in no doubt. Not only in Cyprus was the Church promoting *enosis*, but so also were the clergy on the mainland, where Archbishop Serapheim of Athens and All Greece held sway. Less sophisticated than Makarios, he had a village mentality. While the Istanbul-based Ecumenical Patriarch was the spiritual head of world orthodoxy, Serapheim opposed him throughout his life, convinced the Turks had corrupted the priest. What made the Greek Archbishop dangerous was not merely his power to influence events but also the enormous wealth he had at his disposal. He had paid for EOKA's first weapons. British intelligence officers in Athens knew the organization's members had travelled to Ioannina in north-west Greece to take delivery of the initial supplies. Serapheim and Makarios needed to be neutralized.

From the beginning the new Governor worked to separate the Cypriot leader from the powers in Athens, turn him away from terrorism and persuade him to 'advise his fellow-countrymen to follow his lead in the belief that this might be the quickest and least painful way of getting the people of the Island back on the path of democracy and of restoring to them freedom to think and speak for themselves'. Harding's efforts were not rewarded. He said later: 'I pursued these discussions to the furthest possible limit of conciliation and concession in the hope that Makarios would be induced to denounce violence, and so open the door to co-operation and orderly constitutional progress.'

Makarios Droushiotis, an authority on the life and times of the Archbishop, believed the prelate had almost reached agreement with the British on a transitional self-government solution – which offered Cypriots autonomy, except for defence and foreign affairs, and did not rule out *enosis* at some future date – but failed to follow through 'largely because of Makarios' tendency to amuse himself at the expense of his negotiating counterparts by deliberate vacillation and brinkmanship'. To prove his point, Droushiotis quoted the Ethnarch as saying: 'I always enjoyed driving myself to the brink of the abyss, and then stopping just in time not to fall. The other party, of course, believes that I am about to kill myself. On the contrary, I proceed very calmly, knowing when to put on the brakes.'

AT GOVERNMENT House, a staff low in morale, but eager to change, met Harding. They saw in their new man a vision that had been lacking. Lawrence Durrell, the administration's information officer, was so enamoured with the Field Marshal that in his *Bitter Lemons*, he rhapsodized: 'He had all the deftness and dispatch of a francolin and the keen clear bird-mind of one trained to decisions based in a trained power of will ... Upon the disorder and dishevelment of an administration still wallowing in shortages and indecisions he turned the pure direct eye of a soldier with a simple brief – the restoration of public order, the meeting of force with force; and he was followed swiftly by his soldiers, whose splendid professional bearing and brown faces – still smiling and kindly – brought a fresh atmosphere to dusty purlieus of the five towns. Skilfully and smoothly the chessboard was altered, the pieces rearranged.'

As Harding set about his reorganization, nothing, large or small, escaped his attention. During a walkabout of his premises he was shocked to find the administration's code-books were locked in a safe stored in a lavatory. Working against the clock, he still found time to tour the Island by helicopter, showing the flag, and getting to know ordinary Cypriots in their villages and on their farms. His troops cheered when he visited their shabby camps and heard their complaints. He told them their days of 'boy scouting' were over.

Para officer Sandy Cavenagh remembered the Field Marshal's first visit to his camp: 'His helicopter swung low over the hills and landed in a flurry of dust on the beach ... he shook hands with the Colonel, and all the other officers were introduced. He had met many of them before on other operations. Then he moved to inspect Battalion Headquarters. Each department was covered carefully, a few searching questions, and he passed on. Our turn arrived. A firm handshake and penetrating glance from the kindly grey eyes. "What can you manage to cope with here?" His glance roved over our few pieces of equipment. He must have inspected thousands of Regimental Aid Posts, but gave the impression that this, to him, was a novel and interesting experience.'

Everywhere Harding went he promised better welfare schemes and economic development programmes for the people. But first, there had to be security. The Field Marshal said: 'To put it briefly, the anti-terrorist campaign was designed to cut the terrorists off from supplies and support from outside and to harry and hunt them down inside the Island. This was more like looking for a needle in a bundle of hay than anything I had encountered before.'

In the weeks that followed Harding and Makarios continued their discussions and eventually appeared to have drawn up a plan to which all concerned could put their signatures. There was even a draft statement ready to be presented to the Government's Communal Assembly. The Archbishop had also met Grivas to explain the contents. Droushiotis said: 'Grivas announced to his guerrillas that the struggle was over. They had a souvenir group photo taken. That is the picture of Grivas in the mountains, surrounded by his men, which is today a well known historical image.' But were there a settlement, could the EOKA leader allow Makarios take the glory and popularity, thereby thwarting his aim to become the sole power behind the throne in Greece?

It was clear that from the moment the new Governor arrived, Colonel Grivas had decided to test his authority with an increasing number of strikes against people and property. He had thrown down his gauntlet and waited to see if the British Field Marshal would take up the challenge. Makarios and Harding could talk until hell froze over, as far as the EOKA leader was concerned, because his heart and head told him that Britain would never grant enosis and that – and that alone – was his objective. To achieve it required force, not words, unless he uttered them. His targets would be chosen indiscriminately.

Against a backdrop of a buildup of British

Mufti Dana, the Turkish Cypriot religious leader, welcomes Governor Harding.

Forces, the EOKA leader chose to go on the offensive, often taunting his enemy. In Famagusta, a gang of eight masked men raided a British Army depot. After they had bound the civilian guard they loaded their truck with several crates containing rifles and Sten guns, part of a cargo discharged from the steamer *Halcyon Med*. Before they drove off, they left a note, which said: 'We have received these arms from the British Army and we shall pay for them soon after Cyprus is freed.' It was signed: 'Dighenis, the Chief'. The raid, planned by Pavlos Pavlakis, the local commander, was led by George Matsis, who, with his brother, Kyriakos, would lead the Army a merry chase in the months to come.

America's *Time* magazine reported: 'In the week's worst incident, chivalry caused a British retreat. As British troops approached a village near the Baths of Aphrodite, they were met by a solid phalanx of Island women, Aphrodite's daughters shielding Ares' stone-hurling sons. Thus protected, the men showered stones on the British Tommies, forcing them to retire.'

By nature anti-colonial and fearing the Communist threat, Americans were concerned no less by what was happening in the eastern Mediterranean than their government. President Eisenhower and his Secretary of State, John Foster Dulles, pressed Prime Minister Anthony Eden's Cabinet to find a solution in Cyprus without delay. Whatever was decided, the United States would back HMG, as long as NATO remained intact. Greece was not happy with Washington's position. 'For every Cypriot [Harding] kills or imprisons, free Greece will hold neither Eden nor Harding responsible, but Mr. Dulles, unless he repents at the last minute and stays the hand of Harding,' Greek Foreign Minister Stephanos Stephanopoulos warned, accusing Britain of having 'declared war on the people of Cyprus'.

LEAFLETS AND bombs were EOKA's weapons of choice in the Island's towns, while gangs in the mountains preferred guns and grenades in their hit-and-run strikes against military convoys. The softer the target, the better, whether it offered a threat or not. In November, bombs were thrown for a second time at the Famagusta home of Major G. Benyon, a non-combatant senior Army chaplain. He and his family escaped injury, although their ground floor windows were blown out. Not far away, another civilian pastor's house came under grenade attack, without the bombs exploding. In Nicosia, a bridge linking the capital with villages in the south-west was destroyed, damaging pipes that supplied water to two Greek Cypriot communities.

Field Marshal Harding began to lose patience. Still unable to persuade Archbishop Markarios to denounce EOKA's violence, he began to consider tougher measures to stop the terrorists. On 1 November he notified London: 'One of two courses has to be decided upon. Either there must be offered some prospect of ultimate self-determination, though subject to requirements of the strategic situation and to progress in self-government, or a regime of military government must be established and the country run indefinitely as a police state. No middle course is any longer open.'

In Limassol, EOKA tossed a grenade in the front porch of a Mrs Webb, an 80-year-old British expatriate, who had lived longer in Cyprus than most farmers had seen seasons. Made of that stern stuff so common in old colonials, she complained not about the terrorists but having her night's sleep disturbed. Captain Macdonald paid her a duty visit. 'She bore up wonderfully, but when I went to view the damage she doddered about in a Panama hat, treating the Cypriots, who were overawed, like children. She muttered about Socialists, useless municipal services and ranted at the police inspector who owned her house. He looked a very frightened man! Poor old soul, all she said was probably true, but she was in Cyprus, not England.'

Earlier Macdonald had been at the police station, where he examined fragments of a bomb, bits of which had been dug out of the legs of a British soldier. He was there to check a type of grenade found in possession of a local EOKA youth, but it had been taken away by a Marine Commando officer as a souvenir. Eventually he ran it down to an office at 3 Commando Brigade headquarters, where it was lying on top of the officer's safe. Called an Italian Red Devil, it was still armed. 'I reasoned that since it had not gone off so far, it was safe to move, so I picked it up and took it out to the Land Rover, put it in a sand-filled box, found an open spot away from any houses and blew it up,' Macdonald said. 'I had never seen this type of grenade before but I had an idea how it worked. I must say, my driver, Private Hall was much less confident in my abilities.'

A few weeks later, Private Hall returned to England to get married. After a short honeymoon, he rejoined Macdonald. When he did not appear for duty one morning, his officer found his driver was in the hands of the Royal Military Police. Hall had been arrested after they found him lining up near the camp gates for a taxi, not any one, but one under surveillance, whose owner hired out his daughter to pleasure the local soldiery in the back seat of his vehicle. 'In one door, out the other,' Macdonald quipped as he related what happened next. 'When Hall was marched in front of me on a charge, I asked him what the bloody hell he thought he was doing, to which he replied, "Well, you know how it is, sir." I didn't,' he said. Such were the ways of the bomb squad as they went about their dangerous business.

No longer did British soldiers go out unarmed and alone. If they were married, their wives shopped and their children travelled on buses, always with armed guards present. Where there were married quarters, individuals were rostered in a type of 'neighbourhood watch' to help ensure the safety of civilian families. Pubs and bars now had metal grilles over their windows. Everywhere, more and more EOKA slogans appeared overnight on town walls and also in the middle of main roads, writ large in blue and white letters, the colours of Greece. Street traders no longer greeted the British with bright smiles. Instead they were met with dark stares of resentment.

F. C. Parkinson of 2 Field Ambulance RAMC said: 'One night I was returning from a show at a RAF camp, when a bomb was lobbed into the back of the lorry behind ours. It sped past us as panic set in. Our two escorts opened up with their Sten guns, firing blindly into darkness. We raced back to our camp. The lorry in front did not stop at the camp gate, but crashed through the barrier. Guard duty now affected soldiers in different ways. Most personnel acted as if everything was normal, while others were very scared. One private fired a round of ammunition through nervousness and was placed on a charge. Others were caught sleeping. Punishments varied and mostly involved cookhouse duties at night. I was charged once for not shaving by a Sergeant Major who always took a delight in catching me out.'

On 12 October, there was public recognition of the way British service personnel were performing against the odds. The *London Gazette* announced that the Queen had approved the award of the British Empire Medal (Military Division) to Acting Corporal Myles O'Connor, RAF, No. 264 Signals Unit. The citation read as follows:

On 19 June 1955, a hand-grenade was thrown through a window into a refreshment establishment in Famagusta, Cyprus, where several British Service personnel were seated. The grenade struck Corporal O'Connor and fell to the floor, a short length of ignited safety fuse protruding. Warning all present to take cover, Corporal O'Connor attempted to throw the grenade out of the window, but it hit the window sill and exploded. Although the walls of the room were badly pitted, everyone had taken cover and nobody was injured. In tackling the grenade while the fuse was burning Corporal O'Connor displayed commendable courage and great presence of mind and probably averted grave injury or even loss of life among those present.

SO FAR the only British service dead were the result of various kinds of accident – usually on the Island's dangerous mountain roads. They included Private Sidney Ingram of the South Staffs, Driver Arthur Hampson, RASC, and SAC Percival Anolda. Then everything changed.

On 27 October Lance Corporal Angus Milne of the Royal Scots Regiment became the first soldier to die as a result of an EOKA attack.

While on the road near Chlorakas in the Paphos District, a grenade was thrown at his truck. With his passenger, also severely injured, Milne was rushed to hospital, but his life could not be saved. Captain Peter Macdonald, RAOC, recently arrived in Cyprus, paid a courtesy call to police head-quarters in Nicosia and was shown photo-graphs of the incident. 'Not a pleasant sight,' he said. Milne's parents paid to have their son's body brought back to Blackhall, Edinburgh, for 'a Christian burial'. His father – 'not a wealthy person' – had requested the Government pay the cost of £372, but Anthony Head, the Secretary of State for War, refused. 'I cannot give exceptional treatment without unfairness to many others who have been faced with this problem in similar sad circumstances,' he replied.

The next serviceman to die was Lance Corporal Alan Alderson of the Royal Engineers on 9 November. Four days later, on the 13th, two members of 625 Ordnance Depot in Famagusta were dangerously injured. Private Edward Barton, 20, was shot in the head, and Private Edward Gibson, 19, took a bullet in the stomach. They had been to the cinema and were walking in Hermes Street when they were attacked from behind.

Next day, again in Famagusta, a Royal Navy motor launch on the stocks was blown up, with an old rating on board, who had been sleeping in the bunk above the bomb. The sailor, with 20 years' service in submarines, shouted: 'The buggers are depth charging us.' Unscathed, he stumbled in the smoke mutter-ing: 'I'll be okay as soon as I finds me false teeth.'

On 19 November, Captain Macdonald returned to Kykko Camp near Nicosia after 36 hours without sleep investigating and making safe bombs and explosives placed by EOKA in various parts of the Island. At 14.48, half awake in his tent, he heard 'an almighty explosion'. He donned his hat and rushed outside to find the blast had been in the sergeants' mess. 'I was on the scene in about a minute,' he told the author. 'A bomb in the saddle bag of a bike had wrecked one wall and smashed corrugated iron sheets and wooden planking, tearing open the side of the mess.

'A dead NCO – Staff Sergeant Gilbert Cripps of the RASC – was lying on the ground beside another badly wounded man, who was bleeding heavily. I ran towards the Medical Centre and met a doctor and medical orderly coming in my direction. They went to work quickly on the wounded man, but maybe I could have done something for him earlier. Could I have done anything? I wasn't trained in first aid. I was shocked and angry. It was the first time I had met sudden death.'

Grivas, who always exaggerated his 'victo-ries' by adding two and two and coming up with 22, claimed Cripps' death was caused by an eight-pound bomb, smuggled into the camp because 'security measures were slack and more than 150 Cypriots worked inside the camp area, in addition to delivery men who went in and out during the day'.

For the bomb squad, it was just another day and another bombing. On 19 November, 41 bombs exploded in Cyprus within 24 hours – all directed at British Army camps and installations. Grivas called his campaign Operation *Forward Victory*. In part its ferocity was prompted by the fury of Greek Cypriots at the Supreme Court's dismissal of the appeal by Karaolis against his conviction and death sentence for the murder of PC Poulis in August. Two miles from Famagusta, terrorists bound and gagged three guards at a water supply station manned by the military. Two explosions wrecked the engine room. Another grenade thrown at a photographic studio belonging to an Armenian did £300-worth of damage. The proprietor received slight injuries. The presumed motive for the outrage was that a photograph of Sir John Harding was displayed in the window.

51 Brigade headquarters, too, came under attack with grenades, but the terrorists fled when troops returned fire. Two grenades tossed at Yialousa police station, 60 miles north-east of Nicosia, caused slight damage. Three were thrown at Paralimni police station and a bomb went off behind the British-owned *Ship Inn* at Famagusta. During the night all British forces were placed on 'full alert' for more to come. And so it went on.

A British officer was slightly wounded. Other attacks were reported from widely scattered areas of Cyprus throughout the day. British troops beat off terrorists who attacked an Army encampment at the Mitsero copper mines, 25 miles west of Nicosia, but not before EOKA got away with 1,500 sticks of dynamite, 600 detonators and 3,000 yards of fuse.

On the 20th, the target was the main post office in Nicosia. The explosion was the biggest in Cyprus since the first EOKA bombs went off on 1 April. It went off at 17.43, hurling masonry and shutters yards away, injuring two Greek Cypriot passersby and shattering windows in offices opposite. Wall letterboxes were boarded up and the public asked to use pillar-boxes only. A military officer commented: 'The events of the past two days leave little doubt that the underground organization is controlled and directed by men with experience of terrorism and knowledge of how to make and handle explosives. Such men are not to be found among Cypriots normally. The assumption, therefore, that these people have been trained abroad is not unjustified.' His listeners knew he meant Greece, but he bit his tongue from saying so.

Meanwhile in the centre of Famagusta, British troops and terrorists had fought a running battle in the streets and gardens. Crouching in ditches behind a hotel the terrorists opened fire on a British military patrol car. Men of the Inniskilling Fusiliers returned the fire and chased the attackers through the streets. A British officer was slightly wounded. Reports of other attacks poured into Government House from widely scattered areas of the Island. At the Mitsero copper mines, 25 miles west of Nicosia, British troops beat off a terrorist gang who attacked an Army encampment.

21 November saw EOKA killing another British soldier – Sergeant Andrew Steel, RASC – when terrorists opened fire with Sten guns on his truck in the Famagusta area. Four others were rushed to the military hospital in 'a dangerously ill' state after the attack. In just three days of intensified violence, the terrorists had committed 89 criminal incidents. The death toll continued to mount. 'The British had no answer to this kind of warfare and we were able to strike when and where we liked,' Grivas later wrote in his *Memoirs*.

On 23 November Lance Corporal Roger Downing of 3 Infantry Division Provost Company lost his life in a traffic accident.

Next day, Sergeant James Shipman, RE, was gunned down in broad daylight when he walked along a quiet street in Nicosia, where several service families were quartered. He was struck by a single bullet in the face. Again, there were no witnesses.

In Khandria, an EOKA gang ambushed two Army vehicles on a mountain road. In an exchange of fire, an officer and a soldier were wounded, but a third man, Sapper Robert Melson, Royal Engineers, was killed. Royal Marines sent to the area failed to catch the attackers. Within hours, Craftsman Kenneth Heyes, REME, was added to the list of fatalities. He was caught in another ambush, this time in Petra, and died in hospital from gun shot wounds on 25 November, a Friday. On Saturday, Sapper Peter Percival joined the list of the dead.

SIX MURDERS of servicemen in six days by EOKA was six too many. Harding had to bare his teeth and stop the outrages, even if this meant life for innocent civilians became more difficult. Because the majority would not or could not cooperate with the security forces, they were nearly as guilty as EOKA by default. The Governor saw only one way forward. He must declare a State of Emergency. Robert Holland, the historian, says: 'After some hurried hours spent with lawyers and security advisers, Harding gave a short but sharp public broadcast in which he announced that a State of Emergency now existed on the Island.' It came into force at 17.00 on Saturday, 26 November 1955.

That same evening Sir John and Lady Harding were due to be the Guests of Honour at the Caledonian Society's annual charity ball – a very *pukka* affair – at the Ledra Palace Hotel in Nicosia. During the 50s, this five-storey building was the largest conference and banqueting facility in Cyprus. With more than 200 luxurious rooms, a restaurant and taverna bars, it was popular with visiting politicians, businessmen and, most of all, journalists, their expenses paid by their newspapers. While British intelligence teams were permanently lodged on the top floor, in the basement there was a small room used by EOKA as a bomb-making 'factory', where the hotel's handyman Yannis Pafitis used his off-duty hours to turn out explosive devices.

The hotel, too, was where the good and the great of the Island gathered to celebrate important dates of the social calendar, especially so during the twilight years of Britain's colonial rule. In his time, Sir Winston Churchill's son, Randolph, imbibed more whisky at the hotel than his father had consumed brandy throughout the Second World War at 10 Downing Street.

For EOKA, the ball provided a marvellous opportunity to move against the British establishment and even eliminate key members, including the Governor. The war was becoming a duel between two small men with a larger than normal determination for a scrap. Cyprus was not big enough for both. For the present, Grivas held the advantage as no one knew where to find him, but the Field Marshal's official engagements were publicized in advance and the elusive terrorist leader always knew where his adversary would be and when he would be least protected.

British newspapers on sale in Nicosia.

The local press reports the search for the EOKA leader.

For Grivas, Pafitis was the ideal person to breach the tight security arrangements in place for Harding's scheduled attendance. The handyman was ordered to be the assassin and accepted the role with alacrity. First, he smuggled two grenades into the hotel, using a box of oranges to hide them. Next, dressed as a waiter, he waited for the band of the Royal Scots regiment to start playing. Once guests took to the dance floor, he fused the lights in the ballroom at 23.10 and, in the darkness, rolled his grenades in the direction of the top table, believing the Hardings were sitting there. They, however, had been unable to join the festivities, because the Governor had been far too busy finalizing the details of the State of Emergency, broadcasting the declaration on state radio and talking to London, which was four hours behind the time in Cyprus.

One of the two grenades exploded. Fragments ripped through dance gowns and dinner jackets, but the second, which was American-made, was swiftly collected by Captain Peter Macdonald, RAOC. 'I picked it up and put it in my pocket under the admiring gaze of a distant policeman,' he remembers. Macdonald adds with a smile and a wink: 'The policeman was unaware that it was perfectly safe since the thrower had omitted to pull the pin out.'

It had taken just five seconds for a grand social occasion of grace and manners to become a scene of blood-splattered confusion. Several guests were hit by flying metal and a pierced radiator flooded the floor with water. Among those injured were the ill-starred British Institute librarian Norman Horrocks and the wife of Cyprus Police Commissioner G. N. Robbins, but Lord and Lady Harding were unharmed.

In the 'chaos of sudden darkness, explosive fumes and shattered glass', Pafitis had not waited to see whether his grenades exploded. Instead he ran to the hotel's basement, where he turned on the electricity and carried back sheets and blankets to help the injured. Fortunately there were no fatalities, although Mr Horrocks and Mrs Robbins were taken to hospital to spend the rest of the night.

Once the lights were back on, according to the *Times of Cyprus,* 'the Royal Scots band played *Glasgow Belongs to Me,* and everyone wanted to continue dancing but as the water on the floor made this impossible the 270 assembled Britons, after singing *God Save the Queen* with fervour, adjourned to the refreshment bar'. Stelios, the Egyptian-born Greek barman, was on duty and ready to serve them in his oasis for British officers. Here they were comparatively safe from a bullet in the back, 'fired by some enthusiastic Greek youngster working his way up EOKA's ranks'.

Pafitis and the rest of the hotel's staff were detained and questioned, but released a few days later. What became of the eager grenade-thrower is not known.

Commissioner Robbins heard about his wife's injuries while he was in London consulting with the Home Office and with the Colonial Office about establishing a UK Police Unit in Cyprus. He wanted it to comprise volunteers from the best county constabularies. Amongst these officers' many special duties would be leadership of the local police and the teaching of modern methods as well as providing Field Marshal Sir John

Harding with a personal bodyguard. He was sure any of the new unit's offers would have found those guilty of spoiling his wife's night out.

Next day, with the talks stalled, Archbishop Makarios made his feelings known about the State of Emergency. 'The anomalous situation which has been created in the island is simply a symptom of another situation – that is to say, the insistence of the British on holding rule in Cyprus in spite of the will of the inhabitants,' he told the media. 'It is indeed to be regretted that the British Government are under the impression that they can solve the Cyprus problem by using military measures. But the problem is not solved by such measures. On the contrary, it becomes more acute. So long as it remains unsolved, neither normality nor order will be established. There is only one solution: self-determination for the people of Cyprus.' He made no comment on the attempt to kill the Governor.

Four days later, the Archbishop addressed several thousand worshippers overflowing from inside a small church on the outskirts of Nicosia. His voice, amplified by loudspeakers, talked about the 'end of Cypriot freedom' and the action of a 'doomed' regime. 'Every one of us is now at the mercy of the first policeman or British soldier, who may lead us to an 18b detention camp without trial, without proof of guilt … We cannot even go on strike … We must go on working compulsorily, just as under Fascist rule in Germany and in Siberia … All these measures are being taken simply because Cypriots are fighting for their freedom. Their purpose is to prolong British rule on the island', but, he affirmed, 'after the darkness of slavery in Cyprus the day of liberty will soon dawn'.

IMMEDIATELY AFTER the declaration of the State of Emergency, Britain's 10,000 troops in Cyprus were placed 'on active service' starting 26 November – for an initial period of three months, which could be extended. No more would they be on the Island to aid the civil power, but on a wartime footing, subject to military law and military courts for any offenses committed against the population.

The power of the security forces was vastly increased in the new situation, with its 76 latest regulations. Under these, the death penalty was extended to include anyone found guilty in special courts of being in possession of firearms, ammunition and explosives. Strikes were made illegal if unconnected to a trade dispute and collective fines and confiscation of property could be enforced. All assemblies, with the exception of cinema and theatre audiences and religious services, were banned. Other offences punishable with long terms of imprisonment were the wearing of uniform 'to which the bearer is not entitled'; 'any attempt to seduce Government officials from their duty'; 'unlawful drilling'; and the 'sheltering of any persons engaged in activity prejudicial to the public safety'. Males under 18, convicted under existing regulations, could now be whipped. Carrying stones was considered a crime worthy of a lashing, two years' imprisonment or a fine of £100.

The Governor had power to stop the ringing of church bells or the display of flags, and when circumstances required, he could restrict the movements of persons, deport persons, censor mail and postal packets and control telephone communications.

To enforce the State of Emergency, Harding had his young soldiers, mainly National Servicemen, who were growing daily in confidence and sharpening their skills of observation and initiative under Brigadier G. F. Baker brought from Britain to be Director of Security. Even before his arrival, London had agreed the Governor's request to put more boots on the ground.

In mid-October, the 1st Battalion the Gordon Highlanders from Edinburgh had set up camp in Xeros after a short stay in a camp outside Nicosia – 'an arid plain with a huddle of dejected-looking canvas'. The 1st Battalion of the Royal Leicestershire Regiment – 'the Green Tigers' – arrived by sea from the Sudan to join the Royal Marines in Aghirda, 'a delightful camp in the pines high in the Kyrenian hills'. With the regiment came twins Peter and Barry Watson from Swannington. The 1st Battalion the Middlesex Regiment – 'the Diehards' – veterans of the Korean War, sailed from Liverpool on board the troopship *Empire Clyde* followed by the 1st Battalion the Royal Norfolk Regiment from Colchester.

The 'Diehards' would be the only regiment to serve for the entire duration of the Emergency. 'We arrived for a normal three-year posting and were stationed at Dhekelia, initially at Alma Camp, a tented area – with concrete bases – at the top of the hill,' said Major Donald Carson MBE. 'Two and a half years later we marched, with full pomp and ceremony, down the hill to take over the brand new Alexander Barracks on the sea front – but for only six months!'

Another 'Diehard', Eddie White, told the author: 'Our first few days were spent doing very little. "Get acclimatized," we were ordered. Every morning we were assembled by a sergeant or corporal and made to take off our shirts, 10 minutes on the first day, 15 on the next and so on. Eventually, the Army declared we had "acclimatized". Now, if anyone suffered sunstroke or burned, it was their fault and they would be placed on a charge.

'I remember clearly the first time we set up a roadblock. It consisted of barbed wire and some piles of wood, with gaps between so that vehicles could drive through after they had been searched. Armed, we sat on a wall on both sides of the partial barricade. I had just been promoted to acting corporal and was in charge of the party that night.

'Suddenly a car drove past at speed, ignoring our shouts in English, Greek and Turkish to halt. We raised our weapons and my trigger finger tightened on my Sten. Just before I squeezed, the car stopped and reversed slowly, its driver ready to be checked. After he had gone on his way, a Greek Cypriot woman screamed invective at us. "Bastard Tommy, this is our country, what would you have done if he had not stopped?"

'I replied coldly, "I would have shot him." And I meant it. I was 19 years old and I wanted a bit of action.'

The first test of the Middlesex Regiment's initiative and ingenuity took place in Larnaca during a riot of stone-throwing youngsters, who had succeeded in knocking out one of the civil police officers. Entering the fray, the troops moved forward and the school children ran into the graveyard of the St Lazarus Church from where their catapult marksmen took potshots. The young officer of the 'Diehards' faced a dilemma: to give chase and create a battlefield out of a sacred place or sit back and lay siege. He chose the latter course and waited patiently as his men cooked themselves a meal. Eventually parents arrived and extracted their broods in small hungry and tired groups, after they had surrendered their 'weapons'.

The Royal Norfolks flew into Nicosia Airport in several aircraft and were immediately driven a short distance to 'a brand new tented camp' next door to the Cyprus Broadcasting Station's aerial site, thereafter known as CBS Camp. Men from the Gordon Highlanders had pitched the regiment's tents – or as many as they could find. In fact, the camp was so new, it lacked washing facilities, dining halls, armouries and other necessary buildings. To wash themselves, the first platoons were piled on trucks and taken to Kyrenia to swim in the sea.

On 22 October, 'C' Company, under Major Athill, drove down to Karaolos Camp at Famagusta where it came under operational control of the Royal Inniskilling Fusiliers, commanded by Lieutenant Colonel Freeland of the Royal Norfolk Regiment. Then, in no time, the Norfolks were made the Island Reserve Battalion. For the next few weeks the Battalion was served wherever it was required to boost the security forces' presence. Much of its time was spent in Nicosia where, until its arrival, the 1st Battalion, the South Staffordshire Regiment had coped with the worsening situation alone. Now the chores could be shared.

The first task the Gordon Highlanders faced when they were dumped at Xeros on the north-west coast was to build camp before they took on EOKA. 'The site for this was a barren tract of land close by the immense bulk of the Cyprus Mining Corporation's buildings,' an officer wrote in the regimental magazine. 'From this virtual wilderness was to arise the Aberdeen Camp that today is a proud monument to the skill of the designers and the industry of the soldiers who live in it. Amid the scorching heat which greeted us it was gratefully soothing to the eyes to look out across the sparkling sea only 200 yards from the camp, strangely tinted with brown close to the shore, where the copper dredging drained away; and it was equally pleasant to leave the arid shimmering desert around Nicosia and drive towards the hills.'

Close by in Lefka, the Gordons found, as one officer noted, 'the Turkish inhabitants and those of other remote Turkish hill villages almost embarrassingly friendly, and any visitor invariably departs replete with admirable coffee and pursued by the enthusiastic farewells of a horde of children. As regards the Greek villages, it can be taken as a general rule that the more remote and agrarian they are the less interest they take in politics and are therefore more inclined towards friendliness.'

On 28 October, all changed and the Gordons had their first slight taste of what was ahead. A patrol of the Internal Security platoon was passing through the largely Greek Cypriot town of Morphou/Guzelyurt when they were assaulted by verbal abuse and showers of stones from the local school. As the Scottish troops took countermeasures, they proved there was only so much provocation they would tolerate. The crowds were dispersed, but three of the soldiers came away injured. Then, from somewhere, a single shot was fired and Captain Derek Bowman, MC, the officer commanding the detachment, limped to the side of the action, a bullet in his leg. They laughed that night in the officers' mess over his minor injury: he had maintained his self-made tradition of annually being wounded in October or November.

'Maybe it was a slip of the tongue, but some Labour MP told the Commons that "the situation in Cyprus has got worse since the Gordon Highlanders arrived",' remembered Reg Parnell, a REME Armoury Sergeant, attached to the regiment. 'That person was invited to fly to Cyprus at the CO's expense and repeat it in front of a Battalion parade. It never happened.'

Brigadier Baker, Harding's Chief of Staff, who had been brought to Cyprus from the Imperial Defence College, wasted no time in making root and branch changes to the security organizations that had existed under the previous Governor. His first edict was 'Cooperation is not enough: there must be integration.' Based in a compound ringed by barbed wire and crammed with huts, he took control of every unit – land, sea and air – that had a role to play in his plans to take the offensive against EOKA. His writ also included civilian departments, such as police, immigration, customs and public relations.

At a battalion level, regiments became responsible, with the local police, for riot control in their areas. How they did this was their affair. Most chose to issue steel helmets, face shields, gas masks, batons and metal shields. A photograph of a platoon of the 1st Battalion the South Staffordshires being

'The Dustbin Bandits' on parade.

inspected by Company Commander Captain J. F. H. Gregory appeared in an American magazine with the caption: 'This is the first time in the history of the British Army that Tommy Atkins has had to lay down his rifle and bayonet for a stick and a dustbin lid.' From then on, the South Staffs were proudly known as the 'Dustbin Bandits'.

In the summer 2003 issue of the *Security Affairs Journal International*, retired Colonel Roy Giles outlined his men's methods for bringing order to the recalcitrant. 'My platoon's drill for dispersing a riot or illegal gathering (and all gatherings except funerals were illegal) followed this sequence. I marched my platoon forward in hollow square formation down the street towards the crowd. At a distance beyond stone-throwing range but well within earshot, I would give the order "Platoon, halt." Then, by loudspeaker, "You are an illegal gathering. Disperse or we fire." The crowd would be given time to disperse. If they did not do so, I would carry on: "Platoon – fix bayonets, Wiremen – lay out the wire." Two soldiers from the platoon then would run forward and stretch a coil of barbed wire across the road, some 20 metres in front of us – I may say that in training, we taught this distance as the length of a cricket pitch.

'Then: "Bannerman – raise the banner" – the banner was inscribed in the English, Greek and Turkish languages. "Disperse or we fire."

Next, "Bugler, sound 3 G." This strident and definitely alarming blast, blown by my bugler from the centre of our square, was the equivalent of a warning on a ship's siren. Now came, "Front rank, kneeling position, down" – by this stage, any crowd would be in no doubt that we meant business. Finally, if the riot was still in progress, or the crowd not dispersing: "Front rank, one round at xxxxx – I would nominate a distinctive person in clear view – to kill, fire."

'Each man in the front rank was to fire one round, in a volley, so that no individual could be picked out as the executioner – the same logic as for a formal firing squad. While all this was going on, in the centre of my platoon square, I had a photographer equipped with an Army-issue box Brownie, taking pictures of the changing scene, and a clerk taking notes and timings – doubtless in a shaky hand – of the events and my orders.

'This sequence of clear, orchestrated and unambiguous drill movements had been laid down in our army since 1919 ... Our experience in Cyprus proved the efficacy of this often-rehearsed choreography. Never did we have to open fire to disperse illegal gatherings. The British Army dealt with, probably, thousands of crowd scenes the length and breadth of the island, and everyone involved knew that, once the Army came onto the scene, it was time to pack up and go home.'

Throughout the ages, Whitehall mandarins had lagged behind in providing the military with all that was required to fulfil its mission. Fight on the cheap appeared to have been the motto. Cyprus, in the 50s, was no different from the present day and troops had to 'make do'. 'We had a NAAFI on which we came to rely at Polemidia Barracks,' laughed Lance Corporal Robert Shaw of 35 Field Regiment, Royal Engineers, 'although the elderly staff could have been left there since the First World War.' He continued: 'Needless to say, apart from the Colonel's wife, there were no other women on the site. He and his lady lived in a small hut far away from the rest. The reason for its distance, I discovered later, was because it was also our dentist's surgery and nobody wanted the screams from his patients to be heard by the rest of us.'

The soldiers did, however, experience equipment shortages and had to put up with equally out of date kit. 'I was with LAD REME attached to RASC 40 Company, with the divisional black swan sign, that was one of the first units to move into Dhekelia,' Stuart Beveridge remarked. 'We were very much on the move day and night transporting infantry units in and around Larnaca. We were assigned a large fleet of Bedford QL three-tonners, painted beige, most of which were found in WW2 crates discovered when Tel el Kebir in the Canal Zone was evacuated.' Royal Marine John Best was not untypical of those who bumped into them: 'My first job was to be as a dispatch rider, but I was without a motorcycle to travel around Cyprus. Far too dangerous, said the Troop Sergeant Major. My vehicle was to be a Champ with another Royal Marine at the wheel.'

Foreign observers also laughed when units based in Nicosia were issued with bicycles to race to the scenes of trouble. What they did not take into account was their effectiveness. An officer explained: 'The narrowness of the streets limited the use of vehicles and, as speed was vital, bikes were pressed into service and our patrols could be seen at all hours of the day peddling leisurely or frantically – as the situation dictated – in all directions with rifles slung on their backs.' 42 Survey Engineer Regiment had no rifles at all. On the move from the Canal Zone, the weapons had been sent to a camp in Larnaca when they were needed in Nicosia. Sapper Peter Woodman said: 'Our "armament" on guard duty were pickaxe handles. On mine I burnt the inscription "Anti-EOKA cudgel Mk. 1"!'

Charles Bailey, a Royal Military Policeman, remembered Land Rovers had no protection from bombs thrown at them. 'After one of our Mobile Patrols had been attacked, we were given sandbags to put on the floor,' he recalled. 'Later we ran up a raised hook at the front of the vehicle to stop our heads being whipped off by wire stretched across a road.'

Worse though for the Army's intelligence officers was the shortage of Greek interpreters that could be trusted. EOKA suspects held by British patrols invariably answered questions in the local version of the Greek language and their words were either translated badly into English by a Turkish policeman or by a Greek, who feared for his loved ones, and gave a version the terrorists would approve. In 1955, the British Army could boast only five Greek interpreters from the UK.

'Skilled interpreters were so few on the Island that interrogation of EOKA suspects early in the Emergency presented a severe problem. Ignorant of what was going on under their noses, the British had not raised a finger to correct or oppose the subversion of the children, and when we realized what had happened it was too late,' wrote Para officer Sandy Cavenagh in his book, *Airborne to Suez*. 'This failure to learn the language of a colonial people was an elementary error. At one time the presence of a Greek 'E' in your handwriting was said to be worth a place in the Foreign Office. It would have been as well, for Cyprus at least, if the Colonial Office had used the same criterion for their candidates.'

Second Lieutenant Goodhall, the 1st Battalion King's Own Yorkshire Light Infantry's Intelligence Officer, recalled that the shortage of translators was 'a major handicap for British units operating in western Cyprus when we were at Limni, near Polis. It was a melancholy fact that in the entire Brigade area there was only one British officer or official – apart from the District Commissioner – who could speak modern Greek, which, to put it mildly, severely limited the ability of our patrols' roadblock contingents to communicate with the local population or obtain useful information from them. The lack of interpreters was also a factor in alienating the local population from the Security Forces, especially during the understandably very unpopular cordon-and-search operations against villages.'

KOYLI had disembarked at Famagusta on 20 November and 'D' Company, and its baggage, was transported 110 miles to Limni Mine Camp in the north-west, where it relieved 'B' Company, 1st Royal Scots Regiment. Its arrival coincided with a violent storm of thunder, lightning, wind, rain and hail, but in the Officers' Mess, the substitution of a large glass of whisky for the expected cup of afternoon tea was much appreciated by those in charge. The rest received large cups of *cha*, sweetened with dollops of condensed milk in the canteen.

Earlier, when 'C' Company came ashore, customs officials pounced on crates of their equipment and opened them for inspection. 'Sorry,' said a Greek Cypriot official with all the solemnity of a judge about to pass a death sentence, 'you will not be allowed to bring these items into Cyprus.' He pointed a well-manicured finger at a number of swords, used by the regiment for ceremonial duties. 'Knives of this size are prohibited items for importation by orders of His Excellency, the Governor.'

'Sod off,' huffed an irate sergeant. 'If we can be entrusted with some 600 lethal weapons, I think we can take care of a few bloody swords, mate.' His men stepped forward and carried off their 'dubious' imports.

With the added troops in Cyprus, Field Marshal Harding and Brigadier Baker launched their first week-long, combined operation against the terrorist mountain gangs. Called Operation *Turkey Trot*, it began on 31 October in the Kyrenia range with over 1,700 soldiers involved. Those taking part came from 45 Commando Royal Marines, 1st Battalion the Royal Leicestershire Regiment, 1st Battalion the Royal Norfolk Regiment, and 40th Field Regiment, Royal Artillery, with attendant civil police officers, aided by light spotting aircraft and helicopters.

'The operation was noteworthy for the extreme heat and the fact that we had not been issued with the appropriate clothing for Cyprus,' said Brian Hobbs of the Royal Norfolks. 'The Military also decided to use the operation as a showcase. They invited all sorts of newsreel crews and journalists to view the operation. This was to let the folks back home know they were doing something.'

At the completion of the operation, an Army spokesman claimed it had been an outstanding success, with vast amounts of information gathered about EOKA's tactics and supply systems. He said that no fewer than six terrorist camps had been discovered and he was in no doubt that the operation disrupted the organization in the Kyrenia area. He listed what the troops had captured. There were two rifles, one pistol, two sacks of explosives, daggers, smoke bombs, and a pair of telephone handsets. Also found were police uniforms, including steel helmets recently stolen from Lefkoniko police station, black masks used by the terrorists, and large quantities of canned food supplies.

Whatever spin the Army's PR put on the operation's successes, Governor Harding and Brigadier Baker knew very well that they had only scratched EOKA's surface with *Turkey Trot*. Dighenis was still on the loose, surrounded by some of his most dangerous men. What the operation had proved was that different regiments could work together against the common enemy and this would be the forerunner of many more large-scale operations or 'troop surges' in today's parlance.

Where there had been mistakes, these were remedied by the time of the next assaults on EOKA's mountain strongholds. Meanwhile, Makarios vented his spleen in churches and monasteries and Dighenis scattered cyclostyled leaflets. The most menacing one appeared on 2 December. It warned: 'A special execution group has been formed which will execute judges who pass death sentences on arrested "patriots"' and advised the judges to resign their posts 'forthwith'. Another, addressed to British troops, spoke of 'much harder blows' if they followed orders that were akin to the 'criminal and abominable methods of Hitler and Mussolini'. The leaflet went on: 'Cyprus will then become a big British cemetery.' A third leaflet denied that there were any differences between the terrorist organization and Archbishop Makarios, whom it regarded as the 'holy symbol of the struggle'.

While the regiments waited to hear about their next major operation, their comrades lost their lives in what they considered attacks by cowards, afraid to face them eyeball-to-eyeball in a straightforward fight. Instead they faced a shot in the back and a bomb in the night. On 5 December Royal Marine Terence Roberts met his death with a Greek Cypriot civilian and a policeman when their vehicle came under attack outside the Amiandos mines, a popular target for the terrorists. During a short fight, one of the EOKA men was wounded, but escaped with the rest of his gang.

The same day a Red Cross ambulance came under heavy and sustained fire as it rounded a bend on a mountain road near Troodos. Marine D. Walker of 45 Commando Royal Marines, following in an escort vehicle with four companions, jumped out and went into action, determined to save the lives of those in the ambulance. In the crossfire three Royal Marines were hit. With complete disregard for his own safety, Walker moved the injured men to safety, all the time returning the terrorists' fire single-handedly until a second convoy arrived and he was reinforced. His actions earned him a BEM. The citation read: 'By his courage and example Marine Walker prevented his party from being overrun and his bravery in rescuing three wounded men from an exposed position was of a high order.'

In the House of Commons that same afternoon, Foreign Minister Harold Macmillan ran through all the details of the various talks that had taken place since September, but gave a new emphasis to the Greek Cypriot demand for self-determination, which caused a stir in the ranks of MPs – and later in the minds of the people in Cyprus. Macmillan recalled that Greece wanted self-determination 'this year, or at any rate in a year or two'. Turkey said 'Never' and 'We said "some time"'. He added quickly: 'I mean some time and in certain conditions that would have to be worked out.' The problem had never been bi-lateral, but always tri-lateral with strategic issues, and so solutions would take 'some time'.

There would always be the critics abroad, and some at home, who would blame as guilty of reactionary or Blimpish obstinacy any British Government who did not immediately accede to any demand made upon them, Macmillan said. The Cyprus problem was very different from the normal problems of colonial development. In any future question of self-determination, the first thing necessary was to achieve self-government, and he was sure the Archbishop was too clever not to recognize that. He believed there were the forces that were using terrorism to make sure that the moderates did not get support, but that the extremists would win the day.

For Labour, James Griffiths stopped the waffling walrus of a Foreign Secretary with a single sharp question: if Mr Macmillan had conceded the principle of self-determination, could he not set a target date for it to be decided, because there was much to be gained.

The Conservative majority in the House drowned out any answer, which would not have satisfied in any case.

The Greek press reported the Commons debate on Cyprus in full under headlines proclaiming: 'Britain recognizes self-determination'. In Cypriot quarters, Macmillan's speech was accepted at face-value, but with confusion: they wanted a return to peace, but they had no idea how they would reach it. On one hand, there were the EOKA bombers and on the other, the British Army determined to catch them. Neither Grivas, Makarios nor Harding were about to declare a truce.

Athens looked to Washington for clear answers, but found only obfuscation in the statements of American diplomats. They said they thought that the gap between the British and the Cypriots had 'narrowed', that London recognized the inherent right of the Cypriot people to be masters of their destiny and only military considerations remained: the very issue that had aroused suspicions in Cyprus about Britain's true motives. The State Department assured the Greeks that it would request clarification from the Foreign and Colonial Offices to eliminate any misgivings in Cyprus – and would nudge the British to resume official negotiations.

Still pressed by Whitehall not to take both his gloves off against the terrorists, a frustrated Governor Harding replied to Colonial Secretary Alan Lennox-Boyd: 'I cannot continue to accept responsibility for the Government of Cyprus and for the morale and discipline of the Security Force unless I am allowed to take effective measures to deal with all cases of flagrant sedition and other breaches of the law.'

Before Lennox-Boyd could send a considered, carefully crafted response couched in civil service language, another British life was taken. This time it belonged to Private Peter Ketchen, 19, a driver of the Royal Scots, when a grenade was slung into his truck near Ktima

on 9 December. The same day Army Chaplain Beynon was targeted for the second time as he and his family were eating lunch, but they survived without serious injuries.

If British chaplains were not directly involved in the conflict, under Archbishop Makarios there were few priests and monasteries that were not in the service of EOKA. To reduce their threat, Brigadier Baker ordered 1,000 troops to make a lightning swoop on 24 Orthodox places of worship at dawn on 8 December. To arrive at their target on time, 'B' Company of the Royal Norfolks left camp at 03.00 for Makhaeras Monastery. The men were carried in 14 Land Rovers because the mountain tracks were too narrow and twisting for larger vehicles. The last half of the journey was completed without lights: quite a test of the drivers' skills given the poor state of the tracks. 'The remoteness of these monasteries made them ideal places to conceal gang members, weapons and food supplies, while monks acted as couriers for EOKA and gave

British troops search a Greek priest.

terrorists early warning of our patrols,' explained an officer.

Wherever possible, the rifle-carrying soldiers were accompanied by padres to ensure nothing in the monasteries was damaged. In the course of their surprise search in Lefka, the Gordon Highlanders discovered frightened monks hiding pistols – some in a box marked with a crucifix – sticks of dynamite and other terrorist paraphernalia. They pushed into the Abbot's bedroom and found two pairs of service binoculars and several packets of contraceptives tucked under a pile of well-thumbed 'girlie' magazines. An officer smiled. Turning to his padre, he said: 'I suppose even the most religious of men must be prepared for any eventuality.'

The Reverend McKinnon, the 'militant' chaplain of the Staffordshire Regiment, tackled his monastery assignment with 'tremendous zest for good reason', the regimental magazine observed. 'EOKA has never hesitated to use churches as arms caches and the discovery of 53 sticks of dynamite in a safe in Kykko Monastery set a standard which he has hoped to surpass ever since.' At first he only used a crowbar, but later persuaded the Regiment's Quartermaster to provide 'tools, burglar sets, one' and began taking lessons in small-scale demolitions. He took delight in running his fingers through the beards of any Greek priest whom he considered suspicious, hoping to find a weapon of some kind.

Father Casey was present with members of the Parachute Regiment. 'When we were in the Troodos, he would suddenly show up in his Land Rover, driven by Roy Sanderson of the RASC,' said paratrooper William Bell. 'He liked to say in his Irish lilt, "It's Sunday whenever I show up, so don't worry if you lose track of the day." He knew every man in the battalion by his Christian name – Catholic or not. He had earned his wings and jumped every time we did.'

As the operations continued, in particular in

the Kyperounda area, a priest and a Greek Cypriot policeman were arrested; the latter was believed to be an EOKA informant. Seventy other men were taken into detention.

The priest was found with detonators and 'time pencils' in his possession. In two church gardens a machine gun, a Sten, several magazines of ammunition and quantities of military clothing were uncovered. During a raid, Renos Kyriakides, the brother of the Bishop of Kyrenia, rushed at the troops, holding a revolver in one hand and a file in the other. He was wounded in the encounter. The file contained valuable documents relating to EOKA bills paid by the Church.

In Nicosia, Royal Military Police entered the premises of a religious youth organization in the courtyard of the Phanoromeni Church. The RMPs took away a large number of documents, including EOKA leaflets, against the protests of a priest.

'Mercenaries of the British Government have invaded sanctuaries, like new barbarians, with bayonets and machine-guns, and have defiled sacred places. Such a barbarous act is a shame for the British Government,' preached Archbishop Makarios from a pulpit in the monastery of St Spiridon, near Larnaca. It had been searched two days earlier. In his sermon, the prelate lashed out that 'even the most barbarous conquerors' had respected the privileges of the Church, but they had been 'trampled on by so-called defenders of the Christian faith – British soldiers'. To spread Markarios's words across his flock throughout the Island, Radio Athens broadcast a tape-recording of his angry sermon.

In protest, secondary schools in Kyrenia, Morphou, Lapithos and Evrykhou went on strike. Many went to church to pray for Karaolis's life and then paraded through the streets, waving Greek flags. Twenty-one students were arrested after stoning police and troops.

Grivas saw the British raids and subsequent

demonstrations as another opportunity to reach out to the staunchly religious hearts and minds of Greek Cypriot youth and win more to his nationalist cause, but two days later, while on the run with one of his mountain gangs, he found it hard to understand the Governor's next move.

QUITE UNEXPECTEDLY Field Marshal Sir John Harding banned AKEL, the Island's Communist Party. Satellite organizations, such as AON, its youth body, EAK, the left-wing farmers' association, and POD, the Communist women's organization, were also proscribed, together with the party newspaper. To prevent it appearing in a new guise its printing machinery was seized and taken away in Operation *Lobster Pot*.

Demetris Christofias, who was democratically elected President of (South) Cyprus, has not forgotten the day his party was shut down. 'In the first midnight hours towards dawn of 14 December 1955, British soldiers, backed by police forces, burst into the family homes of cadres and members of AKEL and of the broader Popular Movement. They smashed down doors with rifles, terrorized women and small children, arrested and put the members of AKEL in chains. On that cold winter night they arrested around 135 cadres of the Left and led them at the first light of day to the makeshift prison camps, which they had set up in Dhekelia. It was the first time Cyprus had witnessed such a massive roundup within a few hours.'

Mr Papaioannou, the Party's General Secretary, who had recently returned from an 'enlightenment' trip to London, where he made a violent attack on Archbishop Makarios, was among those arrested. The Mayors of Limassol and Larnaca were also held.

'All of these actions were carried out according to the decree issued by the British colonial Governor Harding. The colonialists closed down the *Neos Democratis* and also closed down the Turkish Cypriot newspapers *Emektci* and *Inkilapsi*, which were published by the Left,' continues Christofias. 'These events shocked Cyprus. There were, however, some bigoted people from the Right such as Themistoklis Dervis and Socratis Loizidis who stated that by banning AKEL the English wanted to defame the struggle of the Cypriot people as Communist!'

As the party was opposed to EOKA, it seemed an odd thing for Harding to do. It can only be explained in light of the Cold War and fear that 'the red menace' would exploit the situation in Cyprus. Several officials said the Communists would not accept any settlement, unless it excluded the presence of British bases on the Island. 'Those buggers want to weaken us to benefit Moscow,' huffed a retired red-faced colonel. 'It's clear, old chap, they're using the damned *enosis* issue to get us out so that we lose our influence in the Middle East. No oil then, as Eden said, and then what? A Britain knackered. Not on, just not on.'

Christofias posited another explanation: 'AKEL, as it is well known, disagreed with the form of the armed struggle, coming to the conclusion that in the concrete conditions prevailing in Cyprus this not only would not vindicate the aspirations of our people but on the contrary it would lead to deadlocks and adventures.'

News of the ban was totally unexpected, and, when it filtered through to workers – Greeks and Turks alike – many downed tools at once. Three hundred paraded outside the trade union headquarters in Nicosia and refused to disperse, until police used tear gas. In Dhekelia and Akrotiri, where the new British bases were under construction, the 2,000 workforce walked out. Hotel staff left guests to serve themselves.

Makarios, trying to straddle both Left and Right horses, denounced the British action. 'Irrespective of the fundamental differences which separate us from those against whom the Government action is aimed, we believe that an ideology can be fought only by another, better ideology, and not by force,' he declared. Grivas was less ambiguous. He still saw the Communists as the 'national enemy'. To any potential defectors from AKEL's ranks, he addressed a specific message: 'We were aware of the fact that all "leftists" do not agree with the attitude of AKEL towards our struggle and that most of them think patriotically as we do and acknowledge the fact that they have been misled by AKEL because of the false promises of its leadership. At this moment, we address ourselves to the "honest leftists" and not to AKEL in general, and call upon them to sever their ties with the leadership of AKEL, which has been proved as not serving the interests of the people of Cyprus. We summon these honest "leftists" to shake off Satan, that is to say AKEL, and to join the ranks of our national liberation movement.'

Pressed for reasons why the Communists had been proscribed, Brigadier Baker's public information team could only try to baffle the hacks with an outpouring of statistics and guilt by association. The first general secretary was trained in Moscow, they said. The present general secretary, Mr Papaioannou, had received his training from the British Communist Party in London and, in the past six years, they pointed out, some 50 Cypriot men and women had left Cyprus and studied in countries behind the Iron Curtain. Many of these, no doubt, provided the cadre of trained Communists in the current party today ... and so on. The truth was simple: AKEL had not participated in a single terrorist act. The Communists also came from both Greek and Turkish communities. Their mantra called for an independent, demilitarized state.

Hindsight suggests the doughty Governor may have been served better had he chosen to keep the Communists more on side and focused his attention only against the fanatical religious right in the tiny shape of the diminutive aggressive Greek Army Colonel who was dancing his way out of his mountain lairs even as the reds were taken from their beds.

CHAPTER SIX

'Misguided, frightened citizens':
reds and condoms

'If unpleasant things must be done, do them all at once, decisively and quickly, and ignore diplomats, who always advise taking things slowly.'

Niccolo Machiavelli

SUNDAY 11 DECEMBER, 04.00: light snow is falling on the Troodos Mountains. Soon it will be knee deep on the higher slopes. In the summer holiday resort of Platres, a convoy of trucks, with lights dimmed, snakes its way out, carrying 45 Commando Royal Marines, bristling with guns. Lieutenant Colonel Norman Tailyour has briefed each man about their mission, a combined operation with the Gordon Highlanders. This is the start of *Foxhunter*. Its aim is to capture or kill the EOKA leader Dighenis, thought to be hiding in a well-defended lair somewhere near the village of Spilia, named after the caves that riddle the area. Camped at the top of the mountain pass above the village, two companies of infantry soldiers of the Scottish regiment, with their weapons checked and ready, are huddled in the chill mist, waiting for the signal to swoop on the red-tiled houses sprawled over the hillside. Some dogs are barking in the distance and they hear a cock crowing.

Neither the Gordons nor the Marines realize that there are nearly 30 heavily armed terrorists watching their every move, ready to guard their 'Leader' to the death. They are divided into three groups led by Gregoris Afxentiou, Renos Kyriakides and Christos Chartas, three of EOKA's most effective operators. In what he calls his cave headquarters, Dhigenis is suffering a cold and a bad

toothache. Last night a dentist from Nicosia was brought to treat him, but to little avail. He has been asked to stay another day in the village, but now his patient might have to go on the run again, if the British come closer.

Spilia has been cordoned. At first light two trucks drive into the village, stop and the Marines pour out and take up positions. A young officer stands up in his Champ and waves a cocked .45 automatic pistol. He instructs his interpreter to warn the inhabitants to stay where they are and not to make any aggressive moves. The interpreter also wishes the populace a merry Christmas. Their Champ circuits the narrow winding streets below balconies weighed down by weather-beaten men and women still in their night-clothes. 'Attention! Attention! Stay in your houses!' the order is barked from the interpreter's megaphone. With his other hand, the interpreter grips the Champ's side to stop himself taking an undignified tumble onto the wet cobblestones.

Gordon Highlanders arrive and spread out, knock on doors and enter homes to start searching. Disgruntled Greek Cypriots stand aside nervously. There is no point in resisting. They know the consequences, but they also know Spilia is a hotbed of EOKA activity and fear what will happen if any terrorists are found hiding.

Through his binoculars, Dighenis watches the carefully planned operation from 'The Castle', his mountain redoubt. He sees two tracker dogs with the soldiers. He analyses the way the troops have 'captured' the village and are spreading out on all sides and concludes that this is an operation to encircle him and his men. They will have to fight their way out.

Suddenly there is a crackle of gunfire that echoes through the valley. A short staccato burst from a Sten follows. A man with a pistol is running, bobbing and weaving his way over terraced gardens, pursued by two commandoes. Bullets follow him from gully to gully, bouncing off rocks.

'I saw him come scampering out of the house and run across the fields,' says Sergeant Tom Cossar of the Gordons. 'I put a couple of short bursts after him and he stumbled and fell, but got up and disappeared with the commandos after him.'

A few seconds later, the man surrenders and is brought back to the village. He groans and whimpers. He has a bullet in his left shoulder. Army medics treat him quickly and then the interrogators take over. He has in his possession some valuable documents. 'This is the heart of EOKA,' says an intelligence officer, gesturing towards the now wide-awake village. Every male adult is led past the injured man, lying covered in blankets in an ambulance vehicle. They are told: 'This is what happens if you join EOKA.'

Then, almost incredibly, a young man is spotted whistling and strolling casually down the road to the village. He has a .303 rifle slung over his shoulder. At first, the soldiers wonder if he is there to lead them into an ambush. They ignore the risk and go after him. 'As soon as he saw us, he dived behind a bush, hid his haversack containing ammunition, then came out again smiling and offering to shake my hand,' says Sergeant Roy Pengal, another Gordon. 'A fat chance after he had perhaps killed one of our lads.'

Without much persuasion, the captive agrees to lead the soldiers to the terrorists' hideout – and Dighenis himself. He can be found in a cave just on the edge of the Adelphi Forrest, he declares. 'Right oh,' someone exclaims. 'Lead on Gunga Din.'

Colonel Tailyour intends to lead his Marines up the sheer hillside, with the newly arrived police dogs. They clamber upwards with their catch, a rifle pushed against his spine. About 30 yards from the top the terrorists open fire from a heavily camouflaged stone-walled pit roofed with logs. Immediately every commando weapon cracks back, pouring a hail of Bren, Sten, rifle, pistol and riot gun bullets into the terrorist position. There are three terrorists in the pit. One of them is Afxentiou, ordered to buy time for his 'Leader' to get away with his bodyguards.

The Marines run for cover and melt into the mist, ducking from boulder to boulder, firing from hip and shoulder. Gunfire reverberates through the rock alleyways. Bullets clip twigs a few inches above their heads and whine as they ricochet off grey stones. Mortar fire is requested and bombs drop everywhere. The first proper battle of the EOKA conflict is taking place. In a pause, the troops surge forward and follow the withdrawing terrorists, with police dogs barking in pursuit.

The EOKA stronghold has been captured in less than 20 minutes. It comprises five man-made caves, roofed, floored and supplied with enough food and equipment for at least 20 people. The standard of construction and layout indicates a high degree of professional skill. At the end of this stage of the offensive, three commandos, including one officer, have been slightly wounded in the skirmish from a mortar round that exploded in nearby trees, falling short after being fired by a platoon in the rear.

The Commandoes leave with loads of equipment found in the main cave and others. Their haul includes:

An EOKA arms cache.

2 Verey light pistols
1 British pattern rifle
50 homemade grenades
1 Schmeitzer sub-machine gun
1 Bren gun
7 magazines
1 bag of shotgun cartridges
1 recapping machine
1,335 rounds of ammunition
28 Verey light cartridges
2 sticks of dynamite
17 detonators
and various other items, such as binoculars
    and cameras.

AGAIN 'DIGHENIS' and his gang leaders had escaped. It was noon and the wanted terrorists were working their way towards Kakopetria, where the countryside offered good cover. 'There was only one main road in our path, and I fully expected to find it patrolled since the Army did not lack fast transport,' wrote Grivas in his *Memoirs*. 'But to my surprise the road was unguarded and we slipped across it, one by one. The winter dusk was falling as we rested briefly on the other side ... Our route led over difficult and precipitous ground and our only guide was the Pole star. In order not to lose each other as we climbed, I and my three fighters, Evagoras Papachristoforou, Harilaos Xenofontos and Lambros Kafkallides, clasped hands. Several times we narrowly escaped a fall, which would have meant certain death.'

At 03.00, 12 December, the gang reached the heights above Kakopetria. The rain streamed down until dawn, when Grivas saw the village was quiet and free of British troops. Not having eaten for 24 hours, he sent one of his men down to fetch food and news. Later, after dark, they came down from the mountain and lodged at a safe house. Here they were told that Costas Zavros, a forestry worker, was the man who brought the Marines to Grivas's stronghold. He was branded a traitor and, on 14 February 1956, was executed by three masked men in Spilia's coffee shop. They were also told that Renos Kyriakides had been captured. He had sacrificed himself by trying to delay the advance on the hiding place of his 'Leader'.

The next day Grivas and others moved on to join the Gregoris Louka group. Together they plotted to find a new command post for 'The Leader'. Day after day, until the morning of 16 December, they kept on the move, moving cautiously through the mountains to avoid army patrols. Tired and wet, they decided to stay where they were at Galata and started to build a new hide. Once the weather improved that morning, Grivas sent one of his gang to renew contact with the other scattered groups. 'The Leader' intended to maintain his iron grip of EOKA. His first courier returned and told him about an ambush that had gone seriously wrong when Markos Drakos's gang hoped to murder Major Brian Coombe, a Royal Engineer officer, near Vouni, and how one of the Archbishop's relatives had died instead.

Major Brian Coombe, GM, Royal Engineers.

THE ROAD between Xeros and Pyrgos was not usually used by EOKA to ambush British convoy traffic, which was why Major Brian Coombe of the Royal Engineers was at the wheel of his Champ vehicle, with his driver, Lance Corporal James Morum, sitting in the passenger seat. They were travelling without an armed escort after a tour of several construction sites in the Troodos Mountains and were heading back to their 35 Field Regiment camp in Nicosia. They were just four miles from Lefka, where there were some Gordon Highlanders pitched up. It was approaching noon and there were no other cars on the road that 15 December morning.

Suddenly machine gun fire burst from the side of the road. Morum slumped, face down, blood pouring from his mouth. Coombe swung the steering wheel and slewed the damaged vehicle round a slight bend, bringing it to stop under the lee of a spur. He could see his driver was dead and all he could do now was fight for his survival. He reached for a Sten gun and two magazines, scrambled to the ground and crawled his way up a slope to look

over the crest to see if he could locate his attackers. He had faultlessly remembered his anti-ambush drill. He spotted four gunmen crouched in a gully, about 30 yards away.

As soon as the terrorists saw Coombe and the short barrel of his semi-automatic machine gun pointing down at them, they scurried for cover, firing wildly in all directions. 'At every glimpse I got of them I let loose a burst of bullets, but the effect seemed to remain purely psychological,' the Major said. 'There were no indications that I had scored a hit, but even without much faith in my skill with a gun it seemed that I must hit something.'

With his Sten gun's ammunition exhausted, Coombe drew his pistol from his holster and waved it in the air with a sense of bluff more than bravado. Unsure of what to do next, he prayed silently for an army truck to drive down the road so that he could flag it down. Every few moments the terrorists fired another volley. In the far distance the Major saw a cloud of smoke coming his way. It was belching out from the exhaust of a civilian lorry overloaded with timber, probably destined for the copper mine works at Xeros.

The lorry coughed to a halt. The driver smiled from his cab at Coombe, but signed he did not understand English. The Major made vigorous hand signals, pointed at the bullet-ridden Champ and his driver's dead body. The Cypriot driver continued to smile, nodded and pointed down the road, then brought both his hands towards chest, perhaps a gesture to indicate 'I will bring help'. Now Coombe remembered Morum's Sten with its loaded magazines.

Coombe began climbing the hillock again, trying to crawl behind where he had last seen the terrorists. By his own admission, he was not as fit as he would have liked and he paused several times to catch his breath. From the other side of the mound, he heard muffled voices and knew the gang was still there. He stood up, pointed his gun and fired again. To his astonishment, the four men raised their hands in surrender. One shouted: 'Don't shoot! Don't shoot!' Two others followed suit and began climbing out of the gully in the Major's direction.

Just as they stood up erect opposite Coombe, the fourth terrorist opened up with his machine gun. The surrender had been a ploy. With no alternative, the Major, his Sten gun held at waist height, squeezed the trigger and fired at the three men. Without pausing, he rushed towards the gully and the fourth man, shooting every round left in his magazine. Then there was silence. The seconds ticked as Coombe replaced his empty magazine and waited for any movement at which he could vent his anger.

'I surrender,' came a cry from below. 'Come out and show yourself,' Coombe shouted back. 'And no tricks this time.' One of the terrorists, who had not been hurt as badly as the Major thought, pleaded for his comrade to be given a second chance, as he was injured. Coombe lowered his weapon, only to find the fourth man leap out of his ditch and race away.

'It was galling to see what had been such a sitting bird flying away out of reach; but three in the hand was worth more than one in the bush, so I just had to let him go,' said Major Coombe. The escapee was Markos Drakos, the man instrumental in the assassination attempt of the previous Governor, Sir Robert Armitage, in the Pallas cinema. He went on to cause the British Army a great deal of trouble until he was run to ground and killed.

Of the three terrorists Coombe had shot at close quarters, one was dead, one was badly injured and the third, the English speaker, was barely scratched. None of them knew that the Major, who sat guarding them, was carrying an empty Sten gun. The dead man was identified as Haralambos Mouskos, Archbishop Makarios's 23-year-old cousin. He had been a fugitive since July with a £5,000 reward on his head. The wounded were Andreas Zakos and Harilaos Michael. Both would be hanged for their crimes.

Zakos, the English-speaking terrorist, struck up a conversation with his captor. He answered questions freely and spoke about how he had enlisted in EOKA after training as a draughtsman in the Xeros mining company. He told Coombe proudly that he was a 'freedom fighter' against the British Nazi occupation of his country. The Major, who had fought in Greece against the Nazis in the Second World War, tried to put the young man straight on several points: 'I explained to him that it was his organization that was the stumbling block to freedom and that if they really wanted their freedom the last way they could get it was by adopting a campaign of murder and terror. I pointed out that, on the contrary, it was the British Army that was fighting to preserve freedom on the Island. In particular I pointed out what we had done for Greece both during and after the war. How we had fought and how we had died in order to give Greece her freedom. Without our aid, I told him, Greece would have been another strangled satellite of Russia like her neighbour Bulgaria.

'I had hoped to talk the man into seeing something of the folly of his ways, to sow some small seed of doubt, so that if he should escape, perhaps he would think twice before continuing his nefarious activities. But he was in no mood for further political argument, and he relapsed into a grumbling whine that I should go off to find help for himself and his friends.'

Help was on its way, although Major Coombe and his prisoners did not know yet when it would arrive. Then, there they were, the Gordons to the rescue, tumbling out of a convoy of military trucks.

'The incident was over: Cyprus had claimed one more victim. Another soldier had lost his life in the service of his country; a life nurtured in a happy family, moulded in a famous school, full of promise for launching out into a chosen profession. A life full of keenness, efficiency and cheerfulness lost without purpose. For the third time the Squadron saluted with military honours at the graveside of a comrade,' said Major Coombe.

The days leading to Christmas were filled with sadness for growing numbers of families back in Britain, as they received news almost daily about their loved ones being gunned down by assassination squads in the Island's towns or bombed by ambushers on country roads. The day before the Coombe incident, Private Douglas Laventure, RASC, was shot down and killed in Nicosia's Ledra Street. He had been in the Army for five months.

Lance Corporal Peter Woodman, his friend, heard the news of the soldier's death on the Forces Broadcasting Service during the afternoon. They had planned to eat lunch together, but had to cancel because Laventure had been chosen to act as an officer's escort. After taking the officer to a house in Nicosia, he and the Land Rover's driver were freed from duty for a couple of hours and thought they would use them Christmas shopping.

Ledra Street was a traffic-free zone. They parked their vehicle elsewhere and walked to a chemist's shop. While gazing in the window, the hat-wearing murderers struck, shooting at the two soldiers' backs. A nearby RAF sergeant, in civilian clothes, saw the act and drew his revolver. He chased the two assailants through the crowds until they took cover behind a parked car. There was a short exchange of fire. One of the attackers – Alecos Pantazis – dropped to the ground, injured, while the other – Isychios Sophocleous – ran off. The wounded man was searched for a weapon before being taken to hospital to have a bullet removed from his knee, but the runaway had taken the pistol. Laventure was dead, his comrade seriously ill.

In Famagusta, pupils staged a riot in their school. The Inniskilling Fusiliers were called to restore order. A youthful Nicos Georghiades watched the ensuing scuffles with particularly keen interest, which drew him to the attention of the police who were assisting the troops and he was arrested with some of the other demonstrators. Michael Davidson, the news editor of the *Times of Cyprus*, was present and insisted Georghiades had been falsely taken into custody. Later the Greek Cypriot teenager appeared in court and received a short prison sentence. On his release he was befriended by Davidson, who would employ him as a keen freelance photographer and journalist. With his camera always ready, he was often first on the scene of a murder. It was only discovered after many killings that he, in fact, was the killer, a leading member of the capital's execution squads. His name became internationally known as Nicos Sampson.

The eleventh British soldier and the first commissioned officer to die in the EOKA conflict lost his life on 17 December during an

A youthful Nicos Sampson recruited by *The Times of Cyprus*.

attack on a police station in Yialousa, in the north-east of the island. He was Lieutenant John Kelly of 40 Field Regiment, Royal Artillery, the son of Brigadier T. E. Kelly. After cutting the telephone lines to the village, the terrorists threw grenades and opened fire. The gunners and police fired back. To bring an end to the matter, Kelly stood up from behind a barricade of sandbags, grenade in hand, took aim, raised his arm and flung his bomb. Barely had it left his fingers, when a bullet struck him down. Mr Kelly and his men from 40th Regiment, Royal Artillery had arrived in Yialousa on a goodwill visit, never expecting to fight.

The fight continued for 15 minutes before the attackers fled in a car. The troops gave chase in two vehicles of their own. Overtaking the gunmen's car, they forced it off the road and arrested all six passengers, one the son of a prominent Famagustan businessman. All were still carrying their weapons.

Former Sergeant Bill Miller of the 40th told the author that when the ground outside the police station was minutely examined in the morning, the searchers found two unexploded British Army grenades, both unprimed. He said: 'Safety rules insisted that our grenades must be kept close to hand, but left unprimed. In the excitement of the situation, clearly these had been thrown that way. This may not have been the cause of our loss, but if they had been primed, they it would have certainly repulsed the terrorists much more quickly.'

The next day, an EOKA execution squad in Nicosia targeted Major Greenaway, the Commanding Officer of HQ 1 Divisional Provost Company. Once again, it was in the afternoon. Once again, the terrorists were back-shooters. Greenaway survived, but paralysed. He was rushed back to the UK's Stoke Mandeville Hospital for urgent treatment.

Then, on the 19th, Sergeant John Routledge of Y Troop 40 Commando Royal Marines lost his battle for life in hospital. He had been severely wounded on 14 December when a homemade bomb was thrown at his Section as it confronted and tried to disperse angry demonstrators in Limassol. They were out on the streets to protest against the arrest of the town's Communist Mayor. The rowdiest of those involved were the 1,200 pupils of the local gymnasium. Routledge's death was followed by another, that of Private Liddle, aged 23, of the RAOC. He became EOKA's 13th victim.

WITH DEATHS came funerals. The British buried theirs with quiet dignity and full military honours in Wayne's Keep Cemetery. Those of EOKA became a procession of wailing women in black, shouting youths with flags and banners, angry men, their fists raised and muttering long-robed priests behind the coffin as it was trundled through winding streets and broad roads to a cemetery. These public displays of mourning had to be given official permission in advance and required the police to be out in force, while troops were held in reserve.

For the funeral of the Archbishop's cousin, Haralambos Mouskos, the only permission granted by Governor Harding was for a small funeral to be held in Phaneromeni Church in Nicosia, with only clergy and up to 50 rela-

The funeral of Haralambos Mouskos, the Archbishop's cousin.

tives present on 17 December. It was the same day Lance Corporal Morum was buried, without his relatives.

The capital grew tense as the time for the funeral service neared. By his death, Haralambos Mouskos had secured a place in the annals of modern Greek history as the first EOKA fighter to die in face-to-face combat, at least in the eyes of Greek Cypriots. Whether they knew or cared about his dishonourable surrender to Major Coombe was not of any consequence today. They wanted him to have a heroic burial, especially the nationalist youths who attended the Pancyprian Gymnasium. From dawn, they had gathered in the courtyard of the Archbishopric to produce scores of wreaths made of white chrysanthemums, tied with ribbons of white and blue silk, a nod to the colours of the Greek flag now banned in the Colony. With added myrtle and laurel, they tried to show their lineage to ancient Athens, the birthplace of democracy.

After Archbishop Makarios completed the religious service, the hearse came out of the Phaneromeni Church and was taken to Metaxas Square, followed by the coffin and its pallbearers, a tradition usually applied only to the great and the good. Under a cloud-darkening sky, crowds spilled into the road, forcing their way past police and soldiers on cordon duty. Flag-waving schoolgirls in uniform were the first to break through. Control was breaking down. An edgy officer, fearing a riot, ordered his men to fire several rounds of teargas grenades. They only made the situation worse, especially after one of the missiles landed on the hearse.

Suddenly the cortège changed direction, rushing down a side street to get away from the acrid fumes before returning in a slightly more ordered form on the cemetery road, still lined by thousands. Many kneeled as the coffin moved on. Others barged their way into the formal procession. What had been intended as a dignified procession was again breaking apart. Eventually the coffin was placed in its grave. The funeral ended with a clap of thunder and an outburst of heavy winter rain. Mourners and security forces returned whence they came, soaked.

Makarios was furious. He called what had happened 'a black stigma in the history of the British occupation of Cyprus'. For the non-Greek inhabitants, in particular the expatriate British on the Island, this was a time for tears or even sound and fury, but more of an occasion to raise a glass to celebrate the death of a terrorist, one closely related to the hated Archbishop.

EVENTS WERE speeding forward without a driver at the wheel. Both Makarios and Harding saw they were losing control. Something had to be done. On 18 December, a member of the Nicosia execution squad threw a bomb at a group of Americans whom he mistook for British civilians, injuring three. Sorry, said EOKA, it was an accident. This incident prompted the State Department in Washington to draw up contingency plans to evacuate US citizens in a hurry if civil order broke down. Secretary of State John Foster Dulles, a Cold War warrior whose only interest was keeping the Red Bear at bay, saw Cyprus as a minor irritant that could infect the body whole that was NATO, unless it was cleansed by a large dose of disinfectant. He instructed Consul Courtney to speak quietly to the Archbishop and Ambassador Cannon to whisper in the ear of Prime Minister Karamanlis in Athens. He wanted the Greek Government to nudge the prelate towards mediation. At this stage, there was no need to involve Turkey. Ankara would accept whatever America dictated as long as the message to behave came with another load of dollar aid.

For Prime Minister Eden, Dulles had little time. He distrusted his style of public school upper-class snobbery and the manner in which he camouflaged his true intentions in the diplomatic argot of the British civil service. Dulles also believed he 'had pushed the British considerably'. For that reason alone, Eden could be left out of the loop until there was some certainty that the players on the ground were ready to play again. Harding, he was sure, was a true officer and gentleman, devoid of political deviousness and would do all in his power to avoid further bloodshed, short of surrender.

'Harding was an unvarnished military professional whose virtues did not lie in dealing with the unfamiliar and baffling,' explains historian Robert Holland. 'The Primate of an ancient Eastern church was very unfamiliar to him indeed, and partly, but not only, for this reason he did not conceal that the process of negotiation was one in which he felt intensely uncomfortable. Makarios' theological habit of chiseling away little gains by protracted argument created in Harding an impression of insatiability which made him uneasy and increasingly impatient.'

Whether the Middle East specialists at the State Department were any more understanding of the way Byzantine minds worked is hard to tell, but, nevertheless, to highlight the view from the White House and the Eisenhower administration, Secretary Dulles advised Karamanlis 'this may be the high tide for Greece on the Cyprus problem and if the Greek Government does not try to ride into harbor now, it may find no such favorable opportunity for years to come'.

Karamanlis took Dulles at his word and sent his personal envoy, Alexis Liaitis, to 'persuade' Makarios to deal with Harding and then talked to Harding, which, by all accounts, became a one-sided conversation when he raised the subject of clemency for Karaolis, the young man sentenced to death for murdering PC Poulis on Grivas's orders in August.

The Turks in the capital watched envoy Liatis's activities with suspicion. *Halkin Sesi*, the newspaper that represented the nationalist position, editorialized that if the British ever left, Turkey should seize the Island by force.

Makarios accepted the appeal from the Greek Prime Minister. Under no circumstances could he afford to lose the mainland's support. Furthermore, his long-term ambitions saw him waving his staff from the steps of the Acropolis to the acclamation of Athenians once Cyprus was united with the motherland. Ideally if this could be achieved without more loss of life, his star would shine even brighter. Not bad for the son of a shepherd. On the other side, if the Dighenis-way won out, the glory would go to the little Cypriot-born Colonel. He, too, dreamed of being the power behind the throne of Greece, every Communist exterminated and he commemorated in marble statues wherever his people looked. No more could he be viewed as both a military and political failure who had suffered defeat at the hands of the Turks in Anatolia. Both needed the bricks to fall from their shoulders.

As Christmas came closer, morale in the British Forces dropped. Camped in unpleasant conditions and with little social life, their thoughts returned to home. Daily they risked their lives on patrol, picked up the pieces after an attack and read about town executions and ambushes on outlying roads, where their mates stood little chance. More often than not, they were confined to their bases. Even when they went out, their lives were at risk from a bullet in the back. That aside, the lowly paid National Servicemen never had any money to spend. They merely followed orders and counted the days until they left Cyprus. If the Island were vital to their country's survival, then they would fight and 'the Cyps wouldn't know what hit 'em, but fuckin' hell, we ain't allowed to sort 'em out,' said one Cockney private. 'Otherwise, what's the bleedin' point?'

The troops had raided monasteries,

rounded up Communists, chased rioting schoolgirls, but to what purpose? Official information pamphlets aimed at the soldiery used phrases, such as 'Unless the attempt of EOKA to dictate to the people of Cyprus by bloodshed and fear can be checked, the chances of democratic development for Cyprus are nil' and 'We are here to ensure control of a British military strongpoint, the maintenance of which is essential to the defence of the free world.' Yes, well?

No doubt 'Fighting John' often felt the same way. Frustrated by not having sufficient numbers of soldiers at his command and barely holding the line with an inadequate police force, he knew 1956 would not become any easier. He was also now very well aware that he was no longer battling a bunch of youthful delinquents, but individuals that were better trained each day – although they had a habit of surrendering at the first sign of confrontation – led by a very tough and resourceful leader. In different circumstances, the Field Marshal and the Colonel could well have spent an enjoyable evening discussing guerrilla tactics. In the New Year, Harding saw more meetings with the Archbishop on the horizon, with more ambiguous answers uttered from his lips. During an earlier session, he had tried to pin down the priest to a straightforward reply. 'I am asking whether His Beatitude is prepared to send me a letter,' the Governor demanded, 'by which it is made clear that he accepts cooperation and he denounces violence. The answer I am waiting for is yes or no.'

The Archbishop looked up at the ceiling for a few moments, knitted his bejewelled fingers together, repeated everything that the two had discussed and then replied: 'I would agree, but not in the way you put it.'

On 23 December, the first news bulletin of the day from the British Forces' Nicosia radio station announced: 'The George Medal has been awarded to Major Brian Jackson Coombe, of the Corps of Royal Engineers, the War Office announced last night. Major Coombe's home is at Invicta Lines, Maidstone, Kent.

> With utter disregard of his own safety, he carefully selected a position from which he could accurately locate and bring fire to bear upon the terrorists, three of whom he saw firmly established 30 yards away. A fourth terrorist opened automatic fire on Coombe from a separate position on the flank. Although outnumbered four to one, he continued to fire his Sten until his ammunition was exhausted. Having returned to the vehicle to get the escort's Sten, he resumed his position. After a further exchange of fire, during which he came under heavy fire from the fourth terrorist, Coombe put two of the party of three assailants out of action. He then directed a further burst of fire on the fourth terrorist. His ammunition being by now again exhausted, he drew his pistol and covered his opponents for 30 minutes ... When assistance arrived some 75 minutes after the action began, Major Coombe had, single handed, killed one terrorist, wounded two and captured one. He displayed courage and initiative of the very highest order, pressing home his attack against prepared positions at only 40 yards range.

Army PR officers hurriedly arranged a press conference for the Major to boast about his achievement. Instead the assembled press corps received a lesson in compassion and modesty. 'The prospect was frightening and fraught with unknown pitfalls, but when the time came I made a straightforward appeal to the assembled company to use their power to promote understanding in place of distrust, and sympathy in place of hatred.'

Speaking in a subdued voice in a hushed conference room, Coombe said: 'I am now going to do something I have never done before and hope never to do again – I am going to preach a sermon. My feeling is that civilians in Cyprus are being cowed by the threats and fear of a handful of murderers at large in the Island. As a result they are afraid to bring these people to justice.

'Last week my driver was killed by one of them, and it was my duty to bring to justice the people who murdered him – aided by my personal bitterness at my driver's death. As a result, one frightened, pathetic young Cypriot was killed and the national reaction to his death has been tragic.

'I feel it is tragic that misguided, frightened citizens should feel compelled to give this man a hero's status and consider that I killed a patriot. This is the thought that is worrying me. You may think I am talking like a grandmother, but there is far too much hatred here and I appeal to you all not to deepen the rift between peaceful Cyprus citizens and equally peaceful British.

'Let there be no jubilation over this tragedy. The fact is that a distasteful job had to be done ... The Cypriots are now acclaiming the dead man as their hero and the British Press is acclaiming me as theirs. This incident, instead of doing good, is separating the two camps over this so-called hero worship. I appeal to all to wipe out this evil in Cyprus so that we save the Island from any more deaths, tears, and sorrow.' Before fielding a few questions from the journalists – not Fighting John's favourite species – the Major quoted the Bible text that he had read at Lance Corporal Morum's funeral: 'And God shall wipe away all tears from their eyes; and there shall be no more death, neither sorrow, nor crying, neither shall there be any more pain: for the former things are passed away' (Revelations 21:4).

Silenced journalists left to file their stories. The Army PR people shrugged and hoped the press would be kind. Major Coombe admitted: 'The gesture carried no weight of authority, but it was some consolation to discover later that the sentiments expressed were received with sympathetic understanding in a great many quarters.'

Field Marshal Sir John Harding sent Christmas greetings to his men. He congratulated them on their discipline, patience, restraint, and good humour in the most difficult and trying conditions. 'You can all take great pride,' he said, 'in the fact that you are playing a full part in helping to stamp out terrorism in Cyprus, and so re-establish conditions in which all people can live at peace, but you must always be alert, ready for any eventuality.'

Those soldiers who were allowed Christmas Day off wore silly hats and waited patiently to be served roast turkey, with all the trimmings, by their officers in makeshift canteens. A few men had hidden some bottles of beer in their tents to celebrate later ... Over the holiday, EOKA and the troops observed an unofficial truce.

On New Year's Eve, Mount Olympus, the highest peak in Cyprus, was capped with snow. When the advance party of the UK Police Unit landed at Nicosia International Airport, it was the first sight they noticed on the horizon. In their light clothes, the officers shivered. Snow in 'Sunny Cyprus' – it had never crossed their minds.

CHAPTER SEVEN

Setting the example on the Cyprus beat

'Ye are a fractious crew, and enemies to all good government.'
Oliver Cromwell

OPTIMISTS WOKE on 1 January 1956 in an atmosphere of depression. Their convictions that there would be a rapid settlement to the Cyprus dispute once Field Marshal Sir John Harding took control as Governor were rapidly fading as the key figures declared their New Year's Day resolutions. Colonel Grivas was the first to reveal his in leaflets that were eagerly read by youngsters on holiday from their schools.

'The year, which has ended, has been the beginning of a hard, bloody, and glorious struggle for the overthrow of the repressive yoke of the repugnant tyrant,' Dighenis said, warning 'we shall continue the New Year with the same decisiveness ... until the tyrant who desecrates churches, seizes the belongings of bread-winners and rapes virgins (yes, even that has been observed) is driven from the land of our fathers ... Let us continue the struggle that awaits us, harder and bloodier ... On behalf of your fighting EOKA, children, I renew our sacred oath ...'

In his sermon, Archbishop Makarios reaffirmed that he not only demanded the right of self-determination – *enosis* – for his Greek Cypriot flock, but the British would also have to give a guarantee that it would be granted by a specific date. He also disclosed that he and Harding had met secretly on 21 November, but the Governor conceded nothing. He suggested that they would not be conferring again unless the Field Marshal had a change of heart. Hence, the fight must continue and more sacrifices would have to be made in the year ahead. His words were supported by a proclamation in Athens from Archbishop Sophronios, delivered on behalf of the Pan-Hellenic Committee for *enosis*. 'The heroic struggle of the Cypriots,' it said, 'was directed resolutely and wisely by Archbishop Makarios.'

The Governor's New Year's Day broadcast was one of firm determination and optimism. He dangled several carrots in front of his listeners to induce them to settle for peace. He said the British Government had set aside more than £38 million for civic improvements on the Island and that he planned to introduce a social insurance scheme for the people. First of all, however, he stressed there must be an end to the violence, followed by the acceptance of limited self-government, with the 'possibility' of self-determination 'in the future'. He agreed that the search for a political solution would not be easy, but asked: 'Would Cyprus, Greece, Turkey and the Middle East and the world generally all at once be safer and happier if Great Britain suddenly abdicated her responsibilities?' This was something Britain would never do.

Turning to EOKA, Harding pointed out

that its acts of violence only made a settlement all the more difficult and distant. Shooting unarmed men and indiscriminate tossing of bombs in public places were acts of brutality debasing both those who committed them and those who connived at them.

'I warn EOKA here and now that their days are numbered and the net slowly but surely is closing around them.' His message was firm and clear: 'No matter what temporary successes they may still gain by murder, raid or ambush, they and their organization will be destroyed. I believe that 99 per cent of the population of Cyprus is longing for this sorry state of affairs to be brought to an end.'

1956 WAS starting much as 1955 had ended, except that more British Regiments would be brought to the Island to fight the enemy and more effective civil policing would be introduced. The arrival of the UK Police Unit would lead the way. Put bluntly, the administration could no longer trust the Greek Cypriot policemen and the widespread use of Turks on the beat posed other difficulties. The latter were definitely dependable and honest, but generally less well educated and more likely to come down hard on any Greek who fell into their hands.

On his arrival Sir John had expressed his view that a civil police force was 'fundamental to good government. Without it there can be no lasting progress in any field of human activity. Here in Cyprus that task has been rendered even more important and more difficult under the conditions of unrest and violence that now exist.' This was why he had pressed Whitehall to find solid British 'Bobbies' to come to the Island.

'Through no fault of its own, the Cyprus Police Force has not yet developed up to the standard required to provide the degree of security needed in a modern civilized country such as Cyprus,' he explained. Now he was able to add: 'Plans have been made accord-ingly and are being put into effect as a matter of urgency.'

The purpose of the UK Police Unit was to supplement the existing force, not act as a replacement. Integration was not expected to be a problem, as the local organization was along the traditional lines of the British constabularies. 'The force Harding wanted to establish was to be a "model" to Cypriot policemen, setting an example of discipline and efficiency, which the Cyprus Police would observe, learn from and (he hoped) seek to emulate,' write David Anderson and David Killigray in their study, *Policing and Decolonization*. 'With no direct experience of policing, his notion of the qualities of the "British bobby" was somewhat idealized, but his concern was more to improve the morale and attitude of the local police than to impose any particular methods of operations.'

The Governor's Police Commissioner, Mr G. N. Robbins, commanded a service of 1,386 poorly paid and poorly trained policemen of whom 37 per cent were Turkish Cypriots. A police constable earned a wage of only £21 per month compared to an unskilled labourer who might expect £26 or more. Robbins' senior officers were mainly British from former colonies, while the rank and file came from both Greek and Turkish communities. By 1958, the Turks in the force outnumbered

The view from the central police station in Nicosia.

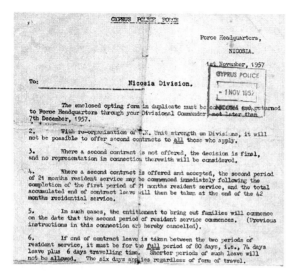

CYPRUS POLICE FORCE

Force Headquarters,
NICOSIA.
1st November, 1957

CYPRUS POLICE
- 1 NOV 1957
NICOSIA

To: Nicosia Division.

The enclosed opting form in duplicate must be completed and returned to Force Headquarters through your Divisional Commander not later than 7th December, 1957.

2.   With re-organisation of U.K. Unit strength on Divisions, it will not be possible to offer second contracts to all those who apply.

3.   Where a second contract is not offered, the decision is final, and no representation in connection therewith will be considered.

4.   Where a second contract is offered and accepted, the second period of 21 months resident service may be commenced immediately following the completion of the first period of 21 months resident service, and the total accumulated end of contract leave will then be taken at the end of the 42 months residential service.

5.   In such cases, the entitlement to bring out families will commence on the date that the second period of resident service commences. (Previous instructions in this connection are hereby cancelled).

6.   If end of contract leave is taken between the two periods of resident service, it must be for the full period of 80 days, i.e., 74 days leave plus 6 days travelling time. Shorter periods of such leave will not be allowed. The six days applies regardless of form of travel.

A UK Police Unit contract.

the Greeks, many of whom, intimidated by EOKA, had resigned. In their place, British expatriates volunteered to be 'Emergency Specials' and kept their eyes peeled for lawbreakers in their neighbourhoods.

While waiting for the British policemen, Harding had used his troops as an aid to the civil power. 'I have had to give definite orders that troops will carry out police duties by providing patrols, riot squads and other appropriate assistance,' he informed London. 'In doing so they will use police methods, e.g. baton charges and other non-lethal methods of dispersing crowds and maintaining order. The troops are being equipped and trained accordingly.' Although he issued a Royal Instruction, which gave soldiers the same legal status as the police, he did not welcome having to order his men into this role.

Now 150 British officers – all volunteers – were in Cyprus, together with several police dogs and their handlers, to take over part of the military's chores. For these 'bobbies' – both men and women – more used to dealing with petty crime and speeding offences than an armed insurgency, their new duties on the Island came as a shock. The dogs were first 'in action'. Within days of arriving, they were sniffing out arms dumps in the Troodos Mountains. The policewomen searched females, escorted women prisoners and were used to staff control rooms, releasing male officers for outside duties. There were no locally recruited policewomen until 1957. In the minds of conservative Cypriots, it was not a job for females, as they would have to mix with men, unescorted by any family members – something quite outside their culture.

The breakthrough came when Guner Ahmet Bigin, a Turkish Cypriot, joined. The 21–year-old was fluent in Greek, learning it from Fanu Denaetriou, a dressmaker, who lived in the Turkish quarter of Kyrenia. When the Cyprus Police advertised for female recruits, Guner was among the first to apply. 'Was Guner lucky that she was the only one chosen out of five candidates? I think not, policewomen are not chosen by a lucky chance, like nurses they are born,' said W/Sergeant Barnes.

Twenty-one year-old Guner's first day on duty was 14 October 1957.

Detective Chief Superintendent Thomas Lockley of the Staffordshire County Constabulary, which had also supplied volunteers, was in charge of the UKU's first arrivals. His officers' terms of agreement were simple: a two-year-attachment, consisting of 21

The UK Police Unit learns to handle small arms.

months' service, followed by three months' home leave, but, in Cyprus, they moved up a rank. Thus, a Constable became a Sergeant, a Sergeant became an Inspector and so on. Harding had expected the Unit to be made up of young unmarried officers with unblemished records and proven experience. Instead he saw a collection of older men nearing retirement who wanted to enhance their pensions. Sergeant Robin Fletcher was one of the younger officers. He explains: 'Our pay was about three times what we earned back home. If we signed on for a second tour, promotion to inspector was almost automatic.'

The new arrivals were soon kitted out in the standard uniform of the Colonial Police: khaki shirts and shorts in summer, with black peaked caps, socks and epaulettes. Winter uniform was 'police blue' high-necked tunics and trousers. The officers were accommodated in hotels commandeered for the purpose. These were guarded 24 hours a day by armed British Army soldiers and Turkish Cypriot policemen.

'We had to carry a short-barrelled Smith and Wesson .38 calibre revolver, a heavy clumsy piece of ironmongery, but necessary for all British policemen, both on and off duty,' Sergeant Fletcher explained. 'On duty we carried a Sterling 9mm sub-machine gun with a 25-round magazine, normally fitted to the gun, which could be fired on either single shot or automatic. The Sterling was another clumsy piece of ironmongery, supported on a webbing strap over the left shoulder, and fired from either the shoulder or from waist level.'

The fresh arrivals were trained in the use of their new weapons at the Athalassa range. They had to learn to 'shoot to kill' instinctively. While there, they were lectured on EOKA's favourite booby traps and explosives by Major 'Bomber' Harrison in his customary cavalier fashion, passing boxes of gunpowder and gelignite for the police sergeants to handle. Just as important was their course of

unarmed combat run by Lieutenant Colonel William Fairbairn. He was the world's leading authority in *defendu*, a method of self-defence rooted in the brutal realities of street violence.

Fairbairn had perfected his skills while serving in the Shanghai Municipal Police force of the International Settlement. The 'open' port city was considered the roughest police beat in the world, rife with every imaginable criminal activity and vice. His colleagues considered him 'a good man in a dust-up'. In 1940, he returned to England, where he was assigned to various elite forces and covert intelligence units as an instructor. In 1956, at the age of 71, the British employed him again to teach riot-control techniques in Cyprus. His student policemen, with whom he frequently demonstrated his methods, discovered to their surprise that he was still fighting fit and that his system of unarmed combat made it possible for a person of average strength and skill to win against most opponents, even those trained in the martial arts.

The UK Unit's day-to-day duties consisted of mobile and foot patrols, alongside the existing Cyprus Police, in the Island's major towns, and attachments as 'wardens' in the Island's detention centres. UKU sergeants took charge of rural stations, known as 'out stations'. British soldiers always guarded these. Besides the uniformed British policemen, there were plain-clothes officers of the Criminal Investigation Branch and Special Branch. They liaised closely with the police departments of the armed forces and conducted joint operations against the 'common enemy'. Mobile patrols were conducted using Land Rovers, driven by a Cypriot, with local officers on board. Foot patrols also consisted of mixed groups. There was also a Traffic Division, which used blue Vauxhall cars with Cyprus Police badges on their doors. Later a Marine Section was formed, as well as Riot Squads, made up of Turkish Cypriot policemen under the command of UKU Inspectors. At first, some British policemen regarded the Unit as an opportunity to enjoy a paid holiday in the sun, but things were to change quickly.

Sergeant Gerald Rooney, aged 24, was the first to be shot dead. He was killed at 08.45 on 14 March 1956 in Ledra Street at the junction with Hippocrates Street, while teaching a new recruit how to patrol a beat.

Just as they crossed the intersection of the two narrow streets, lined by shops tightly shuttered in compliance with a general strike, the assassin, lurking in a hallway, ran up behind the two officers and fired a burst from a Sten gun. Sergeant Rooney fell. The Turkish recruit was hit in his left arm. A Greek Cypriot civilian standing nearby was slightly wounded. A roundup of Greek Cypriots followed. All protested they had seen and heard nothing. Fifty men were detained and police dogs were fetched, but they did not pick up a trail.

Rooney, from the Kent County Constabulary, had been a constable stationed at Chatham. His body was flown home and he was buried with full honours.

Three months later, on 21 June 1956, EOKA shot Sergeant Reginald Tipple, a Metropolitan Police constable, attached to the Pyla/Pile Detention Camp. He had gone shopping to buy his five-year-old daughter a present from Larnaca market. He died on his way to hospital.

'The contradictions in seeking to combine the function of a "hit squad", to be used against EOKA in the towns, and a "model force", setting an example of disciplined modern policing, quickly became evident,' write Anderson and Killingray. 'Following precedents set in Malaya, it had been agreed that the force would be created as a special unit with its own terms of service, and not be integrated within the main body of the Cyprus Police. This reduced the direct influence the UK policemen might have on their Cypriot colleagues, and tended to isolate the unit from the community: in many senses, it became just like another military-style regiment.

'Though undoubtedly reliable and efficient, the unit was not particularly well suited to its task. None of these policemen had any experience of the island and they had little knowledge of its peoples, culture or geography. The British police were often intolerant of the difficulties confronting their Cypriot colleagues, and their establishment as an armed "elite corps" distanced them from the normal routines of police work.

'In June 1956 the officer commanding the first UK Police Unit, Lockley, confessed his "mixed feelings" about the record of the unit. He was reported to have been "ashamed of the behaviour and attitude of a certain element", expressing the opinion that "some of the Home Forces had dumped their unwanted personnel on to Cyprus".

'The speed with which the unit had been recruited and the relatively low numbers of applicants – virtually all who applied were taken – left little scope for finding the higher-calibre constables that Harding had expected. Despite its many shortcomings, the UK Police Unit was crucial to the British during the Emergency. Without the unit, and the other police staff seconded to Cyprus from Britain and various colonial forces, it is doubtful that the security forces would have been able to contain the violence to the extent they did.'

On 31 August 1956, the unit suffered yet another fatality in what became known as the 'Battle of Nicosia Hospital'. It resulted in the deaths of four people. Two EOKA gang members had been taken from prison under escort for medical treatment, where George Taliadoros, a registry clerk at the hospital, relayed the information to Colonel Grivas, who ordered Nicos Sampson to attempt the release of the more hard-core of the two – Polycarpos Georghadjis, code-named *Klimis* or *Cicero*. After Cyprus gained independence, Makarios appointed him his Minister of the Interior. The second prisoner was Nicos Ionnou.

Sergeant Maurice 'Anthony' Eden from the UK Police Unit was one of the escorts and he described what happened: 'At about 10.30, Sergeant Leonard Demmon, who had come out from the Met, and I were moving the prisoners from the X-Ray ward towards what we called the "cage". As we came down the main staircase I was in the lead, followed by our prisoners and a couple of Greek Cypriot warders, to whom they were handcuffed. A third warder was alongside them. Private George Bott of the Leicestershire Regiment was bringing up the rear. At the bottom we had to pass through the "cage" to reach the main hall. Several men were standing about, and a woman was in front of them. I went through first and then I heard a shot.

'I turned and saw Bott fall. He went on firing where he lay. Sergeant Demmon was also shooting back. I fired my own revolver and hit one of the gunmen and continued until he stopped moving. The other terrorist stared at me for a moment, then turned and ran. I chased him, got fairly near, and fired my weapon and knocked him to the ground. Tony, too, ran out of ammunition and, like me, gave chase, clubbing his man on the head, causing his death. I carried on running after another terrorist, but lost him outside. I turned to go back into the hospital to see how Bott and Tony were faring, when I came face to face with yet another armed man, who fired at me through the grill of the cage.

'I ducked behind a pillar, put two rounds in my pistol, and went after him. When I got into the corridor I saw him with Bott's Sterling sub-machine gun. I was sure he would use it, but instead he took off again, disappearing outside the building. I went back to the original scene of battle and found Sergeant Demmon lying face down in a pool of blood, with his pistol in his hand. I would like to say that but for him I don't think I should have been alive now. His shooting attracted all the fire from the terrorists towards himself. Poor Bott, he had died from a single bullet. Two hospital staff were also killed.'

The Greek Cypriot prison warders had put up no resistance. They undid the prisoners' handcuffs and released them to the attackers, allowing them to disappear into the crowds outside the hospital. Within minutes the Army sealed off the area and cordons were thrown across roads as far as 10 miles from Nicosia.

Demmon, aged 23, a Metropolitan constable, came from Orpington police station, where his body was returned for burial. He was subsequently awarded the Queen's Police Medal for Gallantry, a decoration now only awarded posthumously.

Ionas Nicolaou and Kyriacos Kolokasis, the two dead terrorists, came from Yeri village, where their bodies were interred, their coffins covered in the Greek flag and wreaths signed by 'Dighenis'. A third man, Spyros Kyriacou, was injured and taken into custody later. In the shootout, Koulis Kyriakidies, a pharmacist, was badly wounded. Eleni Christophorides and Vereniki Leonidou had carried the EOKA's team pistols into the hospital, hidden under their skirts. Nicos Sampson escaped by car, taking one of the prisoners with him. Not recognizing Polycarpos Georghadjis, he had grabbed the wrong man. He had left with Nicos Ionnou. The latter became a member of a mountain gang until he was recaptured. He was sentenced to death, but he was reprieved minutes before his execution.

After his escape through a back door at the hospital, Georghadjis raced to a safe house owned by Gabriel Gabrielides, a prominent Greek businessman in the capital, who specialized in electrical contracting. He was a leading member of the Nicosia Club, a bastion of 'Britishness', where senior military and police officers relaxed. To them he was known as 'Gabby'. When the club bar closed at midnight, they often accepted Gabrielides' invitation to continue drinking at the well-stocked bar in the basement of his house. The British never knew there was an EOKA hide behind the bar. Gabrielides knew that with his reputation, it was highly unlikely the Security Forces would raid his residence. He was correct and was never found out. The house became EOKA's Nicosia HQ.

From Gabrielides' house, Georghadjis wrote Grivas a letter:

Leader,
I have just arrived at Gavriel's house, very much distressed at the unhappy results of today's events. My escape can only be considered miraculous. The handcuffs seemed to fall by themselves from my wrists, and through a stream of bullets I ran out of the hospital without meeting our men. I had been taken there by six guards: the attempt should not have been made. I await your orders as to where and how I shall offer my services,
Klimis (Cicero)

Following the hospital battle, Governor Harding strongly advised Eden to return to the United Kingdom, with his wife Stella (née Kenny), a policewoman who left the service to be with him in Cyprus. He said EOKA would make him 'a marked man', but the sergeant, a very determined and self-willed person, chose to stay. He was recommended for the George Medal. Tragically however, on 17 December, just one day before the award was confirmed in the *London Gazette*, he died. While playing with his puppy, his revolver – which he always kept loaded and cocked – fell from his shoulder holster. The weapon went off and a bullet shot upwards through his chin. He was flown by helicopter to the British Military Hospital in Nicosia, but was pronounced dead on arrival. 'His body was taken home to the UK and I was chosen, as a friend, to be one of the pallbearers at his funeral, which was held in a cemetery in North London – Barnet – as I recall,' his friend in the Met, Sergeant Hurrell, told the author.

FOUR WEEKS later, on 28 September 1956, the UKU had to mourn two more members: Sergeant Cyril Thorogood (Leicester and Rutland Constabulary) and Sergeant Hugh Carter (Herefordshire County Constabulary). Sergeant William Webb (Worcestershire County Constabulary), the third member of the group, survived the EOKA attack. They were in plain clothes and had just stepped out of a shop after collecting a camera they had ordered the day before. The owner had tipped off EOKA about when they were coming back.

At the junction of Ledra Street and Alexander the Great Street, Nicos Sampson, Athos Petrides and Andis Tseriotis waited for the three police officers. Each was to target a specific individual as they walked in single file on the crowded pavement. Dodging between the traffic, the killers crossed the busy street and fell in step behind the policemen. Sampson drew his revolver and shouted to the others to shoot. He took down Carter and Petrides fired his bullets into Thorogood. Tseriotis hesitated. When he loosed his shots, they hit Webb's arm five times.

Although dying, Thorogood forced himself up on one arm, pulled out his pistol and fired three times, before collapsing in a pool of blood. His bullets missed the assassins, but one hit an innocent Greek Cypriot in the leg. Despite his severe injuries, Webb also began shooting. Witnesses say Sampson slapped Tseriotis across the face and dragged him round the corner where a car was waiting to drive them away. Wracked with pain, Webb slumped on the shop doorstep, still holding his weapon.

Victor Bodker of the *Cyprus Mail* reported the policemen's deaths the next day in his

Sergeant Thorogood returns fire after Nicos Sampson fatally injures Sergeants Carter and William Webb.

newspaper. 'It was a peaceful morning in the *Cyprus Mail* office. The time was roughly 10.30. The printers had not yet arrived and the only noise to be heard was that of the tapping of a typewriter. But suddenly the silence was broken by the sound of eight or nine shots fired in rapid succession.

'I rushed out of the office into Ledra Street. There, practically opposite our office, I saw two men lying on the ground, a third leaning against a wall, revolver in hand. There was not a sign of anyone running away and the gunmen who had shot three Englishmen must have disappeared round a corner within a few seconds of committing their crime.

'I bent over one of the wounded men and asked if he was badly hurt. He could only moan in reply and a Cypriot doctor, George Partelides, who came up at this moment bent over him and said: "He's in a very bad way."

'The second man lying on the pavement was bleeding from the mouth and was kicking his legs in agony and breathing stertorously. I said to the third man leaning against the wall: "Was it one man who did this?"

'He replied: "No, there were three. Get me a taxi."

'A taxi which had apparently brought the men to Ledra Street was there. With the help of a few English women shoppers and some Greek Cypriot men, the three men were lifted into the taxi and driven off to the British Military Hospital.

'A good 15 minutes had elapsed since the shots were heard and no ambulance had appeared. Security Forces arrived on the scene after the taxi had taken the wounded man to hospital.'

Anthony Windrum was junior officer in the Political Office Middle East Forces, an offshoot of the Foreign Office. On the day of the incident in Ledra Street, he had been in Nicosia for exactly one month. His office was directly opposite the British Military Hospital. Suddenly he heard loud tooting from a car and looked out of his window. Ahead he saw a frantic taxi driver trying to gain the attention of the guards so that they would open the hospital gates to allow him to enter with the injured Sergeant Webb and the corpses of Thorogood and Carter. 'EOKA had done its damnedest again,' Windrum said. He was becoming a veteran of the war.

Webb's Greek-born wife was on holiday with their six-year-old son when the incident took place. In 2006, West Mercia Police confirmed that the retired police officer was living 'somewhere abroad', aged 80.

Grivas later defended the methods of his town murder squads: 'Our opponents called us murderers because we struck from behind. Such a charge is, to say the least, naive, because to kill your opponent by assailing him at his weakest point, from the side or the rear, is a tactic as old as . . . Marathon. What would the critics say if a General were to make a frontal attack against a much stronger opponent, thereby leading his soldiers to a useless death? They would of course demand that he be court martialled or at least cashiered.'

The *Cyprus Mail* report continued: 'After the shooting, Security Forces barred all exits from the Greek Cypriot sector of the walled city. A full curfew of the walled city was imposed from 17.00 yesterday until further notice. Moreover all establishments owned and/or managed by Greek Cypriots and situated within the municipal limits of Nicosia and the suburban village areas of Strovolos, Engomi, Ayios Dhometios, Trahonas, Omorphita, Kaimakli and Pallouriotissa were closed from 19.00 last night until further notice.

'The word "establishment" means any bar in a hotel, any cabaret, cine theatre club, coffee shop, restaurant, theatre and any other place of public resort or establishment whatsoever. But hotels may remain open for the purpose of catering for the residents therein.

'The Commissioner of Nicosia yesterday ordered the closing "until further notice" of two shops in Pallouriotissa village at St. Andrew Street. It was at the junction of St. Andrew and Queen Frederica Street that Surgeon Captain C. E. Wilson of the Royal Horse Guards was shot and killed in his car on Thursday last.'

The body of Sergeant Carter was flown back to Herefordshire for burial, but Sergeant Thorogood was buried in Wayne's Keep Military Cemetery.

NICOS SAMPSON, the 25-year-old Greek Cypriot photo-journalist from the *Times of Cyprus*, was suspected of firing the fatal shots but it was not until the following January (1957) that he was arrested at Dhali for carrying arms, contrary to British Emergency Regulations. Sergeant Taylor was one of the UKU officers who helped catch him. An EOKA courier, Lazarou Ioannides, known as *Chateris*, fell into his hands and, during interrogation, confessed he was the link between the 'Kill Group' in Nicosia and Grivas.

Ioannides' information led swiftly to Sampson's capture. After a brief struggle, he was brought to police headquarters in need of medical treatment. 'It was nothing to the treatment he would have required if I had

Sergeant Jack Taylor of the UK Police Unit.

been allowed on the raid,' Taylor told the author. 'He faced me and said, "If I get away from here, you will never leave the island alive." I walked around the counter, took off my .38 revolver and replied, "You are playing in the wrong league. I saw and learned too much in the war for the likes of you to cause me concern. Pass me, and my colleague will escort you from this police station. Don't get by, and you will be killed trying to escape. Don't threaten me." Whilst making this remark, I causally undid my tie, flipped it loose, held it before him and said: "I could strangle you before you moved".' Taylor had been a Royal Marine Commando in the Second World War.

At Sampson's trial, which lasted from March until June 1957, Webb identified him as Carter and Thorogood's killer, but Mr Justice Shaw ruled that identification might have been erroneous as it was not made during a properly conducted identification parade but when the police officer was shown the accused, manacled in irons in a prison cell after his capture.

Michael Davidson, who had hired Sampson to work on the *Times of Cyprus*, gave evidence on his behalf – the man accused of being the 'Murder Mile' gunman in more than 20 shootings. 'I had been seeing Nicos fairly frequently generally when he called at our office,' he explained. 'I'd no inkling that he'd any connection with EOKA.' The gay journalist had always found the young Sampson attractive from the moment they set eyes on each other for the first time in Famagusta.

'Resisting this perversion of British justice, I was accused of being on EOKA's side,' Davidson said. 'Of course I wasn't: I loathed the beastliness of terrorism no less than I loathed the beastliness of hanging. But I was on the side of British decency and fairness, of those British legal standards which Cyprus still had respected: and was appalled by the shame of their being dragged down to terrorism's beastly level. I exposed the Government's mendacity about "ill treatment" in the interrogation cells.' But he had praise for Mr Justice Shaw. 'His departure from the island in June 1957 was England's loss more than the Cypriots': there was almost no one else to uphold Britain's name in the one sphere in which she'd won honour: the law.'

Sampson was acquitted – due to procedural inadequacies. 'Shaw ought to have flung the book at him,' a shocked British Colonel exclaimed. Davidson huffed and puffed even more. 'He was six times tried – if one counts two preliminary hearings, two assize trials, a reference to the Supreme Court during the murder trial of a "confession" which the Attorney General sought to introduce and which Mr. Justice Shaw had rejected, and an appeal to the Supreme Court against two death sentences. For four months he was on trial for his life. Well, what's wrong with that, one may ask – if what was said of him was true: if indeed (which was never proved) he was a murderer many times over? What's wrong with trying to put a rope round his neck, if one believes in the justice of capital punishment?

'There's the point: the motive wasn't justice, it was vengeance. There was no "justice", in the English legal sense, in any of the prosecutions conducted against Sampson; they were makeshift attempts to satisfy a frenetic craving to hang him for vengeance's sake, cost what it might to British principles and British law: an attempt at legalized lynching in which nearly the whole British community joined, from Government House down.'

Eventually, Sampson was found guilty of possession of arms, and for that offence received the death penalty. This immediately provoked further outbreaks of violence and the authorities commuted his sentence to life imprisonment in England.

Not long afterwards, Davidson quit his job on the newspaper Foley and he had set up in 1955. He claimed Victor Bodker, his professional rival at the *Cyprus Mail*, tipped him off that Special Branch was trying to find evidence to charge him with breaking the Emergency Regulations. 'But what charges?' Davidson asked. 'My private life had for long been immaculate; there was no evidence there. And then once more the spectre of the "previous" appeared: what if the Field Marshal and the Attorney General's office had secured from Scotland Yard my "record"?

'In Cyprus the police could easily have hired a couple of young Turks and framed an accusation against me, comfortably supported by my "previous" – that's the way my thinking went. Probably I was wrong; I'm sure the Field Marshal wouldn't have countenanced such a thing; though the police, once they knew I'd been convicted, might certainly have so acted on their own. I dare say I was cowardly: I felt I was too vulnerable to face the possibility of such a case; I decided it was time I left Cyprus. In the first week of August I secured an "exit permit" and slipped away; I didn't feel secure until I was aboard the Italian ship at Larnaca.'

All Davidson's faith in his Nicos was worth naught, because in 1961 Sampson boasted that he had murdered the British police sergeants. He made his confession in the Greek Cypriot paper *Makhi*, which he edited and published. His article described how he and two other EOKA men trailed the three officers and then shot them down from behind. He says he fired shots at all three men. He also took responsibility for killing Sergeant Leonard in Nicosia General Hospital.

One of the other gunmen, Athos Petrides, nicknamed 'the smiling killer' by Webb, became a civil servant in the post-independence government and prospered. Petrides was 17 at the time of the Ledra Street murders. With a smile and obvious pride, the Arsenal FC supporter said: 'We were firing at each other from 10, 20 yards away. It was like the movies. Now I think only God has the right to take life. But I was a patriot, very religious. I didn't hate the English. They were soldiers like we were.'

This was not a view shared by *Halkin Sesi*, the newspaper owned by Dr Kutchuk. It opined: 'Grivas, if you one day come face to face with a Turkish constable, just surrender. Because even in his last breath he will not let you go, because if you take him by surprise his comrades will soon catch up with you. Grivas realize this: Crime never pays. Your day of reckoning is here, approaching.'

Sergeant Fletcher explained how the EOKA assassins constantly adapted their operations in Nicosia to evade capture: 'They were always followed around by a schoolgirl, who carried a pistol in the waistband of her knickers. When they spotted a likely target, they would go down an alley or into a shop doorway and then take the gun, go and shoot their victim, and immediately return the weapon back to the girl. She would leave the area of the murder, knowing that no policeman or soldier would dare put their hand down there, even if she was suspected, which she never was. They always shot their victims in the back, at close range. They never attempted to take on anyone face to face.'

Wounded twice during his tour, Sergeant Fletcher, based at Omorphita Police station, was involved in several mobile patrols that ended in violence. Usually he set off in his Land Rover with two Cypriot Police Constables, one Greek and one Turkish. 'Our area covered the middle class sprawling outskirts of Nicosia, the main road to Kyrenia and several villages a few miles out of the city, spread out across a flat dusty plain, no fences or hedges, where shepherds tended flocks of goats. One such village was Mia Melia, just inside the boundary of our area, with only one Tarmac road to get there, so that having driven out to the village the only way back was to return along the same route,' he said. 'The men of Mia Melia worked in the brickyards next to the village, and piles of new bricks lined both sides of the road, waiting to be collected. The village was said to support AKEL, the Communist Party, and, from the slogans on the house walls, they also appeared to support the right wing EOKA.'

On Monday, 6 October 1958, Fletcher was working the night shift and was in charge of the Mobile Patrol of Sector Three. Because of increased terrorist activity and rioting, two soldiers were also ready to ride 'shotgun' in the rear of his Land Rover to provide additional firepower if required. His police team that night consisted of another British Sergeant, Les Barrs, Constable Ali and Special Constable Mehmet, an elderly Turk, who could not speak much English, but was a good driver and did his best to please. The soldiers were Privates Lane and Tye of the 1st Battalion, the Suffolk Regiment. One carried a Bren machine gun and the other was armed with an FN Self-Loading Rifle (SLR). Because there had been no unusual incidents reported, there was no need for Fletcher to patrol a specific area. Purely as a matter of routine, he chose to visit Mia Melia.

In the control room, staff were moving markers around a huge plotting table, so that the approximate location of all police and army patrols could be seen at a glance. Each marker represented a different radio call sign. Fletcher's was NIC (for Nicosia Division) One. Every 45 minutes, patrols reported their locations and next destination.

There was little traffic on the road as there had been a curfew in force from 19.00. At about 00.45, Fletcher's patrol reached the outskirts of the village. The Land Rover slowed to walking pace as PC Ali shone a searchlight on the road ahead in case a barricade had been erected, designed to make the driver avoid it and cross a landmine. Nothing was out of order. The light was switched off and the patrol continued to the silent village square, dominated by a Greek Church. After a short pause, the patrol turned round and started the journey back to Nicosia. Suddenly, a trail of sparks curved its way from a large stack of bricks towards the vehicle's passengers.

It was a hand-made grenade. It exploded with a loud bang within feet of the Land Rover. Another followed the first. Now there were shouts in Greek followed by the sounds of shots from the direction of the bricks. 'Rapid Fire,' bellowed Police Sergeant Fletcher. Private Lane let loose a burst of bullets from his Bren. Private Rye put his SLR against his right shoulder and released a sequence of single shots in rapid succession towards the attackers. Holding his sub-machine, Fletcher joined the firefight. He had cocked his weapon and taken off the safety catch without thinking.

'From the gun flashes, I saw there were four positions from which EOKA was targeting us. The terrorist closest to Mia Melia was shooting rapidly and I assumed he was using a sub-machine gun, while the others were armed with pistols,' said Fletcher. 'Another trail of sparks suddenly came out of the stacks of bricks and bounced on the road in front of us. Special Constable Mehmet switched off the Land Rover's lights, slammed his foot down and raced over the grenade. Fortunately it didn't explode, but my Sterling had jammed.'

Once the soldiers and police were out of grenade-throwing range, they stopped the Land Rover and jumped towards the verge of the road, sprawling flat on the ground, their weapons pointing towards the bricks. None had been injured. Silence under the stars. Nothing moved. Fletcher whispered to his Bren gunner: 'Give them another blast. Let's see if they move.' The bullets whined into the darkness, and ricocheted off the bricks. The gunner took his finger of the trigger. They all waited. The terrorists had fled. With that it was all over.

'We sent a brief radio message to the control room. Before long, we saw vehicle lights coming at high speed along the road from Nicosia and heard the roar of engines as friendly forces came to our rescue. An armoured car from the Life Guards was the first to reach us, soon followed by police and army Land Rovers,' recalled Fletcher. 'No bodies were found among the bricks, but there were some splashes of fresh blood, so we had hit one or more of the terrorists. When I checked my gun again, I found it hadn't jammed, just run out of ammunition.'

With daylight a thorough search of the village began, using tracker dogs. One of them sniffed a trail and raced ahead towards a dry river bed and then stopped as suddenly as it had started, wagging its tail in excitement, even if it had no idea where to run next. 'All we found afterwards were some 9mm casings near the bricks that confirmed an automatic weapon had been used and an unexploded grenade on the roadside, where we had taken up our defensive position,' said Fletcher. 'None of us had seen it coming. Perhaps the thrower forgot to light its fuse in his excitement!'

During the short-lived exchange, both sides had fired a total of 63 shots. The ambushed had injured one ambusher, a tiny target in the darkness, while the ambushers had missed entirely the much larger Land Rover silhouetted against the sky.

A month later, Police Sergeants Fletcher and Les Barrs were out on patrol in Kaimakli, accompanied by Special Constable Mehmet, a Greek Cypriot PC and two Lancashire Fusiliers, when their Land Rover was 'shredded' by shrapnel – from an electrically detonated mine this time.

'After the Cyprus Emergency was over, and just before I returned to England I met one of the six EOKA men who had ambushed us at Mia Melia. By then, 1960, he was an officer in the new republic's police service,' Fletcher recalled. 'He told me that the "Freedom Fighters" – as they were now called – had expected us to be half asleep and were shocked at the hail of bullets instantly fired back at them. They did not know that we were a joint police/army patrol, and they were very frightened and did not stop running until they were a long way from the village. When I enquired about the blood, he said the leader of the gang had lost a finger, shot off by one of us. This man later lost his head, when a homemade grenade blew up before he could throw it.'

The UKU also had to deal with general criminal activity and learn how to handle resident British civilians. Sergeant Fletcher remembered: 'There were quite a few expatriate British, some of whom were "remittance men" – paid money to stay out of England, by their disapproving families! Others held legitimate jobs, but most of them thought that traffic laws and so on did not apply to them, "because they were British".'

During his service in Cyprus, the UKU's Sergeant Taylor gained first-hand knowledge of EOKA's treatment of Greek Cypriots who did not fully cooperate. Called to investigate a robbery at a coffee shop in Eylanja, he found the village *mukhtar* had been badly beaten. 'His back had been cut to ribbons, when masked men tied him to a tree in front of the village's inhabitants,' Taylor remembered. 'They said he was a traitor and then beat him with whips and a chain. His wife and children were made to watch and prevented from going to his assistance.' Not even his experiences in combat during the war matched what he saw that day.

Unknown to them, two future presidents of Cyprus – Glafcos Clerides and Rauf Denktas – may have owed their lives to Taylor, who had been ordered to give them protection against attack, without their knowledge. 'I was told by the authorities to keep an eye open when Mr Denktas was out in Nicosia, staying a discreet distance behind him and his bodyguard, ready to take action should his life be threatened by any Greek Cypriot extremist. You see, he had prosecuted several EOKA men in court, while Mr Clerides defended them. I am pleased that Mr Denktas has lived a long life, but I hope he slowed down a bit, because he was certainly a rapid walker when he headed for the Turkish quarter.'

On 12 May 1957, Taylor was ordered to meet Clerides at Nicosia Airport on his return from London. The Greek Cypriot lawyer and politician, with his entourage, boarded a bus to take him home. Taylor and his officers drove just ahead in a Land Rover. All along the route to his house, Clerides was greeted by cheering Greek Cypriots, waving Greek flags. 'I was sweating all the way,' the retired Yorkshire policeman recalled. 'I was grateful that armed members of the Mobile Reserve were in position on roofs of nearby buildings, ready to deal with any counterdemonstrations or bomb-throwing incidents by the Turks.'

The next time Taylor and Clerides saw each other was in Nicosia's Special Court on 4 March 1958. Clerides and his father, in their barrister's role, were defending 23 Greek

Cypriot youths charged with various offences under the Island's Emergency Regulations. Taylor was a witness for the Crown and the first to be called to give evidence. Mr Clerides Sr. began the questioning. After he sat down, Mr Clerides Jr. faced the British policeman and repeated most of the questions asked by his father. A third barrister did the same.

After two hours of their non-stop interrogation, the Judge, Justice Ellison, told the Greek Cypriot defence team to get on and stop wasting time. 'He pointed out that though they had questioned me and re-questioned me, not once had I deviated one iota from my original evidence, and he reminded them that I was a British police officer who knew very well the result of committing perjury,' Taylor said. 'Mr Clerides Jr. then flung his law books to the floor.'

Following the tantrum, the usually suave Mr Clerides Jr. asked Justice Ellison for a 15-minute recess so that he could consult with his clients. He returned to say the accused had changed their pleas to guilty. They were sentenced to several terms of imprisonment.

In April 1957, the UKU was increased by 53 policewomen from 34 different county constabularies to combat the increasing violence. A year later Mr J. E. S. Browne took over from Lieutenant Colonel White, who had

Prime Minister Macmillan meets the UK Police Unit in 1958.

completed his two-year detachment in January 1958. Browne, 47, had been Chief Constable of Nottinghamshire since 1949.

On 1 September 1958, Assistant Superintendent Donal Thompson, a New Zealander, was shot in the back and fell dead on the pavement, 'a crumpled symbol of the decision last week by the rebel EOKA to end its jittery truce with the British military government,' *Time* reported. 'Next day, on the streets of the ancient-walled Nicosia (pop. 60,000), the only unarmed Britons abroad were those who had to be: reporters for the jaunty *Times of Cyprus* (circ. 5,400).'

Sergeant Robin Fletcher remembered: 'He had gone out on duty with two Greek Cypriot Sub-Inspectors, in their Volkswagen Beetle car. They stopped in Ledra Street and Thompson was killed as he stooped to get out. Not them, just him.'

The last UKU officer to be murdered by EOKA was Sergeant Stanley Woodward of the Durham Constabulary. His Land Rover hit a land mine on 13 October 1958 while he was on a mobile patrol near Podromos in the south-west of the Island. He died instantly and was buried in Wayne's Keep Cemetery.

No two days were the same for the Unit's members. Since his secondment from the Metropolitan Police in February 1956, Acting Superintendent Eric Holderness had been called out to deal with student riots, terrorist incidents and crowds bent on violence. His responsibility was to patrol the Limassol District with Turkish Cypriot PC Zyghul in their short-wheeled base Land Rover. Their 'manor' included the isolated hospital at the Amiandos asbestos mines. On 8 November 1958, he was on duty late in the evening at the Limassol station, when he received a distraught telephone call from Sister Sue Brewer, one of the hospital nurses. 'They have shot him, they have shot him,' was all she could blurt out.

'I immediately called Zyghul and away we

went.' Holderness said. 'On arriving at Amiandos, we learnt that two Greek Cypriots had called at the hospital, one of them complaining of a pain in his stomach on the right hand side. Dr Bevan was summoned from his home and, as he bent down to examine his patient, the other pulled out a revolver and shot him dead. The killers then ran off, stealing the doctor's car to drive away. The hospital's three nursing sisters were immediately evacuated from the Island in case an attempt was made on their lives, as they would have been able to identify the killers. A sad end to their nursing career in the sun and even a greater loss to the mine's workers who relied on the nurses and Dr Bevan.'

When Cyprus was proclaimed a self-ruling independent republic in August 1960, there was no longer a need for a United Kingdom Police Unit. Over 600 British policemen and women had served. Those who had been in Cyprus longer than three months were awarded the General Service Medal with the Cyprus clasp. Since the arrival of the 'bobbies' EOKA had murdered seven of them and wounded nine. One had died as the result of an unfortunate accident and seven more lost their lives due to other causes.

All the Greek Cypriot policemen who had joined EOKA and been held in detention were released by the new government, given back pay and promised promotion over the heads of those who had stayed loyal to the British.

On his departure from Cyprus, Lieutenant Colonel Geoffrey White, who had held the post of Chief Constable, expressed his appreciation of the UKU's work: 'It was a memorable experience for all who shared in it and the UK police officers were called upon to serve under difficult and dangerous conditions. The way the challenge was accepted has enhanced the reputation of the British Police. Some died, others were killed. All who did their duty in the heat and burden of the day in that small and historical Island have nothing of which to be ashamed and much of which to be proud. The United Kingdom Police Unit has ceased to exist, but the spirit which animated and made it such a potent force shall survive.'

The UKU was the first unit of its kind. Since then, it has become the model for similar formations deployed by the UK authorities in various other 'trouble spots' around the globe – with the appreciation of the international community.

CHAPTER EIGHT

Troublesome bishops:
Archbishop Makarios's exile

PAKHNA VILLAGE, 20 miles from Limassol, was still and shrouded in darkness. 'What's the time, mate?' Private Conaghan directed his whispered question to Lance Corporal Jay. '5.20,' he replied. With Private Watling, the three soldiers from the Royal Norfolk Regiment had been watching the EOKA stronghold all through the cold night. 'Jeez, I could do with a hot cuppa,' one of the privates exclaimed. 'Quiet,' Jay put his index finger to his lips. 'Look – over there.'

Three shadowy figures were moving in their direction from a house in the village. The soldiers checked their weapons and waited.

'Britisher,' hailed one of the approaching Greek Cypriots in clear English, 'I will give you eight pounds if you let us through.'

Jay released the safety catch on his rifle and replied: 'And I'll give you five yards, mate.' Watling and Conaghan raised their weapons. 'Your choice?'

The Greek Cypriots immediately surrendered. They had been carrying a pistol, a Breda carbine, and two Sten guns, with eight full magazines, 150 rounds of 9mm ammunition, and some British Army uniforms. At the local police station, two of them were identified as men wanted for murder, each with a price of £5,000 on their head.

While this encounter between the terrorists and the Security Forces ended without death or injury, the conflict was doing nothing for either side. A political settlement was as far away today as on the day Dighenis opened his battle for *enosis*. In London it was decided to give Archbishop Makarios, as the spiritual leader of the Greek Cypriots, a final chance to disavow violence in return for a settlement.

On 26 February Secretary of State for the Colonies Lennox-Boyd, accompanied by Sir John Martin, the head of the Colonial Office's Mediterranean section, arrived unexpectedly from London. With them was Mr Noel Baker, the Labour MP, who spoke fluent Greek and whose family owned property on the mainland. He was a known sympathizer of the Greek Cypriot cause. Speculation became rife that they were in Cyprus to sort out the final details of an agreement, including the Archbishop's demand for an amnesty for all EOKA detainees and those awaiting execution for murder. Official sources admitted negotiations had reached 'a critical stage'. While the Governor was greeting Lennox-Boyd at Nicosia Airport, 600 men of the Royal Horse Guards, commanded by the Marquess Douro, were disembarking from the troopship *Devonshire* in Famagusta. A band from the 1st Leicesters played them ashore.

Nobody expected a reformed Makarios to sign any agreement without a bit more haggling, but the general belief was that he would finally accept the British offer, with only very minor alterations to satisfy his ego. Yet while the talks continued amicably on the 29th, bombs went off in various parts of Nicosia. The Archbishop immediately blamed Grivas for the mischief and explained that he was powerless to stop the terrorists, unless the British conceded more of his demands. 'The authorities assumed that this outburst was initiated by the Archbishop in order to increase his bargaining power,' wrote Nancy Crawshaw. 'The more valid explanation is that the Colonel decided to remind Makarios that he would not tolerate any further concessions to the British.'

The bombers on this occasion were Andreas Ellinas, Andreas Louca, Christos Paroutis and Michalis Pittalis. The four-man gang had been told to synchronize the explosions to take place at 19.00, but, as was often the case, EOKA timing mechanisms failed. After the 13th and final bomb rocked the capital, Lennox-Boyd shut down the talks. 'God help your people,' he boomed as he left the room. 'Makarios was surprised and tried to back track, but he had stepped over the brink,' Greek Cypriot historian Makarios Droushiotis observes. Greek Cypriots would never again get a better offer to fulfil their aspirations.

'I was very angry,' the Archbishop explained later. 'I did not want the British to think I was so foolish as to try to put pressure on them in this way. I believe the bombs hardened their view and contributed to my exile. I wrote an angry letter to Grivas next day, saying that he had spoilt everything, but the Abbot of Kykko, to whom I showed it, thought it was too strong so I changed the wording.'

After the meeting, which had lasted two hours and 10 minutes, the Government issued a statement: 'The Secretary of State took up points raised by the Archbishop in his letter to the Governor of 25 February and set out personally the position of her Majesty's Government both on constitutional points and on the question of an amnesty (for EOKA members). He made clear the nature of the cooperation her Majesty's Government hoped from the Archbishop.'

An Ethnarchy source riposted that no agreement could be reached on three vital points, which separated both sides – an amnesty; the question of the Greek majority in a house of representatives of a constitutional self-governing system; and the question of control over internal security. Makarios was backed by the official view of the Greek Foreign Ministry. It expressed 'very deep disappointment', adding that when the British used the terms 'wide powers of self- government' they, in fact, had offered the Cypriots very little. The British had proved 'unyielding' on matters of substance. Vague British promises could not be trusted, said Athens. The British could have said the same about Makarios and his advisers.

On the subject of the terrorist campaign, Makarios said he refused to appeal to the people of Cyprus to restore law and order until an agreement had been reached with the British Government. 'Why don't I make such an appeal now?' he continued. 'Because I have nothing concrete to offer the Cyprus people, and an appeal would serve no purpose.' He said the Colonial Secretary had not given a clear answer to his demand that any legislative assembly in Cyprus must have an elected Greek majority, with the Turkish community being represented according to its size on the Island. The Turks accounted for 18 per cent of the population.

Greek Foreign Minister Theotokis chose also to criticize the Turks. He said Turkish opposition to self-government in Cyprus was 'unjustified', 'a violation of the principles of international law' and regarded as 'hostile action'. He concluded: 'I fear Turkish intransigence may influence adversely the creative work of three nations (Britain, Turkey and Greece, all NATO members) and loosen their common defensive efforts.'

With some condescension, Makarios added: 'The Turks are not to blame for the failure of the negotiations. So far as the Turks are concerned, the more the British Government talks of their reaction to my suggestions, the fiercer that reaction becomes. If the Government were to tell the Turks what to do, I am sure they would obey, for they are not bad boys.' He concluded: 'Britain's intransigence has closed the door on negotiations.'

Asked if that meant that matters in Cyprus must now take their course, with unpleasant consequences for everyone, the Archbishop replied: 'I suggest the Governor should be asked that question. He said he might go to Athens soon for discussions with the Greek Government.'

Worse, Grivas now ordered a bomb to be placed on a British chartered aircraft at Nicosia Airport on Sunday, 4 March 1956. 'I approve the placing of time bombs at the Airport yet you do not indicate what length of time you want,' he wrote to his No. 2 Gregorios Afxentiou. 'You should be given a time bomb, which I calculate will explode after two hours because of the reduction in temperature. Take great care in preparing the filling so as not to be unsuccessful.' Fortunately, the poorly manufactured bomb exploded 20 minutes before the families of British servicemen boarded the Skyways Hermes to fly back to the UK, otherwise 68 passengers would have died in the sky above the Mediterranean.

Reg Potterton, ex-Royal Signals, told the author from his retirement home in Fort Lauderdale, Florida: 'I was at the foot of the Hermes' steps waiting to board, when there was just a thud, a gush of flame inside the plane and a wing falling to the tarmac. Afterwards, they took us back to Wayne's Keep transit camp in a three-tonner to wait

The wrecked civilian Hermes aircraft at Nicosia Airport.

Field Marshal Sir John Harding sees the remains of the bombed Hermes aircraft.

for another flight the next day. Someone in EOKA took a pot shot at us on the way there.'

Victor Freeman, a former RAF Corporal, remembered: 'The sound of the explosion shook our billet huts, which were situated a half mile from the civil airport. We interrupted our listening to the cultural half hour of *The Goon Show* and raced up – on foot – to the Airport. A spectacular cascade of flames from the burning fuel surrounded the aircraft. The crew had jumped to safety.'

It was clear now that Makarios could not – or would not – control Grivas and abandon terrorism and intimidation – not only of the British, but his own people as well. Harding was left with no option but to break off his negotiations. He told his advisers: 'The

Archbishop personally constitutes a major obstacle to a return to peaceful conditions. His influence must therefore be removed from the island in the interest of promoting peace, order and good government.'

The Archbishop described as 'chilly' the final meeting between Harding and himself. 'The Governor seemed hardly able to keep calm, and spoke only once, on the question of the police. Mr Lennox-Boyd did most of the talking ... Mr Lennox-Boyd said, "The Governor will be able to explain why we must keep control of the police." Harding said, "You know why," and added that EOKA might continue to work underground and start up again later. I didn't see why, if we came to an agreement ... I didn't like the way Harding put this issue. I was sorry that we had failed to reach agreement, and the meeting ended. I was not too worried; I expected we would meet again. But I noticed that for the first time, Harding and Lennox-Boyd stayed on after I left. At all previous meetings, Harding and I had left together. I believe they decided on my exile that night, and sent the proposal to London.'

The London *Times* concluded: 'Makarios's tactics had long been wily, evasive, and seemingly Levantine. He had behind him a long tradition of Byzantine bargaining which could not have been readily comprehensible to British negotiators and which could be countered only by extreme patience.'

This was the last time that the British talked with the Greek Cypriot leadership, hoping to achieve the pacification of the Island through a political settlement. Had the negotiations continued, there was a distinct possibility that union with Greece – enosis – could have been the outcome, because Sir John Harding was holding out the promise of *self-determination* at some unspecified moment in the future, rather than supervised independence. Makarios, determined to haggle to the last, failed to notice the carrot held in front of his nose.

At the 3rd Annual Conference of the PRIO Cyprus Centre held in Nicosia on 28-29 November 2008 under the title of *One Island, Many Histories: Rethinking the Politics of the Past in Cyprus*, Greek Cypriot academic Demetris Assos agreed: 'It was also the only time when the British government conceded, theoretically at least, the possibility of unitary self-determination, fulfilling one of EOKA's original objectives. This proposal was made at a time when certain officials were contemplating to "tell the Turks that 18 per cent of the [Cypriot] population cannot have an unqualified veto on the remaining 82 per cent".'

A formidable soldier used to straight talking, Governor Harding had lost patience with the Archbishop's evasiveness. He had to go. To remove Makarios meant one of two choices: kill or arrest him. He opted for the latter. He decided to exile the Archbishop, along with several of his closest associates, including the Bishop of Kyrenia, to the Seychelles. And so Operation *Apollo* was launched. First, arrangements for the plane to land in Aden and Kenya, with appropriate security, had to be finalized. The Royal Navy, too, had to be brought into the plan so that they had a vessel ready to carry Makarios and his associates to the islands in the Indian Ocean.

PLANS TO exile – even imprison – the Ethnarch had been considered before. They had been raised several more times since the start of 1956, whenever there was a terrorist killing or some other outrage. Although Dighenis had told the Turkish Cypriots his quarrel was not with them, an EOKA gunman shot Police Sergeant Ali Riza on 11 January as he was returning to his Paphos home. He fired back, but his assailant got away. The policeman died later in hospital. EOKA claimed he was 'executed' because he had been the chief witness at the trial of six villagers from Chloraka, who had been guilty of attempting to smuggle weapons onto the Island.

Turks were outraged and hundreds protested outside the home of Dr Kutchuk, the leader of the recently founded 'Cyprus is Turkish' Party. As Turkish anger bubbled towards boiling point, Kutchuk telegrammed the Governor to condemn this 'unprovoked and cowardly attack' and demanded that the Orthodox Church compensate Riza's widow and children. Unless the killer was caught and punished, he could see EOKA killing more Turkish policemen for doing their duty. That evening someone, possibly a Turk, threw a grenade into a Nicosia restaurant owned by a Greek. It was soon followed by widespread anti-Greek demonstrations. The rift between the two main communities began to widen. Only a tiny spark was needed to ignite a civil war in which the British Army would be caught in the middle.

Not only was the temperature rising in Cyprus, but nearby Jordan was also undergoing upheaval as Arab factions fought to take control and Israel threatened to expand its frontiers, forcing Britain to stand by in case the King called for help. The build-up of forces on the Island grew apace, proving, as far as London was concerned, why Britain needed to hold Cyprus as a base to guard its oil interests in the Middle East. The 1st and 3rd Battalions of the Parachute Regiment were combat ready and were joined in January by the 1st Battalion the Highland Light Infantry. The War Office said the 1st Wiltshires would follow soon. Very soon, 20,000 British soldiers would be available for security operations. Numbers alone, however, would not stop EOKA. *The Times* put it succinctly in a report from its local correspondent. 'By far the greatest weakness in the Island's security, particularly in the towns, is one, which can be overcome only slowly,' he wrote. 'It is the almost complete absence until recently of a Special Branch organization and intelligence sources. Neither of these can be made good by the military forces nor be built up quickly,

particularly once an emergency has arisen. This difficulty is aggravated by the extreme reluctance of ordinary citizens to see anything, hear anything, or say anything, of any crime, though recently more information has been forthcoming.'

Week after week, Harding and Makarios had met, talked and walked away to return another day. The death of the first British soldier of 1956 took place on 14 January, while he was on guard duty. He was Driver William Bootman, aged 18, RASC, at the Golden Sands rest camp. Five days later Captain Peter Lane, RAOC, was slain in broad daylight by two assassins. He had recently arrived in Cyprus from the Canal Zone with his wife and their nine-week-old child. While waiting for a rented house, they stayed in a hotel just inside the city walls. Every morning at 07.30 he walked to a taxi rank 200 yards away to catch transport to his office at Army headquarters. The terrorists had noted his daily routine and took advantage to time their attack to allow them to escape in the rush hour traffic. Grivas boasted about Lane's death in his *Memoirs*: 'Two of Sophocleous's group made the attack while a third kept watch. The officer, hit by five bullets at point-blank range, fell in the road, then got up and staggered a few paces before collapsing, dead.'

Meanwhile, rioting schoolboys tasted the sting of three to seven strokes of the cane on their buttocks. Corporal punishment for guilty youths became commonplace. The teenagers were hauled to Karaolos camp, outside Famagusta, where a Greek policeman performed the act in the presence of a Greek medical officer and a senior rank from the UK Police Unit. At the same time the colonial administration introduced the most advanced social insurance scheme in the Middle East. The scheme provided for marriage, maternity, sickness, unemployment, widows, old age and death benefits.

By mid-February, the Harding–Makarios talks gave rise to some optimism again. 'Negotiations in Cyprus during the past week seem to have reached a point at which some sort of agreement may be in sight. There is, at this stage, no question of signing a detailed instrument which will settle the political future of Cyprus for a long time to come, but rather of an understanding on points of principle, which should allow for a cooling off of passions and a return to more or less normal conditions inside the island-essential preliminaries if the exact path ahead is to be plotted,' reported *The Times*. 'The main reason for this rather more hopeful prospect is that the British Government is now prepared to allow the term "self-determination" to enter the debate.'

The Times did not thunder, but spoke in measured terms: '"Cyprus," as Field Marshal Sir John Harding said in London last month, "is directly concerned with all our military effort in the Middle East." So long as this remains true, there can be no substitute for British sovereignty. This does not mean that the offer of self-government as a first step to self-determination is illusory, but it does mean that Britain cannot for the present hand over to elected Cypriot representatives responsibility for the Island's defence, its foreign relations, or its internal security. Nor can there be any question of leaving the Cypriot Turks to sink or swim in a new self-governing regime. It is normal practice, when self-governing institutions are being tried out, to ensure that the status of religious or racial minorities should be protected by more than the good will of the majority. In the long run it is goodwill which counts, but at the start at least there must be written guarantees that a minority will not be politically eclipsed. In the particular case of Cyprus, the fact that Turkey is only forty miles away and that the Turks rightly feel that Cyprus is an integral element in their own defence makes the need for such solid guarantees self-evident. Whatever happens in Cyprus, the way ahead will be difficult.'

CYNICAL EXPATRIATES folded their copies and laughed. They had heard it all before and would only believe the conflict was over when they saw the ink dry on any agreement.

There may have appeared to be an easing in the political storm, but February found Cyprus battered by gales and bad weather. The RAF station at Mount Olympus, 6,000 feet above sea level, reported a 60-knot wind driving through the valleys of the snow-swept Troodos Mountains. Roads above 4,000 feet became impassable.

'We were snowed-in for two months at Troodos Camp and only those of us in the "Ski Platoon" could get out of camp. I did a few runs between patrols with a Hanson toboggan to get the mail from Platres, a two-day trip on skis. The coldest it got was 59 degrees F below,' Marine Albert 'Taffy' Boyer

Troops dig themselves out from their snowed-in camp in the Troodos Mountains.

Royal Marines set off on a mountain patrol at the height of winter.

of 45 Commando Royal Marines told the author from his home in Victoria, Australia. 'On 8 February we received a signal from 3rd Commando Brigade HQ that a truck had either broken down or was caught in the blizzard and we were to go out and rescue the passengers. We were told to search in the area of a particular map reference – which was on the main road the other side of Mount Olympus, about 12 miles as the crow flies. I was one of a four-man ski-patrol that set out at 16.00.'

The four Marines made very slow progress through the blizzard raging around them at speeds of 70 miles an hour. 'We could only see a few feet ahead. Fortunately the temperature did not drop too low,' Boyer remembered. 'Our main problem was trying to see. Our goggles were useless in the blinding conditions. Conditions worsened on the other side of the mountain, with the wind coming directly from the north. Twice we had to dig snow holes in the side of the slope to shelter until the blizzard subsided. With the wind screaming, we couldn't even hear ourselves shout.'

Twelve hours later the storm abated and the temperature dropped to 40 below. Boyer continued: 'We donned our skis, hoping to make better headway over the freezing snow, but most of the time we were up to our waists and in the end had to wear snowshoes to make any progress. At about 15.00, we discovered the missing vehicle – a 3-ton workshop repair truck. It was snowed-in on a horseshoe bend with a big drop on the far side of the road. As we neared we saw vehicle tracks and footprints. They led back in the direction from where the truck had come. There was nobody with the vehicle, so we followed the footprints. Two miles along we reached a hotel, where a company of the Gordon Highlanders lodged.

'We had a job to convince the sentries we were Royal Marines, because they couldn't see us clearly, as heavy snow was falling again and visibility was down to a few yards. The Gordons had also received signals about the truck and told us that they had sent out a patrol in a Saracen armoured vehicle and a couple of Land Rovers with chains. When they reached the missing vehicle, they spotted two sets of footprints leading to a culvert. There, on the 9th, they had found two dead Marines huddled together under a tree. Both had frozen to death. One was QSM Alfred Wheeler and the other Marine Benet Blakeway. We were shown their bodies laid out in one of the hotel's rooms. They were dressed in civilian clothes and definitely not rigged for walking in inclement weather.

'When we returned to Troodos two days later, we were told Blakeway had twisted his ankle. Unable to walk with the main group, the QSM – only two weeks out of the UK – had stayed with him. The other passengers had made it to safety in a village seven miles away, where the police station was manned by British troops.

'It was ironic that when we checked the truck later, we found it had a special heavy-duty waterproof plastic-lined canopy. On the open side, there were 10-feet long icicles hanging, but inside there was a small, two-ring paraffin stove, with 20 gallons of fuel, plus canned food in a locker. Had they stayed in the truck, they would have been warm and could have easily survived for at least three days. Because of the lack of visibility in the blizzard, the driver must have missed the Gordons Highlanders' hotel, which was only 30 yards off the road.'

IN THE Paphos district, floods isolated several villages. Royal Engineers were rushed from Limassol to build an emergency bridge by floodlight so that food supplies could reach the cut-off areas. While an RAF Anson light aircraft dropped sacks of bread on Prodromos village in the Troodos, cut off by deep snow, three RAF personnel were attacked in a Nicosia Street.

The three men, unarmed and in civilian clothes, were walking and looking at shop windows. The had passed a group of six men wearing raincoats, who suddenly turned and fired five shots with a Sten gun, killing one serviceman outright, while a second fell seriously wounded. The third managed to run nearly 100 yards into a barber's shop, where he collapsed and died. Almost before the firing ceased the street was deserted and the police could find no one who had seen or knew anything. The dead men were two 19-year-olds, Leading Aircraftmen Roger Cox and Corporal Desmond Jones. The wounded man was Senior Aircraftman J. Douglas. Once again the death squad was led by Isychios Sophocleous. Born in 1932, he had worked in the Island's electricity department before committing his talent to EOKA.

The outrage brought the number of British servicemen murdered to 17, of whom two were RAF. The administration officially stated that there had been 17 British people killed and many more wounded by EOKA between 24 April 1955 and 11 February 1956. The total was made up as follows:

Army: 13 killed, 27 wounded;
Royal Air Force: 2 killed, 11 wounded;
Royal Marines: 2 killed, 12 wounded;
Royal Navy: 3 wounded;
Civilians: 3 wounded.

The demands for the Ethnarch's removal grew louder from the British. Unknown to them, a plan was in the making at Government House.

UTMOST SECRECY was vital to ensure maximum success with minimum risk to the operation to exile Makarios. EOKA had to be kept completely in the dark about the Governor's intention, especially the 'when' and 'how' of the operation to arrest the Archbishop. If the slightest hint reached the terrorists, they would generate civil unrest, Makarios might go into hiding and anti-British violence would be stepped up.

Responsibility for carrying out the snatch-operation was handed to Lieutenant Colonel John Commings, the Commanding Officer of the 1st Battalion of the South Staffordshire Regiment. He assigned one of his Company Commanders to plan and put it into effect.

Major Jos Jones, OC Charlie Company, a light heavyweight boxing champion during the Second World War, was tasked with the job. To support him, he was given 1 Platoon of Bravo Company. The latter had recently taken on the chore of guarding Nicosia. Jones later recalled: 'The aim of the exercise was clear, but the proposed methods of execution were not. The point at issue was the likely reaction of the civilian population to the removal of the Archbishop and the amount of force which could be applied if required. How much force could we use to an Archbishop in his own See? What could we do if the Archbishop turned difficult and refused to be arrested? How were we to get into his palace at all and in which room were we likely to find him?

'We knew the palace was an extraordinary ramshackle place, a rabbit warren to search.

Major Jos Jones of the South Staffordshire Regiment.

Would we have to perform a smash and grab or a cordon-and-search job? In fact, we could not guarantee that he would be at home at all for the "lifting" squad. It was a nail-biter of an assignment. We had to get it right if our soldiers' lives weren't to be put at risk.'

Jones's identity has never before been revealed in a public domain. His name was kept secret outside military circles, because there were fears his life would be jeopardized and EOKA sympathizers – with long memories – would track down and hurt his family at their home in England.

(Major Jo Jones died on 25 March 2002 in Tiree, Scotland, after suffering from Parkinson's Disease. He was still shadow boxing with his grandson from his armchair.)

Lieutenant Colonel Paul Crook of 3 Para was also advised to have his men ready for a special operation on a date to be announced.

Before the plan could be finalized, Lady Luck came on the scene to favour the British. Makarios announced he would fly to Athens with the Bishop of Kyrenia to meet Greek political leaders on 9 March 1956. Once this was known, a British official visited the Archbishop on the night before his departure to suggest that when he drove to the airport, only his driver-bodyguard should accompany him. When asked the reason, the official replied that it was for his safety as crowds could cause chaos. Whether Makarios concluded that the British were up to 'mischief', no one can say, but he did pack more than was necessary for a short trip to Athens, including an Anglo-Greek dictionary and some extra ecclesiastical robes.

Meanwhile, British intelligence officers had recommended that Major Jones's men simply meet the Archbishop and his entourage as he was about to board his aircraft at Nicosia airport and quietly escort him to a military plane parked nearby. He would be ordered inside, with others, and the plane would take off immediately. Only when it was clear of Cyprus would Makarios be told his destination: the Seychelles. It all sounded easy and simple, but would prove far more difficult to achieve. If it failed, the political ramifications would be considerable. It was left to Major Jones to work out the details. He decided to intercept Makarios as soon as he passed through the airport's main gate.

There were three major roads leading to the airport. These could be closed easily after the Archbishop's arrest, but they needed to be monitored from dawn, without arousing any suspicions, so that Jones knew exactly which route the Archbishop was using. Because there was considerable military traffic coming in and out of the airport, Jones concluded, a few more vehicles would not be noticed.

He decided to place a platoon along each of the access roads. The soldiers were to hide themselves in army vehicles that appeared to have broken down. Their officers were told to look out for an RAF policeman raising his white armband at one of the airport's checkpoints. This would be the signal that the

Archbishop's vehicle had passed through and he was inside the airport, where his arrest could then take place.

SHORTLY AFTER 09.00 on 9 March, Makarios left his residence on schedule, accompanied by his religious and political followers. On his way to Nicosia Airport, crowds surrounded his car, cheering him on his journey to garner more support for the *enosis* movement from the Athens leadership, little knowing his true destination.

Near the airport entrance Lieutenant Peter Lee, in charge of a 'B' Company platoon, had the bonnet of his vehicle open, pretending he was repairing the engine. As he fiddled, he saw an RAF policeman, 100 yards away, raise his armband. 'Get cracking, lads,' he shouted, ordering his men into action. Their vehicle burst into life and accelerated in the direction of the checkpoint, stopping with a jolt behind a polished black limousine. Weapons at the ready, the platoon surrounded the car's occupants.

Moments later, Lee and his soldiers withdrew, red-faced, once again to take up their original position. The RAF policeman had not signalled the arrival of the Archbishop. He had merely been saluting the Air Officer Commanding who had arrived unexpectedly. He was not pleased by his reception. Major Jones's account reads: 'When Makarios eventually arrived, the system worked, but it was almost an anticlimax. His driver was, I believe, his nephew who had sworn to protect his boss with his life. CSM Martin, however, with his Sten gun, rapidly made him postpone his promise. A British police officer then read the Deportation Order. Makarios took it very well and maintained his dignity, while Brigadier Baker watched.' The Deportation Order was issued under Regulation VII of the Emergency Powers (Public Safety and Order) Regulations.

For Arthur Melton, an RAF airman at Nicosia Airport the day had started as any other. 'We arrived at our squadron work place at our usual start time. An NCO there singled out a couple of us who belonged to a ground crew and told us to prepare a particular aircraft for a flight soon. I asked how much fuel was to be loaded. "Fill all the tanks," he replied. The aircraft had 14 tanks. We immediately realized something out of the ordinary was about to take place as the aircraft would not be able to carry many passengers or a large load of cargo with 3,000 gallons of 130-octane petrol on board.

'At about 11.00, the plane's air crew arrived, began their pre-flight checks, started up the engines and taxied away from us to the end of the runway, where it parked. A short while later we were detailed to take a starter-trolley to the aircraft and wait. An armed RAF sergeant was there already and kept walking around the plane. Just before midday, we saw a large black car moving slowly down the taxi-track, but didn't know who was in it. "That would be Black Mak," said our Sergeant Williams in his West Country burr. "The right holy Archbishop is about to take a long journey by flying RAF".'

Surrounded by British troops, the Archbishop was escorted to the waiting Hastings Mark II aircraft by Squadron Leader Wilfred Pink, who, in retirement, went to live in Newton Poppleford, Devon. 'The aircraft was parked in a secluded part of the airport, far from prying eyes. Mak took it all in his stride and chatted with us about nothing in particular as if he were heading for a jolly picnic, although he still didn't know where,' Pink told this author.

'An officer was waiting at the foot of the steps, and he very politely invited me aboard, like an airhostess,' Makarios recalled. 'Apologetically, he explained that it was his duty to inform me, etc., etc., and would I like him to read the Deportation Order? I thanked him, and said, no, a copy would be sufficient.

The British have perfect military manners. What other nation arranges for its officers to salute you when they come to put you in gaol?' Later, he would act out the officer's behaviour for visitors: 'Rising from the lunch table, the Archbishop, using his Episcopal staff as a regimental cane, gave an exact imitation of the young officer's behaviour, salute and Sandhurst-style halt included. It brought the house down,' said Lieutenant General Sir James Wilson.

While Makarios sat on the aircraft, the British authorities rounded up the others who would join him in exile. Operation *Airborne*, as it was now called, continued on schedule. The airport was closed to all, except airline passengers. Journalists and photographers were kept well away and outgoing telephone calls were stopped. Sir John Harding later issued an order prohibiting until further notice any trunk telephone communications with Greece, except for officials and the security forces. A censor was appointed to check all internal telegrams and those to and from Greece.

The local press was now unable to make contact with its correspondents and had to rely entirely on official sources of information.

The Reverend Papastavros Papagathangelou of the Phanoromeni Church in Nicosia was the next to join the Archbishop at the Airport. Officials described him as a 'most pernicious influence on Greek Cypriot youth ... [who] indoctrinated prospective recruits for EOKA'. Makarios thought he had come to wish him farewell, until he saw the priest's packed bags and his worried demeanour.

Bishop Kyprianos Kyriakides of Kyrenia arrived soon afterwards to be boarded on the aircraft. Then another car appeared and out stepped Polycarpos Ioannides, the Bishop's personal assistant and part-time propagandist. The former editor of the anti-British newspaper *Ephemneris* had served 18 months' imprisonment for sedition – for 'publishing an article with the intention of bringing into hatred the Government of the colony'. His publication was shut down. After he was picked up, shopping in a Kyrenia street, his wife only packed him a small suitcase, believing he would be back home within a few days at most after questioning.

Once again the deportation order was read. Ioannides was heading into exile and would be held at 'the Governor's pleasure'. He replied in Greek: 'It may be the Governor's pleasure – but it's not mine!' Ironically, all the arrangements to fly out Makarios and his entourage had been made by a one-eyed Anglo-Irishman, Group Captain Norman de W. Boult, DFC, AFC. During the Second World War, the Government of Greece had presented him with the Royal Hellenic Air Force Cross for training Greek pilots.

Throughout the deportation operation, Makarios protested only once. He argued that if the Bishop of Kyrenia could be accompanied into exile by his personal secretary, Ioannides, he should be granted the same privilege. The Archbishop's captors returned the Archbishop's benign smile with several of their own. Sergeant Lancaster of the Civil Police snorted. He was accompanying the exiles on their flight. On their way to their ultimate destination, Makarios noticed the policeman did not have a watch. 'My gift to you,' he said taking his off and handing it across. His gold wristwatch could tell the time anywhere in the world.

The Hastings took off at 16.15 local time and headed south-east. 'I doubt he enjoyed the most comfortable of flights by his standards, as we had not configured the aircraft in any special way, other than to place one double-seat on the aircraft's port side, near the tail, and another further back on starboard, possibly for use by his armed escort,' commented Airman Melton. 'As usual bog standard RAF lunch boxes for long flights had been stashed. If he wanted coffee, it could be prepared in the galley. At least he was not seated too far from the toilet.'

In the evening Sir John Harding broadcast his reasons for deporting the Archbishop. He said: 'He [Makarios] has remained silent while policemen and soldiers have been murdered in cold blood, while women and children have been killed and maimed by bombs, while a Cypriot woman was shot and wounded for the second time as she lay in hospital, recovering from a previous terrorist attack, and even while he stood by the coffin of an Abbot in his own church who was brutally murdered in his own monastery. His silence has understandably been accepted among his community as not merely condoning but even as approving assassination and bomb throwing.'

Once the news broke of Archbishop Makarios's deportation, shops closed in Nicosia, Greek taxi drivers stopped work and the streets emptied.

A night curfew was imposed from 18.30 to 06.00, as the Island waited for an EOKA backlash. The Greek Government condemned the Governor for exiling Makarios and his associates, calling his action 'incompatible with the assurances repeatedly given to Greece by the British of their alleged desire to find a peaceful solution to the Cyprus question'. Athens immediately recalled its Ambassador to London and lodged a 'most energetic protest' with the United Nations Security Council. The British action had 'deeply wounded the nation', said a Government spokesman.

Opposition parties in Britain also expressed their disapproval. Mr Hugh Gaitskell, leader of the Labour Party, said, 'This seems to be an act of folly, which will only make the insurgents more determined in their fight for self-determination and therefore encourage terrorist outrages against our troops.' For the Liberals, Mr Clement Davies added that it was 'an act of madness'.

Turkey approved the Archbishop's deportation.

Paras get their orders to search the Archbishopric.

AS SOON as the Hastings took off, members of 3 Para, commanded by Lieutenant Colonel Paul Crook and paratroopers, cordoned off and began searching the Ethnarch's palace in central Nicosia. They hoped to find secret EOKA files, but the wily Makarios had hidden them elsewhere. The troops had to satisfy themselves with ploughing through the Archbishop's papers, piles of religious correspondence and some EOKA propaganda leaflets. The Paras' haul eventually consisted of a four-gallon container of petrol, a pistol (under the robes of a priest) 18 rounds of .32 pistol ammunition in a tin, a petrol bomb, 10 similar ones under construction and boxes of papers. Officials claimed many of these documents gave valuable insights into the workings of EOKA and disclosed information about the organization's methods, weapons, funds and personnel. A letter signed 'Dighenis' said: 'A certain individual poses as a nationalist, but one of our agents believes he is treacherous. This man must be liquidated.'

An official communiqué maintained that one document listed names of Cypriots declared 'traitors' who were to be assassinated. Another said 'there must be <u>reorganization</u> and preparation of our militant groups'. A third suggested Makarios must not be allowed to waver in his negotiations with the British: 'Tell X ... that the leader is unyielding, and that no retreat is possible, not even to the smallest degree, from the proposals of the Archbishop. That is why the leader is in Nicosia now, so as not to allow the Archbishop any retraction whatever.'

Other extracts indicated some indiscipline among the terrorists. In one, 'The Leader' pointed out that in spite of his orders to the contrary, threatening letters were being sent to 'persons who are not traitors, but are actually helping us'. A letter contained the admission that 'Dighenis' was personally responsible for ordering murders, but that the EOKA rank-and-file had committed murders on their own initiative (possibly for private ends or out of brutality). 'The execution of persons for whom my authority has not been obtained will be considered as murder, and those giving orders for the liquidation will in due course be punished.' The letter was signed by 'The Leader', but the name below was illegible. None of the papers revealed the real identity of 'Dighenis'.

The Paras' most intriguing discovery, how-ever, was a bricked-up chamber, which con-tained a skeleton, some hundreds of years old, leading to another of those difficult questions which never get satisfactory answers in Cyprus: whose was it and why had he been hidden so long?

Meanwhile, across Cyprus, the Security Forces encountered a series of illegal strikes at Nicosia, Dhekelia, Akrotiri, Episkopi, the Pisouri plantation, Paphos, the RAF station at Famagusta and a factory in Limassol. There were also some minor street disturbances. The worst incidents included an attack on a Red Cross ambulance. One of the two bombs failed to explode; the other blew up in the hands of the 17-year-old youth who tried to throw it. He died.

TERROR ATTACKS continued in Cyprus – a bomb was thrown at the house of Corporal Plumb of the Middlesex Regiment in Larnaca, damaging the building and furniture, and leaving Mrs Plumb with glass splinters in her face. Their two-year-old son, who was asleep, was thrown out of bed. At the same time, the Hastings aircraft was touching down in Aden to refuel before continuing to its eventual destination. When it next landed, it was at another military airport. The exiles were disembarked and placed in a large limousine with blacked-out windows. 'It was very hot inside, and the Bishop of Kyrenia became distressed and tried repeatedly to open a window. He did not succeed,' Makarios said later. 'Finally we found ourselves in a wired enclosure – some sort of military camp. I could smell the sea. I asked a soldier if this were Nairobi and he replied, looking startled, that it was Mombassa.'

The next day, the Archbishop and his party were boarded on the Royal Navy's *Rosalind*, which sailed for a rendezvous at sea with the frigate HMS *Loch Fada*. Throughout its journey, the vessel was trailed by reporters in several light aircraft. At 18.00 on 11 March, they saw a launch, lowered from the frigate, cross to the *Rosalind* and take bags lowered from the minesweeper's stern. The launch

Archbishop Makarios and his exile party leave Mombassa.

The Royal Navy vessel *Loch Fada.*

Sans Souci, where the exiles were lodged.

returned to her mother ship, and then crossed back to pick up the black-gowned, bearded figure of Archbishop Makarios, followed by his companions. They went on board the *Loch Fada*, the launch was taken in, and the frigate sailed with the exiles on the 1,000-mile journey to Port Victoria, the capital of the Seychelles. While in range of their Kenyan base, RAF aircraft continued to fly overhead.

The Archbishop later expressed his 'deep appreciation of the courtesy and kindness of the officials en route and of the officers on board'. He said he was astonished, and greatly touched, when the Captain gave up his own cabin, so that he, Makarios, could have one to himself.

While *Loch Fada* was still deep into the Indian Ocean, the Seychelles Legislative Council busily enacted emergency legislation to allow the deportees to be held in the islands. Dr Hilda Stevenson Delhomme, elected member for North Mahe, said the colony was deeply honoured to cooperate with the British Government in suppressing EOKA violence.

In Mahe, overlooking Port Victoria, the Greek Cypriot party was placed in the comfort of the Governor's Lodge at *Sans Souci*, under the supervision of Captain P. S. Le Geyt and his wife. Le Geyt had served as a captain in the Indian Army and the Uganda Police. On 14 March 1956 Makarios and the others were told the conditions of their exile.

- Except with special authority, you may not communicate with any person other than the other persons detained with you and the police officers and staff of the Lodge at which you are detained.
- All requests, complaints, and suggestions that you have to make should be made to Captain P. S. Le Geyt who has been appointed as Controller of the Household at the Lodge. All written communications you may wish to send to any person should be handed to him.
- Upon request, daytime visits to other parts of the island will be arranged when possible. These may include visits to shops where goods within reason may be bought on official account.
- During the hours of 18.00 and 06.00 you will be required, except with special authority, to remain within the Lodge and its grounds.

In conclusion, the exiles were told: 'It is the wish of Her Majesty's Government in the United Kingdom, of the Government of Cyprus and of this Government that your period of detention in Seychelles should be as pleasant and comfortable as possible. Adequate funds have been placed at the disposal of this Government for this purpose as well as for your board and lodging and, within reasonable bounds and subject to security restrictions, every effort will be made to comply with your wishes.'

The exiled Archbishop writes a letter home.

In practice, the authorities did not keep their promise. When the exiles asked for olive oil for their diet, their request was turned down. When Captain Le Geyt suggested they supply a croquet set for his 'guests', especially for the overweight Bishop of Kyrenia to exercise, once more they refused. Historian Robert Holland believes 'such small mindedness came as much from official nervousness as from any spite. It was the same nervousness, which at first meant that the perimeter of *Sans Souci* was patrolled by guards with machine guns and the ubiquitous tracker dogs from Kenya ... [there was] concern that an attempt to rescue the Archbishop might be launched from within the Greek community in East Africa.'

While at *Sans Souci*, the Le Geyts tried to make the exiles comfortable within the limits imposed on them. Makarios spent his time trying to improve his English, Bishop Kyprianos constantly complained and Iaonnides pursued his love for gardening, but refused to answer questions in English, although he spoke the language fluently. Only Papagathangelou remained cheerful throughout his stay, often bursting into song to entertain his hosts and staff alike.

Old-fashioned colonial Captain Le Geyt grew to enjoy the Archbishop's company so much that he found it difficult to understand 'why a man with such a sporting nature has not condemned the unsporting tactics of the EOKA terrorists'. Whatever his reasons – fear, obstinacy or commitment to the 'cause' – he could be heartened, writes Holland, 'as it became obvious that, far from destroying his reputation with his own countrymen, exile only served to confirm his status as the leader of the Greek Cypriot people'.

When Makarios looked back at his stay in the Seychelles, he often told his guests: 'That exile seems anything but tragic. Actually it wasn't an exile, it was a vacation. I was given a nice house where I was served and respected. The landscape was marvellous, so marvellous that I wanted to see it again, and I went back as a tourist and even bought a little piece of land near the same house, which the owner, unfortunately, didn't want to sell. The British treated me well and didn't keep me there long – just eleven months.'

Many historians today, with the benefit of hindsight, suggest Governor Harding made a mistake by exiling the prelate from Cyprus, because his absence gave Grivas a free hand to conduct a more vicious terrorist campaign than the Archbishop would have approved.

In his *Memoirs*, Grivas said: 'The exile of Archbishop Makarios meant that I had now to take on the political as well as the military leadership of the resistance. I did not shrink from this double burden: indeed, the additional responsibility gave me greater freedom of action and added strength, just as the Archbishop's deportation, far from quenching the fires of revolt, fanned them into flames. I launched a new offensive designed to transform the whole island into a battlefield. I believed Harding had made the greatest mistake of his career and I took full advantage of it.'

Makarios apologists maintained that he opposed violence and only wanted attacks against government buildings, never individuals. Whether true or not, there was no disputing the fact that Grivas protested the 1959

Independence agreements and, until his death, tried to depose Makarios, culminating in the 15 July 1974 coup by EOKA-B, which ultimately led to Turkish mainland forces landing on the Island five days later to divide Cyprus into separate Greek and Turkish zones, separated by UNFICYP.

Speaking in the House of Commons in May, the Colonial Secretary, Mr Lennox-Boyd, had no doubts about Makarios's exile or Britain's Cyprus policy, whatever the Opposition argued. The Government, contrary to Labour's assertion, was not setting out to create hostility between Greeks and Turks. A wilder or more inaccurate statement had never been made and it was 'nonsense'. Conservative Members cheered their support. One of them, Mr Maclay, expressed the opinion that while the mainland Turks and those on the island were much concerned to see that in any settlement justice should be done to the important Turkish population, infinitely more important in their eyes was the strategic position of Cyprus, so close to the shores of Turkey. Because of this very real Turkish interest and the real difficulties, which it represented, the (Cyprus) problem was an extremely complicated one.

He continued: 'So often some of the beastliness being conducted in the name of democracy – largely against their own people by the gangsters in Cyprus – tends to be forgotten. There is a tendency to describe those people as "Cypriots who are fighting for their freedom". Nothing could be further from the truth.'

Some people thought that the servicemen who had been shot or stabbed in the back, while fulfilling their military duties in Cyprus, could expect this sort of risk. Mr Maclay did not look at it in that way. Nor did he believe that the 68 people in the British Army transport aircraft in which a bomb was placed, and

which was saved by a miracle, would have been fair victims of this conspiracy. Even assuming that all who had gone out as combatants or who were travelling as members of their families were, to put it crudely, fair game, what of the 50 Cypriots who had been murdered – 27 of them civilians – many of whom were killed under conditions of almost unbelievable callousness? If anyone seriously suggested that the Government should possibly surrender to this form of murderous blackmail, then they did not understand the real feelings of the British people.

Following Makarios's exile, Athens withdrew its ambassador to London, Greek state radio stepped up its anti-British propaganda, students in Cyprus forced schools to close down and Church representatives scurried around the Middle East trying to drum up support. In the United States, the Greek lobby asked Congressional representatives to condemn Britain. Nationalists of both sides worked to stir up trouble between the two – not a difficult task.

As was to be expected, British Tommies were ordered to stand between the feuding parties. On 17 March four bombs were thrown at a truck in which men of the Wiltshire Regiment were travelling after being relieved of cordon duties at Lapithos. Private Ronald Gould, aged 23, of the 1st Wiltshires, a victim of the attack, died two days later. He came from Ilfracombe. Another of his comrades had his arm amputated. Gunner Colin Yates, aged 19, Royal Artillery, was killed on 18 March and three others injured in an incident at Yialousa. An ambulance taking them to hospital also came under attack.

The pages of a young British soldier's diary says life continued 'as usual'. He wrote: 'We continued our patrols, stoned by the old ladies of Avgorou or shot and screamed at by the young ladies of Famagusta.'

CHAPTER NINE

'Kill the bloodstained ogre': the valet and the bed bomb

'For Tommy Atkins, there is a job to do, an unpleasant, dirty, bloodletting job.'
Joseph Haff, *New York Times*

ONCE ARCHBISHOP Makarios was settled in exile in the Seychelles, Colonel Grivas, now the undisputed leader of the EOKA organization, needed to quickly demonstrate his power and determination to the Greek Cypriot population as a whole and, in particular, any on the left who disapproved his avowed intention to unite the Island with mainland Greece.

While the wily colonel was personally delighted that Field Marshal Sir John Harding had acted decisively to rid the Island of the Ethnarch and freed him of any political control or rivalry, Grivas saw the Governor as the greatest threat to his terrorist organization. He felt the time was right to deliver a double blow against the British. By killing Harding, he could garner more public support from Makarios's religious followers and, at the same time, strike at the heart of the military establishment.

Grivas encouraged his followers to send 'hate' letters to the Governor. These likened him to Genghis Khan, Tamerlane and Hitler. He was also described as 'this bloodstained ogre whose hands drip with the blood of his victim'. Radio Athens, broadcasting to the Greek Cypriots on behalf of Grivas, increased its vituperative attacks on the Governor. Time and time again, its commentators declared: 'Field Marshal Harding commits tyranny, vandalism, cowardice and incites to treachery.'

After considering various other assassination methods, including planting a sniper on the roof of the Greek Consulate opposite the Anglican Church to shoot Sir John as he came out from Sunday morning service, Grivas settled on what he thought was a sure-fire plan. It was to be implemented on 21 March 1956, this time using Neophytos Sophocleous. He had been recruited by EOKA the previous January.

Earlier, Grivas had warned Harding in a mimeographed leaflet distributed in the capital, 'We will get you, even in your bed', but the feisty Governor retorted: 'If they do attempt it, they will have to deal with my army, and that is no trifling matter.'

ORIGINALLY KNOWN as the 'cat's guardian' at Government House, the 20-year-old Sophocleous had been employed by the previous Governor, Sir Robert Armitage, in 1955. In March 1956 he returned from leave to continue working for the new Governor.

Government House, built in 1932 to replace the old building destroyed in the 1931 rebellion, had been carefully guarded since Sir John Harding's arrival. It was claimed that without challenge it was impossible for any unauthorized individuals to get past the guards, composed of army soldiers, civilian police and Special Branch officers – and a police sniffer dog.

But the Royal Horse Guards on duty at the main gate recognized Sophocleous and didn't search him when he arrived for work as usual on his bicycle. Unknown to them, he was carrying a flat bomb with a time pencil strapped to his body under his clothes. The bomb had been constructed by Iakovos Patatsos and Stavros, both members of Nicosia's execution squads. Because, as a valet, Sophocleous had access to the Governor's bedroom, that was where he took it. In his privately published memoir, Francis Noel Baker, a Labour MP with sympathies for the Greek Cypriot cause, wrote: 'He planted the bomb under the gubernatorial mattress and hopped onto his bicycle, not to be seen again for several years.'

The bomb was described as looking like 'a small brown-paper parcel that might contain a book – except that a small tube protruded from one end'. It was timed to go off during the night. Its mechanism required a constant room temperature of 67°F to function, but unknown to the bomb-makers and Sophocleous, Harding always slept with his bedroom windows open. That night it was colder than usual and the temperature fell well below the required temperature for the device to explode.

Next morning, in a routine sweep of the bedroom, Lance Corporal Welch of the King's Royal Rifles and Guardsman Ball of the Grenadiers discovered the bomb. According to Mr Noel Baker, Lady Harding was writing in her boudoir next to the bedroom when Welch shouted: 'There's a bomb in your bed, my Lady.'

'Don't be so silly,' she replied. 'Let me get on with my letters.'

The two soldiers then called for the young commander of the guard platoon, 2nd Lieutenant Michael Buckley of the Royal Norfolk Regiment, who collected the bomb without fuss, using a shovel. He took it

SPECIAL NOTICE

WANTED

WANTED in connection with the bomb incident at Government House, on 21st March, 1956:—

NEOPHYTOS SOPHOCLEOUS.

Born (Peyia, Paphos District) 1936, height 5' 6", black hair, brown eyes, slim build. Front teeth protrude slightly.

SPECIAL enquiries and observation must be maintained to effect arrest.

When arrested DO NOT INTERROGATE, but inform Police Headquarters (Criminal Investigation Department).

G. H. ROBINS,
Commissioner of Police.

The wanted 'Bed Bomber'.

outside to the garden and popped it into a sandbagged slit trench. Three seconds later, the gelignite charge exploded with a force that 'would have demolished half of Government House itself'. The bomb was of the kind that had destroyed the civilian Hermes earlier in the month at Nicosia airport.

Informed of the bomb, Harding mused: 'That's funny, I slept better than usual last night.' He added dryly: 'I'm told there's a story of a princess who couldn't sleep for a pea under her mattress. It puzzles me.' Sophocleous, meanwhile, escaped to join one of Grivas's mountain gangs, with a price of £5,000 placed on his head. The day after the attempt on Harding's life, all Greek Cypriots on staff duties inside Government House, many of them with years of faithful service behind them, were relieved of their duties. In the evening leaders of the Turkish community came to Government House and congratulated the Governor on his escape.

'For the calm and gallant way in which he handled the difficult and dangerous situation with which he was faced' in removing the bomb from the Governor's bedroom, 2nd Lieutenant Michael Buckley was made a Member of the Order of the British Empire (MBE). Lieutenant Buckley was the son of Lieutenant Colonel G. Buckley, of the Rifle Brigade, who died from wounds in Libya and he had been decorated by the King of the Hellenes for fighting with the Greeks during the last war. Michael Buckley died in October 2005, leaving a widow, Mary Ann.

Lance Corporal Peter Welch, 21, who discovered the bomb, was killed soon after his return to the UK on completion of his National Service. Riding his motor-assisted bicycle he collided with a motor coach in Plaistow, East London. At his inquest at Romford, Essex, a verdict of Accidental Death was recorded,

ENRAGED BY his failure to rid himself of Harding, Grivas issued another of his pamphlets:

We proclaim, WITHOUT ANY MATERIAL REWARD the Gauleiter SIR JOHN HARDING, whose execution is the duty of every patriotic Greek. Instead of monetary rewards, which are given by the vulgar to the vulgar, we shall declare the man who executes him a national hero whose name will be written in letters of gold in the Pantheon of Heroes of the Cyprus Struggle.
EOKA,
The Leader,
Dighenis.

And then he stepped up the conflict, not only against the British, but the Turkish community as well. He may not have killed the Governor, but he was determined to slake his thirst for British blood as soon as possible. On 21 March, terrorists threw grenades at a 15 cwt. truck in Famagusta, slightly wounding Lance Corporals Prosser, Burrows and Smith and

fatally injuring Lance Corporal Bryan Welsh, aged 18, of the Royal Military Police. From Lewisham, London, his ambition had been to become a schoolteacher. He was the 20th serviceman to die since the start of the conflict.

In January 1957, Welsh received the Queen's Commendation for Brave Conduct posthumously. The citation read:

At Famagusta on 21 March 1956, three bombs were thrown by EOKA terrorists, at a vehicle, in which Lance Corporal Welsh, with other members of the Military Police, was travelling. One bomb fell into the rear of the vehicle where it almost immediately exploded. Another Lance Corporal who was in the rear of the vehicle with Welsh, seeing the smoking fuse, shouted a warning before being blown out of the vehicle and severely wounded. The men in the front portion were both slightly wounded, Lance Corporal Welsh was killed. His body was found with his right hand blown off and his arm burnt and charred. At the Inquest the conclusion was reached that Welsh, seeing the bomb close behind the front seats, instead of trying to escape, seized the bomb to throw it out in an heroic attempt to protect his companions. His action probably saved the lives of the two men in the front seat.

His 44-year-old mother said: 'I am very, very proud.'

Before nightfall there were several more attacks. Explosions resonated throughout the capital and the South Staffordshire Regiment sealed off the area around the Archbishopric, while men of the 3rd Battalion, Parachute Regiment, questioned people, searched offices, shops and houses, and prevented anyone from leaving the area. At midnight the final two bombs blasted the Public Information Office and the entrance to Wolseley Barracks, the present Middle East Land Forces headquarters. At Karavostasi, near Lefka, several masked men gunned down and killed a Greek Cypriot ex-policeman, as he was sipping coffee in the local café.

In Limassol, EOKA set a British car on fire, the fourth case of its type since the terrorists began their attacks on servicemen and civilian properties. EOKA had also developed a new weapon, a 20mm cannon shell stuffed with gunpowder. One failed to detonate outside the entrance of a police station in a Nicosia suburb. It was immediately handed to Major 'Bomber' Harrison to examine.

If that were not enough, on the same day Turkish Cypriots in Nicosia demonstrated against EOKA to add to the pressure on the British in keeping the peace. Eleven Greeks were injured and there was damage to buildings. The disturbances were caused because the authorities had curfewed the inhabitants of Vasilia and Lapithos/Lapta, fining them £7,000 for brawling with the local Greek Cypriots and setting the local elementary school on fire.

In Government circles, the blame for all the Island's ills could now be pinned exclusively on the mysterious Dighenis or Grivas. 'A madman, very religious and certainly unscrupulous,' was how Major General Kendrew described him, pointing out his pathological hatred of Communism and the Left. Although banned by the British, AKEL, the main political party of the Left, concurred with Kendrew's opinion. 'When the armed struggle of EOKA began, a tense and unsettled situation was created in Cyprus,' its spokesman says today. 'AKEL disagreed with the form of the armed struggle, coming to the conclusion that in the concrete conditions prevailing in Cyprus this would not vindicate the aspirations of our people but, on the contrary, it would lead to deadlocks and adventures.'

Day after day in March, more and more bombs exploded Island-wide. EOKA was on a roll. The police station at Ayios Epiktitos in the Kyrenia area was attacked. An Army patrol in Ayia Trimithia, near Nicosia, came under fire, injuring one soldier. The target of another bomb was a military vehicle near Ayios Nikolaos.

In a single a day, 27 March, two British soldiers on a mobile patrol were shot and killed in an ambush in Frenaros. They were Lieutenant Samuel Walker and Private Ronnie Bowman of the 1st Battalion the Royal Leicestershire Regiment. The area near Famagusta was immediately placed under curfew while a search was made for the terrorists. None was found. The male population was then gathered together, placed behind barbed wire, provided with paper and envelopes and ordered to supply information anonymously. This tactic, like many others, proved valueless. However, six shotguns were found, with a quantity of cartridges. The guns had been fired recently. Troops and police, using tracker dogs, also discovered two unexploded bombs, three grenades and a 77mm high explosive shell, and a quantity of shotgun cartridges. Sixteen villagers were taken into custody. Four of them were detained, having been taken from their beds – fully dressed.

In Limassol, Elias Maliotis, a 29-year-old Customs official, considered an informer by EOKA, was shot three times in the chest as he stepped out of his car at noon. He was about to collect his young daughter from his sister's house. Maliotis was the second Limassol Customs employee to be attacked in three months. The first was Stavros Makris in January. He survived. EOKA was angry that he had opened a package from Greece, supposedly containing books, but uncovered a shipment of ammunition destined for the terrorists. For his safety, the authorities moved him to Britain

The assassination of Maliotis took place a few minutes after Sir John Harding reported that the cost of lawlessness to the Island's taxpayers in 1956 had been estimated at £2,283,875.

March ended with a bomb loaded with nails exploding in Nicosia's Palace Theatre and critically wounding another soldier. In Kyrenia, there were three explosions. In

Lefka, a mine went off under a military vehicle. No one was hurt and the troops opened fire at a group of suspects standing on a nearby hill. A 13-year-old boy connected to the incident was injured in the thigh and captured. He was the youngest terrorist to be arrested.

On the eve of the first anniversary of the EOKA conflict, a *Times* of London correspondent observed: 'The most obvious impact of the Emergency has been on towns after dark. Where there was once a thriving Mediterranean life in the streets in the evening everything now closes at dusk. It is eerie to walk at night in Nicosia eyed from the street corners by the ubiquitous policemen. Apart from the bitterness, which inevitably follows searches and other punitive measures, however carefully carried out, the troops so far have shown much restraint and even embarrassment over this work.'

But morale remained high among the British forces as Joseph Haff, the Pulitzer Prize-winner of the *New York Times*, discovered when he visited the Royal Warwickshire Regiment at its camp just outside Nicosia, on the road leading to Limassol and adjoining land of the Cyprus Broadcasting Service. The regiment's tents, once coloured a dark service brown, were bleached to light tan by the sun. Corporal John Winters of Coventry, aged 19, told the American reporter: 'Duty here is a lot better than in the Canal Zone. There it was all guard duties. Here we get around on patrols or go out on searches that make life interesting. Our outfit has been lucky so far and not lost any men.'

Private Leslie Stone, also 19, recognized the politics of the situation. 'Britain can't afford to give up Cyprus and the Greeks here know it,' he said. 'Even if the British did pull out the Turks would beat the Greeks in getting down here. If that happened there would be a mighty hot time on the Island. Maybe then the Greeks would appreciate the British way of handling the situation. Most of these people are just terrorized. It's not their fault.'

Joseph Haff concluded: 'Whether Greece is right in her contention that, because there are four Greek Cypriots to every Turk Cypriot, Cyprus should become a part of Greece, means nothing to Tommy Atkins. All he knows is that there is a job to do, an unpleasant, dirty, bloodletting job. And gets on with it.'

British residents, to keep morale high, organized mobile canteens and libraries and compiled lists of families whom off-duty soldiers could visit for afternoon tea or a rest in the atmosphere of a British home. Many of these civilian volunteers would face threats from EOKA. One would be killed – William Jamieson, a volunteer Church of Scotland charity worker – by a mine in Ayios Amvrosios on 1 November 1958. Corporal A. B. Cameron of the 1st Battalion the Highland Light Infantry spoke highly of him: 'He was a great old gentleman, who used to call in occasionally and bring some biscuits and magazines. He would never accept our offers of escorts to his next port of call.' An officer of the Wiltshire Regiment added: 'From all accounts he was an eccentric, who drove a small van. He travelled all over the Island in his mobile canteen to serve tea and cake to British soldiers while they were on anti-EOKA operations.' In his memory, the Regiment has placed his name on a plaque in St Andrew's Church, Kyrenia.

TO CELEBRATE the first anniversary of the 'war of liberation' EOKA wanted to demonstrate its power with added vigour. The authorities in anticipation cracked down with curfews in several towns. Special arrangements, however, were made for those Cypriots who wished to attend services at the Roman Catholic, Maronite and Armenian Churches within the walls of Nicosia, and newspapers were able to publish and circulate as usual. If

EOKA had ideas about showing off its strength in the capital, it failed. There were no incidents. In fact, the authorities went on the offensive. Troops of the South Staffordshire Regiment conducted a thorough search of Kykko monastery, the temporary headquarters of the Ethnarchy, two miles outside Nicosia. Every room and all the inmates were checked. Seven people, but not priests, were detained for questioning and shotgun cartridges, six cartridge-filling machines, a small quantity of explosives and EOKA pamphlets were taken away.

In Famagusta, EOKA continued its anniversary day attacks as Lance Corporal Mick Parry and Corporal Vic Sunderland found to their cost. They had left 51 Brigade Headquarters to collect Lance Corporal Sims from Warburg House. Because it was a gusty and dusty morning, Sunderland raised their Land Rover's windscreen, contrary to the orders of the day, which required it to be down and for Royal Military Police not to wear sunglasses.

After picking up Sims, the trio then turned left through the gate towards the crossroads, where Sunderland, who was driving, indicated that he was going straight over. About 50 yards further on, three hand-made bombs – fashioned from a cast iron drainpipe – were lobbed over a wall to the right of the Land Rover. Two landed on the bonnet, one of which hit the windscreen. One rolled to the left of their vehicle, the other to the right. The third went underneath or to the rear and all exploded. A piece of shrapnel hit Parry's cap and turned it sideways! His right forearm was also injured. Sunderland was wounded twice in the back. Sims escaped unscathed.

On the scene first, Corporal Ernie Guy drove Parry and Sunderland to a First Aid post and from there the two RMPs were transferred to the British Military Hospital, Nicosia. After two weeks' treatment, they were RTU – returned to unit – fit for duty.

Both are convinced that had the windscreen been left down – as ordered – the bomb would have exploded at chest level with fatal consequences. When the unit's CO heard about the accident, his first question was to inquire if the Land Rover was still serviceable.

EOKA had failed in this case to add to their score of 'kills'. In the House of Commons, Mr Hare, Minister of State at the Colonial Office, revealed the catalogue of violence to Members of Parliament. Since the start of the Emergency 24 British soldiers had been killed and 107 injured. In the same period, six Greek Cypriots, one Turkish Cypriot and one United Kingdom member of the police force had been murdered and 29 wounded. Twelve United Kingdom civilians had been injured, 23 Greek Cypriot civilians killed and 35 injured, and six Turkish Cypriot civilians injured. In Athens Savvas Loizides, the representative of the Cyprus Ethnarchy, challenged these figures. He claimed the British Army was concealing its losses. He maintained that well over 100 servicemen had been killed and urged Greece to accord EOKA official status as 'a revolutionary army' – the 'army of Cypriot people defending its freedom against foreign violence'.

Elsewhere the story was different. For the first time in weeks schoolboys caused trouble, this time in Paphos, where a large crowd formed a procession in the grounds of the secondary school, carrying two Greek flags. A couple of student priests were among them. They marched to the centre of the town, where they were dispersed after the arrival of troops and police, but an hour later the youngsters were back again and stormed a police station. They stoned the security forces and threw three bombs. One failed to explode; the others slightly injured a schoolmaster.

For the Security Forces, one of the most difficult tasks was dealing with riots by schoolchildren. Usually they were led by young girls filled with nationalist fervour.

Handling them was a chore the soldiers, barely older than them, found very uncomfortable. In the area for which the Royal Norfolks were responsible, officers devised an appropriate punishment for the youthful demonstrators, which avoided having to make arrests and appearances in the local courts.

If, after a warning, the youngsters refused to disperse peacefully, a platoon, with bayonets fixed and wearing their grimmest looks, came up from the rear and pushed the students forward into the waiting arms of the platoon ahead, whereupon they were lifted bodily and dropped in the rear of a truck, which was driven off at speed. Not knowing what fate lay ahead for them, they quickly lost their desire to be martyrs for the 'cause' and wished they were back at their school desks. Shocked adult onlookers could only gape, wondering where their offspring had been taken. Half a dozen miles along the road, the captives would be unceremoniously dumped and told to make their way home. The thought of a long walk in the hot sun made them wonder if their efforts were really worthwhile – until the next time. As they grew older, many became killers, indoctrinated by trained EOKA leaders.

In Limassol, John Cooke, a government civil servant, was shot dead by a bullet in his back, fired by a teenager in Gladstone Street. During the shooting a Greek Cypriot was wounded. Cooke, a veteran of Dunkirk, was killed three days after his arrival in Cyprus to work as a civil servant for the War Office. The 51-year-old had expected his Island posting to last three years, with his wife joining him as soon as accommodation became available. He was shot by accident, said EOKA, mistaken for a 'British security agent'.

The 'Organization' added that it did not approve murders of civilians, but their words denied their actions, because a few minutes later a bomb was thrown at an English couple, both aged about 50, while they were walking in the street. Both were taken to hospital with slight injuries. It was the second time British civilians had become EOKA targets. Another bomb exploded near a British car, seriously injuring a Greek Cypriot child.

Only one British soldier lost his life on EOKA's first anniversary. He was 20-year-old Private Cyril Hewitt of the South Staffordshire Regiment. His death was caused by a traffic accident.

The day ended with an unusual find reported from the village of Kato Lakatamia. After removing the Greek flag, unknown persons had decorated the elementary school with British Coronation flags and painted pro-British and anti-*enosis* slogans in good Greek on the walls. If these individuals had been found by EOKA, they would have been severely punished. Once an order went out to eliminate those opposed to the 'Organization', it did not matter who they were or what they were alleged to have done.

On 3 April another private, Frederick Downing, of the Royal Warwickshires, died. His death came while surgeons at the British Military Hospital tried to save his life after he had been accidentally shot while on 'prowler guard' at Omorphita Prison the night before. On the Lefka–Pedhoulas road, an EOKA mountain gang ambushed two trucks of the Gordon Highlanders in the afternoon of the same day. An electric mine was detonated under the leading vehicle followed by small arms fire on the second. Private James Falconer was killed. Once again the gunmen escaped.

RAF Airman Kenneth Young was added to the death toll on 6 April. Barely three days later, on 9 April, Private William Asprey lost his life.

IN NICOSIA, the RAF took complete control of airport operations. No Cypriot employees except a few immigration officials were any longer allowed access to the 'secure' area on the airfield. Using newly installed special equipment, all baggage, freight and even airmail letters would be examined from now on. The increased security was prompted by an intercepted letter from 'The Leader' calling on an EOKA member to plant pencil bombs, wherever they would cause most damage and injuries to airline passengers. Customs formalities now would be completed at the Customs House in Nicosia, and all baggage would undergo security scrutiny at the airport, where special apparatus was being installed to assist the control officials in their examination of passengers, baggage, freight, and airmail letters and packages.

To strengthen the land forces, Army Air Corps helicopters were introduced to support them by rapidly carrying troops to troublesome areas and evacuating the injured. A close relationship developed between the members of the three services and many friendships have lasted to the present day.

Meanwhile Royal Navy frigates and minesweepers patrolled the Cyprus coast to stop and search any vessels believed to be smuggling weapons, munitions and explosives to make bombs. Greek Cypriot fishermen were adept at recovering the explosives from the hundreds of tons of shells and mines the British had dumped off the coast near Salamis at the end of the Second World War II. According to Charles Foley of the *Times of Cyprus*, EOKA was willing to pay up to £3 for an anti-aircraft shell, a far more valuable catch than fish.

During the night the frigates and minesweepers covered their portholes and showed no riding lights as they cruised at about 10 knots. They were packed with 'a bewildering assortment of gear to trace and render harmless the many types of mines developed for modern warfare', reported a *New York Times* correspondent invited to sail on board HMS *Fenton* with its complement of 30, including four officers and 26 ratings.

'The first three hours of this patrol were uneventful. The ship ran from Famagusta to Cape Andreas on this occasion and then turned south on the long leg to Larnaca Bay. Lieutenant Richard Todd had replaced the skipper Lieutenant Commander Michael De V. Hart on the flying bridge when the lookout reported two sets of lights far ahead. In the chartroom two "blips" appeared on the radar screen.'

By now *Fenton* was close enough to make out the name *Omona* on one trawler. She was on the list of licensed fishing boats in the area, so she was allowed to proceed. The other trawler's name could not be made out as the weather-beaten Greek letters were too worn to read. Fenton's boat took a boarding party to the trawler. The craft was the *Ayia Phylaxis*. Out of Famagusta, Lieutenant Todd made a walkie-talkie check. The *Ayia Phylaxis* was on the approved list.

'There's a bit of psychology in a search like that,' Commander Hart told the correspondent. 'Those chaps will go into town and spread the word around. They'll tell their friends that the blooming patrols never give them a minute's peace. Of course, that's an exaggeration, but it makes anyone who has a mind to do a job of smuggling for the murder-

The Royal Navy intercepts a Greek vessel to check for arms smuggling.

ers up in the hills hesitate taking a chance. They know the penalty for smuggling firearms is death and none of them is very keen on dying.'

But occasionally the Navy was forced to fire warning shots over a craft that refused to stop to be boarded. One of these was the 5,172–ton Italian liner *Enotria*. The incident sparked a minor diplomatic row, but nevertheless the crew of the coastal minesweeper HMS *Fenton*, unwilling to take any chances, searched her, as *Enotria*'s last port of call was Pyraeus in Greece. The Italian Consul in Nicosia, Signor Victor Mantovani, protested loudly that at the time of the incident, the ship was in Cyprus waters and the Navy could have waited until she docked in Limassol for normal Customs examination. The Consul's cries fell on deaf ears. The liner was allowed to proceed after 90 minutes.

Ray Anderson served on HMS *Walkerton* and *Essington*. 'While we were on patrol at sea, we heard some army lads ashore had their families' school bus attacked and there were casualties. News like this made us take our job much more seriously,' he said. 'We often had the army on board while some of our sailors joined them on shore patrols. I didn't fancy that as their grub disagreed with me. After tasting some, I was rushed into BMH, Nicosia, with an ulcer caused by the food and almost died. We were lucky on our minesweepers because the RN cooks were good. The Army lads loved our food and the daily tot of rum they received.'

The Royal Navy ships were often helped to their targets by reconnaissance aircraft. On 12 April 1956, the Fleet Air Arm (FAA) started operations from Nicosia with three Airborne Early Warning (AEW) Fairey Gannet Mark I aircraft from 847 Naval Air Squadron. The Gannets were also used to direct RAF fighters in interceptions of any unidentified aircraft nearing the Island's air space, but pilots never received permission to open fire.

'Having just left a large training squadron of around 18 aircraft, it was strange to become part of a total complement of only 21 ratings and ten officers, where everyone was extremely friendly, with little outward signs of navy discipline having to be applied to our work,' Ian Howard remembered. He had been posted to the squadron from Malta. 'And, of course, as sailors, we all considered ourselves superior to the other services in Nicosia.'

847 was based at RAF Nicosia. To Howard, it was 'a huge, bustling metropolis of buildings and tents, enclosed by rings of barbed wire, with soldiers and airmen everywhere. Whether walking, marching or in trucks, they were all armed with rifles and small arms. And there were some palm trees. I'd never seen one before!

'The squadron ratings were allocated accommodation with 113 Maintenance Unit, four beds to a room, right next to the mess hall. We spent our first week sleeping on camp beds, until those we were replacing had left for home. Bed bugs seemed to be the most important issue at this stage, with stories of them climbing the walls and dropping on us for their next meal, but I never saw one in my entire posting. Our room had a ceiling fan in its centre and louvred shutters on the window to allow air to enter and cool us during the long, hot summer months, when temperatures often rose above 120 degrees F.

'During the hours of darkness the shutters offered us some security. They, however, did not stop the smell, emanating from the thunder box at the back of our hut. Nor was this a place to visit at night due to its lack of lighting and the rustling sounds that came from within the dark pit used to expel excreta ...'

Ratings worked 24-hour shifts every other day, starting at noon. Their role was to keep two Gannets serviceable and ready, while the third patrolled and returned safely late at night. The Gannets picked up unidentified targets and these were tracked until naval ships arrived at the scene to board and carry out searches. How many weapon smugglers were caught was never disclosed.

'Spares for our aircraft came by sea and arrived at Famagusta, where they were placed in a warehouse guarded by an RN detachment, which was also responsible for the port's defences. They lived in a beachfront hotel nearby,' Howard recalled. 'We made regular lorry-runs from our squadron to collect the parts, even when other military personnel were confined to camp in case EOKA ambushed them. To protect our load, some of us rode shotgun in the rear of the vehicle. It never crossed our minds that we could be endangered, such was our youthful innocence.'

He continued: 'From time to time we were allowed "ashore", but before we visited Nicosia, we drew arms and ammunition from the station's armoury. Our weapons were loaded with a magazine of live rounds, but kept with the safety catch on.

'After three months' active service, we were awarded the General Service Medal, with Cyprus clasp. I suspect there aren't too many of the Royal Navy version around. These have red and white vertical bars on their ribbons, unlike those worn by the Army, which have purple and green.'

ON 20 FEBRUARY 1958, one of 847's Fairey Gannets was on its 'finals', making its landing approach in darkness from the north of Nicosia Airport. The three-man crew had completed another patrol of the sea around Cyprus. Equipped with ASV Mk 19B radar, the aircraft was ideal for long-range detection of surface vessels. It also had VHF and HF radio for both short- and long-range communications with ships, other aircraft and headquarters.

Suddenly the crew heard the aircraft's contra-rotating propellers stutter. They feathered one of the propellers and switched off its Mamba engine in the hope of curing the problem, but to no avail. They were losing altitude far to fast too make a safe landing as the runway came nearer and nearer.

The Gannet hit the tarmac, bounced and broke up, killing the crew – pilot Lieutenant Raymond Greer, 29, Leading Telegraphist Frank Chivers, 22, and observer Lieutenant Edward Wright. It was Wright's 29th birthday.

847 Squadron consisted of only three Fairey Gannets and a complement of 10 officers and 21 ratings. The unit had been based in Cyprus for a year. During the EOKA conflict this was its only tragedy.

'I would like to think the contribution made by 847 Squadron, RN, helped in its own way to prevent many more deaths,' Howard reflected. 'We never discovered the reason for the crash, but it brought great sadness to our small unit, where everyone was so close. These men are buried in Wayne's Keep Military Cemetery in Nicosia, where I hope that occasionally, someone stops before their graves and thinks of them and all the others who paid the ultimate sacrifice, for their service in Cyprus.'

Lieutenants T. M. Luke and D. W. Ashby were luckier when their Sea Hawks of 804 Squadron, flying from the aircraft carrier HMS *Albion*, collided during an anti-EOKA

Governor Harding talks to 847 Naval Air Squadron members.

sortie. They ejected successfully and were picked up from the sea, slightly bruised.

THE 'SMALL WAR' continued unabated. Some days the Army caught its prey, on others EOKA found its targets. The casualty-count mounted on both sides. On 10 April, Sergeant Allan Pinner of the Royal Leicestershire Regiment became the 26th British soldier to be killed by the terrorists, when his convoy of three vehicles came under fire from both sides of the road near Kalopsida. The Leicesters returned the fire, then dismounted and threw a grenade in an attempt to cut off the attackers' retreat, but they got away in the darkness. In retaliation, the authorities punished the whole village by imposing a collective fine of £1,000.

If British troops were taking casualties, so were innocent Greek Cypriot civilians, either killed or injured by EOKA while attacking their 'enemy' in towns and villages. On Sunday evening, 15 April 1956, Assistant Superintendent Kyriakos Aristotelous, a Greek Cypriot officer, was visiting a private maternity home in Nicosia to see his wife and their five-day-old son. Three gunmen – again masked – armed with two pistols and a Sten gun, shot him dead in the doctor's office within calling distance of his wife, and wounded the doctor.

Greek Cypriots pay their share of a 'collective fine' on their village.

Grivas had warned all Greek Cypriot members of the Cyprus Police to resign or collaborate with EOKA. Aristotelous did neither. For remaining loyal to the service, EOKA labelled him a 'traitor'. Because of the officer's high rank, he was especially high on Grivas's list, but throughout his career, he had steered clear of politics and focused his attention on dealing only with purely criminal matters. He was never directly involved with investigations of the terrorist organization or interrogation of EOKA suspects. These were jobs for the Special Branch and he was a straightforward police officer. 'The word "traitor" was used in abundance at that time to justify assassinations,' his son, Jack, told the author. 'In many cases these were driven by personal agendas of the murderers for self gain.'

Had this young officer survived, he might have become the first Cypriot-born Commissioner of Police, his shocked colleagues said. During his comparatively short service of 14 years, he gained no less than 44 commendations from the Commissioner of Police, and two from the Governor.

Mrs Aristotelous was left to bring up her son on a meagre police widow's pension. When Cyprus was eventually granted independence in 1960, the UK Government ended its responsibility for the payment of pensions and transferred its liabilities to the new Cypriot administration, which consisted of several former leading EOKA terrorists. The British took no account of the sensitivities involved in this case. 'My mother fought against this decision,' said Jack. 'Her regular pension payments were restored in 1962 after she petitioned the Queen. Support given to widows of former colonial employees whose husbands were killed during the Emergency still remains patchy and limited to survival on the breadline.'

For the officer's brutal murder, Nicosia and its 50,000 inhabitants were made to pay with a week's 'penance'. By the Governor's order, intended as a mark of public abhorrence of the deed and to help the Security Forces trace the perpetrators, Nicosia and its suburbs were subjected to a collective punishment, which was without precedent. Every restaurant, bar, club, coffee shop, cinema, confectioner's shop, cabaret, and, in fact, any place of entertainment or public resort owned by a Greek Cypriot had to remain closed for a week. Further, no football matches, athletic meetings, races or any assemblies were permitted. Financial experts reckoned the cost to the owners would run into thousands of pounds and several bankruptcies. Unless owned by Britons, Turks or other foreigners, even bars and hotels were banned to non-residents. The London *Times* correspondent saw Nicosia becoming 'a dead city at night'. He noted that 'the attitude of the average Cypriot to this disruption of normal life seems to be philosophical'. The people, he added, 'expected a rough time after the Archbishop's deportation'.

The authorities hoped this draconian order would encourage the people of Nicosia to speak out against the terrorists, but whether they feared for their safety or because they were passive supporters, nobody came forward. And EOKA continued to execute 'traitors'.

The same form of collective punishment was applied to Limassol, after the shooting of Vassos Stefanou in bed. Three youths aged about 18 years of age forced their way into his house in Limassol at 08.15, entered the bedroom where he was with his wife, handed him a letter and, while he was reading it, fired several shots at point-blank range. The 22-year-old Cypriot was considered anti-EOKA because he was employed as a waiter at the Sergeants' Mess at Episkopi cantonment. He died six hours later in hospital.

ON 20 APRIL, dressed in his customary red shirt and spotless white tropical suit,

Theodore Costa Bogdanovitch, GC, was mildly irritated. His dinner was late. The sun had set and the orange glow of evening was turning a dark purple. As usual he was expecting his meal to be delivered at exactly 18.00 from the Greek Cypriot café across the narrow street from where he lived alone in Liminitis. 'Bogs', as he was known to everybody in the area, was the security officer of the American-owned Cyprus Mining Corporation. He glanced at his watch again. It was ten minutes past the hour and still there was no sign of his meal. Not good enough, Bogs thought, and decided to find out why. He strode across his tidy garden, his two boxer dogs at his heels. Reaching the wire fence of his property, he shouted in Greek in the direction of the café. There was no reply. The street was empty. Nothing moved.

Suddenly Bogs was thrown backwards from a punch to his chest, followed by another as he heard the first shotgun blast to be echoed by a second in rapid succession. As he fell to the ground, his white jacket turned red with his blood. Now a burst of machine-gun bullets tore through his body. His dogs crouched next

Theodore Costa Bogdanovitch, GC.

to him, barking at first and then whimpering over their master. The gunshots and the dogs' cries brought a platoon of the Gordon Highlanders rushing to the scene. They were based at the nearby Aberdeen Camp. But the soldiers were too late to save Bogs' life. His last words were: 'Why? They were my friends.' The time was 18.15. The masked gunmen got away.

Two thousand local CMC employees – Greeks and Turks – saw Bogs' murder as a personal tragedy. They mourned because he had a reputation for treating both communities fairly. His acts of kindness were proverbial. Lieutenant Jamie Henderson of the Highland Light Infantry wrote home: 'We are all very sad, as he was a very memorable and likeable old boy.' His sentiments were echoed by others. James Hope, another HLI officer, said: 'Not only were we sad, we were a very angry regiment after that, but there was one final courtesy we could pay him. He was buried with full military honours in the English Cemetery in Nicosia, where his body remains still. Four Highland and two Cyprus Police officers carried him to his final resting place. Buglers sounded the *Last Post*. Men of all nationalities mourned him.'

A senior employee of the CMC, who wished to remain anonymous, told the author: 'I remember being impressed by the funeral put on by the 1st Battalion Gordon Highlanders. All the traditions of the regiment were there with the slow march, muffled drums and the laments and dirges played by the pipers. All this was due to the well-deserved respect he had earned from the regiment in the short time he had worked with them.' Uniquely priests of the Greek Orthodox Church and the Muslim faith took part in the funeral service.

Superintendent Duncan, a British Cyprus Police officer, described Bogdanovitch as 'a gentlemen in every sense of the word and the straightest man I've ever met. Extremely modest, he was deeply religious and generous to a fault,

but he simply could not tolerate anything that was dishonest.' Another CMC employee, who lives today in Nevada, remembered Bogs as 'smart in the extreme'. He added: 'I believe he waxed the ends of his moustache. He came over as a totally military man with a clipped and precise way of speaking. He was always the perfect gentleman.'

Although Bogs was highly respected, only a rare few knew him as a person or much about his roots. To most, he was a man of mystery. Despite his knowledge of local affairs and who was doing what and where, he consistently refused to reveal information to British Special Branch officers. He would only deal with the intelligence team of the locally based regiments and only then if he felt soldiers' lives were at risk from EOKA activity.

'In the mine,' Bogs explained, 'we have Greek and Turkish: both have good people in their ranks, both have bad. All must work, all have families – children, old folk, who must eat. I have seen too much suffering in my life, this is now my home and I want peace for all. Turks and Greeks are my friends. It is better so.' He encouraged Greek Cypriot employees at the mining company not to get involved with the terrorists. And they listened. For EOKA, he was anathema, somebody who had to be eliminated.

But who was Bogs? The author put the question to another former CMC employee. 'About his background, I know very little, but, at the time of his death he was living in what had been a CMC clinic across the road from the Englezos canteen and virtually next door to the police station. This was for security reasons,' he replied. 'Prior to that I remember he lived in a CMC house near the old Assay office on the road leading up to where other CMC staff members lived, near the entrance to Aberdeen Camp. This enabled him to walk his nightly check around Xeros Plant area and surprise sleepy watchmen.'

His colleague added: 'I was told that he had

served the British in Palestine and was awarded an Empire Gallantry medal for the actions he took when communications were lost between his group and headquarters during a battle with the local Arabs. The story was that whilst under fire, he climbed telegraph poles, replaced and repaired wires and restored communications, thereby saving the day.'

Bogs had been born in 1899 in the Serb town of Bogdans, named after his family who founded the place. They were Royalists. 'In childhood it was a happy time. My mother was a very beautiful woman and we had dogs, many dogs,' he wrote to a friend. When his homeland was invaded at the outbreak of the First World War, Bogs enlisted in the Serbian Army at the age of 15. He was twice wounded in battle and decorated for gallantry.

Because of his knowledge of English, he was posted to the British Forces as an interpreter. He remained with them throughout the Salonika campaign and on to Constantinople, which the British occupied at the end of the First World War. There he was placed in charge of the Serbian Guard outside British Army HQ. Eventually the British withdrew from Turkey and the Serbian Guard was disbanded.

By now there was no reason for Bogs to return to his country, enveloped in political turmoil. His father had been killed and his mother was missing. He chose to head east, a stateless refugee. In March 1924, he joined the Palestine Gendarmerie and became Trooper Bogdanovitch, a servant of the British who had been mandated to govern Palestine. On his travels Bogs had learned to speak Greek, Turkish, French and Arabic in addition to his own language and English. Eventually the Gendarmerie was divided into the Palestine Police and the Trans-Jordan Frontier Force. He opted for the latter and was commissioned as a *Mulazim* or Lieutenant.

For the British, life in Palestine was far

Trooper Bogdanovitch (extreme left) in the Trans-Jordan Frontier Force.

from peaceful, with Arabs and Jews trying to take over the region. An Arab Revolt broke out, led by a charismatic leader called Ferzi Quakji. In March 1939, Quakji's brother entered Jordan with a large force trained at bases in Syria. A vigorous battle began between them and units of the Frontier Force, with Arab Legion troops in the front line. Almost immediately Lieutenant Macadam, the Legion's young commander was killed. Bogs immediately took charge of both military groups and their armoured cars. Outnumbered and short of ammunition, he ordered his men into hand-to-hand combat and won the day, personally killing Quakji's brother in the fighting.

Three months later, the British Government awarded Bogs the Empire Gallantry Medal, which, in 1940, was converted to the George Cross, ranking second only to a VC. The citation said that his 'complete contempt of personal danger and the tactical skill he displayed were an inspiration to his men, and contributed in no small measure to the success of the action'.

In 1944 Bogs became a naturalized British citizen. Three years later he retired from the Trans-Jordan Frontier Force with the rank of *Kaimakam* (Major) and went to Cyprus. A year later he was offered the job of Security

Officer with the CMC. 'The resident manager R. J. Hendricks,' said a CMC source, 'hired him in 1948, but even though my job was to administer any and all confidential matters, Hendricks kept Bogs' activities to himself and I rarely saw him. He never came to my office and he never mingled with senior staff at our club in Skouriotissa.'

Bogs only visited the UK once – to watch the Coronation celebrations for Queen Elizabeth II.

Three years after Bogs' murder, as the British were pulling out of Cyprus after independence, the same American CMC manager met the EOKA commander for Xeros at a Queen's Birthday function in Nicosia. 'The EOKA man told me that Bogs' assassination had been planned to take place at the entrance to Pendayia Hospital which Bogs visited at 16.00 each afternoon as part of his security round,' he said. 'An ambush was set up, but Bogs failed to appear. The EOKA man in question had worked for me prior to the trouble and remarked that the ambush was also cancelled because I had turned up at Pendayia in a company pick-up truck and I could have been shot, too, had he not recognized me. So the EOKA men proceeded to Xeros, where they killed Bogs two hours later.'

Today, thanks to James Hope, all Theodore Costa Bogdanovitch's service medals and his George Cross are held in a place of honour in the Gordon Highlanders' Regimental Museum in Scotland. His other medals include: the General Service Medal 1918-62, 1939-45 Star, Defence Medal 1939-45, War Medal 1939-45, Coronation Medal 1953 and the Trans Jordan Frontier Force Long Service and Good Conduct Medal – an extremely rare honour as only 112 were awarded. 'Bogs, we think, would have liked that,' Hope believed. And he would have probably replied with his most-used phrase: 'It is better so.'

Two days later, nine miles west of Limassol, EOKA struck against an army vehicle carrying members of the Royal Artillery. In the ambush, bombs were thrown and shots fired by a local terrorist gang, wounding three soldiers, one of whom died from his wounds on the 24th. He was Lieutenant John Joe. The same day Joe was struck, Lance Corporal Albert Shaw, of 5 Section, 10th Armoured Division Provost Company, was riding as a passenger in a Land Rover driven by another Royal Military Policeman, Lance Corporal Ray Pain. Both had grown up together in Dagenham and had attended the same schools before being called up for National Service. With them was an ACC cook. They were returning to their camp after delivering rations to an outstation. As they passed the ancient ruins of Curium, they came under terrorist fire. Although badly wounded, Pain was able to accelerate the vehicle out of danger and managed to rush to a hospital in Limassol. Sadly, Shaw had been hit in the head and could not be saved. He died the next day, Monday 23 April. The cook returned to duty, uninjured.

TURKISH REPUBLIC Day was 23 April. EOKA marked it by shooting dead a Turkish policeman in the heart of Nicosia at 15.30. There was no better way for the Greek Cypriot fanatics to turn celebrations into hate-fuelled communal riots. The incident began with an attack on a Greek Cypriot officer by two youths on bicycles, who had broken the capital's curfew and entered the Turkish quarter. They fired three shots at their target, but they missed and tried to run off, leaving one of their guns behind in the road. An off-duty, unarmed Turkish Cypriot auxiliary, hearing the firing from the front room of his house, rushed outside and gave chase. One of the assailants turned, took aim and pulled the trigger of a second pistol, fatally wounding the man. The other assassin grabbed a bike and tried to mount, but a 17-year-old girl forced him off and beat him to the ground with her wooden shoes, where an angry crowd held him down until he was arrested. The second young terrorist had run into a Turkish house, where the female owner kept him until police arrived to take him away.

Furious Turkish Cypriots gathered with clubs, bottles and stones, marched into the Greek area of the city and set fire to the first shops they saw. Assistant Police Super-intendent Antony Willis arrived on the scene to stop the clash before it accelerated into a full-blown riot by standing alone between the opposing groups, ordering them to stop until troops arrived to take control.

The same day, Iakovos Patatsos, the primary bomb-maker in the Government House bed-bomb incident, was arrested, when he and another tried to murder a Greek Cypriot policeman outside Nicosia's Central Police station. Nihat Vasif, a Turkish officer, grabbed Patatsos before he could make off on a bicycle, EOKA's chosen means of transport in the Island's towns. Two of the remaining potential assassins were left. Stavros Stylianides, the second bomb-maker, died in Nicosia Hospital on 19 February 1957 after explosives blew up in his Episkopi bomb-making 'factory', three days before they were to be used. His death was declared 'self-inflicted'.

A month earlier, Sophocleous, the Government House bed-bomber, was appointed to head the Marathassa group – 'the first valet to fight as a guerrilla chieftain,' quipped Grivas. Sophocleous was caught a few months later in the Troodos Mountains, during Operation *Bullfinch* on 4 April, but was released in time to say farewell to his Colonel in March 1959 after the signing of the London and Zurich Peace Agreements. In August 1960, Sophocleous, like many other EOKA stalwarts, was rewarded with a government post. The former valet was made a Special Branch police inspector. At the Ledra Palace Hotel, he spotted Mr Philip Noel Baker, the Labour MP,

having a drink on the terrace with another 'hero' – Polycarpos Georghadjis, the new Minister of the Interior. 'How is Sir John?' he asked. 'Please give him my kind regards.' Baker passed them on to the Field Marshal in England.

With the Island's economy under strain and thousands being put out of work by the conflict, a local Greek newspaper, *Phos*, suggested towards the end of April that Bishop Anthimos of Kitium, who represented the exiled Archbishop Makarios as Ethnarch, should request prominent Greek Cypriot citizens, such as the Mayor of Nicosia, Dr Themistocles Dervis; a former member of the Executive Council, John Clerides; the former Attorney-General, Stelios Pavlides; businessman Andreas Araozou; and lawyer Hadjipavlou to call a meeting of representatives of all shades of opinion to discuss methods to bring peace. *Phos* further suggested that Dighenis should order a truce, because the authorities made the restoration of order a condition for conciliation talks.

The named individuals gave their reply to the English language *Cyprus Mail*. It was a blunt refusal to have anything to do with such a meeting unless Makarios attended – and he was sitting in the Seychelles by order of the Governor. Bishop Anthimos added his weight by stating that a solution to the Cyprus problem could only be found by the return of the Archbishop to negotiate on the basis of the principle of self-determination.

To prove that Dighenis had no intention of calling a truce until a time favourable to him, EOKA bombed three buses carrying members of 'The Jimmy Edwards Show' as they drove through Famagusta on their way to entertain an audience of servicemen. Lance Corporal Derek Coleman heard the explosion at RMP HQ. With two other colleagues, he rushed to the scene of the incident, where the leading vehicle had had its front wheels blown off. The passengers, including Jess Conrad and

Jimmy Edwards at Akrotiri with an RAF 'double'. (Photograph by John Boon.)

Lita Rosa, were 'shaken up by their experience, but were quickly conveyed back to HQ where Mr Edwards declared that the military police had saved their lives,' remarked 2nd Lieutenant Maurice Nicholls.

In true showbusiness tradition, the curtain went up on time and the company performed – 'an absolute riot of *ad hoc* and ad-lib entertainment' – to rapturous cheers from the troops.

'The following morning, the lovely Lita Rosa visited one of the RMP billets to express her thanks to the young NCOs,' Nicholls continued. 'It was a delightful and very welcome surprise to have such a beautiful young woman in their midst and apparently a surprise that boosted both morale and testosterone levels.'

On the same day, two youths, aged 20 and 21, were sentenced to life imprisonment for carrying six bombs, when they were arrested at a roadblock in March by a patrol of the Royal Horse Guards commanded by Cornet S. Butler, a son of Government Minister R. A. Butler. If EOKA were determined to terrorize, the authorities were even more capable of doing the same. More and more, EOKA was using impressionable young people to do its dirty work, caring little that, if caught, they could receive death sentences at worst or life imprisonment at best.

In the United States, the Greek lobby was working overtime to garner support by trying to convince citizens that Cyprus was fighting a war against Britain for independence, something that resonated with the electorate's pride in what their forebears started with the Boston Tea Party. It was left to a *Time* magazine reader to put the Island's situation into perspective. John Amsden wrote: 'Privately, the US attitude can be summed up in a question, "what do we do about an ally who frisks nuns and deports an archbishop?" I would be interested in knowing what America would do about nuns who carry concealed weapons and an archbishop who preaches sedition?'

'Terrorism by the EOKA movement in Cyprus has now been going on for just over a year,' an editorial in *The Times* began. 'What progress has been made in stamping it out, and how long is it likely to take? Possibly it is too early yet to answer the second question, but it is important to keep both under review because everything else waits upon them. More than 15,000 troops are engaged in hunting fewer than 500 terrorists.

'This kind of balance sheet in internal

security operations is not unfamiliar. The best that can be said of it is that the terrorism has not worsened ... The worst is that no outstanding terrorist leader has yet been captured. Purely military success in operations of this kind varies proportionately with the sternness of the methods employed. There is no doubt that savage reprisals, which make civilian populations more frightened of the security forces than of the terrorists, are the quickest way to gain the intelligence on which the defeat of terrorists depends. Such methods have rightly been eschewed in Cyprus and would never be countenanced by Britain.

'The measures taken against the civil population of Cyprus have been limited to the imposition of curfews and collective fines and the closing of schools. The cost of this comparative clemency is a serious lack of information about the identity, whereabouts and forthcoming operations of the terrorists, which means that the only successful ambushes in Cyprus are brought off by the terrorists, usually at the expense of the soldiers. The restraint of the latter has been a remarkable tribute to their discipline. The greatest weakness in the island's security has been the absence until recently of a Special Branch organization and intelligence sources, both of which take time to build. The fact has to be faced that our intelligence is unlikely to improve significantly for some time.

'We have refused to compete with the terrorists in violence, which is their first lever on the civil population, and we cannot compete with them in popular appeal, which is their second.

'In general the outlook for the future cannot be said to be bright unless the leaders of the EOKA movement can be caught. Accurate intelligence from the civil population is hardly to be looked for until their desire for peace outweighs their fear of, and sympathy for, the terrorists. Failing this, the soldiers' best hope is luck – the indispensable quality of the successful general.'

Unknown to *The Times*, military commanders were planning to teach the EOKA mountain gangs a sharp lesson. It would come sooner than the terrorists expected, but would luck favour the brave and turn the tables on Grivas?

CHAPTER TEN

Communal troubles start: a not merry month of May

'I do not know the method of drawing up an indictment against a whole people.'

Edmund Burke

THE STIFF peak of his red cap stopped doughty Corporal Len Want's skull from being smashed when he was hit by large piece of concrete thrown by rioters in Famagusta. He was a member of a Royal Military Police patrol that was sent to restrain the angry youthful demonstrators. A short distance away, Corporal Barry Heseltine and Lance Corporal Neville Dawes, two other RMPs, both aged 19, were also trying to control the crowd. A bomb threatened their lives and Heseltine was forced to open fire, first in the air and then on the mob's ring leader. Petros Yiallouros, a Greek Cypriot only a year younger than the British troops, was hit and died from his injuries. A committed member of EOKA, he attended Ammochostos high school. After lessons, he passed messages between local gang leaders and helped move weapons from hiding place to hiding place.

'Loss of young life on either side was always a matter of deep regret,' commented 2nd Lieutenant Maurice Nicholls, another RMP. 'Poignancy was added to this death by the fact that like many Cypriots, the dead youth's parents lived in London.'

EOKA propaganda exploited the student's death to the full, accusing the British of brutality and claiming Yiallouros's last words were: 'Long live *enosis*.'

After a period of prolonged anxiety for Heseltine, the subsequent lengthy Coroner's inquest completely exonerated the soldier and complimented the RMP's high standard of conduct.

Barely had the inquest ended on 30 April before EOKA threw bombs at an RMP two-vehicle patrol, which included two RAF policemen – 'Snowdrops' as they were known. Most of the members of the patrol were injured. Two of them, Lance Corporal Roger Golden and RAF Corporal Laing, RAF Police, were seriously hurt. Corporal (later Lieutenant Colonel) Steve Manning picked them up and put them in his Land Rover. With Lance Corporal George Watts at the wheel, they raced towards the nearest civilian hospital, but his damaged vehicle broke down.

Nicholls described what happened next. 'A passing Cypriot civilian very bravely stopped his car and took the injured to the hospital, racing straight through an armed police road-block in front of the police station at great risk to himself. On arrival at the hospital, the "Good Samaritan" dragged Corporal Golden inside and then returned to his blood-soaked car, drove away and was never seen again.

'He was truly a caring and gallant man who put his own life at substantial risk and demonstrated that even in times of great anguish, fear and hatred, humanity and decency can still emerge as an example to us all,' Nicholls reflected. 'Both Corporals Golden and Laing were evacuated to the UK. Golden made a full recovery while Laing unfortunately lost a lung as a result of his injuries.'

THE SPRING brought out the Cyprus sun roses and transformed the land from green to gold. Butterflies, 50 different types, danced in the air between turban buttercups, snapdragons, oats and wild mustard that carpeted the broad plain between the jagged Kyrenia peaks and the solid mass of the Troodos. The mountainsides dripped with pink arabis and tiny lilac crocuses. Village gardens were awash with mimosa and sorrel blooms. On the surface, Cyprus was Aphrodite's Isle of Love, but not in this month of May. It had opened badly for the Security Forces and love was in short supply.

The Colonial authorities in Nicosia were still not completely sure who was leading EOKA. The organization's propaganda leaflets were signed 'Dighenis, the leader', but was this a single individual or a collective name for a committee? Intelligence gatherers picked up clues and carefully studied whatever the terrorists published, but they could not provide a definitive answer, although all the signs pointed to Grivas, the Cyprus-born Greek who pursued *enosis* with messianic zeal as evidenced by his propaganda. 'His leaflets were written either in the style of a religious tract, likening the struggle to the suffering of Christ and the Resurrection, or in the form of an ultimatum threatening execution and reprisal in the case of any Cypriots daring to defy the Leader's wishes,' wrote Nancy Crawshaw in her detailed analysis of the conflict.

The Times expressed the view of the Establishment when it pronounced sonorously: 'If, as the intelligence reports suggest, he is a retired Greek general with wartime training in guerrilla tactics by British officers during the German occupation, then

he is, no doubt, an opponent well worth capturing. So, to a less degree, are the other wanted men – their numbers are mounting – whose arrests would enrich informers by, in the aggregate, many thousands of pounds.'

Whether Grivas were 'The Leader' or not, Governor Harding was losing patience after the second successful EOKA bombing of a parked aircraft at Nicosia Airport. The Dakota DC-3 belonged to Cyprus Airways and was awaiting servicing. He placed high-level rewards on the heads of the 'most wanted' and offered many inducements for the membership to surrender and become informers. This policy began to pay dividends in due course and splits appeared in the ranks of the organization.

The Times did not know that British forces, guided by informers, had Grivas on the run in the Troodos, even if the mountain gangs were fighting back with hit-and-run tactics.

The Times editorial carried on: 'The desirability of disorganizing resistance by taking key prisoners is as undeniable as are the doubts aroused by this policy of offering reward, accompanied by free passage, by sea or air, to some safe place. What will be the effect on rank and file Cypriots of an attempt – no purpose is served by less than plain speaking – to bribe men to turn informer? Psychological factors enter into the conduct of such operations as those in Cyprus even more than into a campaign between enemies in uniform. Lawful authority can, by action that is repugnant to ordinary decent people, however inevitable it may seem to those responsible, forfeit the good will of the hitherto non-aggressive sections of a population. The terrorist of yesterday may come to be regarded in the eyes of his compatriots as a potential martyr.'

GREEK CYPRIOTS found their 'martyrs' when two young EOKA foot soldiers, Michael Karaolis and Andreas Demetriou, were hanged simultaneously at 03.00 on 10 May 1956 by a masked executioner at the Central Prison in Nicosia after they had received the last sacraments from a priest of the Greek Orthodox Church.

The late Jack Taylor, a sergeant in the UK Police Unit, was present at an execution of a terrorist and gave the author a graphic description of the procedure and those involved. About 30 minutes before a hanging, the Chief Warder opened the condemned cell. The Prison Governor then told the condemned man that there was no last minute reprieve. From behind the Governor a black-gowned, stove-hatted priest stepped forward. He oversaw three guards manacle the struggling victim's arms behind his back. The priest asked: 'Would you like to spend a few minutes with me? Perhaps a few moments of reflection will help you.'

Now the priest took the leading position in the procession from the condemned cell. Two warders held his arms and the third walked behind him. The prison governor and chief warder followed. As they crossed the prison yard, the priest chanted prayers. The sound of metal cups banged against the bars of prison cells grew louder. The inmates began calling 'EOKA – EOKA – EOKA' to the rhythm.

'Inside the execution chamber, painted a ghastly grey, the governor spoke briefly to a pair of civilian witnesses and the condemned man was pushed towards the steps leading to the hanging platform,' Taylor recalled. 'A knotted noose dropped from the ceiling. A tall man in army uniform stood, a black mask covering his face except for his emotionless eyes. On the platform the young man's legs were strapped together. The priest stepped forward and stood in front of him, asking if he wished to make a confession. Once the priest had finished, the Governor told him, "The sentence ordered by the Court that you should be executed by hanging for murder is to be carried out. Your appeal was denied. Have

you anything you wish to say before it is done?" The man said nothing.

'The Prison Governor stepped clear of the trap door and nodded. The hangman effortlessly slipped a hood over the condemned man's head, followed by the knotted noose. This trap door opened. The man dropped, the rope tightened, straightened and jerked for a few seconds. The priest, governor, warders and officials left the execution chamber as the hangman slowly descended from the gallows.

'The chamber was empty as he removed the mask to reveal the weather-beaten face of a long-serving army sergeant. He glanced at the still rope and lit a cigarette, before walking out of the chamber into the prison yard, heading briskly to the warders' mess for a drink. With the others he discussed the execution and speculated about repercussions. The Greek Cypriot priest was not with them. In the Officers' mess, the Governor, Chief Warder, the Coroner and the Commissioner sat, enjoying whiskies and sandwiches, and they, too, discussed the EOKA threat.'

The hangman's identity was a closely guarded secret, but now he can be revealed as Birmingham-born Sergeant Douglas 'Snudge' Lewis of the Royal Warwickshire Regiment, who was posted to the Island with his family. Lewis's son, in an interview with the author, said: 'My father didn't speak that much about his position. He told me only after the death of my mother. He first came into contact with his trade – not actually carrying out – when he was a guard at Shepton Mallet Military prison in 1952. He never divulged the number of terrorists he dispatched.' Shepton Mallet was where Albert Pierrepoint, the most prolific hangman of the twentieth century, oversaw several executions.

The Royal Warwickshire Regiment was responsible for guarding the Central Prison, and in particular the EOKA inmates and those in the condemned cells. 'This became a complete company commitment during the

Sergeant 'Snudge' Lewis.

period between the final dismissal of the appeals of the two murderers and their hanging,' the *Antelope*, the regimental journal recorded. '"B" Company had this task, which was carried out over the four days of mounting tension. Very special precautions had to be taken and as the time of execution came near, a great many normal police and warden duties were taken over by the company.'

Sergeant Lewis's son said: 'He was very aware that he was a wanted man and always carried a Sten gun and side arm in Cyprus. In addition, another armed soldier accompanied him. He was very aware, too, of the dangers to his family, but I don't know if we had any protection. My mother, for instance, came under attack when she was pregnant, carrying me. The individual who carried out the attack was only about 15 and she was saddened at how children were involved in the terrorist movement. I believe my father had no regrets

about what he did, because the terrorist had carried out cowardly acts against British Service personnel. During his working life with the army, my father was firm but fair. The man I knew was very loving.'

Brian Hobbs of the 1st Battalion The Royal Norfolks was 19 when he arrived in Cyprus as a National Serviceman. In civilian life he had been a stockbroker's clerk and one of his first duties was to join the guards at the Nicosia Prison for two weeks over Christmas 1955 – 'the worst Christmas of my life'. His memories of meeting the condemned men are permanently etched deep on his mind. One of Hobbs's charges was Michael Karaolis, 23, the former government civil servant, who had been given the death penalty for the murder on 29 August 1955 of PC Herodotus Poullis, a Greek Cypriot Special Branch officer, in Ledra Street. An avid cricketer at school, his first act after joining EOKA was to blow up the tax office in which he worked. To prevent civilian casualties, he claimed, the bomb was timed to explode on a Sunday.

'We lived in tents in the main courtyard. This was most uncomfortable because of the icy winds coming off the mountains and the constant rain. I was detailed to guard the death cells. The death cells consisted of a block of three, off a small corridor with a barred gate at each end. While on duty, the guard was locked in the corridor and sat outside the prisoner's cell. The building, which had a flat-roof, was in the middle of the main exercise yard,' Hobbs said. 'Sentries were strictly forbidden to talk to any prisoner but I was locked in with him for eight hours a day for a week and at night we talked to him, because there were hardly any inspections, although I had the means to summon help. We went through the transcript of his trial and discussed it endlessly.'

Karaolis pointed Hobbs to the contradictions and discrepancies in the evidence. 'In fact he almost convinced me that he was innocent,' said the Royal Norfolk soldier. 'This was the most miserable Christmas of my life, because Karaolis was quite genial and likeable but, of course, he was hanged the following May.'

In mid-January 1956, the Royal Norfolks handed over their duties to the 1st Battalion The Royal Warwickshire Regiment.

Karaolis, 22, became the first Cypriot to be executed by hanging. Charles Foley, the *Times of Cyprus* editor reported, 'He was a product of the English School, the multi-racial, cricket-playing, Shakespeare reading-mill for producing Cypriot Civil Servants, where every year the Governor presented the prizes on sports day. Karaolis had been a model pupil, a good scholar, a popular prefect, a half-mile champion, and a member of the school cricket team. On leaving school he had taken a minor post in the Civil Service and, according to his colleagues, shown little interest in politics. There were no signs of fanaticism, or of mental unbalance. An uncle recalled that he was prone to faint "at the sight of blood".'

Karaolis's last words were allegedly: 'You should not feel sorrow for me ... since I myself see no reason to feel sorrow for myself. I don't want my family to shed tears for me either.' EOKA made great play with his last wishes to create a legend. The two men were buried in the prison cemetery, with a priest officiating at the service, but no relatives were present. Throughout the night of their executions, nobody had been allowed within 200 yards of the grim building.

(A two-page letter written by French author and philosopher Albert Camus asking for clemency for Karaolis was auctioned in Athens on 7 June 2006 by Greek private collector Nicos Spanos. The Cypriot ambassador to Greece George Georgis remarked: 'The letter was written in 1956, two days before Karaolis's execution. He related the Cyprus struggle for independence with that of Algeria's.')

When news of the hangings was broadcast by state radio at 07.00 Greek Cypriots hailed the two hanged men as 'martyrs' and went into mourning. Nicosia and other towns on the Island became like places of the dead, with scarcely a soul outside. Shops, factories, restaurants and bars closed, their owners intimidated by gangs of youths who warned any shopkeepers they should close or face trouble later. Only Turkish-owned establishments carried on as usual.

The fact that one of them, Karaolis, shot dead a Greek Cypriot policeman, and the other *tried* to kill an Englishman, Sidney Taylor, appeared to be immaterial to most Greek Cypriots, who sincerely believed both men should have been reprieved by the Governor, as a gesture of appeasement and for reasons of political expediency. Under a Royal Ordinance of 1925, Harding had the authority to 'decide whether to extend or withhold the pardon or reprieve of a man under sentence of death whether the Executive Council concurs or not'.

The general opinion among British residents in Cyprus was that Karaolis and Andreas Demetriou certainly had to be hanged if justice were not to become a mockery and the entire Greek Cypriot police force become disrupted. At the same time it was realized that grave consequences might follow and that the number of pro-British Cypriots would decrease, while the ranks of EOKA could increase correspondingly.

From his room in the Pinewood Valley Hotel in the Troodos mountain village of Pedhoulas, 2nd Lieutenant Jamie Henderson of the 1st Battalion Highland Light Infantry wrote home: 'We are all delighted that KARAOLIS & DEMETRIOU were hanged on Thursday, and all hope that a few more of the bastards will follow suit!'

In Athens, Prime Minister Karamanlis rebuked the British Government: 'Unable to count on the British Government's good will and *bona fides*, Greece deeply wounded by today's executions, now turns towards the public opinion of all free nations, confident that faith in the ideals of freedom and democracy has not been estranged from world conscience.' He ended by quoting Euripides' observation: 'Those whom the gods wish to destroy they first make mad.'

The day before EOKA had murdered Royal Marine Lieutenant Timothy Dick, aged 27, near Paphos. The officer was the son of Rear Admiral R. M. Dick.

'I was serving with "P" Troop 40 Commando under canvas about a mile inland from the town of Ktima in Cyprus when Lieutenant Dick, whose engagement to Miss Vincent-Smith had only been announced six weeks before, left camp with P Troop Commander, Captain Neil Maude, a Sergeant and a driver in an Austin Champ to visit the District Officer and Chief of Police in Paphos,' Brian Tarpey said. 'The only way to reach the town was through a street of terraced houses which led into Ktima, a locality that had become known as "Bomb Alley" because of the frequent bomb attacks carried out on military vehicles.

'On that day a bomb was thrown at Mr Dick's vehicle and landed in his lap, killing him instantly and injuring the three other Marines who were with him. The tragedy could have been worse if our officer's body had not taken the full impact of the bomb.'

RETRIBUTION FOR Karaolis' and Demetriou's hanging was swift. EOKA leaflets, addressed 'To British soldiers' and signed 'The Leader Dighenis', announced that the organization had hanged two British soldiers in reprisal. The soldiers were named as Corporal Gordon Hill and Corporal Ronnie Shilton, both of them missing from their regiment, the 1st Battalion the Royal Leicestershire Regiment. Hill, aged 22, had disappeared the previous December, but the authorities had said nothing about Shilton. EOKA, however, claimed it had captured Hill in November and Shilton in April.

'May God have mercy on their souls,' the leaflets added in good English. 'We do not hate British soldiers but we are determined to be free. We are compelled to use for our freedom the same means that are used by the occupation forces for its suppression.' EOKA said their bodies would not be returned 'following the example of the occupation forces towards the murdered Greek patriots ... We shall answer hanging with hanging, and torture with torture.'

An official statement followed almost immediately to challenge EOKA's claims. It said that Lance Corporal Hill had disappeared from his unit on 19 December 1955. 'In February this year, rumours circulated that EOKA held him as a hostage, but no evidence of any sort was found to substantiate the allegation. Private Shilton, of the same battalion, who has on more than one occasion been absent without leave, went absent on 17 April, after being charged and reprimanded for sending home false reports that he had been seriously wounded. He has not been seen since.

'Security authorities have never at any time come across the slightest evidence that EOKA holds these soldiers. EOKA has never previously claimed to hold them ... Nor has EOKA produced any evidence to prove that they ever held these men or executed them on 10 May. The current leaflet is incorrect on the ranks of both soldiers ... Failing the reappearance of the two soldiers, both of whom are missing, it is impossible to say what has happened to them or where they are. The leaflets in question are, however, patently an attempt to make propaganda capital.'

The disappearance of Shilton and Hill would take a surprising turn later.

THE DEATH toll mounted almost every day.

Michael Karaolis.

Andreas Demetriou.

Private Ronald Shilton.

Lance Corporal Gordon Hill.

E.O.K.A.

TO BRITISH SOLDIERS

1.   A few weeks ago we announced the execution of Hostages Gordon Hill and Ronnie Shilton. It is an unpleasant subject, and we would not have returned to it, were it not for the futile attempt of the Military Dictatorship to challenge the truth of our statement; that compels us to some further clarification, if only for the sake of the unfortunate families of the two men, who should not be left any longer uselessly in the anxiety of doubt.

2.   We apologise for having mentioned Hill as a corporal instead of lance-corporal, and the time of his capture as November instead of December. Those were presumably oversights of our press service. Anyway, we are sure we mean the same man: He carried three small metal plates, one oval and two round, on each of which were engraved the number 23137483, the initials "C.E." and the name "Hill G".

3.   We described Shilton as a corporal. In fact, he had stated that he had held that rank before having been deprived of it, some time before his capture; we did not think it worth while to verify the story and mentioned him by what he had said to be his former rank. We are again sure, however, that we mean the same man. (His disappearance, by the way, had not been published by the Authorities - Why?): Shilton said he was the son of an Irish doctor - now in America - and an Italian mother, subsequently divorced. He also said he was born at Santa Margherita twenty years ago. He was approximately 5 ft.9" tall, fair, with the trace of a wound in the back of the neck. Both his arms were tattooed with pictures of flowers and a tiger and names, among which "EVA" (his sister). His sten-gun bore the number 82494.

4.   We may be credited with sufficient intelligence not to make statements which can be proved untrue by the "REAPPEARANCE" of those whom we mention as dead.

5.   We have noted with interest that the Military dictatorship was surprised that we did not attempt to bargain the lives of our prisoners against those of Karaolis and Demetriou. Although we know Harding better than to believe that he cares so much about the lives of his men, we may propose the bargain next time - just to see what happens.

       We are not afraid of death - we shall strike back and fight until we get self-determination for Cyprus.

                        E.O.K.A.
                          THE
                        LEADER
                  D I G E N I S.

EOKA announces the 'executions' of Hill and Shilton.

On the 14th, Colonel Guy Thompson, formerly a director of Cyprus Airways, was found dead from gunshot wounds, 15 miles from Famagusta on the Monarga road. A day later, gunmen walked into Barclays Bank in Limassol and shot dead Julian Wathen, the manager, in his office, without interference from any of his staff.

The same day Grivas exacerbated relations between the Island's Turks and Greeks by sending threatening letters to the leaders of the Turkish Cypriots, Dr Kutchuk and Faiz Kaymak. 'We have learned that you have established an organization named the Turkish

National Party. If the current founders carry on their activities, they will deserve what they will be subject to. If you want the good of Turks, we suggest that they keep away from everything. Otherwise, you will be the next victim.'

To Greek Cypriots who shared a bus with Turkish Cypriot workers employed in the building of the Dhekelia base, the EOKA leader sent a warning: 'We have ascertained that you went to work by a Turkish bus although there are Greek Cypriot buses. You must be ashamed of God and people since you accepted a bus used by Turks. You are wretched, you are Greek Cypriots. Do you not

Corporal Hill And Another Hanged As

Reprisals Says EOKA

CYPRUS TERRORISTS HANG TIGER

Secret Burial Says Leaflet

A Leicester newspaper's front page.

CYPRUS terrorists have executed and secretly buried two British soldiers, one a member of the 1st Battalion Royal Leicestershire Regiment, in retaliation for the hanging of two Greek Cypriots, the Eoka terrorist organisation claimed in leaflets distributed in Nicosia today.

Eoka said the Britons, who had been prisoners for some time, were hanged after the execution at dawn yesterday of Michael Karaolis (23) and Andreas Demetriou (22), who were convicted of acts of terrorism.

THE SOLDIERS WERE NAMED AS CORPORAL GORDON HILL, WHO DISAPPEARED ON DECEMBER 19, AND CORPORAL RONNIE SHILTON. THERE WAS NO IMMEDIATE INFORMATION ON CORPORAL SHILTON, SAID BY EOKA TO HAVE BEEN TAKEN PRISONER LAST MONTH.

regret betraying your country and co-operating with Turks? I order you to stop travelling with Turks immediately. Otherwise, EOKA warriors fall in behind you and spill the blood of a traitor to teach a lesson to you. If ever … Heaven joins Hell, only then we can be friends with Turks. In case you do not terminate all your relations with Turks within three hours after you receive this warning, I will instantly order for your execution.' It was signed 'DIGHENIS.'

Less than two months after the murder of Corporal Welsh, the Famagusta RMP detachment lost another popular NCO, Lance Corporal Colin Keightley, when a bomb was thrown into the compound of Inkerman House, a requisitioned house used to accommodate the NCOs.

National Serviceman Lance Corporal Tony Fish was present at the time and clearly remembered: 'The 13th of May 1956 was a Sunday. The yard at the side of the house served as a vehicle park and located in it were

the "thunder boxes" [latrines], the sign writer's store and garaging. Behind the thunder boxes was a footpath, which ran from the road at the front of the billet, along the side and to a field, which was overlooked by a guard point in the water tower at the rear of the premises.

'No guard was mounted during daytime hours. During the week the area was used for patrols and off-duty NCOs to congregate to receive orders and during tea breaks. On this occasion there were far fewer people around, but Corporal Geoff Allman of the RAF Police patrol was there, with a Land Rover, about to go on patrol.

'Lance Corporal Colin Keightley, Private Norbury – one of our ACC cooks – and "Busty", the Greek Cypriot cook, were sitting together outside the kitchen, preparing vegetables for the day's meals. I was in the yard collecting the floor mats from the Corporals' Mess which had been drying on a fence next to the "thunder boxes".

'As I approached the Mess windows, there was an almighty explosion and I was pushed up against the billet wall. Everything seemed to stand still. There was that smell that always goes with an explosion of this nature. And absolute silence. Just thick black smoke everywhere. My back hurt and I put my hand where I felt the pain. Yes, it was wet. Blood. Frightening, you know how it is – self-preservation. Geoff Allman is there. He looks at me and his eyes widen. Yes, it is blood, he confirms. I'm taken inside to a ground floor bedroom and laid face downwards on someone's bed. I remember a newspaper on the floor below my head. It was rapidly sodden with dripping sweat. I was in a state of funk.

'Eventually I was treated by a civilian, a Mr Munson of 2 Field Ambulance who removed a small piece of shrapnel from a minor wound. The *acroflavine*, which he used, caused more damage because my injury turned septic, apparently due to an allergy.

'Colin Keightley, Private Norbury and "Busty" were all hit by shrapnel from the pipe bomb, for that's what it was. Colin was very badly hurt and taken to the British Military Hospital in Nicosia where he died. The memories we hold can be strange but I will always see Colin in his Davy Crockett hat. The song, *The Ballad of Davy Crockett* was popular at the time. He was an immensely popular man who was genuinely sadly missed. The other two injured in the incident subsequently returned to good health.'

Lance Corporal Wilf Mannion was lying in bed asleep when the bomb blast jolted him awake. 'I jumped up, wearing only "drawers green cellular", pushed my feet into my boots and, without lacing them, wrenched open my locker. My only thought was to lay hands on my already loaded Webley .38 revolver. Keeping a weapon in one's locker was contrary to orders – a serious offence. All firearms were to be kept in the armoury.

'Our small arms instructor in training had remarked that this particular revolver would do just as much harm to your opponent if you took it by the barrel and threw it at him. Needless to say it didn't fill me with a great deal of confidence. Grabbing my firearm, I ran like a bat out of hell down the stairs, my unlaced boots barely touching the treads.

'In the yard, I ran past several shocked and bleeding colleagues. Training and instinct took over. My foremost thought was to capture the offender who had thrown the bomb. I turned right out of the yard into the path to the rear of Inkerman House. I found the narrow walkway deserted and uncannily quiet, except for my puffing and panting – too many fags – and the deafening thuds from my heart. I made my way along to the connecting road. That, too, was deserted. "Where is he? Where is he?" I was all hyped-up, but my enemy was nowhere to be seen. I then spotted the door to a small shrine, an alcove dug into the bank of the road. I could see a Madonna and crucifix. "That's it! That's it! He must be in there!"

'I approached the door, when the reality of the situation suddenly struck me. If the enemy were in the shrine, he could well kill me. What was one more death to him? "What am I going to do?" I thought. Was I going to shoot him? "God, God, don't let him be in there. Please, please don't let him be in there". I flung open the door, still praying. To my relief, the sanctuary was empty. If anyone had been in there, I might well have shot them – innocent or guilty. I was in a surreal world.

'If I had shot and killed someone, I could have been charged with murder, because I hadn't identified the bomber. He could have been black, white, fat, thin, tall, short. I was taking one hell of a chance, a chance, which, at that moment, seemed justifiable. Having failed to find the bomber, I returned to Inkerman House, a warrior dressed in "drawers green cellular", boots munition black, unlaced, and carrying a large black revolver in my shaking, sweaty hand. I proceeded around the corner into the front door of Inkerman House. And there was the bomber under arrest.'

Corporal Fish continued the story: 'Fortunately, as the bomb exploded, an Army 15-cwt truck was passing the front of the billet and instead of stopping, the driver and his escort, both soldiers with the RAOC, used their common sense and drove on past, spotting the bomber as he ran across the field at the rear of our building and straight into their arms.'

The arrested man was Chrysostomos Panayi, an 18-year-old, who came from the village of Askas. He was handcuffed to a shower on the first floor of Inkerman House until the civilian police arrived to take him away to be charged with a terrorist offence. Lance Corporal Ted Millan, who had seen the entire incident from an upstairs window, identified him.

When Lance Corporal Colin Keightley died in hospital on 19 May, he became the 29th victim of an EOKA attack. His father had been flown out by the War Office to be at his bedside. While Mr Keightley mourned the loss of his son, Mayor Dervis of Nicosia opened a telegram from Mr Larkin, The Lord Mayor of Dublin, which asked him to convey to the parents of Karaolis and Demetriou, the 'deep sympathy of the people of Dublin'.

'Together with others I later gave evidence and was present at the special court in Nicosia when Panayi was sentenced to death which involved the Judge donning the black cap, a square of cloth, and sitting with a Priest,' said Corporal Fish. 'Like most of those caught and sentenced to death, he was not hanged and, as far as I am aware, he is a free man. More than can be said of the terrorists' victims. Such is politics.'

Another British soldier, WO2 Ronald Crisell of the Royal Leicestershire Regiment was killed in Plutarchoos St Famagusta, on 17 May when a bomb was thrown and exploded in his vehicle.

The next day Private Raymond Banks of the South Staffordshire Regiment met his death during a riot in Ledra Street. Michael Hill was his platoon commander and remembers the day clearly. 7 Platoon had been called out to restore order. A large crowd met his soldiers – many were schoolgirls, throwing stones and bottles – when they debussed. 'We set up in riot drill formation and moved down the street, ordering them to retreat. Suddenly there was an explosion and Banks was down and others cut. A bomb had been thrown at us,' he says. 'I sent one of my men to a nearby chemist's shop. When he wouldn't open the door, we broke it down. But it was too late.'

The late Ted Badger was one of the regiment's medical orderlies and told the author: 'The ambulance driver and me got to the site as quickly as possible, not knowing what to expect because the message to us simply said "Bomb thrown". We ran to where Banks was lying to give him first aid, but couldn't find a pulse. We placed him on a stretcher and rushed to BMH, Nicosia, but an RAMC officer confirmed he was dead. The most tragic part was that he had only three weeks left to serve.'

Charles Foley, the editor of the *Times of*

Greek Cypriot schoolgirls taunt British troops.

Cyprus, reported that the area in Nicosia where Banks died was immediately cordoned off by troops using barbed wire. Houses were searched and gun posts established on rooftops. He wrote: 'After a seventy-two hour curfew the families caught inside the barbed wire net were taken out and addressed by the Commissioner of Nicosia, Mr Martin Clemens. "Tonight", he said, "a policeman will visit every home in the curfewed area with envelopes and paper. Every householder will write on the paper everything he knows about EOKA, then seal it in the envelopes. All the envelopes will be given to me tomorrow and I will open them myself in private. Here is your chance to help the Police without fear of any consequence." Next day the envelopes were collected: the papers were all blank.'

After nobody came forward to identify Banks's killers, severe penalties were inflicted on the residents and shop and office owners where the outrages took place. With the approval of Field Marshal Sir John Harding, the Commissioner ordered 50 shops, flats and offices to be closed for three months, with their contents removed within 48 hours. The residents were evicted.

Two days later Henry Moseley, a civilian employee at RAF Akrotiri, was shot dead while enjoying a quiet drink in the King's Arms, a British-owned pub in Limassol. From South Wales, he was married with two children. His killers were identified as Michael Thrassyvoulides, Nicos Sophocleous and Christakis Pantelides. Thrassyvoulides, as the head of EOKA's execution team in Limassol, had also been responsible for the death of John Cook in Gladstone Street a month earlier.

In the Troodos Mountains, Private William Perks had finished his evening meal and was in conversation with the other members of his patrol as they settled down for the night. During their banter, the subject of weapons' usage came up. Perks picked up a Browning automatic pistol to prove a point. Thinking it had been unloaded, he raised the gun in the air and pulled the trigger. It fired and the bullet shattered his skull. His mates sat stunned, listening to his death rattles, until a corporal, an Australian, pushed the soldier's eyes back into their sockets and closed the lids. Not all service fatalities were due to EOKA's actions, whatever 'The Organization' would claim later.

RELATIONS BETWEEN Greeks and Turks were now at their worst for 80 years and had steadily deteriorated since EOKA launched its campaign. On 23 May two EOKA gunmen executed a Turkish policeman while he sat next to the village mayor of Polis in a local coffee shop. The incident brought Turkish Cypriots on to the streets of various towns the next day in protest. In Nicosia, demonstrators set three Greek-owned cars alight, broke shop windows and stoned their owners. In Larnaca 200 Turks, armed with sticks, smashed Greek properties. In both places, British troops had to fire tear gas to disperse the mobs and restore calm. Privately many soldiers would have preferred not to intervene and allow the Turks to wreak havoc. In the disturbances, seven Turks and six Greeks were injured, four critically.

EOKA ignored the Turkish Cypriot threats and murdered another Turkish policeman on 27 May. It suddenly became open season for worse battles between the two communities. In clashes in Nicosia, two people were killed. The Nicosia fire brigade was called out 15 times to put out fires started by unknown persons in Greek-owned shops and other premises.

That same day, Airmen Leonard Kinchin, aged 18, and Sergeant Alexander Sutton, 39, were off duty and had travelled to Kyrenia to relax and swim. While on the beach, they saw a young Turkish Cypriot struggling in the heavy seas near Karavas/Alsancak (incidentally the ancestral home village of pop singer George Michael). Both servicemen immediately went to the man's rescue. The Turk was saved, but Sutton drowned in the effort. When Kinchin returned to where they had left their towels, he lost his life by treading on a mine placed there in their absence by EOKA.

At Lapitos/Lapta they saw cruelty at its worst after a pipe bomb of the type favoured by EOKA exploded, killing an eight-year-old boy, tearing the legs off a seven year-old boy and injuring a three-year-old girl. All three children belonged to the same Greek family. A device was thrown into a shop at Famagusta, which was filled with Greek Cypriot women and children. Fortunately it failed to go off. The owner, Cecil Birkle, a longtime resident of the Island, had been the subject of attack before. Andreas Demetriou, who was hanged alongside Karaolis, had shot and wounded his assistant, Sydney Taylor.

Caused by EOKA's continued killing of policemen, mainly Turks, the tension between the two Cypriot communities was being heightened day by day, even in places where they had lived in amity, such as Aphania, 12 miles from Nicosia. Here, for no apparent reason, a pitched battle erupted in which both sides used knives and staves against each other and set fire to houses and haystacks. The fighting stopped only when soldiers from the Royal Warwickshire Regiment arrived. By then one Greek Cypriot and one Turkish Cypriot lay dead. The Turk, an auxiliary policeman, had arrived by chance on his motorcycle just as fighting was at its worst. Angry Greeks spotted him and pounced. Using shovels, they beat him to death.

At the funeral in Omorphita of another Turkish Cypriot policeman, mourners vented their spleen, setting alight Greek properties and killing a foreman at a tobacco factory. A number of Greeks retaliated with pick helves and stakes. Once again it was left to the British to restore peace. Military police broke

up the fight, and the fires did no serious damage. To prevent more of the same taking hold in the capital, the authorities began erecting a wire fence between the Greek and Turkish sectors in the walled city. It had a gate, which could be closed in the case of trouble. The division of Nicosia had begun.

Dr Fazil Kutchuk, chairman of the 'Cyprus is Turkish' Party, usually a quiet man, sent an angry telegram to the Secretary-General of the United Nations, the American Secretary of State, Foster Dulles, and Lennox-Boyd, the British Secretary of State for Colonial Affairs. He told them that Turkish feeling in Cyprus was running 'very high, following attacks by terrorists on our community'. He warned that 'Turks will never be sacrificed on the altar of self-determination', and that on Britain abandoning Cyprus, 'Turkey will immediately step in. So far this knowledge has kept Cyprus Turks within reason and law. We appeal to America to denounce terrorism and back Britain's policy of no settlement until terrorism is vanquished in Cyprus.' Later he met with Governor Harding and discussed the dangers of the communal tension on the Island. After the meeting he issued a statement saying EOKA was provoking his people and that they 'could not be expected to stand by and see innocent Turkish blood flowing'. He said: 'While we will never bow to the activities of the terrorists, our interests require that our policy should be one of level-headed restraint.'

'Relations between Greeks and Turks in Cyprus have deteriorated in an alarming fashion since EOKA began its activities just over a year ago,' said a government spokesman in typical understatement, 'and have now reached a stage which gives cause for serious apprehension.'

As more anti-Greek demonstrations followed in the last days of the month, Bishop Anthimos of Kitium, the acting Ethnarch, blamed the British Government for the Greek–Turkish riots. By their negative policy, he declared, the Government 'has excited passions and created conditions, which render remote a settlement and create complications dangerous for peace and security'. The Bishop attributed the riots to 'certain mischievous Turkish elements' and expressed his sympathy for the 'victims of such barbarism'.

The Government responded that the present communal troubles had been directly provoked by the campaign of murder, violence, and intimidation waged by EOKA terrorists, at whose hands members of the Turkish community had recently suffered death and injury, with the result that the latter had reacted on certain occasions in a manner overstepping law-abiding behaviour. The only answer was to apply an antiseptic to the centre of contagion – EOKA. 'Greek leaders who have failed to denounce the methods of EOKA cannot escape a heavy share of the responsibility for the present communal troubles,' a spokesman concluded.

IN HIS Empire Day address, Governor Harding emphasized that the task of the armed forces in Cyprus was 'to ensure that this Island, with its airfields, its command and signal organization and its other military installations, is protected and secure, and always ready for use'. Speaking on the Forces Broadcasting Station, he said: 'In fact, it is not too much to say that as things are in the world today, use of this small Island is vital to the maintenance and development of the Commonwealth in peace and to its defence in war … At present attempts are being made to undermine the security of this base by a group of desperate, ruthless and unscrupulous men, whose aim it is to overthrow the Government and by terrorism and intimidation to impose their will on all the people here. So far, and because of the great efforts of the security forces here, they have caused no real interference with the use of the base. But to make it fully secure and to enable the people of

Cyprus to live in peace, the campaign against the terrorists must go on until they have been eliminated or forced to desist.'

With Operation *Pepperpot* under way in the Troodos Mountains, the Governor tried to make life even more difficult for EOKA. He ordered that every Cypriot must carry an identity card. The authorities' spin on the measure was that the cards would facilitate the movement of people going about their lawful business and prevent inconvenience caused by roadblocks for identity checks. In reality it was intended to gather intelligence on the backgrounds of every individual.

Registration began immediately in 76 villages in the mountain areas, including Platres and Pedhoulas, normally visited by thousands of inhabitants of the towns, in addition to many foreigners from Egypt and other Middle East countries. Under the new regulation published in the *Cyprus Gazette* nobody could enter these places without a special permit from the local police, thus allowing checks on every stranger. Another decree placed the responsibility on the owners of any premises for cleaning any EOKA slogans daubed, painted, or smeared on them.

Two weeks after Lieutenant Dick was killed, Marine Tarpey was sure he had caught his murderer. Tarpey had been sent to escort a three-ton truck carrying four other Marines. He picks up the story: 'Travelling through "Bomb Alley" I suddenly heard one of them yell "Bomb" as he fired a rapid burst from his Sten gun at an unseen target. Everything occurred in a split second. I heard the bomb hit the canvas cover above my head, but with the truck travelling fast, it bounced off. A second later there was an eardrum-shattering blast as the bomb exploded, then a column of smoke. No sooner had the shockwaves subsided and the truck come to a standstill than I jumped out and sprinted towards the Austin Champ, which had been following at some distance behind. For a second I thought it had been hit, until it appeared through the drifting smoke left behind by the explosion.

'As I ran, I remembered the search we had made in the same area weeks before and turned into the narrow lane between two houses and came out into the field, where I saw a man running towards some trees. I challenged him in English, Turkish and Greek (*Halt, Stamata, Dur*) and when he refused to stop, I raised my rifle and fired. I missed. Convinced he was the bomb thrower, I reloaded my rifle and gave chase until I came out onto the road where the previous "bomb thrower" had made his escape after he had killed Lieutenant Dick.

'It was then I discovered how the first bomb thrower had made his getaway. The man I was now chasing was already in possession of a bicycle and was about to jump on it when he heard my second challenge. This time he glanced round, saw my raised rifle pointing directly at him and let go of the bicycle and then threw his arms up into the air.

'By this time, still in my firing position, I spotted our Champ up the road, along with several other Marines, blocking the man's escape route. He was quickly surrounded. The captured man was taken to Ktima Police Station where he was placed in a cell. On the day of the accused's trial in Paphos, the police set up barbed wire roadblocks outside the court and every vehicle that came near was stopped and checked. Precautions were taken in the packed courtroom in case any threats were made on the judge or witnesses. Armed Marines lined against the walls carried out this duty.

'When I took my place in the witness box, I noticed a group of Greek Cypriots sitting in the front row of seats looking at me with hatred in their eyes. Some were the accused bomber's relatives. I thought, "You lot should be showing remorse for the murder of a Marine officer rather than sorrow for a bomb thrower who no one knows how many times

has made attempts to kill British soldiers."

'The trial was brief. The man was found guilty. My mates were certain I had caught Lieutenant Dick's killer. No further bombs were thrown in "Bomb Alley" that I can recall.'

Meanwhile, *Pepperpot* steamed ahead with added power. The 1st King's Own Yorkshire Light Infantry (KOYLI), part of 3 Royal Marine Commando Brigade, joined the operation. The regiment's Tactical Headquarters and Support Company moved from the heat of Paphos and spent 16 days 'buried away in the forest and enjoyed the cool climate of life at 4,000 feet', says Malcolm Johnson, KOYLI's official historian. 'It was during a search of ruined buildings in a gully that Private Richardson of Lieutenant L. A. Charlesworth's 2 Platoon caught a wanted EOKA terrorist named Nicos Xenophontos, whose premises contained clothing, medical supplies, food and weapons in what appeared to be a bomb-making factory complete with lathes and a variety of modern tools. At his trial in Nicosia, Xenophontos, who had a price of £5,000 on his head, was found guilty of murder and sentenced to death, but was later reprieved.

Operation *Pepperpot* lasted three weeks. All military services were used. Off the coast, Royal Navy vessels stepped up their patrols. On land, British troops, Royal Marine Commandos, RAF helicopters and the police combed the steeply wooded and rugged country along the north-west coast of the Island from Polis to Karovastasi, extending 20 miles inland and struck EOKA a heavy blow.

The authorities claimed that two 'hard core' terrorist gangs had been smashed, another almost completely eliminated and a fourth had lost its leader. Seventeen terrorists were 'in the bag', including two with £5,000 rewards on their heads. EOKA hides were also made unusable and large quantities of explosives, weapons and ammunition found. The hides were well constructed with boarded sides, timbered floors, and corrugated iron roofs, and were well camouflaged deep in the hillsides.

Pepperpot was carried out by the permanent troops of the districts in which they were based – Royal Horse Guards, Royal Marines of 40 and 45 Commando, the King's Own Yorkshire Light Infantry and the Gordon Highlanders. Men of the 1st Battalion the Parachute Regiment, who moved into the operational area at night, left their buses many miles from their objectives and force marched their way across rough and broken country. On 18 May a small Para patrol made contact with a heavily armed EOKA group. Without a fight, its members left their weapons and fled. The Paras harried them through the mountains, and captured them on 20 May. During the next night, another terrorist, armed with a Bren gun and five grenades, was captured without a fight.

To maintain the initiative, British commanders changed their tactics after 21 May. Rather than wide sweeps by the forces, it was decided to concentrate small groups of troops in a smaller area and scour the ground more thoroughly. Even dung heaps were searched and shotguns found in them.

Brigadier M. A. H. Butler praised 'the splendid work accomplished by all concerned'. The RAF helicopter pilots, who had been invaluable, particularly impressed him, he said. His officers and men had been ordered to carry out their tasks with a minimum of inconvenience to the residents of the mountain villages. In fact, they did more. In one hamlet, which was visited only once a week by a doctor, the sick were looked after daily by an Army medical team and an Army ambulance took a pregnant woman 50 miles to a hospital.

The Times correspondent in Nicosia was very impressed. 'It can justifiably be claimed that the security forces have by their operation knocked a major crack in the terrorist edifice, and that the EOKA mountain gangs have suffered serious losses, which they can ill afford,' he told readers back home.

ON THAT optimistic note, Government House determined that a ceremonial parade to mark the Queen's official birthday should take place as usual, with Sir John Harding taking the salute within the grounds of Nicosia's walled city. Here troops checked every square inch with mine detectors. Stringent precautions were put in place to ensure there were no unwanted guests present. Those invited were issued with a special permit and they had to give advance notice of the cars in which they planned to arrive, together with complete lists of passengers. A London *Times* correspondent suggested, 'It is unlikely any Greek Cypriots will attend.' It is worth noting that Charles Foley and Michael Davidson of the *Times of Cyprus* did not receive invitations.

As far as it could, EOKA was determined to spoil the occasion and chose a soft target to attack: a unit of the Royal Leicestershire Regiment, as it returned to the Golden Sands Camp from a Queen's birthday parade rehearsal in Famagusta. Lance Corporal Tony Chester, a three-year regular, of 65 Coy RASC was there. He gave the author his eyewitness account.

'A bomb was thrown into the leading Bedford 3-tonner and exploded, setting the petrol tank on fire. Members of the Leicesters were on board. We, the RASC blokes, were following in a second vehicle and were lucky not to have been caught in the blast. Although 65 Coy was based on the left side of the camp and the Leicesters on the right, we sometimes used the same entrance. The person who threw the bomb must have known that our vehicles would come almost to a stop before turning into the camp. Even though the truck was badly damaged, it continued moving. The driver was badly injured and covered in blood. Many of his passengers had suffered more.

'They had been blasted over the nearby

stonewalls on both sides of the road. One soldier lay in the middle with very severe head injuries; his arm moved up and down, but he was unconscious. I remember a medical officer taking a quick look and then moving on. It was obvious he could nothing for him. Another soldier sat with his back to the wall and we went over to see if he was okay. He had an unlit cigarette in his mouth, but he was dead. Several soldiers were found in the surrounding orange groves, very badly wounded. Our platoon fanned out around to see if we could find any sign of the bomb thrower. Because we had been on parade, we were not armed.

'Office staff came rushing out in a Land Rover and the pay sergeant – whose name I can't remember – rounded up suspects in the immediate area, his pistol at the ready as he took them to the guardroom. They were mostly young men and were lined up in our guardroom, facing the wall, resting against it with only their fingertips. The Leicesters did not treat them too kindly. Those under arrest probably had nothing to do with the bomb throwing – and some would have been Turkish Cypriots anyway – all were taken away for questioning by the police.

'After a team of medics arrived at the scene, Driver Hostad and I were told to put the dead on stretchers and place them in the back of a vehicle. I was only 19 at the time. Prior to this incident I had never seen a dead person, never mind having to pick one up. We were both very reluctant, but we had been ordered and so had no choice. The injured were placed in ambulances and taken to the camp's football field for evacuation by Sycamore helicopters.'

Three soldiers died – Privates John Argyle, John Attenborough and Kenneth Hebb. Twenty-two soldiers were injured, eight seriously.

Of all the wounded, none was probably braver than Lance Corporal M. Harrison of 'C' Company. He had sustained severe multiple injuries, which included bomb wounds to the chest, abdomen, both buttocks and thighs, with a compound fracture of the right femur, and severe petrol burns of both knees, both hands, arms and face. He was flown by helicopter for emergency treatment at the British Military Hospital in Nicosia, where Lieutenant Colonel J. C. Watts, MC, the Officer-in-Charge of Surgical Division, became his consultant.

In the days that followed, Harrison underwent several operations and blood transfusions. 'In eighteen years of war surgery, I have never before seen such ghastly wounds borne with such sustained fortitude. His courage has been an example and inspiration to staff and patients alike and his constant cheerfulness in adversity worthy of the highest tradition of the Army,' said Colonel Watts. Lieutenant Colonel J. M. Milne, RAMC, added his commendation: 'He has fought for his life from the start and although still dangerously ill is slowly improving. His unfailing cooperation and lack of complaint has undoubtedly helped greatly in maintaining morale in the acute surgical ward and the staff have had an eye opener in what sheer guts can do.'

Private Jervis, the driver of the bombed truck, was Mentioned in Dispatches for his courageous action.

Away from the towns, however, EOKA was on the run, quite literally. Its leader would have to find a 'safe house' to escape capture,

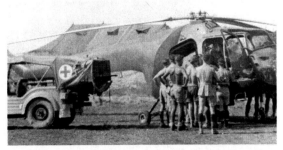

Injured Royal Leicestershire Regiment soldiers are taken from Golden Sands Camp by helicopter for urgent medical treatment in Nicosia.

his daily diary would be found and his mountain gangs began to fall apart, because of informers within their ranks.

The Queen's Birthday Parade took place without incident. Reported *The Antelope*, the journal of the Royal Warwickshire Regiment: 'HE Field Marshal Sir John Harding inspected the parade and took the salute. In the evening at Government House, amidst scenes of almost pre-war Vice-Regal splendour, HE and Lady Harding held their reception. The whole day was one of which one could feel most proud that in a strife-torn city and in spite of gunmen's threats, it was still possible to celebrate Her Majesty's birthday in the time-honoured fashion.'

The Governor takes the salute at the Queen's Birthday Parade in 1956.

CHAPTER ELEVEN

'An act which must be condemned': the murder of a gentle Irishman

'A blow in cold blood neither can nor should be forgiven.'
G. B. Shaw

LEADING AIRCRAFTSMAN John Hollis and Corporal Patrick 'Paddy' Hale arrived at the Homer building at 06.30 to start their day's shift. The sensitive electronics inside had to be isolated from metal objects, such as hangars and moving vehicles, which was why they found themselves located outside the incomplete barbed wire fence on the southern side of the airfield's perimeter. Their job was to use the radio navigational equipment housed in their twin rooms to gather the bearings of radio transmissions from approaching aircraft and relay them to the Control Tower at Nicosia Airport, the base for 2,400 RAF personnel. In emergencies or in adverse weather conditions, pilots often required 'Homing' assistance. That morning, because an underground cable had been cut accidentally by contractors of the Air Ministry Works Department, the two RAF men could not operate the fully automated direction-finding equipment and were using a manual system instead. Neither was armed. Their request to carry weapons had been turned down by higher authority.

At his bungalow at No. 2 Serrae St, Ayios Dhometios, very close to Nicosia's Central Prison, Master Pilot WO1 Jim McCorkle had finished breakfast with his wife Bonnie and was about to catch his bus to the airport, where he would spend his day training Flight

Sergeant Tony Harrison to fly one of the two Sycamore helicopters based there. Designed for civilian use, the aircraft had been bought by the RAF to see if they could be adapted to operate as military machines. McCorkle, who had joined the Air Force in 1940, was one of the pilots charged to test them in Cyprus. He had no idea that his helicopter would make history that day, 16 May 1956.

Senior Aircraftsman Robin Stitchbury, as he left Signals Billet 189, which he shared with LAC John Hollis, felt it would another day of boring routine. As a Ground Wireless Mechanic, his responsibility was to maintain and repair the Control Tower's radio and associated systems dotted around the airport. Because he had done his job well, 'the equipment under my charge was humming along without fault' and he had little to do, unless there was an emergency.

In the neighbouring field 150 yards from the Homer shack, two 22-year-old Greek Cypriots, Michael Koutsoftas and Andreas Panaghides, and Paraskevas Hiropoulis, aged 18, started cutting the ripened corn. They were from Paleometocho, where they had volunteered to join EOKA. Papa Lefteris, their village priest, had administered the organization's binding oath.

The previous day, Panaghides had tried to smuggle a Greek flag into the airport, hoping to raise it as a sign of protest. Although he was known to work as a cook in a nearby army canteen, two soldiers decided to search him. They found the flag and he was ordered to clean his boots with it. He refused and received a slap in the face for his temerity and told never to return. Under his breath, he vowed retribution for his humiliation.

Filled with youthful nationalist fervour and committed to 'the cause', today the three friends had murder on their minds, but their 'soft' target was yet to be decided. First they needed to quench their thirst. The work they were doing was dusty and hot and their tongues were dry. They decided to walk the short distance to the Homer building and ask the RAF occupants for a drink of water. They had seen Yiakoumis Poullou, a shepherd, do it many times without refusal. After all, it was a Cypriot tradition to give drinking water to any traveller who requested it.

Corporal Hale did not hesitate to respond to the Greek Cypriots' request. The young Irish-born airman from County Sligo had grown up in a home where Christian values were paramount and he himself had once

Leading Aircraftsman John Hollis.

thought of joining the priesthood. He filled a glass and each of his 'guests' took it in turn to drink the water. 'It was the sort of thing which the Forces were doing all over the Island and the sort of treatment they themselves are receiving on so many occasions,' reported the *Times of Cyprus*.

An hour later the three men returned – one carrying a scythe – and asked for another drink. The day was getting hot and neither Hollis nor Hale suspected anything out of the ordinary and provided water again. This time the Greek Cypriots sat down in the shade of the hut and watched a sweating team of the RAF Regiment completing a massive barbed wire fence around the airport's perimeter. Once a gap, several hundred yards wide, was filled, the airfield would be encircled and secure.

Hollis, due to attend a pay parade, waited until the labourers returned to their chores, leaving the site at 10.20. Twenty-five minutes later he was back and noticed that now nobody was working the adjacent field. Then, suddenly, around 11.00, from his desk inside he spotted two of the Greeks looking through the hut's north window. Using hand gestures, they indicated they wanted yet another drink of water.

Once again, Hale was the water bearer. He walked out of the hut and saw the third Greek Cypriot had arrived. They greeted him with friendly grins and one after the other they swallowed their drinks. The Corporal glanced upwards. A flight of three Hunter jet fighters was screaming overhead in an immaculate starboard echelon formation, before peeling off in separate parabolic arcs which all terminated perfectly with a squeal of tyres and puffs of smoke, right on the button of the active runway. The trio signified their admiration of the British pilots' skills and courteously, once again, thanked their host for his hospitality.

Hale smiled in acknowledgement and stared for a moment at the distant hangars shimmering in the morning sunshine, their shapes distorted and hazy in the reflected heat. He was pleased to be working away from the blazing sun. He returned to his workstation, sat down at his desk and picked up his headphones to listen to the conversations between airborne pilots and the Air Traffic Controller. He never heard the shot fired by one of the Greek Cypriots at point-blank range. He slumped in his swivel chair and slid to the floor, dead. The gunmen fired two more shots before they bolted. One of the bullets hit the partition between where Hale and Hollis sat. The second punctured the ceiling.

Hollis, hearing the gunfire, had dropped to the floor to protect himself behind his radio equipment, not realizing how narrowly he had escaped death. Seconds later, still keeping his head down, he stretched his right arm forward and ran his hand towards a switch on his radio set. He pushed it down to make a 'flash call' and was immediately in contact with the Duty Controller at the airport. 'They've shot Paddy,' he screamed into his microphone. 'I think he's dead. He's bleeding badly.'

'Now wait a mo,' replied the Controller, his

The room where 'Paddy' Hale died.

voice steady. 'Calm down, laddie and give me all the gen. Who's shot who and where?' Looking through one of the hut's windows, Hollis replied: 'Three men are running away from the Homer toward the fence. They shot Corporal Hale. All I can see is that one has a white shirt, one a green shirt and the other is wearing a khaki shirt. Hurry, they're getting away.'

Speaking afterwards, Hollis added: 'I also saw some RAF Signals men running towards the hut. One of them stayed with me while the others chased the killers.' They were joined by an RAF Regiment mobile patrol led by Flight Lieutenant Revers Stanley, but he failed to capture the terrorists.

About six minutes later an RAF ambulance arrived to take away Corporal Hale's body. He was the 28th British serviceman to be killed by EOKA.

Aircraftsman Ray Ingram was in the Control Tower when the 'flash call' came through. 'I recall that it was badly garbled and we had difficulty in understanding the full portent of the message,' he told the author. 'Another airman and me were rushed out of the tower and taken to the armoury by Land Rover and issued with .303 rifles. After this we were taken to the guardroom at the airport's main entrance and ordered to wait.'

While John Hollis was trying to recover from the shock of the EOKA attack, Robin Stitchbury, with whom he shared a billet, was away from his post, helping his friend Alan Benson clean an old aircraft hangar. After notifying the air-traffic controller of their movements, they had taken the Signals Vanguard pick-up truck to drive out. Nobody expected it would be required later.

THE PRE-FLIGHT checks of the new Sycamore helicopter were complete. Its three-blade rotor had started to turn, slowly at first and then blurring into the shape of a shining disc as it picked up speed. Jim McCorkle and

Master Pilot WO1 Jim McCorkle (extreme right).

his trainee co-pilot Tony Harrison were ready to take off. 'Nicosia Tower, this is Heli Alpha requesting take-off clearance for a training trip to Tymbou,' McCorkle transmitted. The reply that came back shocked him. 'Heli Alpha, this is Nicosia Tower. Reported shooting at Homer building. Investigate immediately. You are cleared to cross the active runway.'

From his home in Canada, McCorkle told the author: 'My co-pilot shot a startled glance at me as I practically stood the Sycamore on its nose in a full-powered transition from a three-foot hover and hurtled our way across the airfield. When we crossed the field boundary, we were skimming the undulating ground at 100 mph.'

'Heli Alpha – three men involved in shooting,' the radio crackled again. 'Last seen running towards gap in peri fence.'

McCorkle scanned the horizon and spotted two figures briefly silhouetted on his starboard side before they dropped behind the crest of a small hill. 'I skidded the chopper around in a shuddering arc and went in hot pursuit,' he says. 'Moments later, the same two figures popped into view again, their running feet throwing up puffs of dust from the arid field. Screeching as low as I dared with my tricycle undercarriage a foot above

the ground, I raced after the fugitives. At the last moment before collision, they threw themselves down. As soon as I passed over them, they were up again running on a different tangent.

'A helicopter can be turned through 180 degrees very quickly, but this time I think we established a world record. A climbing torque turn soon had our heading reversed and down we swooped to harass the runners. Again and again we forced them to drop to the ground, until, completely exhausted, they stayed down.

'I hovered near the two, throwing up clouds of dust and grit from our rotor blades, until they placed their arms behind their heads, signifying surrender. I landed the helicopter just as a ground party of RAF Regiment troops joined us. The Greek youths, their chests still heaving for air, were searched. Their pockets were empty. No weapons. No identification cards. We tied their hands and feet tightly and bundled them unceremoniously into the rear of the helicopter's cabin and flew back immediately to the landing pad closest to the Control Tower. The entire operation from start to finish had lasted just 15 minutes.'

For the first time in history, a helicopter had been used to chase and arrest suspected criminals. But while two had been caught, a third was still on the loose. McCorkle refuelled his Sycamore and took off again to find the missing man. By now the captured men – Koutsoftas and Panaghides – were at the guardroom, awaiting collection by the civil police. They were held by Ray Ingram and another airman, both armed. 'We drove the prisoners in our Land Rover to the rifle range, where we stood them near a wall. Over there, a Turkish Cypriot worker rushed at them, trying to throw punches. Unfortunately, I had to use my rifle butt to push him away,' says Ingram, adding without apology, 'We also used our rifle butts to push the Greeks towards a nearby wall and told them move slowly backwards for about 60 yards, hoping they would attempt to make a run for it, as unknown to them, there was a hidden Bren gun trained on them and we could have cut them down. The men didn't take the bait, unfortunately.'

News of the incident had spread to others at the airport. When Robin Stitchbury returned to his post, he was met by Flight Lieutenant 'Dusty' Miller and his administration assistant, Flight Sergeant Jameson. They were furious and berated him for taking the unit vehicle. 'Where the hell have you been?' one shouted. They pointed out that they had planned to use the Vanguard truck for an inspection visit to the Homer building. Nobody had told them Stitchbury had been given permission by the Tower to go out. There had been a breakdown in communication.

'I was devastated,' said Stitchbury. 'If I had stayed in my workshop, they could have driven to the Homer building and it's likely Paddy Hale would still be alive. I'm sure the terrorists wouldn't have dared to attack a large group of visitors.'

Jim McCorkle and Tony Harrison were back in the air in their Sycamore, flying up and down the search area, methodically checking every square yard of the bleached landscape with its occasional clusters of stunted trees. Here they hovered, there they flew along a dry wadi. 'Our slow crawling flight barely registered on the airspeed indicator, while the cockpit temperature soared,' the pilot recalled. 'The heat was magnified by the cockpit's plastic canopy. Tony and I were soon drenched in perspiration, but that was the least of our problems. An hour had passed, we hadn't spotted any sign of our quarry and our quest seemed hopeless as our fuel-gulping machine drained the 'copter's tanks.'

Suddenly McCorkle glimpsed a flicker of movement in the branches of a tree. There,

crouching in a high fork, was a man. 'Down we plummeted and I slammed the Sycamore onto the ground in a bone jarring landing, with the whirling rotor blades almost cutting into the gnarled trunk of the tree. I jumped out of the cockpit, leaving Tony at the dual controls and dashed to the bottom of the tree, while pulling my side arm from my holster.'

'Come down, you bastard,' McCorkle bellowed at the terrified figure in the tree, 'or I'll blast you.' He hoped the man had heard his shout above the roar of the helicopter's engine. If he had not, he certainly could see the cocked pistol pointed at him. 'Because no terrorist weapons had been found so far, I believed the fugitive could be armed. Yet I had no sense of danger. I was sure I was in control of the situation.'

The young Greek Cypriot removed his white shirt and threw it on the ground and then, bare-chested, struggled through the branches down to the ground. 'What do you want, sir?' he asked. 'I am a bird watcher. That is why I am in the tree.' His excuse was less than convincing, McCorkle thought, and he began to search him. All he found was a box of safety matches – British made. The captive was the youngest of the three killers – 18-year-old Paraskevas Hiropoulis.

Using nylon cord, McCorkle tied Hiropoulis's hands behind his back, placed him aboard the helicopter and sat down next to him while Harrison remained at the controls to fly them back to the airport. Time elapsed between the emergency call from the Homer building to the capture of the final terrorist had been 75 minutes.

IN THE air-conditioned crew room at Nicosia Airport, Harrison and McCorkle began sipping ice-cold bottles of Coke before removing their sweat-soaked flying suits, when a burly civilian entered and identified himself as Detective Inspector Edmond Clive, a member of the UK Police Unit in Cyprus. He had been placed in charge of gathering evidence against the three Greek Cypriots. 'To avoid them getting off in court, we need to find the weapons they used,' he said. 'Would it be possible for you to fly me and my two assistants over the area so that we can find them?'

McCorkle smiled. At least this flight should be less hectic. With the two police assistants sitting at the back of the Sycamore and Inspector Clive in the co-pilot's seat, the helicopter flew over the fields where the first pair of terrorists had hit the ground to escape being hit by the pursuit aircraft. Clive asked to land so that his men could conduct a fingertip search of the ground. Touching down, McCorkle stayed on board and the policemen disembarked to go about their business.

Suddenly one of the officers let out a whoop, pointing at a spot just a foot ahead of the helicopter's front wheel. There, rising from the soil, was the butt of a .38 calibre Smith and Wesson revolver. 'What fantastic luck,' thought McCorkle, as Inspector Clive pushed a pencil through the trigger guard to raise the weapon. He sniffed the barrel. 'Yes,' he said, 'it has been fired recently.'

'Finding the pistol has always struck me as too fortunate and I confess to feeling uneasy about it,' McCorkle admits more than 50 years later. 'At the time I thought, "Now that's amazing. Fancy locating it so quickly" and I suspected that, perhaps, a fix was being planned, but I was so angry about Hale's death that I went along with it and shrugged my shoulders.'

The search continued, but no other weapons were found that day. Nevertheless, Inspector Clive was happy. If ballistic tests proved that the revolver had fired the bullet that killed Corporal Hale, there would be adequate evidence to secure convictions when the case came to court, he concluded. And sure enough, experts agreed that the weapon was the one. Not only had it been used in this murder, it had been used in several other

assassinations after being stolen from a serviceman in an earlier incident.

The next day 300 troops of the Royal Warwicks, the South Staffords and the RAF Regiment uncovered a further 40 weapons during their area search.

Following Hale's murder, a number of RAF personnel vented their anger on the Airport's Greek Cypriots workers, who arrived every morning at the main gate to be searched by the guards. Art Melton of 70 Squadron was one of them. 'I was on duty when we were ordered to cut in half all melons brought by the workers for their lunch. The authorities suspected bombs were being smuggled into the camp, hidden inside the fruit. To do the job, we were each issued with a large carving knife. When the 500 workers came forward, there was a lot of melons to cut. I hated the job, because we smashed the fruit on the ground at the end of our search. Apart from the mess, it was the waste I found deplorable and the loss of goodwill from the locals.'

Three days later, Robin Stitchbury was ordered to clean the Homer building. 'I felt salt was being rubbed into my wounds,' he told the author. He still felt partly responsible for Hale's death. 'While I was there, I found three used shell cases. One of them was badly torn, probably because the revolver jammed, which could explain why the terrorists broke off their attack,' he suggests. Stitchbury became a police officer after completing his RAF service.

AT NICOSIA Special Assizes in June, giving evidence in front of Mr Justice Shaw, Inspector Clive reported how the first revolver was found and that the next day two others had been recovered in the area near the Homer building. Of these, he said, one contained six empty cases and there were five in the other. Senior Superintendent F. W. Bird, who took charge of the weapons and spent ammunition, confirmed that ballistics tests conclusively showed the fatal shot had been fired by the first revolver collected by Clive. The bullets found embedded in the building came from the others. Another witness said he had examined the glass from which the killers had drunk water and found a fingerprint that matched Panaghides's right thumb.

On 18 June, despite a vigourous defence put up by their lawyers – Glafcos Clerides (a secret member of EOKA), Michael Triantafillides, Them. Fanos and Reno Lyssiotis – Mr Justice Shaw found the three defendants guilty of the murder of RAF Corporal Patrick Hale. The judge said: 'The circumstances of the killing show that the murder was cold blooded and carefully planned. I am satisfied that you three reconnoitered the position to make sure that the two airmen were unarmed … You killed Hale when you received kindness from him – he had just shared his drinking water with you … Yours is an act which must be condemned by all right thinking people.'

He sentenced Michael Koutsoftas and Andreas Panaghides to death by hanging. Addressing Paraskevas Hiropoulis, Mr Justice Shaw said: 'You are younger and I think you have acted under their influence and therefore I shall be more merciful to you.' He committed the 18-year-old to life imprisonment. As the three were led away, they sang the Greek National Anthem. All had pleaded 'Not Guilty'.

MICHAEL DAVIDSON sharpened his pencil to report what he saw and heard for the *Times of Cyprus*. He had been the foreign correspondent of the London *Observer* before he was found to be 'over-fond of young men'. Despite his personal proclivities, he wrote fine 'colour' pieces for his employer, Charles Foley. That day he reported: 'I suppose that all the horror, all the suffering and degradation that murder and its consequences can bring was present outside the Nicosia Special Court in those few minutes shortly after six o'clock when it was learned by the waiting crowd that two young men had been sentenced to death for shooting Corporal Hale and a third to life imprisonment.

'I suppose the extremes of love and hate could be felt in those minutes – and the hysteria which their uncontrolled expression means. It was not a big crowd: perhaps 50 all told, with women and men about equal. There were babies in arms too … But the signal for the climactic gush of emotion did not come until three condemned men were led out of court surrounded by police and troops, to be taken to the Central Prison …

'The women screamed and swayed and spread their arms in gestures of crucifixion, the men cheered and hoorayed and clapped their hands as if welcoming the greatest heroes of the age … Tough men came away with tears running down their cheeks. Mere lads, faces pale and drawn, looked with detestation at any British they saw … Young British soldiers by the dozen escorted the prisoners out, youngsters who looked embarrassed by this spectacle of such naked anguish.

'Of course, there was one grief that was not represented in this tormented scene: the grief of the family of Corporal Hale.'

The same day Second-Lieutenant Michael Edmund Buckley, of the Royal Norfolk Regiment, the officer who removed a time bomb from the bed of Sir John Harding, Governor of Cyprus, was made a Member of the Order of the British Empire.

Neither Jim McCorkle nor Tony Harrison were called to give evidence at the men's trial. The author argues that this was probably because their testimony might have contradicted the case by the government's prosecutor, who produced witnesses that either were not present when the accused were captured or gave a version of events which was entirely different from the two helicopter pilots' eyewitness accounts.

One official reason given for not bringing McCorkle to court was because, it was claimed, he had become a marked man for EOKA vengeance. There is a hint of truth in this. Some days after the terrorists' capture, McCorkle caught his regular civilian bus for the airport. En route the bus developed a flat tyre. Rather than waiting and arriving late for work, he got off and hitched a ride from a passing driver. During the tyre change, a bomb was found aboard and was defused without anyone getting hurt.

After the bomb incident, McCorkle was sent to the Isle of Man for officer training. His wife and daughter left with him. He was never posted back to the Island.

EOKA also tried to assassinate Mr Justice Shaw, the senior special judge on the Island. On 25 June, two terrorists seriously wounded him with shots to his neck and head, while his car was held up in traffic in Nicosia. His bodyguard returned fire as the gunmen raced down a side street, where a car waited for their escape. Mr Justice Shaw was saved by a blood transfusion and was soon back at work. Since his arrival the previous November, he had passed six death sentences.

After Governor Harding had rejected last-minute pleas for clemency, Michael Koutsoftas and Andreas Panaghides were hanged with Stelios Mavrommatis, another EOKA killer, on 21 September. Fearing a demonstration, British troops had set up road-blocks on roads to the Central Prison, a low-walled, yellow sandstone building behind a small forest of dusty eucalyptus trees. Inside 170 prisoners shouted 'EOKA! EOKA!' in unison and slammed wooden stools against the bars of their cells.

Earlier Koutsoftas nearly escaped the hangman's noose because Dhigenis had ordered Nicos Sampson to rescue him from a Nicosia hospital where he had been taken for a minor illness. Accompanied by four armed members of his gang, Sampson, the part-time photographer and full-time psychopath, rushed into the building, ordered police guards to release their manacled prisoner and raced him to their waiting car. They sped off at high speed until they arrived at a small village outside the capital. Only then did Sampson discover he had 'kidnapped' the wrong man. Instead of Koutsoftas, he had grabbed Argyros Karadymas, a Greek national, who had been imprisoned for trying to smuggle weapons for EOKA on board the caique St George in January 1955. Karadymas went to join a terrorist gang in the Troodos Mountains.

Some unpleasant facts emerged after the trial that made junior ranks wonder if Hale would have died had the Officer Commanding the local unit of the RAF Regiment provided the armed guards requested by Wing Commander (Flying) for the Homer building. Instead the OC had replied that it was not his responsibility and if guards were needed, the RAF should produce them from its ranks. And they were. 'RAF clerks were given the guard duties. And the Homer teams drew Sten guns from the station armoury before they went on duty. At night, dogs and their handlers patrolled the area,' says Victor Freeman, Hale's working colleague and friend. 'To relieve the boredom of guard duty, I would sit at night and totally strip the gun down to the smallest component, even taking all 28 rounds out of the magazine. Then I would reassemble it. I did this often, sometimes two or three times during a shift. As I was on my own outside the airfield perimeter, it was probably a foolhardy pastime.'

The Homer building continued its vital tasks at the edge of the airport until the British left. The duty staff still offered water, but to only one man: the Greek Cypriot shepherd Yiakoumis Poullou, who was always there, dead cigarette in his mouth, with his dog, a large ram that had a bell fastened to his collar and of course, his sheep, which never appeared to stray. His black bag only carried his daily meal of some crusty bread and a bottle of *Keo* beer.

Andreas Panaghides, the hanged gunman, had a young wife, and Koutsoftas left behind a wife and three infant children. Mrs Patrick Hale, back in England in May 1956, was left caring for her six-month-old daughter, with another baby on the way. Paraskevas Hiropoulis was freed from imprisonment on orders of Archbishop Makarios as soon as Cyprus gained its independence from the British.

CHAPTER TWELVE

Grivas escapes:
the tragedy of *Lucky Alphonse*

'All place shall be hell that is not heaven.'
Christopher Marlowe

IT TOOK only a spark to cause the deaths of more British soldiers in a single day during Operation *Lucky Alphonse* than in any other action conducted in the four-year-long EOKA conflict in Cyprus. The men were killed not by terrorists, but by a fire that swept through the Paphos Forest at the speed of an express train. Even today the number of fatalities remains disputed and mystery surrounds the exact cause of the conflagration. But despite its disastrous finale, the operation virtually destroyed the terrorist gangs in the Troodos Mountains and could be considered by the 20,000 troops as a victory against Colonel George Grivas, the diminutive mastermind behind the Greek Cypriot campaign. Grivas himself barely escaped capture and was forced to hide in a small house in Limassol for almost the whole of the remainder of the 'war'.

Operation *Pepperpot* preceded *Lucky Alphonse*. Launched in May, it involved more than 2,000 troops. Until then, successes against EOKA had not seriously disrupted the organization's infrastructure. Sandy Cavenagh, a Parachute Regiment officer, analysed the British campaign and concluded: 'The pursuit of EOKA by the security forces resembled a display of shadowboxing. Most of the British hammer blows landed on air, as their targets vanished into the forests, the farms, or the dark, twisting alleyways of the towns. For the essential element of surprise was usually denied them.

'Great cordon-and-search operations, involving thousands of troops and great movements of trucks, inevitably sent out vibrations, which were picked up by the sensitive antennae of EOKA, and messages of warning could often be sent off ahead of the darkened convoys twisting through the night. It was the extreme efficiency with which EOKA had permeated every organization on the island, which made this possible. Postmen, telephone operators, contractors, foresters, policemen, all passed on what was required of them in the way of information.'

Directed by Brigadier George Baker, the Governor's Chief of Staff, Operation *Pepperpot* was centered on the Kyyko Monastery, which became a temporary Army headquarters, Kambos village and the surrounding area where Grivas was thought to be hiding. For three weeks, troops, in combination with Royal Marine Commandos, civil police, RAF helicopters and Royal Navy patrol craft to cut off escape routes at sea, scoured the steeply wooded and rugged countryside along the Island's north-west coast, extending 20 miles inland, from Polis to Karovastasi. But Charles Foley, the *Times of Cyprus* editor, maintained that 'The Leader' was kept informed of their movements by priests from the monastery carrying messages to couriers in the capital, who passed them on. Heading the communications network was Archimandrite Lefkosiatis of the Nicosia seminary, who came and went through security cordons, pleading priestly duties.

Troops familiar with the area were deployed on the ground, especially in the area known as the Black Chasms – *Mavron Kremas*. They included men from Royal Horse Guards, Royal Marines of 40 and 45 Commando, infantrymen of the King's Own Yorkshire Light Infantry and the Gordon Highlanders, who were joined by the 1st and 3rd Battalions, the Parachute Regiment, who moved quickly at night, towards the terrorists on the run. Faced with these odds, Grivas was forced to split his gangs into smaller groups to escape in different directions by forced marches at night.

As the Security Forces raced after the gangs, they uncovered their rapidly vacated 'hides'. They were carefully constructed in caves that had boarded sides, timbered floors and corrugated iron roofs, and were well camouflaged deep in the hillsides. They were full of canned food, blankets, clothing, and camp equipment. In their hurry to leave, the terrorists had also left behind large quantities of weapons, ammunition, and grenades, including 41 shotguns, a few light machine-guns, revolvers, 31 bombs, a mass of secret documents, dynamite and gelignite, cartridge-filling machines, pellets, and gunpowder.

With greater efficiency and effectiveness than in the past, by using the terrorists' own tactics against them, the troops were hitting back, capturing many of the Colonel's most trusted associates and uncovering arms dumps. Almost daily the EOKA leader received information that his men were being killed or captured. Some of them, faced with long prison terms or, worse, execution, eagerly became informers.

During their sweep of the mountains,

A hooded informer leads the way to an EOKA hide.

Major J. B. Dye of the Royal Norfolks on the move in the Troodos.

British soldiers were often surprised that contrary to the image projected by EOKA in its propaganda, the terrrorists' bravado vanished the moment they raised their hands in surrender. They wanted nothing more than to please their captors and were enthusiastic to point out other activists, whether they were hiding in the hills or seeking shelter in nearby villages. The 'finger-pointers', as they became known, only asked that they should be hooded when performing their Judas role. In return for their treachery, a few were rewarded financially and sent abroad with new identities.

Faced by a small patrol of the 1st Battalion, The Parachute Regiment on 18 May, a heavily armed group of terrorists dropped their weapons and were captured without a fight. Two were 'hard core' members of EOKA with rewards on their heads. The next night, another man, armed with a Bren gun and five grenades, surrendered. More suspects were arrested in nearby villagers as a result of information supplied by the captives.

Fearing he would be captured, Grivas sent for Antonis Georghiades, one of his most trusted gang leaders and a native of Milikouri, to help him find a safe escape route. Georghiades duly did as he was bid, which Grivas recorded in his diary:

> 27 May 1956: At about 01.00 two couriers arrived with Benakis. When I got up I met him in the new area of our hideout (high up between the road Milikouri to Vassa and Kykko to Panayia). The question of our link to Nicosia and with the food suppliers was solved ... At about 19.00 we left for the new hideout approximately one mile SW of height 4,014 ... After a tiresome and extremely dangerous march we arrived at about 11.15 next day ...

In their escape through the mountains at night, Georghiades tripped and fell more than 20 feet, his backpack saving him from severe injury, but breaking their radio receiver. A little distance along a slippery path, 'The Leader' slipped down a precipice. He survived only because he grasped a bush before he reached the bottom. Foley, who helped Grivas write his *Memoirs*, claimed: 'For a week they camped on a mountaintop in an area called Dipli, while the main thrust of *Pepperpot* spent itself in unprofitable searches. The radio was repaired and they heard official communiqués broadcast by state radio.'

Towards the end of Operation *Pepperpot* the troops were exhausted. They had barely rested for 11 days. 'We were exceptionally well-trained,' John Williams, then a young private soldier, told author Charles Allen for his book, *The Savage Wars of Peace*. 'We were very, very fit and we were led by some very good soldiers. We had rehearsed and trained until we were a well-oiled machine, but we spent nearly all our time in the Troodos Mountains chasing the shadows ... One became more and more frustrated because while we were doing these massive sweeps in the mountains, back in the towns the terrorist was sneaking in and planting his bomb, shooting policemen in the back and making life thoroughly miserable, not caring who his victims were – man, woman or child, policeman or soldier – so long as he got a victim and captured the headlines and gained some publicity for the EOKA cause. I remember feeling so frustrated about it all.' But officers could not conceal their admiration of their men, telling the media that they were first-class soldiers, both in physical toughness and skill in patrolling in the heat in a rugged terrain.

Announcing the results of the operation, an official claimed that 17 'hard core' terrorists, including two on the £5,000 reward list, were being held prisoner. With their capture, and the need to interrogate them thoroughly, commanders closed *Pepperpot* on 28 May to study the information that was pouring in.

BY EARLY June, the authorities were even more confident of finding Grivas in his mountain lair and hoped to bring the conflict to an early end. Field Marshal Sir John Harding, the Governor of Cyprus, now ordered Brigadier 'Tubby' Butler of 16 Independent Parachute Brigade to plan and take tactical command of the largest military operation ever mounted in Cyprus. Called

Operation *Lucky Alphonse*, it began on 8 June and would continue until the 23rd. As events would show, the operation's name was ill chosen.

The plan adopted was to cover a wide area with small parties of men working independently, both on the move and setting up well-concealed ambushes. The 2,000 troops engaged were under the command of Lieutenant Colonel Norman Tailyour, of 45 Commando Royal Marines.

As the troops prepared, they heard the news of how EOKA had tried to murder 18-year-old Roy Garrett, the civilian son of a soldier, on 3 June, when he and two army friends left a camp in Famagusta for a swim. The group was ambushed and Private George Isbell, 19, was killed. The second soldier managed to escape, but young Garrett was captured. The terrorists tied his hands behind him, spun him around until he became dizzy, then shot him at close range in the back. He dropped to the ground and feigned death. When the EOKA men left, he cried out for help. Four Greek Cypriots – a shepherd and three youths – passed him by, all ignoring his plea. By some super-human effort, Garrett crawled eventually to a nearby church, where he was found and taken to hospital.

(The following September, the Security Forces felt they had caught the EOKA youth who had shot Garrett. He was Antonis Vrahimis, the same age as the badly injured lad. Although identified as the person who shot him, the judge suggested that Garrett's eyewitness evidence was insufficient, as he was not wearing his glasses at the time of the incident. Furthermore, the firearms found at the site were free of fingerprints and, therefore, could not be connected to the accused. Told to face the judge, the shepherd who failed to offer help was roundly condemned for his lack of humanity. He left the court and hanged himself. Vrahimis was acquitted, but was re-arrested on other charges.)

On 6 June, two days before the start date of *Lucky Alphonse*, an official report revealed that since the start of the EOKA conflict on 1 April 1955, 98 people, 40 of them Britons, including 35 servicemen, had been murdered by order of Dighenis. Fifteen Cypriots were killed by troops, and six Cypriots died in communal clashes. Four terrorists were killed by their own bombs and two were hanged. During this period, 666 people were injured, including 319 Britons – 290 of them servicemen, 42 Cypriot policemen, and 305 Cypriot civilians.

That same day the name of Thomas Mylrea was added to the list of the dead – the fifth British civilian victim. An English schoolteacher who had arrived in Cyprus two years earlier, he was shot dead in Limassol by an unknown gunman. He fired a shot from his revolver in return, but missed his assassin. A taxi driver drove Mylrea to hospital, but he was dead on arrival. He was married with a child.

OPERATION *Lucky Alphonse* began on schedule, shortly after midnight on 8 June. Summer had come early to Cyprus and the temperature was already hitting the high 80s and the forest areas were tinder dry. At 02.00, Grivas woke to hear a tracker dog barking near his hide. He and his men packed rapidly and marched to a nearby hill from where, at dawn, they saw four two-ton army lorries carrying soldiers up the Milikouri Road. With them were two EOKA informers – code-named 'Botsaris' and 'Bouboulis' – pointing the way. The Colonel's only thought now was to find a way out of the cordon for himself and his men, but where were they to go? Whichever direction they chose to run, they saw more British soldiers or heard their movements. Nevertheless, somehow, they continued to evade their enemy by long marches, zigzagging their way along rough tracks and occasionally crossing roads at night.

'For the troops engaged in seeking out the terrorists, life was hard,' a British Army officer recalls. 'Patrolling such country demanded huge resources of strength and determination while operating cordons or stop positions required immense concentration, especially when units were committed for several days running.' The work was painstaking and laborious. Every re-entrant was searched, every patch of scrub examined. Bren gun positions were set up to fire on fixed lines on every potential escape route so that they could be used at night. The chase was fast and deliberate.

The terrorists were being tracked by the Parachute Regiment in the lead, the Royal Marines and the Gordon Highlanders, all stationed in the Troodos area, supported by the King's Own Yorkshire Light Infantry, the South Staffordshire Regiment, the Royal Norfolk Regiment, the Royal Horse Guards, the RAF Regiment and a small landing party from HMS *Diamond*, which was on anti-smuggling patrol in the waters off Cyprus. They were joined later by 'C' Company of the 1st Battalion, the Highland Light Infantry.

The plan was to swamp the central Troodos region with overwhelming numbers of troops and encircle the area where Grivas was suspected of hiding, moving forward slowly but surely to tighten the noose. The aim was to cut off the terrorists from their village supporters and their escape routes by sea. But it was easier said than done, as an officer of the Royal Norfolk Regiment recalled: 'It was ideal country from a guerrilla's point of view not just to hide, but also to ambush vehicles and foot patrols. The area was thickly wooded and the mountain slopes fell away steeply, with many sheer drops among the rocky outcrops. It provided Grivas with opportunities to hide away in re-entrants, thick with scrub. The terrorists could almost have withstood an indefinite siege, even if located. Water was always avail-able and villagers, whether they liked it or not, would provide them with food.'

Nevertheless in their rush to collect rations, the terrorists sometimes fell into traps set by British forces. During *Lucky Alphonse* a small team of camouflaged Royal Marine Commandos waited patiently one evening above a small mountain village watching the inhabitants through their binoculars. A woman came out and began walking towards a clump of pine trees, where she dropped her heavy load and returned from whence she came. With Sten guns at the ready, the troops moved silently and swiftly towards the spot in time to ambush and arrest a group of terrorists who had arrived to collect their supplies.

With the start of *Lucky Alphonse*, Royal Navy and Army demolition experts began planning a joint underwater operation to eliminate one of the sources of explosives used by Grivas's men. Their task was to remove and destroy a large supply of United States ammunition dumped into the sea about half a mile from Famagusta's old harbour at the end of the Second World War. At the time, experts thought the water was far deeper than its actual depth of 40 feet and the ammunition would never be valuable again. They had not counted on the skills of Cypriot fisherman, who used small amounts of dynamite to blast fish to the surface. Rather than spend their profits on buying explosive charges – and to avoid the security restrictions on possession of these products – it was far easier to salvage unexploded shells and extract the explosive substances.

'The fishermen learned how to handle explosives the hard way,' Joseph Haff of the *New York Times* told his readers. 'In almost every Cypriot coastal village today there are a dozen or more fishermen with missing fingers, hands or even arms, the result of making fuses too short.'

Although civil authorities prohibited the use of explosives by fishermen, boat owners reckoned it was worth paying a fine of £5 when one well-placed dynamite stick could result in a 'catch' worth £100. They also found a ready-made market in EOKA for the surplus charges.

Inland, the Parachute Regiment entered the mountainous operational area around Kykko Monastery from the direction of Nicosia, while 40 Commando Royal Marines moved up the narrow, winding roads from their base in three-ton Bedford trucks. 'Leading the convoy was a young subaltern in an Austin Champ, with a sergeant and two Marines,' Brian Tarpey said. 'Suddenly we all had to stop. Ahead of us was a bridge with a large hole in the middle caused by an EOKA bomb explosion. The Champ was able to cross relatively easily, its wheels balanced on the remains of the structure. But would the damaged bridge carry the weight of our Bedfords? There was only one thing to do. See what happened.

'Carrying our equipment, we all got off the vehicles. Then a Marine went ahead, and waving his hands, carefully guided the first truck, inch by inch, to ensure its wheels remained aligned correctly on either side of the hole until the danger was over. Vehicle after vehicle followed the same procedure and all crossed safely, allowing us to embark again.'

By the time the Marines left the bridge about 15 minutes later, the Champ had raced far ahead, its young officer eager to find out where his troops were to be deployed. The trailing convoy continued its way along a series of hairpin bends, until it rounded the final curve. There they saw the Champ lying upside down against the cliff face. 'The terrorists had planted a mine in the centre of the road on the blind side of the curve and detonated it when the lone Champ passed over, expecting the blast to throw the vehicle into the valley 600 feet below,' explained Tarpey. 'The force of the explosion, however, went in

the wrong direction and the passengers became trapped underneath. It was fortunate for them because the Champ's body acted as protection when the terrorists started shooting from across the valley.'

By now Grivas was running out of places to hide, but he still hoped to find a way out of the mountains and reach a 'safe house' in either Limassol or Larnaca by using a series of hides along the way. To relieve the pressure on him, he sent messengers to his town groups ordering them to create diversionary riots. He hoped many of the advancing troops would have to be withdrawn to deal with these, but to no avail. The messengers had difficulty getting through the cordons and of those that did, many chose not to return.

On 10 June, after a march lasting 17 hours, exhausted and short of supplies, the 58-year-old 'Leader' and his men reached a wooded valley where they decided to fill their water bottles and rest for a few hours in the shade of the trees. During the night they had narrowly escaped death when a patrol, consisting of a corporal and four soldiers, spotted the group 100 yards away on a mountain track. Instead of trailing the terrorists, the soldiers chose to get ahead and set an ambush. They slithered their way down a cliff and reached a deserted wayside chapel in the valley and waited. As soon as Grivas and his men came within range, the soldiers opened fire. The terrorists rushed back into the forest, but the soldiers lost them in the darkness.

For the first time in days Grivas and his gang believed they could relax, but during the afternoon of the next day, Sergeant Jim McCorkle was returning to Nicosia Airport after a routine flight over the mountains in his Sycamore helicopter and spotted Grivas sitting at the edge of a small stream 'with his breeches off, and his legs deep in the water'.

'I was flying low and slow. He looked up, startled and it was easy to see his face clearly,' said McCorkle. 'He then scrambled to his feet, grabbed his riding breeches, and darted under cover of the trees. I immediately climbed higher and made a transmission informing base that I had seen the Number 1 enemy and gave the location.'

Soon afterwards, a patrol from 'C' Company, 3 Para, was directed to the location, approaching through the riverbed with a tracker dog from No. 6 Army Guard Dog Unit, based at Lakatamia, near Nicosia. Grivas said later in his *Memoirs* that he suspected there were British troops nearby, because he had seen fresh footprints and an empty English cigarette pack. If this were true, it leaves open the question of why he went forward in the first place and did not set up a counter ambush. He does not mention the helicopter that over flew him while he was naked in the water.

At about 16.00 the patrol reached the EOKA gang again and there was a brief exchange of fire, but the terrorists broke off the encounter. Grivas and five of his men fled into the woods without their personal belongings, including three automatic weapons and a pair of boots. They also left behind Grivas's glasses, binoculars, a Sam Browne belt, beret and his meticulously kept diary, made up to 9 June, which would prove to be immensely valuable to the intelligence services. Captured terrorists later affirmed that some of the clothing and other articles belonged to Grivas himself, including his shaving kit. There was also a photograph of 'The Leader', wearing a beret.

A young Para officer, Lt M. Swann, added: 'We also found several photos of groups of terrorists. They were particularly flamboyant when it came to photographs of each other and the Security Forces often came across them and even rolls of undeveloped film. Their thoughtlessness provided the intelligence community with clear, useful pictures of many known "players". We enlarged their pictures and sent them to every unit to act as aids in "suspect recognition". Big crosses were drawn across a man's face when he was caught or killed.'

Because he was bald and self-conscious about his height – he barely stood 5 ft 3 inches – Grivas insisted on approving all his photographs. Only those taken from a low angle to make him appear tall were allowed for publication. The pictures also needed to show him wearing a beret and a combat uniform, every inch an underground fighter. In reality, he could easily pass as a typical Cypriot peasant. He did not smoke or drink and suffered from haemorrhoids and bad teeth. Yet there was no denying his strength and stamina. Sir Hugh Foot, the last Governor of Cyprus, described him as a 'little man who looks like a cross between Groucho Marx and Adolph Hitler'.

According to Para Wally Dinsdale: 'The terrorists' kit was spread out in a circle, as if they had just held a meeting.' One of the captured documents was a letter signed by '*Asklypius*' and dated 22 May. The English translation read: 'It is with a great degree of emotion that I write to inform you that they have found all the hideouts. They had a traitor whom they took by helicopter and he pointed out all the hideouts ... They arrested BOTSARIS and one other at Kambos ... They came to capture me four times, but never found me ... It is possible they will come to where you are.

'They have arrested both our chauffeurs, also our cook and two monks. We are in very grave danger. Be careful of all roads – they control them. Do not make use of any roads ... At this very moment there are soldiers outside – only the Virgin Mary will save us.'

Botsaris was Andreas Polyviou, a member of the Markos Drakos gang, while the letter writer, *Asklypius*, was Savvas Aloneftis from Alona village. His greatest claim to fame was to be one of the terrorists seen in the posed photographs of Grivas taken near Kykko Monastery.

The Paras with their haul of captured EOKA arms and ammunition.

The authorities, keen to show the Security Forces were hot on the heels of the mountain gangs or *andartes*, assembled the press in Nicosia, handed out copies of the captured photographs that showed EOKA men posing in forest glades with their weapons, and allowed the journalists to interview some of the Paras who had nearly captured Grivas.

The Grivas diary, published later, gave an insight into the leader's mind. Its content revealed that, despite his ruthlessness, he was a fanatically religious man, obsessed by detail and discipline. One entry showed he had authorized a 10-year-old boy to buy a new bicycle for losing his while running an errand for EOKA. He had also agreed payment of about £5 to another gang member for the expenses incurred from executing a 'traitor'. More importantly, his record of day-to-day activities gave away many of EOKA's biggest secrets and proved conclusively that Archbishop Makarios was more than the organization's spiritual head.

In the 1960s, Grivas recalled: 'There was no attempt to pursue us or to make a thorough search of the immediate area, although several helicopters flew off in the direction of Nicosia – presumably to inform Harding of the incident. So we waited motionless and silent among the trees for two hours, wondering at the majestic clumsiness of the enemy ... A British soldier was posted as a

Captain J. G. Jones, MBE, of the Royal Norfolk Regiment, with a captured EOKA flag.

sentry, almost within touching distance of the tree I was standing behind.'

Two days after Grivas' narrow escape from the Paras, the Norfolks captured seven terrorists from his Paphos group. Two had £5,000 rewards on their heads. The men quickly revealed a hidden arms-dump containing a Bren gun, three shotguns, two rifles and two sub-machine guns. But for every success for the troops, there was a tragedy.

ON 10 JUNE British forces suffered their first fatalities during *Lucky Alphonse*. Private Edward Brooks, Private Ivan Gurr and Private Alan Millington, all from the Parachute Regiment, were killed, and seven injured, when their vehicle overturned on a mountain road near Pedoulas. WO2 J. Forster of 1 Para was the fourth fatality, a victim of a 'friendly fire' incident. He had strayed across the boundary line between his Para battalion and the Royal Norfolks. In the dense Paphos forest, a soldier had sensed movement ahead and fired. There would be more such incidents in the days and weeks ahead.

Another seven terrorists two days later handed themselves to 40 Commando Royal Marines. They had showed no resistance. Corporal Robert Benbow, 19, a National Serviceman, explained that his group encountered them unexpectedly and they 'surrendered at once'.

In London, on the 12th, the Government announced the casualty figures recently published in their official report. As the figures were revealed, Corporal W. R. Holden of the Royal Leicestershire Regiment was dying from a revolver shot fired at him while he attended a Greek cinema, which had been declared 'Out of Bounds'.

The next day – the 13th – the last British troops left Egypt 'quietly and with dignity', according to a British Army spokesman. 'We have done everything we promised to do.' In fact, it was five days before the ending of the

20-month period laid down in the Anglo-Egyptian agreement signed in 1954. The withdrawal party , which sailed from Port Said in the transport *Evan Gibb*, consisted of 11 officers and 68 other ranks under the command of Brigadier J. A. S. Lucey, ending a military link with Egypt that had existed unbroken since 1882. At Navy House, crowds cheered loudly when the Egyptian flag was hoisted 80 minutes after the troops left. From now on, all Britain's Middle East Land Forces would be concentrated in Cyprus.

On 14 June, the second 'friendly fire' incident of Operation *Lucky Alphonse* took place. A 3 Para patrol this time opened fire at an approaching unidentified group. 'We were given orders to "shoot to kill" if anyone crossed a certain point when we were "flushing out",' former Para private William Bell recalled to the author. 'It was a map reading error.' In addition, the troops had not been told that a stop-group from the Norfolks was operating in their vicinity. In the encounter, Lance Corporal David Elliot of Support Company was fatally injured.

Sandy Cavenagh presented a different version of events. 'Press reporters and photographers joined the searchers. The incipient capture of Grivas was big news. In the early dawn a photographer and reporter from the *Daily Telegraph* accompanied one of the 3 Para Company Commanders as he visited his outposts. Suddenly the reporter pointed out a figure crawling off through the forest, wrapped in a blanket. None of our troops were in the area and it must be a terrorist.

'The Company Commander fired one shot with his Sten gun, a notoriously inaccurate weapon. The crawling figure dropped dead. They ran up and were appalled to find the flashes of the Norfolk regiment on the body beneath the blanket. It transpired that the Norfolk soldier, delirious with fever, had left his position and was walking aimlessly around in the forest. During a cordon-and-search you could not afford to walk aimlessly, anywhere.'

Meanwhile, Grivas had split his men into two groups, each searching for a safe resting place. For two days, with Georghiades and Nikitas, he rested outside Kaminaria village. On the evening of 12 June, the latter two approached the village again to acquire food supplies for the next lap of their journey, but British soldiers spotted them. They managed to escape unharmed and re-join Grivas. Together they set off for Trooditissa, five miles away. Hungry and tired, it took them the whole night and most of the morning of the following day to reach their destination, where they were fed by the abbot of the monastery.

That night they slipped across the Troodos–Platres road and reached the southern slopes of the Troodos. After a short rest, they moved again under cover of darkness for Saitta. Waiting for them there was Hadjimiltis, the EOKA leader for Limassol district. He assured them they would be safe in the seaport, but he would have to make arrangements and these would not be completed until 18 June. They should head slowly towards Yerasa via Agios Mamas, where they could rest again. In Yerasa, another EOKA contact would drive them to Limassol.

As the gang made their way, they avoided walking on roads and stayed in the open countryside, parallel to the routes used by Army traffic. However, some soldiers turned off the main road in search of a water point and almost literally bumped into their nemesis. Grivas decided to bluff his way out of trouble. He saluted the soldiers and walked by them with his men, all playing the role of peasants. They were waved on their way.

When the soldiers rejoined their main body, they mentioned the friendliness of the locals. Hearing this, an officer questioned them carefully and came to the conclusion his men had let Grivas go free. Immediately the troops were ordered to focus their search in the direction the terrorists had gone. At this point, Grivas decided to disband the mountain men.

In her account *The Cyprus Revolt*, Nancy Crawshaw wrote that these gangs had served their purpose and 'bestowed upon the revolt the aura of "resistance" and conjured up in the Greek Cypriot mind the heroic epic of the Greek war of independence in a way in which urban terrorism, more generally associated with gangsters and common crime, could never have done'.

More likely Grivas knew that the British had broken the back of his Troodos network and wanted his surviving members to go elsewhere to continue his campaign. After all, the British were hard on his heels. To divert attention from the mountain gangs, EOKA's assassination squad acted on its own initiative and hurled two bombs into *Little Soho*, a popular Hungarian restaurant in Nicosia. It was a serious tactical mistake because, when the bombs exploded, three US State Department employees were seriously injured and a fourth killed. He was William Boeteler, the young CIA station chief, EOKA's first American victim. The others worked at the secret US telecommunications centre just outside the capital at Yerolakkos, one of several Anglo-American signals intelligence-gathering sites in Cyprus.

In his last letter home, Boeteler had written: 'Most every night EOKA drops a bomb on the front porch of some Englishman's home, making a big noise and not much else. Through it all, the British cling grimly to their social traditions; the Queen's birthday was celebrated the other night in all due pomp and splendor, in as heavily guarded a location as you could imagine. The invitations for the affair carried a little note requesting everyone to check their personal weapons at the door. So far, as an American, I'm a man nobody hates, which can't be said by anybody else – except other Americans.'

Troops from the Royal Warwickshire's Luna Park platoon were 200 yards away when they heard the blast and arrived on the scene almost immediately. By a remarkable coincidence, the regiment's Major Fraymouth was with a Forces Broadcasting Service reporter recording a feature called *Night Patrol*.

For Grivas, this was another blow as Greece was trying hard to get the United States to support his campaign for *enosis* or, as EOKA's propaganda put it, 'self-determination'. In Makarios's absence, the acting Ethnarch, the Bishop of Kitium, was to apologize. He issued a statement expressing 'the deepest pain of the Greek Cypriot people at the death of a member of a friendly allied nation, who was an unfortunate victim of the tragedy', which the Greek Cypriot people had always been trying, and were still trying, to end.

A few days later, Grivas managed to distribute another of his pamphlets. He called the incident 'a tragic mistake' and continued: 'On Saturday the American Vice-Consul was killed as a result of a bomb explosion, and other American citizens were injured. We know very well that British propaganda is trying to exploit this sad incident, maintaining that the attack was premeditated. We state categorically that it was a tragic mistake. No Greek bears hatred for the American people, whose liberal feelings must, we feel sure, place the majority of them on our side in the righteous struggle. We are deeply grieved at the death of the American diplomat. We advise foreigners living in Cyprus, for their own safety, not to frequent English places of entertainment, since it is not always possible to distinguish them from the English enemies. – EOKA, The Leader, Dighenis.'

FATE THEN intervened to allow Grivas to break out from the British Army cordon. The very day Boeteler was murdered, a fire started in the forest. The blaze spread and continued through the next day, when a strong wind

The start of the fire in the Paphos forest.

blew up and fanned the flames through valleys and up the mountainsides at alarming speed. Eyewitnesses reported that the fire travelled at 30 mph. 'It was impossible for men to out-run the fire,' said Tarpey. Former Para Bryan Hunter, although watching from a safe distance, adds: 'The noise of the fire was like a Concorde in flight. Trees exploded like shells as their sap expanded in the heat.' The Army immediately blamed EOKA for starting the fire and EOKA blamed the Army. 'Only two things were certain,' comments the historian of the Gordon Highlanders, 'Grivas escaped and the Gordons mourned their 13 dead.'

Elenitsa Seraphim, EOKA's female area commander, provided the terrorists' point of view in her published account of the conflict. She insisted, 'The fire was started deliberately by the British who were hoping to capture Dighenis and his men. The fire grew stronger as it advanced threateningly in the direction of Kykko and it went on raging the next day. Gales hampered the attempts of the men from the Forestry Department and the surrounding areas to extinguish the blaze and the situation began to look hopeless. Our concern for Dighenis and the groups in the area was growing by the minute when suddenly, as if a divine hand wanted to stir up trouble, the wind changed direction and turned the flames towards the British soldiers. Now trapped by the raging fire they rushed frantically to escape, only to fall prey to the flames more quickly. Their vehicles were surrounded and turned into blazing brands.'

With his trusted tracker dog 'Libra' at his side, Jim Head saw the fire start. He was an RASVC corporal attached to Z Troop, 45 Commando, whose OC was Major Halliday. They were usually based at Troodos, but had been moved to Platres. They had been ordered to patrol an area close to the Paphos Forest. He said: 'On Saturday, 16 June 1956, the Royal Marines started what was called "prophylactic" firing of their 2- and 3-inch mortars, aimed at the horizon. They blasted away, then moved on to find another to hit. They began firing at 09.03 and continued until 10.23. Lt Thompson, RM, took our patrol forward to find anyone who might have been "flushed out". To assist him I took my dog Libra with me. I was carrying a small camera for personal use.'

Head managed to snap a picture before Thompson gave him a 'rollocking'. He contin-

Mortar fire during *Lucky Alphonse*.

ues, 'Moving forward it became clear a fire had started. It did not come close to us, but we were ready to move out in a hurry if push came to shove. By nightfall, when I took my turn on guard duty, the forest was well alight. At the end of the next day I wrote in my diary "13 Gordons dead. 25 trapped". On the 18th, three Bedford trucks came through our "camp". They carried some of those who had lost their lives. We all spent a very quiet day, keeping our thoughts to ourselves.'

Roy Baker, too, was with 45 Commando. He was serving as a signaller. 'I was present when the fire started and heard an order given to the Royal Horse Guards to open mortar fire on caves in the mountainside. A faulty HT bomb was launched by mistake,' he said. 'That's how the conflagration began. The trees were tinder dry and any spark would have set them ablaze. I ran like hell after our petrol drum went up like an atomic bomb, mushroom cloud as well.'

Former Para Ken Jewsbury concurred that there was a large mortar barrage, but on a valley, while concentrated heavy machine gun fire raked the mountainside. 'One of these barrages started a fire in the valley floor, when a "Curie", a type of whirlwind, plucked up the fire and carried it at the speed of an express train across the treetops on one side of the valley. The trees then fell as hot burning ash, leaving burning charcoal ash up to a depth of 12 inches in places. The forest floor was so hot it burnt the boots off our feet and the air was sucked from our lungs.'

The author of the official history of the Royal Norfolk Regiment declared, 'Whether or not mortar fire was the cause will never be confirmed, but it was at the time believed by some members of the battalion to have started the fire.'

In Robin Neillands' book *A Fighting Retreat*, Spike Hughs of Support Company, 45 Commando, explained it was common practice for troops to get rid of unwanted ammunition: they would fire their Vickers machine guns and mortars on selected areas that were too difficult to reach on foot, hoping to flush out any terrorists. 'It was good fun for us,' he says. On 16 June, members of Support Company began using their three-inch mortars at the same time as 'A' Troop, 45 Commando, tested its two-inch mortars. 'We were firing away when suddenly we got the order. "Cease firing! Christ! We've dropped a bomb on 'A' Troop! Check ranges and bearings." The radios were red hot. We were nearest to 'A' Troop so we went to their aid. By the time we got there the medics had treated the wounded and there were four or five lads on stretchers. One sergeant of 'A' Troop roundly cursed us and accused Support Troop of causing the accident,' says Hughs. 'Our sergeant was adamant we had not caused it. Whether a two-inch mortar bomb had hit an overhead branch or had exploded as it left the barrel … it was all speculation. Vic Pegler showed his upset by hurling a two-inch mortar on the ground and calling it an "effing bastard toy", the only time I ever saw him lose his rag.

'We manhandled the stretchers up to the top of the mountain, where the casualties were picked up by helicopter and taken to hospital. We were left to pick up the unused bombs and dismantle the mortars and immediately noted that the bombs were well out of date. We also noted that the opposite hillside was alight. "I suppose it will burn itself out," someone said, but I was not sure. The following day the fire had spread and the operation began to collapse.'

Captain A. W. C. Wallace was the Administrative Officer of 3 Commando Brigade, stationed in Limassol. Although his staff was not usually involved in 'front line' operations against EOKA, on this occasion HQ provided a composite platoon of cooks, drivers and clerks. During *Lucky Alphonse* Wallace commanded this platoon and was detailed to take his orders from a major of the Norfolk Regiment. 'On the night of 15/16 June I observed mortar fire on the side of a hill across the valley from my position,' Wallace remembered in a letter he wrote to the author. 'I could see quite clearly the semi-circle of flames spreading from the points of the explosions. It is my opinion that the subsequent forest fire was a result of the mortar bomb explosions and was not deliberately started by EOKA as stories circulating later suggested.'

As the fire spread, Wallace was ordered back into the area to rendezvous with troops from the Gordons and Norfolks, under the command of a major from the Gordons. They were part of a company sent to assist Turkish Cypriot foresters to fight the fire. Former Para Wally Dinsdale added, 'I remember these people passing our location and they carried a blanket, which was their safeguard if they got cornered, as they'd wrap up and run through the oncoming fire.'

At the rendezvous, the foresters were very agitated and worried. When the major from the Gordons arrived, they told him the situation was becoming critical and they needed help to fight the fire. The major replied that the foresters and Wallace's platoon should get to work immediately while he called for fresh troops to relieve the men who were there. 'I took my platoon, with a group of foresters, up the hill away from the fire and began to create a firebreak near the crest, taking my directions from the foresters,' said Wallace. 'I had been promised fresh troops, but when they became long overdue, I went down to the original RV to confer with the major. He was not there and I did not see him again.'

Wallace continued down the road away from the fire hoping to meet his relief and eventually met up with another group of foresters, accompanied by troops from the Norfolks and Gordons. 'They were standing by their three 3-ton trucks. The young officer in charge told me he had been given another task and was not our relief,' he recalled. 'By now the fire was closing on us and the foresters expressed their concern for our safety. Although events seemed to happen very fast, I remember clearly that I had time to walk back towards the RV, but was prevented by a wall of fire crossing the road in front of me. I was forced to return to the group I had just left. The foresters advised us that the situation had become critical and recommended we all follow them up the hill. Someone – I don't know whom – decided it was better to escape the inferno by using the trucks and he gave the troops an order to embark and move off.

'With my driver, I chose to follow the foresters' advice to abandon our Land Rover and headed up the hill. It is very hard to describe the heat. It was almost impossible to breathe and difficult to climb the hill. Near collapse and exhausted, an elder Turkish Cypriot forester saw my plight and helped me towards a burnt out patch of ground. I was left alone sitting there, as the fire swept past me on both sides. Strangely, at no time, did I actually consider myself in danger. It was as if I were a spectator of events, safe in my little world. A forest fire is a spectacular and terrifying experience. It moves very fast, leaping from one spot to another in the blink of an eye.

'Suddenly I heard gunfire and screams coming from the direction the trucks had taken. A little later, through the smoke, I saw two men helping each other on the road. One of them was naked, his clothes burnt off him. By the time I reached the spot on the road where they had been, they were no longer there. I continued down the road, turned a bend and saw where the trucks had been caught in the blaze. It appeared as if they had driven straight into a tunnel of flames. The troops had tried to escape by running up an incline, but failed and their dead bodies were spread everywhere. Without dwelling on the horror of the sight and the effect of the fire, I now realized that the sound I had taken for gunfire was the soldiers' ammunition exploding in their bandoliers worn on their waists. The explosives had ripped out their guts.

'Then, out of the smoke, a group of Norfolks with a senior NCO arrived. Together we began bringing the bodies to the road. There was no urgency, but it seemed the right thing to do. Despite the horror, the young soldiers were calm and carried out their distasteful task in almost a matter-of-fact manner with no signs of distress. Later we discovered that the reason why these soldiers were unable to escape was because their Bedford trucks could not continue down the single-track road as they had been blocked by a scout car travelling in the opposite direction. Surprisingly the trucks and scout car, although hot and smouldering, were still capable of being driven. We pushed the scout car into a gully to try clearing the road. With hindsight, it was a pointless act.

'More troops arrived. With another officer now in charge, I went off to find my own platoon and driver. I had left them in the care of the foresters. Half a mile up the road, I found them sitting, "having a smoke". One of them casually remarked, "We thought you were a gonner, sir." We evacuated to another Marine location and next morning, rested, we drove back through the blackened forest towards Limassol.'

Private Brian Sweeny of 'C' Company of the 1st Battalion the Highland Light Infantry was one of those sent to fight the fire. 'Although more than 50 years have passed – and my memory is not as good as it was – I can never forget the ferocity of that fire,' he said. 'We were given machetes to cut a firebreak. Before long we were exhausted and received orders on our radio – an 88 set – that we were being relieved by another section and to return to the road below us. Just as we got back up to the road, I was collared by our sergeant major and told to run back to the section that had just relieved us to warn them that the fire was about to encircle them. The lad who operated the 88 set hadn't switched it on, and so they couldn't be contacted. I got to the lads and we all made it back to the road safely, where I rejoined my section on a lorry. We drove a couple of miles to a refreshment point, but no sooner were we there than a Land Rover roared towards us, the driver shouting for us to get the hell out. The fire was coming down that road as fast as he was. I'm certain it was travelling far faster than 30 mph.'

Sweeny remembered that Turkish Cypriot forestry workers had come out in force and were waiting, they said, for the wind to change before going into action. One of them told him he had learned his skills in Scotland!

The 1st Battalion, Royal Norfolks, lost five men in the fire. They were Corporal K. R. Haylock from 'B' Company, Privates Robin Beaumont, Clifford Gosling and William Wright from 'D' Company, and Private William Wood of HQ Company. An officer from the Royal Norfolks, who counted the dead, said, 'Those who fled ahead of the fire perished, whereas those who ran at right angles to its path or even into the smouldering areas survived.' Members of 3 Para supported the Norfolks' view when they recovered their dead. A vehicle carrying the 2/ic of 'A' Company, Captain Mike Walsh, and Captain Michael Beagley, and their driver, Private Joseph Hawker, had been caught in the flames. All three tried to escape by running downhill from the fire. Beagley and Walsh did not make it to safety. Hawker survived after falling into a ditch and staying there until the fire had passed, but died later.

Private Hawker was probably typical of all the 'ordinary' National Service lads who died in the fire. It was only four years since he had left school in Brierley Hill, where he lived on a council housing estate with his 48-year-old mother Mabel, four younger brothers and three sisters at 17 Lower Valley Road. His

headmaster recalled: 'Joseph was a nice boy. Quite ordinary in his lessons, but never any trouble.' Until he was called up, he had worked in the local glass works, like so many others in the small Black Country town. His foreman said: 'He was a good boy. We looked forward to having him back.' Weekends had been spent playing cricket and football. Saturday evenings were for dating and dancing in the local youth club. His last letter to his mother said: 'Dear Ma, just a few lines to let you know I'm OK. On Friday night the Battalion went on an operation to screen and question a village in the mountains. We took six suspects, including two priests and the brother of a wanted gunman. I was on guard.'

Father Casey, a Para chaplain, said: 'A wall of flame came at us at about 30 miles an hour. Some of those who were burned had been fighting the fire. Others were taking part in operations against Grivas and his men. A few managed to escape by running up a hill. Others tried to get out of the path of the flames in vehicles, but some of these were caught by the fire. For them it was all over in about three minutes.'

A covert OP was also caught in the path of the fire and the entire four-man crew perished, former Para Ken Jewsbury claimed. Another soldier, Jerry Bastin, remembered riding on the canopy of a 3-tonner as the Paras withdrew. 'There were smouldering trees and bushes on either side. Some of us had buckets of water, which we used to damp down the canvas cover.' Para Bryan Hunter and his men raced to a stream and lay down in the water until the fire had passed. 'There was very little left of our kit when we got out and I hate to think what would have happened to us if the stream had not been there. The chaps from 3 Para weren't consumed by the flames, the heat suffocated them. It was so intense that it had burnt all the oxygen out of the air. When we found their bodies they looked as if they were asleep.'

Roy Barker, Royal Marines, was among those given the task of recovering the dead. He said: 'During the following days, we brought back bodies on stretchers in the back of our Austin Champs.' Others were carried in Bedford trucks. Hospitals were placed on alert and accepted 48 servicemen for treatment for burns. Despite the dangers, the RAF Sycamore helicopters, diverted from their surveillance duties, flew several of the badly injured to the British Military Hospital in Nicosia.

Some helicopters touched down in dense clouds of smoke on a makeshift strip, a short stroll from exploding ammunition and petrol tanks, and their crews unloaded medical supplies and quantities of blood plasma. In two cases, doctors were lowered to the ground by winch to attend the injured. The RAF pilots' assistance was invaluable, landing even where angels feared to tread. One injured soldier was flown out from the bottom of a mountain gully, far from any road. Crews worked round the clock. At night, they relied on vehicle headlights to guide them down. When the War Office heard of the effectiveness of helicopters in Cyprus, more Sycamores were ordered to the Island.

At Nicosia airport, Arthur Melton was a junior technician engine-fitter with 70 Squadron, recently arrived from the Canal Zone re-equipped with the Handley Page Hastings four-engined transport aircraft. The maintenance chief was Flight Sergeant Duffield. 'Our day-to-day activities covered the normal servicing and refuelling of aircraft to ensure they were ready to transport supplies or personnel when required, but at the time of the Troodos fire, we were ordered to work all day and all night removing seats from our aircraft and replacing them with 30 stretchers for the injured troops. Heavy casualties were expected. Our aircraft were to fly them to a destination where they could receive treatment.'

Of all the regiments taking part in

Operation *Lucky Alphonse* none suffered more fatalities than 1 Gordon Highlanders. The Battalion lost 2nd Lieutenant Bruce Kynoch, who had only been with the Battalion for three weeks, Lance Corporal Ferrie, and Privates Burnett, Cockie, Gerrard, William Gray, Ian Gray, Hindle, McRuvie and Simpson, all killed on the second day of the fire, 17 June. During the subsequent four days, Private Dunbar, Lance Corporal Oakley and Private James Smith died from their wounds.

More would have been killed had it not been for the bravery of Lt Stanley Sutton of the Royal Army Medical Corps, who was the RMO, and W02 Leslie Dunn. On hearing reports of the growing number of casualties, Lieutenant Sutton raced his Land Rover ambulance along a mountain track towards the victims, but flames blocked his path and he sought refuge in a small ditch filled with shale. As the blaze passed on, he raised himself only to find his vehicle and equipment completely destroyed.

Despite bad burns to his right arm, Sutton pressed forward on foot to do his best for the injured soldiers. Seeing the men's injuries, he realized they were in a dangerous state and required greater medical care than he could provide alone. He saw a deserted vehicle and went to get help. Again his path was blocked by fire. The wind was constantly changing direction, taking the flames with it. Once more he returned to the injured.

Now, with the help of some survivors, he headed for a spring and filled several cans with water. Close to the water source he spotted another stranded Austin Champ. Hoping it was still serviceable, he loaded the water on board, but the vehicle would not start. He, with the other soldiers, then marched their way back to the wounded with the cans of water. Despite being badly hurt – and without any equipment – he nevertheless continued for the next five hours succouring the wounded. Lieutenant Sutton was made a Member of the British Empire (MBE) because his 'brave conduct and devotion to duty was beyond praise'.

Captain R. Meadows, 45 Royal Marine Commando, was also awarded an MBE for 'leadership and courage of a high order' during the rescue operation. After organizing the evacuation of his own men, he personally carried a wounded man for a mile through smoke-filled undergrowth. He then found a burning armoured car and, regardless of his own safety, he jumped inside, removed cans of petrol, beat out the flames and let the handbrake off so the vehicle could be pushed off the road.

No less brave was WO2 Leslie Dunn of the Gordon Highlanders. In December 1956, Dunn was awarded the British Empire Medal for Distinguished Service. The citation read:

On 17 June 1956, during operations in the Paphos Forest area of Cyprus a disastrous forest fire trapped a considerable number of troops many of whom lost their lives or suffered severe injury in consequence of the flames. When the magnitude of the emergency was first realized, Company Sergeant Major Dunn went at once to investigate and after sending urgent messages for assistance worked unceasingly throughout the day displaying outstanding initiative, good sense and leadership. Undeterred by the smoke and confusion caused by the fire he entered and re-entered the burning area organizing the collection of dead and injured and searches for further possible victims. Showing a complete disregard for exploding ammunition he assisted in pushing burning lorries off the mountain track to clear the way for rescue vehicles. He gave valuable assistance in the organization and loading of a convoy for the evacuation of the victims. His exceptional devotion to duty, courage and resource were an inspiration to those about him.

Meanwhile Grivas was making his way out of the chaos.

AT MIDNIGHT on 18 June, he neared Palodhia village, but heard dogs barking. Convinced he might be heading for another trap, he returned to spend the night with his companions in Yerasa. The next day he was driven to Limassol by 'Fat Costas' and taken to a house where he would stay for several months, resting and recovering his health.

In his autobiography, Grivas detailed his escape: 'Two cars arrived to drive us the last 10 miles to Limassol, where a hiding place had been prepared for Georgiades and myself. The Limassol men had recruited, as one of the drivers, Chief Inspector Costas Efstathiou, better known as "Fat Costas". He was not, of course, told the identity of his passenger. Like most of the police, he did what he was told by the organization and asked no questions.' 'The Leader' arrived in the small hours of the morning and was met by Dafnis Panayides, who had arranged a 'safe house'.

The authorities in Nicosia, still reluctant to reveal the fire disaster, merely released an anodyne communiqué at 00:50 on 18 June, when most reporters were tucked up in bed. 'There have been some casualties, but the number will not be known until a check is made among units working in a remote sector of the operation area where the fire is still burning,' it said. RAF helicopter pilot Jim McCorkle said: 'It was a terrible day. I flew 19 bodies to the military hospital and couldn't face my evening meal when I got back to our hiring in Ayios Dhometios that evening. I was so angry, I wanted to drop a bomb on Mac Hairy Ass, as we referred to the Archbishop. We never did come up with a full count of the dead, did we?'

Frank Pearson of 2 Field Ambulance, RAMC, was assigned to work as a night medical orderly at the British Military Hospital, Nicosia. Previously he had been attached to the Royal Leicestershire Regiment. 'Because the "Tigers" suffered more than their fair share of injuries and fatalities I spent some time in their wards,' he recalled. 'I was ordered to stay with two of the badly burned soldiers and to do my best to make them comfortable. Their parents were rushed from the UK to be at their bedsides. I will never forget having to turn over one of them so that I could put some gauze under his buttocks to allow him to defecate. His hot, sticky back and his agony live on in my memory. Both soldiers died that night.'

The worst of the fire was over and Operation *Lucky Alphonse*, which had started with so much enthusiasm, was ending in a cloud of smoke and deep depression. Flames still licked at the charred pines. Melted mess tins and even letters, which somehow had survived, lay scattered by wrecked vehicles. A shocked British United Press reporter noted: 'As we walked past a line of twisted and charred three-ton lorries, the scout car and an ambulance jeep with burned stretchers sticking out from it, one officer said: "The whole of my company is written off." His men had been busy making a firebreak when the fire travelled swiftly up the valley engulfing them as they tried to drive and run before it.'

Gordon Highlander Corporal Robin McDonald was keen to tell his story: 'We had been fighting the flames for some time, and we thought we had beaten them. But even as I straightened from beating out the last of the flames before me, I felt the wind change on my cheek. Then with awful suddenness, the fire started up again and came roaring down on us in one solid wall. The flames before us leapt from tree to tree and soon the whole area was cracking and popping like a million fire-crackers. Soon we were rushing away from an inferno, which was bearing down on us at 30 miles an hour. Our vehicles turned out of its path, but it was too late. Their tanks went up with a roar and above all the noise came the explosions of the ammunition.'

Stupidity had caused the fire and once it took hold, the rescue operations were less than satisfactorily managed.

Elenitsa Seraphim, the local EOKA area commander, maintained, 'Greek Cypriots cast aside the bitterness they felt towards their rulers who were spreading sorrow and grief throughout the island and tried to put out the fire, rushing to help the soldiers and thus the fire was brought under control and extinguished on 19 June after intensive efforts by local farmers. The government announced that 19 British soldiers had lost their lives and a further 18 sustained serious burns. One of our men who was on the wanted list, code-named *Kyros*, had been trapped in the area surrounded by the Army but he managed to escape before the fire started and reached Larnaca by bus.

'The next day I went to Nicosia and found a pleasant surprise awaiting me. It was a letter from Dighenis who was free again at last. What a relief. I said a prayer of thanks, as did all those of us who knew what he had been through.' Grivas, too, went to his death insisting, 'When a British officer in tears begged the [Greek] Cypriot fire fighters to help, they choked down their hatred of the tyrant and, heedless of the danger, ran into the flames to carry out the dead and the dying.'

Frank Delamere, one of the Gordon Highlanders based at Limni Camp, pointed out that all Cypriots, by law, had to fight local forest fires. 'They were paid as well,' he said. He disputed the statements made by both Grivas and Elenitsa Seraphim. He said, 'Yes, we faced some very frightening moments. Blinded by the smoke and finding it difficult to breathe, we were left to fight the fire by beating. Just beating. There was no water. Just as we put out one blaze, the Greek bastards came up behind us and started another.'

Later there was a Court of Inquiry into the disaster. Captain A. W. C. Wallace, RM, was among those called to give evidence. Part of his testimony also contradicted Seraphim. 'The Inquiry was unsatisfactory,' he believed. 'At one point, I was asked if the Turkish foresters had run away – deserted the British troops. I replied that on the contrary the Turks had given sound advice and repeatedly it had been ignored. I suggested that had their advice been followed and the urgency of the situation been appreciated, the tragedy may have been avoided. I do not recall any mention of this event after the Court of Inquiry.'

The Inquiry's report was inconclusive. It stated there was no definitive evidence to prove whether the fire was started by EOKA to allow Grivas to escape or that it had been caused by the pursuing British troops.

A total of 17 terrorists was captured during Operation *Lucky Alphonse*; the EOKA mountain network was broken and no longer a major threat. Grivas was never able again to play the role of a combatant. From midsummer 1956 until 1959, he controlled the EOKA campaign from a basement in Limassol, only occasionally travelling in disguise to Nicosia to receive medical treatment, usually from his brother, a doctor.

Rumours that he eluded the British authorities by dressing as a woman during his excursions remain the stuff of legend. But Grivas considered *Lucky Alphonse* a major failure in military terms. 'The difference between our strategy and that of the British was striking,' he said later. 'One can describe it by the following simile – one can only catch mice with cunning, and that means one must employ cats and traps.' The British planners did neither.

'Whether terrorists started the fire deliberately or not is hardly relevant. The troops who were caught by the fire were not in Cyprus by their own choice. They were carrying out dangerous and unpleasant duty in the doggedly cheerful way British soldiers always do,' editorialized the Aberdeen *Press and Journal*. 'In this country we may argue about the rights and wrongs of the Cyprus issue, but the soldier has no time for discussion. He has to drive along a road that may hold an ambush: he must walk down a street where an assassin may lurk. The tragedy of the fire brings home to us the extraordinarily difficult and perilous task which our soldiers face in Cyprus. They have shown restraint in the face of provocation, which does credit to the British Army.'

ON 19 JUNE, the dead were laid to rest in Wayne's Keep Military Cemetery on the outskirts of Nicosia. There were three proces-

The victims of Operation *Lucky Alphonse* are buried in a mass grave in Wayne's Keep Military Cemetery.

sions in a single day, each accompanied by Chopin's *Funeral March* played by the band of the 3rd Battalion The Parachute Regiment. Chaplains representing the Church of England, the Roman Catholic Church and the Church of Scotland read the burial services. Detachments from every unit in Cyprus attended, with a complete company of the Gordon Highlanders. Senior officers of the Navy, Army and RAF were also present. Because Sir John Harding was in the UK, he was represented by Captain Nigel Tunnicliffe. The coffins were covered with Union flags, and the dead man's cap and belt lay on each. Sixty wreaths from all ranks were arranged by their graves. The *Last Post* was sounded. Guards of Honour fired three volleys and the Gordon Highlanders played *Flowers of the Forest*.

EOKA showed no respect for the occasion. A Grivas foot soldier delayed the funeral service of the Parachute Regiment's dead for half an hour by hurling a bomb at the cortège as it passed close to the American Consulate. It narrowly missed the Reverend Horace McClelland, the regiment's chaplain, riding in an open vehicle at the head of the procession, behind which was a truck carrying the bodies of two paratroopers.

The bomb exploded at the edge of the road, injuring three Greek Cypriots who were passing on bicycles. There were no service casualties, however. Escorting troops leapt from an armoured car, vaulted a wall and raced into a nearby garden, firing at the fleeing bomber, who escaped. The area was immediately cordoned off and houses searched. Four suspects were arrested later. A British official condemned the attack, pointing out that Reverend McClelland was wearing vestments and the bomber would have known he was a clergyman.

General Sir Charles Keightley, Commander-in-Chief of British Middle East Land Forces, attended the services after flying over the fire-blackened ridges of the Troodos range. 'This is one of the grimmest disasters I have seen for many years,' he said. 'It was caused by a series of fantastically ill-fortuned circumstances. These men died in a selfless effort to restore peace and remove murder, arson and intimidation from this island. Their lives were as much a sacrifice to the peace of the world as if they were killed in battle. The fact that they were re-establishing freedom from fear seems sometimes forgotten, both abroad and at home.'

Long after the emergency ended, Grivas continued to accuse the British of concealing the real number of fatalities and serious injuries. 'The dead numbered more than 60,' he said, basing his conclusion on information given to him by Greek Cypriots on the ground and informants within the police. He denied that seven terrorists also perished. A diary kept by a Royal Marine, however, gave a total of 19 British fatalities. The author of a Grivas biography, published in 1959 with the co-operation of the colonial authorities, confirmed 19. Peter Herclerode, the author of *Para*, claimed, on the other hand, that there were 30 fatalities. The number quoted by the Royal Norfolk's historian was 21. This tallied with the names published in the Honour Roll of *Britain's Small Wars*, a website compiled by former soldiers and the author. None was killed or wounded by EOKA during the operation.

Albert 'Taff' Boyer, Secretary Royal Marines Association of Victoria, Australia, vigorously questions the number of deaths. 'We had definite verification that 44 men died,' he said, adding, 'I was driving a Humber Combat 1–ton truck at the time and ferried injured men from a forest clearing back to the main helicopter landing strip and the Operational Command Post about a mile further back. I recall 22 bodies were recovered. Their remains had to be brushed carefully onto waterproof capes and sheets. The heat had melted them, bones and all.

'I saw only one man come out of the smoke

alive. He was a Gordon Highlanders officer. He was smoking from head to foot; most of his hair, skin and clothes had gone. He was staggering, suffering terrible burns. He dropped in front of us. The intense heat had shrunk his arms, which were still cooking. One of our unit SBAs – Sick Berth Attendants – tried to insert a Biro pen into his throat to make an airway. His own had shrunken to about a quarter of an inch. He died in front of us. It was a relief to see him no longer suffering. This was the worst moment of my life. I have since attended road crashes and many fires in the course of my civilian career but my introduction to such horror at 20 has taken a toll on my mind.

'Much later, when the fire had died down I was present with two other drivers when the search and rescue teams went into the still smouldering trees to look for survivors. Forty-four Gordon Highlanders were still missing, most of them National Servicemen, lads no more than 20 years old.'

IN THE chaos of the fire and rescue attempts, keeping accurate records was the last thing on the minds of most soldiers and, clearly, errors were made later when a tally was taken of the survivors and the dead. Sergeant Bellamy of 6 Platoon, 'B' Company of the Royal Norfolk Regiment recalls that an RASC driver joined them during the worst of the blaze when he had been separated from his vehicle. With the Norfolks, the man picked up a rifle and became an infantryman for the next few days. His name was 'Speedy' Williams.

Meanwhile, his truck had been found by another unit and was being used to ferry corpses to a morgue in Limassol. On the way, the soldiers passed an RASC camp, where a guard recognized the vehicle as belonging to Speedy and wanted to know why he was not at the wheel. The driver pointed at the rear of the truck and remarked: 'He's probably one them dead 'uns in the back, mate.'

Ken Wintle, another RASC driver at 'Speedy's camp took up the story:

'The horror of the carnage affected all of us in our company, even more so when we heard of Speedy Williams' death. His charred body had been found beside his truck. Obviously he had stayed at his post till the end. Speedy was a popular lad, but I felt his loss more than others, because I'd known him before we'd joined the army. We had played football together in West Bromwich before our call-up. It seemed unreal that a healthy young man and friend had gone forever.

'During the next few days, groups of us gathered in the NAAFI, and reminisced about our experiences with our departed friend. An air of sadness hung over the camp, as everyone seemed affected by his death. We thought about his parents, grieving back home. Our Company Commander, Major Lewis, sent them a letter of condolence.

'Three days later, in the evening, just after sunset when there is an eerie half-light that can deceive the senses, I was walking across the disused airfield that doubled as our parade ground, when I spotted a figure approaching in the gloom. As it neared, its shape and outline looked vaguely familiar. Suddenly I recognized it was my late friend Speedy. A feeling of horror ran through me, my hair stood on end and I shivered in my boots despite the warmth of the evening, but there he was at arm's length, grinning fiendishly. I reached out tentatively with my right hand and touched his arm. He was solid, warm, and most important of all "alive".

'"We," I blurted out, "all thought you were dead and buried."

'Speedy explained what had happened. Yes, he had escaped, but another unrecognizable body was found near his truck and everyone assumed it was him. As he'd been on detachment to the Royal Suffolk Regiment, based at Polymedia, at the time, he'd gone back there after his brief spell with the Norfolks. Because there had been little communication between the different companies, a blunder occurred and he had been reported dead.

'"But," I said, "your parents have been notified of your death and burial!"

'He was shocked by the news. "Are your parents on the phone?" I asked, because I was anxious for them to be told the good news.

'"No," he said. "Well, why don't you place a call to the local police station in West Bromwich and ask them to tell your parents that you're alive and well?"

'We rushed to the Company Office, where he made the call. It took some time before he was able to get through, but he eventually convinced the person on the other end of the line that a terrible mistake had been made, and they promised to notify his parents. They had been grieving the death of a son and would now be experiencing another emotional upheaval, but a happy one.

'That night the NAAFI burst at the seams as we all welcomed Speedy back from the dead in a way only good comrades can, finishing up with that old faithful, "For He's a Jolly Good Fellow".'

Compassionate leave was immediately arranged for Speedy to return home by air. While in the United Kingdom a local posting was arranged so that he would not have to return to Cyprus to complete his National Service.

Soon after the search and rescue teams had completed their tasks, the War Office named the dead as follows:

From the Gordon Highlanders:
Second Lieutenant B. A. G. Kynoch, Keith, Banffshire;
Lance-Corporal D. R. Ferrie, Farnham, Surrey;
Pte. R. Burnett, St. Andrews, Fife;
Pte. J. Cockie, Fordoun, Kincardineshire;
Pte. H. G. Gerrard, Gillyfourie, Aberdeenshire;
Pte. W. A. Gray, Birmingham;
Pte. M. Hindle, Preston, Edinburgh;
Pte. I. M. Simpson, Longside, Aberdeenshire;

Pte. G. McRuvie, Aberdeen;
Private A. Dunbar, Aberdeen,
Pte. I. Gray, Aberdeen.

Attached to the Gordons:
Acting Corporal Kennedy, Royal Army Service Corps, Stirling.

From the 1st Battalion, the Royal Norfolk Regiment:
Acting Corporal Haylock, Steeple Bumpstead, Essex;
Private W. Woods, Norwich;
Private C. J. Gosling, King's Lynn;
Private W. G. Wrights, Tillingham, Essex;
Private R. Beaumont Stowmarket, Suffolk.

From the 3rd Battalion, the Parachute Brigade:
Captain H. T. Beagley, whose wife lived in Cyprus;
Pte. J. A. Hawker, Brierly Hill, Staffordshire.

2nd Lieutenant Bruce Kynoch was the only Gordon not to be buried at Wayne's Keep. He was the son of Lieutenant Colonel Kynoch, who owned the famous woollen mills and tweed of that name. He employed some 500 people at Keith in Banffshire. The business disintegrated after his son's death.

Operation *Lucky Alphonse* ended after 16 days of action. Colonel Grivas evaded capture after several narrow escapes, but a complete EOKA gang was captured and the terrorists' supply and communications system with other mountain gangs had been dislocated, never to fully recover. The Security Forces had gained vast amounts of information and captured large quantities of weapons, ammunition, clothing, food, documents and radio equipment in working order. At Kykko Monastery, documentary evidence was uncovered, proving it had been used as a supply and information centre for the terrorists. Five monks confessed their sins and were detained.

There is an ironic postscript to this drama. Later in 1956 a representative of the Canadian Government arrived at Limini Camp to recruit

Demitrakis Constantides, an EOKA group leader, captured during *Lucky Alphonse* with pipe-smoking Major Halliday of the Royal Marines.

for the Canadian Forest Service. 'He wanted volunteers to become smoke-jumpers or airborne fire fighters,' Bryan Hunter recalled. 'Would you believe, he did not find a single applicant!'

DESPITE THE military's mountain operations, nothing much had changed in the towns of Cyprus. In Larnaca, Sergeant William Tipple of the UK Police Unit was shot dead by an unknown assailant. He was about to enter his van to drive to Pyla Pile Detention Camp, where he was attached, when the gunman struck. Tipple, a former Royal Marine, was on secondment from the Metropolitan Police.

Because of the continuing EOKA attacks and the failure of any Greek Cypriots to come forward to assist police investigators, a collective fine of £35,000 was imposed on the inhabitants of the port town. In Nicosia, barbed wire barriers separated the Greek and Turkish sections of the capital, while troops stood ready to stop further communal disorders. In Paphos, Security forces detained Archbishop Makarios's uncle, George Mouskos.

The conflict continued. Sir John Harding returned to Cyprus from talks in London with Prime Minister Eden and his Cabinet at No. 10, immediately starting a flurry of rumours that a new peace plan was in the offing. There were hints of behind-the-scenes moves and of informal talks between Greece and Turkey.

The Chinese whispers took on some veracity by an editorial in the London *Times*: 'There are many promising signs that the Government is planning another attempt to break the diplomatic deadlock in which Cyprus is gripped. They have been miserably slow, and they have years of fumbling behind them, but the moves are not less to be welcomed on that account ... Lord Radcliffe, who has been chosen as constitutional architect for Cyprus, is expected to go there early next month to begin his soundings on the spot.'

The newspaper continued: 'The Greek case has often been heard and will be borne in account, but it is not a bit of use pretending that the Turks have not legitimate interests which must be safeguarded. Their attitude, which is partly based on considerations of strategy and partly (as is that of Greece) on national pride, is understandable. Nothing is gained by under-estimating the strength with which it is held. It is a perfectly legitimate feeling, which must be taken into account at every stage of a settlement. It would be a fatal error to think that Britain could commit itself to some course of action and expect the Turks automatically to "come round" in time.'

And Turkish Cypriots were quick to point this out. Their leader Dr. Kutchuk stated bluntly they would never accept any proposal that gave the Greeks majority representation in any future Cyprus Parliament. It would, he said, place a hangman's noose around the necks of Cypriot Turks. Attacking the reported British plan to offer the Cypriot Greeks self-determination in 10 to 15 years, he said: 'We consider it a great political blunder and treachery to accept self-determination, which means nothing but *enosis*.' Turkish rights could only be guaranteed by a constitution based on equal representation. If necessary, 'we shall again appeal to the Turkish Government to defend our rights and interests'. But ultimately it was up to Greece to stop encouraging EOKA and providing the organization with financial and material support, something Athens categorically denied and heard in Ankara with wry smiles.

Peace in Cyprus remained far off below the horizon and there would be many more deaths before it was reached.

CHAPTER THIRTEEN

Battle of the leaflets and the short-lived truce

I've been down Murder Mile,
Where the people wear a smile,
And would gladly shoot you in the back,
So be careful where you walk,
Look around while you talk,
If you can get home safe you're lucky, Jack.
Rev. Michael Scarrott, RAF

GARETH KARBERRY, 33, a British Customs official, turned the wheel of his car as he came out of a sharp bend on the mountain road, seven miles north of Lefkonico, near Ayios Nikolaos village. Ahead was the coast, where hundreds of British civilians, despite 'the troubles', still spent weekends swimming and relaxing. With his wife, Margaret, 30, he planned to join them. They had passed safely through an area near 'Black Mountain', a place the Security Forces had searched intensively and found several EOKA hides. Some one hundred yards in front of them, they saw a young Cypriot indicating he wanted to hitch a ride. They slowed to pick him up. Immediately there were several bursts of automatic fire from a clump of pine trees on the side of the road. A bomb exploded a few feet away. The car swerved and went out of control, ending in a ditch. The terrorists collected their weapons and ran. Mrs Karberry had died instantly. She was pregnant. Her husband succumbed on the way to hospital. Until this day, 8 July, Grivas had never ordered his gangs to kill a British woman. As soon as the news of the ambush reached British troops, a major sweep of the area began, but the killers had escaped yet again.

This outrage followed a period of comparative calm since the British Government announced that Lord Radcliffe would be visiting Cyprus to help draft a constitution that could lead to limited self-government. Radcliffe had drawn the lines that had created the new state of Pakistan when India was granted independence in August 1947. Lord Mountbatten, the last Governor General, had given him six weeks to lay down the new frontiers.

'It will be Lord Radcliffe's task,' said Prime Minister Sir Anthony Eden, 'to consider the framework of a new liberal constitution for Cyprus, including safeguards for the interests of all communities, and to make recommendations. Her Majesty's Government intends on his return to draw up detailed terms of reference.' The new Constitutional Commissioner added that he wanted 'to see the place and the people; to see how the work of the Government goes on at present; talk to the people on the spot; and listen to anybody who wants to talk to me'.

Clearly Grivas had decided again to demonstrate his capabilities to cause terror, as he had done before, whenever there were attempts to find a solution to the Cyprus problem. With the death of the first British woman notched on his pistol, he returned to his usual hit and run tactics against British servicemen. That same afternoon, a further tragedy occurred on the far side of the Island. Sergeant Allan Smith was leading a Gordon Highlanders' patrol along a dried-up river bed to the north of Morphou when he spotted three men moving about 25 yards away. He shouted a challenge and they promptly opened fire. Smith was shot in the chest and in the leg, but even so managed to fire back almost a complete Sten gun magazine. The terrorists fled, leaving behind their shotguns. Although Smith was evacuated immediately, he died soon after arriving at hospital in Pendayia.

These three murders brought the number of Britons killed so far by terrorists to 48. Of these, five were service personnel.

WHATEVER THE problems in Cyprus, they were about to become considerably less important to the UK Government following the decision on 26 July by President Nasser of Egypt to nationalize the Suez Canal, considered by the British and the French as their property and of vital interest to their security. Sir Anthony Eden and a large section of the Conservative Party were determined not to let him get away with the seizure, even if this meant using force – and Cyprus as a base from which to launch an invasion. Soon the Mediterranean would be filled with warships, loaded with men and munitions, heading for the Island. Allied planes would make Cyprus a vast aircraft carrier in the weeks ahead. How would Grivas react? He knew very well that mounting the Suez operation could not but divert attention and effort from the offensive against EOKA, forcing the Army to provide security for all the extra military facilities that needed to be established.

Because EOKA had lessened its attacks since the end of Operation *Lucky Alphonse* in June to give Grivas time to plan and rebuild his shattered mountain groups, some British servicemen and their families had lowered their guard and began behaving as if every-thing had returned to normal. They became targets of opportunity. In his Limassol hideout, 'The Leader' was also being pressed by his most trusted aides to take hostages, which could be exchanged, they thought, for those awaiting execution in Nicosia General Prison. Kyriacos Matsis and Nitsa Hadji Georghiou – 'one of our boldest girls' – set a honey trap in which they hoped to lure a lonely soldier.

During the next few days Nitsa – code-named *Cassandra* and *Miss Diamanticou* – set her sights on RAF Sergeant Ernest Allen, who found her charms irresistible and agreed to return with her in his car to a house in Ayios Dhometios, a Nicosia suburb, on 17 July. Before long, he was tempted into her bedroom, where he undressed. At that moment, the woman went to the bathroom and returned with three masked men. Their plan was to overcome Allen and drive off with him in his own car, but the airman resisted and he was shot dead in the struggle.

The terrorists now faced a problem they had not anticipated: how were they to remove the body? The house was in a busy residential area and neighbours would notice any unusual activity. Nitsa provided a solution: she told the gunmen to leave casually, without taking the car, and she would report the murder to the police, explaining that she and Allen were jumped by two strangers as they opened the front door. As she was known to 'entertain' males, she expected the police to accept her story. But the police did not believe 25-year-old Nitsa's tale, although she stuck to it throughout her interrogation. According to Grivas, the authorities did not bring her to trial for murder because 'senior officers had been among her visitors and had frequently given her useful information'. Nevertheless they arrested her on several lesser charges, including aiding and abetting murder. Found guilty, she was sent to prison, where she worked in the kitchens. Her relative freedom allowed her, on behalf of EOKA, to pass coded messages to the other prisoners of both sexes.

Released in November 1956, she was re-arrested later and sent to the notorious Omorphita Interrogation Center. Under questioning, she admitted taking EOKA's No. 2, Gregoris Afxentiou from the Pentadactylos Mountains to Kakopetria in 1955, in a car driven by Kyriakos Matsis. Stopped at a British checkpoint, she and Afxentiou began making love in the back seat. The soldiers blushed and waved the car on.

When Governor Harding commuted her friend Nicos Xenophontas's death sentence to life imprisonment, Grivas believed that this was her reward for collaborating with the Security Forces and ordered EOKA to ostracize her. When she was eventually freed on 14 December 1957, many Greek Cypriot women condemned her for having behaved as a common prostitute. Her reply to them was always the same: 'Whoever does not give all for her country, gives nothing.' She died alone in poverty on 10 March 1958, with a Bible resting on her chest.

Sergeant Allen was not the first or the last British serviceman to fall in love with a Greek Cypriot woman. At least two other members of the RAF married during their tours of duty. When their wives were found to be related to known EOKA terrorists, Special Branch told their superior officers and these airmen were shipped out of the Island in a hurry.

AUGUST BEGAN in a flurry of activity with the requisitioning of buildings – described as 'only temporary'- for the additional troops headed to Cyprus. These were the first outward signs of the Suez crisis, although the War Office in London refused to give details of any military movements. In addition two areas of the Island became so-called 'protected areas' under military jurisdiction. Only government employees with special passes were allowed to travel in them. The first, roughly 100 square miles, was in the western mountain area. The second, eight miles from Famagusta, was to be surrounded with barbed-wire fences and signs in Greek, Turkish and English warning intruders that they could be shot on sight. The Government put a smokescreen round how the areas were to be used.

In the UK, battalions of the Suffolk Regiment, the Somerset Light Infantry, Oxfordshire and Buckinghamshire Light Infantry, the Royal Berkshire Regiment, the Duke of Wellington's Regiment, the Life Guards, Grenadier Guards, 16th Light Anti-Aircraft Regiment and 42 Commando Royal Marines, prepared to leave for Cyprus to strengthen forces on the Island and, perhaps, to be used to invade Egypt.

A confident Sir John Harding told the press in Nicosia that EOKA had not affected in any way the full availability of the Island as a base for British military power in the eastern Mediterranean, had not reduced the functioning of the Middle East command and communications centre and had not prevented him from making available special forces for use in any emergency, such as operations in the Suez Canal Zone. On that subject, General Sir Charles Keightley, C-in-C Middle East Land Forces, said: 'We have faithfully carried out our side of the [1954] agreement in fact and in spirit. Given proper leadership Egypt should be capable of exerting a stabilizing influence in the Middle East. As it is, we have to be prepared for anything to happen.'

The Times reported: 'French forces are already in position in the Mediterranean. Reservists have been with the Colours for several months, and there are 400,000 French troops already on a war footing in Algeria. Some of these, together with the fleet at Toulon and many bomber and fighter squadrons in Europe and North Africa, could be sent at very short notice to share the British bases in Malta and Cyprus.

On 7 August France and Britain established a joint military command, with Cyprus as its headquarters, for any attack on Egypt. Work to complete the runway at RAF Akrotiri was accelerated and the disused airfield at Tymbou – the site of today's Ercan Airport in North Cyprus – was reopened for use by the French Air Force. Watching the military build-up from Washington, President Eisenhower urged Prime Minister Eden not to act precipitously with French Prime Minister Mollet, because 'from this point onward our views on the situation diverge'. Put in non-diplomatic language, America was warning Britain that it could not count on any backing from the United States in the event of a war.

Once again British Forces would be expected to go into battle ill-equipped and poorly supported. Malcolm Johnson, the official historian of the King's Own Yorkshire Light Infantry, wrote: 'On arrival in Cyprus, the platoon had not been equipped with the latest modes of military transport, some vehicles even showed signs of having seen service against Rommel's Afrika Corps. One incident could have qualified for inclusion in a Disney cartoon; the driver, however, may not have been particularly amused. Our vehicles were ex-2nd World War and often very ancient. On an operation in a mountain village with a curving, narrow street I saw an 'A' Company 15 cwt truck passing, with the driver waving a stick at me. A closer look revealed that the gear lever had come out in his hand. How he managed not to have an accident I shall never understand.'

For the resident battalions, however, life still went on day after day much the same as before – conducting exhaustive patrols, returning to poor accommodation and confinement in camp when they came off-duty, never knowing when next they might be suddenly called out again. While they had their successes, they often returned with nothing to show for their efforts. A description of a typical small-scale operation was published in *The Green Tiger*, the journal of the Royal Leicestershire Regiment. It appears here unaltered and complete:

Weapons have been checked, First Field Dressings lie snug in hip pockets, the Patrol has been briefed and is to lay in ambush at …

The final cigarette is put out and, in square formation, the Patrol moves off on its night's task.

Yes, you all know the form, but which one of you can predict just what will happen tonight?

It has been quiet for several nights and, maybe, as we move off so too are terrorists moving into position to throw their bombs and to run.

Any fisherman will know just how we feel: we've picked a likely spot, the bait is there, but will we get a bite?

It's the old, old thrill and hope of the hunter that each feels as we move along, but the bait is now British lives and property, the depths of the water is the gloom of an orange grove or the confusion of alleyways, the bite is the bursting of bombs. Will we get a bite tonight?

We have to take a roundabout route to get unobserved into our ambush position and, each man alert, we move quietly along our approach route.

Suddenly, or so it seems, the whine of a fast approaching Jeep is heard. The driver pulls up and says: 'Terrorists seen at—'

We pile aboard, quick messages are passed to Base. We race off.

On arrival all is quiet. A cordon is quickly established and witnesses are interrogated. This is a fairly notorious area for incidents.

A lot of British families live here intermingled with Cypriot families and there are orange groves on three sides.

The report is that two youths have been spotted hiding something in straw on a roof and that two "lookouts" were seen signaling them to get down.

Well, this might be it!

It's a very good spot, there's plenty of bait and we've had many bites here.

The Police arrive and, with Cypriot families

sitting on their verandas in the cool of the evening (they look pretty apprehensive too) the search begins.

The search is meticulous and thorough.

The roofs of each house and shed in the area are checked.

Finally, we all meet around one house, bearings are checked, quick consultations are held. Yes, this is 'IT', no doubt about it.

Check back to the witnesses. 'Yes,' they reaffirm, 'they shouted either Bambi or Bambo' – and then we discover that this is the nickname for Haralambambous. A good clue this, we think. We decide it's even better when we discover that a family named Haralambambous lives in the house we are surrounding AND they have two sons, aged 17 and 18.

The family is all in a huddle outside the house. They seem eager to please. Perhaps a bit frightened too.

By Jove, this is the stuff!

We're on to the house, it's in the right area, 'Hambo' is in the right age group. Is he our fish? Tension rises, everybody is alert: 'Fetch Hambo.'

'Hambo' is produced from the middle of a twittering family group.

'Yes,' he says, 'I was on the roof this evening with my brother.'

Quite obviously this thickset, swarthy Cypriot desperado is our chap. We've now only got to drive the hook home. What is on the roof? Bombs? A Pistol? Ammo?

'Hambo' finishes the sentence and kicks a bundle of grass and twigs at his feet: 'I went up there to pull down this sparrow's nest.'

AGAINST THIS background, EOKA continued to 'execute' Greek Cypriots considered 'traitors'. In one case, masked men dressed as priests and wearing black hoods went into a coffee shop in Psomolophou and ordered the customers to stand against the wall. The owner tried to run through to a back room but was shot in the head and back and died soon after.

During the Second World War the Nazi occupiers of Greece had often taken innocent people from areas where guerrillas were active. When civil war broke out after the country's liberation by the Allies, Grivas, an admirer of German military methods, adopted similar practices. His 'X' gangs often grabbed hostages from ELAS, the Communist insurgents whom he was battling. At a meeting with his EOKA leaders in Cyprus at the start of the conflict he had even considered the abduction of children from service families. Dudley Barker, his biographer, said 'he was basing his campaign on a study of guerrilla activity in Greece during and after the occupation. During the civil war the Communists had abducted thousands of Greek children, taking them over the northern frontiers to hold them as hostages against the Greek Army.' Curiously, when it was suggested that service wives should be kidnapped and have their heads shaved before release, 'The Leader' flew into a fury and ordered his men never again to contemplate such action.

Knowing Grivas's views on hostage taking, the EOKA gang, acting on its own initiative, went out to find him one that he could use as a bargaining counter for the release of the three convicted terrorists who were awaiting execution. The man chosen was John Cremer, a 78-year-old retired civil servant who was known to take a walk along the same route every day. Each evening he gave an English lesson to some schoolgirls in Temblos. His capture was revealed in leaflets scattered in Nicosia. They said the old man was 'a senior agent of British military intelligence' and 'it was up to dictator Harding to show whether he is sufficiently interested in the fate of his spies to spare the lives of freedom-loving patriots for we know that considerations of simple humanity would be insufficient to induce him to use his powers of reprieve'. The message continued ominously: 'If the sentences of Zakos, Michael and Patatsos are not reprieved before noon on Saturday, 4 August, Cremer will be executed. There will be no further warning.' It was signed 'Dighenis'.

Andreas Zakos and Charilaos Michael were part of the gang that had attacked Major Coombe near Soli and murdered his driver Corporal Morum the previous December. The third man, Iakovos Patsatsos, was sentenced to death for killing Turkish Cypriot policeman Nihat Basif in North Nicosia on 23 April 1956. Patsatsos had also helped prepare the timing mechanism for the bomb Neophytos Sophocleous placed under Governor Harding's mattress. All three were awaiting execution on 9 August.

On the day Cremer was due to be executed, Zakos issued an appeal from his condemned cell for the old man's life to be spared. Within hours, EOKA circulated another leaflet that promised he would be released shortly. Just after midnight, a Greek Cypriot resident of Kyrenia heard a voice from his garden say: 'Tell the police that Cremer is in Elea Road.' The man telephoned the local station and a mobile patrol was directed to the spot, which was near the grounds of Cremer's house. They arrived to see a car racing off, leaving EOKA's hostage stumbling in the darkness. Suffering from shock, he was taken immediately to hospital. However, it was not Zakos who persuaded the gang not to kill Cremer, but several priests, who were sure there would be an unfavourable effect on public opinion if an innocent old man were murdered in cold blood.

Next day Superintendent C. E. Riley explained what had happened. He said Cremer was taking his customary evening stroll, when four masked men stepped from behind a tree, threatened him with a pistol, and said: 'EOKA, hold up your hands. We are not going to kill you.' He replied: 'Well, it doesn't much matter if you do at my age.' His captors bound, gagged, and blindfolded him before putting him in a car and driving away. He had no idea where or how far he was taken. When they stopped, he was carried inside a building, where he remained until the night of his release. The gag was only taken off to allow him to eat and drink.

As soon as he had recovered from the shock of his imprisonment, Cremer was flown to England 'for his safety'. On his arrival and reunion with his 100-year-old mother, he told journalists: 'I plan to return to Cyprus as soon as a peace agreement has been reached. I get along very well with both Greek and Turkish Cypriots.' The local community of Kyrenia shared that view. Everyone had a kind word for the old gentleman.

The executions of the three EOKA prisoners went ahead as scheduled, watched by British officials. The prison chaplain, Father Antonis, administered the sacraments before their deaths and conducted a short service over their bodies, while other inmates screamed protests and troops kept watch in silent cordoned streets around the prison. Local press reports claimed the din of the prisoners could be heard as far away as the Ledra Palace Hotel. For months, Harding had complained to the Colonial Office that the prison was understaffed, overcrowded and in an 'explosive state'. The unpleasant task of burying the three men in the prison grounds, therefore, fell to soldiers from the South Staffordshire Regiment. The next morning Greek Cypriots staged a three-day national strike with requiem services held in churches Island-wide.

A WEEK after the executions, Grivas astonished the colonial administration. He announced a conditional truce to hostilities, which he published in cyclostyled Greek leaflets that were circulated throughout the Island. The text, headed 'Declaration', said: 'For 16 months we heroic children of Cyprus have been fighting a bitter struggle for freedom. The opponent, who imposed upon us our national liberation movement by his unjustified intransigence, now makes use of the struggle, described by him as armed force, to justify his refusal of agreement with us. I undertook this struggle, not from personal ambition, but because I envisaged a free Cyprus. To this purpose I will devote all my strength. I am ready to give one more proof of my humanitarian sentiments, just to prevent new bloodshed and to help achieve a settlement between the two opposing sides in fulfilment of the wishes of a Greek Cyprus.

'I wish to declare: If our adversaries are really sincere when they state that under the conditions created in Cyprus by our activities it is impossible to achieve a just solution which we are seeking, I am ready to SUSPEND [sic] the operations of my men, and I am awaiting full corresponding action on the part of England to enable the fulfilment of Greek Cypriot claims as they have been expressed, supported, and outlined for future discussion by our Ethnarch, Archbishop Makarios. To prove my unshakable desire to promote a favourable solution of the work undertaken by Makarios, and to give him once again a chance to solve the Cyprus national question, I order from today a suspension of operations of all forces under my authority. The national organization of Cypriot fighters state, nevertheless, that they will keep their arms ready and at the alert, ready for new sacrifices if these should be imposed on us by any further threat, in the certainty that they have at their disposal the moral and material resources to prevail. (Signed) EOKA, Dighenis, the leader.'

Once again, the British began walking the streets of Cyprus freely, and in the capital long-idle café waiters scurried to serve capacity crowds. For the first time in months there were even queues outside the theatres near 'Murder Mile'. Greek Cypriots reacted with a collective sigh of relief. They hoped the truce would bring an end to curfews, cordons and collective punishments to which they had been subjected since the start of the conflict.

'From one hour to the next a sense of relief flooded the Island which was comparable to nothing I can think of so much as breaking the surface after too deep a dive,' wrote Penelope Tremayne, Red Cross nurse in Cyprus. 'This gave away, more clearly than anything I had yet seen, the fact that very many people were entirely ignorant of, or else uninterested in, what the EOKA campaign was really about. The English, who had been their friends, had suddenly and inexplicably become their enemies. Now there was a stop to that; and – who knew? Perhaps now the whole stupid nightmare would also come to an end. "Fraternization" flowered unexpectedly in all directions. Soldiers, against advice, went to the local cinemas, and found themselves talked to and patted on the back, or offered cups of coffee by total strangers. People who had been at pains not to be seen speaking to the English were now at pains to be seen so. It was all splendid while it lasted ...'

But why Grivas had chosen this moment to declare his truce was the subject of considerable speculation.

Several observers believed his decision may have been prompted by some loss of support for the *enosis* campaign and EOKA's methods. The Greek Cypriot populace, which once gave Grivas almost unanimous approval, had been increasingly distressed by bombings, riots and murders of 'traitors'. In the past weeks, several Greek Cypriots, including an EOKA deserter, had made anti-Grivas broadcasts on state radio and traders were suffering a loss of business – and money.

British expatriates were convinced the reason was that Grivas knew he was losing the conflict and that Harding's stern measures were paying dividends. Others gave a third explanation: EOKA saw an opportunity to squeeze substantial political concessions in return for peace at a time when Britain was caught up in the Suez crisis.

Bishop Anthimos of Kitium, the acting head

of the Greek Orthodox Church, said he was confident that the British Government would now free Archbishop Makarios, as this would be the 'necessary prerequisite for achieving an honorable and just solution in keeping with the will of the Cyprus people'. He stressed: 'As has been repeatedly declared the Ethnarchy unshakably believes that no progress on the Cyprus question can be achieved without the liberation of Archbishop Makarios. Only thus can new developments be initiated. In the absence of Makarios no political initiative will be taken and no negotiations will be held.'

Turkish Cypriots, by contrast, saw the truce offer as an attempt to 'get the British to let down their guard'. In Athens, politicians described the gesture as a political move, prompted by a desire to test the sincerity of the British Government's claim that violence was preventing a settlement of the Cyprus dispute. It was a 'noble decision' said the Greek press.

As a gesture of goodwill, the Cyprus Supreme Court commuted to life imprisonment the death sentence passed on an 18-year-old Greek Cypriot, Chrysostomos Panayi, for a bomb-throwing incident in which a British soldier was killed. It was the first occasion since the beginning of the conflict that a death sentence had been commuted.

At Government House, Field Marshal Sir John Harding called an immediate conference of his advisers to decide his administration's position. In the past he had doggedly reiterated the terms on which Britain would abandon its 'get tough' policy. 'Let the murderers make the first move if there is to be a stopping of violence,' he had said bluntly. Now EOKA had taken up the challenge. 'You must remember,' a British spokesman advised the media, 'that this is only one man's offer, and it comes from pieces of paper scattered in the street. If it is genuine, the Government will certainly not be backward in responding to such a welcome change, but common sense requires that it should heed the old advice, by

their deeds ye shall know them, and we must see whether in fact violence ceases. Sir John throws the entire responsibility for peace on the Island on the terrorist leader.'

'By their deeds ye shall know them' rightly became the order of the day, because some of Grivas's gangs were paying little heed to their 'Leader' and his offer of a truce. On 16 August, Signalman Len Staniforth and his wife were on honeymoon in Kyrenia and saw the 53-ton yacht *Fieldfare* sink in the harbour after a limpet mine exploded just before noon under her starboard bow. The yacht, owned by the Honourable Captain Charles Worthington, the Royal Horse Guards commander of the Governor's escort, was flying the burgee of the Royal Yacht Squadron and the White Ensign.

'Barbara and I were walking down to the harbour when we saw a rowing boat move into the middle and a youth go over the side to swim under the stern of the boat,' Staniforth remembered. 'Just as we were about 100 yards away, there was a sharp explosion and a sudden spout of water towards the rear end. She settled bow first, quite gently until her nose touched bottom and there she sat, her stern pointing to the sky. Later we heard that Craftsman Kopp of REME nearly lost his life because he had been swimming next to *Fieldfare* when the bomb went off.'

Following the explosion, troops of 1 Wiltshires, based at Kyrenia Castle, were stood to and police cordoned off the harbour, while

The *Fieldfare* lies in Kyrenia harbour.

the 2,460-ton destroyer *Corunna* was diverted to Kyrenia at top speed. A seven-ton recovery truck with mounted crane was also rushed from Nicosia to assist with the salvage operation. Captain Worthington, a well-known figure at social gatherings since his arrival in Cyprus in February, flew to the scene by helicopter, to check the damage. He came with his fiancée Camille Crawley, who was staying at Government House while on her visit to the Island.

When HMS *Corunna* reached the harbour mouth, Royal Navy frogmen went to investigate the damage to the yacht. They concluded that the mine had been attached expertly on the exterior, by a bulkhead, where it would cause the most damage. The mine, they said, was of Second World War origin and could be used as effectively on land as in water. Security officials believed EOKA had several of this type, salvaged from the waters off Famagusta, where they had been dumped in 1946.

At 14.30 *Fieldfare* heeled over and sank to her gunwales with about 20 soldiers and sailors left wading in a floating mess of deck wreckage. An official statement described the sinking as a deliberate act of sabotage against British property. Privately officials expressed the opinion that EOKA had hoped to kill Lieutenant John Harding, the Governor's son, who was on leave from the 11th Hussars in Germany and had been on board the night before.

Whatever his personal feelings about the assassination attempt on his son, Sir John Harding did not allow them to colour his judgement over the truce. He said: 'It could prove to be a turning point in the history of the island. The lesson of this past wretched period through which the island has gone is that violence does not pay. It is futile waste.' But he added a proviso: Grivas had called only for a suspension of violence, not its complete abandonment as a political weapon.

Meanwhile, plans to reclaim the Suez Canal from President Nasser continued apace in

Malta and Cyprus. There was non-stop movement of troops between the two islands as units were repositioned to increase their effectiveness in the event that an invasion of Egypt went ahead. On 14 August, 45 Commando left Cyprus to prepare for the assault on Suez. During their stay, the Marines had participated in 64 major anti-EOKA operations and arrested 505 suspected terrorists, 56 of whom were known hard-core terrorists with rewards on their heads.

A WEEK after Grivas's truce offer, Sir John called for EOKA's surrender and laid out his terms. Under these, the terrorists would be allowed to go to Greece without prosecution, but renouncing British nationality, or they could remain in Cyprus and take the consequences of their activity. His offer would remain open until 12 September. The full conditions were published in an official statement:

> In the new conditions created by the decision of the terrorists to call off their campaign of violence, the Government of Cyprus, with the full approval of her Majesty's Government, has decided that it would now be in the public interest to give the terrorists who are still at large on the island the opportunity of extricating themselves from the position into which their action in taking up arms against the established Government of the country has led them.
>
> These terrorists will therefore now be given the opportunity of surrendering with their arms. The offer will remain open for three weeks from midnight tonight.
>
> Details of the manner in which the terrorists should surrender themselves and their arms will be announced during the course of tomorrow.
>
> A terrorist who surrenders during this period in accordance with the procedure to be announced will have the choice of being dealt with in one of two ways:
> (i) He may opt to leave Cyprus for Greece as soon as the necessary arrangements can be made, and subject to certain conditions,

(ii) Or he may opt to remain in Cyprus. Once he has opted for one or other of these courses his decision will be final. If he decides to leave Cyprus for Greece the following terms will apply:

(a) He will be kept in detention pending his departure.

(b) He will not be prosecuted for any crime he may have committed before this announcement, even involving violence against the person.

(c) His option will be conditional upon proof that Greece is willing to admit him.

(d) If a British subject, he will be required to give an undertaking that on arrival in Greece he will apply for Greek nationality and will renounce his British nationality as soon as possible, and that he will not in future claim protection and privileges as a British subject.

(e) On his departure he will be declared a prohibited immigrant and will not be allowed to re-enter Cyprus. If he is not admitted into Greece, he will be treated as though he had opted to remain in Cyprus.

If he decides to remain in Cyprus the following terms will apply:

(a) If there is evidence against him of the commission of a specific offence involving violence against the person, he will be brought to trial.

(b) He will not be brought to trial for any terrorist offence not involving violence against the person committed before this announcement.

(c) Unless brought to trial and sentenced, he will remain in detention until released either by the ending of the State of Emergency or by virtue of an order of the Governor, whichever is the earlier. At a later stage, when the Governor is satisfied that stable conditions of peace and order have been re-created, he will be prepared to declare an amnesty for certain offences committed by the terrorists and their supporters now in prison or under detention.

This amnesty will include those who surrender under the terms of this announcement. It must be remembered that the carrying of arms and the possession of arms and explosives without lawful authority continue to be illegal and are offences punishable with death and life imprisonment respectively.

There will be no relaxation in the efforts of the security forces to enforce the law.

'When I heard the news on our little set in the underground hide at Limassol I told Georgiades that, at least, we did not have to spend time considering a reply,' wrote Grivas in his *Memoirs*. 'I made my decision in the space of time it takes to utter the word 'NO!' and I picked up my pen at once to write our answer. My proclamation was circulated with lightning speed and the British were astonished to find a leaflet rejecting Harding's ultimatum on the streets of every town and village by midday on 23 August.

A Government spokesman said that 120,000 leaflets containing the surrender terms and instructions to terrorists would be distributed throughout the island as soon as possible. The leaflet would instruct terrorists to report to the nearest police station or military unit.

Tom Driver, an Army pilot, helped to airdrop 103,000 leaflets at various times. 'The numbers dropped on a particular locality or area weren't fixed,' he said. 'If there had been a spot of trouble in a particular area, then the numbers were increased. Similarly, such important issues, like "surrender terms", had a much larger circulation and larger quantities. A typical example was Famagusta, which normally received only 2,500, but had 8,000 of the "surrender" issue. Famagusta was an easy run, because the ground there is reasonably level and we let the wind spread them.

Translated from Greek, one leaflet read:

'WHAT EOKA OFFERS:
Blood, sadness, fear, destruction of children, loss of a peaceful life, economic troubles, confinement to your house, terrorism, shootings, that's the bad name they give Cypriots all over the world. WHY? It is now very obvious that the British are deeply involved in Cyprus and they are not leaving. The problems EOKA say they are solving are those it created. It is a big mistake and the people admit it. Grivas is more interested in the personal glory he hopes to get than the happiness of the Cypriot people. WHAT IS THE WAY OUT FROM ALL THIS ANIMOSITY? Stop the killing by EOKA. Forget the use of force and work together in co-operation to give Cypriots the chance to have political independence. Know that the beginning of self-government was rejected and it is impossible to have it in the present conditions. But if all the people work together for the happiness of Cyprus, there will be peace, happiness, and self-government! It is not impossible to abandon the force of arms to work together for the constitution that will give Cypriots the chance to conduct their own affairs. The recognition of this is the beginning of self-determination. But it is impossible under the situation that is in force at present. All people, there are a lot of reasons for happiness on the island. EOKA stop the killings.'

Dropping leaflets for the 18 villages of the Troodos was much more hazardous. The task at times was 'downright dangerous' where the villages either cling to the sides of the steep mountains or lie in valleys between the peaks, rising to heights between 5,000 and 6,000 feet. 'It was almost impossible to make the leaflets go where you wanted them, because quite often the air was rising at such a rate that the leaflets went up instead of down,' Tom Driver recalled. 'When that occurred we had to wait and make test drops at odd times until conditions were suitable.'

Flying skilfully, the aircrews managed to continue dropping their loads, often from an altitude of less than 30 feet. 'In some cases, we dumped a lot from so low down that they landed on a café doorstep,' Driver said. 'Apart from the airdrop proper, we also made free drops of bundles of leaflets to be given out by hand. The leaflets were well wrapped in parcels of 5,000 or so. We just flew low and slow over the marker and pushed them out.'

Then the scientists at Boscombe Down back in the UK devised a contraption which, they claimed, would add to accuracy and cut down on wastage. The device consisted of a cardboard folder in which 50 leaflets had to be carefully packed and tied with a nylon cord. Next the flyers were told to place a small fuse under the space where the lines crossed. The fuse was attached to another length of string, which had to be tied to the aircraft.

Carrying these folders, the pilots were expected to fly a certain distance upwind of the targeted village and release them at six-second intervals. As the folders fell, the line connected to the plane was supposed to pull a pin, which, in turn, ignited the fuse. The scientists claimed that if the pilot were flying according to plan, the fuse would go bang and, hey presto, 200 feet above the ground, out would pop the leaflets from the folder.

The scientists' scheme was a complete failure. Tom Driver explained: 'On one test run, a cord was accidentally pulled inside the aircraft and the whole lot went pop in the cabin. I think the pilot had enough to cope with without worrying about a fire in the back and hundreds of leaflets blowing round and round his controls.'

Aircrews were against the scheme from the start. The folders took time to pack properly, added extra weight to the plane and far too often the fuses failed to ignite. 'In addition, if a village were stuck on the side of a 5,000-foot mountain, it wasn't always possible to get upwind and at the height advised. Worst of all, the device was a fire hazard,' Driver explained. The scientists' device was put away, never to be seen again. 'One Sunday afternoon an aircraft flew over our camp in Limassol and made a drop,' said RAOC Corporal Lawrence Petley. 'We could see the leaflets floating down from the sky, all glittering in the brilliant sunshine. There were thousands of them, but unfortunately there was a slight breeze and most of them drifted down on us. The whole camp was littered with our own leaflets, which didn't please us at all, because we had to spend the rest of our day-off picking them up.'

Charles Foley, the *Times of Cyprus* editor, reported one particular leaflet drop: 'An RAF Auster droned over Nicosia circling round and showering copies of the printed "surrender" instructions on amazed heads below. The call was bellowed through an amplified loudspeaker in pidgin Greek as the plane flew low over the rooftops. People in the streets flung their arms up and cried: "We surrender – now go away." In Detention Camp K a prisoner pinned a "surrender" notice to his chest and walked into the Commandant's office to ask for his liberty and a free air ticket to Athens.'

The Colonial Office in London backed Harding's surrender offer to Grivas and his gangs, pointing out that if it were accepted 'it will help create conditions in which real progress can be made in the introduction of responsible self-government. Lord Radcliffe has already agreed to do all in his power to accelerate his programme and to produce the main outline of his recommendations' on a new constitution for the Island. Privately, Harding never expected a surge of EOKA members rushing to surrender. He told Colonial Secretary Lennox-Boyd: 'The main reason for putting out surrender terms is political. It will regain for us the initiative which for the moment EOKA has seized by its dramatic gesture.'

TALK OF surrender became a red rag to the bull that was Grivas. When the Governor

Grivas responds to the Governor's demand to give up the EOKA struggle.

repeated his offer in a radio broadcast, 'The Leader' charged with a rare sense of humour. He arranged for a donkey, with two wooden guns strapped to its back, to be paraded through Nicosia, with an 'I SURRENDER' placard attached to the animal's rear. The donkey was caught eventually and its placard and wooden guns removed by armed soldiers. Simultaneously two large cloth signs appeared on buildings facing Metaxas Square, entrance to the old walled city, and on the walls of the Sports Stadium. They had been raised by Renos Lyssiotis, Grivas's youth leader in Nicosia. His boys and girls had spent the night painting the slogans – 'ALL FIGHTERS ARE AT THEIR POSTS', 'Second week and EOKA is holding firm' and 'Not a single surrender to date'. The signs were torn down to the jeers of Sunday night strollers.

At the same time another of Grivas's leaflets appeared on the streets. Written in Greek, his message was headlined: 'Victors, do not surrender.' Grivas continued clearly and to the point: 'As military commander of the fighting Cypriot people, my reply to the Government's surrender terms is "No, come and take it!"' Dighenis was quoting the classical Greek hero Leonidas, who defended the pass at Thermopylae against the forces under Xerxes in 480 BCE, and replied to the Persian king's call to surrender with those words. Having laid down his challenge, Grivas added a threat: 'It is impossible to halt our campaign unless a final agreement is reached. The British Government's demand shows a lack of sincerity, and indicates shortsightedness. But to indicate once again my good will and desire to prevent bloodshed, I declare that if by the 27th of this month the wretched surrender order is not withdrawn and negotiations on the basis of Archbishop Makarios's terms are not begun, then I am relieved of obligations concerning the truce which I declared of my own initiative, and shall resume freedom of action.'

A second leaflet, in English, was addressed directly at British service personnel: 'We have offered you peace and we have kept our word about the ceasefire. In return for this noble gesture your Government is pushing us to war against you. They asked us to surrender: we replied "No." The British Government and Harding have proved to be insincere and are

The Greek people as a Greek, Greek-feeling, Greek Orthodox, Greek speaking people belong to the Western world. The western mentality, the western civilization, the western interest are their own. The best proof for this is the Cypriot claim for self-determination. For the right of self-determination is a fundamental right which has been brought into expression and sanctioned by the Western Nations. Were not the western powers who spoke about it and made a "credo" out of it during the last world war? Were not the Western Nations that invited every freedom-loving human being to join them in their effort to fight against the dictatorial oppression of the axis, in order to defend and preserve freedom, the fundamental human and national right, the dignity of the human being? If this is so, and there could not be any doubt about how is it to be explained that one of the leading western nations, Great Britain, denies the application of these rights? Because no one can deny that Great Britain or rather the Conservative British Government is refusing Cypriots their freedom, their right to determine their own destiny and future, that it is trying to suppress their national wishes and annihilate their dignity as human beings.

May be one world object, that Great Britain is been obliged to change its attitude towards these fundamental ideas which were sanctioned by the Charter of the United Nations, that it no longer believes in their value. This is not the case. Because the Conservative British Government avails itself of every possible opportunity to appear as the most fervent defendant of these ideas and values. It suffices to recall the emotion shown by this Government when Soviet troops suppressed the Hungarian people's uprising. Right they were but are they right to do in Cyprus what the Russians did in Hungary? In connection with Cyprus the British Government say that there will be "sometime" self-determination for the Cyprus people. They said it three years ago. When the question of the unification of Germany is at stake that is in a case where the Russians are the offenders the Conservative Prime Minister of Great Britain states that unless the Soviet Government are prepared to grant the fundamental right of self-determination to the German people, there will be little chance for other important differences between East and West to be settled. Are the Cypriot people not entitled to say after what they have experienced under British rule that unless the British Government grants them the right of self-determination there is no chance for the establishment of friendly relations between the Island and Great Britain?

P.E.K.A.
Political Committee of the Cyprus Struggle).

A message from Grivas to British forces.

thinking ill ... We are not responsible if more English blood is shed again – plenty of blood this time.'

At Government House, Sir John had received an emergency Top Secret telegram from the Secretary of State for the Colonies. It said that the British Government would be releasing English translations in the next few days of extracts from captured EOKA documents and Grivas's diary. These had come into the hands of the Royal Horse Guards and Royal Leicesters on 20 August during a cordon-and-search operation of Lysi. Their discovery suggested there was a traitor at the heart of EOKA, because a month earlier an anonymous letter had been sent to the Security Forces to say that a quantity of arms was due to be moved from a specific area of the village that same night. Only later was the writer of the letter identified as a man named Paschalis Papadopoulos. Many Greek Cypriots believe he was a highly paid informer for the security services.

As all available troops and police were already engaged on another operation, only one troop of the Royal Horse Guards was available to investigate. At about 20.30 on 19 July, two troopers spotted three men come out of the village and enter a small hut. The full patrol followed the Greek Cypriots and saw them digging up a large glass jar containing a .45 revolver and a quantity of ammunition. The men's arrest led to the discovery of a number of other arms caches, including 18 filled pipe bombs, 50 filled cartridges and a quantity of empty shotgun cartridges, eleven shotguns, some lead, and eight time pencils.

When more soldiers became available Lysi was 'turned over' in the following days. During one raid, an underground hide was found.

It consisted of a chamber about ten feet square with a boarded-up entrance, made to resemble a manhole, and covered with backyard rubble and firewood. The only other connection with the outside world was via an underground drainpipe running from a nearby house to the hideout and through which food or messages could have been passed. 'As we embussed there was a loud explosion and a tall column of dust and debris shot up from the centre of the village,' said a member of the Royal Leicesters Headquarters Company sent to support the Horse Guards. 'The police had demolished the underground hideout that they had discovered.'

Finally, on 20 August, came the most important discovery of all: the secret EOKA papers and the Grivas diary stuffed in several glass jars buried deep in the ground. Credit for the find went to 19-year-old Troopers Maurice Bowler of Leeds, Arthur Hobbs of Liverpool, John Freestone of London and Thomas Ansell of Nottingham, all National Servicemen. Corporal Greaves and Private Downing of the Royal Leicesters also contributed but were overlooked in the excitement. 'We contributed quite a lot that week,' one of them said later.

These documents, amounting to more than 250,000 words, would conclusively prove that Archbishop Makarios was EOKA's real leader and Grivas took his orders from him. To

A page from the captured Grivas diary.

A translation of a captured EOKA document.

The bottle that contained the Grivas diary.

discuss the future of Cyprus with the prelate, as Grivas demanded, would be a victory for terrorism. The Government hoped that the international community would now understand the real nature of the conflict and why Britain must win. Certainly, there were many in the United States who saw the head of the Church of Cyprus in a new light and were less sympathetic to his 'cause', something he had promoted to great effect during his frequent visits to America.

The discovery and publication of the documents surprised and shocked Grivas. Still keeping a diary, he wrote: 'The first impression is deplorable. The morale of the people has suffered a shock. To raise it again I have given orders to area commanders to consider it as if it were a matter of no consequence. I have put out leaflets saying that the whole story of my journal has been fabricated by the British in order to distract world attention from the situation in Cyprus, which they themselves have created.'

He added: 'There was no doubt in my mind, after the insulting demand for surrender and the publication of my diary, that Harding wants to provoke us into a fight to the finish.'

(Grivas later claimed that 'the inquisitors of the intelligence service' had forged the diary, with the assistance of its paid informers in Athens. In a letter to several British newspapers, he wrote: 'I shall in time reveal the way that the diary was forged with the help of persons who are now under the protection of the British.' Dighenis, like the translators in London, knew every line was genuine.)

To a tough soldier like Harding it was clear: if Grivas refused to accept his surrender offer, then the fight must continue with added vigour. The pride of two implacable personalities was now at stake. The Governor acted first by cordoning Dr Themistocles Dervis's surgery and house. Dervis, the Mayor of Nicosia, was ordered to accompany troops as they searched his premises. At the same time police officers took the keys of the Municipality building in Metaxas Square.

At the airport, Renos Kyriakides, brother of the exiled Bishop of Kyrenia, was put on board a flight to London, where he faced interrogation on the contents of the Grivas diaries. In Larnaca, a restriction order was served on the Bishop of Kitium, the senior Orthodox priest on the Island. From now on he would be confined to his official residence, unable to leave or see visitors without police approval. All his correspondence would be subjected to examination by the security forces. This action was taken because Sir John accepted the evidence in the captured EOKA

documents that the bishop was personally implicated in the organization of terrorism and the supply of funds for the purchase of weapons.

The clock ticked towards midnight on 27 August. By 19.00 shops in Nicosia had their shutters drawn down. Ledra Street, the capital's 'Murder Mile', was once more deserted. Since the truce, people had regained their confidence to shop in a carefree atmosphere and stay up late to enjoy the pleasures of bars and restaurants. Traders had seen a boom in their profits. Would Grivas now resume the conflict all over again? For the security forces, the answer was a clear affirmative. Within hours of the truce ending, they were finding and disarming bombs across Cyprus. As night followed day, the terrorist activity would continue.

Before August ended, a British Army officer was shot at five times in the Greek quarter of Nicosia, and wounded in both arms, while walking with his wife. Both were wounded and taken to hospital. At a village police station, terrorists engaged British troops in a 20-minute gun battle. The same evening, a serviceman and two army wives were slightly injured during an EOKA attack in the capital's suburbs. In Famagusta port, the British ship *Charles McLeod* was holed by an explosion caused by a limpet mine attached to the vessel's hull while it was in port. It tore a hole in the ship's side, causing a fuel leak. There were no injuries to the crew.

On 1 September, a stand-by section of the Royal Norfolk Regiment under Sergeant Norman Folkard was sent out to the village of Kolossi to investigate an EOKA crime. En route the vehicle in which the group was travelling skidded on loose stones and overturned. Folkard and Private Kenneth Squires were killed outright and 12 other members of the patrol were injured.

The next day, Grivas tried to destroy the printing presses on which the Governor's 'surrender' posters were run off by their thousands. The first EOKA bomb exploded in the building, causing considerable damage, but were there any more timed to go off? Acting Sergeant John Proudlock of the RAOC volunteered to find out.

In July 1957, he was awarded the George Medal. The citation read:

On the night of 2 September 1956, a part of the Government Printing Establishment in Cyprus was destroyed by a bomb. A second suspected bomb was seen in a hole beneath a machine. On being called, Sergeant Proudlock entered the building, from which all others had been withdrawn, and although he could reach the bomb with only one hand, removed it and carried it outside. He then extracted the time pencil, in spite of the fact that it was jammed. The bomb was powerful and very dangerous for it might have exploded at any time. Sergeant Proudlock well knew this. Sergeant Proudlock has disarmed fourteen time bombs. He has been on call by night and by day and has never failed to perform his difficult and dangerous duties with courage and devotion.

CHAPTER FOURTEEN

Suez, *Sparrowhawk* and the fountain bombing

'He who seeks vengeance must dig two graves: one for his enemy and one for himself.'
Confucius

THE GRIMY troopship *Athos II* flying the French Tricolour smoked its way into Limassol harbour. On board were 1,400 blue-bereted paratroopers in their leopard-skin combat uniforms and 1,300 airmen. EOKA meant nothing to them. Suez was the only word on their minds. They were battle-hardened veterans who had served in Indo China and Algeria, confident they could care for themselves without any protection from the British. For them it only mattered that the *Bacchus*, a 3,226-ton tanker, sloshing with wine, anchored safely without spilling a drop. All they needed from the British were efficient stevedores and so 'C' Company of the Leicesters was 'volunteered' to fill the role. For a week, the soldiers unloaded stores from the French craft at Famagusta docks and else-where. They also became experts in handling tons of high-octane gasoline, landed on open beaches from Z craft for the French Air Force. 'We had the greatest difficulty,' said an NCO, 'in making our gallant allies understand the meaning of *defense de fumer*.' To prevent

French troops arrive in Cyprus.

dehydration from the blazing late summer sun, each soldier is reputed to have consumed an average of 38 bottles of Coca-Cola every day.

From his underground hideout in a house 100 yards from the main Limassol bypass, lined with pomegranate trees, Grivas saw the road jammed with French Army trucks moving towards the port, while British lorries laden with ammunition and equipment headed in the opposite direction towards camps outside Nicosia, where many of the newcomers would be stationed. There were military policemen everywhere erecting new road signs that said *Tenez la Gauche* (Keep to the Left). The house belonged to Marios Christodoulides, a young clerk employed by the Ottoman Bank at its branches inside the Episkopi base. The British called him 'the right kind of Cypriot'.

Always a cautious man, Grivas considered all his options in the new conditions and discussed them with his personal assistant, Antonis Georghiades, with whom he shared his hiding space. From dawn to dusk – and sometimes beyond – 'The Leader' dictated his thoughts and his aide dutifully tapped them out on a battered typewriter. Together they churned out a constant stream of orders to gang leaders and leaflets for public consumption. In the rare pauses in his stream of consciousness, Grivas looked out of the window at the Union flag fluttering over the army school within walking distance.

(Georghiades, who had run the EOKA gang in his home village of Milikouri, survived the EOKA conflict and was known to be running a small photographic business in Nicosia in 2008. According to a reliable source, he was not welcome back in Milikouri and not honoured by the inhabitants for his contribution to 'the struggle'.)

Grivas decided to stay neutral on the political issues surrounding the Suez crisis but saw that there was no better time than now to seri-

ously disrupt British involvement by targeted sabotage at the new military bases, more town assassinations and a greater number of convoy ambushes. For the French, he would make life as easy as possible. Under no circumstances were his men to attack them, he ordered. Rather they should befriend them, win their support and offer to buy their surplus arms.

At the age of 26, Grivas had won a scholarship to study at the *Ecole de Tir* and the *Ecole d'Infanterie* at Versailles. He had also been attached to the 8th French Army Division for an advanced military course before the Second World War. As he could speak the language, he drafted a leaflet in basic French, which said that as long as the troops did not provide any anti-EOKA assistance to the British, they would have nothing to fear. He wished them a happy stay in Aphrodite's Isle and a safe return home. In addition, he addressed letters to General Jean Gilles, commander of the French airborne

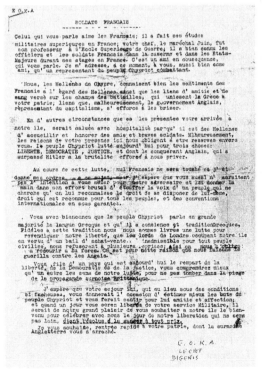

Grivas sends a message to the French troops.

forces, and Admiral Barjot, the Deputy Commander-in-Chief of Allied Forces, based at Akrotiri, informing them of his intentions.

Grivas's letters and leaflets had the desired effect, because within days the French were behaving like tourists, strolling freely around the Island in their off-duty hours and enjoying the nightlife in the towns. Their behaviour irritated British soldiers who were banned from such activity. Foreign newspaper reporters gathering in Nicosia to cover the Suez operations quickly placed large stickers on their cars in Greek and English giving their nationalities in the hope the Colonel would include them in his pro-French policy. A German journalist went further. He pinned a cardboard placard on his vehicle, with the plea: 'Don't shoot. I am German!'

Whatever Grivas may have felt for the French troops, the Athens-based Greek committee for Cypriot self-determination did not share his view. The Greek Primate, Archbishop Dorotheos, headed it and he sent a strongly worded protest to the French Government demanding their removal. Dr Vasos Papadopoulos, Limassol's deputy mayor, was also against them. He telegrammed the Governor to say they were 'detrimental to the Island's economy and will send the cost of living higher'. He wanted them to go home as soon as possible.

Suffragan Bishop Yennadios of Salamis, the acting head of the Ethnarchy Council, the ruling body of the Orthodox Church of Cyprus, joined the protesters by insisting that the presence of French troops had widened the gap between the colonial government and the Cypriots by serving aims alien to the desires of the Cypriot people. 'This act proves that the British are not seriously concerned in finding a solution to satisfy the desires of the Cypriots for self-determination,' he argued in a perverse demonstration of logic.

Cypriot farmers and wine producers, too, expressed disapproval. They objected to the French bringing their own wines with them and considered their action an insult.

Royal Engineers everywhere were under pressure to get military facilities ready. At Akrotiri, 37 Regiment laid a 1,250-foot-long ship-to-shore aviation fuel pipeline, storage tanks and pumps. Nick Carter, a reservist, posted to 47 GHQ Survey Squadron at Episkopi, had the job of supervising the production of up-to-date maps of which there was a shortage for the troops destined for Egypt. Every day his team had to make changes as fresh details were flown from London by Canberra aircraft. Given just seven days' notice, another RE group had to erect a camp at Pyroi, 14 miles south of Nicosia, to house a complete French brigade. To meet the deadline, they had to use local labour, 'recruited in a somewhat unorthodox manner, with the aid of village bus drivers, who rounded up anyone they saw until their buses were full'.

To make the French feel 'at home', the British Forces Broadcasting Station in Nicosia launched a records request programme for them, introduced immaculately in their own language by Mary Tipler, a sort of forces' sweetheart with a touch of garlic.

On 9 September, French troops learned a little about what their British allies had to endure in Cyprus. Contrary to Grivas's strict orders, an EOKA gang mounted an ambush of a French convoy on the Famagusta–Nicosia road. The French troops returned fire and there were no casualties among their ranks. They now realized they were no longer immune because they flew the Tricolour on their uniforms. (Curiously, Grivas neglects to mention this event in his *Memoirs*.)

WITH MILITARY attention focused on the Suez crisis, EOKA operations became ever more daring and British casualties mounted. The Norfolks' garrison in Limassol was not only kept extremely busy with a constant succession of murders, bombs and alarms of different sorts, but was forced to take on additional duties: guarding ammunition ships in port and escorting lighters carrying stores from ship to shore. Early in September yet another duty was thrust on to the Battalion. It was required to provide a company to guard construction work at Episkopi-Akrotiri cantonment where the new GHQ, Middle East Land Forces, was being built and where EOKA supporters were doing a lot of damage.

Despite the Norfolks' presence, there was no shortage of cases, which included the burning down of the almost completed residence for the C-in-C Middle East Land Forces. The fire brigade could only save the kitchen and garage. The house was to have accommodated Lieutenant General Sir Geoffrey Bourne, who was replacing General Sir Charles Keightley in October.

Greek Cypriots were employed to do the building work and while every effort was made to control them it was not always possible to prevent such acts of sabotage. In one incident, 2nd Lieutenant D. C. L. Earle of 'C' Company was lucky not to be hurt when he was caught squarely in a bomb blast, which hurled him backwards. In another, 2nd Lieutenant D. R. Burns, also of 'C' Company, was told to investigate a mysterious box found in a cave. Not expert in dismantling bombs, Burns was advised to step away while Staff Sergeant Joseph Culkin, of the RAOC, handled the object. Unknown to him, it was booby-trapped. The moment his fingers touched it, it exploded, killing him. Captain Peter Macdonald, who knew him well, observed: 'There wasn't much left of him to put in the coffin. I watched being lowered into a hole in the military cemetery in Nicosia a few days later.'

Much as before, however, more British fatalities were being caused by traffic accidents than by EOKA. One of the worst occurred on 7 September when an RAF truck overturned after hitting a culvert near Famagusta, injuring 20 airmen and causing the deaths of Sergeant James Hunter, LAC Kenneth McNulty and Airman Anthony Davis, a day later in hospital. Two days later, there was another British fatality: Gunner Thomas Thompson of the Royal Artillery.

On 8 September, Tassos Sophocleous, who ran the terrorist groups in the Kyrenia District, agreed a raid on the police station by the Castle. Dinos Haralambos, the school caretaker, led the group, consisting almost entirely of schoolboys from the Gymnasium. Armed with a Sten, four revolvers, three shotguns and 15 home-made grenades, the 12 teenagers stormed the building at 03.00, forcing the guards to surrender, but only after a Turkish policeman had wounded two of the attackers. Before they escaped, they grabbed two Sterling sub-machine guns and as much ammunition as they could carry to their two waiting cars. By chance, two paratroopers saw them loading the vehicles and opened fire. In their hurry to get away, the young terrorists dropped most of the stolen ammunition.

The day before Harding's surrender offer to EOKA expired, Lance Corporal Roy Newsome of the RASC and REME Private George Roberts were added to the list of British service deaths. An official curtly said: 'The offer will not be extended. No surrenders have taken place.' EOKA answered by planting five time bombs in the Dhekelia military hospital, which was under construction. They were put in position by Andreas Koumides, who was employed at the site. Three of the bombs exploded in succession between 05.00 and 11.00 and caused damage to valuable laundry machinery and equipment. Nobody was killed, but several soldiers were injured. About 350 Cypriot workers immediately stopped work and went home.

The next day Private Norman Eggleton of the Royal Norfolks lost his life. On 15 September Corporal Paul Farley of the RAOC was shot dead in Ayios Dhometios. A day later Captain Francis Hellier was murdered while he was out shopping. The death toll mounted relentlessly and the Security Forces were failing to capture the culprits.

In Nicosia Prison another three convicted terrorists awaited execution. Grivas had warned that if they were hanged, he would exact vengeance in the old-fashioned way of an eye for an eye. Harding was not to be cowed and he rejected the prisoners' last-minute appeal for clemency. Early in the morning of 21 September, Michael Koutsoftas, 22, and Andreas Gregori Panayides, 22, convicted of the shooting and killing of Corporal Patrick Hale of the RAF on 16 May, and Stelios Mavromatis, 23, who, on 15 March, fired at LAC Lawrence Leith and Senior Technician N. A. Kitchen, met their maker.

In protest against the hangings of 'national heroes who died fighting for the sacred cause of freedom' Greek Cypriots began an 'unofficial' general strike throughout Cyprus. Factories, offices and newspapers closed.

Shops, except those selling food, remained shut and workers again 'took a holiday'. The gulf between British residents and Greek Cypriots grew wider. Nobody doubted there would be repercussions.

The first 'eye' Grivas took was RAF Corporal Mervyn Whurr, 22. Because his duty hours in Nicosia were usually 07.00 to 13.00, he often went to Kyrenia for a swim in the afternoon. On the 24th, he had agreed to join his friend Jim Fail in the port town. They had both arrived in Cyprus within days of each other and came from the same UK town – Sopley.

'For my trip to Kyrenia on this occasion, I took the coast road, travelling east from Kormakiti village, where I had filled our bowser with water,' Fail told the author. 'As I neared the town, the place was crawling with soldiers and civilian police. I was waved through to the place where Mervyn and I were

to meet. Here I discovered that he had gone into the sea for a swim. While he was away, EOKA had planted a bomb under his towel. It detonated the moment he picked it up to dry himself. He was rushed to BMH in Nicosia for urgent treatment, but died there soon afterwards. On returning to Kormakiti, I had to break the sad news to his other mates.'.

The next day Royal Artillery Sergeant Andrew Hay, 25, a married soldier, was killed when his truck drove over a mine in the Paphos district. Eleven of his comrades were injured. Barely a few hours later, Driver James Neil of the RASC died in another incident.

On 26 September the Royal Horse Guards lost its doctor, Surgeon Captain Gordon Wilson, 29. 'I was orderly when the doctor drove off from camp into town to attend a Greek family,' said Trooper Graham Williams, who was at the Blues and Royals' armoured section HQ. 'He was a National Serviceman from St Andrews.'

As Wilson pulled up at a road junction, his killer pushed a pistol through the driver's side window and squeezed the trigger, before running back to his two female accomplices at a nearby café, who took his weapon and walked casually away.

According to a member of his regiment, 'not one Cypriot, of whom there were many within 100 yards, went to his aid'. 'An hour later they brought back his clothing.' Lieutenant General Roy Redgrave added: 'Whenever a soldier was murdered we were all shaken, especially so when it was someone as popular as our Medical Officer. Wilson was married with a young son.'

The principal assassin was again Nicos Sampson. Ironically, it was a Blues and Royals patrol that eventually caught him some months later.

TWELVE DAYS after his arrival in Cyprus Private Colin Read of the 1st Wiltshire Regiment became another victim in Grivas's

A rifle salute at the funeral of Surgeon Captain Gordon Wilson.

roll call of vengeance. He was killed in an EOKA ambush. Bristol City Football Club lost a forward and Hazel Jefferies her fiancé. The next morning the postman delivered his last letter to her. Pat Beasley, his manager, said: 'Colin was one of the most promising players we had on our books. He was big and strong and certainly would have made the grade as a League player when he came out of the Forces.'

Read had volunteered to be one of a pair of escorts for a WVS helper, Mary Holton, who had been visiting the Wiltshire Regiment at Aghirda Camp to organize film shows and was returning to her Kyrenia hotel on Saturday night, 28 September. She was in the first Austin Champ, driven by Private Woods, and Read was in the second, with Private Flower at the wheel.

Not far from Bellapais on their right, there were two steep 'S' bends, 150 yards apart on the Nicosia–Kyrenia Road. Just as their vehicles reached the space between them, they slowed to a crawl and came under rifle and Bren gun fire from a gully on one side and a ridge on the other. Before anyone could find cover, a mortar bomb landed and exploded. The blast threw Read on to the ground. His Champ skidded and overturned in a ditch.

Severely wounded by a bullet in his neck, Private Woods nevertheless pressed his foot on the accelerator and raced to the nearest Wiltshire Company, which was based near Kyrenia Castle. At the main gate, he stopped his vehicle and collapsed from blood loss and shock. His passenger, Mary Holton, was dead.

When the 20-year-old Private Read's body was collected, medics found he had been shot

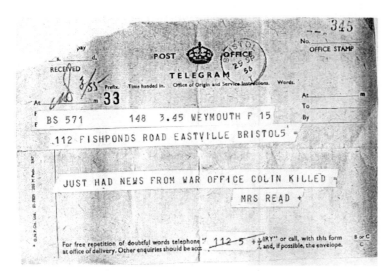

The telegram sent to
Colin Read's fiancée.

through his ribs. A second bullet was pulled from a leg. 'I think it was merciful that if he had to die in this tragic way, he died immediately and was spared the pain from a lingering death,' Major F. R. E. Turner of A Company wrote to the young soldier's mother. 'He was a very promising soldier ... I was considering making him a junior NCO as I thought so highly of him.'

Bert Smith was a pallbearer at Colin Read's funeral at Wayne's Keep Cemetery. Aged 71 and living in Ozankoy, North Cyprus, in 2009, he remembers: 'I shared a tent with him and knew him well. It could have been anyone escorting Mrs Holton that day, but it happened to be Colin who volunteered.'

Mary Holton, the 48-year-old widow from Scotland, was greatly mourned by the WVS. 'There are probably few gatherings of British Army personnel in the world where her name was not known and loved. She had given most of the past 12 years to the Army, serving in Egypt, Malaya, Korea and Japan. Sometimes she was with the troops, sometimes with their wives and children, but always with the same quiet understanding and distinction in her work, with the same interest in good conversation and the ability often to lift it out of its normal deadly rut, always with the same

enjoyment of a party,' a friend said. 'She was told in Germany, not very long after the war ended, that she was to be recommended for an award in appreciation for some outstanding service, but she asked that her name should not go forward, saying that others deserved honour so much more than her. Returning recently, after a very severe operation, to the life she chose after the death of her husband, she would, I think, still have refused any honour other than the awareness that she had striven to serve and had given of her best.'

Grivas said later that the murder gang consisted of nine men, six on one side of the road and three on the other. The bullets that ripped into Mary Holton and Colin Read were fired from a Bren gun manned by 18-year-old Vassos Petronas. After the ambush, he escaped and hid in Bellapais for a few days.

The next day an assassination team in Nicosia murdered two British police officers – Sergeants Cyril John Thorogood, 29, and Hugh Carter, 25 – and wounded a third, Sergeant William Webb. In Larnaca, Sergeant Wilfred Jepson, 43, of the 14/20 King's Hussars died in hospital from his wounds caused by another EOKA attack as he was returning from church with his wife and child. Petrakis Kyprianou, 17, was his suspected killer. Expelled from the American Academy for trouble-making, he joined EOKA at the age of 15, taking his oath in the town's St John's Church. During his year-long membership, he led hand grenade attacks on military convoys and executed so-called 'traitors'. He vowed he would not be taken alive. On 21 March 1957, the Security Forces shot him dead.

Since the start of the conflict in April 1955, 61 British citizens had been killed, 52 of whom were members of the Security Forces. Coupled with the deaths of Read and Holton, these latest EOKA outrages sparked an outburst of fury in the British community and demands for the Governor to punish the Greek Cypriots in general for the terrorist actions. On 29 September RAF Corporal Leslie Wilkins was shot dead as he chased a gang member.

Harding responded to the murders with the harshest curfew ever ordered in the capital and the start of the largest mass military operation since *Lucky Alphonse*. It was code-named *Sparrowhawk*.

At dawn on the morning of the 30th, vans roared through the Greek quarters of Nicosia to announce the new curfew. 'Anyone who dares to come out will be shot,' blared their loudspeakers. Not only would people be confined to their quarters, but they had to pull down the shutters and not sit on any balconies. There would be a complete city lockdown for 23 hours a day, enforced by British and Turkish police patrols. People would be allowed out of their homes between noon and 13.00 for shopping.

'This time hardly any warning was given, so few families were able to stock up with essentials. Access to the municipal market was barred even during the short intervals allowed for individuals to emerge from the airless interiors of houses and apartments to fetch water and other necessaries,' said Robert Holland.

British and foreign residents were not exempt from the restrictions and complained that they were being penalized for crimes for which they were not responsible, and which they abhorred. Their bitterness grew when they heard that a deaf and dumb English girl in the area had difficulty getting permission to leave her house to catch the boat on which she had booked a passage. By contrast, *The Times* correspondent reported: 'Greek Cypriots themselves do not seem to be unduly perturbed, for many were smiling and chatting on the streets today during the shopping interval. What is certain is that nobody will come forward to admit he knows who the murderers are, because the fear of vengeance by EOKA on "informers" is too great among the general public.' In Kyrenia, all places of entertainment were ordered to close until further notice.

'The whole point of the ceaseless patrolling by Security Forces, the close regulation of movement (so that even to appear on a balcony was hazardous), and the interrogation of household heads in screened-off compounds, was not to catch the murderers, who had quite obviously got clean away, but to induce in the people at large a sense of guilt, of complicity in terror, and hence a radical "change of heart",' wrote Robert Holland about the curfew. 'Harding had always warned Makarios that life would be very unpleasant if the troubles continued, and unpleasant it certainly became.'

The last day of September was marked by the death of another British serviceman: REME Craftsman Leslie Smale. The curfew ended eight days later. It was celebrated by EOKA with the successful ambush of an RAF water tanker at Paralimni, which killed LAC Donald Hayes, 19, a National Serviceman from Croydon, and injured another. An official statement said that an electrically detonated mine exploded in the middle of the road in front of the vehicle and the driver was hit by terrorist fire.

AFTER THIS spate of daily murders, all hoped Operation *Sparrowhawk* would produce better results than the surrender offer and curfews. It was launched to bring an end to the EOKA gangs that operated in the Kyrenia Mountains. Wanting to capture Private Read and Mary Holton's killers, the troops went about their business with increased determination. They were keen to make murderers pay, even if they did not know or care who they were: any terrorist would do.

The 16th Independent Parachute Brigade, commanded by Brigadier 'Tubby' Butler, took the lead with the support of a squadron of Royal Horse Guards, a battery of 40th Field Regiment, Royal Artillery, a detachment of Cyprus District Signal Regiment, two companies of the King's Own Yorkshire Light Infantry, and two more from each of the Wiltshire Regiment and the Highland Light Infantry. The Royal Navy cut off escape routes by sea, while RAF helicopters dropped small snatch squads in the difficult terrain. Air Observation Post Austers were also deployed, controlled by flying Gunners. Three thousand service personnel were involved. The Brigade's tactical was established at Ayios Amvrosios, together with interpreters, cages, screening teams and a platoon of police and intelligence personnel.

With the entire area cordoned off, the noose tightened on the three EOKA gangs – 20 terrorists in all – believed to be operating in the area. Village after village was subjected to curfew, searched and their inhabitants quizzed by officers and men of the Intelligence Corps. Members of the Women's Royal Army Corps Provost Company politely patted females down for hidden weapons. Army dogs and their handlers trekked mile after mile with the soldiers. At night 188 Battery (Radar and Searchlight) Royal Artillery illuminated the mountain passes to make it difficult for terrorists to make a dash from the cordoned area under cover of darkness.

To minimize the inconvenience of the local shepherds under curfew, special measures were taken to protect their flocks. Every day the Army used a helicopter to scour the 300 square miles of operational area to round up strays and ensure they were fed and watered. One company commander had 20 flocks in his charge during *Sparrowhawk*. The tending of sheep was not part of normal military training but not an animal was lost. The Army also brought food and supplies to where they were running short. In addition, a team of 10 medical officers tended the sick and elderly they came across.

As the army patrols moved forward, they left behind small teams in ambush positions to deal with any terrorists who might evade the main sweep. Their locations required a high degree of coordination with the other units in the area. 'The object was to drive the terrorists out of the Kyrenia Mountains,' said Para Wally Gee.

'It was a hard slog from one end to the other and although our troop made no real contacts, we did have some spectacular finds of pipe bombs, ammo, guns and just about all kinds of illegal arms. Our troop had no casualties, but on 4 October, a tragic mistake took place: Sapper "Bomber" James Brown, a Scouser, was killed and another Para, Tom Green, was seriously injured after they strayed across a prohibited line. From what I can remember we were all supposed to go to ground by 18.00, but somebody thought his patrol could make it back to base camp, as they were only a few minutes after that time.' Today these casualties would fall under the heading of 'friendly fire' or a 'blue on blue' accident.

Outside the cordoned-off area, Grivas maintained his assaults on police stations, usually heavily guarded by British troops in support of the local constables, now mainly Turkish. Because some stations were less protected due to the Suez buildup, EOKA was quick to spot any weaknesses in their defences, especially where buildings were being modernized and workers could bring in bombs under loads of bricks. When three exploded at one station under construction, RAOC Sergeant Anthony Trevor, an expert in defusing explosives, was brought to the scene to evaluate any potential risks before work resumed. For his efforts, he was awarded a George Medal.

The citation read:

At 09.00 hours on the 7 October 1956, Sergeant Taylor, RAOC, the Ammunition Examiner attached to an Infantry Brigade, was called out to deal with time bombs located in a practically completed new Police Station. On arrival he was informed that three bombs had already exploded, the last of which had gone off some ten minutes before, doing considerable damage, and that it was thought there might be others. Sergeant Taylor at once entered the building and regardless of his own safety searched the various rooms, eventually finding a fourth bomb concealed in a wall beneath the stairs. A time pencil protruded from this bomb but Sergeant Taylor, although he knew it might go off at any moment, removed the pencil, and having great difficulty in getting it out, broke the end off the detonator in the process. He then removed the bomb and while he was doing so the striker in the time pencil operated harmlessly in his hand. Had it not been for his extreme devotion to duty, and his prompt and unhesitant action, not only Sergeant Taylor himself, but several others would have been blown up and considerable damage would have been caused to the building. During the past six months Sergeant Taylor has dealt with no less than ten similar time bombs and many home made bombs and grenades, which he has been called out to examine and render safe.

Busy as they were fighting EOKA and preparing for action against Egypt, most soldiers still believed there would not be an invasion, but in London and Paris, politicians were determined to grab back ownership of the Suez Canal, with or without US support.

Military historian Correlli Barnett wrote: 'So Britain's only ally in the planned attack on Egypt would be France, also a onetime first-class power refusing to face the reality of second-class status. The cynical French, however, had a cunning plan, which could not possibly fail. On 1 October, they secretly struck a deal with the Israelis for a joint attack on Egypt.

'It made brilliant military sense: after the Israeli army had advanced westwards across the Sinai desert towards the canal, the French (and British) would land at Port Said and take the beaten Egyptian army from the rear flank. The threat of an Egyptian invasion of Israel would be eliminated, Britain and France would regain control of the Canal; and, as a bonus, Britain could reoccupy her huge base in the Canal Zone. The supreme prize would lie in the downfall of Nasser himself.

'Should Britain join this cynical conspiracy? It was alien to the whole moral ethos of Eden's own career as a pre-war apostle of the League of Nations and a postwar founder of the United Nations Organization. So his were now the dithers of a bishop nerving himself to enter a brothel. But on 24 October 1956, after cloak-and-dagger meetings with French ministers, Eden secretly committed Britain to the Franco-Israeli plot.

'The Chiefs of Staff had long had their own misgivings. What about the aftermath, they asked, with the allies saddled with a war-damaged Egyptian economy and a disrupted society? Land Force Commander General Sir Charles Keightley had personally asked Eden the fundamental question: was Britain going to be better off after a successful operation? He got a severe ticking off, but no answer.'

Members of 2 Para were the first to succeed in capturing a complete EOKA gang during Operation *Sparrowhawk*. Yomping their way through the mountains, they saw an isolated farmhouse on a bluff near the Turkish Cypriot hamlet of Trapeza. As they approached, there was surprisingly no activity around the building. Inside they found an elderly Greek Cypriot couple, who appeared nervous. The troops went through every room and found nothing incriminating, but while Privates Pearce and O'Donell were examining the barn outside they accidentally brushed against a winter coat on a hanger. As it moved to one side, they noticed a small hole that had been hidden. They shone a torch through it and a man's face peered back at them.

Alan Staff of 'C' Company said the terrorist 'must have been given a real turn, because Pearce, a reservist, fired his 9mm pistol into the hole'. It was answered with a cry of 'Don't shoot! We'll come out.' Six partially clothed men exited, arms raised. They had been hiding in a space no more than three by eight feet.

Staff continued: 'We were getting quite matey, when the police arrived, Special Branch chaps, and they were bastards. They really knocked these blokes about. I could hear them crying. None of us liked this.'

Another Para was less sympathetic. 'These men, and others like them, are fearless enough when they are operating in the rabbit warrens of narrow streets in the towns or when darkness protects them in the mountains,' he said dismissively. 'There is no indication yet of any real courage in their make-up when they come face to face with us.'

Under interrogation the six captives 'sang like canaries' and provided information that led to the arrest of another 18 suspects and the breaking up of gangs in Ayios Amvrosios, Kalogrea and Kartja.

An inch-by-inch search of the farmhouse ground by Private Robert Taylor revealed several buried oil drums filled with weapons, clothing and foodstuffs. It was the largest haul to be collected since the start of the Emergency. The Paras also found a second hide with bedding, cans of food and two radios. A terrorist could have stayed in it for weeks without discovery. The farmer and his wife pleaded complete ignorance about the EOKA stores and claimed they had never before seen the prisoners.

Among the Para captives were Andreas Charalambous, Fotis Christofi and Tassos Themistocleous: all three belonged to the gang believed to have planned and executed the ambush in which Private Colin Read and Mrs Mary Holton were killed. None was sentenced to death, although forensic evidence proved that one of their machine guns had been used in the St Hilarion ambush. Because the prosecution could not prove any of them had pulled the trigger, they escaped the death penalty and received life terms instead, to be served in Dartmoor Prison. When the EOKA conflict eventually ended, they returned to Cyprus as free men.

BEFORE *SPARROWHAWK* ended, soldiers made a grisly discovery: the partially buried body of Lance Corporal Gordon Hill, one of the two Royal Leicesters who had gone missing, posted 'absent without leave' in December 1955. The other was Private Ronald Shilton, taken hostage by EOKA on 17 April. Hill's Sten gun was found with him. Ballistic tests showed the terrorists had used it in several attacks.

EOKA had claimed both Hill and Shilton had been hanged on 10 May as a reprisal for the judicial executions of Michael Karaolis and Andreas Demetriou. Grivas had announced his action in a leaflet. Because there were discrepancies in the descriptions given, the authorities doubted the men had been held hostage. To prove the soldiers had been killed, the EOKA leader issued a second leaflet. It said:

TO BRITISH SOLDIERS
'1. A few weeks ago we announced the execution of Hostages Gordon Hill and Ronnie Shilton. It is an unpleasant subject, and we would not have returned to it, were it not for the futile attempt of the Military Dictatorship to

challenge the truth of our statement; that compels us to some further clarification, if only for the sake of the unfortunate families of the two men, who should not be left any longer uselessly in the anxiety of doubt.

'2. We apologise for having mentioned Hill as a corporal instead of lance-corporal, and the time of his capture as 7 November instead of December. Those were presumably oversights of our press service. Anyway, we are sure we mean the same man. He carried three small metal plates, one oval and two round, on each of which were engraved the number 93137483, the initials "C E" and the name "Hill G"

'3. We described Shilton as a corporal. In fact, he had stated that he had held that rank before having been deprived of it, some time before his capture; we did not think it worthwhile to verify the story and mentioned him by what he had said to be his former rank. We are again sure, however, that we mean the same man. (His disappearance, by the way, had not been published by the Authorities – Why?): Shilton said he was the son of an Irish doctor – now in America – and an Italian mother, subsequently divorced. He also said he was born at Santa Margherita 20 years ago. He was approximately 5 feet 9 inches tall, fair, with the trace of a wound in the back of the neck. Both his arms were tattooed with pictures of flowers and a tiger and names, among which "EVA" (his sister). His Sten gun bore the number 82494.

'4. We may be credited with sufficient intelligence not to make statements which can be proved untrue by the "REAPPEARANCE" of those whom we mention as dead.

'5. We have noted with interest that the Military Dictatorship was surprised that we did not attempt to bargain the lives of our prisoners against those of Karaolis and Demetriou. Although we know Harding better than to believe that he cares so much about the lives of his men, we may propose the bargain next time just to see what happens.

'We are not afraid of death – we shall strike back and fight until we get self-determination for Cyprus.'

EOKA
THE LEADER DIGHENIS.

Not for the first time, Grivas had lied. A Coroner's Court pronounced Hill was killed by manual 'strangulation', not hanging, although the exact date of his death could not be established. His murder had nothing to do with the executions of the terrorists. In the case of Shilton, his death was caused by a spade crashed on his head after his captor bungled an attempt to shoot him. The spade was the same one that he had been forced to use to dig his own grave. His corpse would be found on 2 February 1957, buried in a field near Famagusta.

The full story of Shilton's murder would emerge at the trial of his alleged killer, 21–year-old Michael Rossides, a terrorist with a £5,000 price on his head, who was captured in Larnaca.

In court Rossides gave a graphic description of the events leading to the soldier's death. He said 29-year-old Shilton had been brought to his Liopetri house in civilian clothes. 'I was told to guard him and was given £10 to feed him. Because I had only one bed, we slept together.' When the day came for the murder, he refused at first 'because I had become his friend'. After a short pause, tears rolling down his face, he continued: 'Ronnie noticed I was refusing to shoot him. He asked what the matter was. I told him. He said, "All right, kill me. Soldiers must obey orders, as I used to." A man known as Ziam then put his revolver to my back saying: "If you don't obey I'll execute you." I fired and collapsed. Ziam did the rest. Be sure that as from that day I continually lost my sleep and I see Ronnie's ghost in front of me. I have been haunted by his vision. I ask God's forgiveness.'

Rossides later retracted his confession.

Grivas, continuing to delude himself long after the conflict had ended, claimed that Operation *Sparrowhawk* was not a success and did not stop the Kyrenia gangs from functioning under a new commander, Kyriakos Matsis, who had just escaped from detention.

Nancy Crawshaw disagreed. 'The operation paralysed EOKA in the Kyrenia Range for a long time to come,' she noted. 'During October the organization kept up the pressure by means of sporadic incidents in other parts of the Island concentrating mainly on the Cypriot civilians. Fourteen were killed by gunmen in three weeks. Five of the murders took place in coffee shops, two in barbers' shops and one at a wedding reception. The presence of spectators helped to further the process of intimidation, so whenever possible EOKA chose public places for its executions.'

HARDING AUTHORIZED another leaflet drop on known EOKA areas and throughout the Island's main towns, determined to exert as much pressure as possible on Grivas before he lost more of his internal security troops to the Suez buildup of forces. The unsigned leaflet said that even if the terrorists committed '20 times more murders and threw 20 times more bombs', Britain would not give way to their demands. There were 'bigger and more serious problems' that needed a solution than the question of independence and self-determination. The message was clear: 'Due to the restless situation in the world, and especially to Middle East troubles, Britain for strategic reasons must have control over Cyprus. It is in the interests of Cyprus, Greece, Turkey, and all western Powers and the free world that Britain should have Cyprus as a powerful military base.'

After the leaflets fell from the sky, Cypriots looked up again and now saw scores of French paratroopers drifting slowly on to the plain north of Nicosia in the first of their practice jumps in preparation for the invasion of Suez.

Protection of the growing arms and explosives stores now became a priority. For 28-year-old Captain Peter Macdonald of the RAOC the challenge was 'in the stratosphere'. The amount of munitions under his control had risen from 1,500 tons to 15,000. Their storage site at Lakatamia expended proportionately. 'I have never understood why EOKA did not slip a time pencil into a box of plastic explosive, when it was being handled by Cypriot labourers at Limassol docks,' he said. 'Not only did the size of the depot increase, so did its numbers. Army Emergency Reserve officers and soldiers arrived from the UK and I, a captain, ended up commanding a major, Arnold Groves, and his unit as well as my own, a somewhat unorthodox situation.

'French forces too arrived in droves, landing in Nord Atlas transport planes on the disused wartime airfield at Tymbou and transforming it in short order into a major base. Then their ammunition began to arrive and was put into the same perimeter as ours. I thought the French army was very impressive, highly experienced and professional, especially Les Paras and the Foreign Legion. The two elite corps quickly found the red light district in Nicosia and now and then flogged their weapons in order to fund their visits to it. Furthermore, a lot of the legionnaires were German ex-soldiers, who had few qualms about disposing of carbines that could be used against the British.

'We took some French officers into our little mess, where for several nights we much enjoyed each other's company. As you would expect, they provided the wine. Then with no word of warning one evening they did not arrive for dinner. When, the next morning, I asked why, one of them shamefacedly admitted that they had no money with which to pay their mess bills. He and the others went back to sharing food and company with their Warrant Officers in a tent at the far end of the ammunition lines. Then, just as quickly as they had arrived, they all went away. No doubt there are a few Gallic Cypriots with a special taste for wine enjoying life on the island today.'

IN LATE October, Grivas enlisted four high school students in Lefkoniko to perpetrate one of the worst atrocities of the four-year conflict. The 1st Battalion of the Highland Light Infantry was camped nearby and its soccer team was invited by the village elders to play a game against a local Greek Cypriot XI as a gesture of goodwill on Sunday afternoon of the 23rd. When the Scottish lads of 'A' Company arrived at the ground, their opponents were not to be found, although there was a turnout of smiling children and their teachers ready to watch. Rather than disappoint the small crowd and waste the afternoon, the soldiers decided to have a rough-and-ready knockabout amongst themselves. The onlookers cheered, jeered and generally appeared to be having a good time.

When the referee blew the final whistle, the crowd moved quickly away from the pitch. Still in their football kit, several of the players, now very thirsty, made a dash to the village fountain for a drink. As they dipped their faces in the water, they did not notice two schoolgirls raise and wave a white handkerchief. Less than a second later, an explosion ripped the soldiers apart. Private Matthew Neely, 19, was disembowelled and died instantly. He was due to complete his National Service in two weeks and was counting the days to returning home. His mate Private John Beattie, also 19, died the next day in hospital. A third soldier, 18-year-old Private Benjamin Doherty was repatriated to hospital in Scotland, but failed to recover and lost his life on 6 December.

An official press release stated: 'As the smoke cleared the villagers hurried off the field in a mad rush to get away. A military vehicle quickly followed after them and a bomb was thrown at it. Fortunately this bomb failed to cause any further casualties or do any damage. One hundred and fifty persons were taken in for questioning shortly after the incident occurred. This number has now been reduced but police investigations are still continuing and another suspect was detained yesterday morning.'

Former HLI Private Alistair Cameron said: 'It was indeed the saddest day of our service. I was probably closest to Matt Neely, one of the cooks who was in the next tent to me.'

The night before the explosion, Georghios Ellinas and Petros Karmbis, both teenagers from the local high school, had dug a long trench from a nearby olive grove to the village fountain, where they hid an electrically detonated bomb. They then laid a wire in the trench, covering it with soil as they went, to a battery-powered switch 400 yards away, where they sat out the Sunday afternoon game. Earlier they had shared their plans with their teachers and arranged two schoolgirls to signal them with a handkerchief when the soldiers went to drink.

When news of their comrades' deaths reached the HLI camp, two platoons left and stormed into Lefkonico. The Brigadier ordered their immediate return, but Lieutenant Colonel F. B. B. Noble did not comply. The soldiers smashed shop windows and destroyed bars. Any Greek Cypriots who stood in their way were punched to the ground and given a hefty kicking. By the time they had finished venting their fury, the main street looked as if a tornado had struck. 'A' Company did not experience any more serious EOKA incidents.

The next day, the village's 73-year-old Mayor, Loucas Gregoriou, gathered the press around him and claimed that the damage caused by the soldiers amounted to £3,000. Michael Pappa Demetriou, his clerk, produced several schoolchildren and other witnesses, who said that they had been robbed, ill-treated and terrorized by the Scotsmen. Kyriakos Houtri, 25, said: 'I was caught by the hair and pulled down. They started kicking me, before placing my head in the fountain as they tried to drown me.'

A British correspondent asked: 'Mr. Mayor,

what are your views about the EOKA bomb outrage?'

Mayor: 'I know nothing about that. Anyway, it was fired from outside the village.'

Correspondent: 'Do you condemn violence?'

Mayor: 'That is not relevant.'

Meanwhile, Greek reporters scurried about gathering allegations of unrestrained brutality to report in their journals, but would play down the reasons why there was a breakdown in discipline that Sunday evening. One of those they quoted extensively was a Londoner, Mrs Betty Davy, a mother of three, whose husband was a Greek Cypriot. She gave them just the kind of copy they were after. 'I was not proud of the British soldiers yesterday,' she said. 'They came to take my husband away, but I spoke to them and they realized I was English.'

When Colonel F. Noble, the HLI's Commanding Officer, heard about the Mayor's demand for compensation, he replied: 'The murder of Private Neely is probably one of the most dastardly murders EOKA has committed. It was premeditated and aimed to catch soldiers when they were at play. If three thousand pounds is being claimed for alleged damage caused by troops it is infinitesimal when compared with damage caused by EOKA to my soldiers.'

Governor Harding put it more bluntly: 'The people of Lefkoniko have reason to be thankful that it was British troops with whom they had to deal on that day.'

The US Consul in Nicosia reported to his masters in the State Department in Washington that the 'extensive and sustained drive' against EOKA was proving unproductive and ordinary Cypriots were 'getting rougher handling' by the Security Forces. The American Government, already displeased with London over the Suez crisis, began to think it should get more involved in the Cyprus problem and lend less support to the way the Colonial Office conducted its business. It would not be long before the United States would become the major influence in the Middle East, leaving British credibility at rock bottom.

In 1956, it was not the custom of the British Army to bring back the bodies of soldiers killed abroad and so the Neely family in Glasgow raised the £119 from friends and neighbours to bring their son home. A month later he was buried in the city's Necropolis. On the 50th anniversary of Matthew's death, his two sisters, Nan and Margaret, laid a small plaque at the grave that simply said: 'Gone but not forgotten.'

An official list published on 24 October disclosed that since 1 April 1955, 51 servicemen had been killed and 191 wounded; 24 police had been murdered, of whom six were English, and 59 wounded; and 90 civilians had died at EOKA's hands, of whom seven were English, and 120 wounded. During the same period there had been 560 major and 449 minor explosions, while 404 bombs failed to explode.

That same day Gunner Albert Balmer arrived to start his tour of duty on the Island. Within hours, he was assigned to guard his new camp's barbed-wired perimeter on his very first night. Next morning, after breakfast, his duty would continue because several of the 'old hands' had been given permission to have a day off on one of the sandy beaches of Famagusta. 'I really felt sick as a pig,' said Balmer. 'I couldn't swim, but at least I would have seen a bit more of Cyprus. Anyhow, the truck turned up at the gate at 10.00, all full up, with a Champ in the lead and an officer named Jones on board in charge of the detail. Away they went. No more than 30 minutes later, a distant rumbling could be heard coming from the direction of Yialousa. Being an artillery unit we knew immediately that it was an explosion. All we could do now was to wait for information.

'When it did come, the news was bad; the swimming detail had been blown up outside Yialousa police station resulting in one dead and 18 wounded: three critically, four seriously and eleven slightly.

'All available personnel were pushed into service of some kind. It wasn't long before ambulances – not just our own – came speeding past the camp gate, going to the scene of carnage, then ferrying the injured back to hospital as fast as they could go. The very badly injured had to be airlifted by helicopter.

'Things happened so fast I can only remember helping two men into the air ambulance. One, although blood-splattered, seemed to have internal injuries, but the second man was covered in blood at his head and shoulder with a huge bandage around his neck.

'Most of the camp was in a very sombre mood, and it was very hard to find a smiling face. So this was it. Welcome to Cyprus, boys; well, not any more – we had all become men within one long day.'

In another attempt to disrupt British preparations for aerial attacks on Egypt, Grivas sanctioned an act of sabotage by a Greek Cypriot employee at RAF Akrotiri. Three days before the start of Operation *Musketeer*, the man passed security checks at the main gate while carrying four time bombs hidden in a basket of grapes. Once inside, he made for a storm drain and crawled underground on his hands and knees until he sensed he was directly under the runway, where he started the bombs' mechanisms. The job had taken him six hours. When he emerged, he returned to his workplace and left at the end of the day as usual. At midnight, the bombs went off. It took engineers working overtime to repair the damage before the first RAF attack aircraft were scheduled to take off. With typical exaggeration, Grivas claimed the base was put out of action for several weeks.

AS OCTOBER drew to a close, the troops of 3 Para who had been part of Operation *Sparrowhawk* were brought back to Nicosia. 'We trekked back from the cool mountains to our hot, dusty camp next to the airfield where it was apparent that there was a lot of activity and many more planes,' wrote Brigadier Paul Crook recently. 'I was told to prepare for an airborne operation but I was not told where or when ... We envied the French with their equipment which was light and much more suitable for airborne operations than ours. Also they had a more realistic and practical attitude to their transport planes. They treated their Dakotas like unit trucks and lived with them and slept under them where appropriate.'

Charles Pepper, an REME Sergeant, also envied the equipment the French had at their disposal. 'While their transport aircraft with rear loading doors flew above us, we were practising our loading and landing techniques on a fuselage of a Hastings mounted on blocks and a steep ramp to its side-loading door,' he recounted. 'Our Champs were driven up the ramp, where, inside the fuselage, a group of men grabbed the vehicle and manhandled it along. Watching this ridiculous caper made me smirk as we were burning clutches at a fast rate and generating smelly blue smoke that could be seen for miles!'

Gordon Burt of 1 Para added: 'The sad thing was that we were jumping from their aircraft since we didn't have enough of our own for training. It put us to shame to see the French turn up with 30 or 40 Nords lined up on their airstrips and we hardly had any aircraft, just a couple of Hastings and a couple of Valettas, and I'm afraid that was it.' However, help was on its way. Gerry Catling, a BOAC pilot, was expecting to take leave and get married, when he was told to head for Cyprus with the flight manual for the new Britannia 102 aircraft, which was still not in service, but would be used, he was told, as a transport for British soldiers destined for Egypt. He had never flown or even seen one.

At Akrotiri, the RAF Regiment's 37 Squadron was taken off internal security duties and assigned to join 27 Squadron in preparing the anti-aircraft defences. The recently completed airfield was now fully functional again, despite several EOKA attempts to bomb the runway, and every hour Canberra and Valiant bombers from the UK were landing and lining up like cars in a super-market car park.

Meanwhile there was increased British naval activity in the eastern Mediterranean. Most of the ships of the Mediterranean Fleet had sailed from Malta, said the Admiralty, to take part in a 'communications exercise'. Three French naval vessels – a convoy vessel, a tank-landing ship and a tugboat – arrived at Famagusta, raising the number of French ships at the port to nine. RAF Sergeant Eric Irving was one of the many military personnel rushed to Cyprus. He told the author from his retirement home in New Zealand: 'As we flew over the Mediterranean we knew something was up: from skyline to skyline, there were Royal Navy vessels, all heading East. I remember thinking it was an awesome sight, all that fire power.'

American vessels were also present and their task was not to help the Anglo-French fleets, rather to hinder, some people believed. 'One unexpected diversion was the appear-ance of units of the US Sixth Fleet, which signalled HMS *Ocean*. "What ship? Where Bound?" – to receive the reply from *Ocean*, "What Fleet?" HMS *Meon* then signalled, "Why don't you join us?" "No thanks, we'll hold your coat" came back the reply, and the Sixth Fleet ships altered course and sailed away,' wrote Robin Neillands in his book, *By Land and By Sea*.

It was estimated that the French soldiers in Cyprus now numbered 4,000. Eric Irving was billeted close to some of them. 'Their para-troopers were in tents close to ours and used the same ablution block. We were warned to keep clear of them as the smallest smart remark could trigger an incident. Only a fool would have tested them. They were all over six feet tall, lean and fighting fit. All had shaven heads. They were extremely aloof and never glanced in our direction, even when they were washing next to us. They reminded me of General De Gaulle,' he remembered. 'Two mornings later, they were gone. Not even their tents remained. They had slipped away, silently in the night.'

The French were always surprising the British by their behaviour. Dudley Martin of 3 Infantry Workshops, RASC, recalled: 'The Legionnaires near us marched from Larnaca to Akrotiri overnight in full battle order – rather them than me. And that was on a road where EOKA was always detonating mines.'

BOAC pilot Gerry Catling, booked into the Ledra Palace Hotel, along with the 120 gentle-men of the foreign press, noted the difference in mess etiquette between the British and French officers. 'Whereas the British very properly hung their belts and side arms in the cloakroom before entering the dining room, the French placed their loaded sub-machine guns on the table beside their soup spoons,' he laughed. 'If you were sitting opposite one of them, it was a great incentive to finish your meal quickly and not linger for coffee and liqueurs. This armed camp existence went on for about a couple of weeks until President Eisenhower pulled the plug on the British and French and the operation went into reverse.'

Although on leave in the UK, Jim Fail of the RAF had been ordered back to the Island to set up a Mobile Radar Signals Unit at Kormakiti, which would act as an early warning system. 'Our radars were on maximum alert in case the Egyptian air force decided to counter-strike,' he said. 'Isolated as we were, none of us knew all the facts or the complete story until long afterwards.

Nevertheless, rumour control and the grape-vine worked overtime.'

THROUGHOUT THE Island, the public was told to take precautions in case the Russian bombers of the Egyptian Air Force launched a surprise attack against Cyprus. There were whispers that Soviet pilots would be at the controls of the aircraft. Charles Pepper of REME feared for the safety of his headquarters. 'It lay at the end of a straight road, which was ideal for aircraft to line up on to pay us a visit,' he told the author. 'I found it rather unsettling as I had been machine-gunned several times as a child during Nazi air raids on the Isle of Wight, where we lived. But nobody seemed worried at our camp and no safety arrangements were made. The best I could do was to get the lads to duck behind our concrete inspection ramps if there were an attack.'

In her book *Below The Tide*, Pamela Tremayne explained the Red Cross's prime pre-occupation was how to deal 'with refugees: expected arrivals, non-arrivals, actual, unannounced, arrivals, erratic departures'. With the influx of troops and the anti-terrorist campaign, the British Military Hospital in Nicosia was bursting at the seams. Originally built during the Second World War as a 200-bedded hospital, dispersed widely to minimize casualties from aerial attack, and devoid of such amenities as adequate sanitation, or covered passages between wards, conditions were far from ideal. But a crisis expansion of 520 beds was achieved, in spite of some inadequacies in staff and equipment.

Said Pamela Tremayne: 'The question of air-raid precautions arose; and we were asked to help in the laying on of teams of volunteers to man first-aid and anti-fire posts at points about Nicosia. Volunteers were collected; and not only these, but also buckets, spades, sandbags, bandages, stretchers, and other relevant objects. We asked if we should submit a plan for the positions of the posts? No, an expert in ARP had arrived from London, and had already settled all that. After a decent interval, we asked if the plan could be shown to us, so that our volunteers could be posted? No again: the location of the posts was top-secret, and would remain so until air raids actually began. This made the volunteers look rather silly; and it was discouraging to think of the amount of telephoning and dashing about that would be necessary, when the first air-raid siren blew, before they could be got on to the job.'

A few nights later the Island's sirens wailed. Someone, somewhere had spotted an unidentified aircraft flying far off the coast of the Karpas peninsular. 'We put on our clothes and stood in the starlit garden, gaping like ninnies at a silent and untroubled sky in Nicosia,' Tremayne noted. 'No droning black dot appeared: nothing disturbed the stillness in the slack of the night. We grew cold, and went indoors again. After about half an hour the long, queasy moan of the "All Clear" set us free and we went back to bed.'

At Karaolos Camp, for the Royal Leicesters there was an atmosphere reminiscent of the early days of the Second World War, but when eventually the sirens did go off, 'no one moved from his bed', the regimental journal recorded. 'Blackout curtains were quickly rigged up, slit trenches were dug between the huts and tents, and an energetic start was made in building sand bag blast walls. Enthusiasm for this, however, was damped by Drum Major Bradburn's revelation at the end of a day's intensive work on the wall outside the M I Room that, continued at its present rate, it would take three weeks to complete to specification!

'For those of us who were in the Army in September 1939, the sight of the Battalion digging air raid trenches was strangely familiar. Thoughts ranged far and wide, in a welter of conjectures, seeking the immediate future of misguided and tortured humanity. Was it a question of "Once more unto the breach, dear friends, once more?" Would Russia actively intervene in the Middle East? Would Egyptian planes bomb Famagusta? Whatever happened our one thought was to prepare ourselves for all eventualities.'

Alas, trench digging and companies moving were not the only distractions of that eventful day. Major General A. H. G. Ricketts, CBE, DSO, late GOC Cyprus District, was leaving Famagusta and 'D' Company, with the Regimental Band, was finding a guard of honour on the quayside for the departing General. There is no confirmation that the Officer Commanding the Guard, when asked what action was to be taken if an air raid developed on the docks, ordered that the guard would remain at 'Present Arms'.

Unknown to the people of Cyprus, the aircraft that set off the sirens was an American U-2 spy plane ordered to monitor British, French and Israeli preparations to invade Egypt, despite US opposition. Gary Powers was one of the pilots who particularly reconnoitered military activity in Cyprus. CIA documents prove that on 27 October, a U-2 launched from Wiesbaden, Germany, photographed the British bases in Cyprus. Its high-resolution photographs revealed large numbers of British and French bombers and transport planes parked beside the runways. Concentrations of troops and equipment were also revealed. Another U-2 flying from Incirlik airbase in Turkey detected a squadron of French fighter-bombers parked at an Israeli airfield. Its photographs nailed the lie from the British and French Prime Ministers who insisted that Operation *Musketeer*, as their invasion would be called, was purely and simply an action to safeguard the Suez Canal from Israel's war against Egypt.

On 30 October, the people of Cyprus were officially warned that the Middle East hostilities might spread to the Island, but that the only danger would be of small-scale attack from the air. People were advised to avoid large towns, to keep water tanks full and to store sufficient food for two days. A postal and telegraphic censorship was imposed, long distance telephone calls were banned and the press would be prevented from publishing certain information. Those wishing to leave for abroad would have to apply for exit permits three weeks in advance of their departure date.

British forces now totalled 45,000 men, with 12,000 vehicles, 300 aircraft and 100 warships. The French added 34,000 men, 9,000 vehicles, 200 aircraft and 30 warships. Whatever the folly of the Anglo-French politicians to go ahead, the troops were itching for a scrap, apart from a few disgruntled reservists recalled to the colours. Occasionally they added to the burden carried by the Security Forces.

Many of those in the Royal Engineers 25th Port Operating Regiment were reservists and in civilian life had been stevedores. 'And a pretty bolshie and undisciplined lot we were,' Robert Gretton commented in *Six Campaigns* by Adrian Walker. 'From the start it was clear that our officers and NCOs didn't have a lot of say or control over us. We more or less took leave when we wanted and showed up on parade in scruff order.

'For several weeks we had nothing to do and began to think that the Suez thing would come to nothing. Morale was steadily getting worse and we were becoming more difficult to handle. Then, suddenly, we were summoned into the biggest tent on camp and told General Somebody-or-Other was going to talk to us.

'The General was late and while we waited our bolshiness began to grow. We began to throw pebbles at the NCOs. When the General arrived we greeted him with boos and a shower of larger stones. He looked alarmed and obviously was wondering whether to go straight out again, but the Sergeant Major encouraged him to stay. He stood on a chair to address us. "I want you men to know you're doing a valuable job," he said, but his words were drowned out by shouts of derision and he scuttled out of the tent. We were immediately sent on leave to stop us pulling the camp apart.'

Twenty-two-year-old Lieutenant John P. G. Moss-Norbury recalled that the reservists of 2 Para could be particularly troublesome. 'One of our patrols was called to an open-air cabaret where there was trouble with some of them,' he said. 'When our Q driver, Lance Corporal Hollaway, entered the premises, a Sten gun was pushed into his stomach by one drunken red beret who wanted "out" of the army. But after some quiet discussion, our man was able to disarm him and take him away to somber up. When Hollaway came back to the duty room I saw he was as white as a sheet. He was a good soldier and went on to become Regimental Sergeant Major.'

In the purple light of early dawn on 31 October, Canberra and Valiant bombers from RAF Akrotiri and RAF Nicosia roared into the sky and raced towards their destinations in Egypt. Pathfinder aircraft had already illuminated their military targets at Almaza and Inchass near Cairo, and Abu Sueir and Kabrit,

Aircraft prepared at RAF Nicosia Airport for Operation *Musketeer*.

former RAF stations in the Canal Zone. Pilots reported the Egyptian defences were caught by surprise. Flight Lieutenant John Slater was the pilot of the first Canberra to drop its bombs. 'There was a certain amount of wildly directed flak reaching up to 8,000 feet,' he said, 'but no fighter opposition. The weather was clear and there was no sign of activity on the ground. Our bombing runs were jolly smooth and I can say the raid was successful.'

An official communiqué said all aircraft returned safely.

President Eisenhower condemned the action. This armed attack was an error, he said, and could not be reconciled with the principles of the United Nations.

Operation *Musketeer* had begun. It would be short-lived.

CHAPTER FIFTEEN

Fall in for
the Suez misadventure

'For it's Tommy this, an' Tommy that, an' "Chuck him out, the brute!" But it's "Saviour of 'is country" when the guns begin to shoot.'

Rudyard Kipling

CONTROVERSY NOW raged in the UK over Prime Minister Eden's decision to launch Operation *Musketeer*. There were angry anti-Government demonstrations at home and rumblings abroad among the reservists who had been called up. In Cyprus, military personnel struggled to coordinate plans with their French allies, organize fighting units, find equipment and ensure ports of departure were safe from EOKA, while still maintaining internal security. Many observers claimed that the sudden rush of activity was nothing better than organized chaos.

Despite the bombing raids by the RAF, General Sir Charles Keightley, the overall commander, admitted that the Egyptian Army was still 'a cohesive force', but claimed all was ready for Phase Two of the 'limited action'. America's *Time* magazine dampened any enthusiasm by reporting: 'From the first instant of combat, it became apparent that the Anglo-French could not hope for a quick victory without bloodshed.'

The political hope in London and Paris was that air strikes alone, combined with the Israeli sweep across the Sinai, would persuade

French forces ready for the invasion of Egypt.

Egypt to surrender, or to overthrow Nasser. Although the Israelis had reached the Suez Canal in just three days, the Egyptian Army had consolidated its remaining fighting units on the far side and showed no signs of giving up. By the fifth day, the Canberras, Venoms and French Corsairs had destroyed the Egyptian Air Force on the ground and started softening up strategic points that could hinder the Allies' landings. They had been taking off and landing at a rate of one a minute from Cyprus airfields.

Whatever their personal feelings, all the pilots except one followed their orders, but Flying Officer Dennis Kenyon, 24, slumped the nose of his Canberra into the runway at Nicosia Airport. With his squadron he was due to bomb Inshass airfield outside Cairo. Four minutes later, Pilot Dennis Raymond Kenyon faced Squadron Leader Norman Hartley.

'What's the matter, Dennis?' Hartley demanded. 'Did you push the wrong button?'

The pilot threw his helmet on the ground and burst into incoherent tears. Former Canberra navigator Dilwyn Harwidge explained: 'Kenyon had apparently requested his Squadron Commander not to send him on the bombing mission, since he had serious doubts about the morality of bombing targets where civilians might be killed due to what he considered a misconceived policy by Sir Anthony Eden. His squadron commander, however, insisted he fulfil his role during the engagement. While lining up for take-off, he retracted the undercarriage, disabling the aircraft.'

Retired Squadron Leader Dennis Bird considered Kenyon's action was unforgivable. 'Many of us in the RAF at the time had similar misgivings about the Suez operation,' he said, 'but the pilot's action was entirely wrong. His aircraft was carrying a full bomb-load, and by in effect crashing it on the runway he put at risk the lives of his crew, and those of the other bombers taking off behind him.'

RAF Corporal Alan Wilson witnessed the incident: 'I was serving on the pilot's City of Lincoln, 61 Squadron,' he recalled. 'The aircraft was not a write-off. We were told to stand back while it was supported on jacks and the armourers removed the bombs.'

At his court martial, Kenyon insisted he had just pushed the wrong button by mistake. He was upset and nervous, the cockpit was dark, he felt hurried because the briefing had run behind schedule, the flap and undercarriage buttons were close together. He said: 'I have no political or religious views; I gave that reason merely because I was dreadfully worried over my tragic mistake. It was far better, I thought, to say I had intentionally caused the Canberra damage rather than to say I had made a mistake and was incompetent.'

The prosecutor pointed out that Kenyon by his own admission had been unable to sleep or eat for days and charged that he had wrecked his plane out of simple fear. After deliberating for an hour, the court martial found him guilty of acting 'willfully' to avoid carrying out 'a warlike operation in the air when under orders'. He was sentenced to dismissal from the RAF and a year's imprisonment.

While this was going on, RAF radar stations searched the skies for enemy aircraft. On the ground anti-aircraft guns were ready to fire. But Nasser's Russian Ilyushin bombers never came. At Allied HQ, French Admiral Barjot was pressing the British to get cracking with the land invasion, but General Keightley stalled for time.

CONFUSION AND chaos appeared to reign wherever the troops were ordered to gather. At the Ox and Bucks Light Infantry camp near Limassol, the regimental journal recorded: 'When events in the Canal Zone crisis were coming to a head, we were already steeled to meet most of their communications with the necessary good humour. However, we were a little taken aback to receive a signal on 1

British Paras prepare for the Suez invasion.

November informing us that a state of war existed between the United Kingdom and Egypt.'

Lieutenant Colonel Paul Crook, the Commanding Officer of 3 Para in Cyprus, was still trying to find enough space on aircraft for his troops to parachute into Egypt. 'The number of serviceable transport planes changed right up to the last minute,' he recorded. 'Finally there were 18 Valettas, 7 Hastings for personnel and 7 Hastings to drop heavy equipment.'

With an eye on public relations, he added: 'Although each seat was very precious I agreed that one should be allocated to a member of the press on the understanding that he had some knowledge of parachuting. Somehow Peter Wood of the *Daily Mirror* managed to con his colleagues that he was an experienced parachutist and so got the vacancy. He was a big man and unfortunately not a parachutist at all. In the event he had a heavy landing, damaged his ankles, and evacuated himself on the first available helicopter.

'I was upset by all this as I am always in favour of working openly with the press and felt that a representative accompanying me on that first day could have told the true story of our humane treatment of the Egyptians and dispelled the baseless lies and figments of imagination that were put about afterwards by people who weren't there.'

To carry the Brigade HQ team Viking aircraft 'were dug out of mothballs'. 'We were to fly in at three heights stacked at 500, 600 and 700 feet,' said John Rymer Jones.

On Saturday 3 November Crook thought he had received his final orders. His men were to drop on the following Tuesday. Then the start date was brought forward again. They would start on Monday. His camp was sealed and the Paras prepared. Crook insisted his men were not interested and took no notice of 'the ranting of politicians and others at home. They preferred listening to the *Goon Show* than *Yesterday in Parliament*. Not that there was much difference.'

The Paras carried weapons containers filled to capacity. Some troops could barely lift their loads. 'To save weight I took the decision to discard the reserve 'chute which we normally wore,' said Crook.

John Rymer Jones expected to be sailing to Egypt, but ... He explained: 'On the night of 3 November I was with a large group from Brigade HQ, three to four dozen officers and soldiers. We had embarked with the invasion fleet being assembled at Limassol, only to see a launch approaching in the early hours ... Captain Sid Cooper was aboard bearing the message that certain elements of Brigade HQ were to go back to Nicosia and parachute in with the 3rd Battalion the next morning. We were briefed on the night of the 4th ... We of Brigade HQ were to parachute in at 05.00 in two aircraft.'

British Forces had been told to expect 40 per cent casualties during the early phase of the operation.

The same day, the main body of 63 Parachute Company RASC sailed for Egypt, without its vehicles, and arrived just before a ceasefire was announced. In order to fulfil its tasks after landing, the Company requisitioned civilian transport – Coca-Cola vans and air-conditioned tourist buses.

Meanwhile, with the world's attention sharply focused on events in the Middle East, the Soviet Union sent its army into Hungary to put down the anti-Communist revolution, which the West had long encouraged, but now could do nothing to help.

Throughout the early hours of Monday, 5 November, a steady stream of trucks filled with men wearing maroon berets arrived at the airfield, bathed in the glow of orange floodlights. Gathered in small groups by the lines of aircraft, they made last-minute checks of their equipment. Officers moved among them making adjustments to the parachute harnesses of their men. The Paras were then given permission to step away to a safe distance from the planes for a final cigarette before takeoff. Finally came the order: 'Fall in – in stick order.'

PRECISELY AT 04.15, with Paras and equipment on board, one after the other engines coughed, spluttered and roared into life. With propellers spinning in a blur, the aircraft moved almost delicately into position to take off. Suddenly they were racing down the runway under full power at 15-second intervals and lumbering into the air for the three-hour flight to Port Said. Their objective was the capture of El Gamil airfield. It would be the first and last combat jump by a battalion group since the Second World War.

At Tymbou, north of Nicosia, the French Noratlas aircraft were joining up with their British allies. By 05.15, the last clusters of red and green navigation lights in the sky had disappeared. Silence descended and empty trucks returned to their camps.

'The RAF only had enough planes to drop one battalion and its supporting units. 1 and 2 Para left by sea in a large number of extraordinary ships. Crazy, isn't it? – All that training wasted. I went in some old tub, I can't remember what it was,' laughed David Hartley, an RAMC attached to the paratroopers.

Several of the vessels moving troops were flat-bottomed Z barges that could pull up to the quay at Famagusta. Lieutenant Rodney Farkas of the minesweeper HMS *Fenton* said: 'I witnessed one loaded with a full military band. I just prayed that the weather would hold until they boarded whatever ship was waiting for them somewhere anchored in the bay.'

2 Para arrived in Port Said on board the troopship *Empire Parkeston* during the afternoon of the 6th. Due to sniper fire from shore, the battalion's landing was delayed. By the time they were on shore, unpacking their equipment for battle, a ceasefire had been declared.

'Excitement was high throughout our camp during the days of the Anglo-French landings at Port Said,' the Ox and Bucks journal continued. 'Our friends and next door neighbours 2 Parachute Regt were fed entirely by us for several days before they actually sailed for Egypt. The officers' mess wireless was the centre of attraction for every news broadcast and Captain Bryan Balls was made to change the times at which his control wireless set called to prevent them interfering with the hourly bulletins.'

'During *Musketeer*, we realized just how poorly the British Army was equipped,' said ex-Para Bryan Hunter. 'Our rifle was the very accurate Lee Enfield bolt-action .303. In good hands it was deadly. Most of our lads could use it very well. It was robust and could take a lot of punishment and yet it always worked. But the rifle had hardly changed in 80 years. Because it was bolt operated, it was slow, its magazine held just 10 rounds. Matched against other infantry weapons it was an antique.

'But in Suez, we saw the AK-47 for the first time, the standard infantry weapon of the Egyptian forces. As they withdrew ahead of our advance, they had thrown them away, with boxes of ammunition, in the hope that the civilian population would collect and use them against the foreign invaders. We were rather impressed by the AK-47 and soon we were all equipped with them. Now we could fire single rounds manually or loose off 30 from the magazine when switched to automatic. The Egyptians' bullets had different coloured tips. If I remember rightly, red was for tracer, green was for an explosive bullet and blue was for armour piercing. We found Egyptian magazines filled with a mix of types.'

Hunter's platoon of Paras also 'liberated' a large Mercedes saloon into which they slung their old rifles, other kit and as much AK-47 ammunition they could find, and continued their advance in style.

Meanwhile 500 men of 45 Commando were making history by taking part in the first-ever British heli-borne assault. They were airlifted by helicopter from two light fleet carriers – HMS *Ocean* and HMS *Theseus* – and landed on a patch of waste ground beside De Lesseps' statue in Port Said. Royal Navy, Army and RAF Whirlwinds and Bristol Sycamores had carried the troops into combat and then switched to a casualty evacuation role, with one Royal Marine, injured in the fighting, returned to his ship just 20 minutes after leaving. The CASEVAC missions continued and included the rescue of a Royal Navy Sea Hawk pilot from where he had parachuted, 30 miles inland.

On their way, however, to link up with 3 Para at the El Gamil airfield, the Marines came under 'friendly' fire, when a Fleet Air Arm Wyvern fired rockets into their landing site, just as they were laying out identification panels on the ground. One Marine was killed and 15 others wounded, including an intelligence officer and Colonel Tailyour, the CO.

The next day, 24 hours after the Paras secured El Gamil airfield, tanks stormed ashore at Port Said and Port Fuad from an armada of ships that had assembled off the coast of Egypt during the night. Royal Navy ships had been cautioned to expect 6-inch guns on shore to bombard them. The British had left the guns behind when they withdrew from the Canal Zone. As it happens, they were

not fired. The Egyptians had been supplied with 4.5-inch shells.

'HMS *Tyne* was our command ship that was to direct operations at the sharp end of the landing,' Corporal Montgomery remembered. 'She had been sailing up and down the Mediterranean for some weeks and it was impossible to keep in contact for any length of time. As soon as a new frequency was settled on, it started to fade and those in charge reported back that the shipboard equipment did not seem up to the job.

'When the troops went in, she dropped anchor and with her stationary things were a bit better. Nevertheless the classified signals that did get through by radio were taken ashore by boat and delivered by hand.

'We had the *Tyne* and the French had their own vessel. The French commander, an excitable bloke, decided to see the action first hand and went ashore. While there he decided that in case of an aerial attack, our two ships should move apart and go out to sea. When it came time for him to return on board, his ship had gone, as ordered. He spent the next several hours at the height of the battle wandering up and down the beach looking for it.'

Roy Sanderson of the RASC thought the whole operation was a fiasco. 'We left Cyprus for Egypt on an LST and returned the same way,' he remarked. 'We didn't disembark until the afternoon in Egypt and come nightfall a Scots lad and myself laid out a scrim net like a large Dutch blanket in the back of his lorry and got our heads down. The next morning, when we rose, the Scots lad was complaining bitterly about the lack of sleep. I asked him why. There had been shelling overhead, nearly all night, he replied. He was amazed when I told him I had not heard a thing. The noise, he said, had been horrendous.

'Later in the day, we moved out and relocated in a walled shopping arcade with large doors at each end. In the centre of this open air market place, there was an unexploded missile from one of our aircraft sticking out of the tarmac. That evening I was on the roof doing guard duty and someone came round with a handful of mail for me. My 22nd birthday was nearly at an end and I had not even realized it.'

In Cyprus, a Royal Engineers Field Park Squadron was taken to Limassol from its camp, which the Royal Norfolk Regiment was expected to make its Battalion HQ. The Engineers were boarded on one of the Egypt-bound vessels and waited to sail. A day later they were taken off and returned to take back their premises from the Norfolks, who, in turn, had to march back whence they had come. The problems that resulted from these moves took two weeks to resolve.

At the southern end of the Suez Canal, HMS *Crane* was patrolling the Red Sea on 3 November. She was attacked, not by the Egyptians, but first by a flight of Israeli Air Force Mustangs dropping napalm bombs, which inflicted no damage. Soon afterwards IAF rocket-armed Mysteres swooped and fired their weapons in the belief that *Crane* was an Egyptian ship. Royal Navy gunners fired back, knocking out one of the jets and damaging a second.

Corporal Montgomery continued to contend with other difficulties. 'As our forces advanced down the length of the canal, there was a magnetic storm that wiped out all communications for a couple of days,' he recalled. 'The first message to get through afterwards from Episkopi was the one calling a halt to the campaign. If the storm had lasted another day, we would have got to the far end and the whole strategic outlook would have changed leaving us in a much stronger position.'

Throughout Operation *Musketeer*, Montgomery was in daily radio contact with GCHQ in Cheltenham, setting up links for the top brass at Episkopi to report events to London. 'One evening, we had set up a confer-

ence line, but the officers were delayed and so the civvy mech at the other end and I chatted. I remember him moaning about petrol rationing and the difficulties he faced getting home at the end of his shift.'

In the Seychelles, sitting in exile, Archbishop Bishop Makarios was very upset, said his host Captain Le Geyt. 'For the first time I found him quite angry, and he enquired why no mail had arrived. I said "Surely you have heard about the recent military operations at the Suez Canal?" and added that we, also, had received no mail from England. He then smiled and said he understood the reason.'

FOR A week, there had been little EOKA activity, but on Friday 2 November, the organization launched Island-wide attacks to pick off less protected members of the Security Forces. They had been depleted of 6,000 men because of Operation *Musketeer*. Sergeant Edward Smith of the Royal Engineers was shot in the back and killed while walking in a street on the 3rd. A dawn-to-dusk curfew was immediately imposed on all citizens in the town, irrespective of age.

The next day, Airman Albert McKinley from Wallasey in Cheshire was murdered as his truck travelled through Paralimni. The driver, a passenger and he had been visiting the village's annual fair. Tom Macleod, who knew McKinley well at 751 Signals Unit in Cape Greco, told the author: 'Herb was standing in the turret between the driver and passenger, when a single shot, fired from the top of the Church, hit him in the heart. After his death I was moved into his tent, which was already occupied by a couple of Scotsmen. Whenever we were sent to Paralimni after his murder, we got out of our trucks and walked slowly through the village, carrying our Sten guns or .303 rifles with a round up the spout and watching each other's backs. The Greek Cypriot males carried on sitting on their porches, pretending they couldn't see us. But the women followed as closely as possible, spitting and calling us "English bastards" and "Pig English". Coming as I do from Glasgow and being a wee guy, I found it difficult to keep my temper and not strike out.'

But the greatest threat now was EOKA's use of electrically detonated mines on a wide scale. They were planted on roads, in trees and under bridges. 'Their great advantage was that they could be fired from a distance by means of a battery and an electric wire,' said Grivas. 'The enemy had little chance to hit back before our men escaped.' The new weapon had been successfully tested in October to kill the three Highland Light Infantry soldiers in Lefkonico after their football game.

WO2 William Cutsforth of the Royal Artillery, from Troon in Scotland, was a victim in the Paphos area of the new mine. Because it was the height of the grape-gathering season, trucks over-filled with ripe fruit frequently dropped parts of their loads on the roads, which drivers ignored and drove over. Savvas Papaefstathiou decided to hide one of the mines in a pile of rotting grapes and wait to detonate it. Cutsforth arrived and was blasted to pieces.

On the Limassol–Polemidia road, Corporal Richard Chittock of Ipswich and Private Malcolm Cook, 18, from Great Yarmouth, of the Royal Norfolks also became victims. They were returning with Lieutenant M. L. Henderson, the Regiment's Intelligence Officer, from a house in Limassol that they had been guarding during the day. As they drove through Berengaria village, the mine was triggered. Out of control, their truck careered down the road, finally stopping. Henderson and four other passengers survived, although injured.

Private Frederick Bayliss, from Bristol, of the Royal Berkshires was killed by the same means on his way to Episkopi. On 6 November another electrically detonated mine exploded under a bridge near Limassol as military personnel were crossing. Four members of the RAF were injured, but Corporal James Smith lost his life.

In Nicosia, the assassination gangs put aside their revolvers temporarily and threw bombs at military vehicles, killing WO2 Charles Martin of the HQ staff in one attack and Signalman Ken Spragg, 20, in another. The next day Gunner Adrian Johnson's truck was ambushed at Kalopsida, killing him and injuring another soldier. In three days, EOKA had murdered 14 people.

EOKA used a parcel bomb disguised as a book on 6 November to kill its next victim. He was Douglas Williamson, an Assistant District Commissioner based in Platres, whom Grivas regarded as an intelligence operative deserving death. He was blown apart when he opened the package. He was the 77th Briton to be killed in the Emergency. From then on, the authorities checked every parcel that came through the mail.

The anti-EOKA campaign was going badly for Sir John Harding, but for the British Government, especially Prime Minister Eden, the Suez operation was a debacle. Washington had warned against Operation *Musketeer*, but No. 10 Downing Street had chosen to go ahead anyway. To show his displeasure, President Eisenhower punished Britain by selling off America's stocks of sterling. The Bank of England tried to stop the drain on the pound, but failed. Only a massive loan from the International Monetary Fund could prevent disaster, but America would not allow one, unless the UK Government called a cease-fire, as the UN demanded. The Chancellor, Harold Macmillan, had the unpleasant task of telling Eden that the country was almost broke. To continue with the Suez operation would lead the nation to economic disaster. The public was already angry about the introduction of petrol rationing and would not tolerate the devaluing of their hard-earned income and spending power.

At the same time, NATO HQ was alerting

its partners – and the Allied Command in Cyprus – that Soviet jets had been seen flying over Turkey, heading for bases in Egypt and Syria. It was also believed six Russian submarines were operating off Alexandria. The French commanders were more gung-ho than their British military counterparts and were prepared to fight off any threats from Moscow.

'We were all told to prepare for possible air attacks and I was now remembering back to the days of the blitz of London when I was a child living constantly through air raids and bombings,' said REME Sergeant Lawrence Petley, who was at Episkopi. 'There were no air raid shelters near us. We lived in tents on a hill and were completely exposed. Hopefully the new Royal Artillery Unit would protect us from air attacks if they occurred.

'I looked around the camp and decided if we were attacked by aircraft I would take cover in one of the water drainage trenches, which ran through our camp. They were deep and muddy, but I thought they would give a little protection.

'But who was likely to attack us? The general feeling was that it would be the Egyptian Air Force. I immediately felt better and safer and confident, because having spent a year in Egypt, I had never been impressed with what I had seen of their military capability or discipline. War with Egypt? I didn't think it would take too long to finish.

'At the same time it was announced to us that all *regular* troops due for demob would remain in the Army until further notice. Only National Servicemen would be going home after serving their two years. I had made a personal demob countdown calendar, eagerly crossing off the days as they passed, but the calendar was useless now, so with great disappointment I tore it up.'

At Akrotiri, 3 LAA Wing of the RAF Regiment stood by to repel any hostile aircraft entering the airspace above the long runway.

Fighter aircraft are fuelled and armed at RAF Akrotiri to combat any air threats over Cyprus.

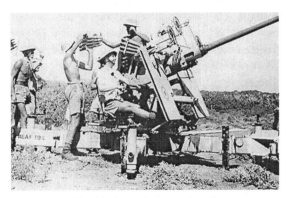
Stand by to repel enemy aircraft.

When it was being built, all the excavated earth had been piled along the entire length on the north side, between the camp and the nearby salt flats. In places the mounds were a mile wide and up to 50 feet high. Buried underground were living quarters and lavatories for those men on duty. These anti-aircraft defences were so well camouflaged that all that could be seen was the occasional barrel of a Bofors gun draped in netting. Camp guards often walked past the positions without noticing them.

An army officer, who did not wish to be identified, told the author: 'My troops didn't know they were there until I pointed them out. The gunners seemed to have a servicing force of RAF armoires that moved about from gun to gun, stripping them down into little pieces, gauging them, servicing them, greasing them, and then putting them back together again. Apparently, the Bofors were tested twice a year off the cliffs. At no time during the Suez crisis were they fired in anger.'

THE WORLDWIDE opposition to the Suez campaign reached its climax at 09.45 on Tuesday 6 November, when Israel agreed a ceasefire. Britain unilaterally followed suit without informing France in advance. On hearing the news that Eden had ordered a stop to the fighting, General Beaufre, the commander of French troops, is reported to have said: 'I was in a suppressed rage, and at that moment I considered the possibility of disobeying.' The French, who had advanced 23 miles along the Canal, could not continue alone.

At 23.59 on 6 November, the Anglo-French ceasefire came into force. The United Nations ordered the allied forces to leave the Canal Zone. By year's end, UN Blue Berets had replaced them.

In the United States, voters had re-elected Eisenhower as President for a second term.

By midday of 7 November, Egyptian gift sellers were back on the streets offering their wares to the 'invaders' as if they were tourists.

None of the aims of the British and French Prime Ministers had been achieved. Nasser had blocked the Suez Canal by sinking ships in the waterway and consolidated his power in Cairo. Eden had brought Britain near to bankruptcy and the nation's influence in the Middle East was never at lower ebb. In Cyprus, EOKA had killed more British citizens than Nasser's forces had managed during Operation *Musketeer*. The troops were angry. They had done more than could have been expected of them, lost comrades, were near fulfilling their military objectives and now were denied victory.

The Times correspondent in Nicosia reported: 'The failure to allow them to complete the job has produced a sense of frustration and confusion among many senior officers here, as well as among many of their subordinates. This frustration at the way in which the allied operation was ended has produced a degree of bluntness and criticism in private conversation which is as widespread among responsible service officers as is the criticism among Foreign Service officials connected with Arab affairs of the manner of its launching.

'Senior officers in excellent positions to judge say that it is probable that within another 18 or 24 hours the whole length of the canal would have been in allied hands – with all that that would have meant diplomatically and in freedom to get ahead with clearing operations – and that if they had been allowed only another eight or 12 hours they would have been in or beyond Ismailia and have had several useful airfields in their hands.'

'All the time we were in Egypt I don't remember seeing an Egyptian soldier, but we did see a lot of people who'd clearly changed their clothes fairly rapidly, because we found their uniforms, and in one case they were actually still warm,' Sapper Robert Gretton

Egyptians surrender to British forces.

recalled. 'As well as uniforms, there were boots and rifles and even grenades. There were men sitting around wearing new-looking *jellabas*. We thought they were soldiers, so we rounded them up and passed them back, I suppose, for internment. But I never saw an identifiable enemy.'

During the next few weeks, the Anglo-French forces began their withdrawal. British troops were either sent home or returned to Cyprus to continue anti-EOKA operations, but it would be several months before Governor Harding's garrison was back at full strength. The last troops left Egypt on 22 December.

Soldier magazine summed up the Suez misadventure in a few, short sentences: 'In a way, it was like one of those exercises in which an umpire with a white armband comes along at the most exciting moment and orders both sides to stop fighting. That is always a disappointing moment, especially for the side which knows it's winning. The "umpire" this time was the United Nations' force in its white Jeeps, white railway coaches and white aeroplanes. It was a strange experience for the British Army, having gained a foothold by assault, to hand over control to a somewhat bewildered, but game, international force drawn from small states the world over.'

By 9 January 1957, Prime Minister Eden could no longer stand the storm of criticism surrounding his actions over Suez. With his health failing, he resigned the premiership and was replaced by Harold Macmillan.

OPERATION *SPARROWHAWK* in October had wrong-footed EOKA, but the Suez events returned the initiative to Grivas. 'I have little doubt that if it had been possible to continue active operations against them on that scale for several months, their defeat would have been completed,' Grivas admitted. 'After the collapse of the Suez operation, British troops poured back into Cyprus and I reduced my pressure, leaving it mainly to the execution groups in the towns to keep up a war of nerves: so many street killings took place in the centre of the capital that the London newspapers took to calling it "Murder Mile".'

But there were soldiers who were not in awe of his assassination squads, as Barry Smith, an infantry regiment private, remembered: 'I was once in a Land Rover with an RAF Regiment sergeant, when a bomb, which was meant for us, went off after we had driven past it. We saw two men running away, carrying rifles. The sergeant gave me his .38 to hold and ran after them. When he caught them, he smashed their heads together and said: "Don't f---ing try to kill me again." I don't know if the sergeant was crazy or very brave.'

With failure on all fronts, the month went down in history as 'Black November'.

Bringing the soldiers back to Cyprus appeared to pose as many problems for planners as getting them to Egypt had in the first place. *The Knot*, the journal of the South Staffordshire Regiment, noted: 'Although not directly involved in the Suez operations, we stood, as it were, on the touchline; and, when calls for help of various kinds came from our friends in the Parachute Brigade, and others too numerous to mention, we were not found wanting. Indeed, we considered it an honour

British troops leave Port Said.

to be asked to send our Regimental Band to Famagusta to play ashore the 3rd Parachute Battalion on returning from their gallant exploits at El Gamil airfield. The fact that on arrival (9 November) they had to be hurriedly diverted to the port of Limassol, some 70 miles away, owing to a change in plan, in no way detracted from that honour, but is, perhaps, an indication that movements were running true to form.'

Early in the morning of Wednesday the 7th, the men of 1 Para, including Bryan Hunter, had marched to the docks in Port Said and boarded HMS *Ocean*. 'Here we were ordered to leave all our ill-gotten gains on the quay. We took this to mean our beloved Mercedes,' he says. 'Once we had parked the vehicle, one of the lads turned to a sailor and said: "Whatever you do, be careful with that car as it belongs to our CO." Dutifully he stuck a label on the Merc's windscreen. On our arrival in Cyprus, the Redcaps and a group of civilian CID officers met us, all demanding we hand over our AK-47s, with their ammunition. Under protest we obeyed and lost a fine piece of kit, which could have been put to good use against EOKA.

'A few days later our CO was in a right flap, because he had received a message from the Suez docks saying his Mercedes was there, awaiting collection. His clerk told us the CO had tried to disown the vehicle, but was told it was down to him and he must collect it forthwith. His driver went over and brought it back. The CO now had in his possession some very expensive loot. After threatening us with a fate worse than death for looting, he had become the worst offender. To his credit, he chose to sell the car and add the money to Battalion funds. So ended 1 Para's involvement in the Suez invasion of 1956.'

With some bitterness, Colonel Paul Crook remembered the reception his men received on their return to Cyprus. 'We arrived off Famagusta at dawn, but we were not allowed to disembark at Limassol until late afternoon. By then a reception party consisting solely of a Military Police Officer and some Redcaps [Military Police] was awaiting us. Everyone else was too busy it seemed. The Provost officer informed me that he intended to search us for weapons.

'I watched for a while as my battle-experienced soldiers were subjected to a humiliating total body search by raw, unseasoned military personnel who had never seen a shot fired in anger. The sight of my men being treated as common criminals became too much for me and I exploded. I ordered it to stop. The Provost officer remonstrated, insisting that the searching had to go on. I refused to allow it and said that I would take the consequences. I had defied the might of the Provost machine, a dangerous thing to do. I more or less got away with it but it was not forgotten and we featured in their black books. After this "welcome" it was back to Tunisia Camp.'

Gordon Burt, another Para, returned to Cyprus on the aircraft carrier HMS *Hermes*. 'She drew up as close as she could to the beach and we were told to get on board. Once we were at sea, we were ordered to throw all our ammunition overboard, because the captain did not wish to proceed with loose ammo on his ship,' he said. 'We then spent two weeks expending all loose ammunition because it couldn't be packed up. Myself and six others from my platoon threw hand grenades till we were sick of hearing them. Then, I'm afraid, we had the reservists with us who had been called back for Suez. Their main interest then was to get home because, as far as they were concerned, the emergency they had been called up for had finished. But, of course, this didn't happen and we were then sent on anti-EOKA terrorist duties. Morale was pretty low that we had been withdrawn. Word was filtering back from home about the political opposition surrounding Suez. We had gone there to do what we thought was a job for our country, but we weren't really prepared for it. We didn't have the transport, whether it was air transport, ships or vehicles. It was a very shoddy operation.'

David Hartley, a doctor attached to 1 Para, shared Burt's opinion. 'We came back from Suez on HMS *Bulwark*, an aircraft carrier and I had my first bath for ten days. I was very impressed by the courtesy of the Royal Navy. They filled the ship up with thousands of soldiers and made us very welcome. We went back to Famagusta, I think; I really can't remember. There was a terrible feeling of anticlimax about Suez, of a job not properly done. I felt pretty angry towards politicians in general; not just ours, but the whole lot – the Egyptians, the French, the British – everybody. That common soldiers had killed each other because politicians had ballsed it up; that made me very angry.'

Many French troops, angered by the British Government's decision to halt the invasion, returned to the Island and showed their disgust by selling their weapons to any terrorists they could find and used their ill-gotten gains to support the economies of the red light districts.

Other units remained longer in Egypt to ensure a smooth transfer to the UN Force that had been sent to replace them. Robert Gretton's 'bolshie' Royal Engineers were amongst them. 'When we finally set sail, we were on a little flat-bottomed boat, not a landing craft, and we were all terribly sick. I think this was just before Christmas, so we'd only been in Egypt something like a maximum of four or five weeks. As we approached Cyprus, we were given a very stiff talking to by an officer who was in an infantry regiment, warning us that the security situation was very bad, and that we could expect bombs and shooting and, generally, things would be much worse than in Port Said. Our morale, of course, then rocketed down. Everyone said, "Why aren't we going home?" We were in a

really recalcitrant mood, but we were so seasick we could hardly raise a shout.

'When we landed at Famagusta – thoroughly scared – we were told that we were going to join 35th Field Engineer Regiment. This meant proper soldiering duties. We weren't too keen on that, and we let it be known to any officer or sergeant who dared to come anywhere near us. By then, we had acquired a fairly unsavoury reputation as an unruly and ungovernable lot. My memories are pretty sketchy, except that we seemed to spend a lot of time doing patrols, but not knowing quite why we were patrolling.'

WITH AN end to the Suez disaster, Harding and Grivas went head-to-head again, each determined to destroy the other. While EOKA could still maintain the pressure by its hit-and-run tactics and murder squads in the towns, the colonial administration's intelligence gathering and interrogation teams and techniques had much improved. They would lead the Army to gain the upper hand in the year ahead. At the same time, the UK Government was studying new proposals for a settlement drafted by Lord Radcliffe. Both would dramatically change the future of Cyprus. Until then, there was no stopping the daily murders by the terrorists to which Harding's only response was to arrest and hold even more Greek Cypriots in detention camps.

By 6 November, 196 people had been killed by EOKA, of whom 114 were Cypriots. The figures rose steeply during the next three weeks.

On 8 November, Grivas's orders to murder the head of the specialist hospital in Kyperounda were carried out. The victim was Dr Charles Bevan, a man who had put ambition and financial gain behind him in devoting his life's work to the care and cure of tuberculosis on the Island. Of him, Lord Winster wrote: 'Nothing can emphasize more the tragedy of Cyprus than that such a unique and gifted friend of the Island should come to his end in such a way.' Another friend told *The Times*: 'His death is particularly tragic in view of the long years of devoted service he had given to Cyprus and the love and understanding he always showed for its people. He will be deeply mourned by people of all races: there can hardly fail to be a considerable revulsion among his many Cypriot friends against so wicked and senseless a killing.'

But what had motivated the EOKA leader to 'execute' the good doctor? Simply a rumour that he was collaborating with the Security Forces by using truth drugs on suspected terrorist prisoners – and in Cyprus rumours travel faster than a forest fire in summer and can generate as much heat. Elsewhere such an outrageous suggestion would have been cast aside without a second thought, but in Grivas's head it grew into fact.

After the murder, a company of the Gordon Highlanders was rushed from the Troodos Mountains to scour the area for suspects. Reg Parnell, who was an armoire, was conducting a quarterly inspection of the troops' weapons when the order came to 'Stand To!' As the regiment's three-ton trucks were about to drive off, he noticed that one was carrying a draft of soldiers that had arrived only hours earlier. 'I could tell from their smart brand new uniforms,' he said. 'I decided to join them so that they didn't do anything dangerous.'

At the hospital, locally recruited staff told the Highlanders that the terrorists had escaped and hidden on top of a particular hill, which was pointed out. An officer speculated that the information could have been given to draw his men into an ambush and so he asked Parnell to fire flares to illuminate the hilltop before advancing. 'Two of the new arrivals prepared the two-inch mortar, but couldn't get the bombs to drop down the barrel,' he recalled. 'They had forgotten to first remove the bombs' safety caps. I took over and for the only time in my 25 years' service went into action. Of course, by this time, if there had been any terrorists, they were long gone.'

Later Dr Bevan's shooter was identified as Evagoras Papachristoforou, who himself was 'executed' by EOKA for allegedly becoming an 'informer'. His father, a priest interned at the Pyla Pile Detention Centre, was refused permission to attend his funeral.

Death followed death in 'Black November'. Grivas boasted: 'The high point was the full-scale ambush mounted by Markos Drakos and his group of 12 men on the mountain road between Lefka and Pedhoulas. The guerrillas took up their positions overnight and found a target soon after daybreak [on 12 November], when the lookout signalled the approach of three lorries loaded with soldiers moving down to the coast.

'As the first vehicle appeared round the bend, Drakos's men sent a hail of automatic fire down the hillside, wounding a driver and an officer sitting beside him. Both this and the second truck went off the road, but the soldiers climbed out and returned our fire, while the third lorry sped on to a safer position: here the soldiers dismounted and began to shell the EOKA men with mortars. During the next 20 minutes our Bren gunner killed the sergeant firing the mortar with a shot from over 500 yards. The group then withdrew, leaving one dead and four wounded soldiers behind them. We had no losses.'

The dead soldier was Sergeant Alexander Dow, 25, of the Gordon Highlanders. He became the 82nd Briton to be killed since the Emergency began.

Civil or military, it did not matter to the terrorists as long as their targets were British. To prove their point, they attacked British businessmen A. S. Hallam and J. V. Miles, both architects, in Nicosia as they were leaving their office. Hallam was a leading member of the British Residents' Association. Their deaths made 14 November the worst day for murders since the EOKA campaign began. The next day, Alan Grice, another civilian, was blasted to pieces when he drove over an electrically detonated mine in Limassol.

Speculation mounted that either Grivas was dead or gravely ill as his gangs seemed out of control and appeared to be choosing their targets at random, especially when their guns were turned on 27-year-old Angus Macdonald, who had arrived only the week before to join the *Times of Cyprus* from *The Spectator* in London. He was using journalism, his friends said, as a steppingstone to Parliament and intended to run as a Conservative candidate at the next General Election.

Until Macdonald's murder on 16 November, Charles Foley and his editorial staff had never been attacked. The rival *Cyprus Mail*, however, was under EOKA threat. The captured Grivas diaries showed Dighenis had ordered his 'killer group' to 'liquidate' the newspaper.

Foley's reaction to his reporter's death was almost an apology for the EOKA action. He explained: 'Sampson saw the young Englishman walking the streets and assumed him to be a "special constable", like two British businessmen who had been murdered earlier. But whereas the latter were armed and were outspoken opponents of EOKA, Macdonald carried no weapons and had written articles highly critical of official British attitudes. The assassination embarrassed Cypriot leaders; there were complaints inside the EOKA hierarchy and Sampson's star began to fade. The young journalist was his last British victim.'

Ironically, Macdonald's last published piece argued 'Those who advised the Governor in August to put an end to the truce by demanding surrender terms because, they said, EOKA was beaten, bear some responsibility for the men who have died since.' As a reserve officer, he was buried with full military honours in Wayne's Keep Cemetery. An escort from the Gordon Highlanders fired a volley at the graveside.

BLOOD STREAMING down his face, a piece of metal sticking out from his forehead, the Sergeant Major of 21 Medium Regiment Royal Artillery screamed orders to the soldiers who were still on their feet. At just after 20.00, in the middle of a crowded Tombola session, a time bomb had blasted apart their NAAFI, a commandeered taverna at Coral Bay on the outskirts of Paphos. 'I was lying on my bed in our tent when I heard the explosion,' said Gunner Colin Gray. He had arrived in Cyprus in mid-August, just after his 20th birthday.

Gray continued: 'With others, I ran to the armoury, where we drew our rifles and belted like hell to the NAAFI, about 300 yards away. The place was in a right state. The first bloke I saw was Gunner Ernie Hargreaves lying on the floor, yelling in pain. I could see he was in a very bad way. I called across to my mate Gunner Nobby Clarke from Southend to give me a hand. We each took hold of one of Ernie's arms and tried to lift him. As we did, he yelled, "My stomach." It had a gaping hole. We shouted for a stretcher and carried him to the first aid station. There we saw our Troop Bombardier, Emlyn "Taff" Francis, lying on a bed. He was in a very bad way, too.'

Gordon Patterson, one of the ACC cooks, who escaped injury, also helped to carry out the wounded. Francis was one of his friends and they had chatted a few minutes earlier. He told the author: '"Taff" got married by special licence on board the aircraft carrier HMS *Ocean* at Devonport docks just before he sailed for Cyprus.'

Francis and Hargreaves, 19, were dead a few hours later. All the Greek Cypriots employed at the camp were dismissed the next day. Bombardier George Roberts, another of the 14 injured soldiers, succumbed in hospital on 22 November.

Special Branch officers concluded that a Greek Cypriot camp orderly from Peyia village, who had disappeared, had planted a pencil bomb inside one of the tubular metal tables in the NAAFI. The troops speculated that the local manager was to blame.

'Because of this attack, we made life a little difficult for the Greeks,' Gray admitted. 'When we did house searches we forced them to take everything out of their houses – and I mean everything. On roadblocks we made them empty their tipper lorries, which were full of grapes, onto the road. I'm afraid we pushed them around a bit. I've been back to Paphos on holiday and visited the locations of my past, but I find the Greeks have a very distorted view of their recent history.'

Two youths on a motorcycle slowly followed Private David Coulter of the RASC and his companion, a Turkish Cypriot auxiliary policeman, as they walked on the pavement of a crowed narrow street in Limassol. Against the cacophony of tooting car horns from impatient drivers and the ringing bells of cyclists trying to negotiate their way through the traffic, they did not pay much attention to the phut-phutting of the motorbike that drew alongside them. Nor did they notice the pillion passenger Michalakis Thrassyvoulides, who led EOKA's assassination squad in Limassol, pulling a pistol from his belt. Only the policeman heard the fatal shots that killed his friend and wounded him. The young terrorists, dodging the traffic, raced away in a cloud of exhaust fumes mixed with the smell of cordite. It was 18 November 1956. Private Coulter left a wife and five young children to mourn him.

Thrassyvoulides was arrested later and appeared in court, but Mr Justice Shaw ruled that the prosecution had not proved its case and so the killer walked free.

'Attacks of this kind in Limassol were, of course, a threat to my security, since my house was only a mile from the centre of town,'

Grivas opined, 'but I decided there was an equal risk attached to keeping the area too quiet, which might arouse British suspicions.'

After the latest EOKA outrages, the authorities imposed a dawn-to-dusk curfew for all males under 27 in the Island's main towns, with tougher restrictions applied in Nicosia. For 7,500 inhabitants over the age of 18 in Limassol, there was a collective punishment – a fine to which each person would have to contribute at least £3, although in some cases a payment of £175 was required.

DESPITE THE onslaught of bad news, gleefully reported in the Greek press and in the *Times of Cyprus*, the tide began to turn against EOKA as the Security Forces introduced more heavily-armed 'Q' patrols that carried out sudden raids and gathered intelligence.

Historian Robert Holland explained: 'The Q patrols consisted of Greek Cypriots, sometimes turned EOKA members, more often criminals recruited from the Greek Cypriot community in Britain, Turkish Cypriots and British personnel. They had the advantage of personal knowledge both of the areas they operated in and of the men they were hunting. An added advantage was that they were only loosely bound by the constraints of police or military discipline and so behaved with much greater ruthlessness ... There is no doubt that they successfully carried the war to the guerrillas and played an important part in forcing EOKA on the defensive.'

Outside the towns, the Security Forces were arriving on the scenes of incidents far faster than before by helicopter. The RAF had formed 284 Squadron, with six of its Sycamores at the disposal of the military. Three others and a Whirlwind flew in support, fulfilling search and rescue duties.

There was also an effort to 'silence' the *Times of Cyprus* by charging editor Charles Foley under Section 43 of the Emergency

Regulations for publishing a report 'likely to cause alarm and despondency and likely to be prejudicial to the maintenance of public order'. The law gave the Governor the power to suspend any publication, which, in his view, prejudiced 'the success of measures taken to bring about an end to the State of Emergency'. Fearing for their own newspapers, all the other editors in Nicosia supported Foley. Their protest concluded: 'In view of the above circumstances there can be neither objective reporting of facts nor fair and helpful comment until the regulation is withdrawn, amended, or hedged about with safeguards for the freedom of the Press.'

After a long-drawn-out legal battle, with Foley represented by Glafcos Clerides, a secret member of EOKA, and an imported team of top lawyers from London, the editor was fined £50.

Although there were good reasons for Sir John Harding to put pressure on Foley, there seemed none for EOKA to kill another of his reporters, 30-year-old Donald Fox, as he stood outside a cinema in Catsellis Street in Kyrenia on 9 December. He had only joined the *Times of Cyprus* as a sub-editor 10 days earlier after leaving the London *Evening News* for which he had been covering Operation *Musketeer*.

Foley wrote later: 'The Anglican Archdeacon advised over the telephone that the funeral should be held at once ("odd things happen in this climate") and recommended that a coffin should be bought in Kyrenia ("better as well as cheaper"). The body was brought to Nicosia for burial. The Governor's aide appeared, top hat in hand, among the small group of newspapermen who were Fox's only friends in Cyprus. There was no time for relatives to come out, no time even to trace them.' Readers began to wonder if Foley was being sent a warning by Grivas.

By December, EOKA, too, was taking a lot of punishment from the Security Forces. The Organization's arms smuggling ring of 44, including Customs officials, was broken up in Limassol. In another operation, lasting seven days in south-west Cyprus, 52 EOKA gang members were captured in their lairs. But for all the Greek Cypriots who demanded *enosis*, their political machinations appeared to have backfired with Lord Radcliffe's plan for the future administration of the Island. It recommended that if the people were given the right to self-determination, that right must apply to both communities. In other words, Greeks could vote for union with Athens, but so could the Turks for union with Ankara.

For the first time, a new and frightening word for Greek Cypriots entered the political debate: *partition*.

CHAPTER SIXTEEN

Death of a terrorist: the birth of a legend

'It was like a jolly big shoot, and my men acted as beaters.'
Brigadier J. A. Hopwood

THE AFTERNOON sun was groping its way through a blanket of rain-laden grey clouds when Gregoris Afxentiou, EOKA's second-in-command, met his death in the 'Valley of the Knife' as a bone-chilling wind whipped the Troodos Mountains and the sounds of machine gun fire and explosions echoed around their peaks. It was Sunday, 3 March 1957, a few minutes after 14.00. For eight hours, Afxentiou and his gang of four terrorists had defied a cordon of 60 British troops who had tracked him for days and in the early hours of the morning found his hiding place not far from Makhaeras monastery.

From the start of the EOKA conflict, Afxentiou had been a formidable opponent and the British placed a reward of £5,000 on his head. While he had escaped from British hands and eluded capture on numerous other occasions, sometimes by just a matter of minutes, he must have known that now he had two choices: either surrender or die in what would be a one-sided battle.

Afxentiou chose death and so created a legend. His stand has become one of the epics of Greek history, taking its place alongside Koungi, Arkadi, Thermopylae and Gravis in exaggerated speeches and books about his life. For Greek Cypriots he remains their revolutionary hero *sans peur et sans reproche* and pre-eminent in the struggle to liberate Cyprus

from British colonial rule and unite it with Greece. 'It's a pity we have to kill people like that,' Frank Dewsbury, a former member of a Special Operations Group, told the author. 'This statement may make me sound like an EOKA sympathizer, but I respect good soldiers and brave men doing a hard dangerous job whatever their nationality or cause, and most professional military men feel the same.' Lt Colonel Britten of the Grenadier Guards who was present at the time of Afxentiou's death also observed: 'He fought back bravely, determined to sell his life dearly.' During an earlier attempt to capture Afxentiou, another British officer told his father: 'As a soldier, of course I want to capture him – he is an arch-terrorist and it's my duty. As a man, I want to congratulate you on having such a splendid son ...'

Afxentiou commanded respect from his supporters and the British Army alike because he was the only military-trained member of EOKA, apart from the leader Colonel George Grivas, who spent most of his 'small war' hiding in Limassol. Afxentiou, by contrast, led his inexperienced men from the front and fought his opponents openly.

GREGORIS PIERIS Afxentiou was born in Lysi village on 22 February 1928 and received his education at the Famagusta Hellenic Gymnasium. He went to Greece in the hope of entering the Hellenic Military Academy in Athens, but was turned down. Nevertheless he joined the Greek Army in December 1949 as a volunteer and attended a reserve officer's academy on the island of Syros. He reached the rank of a second lieutenant or *Anthypolokhagos*. But his father needed him back home and so he returned to the Island and the family's small farm to work as a truck driver. Soon afterwards he became engaged to Vasiliki Panayi, his longtime village sweetheart.

Filled with Greek nationalism, once Afxentiou heard about the insurrection planned by Archbishop Makarios and Colonel Grivas, he enlisted in the ranks of the guerrillas, most of whom the leader considered of 'poor quality', but when they met for the first time in 1955, Grivas saw a man he thought he could mould as a young fighter. He took Afxentiou to Palouriotissa village in early February and put him through a concentrated course in leadership and sabotage. During the training the two men often discussed life at the Athens Military Academy.

On the opening night of the EOKA conflict – 31 March/1 April 1955 – Grivas assigned Afxentiou the task of blowing up the Cyprus Broadcasting Station in Nicosia. His mission successfully completed, Grivas ordered him to return home and go about his business as usual. By the next day, however, the police had identified him and he went on the run to become leader of a mountain group near Kyrenia. He was given the code-name *Zidros*. For several months, he taught his men how to use weapons and the techniques of guerrilla warfare among the peaks of the Pentadactylos Mountain range.

Afxentiou believed in meticulously planning his attacks against the British. Grivas, on the other hand, wanted quick results, but his protégé was determined not to waste lives needlessly nor do anything that dishonoured his sense of military honour. The Colonel often reprimanded him for 'lack of energy'. Grivas said later: 'Afxentiou would bow his head and say nothing, but he could never be hurried against his will.'

Unlike Grivas, Afxentiou also showed compassion for those who became informers. Against orders, he refused to execute a man who had betrayed his group. Because the man's wife had just given birth, he ordered his gang to release him, but warned him to never repeat his offence, as mercy would not be shown again. 'You are too kind hearted,' his men chorused. Afxentiou replied: 'I'm a fighter, not a butcher.'

Afxentiou also believed in education and encouraged his men to read books and study when time allowed.

During the build-up to the first organized ambushes of British patrols and convoys, Afxentiou secretly married Vasiliki Panayi on 10 June 1955. The wedding was organized as if it were a military campaign. Accompanied by a friend, the girl was taken by an EOKA member to Nicosia and from there to a little monastery not far from the American monitoring station near Karavas. The wedding took place with Afxentiou's gang guarding the monastery walls. The ceremony over, he returned to the mountains almost at once and his wife went back to their village. A month later, they met again for a few days. That was the last time they saw each other.

Mr and Mrs Afxentiou.

After Operation *Lucky Alphonse* in 1956, when Grivas escaped and settled in Limassol, Afxentiou was placed in charge of guerrilla activities in the whole central area of the Troodos Mountains. His main task was to coordinate and re-organize the mountain gangs the British had broken up and scattered. He tramped the rugged area meeting leaders and gathering recruits, some of whom had escaped from detention and soon the *antartes* were back in action. Until the end of the year, Afxentiou's hit-and-run methods against military convoys on the Nicosia–Limassol road caused the British a lot of trouble. He soon became the authorities' 'Most Wanted' terrorist. But his time was running out as the British began to receive better intelligence.

In December 1956, the security forces had smashed the terrorists' arms-smuggling ring in Limassol. In his *Memoirs*, Grivas admitted his worries about the British counter-offensive. 'Trouble began when the Limassol smuggling network was broken and the EOKA customs' team arrested, along with several important

The 'Wanted' poster for Afxentiou.

Limassol leaders, including three men who knew my whereabouts,' he wrote. 'These were Manolis Savvides and Andreas Papadopoulos, who had helped to build the hideout I was living in, and Dafnis Panayides, whose house I had stayed at from June to September of that year. If any of them broke down under torture my life was in grave danger.'

Arms and munitions would now be in short supply for EOKA. This was proved later in a captured letter from Grivas. Writing to a gang member with the code-name of *Polynikis*, he warned: 'You must economies [*sic*] in pistol ammunition. You are the only ones who waste it. Our reserves are now exhausted.'

THE GREEK Government rejected outright the Radcliffe proposals that had raised the possibility of eventual double *enosis* for Cyprus. Foreign Minister Averoff said: 'The vague reference to self-determination made in the House of Commons connected with an idea about the Island's partition, instead of leading to a settlement of the issue adds new and complex problems.' By contrast, Turkish Prime Minister Menderes found they constituted a basis of discussion. Washington believed they showed abandonment of previous British intransigence and steps toward a friendly settlement of the dispute, but disapproved of the notion of any 'forcible vivisection' of Cyprus. Eisenhower's primary concern was the unity of NATO, more so after the disaster of Suez and the Soviet aggression in Hungary. Governor Harding was against any division and privately suggested Whitehall was behaving in an underhand manner. The partition dispute drowned out all the other recommendations, which had merit.

Nevertheless, Criton Tornartis, the Cyprus Attorney General, and Radcliffe's aide Derek Pearson, left secretly by air for Mombassa, where they boarded a cruise liner as 'Mr Symes' and 'Mr Black' for the Seychelles to discuss the proposals with the exiled

Archbishop Makarios. Their undercover activity came to an end when someone in Mombassa recognized Pearson and phoned Charles Foley, who immediately published the information in his *Times of Cyprus*.

The two UK Government envoys, however, were not empowered to negotiate. They could only gather Makarios's reactions to the Radcliffe Report and establish if he was ready to denounce violence ahead of any possible talks. Captain Le Geyt and his wife made sure they had an enjoyable Christmas dinner together. His efforts included a Christmas tree, candles, paper hats, crackers and glasses filled with Cypriot wine. In the days that followed, they went on picnics and saw the sights, always continuing their conversations in a convivial atmosphere, but without reaching any conclusions.

The Archbishop once more would not give a straight answer. He also wanted to end his 'holiday' and to return to lead the Greek Cypriots, who were in thrall of Grivas. Dialogue exhausted, the messengers were told on 9 January to catch the next mail boat out of Mahe. The mission had become another exercise in futility.

The next day Sir Anthony Eden resigned as Prime Minister. His departure from No. 10 Downing Street was met with satisfaction in Athens. The press called him the 'most hated Englishman of those who ever hurt Greece' because of his Cyprus policy, but the public was cautioned against thinking that his successor, Harold Macmillan, would change anything, as 'his accomplices in this lunatic foreign policy remain in power'. The Greeks were still smarting at the thought that the Island could be partitioned. In London, the Cabinet believed that it could now negotiate from a position of strength for a settlement.

IN JANUARY 1957, British counter-insurgency tactics improved dramatically when Major General Joe Kendrew took over

and combined the posts of District Commander, previously held by Major General Ricketts, and Chief of Staff, a role Brigadier Baker had filled. Baker was now appointed Director of Operations.

Rather than throwing vast numbers of troops at the enemy in large-scale operations, Kendrew and Baker increasingly used the so-called Q patrols to gather intelligence in EOKA dominated areas and then followed up with small, fast-moving teams – often carried in helicopters – to snatch and grab suspects. The Q Patrols consisted of civilian police officers, Greek Cypriot informers and specially selected soldiers, none probably more effective than Captain Lionel Savery. At considerable danger to himself, he often roamed the mountains alone disguised as a villager recording what he saw.

Occasionally Savery took part in a Q Patrol operation. On New Year's Eve, tipped off by an informer that Grivas was hiding in

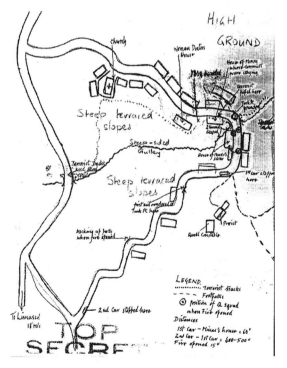

The map of the Zoopiyi village operation.

Zoopiyi, he led a patrol into the village, using an old taxi as cover. Grivas wasn't there, but Afxentiou was. A firefight broke out, but Grivas's No. 2 escaped with a bullet wound. However, his friend, Michael Georgallas, was killed.

Coupled with information gained by Savery from captured EOKA men and the intelligence coming from the Special Operations Group, a clear picture was emerging about where Afxentiou and his men were headed. There were also SAS men following the terrorists from hide to hide. Frank Dewsbury said: 'If recognized by SOG, they were allowed to continue under continuous surveillance, with the hope that they would lead us to their safe houses, other terrorists, arms dumps and hopefully Grivas himself.'

At the start of the New Year, Brigadier Baker launched Operation *Black Mak*. With every passing day in January it gathered momentum as the Army, RAF and civilian police worked together. The operation's primary objective in the mountains was to capture or kill Markos Drakos, Polycarpos Georghadjis and Afxentiou. At the slightest sign of EOKA movement, the RAF flew troops to the spot, carrying them three at a time in 12 brand new Sycamore helicopters based at Nicosia Airport. If there were no safe landing place, the soldiers descended by rope, a technique they had developed in Malaya against the Communist insurgents. By now the authorities had also declared parts of the Troodos 'prohibited areas', where small hunter units of the Army could shoot strangers on site.

First of the terrorists to fall in this new campaign was Markos Drakos (code names: *Lykourgos* and *Mavilis*) on the night of 17/18 January. The 1st Battalion Royal Suffolks, based in Kakopetria, had been deployed to set up positions in the mountains to ambush any Greek Cypriots using tracks at night. The soldiers had intelligence that several terrorist groups hid in the mountains by day, but slipped into villages after dark to gather supplies and security information.

A patrol led by Corporal King, Privates Brasset, Cooper, Sells, Wilson, Woods and Lance Corporal Fowler of 'D' Company was sent out to establish an ambush position near Evrykhou village. In the late afternoon, as darkness fell, they found the ideal spot. It overlooked a track by an outcrop of pine trees. A short distance away, they set up camp. Here they cooked their evening meal and planned to sleep the night in bivouacs. King had split his men into two groups that would rotate every four hours, one at the ambush position, the other resting. Suddenly a storm started. A biting wind cut through their clothing. Sleet and snow cut visibility down to a few yards.

Around 19.00 hrs, Corporal King's ambush party heard several bursts of automatic gunfire in the distance. They took this to mean that another patrol had encountered an EOKA group. Moving his gang and weapons under cover of a heavy mist through the 'no-go' land, Drakos had failed to see he was walking his men into a carefully prepared ambush.

Four hours later, it was the Fowler team's turn to relieve King's group and while they were changing over, Private Wood spotted a lone figure on the track, eight yards below. He said: 'Suddenly he was there, standing in front of me. At first neither of us moved. Then he fired his Sten and bullets whizzed past me. I raised my Sterling sub-machine gun, took aim and fired back.' The figure ran behind a tree and resumed firing. Spotting the flashes from the stranger's weapon, the entire patrol concentrated their attack on the tree, hitting their target. A body fell on the snow, but the soldiers heard another man cry out and a flurry in the bushes.

Tefkros Loizou, one of the terrorists to escape, later described the encounter: 'Three times we came across English soldiers. The first time we exchanged fire. The second we didn't. The weather was very bad. Suddenly there was a streak of lightning. In that moment Drakos and an English soldier spotted and shot at each other. I was next to him. I saw him fall. The rest of us changed direction and managed to get away.'

The Suffolks stayed in their positions till daylight when they moved out of their hide and searched the track, where they found the dead man. His body contained 13 bullets. He was later identified as Drakos, Grivas's third-in-command. According to historian Doros Alastos, the final bullet came from the terrorist's own weapon. A few days later a Sussex officer visited Drakos's mother and handed her a roll of photographic negatives of her son that had been found in his possession.

Born in Kalopanayiotis in 1930, Drakos had launched the first organized attack on British Forces. It took place in the Mersinaki area in mid-December 1955. Before joining EOKA, he had worked for the Hellenic Mining Company. He always carried a copy of the Greek New Testament, which had been printed in the UK, but this disappeared. Alastos suggested that, perhaps, some serviceman may have taken it as a memento.

For the Suffolks, after nearly five months of continuous hard work with little to show except small finds of explosives and ammunition, the death of Drakos was considered due reward for their efforts. 'This success, which was followed by messages of congratulations from HE the Governor, C-in-C MELF, the Director of Operations, and many others, had a tremendous effect on morale in the Battalion and everyone looked forward to further successes in the near future,' reported *The Suffolk Journal*.

For their part in the ambush operation, Corporal King, Lance Corporal Fowler and Private Woods were Mentioned in Dispatches.

Three days after the death of Drakos, George Matsis was killed in Kannavia. The highlight of his EOKA career had been raiding

George Matsis.

The house in Kannavia where Matsis hid and died.

a British arms store in Famagusta and getting away with Sten guns, ammunitions and grenades, part of the supplies removed from the Canal Zone in Egypt. When his death was announced, Athens Radio urged 'all Cypriot children should try to be like him. Troodos is in silence; not even the birds are singing', and said Matsis was 'beloved of the gods'. In his diary, Grivas noted: 'EOKA has lost a brave and honest soldier. May his memory be eternal. His self-sacrifice and patriotism will be an example to all.'

On the same day that Matsis died, 2 Para was striking hard against the EOKA gangs in the eastern Troodos. With the aid of huge flares, 30 parachutists made night descents from helicopters, despite the wind gusting at 50 knots, on to several high points in the Adelphi Forest and at Omodhos, a shiny white vineyard village of small, neat houses and narrow streets of cobblestones. A Parachute Regiment officer entered the cottage of the village police constable. Sitting in front of a blazing fire, the constable was helping a child with his homework, while his wife tended a baby in a cradle. Another child crawled on the floor and a grandmother was setting the table. But this calm family scene didn't fool the young lieutenant. He noticed the fire had only just been lit. Kicking it apart, he found the hearthstone moved. Underneath was a shaft leading down to a room in which eight men were hiding. They came out one by one, hands raised. The much-wanted Argyrious Karademas, Greek arms smuggler, trained saboteur and prison breaker was among them.

The last man to surrender was Polycarpos Georghadjis (code-names: *Klimis* and *Cicero*). Georghadjis had been part of the terrorist organization from its start. To his supporters the 26-year-old was known as 'Houdini' for his numerous escapes from custody. Grivas considered him so important that he had arranged his escape from Nicosia General Hospital on 31 August 1956, during which Sergeant L. A. Demmon of the UK Police Unit was gunned down. Georghadjis's position in EOKA had given him the right to 'execute' anyone he deemed a 'traitor' within its ranks, a power he exercised with relish.

In a single week of Operation *Black Mak*, the Paras eliminated 21 'hard-core' terrorists, three with rewards of £5,000 on their heads (which the soldiers were ineligible to collect),

and captured 2,000 rounds of ammunition and 46 weapons, including six Thompson sub-machine guns and two 3.5 bazooka rocket launchers. Their prisoners quickly became informers. One of them talked to the intelligence officer of the Duke of Wellington's Regiment that was about to lend its weight to the action and had moved up to Kaphedes. For several days and nights Private Davis of 'A' Company, an ex-Mexborough miner, had lived alone on the bare hillside in a newly issued bivouac tent above the village, feeding back information. The 'Dukes' joined him during the darkness of 18 January, expecting to cordon off and search Kaphedes. Instead, based on new information from the informers, it was decided to move to another destination 40 miles away deep in the mountains of the Troodos massif.

At dawn, the Dukes, in a convoy of RASC trucks, weaved their way up frightening and precarious tracks. As they passed through villages, snugly tucked into the mountainside, church bells rang warnings of their arrival. Said an officer: 'As we toiled to our objectives, we created a Sunday atmosphere.'

At their destination – the villages of Sarandi and Lagoudhera – 'A' Company ringed them and established OPs (observation posts). And still the questioning of the talkative terrorist went on, by Special Branch, leading on 21 January to a meticulous investigation of the house in which Sarandi's priest lived. He pleaded illness, but Lieutenant David Gilbert-Smith, supported by Special Branch officers, lifted the priest in his bed to his sunny veranda and the search went on. A pile of logs was moved from the floor of a small room, but there was nothing underneath except a mound of earth. Then Private Davis stirred the pile of earth with his foot and he saw the rim of a wooden box. He prodded at it with his bayonet and it sounded hollow. Underneath he found a hide. Gilbert-Smith lowered himself into the orifice and exclaimed 'Ooer' or words to that effect, because in the light of his torch he saw three cowering men, who were dragged out. They had been hiding with their weapons, ammunition, explosives and orders from Grivas. Like other captives, the priest and the terrorists began revealing all they knew.

Grivas recognized the grave blows his organization was receiving. 'Two guerrilla groups had been wiped out at a time when we were short of good men,' he admitted. 'But I was sure the tide would soon turn, and Afxentiou shared my faith. He wrote to me after these arrests: "I understand the size of our misfortunes, but we will not retreat; on the contrary, we shall throw ourselves into the fight with greater determination than ever and fill the gaps that have been created. Our faith in victory is unshakeable."

'I told him, in my reply, to take great care, regroup and return the enemy's blows so that we could show we still had plenty of fight left in us. I wrote: "In time of trial the true fighter shows how he can face trouble with courage and calmness. If our ranks have been thinned, they must remain unbroken. The gaps will soon be filled and the Organization will continue its mission. If everyone stays at his post and does his duty the wheel will turn once more in our favour."'

To add to Grivas's woes, town gangs were being rounded up as well.

Special Branch officers in Nicosia had caught Lazarou Ionnides, a member of EOKA's execution squad in the capital. Under interrogation, he had agreed to become an informer for the police. He revealed that Nicos Sampson had been wounded by a bullet in his leg during a botched attempt to kill a Turkish constable and was recovering at a house in Dhali, 12 miles away. On 30 January, troops of the Royal Horse Guards quietly cordoned the village and UK Police Unit Sergeants Gordon Willard, Joe Mouncey and Jeff Leach swooped.

As they broke down the door of the house, Sampson rolled off his bed and tried to reach a Sten gun, but was prevented by a kick in his stomach and a policeman standing on one of his hands, breaking a finger. Pinned on the walls of the room were several of his 'Wanted' posters.

At the Blues and Royals' camp Trooper Graham Williams was on orderly duty. 'One of the UK Police Unit rang to ask me to get hold of the nearest officer,' he remembered. '"We've got him," he said. "We had a lorry load of men and they surrounded a farmhouse where Sampson was sleeping. We took him back to police headquarters. The lads may have given him a wee doing." I replied, "You should have shot the bastard."'

Handcuffed and lying on the floor of an open truck, Sampson was brought to Police Headquarters in Nicosia for interrogation. News of his arrest spread quickly and he became an object of curiosity. A duty sergeant tried to stop his fellow officers from seeing Sampson in his cell, but was told 'if it wasn't for these people doing more than their job, he wouldn't be here – now allow us in'.

Sergeant Jack Taylor, on entering the room, saw Sampson 'seated, huddled and wrapped up in a blanket, glaring at us sullenly. I told my crew, "This is the famous EOKA killer who shoots people in the back, get a good look at him, for if he ever escapes, we will make sure he never comes back here."' Later that night, he signed a confession in which he listed 15 murders for which he was responsible. When he appeared in court, however, his defence lawyers contested the document, arguing the content had been extracted under torture.

Mr Justice Shaw, George Bernard Shaw's nephew, accepted that the confession had been made when Sampson was not in a fit condition, having been brought to Nicosia without protection during a heavy rainstorm and not having been treated for the minor injuries caused by his arrest. The confession was rejected and the prosecution case for his murders collapsed, but he was found guilty on other charges that carried the death penalty, including 'attempting to discharge a firearm' at the arresting officers, who were later awarded British Empire Medals.

Sampson's capture was soon followed by the arrests of Andreas Chartas, the capital's overall gang leader; Nicos Koshis, his deputy; Andreas Rigas and Andreas Houvartas, both EOKA 'enforcers'; Rita Kallinikou, Grivas's chief courier; and her assistant, a young theologian, Phidias Kareolemos. Sampson gave all these individuals away.

On 1 February, George Papaverkiou and Takis Sophocleous, obeying orders from Grivas that groups should attack at whatever cost to themselves, went out to ambush a convoy of seven army trucks. They blew up the first vehicle, but a hail of bullets from the soldiers in the other vehicles cut down the two 20-year-olds. On 3 February, EOKA avenged its losses by killing Corporal Ernest Warren of the Royal Electrical and Mechanical Engineers in an ambush in Athnea. He became the 100th British victim of the conflict.

Despite the continuing successes of the security forces, Grivas attempted to raise popular morale by claiming the British were concealing their own casualties, and kept up a barrage of leaflets denouncing them of being 'vandals', 'torturers' and of using 'brutality' in the detention centers, which the US Consul-General was invited to visit 'in order to see the deeds of your allies'.

But the pressure on EOKA did not let up. In February, 16 Para Brigade handed over its responsibilities in Operation *Black Mak* to 40 Commando, while north of Paphos, the Lancashire Fusiliers arrived from the UK and pitched camp to reinforce Royal Artillery units. The Duke of Wellington's and Grenadier Guards now wanted to claim the biggest catch of all: Afxentiou.

IN NICOSIA, General Kendrew held a press conference to announce the Army's successes. His Brigadier, J. A. Hopwood, pink-cheeked and wax-moustached, said: 'It was like a jolly big shoot, and my men acted as beaters.' He went as far as thanking Grivas 'for the wonderful training opportunity afforded my men'.

Kendrew's 'beaters' next caught up with the No. 3 on Britain's 'Most Wanted' list: Stylianos Lenas. A plumber by trade, he had been active from the first day of the EOKA campaign when he had attacked Wolseley Barracks in Nicosia. He had earned the nickname of *Krupps* for his bomb-making skills. With Yannakis Paftis, he had perfected EOKA's first hand grenade – a water pipe junction fitted with a heavy base plate and a screw cap, filled with sharp metal fragments and the explosive charge, while the fuse protruded through the cap, and could be lit by a burning cigarette. Later he became adept at making Mk2–type hand grenades.

At first light on 18 February, Lieutenants Marshal and Haynes, leading 8 and 9 section patrols from 40 Commando, continued their search for terrorists in the Troodos Mountains. They were unaware that Lenas was hiding nearby. Haynes had a sniffer dog with him. Suddenly, the animal began to dig furiously into the soil and uncovered a cache of canned food and ammunition.

Don Ligertwood, a fourth generation Royal Marine, describes what happened next: 'We reburied the foodstuffs and set up an ambush position behind a large fallen tree. A few hours passed and three men approached. Mr Haynes broke cover, stood up and shouted: "Halt – Stamata – Dur".

'Three shots rang out. Our officer fell backwards, with a single shot through his head. We immediately returned fire, using our newly issued FN semi-automatic rifles. Two terrorists died immediately and the third was seriously injured. The bodies of the dead were a mess.

We had to tie them by their wrists and ankles to strong branches to take their remains to the nearest police station. I remember they were still dripping blood when he placed them on the station's tiled floor.'

The surviving terrorist was rushed to the RAF Akrotiri hospital for urgent medical attention, where he was identified as Lenas. He died six weeks later from his injuries.

Ligertwood continues: 'Mr Haynes was a very smart officer, one of the best with whom I have served. I will never forget the day he died.'

Meanwhile, the other four members of the Lenas gang had run into Lieutenant Marshal's foot patrol. There was a vigorous exchange of automatic fire and two terrorists were killed on sight. One of the dead was Soteris Tsangaris, a high value wanted man. The remaining two, Demetrios Christodoulou – also known as Demetrakis – and Panayiotis Aristides, surrendered. After they were disarmed, they chose to run. Christodoulou was killed in the attempt, but Aristides got away into the forest to survive another day.

'The search for terrorist weapons was a time-consuming but essential exercise,' wrote Major J. C. Beadle, MBE, MC, RM, in his book, *The Light Blue Lanyard*. 'During the latter part of February, patrols from "A" and "B' Troops netted two revolvers, hundreds of rounds of ammunition, four 12–inch mortar bombs, four shot guns, a grenade, seven home-made bombs, an anti-tank mine and several sticks of dynamite.' When Operation *Black Mak* concluded at the end of the month it was rated by the British the largest and most successful campaign yet against EOKA. A total of 17 hideouts (not all of them occupied) had been found, behind bookcases and false walls and down hidden trapdoors. One contained 300 cans of food, including Scotch salmon. What made the soldiers' task simpler was that Cypriots were talking – a sign, in the eyes of Field Marshal Sir John Harding, that 'they are weary of fruitless terrorism'.

The all-out assault on EOKA continued remorselessly with units from 3 Infantry Brigade, including men of the Royal Berkshires, Ox and Bucks, South Staffordshires, Lancashire Fusiliers and Grenadier Guards.

On 28 February, 1 Duke of Wellington's No. 11 and SOE Platoons, under command of 'D' Company, were deployed in the vicinity of a forest rest house and a nearby deserted cottage, three miles to the north of the Makhaeras Monastery, which dominated the countryside from its position 2,000ft high on the slopes of Mt Kionia. Governor Harding's Chief of Staff, Brigadier Victor Balfour, said: 'We knew that when Afxentiou was in trouble, he invariably came to the Makhaeras area.'

At first the British troops suspected that Afxentiou and his men were hiding inside the monastery. Now two terrorists confirmed their suspicions. They had been captured in Omodhos by Captain Lionel Savery and switched sides to become willing informers. They were immediately taken to Platres, four miles away, for further questioning by Lieutenant D. S. Gilbert-Smith, MC, and 2nd Lieutenant P. Naylor.

The informers, one of whom had been a member of Afxentiou's gang, pointed out caches of ammunition, explosives and food, and, more importantly, told the two officers that Afxentiou had, in fact, lived in the Forest Rest House for long periods in the past and that on these occasions, supplies had been brought up from the Monastery on mules, led by a man named Petros, who was employed there. This lead was what the regiment most needed. Planning for Operation *Whisky Mak* began in utmost secrecy. Even the troops and junior officers were not informed until the last minute about where they would be heading. The operation would end with Afxentiou's death.

Petros was arrested on Friday, 1 March and sent to 3 Infantry Brigade HQ for questioning. He produced information which led next day to the discovery of two pistols a short distance outside the monastery walls and then, at approximately 16.30 the same day, the Dukes received a signal from Brigade ordering a snatch party to stand by and stating that a guide was being brought by road to Battalion HQ. Captain J. Newton of 1 Dukes assembled a small party and was ready to set off when Major Rodick arrived with Petros. He agreed to lead the party to a hide to which Afxentiou and his four gang members had moved from the monastery at 22.00 hrs on 27 February, and where he thought they still were.

It was immediately apparent that Captain Newton's patrol would need to be strengthened, as almost certainly Afxentiou would fight if cornered. Major D. M. Harris, in whose company area the hide was said to be located, was given command of the operation.

Unknown to the regiment, Afxentiou, with a 25-man gang, had been the guests of Abbot Irineos who was in charge of the twelfth-century monastery, for several weeks. He had stayed there to convalesce from the bullet wound he had received during his escape from Zoopiyi when a snatch squad arrived on New Year's Eve. Visitors to the monastery had not noticed Afxentiou disguised as a senior priest, one of four who lived there. There were also four young deacons and three novices. Abbot Irineos had even given his bed to the guerrilla leader to rest. Most mornings, the gang left before dawn to improve one or other of several nearby hideouts they were building, but, according to Irineos, on the night of Friday 1 March they left early, round about midnight.

The Makhaeras Monastery and Abbot Irineos, for historical reasons, were not under the jurisdiction of Archbishop Makarios, who was still in exile in the Seychelles, but Irineos operated an effective communications network to keep Grivas informed of what was taking place in the vicinity. Irineos, who spoke excellent English learned during his RAF service in Nicosia during the Second World War, told the Greek Cypriot historian Doros Alastos why Afxentiou suddenly left. 'There were rumours that there'd been another betrayal,' he said. 'When they'd left, I sat writing my report – for higher up, you know.'

Late that Friday evening, his report complete, Irineos prepared for bed, 'when he heard the sound of approaching cars. He threw the report in the stove, sprinkled pepper outside his room to throw the dogs off the scent, and hastily jumped between the sheets. Soon the door burst open,' says Alastos. An officer of the Duke of Wellington's Regiment entered. He shouted: 'We know you've got him here. It's too late for any of your lies.'

The Abbot protested about the invasion of his monastery, but was told that he and the place would now be guarded by British troops round the clock and it would be easier for all if he talked. He still steadfastly refused to answer any questions, Meanwhile, his monks, priests and novices were rounded up from their cells in the two storeys of cloisters that surrounded the courtyard. They were brought together and locked in a single room.

By first light the monastery had been taken over by 1 Duke of Wellington's Regiment and became its operational headquarters, and soldiers began to search inside and the surrounding slopes outside. They found nothing incriminating or clues to Afxentiou's whereabouts.

'When we were sure Afxentiou was no longer in the monastery, we could only make two guesses,' said Brigadier Balfour. 'Either he had gone out of the area or else he was underground. And since we had started *Whisky Mak*, we decided to continue on the assumption he was still around.'

(The authorities in Nicosia later discovered that Afxentiou and Abbot Irineos had received a warning phone call from a source in Nicosia about the 'top secret' operation to capture EOKA's No. 2. An investigation was conducted, but the informer was never found. The informer was George Lagoudontis – code-name *Kiotis*. He was a Special Branch Inspector based in the Operations Room at Police HQ. Using hidden microphones, he tape-recorded conversations between officials, including an Army Brigadier and an Assistant Chief Constable, at meetings held every day at 09.00.)

That evening, towards sunset, Petros, the shepherd, revealed the approximate position of where he thought Afxentiou was hiding. He had resisted threats, but not the financial reward he was offered. After careful consider-ation Lieutenant Colonel G. Laing, Com-manding Officer of 1 Dukes, directed that Afxentiou was to be taken at first light the next day – 3 March, a Sunday – as he consid-ered that a march across unknown country with no moon, heavy rain and with a guide (Petros), whose reliability was an unknown factor, might well fail to reach the correct objective or prove so noisy that the quarry would have time to escape. He said he had a strong feeling that if Afxentiou were intending to move that night he would already have done so and that, therefore, nothing would be lost by waiting until dawn.

PLANNING THE move forward proved extremely difficult as neither Major Harris nor anyone else knew the area in which Petros stated the hide would be found and Petros himself proved extremely dull and slow-witted, with absolutely no idea of distance or time. In addition he spoke no English so that all questioning had to be done through an interpreter. As an example of the difficulties encountered, Petros stated again and again that the hide 'is somewhere between up there and down here', pointing to the mountain slope towering above him and stretching hundreds of feet into a deep valley. Pressed to be specific, he said it was in a small isolated wood. When it was eventually found, it was concealed in thick scrub and brushes with not a tree near it.

Having established the approximate location of the hide a plan of attack was rapidly drafted and agreed by the Regiment's Commanding Officer.

A cut-off party set off at 04.00 and took up a position approximately 100 yards north of the hide, covering the track and a stream which flowed down from the suspected location. This was considered to be the only likely, or indeed practicable, escape route. They were followed at 04.55 by two snatch parties and two Bren gunners who approached the hide from the east. About 300 yards from the hide, the Bren gunners took up positions to cover the general area, while the two snatch parties separated and approached their objec-tive in a pincer movement from north and south. In addition, a small party, under RSM Randall, moved off at first light and took up a position on the slopes on the opposite side of the valley, in case anyone should attempt to escape in that direction and to observe any unusual movements. The planners confidently felt that no one would attempt to breakout up the valley to the north, as this led back to the monastery, where Battalion HQ was now located, or directly into the area occupied by 'B' Company.

Finally, Colonel Laing arranged for a heli-copter carrying Major Davis and a soldier to fly over the area to be in position to follow any escapees and stop them by fire from the air.

After an extremely difficult cross-country march over precipitous slopes, at approxi-mately 05.30, just before first light, point X was reached The troops expected that they would be able to see the exact location of the hide from this position, but the contours of the ground made it impossible. As the light increased, however, Petros was able to point out the general area of the hide some 300 yards down the slope to the front. Parties 'A' and 'B' now worked round the flanks to the area indicated by Petros. They met up at approximately 06.00 and were joined by Major Harris, coming down the slope from the two Bren gun positions. At this point Petros lost his nerve and decided not to go any further. He told his escorts that he was unable to identify the exact location of the hide, only the approximate area.

A quiet search of the general area began. Almost immediately Corporal Trinder of 'B' party noticed a small track running up the hill from the lower path. He followed the track for about 10 yards and then spotted footprints. He looked more closely and noticed that the branches of the bushes to the right of the path had been tied down to form an archway about four feet high. He walked inside to investigate and saw some unusually large stones on the ground. He moved them carefully aside and found the mouth of a 40-gallon drum lying on its side, buried in the slope of the hill. There was a 2-inch mortar wrapped up in brown paper inside the drum. Corporal Trinder's finds confirmed that terrorists were, or had been, in the immediate area, and led to the next stage, the discovery of the hide. The helicopter began circling. It signalled back a request for a platoon to cordon off the area while those present on the ground conducted a more thorough search.

It was approximately 06.15 and Captain Newton began walking the small track from where the oil drum had been hidden. From his footfalls he felt the ground below was hollow. Corporal Trinder agreed. Moving aside another unusual-sized stone, he found the entrance to a tunnel no more than 18 inches wide and 18 inches high. The two soldiers looked inside and saw clothing, but nothing else. They concluded the place was empty. Shortly afterwards they were joined by some other soldiers and the unit's interpreter. Then they heard voices from deep inside.

2nd Lieutenant John Grant immediately ordered the cave's inmates in Greek: 'Come out of the hide, leave your arms behind.' Realizing his hiding place had been discovered, Afxentiou ordered his four comrades to surrender. 'We can't do anything,' he told his gang. It was useless for them, he said, to throw their lives away. He himself would stay and fight it out. They asked what he planned and he replied: 'I must die ... I must die ... I must die.'

A shout of 'Endaxi' (OK, alright) came from the hide and four men crawled out slowly into the morning light. They offered no resistance. They were Avgoustis Efstathiou (also known as Matrosis), Andreas Stylianou, Feidias Symeonidis and Antonis Papadopoulos. Each was paraded in front of the press who had been invited by confident officers to watch the capture of the terrorists.

Efstathiou told the journalists: 'They found us this morning at 3.30 and when we heard a helicopter we knew we hadn't a chance. We were all asleep except Afxentiou. A clatter of stones woke us up. Someone was sliding down the slope above us. Then we heard a shout: "Come out and surrender – leave your weapons behind." Afxentiou told us to go and we obeyed. I was surprised when he didn't follow us. Perhaps he expected the troops to be satisfied with four of us, giving him a chance

Avgoustis Efstathiou surrenders.

to escape. Perhaps he had already decided to fight it out. I'm not sorry it's all over. I've been 14 months in the mountains. But I have never killed anybody. I'm a patriot.'

Then there was a sudden burst of automatic fire from the hide entrance. The first bullets went aimlessly into the bushes. 2nd Lieutenant Grant shouted again in Greek for the hide's occupant to give himself up. Corporal Peter Brown added: 'It's all up. You may as well come out. You are surrounded.' Afxentiou answered by firing his Sten directly at Brown and knocked him backwards, mortally wounded. Captain Newton moved closer to the hide's entrance, threw in a grenade, the only one in the unit's possession, and ran quickly away before it exploded. There was a big bang, the ground trembled and smoke poured from the roof. 'You've killed him,' screamed Efstathiou. There was silence from inside. The only sound came from the falling rain and the clatter of a helicopter hovering above. 'It was too dangerous to go near the hideout,' said 2nd Lieutenant Grant. 'We just sat round and kept an eye on it. Every now and again a grenade would come hurtling out, and sometimes a burst of fire.'

On the track above the hide, officers held a council of war. Having lost one man, they agreed not to risk any more lives.

2nd Lieutenant Middleton, who headed the detachment, grabbed Efstathiou by his collar and pushed him forward, ordering him back inside to persuade Afxentiou, if he were still alive, to give up without causing any further casualties. If his leader were dead, he was to bring out the body. Reluctantly Efstathiou did as he was told. Fearful for his own life as he approached, he shouted: 'Chief, don't shoot. It's me, Matrosis.' He went inside and found Afxentiou losing blood from severe neck and knee wounds. Nothing happened for several seconds and then the troops heard a single shot and wondered if Afxentiou had killed his comrade. Suddenly Afxentiou shouted out in

English, 'Now we are two. Come and get us.' In Greek, he defiantly added: '*Molon lave*' or 'Come and get.' This was a response given to the Persians by the Ancient Greek King Leonidas I during the Battle of Thermopylae.

All hopes of a peaceful resolution ended as Afxentiou and now Efstathiou fired at the soldiers.

Inside the hide, according to Efstathiou, the two men discussed the prospects of their survival and the part they had played in the EOKA conflict. He claimed Afxentiou told him: 'The flame we lit years ago has spread through the hearts of all Greeks. Nothing can extinguish it now. Freedom will not be long in coming, for our death will fan the flames still higher.'

The minutes passed and the two considered how to escape. Afxentiou said he would throw a phosphorous grenade towards the British soldiers and then they could rush out, firing, and head into the forest and hide until darkness fell. The grenade was hurled, exploded and yellow smoke obscured the entrance, but Efstathiou's Sten gun failed to fire. In his panic, he had left the safety catch on. Major Rodick, Corporal Trinder and Lance Corporal Martin returned fire and kept it up until the smoke dispersed. Neither Afxentiou or Efstathiou had managed to get away.

In the ensuing confusion Lance Corporal Dowdall tried to drag Corporal Brown's body away from the hide, but after moving him a short distance came under more heavy fire from the two terrorists and had to abandon his attempt.

The two Duke of Wellington's Bren gunners were now called forward and put in position, approximately 30 to 40 yards above the hide, covering the entrance. The officers took stock and made the following appreciation: first, the captured terrorists had told them that Afxentiou had two machine-guns, a large quantity of ammunition, three pistols and a number of bombs in the hide with him. Secondly, previous information, and Afxentiou's present actions, indicated that he was likely to make a suicidal last stand with the object of killing as many as possible. Furthermore, it would be quite easy for him to lob a grenade out of the entrance, which could cause severe casualties to anyone standing on top of or above the hide, while doing little or no damage to those inside. Thirdly, the hide was surrounded and escape virtually impossible. In these circumstances, the risk of remaining on the hide's roof was considered unacceptable and so the party withdrew to the upper track, while deciding how to capture or eliminate the enemy.

At 07.15, the Commander, 3 Infantry Brigade, and the Duke of Wellington's CO arrived by helicopter. They ordered the death of Afxentiou before any further casualties were suffered. The best means to achieve this objective were either to burn him out using petrol or by detonating a heavy charge on top of the hide. A request was made for 50 gallons of petrol and *avgas* (aviation fuel) as well as the assistance of a Royal Engineer.

The petrol and *avgas* cans were loaded on Sycamore helicopters and flown to a landing site close to the terrorists' hide.

No. 10 Platoon, 'D' Company, arrived at the scene at 07.45, and formed an outer cordon, with two additional Bren guns covering the immediate area of the hide. Meanwhile, four patrols from 3 Company, Grenadier Guards, attached to 3 Brigade for the operation, set out for the battle site, with 1 Company holding the cordon. Royal Engineers set up searchlights to illuminate the area by reflecting their beams off low cloud. Extended lines of Guardsmen waded through undergrowth as rain continued to pour down. Lieutenant Colonel Britten's party, which included Major P. H. Haslett, Lieutenant W. L. A. Nash, and RSM C. White, travelled in two Land Rovers. During the short lulls between exchanges of fire, bushes around the hide were cut down.

At about 09.00, a mule-train arrived carrying petrol and this was thrown over the suspected area from the upper path and ignited, slightly south of the hide's entrance, but failed to burn out the terrorists. Rain, interspersed with showers of hailstones, had stopped the bushes burning properly. Fifteen minutes later an RE officer reached the scene of the operation with various explosives. He decided that 6lb of 'plastic' would be enough to blow away the hide's roof. The explosive was detonated, but the roof stayed firmly in its place. For their part, the men inside threw out more grenades.

During the next three hours there was a standoff between the well-protected terrorists tossing the occasional grenade and the attacking British forces laying down harassing Bren gun fire.

At noon, *avgas* and more petrol arrived and this was thrown with great effect by Captain Hoppe onto an area a few yards further north than that previously fired. The petrol flowed down the slope and down cracks into the hide, soaking the terrorists. As soon as it was ignited, a sheet of flame engulfed Afxentiou and Efstathiou.

'Don't be afraid,' Afxentiou shouted as he tried to put out the fire. The British troops heard screams from the hide and watched a man, his hair ablaze, stagger out into a neighbouring clump of bushes. The combination of grenades, explosives, tear gas and *avgas* appeared to have finally settled the matter. The DWR's four Bren gunners immediately opened fire. Watched by troops, civilian police and the press, the ammunition exploded seconds later.

Now, under the command of former rugby international Captain Dennis Shuttleworth, a small party armed with Sten guns moved forward and were directed to the smoking hide by Captain Newton. Shuttleworth volunteered to lay another charge above the entrance.

Foot by foot he edged himself down the mountain slope. One false step and he would have slid past the hideout and become a sitting target. Slowly and precisely he put a 'beehive' shell in position. Gingerly he crawled back to the track, trailing a length of fuse behind him. Someone produced a box of matches from a sodden jacket.

Shuttleworth lit the fuse. A shattering roar reverberated throughout the mountains. The Grenadier Guards heard it in Makhaeras monastery. It was 13.30.

Shuttleworth's men threw a tear gas bomb inside and sprayed gunfire through the entrance. The man who had run out earlier in flames was found lying in bushes not far away. He was in extreme pain and terrified. It was Efstathiou. 'Do not shoot, I surrender,' he repeated.

Before being removed for medical attention at RAF Akrotiri, he insisted Afxentiou was dead. His statement could not be verified immediately because the hide was still burning. The area was cordoned off and the flames put out. As there was a possibility that some munitions remained inside, the CO of the Duke of Wellington's Regiment decided a proper search would take place next day, when Afxentiou's remains would be recovered for identification. 'The Battle of Makhaeras' was over at 14.00.

That night Grivas was told of Afxentiou's death. He replied coldly: 'Why are you so sad? People get killed in a war, and that is what we are fighting. We shall have many more as brave as he.'

By Monday, 4 March, the news of Afxentiou's last stand was known Island-wide. The operation had played out in front of press reporters and newsreel cameramen, who had been allowed to interview officers and captives alike, in the hope that EOKA would believe its time was up. Instead the media coverage contributed to the making of a legend.

At his native village of Lysi, shops closed for the day and the authorities were forced to impose a curfew on males from 12 to 27. In Famagusta town the gymnasium's schoolboys refused to attend classes as a mark of respect and because one of their teachers, Antonis Papadopoulos, was one of those who had been captured.

During the search that took place on 4 March, Afxentiou's charred body was finally recovered. One leg was completely severed and there was a gaping hole in his skull. Alongside him was a copy of Kazantzakis' *Christ Recrucified*; its flyleaf bore the name of Abbot Irineos. Afxentiou had borrowed the book when he left the Abbot's room in the monastery. The book with Irineos's name was the final confirmation that the Abbot had collaborated with EOKA. He was detained. (The author wonders how the book survived the blaze and suspects this information was fabricated.)

Pieris, Afxentiou's father, was allowed to see his son's remains in the mortuary, but showed little emotion in front of his military escorts. He told them the remains were not those of his son and insisted he was alive and continuing the struggle. Later, Pieris broke down in tears and confessed to friends: 'I knew it was him, but I didn't want the dogs to see me crying.'

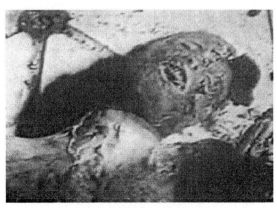

Afxentiou's charred remains.

The pathologist at the British Military Hospital, Nicosia, conducted a post mortem on the body. Later at the Coroner's hearing, Mr Justice Ellison was satisfied beyond any doubt that the terrorist had died from a gunshot wound through the skull, that death was instantaneous and had occurred before the body was burnt. The evidence suggested the bullet had been fired directly at the head. Efstathiou, called to give evidence, changed the story that he had told his captors, saying instead that Afxentiou was still alive when he had escaped the hide. Under cross-examination by counsel for Afxentiou's parents, he insisted his leader had never contemplated suicide.

The Coroner's verdict was that Afxentiou died from a gunshot wound caused by a bullet's explosion due to the intense heat in the hideout, but many people believe death was at Afxentiou's own hand. It was, they said, his way of ending his life, rather than dying on the gallows.

The authorities knew that if Afxentiou were to have a public funeral, it would end in riots and probably deaths among mourners and the forces of law and order. They decided instead to bury his body in an unmarked grave in the grounds of Nicosia's Central Prison, alongside those of hanged EOKA members. His grave remains there, a shrine honoured by Greek Cypriot youth, educated to believe him a martyr in the cause of freedom.

Field Marshal Sir John Harding, the Governor, however, shed no tears. In his address to his soldiers, on 4 March 1957, he said: 'These successes have made a very big impact on the whole campaign and they have come at a very opportune time. Well done, very well done indeed.' Whatever may have been the mood of the Greek Cypriots about Afxentiou, Grivas was very aware that his organization had been wrong-footed by Operations *Black Mak* and *Whisky Mak*, whatever stirring words he spread.

Both sides now stepped up their propaganda campaigns. The Government-controlled radio station, said Grivas, was quoting 'forged letters attacking us, purporting to come from anonymous priests, sorrowing mothers, bereft widows and "true patriots". We countered this poisonous rubbish by leaflet and word of mouth. I ended a typical proclamation with the words: "Let us give one more slap to the unblushing cheek of the tyrant. Let us write across the length and breadth of our country, All for the freedom of Cyprus!"' Until his death in January 1974, Grivas was never found short of bombast.

THE MAKHAERAS Monastery was no longer a hiding place for EOKA terrorists on the run. When the Duke of Wellington's Regiment pulled out, 1 Battalion Grenadier Guards became the occupiers. Eleven guardsman took charge, under the command of Lieutenant Robin Dixon, the son of Lord and Lady Glenloran. The guardsmen were rotated weekly, because this duty was much sought after the heat of the central plain round Nicosia, where they were usually camped. Abbot Irineos appeared happy to have them, but the soldiers wearing shorts shocked the more elderly monks. As the days passed, the authorities added to the monastery's population by transferring a dozen priests from detention centres where they had been held under the Emergency Regulations for aiding and abetting terrorists.

Charles Foley, the editor of the *Times of Cyprus*, a newspaper not unsympathetic to the independence struggle, aptly wrote: 'Both in town and countryside small, highly mobile forces penetrated EOKA's defence with great resourcefulness and few inhibitions. They had seized the element of surprise and were hoisting EOKA with its own petard.' But Grivas promised the battle would continue with greater intensity in spite of the organization's losses and appointed Antonis

Georghiades as his second-in-command to replace Afxentiou.

After Cyprus gained independence, the Greek Cypriot historian Nicos Pittas declared: 'If we were truthful with ourselves, we would admit that for all their bravery and idealism, the EOKA fighters were engaged in a struggle for a goal that was strategically misguided and unachievable, using methods, including terrorizing civilians, that were extreme and unnecessary and in many ways counter-productive to achieving the realistic goal of an independent and democratic bicommunal republic.'

Today there are many streets in Cyprus named after Afxentiou. A monument has been erected to his memory and a small museum dedicated to him in the Makhaeras Monastery. His hideout, one kilometre below, has become a shrine and a place of pilgrimage called the *Krisfigeto tou Afxentiou*. A massive figure of him, legs akimbo, stands high above, guarded by a huge sculpted eagle. In London, the Greek Cypriot community pays annual tribute to Afxentiou at a memorial service in the Church of St Demetrios in Edmonton.

The Duke of Wellington's Regiment continues to remember the loss of Corporal Peter Brown from Leeds and two staunch members of the Police Special Branch: Bill Sharp and Joe Mounsey, who so often accompanied the Battalion on its searches for terrorists. Bill Sharp became a Detective Chief Superintendent in the Devon and Cornwall Constabulary, and Joe Mounsey a Detective Chief Inspector in the Lancashire Constabulary. Mounsey was with 1 DWR when Afxentiou's hide was found. In the early 1960s he was an investigating officer in the Moors' Murder case. Of the four terrorists who survived the battle, all received long prison sentences, but were released when agreements were reached for the independence of Cyprus.

Andreas Stylianou kept a very low profile after independence, returning to Lagoudhera, his home village, to resume his life as a farmer.

He began his EOKA career as a courier in the Madari area and joined Afxentiou in October 1956. He gave his first interview on 3 March 1987, 30 years after Afxentiou's death, at a school gathering. His account of the Makhaeras operation appeared in a 10-page booklet by Spanos, the official EOKA historian. Stylianou was still alive in 2008.

Phidias Symeonides, a very proud man, also withdrew from normal life, and built a small house on the outskirts of Nicosia at Anthoupoli. He earned a bare living by working occasionally as a waiter at the *Spanos* restaurant in Ayios Dhometios. Asked why he did not seek any favours from the Greek Cypriot authorities – as many others did – for the 'services' provided as an EOKA fighter, he always replied: 'They know where I am and if they want to help me they know where to find me.' He became very ill and wanted to move to the clear air of the Troodos. Several days after his death, his body was found lying in the yard of his house, completely forgotten by the Makarios Government.

Antonios Papadopoulos is no longer alive. An athlete and a skilled footballer, he became the captain of Anorthosis, a Famagusta football team. A stadium in Larnaca commemorates his name. The man who had a £5,000 on his head ended his days as a school headmaster.

Augustus Efstathiou, a onetime hawker in Ledra Street, was rewarded by a senior position in the Republic's new Cyprus Police Force and lives on a state pension today. He has become a celebrity in Greek Cyprus by exploiting his connection to Afxentiou, making speeches and appearing regularly on television. He declined to be interviewed by the author. A friend suggested he was concerned his 'image' could be harmed.

Mrs Vasilou Afxentiou was ignored by EOKA after the conflict was over. To survive, she worked in the fields of their village and later as a housemaid and cleaner. She later re-married.

The various Duke of Wellington parties named above were organized as follows:

Commander: Major D M Harris.
Party 'A' (Snatch Party): Lt E. J. H. Dasent, Sgt. J. Mounsey (Special Branch, Cyprus Police), Petros (guide), 2/Lt G. Middleton (RNF interpreter), Cpl. Brown, L/Cpl. Dowall, L/Cpl. Martin
Party 'B' (Snatch Party): Captain J. M. Newton, Major E. L. Rodick (Com. Intelligence Wing), Inspector W. Sharpe (CID, Cyprus Police), Cpl. Trinder, Pte. Riley, Pte. Bramham
Party 'C' (Bren Gunners): Lt C. M. Wood, Pte. Seymour.
Party 'D' (Cut-off Party): 2/Lt. T. D. Sugden and two ORs.

When Afxentiou's hide was searched, troops found:

2 × Thompson sub-machine guns;
6 × magazines (4 full and 2 half-full);
1 × Brevete automatic pistol and one magazine;
1 × Bretta automatic pistol and one magazine;
1 × Smith and Wesson .38 pistol;
3 × homemade grenades.

Rounds:
55 × .45mm;
19 × .38mm;
12 × 9mm;
2 × spent .45mm.

1 × head, body, fins 2-in. Hemor bomb (exploded);
1 × American bayonet;
1 × belt, with holster and ammunition pouch;
2 × pairs binoculars;
and, strangely 1 x dental plate from BMH, Nicosia.

CHAPTER SEVENTEEN

'Millionaires' Row
the Dachau of Cyprus

'Laws are dumb in time of war.'
CICERO

MILITARY OPERATIONS during the first three months of the year could not have gone better in bringing EOKA near to defeat, but it was very different on the political front. The Radcliffe Report had not persuaded anyone in or outside Cyprus to take it seriously. At best, it was considered a last despairing effort by Anthony Eden to leave No. 10 Downing Street with some sense of achievement, but, as Harold Macmillan had become Prime Minister, the decision-takers chose to see what offers he would place on the table. As far as the Greek Government was concerned, it wanted the international community not to look at British successes in the war against terrorism, but to see Cyprus as an occupied state with the occupiers behaving no better than the Nazis in the Second World War.

Early in the campaign, Grivas ordered EOKA members to collect torture claims, because denigration of the Security Forces fanned local resentment and he wanted to create a dossier to be used against the British Government at international fora. He called it his 'Black Book'. He stressed the importance of accuracy, but, following in The Leader's tendency to exaggerate his victories, his men's reports lacked credibility.

Backed by Athens, Michalis Pissas, a right-wing trade unionist and member of the Ethnarchy Council, led the charge of accusers with the publication and distribution in the United States of a booklet entitled *The Truth About Concentration Camps in Cyprus*, which he had written. The Cyprus Federation of America released it alongside *Violation of Human Rights in Cyprus – A Factual Documentation*. Both publications became subjects of radio and television programmes and convinced many Americans that the Security Forces were using torture to extract confessions from their prisoners and keeping them in inhumane conditions.

The matter was 'internationalized' by Greek Foreign Minister Averoff at the United Nations in New York, where he told delegates

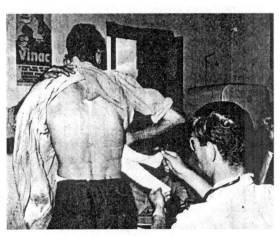

A doctor examines a Greek Cypriot who alleges police brutality.

The cover of the Greek book claiming British
torture of EOKA prisoners.

that he had 237 handwritten statements by
Greek Cypriots who had been tortured. The
documents were 'horrifying and dreadful' and
he promised that he would show them to the
Secretary-General. The British Ambassador
dared him to publish them in full or withdraw
the smear. Averoff did neither.

Pissas knew the truth was very different. A
committed supporter of EOKA, he had been
rounded up soon after the start of the conflict
and held at the Kokkinotrimithia Detention
Centre, where he became spokesman for the
inmates' committee. After a request from the
International Confederation of Free Trade
Unions, based in Brussels, the authorities had
released him on condition he did not return to
Cyprus. He chose to move to Athens. There he
had studiously campaigned to spread allegations of atrocities.

Understandably the colonial authorities
denied them just as vigorously. A spokesman
pointed out that neither publication gave any
details of the dates and places when the
offences occurred, or the name of any unit

involved. He also pointed out that a delegate
of the International Red Cross had given a
clean bill of health to the 'satisfactory treatment of detainees', which was 'in conformity
with general humane principles'. Whatever the
reality, the accusations stuck and politicians in
the UK and the US were happy to spread
them, much to the anger of the soldiers on the
ground, who saw EOKA's brutality on an
almost daily basis.

'Many of EOKA's defeats were due to
betrayal,' wrote Nancy Crawshaw. 'And it
was natural that those responsible should seek
to justify their actions to the Organization by
pleading torture. The atrocity campaign
served a legal as well as a political purpose.'

Of the accusations against the UK Police
Unit, Governor Harding replied: 'A very large
number of the police officers who are accused
of such monstrous conduct are in fact
members of the United Kingdom police forces
whose traditions of restraint and humanity
have long been the admiration of the civilized
world. It must appear unlikely that such men,
with their years of training and experience,
should on arrival in Cyprus apparently turn
into typical members of Hitler's Gestapo and
on their return home as quickly resume their
well-known and respected role.'

General Sir David Fraser served in Cyprus
as Second-in-Command of the 2nd Battalion
of the Grenadier Guards. In his memoirs, *War
and Shadows*, he discussed the treatment of
EOKA captives. 'Nobody – certainly not I –
thought their prisoners should be treated with
kid gloves. There were, however, limits (and
some pretty respectable guidelines issued by
the authorities) ... One has to find one's way
to certain principles in such matters. The letter
of the law is seldom a sufficient guide – and
certainly not a sufficient defence if defence be
needed.'

Before any operation he addressed his
troops on how they had to behave: 'What
mattered most, I said, was that when the

Cypriots themselves, or their descendants, asked each other "What sort of people were the British?" The answer should not be one of which to be ashamed.'

General Sir Roy Redgrave, who, as a Major, commanded one of the three Blues and Royals armoured car squadrons in Cyprus, explained to the author the basis of some Greek Cypriot allegations. 'I was told to go to a very big pro-EOKA village, with two churches, to remove all the signs on the walls. I wondered how I was going to do it as I barely had 100 men. I went and had a look at the place in daylight with a police sergeant, who showed me the offending signs, which didn't mean much to me as they were written in Greek. They were in six places and I thought the best way to get the job done was to get in and get out in 10 minutes before the hornet's nest stirred,' he said.

'We found some huge buckets, filled them with a tar-like cleansing substance, brooms and brushes and split the troops into groups. Then we roared into the village at just before 10 o'clock on a Saturday night, when we knew the cinema was full. We dragged any idling male from the street and even took away the barber from his shop, where he was busy shaving a fellow. They were given the brooms and brushes and told to obliterate the mess. The job was done and we got out just as the church bells began to ring. Afterwards, of course, we were accused of the most appalling atrocities, of pouring tar down the sleeves of the poor people rather than waste any.'

Athens Radio, calling itself *The Voice of the Fatherland*, and Greek newspapers, of course, spread the atrocity claims without checking the facts. 'EOKA states that British interrogators examining suspects subject them to tortures such as flogging, or force them to stand on nails or on ice and inject them with narcotics,' reported one publication. Another quoted Makarios as saying British troops 'used methods that were not far from the

things I experienced during the German occupation of Greece. Doctors have verified the marks of beatings received by persons from whom soldiers tried to extract information.' As Ethnarch he was bound to be believed by his flock, especially when he added, 'I examined personally the marks a former prisoner had on his body. He said he had been beaten by a heavy piece of chain. I have also been informed that the British use a kind of truth serum on prisoners.'

That is not say there were no cases of brutality, as British servicemen would be the first to admit. With more than 30,000 stationed on the Island, inevitably all were not saints, but what they did must be judged in the context and the character of the people with whom they were dealing. As far back as the 1931 Rebellion, Governor Storrs noted: 'The Balkans and Levant are past masters in the craft of manufacturing atrocities. How toughly soldiers treated their captives often depended on the number of casualties their unit had suffered and the degree of provocation.'

Years later Sir Roy Redgrave reflected on his service as a Major in the Blues and Royals. 'I had never considered the moral issue of how much mental or physical pressure should be put on a suspect to get him to talk. Interrogation methods used by German SS officers during the War on Allied agents and Resistance members were, I considered, despicable,' he said. 'Yet here we were trying to prevent our friends and innocent civilians being shot or blown to pieces. Usually if terrorists were caught red-handed, so to speak, they were so scared they might be shot that they volunteered a lot of information. If the police could act upon this within the hour it often resulted in another arms find and arrest.'

For young soldiers, many still teenagers, every confrontation with the terrorists brought ambiguity. 'Reputations varied with different regiments. The South Staffordshires were noted for the gentleness of their tactics in dispersing riots; the Royal Marine Commandos for their ability to get on with the villagers. The paratroopers, usually called upon to deal with the most critical situations, were associated with roughness in carrying out their orders,' Nancy Crawshaw opined. 'The great majority of British soldiers carried out their duties under conditions of strain with exemplary patience and restraint.'

'I saw many acts of kindness on the part of individual soldiers but I also witnessed brutality,' admitted a member of 284 Squadron who flew as a helicopter crewman with the Army on operations. 'I saw a suspect being interrogated through an interpreter. He had a big biscuit tin placed on his head. On each side of the suspect stood soldiers with stakes or axe handles. The questioning was carried out while two soldiers with clubs banged the front back or side of the biscuit tin on the suspect's head. To be honest, at that time I shared the collective mindset and was not outraged by this.

'The "Cyps" hated us and we them! Little children in Nicosia would throw stones at us as we walked past them. On my first day in Nicosia I was walking around the Wall when a tangerine bounced off the back of my head. When I looked around I saw a crocodile of schoolgirls in blue uniforms accompanied by a woman teacher walking innocently on. These kids couldn't have been more than 10 years old. Such was the atmosphere of hatred in which we worked and they lived. Even the bloody dogs hated the Brits!

'Such an atmosphere brutalizes everyone. I stand in pious judgement of no one. I was a young man with a gun and a mind full of macho young man's fantasies. I even had a shoulder holster for my bulky Smith and Wesson pistol, which made me resemble Quasimodo more than James Bond!'

Interrogations, however, were mainly the responsibility of the civilian Special Branch

and MI5. They generally took place at centres in Lefka, Ktima, Platres, Ayios Memnon and Omorphita and were reserved for high value suspects.

When two British Army officers – Captain G. O'Driscoll of the Intelligence Corps and Lieutenant R. A. Linzee of the Gordon Highlanders – were accused of 'assault occasioning actual bodily harm' to a prisoner they were questioning and of 'conspiracy to prevent the course of public justice', they faced a court martial on 4 April 1956, were found guilty and dismissed from the Army.

On 16 April, the British Ambassador to Athens sent a confidential message to the Governor. Marked 'Immediate', it said 'Andreas Koronidos is giving a press conference this morning in order to describe the torture to which he is alleged to have been subjected in Cyprus by O'Driscoll and Lindsey [sic]. I assume the substance of K's allegations will be available to you from news agencies. I propose to issue a statement to the press in order to put this affair in its right proportions.'

Whenever a soldier was believed to have

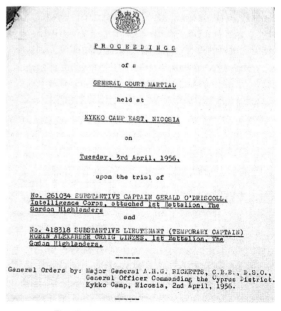

The first page of a Court Martial report.

transgressed, the authorities investigated and, if there appeared any doubt, the man involved was brought in front of a court martial and the trial was always published, as happened to Sergeant John Smith. In February 1956, his squad fired shots to break up a riot in Limassol that resulted in the death of Andreas Kolossiatis, 22. At the inquest, a verdict was returned that death had been caused 'under circumstances amounting to manslaughter'. His court martial heard the evidence and concluded Smith was not guilty.

DURING THE Emergency Peter Hamilton was a security adviser on the Governor's staff for three years. 'From the start, we didn't put a full interrogation effort into the job,' he said. 'The Cypriots were very close to us. I think the British were handicapped very much by liking these people who were quite prepared to die for their cause. Late in the day, some able British investigators were brought in, but they were not Greek speakers and the quality of interpreters was not sufficiently high for such a delicate operation.' Hamilton believed that if the intelligence role had been handed over to the Army, Grivas could have been caught and the Emergency quickly brought to an end.

In December 1956, the Cyprus Bar Association submitted a long list of complaints to the authorities. As a result, a police superintendent was convicted of a minor assault, a Turkish auxiliary constable was sent to prison for three years for wounding two Greeks with a pistol, and an assistant police superintendent was fined for using more force than was necessary when he carried out an arrest. Had Governor Harding agreed to an independent inquiry, perhaps its findings would have cleared the forces of the charges of which they were accused, but he firmly believed that while it gathered information from witnesses, military operations would be hindered and the morale of his soldiers damaged.

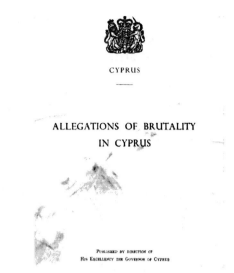

CYPRUS

ALLEGATIONS OF BRUTALITY
IN CYPRUS

PUBLISHED BY DIRECTION OF
HIS EXCELLENCY THE GOVERNOR OF CYPRUS

The Cyprus Government's answer to Greek charges.

Although an inquiry was rejected, the British Government published a White Paper – *Allegations of Brutality in Cyprus, 1957* – about its own findings. It said: 'The Governor has publicly stated that while it would be unrealistic to rule out the use of physical force when effecting the capture of a dangerous terrorist, this was quite a different matter from calculated violence to obtain information and he has said that all allegations of this kind had been and would continue to be properly investigated.'

Harding declared: 'If the price of immediately clearing the Security Forces of these allegations is to impair their ability to deal effectively with fresh outbreaks of terrorism and to gain information which will assist them in protecting the public from murder, violence and brutality, then the security forces will continue to place their duty first. They will be content that one day they will be vindicated.

'Meanwhile Her Majesty's Armed Forces and the police in Cyprus will rely on the worldwide knowledge of their traditions of humanity and decency to convince the public of the free world of the falsity of allegations which emanate from men who have no scruples in aiding and abetting murder.'

The White Paper systematically revealed the results of investigations into the scores of accusations levelled at the authorities. Time and time again, lawyers known to have EOKA connections had made them. Renos Lyssiotis, one of the lawyers, was notorious for raising torture allegations whenever he defended his clients in court. A typical case, which Makarios and others publicized at every opportunity, involved Maria Anastassiou Lambrou, who miscarried while in police custody.

She was 17 years old, unmarried and had been attending a local Greek Cypriot medical practitioner prior to her arrest. There was medical evidence that she had had a septic abortion. Immediately after her miscarriage at the police station, she was rushed to the Nicosia General Hospital where two Greek Cypriot doctors examined her. She made no complaint of ill treatment to them.

Interviewed some days later by Lyssiotis, she was then apparently ready to accuse the police of striking her on the face and neck and implied that this was the cause of her miscarriage. The investigation of this case was not simplified by the fact that the medical report by the Greek Cypriot Government doctor, who first examined her, 'disappeared' after being taken to her original gynaecologist for cross-checking against his records. The same doctor subsequently produced three medical reports, each substantially different in content, for the investigators. After questioning, he admitted that there was no evidence to support the girl's allegations that physical violence had been used against her.

(Lyssiotis was later detained when it was discovered he was an EOKA activist, who had encouraged youth in Nicosia to paint sheets with the slogan ALL FIGHTERS ARE AT THEIR POSTS and hang them on the capital's sports stadium when Harding called on the terrorists to surrender in August 1956.)

In another case, two priests who were held in detention were approached by the camp's unofficial EOKA Committee and told to fabricate allegations of ill treatment, which could be directed against the police. One of the priests subsequently went to the authorities of his own free will to say he had never been ill-treated and signed a statement to that effect. He added that he had told the Committee that it could put forward complaints on his behalf if it liked, but that he himself was not prepared to do so.

A lawyer in Nicosia, in a different case, handed the Government a highly circumstantial account of gross ill treatment, which he alleged had been inflicted on yet another priest. The latter, when asked privately about the complaint, appeared both frightened and embarrassed. He had never been touched by the Security Forces, but was pressurized by EOKA to say he had. 'I cannot forget what happened to the Abbot of Chrysorroyiatissa,' he said. The Abbot of Chrysorroyiatissa was murdered by EOKA in his own monastery in February 1956.

Next a youth stated at his trial that he had been slapped and punched by the police while held in custody. After his conviction however, he wrote to the Governor: 'From the day that I was arrested till now ... no force was used against me. Here in the prison the prisoners are insulting me and call me a traitor. They do not speak to me and are always asking for a chance to beat me. I warmly request you to take me away from Cyprus. At least be sorry for my mother who will die by her grief because they threaten her daily that they will kill her.' When Grivas failed to terrorize a particular individual, he vented his fury on their relatives.

In the House of Commons Selwyn Lloyd spoke about the claims made by Loulla Kokkinou, who had told the Greek press that she 'lost front teeth after a rough blow by her sadist tormentor'. In truth, however, her dental records showed her one and only missing tooth had been extracted in June 1955 and she was arrested in May 1956.

Despite the Government White Paper's effective demolition of the case against the Security Forces, Greek Cypriots preferred to still believe their own leaders. Nor did the *Times of Cyprus* help the British case by splashing a highly critical article on its front page. In the absence of Charles Foley, the editor, Michael Davidson, the paper's co-founder, penned the piece. 'I analyzed it, sentence by sentence, with Glafkos Clerides; and then wrote a detailed reply, taking each paragraph in turn and surgically exposing the fallacies. It was, I think, a clever piece of analysis; and it destroyed the White Paper,' he said later. 'Government House was in a rage; it was reported to me that either the Field Marshal himself or one of his closest collaborators – I was unable to find out exactly – exclaimed: "We're going to get that man!" Neither I nor Foley and his wife were that year asked to Government House, to drink the Queen's health on her Birthday!'

'If the Cyprus Government could do no wrong in most British eyes, neither could Grivas among the Greeks. Excesses and mistakes could not be acknowledged,' wrote Charles Foley. 'When MacDonald and his successor Fox were killed, the Greeks at once said they were both British agents, using the newspaper as cover for their true role; since Dighenis himself ordered all "executions" no further proof was needed.' Such was the nature of the Greek-speaking community.

Even after the White Paper's publication, Archbishop Makarios still claimed he had evidence of 317 torture cases. In one example, he said two churchmen had been arrested on suspicion of being connected with EOKA and, according to him, they had been beaten, pulled by the hair and beard and generally insulted. In another, he maintained that matches had been put in the beard of a priest and then ignited. Again, like Pissas in his

booklet, no substantiating evidence was produced. Smearing reputations by hearsay became a common weapon in EOKA's armoury.

After the conflict was over, John Reddaway, one of Harding's key advisers at Government House, commented: 'How effective an independent enquiry into the allegations *en masse* would have been in establishing the truth is hard to say. There were of course enquiries into certain specific incidents. But the opinion among those in charge of security operations in Cyprus seems to have been that any sort of generalized enquiry would do more to publicize unfounded allegations than to establish the truth.

'But what such an enquiry would have shown is that there was no truth in the accusation that the authorities condoned and turned a blind eye to atrocious misconduct. The evidence has been fully and fairly set out in one of the most authoritative histories of this period yet to be produced. The conclusion reached is – the allegations gained ground with the Government's refusal to hold an independent inquiry. This would almost certainly have revealed some abuses. But it would have put the campaign into perspective. Instead of which many of the allegations came to be accepted at their face value and recorded as fact.'

Even if there had been the independent inquiry, which Charles Foley of the *Times of Cyprus*, Greek Cypriot lawyers and left-wing Members of Parliament, such as Barbara Castle, demanded, it is doubtful that it could have established the complete truth. The interrogation of captives and suspects was conducted in private in order to ensure the secrecy of any disclosures that were made and to protect the person under interrogation from being punished as a traitor by his associates later on.

'Rarely, if ever, is there any independent testimony about the way in which the interrogation was conducted,' Reddaway explained.

'Since intelligence was the key to defeating terrorism, the interrogator could be tempted to justify to himself the use of force against suspected terrorists on the grounds that the information to be extracted would save lives by bringing terrorism to an earlier end. The objection is of course not only humanitarian, but besides the violation of human rights, the use of illegal methods of interrogation strikes at the root of any system of justice.

'As for the person under interrogation, he was very likely afterwards to allege ill-treatment in order to claim credit for withstanding it, to protect himself against accusations of treachery and to blacken the reputation of the regime. For his part the interrogator was bound to maintain that no unlawful pressure was used and that the person under interrogation readily volunteered information … Rough handling of prisoners by soldiers in the heat of battle is understandable and cannot be wholly prevented; but it is different from the systematic use of ill-treatment against persons under interrogation.'

'Rough handling was used in Cyprus, but only in isolated instances. Nevertheless it was there,' said Peter Hamilton. 'There were stories about people sitting on blocks of ice and being told, "You sit there till you tell me", but I simply don't believe it.'

The wilder the accusation, the more it was believed and spread by the media, in Cyprus and the UK. Charles Foley was more guilty than most in his coverage. It prompted Mr. Justice Shaw who presided at the trial of Nicos Sampson to issue a public statement, which read as follows:

'In the *Times of Cyprus* of 29 May, under the heading "Out of the mouths of Government Spokesmen" reference was made to the case of the Queen against Nicos Sampson which I recently tried. The writer of this article states that a certain passage in my judgment indicated that I believed that the police consciously intended to cause Sampson to

talk, and he also states that he does not think that my ruling wholly acquits the police of the charges of deliberate ill treatment after Dhali.

'My ruling must speak for itself, and I do not consider it satisfactory that anyone should try to interpret it by quoting extracts and giving their views as to what I meant. The proper course is to publish the ruling in full. I am glad to see that this is now being done.

'There was a clear finding that apart from the circumstances in which Sampson was made to travel from Dhali to Nicosia and the failure to provide him with dry clothes and medical attention on his arrival at Nicosia, there was no ill-treatment of any kind, and all allegations of torture were found to be untrue.'

Iris Russell, who shared an office at the *Times of Cyprus*, undeterred sent a scathing attack on the Security Forces for her London newspaper, the *Sunday Dispatch*. It was headlined: 'This British Terror Must Be Stopped.' Her article said: 'I have little doubt that force has been used to extract confessions or information from arrested Cypriots, even though many allegations of ill-treatment have been grossly exaggerated. What is, perhaps, the most disturbing factor is that almost every Briton in Cyprus condones the use of such measures.

'The first rumours of ill-treatment and third-degree spread early last year, and substance was given to them when two British interrogators faced a court-martial on charges of beating-up Cypriots. In April last year two officers were found guilty and cashiered. Ever since it has been a matter of deep regret in British official circles that the case "was ever allowed to come to court". I have heard many British Army and police officers declare their disapproval of the "disgraceful" way those "two brilliant officers" were treated. Their sackings had been the utmost loss to the anti-terrorist campaign, they say, and unhesitatingly justify their "methods".

'I have heard British paratroopers recount with relish instances of "mild third degree" they used to extract information during anti-terrorist operations in the mountains. They always justified their actions: "They are murderers and we want information."

'For you at home in Britain, 2,000 miles from the anguish of the island, the question remains: "Can this sort of thing be tolerated?" It was disturbing to see so many Britons angered by British justice when Nicos Sampson was acquitted. Maybe it is time these Britons returned home.'

An officer of a Parachute Regiment was unsure whether to laugh or cry when he was charged with cruelty: 'I was one of the people accused of burying Cypriots up to their necks in sand on Famagusta beach and putting jam on their heads to attract the ants – something straight out of the *Boy's Own Paper*. Goddammit, I've never done anything like that, but all these things were very often repeated and, you know, if you throw enough mud it sticks.'

'To appreciate the true position of the Cyprus problem those armchair critics, Members of Parliament and church leaders who air their views should either go out and see for themselves or find something else to talk about,' retorted Ivan Smith, editor-in-chief of the Hampshire and North-West Surrey Group of Newspapers, after spending time with the Paras. He condemned journalists, such as Iris Russell, for their reports.

'Their utterances so far have not only aggravated the position, but have made much more irksome and dangerous the internal security duties of the armed forces now trying to control the EOKA fanatics of the age and sometimes of the mentality, of our own Teddy-boys, led by a mere handful of extreme nationalists. The national and foreign press representatives who spend their time alternatively between Cyprus and Israel are normally content to keep out of the way of trouble by working in the snugness of luxury hotels in Nicosia.

'It is this policy adopted in the past by so many correspondents that is responsible for an untrue picture continually being painted by the less reputable national newspapers. These warped views get into print and are eagerly snapped up for propaganda purposes by the anti-British newspapers.

'When Derbyshire miners send £250 to the known murderers, snipers and bomb-throwers, who, because of insufficient evidence for presentation in our courts, are quite rightly put into an 18b detention camp guarded by men of the Parachute Regiment, both Greeks and Cypriots can be forgiven for marvelling at the mentality of those at home.'

TO TRY to counter the anti-British propaganda, the authorities frequently invited foreign correspondents to visit detention centres, see whatever they wanted and to pick and privately interview any prisoner. Amongst those who checked conditions at Kokkinotrimithia or 'Camp K' were *Picture Post* reporter William Richardson, with his photographer Jack Estan, A. C. Sedgwick of the *New York Times* and editor Ivan Smith from a Hampshire press group. Their reports contradicted the broadcasts from Radio Athens, the articles by Charles Foley and Iris

Kokkinotrimithia Camp.

A Greek internee at Camp K keeps up with his studies.

Russell, and the critical comments made in Parliament and at the United Nations.

'Camp K', eight miles from Nicosia, was formerly an isolation hospital, which was reconstructed on the three-acre site to house around 250 detainees under 18b Regulations that allowed the authorities to hold individuals under suspicion of terrorist activity but without trial. The camp had a double fence, which was patrolled by two German shepherd dogs – Hector and Hercules – trained to attack any thing between the wires.

William Richardson of the *Picture Post* had listened to the broadcasts from Athens Radio, one of which compared the centre to Nazi concentration camps to invoke images of the Swastika and the cruelty that went with it:

'All those who have lived through the horror of the Nazi occupation in Europe shudder at the sight. One thinks he is once again in front of Dachau and Buchenwald. People in rags and skin and bone often approach barbed wire to face the outside world. Every morning, in rags and exhausted, men and women are lined up under the sullen gaze of their British jailers. Misery prevails. The camp reminds one in every aspect of Buchenwald and Auschwitz. Only crematoriums are lacking. Same gaunt faces, same barbed wire, same final objective – strangling of freedom.'

'To any who saw those concentration camps in the last thin days of the war, to anyone who really did experience the stench of burning flesh and the sight of walking skeletons, these are grave accusations. As a war correspondent, I did have that experience,' wrote Richardson with undisguised anger. 'The very mention of their names brings back the awful nightmare of suffering without precedent, which is obviously what Athens Radio intended. To use this comparison lightly would be a moral sacrilege against the memory of the victims.

'Having known the real meaning of Dachau, we went out to Camp K through the heat of an August afternoon. Camp K is certainly surrounded by barbed wire. It has guard towers with machine-gunners posted in them. There the analogy with anything Hitlerian ends abruptly, as we discovered.'

Superintendent Timothy Driscoll from the Metropolitan Police, who was responsible for running the centre, told the journalists: 'We are here to give the same sort of humane, just treatment and respect for the individual we would give to anyone incarcerated at home.' He was assisted by 13 other British policemen, eight Greek and eight Turkish Cypriot warders and perimeter guards from the Army.

'All the men are compensated for their incarceration,' O'Donnell added. Single males, he said, received a minimum of £5 monthly out of which they could shop at a *Naafi*-type

Kokkinotrimithia Camp.

Angry prisoners at Camp K.

store operated by detainees themselves. Married men with families could draw up to £35 a month. An interned shepherd said that before he arrived at the camp he had never earned more than £3 a week, but now was being paid almost £8 a week, including allowances for his wife and children, for doing nothing. There was no compulsion for the inmates to work. Those that did, added Corporal Ken Harrison of the King's Own Yorkshire Light Infantry, did it for fun and to avoid boredom.

The prisoners decided their own menus and traditional Greek Cypriot food was bought for them from outside contractors. They were allowed one adult visitor a week, who could bring 'a reasonable number of children'. There was no limit on their incoming mail and they could send 12 uncensored letters a month. There was a Greek Cypriot doctor available round-the-clock to see them within 10 minutes.

The detainees' day began at 06.30 with breakfast served an hour later, lunch at noon and dinner at 18.00. Greek music played on the camp's loudspeaker system. An elected committee composed of two representatives from each compound met daily with Superintendent O'Driscoll to deal with any complaints and requests. According to him, the Red Cross had donated £1,000 for recre-

ational facilities, such as table tennis tables and dart boards.

'That is the dread story of British Hitlerian methods in Cyprus,' reported Richardson. 'As one enlightened detainee said to me half-humorously: "It's more than a camp. It's almost a Welfare State".'

Ivan Smith decided to call the camp 'Millionaires' Row'. 'When I was conducted around, the insolence of most of the occupants was obvious,' he reported. 'They sat in summer lounge chairs, eating the expensive foods they are permitted to have sent to them. They talk in Greek and an interpreter stands near to report on the conversation, but as he is a Greek who probably, as most do today, fears for his loved ones, there is no guarantee of co-operation. It is firmly believed that the detention camp is a hot-bed of intrigue, and that from it detainee EOKA leaders send back, through the visitors, instructions for the bombing and shooting that continually flares up after a temporary lull.'

The *New York Times* representative, with no axes to grind and with an American readership influenced by the Greek lobby to inform, wrote: 'We were permitted to ask whatever questions we wished. What was expressly forbidden, however, was for a correspondent to conduct an interview in Greek,

A priest blesses Camp K prisoners.

Interned priests at Pyla Camp.

the only language most of the inmates understood. "Security" was given as the reason for
the prohibition. All the inmates were eager to
tell their stories. The point they made again
and again was that they were serving prison
terms for no offence but for favoring the
Cyprus right to determine its own political
future. They said that if there were more
serious or tangible reasons for depriving them
of their liberty they had not been informed of
them. Some of the charges made by Athens
Radio could not be even remotely substanti-
ated. One was that women inmates were
among those ill-treated. There are no women
inmates.'

He continued: 'A committee of three
inmates was produced for the correspondents,
One did most of the talking. He said that
Athens Radio was correct in stating that on
occasions the inmates had been beaten and
otherwise tortured but not, he said, in camp
and not by camp personnel. He charged that

the soldiers performing guard duties were in
the habit of calling out insults to the inmates
and making threatening remarks to them. He
asserted that the inmates sometimes had guns
pointed at them, presumably to make the
threats against them more realistic. The mere
fact that any inmates were allowed to be as
outspoken as they were seemed to argue
against the similarity of this camp with such
institutions as the Nazis established during the
war.'

During other press visits to the detention
centres, some of those held wrapped their
arms in 'blood'-stained bandages in an effort
to deceive reporters. When the bandages were
removed, there were no injuries and the
'blood' turned out to be tomato sauce. Dave
Cranston of the Royal Ulster Rifles substanti-
ated this story for the benefit of the author.

Many British soldiers resented the way their
Greek Cypriot prisoners were treated and
when they were assigned guard duties at
Camp K went out of their way to annoy them,
as Bryan Hunter, an ex-Para, confessed: 'At
night we thought it was very wrong that the
EOKA suspects were nicely tucked up in their
beds while we were stuck in the goon towers
to guard them. So we filled our pockets with
stones and threw one at their Nissan hut roofs
at 15-minute intervals. All through the night
there were bangs, followed by a series of
smaller bangs as each stone rattled downwards. My guard position was on the first
floor of the water tower. The Paras caused so
much trouble, the authorities requested we
never return to the camp after our first
guarding duty. Thank Goodness.'

After the conflict, Greek historian Doros
Alastos interviewed several former inmates of
the Kokkinotremithia Detention Camp. He
wrote: 'It was a self-imposed, inflexible rule
of the detainees to stand to attention and sing
the Greek National Anthem just before being
locked in for the evening. To them it was an
assertion of faith and, in the circumstances,

A Greek Cypriot reconstruction of Camp K for tourists.

obtain from them statements of ill-treatment in the hands of the Security forces.

'My orders were to obtain such statements by threats, if necessary, from the persons concerned. The resultant full-scale fabrications, which I was to obtain, were to be further improved upon and edited by me, and to be incorporated in my weekly reports to Grivas. And this is what I did, week after week, month after month.'

Immediately after these admissions, Grivas forced Ashiotis's father to publicly disown his son in paid advertisements in the local press.

highly symbolic. Some of the camp guards, Turks, found this entertaining. To relieve their own boredom they made cheap fun of the little ceremony with catcalls and ribald insults. But they were not allowed to get away with it for long. One evening, by prearranged plan, all the guards who behaved in this crude way were pelted with eggs, tomatoes, and anything else at hand. The incident was reported to the Commandant. The Camp Committee protested that the guards' behaviour constituted a national affront and asked the Commandant to ensure that this, to them, sacred moment was not made light of. To his credit, he ordered the guards to stand to attention whichever country's National Anthem was sung.'

(Today's Republic of Cyprus has rebuilt Camp K in the style of a German concentration camp for school children to visit so that the myths of EOKA are maintained.)

When Michael Ashiotis, an EOKA gang member, voluntarily gave himself up to the authorities, he explained how Grivas engineered claims of cruelty. 'Many months ago, in common with other EOKA area commanders, I received unequivocal instructions from Grivas that I was to approach, directly or indirectly, all persons in my area who had been in the hands of troops or police, or who had been in places of detention, and to

WHILE ON the international front the political debate continued and Harding scored military victories against EOKA, Grivas's execution squads were adding to the death toll during the first three months of 1957. In early January, they killed Herbert Pritchard, an engineer who worked for Cable and Wireless in Nicosia; Cecil Cook, a district education officer in Famagusta; and Royal Navy Writer Philip Bingham outside the Post Office's parcel office in the capital.

Whatever British troops and the Governor did in Cyprus, following the Suez debacle, Parliament's left-wing Labour Members of Parliament and their supporters in the media grabbed every opportunity to attack the new Macmillan Government for its handling of the conflict, especially the powers it gave Field Marshal Sir John Harding as Governor to arrest and detain EOKA suspects without trial, impose press restrictions and deny public inquiries into the Greek allegations.

'What have you got to hide, Sir John?' screamed a headline in the *News Chronicle* above an article by the highly respected journalist James Cameron, who wrote: 'More and more as the dismal days drag on is the situation dominated by personal factors in the Governor's mind – his personal feud with Archbishop Makarios, his personal stake in the capture of Grivas, his personal necessity to prove the unprovable: that Cyprus can be held by force.

'While face is saved, Cyprus rots. Anglo-Greek relations deteriorate, the Mediter-ranean NATO becomes more and more meaningless and thousands of British troops lead a futile and exasperating life among people who two years ago were their friends and who now will probably never lose their enmity for a generation.'

If the Governor felt in need of some support, he received it from *The Times* in an editorial. The newspaper said: 'Sir John Harding's battle against terrorism has at last begun to yield dividends. This would probably have happened before except for constant interruptions in order to prepare for eventual-ities at Suez. The publication of the Radcliffe report has provided an interim solution, which ought to be acceptable to all. It gives to the Greeks a majority in the Legislative Assembly, which is what they always claimed. It gives to the Turks, by whom it has been favourably received, adequate safeguards for their minorities. And it gives to Archbishop Makarios the chance to play a role in a diarchy ... The Suez crisis, and Britain's reap-praisal of her defence needs, must certainly lead to a reappraisal of her needs in Cyprus. It could be that Britain's own strategic stake in the Island became less important, but that of NATO remained unaffected.'

Just as the press was divided, Prime Minister Macmillan presided over a split Cabinet – those who wanted to show Britain still had muscle after the failure at Suez and others who pressed for Makarios's release from exile so that political negotiations could be resumed. For the moment, Macmillan put Cyprus to one side and concentrated on his forthcoming meeting in Bermuda with President Eisenhower at which he hoped Anglo-American relations could be restored without the Island's problems becoming an issue.

The US State Department, however, deeply concerned that after Suez the Middle East was increasingly looking to the Soviet Union for support and NATO was being weakened by the differences between Greece and Turkey over Aphrodite's Isle, wanted a quick settle-ment and was pressing Greece to be coopera-tive in this endeavour. Privately Athens responded by demanding that the EOKA leader stop his activities and allow time for Macmillan and Eisenhower at their Bermuda conference to discuss Cyprus to see if they would progress the situation in a conciliatory manner.

UNAWARE OF the discussions between Greece and the United States, Governor Harding rejected an appeal for clemency by the father, a policeman of 30 years' service, of 19-year-old Evagoras Palikarides. His execu-tion went ahead as scheduled at 00.15 on 13 March. He was the first person to be hanged for carrying a firearm since the death penalty was made mandatory for this offence under the latest Emergency Regulations, and the ninth Cypriot to die by the noose. Sir John, however, did commute to life imprisonment the death sentence passed on Stavros Demetriou, 18, who had pleaded he did not know of the new law.

The timing could not have been worse for Grivas, but under pressure from the Greek Government he was obliged to order a cease-fire on the day after Palikarides' execution – 14 March 1957. The news was spread in one of his frequent leaflets. Translated into English, it said, 'Complying with the spirit of the United Nations, which has expressed the desire for a peaceful and just solution of the Cyprus problem in accordance with the prin-ciples of the United Nations Charter, and in order to facilitate the resumption of negotia-tions between Britain and the real representa-tive of the Cyprus people, Archbishop Makarios, our Organization hereby declares itself willing to order a suspension of operations as soon as the Archbishop is released.' It was signed 'EOKA, Dighenis, the Leader.' His decision would give the Island a respite from violence.

Earlier the *Times of Cyprus* had predicted that Palikarides' execution would put an end to all hopes of an early relaxation of tension and would swell the ranks of those Greek Cypriots who regarded the British administration of the Island as 'brutal and tyrannical'. The Grivas statement suggested different possibilities and questions.

Military commanders were convinced that Grivas knew EOKA was being beaten and was merely buying time to regroup his men. It was a view shared by Dr Kutchuk, the Turkish Cypriot leader. He sniffed: 'This is nothing different from EOKA's first truce offer. It is merely another delaying tactic to help relieve EOKA from the hopeless position into which it has fallen. This is further proof that Grivas himself now realizes that his organization has been shattered to the roots.'

Later Grivas admitted that he used the truce to fill the gaps in his ranks and to re-arm. 'I also gave careful attention to a list of unmanned targets which our saboteurs could attack without technically breaking the ceasefire,' he said. 'They would do so on my orders only if reasons of prestige, such as the execution of one of our men by the British called for a gesture on our part.'

The Times in London urged the British Government 'to put a lever in any crack that seems to appear in the Cyprus deadlock. Such a crack there is now, though it is hard to analyse what exactly has caused it. No doubt the mildness of the General Assembly debate and resolution has been partly responsible; so, certainly, has the growing weakness of EOKA, of which there is fresh evidence in the conditional offer to suspend operations.'

For its part the Government of Cyprus was confident that EOKA was on its last legs and

reduced drastically the rewards on the heads of terrorists. It was a blow to Grivas's ego that the reward for his capture fell from £10,000 to £5,000.

The Security Forces, truce or not, kept up their efforts, capturing more weapons, munitions and wanted EOKA terrorists, including Christou Rossides, a district leader and operational commander of a mountain group, together with two members of his gang. In the same operation Petrakis Michalakis was shot dead. He was wanted for the murder of a Sergeant Wilfred Jepson of the 14/20 King's Hussars on 28 September 1956 in Larnaca and the murder of a Greek Cypriot journalist the previous April.

THE BERMUDA conference began a week after the truce announcement on 21 March. Macmillan hoped to return home with a promise from America that it would supply Britain with Thor missiles and other technologies and he could placate the hawks in his Cabinet. To the surprise of the Prime Minister, Eisenhower brought Cyprus to the forefront of the discussions. He had received a direct appeal from the King of Greece to have Makarios released and the Republican administration had promised to 'speak boldly to the British' on the matter. And Eisenhower did. He told Macmillan that he saw no value to anyone by keeping the Archbishop in exile and he should be 'turned loose on the world'. By this action, the British would see, he said, 'that they were trying to reach a solution to the problem'. Macmillan was unable to refuse the President's request, but knew some of his Cabinet members would not be happy.

Immediately after Grivas made his truce offer, Sir John Harding left for London to seek guidance from Alan Lennox-Boyd, Secretary of State for the Colonies. He was told that Makarios would be released, subject to a few technical details, which needed to be agreed, as soon as Macmillan returned from Bermuda.

Harding knew that victory against EOKA was now lost to him. Soon afterwards, Makarios told London he would denounce violence subject to two conditions: firstly, he would recommend 'the pacification of Cyprus', but only after he was released; and second, the British must call off all military operations against EOKA, otherwise he could not vouch for a permanent peace.

From the Seychelles, Archbishop Makarios released the following statement:

The resolution of the United Nations calling for a resumption of negotiations for a peaceful, democratic, and just solution of the Cyprus problem in accordance with the principles of the United Nations Charter is a starting point towards a final settlement of the issue.

We understand this resolution as an expression of the wish of the United Nations for bilateral negotiations between the British Government and the people of Cyprus.

The EOKA organization, conforming to the spirit of the United Nations resolution, and in order to facilitate a resumption of such negotiations, declares it is ready to suspend its operations at once if prisoners were to be released.

Thus, a new situation has been created opening the way for the restoration of peace in the island.

The British Government, however, was not satisfied with this truce offer by EOKA because its leaders declared only a suspension and not a cessation of operations.

I would be extremely sorry if the road to peace thus now opened were to be blocked by this argument.

In my sincere desire to see peace restored in Cyprus I appeal to the EOKA organization and to the British Government as well. I appeal to EOKA to declare the cessation of all operations given that the British Government will show a spirit of understanding by abolishing simultaneously the present State of Emergency.

To Sir John Harding he wrote:

To this end I repeat here what I wrote in my letter dated 2 February 1956, to the Governor of Cyprus: 'Such pacification will be brought about, more quickly than by anything else, by the policy to be followed simultaneously by your Excellency.

'This should be a policy of appeasement capable of inspiring the citizens with a feeling of freedom and safety. Thus, emergency military measures and emergency legislation should be revoked and an amnesty should be granted for all political offences.'

As regards my intention, the Colonial Secretary stated that after I have made a public statement calling on EOKA for a cessation of violence then I would be free to go anywhere except Cyprus.

I wish to make clear that my personal release will never be an object of bargaining.

As spiritual and national leader of the Greek people of Cyprus I had, and always will have, as my first concern the interests of the people, and not my personal welfare. But I feel most deeply that my return to Cyprus will create a response from the people of the island, and this will be a factor, which should not be underestimated.

The Colonial Secretary stated also that the Government felt that it was better to tackle the international aspects of the problem first by discussion in NATO, but hoped to proceed with constitutional discussions later.

A statement of the Greek Government, interpreting rightly the spirit of the United Nations organization resolution, has already given the reply that it would not be willing to take part in discussion on the Cyprus problem within NATO and that talks should be resumed directly between the British Government and the Cyprus people.

I sincerely believe that if the British Government thinks any Greek Cypriot could be found to negotiate in my absence; that would be a waste of time. Finally, I express the hope that the British Government will understand and appreciate my sincere desire for the restoration of peace in the island.

I also express the wish that the way now

open will lead towards peace in the light of a spirit of mutual trust and understanding.
Mahe, Seychelles,
22 March 1957.

On 28 March, Lennox-Boyd's reply came in a statement in the House of Commons: 'While the Government cannot regard this statement as the clear appeal for which we asked, nevertheless we consider that in present circumstances it is no longer necessary to continue the Archbishop's detention. I have accordingly instructed the Governor of Seychelles, with the full agreement of Sir John Harding, to cancel the orders for the detention of the Archbishop and his three compatriots and to arrange passages from the Seychelles by the first available vessel.'

However, the Archbishop would not, at this stage, be allowed to return to Cyprus, but he was free to come to London, to see anyone, and to discuss anything. To promote a rapid return to peaceful conditions on the Island, Lennox-Boyd continued, the Governor was prepared to offer immediate safe conduct to Grivas and his EOKA men still at large.

There was no question yet of an immediate abolition of the State of Emergency or of an amnesty in Cyprus for those imprisoned for terrorist offences. This included Nicos Sampson sitting in the death cell of Nicosia Prison. According to Charles, he had already been shown the execution shed and the coffin for his body.

As the second year of the EOKA conflict came to an end, the statistics on the dead and the wounded were released. They showed 263 people had died and 708 had been injured. Of those killed, 78 were British servicemen, nine were British policemen and 16 were British civilians. There had been 1,382 explosions. EOKA's losses amounted to 51 killed, 27 imprisoned and about 1,500 suspects held in detention.

With the start of the third year, there may not have been a peace agreement, but there was the semblance of normality again throughout the Island.

In London, Prime Minister Macmillan could smile again. He had returned with America's promise to supply the UK with Thor missiles.

CHAPTER EIGHTEEN

Love and marriage:
an uneasy truce

Fairest isle, all isles excelling,
Seat of pleasures, and of loves;
Venus here will find her dwelling,
And forsake her Cyprian groves.
John Dryden, Song of Venus

*O*LYMPIC THUNDER, a Greek oil tanker, stormed her way through the waves of the Indian Ocean, steaming at full speed towards her next destination. Her captain had received a radio message 800 miles off the Seychelles to change course for the port of Mahe to collect Archbishop Makarios and his three companions in exile. At just before midnight on 5 April, the four Cypriots stood in the gardens of *Sans Souci* and watched the vessel's blaze of lights approach and the ship anchor before returning to pack their bags. Earlier in the evening they had given a farewell party to their hosts and staff of the Governor's Lodge, which had been their home for a little more than a year.

The Seychellois brought their families, all dressed in their Sunday best. Makarios gave each of them a small gift of cash after 'rushing to and fro with trays of food, fetching chairs, serving drinks and listening to the music with a beaming smile', said Mrs Le Geyt to whom he presented a wrist watch. For her husband, Captain Le Geyt, there was a Parker 51 pen and pencil set. To His Excellency Sir William Addis, the Governor of the Islands, he sent a message to thank him for putting his country residence at their disposal and stressed that he and the three others had absolutely no complaints about their treatment.

Makarios went further in his letter to the editor of *Le Seychellois*, the local newspaper. 'I have visited many places all over the world and it is no exaggeration to say that the Seychelles Islands contain the most beautiful places I have ever seen ... Before leaving I want to say, on behalf of my colleagues and myself, how grateful we are for the kindness and consideration with which we have been treated here by all those with whom we came in contact, and by the people employed in the *Sans Souci* household.'

At an earlier press conference, Makarios had declared that only he and the British Government could discuss and settle the Cyprus question. He categorically rejected suggestions that the Turkish 'minority' should participate in the negotiations, although its rights could be 'internationally safeguarded'. Any suggestion for partition of the Island, he said, would bring 'disastrous consequences'.

At 09.00 the next day, the gates of *Sans Souci* were thrown open and the cars taking the exiles drove to the Long Pier in Mahe to catch a launch to the *Olympic Thunder*, now bound for Mombassa so that the Archbishop could catch a flight to Athens. In his luggage, Makarios had put a coco der mer, which would eventually decorate his office at the Archbishopric in Nicosia.

When the prospective release of the Archbishop and his companions – Kyprianos, the Bishop of Kyrenia; the Reverend Papastavos and Polycarpos Joannides – was announced on 28 March by Cyprus Radio, church bells pealed in all the Island's towns, Greek flags were raised, motorists honked their horns and crowds gathered in the streets, ignoring curfew regulations. Greek Cypriots went out of their way to embrace British troops, to their surprise, but the mood changed the next day.

Angered by the constant chanting of 'EOKA – EOKA!' and the carrying shoulder-high by some demonstrators of individuals made to look like Grivas, British soldiers tore down Greek flags and Makarios posters. To prevent the crowds' enthusiasm turning nasty, the authorities banned access to Metaxas Square, enforced the curfew on all males under the age of 27 and warned Emergency Regulations would not be eased until there had been a long period of calm.

The Turkish Cypriot leadership, however, expressed astonishment that the prelate had been given his freedom without condemning EOKA and that Grivas was being offered safe

conduct to leave the Island with his terrorist gangs.

'The political significance of this action will be judged by the future attitude of the British Government,' said Prime Minister Karamanlis, the Greek Prime Minister. 'I hope that the decision to free Archbishop Makarios is an indication of the British Government's desire to seek a peaceful but just solution. Such a solution would lead, among other things, to the restoration of the old friendship of our two nations.'

ARCHBISHOP MAKARIOS arrived in Athens on 17 April, with his fellow exiles, feeling airsick. They were welcomed at the airport by Foreign Minister Averoff, other Cabinet Ministers and Archbishop Dorotheos, the Greek Primate, and driven to the heart of the capital in an open white Cadillac past cheering crowds. In Constitution Square, Makarios addressed them from the balcony of the not-so-aptly named Hotel Grande Bretagne: 'Neither Middle East oil, nor western defence, nor Turkish opposition shall deter the Cypriots' claim to determine their own present and future. We will continue and intensify our

Makarios arrives at Athens Airport after his exile.

Makarios acknowledges his welcome from Athenians.

struggle until the application of the principle of self-determination to Cyprus,' he said. 'From this sacred land I send greetings to the Cypriot people: to all those who are on the front line and others in the rear. I am confident that the Cyprus issue will reach its final phase – self-determination. This is guaranteed by the irrevocable resolve of the Cypriot people to shake off the British yoke and live free.'

The crowds chanted back: 'EOKA! – *Enosis*!' and 'Death to Harding'.

In Cyprus, Grivas had not responded to Harding's offer of safe conduct and so the Security Forces continued their search for him and his mountain gangs. But in the towns, British servicemen and their wives were again moving freely and mixing with Greek Cypriots on the friendliest of terms. *The Times* correspondent reported: 'Greek Cypriots realize full well the advantages this brings them, and the most unpopular man in Cyprus will be he who starts trouble again.' In a gesture of

goodwill, the Governor commuted the death sentence on Christos Kyriacou to 10 years' imprisonment.

By 16 May, the Headquarters of British Forces, Middle East, was operational in Episkopi, a base that was rapidly expanding in size, suggesting to the population that Britain had long-term plans to stay, whatever politicians declared in London. Makarios, in Athens, rejected suggestions that NATO should get involved in solving peace settlement issues and countered that he would accept placing Cyprus under a UN mandate. Dr Kutchuk, for the Turkish Cypriots, said: 'We shall not negotiate except on a basis of partition, and we will not discuss the Radcliffe plan or any other projected constitution,' and added that the Turks were pleased to see that Britain and the United States seemed to be coming round to that standpoint.

He denied that he had ever tried to foster disturbances in Cyprus, or that he had been warned against doing so by Sir John Harding, the Governor, and he remarked that, though there was no civil war in Cyprus today, nobody could tell what might happen. He believed that the Cyprus problem had reached international proportions, and could not be solved locally.

At Episkopi, Ron Barnett, a Royal Engineer Clerk of Works, was supervising some of the building operations, with two locally recruited workforces under his command. In one, there were 30 Turks, and in the other, 40 Greeks, each with a foreman drawn from their own communities. 'There was definite animosity and some dislike between the two groups,' he said, speaking to the author. I could never put Greeks and Turks together on a job, no matter how important completion times were. Also I could never put a foreman in charge of the other group. Nor could I bring to work Greeks in a truck with a Turkish driver or vice versa. Both groups gave me the same excuse – that the driver would take them to his village where his people would attack the passengers. I also had to treat both foremen exactly the same.'

Barnett continued: 'I had strong suspicions that there was some connection between the Greeks and EOKA, because if I told their foreman I planned to go to the Troodos that same day, perhaps calling at Platres en route, he would protest that he could not accompany me because his current work needed his urgent attention. Later I'd hear there was an incident or explosion that day on the road. Next day he would say, "Okay, today we go to Troodos, it will be OK." It usually was.'

During the period of the truce, Barnett was passed an EOKA document, which showed his car's registration number was on the terrorists' list. 'It was to give me safe passage to where I was heading and the frequent café stops the foreman always wanted were to check our progress on the journey and alert any gangs ahead of us.'

Meanwhile, in Athens, the American Ambassador urged the US State Department to convince the Macmillan Government to allow Makarios to return to Cyprus for negotiations, because the longer he stayed in the Greek capital, the more he would be drawn into the machinations of local politics and these could have a bad effect on what happened on the Island, but Macmillan was not in a mood to be persuaded any more than the Governor.

AS THE truce continued, regulations concerning troops leaving camp in their leisure time were relaxed, but they still had to go out in groups of at least two – and armed. Based at Episkopi, Lance Corporal 'Taffy' Fussell and Corporal Clive Hickson of the RASC decided to spend an off-duty Saturday exploring nearby Limassol, with Taffy carrying a revolver from the unit's armoury.

'We roamed up and down various side roads until we came upon a school playground, surrounded by a two-foot high wall on top of which stood spiked iron railings,' said Hickson. On the far side of the playground a small boy appeared stuck on the railings. We raced to his aid. As we approached the youngster gazed at us innocently with bright brown eyes. Fortunately things were not as bad as we'd originally feared. No blood was visible and he didn't appear to be in pain. The spike of a railing had gone up his short trouser leg and protruded from his waist belt. It seemed a miracle that he had not been hurt. He was however stuck several feet off the ground, unable to budge.

'Taffy climbed onto the wall and placed my shoulders under his backside and held him firmly around the legs so that he'd have both hands free to lift the child. "It's OK Ken, you can release me now I've pulled him free."

'"Are you sure mate?" I asked. "Because those spikes look very dangerous."

'"Yes, it's alright," he replied. I stepped

back to get a better view and heard Taffy whispering to the lad prior to dropping him gently to the ground. As the boy landed Taffy gave a groan. "What's up mate?" I asked. "The little bugger," he grimaced, "pushed me as I loosed him. My foot slipped and one of the spikes has gone into my arm."

'"Listen Taffy," I said, "I'm going to lift you off the spike. If you faint I won't be able to do it on my own. So grit your teeth, mate." He groaned as I manoeuvered him down and sat him on a nearby doorstep.

'"Don't move. I'm going to get you a lift to the local hospital," I said.'

Hickson ran to a road and waved down an approaching car to stop. The driver and his passenger were Greek Cypriots who agreed to take him and Taffy to the nearest hospital for treatment.

'In the Casualty Room, Taffy was attended to by two doctors and a nurse. They'd removed his jacket and his white shirt was a mass of red,' remembered Hickson. 'His shoulder holster and weapon lay on a nearby locker. When the doctor told me that my friend would have to stay overnight in hospital for observation, I instinctively reached out and picked up the holster and revolver. The young doctors and nurse showed where their political sympathies lay. They then left the room, allowing me to talk to Taffy in private. "Listen mate," I said, "I've taken charge of the weapon you got from the armoury, because it may get pinched when you fall asleep. I'll hand it back when I get back to camp."

'Taffy then revealed he was on "affectionate terms" with Maroulla, a Greek Cypriot typist in their office. "On Monday will you tactfully inform her what's happened, because she'll be worried when I don't turn up for work."'

After phoning the Duty Officer at their camp to explain what had happened, a Land Rover was sent to collect Hickson. The next day Taffy Fussell was transferred to the British Military Hospital in Akrotiri.

On Monday morning when the civilian staff arrived, a puzzled Maroulla approached. 'Corporal Ken,' she said, 'where's Taffy?' He told her about the accident and she burst into tears. An officer and the Chief Clerk told Hickson to take the girl to visit Taffy and they would arrange a Land Rover to transport them daily to see Taffy until he recovered. When he was discharged from hospital he was declared unfit for further military duties. Immediately he and Maroulla announced their engagement, their marriage approved by the authorities because they would be leaving Cyprus. A simple wedding was held in the military chapel with a more elaborate religious ceremony and party held in the wife's village.

'The military authorities granted us special permission to attend the event. Although our contact with local people was limited to those at work, I found them polite, courteous, and most religious,' says Hickson. 'On the wedding day we dressed in our best uniforms and set off in an old sturdy coach, together with local workers returning home. An hour later the coach stopped in the main street of a primitive but attractive village.

'As the couple alighted, a large cheering crowd hustled them along the main street and off into a side street, uphill to the local church. We stood in a group wondering what we should do, or where we should go. For it seemed as if everyone had forgotten about us.

'Minutes later, we glimpsed the flash of a white wedding gown in the middle of the crowd, where the couple was being jostled with sheer enthusiasm. As the crowd neared the church it grew larger as more people poured from their homes to join the bustle and excitement that the wedding had generated in this small village.

'We followed behind cautiously. If we hadn't known otherwise we'd have thought a riot was taking place. People elbowed, shoved and shouted at each other to get nearer the couple and impatient for the ceremony to begin.

'As we'd never been inside a Greek Orthodox Church before we assumed that it would be similar to our own churches, a quiet place of prayer. We tucked our berets under our epaulettes and entered the dark interior. Everyone was talking excitedly. Above our heads ran a balcony packed with children, who ran along its length screaming and shouting and obviously enjoying themselves.

'As was the custom for that village, all unmarried young men walked the couple in the direction of the pulpit, which stood some 12 feet in the air. From it a young priest rang a hand bell and shouted lustily at the congregation. When no one paid him any attention I thought he'd burst a blood vessel as his face grew redder and his words more furious as he worked himself into a frenzy.

'Our group of soldiers stood at the rear with backs to the wall. Eventually hush descended and all eyes centered on the three main characters. An elderly priest in black costume and hat conducted the Greek wedding rites in a quiet dignified manner. As he smiled to reassure the couple, white teeth contrasted starkly with his black moustache and beard.

'Before the ring was blessed by the priest and fitted on Maroulla's finger, all the best men passed it between themselves. This was done hastily as the ceremony could not be concluded until it reached the priest. I could see a slight smile on his lips.

'Then like something out of a Hollywood musical, a beam of sunlight poured through a narrow window and struck the top of his head and gave him the appearance of having a halo. It was quite extraordinary, and added a seeming holiness to the whole procedure.

'As the ceremony reached its climax, there was total silence. Then a perceptible hum of noise grew louder until once again it was party time. A large roll of ribbon was tied to the couple's foreheads and unravelled behind them. This was the signal for people to write good luck messages to the couple. Maroulla glanced around the hall and spotted our small group of soldiers. She snatched the pen from the hands of a reluctant guest, and with Taffy holding her hand she shoved her way through the crowd to where I stood. "Lance Corporal Ken," she said, "I want you to write next." No sooner had I added my message then my mates all clamoured for the pen.

'Then the Greek Cypriots began to pin paper money to the bride's dress. Our small group of soldiers contributed to the custom. During the ceremony the church doors had remained wide open, and now the jolly crowd surged outside into brilliant sunlight. We followed behind to the wedding feast, a sumptuous spread with tables groaning under the weight of food, delicacies, and assorted bottles of wines.

'With the newlyweds occupying the honoured position, various members of the family, village officials and friends sat nearby. Our group sat well away from the couple on a table to ourselves. We were totally overwhelmed by it all, but eagerly tucked into the food and soon couldn't eat another morsel, or drink any more wine, despite being pressed to do so by many people. Time seemed to pass quickly and by the time we were outside again, the night sky was alight with bright shining stars. In our slightly inebriated state this seemed to add a magic sparkle to the moment.'

Robert Holland, the historian, wrote: 'It is notable that purely human relations between the great bulk of British servicemen and the general population had never lost the basic decencies. The *Times of Cyprus* not infrequently carried the photograph of some smiling British soldier with his newly conquered Greek bride, surrounded by quizzical in-laws from the village; one can only guess who pacified whom in the end.'

The wedding of Maroulla and Taffy Fussell, however, was very different to those of RAF Corporal John Elliot and Senior Aircraftman John Cooper, who married their Greek Cypriot wives in Nicosia and were living with their in-laws. Although not publicly stated, Special Branch had discovered that the RAF men's new families were related to senior members of EOKA.

The same day this information came to the attention of the Security Forces, Elliot and Cooper were hustled out of Cyprus to new postings. One found himself on the way to Malta, the other to El Adem in Libya. The authorities told nosey reporters that it was not intended to separate the two airmen from their wives permanently. They could send for them as soon as married family accommodation was available at their new stations.

The author tracked down one of the former airmen in 2008 to his UK home. He confessed he had never made contact again with his Greek Cypriot wife, and had re-married on his return to England. 'I don't know what our kids will say when they discover my past,' he said. 'I'm concerned how they will react to a previous unknown marriage, but we don't really control our lives. As a two-year RAF conscript, you just toe the line and follow orders.

'Yes, we were spirited away by Special Branch. Our Greek wives were related to Afxentiou and Stylianides. SB decided it was better we were moved elsewhere. That way there couldn't be any embarrassment for the RAF. Fifty years on, it all sounds very James Bond, but at the time we did tremble at times. I never kept in touch with any of the lads after leaving Cyprus and I've never been back. As you know the Greeks have long memories.'

G. W. Young of *Reveille* magazine, which circulated widely amongst the British troops, warned: 'The rule is that if a man is seen out with a girl more than once or twice, he is regarded by everybody as intending to marry her. If he doesn't, he is automatically a dirty dog. "Sign on the dotted line, please," he is invited. It can be dangerous to refuse. These engagements – as some British servicemen have found to their cost – cannot be lightly broken. One airman, who, it is alleged, tried to do so, is currently being sued for breach of promise. A local lawyer told me: "In the past year I have heard of about 10 breach of promise cases brought against British servicemen. Some of these men almost certainly didn't realize that they were engaged. Damages between £50 and £100 are awarded in successful claims – and most of them are successful. Not all families keep cool enough to do it through the courts: a temperamental brother of the girl has threatened more than one British serviceman with a violent end."'

Former Sapper Eric Reed was almost caught in the tender trap. He explained: 'A member of our survey team was a Greek Cypriot and he introduced me to one of his relatives, a beautiful girl called Androula with whom I established a warm friendship. Of course, we never saw each other alone because local custom dictated there had to be a chaperone present. Then news of our relationship reached the ears of my OC. He summoned me to his office for a private chat. He warned me that EOKA often enticed innocent servicemen into their "honey-traps". Once caught, the soldiers were either kidnapped and held hostage or blackmailed into revealing sensitive information. He recommended I break off my friendship.

'A few evenings later I ignored his advice and left camp, claiming I was visiting friends in Berengaria village, but, of course, my destination was Androula's home in Limassol. When I arrived in the town, it was alive with RMPs, but I managed to evade them, probably because, due to my Welsh roots, I have olive skin and dark hair and I could pass for a Greek Cypriot. I expected a friendly welcome from Androula, but I wasn't allowed to see her. Her bother, with the body of a Rambo, greeted me instead and told me to get the hell away. He wanted his family to have nothing to do with me, claiming that if the RMPs spotted me, they would all be dragged off for questioning.

'Downhearted I left and went to a bar nearby to drown my sorrows in the company of some Greek Cypriots to whom Androula had introduced me. The drinks flowed and time passed quickly. Just as I was about to leave, the bar was stormed by a group of RMPs, looking for soldiers who were in town without a pass. The Greeks crowded round me as if I was one of them, not giving me away. The RMPs left and I managed to return to camp safely.'

Said an Army spokesman, who had attended several weddings between servicemen and Greek Cypriot brides: 'A man here inherits up to 300 in-laws when he marries a Greek Cypriot. He is expected to know the lot – even the cousins umpteen times removed.' Androula's brother, unknowingly, had saved young love-struck Reed from Hades.

In 1955, 36 servicemen married Cypriots. A year later, 1956, the figure fell to 25, and in 1957 it was almost 40.

YEARS EARLIER, long before EOKA, John Gow, an RAF airman, had fallen in love with Panayiota Theofanous, a soft-voiced housemaid in Nicosia. They had become engaged, and, according to Greek Cypriot custom, were allowed to sleep together before marriage. Panayiota became pregnant and delivered a baby boy with bright blue eyes. Sadly Gow was not at her bedside in hospital when the baby was born. He had died in an air crash six months earlier. On the same day, in an adjacent bed, Mrs Theodosia Shatis, the wife of a Greek Cypriot shepherd, had given birth to a baby boy, too, except his head was thatched with curly black hair.

The British nurse in charge of the maternity ward showed the proud mothers their babies and then took them to their nursery cots to sleep. Next morning, the mothers were reunited with the children, except each protested theirs had been swapped for the other. Their protests were ignored and three days later Mrs Shatis left with the 'blue eyes' and Panayiota was left with the other boy.

Although Mr Shatis wondered how his child had blue eyes, he accepted him and, as his farm prospered, he thought his luck came from the boy's colouring. Time and time again, Panayiota brought the dark-haired baby to the Shatis's home asking for her child back, only to be refused. Eventually, she took her claim to court and placed it in front of District Judge Zekia Bey. She showed him pictures of her dead blond fiancé. Then Mr and Mrs Shastis, both-dark haired and swarthy, argued their case that 'blue eyes' was theirs.

Without the wisdom of Solomon, Judge Zekia had to decide. One look at the two claimants and he knew the babes had been swapped and ordered the changelings to be returned to their rightful mothers. A week later, a joyful Panayiota was off to Scotland to bring up 'blue eyes' with Gow's welcoming family. Mr and Mrs Shastis spent the next few months learning to love their new child. In matters of love, Aphrodite's Isle could sometimes break hearts.

WHILE OFF-DUTY military personnel were able at last to visit the tourist sites of the Island, EOKA was never out of mind as long as Grivas remained free. For his organization to exist, it had to terrorize or collapse. To avoid breaking the truce, it continued to murder 'informers' to remind the population not to waver in its support.

The Greek Government had hoped Grivas would accept Harding's safe-conduct offer, but the EOKA leader was furious that Athens could have even contemplated such an idea when there was still no acceptance by the British to allow Greek Cypriots the choice of *enosis*. Makarios wrote to him: 'The ceasefire is an excellent idea and the one remaining question is whether it should be made permanent ... from what I hear it seems that we must find a means of bringing all fighting to an end, without, of course, injuring your prestige in any way.'

Grivas, who had never thought too highly of Makarios, blasted back that in his view Athens had failed to make good diplomatic use of 'our struggle' and had 'behaved like mendicants, asking for favours instead of putting forward dignified demands'. He continued: 'The Government cares only for its alliances with people who grovel for our help when they are in danger and spurn us the moment that the danger is past. I do not know what information you have been given about Cyprus by the self-appointed advisers who have rushed to Athens to gain your ears and surround you with the poison of the towns, but I ask you to make no decisions until you have taken the opinion of those who represent the fighting people here. As for a permanent ceasefire, that is unthinkable before conditions for a favourable solution are ensured. If your opinion is different I shall not oppose you because the responsibilities of the struggle dictate that we should work in harmony.'

Not for the first time, Grivas, Makarios and the Greek Government were disagreeing. At the same time, the Archbishop was under pressure from the Athens authorities to act in a more conciliatory manner towards the British, while extreme nationalists, including Orthodox priests, were telling him that he had already conceded too much to the Colonial power. In the background, the Turkish voice in Cyprus was becoming louder and was determined not to be ignored.

Whatever boasts Grivas made, he knew the British were winning the military fight outside the towns. On Good Friday, 19 April, EOKA suffered another setback when Georghios Demetriou, an area leader in Lefke, was captured, with his gang of seven, by 2nd Lieutenant B. Marriot of the Suffolk Regiment's Support Company Machine Gun Platoon. They were spotted resting in a shady glade of the lower Troodos area. Marriot called on them to surrender. Corporal Moyse went forward, his Sten gun cocked. Demetriou raised his hands in surrender and the rest followed his lead without a shot being fired. The others included Mikis Kyriacou Firillas and Neophytes Sophoclous, both with prices on their heads.

By midsummer, politicians in London were convinced that Governor Harding would never negotiate with Makarios and had fulfilled his mission as a military commander to subdue EOKA. The time was right, they felt, to have him replaced at the end of his two-year contract by a civilian who could look at the Island's problems with fresh eyes, ease the Emergency Regulations, release political detainees, give amnesty to several prisoners found guilty of EOKA offences and resume peace talks. Greek Cypriots suggested that EOKA had achieved its main objective, to draw the world's attention to Cyprus, and would not break the truce. They argued that as long as there were a military administration and the UK Government did not resume negotiations with Makarios, there could not be long-term peace. There were still occasional curfews, but, in Nicosia, the barbed wire barricades dividing the walled city were removed.

DESPITE THE truce, British service lives continued to be lost by accidents on the Island's treacherous roads, mines that had been laid earlier, so-called 'friendly fire', accidental self-inflicted injuries and medical conditions. RAOC Lance Corporal James Breheny did not survive surgery at BMH, Nicosia on 9 July. Two days later Sapper John

Hollely drove over a landmine. Corporal Derek Delaney and two of his RAOC friends, one of whom was Ronald Fryer, died when their truck overturned near Dhekelia on 16 July. The day after, Lance Corporal David Perry of the Royal Military Police was killed in a traffic accident in Nicosia.

Other traffic accident victims were Able Seaman Peter Fowler of HMS *Delight*, who was hit by a car as he was standing with other seamen outside the South Staffs' camp on 18 March; Private D. Bullock of the Duke of Wellington's Regiment on 10 May in the Troodos Mountains and Private Ian Collins of the Royal Berkshires on the 23rd. Driver Geoffrey Tuffee of the RASC died on 21 June. On 6 July, Corporal John O'Gorman of the Royal West Kents crashed his Land Rover in the Karpas.

Private Clarence Harker of the Duke of Wellington's Regiment, aged 19, was accidentally shot in a 'friendly fire' incident while on duty in the Troodos on 12 May. Sergeant W. E. Critchley mishandled his revolver on 8 June and killed himself. Another UK Police Unit officer, Sergeant A. J. Coote, died the next day in an unrelated incident.

The RAF, like the Army, counted its deaths too. When Canberra bomber WH114 crashed into the sea off Akrotiri seconds after take-off on 8 July there were no survivors. The dead were Flying Officers Robin Parsons and Hugh Whittle, with LAC Donald Thickbroom. In other non-EOKA related incidents, the RAF lost Flight Lieutenant Jack Thompson the day after Grivas announced his truce in March; Corporal Jeremy Head died on 17 June and LAC David Turnbull on the 21st.

Adding to the toll of fatalities, there were Grenadier Guardsman Christopher Rathburn on 10 April; Lance Corporal Bernard Foxton of the Royal Horse Guards; Sergeant Hugh Brodie of the Royal Army Education Corps, who died on 4 June; and RSM Victor King of the Grenadier Guards on 31 July.

The most dramatic and shocking death was probably that of QMS Graham Casey on 31 May in a training exercise in which Marine Commando David Henderson participated. The Royal Marines were learning how to drop down ropes from Sycamore helicopters that would be used to rush them into action wherever they were needed on the Island.

Henderson knew the full story: 'At Nicosia airport the RAF pilots could hold the helicopters steady, as we dropped down, but at higher altitudes in the mountains it was a different matter. The approach would be fine and hover would be achieved, but without warning, the craft could drop a foot or two like a stone or swerve off to the side, so any poor sod on the rope at the time was either dropped with a thump on the deck or dragged through the treetops. But the pilots got the better of the sideway waltzing and off we set to the training area. It consisted of a small field with a surrounding low wall on which we all sat awaiting our turn.

'I completed my descent with my squad and had just returned to the wall when I became aware of some commotion around the helicopter. Apparently it had come down with the rope trapped under one wheel and its ground

The funeral of Peter John Fowler, RN, at Wayne's Keep Military Cemetery.

crew was signalling the pilot to take off again so they could pull it free. We heard the engine speed up and the craft rose up a few inches but then it went into the most violent sideways vibrations with the pilot being thrown from side to side and trying desperately to keep hold of the controls.

'The ground crew flung themselves flat on the earth and we all followed suit, reckoning that if they thought they were in danger, why wait to find out? Hellish sounds echoed around us as the craft thumped down and fell over on its side, with the rotor blades still turning, threshing and gouging the rough soil. We pressed our faces further into the mud as pieces of the blades and stones screamed over our heads. Slowly the noise died down until all that we could hear was the engine still banging on. The pilot struggled back into the cockpit and turned it off.

'Very slowly we got to our feet and looked around to see if anyone had been injured. At first glance and after a rough count of heads, it seemed that we had all got off without a scratch, with the exception of the QMS who was sitting close to the wall, which was dripping a sticky substance. Suddenly one of our men threw up and exclaimed: "Oh Christ, his legs! Where are his legs?"

'A section of the helicopter's rotor blade had hit the QMS with such force that it sliced off his legs. The substance on the wall was what was left of his bones and muscles. As we stood shocked and gawped, our officers and NCOs reached him, laid him on his back and placed tourniquets on the stubs of his legs. It was too late to save him. He had died from shock.

'When a medevac helicopter reached us, a high-ranking RAF officer was on board with the first aid boys. He made the pilot of the crashed helicopter fly them all back to Nicosia in their craft so that he could regain his confidence.

'On our way back to Platres, we didn't say a word. At camp, our sergeant had the canteen opened after a heated exchange with the NAAFI manager. That evening we tossed back quite a few beers and Keo brandies, but our minds remained filled with the images we had seen. One by one, we silently drifted off to our rooms.'

THE POLITICAL roundabout went on spinning with statement and counter statement coming from the three governments that wanted their interests guaranteed before any face-to-face discussions took place. In Nicosia, Dr Kutchuk, after taking guidance from Ankara, rocked the four months of relative calm by declaring on 24 July that he wanted Cyprus to be partitioned along the 35th parallel, with the Turks taking everything north of the line. It included Nicosia. He added that Turkey was being magnanimous as it had the right to claim the whole Island. As far as he was concerned the Radcliffe proposals were in the garbage bin and negotiations would have to start on the basis of what he now advocated. He said that he relayed his views to both London and Washington.

As Grivas honoured his word, Governor Harding progressively eased the Emergency Regulations, including revoking the law which allowed the death penalty for anyone caught with weapons or explosives. Then, for the first time since March, an EOKA leaflet appeared on the streets on 8 September. It was signed 'The Leader Dighenis' and headed 'No human force can suppress our struggle while the British are still in Cyprus'.

In characteristic style, Grivas accused the British of arming the Turks against the Greeks and encouraged Turkish mobs to attack them to create an atmosphere of division. He called on his followers not to reciprocate – 'EOKA will give an answer when it sees fit'. He claimed: 'It is only when the British have left Cyprus that peace will come to the Island's two communities, which have so far lived in harmony.' He ended his bombast: 'If it becomes necessary I shall appeal to the Greek nation and the political world of the free fatherland urging them that in view of the Anglo-Turkish conspiracy against us they should actively partake in our struggle and revise their alliances according to Greek interests alone. I am confident that my voice, the voice of a fighter well known to the Greek people, will undoubtedly be heard.'

Athens responded with a rebuke for 'The Leader'. In a public announcement the Greek Government said it would not tolerate his interference in homeland politics. The nation's foreign policy was not decided by his 'heroic organization' or any province: it was determined by the elected Government, which protected the country's wider and permanent interests. Grivas, evermore the megalomaniac, replied in another leaflet: 'We are stronger than ever.'

In August, Michael Davidson, the deputy editor and co-founder of the *Times of Cyprus* decided it was time to move on to new pastures. He was disillusioned, he said, by watching Cyprus 'decay into medievalism under the Harding administration' and the lack of justice in the Island's Special Courts. At the age of 61, he went to Aden to report another 'small war'. His departure from the Island went unnoticed by the authorities.

THE SECURITY Forces continued their operations, but there were more British military personnel prepared to risk tours of the Island, even on foot. National Service conscripts Alastair White and Pete Wynn were both based at Episkopi. For a week in late September, they trekked the countryside, living 'rough' or finding overnight accommodation where they could. On their return, White wrote a long letter home about his experiences. These are extracts from that letter, which he passed to the author.

Episkopi,
1 October 1957.

DEAR FOLKS,
Well, I've just spent the most fabulous week in my life. I made sort-of notes on the journey, and will try to form a comprehensive account of our trip, but some of it is a bit beyond my powers of description. The two of us left Episkopi about 14.00 on Sunday, 22 September, armed with little more than two blankets and a tin of sardines and headed off in the general direction of the hills.

Everywhere we went we found the Greeks very hospitable, real country folks like ourselves. Either that or two-faced twisters. After about two hours hard walking uphill, we arrived at the village, where a farmer friend of my companion lives. It's a typical southern Cyprus farming village – stone houses, flat roofs, all white washed and scattered about higgledy-piggledy; hens, goats and sheep running around all over the place.

When we reached the cottage of Pete's friend, Christos Kontandinos, he made us very welcome. His house is a single-roomed, stone-built, no-window affair with simple furnishings and containing all his worldly goods, including his hens. We spent the night there.

At the start of the evening meal Christos offered me a glass of clear liquid, which I thought was an aperitif. Not wanting to hurt the old boy's feelings I downed it after a ritual

Alastair White and Christos Kontandinos.

Christos Kontandinos and his family host a dinner for Alastair White (extreme right).

of clinking glasses and all that rot. Boy, did I feel it! It was as if my inside was on fire. It served its purpose, however, for I ate like a wolf. I think I had been poured a treble of *Zivania*. This is a traditional Cypriot spirit produced from the residue of grapes that have been pressed during the winemaking process. It's colourless and vicious. Christos, of course, didn't speak a word of English, and we knew no more Greek than 'good morning', 'goodbye', and 'thank you'. But it's amazing how we can converse by sign language, and more often than not, generate a great deal of amusement. Partly by gestures and partly by telepathy, we gathered he was setting off at 02.00 for Vouni, where his missus was and so we elected to go with him ...

We arrived at Vouni just as dawn broke at 05.30. It's in the heart of the grape-growing country, where EOKA is very active. The village has about 2,500 inhabitants. The village was a fine sight in the morning mist, with the people all setting about their daily chores. At first we were greeted with incredulous stares and the people shouted '*Anglicos! Anglicos!*' For the next week, everywhere we went people stared, as often as not in a not-too-friendly way. But

after we used our few well-tried Greek phrases, they thawed a little and wanted to know from where we had come, they would ask us where we were going and much more ...

After meeting Christos's wife we went to the coffee shop. The coffee costs two pence a cup and with it you get a glass of water. You pour some of it into the coffee, sip a little water, followed by the coffee and the rest of the water. It's a ritual that both Greeks and Turks perform. I really go a-bundle on the coffee. It's totally different from *Nescafe* or any of that rubbish.

After the coffee, we went to the local butcher to get some meat. There was a big group hanging round outside. Soon two men marched down the street carrying a newly-slaughtered sheep around their necks. Everyone rushed to grab the best part of the poor beast. For the next 15 minutes, there were loud arguments and the sound of chopping. At last Christos emerged from the shop with about two yards of the sheep's guts trailing behind him.

Christos took the meat home to prepare, accompanied by us. When the meal was ready, we were given a chair at the table and fork and invited to dig in. The meal lasted till after 16.00.

Six hours of solid eating and drinking. When it was all over, the family pushed back the table and gave us a selection of Greek songs – you know that queer, off-key stuff you hear on short wave radio. Of course, we applauded politely and said 'very nice', et cetera, et cetera … Then they insisted we get up and sing. I didn't know the Greek for 'sore throat', so after a hasty conference, we decided to give our hosts a spirited rendering of *Nellie Dean* and *On Ilkley Moor Ba'tat* and were rewarded mightily with great applause.

The marathon meal over, we continued our village tour. As the sun went down, we returned to Christos's house, expecting to go to bed. But no, we were met with another meal. Meat, spuds, beans, rice, bread and wine. As you can imagine, having been up and about since 01.00, we were ready to go to bed and made signs that we would sleep in our blankets on the deck. These hospitable folks, however, insisted we sleep in their beds. Too tired to argue, we climbed in. There were two double beds in the room. The two of us in one, the farmer, his wife and their two daughters in the other. Six to a room and two beds. And I slept like a lamb!

Came next morning and we were up and off to the coffee shop for an early morning constitutional and began the long trek towards the Troodos. We covered the first half by bus. And what a bus! It was no more than a large van with four seats shoved into the back. They told us it could carry 19 people. I counted there were 28, including us, dozens of baskets of grapes, earthenware pots, bread, wooden stakes and goodness knows what. The roads are just dirt tracks, and we were bumped and jarred something horrible, but there was no danger of falling out – we were wedged in so tight. I'll never forget that journey.

Suddenly we found ourselves on the main road towards Troodos. What a difference! Tarmac surface, huge *Walls* ice cream billboards, stalls selling cold *Coca-Cola* and English-styled shops on the route. After the isolated villages we had seen, I felt they tainted the simple purity and beauty of the countryside. But we had to stick to the main road, as it was the only feasible way up, so we slogged

onwards. At dusk we found a grassy knoll to spend another night beneath the stars. We had an almond tree to ourselves, so almonds were on the menu that night!

It was now four days since we last spoke to an Englishman, four days relying on our pidgin Greek. We were about 2,800 ft. up and heading in the general direction of Mount Olympus, 6,403 ft. above sea-level. Supper finished, we started to collect brushwood for mattresses, and at seven we rolled over and dropped off.

We rose at 06.00 after 11 hours' sleep and I changed my sox. They were solid with sweat and dirt. Breakfast consisted of mackerel, cheese, bread and water and then we were off, striding cross-country, taking a short cut to Platres. The route followed the side of a steep valley, which reminded me of Glen Nevis. We crossed the top of a 200 ft. dam. It was sensational.

We pressed on to Platres, which we reached in about half an hour to find it was bustling with troops and gunfire echoing up in the hills. Had the 'troubles' started again? We were soon put at ease, when we learned the gunfire was caused by a rifle club practising.

Platres is a lovely place, a real tourists' delight. The buildings are magnificent, resembling Swiss chalets, but with a style of their own. Pine trees all over the place. The presence of troops had its effect on prices. We had a coffee costing us 50 mils as compared with 10 mils in the villages.

On we went again, next stop Troodos. The road became steeper and for the rest of the day we slogged our way up and up. It began to get cooler and big clouds gathered. We even had about 30 seconds' rain. The scenery was fabulous. As we got higher and higher, we could see right across the island. At last, we reached Troodos village in the late afternoon. It was now decidedly chilly. We were a bit dubious about spending the night in the open air, 6,000 ft. up. There was a forces' leave camp up there so we hoped to spend the night there. Holiday camp, it was not. Barbed wire all round, policeman at the gate and guards patrolling everywhere.

We went to the reception desk and waited

about an hour to be informed by a snooty woman it was a place for 'officers only' and we should 'clear off' forthwith. So we departed thinking very naughty things about NAAFI 'holiday' camps! Next we tried a local hotel, but it had closed after the summer season.

There was only one thing to do: cadge a bed at an army camp in the area. We found the Royal Marines. They were real good, tough, blokes and gave us safe refuse. They thought we were nuts, of course, walking around the Cyprus countryside place without being ordered. The top of Mt Olympus was only 500 feet from where we were.

Anyway, next morning we rose before the lark and made our way upwards through the pines to the radar domes on top of Mt Olympus. but we were stopped from going all the way to the top by an army sentry from the signals' facility, which was based on the peak of the mountain. So we just hung around and waited for the sun to rise. It was blooming cold. We were above the level of the clouds and when the sun came up, the colours were terrific. I wanted to take a shot of the sun cleaving the horizon but found I was down to the last exposure. By the time I changed films, the sun was half way up the blinking sky.

We packed and made off straight away, down the other side of the mountains – going north. About a mile later, we stopped for breakfast – a tin of grapefruit, sardines, bread, cheese and water. I must say I felt quite fit on this diet. It was our staple food for about a week. Halfway down, we rounded a bend and saw quite an unexpected sight. Stretched below us, extending for miles, was a huge open-cast asbestos mine. I've never seen anything like it before. I can't say I knew asbestos was mined. As we walked, pine-covered slopes gave way to green, fertile valleys. We stopped awhile and watched a village potter at work. Fascinating. It was much warmer now and a distinct difference from the previous night on the mountains.

Next day we were given a lift on an army lorry. The driver was headed for Famagusta, a distance of about 100 miles, so we decided to go there too. In Famagusta we found another NAAFI-run leave camp – called 'Golden Sands' – where we stayed a couple of nights. It was a grim and miserable place, but we put up with it. Goodness knows how these army blokes can stay there a fortnight and love it. But they do.

I hired a bicycle and went to the town. The bike was about seven sizes too small, had a slow puncture, handlebars that were loose and then the brake cable snapped. Worse, I got lost and was pulled up for riding down a one-way street. Quite a rollicking evening in all.

Monday morning we decided to head back to camp. After a frugal breakfast, which we supplemented with bread and marge purloined from another table when the bloke wasn't looking, we found a lorry travelling to Episkopi, jumped on it, and here I am. It's taken me two-plus days to write this blinking letter – and I've got to write the same to Margot, Richard, Stan, Ian, Dave, to name but a few. So if you don't get another this side of Christmas, you'll know why.

Alastair.

ON 21 OCTOBER the news broke that Field Marshal Sir John Harding would be giving up his Governorship of Cyprus to be replaced by Sir Hugh Foot, who would take up his duties on 1 December. He was known for his liberal outlook. The UK Government stressed that his appointment was not a political one and his administration would pursue well-known existing British policy. Greek Cypriots hoped Foot's arrival would end the Emergency Regulations and herald the return of Archbishop Makarios. Dr Kutchuck of the 'Cyprus is Turkish' Party (*Kibris Turktur Parti*) said the prelate's return would 'encourage and provoke the Greeks to show hatred to the Turks', who would not sit idle in the face of attack. He expected Sir Hugh would 'take the initiative in effecting the partition proposal, which is the only permanent solution to the problem'. His party's slogan was '*Ya taksim ya olum*' (partition or death).

Grivas, again in a leaflet, his favourite means of communication, advised Greek Cypriots to neutralize 'the traps' that Sir Hugh would bring. They should stand firm and their slogan should be 'All or nothing, now or never'. The Cyprus problem could never be solved without Archbishop Makarios and then only on a basis of self-determination. All other proposals, such as self-government or independence, the leaflet said, must be rejected outright.

Many informed Greek Cypriots were depressed by Grivas's latest statement. They wanted to show Sir Hugh the friendly face of Aphrodite's Isle and here was Dighenis threatening the new Governor that unless he – Grivas – got his own way, he would resume terrorism. They wondered if Makarios would soon find out that the EOKA leader had become the tail that wagged the dog.

On 4 November Sir John and Lady Harding left Cyprus for the last time on board an RAF Comet from Nicosia Airport. The RAF Regiment provided a Guard of Honour. Harding said he had given up the post of Governor not because of any differences with the UK Government, but because he had completed his contract and his mission. The Security Forces, he pointed out, had proved, by their skill, courage and perseverance that terrorism could be mastered and stopped from dictating policy. He was asked if he felt that any of the measures he had taken had been too stringent. He replied: 'Certainly not. I was up against a ruthless, brutal, and implacable organization supported by an unscrupulous Church, and I do not believe the job could have been done in any other way ... The security organization is such that it can deal effectively and properly with any further outbreaks of terrorism. I hope no one will be so rash and wicked as to start this business again.'

An anonymously written poem published in the Cyprus Police magazine expressed the view of all those who wore the Queen's uniform:

As Governor to this small island came
A soldier, battle-scarred, but very great.
Not great in stature, nor as just a name
But for his courage and simplicity.

True as the steel, worn nobly at his side.
Straight and unwavering as an arrow's flight.
Firm as a rock, beset by every tide.
In spite of hatreds and hostility.

Amid the strife, he led us on unswerved
Making decisions hard for any man.
Encouragement he gave to all who served
Regardless of creed and nationality.

Thank you Sir John and you Kind Lady too.
For we and all our comrades in this isle,
Are better men for what we learnt from you.
A perfect Knight of great gentility.

AFTER GOVERNOR Harding left, Grivas continued to 'punish' or eliminate Greek Cypriots who either offended him or belonged to AKEL, the Communist Party, but even in 2009 nobody was quite sure when he ended his 'truce'. The authorities reckoned it was over on 21 November, when an explosion blasted a hole below the waterline of the *African Prince*, a British merchant ship, loaded with copper ore from the mines overlooking Morphou Bay. Fortunately a Royal Navy destroyer was in the vicinity and her crew made only a short delay.

Then, on 27 November, there were two far more serious incidents. In Limassol, Superintendent E. N. Peirce of the Special Branch was shot and seriously injured in a carefully planned attack. Because his police car was always followed by a Land Rover with armed policemen, Grivas said three gang members were involved. 'The first man forced Peirce to a halt by riding his bicycle in front of him; the second was ready to give covering fire if anyone tried to interfere; and the third, a youth of fine spirit called Pavlos Pavlou, ran up to the car pulling out his gun,' Grivas said. 'Once more a sixth sense warned Peirce: he turned suddenly towards his executioner just as Pavlou fired through the open nearside window, and received the bullet in his right eye. Our men ran to their bicycles and made off in the stampede. His career was at an end and I slept the better for it.'

Was this the moment that EOKA hostilities resumed? 'No,' replied Grivas, 'it was merely a necessary interruption.'

The second incident occurred at RAF Akrotiri a few hours later. In a series of explosions, four Canberra bombers and a Venom fighter were put out of commission completely and their hangar seriously damaged by fire. No one was injured. A witness to the explosions was Corporal Ron Deane, whose job as a radar mechanic was to inspect and service 'the clapped out WW2 kit'.

He remembered: 'Apart from tinkering with the controls to get the equipment in working order, I used to top up the generator with fuel. It was the generator truck that took the first hit. I was standing in line with two other NCOs about to enter the camp cinema to see that gorgeous Liverpool lass Yana, when BANG! I jokingly quipped, "I hope that means I can have a day off tomorrow."'

The press claimed that this was the most expensive sabotage attack in the 30-month history of the EOKA conflict. The cost was estimated at more than £3 million.

RAF firemen bring the hangar blaze under control.

The remains of one of four Canberra bombers destroyed in the hangar fire, 'the most expensive sabotage attack' in the history of the conflict.

Grivas said the sabotage had been carried out by two electricians employed at the base – Yangos Kaponas, code-name *Pericles*, and 17-year-old Andreas Vassiliou, who told him how they did it. According to Kaponas, he had smuggled in two bombs – no larger than oranges – one hidden in a bag of grapes and the other in a pot of pork jelly, a Cypriot delicacy. Inside the base, he passed the bags to young Vassilou. When a guard was looking elsewhere, he dodged behind the Canberras and attached the bombs. They were set to go off at midnight, but failed.

The next day, Vassiliou was very nervous, not knowing if or when the bombs would detonate. He was the first out of the hangar

The RAF Akrotiri fire, which EOKA claimed to have started.

when the end of work whistle blew at 16.00. With other contract employees he headed for their contractor's office to complete their time sheets. Just as they got there, they were lifted off their feet by the first explosion. When the police arrived, he was amongst those arrested, but, as nothing could be proved against him, he was released and continued to work for the RAF for the next two months before heading to the hills to join an EOKA mountain gang.

'Sorry to disillusion you, but there were no EOKA bombs, as I am aware,' the late Jock Devlin, a man with 41 years' RAF experience, wrote to the author. 'The servicing crew that had refuelled all the aircraft in the hangar forgot to close their fuel caps. As you are no doubt aware, the explosion happened as sunset was approaching, when there were hundreds of security lights in use. One of the lights on the Canberras' hangar wall had a problem and caused a spark. High-octane fumes do not mix too well with electric sparks. The explosion and destruction were the result.'

He continued: 'My info came from the station's security officer. The RAF chose not admit the truth and run the risk of accusations of incompetence and so allowed EOKA to claim responsibility and take the blame. Nevertheless, the serving chief got a bollocking!'

It is worth noting that even Grivas in his *Memoirs* is cautious in claiming the incident had been sanctioned by him and only quoted what Kaponas allegedly claimed. In today's EOKA list of heroes, the latter's name is not given.

As far as the British Government was concerned, the truce was well and truly over. 'During the last few weeks,' John Profumo, Parliamentary Under-Secretary for the Colonies, told the Commons, 'the terrorists have renewed their campaign of violence. EOKA has not, in fact, carried out the pledge it gave when Makarios was set free. It has not stopped terrorizing and intimidating the people of Cyprus. It has merely changed the pattern of its operations. During the last two months there

have been six victims of EOKA killers – all Cypriots; four major acts of sabotage; a Turkish girl wounded and her fiancé murdered by her side; and two days ago an English police superintendent was seriously wounded.'

To add to the Government's woes, leaflets appeared in the main towns of Cyprus from a new underground organization called the TMT – *Turk Mukavemet Teskilati* (Turkish Defence Organization) – 'to protect the Island's Turkish community against any kind of attacks'. Headed 'Bulletin Number One', the leaflets called on Turks to 'stand by for our instructions'.

For some time Turkish Cypriot leaders had debated how they should counter EOKA's *enosis* demands. They knew that without material support from Turkey any counter-organization could not be effective. Rauf Denktas, one of the Colonial administration's prosecuting counsels, Kemal Tanrisevdi, and Burhan Nalbantoglu travelled to the mainland, discussed the situation and returned with Ankara's support.

As a result, Riza Vuruskan, a Turkish Army Colonel, was sent to Cyprus. Over several months, he secretly shaped the Cypriot Turks into a disciplined, armed body along lines not dissimilar to those of EOKA. The TMT's objectives were three-fold: to stop *enosis*, to protect Turkish Cypriots from EOKA attacks and to create conditions for *taksim*, partition of the Island. *Mucahits* – fighters – were recruited, trained, armed and their actions coordinated from the center by Vuruskan. Like EOKA, the TMT was anti-Communist and did not deal kindly with 'informers'. By the time EOKA finished its war with the British, this new organization would push Turks out of 13 mixed villages and murder 84 individuals who had Greek Cypriot associations.

WHILE TURKS and Greeks squabbled over the ownership of Cyprus, a Dr Aris Shevki de Lusignan, a 56-year-old British subject of French-Turkish extraction emerged from his

Turkish Army Colonel Riza Vuruskan, the founder of the *Turk Mukavemet Teskilati* – TMT.

Islington, London, home to demand 2,000 ducats a year from 1914, the last time, he said, his family had been paid.

As a direct descendant and sole surviving heir of the de Lusignan family, his claim, he said, could be traced back to when his ancestor, Guy de Lusignan, bought the Island from Richard the Lionheart. His family had ruled Cyprus until 1492. When the Venetians took over that year, they agreed that the Lusignan family would be entitled annually to the money to the last heir, he explained. He added that even when Cyprus was completely absorbed into the Ottoman Empire in 1573, the Turks continued to pay and still did after leasing the Island to Britain in 1878. The payments stopped only when the British made Cyprus a colony by the Treaty of Lausanne. Logically, Cyprus should belong to him, said Dr Lusignan.

Before the doctor's claim could be tested in court, two other claimants to the Island came forward. A Mr George Menie, a French citizen, lodged his case with the United Nations, while the third person, who chose to remain anonymous, was a resident of Famagusta.

Mr Menie insisted that his ancestors' ownership of Cyprus pre-dated Richard The Lionheart's invasion in the twelfth century and he threatened to raise an independent army, if necessary, to take it back, after which he would build a casino to rival the one in Monte Carlo. The third person maintained that he belonged to the Themistocles' dynasty that had ruled Constantinople and so he was the rightful ruler of Turkey and, therefore, Cyprus, too.

All three claimants were convinced they could bring lasting peace to the Island, but for the time being, more pressing problems lay on the Governor's desk in Government House, where, soon, Sir Hugh Foot and his family would reside.

A TMT Leaflet warns Greek Cypriots not to attack Turks.

CHAPTER NINETEEN

'Nobody cared about Cyprus': the British boycott

'There is nothing Cypriot about Cyprus except its name. In this beautiful beleaguered island you are either a Greek or a Turk. From the leaders of the two communities downwards the chasm of suspicion and hatred, which separates them, is frighteningly wide.'
Anthony Nutting, Foreign Office Minister

SIR HUGH FOOT was caught in a forest of nettles even before he landed at Nicosia Airport with his wife and eight-year-old son on 3 December 1957. When his aircraft stopped briefly in Malta to re-fuel, the Governor designate was passed a telegram from the foreign and local newspaper correspondents in Cyprus, telling him that they planned to boycott his arrival 'owing to the totally inadequate facilities for the press to attend the swearing-in ceremony tomorrow, in spite of the invitation to 172 others', and 'the unco-operative attitude of those responsible'. As a consequence, said the gentlemen of the press, they had 'no option but to forgo the entire arrival, including the afternoon press conference'.

Those who had studied the tall 51–year-old diplomat, who came from a distinguished Cornish family and whose siblings – Michael and Dingle – were active politicians on the left, would have known how much he enjoyed pomp and circumstance and the attention of the media. Not surprisingly, by the time he arrived, the local authorities had agreed to allow the facilities the correspondents wanted and they were present to flash their cameras as he stood smiling and waving on the footsteps of his aircraft. But the oath Sir Hugh expected to take, wearing his plumes and feathers, within the Venetian walls of old Nicosia's

parade ground in front of a large audience of seated guests, was not to be. Government officials told all concerned that the ceremony had been transferred to a smaller venue – a room in Government House – because the winter rain had waterlogged the parade ground. The truth was different: all the Greek Cypriot guests had turned down their invitations and there would have been too many embarrassingly empty seats on show.

Without having to change from his ordinary dark suit into any more formal dress, Sir Hugh was sworn in before a selected collection of civil servants and became the latest – and it would prove to be the last – British Governor of Cyprus. Then he was off to meet the press, radiating optimism.

The Foot family at Government House.

Governor and Lady Foot.

A cheerful Sir Hugh Foot.

'I come with an open mind and no prejudice. We can together find a way out of our
anxieties and perplexities. I am sure nothing
but disaster can come if we neglect the opportunity now before us,' he nodded at the seated
Greek Cypriot scribes. 'At all times I shall be
accessible to those of the Cypriot people who
want to see me. I believe that an overwhelming majority of the Cyprus people will wish to
accept the offer of friendship and understanding and cooperation, which I make.' For the
benefit of the ferrets from Fleet Street, he
dropped his smile and added: 'If there are
those who reject it and resort instead to
disorder and intimidation, they will succeed
only in delaying progress towards a just settlement and making Cyprus suffer.' That was the
kind of comment that would resonate well
within the corridors of No. 10 Downing
Street, he thought.

Standing behind the rows of journalists
bespectacled John Reddaway listened unim-
pressed. He had been Field Marshal Sir John
Harding's tail-wagging Rottweiler, but feared
he would have to show his teeth to the new
Governor, who, he was convinced, had arrived
with a library filled with platitudes, but no
real understanding of the situation.

As a young man, Sir Hugh had been posted

to Cyprus for the first time in 1943. Only a
few weeks later, he assumed the acting
Governorship at the age of 35, when the
incumbent, Sir Charles Woolley, returned to
the UK on leave. And sure enough, he brought
up the subject at his press conference. 'I refuse
to believe that the Cyprus I knew is going to be
permanently a burden of bitterness,' he said.
He promised immediately to meet and greet
the local people, as well as their leaders,
before coming to any conclusions and suggestions for solutions.

Robert Holland, the historian, considered,
'Long-standing advisers like Reddaway feared
that Foot would start under the fatal illusion
that Cyprus was the same place he had left
years before.' On the other hand Reddaway, as
he points out, 'arriving in Cyprus in 1938, had
discovered much more than his *metier*; he
found a place he loved and to whose interests,
as he understood them, he was prepared to
devote his life. Not only did he learn Greek, he
married one in Phaneromani Church in
Nicosia, scene of some of Makarios' most
fervent speeches after he became Archbishop'.

General D. A. Kendrew, the Director of
Operations, and his military commanders,
too, had grave doubts. They viewed Foot's
self-belief that he could charm the various

factions into peace as illusory and thought that it would, in fact, only exacerbate the security situation by leading Turks and Greeks alike to think he was on their side and were free to act as they liked.

The very next day, the new Governor began his travels, whirling around the Island until 12 December – 'to see for myself' – and asking for 'a credit of time', but, as Holland argued, 'Sir Hugh was not sent to Nicosia because of any new panacea, but to buy a bit more time and space. Neither in Ankara or Athens was the response to Foot's elevation promising. In the Turkish capital it was distinctly threatening. "Ominous" was one official description of developments, coupled with a call for immediate partition. From the Greek capital a British journalist reported the feeling that not much could be expected from a Governor appointed by a Conservative Government "whether his name be Harding or Foot, or as Sergeant Buzfuz said in the Pickwick trial, Nookes or Stokes or Stiles or Brown or Thompson". In contrast, Makarios maintained a tactful silence.'

Not so Colonel Grivas. His response to the Governor's plea was a leaflet in which he offered a 'handshake', if he allowed Makarios to return. 'Cyprus is a volcano,' Dighenis said. 'Your attitude will decide whether it will erupt again or remain silent.' Privately, Grivas had no respect for Foot. 'I regarded the self-created aura of "liberalism" surrounding him with distaste: I was sure it was fraudulent,' he wrote. 'I offered the hand of friendship – if his hands were not already tied by the Colonial Office. Having given this proof of my goodwill I sat back to await developments; if, as was all too likely, Foot's promises came to nothing, we could renew the fight with the people's full approval and the understanding of the world.

'I knew how to deal with the open enemies of Cyprus, but our "friends" were more troublesome: professed liberals like Foot, professed democrats like the British Labour Party, professed allies like the Greek Ministers, changed course with monotonous regularity until it sometimes seemed that all three were combining against us.'

Sir Hugh Foot, in his memoirs, spins a very different account of those early days. 'As soon as I had taken the oath of office on the day of my arrival I sat down with General Kendrew and the Deputy Governor (George Sinclair) and the Administrative Secretary (John Reddaway) to tell them what I had in mind. I called on the surprised Greek Mayor of Nicosia, Kiki Dervis, at his home; walked through the streets of Nicosia; and saw the Turkish leaders repeatedly.' He told Dr Dervis: 'Things are bad – very bad, but give me a break and I know we can find a way.' Yes, replied the Mayor, bring back the Archbishop and allow us self-determination.

Addressing the Turks, he said that the Security Forces were 'constantly on the watch to see that their interests were being properly safeguarded'. All well and good, countered Dr Kutchuk, but we demand partition.

Warm-hearted and genuine Foot may have been – deluded was what others thought – as he enjoyed the applause of onlookers when he arrived at the 'Mason-Dixon Line' that separated the Turkish and Greek quarters in Nicosia or read that a Greek Cypriot woman

The 'Mason-Dixon Line' is established in Nicosia to keep Greeks and Turks apart.

had told the *Times of Cyprus* that 'he must be a good man, because he isn't a bit afraid', but his advisers wondered whether he was keener on popularity than problem-solving. Reddaway told him bluntly: 'The attitude of the Greek Cypriot community towards any course of action will be dictated by EOKA rather than by the degree of confidence they may have acquired in Your Excellency.'

Holland wrote that the Governor's advisers stressed that policy 'had to be conducted on the basis that Greek loyalties had been lost to the gunmen of EOKA and could never be recovered. But the contention that the loyalty of the great majority of the population had been forfeited beyond recall went against Foot's grain. The winning of confidence and goodwill were to him what colonial government was all about. It was also what he was good at.'

And so he continued with his walkabouts, waving and smiling, and assuring all sides they were on the path to a better tomorrow. He had no doubts about his personal safety and recalled later that an Army officer had once asked the Commissioner of Police why he went through streets 'unguarded' and received the reply: 'The Governor at the moment is the safest man in Cyprus.' Foot added: 'It was true. I was not facing the daily danger, which confronted our soldiers and police – or even British civilians. No Greek or Turk was going to attack the Governor who had just arrived. They wanted to see what I would do. Many of the leaders remembered me from the time when I was in Cyprus before.'

Although Foot worked unflaggingly to build what he called 'bridges of trust' by racing by helicopter to distant villages to hear farmers' complaints, riding his horse through others, apparently unaccompanied by ranks of bodyguards, lighting candles 'for peace' in an Orthodox Church or appealing in person to surprised shopkeepers in the tense Turkish part of Nicosia and then strolling down Ledra

Sir Hugh Foot often rode to Cypriot villages.

Street – 'Murder Mile' – to shake hands with passing Greek strangers, his 'credit of time' was running out. By 10 December, it was exhausted. 'The credit of time you asked for has run out and so has my patience,' Grivas announced in another of his leaflets. 'The fight must go on ...'

Prompted by EOKA, 1,500 teenagers went on the rampage in Nicosia, shouting '*Enosis! Enosis!*' The trouble began when students assembled in the courtyard of the Pan-Cyprian Gymnasium and started singing Greek national songs and chanting slogans. Police and troops arrived on the scene, fired a couple of warning tear gas shells and the headmaster, Dr Spyridakis, then assembled the school in the courtyard and told them to go home. Most did, but an unruly batch stayed behind and climbed to the roof to continue their demonstration. When police reinforcements arrived the battle began in earnest. Stones and bottles were rained down from the roof and an attempt by the police to storm the building was driven back by a tear gas bomb thrown by the mob inside. Eventually the police did force a way in.

Meanwhile the trouble had spread to other parts of the town, and a Greek shot a Turkish policeman. Though not seriously injured, the

Turks heard he had been killed. They gathered in Ataturk Square and advanced on the Greek quarter, wreaking vengeance on shopkeepers and others. Trucks were overturned and set on fire, windows were smashed, and shots fired at random into the air. Outside the offices of the *Cyprus Mail*, David Lewis, the paper's assistant editor, lay on the ground as bullets crashed into the walls of his office. Eventually the police brought the situation under control.

The trouble was not confined to the capital. Under the shadow of Othello's Tower in Famagusta, Greek Cypriots clashed with police in a two-hour battle. At Ephtakomi, someone defiantly flew a Greek flag. Attempting to tear it down, a British patrol was stoned by the villagers.

Sir Hugh Foot, only a week in Cyprus, was shocked by how easy it was for intercommunal trouble to flare without apparent cause. But still he could not believe that this could be the start of another EOKA campaign, just a setback for the 'clear run' he had expected. With 100 people hurt and 68 under arrest, the Security Forces forced him to agree a curfew, leaving the streets empty except for military patrols and tiny coteries of Cypriots standing in doorways, sullen, watchful and bewildered.

The next day the trouble continued. A convoy of army vehicles was ambushed and stoned by students. One soldier suffered bad head wounds. In two other villages – Ayios Amvrosios and Lapithos – more crowds of angry youth attacked patrolling soldiers. In Polemi, Turkish Cypriot policemen fired on rioting students after their car ran into an improvised roadblock. Another clash was reported in the village of Yailousa.

Undeterred, the new Governor decided to walk through the old town of Nicosia, to make a personal assessment of the areas where communal clashes occurred. Accompanied only by Commissioner B. J. Weston and a couple of his own entourage, he moved freely, talking to Greek and Turkish shopkeepers.

Here and there Greek Cypriots stopped to complain about damage caused by Turkish rioters. He told them he would bear their complaints in mind. He then went to a shop and ate several pastries. One man came forward, shook hands with the Governor and said: 'We want union with Greece.'

Sir Hugh Foot replied: 'I want to hear what everyone wants,' and continued his tour. Gradually, as people realized who he was, there was spontaneous clapping and cheering and those following him grew into a crowd. There were shouts of 'Bravo, Foot' and Greek Cypriot women extended their hands towards him. Girls on a balcony returned his wave. As a further gesture of goodwill, he visited the Central Prison and talked to 12 female inmates, held as suspected terrorists. He ordered the release of two of them, arguing their continued detention was inadvisable on medical grounds.

The crowd's enthusiasm for Foot's demonstration of a new style of Governorship lasted all afternoon, but as dusk fell, two bombs exploded at Nicosia's Kyrenia Gate, while in Kyrenia itself, grenades were thrown at a police patrol. A mobile reserve had to be rushed to the scene to disperse the crowd with a baton charge. Twenty-one students, 15 of them girls, were detained.

The US Consul watched these developments with a wary eye and kept Washington informed. He said that Sir Hugh had bought some 'precious time and goodwill', but that it would count for nothing if he failed to make a breakthrough within a month with a new settlement plan, stamped with the authority of Whitehall. He warned that the Governor's mission, as it was, would collapse 'with the gravest consequences for everybody concerned with Cyprus'.

GRADUALLY THE 'spontaneous' daily demonstrations levelled out as Christmas approached and the Governor settled down in his office to draft his impressions for his masters in London to read when he returned in the New Year. He was convinced that his policy of meeting and greeting Cypriots in their environment was paying dividends. It was, after all, the start of the season of goodwill. He could even quote parts of the latest EOKA leaflet in which Grivas said he was 'sticking to the rules of the truce' because Greek Cypriots were 'honourable and sincere people'. So far the terrorists had not murdered any Britons for nine months.

The next day the Security Forces shot dead Theodorus Georghiou, the 35-year-old EOKA leader in Styllos, after he tried to break out of the cordon placed around his house. When troops searched the farmer's premises, they uncovered a miniature arsenal of small arms and bomb-making material.

This operation was contrary to a promise Foot had given to the US Consul when they got together earlier and he had asked for support in arranging a meeting for him with Makarios in Athens. In return the Governor said he would 'lean over backwards to avoid exacerbating the situation through incidents involving Security Forces'. His pledge was not shared with where it mattered most: John Reddaway and General Kendrew, probably because the latter would have opposed it. The Army preferred the stick to Foot's carrot in dealing with the insurgents, while Reddaway knew that any discussions between the Governor and the Archbishop would make the Turkish Cypriots think the British were selling out to Greek demands.

Against Reddaway's advice, Sir Hugh, always trusting his own instincts more than the knowledge of others, delivered a Christmas present to the Greek Cypriot community by announcing the release of 89 male detainees from Camp K and 11 women held elsewhere. In addition, he said that 12 men held in a monastery near Nicosia were free to leave and that restrictions on the move-

Greek Cypriots released from detention by Sir Hugh Foot.

ments of 600 more would be relaxed. (In his memoirs, he claimed: 'I ordered the release of 600 of the 700 in Detention Camps.')

The Governor ended his broadcast with the words: 'I earnestly call on everyone who occupies a position of influence in either community to help me, to say no word which might increase friction, to take positive action for the full restoration of friendly understanding ... Let the New Year be a new year of new hope.'

Across the Island, church bells rang non-stop for almost 24 hours. Convoys of taxis collected the released prisoners and ferried them to Nicosia, where the Greeks thronged Metaxas Square and celebrated in a carnival atmosphere. Amid cheers, the freed females were carried shoulder-high into the Phaneromeni Church, where they formed a circle near the altar and sang Greek nationalist songs, the choruses of which were punctuated by shouts of 'Long live Makarios' and '*Enosis*' from a congregation of 3,000.

Hearing the news of the releases, the morale of British troops fell as fast as the apple onto Newton's head. Why should they risk their lives in capturing terrorists if the Governor then set them loose, probably to start fresh attacks? Civilian expatriates wondered the same and thought the answer lay in the

Governor's weakness for making grand gestures without considering the consequences.

As if freedom for EOKA suspects were not enough, on Christmas Day Sir Hugh visited the Bishop of Kitium, the head of the Greek Orthodox Church in the absence of Archbishop Makarios, to wish him a Merry Christmas, although it was the same church that provided the funds that paid for the weapons used against the British Forces. His next stop was to the Pyla/Pile Detention Camp to see the inmates. 'It was necessary,' he said, 'to shake everyone out of the sense of gloomy hopelessness which had descended on the Island.' The prisoners were more surprised to see him than his critics who heard he was there.

Foot greeted them like old friends and met the committee elected by the detainees and apologized that he could not release them all until EOKA extended its truce indefinitely to allow a final solution to be found for the Cyprus Problem. He was heading back to London shortly to share his new-found knowledge of the Island's difficulties and hoped to return to grant them and Cyprus freedom, he said. They cheered his words and he beamed his appreciation. With a wave, he said: 'I regret I cannot wish you a Merry Xmas, but I do wish you a Happy New Year.'

That evening Sir Hugh addressed the troops in a radio broadcast. He urged them to take a 'line of positive friendship' towards Greek and Turk alike. 'We must go flat out on the course and not spoil it by half measures,' he said. He agreed this policy might be dangerous in view of past violence, but he continued, 'we are not going to get out of the mess we are in without taking risks'.

His audience was not convinced; nor was Grivas. He noted in his diary: 'I continue to believe that the Governor is a cunning and dangerous diplomat who is trying to win the people over and estrange them from EOKA.'

Boxing Day found Aphrodite's Isle returning to its pre-Christmas ways. At the north Cyprus village of Ayios Ambrosios, Vassilis Michael, aged 40, was beaten to death; near Famagusta, in east Cyprus, Andreas Epiphaniol, aged 22, was stabbed outside his house and died in hospital; and in the west Cyprus village of Loutros, a chauffeur, Christodoulos Solomiou, aged 40, was hacked to death with axes while he was in bed. For EOKA the holiday was over.

In Nicosia, Dr Kutchuk, the Turkish Cypriot leader, repeated that partition was the only peaceful way forward. There was no comfort for Sir Hugh coming from Ankara either. Mr Menderes, the Prime Minister, on his return from a NATO meeting, backed Kutchuk and added that partition was the only way to restore friendly Turco-Greek relations. For the British Forces holding the ring between the two communities and, at the same time, hunting down EOKA, came the news that they would be remaining on active service for at least another three months.

FOOT HAD arrived in Cyprus at the start of December convinced that if the debate on the Island's future were removed from the international area and left to the British and Cypriots alone to sort out, a trouble-free, mutually acceptable formula for self-government and independence could be agreed. There were only four essentials to the success of his plan: 'A period of five or seven years before any final decision; an end to the Emergency; the return of Archbishop Makarios to the Island; and, negotiations in the Island with the leaders of the two communities to evolve a system of self-government.'

On New Year's Eve, the day before Sir Hugh left for London, General Kendrew handed him his thoughts in writing about the security implications of the Governor's 'peace plan'. The document did not make pleasant reading. Pulling no punches, Kendrew said

Foot had not taken a realistic view. He argued that whatever gains Foot had made with the Greeks, there was a corresponding loss of faith among the Turks. 'It is no use assessing what is to be done in terms of the real damage to the Turks, it must be assessed in terms of how they choose to see it [the plan],' the General pointed out.

He contended that Foot's recent actions were giving EOKA the opportunity to rebuild and, simultaneously, weakening the Security Forces who relied heavily on the loyalty of the Turks and especially those who now formed the bulk of the police. The Governor had to face the facts that before any settlement, peace had to be established and this meant defeating the terrorists sooner than later. His troops could not sit on their hands until it was too late for them to perform their duties effectively.

The latest EOKA leaflet, signed 'Dighenis' validated Kendrew's argument. It stated unequivocally: 'If our wishes are not met, we will start an armed struggle soon ... we will not be misled by the machinations of the British diplomacy, we will not accept any agreement and will not lay down arms until liberty dawns over our island.

'We offered our adversary peace or war, we wait calmly and resolutely; if our wishes are not met we shall start an armed struggle soon, in spite of hysterical shouts by the Tories, which are accompanied by suspicious shouts by some fellow travelling Labour politicians. I attach no significance to spectacular demonstrations by the Cyprus Government, which, on the contrary, I consider traps. I expect deeds leading to a solution of our national question. These deeds will determine whether the New Year will see the dawn of the fulfilment of our aspirations or the beginning of new struggles.'

How keenly Foot listened to his Director of Operations is open to speculation, but it appears that he did not. Appearing cheerful and jaunty as ever, he faced the media as his aircraft stood ready at Nicosia Airport to fly him to London on New Year's Day 1958. His pitch: if the Greeks, the Turks, the Cypriots and the British themselves would all show restraint, Britain's new plan for self-government on the Island could be made to work.

Like some biblical prophet, he towered above the seated scribes and declared: 'On our journey to the Promised Land we are not yet at the Jordan. We are just about at the Red Sea. The waters of despair may part for us to go over. And when we have gone over they may swallow up the pursuing forces – the fears and animosities of the past. But we still have a long way to go and hard times ahead.'

In London, Foot mapped out his road to peace for the benefit of Prime Minister Macmillan and other Cabinet Ministers. His objective: to agree upon a set period of self-government for Cyprus, after which the Greek majority could decide in favour of union with Greece if they still wanted it. The ministers heard what he said, but their minds were focused on the General Election later in the year and they did not want Cyprus to become a point of contention with the Labour Party. So they nodded and Sir Hugh left assured that his plan had been 'accepted in full'. He wrote: 'The time-table was worked out. I would go first to Ankara to talk to the Turkish Government, then to Athens to explain the new policy to the Greek Government and to Archbishop Makarios, then back to Cyprus to announce the policy and the end of the Emergency.

'I knew of course that the Turks, who were to be approached first, would strongly dislike some aspects of the policy, and I wrote to the Deputy Governor on 7 January from London to say that everything would depend on whether the British Government would stand up to the Turks. But I thought that our absolute assurance that no final decision on the future of the island would be made without Turkish approval might outweigh their objections. They were in fact being given an absolute veto on long-term policy. Much more difficult to persuade Archbishop Makarios and the Greeks, it seemed to me. But the return of the Archbishop to Cyprus, the ending of the Emergency, the promise of self-government might be sufficient to sway them.'

Unknown to the Governor, however, General Kendrew had secretly sent his critical paper to the War Office, where it was taken seriously. In private, the Cabinet was divided. Most members were inclined towards more talks with the Greek and Turkish Governments before any discussions with Makarios. Others were dubious that security measures should be relaxed until agreements were in place. All believed Foot was being 'a little bright-eyed about it all', but one official mused: 'You never know, perhaps it's just exactly the kind of faith that is needed.' A few days later, he was proved disastrously wrong.

When Foot returned to Cyprus on 18 January he had nothing concrete to offer the people or suggest to his advisers. Some of the jauntiness in his stride had been lost in the streets of London. He could only ask his friend, US Consul Belcher, to pass a message to Makarios asking him to stop Grivas from ending the truce as this would 'slam the door' on hopes for the self-government of a united Cyprus.

The Governor was starting to see the sparks of a three-way struggle that were about to ignite another full-scale explosion of fear and hatred, whatever the thinking in Whitehall. The TMT was building up its resources to fight Grivas and show the British it was as resolute for partition as the EOKA leader was for *enosis*.

Whether Grivas saw TMT as a greater threat than the Greek Cypriot left wing is a moot point. In January he took the leash off his dogs of war to savage 'informers' and 'traitors'. On the 21st, they murdered a carpenter in a coffee shop at Komma tou Yialou and another Greek Cypriot, Michael Petrou, in Lysi. Both belonged to the Pancyprian Federation of Labour (PEO). Typical of EOKA's barbarity was the manner in which Savvas Menikou was murdered. He was tied to a tree in the center of Lefkonico, while church bells rang to call out the villagers to witness the spectacle of teenagers stoning him to death in front of his wife and children.

The next day the trade unions called a 48-hour strike in angry protest. Its leaders shouted: 'The working class must in a body express its indignation over these brutal crimes.' Union demonstrators took to the streets of the main towns holding banners that denounced EOKA as terrorists and fascist thugs. About 3,000 union members marched through Nicosia. At one stage it looked as if their parade would degenerate into a riot, but their leaders maintained order. 'They appeared to be a compact, well-drilled force,' *The Times* reported, 'but there was no mistaking the angry indignation of these men, who are deeply incensed over the killing of their colleagues. At three points the procession stopped by prearrangement and the demonstrators, on bended knee, observed a one-minute's silence for their dead colleagues.'

A smaller left-wing parade was stoned by schoolboys in Trikomo, Grivas's birthplace. Four people were injured, including three women who were openly shouting 'Down with Grivas and EOKA', an utterance as rare as a raindrop in the Gobi desert during the three years of the Emergency. It was the first time that Greek Cypriots had ignored the intimidation they had endured since the outbreak of the conflict.

Andreas Zhiartides, the 39-year-old leader of the PEO, was gaining the reputation of a man capable of challenging Makarios's authority in Cyprus by pointing out the chasm that existed between his supporters and those of EOKA, backed by the Island's bishops. 'I appeal to the people to condemn these acts against our organization,' he told an audience in Limassol. 'I appeal to the Ethnarchy and other organizations to speak and not be silent, otherwise they will be responsible for anything that may happen on account of these incidents.'

In Athens, Makarios received a telegram from the PEO. It warned that Cyprus was on the verge of a civil war between Greeks and said that he must use his influence to stop it. It was followed by an appeal addressed to the Island's mayors and the Ethnarchy by the widows of the murdered men.

'We, the death stricken widows whose husbands were murdered by the masked men on the night of 21st January, we who shed the bitter tears for the loss of our protectors consider it necessary to forward an appeal to every Greek Cypriot, and generally to the responsible political leaders of the country.

'The death of our beloved ones fell upon us like a heavy block of stones. Our eyes are still wet with bitter tears. We never thought that murderers would be so cowardly and without any reason make us dress in black, and deprive our children of their father.

'Do the murderers not understand that the method of political murders is fratricide? Do they not realize that to achieve the extermination of the Left-wing party and the Trade Union Movement thousands of women will be dressed in black, and that thousands of innocent children will be deprived of their fathers? Do they not realize that such madness will lead us to civil war?'

From Athens came Makarios's measured reply: 'We are grieved that recent events tend to present the Greek population of Cyprus as divided. It would indeed be tragic if, as a result of misunderstanding or tendentious impressions, the unity of the Cypriot people were disrupted ... Disunity, especially at this critical stage, will only serve the interests of British colonialism.'

Andreas Zhiartides ordered his members back to work and cancelled further demonstrations, but sent out a coded warning clearly intended for the EOKA leader. 'It appears, however,' he said, 'that there are some Cypriots who – instead of concerning themselves with winning our political demands abolishing the Emergency, bringing back Archbishop Makarios, releasing detainees, gaining an amnesty for political prisoners, and remaining civil liberties – are interested only in exterminating all those who do not belong to their political group. That is what the two political crimes show.'

Grivas realized that EOKA had taken a step too far and while he was not willing to stop killing those who opposed him, he could not afford to lose the support of the Church and Athens. He was now forced to justify his actions, something he abhorred. He defended his murderers on the grounds of self-defence, argued that the deaths were not due to a difference in political ideologies and accused AKEL, the Communist Party, of 'collaboration' with the British for causing divisions between the people.

AKEL's answer was quick and to the point: the party challenged Grivas to agree to an independent investigation of the incidents and accept the findings. If any AKEL member were found to be a 'traitor' and 'guilty of treason', they would be discredited, expelled and left to face the consequences. EOKA did not reply.

On 26 January, Foreign Secretary Selwyn Lloyd ordered Foot to join him in Ankara to sell the latest peace plan to Turkish Prime Minister Menderes and his Foreign Secretary Fatin Zorlu.

'Once in Ankara when we had sat up most of the night drafting a statement of the British position and when we had gone back to the final conference with our Foreign Minister, Selwyn Lloyd, and our Ambassador in Turkey, Sir James Bowker,' Foot wrote, 'Zorlu flicked through the pages of the document and threw it contemptuously on one side without even reading it.' The Governor concluded that he was 'the rudest man I ever met'.

Robert Holland, the historian, added: 'Rarely, if ever, can the Governor of a British colony have been treated with such calculated contempt by a foreign government, and a supposedly allied one at that. Yet what happened in Ankara was mere shadow-play to the main event in Cyprus. No sooner was Foot virtually incarcerated in the Embassy in Ankara, than serious mayhem broke out in Nicosia.'

THE DAY Foot arrived in Ankara, the first of two Turkish Cypriot demonstrations began, but rain stopped play and everyone returned home drenched and waited until the sun shone next day at dawn. By sunset, central Nicosia was a bombed-out battleground under curfew and out of bounds to service personnel. Five Turkish Cypriots lay dead – three shot by the Security Forces when the Suffolks, Glosters and members of the Royal Artillery's 43rd LAA were called up to quell the riots. At least 100 people were injured, of whom 40 were servicemen, two buildings lay smouldering and the Turkish Cypriot policemen were

Turkish demonstrations grow larger.

found wanting, reluctant to stop their kinsmen.

The trouble started at 08.30 when youths raised Turkish flags in Ataturk Square and stretched a large banner across Kyrenia Street outside Dr Kutchuk's house, proclaiming partition. At midday, senior police officers asked his deputy, Osman Orek, to persuade a growing crowd of 1,000 to disperse peacefully. At the Kyrenia Gate, he stood on the old city walls and shouted: 'Our just claims on the Island are in the hands of our leaders who we trust. We have raised our voices and made our protest known to the world. Now let us all go back to our daily work and keep calm.'

A stout Turkish woman waved a blood-soaked handkerchief and screamed back: 'We Turks are not afraid of losing our blood.' Students began singing Turkey's National Anthem. A youth pointed at the Arabic inscription carved in the Gate, which said, '*Oh, Mohamed, give these tidings to the faithful: victory is from God and triumph is very near. Oh, opener of doors, open for us the best of doors.*' In accented English, he told a foreign reporter: 'The only door to a settlement will be partition.'

Later in the afternoon, Rauf Denktas, one of the founders of the TMT, addressed

Turkish Cypriots riot in Nocosia in January 1958.

Turkish Cypriots demand *taksim* – partition.

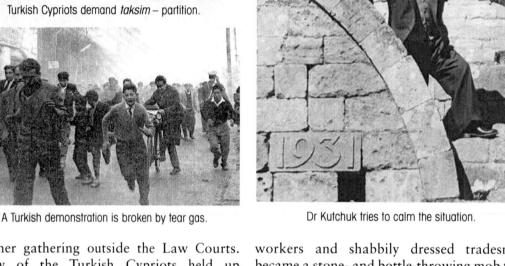

A Turkish demonstration is broken by tear gas.

Dr Kutchuk tries to calm the situation.

another gathering outside the Law Courts. Many of the Turkish Cypriots held up placards with the words 'Out with Governor Foot' and 'Long live Harding'.

Denktas's star was in the ascendancy and the people listened intently to his words, but remained calm, until an Army Land Rover careered out of control and smashed into elderly Mehmet Ali, a street sweet seller, and a woman. Ali died in hospital from a fractured skull and spine, and the woman also died. Events kaleidoscoped into a pattern of fury and savagery, as the crowd chased the Land Rover, forcing a young soldier to fire his Sten gun in the air to allow the occupants to escape.

The crowd now turned their attention on the Divisional Police Headquarters in Ataturk Square, which was surrounded by a thin khaki line of nervous British troops. Shawled women, uniformed schoolgirls, white-collar workers and shabbily dressed tradesmen became a stone- and bottle-throwing mob that defied tear gas and smoke bombs and quickly gained the upper hand. The Army was forced to withdraw in the face of more than 2,000 rioters, some lobbing Molotov cocktails at military vehicles, setting them alight. Turkish police were noticeable by their absence.

Eventually Inspector Kemal of the Mobile Reserve stepped out from the police head-quarters and was immediately picked up and carried shoulder-high by the students in the front line for the crowd to see. They then dropped him on his feet and kissed him on both cheeks. An angry Chief of Staff, Brigadier R. V. Fitzgeorge-Balfour, arrived on the scene and ordered his men to counter-attack. They assembled and quick-marched out in Indian file from the main entrance to the Law Courts, their wire shields raised and batons raised, followed by a gaggle from the Mobile Reserve.

Throughout the afternoon troops and young rioters played hide and seek through the narrow streets, while Turkish policemen hung back in small groups watching. When a stone hit one of them, the thrower rushed up to apologize to his victim. Looking on, Inspector Kemal sighed: 'All this ... all this from the mistake of one driver.' He gloomily waved his arm over the scene. Several times they ignored orders from UK Police Unit officers, even when they were threatened with charges of dereliction of duty. In the ensuing battle, an army sergeant climbed on the roof of the Tekke of the Whirling Dervishes and pointed his pistol at one of the Turkish youngsters who was hurling stones with pinpoint accuracy at the soldiers.

'The little bastard just laughed. He knew I wouldn't shoot him,' the soldier said later. 'Then five shots rang out. I saw him – he was one of the best-dressed men in the mob. He wore a belted gabardine raincoat. He pulled out a .38 revolver, knelt and fired five shots at my men. Fortunately he missed.'

Then a taxi raced towards a line of soldiers blocking the street. He ignored their shouts to stop and forced them to leap aside and open fire. The driver escaped death, but three of his four occupants, including Mustafa Ahmet, 20, and Ibrahim Ali, 19, were killed. The fourth was taken to hospital, where one of his fingers was amputated.

By 18.30, the tear gas had dispersed. The only clouds over the city came from the smoking ruins of a Greek-owned garage and the Ardath Company's cigarette factory near Ataturk Square, where three fire engines were still spraying water. Peace had been restored. The worst riot since the start of the Emergency was over. It was now up to the officer in the Land Rover that caused it to explain himself. The Major, a Staff officer at 50 Brigade HQ, said: 'At Kyrenia Gate my car was heavily

stoned and the window smashed. I could not go back, so I went forward, but found another crowd in front of me – a vicious crowd. Then on the spur of the moment I did the one thing I thought was right. I told the driver to put his foot on it.'

The authorities lifted the curfew the next day, after a meeting between representatives of the Turkish community and negotiators of the Security Forces held to discuss the restoration of normal life in the Turkish section of the city. The Turks undertook full responsibility to ensure normality prevailed and guaranteed that there would be no further violence, but one of them remarked that 'if EOKA renewed its campaign of violence, he doubted whether the Turks would be on the side of the Security Forces'.

The agreement came in time for thousands to attend a mass burial of the Turkish dead, in accordance with Colonial Government's promise not to station troops along the route of the cortège.

All morning Turks began arriving from outlying villages and joined town dwellers at the Selimiye Mosque for the funeral service at noon. Afterwards, the dignified crowd left in a quiet procession ahead of the dead, led by community leaders, relatives and two Turkish policemen on to Ataturk Square and through the Kyrenia Gate to the cemetery two miles from the north of the capital. The coffins followed, carried by four young men dressed in the colours of the football teams two of the dead had supported.

George Sinclair, the Deputy Governor, observed from a distance and commented: 'It is sad to say this but I believe my Government in London has just realized how serious the Turkish Cypriot community is in its opposition to *enosis*. A new page has been turned in our thinking!'

Rauf Denktas insisted the Turkish Cypriots had staged a 'peaceful' demonstration against *enosis* and in favour of partition, adding: 'The

British responded to it by doing what they had not done to the Greek Cypriot anti-British demonstrators for three years [from 1955 to 1957]: they shot dead seven [his figure] Turkish Cypriots who were doing nothing unlawful.'

In London, *The Times* editorialized: 'The Cyprus issue has today reached the point at which its possibilities and its dangers alike are at their maximum. Whatever Sir Hugh Foot may or may not achieve, he has shifted a logjam and the logs are beginning to tumble down the river – whether into calmer or rougher waters no one can as yet foretell ... The reactions in Cyprus itself have been more ominous.

'They have been both novel and violent. There were demonstrations by the Turkish Cypriot community, as opposed to the Greek, against the British Government. Now right-wing Greek Cypriots have apparently begun murdering left-wing Greek Cypriots. Both these developments are intelligible if there is an assumption in the Island – as there certainly is – that a settlement is pending which would be favourable enough to Greece for the Greek Government to accept it. Not only would such an assumption provoke the Turks. It is conceivable that Grivas, the leader of EOKA and a fanatical right-wing nationalist, might have his own reasons at this point either for getting rid of leftist elements or, since he has a vested interest in violence, in terrorizing any Greek Cypriots who might seem prone to accept a settlement.

'But, however dangerous and disconcerting the renewed violence in the island, what passes in Ankara is now more important. Though the details of the so-called Foot plan are a matter for conjecture, the gap between British and Turkish policy is not. On the matter of partition Turkish insistence goes a good deal beyond British assurances.

'As has been said many times before, there can be no solution of the Cyprus question unless all parties are willing to concede some-thing. Great Britain has come a long way from the days of the "never, never" policy. Circumstances have certainly influenced Britain. Her strategic needs have changed. Any arrangement that would allow her to maintain bases in the island under conditions of peace and security would now suit her national needs and international obligations. But the other parties must come part of the road to meet her. No settlement can be reached on the basis that either *enosis* or partition is the sole outcome of self-determination.

'The arguments for reaching a settlement now are surely overwhelming. All should reflect that an indefinite prolongation of the dispute can lead only to chaos in the eastern Mediterranean ...'

SIR HUGH left Ankara humiliated on 31 January and arrived in Nicosia without any standing in the eyes of the people and his staff at Government House, but like other experienced colonial administrators from the start of the British Empire, he was pragmatic and endowed with chameleon qualities to change his outlook. Reddaway and Kendrew could not have been happier.

Two days later Foot went on the radio and read a tough script prepared by Reddaway. From now on, said the Governor, his first priority was defeating EOKA and bringing violence to an end, even if it meant 'dislocation of everyday life' and that 'innocent people have to suffer'. He made it plain that the Security Forces would use every means at their disposal to subdue those who acted against peace. While EOKA was uppermost in his thoughts, the TMT was advocating a policy of passive resistance and non-fraternization with the British.

From London, Foot received orders that he must demonstrate even-handedness between Greek and Turk. To prove this point, he should prepare to visit Archbishop Makarios in Athens now that he had visited and talked to the Ankara leadership. The edict did not appeal to him. He did not want a reprise of the indignities he had endured in the Turkish capital. Whatever his doubts and the local advice given by Reddaway and others, Foreign Minister Selwyn Lloyd was heading to meet Prime Minister Karamanlis and demanded Foot join him,

In Athens, Lloyd, in smooth diplomatic language, told the Greek Government that unless it supported British endeavours, Turkey might use military means to enforce its demands and the outcome inevitably would be partition. Shaken by the mention of war, the ministers were forced into a corner to think. As a sop to the British, they offered a meeting with Makarios. Lloyd did not think it appropriate for him to meet the prelate and pushed Foot forward, explaining that he, after all, was the Governor of Cyprus and the two could relate better to each other on the current situation on the Island.

In the best traditions of cloak and dagger operations, the Governor was smuggled into the Hotel Grande Bretagne through the back door and up the stairs to the Archbishop's suite at five minutes to midnight. Unlike Fatin Zorlu in Ankara, Makarios was courteous and conciliatory. It was, after all, the 13th of the month and 13 was his lucky number. The two men even agreed that Cypriots alone should decide the future of Cyprus, something Foot had always argued. 'He [Makarios] said that if he had not been exiled, a solution would already have been found,' Foot noted.

'There was an undercurrent of sympathy between the two men,' Holland wrote. 'A more natural one than had existed between Makarios and Harding, since they were both, in their different ways, politicians manqué. But neither was really at the centre of power, and all they could do was to go through the motions.'

Their 30-minute meeting ended with Makarios promising to restrain Grivas and blessing Foot on his way out of the room. The Governor was then forced to run the gauntlet to the airport and his RAF transport aircraft to escape a horde of Fleet Street's finest, who had been tipped off, probably by a member of the hotel staff.

A more determined Foot returned to Cyprus. His wife recalled: 'The honeymoon period was over and the Greek Cypriots began to revile us as they saw they could not persuade us of the "non-existence" of the Turkish problem.' Two months after his appointment as Governor, his original proposals had 'utterly failed' and the situation was far worse than before, he acknowledged. Gone was his original idealism.

[He] spent many hours at night lying wide awake in the dark ... thinking, thinking, examining every facet of the complex situation ... not Turk and Greek in Cyprus only, but the small chessboard with the Turkish and Greek pieces and the hands of other nations moving them – Athens and Ankara, Washington, London, Moscow ... all for remote purposes, with nobody apparently concerned to help this little Island and its tormented people to be delivered from its agony,' Lady Foot wrote. 'Nobody cared about Cyprus ... not, it seemed, even the Cypriots themselves, who had got carried away by the excitement of international intrigue and were so little sure of what they really and truly wanted for themselves.'

Sir John said: 'I realized that we had reached the end in the road in asking the Turks and the Greeks to agree on a plan.' He would not pussyfoot any more. 'Now we must decide what we would do, and not ask them but tell them.' In his memoirs, he explained his new approach: 'If the Greek and Turkish Governments wouldn't come to the conference table, and if we couldn't shift the negotiations back to Cyprus by ending the Emergency and bringing back the Archbishop, very well, we would work out a detailed constitutional programme ourselves.

'And this time we wouldn't ask everyone or

anyone to agree. We would make it clear that whether they agreed or not we would go ahead with our plan. We would not allow violence or anything else to deflect us from it. This time we would ourselves take and keep the initiative. Within two months we were ready with our new proposals.'

BEFORE THESE proposals were placed on the negotiating table, there would be much more violence and more tragic deaths of British servicemen. On 26 February, HMS *Alamein*, a battle class destroyer, was patrolling off the coast of Cyprus, stopping and searching vessels for illegal arms and terrorists, when a tragic accident occurred with the loss of three sailors. She had been doing her job for six months.

'There wasn't a full-blown "war" at sea, but day after day was spent at Damage Control State 2,' said a member of the ship's company. 'That's one step down from "Action Stations". Some vessels didn't like being told to heave-to and wait to be boarded and tried to outrun us, but *Alamein* was capable of 35 knots and so we caught up easily. A shot across their bows convinced them of the futility of trying. A few of the gunrunners sometimes answered with small arms fire and we had the scars on the upper deck to prove it. I never considered the rules of engagement. That was the skipper's job. He led, we followed.'

Crewmen with whom the author has talked have conflicting accounts of what exactly happened that fateful night, but all agreed that after searching a suspect ship, the 10 members of the boarding party were being hauled back on *Alamein* in their motor launch when, halfway up, a cable snapped and the sailors were tipped into the sea.

'I was the senior Plot and Radar Petty Officer and the incident took place during my watch,' Tom Redman said. 'I was also in charge of the safety of the boats and men in the boarding party. They were fully armed with

rifles and heavy Lanchester machine guns and kitted out with webbing and ammunition. They also had the use of life jackets – the old, green, cork-filled type. They were very awkward and cumbersome. When the after-fall parted, only two of the sailors were still in the boat, one on board and the other hanging from the jackstay, his legs trailing in the water. The irony was that the sea was flat calm, but we were sailing at 12 knots and those who went into it were soon out of sight.'

The coxswain of the boarding party added: 'At the time, our ship was darkened in an action state. There was panic, screams and cries for help. Searchlights were turned on and the ship's whaler was lowered with two oarsmen. I was one of the first to be picked up. We then pulled out Able Seaman Peter Allengame, who appeared to have drowned. But we made every effort during the next two hours to revive him. We collected the other survivors, but couldn't find Petty Officer Thomas Meyrick and Telegraphist Anthony Gibbs. Their bodies were never found, although the PO's pistol was recovered. Gibbs is still down there, with his radio equipment strapped on.'

Able Seaman Allengame was buried at sea. HMS *Alamein* sailed for Beirut, where the crew mourned the dead.

AT HIS Limassol hiding place Grivas was still plotting. He saw EOKA, although reorganized, losing ground. He was gradually forfeiting his support in Athens, Makarios was prevaricating and his gang leaders were restless to break the truce and start the battle again. 'It was clear by the end of February that we could hope for nothing from Athens, but before I could carry out my threat to part company with the Greek Government it resigned over an internal crisis on 2 March,' Grivas wrote.

In an attempt to regain some of his popularity, he began to present EOKA as warriors of Christ, championing freedom and stopping atheistic Communism from taking over

Cyprus and the world. Filled with Messianic zeal, he typed his next leaflet:

'Christ is the leader of all fighters. He is the leader of all heroes because he himself became the greatest hero during his terrestrial life. Our captain Jesus is championing our struggle. He is inspiring, strengthening and fortifying us ... Where can we turn our eyes now that all our erstwhile Allies have closed their doors to us and have kicked us out into the four winds? We can only look to our eternal and real friend, the Saviour Jesus, for help.'

Passive resistance would be Grivas's latest weapon of choice in his new battle on the side of God. In late February, he informed Greek Cypriot wholesalers to stop importing any goods from the UK that could be manufactured in Cyprus. On 4 March, he ordered an Island-wide boycott of all British products. He demanded that the populace refrain from smoking British cigarettes, drinking Scotch whisky or entering the football pools, 'which give the English £50,000 a week unnecessarily'.

PEKA, Grivas's political wing, urged that women must learn to use locally woven, finely striped Cypriot peasant *alatzies*, silks and cottons for their clothes. 'In this different form of our liberation struggle, of equal importance and greatness, the Greek daughter of Cyprus will take the leading role and set the example,' proclaimed the zealots. 'She must throw her weight into this great battle for Cyprus and keep her home, her office or her factory clear of all British-made products ... Therefore we propose a decent and proper appearance ... let her prefer local fabrics.'

Grivas's faithful and youthful inductees declaimed: 'It is a disgrace to see Greek women imitating foreign city women of suspect morality and social learning, as we see them in the cinema, in the way they smoke, gamble in their shameless way of dress, their manners ...' A Greek Cypriot fashion journalist, Lana Mataff, recorded how the rules

were enforced: 'EOKA boys on their motor bikes, some in *alaja* striped cotton shirts, roared around the Nicosia streets, pulling down the very fashionable imported paper nylon petticoats worn by the trendier teenage girls to humiliate the wearers and discourage this "British fashion trend".' Those who obeyed developed what the *Times of Cyprus* named 'the passive resistance-style'.

Overnight, British signs were removed or painted over, British goods went unsold and importers suffered economic hardship, which was preferable to threatening phone calls at midnight and thrashings from Greek Cypriot teenagers. Youngsters even informed on their own parents if they spotted a bottle of Gordon's Gin or a packet of Capstan cigarettes in their houses.

In Famagusta, several expatriates and service families organized a counter-boycott by refusing to enter Greek shops or restaurants and trading only with non-Greeks. They achieved nothing, but gained satisfaction from their small patriotic action. The authorities also cancelled orders for Cyprus beer in NAAFI establishments.

The trade boycott was accompanied by snap strikes and intensive 'selective sabotage' of military facilities, such as pumping stations and NAAFI warehouses. 'Killing would be sanctioned only for the purpose of reprisal,' Grivas told his gang leaders. 'Night after night the destruction increased as we blew up water supply lines, food stores and any other Government property that offered itself. At the start of the attacks I chose every target myself and often the time so that I could vary my tactics constantly. By 31 March, however, things were going so well that I gave group leaders a free hand.'

The sound of bombs exploding somewhere in Cyprus became a daily occurrence in March and April. The damage was costing the administration tens of thousands of pounds. The economic costs were becoming unendurable.

CHAPTER TWENTY

Grivas ends the truce:
the madness of Geunyeli

Never attribute to malevolence that which can be explained by incompetence.'
Napoleon

THE THIRD ANNIVERSARY of the EOKA conflict was marked by five bomb explosions in Famagusta and the cold-blooded murder of a Greek Cypriot in Nicosia's Ledra Street. The cargo ship *Grecian* was saved when a limpet mine was found and disarmed. The murdered man was Christos Enslezos, a 55-year-old timber merchant and a father of two children. He was 'executed' because Grivas thought he had become an 'informer' to secure his freedom from detention in Governor Foot's Christmas release of prisoners. The bombs began exploding shortly after midnight and continued at regular intervals at different locations until 10.00. So far EOKA had kept its promise not to attack individual British service personnel intentionally, unless it was in reprisal for a Greek killed by the Security Forces.

What Sir Hugh Foot did next could have lost him his job and his life and caused the British government grave embarrassment. In complete secrecy he wrote a personal letter to Colonel Grivas, inviting him to a face-to-face meeting at a place of the EOKA's leader's choosing. It was a highly dangerous, high-risk initiative. 'I didn't tell anyone, not even my closest military and civil advisers, for the simple reason that if I had consulted them they would have prevented me from doing what I proposed,' the Governor said. 'I knew the

danger of what I did. I knew moreover that Lennox-Boyd would be furious if he ever got to know. Nothing annoys him more than not being told what his subordinates are up to. I knew too that what I had done might well be made public by Grivas.'

'But I thought that Grivas might possibly be flattered by the idea of a secret meeting with the Governor. His vanity and sense of melodrama might do the trick and although he would stick at nothing, I believed that if I did go alone and unarmed to meet him, his honour, as a soldier, would not allow him to double-cross me.'

His letter, dated 10 April, said in part: 'I am convinced that if the present campaign of sabotage continues disaster will result for all the people of Cyprus. In their name and interest I call on you to save them from that disaster by ordering the campaign of sabotage and violence to cease ...

'If it would help I am prepared to go to any place at any time you nominate to meet you and urge you to act on this call. I would come alone and unarmed and give you my word that for that day you would be in no danger of arrest.'

To deliver the letter, Foot contacted Glafcos Clerides privately. The articulate young barrister defended Greek Cypriots accused of terrorist activity and it was known he had Grivas's confidence and the means to contact him. Clerides believed the Governor was a sincere man and well intentioned. He agreed to have the message delivered. Events, however, intervened and added urgency to both the Governor's hopes and fears.

USUALLY GUNFIGHTS were kept on the silver screen of Famagusta's three-storeyed Hereon cinema, but on 14 April, two of EOKA's finest took their revolvers into the street, spotted 61-year-old William Dear and fired five shots at him in broad daylight, before firing a sixth in the air and disappearing into the milling crowds out shopping. The Englishman fell 10 yards from the box office, severely wounded in his chest, abdomen, face and hand. After an emergency operation, he died in a British Military Hospital at midnight two days later. Before he entered the operating theatre, he told investigators the names of his two assassins. Dear was the first Briton to be murdered since Grivas had ordered his 'truce' 13 months earlier. His wife lived in north London.

The day before the Colonial Secretary, Allan Lennox-Boyd, had been asked in the House of Commons how many British servicemen, Cypriot civil service employees and civilians had been killed in Cyprus since 1 January. He replied: 'Eleven Cypriot civilians. No British Service men, police, or civilians, and no Cypriot Service men or police. Four of the Cypriots were killed by other Cypriots, and over the whole period of the trouble, 265 people have died, 142 of them Greek-speaking Cypriots killed by other Cypriots.'

Dear, a member of Special Branch, was a known interrogator of EOKA suspects, all of whom 'The Leader' accused of using torture to extract confessions. He had often warned Dear that he was in the top five of his list for assassination, but the police officer scoffed that there was no terrorist who would dare shoot him face-to-face. His boast proved fatal, because two did.

Other interrogators, of whom there were 12, all had a working knowledge of the Greek language and were paid £1,750 a year for their services. Most tried to keep their identities secret, although detainees soon knew them and passed on their names and descriptions to their lawyers or families.

When the Security Forces arrived and cordoned off the area, the first place they searched was the cinema, where Georghios Kaliyorou, 20, the projectionist, had a bedroom. He had disappeared after the shooting and was a suspect. In his quarters the police found a store of explosives, oozing nitro-glycerine, too dangerous to move. RAOC experts asked permission from the Governor to blow them up *in situ*. Sir Hugh gave it without hesitation. Georghios Papageorghiou, the cinema's plump owner burst into tears. He had recently spent a small fortune modernizing the place and now his pride and joy was to be blasted apart. 'Let me carry the bombs out,' he begged. 'Someone carried them in. They can't be all that dangerous.' His pleas were ignored.

Throughout the day the hunt for Dear's killers went on as far as Boghaz. Royal Engineers set up roadblocks. Hundreds of Cypriots were stopped, undressed and searched. Carrying screwdrivers, spanners and jacks, soldiers dismantled and re-assembled cars at a rate of 50 an hour. They took off wheel caps and headlamps, pulled out luggage and crawled under the vehicles.

As dusk neared, houses and shops close to the cinema were cleared, adjoining streets cordoned off and a warning siren sounded. At precisely 18.51, the bombs were detonated. The explosion rocked old Famagusta's north wall. The building collapsed on itself, snapping telephone poles and crushing hundreds of seats. The Hereon cinema was no more. 'An act of retribution,' Greek Cypriots shouted as all the town's theatres closed for the night in protest.

The next day Georghios Papageorghiou

threatened to sue the UK Government for compensation and promised to re-build the cinema immediately. British soldiers, who had been guarding the rubble overnight, handed him the keys of the front door and told him to carry on.

Alekos Constantinou and Panayiotis Georgiadis (code-name *Icarus*) were Dear's killers and escaped to Kourdali. Their lives were short-lived. On 20 June, they, with two others, were making bombs when there was a mighty explosion, destroying the house in which they were hiding. The terrorists' bodies were found in pieces; some fell in a field 50 yards away. Mystery surrounds the details of exactly what happened, but a 'Black Ops' officer told the author that his team intercepted the group's material and set the timers of several fuses running. Even EOKA today admits that their deaths took place in 'unknown circumstances'.

The remains of the four men's bodies were taken to Nicosia General Hospital. 'Scenes of extraordinary emotion took place at the time of delivery of the dead, on whose bodies the Greek sisters of the hospital laid wreaths on behalf of the medical and administrative staff,' reported a Greek Cypriot newspaper. 'One nurse made a valedictory speech to the dead men. "Your names," said the nurse, "will be recorded on the list of martyrs to the liberation struggle of the Greek Cypriot people, who with a sense of pride reveal themselves before your sacrifice, heroic children of the motherland" ... At about 18.00 the coffins of the four immortals arrived at Spilia where flags at half mast and laurel wreaths hung on posts ... There, on their knees, the communities of Spilia, Kourdali and Kannavia and the inhabitants of the villages of Kyperounta, Livadia, Polystypos and many others greeted with cheers and enthusiastic speeches the coffins borne upon the shoulders of lusty youths, and covered them with Greek flags.

'For some time the terrible accident that left four men dead was surrounded by a sense of mystery regarding the identities of two of the dead, since only Patsalides and Anaxagora were identified immediately. The identity of Panayiotis Georgiades became known while Mass was being performed for all four, while the body of Alecos Constantinou was identified by his tragic mother three days after the dreadful event.'

What remained of Constantinou was buried in Famagusta. An only child, the 22-year-old had lived in the city with his mother, spoke excellent English and worked for the British Army in Dhekelia. He was completely trusted and often brought off-duty soldiers home for dinner.

GRIVAS CLAIMED that Dear's assassination was a warning to the Governor to step back from the military's anti-EOKA actions, which were starting to pay dividends and causing significant problems for the underground organization as it tried to fight against left-wing Greek Cypriots, hostile Turks and the British.

It was not until the 20th, after Dear's burial, that Sir Hugh's letter reached Grivas, with an accompanying, well-reasoned note from Clerides wearing his best lawyer's hat. He advised the Colonel not to meet the Governor as he was acting without the authority of the British Government, but suggested that the truce be continued for another two or three months to give time for negotiations to be resumed with the new government in Athens and to placate international public opinion, but conditional on a fixed time limit for a final settlement.

Clerides also pointed out that General Kendrew was opposed to Makarios's return to Cyprus and wanted the Emergency Regulations to be enforced more rigidly. He added that the letter must not fall into the hands of anyone else in the organization. It would be best, therefore, if it were photographed and the original returned as undeliverable. Grivas agreed the latter, but made no comment on extending the truce or stopping his campaign of sabotage. He did not trust Foot and thought the letter a ruse by Special Branch and the intelligence services to find his hide out. He refused to believe he would receive immunity from arrest even for a day.

Security measures in Cyprus were intensified the same day. Troops stopped over 400 vehicles at Boghaz and rigorously searched them, but the sabotage continued unabated. At Camp Elizabeth, near Nicosia, two tents were set on fire in 10 minutes. Damage to personal property was estimated at £450. There were also bomb explosions in the Episkopi cantonment.

With no reply from Grivas, Foot twice more sent out the same letter through other backdoor intermediaries, adding his appreciation that EOKA had continued the truce so far. This time, the Colonel replied in another public leaflet. The truce, he said, would end, if the British did not stop the ill-treatment of detainees.

To prove the administration held prisoners in good conditions, the Governor invited Clerides to tour Camp K with him and see for himself. As expected, Clerides reported back to 'The Leader' what he had seen. Grivas now added another condition: the truce would last if he approved the new peace plan that was rumoured to be the reason why Sir Hugh was visiting London shortly.

'I am not bluffing, as this is contrary to my character. I do not give in to threats, because courage and fortitude are our main virtues. But I simply warn,' he said in another leaflet. 'As a humanitarian I want to avoid more bloodshed, which this time may be much greater. As commander I have to obey the voice of Cyprus – which commands me to fall or to free her. I ask that they should soon take the initiative in starting negotiations.'

Twenty-four hours earlier a similar warning came from the TMT, which claimed to be 'on the verge of launching a struggle for liberation' and that 'all the Turks of Cyprus are ready to sacrifice themselves and their blood'. In Britain, Nedgati Sagher, the chairman of the London branch of the 'Cyprus is Turkish' Party told a crowded press conference that he had made representations to the British Government to have the Governor 'displaced'. Foot had infuriated the Turks who saw him as trying to pacify EOKA by making deals behind their backs at their expense.

At Government House, Sir Hugh locked his letter to Grivas in the safe of his study. Another of his headline-grabbing initiatives had collapsed like a punctured balloon. Instead he had to summon General Kendrew and his military advisers to discuss tightening security.

ON THE eve of the Governor's departure for consultations in London, Grivas ended the truce and sanctioned another attack, this time against the Royal Military Police. It was carefully planned and executed on 4 May in Famagusta with cold-blooded efficiency.

'I was acting as Duty Sergeant on Saturday morning and it was part of my brief to make out the weekend roster. That weekend we were short-staffed and our duties outnumbered the RMPs available,' explained Charles Bailey. 'After several phone calls, I eventually pulled a roster together, but our OC, Major Blakesley, then asked for two plain-clothes patrols, consisting of two men each, for the next day, Sunday. I had to find more volunteers.

'I thought Lance Corporals Cameron and Turvey would be up for the job. Both were National Service soldiers and would appreciate the extra few shillings paid to those operating in plain-clothes. In addition, I knew they did not get out very often. They belonged to the Provost Unit of the 51 Infantry Brigade Group. As I expected, they jumped at the offer. Because my duty lasted 24 hours, I knew I'd still be present at 08.00 on Sunday to make sure everyone reported and the handover went smoothly. To allow colleagues some rest, I was only able to provide six-hours' "cover" for one of the plain-clothes patrols.'

Although Famagusta seemed quiet at the start of Sunday, a few hours later there was a spate of minor riots in the south of the city, started by youths distributing EOKA leaflets. Uniformed Redcaps were sent to stop them, including those giving 'cover' to Cameron and Turvey in an area which was 'out of bounds' to off-duty troops. Unnoticed by the two young military policemen, a car had been following them. As soon as they were alone, it raced past, its occupants firing. One of the pair shot back, but fell fatally wounded in the road. The other dropped and fell back dead, his body resting on the garden wall of a house.

'My patrol rushed to the area of the incident,' Bailey said. 'It was now clear that the riots had been created to divert our attention from where EOKA planned its ambush. We found our men both had been shot in the back. As usual, nobody admitted to seeing or hearing anything. The perpetrators of the crime were never caught. Even after all this time, I'm still haunted by that day.'

Lance Corporals Bill Smith and 'Lofty' Phillips were assigned to recover the bodies. Smith remembered: 'In the silence of the mortuary, we could hear the wrist watch of one of the dead still ticking. For our lads, time had run out.' Cameron and Turvey were within weeks of their demob and return to the UK. They had become the first British servicemen to die since January 1957. Before flying to London, Sir Hugh Foot reimposed the death penalty under the Emergency Regulations.

Barely was the Governor's aircraft in the sky, when Grivas admitted EOKA's responsibility for the latest outrage and declared: 'If the British Government plans to exploit the Turkish factor to our disadvantage or allow Turkish bases in Cyprus, then it is playing with fire. In our struggle we will not be alone any more.' There had been rumours that Sir Hugh was going to London to discuss yet another peace plan, which, this time, involved the mainland Turkish Army.

The TMT, too, distributed a leaflet, equally fanciful, stating that Sir Hugh was about to put forward 'pro-Greek' ideas that were centred on a 'private agreement between EOKA and Governor Foot'. Following Grivas's style, it gave the British a warning: 'For Turkish Cypriots it is unnecessary now to await orders for new all-out action in case Foot returns from London with an unsatisfactory solution, or tries to impose one on the Turks, who demand nothing short of partition. Give the British all kinds of difficulties in towns and villages. This is a general order. Separate instructions will be given about killings.'

The TMT's next proclamation was directed to the patriotic young: 'Oh Turkish Youth! The day is near when you will be called upon to sacrifice your life and blood in the "PARTITION" struggle – the struggle for freedom ... You are a brave Turk. You are faithful to your country and nation and are entrusted with the task of demonstrating Turkish might. Be ready to break the chains of slavery with your determination and willpower and with your love of freedom. All Turkdom, right and justice and God are with you. PARTITION OR DEATH.'

IF THESE EOKA and TMT leaflets were not enough to make the Island's population spin in fear and confusion, a third found its way on to the streets of Nicosia. It purported to come from a new underground called 'AKOE', the EOKA acronym in reverse, and was supposed to stand for the 'Anti-Killers Organization of Expatriates'. It was hand-scripted in block letters, cyclostyled and said:

CALLING ALL BRITONS
DO NOT BUY FROM GREEKS
IF YOU GIVE MONEY TO A GREEK YOU
ARE GIVING SUPPORT TO EOKA
DO NOT ENTER A SHOP WITH A GREEK
NAME
CHANGE YOUR STALL AT THE MARKET
SUPPORT THE PRO BRITISH MINORITIES
BOYCOTT GREEK SHOPS – BUY BRITISH
  AKOE

A second AKOE leaflet followed:

EXPATRIATES, *what are you doing about it?*

One hundred and six of your comrades, husbands, sons and brothers have been murdered – shot in the back – by EOKA's dastard [*sic*] gunmen.

No Greek Cypriot, be it barman or business-man, chemist or café proprietor, hairdresser or hotel keeper, sewing girl or shopkeeper, has ever 'seen' an expatriate murdered, even when the outrage was perpetrated in broad daylight and in a crowded street. This proves the contention of Dr DERVIS, Mayor of NICOSIA, that all

177/58

CALLING ALL BRITONS

DO NOT BUY FROM
GREEKS

IF YOU GIVE MONEY TO A GREEK YOU ARE GIVING SUPPORT TO EOKA

DO NOT ENTER A SHOP
WITH A GREEK NAME

CHANGE YOUR STALL AT THE MARKET
SUPPORT THE PRO BRITISH MINORITIES

BOYCOTT GREEK SHOPS
BUY BRITISH

A.K.O.E.
ANTI-KILLERS ORGANIZATION OF EXPATRIATES

An AKOE leaflet.

Greek Cypriots are EOKA. Why not take the Doctor at his word?

The braggart GRIVAS and his EOKA poltroons have threatened the Government with 'total war'. Why not take *them* at their word too?

In war 'trading with the enemy' is a crime. Government cannot be expected to pass the requisite legislation, but *YOU* and your friends can stop dealing with Greek Cypriot shops, firms or establishments and give your custom to Moslems, Maronites, Armenians or expatriates, and as far as possible refrain from buying goods manufactured by Greek Cypriots. In this way you can hit back at these gutless yellow-bellies in the place where it hurts them most – their pockets.

'Anti-Killer' Organisation of Expatriates

Please read this and pass it on to a friend of BRITAIN.

It seemed that whoever was behind this anti-EOKA outburst did not realize that AKOE also stood for *Apeleftherotiko Kinima Omofilofilon Elladas* or 'Greek Homosexual Liberation Movement'.

Government House was not quite sure how to react. On 9 May, Mr K. J. Mills sent a copy of the clandestine document to Mr A. S. Aldridge at the Colonial Office with the comment: 'We have no knowledge of origin of this leaflet and although vigorous enquiries are being pursued no information has been obtained. I will of course do everything possible to put a stop to this damaging nonsense.'

The administration may have called it 'nonsense', but the Greeks and Greek Cypriots took AKOE very seriously, especially when it produced a poorly written Greek language version, which was equally badly translated back into English as follows:

Because of the request that we change our name we have accepted the recommendation of the true friends of Cyprus that hate the EOKA and what it represents. From now on, we adopt the simple title 'the Anti-EOKA'.

This name includes everyone who is on the island and understands and comprehends the damage caused by EOKA and openly or secretly hates EOKA. The AKOE was created because there was a need to publish our beliefs and we did publish them. Our aim is not to cause villainy as some people claim. We only want to make the population understand that when they use Cypriot products, buy from Greek shops, visit Greek cafes and restaurants, or fill up with petrol from Greek service stations etc., they put money in the hands of Greeks that were been unable to resist EOKA because of their threats of violence.

We are all Anti-EOKAs. We love peace. We do not believe in the use of military force for the achievement of our aims. We do not believe in the use of any form of violence. We warn all our members that we are opposed in any action, which would lower us to the level of EOKA.

Our aim is to unite everyone opposed to EOKA and for this reason we believe that the use of name 'expatriates' is a mistake because the majority of the men of Anti-EOKA are not expatriates. For this reason, we are pleased to accept in our organization all the peaceful Cypriots, even if they are Orthodox, or Mohammedans, or Armenian, or Maronites and of course every member of the British Empire.

We also seek the complete boycott of all the shops from which English-language signs were removed. If you do not see the name of a shop, bar, cafe or hotel written in English, the householder of this shop is a collaborator of the EOKA and he should be boycotted.

The Anti-EOKA

Before long, the Athens press was giving credit to the organization for causing the Greek Cypriots all sorts of pain.

One report stated: 'The explosion of a bomb early this morning in the garden of the Kykkos Monastery, outside Nicosia, was caused by the "secret British organization AKOE". The bomb caused no injuries or damage to property. Greek Cypriots have said that the letters AKOE were found daubed on

The work of British soldiers?

the walls of the monastery about 20 yards from the site of the explosion, just half a mile from the Government House.'

After AKOE came the ICO and Cromwell, both claiming to be movements out to undermine EOKA. ICO, which was said to stand for 'Immediate Counter Offensive', produced only one leaflet. 'The only thing we can say is that it was in no way inspired by us,' laughed a spokesman for the administration.

The latest 'British organization' threatened force. 'Bringing offenders to Court is no good any more,' ICO said. The only way to deal with Greeks was 'to make this race fear the security forces'. The Security forces 'should not stand round like sheep and watch your comrades slaughtered. Retaliate and make the

A leaflet from Cromwell.

Government realize that sterner methods are needed when dealing with savages. The Greeks will be intimidated by our members whenever the opportunity presents itself. This will make some stubborn Greeks realize that terrorism is not a game. We have so far all tried, soldiers, police, expatriates alike to put an end to violence and intimidation with the minimum of force and with politeness. This method apparently does not work. It seems the only thing Greek people understand is force.'

With 'Cromwell', there were now three anti-EOKA groups – or individuals – claiming to represent groups of Britons, civilian and military, prepared to take the law into their hands. They urged the British community to attack the terrorists without mercy and to buy only British products, a response to the EOKA-ordered boycott of British products. Of all, 'Cromwell' became the best known and the most militant in its output.

Copying Dighenis, the 'Cromwell' signature was supposed to represent 'The Leader'. The name had been adopted from the original Oliver Cromwell, whom Thomas Carlyle called the 'last strong man' to govern England after he had launched war against the monarchy and deposed and executed King Charles I. He considered himself a patriot, as did the 'Cromwell' of Cyprus, who believed the Governor was not doing enough to bring an end to EOKA. For him this meant taking Grivas head-on, using the Colonel's ways and means to intimidate his active and passive followers.

For every Briton killed, 'Cromwell' demanded swift retribution by killing two or more Greeks in cold blood. If Grivas bombed a British establishment, he wanted the equivalent amount of Greek property destroyed. Greeks, he said, would have to make a choice between the forces of law and order and those who demanded *enosis* and the end of colonial rule. Once he set its 'Ironsides' loose, his brand of terror would be more fearful than EOKA's.

'Cromwell' acquired an inflated reputation as soon as the Greek Foreign Minister accused his vigilante group of consisting of British soldiers and policemen, who 'indulge in criminal activities against Cypriots with full immunity'.

The Governor and his staff were unanimous that 'Cromwell' and the others had to be stopped to avoid total chaos in the Island. Senior military commanders came to a similar conclusion, but there was no evidence that any of them had done more than distribute a few leaflets in city centres. However, many junior servicemen wished 'Cromwell' every success. They had lost friends and seen EOKA's terrorism at first hand. They were not in a conciliatory mood. They were convinced they could beat Grivas and his men, given half a chance. Many in the officer corps thought Foot was 'too soft' and 'a wishy-washy liberal'. Over drinks in the bar of the Ledra Palace, others speculated that 'Cromwell', AKOE and ICO were part of a 'black' psychological operation created by the intelligence community.

Unconnected to MI5 and MI6, Army intelligence officers investigated and, not surprisingly, found British soldiers were in league with 'Cromwell'. They had duplicated his pamphlets on military duplicating machines and scattered them while on patrol. Worse, some had provided arms and ammunition to expatriates, according to unproven reports. If those behind 'Cromwell' and ICO were discovered, their names have never been revealed. Whether they belonged to the Security Forces or were determined civilians, their identities remained secret – except, perhaps, to the security services.

Strong rumours existed, however, that 'Cromwell' was the creation of someone in the Royal Horse Guards because the regiment could trace its origins back to a force raised by the original Cromwell prior to the invasion of

Scotland in the seventeenth century. Major General Roy Redgrave dismissed this theory.

AKOE was definitely the creation of one man, a corporal in the Royal Signals, it was said. In late 1958, he was caught distributing AKOE leaflets, court-martialled, found guilty and sentenced to nine months' detention in a military prison and reduced to the ranks. His case raised serious questions in Parliament.

The corporal was 22-year-old Brian Ford, married with a three-month old baby. Standing smartly to attention, he pleaded guilty to duplicating the leaflets, as charged, but never admitted to AKOE's creation. 'The whole thing was a practical joke rather than anything else,' he said. 'I realize now it was irresponsible and foolish. I am sorry.' His counsel, a Captain Williams, told the court that the accused had served in Cyprus for more than two years during which he had been involved three times in terrorist incidents and escaped death in an EOKA ambush in Ledra Street. Recently, he added, EOKA had threatened to burn down his family housed in Trichonas village and kill his wife and baby. It was against this background that Ford believed he should counter EOKA's leaflet campaign with one of his own. His defence cut no ice. When sentence was passed Ford's face went ashen and he shook visibly as he was marched away.

A few weeks later, Christopher Soames, the Secretary of State for War, was pressed in the House of Commons by members of all parties to explain why Ford had been sentenced to nine months' imprisonment when Greek Cypriots were merely fined a few pounds for distributing EOKA material.

Mr Soames gave a dusty reply: 'Ford was convicted after pleading guilty to distributing leaflets inviting members of the Forces to intimidate Greeks with violence. The leaflets also accused a judge of being on the pay-roll of EOKA. Ford was sentenced to nine months' and reduced to the ranks. The sentence was first reduced and then remitted on review. In view of the offence he was not harshly treated … The remarkable record of our troops in Cyprus is itself a tribute to the high standard of discipline in the Forces, and it would be fatal for that discipline if we created the impression among servicemen that they could disobey orders or break military law during the process of emergency, in the expectation of having convictions set aside by an amnesty at the end.'

The row in the House of Commons was heard in Cyprus, where the C-in-C MELF then waived Ford's sentence altogether and he was released to rejoin his wife in the UK.

Disgruntled troops confined to camp, except on duty, short of entertainment and usually living in poor conditions, needed outlets for their frustration and wondered why they were in Cyprus, wasting the best years of their lives. 'Nothing was ever explained to us as to why we were there – we were just sent and told what to do,' said Geoffrey Saunders. A National Service corporal, he served with the Ox and Bucks Light Infantry. 'There was no lecturing as to what the EOKA terrorist was all about, and why he wanted union with Greece or why the Turks wanted their section of the Island. Nothing was actually explained, so there was no political side to it at all. You were paid X amount a week for the job you were doing for the British Army.'

To relieve their boredom some soldiers began churning out other specious papers to the annoyance of senior officers. Len Staniforth, a Pay Corps clerk attached to the Royal Signals in Famagusta, said his team put together a spoof document to tease National Service conscripts who were thinking of joining the regulars. It was headed ORAEL – the Other Ranks Anti-Establishment League – and threatened them with more drill and duties, inspections and the painting of white stones on the edge of the parade ground.

Came the time to choose a name for 'The Leader' to sign, Staniforth wrote 'J. Other Rank'.

'When the leaflet was copied and distributed, the shit hit the fan,' he told the author. 'I was arrested and charged with Mutiny and Sedition, under Section 6 of the Army Act. The charge was extremely severe because our CO had an antipathy towards the Pay Corps caused by the misdeeds of my predecessor and a lady related to the aforementioned officer.

'My defending officer at my subsequent Court Martial was Captain The Honourable James Clyde of the Intelligence Corps with a Law degree. Between us, we gathered a number of other leaflets produced by various other local units. One, I recall, was headed LEKA – written in Greek and standing for "Piss on Greeks". After some discussion, the charge was reduced to "Conduct Contrary to Good Order and Prejudicial to Discipline" and I got off with "a severe reprimand". Then I re-enlisted in the Army!'

Before his death, Owen Kitchener, a Royal Artillery sergeant in Cyprus, also remembered the humour the troops enjoyed at EOKA's expense. He said: 'When we patrolled villages, we saw fresh graffiti on walls, put there by EOKA as a warning to the villagers not to cooperate with the Security Forces. Often one of us would sneak in and write on the wall, "HAVE NO FEAR KILROY WAS HERE. WE ARE COMING TO GET YOU" or "CROMWELL WILL GET YOU". Quite frankly, we thought "Cromwell" was just a "Kilroy" look alike or a Turkish Cypriot hoax.'

IN MAY the Army stepped up its campaign to find Grivas. Sever the head of the EOKA snake and calm would be restored for discussions about self-rule and independence to restart was the reasoning. Operation *Kingfisher*, involving as many as 2,000 troops at the start, continued under various names late into the summer. The historian Robert Holland observed: 'It was as if the iron law of Field Marshal Harding that there could be "no middle way" in Cyprus, having been for a while confounded or at least obscured by the impulses of Foot's counter-principle of "generosity", was slowly but surely re-exerting its grip.'

Three battalions – the Argyll and Sutherlanders, 40 Commando and the Ox and Bucks Light Infantry – combed the lower reaches of the Troodos Mountains, six miles north of Limassol. The area consisted of precipitous ridges and valleys, boulder-strewn and covered with low thorn scrub. Goat tracks and footpaths were impassable to vehicles. RAF helicopters were the only means by which rations and water could be supplied.

Two particular villages – Phasula and Mathikoloni – became the soldiers' prime focus of attention. The inhabitants were screened, but they revealed nothing. Yet paid informers insisted Grivas and his key lieutenants were definitely hiding in the locality. They were purposely deceiving the regimental intelligence officers, because they knew Dighenis was conducting his war from the safety of a house in Limassol, within walking distance of a British Army school. To add to the deception, Athens Radio broadcast that the EOKA leader was seriously ill, possibly injured in an attempt to break through the ring of troops. It was one of several baseless reports in the media. Telegraphed a *Daily Express* correspondent: 'It was whispered to me tonight that Grivas is a very sick man, and may not have long to live.' He was alleged to be suffering from a chronic heart ailment and was being treated by an Athens heart specialist. There were stories, too, that the little Colonel had shaved off his moustache and was living in a monastery disguised as a woman, and often served coffee to visiting soldiers.

Nothing spread faster in Aphrodite's Isle

than rumour. Truth disappeared in the harsh light of day. So the village cordons were maintained and ambush points established – just in case. 'Life was not without its hardships,' wrote an Argyll officer in the regiment's journal. 'The long night of watching and waiting would be followed by a day of intensive heat, which made sleeping difficult. After the second week of continuous night work the efficiency of the soldier began to suffer. Imagination began to play weird tricks on reasoning, and the crack of cooling rock or the soft thud of a carob leaf dropping to the ground was often mistaken for the presence of a terrorist.' Because up to 12 ambush positions could be active at one time, there was an elaborate command and control system involved to avoid 'friendly fire' incidents. Often RAF Shackletons were requested to drop flares to illuminate the area when terrorists were suspected to be on the move.

Based on their experiences in previous large-scale operations, the soldiers had developed a healthy respect for the terrorists' fieldcraft in the mountains. 'On approaching a cordon they would move painstakingly slowly, crawling on their hands and feet, and pausing to remove the smallest stones and twigs ahead of them, which might make a noise and give away their presence,' an officer explained. 'A favourite ruse of theirs was to lob small stones in the direction of the cordon posts in order to draw fire and locate their positions. When fired upon the terrorist would act with surprising coolness. In most cases they would drop back for about 10 yards and move slowly on a course parallel to the line of the cordon with a view to making another attempt in a different place.'

One night the Argylls spotted an unexplained light coming from an unguarded area and they thought it was escaping from a crack in the rocks, possibly from an underground hide. Royal Engineers were summoned and the hillside was taken apart layer by layer by

bulldozers and explosives. 'The limestone cave area was left as if it had been struck by an atomic bomb,' said an officer. 'After that no further terrorist movement was seen or heard, and it was presumed that the terrorists had either been killed or buried as a result.'

The search continued for Grivas without success and the troops fell back on jaundiced humour to keep their spirits high. A Private Watson suggested they should leave cans of mutton, cooked in a Greek style, outside every cave they came across and keep a hidden ambush party within sight of the entrance. Another recommended that *Me and My Shadow* become his regiment's march.

Higher up in the Army's command structure, fractures began to develop between the political masters at Government House and senior officers. The latter wanted to take more robust action and bring the fight to Grivas on their terms, rather than allowing him to keep the initiative by striking at targets of his choice and in his time.

'So politically explosive had the Cyprus situation become that we soon learned to be extremely wary of both the civil authorities and politicians. A minor but typical example of the trouble that could be caused by soldiers obeying instructions laid down by civilians took place in a small village near our camp,' Colonel 'Mad Mitch' Mitchell wrote in his autobiography, *Having Been A Soldier*.

'Alastair Campbell – one of my company subalterns, son of Brigadier Lorne Campbell who had won the Victoria Cross commanding the 7th Argylls in the Western Desert, took his platoon into this village to investigate reports that banned EOKA slogans had been painted on the wall of the church. He tactfully but firmly told the headman that these were illegal and must therefore be removed. He would have to order his men to paint them out, so defacing the outside of the church further. He returned later in the day to find that, far from having been removed, yet more slogans had been added. Again, he warned the headman saying that this was his last chance.

'Early that evening, Alastair returned a second time. As his platoon entered the village, doors slammed and slops were thrown at the Jocks from upper windows. In the centre of the village, opposite the church, which was still defiantly covered with the offending slogans, the coffee shop was crowded with men waiting to see what the British would do. They did not have long to wait.

'Alastair ordered his platoon to go round the shops and collect every sort of paint, ink and creosote they could find and mix it together in buckets. This done, they proceeded to cover the outside of the church with this murky mess. This was, of course, the only way this particular regulation, laid down by the Colonial Government, could be enforced.'

Colonel Mitchell was later summoned to explain and justify his men's actions. In the eyes of the soldiers on the ground, this was uncalled-for interference, which could explain why some of them showed their support for the aims expressed in the 'Cromwell' and AKOE leaflets. But the Argylls had the last laugh: 'The Jocks, with typical relish, had not only painted out the slogans but added a few of their own like "Home Rule for Scotland" and "Rangers for the Cup".'

THE SITUATION was getting out of hand. Not only were Greeks and Turks in Cyprus killing each other as EOKA and the TMT battled to enforce their political positions for *enosis* and *taksim*, but there were also anti-Greek demonstrations in mainland Turkish cities and Greece had withdrawn its soldiers and their families from the NATO headquarters in Izmir, Turkey.

Intercommunal hatred had reached an unprecedented pitch of tension. A peal of church bells was sufficient in many parts of the Island to bring hordes of Greeks into the streets, clad in pyjamas and armed with sticks, to resist Turkish 'invaders'. The Greeks protested that in Nicosia 50 Greek rioters were arrested, but only 30 Turks. The Greek Mayors of the main towns spent two hours with Sir Hugh claiming that the Security Forces were providing insufficient protection to their people it might be necessary for them to organize their own self-defence. Turkish representatives arrived in the Governor's office a few hours later demanding protection from Greek attacks.

Sir Hugh cancelled the Queen's Birthday parade and reception and Andreas Zhiartides, the leader of the left-wing Pancyprian Federation of Labour, cabled UN Secretary-General Hammarskjold calling for United Nations intervention to stop Turkish violence.

Six months earlier Foot had arrived with high hopes of finding a liberal and acceptable solution to the Cyprus Problem and was now forced to request more troops from the UK to add to the 20,000 already involved in internal security duties, which was why on 12 June the 16th Parachute Brigade was preparing in Aldershot to fly to the trouble-wracked Island on the verge of civil war.

It was a day on which Turks would massacre Greeks outside a village whose name has become a byword for all the fear and hatred that had developed between the two communities.

In 1958, the village – hamlet would be a better description – was little more than a few houses and a couple of shops on either side of the road to Kyrenia, about 12 miles from Nicosia. Most people passed through without noticing its existence. On maps it was marked as Geunyeli. Students of Cypriot history may have paused to ask why it was nicknamed the 'village of bandy-legged men' and over Turkish coffee heard a fable that before the Second World War, visitors could place orders with the inhabitants to murder for a price of £10 – if it were just an ordinary killing.

Hearsay suggested that the murders always involved inter-family feuds. It was frowned on to use the locals to kill for business reasons. By coincidence, most of the Turks of the village were professional butchers.

In the few days leading to the 'Geunyeli Massacre', Greek Cypriot groups had been descending on undefended Turkish hamlets in the rural areas of the Nicosia plain to take hostages, kill others and destroy as much as they could before an army patrol arrived to stop them. Units of the Grenadiers and the Blues and Royals were finding it increasingly difficult to prevent these widespread incidents and were relying on intelligence to pick out in advance those places where attacks were expected.

At midnight on 10 June, the Turkish *Muktar* of Skylloura contacted a Blues and Royal Officer and claimed a Greek assault was imminent. Troops were sent immediately to investigate. At 05.30, they found 175 armed Greeks hiding in a dry water course a few hundred yards from the village. They were disarmed and sent back whence they came in the nine buses that had brought them. Next day, Ayios Vasilios came under threat, but an armoured car patrol of the Royal Horse Guards spotted two buses and three cars filled with almost 200 Greeks approaching and arrested the lot after removing their weapons and confiscating their transport. They were told to walk back to their home villages and warned not to return.

By now Turkish communities in the countryside were arming and preparing to copy the Greek tactics, causing more difficulties for the Security Forces, who were also dealing with riots and curfews in the urban centres. 'This pattern of events continued all day on 11 June and, as no end seemed in sight, I had to make sure some of my troops got a moment's rest and cars and radios got serviced. The Regiment was motoring over 6,000 miles each day trying to keep things under control,' said

General Roy Redgrave, a Major at the time, commanding 'B' Squadron.

The Royal Horse Guards had spent 10 days non-stop in the field away from their base at Camp Elizabeth, which stood on 'a solid rock plateau, where the latrine pits were blasted out with explosives'. It was 'a dreadful place', Redgrave thought. 'It was, I suppose, typically British that we should live in such conditions, spend days and nights in the wilds trying to arrest terrorists and their helpers, only to discover that they were then placed in accommodation which was infinitely superior to ours. I doubt whether any other nation in the world took such trouble over the welfare of people held without trial. Sir Hugh Foot was determined not to offend the Greeks.'

Hardly rested, Redgrave and a troop of his men were called out again in the morning of 12 June to give assistance to Sergeant Gill from Yerolakkos Police Station and an RAF Squadron Leader who were desperately trying to prevent a battle between a line of Turks on one side and Greeks on the other in Skylloura, where 48 hours earlier the same Greeks had been ordered home.

When Redgrave and his men arrived with two armoured cars, most of the Greeks had fled, but 35 were still there. With them pacified and disarmed, he decided, for their protection, to put them on their own bus and escort them under arrest to Yerolakkos to be charged by Sergeant Gill under the Offensive Weapons Law, but Assistant Superintendent Trusler recommended they be taken instead to Nicosia's Central Police Station.

If the local Turks were in an offensive mood here, it was nothing compared to their unleashed anger in the capital. As the Royal Horse Guards' convoy reached the city ring road, Redgrave received a frantic message. 'For God's sake don't bring those people here,' crackled a voice over the radio. 'We have a Turkish riot going on at the moment and if those Greeks come here they'll eat them!'

Rather than aggravate the situation and with no time to lose, he made a snap decision that he came to regret.

'I wondered what the hell to do, so I said to the convoy, "Take the next turning off and get away from Nicosia." We drove through two Turkish villages – the Greeks hung their blue and white flags up and the Turks their red flags, so you knew which was a Greek and which was a Turkish village – and when we were clear of Geunyeli and the Greeks could see their village, I planned to stop and make them all walk home across the fields. 'Fortunately Lieutenant Peter Baring's troop was already in the area, together with a platoon from No. 1 Company of the Grenadier Guards, and they reported that all was quiet,' Redgrave said.

North of Geunyeli, Redgrave handed over his prisoners to the Grenadiers, while his men kept a watch on the Turkish hamlet. A quarter of a mile away, 2nd Lieutenant R. S. Corkran unloaded the Greeks from his three-ton trucks and ordered them to get home as best they could. The Guards' officer watched them disappear over the brow of a hill, before leaving to patrol elsewhere. Once he had gone, the freed men and youths chose to take a short cut over some cornfields waiting to be harvested. Later, one of the Greeks, a 14-year-old boy, would allege: 'The English officer said, "Get out." We said, "We cannot, this is a Turkish area, they will kill us. Why not take us to our village?" But he said, "Get out, you bastards, you can walk." Then he started pushing us off.'

At about 14.00, Redgrave's troopers saw huge clouds of smoke rising about 800 yards away and drove rapidly in the direction of the fire. What they saw shocked them. A group of Turkish workers in the cornfield had spotted the Greeks and attacked with 'utmost savagery', using clubs and knives after one of them had shouted an insult in a show of bravado. They then ran literally for their lives.

Some escaped, but most did not. Four were killed and many others badly mutilated. One of the survivors said: 'If it had not been for the armoured cars, we would all have been slaughtered.' Trooper Graham Williams remembered: 'Hands and fingers were all over the place. An officer, green in the face, was holding a head and asking if any of us had seen a body to fit it.'

Driving to his home in Kyrenia, Major P. J. C. Ratcliffe, accompanied by his driver and radio operator, broke his journey and joined the Horse Guards, who were doing their best to care for the wounded rather than pursuing the Turkish murderers. He contacted his headquarters at Tunisia Camp for medical assistance. After hearing his report, Lieutenant Colonel A. G. Heywood of the Grenadiers sounded a general alarm. Within the hour, it had deployed and cordoned off the area. A helicopter arrived to fly out the critically injured.

Meanwhile, the Turkish males of Geunyeli were rushing to the bloody scene, encouraged by two men on motorcycles, perhaps from the TMT, who gripped knives in their teeth. Soon there were reports of Greeks heading in the same direction to seek retribution.

'Then we had the most tremendous cops-and-robbers' afternoon chasing the Turks in our scout cars. Although we had the invaluable support of an Auster spotter plane, it was a hair-raising job, blocking every column before it could make trouble over such a wide area, and only our mobility and excellent communications made it possible,' Redgrave opined. 'We were getting very tired indeed. There was no let-up in sight and then the Greeks accused us of plotting the whole incident in advance with the Turks.'

At Nicosia Hospital, the Greek injured were arriving in a convoy of ambulances, escorted by the Army and Civilian Police. As the laden stretchers were brought inside, Dr Paris said 'Someone started a frightening descant; a high-pitched wail descending to a tremulous groan – the keening for the dead, with a background of '*Aman, aman*', a Turkish word used by the Greeks for dismay.' Soon the surgical wards were filled to overflowing, with blood everywhere on the corridor floors.

The Irish doctor saw heads and bellies split open and limbs half hacked off. While every Greek doctor and nurse dealt with their wounded, he noticed a Turk was being ignored. 'I told them to do their job,' Paris wrote later. 'They pretended not to understand my English. I then ordered them in Greek, and most sullenly they did what I asked. I did not want to get involved in politics, but a Greek Cypriot sister was making political speeches in the corridor. Another ran up to me and said, "Tomorrow we will all be fighting the Turks and you British too – we will lay down the scalpel and pick up the knife!"'

Paris noted that a local doctor was also haranguing an English nurse. 'Look what the Turks and the English have done,' he shouted in her face. She stayed calm, raised an eyebrow and replied: 'I saw the victims when EOKA put a bomb in a lorry of British soldiers. It was far worse than this. You only laughed then. I am doing a nurse's job for you. I can't waste sympathy.'

Guardsman G. W. Brinsford (left) and a comrade rest after seeing the horror of Geunyeli.

Late in the afternoon, Governor Foot, Director of Operations General Kendrew, Chief Constable Browne and District Commissioner Weston went to Geunyeli on a fact-finding mission. Even so, the authorities issued conflicting statements that failed to allay the unprecedented pitch of anger in the Greek community as rumours spread across the Island, exaggerated many times in the telling of what had taken place. Typical of the wild claims was the one given by a young survivor to the local press: 'We ran and ran, but the Turks were everywhere. They came out of the cornfields in their hundreds with knives, axes and meat cleavers.'

As darkness fell, the mood in Cyprus turned black. Throughout the night, using searchlights, troops continued to search for victims. At 03.00, SAC Nigel Rouse and other members of 28 LAA Squadron RAF Regiment were woken and told to get ready for a special operation, without being given its nature or location.

'We kitted up in khaki drill uniforms, webbing belts, our ammo pouches and personal weapons,' he said, sharing his memories with the author. 'We drove through Nicosia, heading north. It was some time before the convoy came to a halt. In the predawn light, we saw a Turkish Cypriot village a mile or so ahead. It was Geunyeli, which was still under curfew from the day before. The senior ranks gathered for a "pow-wow" with some "pongos" – army – officers. Then we entered. It was still and silent when we entered. There was not a soul to be seen.

'Our CO took over the local school and established a command HQ inside. With our sergeants, we were ordered to round up every male inhabitant and confine them in the school's playground, sitting them in rows. The village women and children were allowed to remain in their houses, though some did come with their men folk, leaving older women behind.

'As the CO's signaller, I stayed with him at the school, while patrols, carrying sheets, were sent to the surrounding fields to retrieve the remains of the Greek Cypriot dead. A couple of sergeants, who had seen action in previous postings, became physically ill on returning to HQ.

'I still clearly remember how the Turks cheered every sheet-wrapped bloodied body brought back. None expressed regret or showed a sign of remorse. The villagers clearly felt they had done nothing wrong.' But not all: Lieutenant Colonel Britten and a police-woman found a young English woman. She had recently married a Turkish Cypriot in Birmingham and only the week before started her new life in the village. Where did her destiny lie now, she wondered?

To prevent a complete breakdown of law and order in the district, all assemblies, including funeral and marriage processions and cinema shows were banned. British families were advised in broadcasts to stay indoors. In Nicosia, the barricades along the 'Mason-Dixon Line' were strengthened with iron and barbed wire. More soldiers patrolled the city and spotter aircraft flew overhead.

At Government House, Sir Hugh Foot summoned the Chief Justice, Sir Paget Bourke, to undertake a formal enquiry.

To keep Greeks and Turks apart in the vicinity of Geunyeli, Cornet Auberon Waugh and his troop were ordered to guard the area with their four Daimler scout cars. During one of their patrols, the young officer shot himself accidentally with six bullets from his own .300 Browning machine gun. He was hit in his chest, shoulder, arm and left hand.

He joked later: 'I was rather worried and thought I was probably going to die, as every time I moved the blood pouring out of holes in my back, where the bullets had exited, made a horrible gurgling noise. To those who suffer from anxieties about being shot, I can give the reassuring news that it is almost completely painless. Although the bullets caused considerable devastation on the way out, the only sensation at the time was of a mild tapping on the front of the chest. I also felt suddenly winded as they went through a lung. But there was virtually no pain for about three quarters of an hour, and then only a dull ache before the morphine began to take effect.'

Waugh continued: 'Corporal of Horse Chudleigh came back to me, saluted in a rather melodramatic way as I lay on the ground and said words to the effect that this was a sorry turn of events. He was a tough Bristolian parachutist and pentathlete. On this occasion he looked so solemn that I could not resist the temptation of saying: "Kiss me, Chudleigh". Chudleigh did not spot the historical reference and treated me with some caution thereafter.'

He was taken to the BMH, Nicosia, where Lieutenant Colonel John Watts, MC, and his team, one of whom was a young Professor Norman Browse, removed Waugh's shattered spleen, which did not improve his temper but left him in considerable pain. Some years later, Browse wrote to the *Daily Telegraph*: 'His life was saved by the superb skills of a team of Royal Army Medical Corps surgeons and anaesthetists, of which I am proud to have been a junior member ... Sadly, the level of expertise provided for Waugh in 1958 has been seriously undermined by massive cuts imposed upon the Armed Forces medical services by successive governments.'

Waugh's mother, Laura, was rushed from the UK to see him, leaving her large wardrobe at home, which caused her to fret when she was put up at Government House as the Foots' guest. In a letter to her husband, she wrote: 'I have today seen the doctors. They say they think Bron has a very good chance indeed of survival, having started with they thought none. The next two or three days are critical. After that he will be on the danger list for another 10-14 days ... I am not allowed to leave GH without an escort with a machine gun. I have bought myself a dress because I realized I could not continue without one. It cost £7, but will do for Munich if I get there. Poor Lady Foot can never leave GH because she is not allowed out without a guard of 12 machine gunnists and she says that makes it intolerable.'

She added an insightful comment about life at Government House: 'Randolph [Churchill] is in Nicosia and came to dinner last night. He was very drunk, maudlin, sympathetic and loving about you [her husband]. As you may guess he succeeded in giving great offence to the Foots (1) by smoking in the middle of dinner, so that Sir Hugh decided he could not propose the loyal toast (2) by his general drunkenness (3) by shouting and yelling for the prettiest girl present to sit by him during the special cinema performance (4) by barracking the cinema (5) by leaving in the middle of it and taking an affectionate leave of me, but not bothering to say goodbye or thank their Excellencies.'

After a long and miserable stay in the BMH – for himself, the other patients and the medical staff – Waugh was transferred to Westminster Hospital. 'Auberon Waugh was a difficult patient,' Browse concurs. 'He had to stay in our basic intensive care area, which was in the general ward but kept demanding to be in the Officers Ward. His mother was equally demanding.'

After 12 more operations and nine months later, Waugh was discharged from hospital and invalided out of the Army. He never fully recovered from his injuries.

On 17 June, Valerie, Major Redgrave's wife, wrote her parents a letter from her Kyrenia house, trying to calm their fears about the situation. 'This is going to be very short, because the temperature is 105 degrees and it's too hot to do anything but wallow in the sea,' she penned. 'The husbands manage to get home occasionally (about every three or four days). I have even got my own pistol, which is exciting.

'Poor old Roy is very worried as he was responsible for that awful incident at Geunyeli when six Greeks were massacred and had their heads and arms and balls etc cut off by the Turks. There has got to be a public inquiry, but he's got everyone on his side from the Governor and the C-in-C downwards. I think it will be all right. Today was the day we were supposed to have the announcement. Once again it has been postponed, which has infuriated the whole island.'

The enquiry eventually started at the end of June – 'the most appalling Court of Enquiry run by the Chief Justice in which all my troops were involved' was how Redgrave described it. Thirty-seven witnesses gave evidence over eight days. Much of what was said conflicted. 'Although we were completely exonerated it was incredibly unfair as we were being quizzed and getting awful stick in the papers and all the time, day and night, the Greeks and Turks were relying on us to stop them killing each other,' Redgrave added.

Colonel Grivas rejected Sir Paget Bourke's findings and denounced them as a 'new conspiracy' engineered by 'Mr Foot and his blood-drenched assassins'. Soon afterwards, he announced 'open season' on all EOKA's opponents, civilian and military, Turk and Greek.

According to Oliver Lindsay, the editor of the *Guards Magazine*, a few weeks after the massacre, a Grenadier officer, driving through Geunyeli, had a puncture. 'He got out of the vehicle with considerable trepidation, aware of the recent murders. But the Turks produced chairs and coffee while the tyre was changed.'

Against this background, the latest grand plan for peace was about to be announced. It was called an 'Adventure in Partnership'. It was stamped with the authority of Prime Minister Harold Macmillan and had the backing of the 12–nation Atlantic Council, but the question uppermost on everyone's lips was: how would Ankara, Athens and, most importantly, the Greeks and Turks of Cyprus, particularly the egotistical Colonel Grivas, react to it?

CHAPTER TWENTY-ONE

A shot rings out and someone falls: an adventure in partnership?

'The whole problem with the world is that fools and fanatics are always so certain of themselves, but wiser people so full of doubts.'

Umberto Eco, *The Name of The Rose*

SIR HUGH FOOT sat in front of the carefully positioned microphone in the small studio of the Cyprus Broadcasting Service, touched the pages of his long script and waited for the red light on the wall to go on. He was about to address the people of Cyprus and the British Forces. Not since the build-up for the Suez invasion had so many troops been concentrated in the misnamed Island of Love. There were 15 infantry battalions, three parachute battalions, one cavalry regiment, one artillery regiment, and a Royal Marines Commando – 37,000 troops – waiting to know their future.

Although the terrorists probably numbered no more than 500, their unpredictable hit and run operations, never twice in the same area on the same day, gave them the initiative, leaving the Security Forces to react and stretching their resources to the limit. Frustrated, tired and seeing no end in sight, they were also caught in the middle of the war between the Greeks' EOKA and the Turks' TMT. No longer was either Island community to be trusted. Cyprus had become a powder keg. Was there any way to stop the fuse being lit?

The Governor knew his masters in Whitehall were despairing. In the eyes of military planners, Cyprus was of less strategic value than before: the failure of the Suez

campaign had proved this. All Britain needed were a few secured bases from which they could operate now that the United States had become the dominant military and economic power. Washington dictated how Western interests were defended in the Middle East and it ruled NATO, which it determined must not be weakened by Greece and Turkey's differences over a tiny island at the eastern end of the Mediterranean, at a time when the Soviet threat in the region was becoming more apparent. Washington wanted London to find a quick formula that satisfied Athens and Ankara, without a loss of face in the two capitals, and for Britain to cut and run with a degree of dignity. Cypriots had committed themselves to their 'motherlands' and must learn to live with the consequences.

Prime Minister Macmillan, keen to strengthen Anglo-American relations, was a shrewd politician with his finger on the pulse of Britain's economy and his eyes set on winning the forthcoming General Election for the Conservatives. As a former soldier, awarded the Military Cross for bravery, he knew EOKA could not be defeated and the cost was too heavy to even try any longer.

His 'Adventure in Partnership' plan could be the answer to all his domestic problems. It had to be accepted by the parties involved or they could snarl and bark like hungry dogs over the bone Cyprus had become, because, as far as he was concerned, Britain's patience was exhausted. With this in mind, he had given advance copies of his plan to the governments of Turkey and Greece, NATO, the Atlantic Council and the United States to mull over. Dressing it in his customary soothing charm, he had unveiled it in the House of Commons on 19 June and received a favourable reception. It was now up to Sir Hugh to sell it in all its complex intricacies to the Cypriots.

The Governor cleared his throat and saw the studio clock tick forward to the top of the hour. The red light flashed. He was on the air.

'This is the most important day in the history of Cyprus. The Prime Minister in the House of Commons announced a new policy for Cyprus this afternoon, and I am very glad to be able to speak to you about it tonight. It is a new policy, it is a just policy. For Cyprus, it is the policy of "all the advantages",' he said, reading his script in sonorous tones. 'What is the new policy? It can be summed up in three sentences. First, we want to give the best possible deal to all the people of the Island. Second, we want to bring the three Governments of Great Britain, Greece and Turkey together in a joint effort to make sure they get it. Third, we believe that this can only be achieved by Great Britain giving a definite and determined lead to break the vicious circle from which Cyprus has suffered so long.

'It is a policy we can believe in and which we can all support wholeheartedly. It is a policy based on good principles – the principle of doing our best for the people and the principle of partnership between allies. This is not just another idea to be shot down. It is not just another suggestion to be argued about. This is the policy which we are convinced is the right one. I am sure that this is the only policy which can save Cyprus.'

As he turned the typed pages on the table, Sir Hugh became more biblical: 'There must be a beginning of every matter, but the continuing unto the end yields the true glory. The beginning is today. Today we resolve together to see it through to the end.' Slowly he went on, reading paragraph after paragraph, without reaching the details his listeners were eager to hear.

'I shall presently read to you the statement of new policy which the Prime Minister made in the House of Commons this afternoon. Since it will take me a little time to read in full, I shall first summarize the new policy in three sentences,' he continued.

'First, Cyprus should enjoy the advantages of association with the British Commonwealth and with Greece and Turkey too, with Greek Cypriots having Greek nationality and Turkish Cypriots having Turkish nationality and all retaining British nationality as well.

'Second, Great Britain will welcome the co-operation and participation of the two other Governments in a joint effort to secure the peace, progress and prosperity of the Island.

'Third, there should be a representative, democratic system of government, with the Greek and Turkish communities controlling their own communal affairs.

'These are the principles on which the new policy is based.'

When his broadcast came to an end, it boiled down to Prime Minister Macmillan offering separate 'communal assemblies' to the Greek and Turkish Cypriots to handle their own local problems, education and religious affairs; the communal assemblies would in turn elect a Central Council to act as a kind of cabinet under a British Governor. Representation on the Central Council would be in rough proportion to the population.

The plan would give the Greek and Turkish governments a sense of participation – and of responsibility – in Cypriot affairs; Athens and Ankara would each send a representative to take part in the Central Council's meetings, raise questions with the Governor and submit disputes to an 'independent tribunal' if they thought any legislation was discriminatory; the Council would include four Greek Cypriots and two Turkish Cypriots drawn from the Houses of Representatives; and Britain would remain responsible for the Island's defence and its internal security, acting in consultation with the Greek and Turkish Governments.

'To allow time for the new principle of partnership to be fully worked out and brought into operation under this plan in the necessary atmosphere of stability, the international status of the Island will remain unchanged for seven years,' Foot intoned from his script. In short, Britain would stay in Cyprus at least until 1965. There was no promise of 'self determination' in the document.

The Macmillan Plan was filled with paragraphs to please the Cypriot communities and their 'motherlands' – the promise of an end to the Emergency Regulations, the return of Makarios, a favoured economic status, the right for the two communities to administer themselves, the direct involvement of Turkey and Greece to guide them – but there were minefields for the readers to tiptoe through and any miscalculation could blow it apart. Likely to be the most dangerous passage came towards the end: 'Indeed, if the Greek and Turkish Governments were willing to extend this experiment in partnership and co-operation, Her Majesty's Government would be prepared, at the appropriate time, to go further,' it said, 'and, subject to the reservation to the United Kingdom of such bases and facilities as might be necessary for the discharge of her international obligations, to *share* the sovereignty of the Island with their Greek and Turkish allies as their contribution to a lasting settlement ...'

Foot's long address closed with well-rehearsed optimism. 'If it is accepted by the Greeks, we can proceed to the practical work of preparing and working for a system of representative government. If it is accepted by the Turks, they will have the firm assurance that, under the principles of participation by Turkey, dual nationality and communal autonomy exercised through their own House of Representatives, their rights and interests throughout the Island will be effectively secured.

'No one need lose. Everyone stands to gain. No one on either side needs to renounce principles, which they have long advocated or defended. But here is a new road, a road which leads away from fear and despair – a road which can lead to justice and security for all the people of Cyprus. We shall not be deflected from it by violence or by any temporary setback or opposition. I am convinced that sooner or later this is the road which we must travel together. I am eager to get started on it at once. I call on everyone to come together now and make a new start to which we can all dedicate ourselves to a confident and sustained effort to save and serve Cyprus.'

The red light went out. Sir Hugh sighed with relief. At Government House, he re-read a letter from his father, a Methodist lay preacher, then took the Bible from a bookshelf and turned to the passage his father recommended – Corinthians 4, Verse 8: *We are troubled on every side, yet not distressed; we are perplexed, but not in despair; persecuted, but not forsaken; cast down, but not destroyed.* For his reply, he remembered Romans 5, Verse 3 and sent it as a cable to the family home in Cornwall: *And not only so, but we glory in tribulations also: knowing that tribulation worketh patience; and patience, experience; and experience, hope.*

From the hot summer sky of Cyprus, RAF aircraft circled and swooped like hungry vultures, spewing leaflets in Greek and Turkish on the heads of the people to explain the benefits the plan offered. Early whispers heard by diplomats in the three capitals concerned suggested it would be rejected, with qualifications. In a concentrated diplomatic effort led by the United States, 13 NATO members pressed Turkey and Greece to consider the plan in detail and withhold any actions that could split the alliance.

WITHIN HOURS, however, it appeared the plan was a non-starter, like all its predecessors, only this time the naysayers spoke more softly, except for Grivas. 'Chew your plan and swallow it,' was his message to the Governor. Makarios, for his part, rejected the plan as it stood on the grounds that it would constitutionally divide Cyprus, 'thereby creating a focus of permanent unrest', but, for the first time, he did not oppose a 'transitory state of self-government'.

Turkey's leaders grumbled, but felt it could, with 'some realistic modifications', allow for partition by 1965. Patience was one of their virtues. Constantine Karamanlis, the Greek Prime Minister, was prepared to enter negotiations without the British having to give an advance promise of self-determination by a specified date. He was fed up with Grivas trying to dictate the state's foreign policy and saw the country's long-term interests as a friend of Turkey. Opposition parties shouted 'Sell-out!'

'The voice of wisdom says that the British plan for a settlement, whether satisfactory or not, must be accepted as soon as possible. We may bargain, or try to improve it if we can, but we must accept it,' wrote the editor of *Mesoghios*, a newspaper that usually reflected the Government's position on most subjects. 'Can we overpower the Turks and cross the river Evros one day to twist their necks? If not, we must shut up at present, and accept whatever is offered us.'

The ministers in Ankara and Athens knew full well that their countries could not survive without large amounts of financial aid from the United States and, if Washington wanted a resolution of the Cyprus problem, then, perhaps, there was room for them to sort out

the matter behind the backs of the Cypriot people and the British and benefit themselves in the bargain. This thought began to percolate slowly behind locked doors, but would emerge by the end of the year. For the moment, EOKA and the TMT could settle scores and Britain would have to shoulder the pain. No Empire in its final days had escaped that fate.

The Times in London reasoned: 'The Greeks should reflect that *enosis* is no longer a practical possibility. It was a solution which could have been brought about peaceably only if Cyprus, as Britain had originally intended, had been able to develop by the ordinary processes of British constitutional evolution into an independent unitary State. The plan suits British interests in that it offers a fair and peaceful solution and it enables Great Britain to retain its bases in the island for another seven years. What happens after that none can say.

'It is a plan in favour, not of the Turks, nor of the Greeks, nor of the British, but of the Cypriots themselves. That is as it should be, and the Greek and Turkish Governments should reflect on the consequences of rejection. Turkey gains straightaway the substance of part, at least, of what she has sought, without the strife and bloodshed that any other course would entail. No one questions that she is a strong and united Power, or that Cyprus lies geographically within her grasp. But the calculation – raised by some Turkish extremists – that she could really use this force for annexation of the Island in the existing international atmosphere is surely an illusion. The Greeks can hardly now reckon that they would get a better settlement if they waited for a general election in England.'

On 25 June, Sir Hugh Foot left unexpectedly for London in an RAF Canberra bomber to deliver a first-hand report on the reactions in Cyprus to the Macmillan Plan. On landing, he told the waiting press: 'We never expected that it would be immediately agreed. If agreement had been possible it would have been announced long ago. It was because agreement was not made that we had to announce our own policy and the immediate reaction is not unexpected in any way. We want to give an opportunity to the people to cooperate and we believe this can be achieved.' Asked again if he would try to meet Grivas, he replied: 'I will do anything that will bring about the end of violence, and a just solution in Cyprus.'

During his absence, there was relative calm on the Island, as a result of which Foot lifted the night curfew that had existed in the main towns since 9 June. Almost immediately, there were communal clashes and murders once more. The result was a new law to punish more severely those who incited violence.

AKEL, the Cyprus Communist Party, saw benefits in the Macmillan Plan and came out in favour of independence ahead of self-determination. Unknown to the left-wingers, Grivas had set up a special nationalist unit to deal with them. He called it YAKA – the Service for Countering Communist Reaction. The breach between the two factions was bringing the risk of wholesale battles inside the Greek Cypriot community. An incident in Milia village demonstrated the possibility. The left-wing inhabitants had formed a 'home guard' to fight off marauding Turks, but instead were ambushed by Grivas's men, who killed two and injured 20 others.

JULY STARTED with a running gun battle at night between a terrorist gang and the Security Forces in a mountainous area, 25 miles south-west of Nicosia. It was reported to be the fiercest clash in 18 months. During the operation a vehicle was stopped and found to be carrying large supplies of ammunition. By the next day 20 suspects were 'in the bag'. There were no service casualties. Elsewhere there were minor incidents involving Greek and Turkish villagers.

Then, five days later, a Royal Horse Guards patrol searching for Andreas Karios, a wanted terrorist, ran into trouble in the village of Avgorou. The routine patrol, consisting of four armoured cars, each with a crew of two, from 'A' Squadron, had arrived at lunchtime and stopped at the local coffee shop, where a youth was busy erecting a large board with instructions signed 'EOKA'. He was ordered to remove it. He refused and the troops arrested him. Immediately an angry mob, mostly women, rushed from their houses, grabbed the boy and spirited him away. The patrol commander then withdrew his men and took up positions at the entrance and exit of the village after calling for reinforcements. Led by Cornet I. A. D. Pilkington, three more armoured cars arrived with 24 troopers on board a personnel carrier. A house-to-house search began for the youngster.

Tempers flared and the Horse Guards came under attack from more than 200 villagers, who bombarded them with bottles and rocks, some weighing as much as six pounds. At this stage, the patrol commander, Lieutenant H. D. Blake, abandoned the search and ordered his men to grab the rioters' ringleader. By now, scores of youngsters were clambering over the patrol's armoured cars. When a brick crashed through the windscreen of the officer's vehicle, striking the driver's face, Blake raised his Browning machine gun and fired a burst of 15 rounds into the air to disperse the crowd. Bullets ricocheted off walls and the mob scattered, leaving behind two dead. One of them was Mrs Loukia Papagiorgiou. She was six months pregnant and the mother of six children. When it was all over, 13 others were wounded and 22 troopers injured. They were taken to hospitals for treatment. That evening the Royal Horse Guards pulled out and handed responsibility for the village's curfew to the Royal Ulster Rifles.

Mrs Papagiorgiou's death was a great EOKA propaganda coup as the villagers

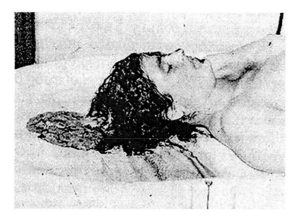

The body of Mrs Loukia Papagiorgiou.

shouted claims that the British had shot her dead. Police, who went to investigate the incident, were met by a hostile reception and no one in Avgorou was willing to give evidence. Although an independent pathologist reported she had not been killed by any bullets, but had been hit on the head by a rock, Grivas did not believe him and promised to retaliate. He sent wreaths to the dead Cypriots' funerals with the message: 'I shall avenge your blood' – and he was true to his word. He laid out his intentions in a leaflet distributed in Famagusta. It was a warning to the British and the Turks. 'If a Greek is killed by a Briton, we shall kill a Briton; if a Greek dies as a result of the Anglo-Turkish conspiracy, we shall also kill Britons; if a Greek is killed by a Turk, we shall kill a Turk in return,' it said. 'If Greek property is destroyed by the British, we shall retaliate by sabotaging British property; if Turks burn Greek property we shall burn Turkish property. The British plan might as well be relegated to the wastepaper basket. The British sword will never put the plan into effect; we shall continue our struggle for self-determination.'

Within hours a Turkish Cypriot and a Greek Cypriot were found dead in different parts of the Island. The Turk, from Lassa village, had been beaten to death by a Greek mob. The dead Greek was shot on the roof of a house near Kyrenia.

After an official inquiry into what took place in Avgorou, Sir Hugh told reporters: 'Throughout the incident Mr Blake acted with great calmness and restraint, and the moment of opening fire was delayed as long as possible, and was then only done by himself personally to save the lives of his men and to protect his vehicles.' The same day, 8 July, Grivas kept his promise to take a life for a life. Not only that, his vengeance was taken out on the Royal Horse Guards.

Sent to buy mess groceries in Hermes Street – Famagusta's 'Murder Mile' – Cornet The Honourable Charles Stephen Fox-Strangways, son of Lord Stavordale, and driver Trooper John Proctor parked their Land Rover outside

Cornet The Honorable Charles Stephen Fox-Strangways, son of Lord Stavordale.

a fresh vegetable shop and walked inside. Both were 20-year-old National Service soldiers. An EOKA terrorist saw their backs to the entrance and fired. The young trooper was killed instantly, but the officer turned, fatally injured and before dying fired a single shot at his attacker, who fled. Roy Redgrave, then a Major, remembered: 'We were ordered to keep tight control, because there was a risk that the fury felt that afternoon might be vented on the nearest Greek Cypriot.'

Fox-Strangways had been due to return home in six weeks' time. A friend said: 'In one of the last letters he wrote, only a few days before his death, he complained of how bored he was of "playing soldiers" in Cyprus and how he longed to be home again in England. But Stephen never "played" at being a soldier – when necessary, he really was one. If there was a job to be done – a patrol, a roadblock or something like that – however routine and tiresome it was, he would tackle it with terrific verve and enthusiasm and make the very most of whatever it might be. Yet when it was finished, he would still have unlimited energy to set out to enjoy the rather limited entertainment which could be found in Cyprus.

'Above all, he could laugh at anything and everything. That, together with his infectious enthusiasm and immense *joie de vivre*, will make him sorely missed by all who knew him.'

The parents of Fox-Strangways paid to have the bodies of the two soldiers brought back to the UK for burial. Trooper Proctor lies today in peace in Handsworth Cemetery, not far from where he played as a youngster in the streets of Birmingham. The inscription by his mother on the grave's headstone says simply: 'Treasured memories of my dear son John Roy Proctor killed in action Cyprus July 8 1958 in his 20th year. Until we meet again.'

Allan Pope, a trooper comrade of his at the Blues and Royals' Camp Elizabeth in Cyprus keeps the grave tidy.

In the House of Commons, Colonial

Trooper John Proctor's grave in Birmingham.

Secretary Alan Lennox-Boyd told Members of Parliament that between 1 June and 22 July, 95 people had been murdered on the Island. He spoke of 'violence between Greeks and Turks ... during which 51 have been killed and over 80 wounded'. Praising the Security Forces, he went on, 'The ceaseless activities of the Security Forces alone have prevented the slaughter from assuming even more serious proportions ... the Governor is faced with the gravest threat to peace in the history of our administration of Cyprus.'

THE BOYCOTT of British imports by EOKA continued, but now the TMT ordered Turks to boycott Greek goods. Turks caught smoking Greek cigarettes or using Greek shops would be punished, its anonymous leader warned. Turks known to have deviated from the 'nationalist' line were thrashed by gangs of Turkish youths. Before long every inhabitant would have to join one organization or the other or else become a 'traitor' and risk death. The Governor decided to proscribe the TMT and rounded up a total of 50 known members and placed them in detention.

Meanwhile, the British suffered another tragedy. Early in the morning of 13 July, Royal Marines of 45 Commando were boarded on helicopters at Nicosia Airport to fly to a location near Akanthou, where EOKA was reported to be active. 'When we arrived at our destination, we had to get off fast and the helicopter left without the usual "thumbs up" sign from the last man,' said Marine John Marston. 'I noticed another helicopter landing on the opposite hill.

'Our sergeant – Dave Baldwin – signalled us to move forward. A few seconds later he pointed at something and fell flat on the ground. Twigs and leaves suddenly started to fall in front of me and I heard crack, crack, crack in rapid succession. The Marine next to me and I dived behind a rock for cover, when I heard David Witham cry out in pain. We couldn't tell from where the shots were coming, but we kept our heads down as more bullets headed our way. My hand was hurting and weeping from the rope burn caused when I dropped from the helicopter. Ants were feeding on the liquid.

'The shooting stopped as suddenly as it had started. There was a lot of shouting, but it was drowned by the sound of a helicopter which had arrived. It had brought a doctor to treat the injured. He asked us to protect him while he examined Sergeant Baldwin and Marine Witham. He said Baldwin was dead and Witham was critically injured. From out of nowhere, another Marine patrol arrived. Like us, they had lost their berets in the confusion.

'When our troop reassembled, every member was very subdued. Someone – an officer, I think – joined us and took our statements about what we thought had happened. Because of the incident, we could return to the UK if we wanted, he said. We declined. None of us had heard before of Marines returning home after coming under fire. What the officer did not say was that our own forces had attacked us. We didn't discover the truth until much later in the day. Witham died from his injuries.' Another Marine, Harry Bostock, also did not survive and lost his battle in hospital on 15 July.

The parents of the Marines were never told the exact circumstances of their sons' deaths. It was not until 2004 that Baldwin's grandson was able to visit his grave in Wayne's Keep Military Cemetery and bring home a photograph of its headstone.

SIR HUGH Foot, as the situation worsened, was forced to remove his velvet gloves and bring down a mailed fist to enforce his authority. On 20 July, he cracked down with the toughest measures Cyprus had ever known. He banned all movement on the Island for civilians, including foreign news correspondents; cut all telephone communications; and imposed total censorship on press and radio.

At dawn, all available troops and police began a major roundup of Cypriots, including Turks. They cordoned off towns and villages and by dawn were knocking on doors to tell the occupants in the house to dress and accompany them. By day's end nearly 2,000 Greek Cypriots were held behind barbed wire. They included the Mayor of Limassol and several prominent lawyers, doctors and teachers. The arrested Greeks and Turks were placed in separate detention centres.

'The long-term holding of detainees without trial had long been a major grievance amongst Greeks, second only to the treatment of the Archbishop. This doubling of the Greek population in the camps was a shock. It was interpreted as part of the natural logic of the Macmillan Plan: designed to make things so miserable for most Cypriots that they settled for whatever was offered to them. This was, indeed, pretty much the truth,' said the historian Robert Holland.

Only after the arrests was press censorship lifted and telephone communication restored. The ban on travel was eased, but not between the hours of 19.00 and 04.30. The liberal-minded Sir Hugh Foot had acted more severely than Field Marshal Sir John Harding ever had, but his draconian measures did not stop communal clashes and murders. If anything, they intensified in the days that followed. Prime Minister Macmillan's 'Adventure in Partnership' was becoming a pattern of futility.

The situation on the Island grew extremely grave. Dr Kutchuk, the Turkish Cypriot leader, said the Turks had 'no more confidence in England'. Speaking to the press, he revealed that he had appealed to the Turkish Government to intervene. Intervention, he added, should take the form of the dispatch of a contingent of Turkish troops to Cyprus to protect Turkish Cypriots. Rauf Denktas declared that the refusal by Britain to allow such Turkish intervention would have the most serious consequences. The Turks were desperate, he insisted. 'England is incapable of protecting the Turks in Cyprus and desperate people will resort to desperate remedies.'

Day after day the two sides found excuses to kill each other, leaving the British to pick up the pieces, while they were booed, hissed and stoned.

TROUBLE HAD blown up in the Middle East at the same time after the monarchy in Iraq was overthrown by a group of rebellious Army officers. Nearby countries called for British and American military aid to stop the same happening to their leaders. US Forces were landed in Lebanon. Nearby Jordan, its oil pipelines from Iraq cut and facing an imminent uprising planned by Egypt and Syria, also needed urgent help. While the US Air Force promised a 'massive sky-train' to satisfy the country's fuel requirements in the short term, 2,000 British soldiers of the 16 Independent Parachute Brigade were landed in Amman to guard the King.

American Globemaster aircraft began a major airlift, using Nicosia Airport, supported by RAF Hastings and Beverleys, with Hunter fighters providing cover. In Turkey and Libya, Anglo-American Forces were readied for action. The British military buildup was

A United States Air Force Globemaster at RAF Nicosia.

complete when there was the equivalent of two army divisions in the Middle East and Cyprus.

Off the coast of Beirut, the US Sixth Fleet of 44 warships gathered, including several aircraft carriers. The Royal Navy carriers, HMS *Eagle* and *Albion*, and the cruiser HMS *Bermuda* were on their way to join them.

At the time Private A. G. Lawrie was 'in the deep end' of this activity, working in the Staff Message Control Centre at the General Headquarters of the Middle East Land Forces at Episkopi. 'The SMC was part of the heavily guarded Signals' complex, within two other guarded perimeters,' he recalled.

'All the signals that came to GHQ passed through our office. Now I knew why I had been "positively vetted". There was all this secret stuff of the highest order, which made life really exciting and interesting. We got to know what was happening on the military and political fronts. The Diptels – diplomatic telegrams – were among the longest, just as you would expect from civilian political employees. I became adept at spelling Dag Hammarskjold, the UN Secretary-General's name. One of his quotes that I remember was, "Constant attention by a good nurse may be just as important as a major operation by a surgeon". I was quite disappointed by the end of the crisis in October.'

There   was   a   clear   view   of   the

Mediterranean from where Corporal Ken Wintle of the RASC was camped. Usually there was not much to be seen, 'but then one morning I glanced seaward and was astonished to see a group of ships anchored a mile or so offshore,' he told the author. 'Despite their greyness they looked sleek and clean cut. Most imposing of all was the aircraft carrier – the USS *Forrestal* – that dwarfed the rest of the US Sixth Fleet.'

A couple of hours later, while Wintle was standing on the porch of the company office, he saw a small helicopter, clattering noisily overhead and getting lower. 'To my astonishment it settled on a patch of grass behind our Records Office and at the side of the Admin Office. Settling on such a small spot was a credit to the pilot's skill,' he went on. 'When the dust cleared, I could see a large yellow Mickey Mouse painted on the side. An American colonel alighted, wearing leather flying jacket, khaki drill trousers, peaked hat, and dark sunglasses. Strapped conspicuously to his waist was a large .45 revolver sagged to one side. He approached and towered a good six inches over my 6-foot frame. He looked like John Wayne, and I felt quite excited.

'"Hey Corporal," he said in a slow American drawl, "I've come to see your boss. Can you show me the way?"

'It was just like on the films. "This way, sir," I replied saluting smartly. He responded with a nonchalant flick of his hand. I admired the pilot's navigation because he'd landed a few yards away from our Commanding Officer's office. Leading the way, I knocked on the door and entered.

'"An American Colonel has just landed in a helicopter, sir, and wants to talk to you." My words gushed out because of my excitement. The American officer went inside, as I held the door open for him. My Colonel spoke: "Make sure we're not disturbed."

'There was now a great deal of excitement amongst the military staff. Office personnel gathered to question me, no doubt they thought I was privy to Top Brass conversation. When the RSM appeared on the scene they all disappeared. He prowled the veranda like a watchdog and no one was tempted to venture near. Meanwhile the pilot stayed in his machine not even bothering to stretch his legs. We never got to know what the two colonels discussed, but we felt honoured that we might be working with the Americans.'

At No. 751 Signals Unit at Cape Greco, the British and Americans were already pulling together. Overlooking the main shipping lanes between Cyprus and Lebanon, the RAF radar screens showed the US Navy flotilla clearly, while still far out at sea. 'For a few days, the ships anchored off the south coast and we had some interesting interception exercises with our Hunters and Javelins from Akrotiri and the Americans' Crusaders and Skyhawks,' SAC 'Fergie' Ferguson, recalled. 'Occasionally the US flyers buzzed our camp as a "thank you" for our efforts.

'On one occasion a "lost" American transport had to be escorted to Nicosia because it would not answer the Javelin that was shadowing it. It turned out that the aircraft's radio had failed and the crew was nervous that the RAF would knock it out. As our aircraft were usually armed that could have happened. Our excitement was usually reserved for when we plotted Russian aircraft either following the Navy exercises or flying along the coast of Turkey towards Lebanon.'

Throughout the Middle East crisis, the Tactical Air Control Centre at RAF Nicosia was stretched to its limits as British reinforcements arrived in a variety of aircraft – civil and military – including unsuitable Shackletons. 'When the soldiers disembarked, they looked dazed and shell-shocked,' recalled LAC Colin Whiting. 'Our bomb dumps personnel worked overtime, providing the explosives required for these Middle East operations.'

The US Air Force also based its planes at the

airport, their crews horrified by the quality of the food in the RAF canteens. 'The Caywood mess – under canvas – was the worst for miles,' said SAC John Thorpe, shrugging his shoulders. 'Dysentery was rife. The Globemaster ground crews refused to use it. The were only willing to try food sent over from the officers' mess.' In the end, they preferred to prepare their own meals from their K-ration packs.

FOR THE moment, defence chiefs in London and Washington took their eyes off Cyprus as far as the EOKA conflict was concerned to deal with more dangerous problems that could involve the Soviet Union and cause Western oil interests to be lost. Sir Hugh Foot and Major General Kendrew were left alone to take care of the Island and its security. Along the length and breath of the Island, death and mayhem continued.

In a single day at the end of July, the authorities recorded three men killed in Limassol, one in Kyrenia and a Turkish shepherd shot in the head in Kellia, followed by a Greek shepherd in Athienou; a Greek Cypriot rural constable kidnapped and 'executed' by three masked men in Karmi; woundings of two in Nicosia; a bomb attack on a police vehicle in Ayios Antonios market;

and arson attacks in Ktima, Paphos and Khlorakas. Excluding these incidents, between 1 and 20 July, 29 Greek Cypriots and 31 Turks were killed, and two servicemen. In addition, there were scores of injured.

On 30 July, Karl 'Ginger' Atkinson, a driver with the Royal Ulster Rifles' HQ Coy, lost his life when his vehicle skidded off the road while he was travelling through Lysi. Local youths had stoned his windscreen, causing him to crash and he died slowly a few yards from the village's water point. Not one villager came to his assistance. His body was found later by a foot patrol.

The month ended with the death of Staff Sergeant Ronald Kirby of the RAOC as he tried to disarm a bomb on a road in the Famagusta district. At the start of August, the grim reaper continued his relentless harvest of death. On the 2nd, Andreas Yakoumis, a 17-year-old garage mechanic, was given two revolvers by his friend Yannakis, who said: 'You take one of these with six rounds and go and kill an Englishman.' The first 'Englishman' he saw was Sergeant Reginald Hammond, who was buying his two-year-old an ice cream from a street trader in the Nicosia suburb of Ayios Dhometios.

Yannakis aimed, fired and shot the father dead, then fled leaving the little boy crouching

Sergeant Reginald Hammond lies dead in a Nicosia street.

Sergeant Hammond's grave in Wayne's Keep Military Cemetery.

over his father, crying: 'Daddy, daddy.' When a patrol arrived, a soldier asked for a handkerchief to stem the blood oozing from Hammond's head. Bystanders ignored his plea and scurried off, leaving the street deserted. Mrs Hammond was left a widow, expecting their second child.

Two days later the young murderer was caught and admitted: 'I killed him.' Much later, when tried in court, Yannakis was freed on a legal technicality.

The next day, Lieutenant Colonel Frederick Collier of the RASC was off duty and relaxing by watering the garden of his house in Limassol at 18.00, when EOKA struck again. According to Grivas, the attack was led by Pavlos Pavlou, the man responsible for severely injuring and bringing an end to the career of Special Branch Superintendent E. N. Peirce. Pavlou shot one bullet into the colonel's back at short range and, as he fell, fired three more into his body. 'I sent him my congratulations on this attack,' said Grivas.

The soldiers in Collier's command attended his funeral at Wayne's Keep Military Cemetery. They had collected voluntary donations to buy a wreath, which Corporal Reg Kelly carried and presented to the colonel's widow. Brigadier D. J. Sutton wrote later: 'The mood of the men at that time was difficult to contain.'

The deaths of Collier and Hammond brought the total of military fatalities caused by EOKA to 86. *The Times* thundered: 'Terrorism in Cyprus has sunk to new depths of foulness. The gunmen are murderers of the most cowardly kind ... They may call themselves nationalists. But they are thugs ... Apparently there are groups who are out to destroy any chance of a truce and a search for peace. But the result of the murders, though by no means unique in their cruelty in Cyprus, is to blacken the Greek case.

'Many will feel that it forfeits its right to be heard at all if it is linked with murderers. The possible effects of such shootings on the British troops in Cyprus must also be taken into account. It is easier for the civilian at home to forget these things than for the dead men's comrades, but in spite of all the provocations discipline has remained good. This reflects great credit on the British Army. But such terrorism can lead only to more intense drives to root out the gunmen in which innocent Cypriots will inevitably be affected by the curfews, searches, and detentions of suspects. That may suit the policy of the terrorists, who are as indifferent to the well being of their decent fellow citizens as they are to the lives of their victims. But it will not lead to peace.'

And, true to form, more curfews were imposed and more large-scale operations mounted to root out the terrorists, wherever they could be found, but black clouds of depression hung over Government House. 'One of the most frightening aspects of Cyprus life is fear itself,' reported a newspaper corre-

Sergeant Hammond's funeral.

spondent. 'No one knows who may be the next on the list for sacrifice on EOKA's unholy altar, and sound, sensible people firmly believe that more assassinations of Britons can be expected, and govern their lives accordingly.'

When Corporal Michael Scarrott of 113 Maintenance Unit, RAF Nicosia, who became a padre after his National Service, and his eight-man team was not filling 45-gallon drums with aviation fuel destined for Jordan, he wrote poetry. The murder of Sergeant Hammond so shocked him that he wrote:

All is quiet and the sun is hot,
Someone walks down the street,
A shot rings out and someone falls,
While somebody makes a retreat.

Nobody bothers to see if they can help,
He just lies there on the ground,
His body all bleeding stains the sand,
He's dead, he can't make a sound.

There's always an ambush outside the camp,
A few shots and somebody dies,
While over the sea there's a mother,
A sweetheart or a wife that cries.

Then, on 4 August, a day on which six people were killed, Grivas made an extraordinary announcement in a leaflet distributed at dusk. He declared the immediate suspension of EOKA operations against the British and Turkish Cypriots to give peace a chance with fresh negotiations. He reserved the right, however, for the terrorists to resume their activities if the authorities continued their 'provocations'. Once again, the wily Colonel had placed Sir Hugh Foot in an invidious position: whether to ignore Grivas's 'truce' or step up the vigorous operations being conducted by the Security Forces. The Governor was left to consider an old Greek proverb: 'A fox is not twice caught in the same snare.'

There was no comment from Government House. From Athens came a message from Makarios: 'We trust the offer will meet with due response and that there will be no provocation nor any attempt to impose the [Macmillan] plan already rejected by the Cyprus people.' Neither the Archbishop's words or Grivas's offer impressed the Turkish deputy leader Rauf Denktas. He shrugged his wide shoulders and boomed: 'If Grivas is sincere about his offer, he should take the opportunity given to him by the Government and leave Cyprus and disband EOKA. He will see that upon doing this violence in Cyprus will cease with immediate effect.' Nevertheless, the next day his TMT organization ordered a cessation of violence 'until further notice'.

The Times reported: 'The relief of Cypriots living in "danger areas" approached jubilation as hour followed hour without any reports of violence.' In an editorial, the paper shared the view of many British expatriates: 'What Grivas's motives for the move may be is largely matter for conjecture. This is the third time he has made a truce offer – acting in one case from strength, in the other from weakness. It is impossible to say into which category the present occasion falls. His reasons may be purely tactical. But the probability is that they reflect in some way the appeals for cessation of violence, which have been made recently, at Mr Macmillan's invitation, by Archbishop Makarios and Mr Karamanlis (the Greek Prime Minister) ... At any rate, there seems a good chance, if the offer is genuine and if the Turks respond to it, that the immediate threat of cataclysm has been stayed.'

In Cyprus, the Governor lifted the night curfews and eased travel restrictions, but the Army continued to search for terrorists. Nicosia residents had been confined to their homes after dark since 7 June. The curfew law had applied equally to off-duty Britons, but there was less cheer in their quarters. They were sceptical that the 'truce' would bring rapprochement.

Weekending at his Sussex home, Prime Minister Macmillan read the cables from Cyprus and concluded the time was ripe for him to visit Athens and Ankara in the hope that one quick, bold move, at a time when both sides were weary and fearful, might clear up the bloody mess the Island had become in less than two months. Like the Governor, the Prime Minister was a showman, but a much

shrewder and pragmatic politician, while Foot, said Stephen Hastings, the MI6 resident on the Island, was 'conditioned more by the radical left-wing thinking of his family than by a dispassionate assessment of his country's interests'.

Arriving at Athens' Ellinikon Airport, on 8 August, Macmillan was met by Greek Prime Minister Karamanlis. They shook hands firmly and Macmillan remarked that the Greek leader's hair had turned greyer since their last get-together. 'Yes,' quipped the other back. 'It's caused by the Cyprus problem.' For the next two days, the men were locked in meetings around a green-draped table in the Anahtora Palace, joined by Sir Hugh who had held separate discussions with Archbishop Makarios.

Before the British party travelled on to Ankara, it was clear there had not been a meeting of minds. The official Greek spokesmen merely used the well-tested phrase – 'there was a sincere exchange of general opinions', while a British representative added that Cyprus figured 'particularly in relation to the importance of this question for the coun-

Prime Minister Karamanlis of Greece welcomes British Prime Minister Harold Macmillan at Athens Airport.

tries of the West in the present international situation'. He did not mention that a US delegation, led by President Eisenhower's personal representative in the Middle East, was on its way to twist Athenian arms for a quick settlement. Yet amid the general trend of pessimism there were optimists who pointed out that many elements of the Partnership Plan were conducive to compromise.

MACMILLAN AND Foot landed in Ankara on the evening of the 9th and immediately conferred with Prime Minister Menderes and Foreign Minister Zorlu and continued their session the next day after the British PM laid a wreath on the tomb of Kemal Ataturk, the founder of the Turkish Republic. It was a gesture that caused an 'excellent impression', said a reporter, adding, 'the political atmosphere is more propitious to a solution than at any time since the recent violence in Cyprus began'. But, yet again, officials refused to specify any points on which there was agreement.

Although due to fly back to London on 11 August, the PM diverted his RAF Comet to land at Nicosia. During his brief unexpected stop, Macmillan was keen 'to show the flag' – and himself – and so he made a lightning trip to Lysi to meet members of a regiment that he had joined 46 years earlier – the 3rd Battalion Grenadier Guards. Those not on operational duties were told to 'smarten up' as an unnamed VIP was on his way. Sergeant Terry Buchanan, a National Serviceman assigned to Army Public Relations, was rushed 'under a cloak of secrecy' to the Guards' camp and asked to 'take some good photos'.

A helicopter landed on the football pitch and out stepped the Prime Minister and the Governor to be greeted by Lieutenant Colonel P. C. Britten, the Commanding Officer, with whose father Macmillan had served in the First World War. Buchanan snapped away, using his Rolleiflex camera. 'The officers,

NCOs and men looked in splendid shape,' said the PM in his memoirs. 'I spoke a few words to them. I found all this very moving, and I almost broke down in speaking, for it all recalled so many memories.'

'At the end of his visit to his former regiment, we stood alongside his helicopter awaiting his departure,' said Buchanan. 'As I was preparing to take the final photograph, to my left and in line with me were a general, a brigadier and a colonel. Harold Macmillan looked at the line, pondered, then strode directly towards me and shook my hand. The roar that went up from the surrounding troops was deafening. The look that came from the adjacent officers was intimidating. The three officers had failed to recognize the instant raising of morale that this simple gesture had made to the surrounding squaddies.'

Without pausing for refreshments, Macmillan flew off to greet the 1st Battalion, the Queen's Own Royal West Kent Regiment in the Karpas.

After listening to service chiefs at the Episkopi Base, the helicopter raced the Prime Minister back to Government House to meet the Mayors of Nicosia and Kyrenia, Dr Dervis and Mr Demetriades for precisely 50 minutes. Thirty minutes later Dr Kutchuk and Rauf Denktas entered the conference room to express their views. The Greeks had complained about the 'partiality' of the Security Forces, and the Turks expressed their unhappiness at the 'inadequate protection for their life and property' during their 60-minute encounter.

Macmillan, for his part, kept to the same script for both his audiences. He informed them that the 'Partnership Plan' would be implemented and urged them to accept the seven-year 'cooling off' period it proposed. 'If these years are years of decent, honourable progress, how much easier it would be to reach the next stage, whatever that might be,' he said in calming tones. He explained that the Greek and Turkish Governments were in agreement with his suggestions and spoke of 'the honourable ambitions and hopes that the people may nurture'. He admitted he was unable to tell what the next phase would be and that he was not discouraged at returning home without signing any treaties on this occasion. Before a lasting agreement, 'the right thing to do is to end terrorism'.

In the evening he met the men and women from the UK Police Unit and thanked them for the sterling work they were doing on behalf of Britain and Cyprus. At 01.40, the Prime Minister's Comet took off with him on board. 'In spite of all the conflicting reports, some progress seems to have been made,' reported *The Times*. 'Mr Macmillan now returns to consult with his colleagues about the next move.'

Soon after Macmillan's departure, his 'Adventure in Partnership' was modified. The Government announced that the mainland Greek and Turkish representatives would not have a seat on the Executive Council of the new-style administration, but they would have 'direct access to the Governor and such facilities as they need to carry out their functions. Accordingly, Her Majesty's Government invites the Governments of Greece and Turkey to appoint their representatives with effect from 1 October.'

Following the changes, Sir Hugh Foot commuted the death sentence imposed on Christos Constantinou to 10 years' imprisonment.

EVERYTHING DEPENDED now on how Grivas would react. He faced a war on three fronts – against the British, against the Turks and against the left-wing Greek Cypriots. Would he return to his campaign of terrorism or allow the Macmillan Plan or take form? Based on his record and character, his tensions with the Greek Government and differences with Makarios, the probability was he would decide in favour of continued violence.

To the surprise of many, the first denunciation of the plan came from Makarios, with AKEL supporting him. The Archbishop and the Communists had given the perfect excuse for Grivas to send out a clarion to his followers to standby for action, without appearing to be at odds with either the prelate or the left-wingers. His first leaflet since the start of his latest truce warned: 'We will not succumb to the Anglo-Turkish conspiracy. Our island is Greek. We accept no compromise. We demand clear self-determination ... No power is capable of subjugating us and imposing the abortive British plan for our enslavement to the British and the Turks. Greek Cypriots, be ready for a great battle against the plan. No one should cooperate in any effort for the imposition of the plan and all must carry out the orders of leadership ...'

By contrast, Turkey suddenly reversed its position. The Foreign Minister announced his country had not abandoned its partition demands, but fully supported the new British plan, because 'it is reconcilable with our thesis'. He said Turkey would not hinder Britain's efforts to find a solution to the Cyprus Problem, but, he hinted, Turks only wanted to make sure the Island never became a Greek possession as it was so close to the nation's southern shores.

For British troops, there was no pause. They maintained their routine of daily patrols, cordons and search operations and guarding remote police stations, never knowing what might happen from one second to the next. Sergeant Ray 'Steve' Stephens of 29 Field Regiment, Royal Artillery, gave the author an example of how things could change from relative calm to the chaos and pain in the blink of an eye after an ambush. These are his words:

'It was 18 August and we went out on patrol to Lefkonico, with two Land Rovers and eight men in all. We called in at the village police station, which was manned by men of the regiment and not policemen. They had nothing of interest to report so we continued on our way. We travelled along the road in the direction of the Kyrenia hills. I noticed two army trucks coming down the road towards us. Suddenly there was one almighty explosion. The leading truck flew into the air and landed on its top. The other went off the road. We were at the ambush site in a minute or so.

'My Bombardier second-in-charge spotted some men running across a field and gave chase, The terrorists fired back and we replied twice as hard, but didn't hit or capture any of them. After this quick exchange, the bombardier saw that a bullet had torn though his cap, just above the badge.

'Meantime I was trying to comfort the injured men in the overturned three-tonner. One young lad was gravely injured with a large hole in the back of his head. I could tell his chances of survival were nil. He died there and then in my arms. I radioed for a chopper to take him and the injured to BMH in Nicosia. I was told later the dead lad was Gunner Graham Baldry, who had been in Cyprus just two weeks.

'We could have just as easily been the target and taken the hit from the electrically detonated mine, hidden by EOKA in a culvert under the road.'

Were EOKA gangs acting on their own? Had Grivas lost control of his men or was another 'truce' at an end? Cyprus waited anxiously for what next would happen. An uncertain lull fell over the Island, only to be shattered by a 'fierce battle' between the Security Forces and an EOKA gang on 23 August in the troublesome Lysi village. The blood-letting had started again in earnest. The people braced themselves for more to come.

The events in the Lysi area began to take shape in late July when a platoon of the Royal Ulster Rifles captured two EOKA couriers outside Vatili police station. They were handed over to Special Branch for interrogation. The men told of several wanted terrorists hiding in the village. As a result, Operation *Swan Lake* was mounted. It lasted two weeks. Not only was Lysi cordoned off and searched, but so were the neighbouring villages of Asha and Vatili, known as the 'Poison Triangle'.

During the operation one of the Royal Ulster Rifles' patrols set out from Karaolos Camp on 1 August in a one-ton vehicle and an Austin Champ, dropping off ambush parties at various points. On their return journey a pipe bomb exploded behind the Champ, in which the passengers were Captain J. B. Wadsworth, his driver, radio operator Tom Rigby, and Rifleman Billy Reid. As the debris fell, they came under fire from both sides of the road. Lying flat, they replied, aiming at the muzzle flashes of the enemy and firing only single shots at a time because they were short of ammunition and could not waste it. Just as the exchange ended, their one-ton truck raced off. Later the driver told Reid: 'When I saw you lying by the roadside, I thought you were all dead and made my getaway!'

Neither the gunmen nor their weapons stores were found, but members of RUR's 'B' Company remained in the vicinity and established a string of ambush positions. They waited for several nights to see if the wanted men would fall into their trap. The Rifles had lost one of their soldiers to EOKA activity on 30 July in Lysi and were determined to repay in kind.

On 23 August their patience was rewarded. At about 21.30, Corporal Beach and his ambush party saw four men pushing two bicycles on a track that cut through their position. The men were challenged and immediately fired back, wounding Rifleman Hagan and a patrol dog, 'who lost several inches of his tail'. Both made a full recovery. The Rifles shot back and were joined by Corporal Austin and his party, who had been hiding 250 yards away. In the ensuing firefight, over in minutes, three terrorists were killed. Loaded on their bicycles was a large cache of arms being taken to a new hide. 'We had our kill and our tails were up,' exclaimed one of the soldiers.

According to Grivas, the leading terrorist was killed as soon as the Rifles spotted the group. The second, Michael Kallis, wounded Rifleman Hagan before dropping dead in a hail of automatic fire. But, while mortally wounded, wrote the Colonel, Kallis hurled a grenade and killed five soldiers. The third man met his death when he tried to escape. 'If all his men were killed, who gave him such detailed information?' asked former Corporal Dave Cranston, one of the Rifles. 'His account, like most of his claims, shows a degree of inaccuracy bordering on the ridiculous.'

Expecting a violent response from EOKA, the Security Forces stepped up patrols in the main towns and launched another major operation in the Morphou area, involving more than 1,000 soldiers.

In Valva, they ran down Michalakis Parides, code-named *Laios*, after a tip-off from an informer. On 27 August he was found hiding in the house belonging to Christos Karageorgis, a schoolteacher. Ordered to surrender, he refused and fired a shot at the troops. They returned fire and he was killed. On his death, Grivas said: 'He fulfilled his mission in an exemplary fashion.' A 'fighter' from the start of the conflict, Parides kept changing his appearance and had used a forged ID card to move around. He was first captured after throwing bombs in the Larnaca court, but later escaped in December 1957 from Nicosia General Hospital, where he had been taken for a nose operation. He then returned to Larnaca to become an area commander.

With four leading terrorists killed within a few days, it was clear Grivas was losing as the Security Forces intensified their efforts, but they knew his gangs would strike back as sure

as the sun rose. His first move was to organize a grand show of nationalist fervour. On EOKA's explicit orders – conveyed partly by leaflet and partly by word of mouth – thousands of Greeks turned out to attend memorial services for the dead men. In towns and villages, priests extolled the gallant deeds of EOKA and denounced the supposed villainy of British rule. Greek flags were everywhere, hanging at half-mast.

The main rallying point in Nicosia was the Phaneromeni Church, where 5,000 Greeks heard Bishop Anthimos of Kitium proclaim the Greek determination to fight on in the face of British attempts to impose a settlement in the shape of the Macmillan Plan. 'Nothing can stop us,' he shouted to a background of ear-splitting cheers and thunderous applause. 'No plan or solution can be imposed without the consent of the Greeks, who make up four-fifths of the Cyprus population.'

On 1 September, the 'Murder Mile' assassins of Ledra Street struck again to uphold Grivas's policy to kill a member of the Security Forces for every death of one of his men. His first victim was Warrant Officer Francis O'Hagan Sloane of the RAF. The 44-year-old Air Traffic Controller and his wife were holding hands as they walked to Mass. His wife was injured in the attack. The three gunmen escaped in a taxi, which was found two miles away. Usually witnesses never came forward to a street killing, but on this occasion a Greek Cypriot chose to help the police. To keep his identity secret, a hood with slits for his eyes was placed over his face, an overall covered his clothes and sandals replaced his shoes as he walked past the hostile gaze of rows of tight-lipped youths that had been rounded up.

The next day, the same EOKA execution squad shot dead Assistant Police Super-intendent Donald Thomson, a married New Zealander with two children. With three bullets in his back, he lay crumpled on the pavement, flies buzzing over his body. The street was suddenly empty. The angry Governor slapped another curfew on Nicosia. Most expatriates and soldiers feared that the EOKA truce was over and indiscriminate attacks against Britons would be resumed along the lines of Grivas's campaigns of 1956 and 1957. Greeks thought that there was little chance left for the authorities to grant Makarios the right to return to the Island for the peace negotiations he would lead on their behalf.

WHILE THE Greek Cypriots of Nicosia shut their shops and sat glumly on doorsteps, Turkish Cypriots carried on business as usual in their half of the capital, north of the so-called Mason-Dixon Line, but 10 miles south-west of Famagusta, a fight to the finish was taking place between the Royal Ulster Rifles and an EOKA gang consisting of Andreas Karios, Christos Samaras, Photis Pittas and Elias Papakyriakou, all with prices on their heads.

In the blackest hours before a late summer dawn a routine cordon-and-search operation had begun in the dusty peasant village of Liopetri in Eastern Cyprus. The following account is drawn from an article published in the RUR journal, when the facts were still fresh in the minds of those whose who took part.

The operation was mounted by 'A', 'B', 'S' and HQ Companies of the 1st Battalion, the Royal Ulster Rifles, with Minden Battery, 20 Field Regiment, Royal Artillery, under command. The troops were dropped from vehicles about three miles from the village, and marched stealthily from equidistant points to the north, east and west of the village. John Rickards, a 19-year-old from Lancashire, was a National Serviceman with 'five months to do'. He shared his memories with the author. 'For this particular operation we were dressed and equipped lightly – known

Aerial view of the Liopetri cordon.

as a "soft shoe patrol" – carrying FN rifles and only 15 rounds of ammunition.'

Ten minutes after the cordon had been mounted at 03.00 hrs a small van was spotted leaving the village to the west. A Rifleman of 'A' Company challenged the driver. Instantly a group of men appeared from behind the vehicle and opened fire with automatic weapons. The fire was returned and the gunmen turned on their heels and made off back into the village. Because it was dark, it was impossible to track them, but the van's driver was arrested and handed to Special Branch officers. He was identified as Elias Samaras, the brother of one the terrorists believed to be hiding in Liopetri.

At 03.45 the Rifles entered the village, ordered all men and boys from 14 to 60 years of age out of bed and confined them behind a wire fence in the grounds of the local school to await questioning, starting at first light. The area where the RUR and the terrorists exchanged shots was searched shortly after dawn. Casings from 9mm rounds and a loaded magazine for an M.3 automatic rifle were recovered.

The sun was well up by the time Elias Samaras told his Special Branch interrogators that he had lost sympathy with EOKA's aims and its 'harsh' actions against fellow Cypriots. He agreed to act as an informer and lead the troops to where there were arms caches hidden in the village. More importantly, he claimed, he knew the terrorists' hideout. There were three of them, he said. It turned out there were four.

At 15.00 Samaras first took a party of RUR soldiers to a house which contained the remains of a demolished hide and then on to two recently constructed hides, about three miles outside the village. Officers began to think their informer was trying to mislead them and buy time for his comrades to escape. He was told to get a move on. Just as dusk began to fall, he led the RUR intelligence officers to the cemetery, where a box containing four bombs was excavated and a further three bombs were found under the floor of a coffee shop on the other side of the road. Throughout the night a sort of treasure hunt ensued with Samaras eventually leading them to a chaff house. He insisted the terrorists had hidden there and could still be inside.

At dawn, after mess-tin ablutions and breakfast eaten on the dusty plain, the decision was taken to clear the chaff. A section of 'B' Company started raking, only to be met by a volley of bullets from within. Rifleman Bolger was slightly wounded and Lieutenant Boyd fought a rearguard action back through the doorway. The cordon was thickened, fire was poured in through the doorway, and Corporal Fleet of the Intelligence section called out in fractured Greek for the gunmen to surrender. Thirty minutes went by without

any activity, but then a terrorist crossed the doorway and was hit – 'taken out'.

Further exhortations to surrender were answered by bursts of bullets aimed at the soldiers. 'Later on, somebody turned up with a box of Mills hand grenades, and in the confusion things quickly escalated into black farce,' Rickards recalled.

Lieutenants Boyd and Gallwey lobbed 36 grenades before someone shouted, 'these things aren't going off' – or words to that effect. 'The truth was that they hadn't been primed, and a call went out for a coin to remove the base-plate to fix the detonator. What a time to run out of loose change! Overall, the grenades were to turn out to be rather ineffective anyway, with many falling short of the target. Their only long-term effect was to cover us all in dust and pepper us with tiny slivers of shrapnel, which we proudly had pulled from our backs days later,' said Rickards.

Captain Lucy recommended a change of tactics and weapon. He wanted to fire 3.5 rockets to bring down the walls of the house. A radio message was sent to 'B' Echelon requesting the necessary equipment. Eventually rockets and launcher arrived 'For what seemed like ages we waited behind a wall,' Rickards commented. 'Cigarettes were passed around. From time to time, we could hear the conversations of the officers and NCOs, who had now begun to arrive from various parts of the village. For a couple of hours there was stalemate.'

CSM McConnell of 'B' Company and another soldier volunteered to make up the rocket-firing pair. Rickards continued: 'The plan was to breech the wall of the barn with 10 anti-tank missiles and then for us to storm through the gap, with the section led by 2nd Lieutenant Boyd. Designed to penetrate steel, the rockets were fired at point-blank range, but failed to dent the two-feet thick wall made of mud bricks. Besides the deafening noise, all they did was to produce large quantities of dust.'

After eleven consecutive rockets, fired from varying angles, the building remained secure, but into the dust storm raced Lieutenant Boyd and his 16 men, including Riflemen Bowes and Rumbell, Driver Kinsella and Lance Corporal Smallwood. When they were silhouetted in the doorway by the bright morning sun, they became easy targets. Despite heavy fire from within, Boyd and four others tried to establish a position by the doorway on the building's veranda. A terrorist followed them out, letting off a burst from his sub-machine gun and hitting the junior officer in the leg. 'The situation became a mixture of shouts, shots and spinning bodies,' Rickards said. 'Corporal Shaughnessy had his weapon knocked from his hand and now faced a terrorist who advanced on him. Keen to keep his life, he grabbed a piece of loose masonry and crashed it on his enemy's head, then sprayed him from the man's own French-made sub-machine gun.

'Our attacking party was now in disarray. Rifleman Daniel Kinsella was propped up against the side of the door, with a fatal head wound. Mr Boyd squirmed on the patio, his leg shattered. Rumble was crawling away with serious chest wounds. Others had withdrawn with less serious injuries. Some of us rushed forward to get the injured out. I remember being more shocked at having to drag Mr Boyd through a prickly thorn bush, as if he wasn't already injured badly enough.

'Rifleman Rumble's chest was pumping blood. One of our sergeants ripped open his shirt and stopped the flow with his fist. Kinsella wasn't moving and he didn't respond to our calls. He was dead by the time we were able to pull his body out.

'The wounded needed water and something to drink from. Hyped-up and covered in blood, I kicked open the door of the nearest house. In the corner of the front room, there was a terrified mother with two tiny children clinging to her. "I'm sorry," I said, "we need a glass", as I helped myself from a cabinet and beat a retreat from the petrified threesome.'

In the meantime Lieutenant Gallwey dashed through the heavy fire on to the veranda to take command of the situation. He pressed home the attack against the desperate EOKA men. 'The next move was to push a tear gas canister through one of the building's ventilation holes. Suddenly a man came running from the house, gun in hand; he didn't last long.'

Under cover of the new attack the Commanding Officer and Lance Corporals Gill and Dillon scrambled onto the roof, poured in petrol and set it alight. The flames and smoke drove out the terrorists who chose to die rather than give themselves up. 'When the end came, it came quickly,' said Rickards. The battle of Liopetri was over just after midday. In a matter of hours the Riflemen had tasted EOKA's fanatical determination. RUR officers learnt the cool, selfless heroism and initiative of the men under their command.

'To the professional soldiers, this had been a small incident, compared with other military involvements,' concluded Rickards, 'but for others like me who were basically civilians in uniform, it had been a taste of life and death in that short informative period known as National Service.'

The dead terrorists were identified as

The end of the Liopetri battle

Christos Samaras killed at Liopetri.

Christos Samaras, Andreas Karios, Photis Pittas and Elias Papakyriakou.

Elias Papakyriakou had taken part in several grenade attacks on British Forces in the Famagusta area. His proudest achievement was stealing automatic weapons from French troops who were in Cyprus, following the Anglo-French Operation *Musketeer* against Egypt. Later, with others, he attempted to sabotage water supplies in Vatili.

Andreas Karios, one of eight children, had led an operation against an electric power station, which failed and caused Modestos Panteli to electrocute himself on the first day of the conflict. He had been arrested in November and held in the Pyla Pile Detention Centre from which he had escaped in March with Photis Pittas. He was a teacher by profession, and had taught at a primary school in Achna and became the deputy commander of EOKA's Lysi gang.

Christos Samaras, code-name *Xanthos*, had been sent to Liopetri to recruit and train local EOKA members. His brother Elias was the informer who had brought the RUR to the barn.

The Security Forces sent Elias to the UK with a new identity and funds sufficient for him to start a fresh life. Within 17 days, he had used up the money on alcohol and, riddled with guilt, returned to Cyprus, where he gave himself up to EOKA and asked Grivas for forgiveness. The Colonel ordered his immediate execution, which even his parents approved, and refused the man's last request to say farewell to his wife and young children.

Nevertheless he implored the EOKA leader to 'protect them and speak to them like a father'. He ended: 'Leader, I pray that God may protect you from all evil and lay his hand upon you, so that you may guide our shattered ship into the haven of eternal freedom. I also wish all members the peace and protection of God our Father. And one thing more: rather than fall into the hands of the enemy, let them fall glorious and honoured. Enlighten them to do their duty, and especially to do God's will, so that he won't punish them like me.' He was given the last rites and then shot dead.

News of the treachery reached Georgios Karios, Andreas's brother, who swore to avenge the Liopetri deaths, although he was held in detention. Some weeks later he escaped and fled to Astromeriti to hide, but another informer betrayed his whereabouts. In a fight with the Security Forces, he was wounded, and he died in Nicosia General Hospital nine days later on 28 October.

Corporal 'Paddy' Shaughnessy was awarded the Military Medal for his bravery in the Battle of Liopetri.

When the smoke cleared, Grivas communicated in his usual fashion. 'We offered peace, but our enemy thought we are weak and provoked,' said his leaflet posted first in Famagusta. 'Every time he [the enemy] murders he will bear the consequences.'

CHAPTER TWENTY-TWO

An end to *enosis:* the diplomatic Mata Hari

'Vanity disappointed will always find an enemy on whom to bestow the utmost hatred and dislike.'

Sarah Fielding

BARBARA CASTLE, the Labour Member of Parliament for Blackburn, Lancashire, known as 'The Red Queen', slipped into the rock pool at the Dome Hotel in Kyrenia and let the limpid water of the Mediterranean embrace her. Suddenly she was a little girl again, giggling and splashing her companion, Peter Benenson, the lawyer who later founded Amnesty International. From the terrace, Ted, her husband, and Charles Foley of the *Times*

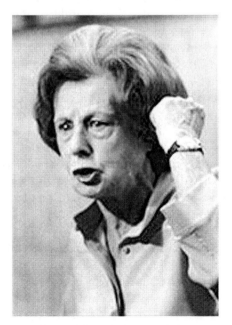

The 'Red Queen' raises passions.

of *Cyprus* and his wife watched from their deckchairs, sipping their second Brandy Sours.

It was the first time on this mellow Sunday in September that Mrs Castle had been able to break her busy schedule for a few hours of unguarded relaxation. Since early morning she had been on the move, stopping only for a meeting with the Governor before travelling to watch the results of a cordon-and-search operation by British troops and to hear the complaints of Greek Cypriots who accused the administration of cruel treatment of prisoners held in harsh and inhumane conditions.

'As we milled about in the water and looked across its perfect blueness at the distant hills of Anatolia, we agreed what a tourist paradise and gold mine the island could be if only the Emergency were removed,' Mrs Castle noted in her diary. 'Foley was a tall, elegant, witty man and an excellent host, always ready to entertain the succession of Labour and progressive notables who passed through the island in the search for a solution to the Cyprus problem.'

With the sun well over the yardarm, she came out of the sea, dried and dressed herself and then left the hotel with her group of admirers for a late lunch in the garden of an open-air restaurant under lemon trees. 'As I sat drinking the local wine in the dappled sunshine of the lemon trees, I thought what a tragedy it was that this predominantly Greek island with its little villages in the hills, where one ate black olives and drank the rather strong, resinous wine, had become the pawn of hard, militaristic, international politics,' she wrote.

It was almost sunset when Mrs Castle and her husband began their journey back to Nicosia and their suite in the Ledra Palace Hotel. A trio of hand-picked Turkish Cypriot police outriders on motorcycles escorted their black limousine, provided by Sir Hugh Foot. Just below St Hilarion Castle, the travellers were flagged down at a British Army check-point by a young second lieutenant. Barely had the car stopped, when a series of shots were fired from above. The car's tyres and lights were blown out and the engine cover peppered with holes. The gunmen had taken great care not to hit the passengers' compart-ment. Not one person suffered a scratch.

One of the Turkish policemen immediately radioed his headquarters and a second car was rushed to collect the fear-struck travellers, by now surrounded by the troops. While they were waiting, MI6 officers in a 'black bag' operation were searching the Castles' room for any incriminating material that would link her to EOKA. Her personal papers were photographed and the pictures sent to London for detailed examination. They also carefully packed the couple's suitcases so that they could take them to the airport immediately – 'for her safety' – and place them on the first available flight out of Cyprus, which happened to be bound for Athens.

A British undercover Special Operations Group had organized the ambush, a former member revealed in a conversation with the author, conducted in strict confidence and with the promise that his identity not be revealed. 'It operated independently of any overt contact with the Cyprus Establishment – Civil or Military,' he said. 'So far as I was aware, the Governor was not in my chain of command, which was nice and short!'

The officer explained: 'Several other chums and I commanded motley crews drawn from all the Services, and dressed as civilians – unshaven, and unwashed – and secretly armed to the teeth, pottering around the Cypriot coastline in a varied selection of decrepit-looking, heavily disguised, civilian craft, and interdicting terrorist smuggling. "Enemy" small craft were sunk where intercepted, along with their cargoes. Officially, we were all – officers and men – attached to bases located elsewhere, not in Cyprus, which never saw us officially. My mail was routed via a German BFPO, for example. We never wore uniform when "in-Theatre"; and when on leave we came and went as civilians.

'Our Boss was a Brigadier – dead now, God rest him – of decidedly "buccaneering" antecedents and an awesome whispered Special Forces' reputation, who was supposed to be tending his roses back in Hampshire, according to the Army List. He seemed to wield the kind of awesome powers one associ-ates with a Theatre Commander – but offi-cially he and we did not exist. At least two smaller units – one drawn from the Cyprus Special Constabulary – were working out of St Hilarion Castle that I am certain of, and there were probably others as well elsewhere.

'Mrs Castle's panic-stricken departure was accompanied by the heartfelt and gleeful cheers – I suspect – of every single British Serviceman in Cyprus – even those who voted Labour. We were all sickened at the way she spouted off, supporting EOKA and blaming the Military for everything.'

FROM THE moment Mrs Castle had arrived in Cyprus the previous Wednesday, 17 September, she had either been watched or accompanied by the Security Forces during her travels. Both as a Member of Parliament and Vice-Chairman of the Labour Party, she warranted special treatment and access to Government House. One of her guards was 18-year-old Lance-Bombardier Wallace Donald of 29 Field Regiment, Royal Artillery, who retired as a Major. His job was to take up a position on a high point ready to 'take out' any threats when she visited a particular place. He was not with her on the day of the Hilarion Castle ambush. From his home in Thetford, Norfolk, he said he remained angry over her attacks on British troops.

In Athens, Ankara and Nicosia, she was well known as a supporter of 'nationalist' causes and as a sharp critic of the forces of law and order in Britain's remaining colonies. She had often promised that when Labour came to power, her party would grant Greek Cypriots the right to *enosis*.

The next day she found Nicosia under curfew after gunmen wounded a married airman and US Vice-Consul J. P. Wentworth within an hour of each other. Both were rushed for treatment to the British Military Hospital. The airman had been with his wife walking down the road near their home, pushing their child in a pram when the terrorists fired at them from a passing car. Two Turks were also attacked and injured. The Turkish community reacted by setting fire to the Ayios Jacovos Church and two houses in a quick fire-raising rampage.

In her autobiography, *Fighting All The Way*, Barbara Castle wrote: 'Most of us in the party had an instinctive sympathy with the Greek Cypriots ... I had never been to Cyprus myself, but I knew that 80 per cent of her population of half a million was Greek and only 17 per cent Turkish, so her culture was basically Hellenic and Christian.'

Hugh Gaitskell, however, and others in the Labour Party leadership who were giving reluctant support to the Macmillan Plan, saw Mrs Castle as a loose cannon and were unhappy that she planned to visit the Island, fearful of what she might say while there.

Unable to prevent her, they nodded their approval subject to two conditions: she must fund her fact-finding mission from her own resources and she must visit the Greek and Turkish Governments to hear their points of view as well as those of the Turks and Greeks in Cyprus.

She agreed, but, in *Red Queen*, her authorized biography, by Anne Perkins, the author wrote, 'through Labour's international officer John Hatch, who had been working on his own plan for an independent Cyprus, Barbara was invited to Athens by Archbishop Makarios ... Barbara decided to make a tour of the region, funded partly by the Greek government, not an unusual move by a backbench MP but one requiring some caution and a careful assessment of the motives of the sponsor.

'The Greeks were looking for a way to derail the Macmillan Plan. Delay through diplomacy was one arm of the strategy; the second was to smear the name of the colonial power. It seems likely that she went not only to talk to Makarios, but as a guest of a Greek government that hoped she might undermine the British position by investigating allegations of brutality made against British troops.'

Mrs Castle arrived in Athens on 14 September where she was feted by Government Ministers and Archbishop Makarios. 'It was the first time I had met the "wily prelate" whom everyone had warned me against. He sat there, a dignified figure ... he said he feared that the British Government had made up its mind to go ahead with the Macmillan Plan whatever compromises were offered it.'

On the night before her arrival in the Greek capital, Private David Morrison of the Argyll and Sutherland Highlanders was shot dead and three others were injured in a remote area of Paphos when their vehicle was ambushed by EOKA. The whole area was cordoned off soon afterwards and a search began for the terror-

Their eyes and minds meet: Barbara Castle, MP, and
Archbishop Makarios in Athens.

ists. In this second action a Greek Cypriot, Charalambous Neophidou, was killed in Kathikas when he stabbed two servicemen.

After Athens, Mrs Castle flew on to Turkey – 'in a dirty little local plane of the Turkish airline', she wrote, adding, 'It smelt, because Turkey is obviously too poor to afford paper bags for people to be sick in and the person who had occupied my seat before me had had no choice but to be ill down the seat in front. At the frontier a particularly brutal Customs officer purloined most of my cigarettes, and an American who took the next seat as we continued in the plane was muttering in fury, "This country could not last a minute without aid and look how they treat you. Just down-right arrogance."'

The Turks, she said, did not believe that the Greek Cypriots would ever give up *enosis* as their objective, but Government officials assured her that Prime Minister Macmillan had given them written guarantees that his plan was only the first step towards partition and so, if they were denied the whole Island, they would settle for *taksim* – the division of Cyprus into Turkish and Greek portions, double *enosis*, in other words.

'I grew irritated as I began to realize the House of Commons was being misled,' Mrs Castle wrote. 'Macmillan had assured MPs that his plan was an alternative to partition. Now it was clear that the Turks had been promised that this was the road to it. Once again the Government had deliberately lied to Parliament.'

Seething with anger, she reached Cyprus 'determined to concentrate on my prime objective: the destruction of the Macmillan Plan'. Her meeting with Sir Hugh Foot also shocked her. She claimed that he told her: 'I do not mind so much if the soldiers get a bit rough when they are engaged in hot pursuit. What would worry me is if they started to do it in cold blood.'

At the Ledra Palace, she said, she had listened 'to a stream of complaints about the brutal handling of Greek Cypriots by the troops' and compiled 'a great dossier' to present to the authorities. She added: 'The rest of my short stay was meeting Greek Cypriots and listening to their woes.'

Although she was an assiduous diary keeper, Mrs Castle's jottings of her visit were highly selective and may have been edited and re-written much later in her life, a view expressed to the author by her authorized biographer. 'I saw Barbara's diary for her trip to Cyprus, which I think she had typed up more or less contemporaneously, although she did do a lot of editing,' Anne Perkins confirmed.

Asked about the alleged ambush, Anne Perkins said: 'Of course, she made no mention of the episode you describe. Everything else fits – the day spent with Foley, who I can well see not being popular as editor of the very anti-military *Times of Cyprus*. This could be because the ambush didn't happen or because she did not want to acknowledge that her stand was very unpopular with the soldiers.

She liked to say – and I have seen one letter supporting this view – that some at least privately agreed with her. Against the ambush theory is the fact that she relentlessly exploited her life in later years – admittedly editing as she went – and I would have thought she'd have seen the money in this.' Mrs Castle did mention that after her afternoon in Kyrenia with the Foleys, there was 'a mad dash to the airport'.

Graham Robinson, ex-RAF, told the author: 'I seem to remember she was forcibly removed from the Island as she had been having tea with some EOKA bigwig or someone else equally unacceptable. She was collected up from wherever she was and her bags picked up from her hotel and then both taken straight to the airport and put on a plane to Athens.'

Soon afterwards, another British soldier was seriously wounded by a mine that detonated under his vehicle in the north-east of the Island. In the west, a British policeman was injured in another incident.

Mrs Castle's diaries and her books also did not mention several other incidents, which former members of the Security Forces swear took place. The late Rabbie Burns of the RAF Regiment became irate when the author mentioned her name.

'The thing that really pissed me off was when she came out on a fact-finding jolly and we were ordered to go and find her and bring her back from a meeting with EOKA sympathizers in Ayios Khivides in the Troodos Mountains,' he said. 'She and her hubby were half pissed when we got there. She was not amused when we pulled her out and returned her to the Government House. Then, three days later, the same lady got up on the stage at Nicosia Football Stadium to address the troops who were assembled and slagged us rotten for hurting the poor Greek populace. I bloody ask you!'

In his autobiography, *Balkan Blue*, Major General Sir Roy Redgrave observed: 'Morale among the soldiers was not much helped by the MP Barbara Castle who visited the island. She appeared generous in her praise for Greeks and seemed to criticize the Army, which greatly upset the Gordon Highlanders who had suffered many deaths in a forest fire, which had been deliberately lit around them by EOKA.

'Meanwhile we were now well aware that the word of any Greek was initially going to be considered more credible by our political masters than anything said by the Security Forces, so we carried out our duties.'

Former paratrooper Frank Dewsbury was more vehement when he talked to the author. 'One terrorist told the infamous Labour MP that he had been badly beaten during interrogation. He claimed we had pushed sticks up his backside, nearly suffocated him with wet rags wrapped around his face and given him electric shocks via his genitals and so on.

'Nosy Parker Castle believed him, making such a song and dance about it in interviews on radio and press reports, she became as good as 50 terrorists to the cause of *enosis* and EOKA. We reckoned for her to have said those things against her own country's military, she must have been having a shag with Makarios, Grivas or some Greek idiot who fancied her.'

Talking to the author, the late Sergeant Jack Taylor of the UK Police Unit revealed another incident that was excluded from her diaries. When Mrs. Castle asked to see how the police dealt with trouble, he took her to the Pancyprian Gymnasium, where pupils habitually caused trouble. She said she wanted to talk to some of them, but they refused, closed the school doors and continued to demonstrate.

Taylor, and another officer, shot off the lock of the main entrance and entered the building, forcing the demonstrators up the stairs and onto the roof, where they had collected stones, bottles and petrol bombs which they began throwing in all directions. In the mêlée a student aimed a stone at Mrs Castle and found his target. She had to have medical attention.

'Maybe it proved that British police officers don't turn the other cheek, but hit back hard,' Taylor laughed. 'The "higher-ups" thought my anecdote had better be deleted from my book.'

Sergeant Robin Fletcher, another member of the UK Police Unit, argued that because she called soldiers 'animals' and accused them of 'raping Greek Cypriot girls', some of the Army's fatalities 'can be attributed to her'.

From his home today in Australia, Gerry Martin, a former corporal with the Wiltshire Regiment based near St Hilarion Castle, contacted the author and seethed with anger: 'Barbara Castle did more to lower morale by her vicious reports of mistreatment of the locals, which in our area were completely false, than the murderous attacks by EOKA on our squaddies and their families. Many an ouzo toast was offered in the Corporals' Mess after her press releases for her bloody ship to sink. Having a nice Church of Scotland fellow (William Jamieson), who visited us often, blown to bits, and our 'B' Company mate Bill Weaver shot and paralysed for life soon after her visit, didn't go down well either.'

Equally bitter was the Argyll and Sutherlanders' Company Commander, Colonel 'Mad Mitch' Mitchell. He remembered how Barbara Castle went to Kathikas village, where one of his men, Private Morrison, had been murdered. 'Soon enough the Greek Cypriots were regaling her with tales of our "brutality". She visited the area at the invitation of a Greek mayor and a parade of those allegedly injured by the Argylls was held for her benefit. In a nearby detention camp, she was allowed to interview detainees in the presence of the Commissioner of Paphos and an Argyll NCO. Yet she did not visit our Battalion Headquarters, as we expected, to hear our side of the story.'

Another eyewitness to Mrs Castle's behaviour was Dave Cranston of the Royal Ulster Rifles, who was part of a cordon-and-search operation with the Paras and the Royal Scots Fusiliers at Paralimni village, a hotbed of EOKA activity. 'Just before dawn, the male occupants were invited to leave their beds by the blowing of Reveille and Defaulters at the Double by buglers of RUR,' he says. 'As they proceeded to the "cages" they were aided by *The Post Horn Gallop* to liven them up.'

The operation was launched after an armoured car had run over an electrically triggered mine. To watch what took place, there were several officially invited reporters present. Suddenly, about two hours after the start of the operation, according to Cranston, there was a surge of activity at the edge of the cordon, created by the arrival of 'a very smart limo, complete with heavy escort'.

'The vehicle halted and out stepped the smartly dressed red-headed one, accompanied by a couple of smart-looking gents,' Cranston remembered. 'She was introduced to the CO, Lieutenant Colonel T. N. S. Wheeler, and the first words she uttered were "I would like to meet the detainees". She said nothing to us, the other peasants present.'

The detainees were held in the village schoolhouse, awaiting questioning. 'The CO, other officers and WOs escorted the Rt. Hon. lady and her entourage there,' Cranston continued. 'Because I was Colonel Wheeler's radio operator I went along with the crowd. The sentry at the door saluted smartly and swung open the doors. "Jesus Christ!" I exclaimed. "Somebody is in the shit for this." The floor was a mass of moaning figures, most of them wearing bloodstained clothing. A few had bloody bandages on their heads and arms.

'There was a stunned silence for about a minute. Then the Rt. Hon. Barbie turned around, stormed towards the door, where she came face-to-face with me and shrieked: "You're animals, barbarous savages! I'll see you are all punished for this." With that she was back in her limo with her entourage and vanishing up the road in a swirl of dust.

'Colonel Wheeler was nobody's fool and told the senior Greek Cypriot police officer present to bring his men into the building to strip off the detainees' bloody bandages and clothing. Surprise, surprise, no wounds were found. The gentlemen of the press were invited to photograph the "victims". No surprise that the Greek Cypriot newspapers didn't print the pictures.'

The investigation that followed revealed that there had been several dead chickens in the schoolhouse kitchen. They had been killed the night before and were awaiting cleaning. The detainees had drained the birds' blood and smeared it on themselves to simulate 'beatings by the Brits'.

'I don't know if Mrs Castle was ever told the truth, but certainly no apology came our way,' said Cranston.

A few days later, one of the US Navy personnel at the Yerolakkos communications monitoring station sent the Royal Ulster Rifles a poem:

The time has come, the British said,
To speak of proper searches,
We'll herald them with pipe and flute
And announce them from the churches.

We'll play it all the British way
For it isn't really cricket,
To be so beastly to the boys,
Who are on a sticky wicket

Bring out the bagpipes and the drums,
Give a flourish of the trumpets,
We'll pass out proper questionnaires,
Then we'll all have tea and crumpets

Oh we British are so mannerly
We've put away the birch,
So let's off to Paralimni boys,
With a hey nonny no
To the search.

Before the 'Red Queen' and her husband were whisked out of Cyprus, she never talked socially to any service personnel. Geoffrey Bown, a Royal Army Medical Corps radiographer, at the British Military Hospital in Nicosia, saw many of the dead and treated the injured. 'Mrs Castle?' he laughed. 'I remember her coming to Cyprus and running down the forces, but she certainly didn't visit BMH while I was there. Nor did I hear of her visiting any army camps. She was too busy hobnobbing with the Greeks. But the politics of the situation didn't bother us a great deal. We were there to do a job, and we did it to the best of our ability.'

AT ATHENS airport, senior officials of the Greek Government met Mrs Castle again. They informed her that Archbishop Makarios wanted to meet her again – 'within the hour'.

'Mercifully, I had managed to change into something moderately respectable on the plane. But I had not had time to wash the salt off my face (from swimming in Kyrenia) and had to content myself with putting another layer of powder on it instead,' she wrote in her diary. 'Thus patched up I walked into Makarios' room at the Ethnarchy to find a battery of television cameras awaiting me.

'I sat there, wishing the ends of my hair had not started curling all the wrong way after my swim. He [Makarios] is an expert in this kind of thing, managing to appear as though he is smiling straight at you while really curious shutters are going up and down over his eyes. Nonetheless I like him.

'His gentleness, coupled with a steeliness of purpose, was very impressive. I do not think "wily" is the right word for him. He obviously cares deeply for his Greek Cypriots and is always thinking out his next moves on their behalf. His almost film-star poise – he arranges his robes and his hat with the elegant motions of a model – is misleading for it disguises what I think is a very real sincerity.

And if he uses his wits, who can blame him? It is the only weapon a small power has against a big.'

Perhaps overcome by her obvious attraction to the prelate, Mrs Castle told him that Prime Minister Macmillan had promised the Turks partition, something revealed to her in confidence during her visit to Ankara. To avoid the division of the Island, she advocated that he, Makarios, renounce *enosis* once and for all and allow her to take back his statement to London. He agreed, but wanted it to appear in the form of a question and answer session.

Mrs Castle claimed in her autobiography that she rejected the Archbishop's suggestion, because 'it would look as if we were playing party politics. The only course was for him to volunteer a statement, which he eventually agreed. I was sent away to type out on my little portable, which I carried everywhere, the statement I believed he should make, which I was to bring to Makarios for approval the following morning. So I typed away until 11 p.m., tired, hungry and still caked with seawater ...

'The next day went like a fantasy. Makarios agreed my draft statement with slight amendments. I had, before coming, entered into a rough arrangement with the powerful American agency BUP, whose editors got very excited when I relayed Makarios' statement to them over the transatlantic line.'

Although Mrs Castle emphatically denied that she accepted Makarios's idea for a question and answer session, her memory must have failed her on two counts, because, firstly, BUP was the *British* United Press and so a transatlantic call would not have connected her to the news agency and, second, the news agency released the text of a full *interview* on 23 September:

Q. *The British Government is clearly determined to stand by their invitation to the Turkish Government to send a special representative to* *Cyprus on 1 October. What do you think will be the effect of this?*

A. I am sure that the arrival of the Turkish representative will be met with such strong Opposition that a very dangerous situation will arise, with far-reaching repercussions affecting not only Cyprus but the NATO alliance and the security of the whole area.

Q. *What is the objection of the Greek Cypriots to the arrival of this representative?*

A. We know that the British Government is planning to give the Turkish Government sovereign rights in Cyprus, either through partition or by some other means. This will make a solution of the Cyprus question impossible. It has always been our view that the problem of Cyprus is one for discussion between the Cypriot people and the British Government. By its policy the British Government has unnecessarily complicated the situation and turned it into a dispute between the Greek and Turkish Governments in which it is trying to pose as arbiter. But in our view it is wrong to involve third parties in this way. That is why we would oppose the arrival of a representative of the Greek Government just as much as of the Turkish Government.

Q. *In your view, therefore, the right way to solve this problem is to take both the Greek and Turkish Governments out of the dispute?*

A. Yes.

Q. *How do you suggest this could be done?*

A. I have been giving earnest consideration to this question. I am anxious to find a way in which peace can be restored in Cyprus and bloodshed on all sides be stopped. I therefore suggest that after a fixed period of self-government Cyprus should become an independent State, which is linked neither to Turkey nor to Greece.

Q. *This means that you would be prepared to accept independence with conditions attached?*

A. Yes. I would be prepared to accept the status of independence for Cyprus on the condition that this status shall not be changed, either by union with Greece, by partition, or by any other way, unless the United Nations approves such a change.

Q. *So the United Nations will guarantee the independence of Cyprus?*

A. Yes.

Q. *What safeguards would there be for the Turkish community in Cyprus?*

A. If my proposal is accepted, full safeguards for the Turkish community would be negotiated.

Q. *Would your suggestion debar the Cypriot people from deciding to remain in the British Commonwealth if they so desired?*

A. No. Membership of the British Commonwealth would not be incompatible with the status I propose.

Q. *What should be the first step in implementing your proposal?*

A. The British Government should sit down with representatives of the Cypriot people to work out a constitution for self-government. When this has been drawn up, it should operate for an agreed period, after which the status of independence will come into effect.

Q. *What would be the strategic consequences of your plan?*

A. I am sure that an independent and peaceful Cyprus would make a better contribution to the defence of freedom than can a Cyprus torn by colonial or civil war.

Q. *Do you think your proposal will bring peace to Cyprus?*

A. Yes. I am sure that once this problem is no longer complicated by the introduction of third parties into the dispute, confidence and harmony between the Cypriot people can be restored.

Later Mrs Castle would say: 'The BUP had done its stuff and there were splash headlines about Makarios' change of line, accompanied by pictures of us looking into each other's eyes. I did not mind overmuch that the whole idea was put down to Makarios. This after all was the condition I had insisted on with him. But I was a bit peeved later when BUP declined to contribute a penny towards my expenses because I had refused to give them an exclusive, insisting that the story should get the widest possible coverage. But I was buoyed up by the knowledge that what I had achieved was completely in line with Labour's policy.'

Whatever else may or may not have happened between Mrs Castle and the Archbishop, she had managed to extract his commitment to the independence of Cyprus rather than self-determination – *enosis* – as the basis for any future negotiations, thereby causing problems for the implementation of the Macmillan Plan and 10 Downing Street.

Anne Perkins, the author of Mrs Castle's authorized biography, commented: 'Barbara was stunned with her success. She tried to identify a motive. "I still cannot believe all this international manoeuvring has been channelled through me. How did it happen? Why was I chosen?" Nonetheless, she couldn't resist the image of herself as "a diplomatic Mata Hari envoy".

'Barbara flew home anticipating a hero's appearance at party conference as the woman who had saved Cyprus – and, incidentally, British soldiers from further fratricidal conflict – by persuading Makarios to abandon *enosis*. To her dismay, the charge of brutality beat her back to London; even more damagingly, the reaction of a right-winger Jim Matthews, the trade unions' representative on Labour's National Executive, also preceded her arrival home.

'Barbara had dismissed Matthews, privately, months earlier as an "exhibitionist loudmouth". He was an old soldier, and a recent bitter critic of Barbara's conduct in the dispute over *Industry and Society*.

'By the time she arrived back in London, Matthews' attack on her "deplorable" remarks about the behaviour of the British troops was headline news. Instead of the hero returning with olive branches with which to garland the Left, she found herself a political pariah. However much of a *cause célèbre* the ill-treatment of Cypriots was among the Left, the largely Right-wing press was in no doubt that it was disloyalty verging on treachery to criticize troops who went in daily fear for their lives and lived cooped up in camps, effectively under curfew.'

Hours before Mrs Castle returned with Makarios's offer and her dossier about mistreatment of Greek Cypriots, Sir Hugh Foot had ordered a mass release of 130 detainees, including 11 Greek Cypriot females held in Nicosia Prison. He also lifted the curfew. His surprise actions 'aroused scenes of intense jubilation', reported *The Times*.

Hugh Gaitskell, the Leader of the Opposition, meanwhile, quickly disassociated the Labour Party from Mrs Castle's criticisms of British Forces, even though she backtracked and said her attacks were not against the rank and file, but their political superiors. He pointed out that her visits to Turkey, Greece and Cyprus were made in a purely personal capacity and not as a representative of the Party.

Jim Matthews castigated Mrs Castle: 'Having had some experience of the sort of things tolerated by our troops now in Cyprus, I can well understand their feelings when comrades are shot in the back and stabbed by the very people they are trying to assist. It would be better if she were to try to understand the difficulties experienced by our troops in that island.'

Clearly stung by Matthews' rebuke on the eve of the Party's annual conference at which she hoped to be voted Chairman, the fiery lady opened her mouth again by saying she stood by her original comments on the rough handling by British troops. She understood, she said, the feelings of soldiers who had lost a comrade and she did not blame their attitude but that of the authorities who encouraged them to believe that every Greek Cypriot was a potential enemy. When she visited Paralimni, she had seen how cruelly detainees were treated and drew the attention of the CO to their condition. He, she claimed, replied 'that the detainees got no rougher treatment than his own men'.

'I believe it is wrong for detainees of various ages and conditions of health to be expected to stand the same treatment through drill or parades as tough, young soldiers,' she told reporters. She never mentioned that she had not talked to the detainees at Paralimni, that they were held there only temporarily and that prisoners were never drilled as soldiers. Her statements were based exclusively on hearsay and what Greek Cypriots had said to her in the comfort of the Ledra Palace Hotel.

Asked about Matthews' comments, she replied: 'When he hears this information, which was hitherto unpublished and when he realizes I am lodging my complaint against the authorities and not individual soldiers he will withdraw his statement. Of course, I understand the troops getting angry. They are living in a state of frustration and strain. I want to remove them from that strain.'

When the Labour Party Conference came to debate foreign affairs, Gaitskell refused Mrs Castle the opportunity to talk about her Cyprus experiences, although she grabbed the chance of addressing a fringe meeting of the Movement for Colonial Freedom, expecting to receive the applause she felt she deserved. Instead she was constantly heckled and jeered by a band of Empire Loyalists, until she had to leave midway through her speech.

But why had Makarios, the master of sophistry, dropped his demand for *enosis*? The simple answer was that the British Government had warned Athens: 'If terrorism breaks out again in Cyprus, we cannot afford indefinitely to devote military resources to its repression.' The Greek Government took this to mean partition of the Island and complete withdrawal of the colonial authorities and security forces. If the British withdrew as hurriedly as they had from the Indian subcontinent, the Karamanlis administration foresaw the two Cypriot communities going to war in an attempt to grab the whole in the cause of nationalism, and drawing mainland Greece and Turkey into the conflict. It knew it could never achieve military victory against the

Turks, and would probably be booted out of NATO and run the risk of the Soviet Union taking advantage of the situation. Grivas and EOKA had become a liability.

If Athens could persuade Makarios to choose independence over self-determination, there was a chance that the Macmillan Plan would have to be dropped and partition would not happen, however much the Turks shouted. Either the Archbishop accepted the realities of the situation or he would be left out in the cold. He had no other option, but to do as he was bid.

IN CYPRUS, the community leaders reacted quickly to the new Makarios proposal, summed up by *The Times* as 'explosive hostility from the Turks, parrot-like endorsement by Greeks and caution, tinged with scepticism, by the British'.

Grivas, in his *Memoirs*, declared: 'It was a complete surprise to me, and I confess to being upset and shocked. The Archbishop had no mandate to depart from our basic claim for self-determination – the right to choose our own future and join our Greek motherland ... His failure to prepare the ground with the Cypriot public in advance also showed a dangerous lack of psychological understanding; I was forced to take immediate action to reassure the Organization.' When Makarios eventually explained his reasons in a letter, Grivas replied: 'We are fighting at this moment to prevent the imposition of a monster on the backs of the Cypriot people and we are not succeeding, thanks to Greek policy ... After three and a half years of unprecedented sufferings, death and disaster, and acts of heroism, we are turning the people over to a slavery more oppressive than the one which they now suffer, a slavery to two masters instead of one, with every probability that they will never emerge from the tomb into which we have thrown them. Which of us among the leaders will dare to face the

Cypriot people? Which of us is worthy to survive such shame?'

Dr Kutchuk, speaking for the Turks, suggested Makarios was merely delaying the day for *enosis* and he would continue to support and help carry out the Macmillan Plan. He gave his views to the Turkish newspaper, *Hur Soz*, and added his impressions of Mrs Castle: 'I regret to say this lady acted as if she were an official representative, or rather the hired spokesman, of the Greek Government.'

More neutral observers considered the Archbishop's renunciation of *enosis* as a hopeful sign, which the British Government should acknowledge. They noted that in many respects the Makarios proposal covered different ground from the British plan and that the two were not necessarily irreconcilable. They also thought pressure now could be put on the Turks to renounce partition; once that partition bogey had been removed all sorts of new things might be possible. Official circles simply wanted Makarios to make some accompanying gesture to end violence before taking his offer at its face value.

Sir Hugh flew to London again in a last-ditch stand to break the deadlock. He wanted Whitehall to agree to Makarios's return so that he had an acknowledged Greek Cypriot with whom to negotiate. The Archbishop, he thought, would be able to restrain EOKA. Colonial Secretary Lennox-Boyd categorically refused. Macmillan suggested a compromise: Foot could assure Cypriots that the prelate would be allowed back – but at some indefinite time. Right now, he reminded the Governor, his duty was to push ahead with his plan whether Greeks liked it or not. Sir Hugh returned to the Island with sad eyes and a heavy frown.

Then, on 26 September, Grivas made an audacious attempt to assassinate Major General D. A. Kendrew, the Director of Operations, as he left his office for an urgent meeting at Government House. Lady Foot described him as 'a great, burly, square man with blue, blue eyes and the DSO and three bars – and the gentle heart and ruthless hatred of the enemy. The uncomplicated general the boys and the soldiers loved. What was it that endeared him so much to the soldiers and the children? Simplicity of mind and generosity of gesture.'

Lance Corporal Norman Daniels of the Royal Military Police took up the story: 'That Saturday started like any other day for our unit. It would end with the death of one of our members. We belonged to a small detachment of Royal Military Police – The Cyprus District Provost Unit – based at Wayne's House, General Kendrew's residence. It was located a few miles from Nicosia's walled city. Our sole function was to provide him with 24-hour protection against attack from EOKA.

'Our unit worked on a rotation basis, providing cover at the doubly compounded residence and escorting the General wherever his duties took him. On the day in question I was assigned to the rear Land Rover (registration 43 BR 57), one of four in the vehicle that escorted the General's dark green Humber Pullman, which was specially reinforced with steel plating and bullet-proof windows. Another Land Rover with RMPs travelled ahead of his car.

'We had left Wayne's House early and gone to the Secretariat building where, as usual, the General disappeared into his office within the inner protected compound. We waited outside. Suddenly, without any warning, he came out again, jumped into his Humber and swept through the entrance and turned right in the direction of Government House. Again, as usual, Andreas Giorgiou was at the wheel. We often wondered why a Greek Cypriot was employed by the military for such a sensitive and prestigious role, when there were RASC drivers available. Andreas was a quiet chap and seemed quite inoffensive, but he always

Andreas Giorgiou, General Kendrew's Greek Cypriot driver.

took the same route, which broke all security rules.

'I had a Bren gun mounted on the floor of our Land Rover. In addition, like the others, I carried a .38 Smith and Wesson revolver in my holster and a Sterling sub-machine gun on a shoulder strap. My mate "Dinger" – Lance Corporal William Bell – was our driver. Sergeant Cameron, our unit NCO, was in the front passenger seat. Lance Corporal McLeod was in the back of the Land Rover with me.

'We stuck on the tail of the General's car. It was about 09.30. As we sped up the dual

Lance Corporal William 'Dinger' Bell.

The Royal Military Police Champ slammed into a wall after the mine explosion.

The scene after the attempt on General Kendrew's life.

carriageway of Demseveris Avenue, we commented on how little traffic there was. Then, suddenly, our open-topped Land Rover was thrown in the air and we heard an almighty explosion. The next thing I was picking myself off the ground in a shower of dust.

'Our vehicle was perched crazily on a stone wall at the side of the road. I tried to cock my sub-machine gun in case the ambushers tried to follow their mine blast by shooting at us, but my weapon had jammed, damaged by the impact. I looked for the Bren gun, but it was nowhere to be seen. Fortunately, EOKA had done the deed and scarpered. What happened next is a bit of a blur. I may have been suffering shock.'

The electrically wired mine, one of the largest used by EOKA, had been placed in a water culvert about three feet under the ground, surrounded by packed explosives. It had been detonated from a chicken house in a nearby garden, belonging to M. D. Nicolaides. When it was fired, it blew a gaping hole several feet wide and deep where Demseveris Avenue met Kanaris Street and tossed the Land Rover 20 feet into the air. Where Lance Corporal Daniels fell was about 175 feet from the shattered vehicle.

Grivas had often threatened in his leaflets to kill the General and this was his best, last

chance, as Kendrew was leaving Cyprus at the end of his two-year tour of duty. Dighenis's men miscalculated and had triggered the device a few seconds too late to hurt their target, allowing his Humber Pullman to escape without any damage and race away at speed to the safety of Government House. Sir Hugh was the first to clasp him by the hand and congratulate him on his escape. Kendrew himself did not refer to the obvious fact that he had been the target. 'Two of the boys caught it badly,' he said afterwards,

'Apart from some bruising, I wasn't injured. How I shall never know,' exclaimed Daniels. 'Then I saw "Dinger", trapped by his legs, his head on the ground, hanging out of the driver's side of our Land Rover. From somewhere, Sergeant Cameron and Lance Corporal McLeod joined me. He was in severe pain from a back injury. Another Land Rover was heading towards us with two chaps from the Royal Signals. They stopped and we managed to put "Dinger" in the back of their vehicle. As we drove like hell to the BMH, I cradled my mate's head in my lap. The journey seemed to go on forever and he needed medical help fast.'

Lance Corporal Bell died the next day from his injuries.

The Nicosia duty battalion, the Royal

Suffolk Regiment, mounted an immediate cordon-and-search operation in the area where the incident occurred but, as was so frequently the case, no trace of the culprits was found.

'General Kendrew left Cyprus soon afterwards. My mate, "Dinger", did not,' Daniels remarked, a hint of bitterness in his voice. 'He had been waiting for a flight back to the UK at the end of his two-year conscription as a National Serviceman. He had only two days left and had volunteered to drive that day to relieve the boredom. His family in Glasgow had planned a combined homecoming and 21st birthday party for him. I was one of the eight coffin-bearers at his funeral. General Kendrew attended.'

The night before his death 'Dinger' had been to a cinema with his mates. 'On the way back he entertained us all in the back of our truck,' former Lance Corporal Bill Smith said. 'He was prancing and dancing, mimicking Elvis, playing an imaginary guitar. He would throw the guitar in the air, catch it and play left-handed, throw it back in the air and on the drop, play right-handed. I can see him yet wearing a canary yellow-coloured jumper. "Dinger" was a great lad who loved life.'

On 27 September, Sir Hugh Foot, the Governor, declared that a commission was being established to examine the question of setting up separate Greek and Turkish municipal councils on the Island. The general principle of separate municipalities, strongly urged by Turkish Cypriots, had been conceded under the Macmillan Plan, which provided for them to be set up 'where local circumstances make it desirable'.

Three days later, on the 30th, the British Government revealed that Burhan Ishin had been appointed Turkey's representative in Cyprus under the Macmillan Plan. Ishin, a career diplomat, who had been his country's Consul General in Nicosia, was not the type of man to allow the grass to grow under his feet

and he was an expert in blending firmness with tact.

At the same time security precautions were reinforced as Greek workers went on strike in protest. In London, 500 Greek Cypriots marched from Mornington Crescent to deliver a letter at 10 Downing Street. It called for the restoration of Anglo-Greek friendship and an independent government for Cyprus – where masked gunmen destroyed the police station in Kambos, while at Irini, near RAF Akrotiri, a military ambulance came under fire.

The Greek Cabinet in Athens, meanwhile, was studying a final message from Macmillan. He plainly stated that his plan to restore order and develop representative institutions would go into force, no matter what. He dismissed the Makarios proposal as 'falling outside the scope of the immediate problem', although it could 'remain open for consideration along with any other for a final settlement'.

From his suite in the Petit Palais hotel in Athens Makarios warned: 'If the Turkish representative goes to Nicosia and Sir Hugh enforces the Macmillan Plan, it will be the beginning of the biggest trouble yet.'

Charles Foley, the chain-smoking editor of the *Times of Cyprus*, added his opinion to the outpourings of the others. 'I have sympathy,' he said, 'for the Cypriots as a civilized people who have for generations been denied the ordinary rights of self-rule and freedom. If we Englishmen can't settle a simple matter like Cyprus without getting in deeper every day, we might as well get out of business as leader of the Commonwealth.'

From RAF headquarters the order went out: 'Keep your eyes open ... be ready to shoot at once and shoot to kill.'

A new hunting season was about to begin. The crucial date was 1 October.

It began with an Island-wide strike by Greek Cypriot workers, while Turks enjoyed the day as if it were a national holiday. A *Times* correspondent reported: 'The two sectors of Nicosia this morning presented an odd contrast, the Greek area being deserted and enveloped in gloom, the Turkish area being bedecked with flags, and gay with excited schoolchildren performing national dances. To some observers the celebrations by one side and the protests of the other seem slightly absurd, for little of substance has happened to make matters better or worse than they were 24 hours ago.'

The first shots were fired the next day, killing John South, a civilian employed at a radio monitoring station. In typical EOKA tradition, he was shot in the back by a gunman in a passing car in one of Larnaca's main streets. His murder was how Grivas marked the inauguration of the Macmillan Plan.

The next three months in Cyprus would be the darkest in the Island since the start of the Emergency.

CHAPTER TWENTY-THREE

The Cutliffe murder: 'A disgrace to humanity'

'To shoot down your enemies in the street may be unprecedented, but I was looking for results, not precedents ... For my part, I always drew the line at unnecessary cruelty.'
Colonel George Grivas

MARGARET CUTLIFFE, 18, screamed. Her mother, Catherine, was about to die, murdered by EOKA. Of all the terrorist actions during the four-year long conflict in Cyprus, none would generate so much shock and hatred of Greek Cypriots by British soldiers, politicians and even those who had showed sympathy for the freedom of the Island from colonial rule.

Catherine, the wife of a sergeant in 29 Field Regiment, Royal Artillery, was out shopping with her daughter and a friend, 20-year-old Mrs Elfriede Robinson, a German national married to another sergeant. They had set out to buy Margaret's first evening dress – to be worn at her first formal dance.

It was Friday afternoon, 3 October 1958, just after 13.00. And the streets of Varosha, the modern section of Famagusta, were quieter than usual.

An eyewitness remembered: 'As the three women emerged from a shop in Hermes Street, Margaret loitered, holding her new dress. Suddenly she screamed. Two youths, waving pistols, were bearing down on her mother and her friend who were ahead. The first gunmen fired three shots at Mrs Cutliffe at point-blank range. She fell to the ground, fatally injured, hit in the back. He discharged a further two shots at her body. Margaret, the daughter, threw her handbag at him. The second youth shot Margaret's friend with a single short. As she staggered and fell, critically injured, he fired another. Blood splattered the dusty pavement. As soon as the shooting began, the few Greek Cypriots in the street scattered. The gunmen did the same. Nobody had seen or heard anything.'

Mrs Cutliffe died, holding Mrs Robinson's hand.

While the women lay on the pavement, some Greek Cypriot children appeared and emptied Mrs Robinson's purse. A nearby shopkeeper telephoned for the police.

It was reported later that one of the gunmen had already played a role in previous executions. For the second, this would be his first assassination. They had sought a target for three days without success and they were about to abandon the attempt when the three women entered a small dress shop across the street.

By some miracle, Margaret was unhurt. Later she said: 'I saw Mrs Robinson fall down and then Mummy. I turned round and saw one gunman holding the revolver tight against his chest with both hands. He stared at me with black, blazing eyes. Then he shot at me. I felt a shot pass between my arm and my body.'

Mrs. Cutliffe was the mother of five children, the youngest 15 months old.

The flag flies at half-mast at the Royal Ulster Rifles' camp following Mrs Catherine Cutliffe's murder.

THE SHOOTINGS came as the climax of 24 hours' sporadic violence and disturbances across the Island. 'It was a deliberate and brutal crime and was the first time that an English woman had been killed in this way,' noted Peter Paris, the doctor employed in Nicosia's General Hospital. He was driving through Varosha en route to the capital when the murder took place.

Brian Lovett was a Lance Corporal in the Royal Military Police, attached to 51 Brigade Provost Unit, Famagusta. 'The whole street and surrounding area was out of bounds to serving military personnel, but not their families,' he said, 'because two members of the Royal Horse Guards had been killed by EOKA in Hermes Street, while buying groceries. The wives of servicemen were never expected to be a terrorist target.' (The latest outrage occurred almost exactly opposite the grocer's shop where Comet Fox-Strangways and Trooper John Procter, the two Royal Horse Guards met their deaths on 8 July.)

Police and troops were on the scene in a few seconds. Arrangements were made to remove Mrs Cutliffe's body, while Mrs Robinson was rushed to the nearest British Military Hospital for emergency medical treatment. Margaret, the daughter, was taken away, protected by armed soldiers, to join her father and siblings.

Lieutenant Colonel Wheeler, the Commanding Officer of the Ulster Rifles, joined them within minutes of the arrival of the emergency services. Several troops were with him. One of them, Dave Cranston, told the author: 'We saw the blood on the street and felt the anger rise. We had done the "Firmness with courtesy" routine and where had it got us? We were dealing with psychos. Had the CO not been there, I think we would have gone looking for trouble.'

The Rifles were co-sited with 29 Field Regiment at Karaloas and they knew each other.

Within six minutes of the shooting, sirens sounded to announce the start of a curfew to lock down the city. Minutes later the word got back to the camps. 'I remember the shock and indignation – that someone had shot any of our women. It was an unofficial thing that we never touched any of their women and the Greek Cyps never touched any of ours. It seemed to have worked okay until that day,' commented, Nigel Coplin, 'a gungy gunner-driver' of 79 Kirkee Battery, RA.

The Security Forces quickly put a ring of steel round Varosha. Bob Williams, a Gunner in 29 Field Regiment and Alma Battery Commander's radio operator, was standing outside the Regimental offices with the BC's driver, waiting to visit out-stations, when their officers raced out and ordered them to immediately set up a roadblock on the Salamis Road, the first of many that afternoon.

Unaware that his pregnant 20-year-old wife Elfriede was lying critically ill in the British Military Hospital, Dhekelia, Sergeant Patrick Robinson, 26, was in charge of another rapidly organized roadblock near 4-mile point, with others from 29 Field Regiment. For two hours he knew only that two women had been attacked, but not that Elfriede was one of them.

Bob Williams said: 'After about half an hour the Battery Commander arrived at the roadblock and told us what had happened. We were sent to pick up Sergeant Robinson and take him to the hospital to be with his wife. We then went down to Famagusta, where our Regiment and the Ulster Rifles were picking up every male between the age of 12 and 60 plus, putting them on trucks and taking them to our camp at Karaloas for interrogation.'

Sergeant Cutliffe was informed of his wife's death while he was having 'a short back and sides' from the camp's Turkish Cypriot barber. The author found him in the Karpaz village of Kaleburnu or Galinoporni, as it was known in Greek. An elderly man of indeterminate age, he sat stooped on a battered chair, his hands resting on a large walking stick in the village's only café.

As if it had happened only yesterday, he remembered in fractured English: 'I was giving Mr Cutliffe a haircut, when another soldier entered and whispered that his wife was dead, shot in the back of her head by an EOKA. His face turned white and he rushed out. At first EOKA tried to blame us – the Turks – for her murder.' He described Sergeant Cutliffe as a small man, about 5 ft 4 inches in height, 'a bouncy chap, very popular'.

'They were bastards, those Greeks,' the old man shouted, his words carrying the tones of somebody who could have been a British soldier himself. 'There was never trouble between us and the British.' He was very proud that half his family lived in the UK, 10 relatives to be exact.

Den Harvey, a REME corporal, lived in married quarters with his wife, Pamela, and their two children, aged two and six. Attached to the administration staff of 9 Infantry Brigade, he had just completed a 24-hour guard at Karaolis camp and was asleep in the family apartment in Famagusta. His wife Pamela recalled: 'Suddenly I heard his name being called. I looked down from the balcony and saw an NCO. "What do you want with Den?" I shouted back.

'"Sorry, but he's back on duty. Two women have been shot in Famagusta."

'Den was already dressing. "Keep the doors and shutters closed," he said as he raced to join his colleague.

'Just minutes later, there was a loud knock on the glass window of our front door. I opened it slowly. Andreas Vaiyas was standing there. Our Greek Cypriot neighbour was very frightened and pleaded to be let inside.

'"The soldiers are rounding up all Cypriot men aged between 14 and 45," he said. "They want to question us."

'An Army truck arrived. Two armed soldiers saw Andreas and bundled him into the back, where another soldier was pointing his rifle at about six other Greek Cypriots, all standing with their hands wrapped round their heads. The truck pulled away and the Greeks fell down, knocked off balance. More

Army trucks followed, packed with Greek Cypriot men. They were shouting a lot.'

That morning Pamela Harvey herself had been shopping in Hermes Street, 'a long and narrow thoroughfare, with a sharp bend about half way along. Where it met another road, there was an Indian sari shop on the corner where I often bought some exquisite materials. I returned home just after one o'clock, ate a snack lunch with Den and then began catching up on the ironing. I will never forget 3 October 1958.'

Joan O'Brien, aged 10, the daughter of an Intelligence Corps officer, was with Toni, her twin, visiting their friends at a house not far from the walls of the old city. Suddenly a Land Rover arrived with armed soldiers to take them home. '"There's a curfew," they said. We were quite frightened, because we couldn't understand why,' she told the author. 'But we went anyway. Being army brats, we did as we were told.'

She continued: 'On the way, I saw lots of soldiers on the streets and Greek men spread-eagled against walls being searched. Someone said two wives had been shot and I wondered if one could be my mother. I was so happy when I saw her again at home. She was very upset, because she had known Mrs Cutliffe.

'The Salamis road outside our house was very quiet, until a convoy passed. Every one of the open-top Bedford trucks was filled with Greek Cypriots. Many of them were lying on top of each other and I was sure they'd suffocate.

'I looked towards the old city and saw crowds standing on the walls, waving huge red and white Turkish flags. I felt sad and frightened and wanted everything to be back to normal. But what was "normal" about life as an army kid in Cyprus during the Emergency?'

For the remainder of her stay on the Island, Joan O'Brien always carried a nail file and a pair of scissors hidden in a Cadbury's choco-late box – 'just in case we were attacked by terrorists'.

AT GOVERNMENT House in Nicosia, Sir Hugh Foot was working in his office when he was told that two British Army wives had been shot in the Greek quarter of Famagusta.

'One was dead, and the other not expected to live,' he wrote in his book, *A Start in Freedom*. 'This was the culmination of all the terrible events of the past few months. I knew that it would be impossible to hold our troops. I called for a helicopter and spoke to General [Joe] Kendrew]Director of Military Operations]. We were in Famagusta within two hours of the killing ... but already the troops had gone wild ... hundreds of Greeks were being treated for wounds inflicted indiscriminately by the furious soldiers.'

While Sir Hugh and General Kendrew were airborne, they received an urgent signal from the brigade commander. He believed that the murder could be a deliberate attempt by EOKA to provoke the Security Forces into actions that would derail the forthcoming NATO and UN discussions on the Island's future. Any retaliation, he suggested, would not help in the search for the culprits of 'this dastardly crime'. The signal arrived too late. Soldiers were already taking the law into their own hands. They wanted immediate justice.

In her living room in Government House, Lady Foot was ending a meeting about a Cypriot children's charity and was due to attend the farewell party for the Kendrews, who were leaving Cyprus shortly. 'I dragged myself upstairs and picked up the receiver and spoke to Norah Kendrew,' she wrote in her diary. 'Her voice sounded faint and weary. "I am sitting," she said, with pathetic inconsequence, "surrounded by a sea of food-trays and glasses all ready for the party. The smell of anchovies is terrible. Thank God our ADC has done some swift work and everybody is being warned. I am hoping no one will turn up unknowingly."

Sir Hugh Foot hears senior officers of the Royal Ulster Rifles and Royal Artillery explain what happened on the night of Mrs Cutliffe's killing.

'I cannot remember what else we said. We had got beyond looking for words to say what we felt ... We could not bear to say anything about the horrible act. I think we speculated half-heartedly as to whether the Military Hospital would have any use for her food.'

Bill Packham was a National Service Lance Bombardier in 29 Field Regiment, Royal Artillery. 'I was the Duty Store man – the local "Mr Fixit" – on that day and began issuing riot batons to anyone who wanted one,' he told the author. 'As feelings were running pretty high, no one was allowed out of camp, except those who lived in married quarters.' General Kendrew had sent the order, but the fury of British soldiers was flying through the camp and to other regiments faster than a forest fire in the Troodos Mountains, and it was too late to restrain all the troops.

Thirty minutes after the shootings, Lance Corporal Chas Baily of 227 Provost Company was ordered to round up every Greek Cypriot male – anywhere. He recollected: 'I was given a 15 cwt. truck and a driver, but no escort in the back. We knew where most of the troublemakers lived and off we went. By the time we reached our first destination, arrests were already underway. In about three-quarters of an hour, my truck was full, with bodies lying on top of each other. The ones at the bottom were in a bad way, I am afraid to say, but because of the circumstances, we were not really bothered.'

Baily's 'catch' was first taken to Famagusta Police Station 'for sorting out, those to be detained for questioning and those who were detained because they were males'.

The late Rabbie Burns of No. 2 Field Squadron RAF Regiment, had been on a regular run from Nicosia to Famagusta to collect munitions from the docks. On arrival, he and troops from 62 Field Squadron RAF Regiment were mustered to assist in the search for the two EOKA gunmen with the Support

Company, Royal Ulster Rifles. 'We mounted our Land Rovers and drove down to the Central Police Station in Varosha, which was to be our base for the incident and our Officer reported to the major in charge, Major H. Hamill,' he remembered. 'Our party was split up into a Land Rover crew with each of the sections of the RUR and given streets to search and told that all suspects had to be returned to base for interrogation.

'We started our house-to-house search and were not very polite or mannerly. If we had a problem entering, we smashed down the door and tore the house apart. We questioned the males rigorously, while looking for arms, ammunition and any EOKA literature. The males were put on a truck and conveyed to base. During our search of properties, we found and confiscated a lot of small arms and ammunition.

'When I got back to the police station, I was ordered to stay and operate a radio 19-set, as I was a trained signaller. There were Police officers and SIB men everywhere, questioning the men being brought in. I saw a suspect tied to and seated on a cane chair with the base removed. A carpet beater was put on the lower rung of the chair and stood on and the beater then hit his "wedding tackle". It wasn't long before he sang like a canary.

'I must stress here that our troops had reached a high state of fury, finally triggered by Mrs Cutliffe's murder. It was the culmination of all the resentment of the terrorist actions that had preceded this event.'

Baily did three trips to the police station, his truck filled each time. He was then told to head for Famagusta docks where Greek Cypriots were still working, but their Turkish Cypriot co-workers had warned the police they intended to 'get them' unless they were removed. He collected the 15 Greek Cypriots and headed back to the police station, passing through the old city, which was entirely populated by Turks. Here he was stopped by a large crowd and 'invited' to step onto the road, which he and his driver did.

'After being ushered round a corner, we had a conversation for about a couple of minutes about the murder with one of the Turks, and then went back to our vehicle. Low and behold there were no passengers. I asked where they were and only got shrugs. You know exactly what I mean: suddenly no one understands or speaks English,' Baily said.

An air-direction frigate HMS *Salisbury* was anchored off Famagusta. After carrying out week-long anti-gun-running patrols around the Island, crew members were rotated to spend a few days at the Army's rest camp on the outskirts of the city. Reg Pope, 19, was one of the ship's Able Seamen (Gunnery). He heard the news while sunbathing on the camp's beach.

'I don't think the Greek Cypriots know just how close they came that day to being killed en masse. Even on board ship there were mutterings of "shore bombardments",' Pope reflected. 'I saw some Greek Cypriots being brought in for questioning by an army patrol, and one of the prisoners approached his escorts and pleaded his innocence. He was not treated gently.

'On the whole we got on very well with the army boys. In fact, they said we could wreck their canteen in Dhekelia anytime we were ashore, as long as we included them in the fight! Seriously, we had nothing but admiration for the thankless job the lads were doing. Some of our crew even joined them on town patrols and we returned the favour by taking them to sea occasionally. Only the Greeks gave them problems. The Turks were quite well thought of.'

Sergeant Ray 'Steve' Stephens added: '29 Regiment nearly lost it that day.' He and his wife were the Cutliffe's next-door neighbours in Famagusta and they knew them well. 'Most of the men were confined to camp, but a good number went into Famagusta to help find the killers. They lost control and smashed their way into Greek Cypriot houses. They stopped and searched young Greek Cypriot men at random.

'I had only just arrived home myself when there was a bang at my front door. Two soldiers were trying to break in. They were surprised to see me there, pointing a Browning Automatic at them. We lived among the Greek Cypriots, and it didn't help any that day.'

He added: 'The Cutliffes were very nice people – no doubt about that – very friendly good neighbours, who did not really enjoy the social scene as much as us. This was due in part to Taffy's job as an Officer's Mess Steward/Caterer. He just did not have the time, and rarely visited the Sergeant's Mess. Mrs Cutliffe was a stay-at-home person, only really going out on shopping trips.'

DR PETER Paris, meanwhile, was halfway to Nicosia. 'On the road out of Famagusta, an old hack jalopy with a broad white stripe on

Injured Greek Cypriots arrive at hospital for treatment for their injuries.

it came hurtling down the road towards me. It screeched to a stop, overloaded with journalists, some of whom I knew. They were shouting at me. One of them leapt out of the back before they had stopped. "Hey, Doc, what gives?"

'"I don't know what gives – you tell me!" I replied.

'"Some Englishwoman was shot out shopping in Famagusta. They say the troops are going to town on the Greeks. What have you heard? Did you see anything?"'

As the afternoon turned to evening about 350 Greek Cypriots had been rounded up. 'They were dropped off in the RUR lines and made to run the gauntlet between 200 squaddies with batons, before they were put in the "snake pit"', said Bill Packham, although most members of 1 RUR denied allegations of brutal treatment of those arrested.

Dave Cranston, however, acknowledged: 'There is no disguising the fact that a degree of force was used during the roundup of the Greek Cypriots. I have the utmost sympathy for them and their families and will not try to make excuses for the behaviour of some of our troops. I will merely state that during my tour of duty in Cyprus I saw very few acts of gratuitous violence used by British troops ...

'I had seen the callous behavior of Greek Cypriots towards their own people and how they walked past injured British troops and civilians, mere children, but there are no words to describe this murder. Even after all these years it makes my blood boil thinking about it.'

Packham continued: 'The "snake pit" was a compound between 29 Field Regiment and the RUR lines. It was an old quarry approximately 30 feet deep, surrounded with barbed wire and guarded by three Bren gun posts. Access to the pit was by steps from the RUR position. During the evening I went to 29 Field's Main Gate and listened to what was going on. I saw bodies laid out in rows, with

A priest addresses the detained Greek Cypriots males in 'The Snake Pit' after the Cutliffe murder.

188 Radar and Searchlight Battery, Royal Artillery, illuminated 'The Snake Pit' at night.

the Medical Officer and medics attending to the injured Greek Cypriots.'

As darkness fell the 188 Radar and Searchlight Battery RA was ordered to provide 'instant daylight', with sweeping beams across the quarry. If the Greek Cypriot males resisted arrest, their reactions were mild compared to their women folk, according to 'John' of the RAOC, who was one of those involved in the roundup. He remembered: 'The women were very hostile. While we were loading some Greeks onto a lorry outside Paula's bar in Fama-G, this crazy girl of about 18 came forward and flung her arms round the second lieutenant in charge, a young chap

from the RUR. We pulled her away and found she was wired up to explosives. Luckily they didn't go off. You should have seen the young officer's face!'

'John' also claimed that some of the damage in Varosha was caused by Greeks themselves on a looting spree, putting all the blame on the British.

At about 19.00, Provost Lance Corporal Chas Baily heard that Sir Hugh Foot and General Kendrew were about to land in Famagusta by helicopter. 'With no more ado, we rounded up as many squaddies as possible and told them to pass the word and got everybody cleaning up the main roads. We knew from past experience no one would look down side roads,' Baily recalled. 'The streets were a right mess. Blood, bits of clothing, odd shoes, shopping. The place looked like a rubbish tip. Ambulances were everywhere, the hospitals were full, and surgeries the same. Some injuries were serious, but most were cuts and bruises, and quite a few broken bones. All the married men realized it could have been their wives who had been murdered. By the time HE arrived there was not much out of place.'

Acting as his CO's radio operator, Dave Cranston of 1 Royal Ulster Rifles was still with Lieutenant Colonel Wheeler, when Sir Hugh touched down, and heard him call the avenging troops 'animals' and promised he would have the Rifles 'off this Island by Christmas'. Perhaps the Governor had not been told that the regiment had just suffered the loss of a staff sergeant, James (Frankie) Lane, killed by a single shot in Varosha that night. He was 23 years old and came from Renelaugh, Dublin. 'His injury was caused by a round fired from a Sterling sub-machine gun when it was dropped by a member of the Security Forces during a busy exit from a crowded vehicle in the middle of an incident,' said Cranston. 'He was a very good soldier and a great loss to his platoon and the regiment.'

Geoffrey Bown, a radiographer at the British Military Hospital, Nicosia, was on duty when Sergeant Lane's body arrived, the victim of another 'friendly fire' incident. He remembered: 'I spoke to the blokes who brought Lane to the BMH. Their rifle straps had more blood than Blanco on them, so I don't think they were very gentle. The Ulsters had the reputation of being one of the roughest regiments on the Island. I'm pretty sure the Staff Sergeant was dead on arrival – otherwise we would have X-rayed him.'

AT 22.00, a dozen members of 615 Signals Troop, 625 Ordnance Depot, stormed into the city and rounded up more than 250 Greek Cypriot males aged between 16 and 40. These men were kicked, punched and ordered to form a column, after which they were marched down Famagusta's main street, past the Law Courts and Municipal Building, towards the old walled city. There they were forced into the moat.

RASC Sergeant Bill Andlaw was present. He claimed 'it was common knowledge that EOKA planned to kill a Brit that day'. He said: 'The information came from a Greek Cypriot informer who worked in the NAAFI, despite him being a senior member of EOKA.'

He described the scene at the moat: 'Turks gathered on the parapets above the Greeks and began stoning them with boulders, while we watched. Around midnight the Greeks were boarded on Army trucks and taken away. Although we were acting on our own initiative, as were others, I believe local officers made no effort to stop us exacting vengeance.'

Around nightfall, Margaret Cutliffe and her father arrived home with an armed escort that would remain on guard at the house, partly to protect them from harassment from journalists, but more importantly from hostile Greeks. British journalists were already writing their 'stories' hoping to meet their London newspapers' deadlines, four hours behind Cyprus time. Charles Foley, the editor of the *Times of Cyprus*, one of the two English language newspapers on the Island, had already decided he would have his reporters write about the 'brutality' of British soldiers rather more than about the brutal murder.

'I was at some semi-official, almost exclusively Anglo-American cocktail party when the news arrived,' wrote Charles Foley in his memoirs. 'There was a sickly silence. Then voices rose again. Men who had left their wives at home strapped on revolvers and finished their drinks, there was the sound of cars starting up outside, and over the confusion a voice shouted: "This is it!"'

Back in Nicosia, Dr Paris stopped at the Ledra Palace Hotel. 'To get the real news one went to Savvas, the hall porter,' he recorded. 'He took all the messages, cables and telephone calls, helped decipher almost any language, and distributed EOKA leaflets – all for a fee. What with running his own car-hire and information service, he must have made a pile. I couldn't find him in the foyer but I pieced the facts together . . . It was a bad affair, but Cyprus was a bad place, and the Army had some justification.'

He added: 'But when the journalists, hotfoot and hot-rod, from Famagusta, went to file their stories back to England, the cable system, conveniently for authority, had mysteriously broken down. No word could go out about Famagusta until the fault was repaired. This line started working again just before dawn the next day when the news was too late to be printed in the English morning papers, except the very last edition of the *Daily Telegraph*.'

In Famagusta, while the mayhem in the streets continued, Sergeant Stephens says: 'The armed escort remained at David "Taffy" Cutliffe's house through the night, because the authorities feared EOKA might try to kill Taff's daughter, as she was a witness to the shooting and might be able to identify the killers.

'At about 02.00 that night, my family and I were wakened by the sound of gunfire at the rear of our house. It really scared my wife and children. I managed to get them under the bed. Bullets were flying everywhere. I decided to find out what was going on. I knew, of course, that the guard at the Cutliffes' would be involved. I went out, climbed on my roof, armed with my Browning Automatic. I could see one of the guards at the rear of Taff's house. I shouted, "What's up, mate?"'

'Lance Bombardier Pete Best, RA, called back: "Don't worry, Sarge, it was a false alarm. No one was hurt, that's the important thing."'

For the Governor, Sir Hugh Foot, and General Kendrew, their visit to Famagusta had helped to reduce the number of reprisals, but he feared for the future. 'I could see nothing but hatred and violence ahead. We were fighting against violence but at the same time we had to deal with false accusation and false rumour. The manufacturers over-reached themselves. They tried to put it about that the attack on the women had been carried out by the British in order to put the blame on the Greeks,' he wrote.

Lady Foot, in her memoirs, *Last Exit*, writes: 'M. [Sir Hugh] and General Joe [Kendrew] drove back from Famagusta by car on that black night. Their miserable and haunted faces are too clear in my mind still. M. prowled about in agony – dreadful pictures of the day's violence rising up before him. The utter, hopeless waste of violence obsessed our minds. To what purpose had this woman died? And why was that woman agonizing in hospital – her body riddled with bullets? ... To what purpose the bleeding heads of old men, Turk and Greek, caught in the flood of fury ... We sat down at a little table upstairs and somehow ate our dinner. Only a few hours' sleep interrupted by telephones and comings and goings. And then it was morning and the day had to be faced.'

LANCE-BOMBARDIER Bill Packham said: 'I went to the Cutliffes' house the next morning, with supplies for the guard that had been posted there. Famagusta was a mess. Windows of houses, shops and cars had been smashed. Some cars had been burnt out. In camp BQMS Potter came to the stores' section and said he had enjoyed himself. The butt of his Sterling machine gun was bent and covered in bits of skin, hair and blood.'

Lance Corporal Bernie Sharkey of the Ulsters was very clear on this point: 'The whole battalion was involved. It got so bad that some of my mates and I decided to look after the women and children, to whom we gave some sweets and comfort.'

'Several shops had been looted. During the next few days, there were stolen radios on sale in the camp,' Packham added. Sharkey backed Packham's recollection: 'In the process of the raids in the town a lot of businesses were damaged and "souvenirs" taken – kitchen appliances, radios, cigarettes. We got the tip-off that we were going to be raided by the MPs so everything went down the latrines. Most of the married quarters had new equipment. One sergeant was busted down to corporal, but was later reinstated after a suitable length of time – he was a good soldier.'

Rawle Knox, *The Observer*'s correspondent in Cyprus, told the paper's readers: 'New precautions against the apparent undiscriminating EOKA war were taken by the forces. Housewives shuttered their windows against bomb-throwers. The RAF ordered men not living on base to sleep with guns tied to their wrists. Shopping expeditions after dark and visits to all places of entertainment were banned.'

Married soldiers who were not needed for active patrol duties were also told to stay indoors with their families. Meanwhile the day and night curfew on all Greek Cypriot men and women born between 1 January 1932 and 1 January 1944 was to be maintained until further notice in Nicosia, Famagusta, Limassol, Larnaca, Ktima and Kyrenia.

With all service families now confined to their quarters, Packham spent the following week delivering their groceries. 'By Saturday morning, the Irish lads were confined to camp, but the results of their labours could still be seen,' observed Bryan Chinn. He served at the nearby RAF communications monitoring station at Ayios Nikolaos, where he was part of the MT Section. His job involved working with the 20 Movements Unit RAF, based at Famagusta Docks. 'At the docks,' he said, 'the Turkish stevedores insisted we should have machine-gunned the lot [of Greek Cypriots]. George Yiassos, our liaison with the shipping agent, worked in our compound. He did not appear for some time after this incident.'

There was the tightest curfew ever in Famagusta. Nobody moved, there were soldiers everywhere. They were controlling the situation and calm was slowly restored. As local units were pulled back to their camps, British replacement troops from elsewhere in Cyprus were rushed to take over the cordons round the city. The Paras were the nearest. They had been carrying out an operation in Ayios Nikolaos to identify and illuminate an EOKA cell causing problems for the re-supply of the RAF radar station.

'The day after the news broke, we were involved in the cordon,' said Major J. W. Graham. 'We did not join those regiments in Famagusta and felt peeved. There was a great deal of anger, but as far as I could see this did not affect our discipline as we watched an endless stream of military buses and 3-ton trucks passing through our roadblocks, carrying them from Varosha to the Special Branch interrogation centre and returning them back into town.'

As the Paras headed to their positions, they passed below the high walls of the old city. 'Massed ranks of Turkish men lined the parapets waving and shouting at us,' commented Lance Corporal Phil Tompkins, one of Major J. W. Graham's men. 'The Turks were making throat-cutting signs with their index fingers and pointing us into the Greek area. Our troops, in Company strength, were dropped from their wagons in groups of about four or five Paras, with an NCO in charge, and ordered to set up VCPs [Vehicle Check Points] and stop every vehicle entering their area of our responsibility.'

Later on Major Graham visited Tompkins' post and ordered him and Private Tony Surtees to patrol the immediate area up to the next Para position. Tompkins picked up the story: 'He came across a bus depot, which contained at least five wooden panelled Greek buses. They were all ablaze from end to end. The nearest bus was half consumed by flames, but the front was only filled with smoke. To our horror we found a big, fat elderly Greek man in the driver's seat. We thought he was dead, but pulled him out anyway. We then found he was as "pissed as a rat" and had fallen into a drunken sleep. It turned out he was the night watchman.'

Meanwhile, according to Charles Foley, 'the killers themselves were hiding in the orange groves north of Famagusta. Here they buried the guns in glass jars – covered with rubber to baffle detection devices – and changed their shirts in case the colour had been noted. By now the authorities had issued a description of one of the assassins. He was said to be aged around 25, with a height between 5'7" and 5'8", well built and of light complexion – fair, bushy, wavy hair. He had been wearing an open-necked, faded blue T-shirt and shorts; 'no socks – sandals and with plump legs.'

In Nicosia, Greek Cypriot Mayor, Dr Them. Dervis put up a reward of £5,000

Sergeant Patrick Robinson and his wife, Elfriede, on their wedding day.

leading to the capture and conviction of the killers. Cynics were sure it was a ploy to deflect blame from EOKA and that he knew full well his money was safe.

AT THE British Military Hospital, Dhekelia, Mrs Elfriede Robinson had survived a series of operations and woke to find her husband, Patrick, sitting at her bedside. Lieutenant Colonel John Watts, MC, FRCS, the lead surgeon, had removed three bullets that had entered her right buttock, fracturing bones. One .45 bullet was lying subcutaneously in the left thigh and another one was removed from the abdominal cavity. 'She was in extremis when she was admitted,' Colonel Watts noted. 'But after a transfusion of three pints of blood was taken to the operating theatre and a laparotomy performed.

'Passive haemorrhage was encountered, eventually traced to the inferior mesenteric vein that had been divided by a .38 caliber bullet, which was lying free in the abdominal cavity near the spleen. A further five pints of blood were given in the theatre during operation. Recovery was complicated by an intestinal obstruction and abdominal dehiscence

necessitating a further operation, but eventually she made a good recovery.'

Speaking in retirement from their Hildesheim home in Germany, Sergeant Robinson told the author: 'Colonel Watts was a brilliant surgeon. My wife spoke very little English as we had only been married a few months and he spoke very good German and was able to explain what he had to do and this gave her great comfort.' As a result of her injuries, Mrs Robinson lost her baby.

Late on Saturday all the arrested Greek Cypriots were released – with the exception of two youths. Were they the killers? Official spokesmen replied: 'Investigations are not yet advanced enough for me to say.' By Sunday, Greek Cypriot newspapers had launched a full-scale attack against the behaviour of British troops. Foley's English language *Times of Cyprus* marched with them.

'The Greek Press as usual overstated its case,' Dr Paris remembered. 'The front page had a picture across the width of the paper of about twenty men standing up with bandages round their heads. It was most dramatic and must have looked bad in other newspapers around the world. A bandage round the head is the same for a fractured skull or for a small cut on the forehead; if they were standing up they were unlikely to have fractured their skulls.'

The *Times of Cyprus* was particularly virulent. Sunday's edition, under the banner headline, 'The Famagusta Story', quoted the Greek Mayor Andreas Pouyouros who fulminated against the actions of the British, which he called a 'reign of terror'. The newspaper's staff reporter described what he had witnessed. 'Their heads swathed in bandages, scores of dazed Greek Cypriots sat on benches outside Famagusta Hospital's casualty ward on Saturday as ambulances toured the town to pick up the injured who had not been treated during the night. A team of four doctors, 12 nurses, four sisters and four male orderlies had worked almost non-stop since 6 p.m. on Friday, when the first 250 came in.'

According to Mayor Pouyouros, who had been sealed in his house (no curfew passes were issued on Saturday) platoons of troops broke into scores of homes – 'many of them nowhere near the incident'.

'It was a reign of terror and the most terrible night we have ever had,' the Mayor told Greek journalists. 'It lasted from 5 p.m. until about 8.30. I had calls continuously from people complaining of injury. More than 40 telephoned from the Byzantium Hotel. I think there are still many others in private houses, perhaps afraid to call for help. Other reputable witnesses standing on the roof of the hospital next to the police station say they heard the screams of those being interrogated. A state of fear and terror reigned in our town. What happened last night exposes the British Government in the eyes of the civilized world. The security forces' behaviour was maniacal.'

Earlier the Mayor had called Famagusta's Acting Commissioner twice, demanding that the troops stop. Even if he had had the authority, Commissioner Sheridan was not interested. 'Considering the offence the troops' attitude was understandable,' he commented.

A few days later Mayor Pouyouros would demand financial compensation from Britain for injuries suffered by the citizens of Famagusta. Unless the Secretary of War, Mr. Christopher Soames, agreed to pay out of court, legal proceedings against him would be considered, he threatened. If necessary, he would sue through the International Court in London. Two weeks later, however, Lieutenant Colonel Wheeler, the Commanding Officer of the Ulster Rifles, sent a cheque for £91 to the owner of the Hermes Street shop outside which Mrs Cutliffe died. The money was compensation for depredations by troops during the search operation. In an accompanying letter, the Colonel wrote: 'I am satisfied that the following articles were stolen by men

of this regiment from your shop ...'

In Nicosia, the Hippocrates Medical Association and the Greek Cypriots' Human Rights Committee, one of whose members was Sir Panayiotis Cacoyiannis, cabled Mr Sheridan, requesting permission to enter the curfew-bound city to carry out their own investigations. Permission was refused.

THREE GREEK Cypriots died during the roundup. 'This morning we saw the last to die – Andreas Loukas, 19, of Ayia Napa village – wheeled to the mortuary, a red blanket over his face and body,' the *Times of Cyprus* reported. 'There he joined Panayiotis Chrysostomou, 35, from Stylia, and a local 13-year-old-girl, Joanna Zachariadou.' In *The Cyprus Revolt*, Nancy Crawshaw, the author, noted: 'An army chaplain at brigade headquarters found Panayotis Chrysostomos dead, with seven broken ribs. Arrested at home, the father of six children, he was at 37 well over the age-limit of the suspect group.'

'A few hours later another man, Andreas Psaras, 39, arrived from Famagusta at 2.30 p.m.,' continued the *Times of Cyprus*. 'He was said to have been shot in the chest during last night's searches. Doctors said he had a miraculous escape from death – but he was still on the danger list.'

An official statement contradicted Greek claims of thousands of arrests and injuries. The authorities insisted 650 were arrested, and 250 had been injured, of which 16 were detained in hospital and seven 'were found to have sustained serious injury'. It added: 'A full investigation into these incidents is proceeding.'

The growing divide between Greek and Turkish Cypriots was highlighted by the manner in which the two sides covered these events. While both *Halkin Sesi* and *Bozkurt* splashed news of the murder on their front pages, the Turkish headlines could not be more different. 'EOKA savagery and butchery has now reached the lowest depths of degradation,' said one and another blasted 'This is the peak of barbarity.'

Halkin Sesi placed the blame on Greece because, it said, captured EOKA arms and munitions had been provided by NATO for Greece, and somehow had arrived in Cyprus. *Bozkurt*, too, criticized the 'misguided' Athens government for allowing Archbishop Makarios – the 'village priest' – to remain in Greece. If the country wanted to recover its reputation, 'lost in world circles when it sided with EOKA's terrorism and savagery', the prelate should be banished.

Charles Foley equally had no doubts. He editorialized in his *Times of Cyprus*: 'No-one is free of blame, and the bell will toll for all. But the heaviest guilt is borne by those (the British) who bestowed liberty on naked savages in Africa while denying the promise of freedom to the fully civilized and educated population here ... Once more, in Famagusta, the troops vented their rage on all and sundry, causing an Island-wide revulsion and bringing the danger of reprisals. The murderers escaped. One is described as of light complexion, with fair, bushy hair. Why should he be a Greek? Whoever may profit from this loathsome deed, it cannot be the Greek Cypriot majority.'

Foley's opinion triggered all kinds of rumours that Greek Cypriots were innocent of Mrs. Cutliffe's murder. The killing was by a jealous lover, many suggested. Others pointed the finger at the intelligence services, who, they claimed, wanted to cause trouble, generate hatred for Greeks, while favouring the Turks, and prevent *enosis*.

George Grivas, whose *Memoirs* Foley edited, pleaded ignorance about the murder. 'The news was as much a surprise to me as to anyone else; I could not imagine how it had come about and I had to wait until my leader in Famagusta, Costas Christodoulides, could get a report through the curfew which had come down on the town. It seemed that he knew nothing about the affair and to this day no one knows who the killers were. While nobody could rule out the possibility of some misunderstanding or of some hot-headed Greek seeking to revenge the frequent attacks on the women of our community by the army, there was no evidence whatever that EOKA was involved; indeed, the woman in question, Mrs Margaret Cutliffe, might have been the victim of some crime of spite or passion.'

According to Grivas, the Security Forces had killed or wounded 18 Cypriot women and children since 1955, and the latest 'murder', at Avgorou, had aroused bitter feeling. He insisted: 'EOKA harmed only those who harmed us; I never ordered an attack on a woman or child throughout the struggle and anything of the sort would have been severely punished.'

But in his *Memoirs* Grivas neglected to mention that his Famagusta commander, like all EOKA members, would not have dared to act on his own initiative for fear of retribution. Immediately after the death of Mrs Papagiorgiou, in Avgorou, the leader had declared unambiguously: 'The order is an eye for an eye.' Mrs Cutliffe's murder and the wounding of Mrs Robinson satisfied his injunction.

Yet if Grivas denied culpability, so did Archbishop Makarios sitting in Athens, still prevented from returning to Cyprus. He issued a press statement deploring Mrs Cutliffe's death 'along with the ensuing bloodbath against the Greek population of Famagusta perpetrated by the security forces, [which] was abhorrent to all honest and brave people. I am certain that the Greek Cypriot people bear absolutely no responsibility for the death of the Englishwoman. It is other suspects who have blood on their hands. However, the blood of the Greek Cypriots of Famagusta will be an eternal blight on the history of those who killed innocent children and tortured to death unsuspecting citizens.'

ON THE day Mrs Cutliffe died, the Archbishop had urged Greek Cypriots to 'react vigorously' to Prime Minister Harold Macmillan's plan for peace. 'Unite like one man, regardless of ideological affiliations, to fight against it,' he had said. It was the outcome of unlawful Anglo-Turkish collusion. Obviously the EOKA terrorists who shot down Mrs. Cutliffe had taken the Archbishop's message to heart, determined to scupper the plan by any means.

Sir Hugh Foot swiftly countered the Archbishop's call: 'It is a tragic thing that the religious leader of the Greek community in Cyprus should so seriously deceive and mislead them ... For long past I have urged him to abandon violence and help bring the Emergency to an end and to return to Cyprus to work for a peaceful and just settlement. But the obstinate pursuit of violence has barred the way. Our first obligation is to stand against violence and rid the Island of the hatred and fear which have brought so much suffering and misery. But our main purpose is to find a just settlement. We offered the Turkish community security. It was right to do so. In spite of all the misrepresentation there is nothing in our policy that will adversely affect the interests of the Greek Cypriots. Certainly there is nothing in it to excuse murder and incitement to murder ...'

EOKA, nevertheless, claimed Mrs Cutliffe's death was 'part of a plot by the British to orchestrate attacks against Cypriot citizens on the pretext that it is they who are guilty of these crimes'. The aim, said EOKA, was to frighten Cypriots into accepting the British plan for the self-government of the Island.

Charles Foley spoke to Bishop Anthimos, the Archbishop's deputy. The shooting of women, the priest said, was monstrously out of harmony with the Greek tradition of chivalry towards the other sex. It was inconceivable that any Greek Cypriot should commit an act which would only damage the national cause. Athens Radio further stirred the pot. EOKA has shown 'great determination in continuing the fight for freedom', it broadcast. 'Bombs have been thrown in all parts of the Island. Two women, the first since EOKA started its campaign against the English, have been shot by patriots of EOKA.'

On 6 October Britain resumed the jamming of news broadcasts transmitted to Cyprus from the Greek mainland station, which had stepped up its inflammatory attacks against the Security Forces, freely accusing troops of 'Hitler-type' atrocities.

WHILE GRIVAS, Makarios and the Greek media played the political blame game, the official inquiry investigation continued. It soon became clear that Mrs Cutliffe's murderers had not acted spontaneously and that the attack had been carefully planned and the local population forewarned. Shops had put the shutters up early that day, the streets were almost deserted, and there were no young people to be seen – all this on a Friday, the busiest shopping day of the week. Intelligence sources came to the conclusion that it was a premeditated attack and the locals had been informed.

The Observer's Rawle Knox had no doubts that the gunmen were fulfilling a planned EOKA operation. 'One would clearly like to believe the Greek Cypriots who are telling one today that the shootings were the act of utterly irresponsible or hate-crazed youths,' he reported, 'but on Friday night Famagusta streets were strewn with EOKA leaflets – the first ones of any consequence to be distributed since 1 October.

'The leaflets accused the British Army of using "cowardly means unworthy of a proper army" (including rape and torture of women), of being, despite their numerical superiority, afraid to face the armed men of EOKA who had always fought an honourable guerrilla war.

'Since a curfew was almost immediately imposed on Famagusta after the shooting, the leaflets can only have been prepared beforehand. As they obviously appear as an attempted justification of the killing, one must assume that it was part of calculated EOKA policy. The vengeance, which almost every Briton resident in Cyprus would consider quite justified, has been brought upon the head of the Greek Cypriots of Famagusta apparently within the calculations of EOKA.'

In Britain, Kennett Love of the *New York Times* reported, 'Conservative party leaders and newspapers were urging the Government to take harsher repressive measures against the Greek Cypriots. They insisted on unwavering implementation of Prime Minister Harold Macmillan's plan for rule of the Mediterranean island colony, which evoked a new wave of violence when it went into effect last Wednesday (1 October).'

The *Sunday Times* warned against vacillation on Britain's seven-year 'partnership' plan, which Greece had rejected and Turkey accepted. Opposition speakers and newspapers demanded suspension of the Government's plan. They called for negotiations on a proposal for Cypriot independence made by Archbishop Makarios.

A cartoon in the *Sunday Express* depicted two British soldiers advancing on Archbishop Makarios, shown standing with a smoking pistol by the body of a woman shot in the back amid the groceries scattered from her fallen shopping basket. The Archbishop was saying: 'Don't you be tough with me – or I'll complain to Barbara Castle.'

To assist the local authorities to find the killers, two senior Scotland Yard detectives were flown to the Island to assist the Security Forces. Both Chief Detective Inspector Butler and Detective Inspector Vibart had consider-

able experience in the investigation of gang violence and interrogation of suspects. They returned to the UK two weeks later after completing their study of the police methods used against EOKA.

While the media spotlight remained on the Famagusta area, EOKA continued its terrorist campaign elsewhere. Forest stations were targets in several areas on Friday night and explosions caused considerable damage. The same evening Greek Cypriot bus passengers travelling from Famagusta to Tavros village were in shock, after an electrically detonated mine exploded under their vehicle. The driver, Serghios Ioannou, was injured. At Platania station, near Amiandos, two masked gunmen held up employees at gunpoint and put explosives in the building. They then blew up the charges, and vanished. Two soldiers were injured, both National Servicemen. Private J. E. Lewis, 22, of Newport, Monmouth, was reported 'seriously ill' while Private N. J. J. Coulthard, 20, of Cardiff, was 'dangerously ill'. At Akrotiri village, near the RAF base, three airmen were injured when a bomb exploded.

Some ambushes failed, however. On 4 October, soldiers driving through Avgorou narrowly escaped death when four bombs were thrown at their vehicle. One landed in the back. A soldier picked it up and flung it out. It exploded as it hit the ground. The other bombs exploded nearby, the shrapnel injuring the two EOKA bombers.

'Up to this point I think most soldiers in Cyprus were pretty easy going with the Cypriots – both Greeks and Turks – but attitudes hardened towards the Greeks,' explained Brian Packham. 'My job in 8 Bty Stores was to supply out-stations with what they needed or wanted – beer, cigarettes, soft drinks, mail and so on. I was happy to leave camp, while other store men preferred staying inside. So I did most of the runs, irrespective of whether it was day or night. In my case, as I did a regular supply-run to out-stations four days a week, I made a point of stopping and searching all vehicles. If I found they carried Greeks, they were given a smack in the mouth. If they were Turks, they were allowed to go on their way in peace. I am not proud of what I did.

'On the Sunday after Mrs Cutliffe's murder, I had to take aviation fuel in jerry cans to Lefkonico, which was our principal out-station. Before I set off I went around the billets asking for escorts. Six soldiers volunteered and we were armed. After delivering the supplies, we stopped in a Greek village on the Lefkonico–Trikomo Road and decided to raid the local coffee shop. We made the Greeks line up against a wall, while beer from the shop was loaded on our truck. We tore down any Greek flags we saw and took them to camp. We shared out the beer with the blokes. Again, I am not proud of what I did, but there was a lot of anger about.'

All the while the Greek Cypriot population refused to believe EOKA committed the Cutliffe murder, but if EOKA did not, who did? The local rumour mill began grinding out stories that the assailants were blue-eyed and blond, so how could they be Greek Cypriots? What justified this description remains a mystery.

On 9 October EOKA distributed another leaflet, which carried a thunderous harangue against the British troops who carried out the search for the young murderers and tried to fog the issue of blame. EOKA said the assailants were linked with those who attacked Mr J. P. Wentworth, the American Vice Consul, in September, another crime which the organization disavowed, and it insinuated that the gunmen in both attacks were not members of EOKA. And it tried to throw a smokescreen over the actual murder. After denouncing the mass arrests, alleged ill treatment and 'cannibalistic invasions of towns and villages' by British troops it concluded: 'We ask, though we are certain the

Government will not tell us the truth, who killed the Englishwoman? Let the Tories hear this once more. No force can bend us. We will resist to the end.'

Significantly at no point did the leaflet explicitly deny that EOKA had actually carried out the Cutliffe murder, nor was it signed as was customary by Dighenis (Grivas), although it bore EOKA's stamp. An official spokesman immediately and emphatically repudiated the leaflet's insinuations. 'Not one iota of evidence has come to light to suggest that it was carried out by anyone other than EOKA terrorists,' he said. 'It is clear that these delayed attempts to blur the issue are intended to shield EOKA from the outcry against them on account of the hateful crime.'

WHATEVER THE bigger picture of the Cyprus situation, for the present the authorities focused their attention on Mrs Cutliffe's funeral, which was scheduled for 6 October, a Tuesday. She was to be accorded full military honours and buried in Wayne's Keep Military Cemetery in Nicosia. Despite security warnings for them not to attend in case EOKA chose the high-level gathering to attack, Lady Foot and Norah Kendrew were determined to be present.

In her autobiography, Lady Foot wrote movingly: 'We drove together to the Military Cemetery, neat and quiet and impersonal in the great arid plain. The military had just been burying a serviceman. One of our ADCs was still there ... It was very hot. The officer in charge of arrangements for the funeral came up and met us – we saw others we knew. Close to the open grave I was touched to see a group of women ... what women? I don't know, they were led by Mary G., the wife of a British brigadier. But that morning she was not there as such but as a member of the [Roman Catholic] Church to which Mrs Cutliffe had belonged.

'Coming out of early Mass that morning

she had looked around at the women coming out of Church and said, "Shall we go?" And they had silently followed her. They wore lace scarves on their heads. I thought they are not all British. I thought – they are women of the same Church coming to pay their respects and to mourn.

'I saw the coffin being borne in through the gate of the cemetery, carried by young men with faces like stones. And behind the coffin a slight girlish figure completely covered by a black satin shawl ... her face heavily veiled, the shawl enveloping her from head to knees. I noticed how slender and somehow hopeless her ankles looked, the high heels in the sand and sinking; her shoulders were shaking not with sobs but with a sort of constant shiver as in an ague.

'We gathered in a straggly sort of way round the grave ... the coffin approached with agonizing slowness, the heat beat down upon us, I saw Sergeant Cutliffe, the dead woman's husband, concentrating on supporting his daughter, behind her the tall young sergeant who was to become her husband. As the priest read the prayers at the grave, I glanced anxiously at fragile, gentle Norah Kendrew.

'The heat really was intolerable and I had that strange floating sensation of one who is about to lose consciousness ... I fought against it and kept my eyes fixed on the tragic little figure in the black shawl.'

The press had been warned not take any photographs that showed Margaret Cutliffe, a key witness in identifying her mother's killers, and herself a possible terrorist target. 'But in any case they could not have done so,' reported the *Daily Mirror's* Reginald Peck. 'Besides being dressed in black, she wore a black chiffon scarf over her face and heavy black satin stole that completely covered her head and face.'

Father James Fitzgerald conducted the service in Latin. It was his second funeral of the day. Earlier he had buried Staff Sergeant Lane of the Royal Ulster Rifles. Margaret Cutliffe reached for her father's hand. Her fingers and his entwined and so they remained throughout the ceremony. Sergeant Robinson, one of the pallbearers, remembered tears streaming down Sergeant Cutliffe's face. 'He was a completely broken man,' he said.

Ray 'Steve' Stephens of 29 Field Regiment, RA, reflected: 'The Army and my regiment did her proud that day. A good send-off with regimental and union flags flown at half-mast. The bearer party – of which I had the honour and privilege to be a member – wore uniforms with medals gleaming in the sunlight.'

Later in the day there would be yet another funeral with full military honours. It would be for Fusilier W. V. Uphill, a regular soldier, aged 20, of the Royal Welch Fusiliers, who died of injuries after an ambush near Amiandos village late on the Saturday night.

A FEW DAYS after her operation, Mrs Robinson was taken from hospital to a line-up of young suspects. The authorities hoped she would be able to identify her attackers. If they were there, she was unable to pick them out. She told the author that much later she remembered one of the attackers had worn dirty shoes, but then it was too late. She had

HOODED MOURNER RISKS CYPRUS TERROR

The *Daily Mirror's* front page coverage of Mrs Cutliffe's funeral. The picture shows Sergeant Cutliffe with his daughter, Margaret.

first noticed the youth while the Cutliffes and she were in the dress shop. He came in, stared at them and left. 'When I was shot down, I turned round and saw the same guy.' She was convinced there were three people involved, not two. But none of them had blond hair, making nonsense of EOKA's claims that the real killers were British *agents provocateurs*.

On 24 November, at the end of the week-long inquest at the Coroner's Court in Famagusta into the deaths of Mrs Cutliffe and three Greek Cypriots, Mr Justice Trainor summed up in scathing language. This was, he declared, 'the most horrible, dastardly murder it has ever been my lot to inquire into, one which filled me with disgust, as no other case has'. He found Mrs Cutliffe died of haemorrhage from wounds received in circumstances which amounted to murder, by persons unknown. Of the evidence given by Mrs Robinson and by Margaret Cutliffe, Mr Trainor said: 'I found it hardly possible to believe. A brute approached two women on the ground and laughed at them. I only think he must be mentally deranged. It is awful that there should be alive in this town a person capable of such monstrous conduct.

'I cannot help remarking on the behaviour of the people on that street that day. I suppose there must have been people on that crowded street that day, who can boast of being Christian. I have never known such an un-Christian thing in my life. These people are a disgrace to humanity.'

The gunmen were never caught, but the author has gathered circumstantial evidence which points at one of them being a Greek Cypriot, who became an officer in the Greek Army after Cyprus was granted independence. He has held several senior posts in the South Cyprus administration.

The Robinsons left Cyprus in early November, never to return.

Catherine Cutliffe's daughter married Sergeant 'Gabby' Haynes, who became RSM of 4 Regiment RA, based in Osnabruk, Germany. Her husband retired from the Army in the 70s. She never fully recovered from seeing her mother murdered. Neither wished to be interviewed by the author. David 'Taffy' Cutliffe retired to South Wales to run a public house.

IN THE weeks ahead EOKA stepped up its attacks. Grivas achieved his aim in stopping the implementation of Prime Minister Macmillan's peace plan or 'Adventure in Partnership', but he was on a downward track to lose the 'war'. Archbishop Makarios pulled the rug from under the Colonel's boots by presenting an unexpected proposal: he dropped his old demand for *enosis* and asked only for independence for the Island. He had had secret talks with the Greek Government and told Grivas that EOKA's campaign was losing the support of Britain's Labour Party and the United States. If EOKA insisted on union with Greece – and nothing else – the Turkish Cypriots could eventually achieve partition of the Island.

The Greek Government concurred. The Cutliffe murder had changed the whole political climate. Foreign Minister Evangelos Averoff even urged Grivas to condemn the crime unequivocally and, furthermore, to declare a ceasefire before the next meeting of the United Nations' General Assembly in November. Grivas refused and Athens began negotiating the Island's future without his views being taken into account. Grivas continued his campaign, sticking to his demand for *enosis*.

On the British side, there was no desire to follow up the Makarios proposal. Ministers saw it as just 'another trick' by the wily Archbishop. They wanted to settle the Cyprus dispute, using the Macmillan Plan, despite the Greeks' opposition.

But even after independence had been granted to Cyprus, the Greek Government continued to insist the murders of Mrs Cutliffe and Mr John P. Wentworth, Vice-Consul in Nicosia, shot by gunmen on 18 September 1958, were not initiated or conducted by EOKA. On 3 March 1959, at a meeting with US State Department officials in Athens, Foreign Minister Averoff said he could assure them that Mrs Cutliffe was shot because of a love affair. 'The Greek government knew this at the time, but could not publish it because once the woman was dead, it would have been regarded with disbelief in the emotional climate of the time,' a minute recorded. 'Mr Averoff then said in a further aside that one day he would let us have access to some of the secret files on Cyprus ... This whole story will be told in time, but the time is not yet.'

According to the official minutes, the US Ambassador 'interrupted him to ask if he could tell us the story of the shooting of the American Vice-Consul. He said he was sorry he could not tell me anything more except that it was not a Greek who did it, but it was done by "those who wanted to create antagonism between the Greeks and the Americans". He refused to be drawn out in the matter, merely saying we would be told in due course.'

No furhter information has ever been realeased.

CHAPTER TWENTY-FOUR

'We shall defeat the assassins': an outbreak of peace

*'Few and short were the prayers we said
And we spoke not a word of sorrow;
But we steadfastly gazed on the face that was dead
And we bitterly thought of the morrow.'*

Charles Wolfe

THE STYLUS tore through the grooves of the record, its screech amplified by the loudspeakers of the jukebox, but it was drowned out by the screams of the injured in the RAF NAAFI canteen, its timber frame shattered and its corrugated metal roof holed in several places by the blast of a time bomb. The airmen had been listening to the Everly Brothers' *All I Have To Do Is Dream*. At the Astra cinema down the road, the early Saturday evening screening of *Ice Cold in Alex* had just ended and the audience was leaving, hoping to emulate the movie's final scene, where John Mills, Anthony Quayle and Sylvia Simms drink a chilled lager. It was 21.03 on 8 November and the NAAFI on the Caywood domestic site was packed.

Senior Aircraftsman Peter Turnbull of the RAF Regiment, serving with No. 26 LAA Squadron, had just finished his beer with a friend, an aircraft fitter. They had been sitting on the sofa in which the bomb was hidden. The fitter had gone to start his shift and Turnbull was returning to his tent to write a letter home to the girl who would become his wife.

'I had left the canteen by the side door and had walked about 15 to 20 yards, when – KAAARRANG – and I found myself flat on my face and my ears singing,' said Turnbull. 'I picked myself up and remember hearing shouts and yells from men running from all directions towards the canteen. They passed me and I turned and saw smoke and dust pouring out of gaping holes in the metalwork. There were large nails sticking up in neat rows. In my 29 years of military service that was the closest I came to meeting the Grim Reaper.'

Turnbull, still dazed, staggered to the NAAFI's cookhouse. 'The duty cook was scared out of his wits and pointed to a hole in the wall. A shard of metal had passed through two sheets of corrugated iron. The bomb must have been placed by one of the four Greek Cypriots who worked in the place, acting on EOKA's instructions. That evening they had tried to keep out of sight and we had complained about their slow service. The lads were fed up with them not clearing empty glasses and not serving the hot sandwiches we ordered. We knew they disliked us, taking their lead from the manager who hated our regular search duties at the entrance to the camp and at Ayios Dhometios, where he lived. I admit, we caused him a lot of inconvenience, but we had a job to do.'

Turnbull's supposition was credible as the NAAFI premises were always searched prior to opening and again at closing time to ensure no surprise packages had been left by EOKA to cause problems.

John Thorpe, an RAF driver, was on the premises when the explosion took place. He was sitting with friends directly opposite the sofa where the bomb had been hidden. 'Those sitting on it absorbed the explosion, saving other fatalities,' he reckoned. 'The two chaps who died were facing away from us. Parts of their bodies splattered the walls. It was a gruesome sight. Flies started to converge on them. In those days, I smoked. Didn't we all? I had been to the cinema, where we weren't allowed to smoke and came to the NAAFI where we could. What I saw was a high price to pay for a beer and a fag.'

The bomb had killed two airmen and severely wounded seven others. The dead were SAC Charles Bray, 23, and LAC Albert Sargent, 22. Bray, a National Serviceman, had been stationed in Hong Kong and was in transit to be demobbed in the UK. In the chaos that followed, the late Flight Sergeant 'Tubby' Grimshaw went to the aid of the injured. For his effort to save lives, he received the BEM for his bravery.

'While not in the NAAFI at the time, I was one of the RAF Regiment personnel who stood guard inside the place after the explosion,' Clive Hickson added. 'I was with No. 2

The interior of the RAF NAAFI after the EOKA bomb explosion.

Field Squadron. Our main duty was to protect the airfield and I was on guard at the time. We immediately went to the NAAFI to assist in cordoning off the area and to search for any further bombs. Afterwards I was taken to another building near the perimeter, where I guarded the Cypriot NAAFI employees who had been incarcerated there. This was partly to detain them and partly for their safety, because they had been beaten by enraged servicemen who had seen their comrades blown to pieces.

'I was told that one of them had been severely beaten in the kidneys and he groaned piteously all night long. He was evidently in great pain.'

'He was the NAAFI's cleaner and it was assumed he was the one most likely to have planted the device, but I don't think he did,' agreed SAC Turnbull.

Hickson continued: 'Nobody, not even British medical personnel, came near the building to render even rudimentary first aid to these people. I was, I must admit, ashamed at being able to do nothing and knowing that our medical officers were ignoring their Hippocratic oath. These Cypriots were probably as much victims of the murderers as were our boys.'

LAC John Crouch arrived that night at 751 Signals Unit at Cape Greco. He was fresh out from England.

'Where have you come from?' asked the camp's only RAF policeman at the gate.

'Transit, Nicosia,' replied the newcomer.

'Christ, you're lucky. EOKA's bombed the NAAFI. We hear some people have been killed.'

'Welcome to the Island, I thought,' Crouch said.

SINCE PRIME Minister Macmillan's 'Adventure in Partnership' plan was put into operation on 1 October, a total of 44 people had been killed and about 370 injured. Of those who lost their lives, 17 were Greek Cypriots killed by EOKA; 11 were terrorists shot by the Army; six were British civilians and 10 were soldiers, as a result of ambushes or electrically-detonated mines laid on roads used by military vehicles.

Among the civilian dead was retired naval commander John Smith, 76, killed instantly when his legs were blown off in a terrorist act at Ardhana on the 12th. His wife was seriously injured in the attack and was taken to the Dhekelia military hospital. The couple had lived in Cyprus for many years and were travelling by car to Kantara, where they had a summerhouse.

Sergeant Warder Arthur Dallen was murdered four days later after walking across a field to visit Greek Cypriot friends in Kokkinotrimithia village. He was carrying a small present for their young daughter. As he reached their front door, two masked men emerged from the garden and pumped bullets into his body. He had just returned from a holiday in England and was due to become an officer in the Cyprus Prison Service. The 55-year-old was the holder of the British Empire Medal, awarded for his service in Malaya as a Company Sergeant Major in the Royal West Regiment and worked at the nearby detention centre. Despite the dangers to them, the Greek Cypriot family attended his funeral.

Dallen was the 119th Briton to be killed since the start of the Emergency. His death was followed by that of Frederick Sharman, a businessman. He was shot on 24 October, as he entered his car in Nicosia. He had first come to Cyprus in 1913. He ran an import–export agency and lived in the capital.

On 31 October, the day after Grivas hinted at another 'truce', EOKA perpetrated a pointless brutality. The victim was 17-year-old Brian Preece, a NAAFI clerk, who was shot dead in Famagusta on his way to work at the Golden Sands Leave Camp. He was the son of Sergeant L. A. Preece of 65 Company, RASC,

Several hours later his body, lying in an orange grove, was discovered by a passing patrol.

The journal of the Durham Light Infantry commented: '"Truce", however, is a convenient word, which Grivas has used before. His fondness of the term really means: "Would the Security Forces please cease all activity so that EOKA can re-group and re-equip?"'

The service fatalities in October included RUR Staff Sergeant James Lane on 3 October, during the Greek Cypriot roundup after Mrs Cutliffe's murder.

Two days later Signalman Robert Bunton was killed. The same day, two military vehicles were ambushed with bombs, grenades and small arms fire outside Amiandos village and Fusilier Walter Uphill of the Royal Welch Fusiliers died from his injuries. On the 6th, a Royal Marine patrol came under attack near Lefkonico and Essex-lad Marine Raymond Greening, 18, lost his short life. In another ambush at Kalhassa, three servicemen were wounded. As they were rushed to hospital, their clearly marked Red Cross ambulance also came under attack.

At Kantara, Private Jimmy Gould and Corporal Bernard Peters of the 1st Battalion Welch Regiment ran over a pressure mine. Gould died instantly and Peters succumbed to his injuries on 7 October.

Fifty years later to the day, Peters' comrades clubbed together to have a calligrapher put his name into a memorial book at the Chapel of Llandaff Cathedral in Cardiff. He became the first Welch Regiment soldier from the Cyprus conflict to be placed in the book. Graham Newbury, who served alongside the corporal, said: 'He was a hell of a nice guy, one of those people who was laughing all the time. We felt it was the most fitting way to remember such a brave soldier.' Rhos Brown, another of his comrades, added: 'He was a smashing kid who fitted in great right from the start. I think it's a testimony to him that we still remember him. It took a lot of effort to get permission to place him in the memorial book so we're really pleased.'

Corporal Peters was originally buried in Wayne's Keep Military Cemetery, Nicosia, but the steelworkers of Llanelli, where he and his father used to work, paid for his body to be returned to Wales so that he could buried in his home town.

On 8 October, another ambush took Lance Bombardier Earnest Barclay's life at Lefkonico. He belonged to 25 Field Regiment. Although not an EOKA target, Rifleman John White of the Royal Ulster Rifles died the same day, while driving a Champ on the approach to the roundabout near the entrance to Famagusta's walled city. His vehicle overturned and its long radio aerial looped round his body and pierced his chest.

The relentless toll of death appeared unstoppable. At Prodhomos, Sergeant S. Woodward from the Durham Constabulary, seconded to the UK Police Unit, was ambushed and killed on the 13th. Trooper Lawrence Birch of the Blues and Royals ran over a mine in his Ferret armoured car and died in the explosion near Ayios Nikolaos on 21 October.

The next day Alexander Macdougall, 20, of 45 Marine Commando Royal Marines was ambushed in Kyperounda. Four of his comrades were injured. In the exchange of fire, one of the ambushers was killed. Soon afterwards the Royal Marines began their search for the killers. Aided by dogs, especially flown by helicopter to the area, the terrorists were tracked to their hiding places and three were arrested.

On the 25th, Private Peter Jenkins of the RASC, attached to 25 Field Regiment, lost his life when a bomb went off outside Yialoussa police station. Private Alan Britton of the Durham Light Infantry died on the 28th, 'Oxi Day' which Greeks celebrate with great jubilation to mark the occasion when Greece refused to surrender to the Axis Powers in the Second World War. To ensure there were no riots in Nicosia, the 1st Battalion the Suffolk Regiment stood ready to intervene, but trouble was avoided.

On 30 October Major Edwin Andrews of the Royal Artillery and his driver, Gunner Anthony Jasper, an army regular, were killed by a pressure mine at Cape Elia. They belonged to 188 Radar and Searchlight Battery. 'It was a lovely afternoon and we joked with Tony about how lucky he was to be going out on this detail,' said Gunner David Nicholas. 'We spent most afternoons lazing about the camp with nothing to do. Then, about an hour later we were informed that both men were dead, just outside one of our sites. Every time after that incident, an AEC Matador filled with sandbags was reversed the few miles to the main road and then reversed back to the camp, to make sure the track was clear of mines. Driving behind the Matador wasn't very pleasant as the dirt track threw dust everywhere, but it was better than being killed and we didn't complain.'

Of those injured in October, about 90 were British nationals, nearly all members of the Security Forces, but 25 'active' terrorists, including a group leader, had been captured. Service fatalities would have been far higher had EOKA destroyed a Comet airliner due to take troops and their families home on 29 October, but the bomb exploded prematurely. It had been hidden in an airman's hand luggage and went off near the aircraft before it was taken on board. Ten airmen were wounded.

GRIVAS HAD ordered his gangs into action at the beginning of the month and they were striking in towns, remote villages and at the British base areas. He had pulled out all the stops to prevent the 'Adventure in Partnership' from succeeding. In his efforts he was supported by a campaign of new anti-British broadcasts of unparalleled virulence from Radio Athens aimed at Greek Cypriots. Sir Hugh Foot was described as a 'Nazi gauleiter' while Hitler was extolled as 'a saint in comparison with British crimes in Cyprus'. A Government official called the broadcasts 'a daily dose of muck'.

Major General Kenneth Darling had replaced Kendrew as Director of Operations and he planned to give Grivas a dose of his own medicine. 'The only EOKA terrorists I am interested in are dead ones,' he told his troops. An extrovert, he enjoyed meeting the press, and using correspondents, including those representing Greek publications, to pass his messages to Dighenis on the front pages of their newspapers. At one of his first press conferences he spoke frankly that it was 'the duty of every soldier, whether cook, clerk or store-man to kill terrorist murderers' and he wanted every 'butcher, baker, or candlestick-maker' to become 'a good marksman'.

His remarks infuriated Grivas, who noted in his *Memoirs*: 'Major General Kenneth Darling was a man of small stature who tried to make up for his lack of inches with a boastful tongue. He assumed every Greek was a possible EOKA supporter – and he was probably correct. His press conferences were taken up with victory claims and abuse. His language shocked even some of his fellow-officers. "We've got those bastards on the run," he said repeatedly. He may have convinced himself, but he convinced no one else, for everyone could see that the army under his command was taking the greatest beating it had yet suffered, worse even than the humiliation we had inflicted on it during the month of "Black November", two years before.' More likely, it was the EOKA leader who was the deluded one, because the war he had resumed was turning against him.

Whatever his personal feelings, Sir Hugh Foot was persuaded by Darling to impose new and drastic security regulations to combat the mounting wave of terrorism, including the reintroduction of certain emergency measures, which had been revoked a year earlier. Under the new regulations, the system of 'danger areas' was reintroduced, and people entering or remaining in these areas were warned that they would do so at the risk of their lives; the security forces were empowered to take immediate armed action – shoot on sight – against any unauthorized person found in those areas, which would be clearly marked by warning notices; powers of postal censorship were reintroduced so as to check the smuggling of arms by parcel post.

Simultaneously, General Darling was having the administration's intelligence-gathering systems reorganized from top to bottom by John Prendergast, whom he had brought to the Island from Kenya. Prendergast concentrated less on known terrorist suspects and much more on those believed to be Grivas's message couriers, with the aim of gaining control of EOKA's communications and of tracking 'The Leader' to his lair. Darling called Prendergast his 'key to the box of tricks'.

The General also encouraged the Army to deploy EOKA's methods in a counter-offensive. To draw the terrorists into the open, new ruses were developed. 'A guerrilla might see a soldier, apparently dead and covered in blood, lying with a weapon beside him, and find himself ambushed as he attempted to retrieve it,' wrote Major Gregory Blaxland. 'Another might see a soldier lackadaisically riding a donkey and find himself held up at close quarters as he followed the trail of this tempting quarry. And in the towns and villages there would be no tramp of foot at night, nor whine of military vehicle, but the soldiers would be there, out of sight and out of hearing. In fact, military vehicles were forbidden to move at night to reduce the chances of them being caught in an ambush.'

ON THE international front, NATO was increasingly worried by the explosive situation on the Island and the deteriorating relations between Greece and Turkey, which, according to Greek Foreign Minister Averoff could 'hardly be worse – barring war'. He suggested an international body should decide the military status of the Island so that it could never be a threat to Turkey; that there should be a Greece–Turkey–Cyprus Customs union; and that Turkish Cypriot interests could be protected by a UN representative permanently based in Cyprus to guard Turkish Cypriots after independence. He rejected Turkey's ongoing demand for partition.

Averoff asked: 'What would happen if in the process of reprisals and counter-reprisals Turkish mobs burnt a Greek village in Cyprus? People in Greece would get frantic, and the blood and fire of Cyprus would spread outside it.'

As NATO's permanent council debated the Cyprus Problem, the organization's Secretary-General Paul-Henri Spaak recommended that Prime Minister Macmillan should amend his plan and drop the idea of having mainland Turkish and Greek representatives as 'advisers' to Government House. He thought a new round table conference should take place with him acting as a mediator. Turkey gave his ideas a firm 'No'.

Washington expressed its 'gravest concern' over the tension between NATO's southern partners, where annually millions of US taxpayers' dollars went in economic and defence aid. The American Government reminded the Greek and Turkish leaders that if their NATO ties were severed, the House Appropriations Committee would find it hard to allot more funds if there were the slightest suspicion that they were disloyal allies.

After arguments over who would attend the NATO conference, agreement was reached that it should take place in Paris in December.

Archbishop Makarios, as was his wont, said he did expect NATO to solve the problem: 'To be constructive a conference as proposed by NATO should advance beyond Mr Macmillan's partnership plan and discuss the final status of Cyprus.' He told reporters he would be willing to discuss the question of British or NATO military bases in Cyprus in conjunction with a final political settlement. If NATO's mediation failed, he said: 'I believe the Greek Government would proceed with its appeal before the United Nations. During that period, however, the allied ties within NATO will perforce be loosened and there will be an absence of harmony and good relations.'

The Athens Government had supported Makarios and Grivas from the beginning in their demands for *enosis* and provided resources for them to continue the EOKA conflict, but now ministers were privately wondering whether the two Greek Cypriots were growing too big for their boots and trying to dictate Greek foreign policy, perhaps with the long-term aim of entering mainland politics ... and then what? There would have to be fresh thinking to prevent wild cards being played.

In Cyprus, nevertheless, November started as grimly as the previous month. The Governor warned that 'no one should offer an easy target to the EOKA killers ... You are all in the front line now. No one should say, "It can't happen to me".' Even as his statement was broadcast, the Security Forces were hunting for those who murdered elderly William Jamieson, who provided tea and comfort to servicemen from his Church of Scotland canteen truck. Jamieson was much admired by the troops for his courage. He would appear wherever they were on operations, unaccompanied and unarmed. The attack on him had taken place in Ayios Amvrosias.

The three other civilians murdered in the first week of November included Charles Woods, who had lived in Cyprus for 30 years and was known as a warm friend of the Greek Cypriots. The gunman, as usual, vanished into thin air.

'Lunch was late. The men came one by one up to my room and brought news. Bad news. I came to dread their coming. They always waited for me to ask: "Any horrors?" Yes, horrors. Little Charlie was shot round the corner this morning while he was waiting for a lift. Who? An old English gentleman, he lived in retirement in the village round the corner,' Lady Foot noted.

'His daughter was married to a Cypriot. He used to go to the Club every morning and help with the accounts. No, he never had anything to do with politics. He was over 70 and a humble little man. The villagers loved him. Yes, his only crime was to be in the same place at the same time every morning – waiting for a lift. He was a soft target. Why? Nobody knows, nobody ever will know. Just another notch in the EOKA stick that marks another British life – just any British life.'

On 3 November, Lieutenant David Spurling, the 23-year-old son of Major General J. M. Spurling, serving in 45 Commando, was killed in the Troodos Mountains.

On 6 November, Joseph Brander, manager of Barclays Bank in Limassol, was EOKA's next victim. He was hit by two bullets fired from a .45 automatic and died instantly on the steps of the bank. He left a widow and two young children. His death squashed any speculation that Grivas was on the point of declaring a 'truce'.

The next day Wilfred Benson, the acting manager of the Ottoman Bank in Nicosia, was struck by EOKA using the same technique and choosing another bank official as a 'soft' target. At 14.00 six rounds hit him from close range as he was about to settle in the driver's seat of his tiny Fiat to drive to the hotel where he and his wife Irene were living. She had given birth a few days earlier to a son, Nigel. On hearing the news, she collapsed and was comforted by her parents, the Reverend and Mrs Thomas.

Polycarpos Georgadjis, a bespectacled man of seemingly peaceful demeanor, was the leader of the EOKA gangs in Nicosia. With Grivas's approval, he had the authority to sanction each murder while he hid in Gabriel Gabrielides' home, a place where off-duty security officials enjoyed after-hours drinking at his well-stocked bar.

Lorryloads of soldiers of the Suffolk Regiment rumbled down the narrow alleys, cordoning off the area around the murder spot. An officer, gun in hand, remarked: 'We called too late and we are too thin on the ground.' A police dog tracked the killer's scent through a building site in the walled city, but lost the trail when it reached a road. General Darling arrived on the scene to direct the hunt.

The London *Daily Express* reported: 'This latest shooting has increased the fury and frustration felt by Englishmen on the island. More and more people are accusing Government House of not doing enough to protect British civilians' lives. Police told me the only solution would be to drive all British civilians to and from work and under military escort.'

British residents pointed out that, while up to a month before, automatic curfews and searches followed such attacks, after the last murders there were no curfews and few, if any, troops taking part in roundup operations. Their complaints reflected a deeper feeling of lack of contact between their loosely knit community and the Governor. They also disapproved of Sir Hugh's policy to hold the balance and find a compromise between Greeks and Turks at the relative neglect of the Security Forces. Their largely emotional distrust began to be voiced and, the next day, 400 civilians gathered at one of Nicosia's main barracks to voice their concerns to the Governor's District Security Committee.

At this extraordinary gathering, probably unique in the Island's history, various personal security problems were frankly discussed. The civilians said the situation had now reached a pitch of terror unprecedented during the three and a half years' violence. They demanded new and drastic measures to counter the killer gangs.

General Darling replied that all British civilians could now have guns if they desired them – women excepted. If they did not know how to use the weapons, the Army would teach them. His offer met a mixed reaction: some welcomed it, but others, working alongside Greek Cypriots, and who had survived unscathed so far, argued that to go around armed was likely to make them targets. They questioned whether anyone would be 'quickest on the draw' when matched against EOKA's trained assassination squads. 'We are defeating the ambushers and we shall defeat the assassins,' the Governor declared optimistically.

The United States Consul-General in Nicosia said that Americans would not be armed, but he urged all US citizens to take security precautions.

General Darling was sure the arming of British civilians was part of 'getting to grips with the bastards', but warned, 'any Englishman who wants a gun may have one. But he must know how to use it. They're not a ration of potatoes.' And so began the distribution of .38 revolvers to the civilians in a tent set up on the edge of a disused garbage dump on the outskirts of Nicosia. Each individual was given a crash course in their weapon's use by firing at a life-sized tin terrorist 15 feet away. Their instructors studied the hits and misses and told them to return for much more training, crossed their fingers and advised: 'The thing is to always look behind you.'

Then came the bomb blast at the NAAFI at RAF Nicosia. When Sir Hubert Patch, the Commander-in-Chief Middle East Air Force, heard the news, he immediately demanded Sir Hugh Foot dismiss all Greek Cypriot NAAFI employees. At first the Governor demurred. Hundreds would be put out of work, he said, but next morning, 4,000 Greek Cypriot

Dismissed Greek Cypriot NAAFI workers leave.

employees were dismissed and banned from entering any camp, barracks or NAAFI establishment. Grivas was hurting his own people almost as much as the British community.

ALAN GILFILLAN of the RAF Police served at Akrotiri. 'On the morning of the dismissal order, I was sent down to a point about 200 yards outside the camp's entrance and main guardroom on the Limassol road,' he remembered. 'My unpleasant task was to stop the busloads of Greek Cypriot workers and tell them their services were no longer required. Many of them were women. They worked for officers and senior NCOs as maids and had grown close to their families. All of us expected a riot and were ready for it, but none ensued. Instead there were floods of tears from the females and much wailing from the males. EOKA had not done them a favour.

'Once they knew their fate, they were ordered to reverse their buses and return from whence they came. To ensure they did, we were accompanied by a couple of locally recruited RAF Auxiliary policemen, who were used to checking the workers' ID cards every morning and were known to those on the buses. One of the auxiliaries was a Turk, the other Greek. Both were armed with Greener guns.

'The Greener, not noted for its reliability, fired a large brass cartridge, equivalent to those used in 12–bore shotguns. Each was filled with double-0 buckshot that could cause a lot of damage. Fortunately I never saw one used in anger. To load the weapon, a lever below the stock had to be pulled down and a single cartridge fed into a slot at the top. From that moment, the weapon had to be treated with great care to avoid an accident, as its safety catch was not very secure. When we were on duty with the auxiliaries, we made certain they kept their "one" cartridge always in their pockets, not loaded in their guns.

'Back in camp, the Greek auxiliary policeman was also told his fate. He, too, had to join the ranks of the unemployed.

'To this day I cannot understand how Greek Cypriots were ever allowed to work on the camps given the situation,' wondered former SAC Graham Robinson, an Air Movements Clerk at RAF Nicosia. 'Greek Cypriots seemed to be grasping and untrustworthy whereas the Turkish Cypriots were far more honest. My opinion hasn't changed. After the NAAFI bombing, there was a rush to the armoury with the intention of taking revenge in Nicosia. Everyone was incensed by the cowardly actions of the EOKA terrorists. If we'd been allowed out, there would have been a massacre.'

After the sackings, EOKA struck back at two unfortunate British NAAFI officers, while they were inspecting their butchery's cold store in Famagusta. Just as they were leaving at the end of their working day, a gang of terrorists pushed them back inside, padlocked the door, switched off the lights and left.

For the men inside, clothed in open-neck shirts and light slacks, their chance of survival in a temperature of minus 10 degrees Fahrenheit was none, if they waited until morning for staff to open up. The prisoners looked around and saw a large meat cleaver. With it, they took turns to cut a hole 18 inches square to allow them to shout until someone

heard and rescued them. 'Had that cleaver not been there,' said one of the men, 'the stocks of meat would have been increased overnight by about 300 lb.'

Forty-six canteens, 17 shops, three clubs, two leave centres and several bakeries came to a standstill with the shortage of staff. 'It caused chaos,' writes Harry Miller, the author of *Service to the Services*. 'Garrison and British NAAFI wives helped to maintain vital

Volunteer NAAFI workers set off from London for Cyprus.

Miss Rowlands, an eager volunteer, is pleased to wear her new NAAFI uniform.

services. Headquarters issued an SOS for 500 volunteers.' A NAAFI boss, Mr. H. P. T. Prideaux said: 'Either men or women can carry out most of the jobs, but the troops would rather see a pretty girl about the place than a man. They are an important factor in maintaining morale. A soldier prefers a girl to serve him his cup of tea.'

NAAFI offered the volunteers six-month contracts. The danger of the work was recognized and this would be adequately reflected in a bonus added to the normal rate of pay. Full board and lodging would be provided free as would working clothes and passage. A male canteen attendant would receive a minimum of £8 10s a week, with a separation allowance of £2 10s if he were married. The minimum for girls at 18 years would be £7 15s. Both these figures included a bonus of £3, and the wages would be tax-free.

One of the difficulties was accommodation because this step was totally unexpected, Prideaux conceded, but he promised that no one, particularly young girls, would be sent out to Cyprus unless satisfactory arrangements could be made for their quarters and safety. He hoped that they would be able to fly out the first replacements within the next five days.

Within 24 hours, 17,000 – mostly young women – had applied. Officials were flabbergasted by the stampede to fill the posts. Telephone operators dealt with 600 calls an hour, while clerks ripped open hundreds of postal applications. They came from all parts of the country. 'Whatever the applicants' backgrounds, they were all filled with patriotism, a desire for adventure and a longing for the sun,' reported *The Times*. A NAAFI official said: 'The girls who have been coming in today have been of all types and classes, with quite a lot of well educated girls who are willing to take jobs at a much lower figure than they are getting now.'

'There were plenty of young women in fur coats on a cold afternoon, and some of them looked as though they had stepped out of the pages of *Vogue*. And there were others who could be said without any lack of chivalry comfortably to exceed the upper age limit of 45. There were women with excellent jobs in banking, Fleet Street, and the professions, and at least one Bachelor of Arts, all willing to do any job that was offered,' *The Times* told readers. 'It's very British,' said senior NAAFI official Aidie Fraser.

'There's a job to be done, and they want to have a crack at it. And nobody's fussy about what they do.'

Sir Winston Churchill's Austrian cook was one of the volunteers who wanted to serve tea and buns to the troops. At his Chartwell home in Kent, Mrs Josephine Schwarz, 42, said she wanted to repay the debt she felt she owed the United Kingdom. 'England gave me a home when I was homeless, starving,' she said. 'Now at last I can be with the English on the same side. I want to join the struggle. I want to go to Cyprus to look after the boys out there. I've not told Sir Winston or Lady Churchill yet. It will be a shock for them, I know.'

The Barry & District News reported enthusiastically that one of those chosen was 'Miss Hilary John, the 19-year-old daughter of Mr and Mrs H. John of Evelyn Street, Barry Dock ... She leaves London Airport on Friday morning for Cyprus, where as a shorthand typist, she will be one of the volunteers for the new all-British NAAFI staff.'

Harry Miller said: 'The Passport Office and medical officers worked extra hours to speed 300 on their flight to the war zone. They also had to be fitted out with brand new uniforms. The airlift was the most costly single item in a total extra cost to NAAFI of £200,000.'

Major General Sir Randle Feilden, NAAFI's Managing Director, announced in London: 'We have enough volunteers to meet our requirements for any foreseeable task in Cyprus. Even so, our original target of 500 may have to be increased. I would like to thank the public for the magnificent response to our appeal. The promptitude with which 17,000 men, women and girls have offered themselves for a task which they recognize will be no picnic is a token of the country's overwhelming support for and confidence in our troops in Cyprus.'

On 16 November, the first batch of 43 new NAAFI employees left Blackbushe Airport in Hampshire in a Viscount aircraft. When they landed in Nicosia, the first to step out on the runway was 21–year-old Sally Anne Heath of Hillingdon. Rosemary Parrott, the nine-year-old daughter of an RAF officer, presented her with a bouquet of roses, before the volunteers left by road for Famagusta.

'I was one of the RAF Police on duty at Akrotiri the night when a batch of them arrived by bus from Nicosia and we had to check them into camp,' Gilfillan remembered. 'As virile young men, mainly in our late teens, we had been eagerly looking forward to meeting the ladies. That feeling of anticipation vanished the moment we saw them. Most were older than my mum and those that weren't would scare a police dog. Whatever the reason, none was billeted at RAF Akrotiri. They were put up overnight at the WRAC camp and in the morning they were distributed round the Island's military establishments.'

'They were a very mixed bunch of women brought out from Blighty to run them,' added Ruth White of 27 Independent Company, WRAC, at Episkopi. 'After the initial teething problems, several of them were found unsuitable.'

A 'Rock Ape' – a member of the RAF Regiment – remarked: 'The girls who came, we thought, must have been after husbands. There were about 20 girls and 10 million guys. Quite a queue for a date. 'Fraid I didn't wait for my turn to come around.'

The first arrivals were sent to the Golden Sands rest camp near Famagusta to start work immediately.

John Thorpe, based at RAF Nicosia, said: 'The womens' billets were enclosed in barbed wire and I never found out if it was to keep them in, keep us out or protect them from EOKA.' Clive Hickson continued: 'Their quarters were in a group of buildings which were declared seriously "out-of-bounds" to all the men there, but the girls used to hang their undies out to dry on a washing line in full view of the guys. One night, all undies were stolen. That was when the barbed wire was put up around the whole building. It became a miniature Fort Knox. Must have really pissed off the NAAFI girls.'

Lucy held that living was
A grand old thing to do
And lived it up each Friday night
Till nigh on half past two.

There was no drink she had not drunk;
No sin she had not tasted;
No make of car she had not smashed;
No soft drink but she laced it.

Now ministers of every faith
Had pledged themselves to save her
'Redeem!' they said. 'The wickedest,
Transform their bad behaviour.'

They pestered her to give up liquor
'Do quench your thirst,' they said,
'With sparkling water from the tap.'
But Lucy shook her head.

'And men are dangerous,' they said,
'For such a girl as you.
Get yourself one good boy friend
And don't branch out to two.'

'Don't race about in fast sports cars
With men as fast beside.
The paths of sin are primrose-lined
And comfortably wide.'

'Come wash off all your sins,' they urged.
'From black, be white instead.'
She poured a glass of cool, straight gin
And 'Bottoms up!' she said.

For three years more did Lucy live
A life of deep delight
Until the Good Lord showed his hand
And changed our Lucy quite.

The cry went up from all the Press
That girls should volunteer
To serve in Cyprus with the NAAFI –
The call of duty clear.

Now Lucy had a painful head,
She'd mixed her drinks that day.
'Hell, this place stinks!' she cried aloud,
'I'd like to go away!'

That very morning she signed up
To be a NAAFI girl
And found herself in Cyprus camps
Behind a counter till.

And here's the moral of the tale
I've struggled-to re-tell.
Scarce two weeks had Lucy worked
Till she was changed as well.

For where the ministers had failed,
With all their talk of Heaven,
The National Servicemen achieved
By examples of clean living.

                ANONYMOUS

Ten years later, an RAF serviceman returned to Cyprus for a second tour in 1968 and recalled seeing the sacked Nicosia canteen manager running a NAAFI beach outlet at Lady's Mile at RAF Akrotiri. 'He did not recognize me naturally, but there was no doubt in my mind it was him,' he said.

IN NOVEMBER 1958, name after name was added to the long list of deaths: Lance Sergeant George Rissbrook of the Grenadier Guards on the 2nd; Sergeant Basil Hill, another Grenadier, on the 5th; and Private John Robertson of the Durham Light Infantry on the 9th. He was killed in a hail of gunfire and two others injured as he was driving his truck on the road south of Kedhares. Corporal Derek Humphreys of the Royal Welch Fusiliers drove over a pressure mine on the 12th on the Polystipos–Khandria road and his vehicle was blasted into a ravine. He died; seven others survived. Humphreys had been awarded the Military Medal in Malaya for gallantry. In the days that followed Gunner Robert Taylor, Private James Boyle of the RASC and Private Michael Button of the Welch Regiment died.

Ten British soldiers were killed in the first fortnight of November by terrorist ambushes and road mining, mainly in the Troodos Mountains and other remote areas. EOKA, too, was suffering. Several terrorists were killed in gun battles and roundups, and a big quantity of arms and ammunition was seized during searches at the village of Karavas, in the Kyrenia district. The arms were found buried in the orchard of a priest who had previously been interned for acting as an EOKA courier.

General Darling's tough intelligence-driven strategy had started to pay dividends. 'Softly, softly, catchee monkey,' he quipped. London was providing him with modern equipment and anything else he needed. 'Prime Minister Macmillan took a personal interest in the provision of bullet-proof jackets,' wrote Robert Holland. 'Junior Colonial Office Minister, John Profumo, oversaw a special executive to speed up the flow of military material to the Island.'

Terrorist gangs were being decimated, arms dumps were being found and Grivas's communications network had been compromised. There was optimism amongst the Security Forces that they were closing on him and his key personnel. Greece's support for 'Dighenis' was waning and his differences with Makarios were widening. He was becoming embittered that his military supplies from Athens had become a dribble and cries for *enosis* were becoming less strident as Greek Cypriots felt the economic crunch caused by his boycott on trade with the British and the unemployment caused by his actions.

In a letter to the Bishop of Kitium, Grivas complained: 'Nothing has been attempted beyond a lot of windy speeches and an exchange of notes; thus is the enemy encouraged in the direction of new excesses. One day history will name those who stood by while our men suffered and our cause was put in terrible danger. If I survive I shall be their chief accuser.'

On 19 November, the Security Forces delivered Grivas another blow by finding the hiding place of 32–year-old Kyriakos Matsis, the Kyrenia area gang leader. Matsis was one of his few friends – or perhaps it is more accurate to say that they had admiration for each other. More importantly, the two were in direct contact and Matsis was the organization's 'quartermaster'.

Earlier a unit of the Queen's Own Royal West Kent Regiment had cordoned off Ayios Yeoryios in the Kyrenia Mountains, where they captured Andreas Sophocleous hiding in a well. During the raid, 30 others were arrested and large quantities of arms and explosives discovered. Within hours, Sophocleous squawked like a parrot, revealing where Matsis was holding out. The information was passed to the Wiltshire Regiment, which was in the area. Meanwhile, the Queen's Own went on to Bellapais, a hotbed of EOKA activity, and curfewed the inhabitants.

Lieutenant Colonel George Woolnough directed the operation to capture Matsis, who had been arrested before in January 1956, but had escaped in the September of that year from Camp K to rejoin his Kyrenia group. He had claimed that during his confinement, Field Marshal Sir John Harding visited him and offered £500,000 and a new identity abroad if he revealed where Grivas was hiding. He is reputed to have replied: 'This struggle is for virtue, not for money.' A graduate of Thessaloniki University, he was one of EOKA's few intellectuals with a proper education. He had a price of £5,000 on his head.

The Wiltshire soldiers followed the directions they were given, starting on the north coast, and and crossing the Pentadactylos Mountains until they reached Kato Dhikomo, which they surrounded. Matsis, said the captured Andreas Sophocleous, could be found in one of the village's tiny houses.

At 12.15 the troops entered the first house they reached, a four-room building, with newly laid tiles on the floor. They tapped each tile in turn. If they heard a hollow sound, it indicated a space underneath. In a rear bedroom, using his bayonet, a soldier marked out a square of tiles. 'Here, sir,' he shouted. 'I think we've found him.'

'Matsis,' shouted Major Herbert McRitchie, attached to the Wiltshires from 1 Para, 'Come out now, with your hands up. No tricks or you're dead.'

'Sir, there are two men with me,' Matsis replied. 'I'm sending them up first. They are unarmed. Don't shoot.'

Everyone stepped out of the room and stood outside, their guns at the ready and trained on the door in case the terrorists made a break to escape. An interpreter told Matsis that the soldiers were ready to receive his men. The tiled trapdoor was slowly raised and the two climbed out, arms raised, eyes blinking in the light. They were grabbed and handed to Special Branch officers.

Bending over the hide's entrance, McRitchie spoke loudly. 'Now it's your turn to come out, Matsis,' he said. The terrorist's muffled reply was in Greek, which the interpreter translated. 'He says he will not surrender. It will dishonour him.'

A smoke grenade was lobbed into the hide.

'Tell him to surrender NOW, because the next one will be a live explosive.'

'No,' Matsis yelled back. Five seconds later an army grenade exploded in the hole. A second was tossed inside, just in case ...

The soldiers found Matsis's smashed body lying a couple of yards away from the entrance to the hidden basement. His right leg was severed at the hip, his head shattered and his chest filled with shrapnel. To his side, there were two rifles, one by his hand. His binocular case, made by Dolland of London, had survived intact. The three terrorists had hidden in a space no more than six feet long and under five feet high.

At an inquest later, the coroner ruled that Matsis had committed suicide. His remains were buried in the grounds of Nicosia's Central Prison. Where he died subsequently became a place of pilgrimage for Greek Cypriots. 'I knew Matsis well and his loss was a deep personal grief to me. I remembered so well when I had first been impressed by his strong and selfless character. It was in September 1955, on a day when he had brought messages to the house where I was living at the time in Kakopetria, the mountain resort in the Troodos,' wrote Grivas in his *Memoirs*.

General Darling congratulated the Wiltshires. 'An absolutely splendid effort,' he told them. Speaking to the press, he said: 'My men have been first class under conditions requiring great patience and endurance. It was a terrific show and only the beginning.'

FOR GRIVAS, his campaign was near its end and his thoughts began to turn towards calling another 'truce', but for the moment he called it 'a temporary order to halt the campaign in order to give the United Nations the opportunity to peacefully resolve the Cyprus issue on account of the machinations of our opponents to intensify our struggle'. His latest leaflet was filled with rambling, incoherent sentences and exaggerated claims. He maintained that 85 soldiers had been killed and 155 others injured in EOKA attacks during a period of 45 days. His losses were negligible, he said. He declared: 'In order to show that we have no desire to raise any obstacles to the UN, we have ordered a halt to all of our activities, although we will of course respond to any aggression of our enemies.'

A military spokesman, without mentioning the EOKA leaflet, announced that during November, 56 terrorist suspects had been captured, two had surrendered voluntarily and nine had been killed. During the latest operations, several Greek Cypriot policemen were among those arrested. The morale of the troops, he said, had never been higher. In London, Dr Fazil Kutchuk, the Turkish Cypriot leader, praised British forces for 'acting in a most humane way in the face of Greek terrorism and barbarism'.

On a surprise visit to the Island at the end of the month, Field Marshal Sir Francis Festing, Chief of the Imperial General Staff, broadcast to the Security Forces. 'The British soldier's great strength has always been his fairness, kindness and good humour under all provocation,' he told them. 'Please do not think I do not realize how sorely your tempers have been tried in recent months ... I realize you have to put up with sub-standard accommodation, lack of amenities, the strain of constant watchfulness, and ceaseless work night and day. I have been greatly impressed to find that under such difficult conditions your spirit is excellent. I did not expect it to be any otherwise.'

During November Lieutenant John Morrison of the Middlesex Regiment was awarded the Military Cross 'for gallantry and determined leadership in command of a patrol ambushed by EOKA terrorists' and Military Medals were given to Corporal Patrick Shaughnessy of the Royal Ulster Rifles for 'courage, initiative and devotion to duty' and to Fusilier Royston Sanders of the Royal Welch Fusiliers and Private P. Dillon 'for courage, coolness, and determination in the face of terrorist attacks in two ambushes' in Cyprus.

At the United Nations, Greece had failed to persuade members to support its Cyprus policy during eight days of intense debate. The UN voted instead to support a resolution that merely agreed the development of self-government and free institutions and called for negotiations between the three Governments concerned – Britain, Greece and Turkey – and representatives of the Cypriots on the future of the Island. It did not denounce the idea of partition that was anathema to Greek Cypriots, who saw it as a Damoclean sword hanging above their heads.

Blame for the Greek failure to win the day was placed four-square on Washington. Said Foreign Minister Averoff: 'The American delegation finally sided openly with the British–Turkish view and against justice and freedom. There is only one comment to this – "The Greek people will not forget".' Anti-American feeling swept through the Greek Cypriot community. 'Betrayal' was the word most heard.

Meanwhile, General Darling kept up the momentum against the terrorists. In another of his operations in north Cyprus, four active EOKA members were killed and 90 suspects arrested. Helicopters were used more and more to drop troops near terrorist strongholds and light aircraft flew ahead of patrols to give them advance warning of potential ambush sites.

On 8 December, Lancashire Fusiliers from 'B' Company were under the command of Captain Wilson, seconded from the SAS, and carrying out a routine roadblock, checking vehicles coming and going and from Nicosia. One of the Fusiliers, who prefers to remain anonymous, told the author: 'Just as we had stopped a bus and were getting all the passen-gers off to search, a small plane came low towards us. The pilot must have been very interested in what was taking place, because he circled and came back for a second look. Unfortunately he came in too low, hit overhead electricity cables and touched the roof of the bus.

'The plane lost speed and I knew it was not going to gain height, so before the plane crashed in a nearby field, I threw my rifle to the ground and started running towards it, even though I had been trained that the rifle was my best friend – and to lose it was a serious offence.

'Before I arrived at the crashed aircraft, two Royal Horse Guards in a scout car – who were on reconnaissance with "B" Company – reached it first.'

The pilot of the Auster aircraft was Captain Terence Mulady of the Queen's Royal West Kent Regiment, attached to 653 Squadron of the Army Air Corps as adjutant. 'He was flying low, without an observer, as an escort to an army convoy,' Gunner Jones of 10 Recce Flight, adds. 'Soldiers rushed from their trucks to get him out from the burning aircraft.'

Corporal Jeffrey Marklew and Trooper David Baxter were the two soldiers first on the scene. Marklew immediately ran into the flames to rescue the pilot, but he could not open the door of the aircraft and was blown away from it by an explosion of burning petrol. Undaunted he again entered the blaze, shouting encouragement to the pilot and tried to pull him thorough the window.

'This he was unable to do, because the pilot's clothing, drenched with burning petrol, came away in his hands,' states the official report of the incident. 'Corporal Marklew then leaned into the cockpit through the window and took hold of the pilot under the arms and, with Trooper Baxter pulling, succeeded in dragging the pilot from the aircraft.'

Captain Mulady, however, slipped from

their grasp and rolled under the burning fuselage. Although by now suffering from burns, 'Marklew plunged under the tail plane and pulled the pilot out of the flames for a second time. He then continued to make every effort to tear off and extinguish the pilot's burning clothes until further assistance arrived.'

The Lancashire Fusilier now tried to help. As the three soldiers dragged Mulady from the flames, his wristwatch and strap came away in the Fusilier's hand. 'Without thinking, I put the watch in my pocket. We were still carrying Captain Mulady when the Auster exploded.

'We went to the British Military Hospital in Nicosia with the pilot to have our minor burns treated. On our way the captain repeatedly requested to see a priest. He was in a terrible condition. After we reached the BMH, I remember very little, except that my burns were dressed as I sat by the pilot's bedside. The doctor was a lieutenant and the pilot again asked him to get a priest. The doctor appeared to ignore the request. Instead, he insisted that I tell him my name and those of the two troopers. He next demanded the pilot's name, rank and serial number to which the pilot replied: "I am the Adjutant of Acquateria." Now the doctor told a nurse to get him a priest.

'The two Horse Guards, who had been outside, drove me back to my battalion. Next morning, while checking the combat trousers that I had worn the night before, I found the pilot's watch in one of its pockets. Immediately I took it to Captain Wilson. He told me the pilot had died at midnight. Nothing was said about the rifle I had left behind.'

'You could not have met a nicer officer than Captain Mulady – he was a true gentleman,' Gunner Jones remembers. 'He bought us a TV set for our NAAFI at Kermia Camp.'

Later, Corporal Jeffrey Marklew was awarded the George Medal. His comrade from the Royal Horse Guards, Trooper David Baxter, received a Queen's Commendation for Brave Conduct.

At a time when the battle against EOKA was at its height, it was ironic that the next British service fatality was caused by a traffic accident, when, on 15 December, a local bus smashed into Royal Lance Corporal Robert Leitch's Land Rover. The Royal Military Policeman was killed instantly.

AS CHRISTMAS neared, nobody knew that the Foreign Ministers of Greece and Turkey had met accidentally in a corridor in the UN building in New York after the General Assembly debate and spontaneously agreed privately to work for a mutually satisfactory solution to the Cyprus Problem. They shook hands as friends and went their separate ways. Their cordial relations continued when they met again in Paris on 17 December at the conference convened by NATO. They found their national interests coincided and the broad terms of a compromise were drawn up, but there were issues outside their control that needed to be settled quickly: the first involved the two terrorists awaiting execution in Nicosia and the second was Grivas's intransigence over the question of *enosis*. The two politicians had agreed *enosis* was no longer an option and nor was partition.

Late that evening, Foreign Ministers Zorlu and Averoff met Selwyn Lloyd, their British opposite number, and asked him to stop the hangings due at 00.15 on the 18th. They said that if the executions went ahead, hopes of a peaceful settlement would be dashed again. Lloyd immediately notified Prime Minister Macmillan and Colonial Secretary Lennox-Boyd of the request. A telephone call to Cyprus was booked, but the lines were busy.

The previous day the cases of the two men – Costas Constantinides and Yiannakis Athanasiou, a member of Nicosia's killer squads – had come before the Executive

Foreign Minister Selwyn Lloyd (centre) with his Turkish and Greek opposite numbers at the Paris NATO meeting on 17 December 1958.

Council and Sir Hugh Foot had signed their death warrants. Their executioners were on their way from the UK to tie the nooses. To minimize trouble, the prison was cordoned off. The Director of Prisons, Denis Malone, was ready to see the job done.

With London four hours behind Nicosia, Lennox-Boyd's telephone call came through to Government House after Sir Hugh had gone to bed. Fortunately, Lady Foot was still awake and heard one of several telephones ringing in the Private Secretary's office. Told that Downing Street was on the line, she rushed to wake her husband. It was 20 minutes to midnight. By the time the Governor and the Colonial Secretary finished speaking, 10 minutes had elapsed.

Sir Hugh dialled the prison number and reached Malone. 'I'm coming to see you – now,' the Governor said. The prisons' director suggested they meet in half an hour.

'Why?'

'Because the hangings will be over by then.'

'You don't understand,' Sir Hugh shouted. 'I'm coming to stop them.'

It was midnight. The mood in the capital was as sinister as anything the Island had known since the start of the Emergency, with EOKA threatening reprisals and a demand for a national strike.

'I went to the Nicosia Prison. Outside I spoke to the Army Commander on the spot. It was a weird scene in the light of the yellow arc lights. And as I approached the prison entrance I heard the terrible din being made by the prisoners. They were shouting and screaming and banging on the doors and floors of their cells,' Sir Hugh wrote in his book, *A Start in Freedom*. 'I went in, saw Malone, the hangmen and the Greek priest, and as I did so the din suddenly stopped. There was absolute silence. By some strange telepathy the prisoners realized that something new had happened. I went back to Government House that night taking the death warrants with me with a sense of overwhelming thankfulness and rejoicing. Divine providence? I don't know. But it was a near thing.'

Had the executions been carried out, they would have been the first since March 1957. Constantinides and Athanasiou's death sentences were commuted to life imprisonment. When their reprieves became known in the morning, unable to explain the reasons why the executions were stopped at the last minute, Sir Hugh Foot was castigated in the

British newspapers, who accused him of either vacillation or blatant publicity seeking by 'playing with people's lives'.

The next day Greek Consul Frydas in Nicosia reproached Grivas for continuing his campaign at this sensitive time. Political developments, he said, outweighed any actions the Colonel might want to take. Foreign Minister Averoff also pointed out that EOKA operations were losing the support of the people and world opinion was growing fed up with the ongoing struggle. It was time to stop to give peace a chance. How to justify another 'truce' was up to him.

An angry Grivas replied to Frydas, telling him to inform their 'friends in Athens' that if they disapproved of his policy, 'then our ways must part: my honour allows no compromise'. He continued: 'I must protest against being confronted with proposals for dealing with the military side. I have already made it clear both to you and the Archbishop that I want no advice on how to go about my work … All I see is unwillingness to back me up. What is the reason behind this? If they hope to make me give in, they hope in vain. I am ready as always to fight to the last bullet.'

On 21 December, Britain, Greece and Turkey agreed to enter negotiations through diplomatic channels to provide Cyprus with 'a form of independence', partition and *enosis* excluded. All Britain wanted was the retention of two military areas, once Cypriots ran their own affairs. Episkopi and Dhekelia were obviously earmarked.

Two days later, Sir Hugh Foot, as a Christmas gesture, lifted the curfew on youths in Nicosia. He then released 350 Greek Cypriots from detention and commuted six death sentences to life imprisonment. Three men, Nicolas Ioannou, Costas Papaiacovou and Yiannis Katsouri, had been sentenced for discharging firearms at Turks during the intercommunal trouble of the summer. The others, Pavlos Panayiotou, Andreas Angelides and Demetris Koutalianos, had been found guilty of unlawfully having firearms under their control.

Under pressure from Athens, Grivas had been forced into a corner with little room to manoeuvre He had to find some wriggle room. 'After careful thought I had decided that we should offer some response to the UN appeal for the creation of a peaceful atmosphere in which talks might proceed. At last, on Christmas Eve, I put out this proclamation:

LET THEM CHOOSE
The member states of the United Nations will judge between our attitude and that of the Tory Government in Britain. We have always respected UN decisions and will continue to do so. Accordingly, we shall now halt our activity for as long as the other side does so as well. Let us see how the British propose to act.

We offer an opportunity for a solution in an atmosphere of peace. What will the enemy do?'

As Grivas's latest leaflets were picked up and read in the Island's towns, Winifred Scaife was wrapping presents in the front room of her home in Wesham that Christmas Eve morning, Back in the summer she knew she would have to celebrate the Yuletide season without Alan, her 28-year-old medical orderly husband, a Senior Aircraftsman in the Royal Air Force. She was wondering whether she should send him a crew-neck pullover of heavy ribbed fisher knit, which she had bought for 26 shillings and nine pence. Although not a prince's ransom, she could not afford for it to be lost in the mail somewhere en route to his RAF station at Ayios Nikolaos, near Famagusta in Cyprus. She decided eventually to keep it until he returned home on leave the following April.

There was a knock at the door. It was the local postman with another pile of Christmas cards. She flicked through them quickly to see if there was one from her husband. And there it was. But Alan was dead, killed four days

Aircraftsman Alan Scaife, one of the last British servicemen to die in the EOKA conflict.

earlier on 20 December 1958, in the cab of his water tanker, with another RAF servicemen, LAC Thomas Boaden, 19. Their vehicle had run over a pressure mine on the road near Galoundpetra. The servicemen were on their way to deliver Christmas presents, rations and fresh water to an RAF outpost in Cape Andreas at the tip of the Karpas Panhandle. Both men were starting their fifth month of duty on the Island. A third member of the party, SAC Carney from Cumberland, had his life saved by the surgeons at the British Military Hospital, Dhekelia.

Mrs Scaife said later: 'My Christmas card was sent by Alan from Nicosia on Tuesday, the same day as he was posted to his new camp. He always told me the EOKA terrorists were cowards. He said they won't stop and fight. They just leave bombs and mines in the road or wedge guns between rocks to fire when a vehicle passes.' Her husband was a regular airman and apart from breaking his service for a year to work for English Electric, he had been in the RAF since he was a boy. He was a native of Durham.

The two servicemen were buried in Wayne's Keep Military Cemetery. The Reverend Douglas Northridge from RAF Ayios Nikolaos conducted their funeral.

For the first time since the start of the Emergency the airmen's murders were condemned by the Bishop of Kitium in a public statement. In his *Memoirs*, Grivas did his best to remove himself from any blame for their deaths. 'Even if I had wished to do so I could not have prevented this attack: it took place almost 100 miles away and no messenger could have got there in time to cancel the plan. To Mr Frydas's violent objections about this and another reprisal, which took place at Agroso, I replied expressing surprise at the tone and contents of his protest:

> The two groups which struck at the British acted within the spirit of my orders. The Gallinopetra action was taken after the army had cut off villages there for a fortnight and ill-treated the inhabitants: it was perfectly justified. In the other instance at Agros the villagers were also villainously ill-used by soldiers so the group there were also entitled to retaliate: you must also remember that Rotsides (one of my veteran guerrillas) was killed by the army in this area recently The instructions suspending activity, which I issued after receiving Mr Averoff's request, had not yet reached these two groups, so in any case their actions were in order.

'I went on to express my indignation that the Consul should ask us to answer for the deaths of two airmen, whereas it was the British who should have been arraigned for murdering Cypriots.'

In his book *A Start in Freedom*, Sir Hugh Foot wrote: 'They were the last RAF casualties of the Cyprus Emergency. But we did not know that at the time. On Christmas Eve 1958 there was talk of EOKA calling for a truce, but we were by this time too cynical and too hardened to believe it.'

Throughout Christmas Day, Cyprus celebrated. At church services in towns and villages, an encyclical from Archbishop Makarios was read out. In this he referred to achieving national claims, but did not mention *enosis*, self-determination or independence. At the Phaneromeni Church in Nicosia, the service was marred only by the EOKA leaflets, signed Dighenis, that fluttered down from the gallery and told the congregation: 'We are ready for a long armed struggle if Britain continues her intransigence ... We hope the British Government will not look on this gesture [the truce] as one of weakness because she will come out of this illusion with a surprise.' In his broadcast, Sir Hugh Foot pointed out that this was the first peaceful Christmas in five years and said: 'We welcome the peaceful situation, but feel that what we must guard against is over-optimism.'

While Cypriots remained in a holiday mood with Greek Cypriot crowds milling around Ledra Street and Metaxas Square, British military operations continued. In the Turkish quarter of Nicosia, thousands thronged Ataturk Square. A fatted calf was killed and a band played as Dr Kutchuk and Mr Denktas, their leaders, walked through the crowds, shaking hands.

For the family of Trooper Peter Livingstone of the Royal Horse Guards there were only tears. He lost his life on the last day of 1958.

1959 STARTED optimistically. Curfews were lifted and more detainees were released as talks between Greece and Turkey began to cover the details of a Cyprus settlement. In the snow, mud and mire of the Troodos Mountains, large numbers of British troops trudged their way through villages and farms in sub-Arctic conditions. The operations applied General Darling's guiding principle that 'troops must be put out on their feet, prodding, exploring, and above all observing'. A military spokesman compared the new

tactics with 'big game hunting'. He explained that 'a particular part of jungle is stealthily explored, then after perhaps days with nothing to show for it, there is the scent of something; and, suddenly, who knows, the tiger himself may bob up from nowhere'.

Whether by design or accident, these operations coincided with the worst snows of winter in the mountains: a time when the terrorists' movements were physically circumscribed, and when Grivas and his henchmen probably least expected British soldiers to turn up. Replying to Greek Cypriot criticism that the military was not observing the 'truce', Sir Hugh Foot declared bluntly: 'There will be no bargain with violence ... We shall never issue a licence for terrorism to intimidate and ruin innocent people, to import and transport arms, make bombs, plot and prepare murder.' He wanted not a temporary truce, he said, but permanent peace, which would permit the complete abolition of the Emergency, the closing of detention camps, and the return of Archbishop Makarios. 'Violence must be abandoned for good,' he concluded. His stern statement was very different in tone to those the Governor made on his arrival in Cyprus in December 1957. His experience of conflict had hardened him. Now there was little difference between him and his predecessor, Field Marshal Sir John Harding.

On every front Grivas was being isolated. In Paris, Foreign Ministers Averoff and Zorlu were making surprisingly fast progress on their plan for peace. Macmillan's 'Adventure in Partnership' had been overtaken as the Turkish and Greek representatives called for a meeting in Zurich in February for their Prime Ministers to sign their agreement. Cypriots would not be invited to attend to argue, interrupt and generally spoil the genial atmosphere by nit picking. Once their document was complete, they would present it to the British Government for final approval – approval they were sure to get. On 10 February, in just

Foreign Minister Zorlu of Turkey and Foreign Minister Averoff of Greece start the process to end the EOKA conflict.

six days, the future of an independent Cyprus was settled.

When Makarios was told in Athens, he replied: 'The agreement reached lays the foundation for an immediate and final solution to the Cyprus issue considering that Cyprus will become an independent sovereign State. The rapprochement of the Governments of Greece and Turkey over the Cyprus issue in a spirit of good will and understanding will pave the way to a new period of freedom and welfare both for the Greeks and Turks of Cyprus.'

After four years of tribulation, Cypriots breathed a sigh of relief, but there were no public celebrations. Too often in the past hopes had soared only to be dashed within

hours. On all sides, people wondered: would Britain endorse the Zurich proposals?

The Governor authorized the re-hiring of Greek Cypriots at British establishments. Military operations were ended with the capture of the last known terrorists – or as they would be soon be called 'freedom fighters' – 'without the discharge of a single shot'.

At last the rebellion was over.

Soon once again we'll pack our kits, and go
From yet another land we've just begun to know.
I wonder what we'll think about next year
Sitting and talking o'er our sauerkraut and beer.

I think we all remember only the best things.
And glancing at that medal on our chest,
We'll boast of Murder Mile, and Omorphita,
And how our camp at Kermia got daily neater.

And K T guards, and Luna Park, and thirst.
Bitter cold or flaming heat, which is the worst?
We had them both in Cyprus, it was hell!
'Twas Active Service there, of course, as well.

So we'll boast on, and talk of Forest Ops,
And Tanzimat Street, and clashes with the cops.
And the recruits will think 'what fun they've had!'
For we'll have forgotten all that was really bad.

That summer heat, and sweat. That thirst.
Those sleepless nights, and how we tossed and cursed.
Those constant guards. The boredom and the strain
Of doing something time and time again.

All these forgotten. Remembered only the fun,
The swimming, the Greek girls, the beer, and the sun.
For that is the way of the British Army.
No wonder the rest of the world think us barmy!

MAJOR L. T. CAPEL, OC 'B' Coy 1 Glosters

CHAPTER TWENTY-FIVE

Cyprus gains independence: sunset on the Empire outpost

'History is almost too profuse in this island.'
BYRON

A FANFARE of military trumpets and a 21-gun salute fired by 42 Field Regiment, Royal Artillery, heralded the start of a new day in Cyprus, one of the hottest of the year. As the sound of the last shot echoed across Nicosia, the independent Republic of Cyprus was born

The flag of the independent Cyprus Republic is raised to a fanfare of trumpets.

and the British flag was slowly lowered outside Government House. The date was 16 August 1960.

'Since shortly before sunset,' reported the *Times of Cyprus*, 'an army of Greek Cypriot youths, armed with ladders, scaled lamp-posts and buildings, hanging streamers of Greek flags across the capital's streets. Rows of coloured lights spanned Metaxas Square and other avenues. A visitor described Nicosia as "a fairyland".' Meanwhile, in the Turkish section of the capital, thousands of Turkish Cypriots came to town by bus, car and bicycle to be present when power changed hands.

At Government House, Sir Hugh Foot held a small dinner party. Reginald Choules, a driver at MEAF HQ, brought one of the guests to the house. 'I ate the same dinner as the officials,' he said. That night in 1960, 20,000 Cypriots, wild with excitement, jammed the streets outside the capital's Council building and tried to break through a police cordon to get closer to see Sir Hugh Foot, the Governor, Archbishop Makarios, the country's new president, and Dr Fazil Kutchuk, the Turkish Cypriot vice-president. The two community leaders entered the building seconds before midnight as British subjects and left as citizens of a new state. While dignitaries accompanied them, the Cyprus Police Band played outside. One of the first tunes to reach the ears of officials was *With a Little Bit of Luck* from 'My Fair Lady'.

Two British Members of Parliament watched the formalities. One of them, Francis Noel Baker, was the Archbishop's guest, while Dr Kutchuk had invited the other, Patrick Wall, a former Royal Marines officer. Said Noel Baker: 'So it was that I found myself sitting in the gallery on this stiflingly hot night ... as ADCs staggered in with pile after pile of documents and maps, each to be signed in turn by His Excellency the Governor, His Beatitude the Archbishop, His Excellency Dr Kutchuk and the Greek and Turkish Consuls-General. It went on for hours, and I wondered if it would ever end.'

In fact, pens scratched away on 87 separate documents for over an hour beneath an outsize painting of Aphrodite rising from the foam. These treaties gave Cyprus independence, but not *enosis*. The British received two Sovereign Bases in perpetuity and both Greece and Turkey were allowed to station military contingents on the island and had the right to intervene in the event that there were any risks to the Republic being undermined. Later, President Makarios warned the British that the usefulness of the military bases would depend on 'the friendliness and cooperation of the Cypriot people'. He said he would object to a nuclear stockpile on Cyprus, and added: 'Nor would we agree to the use of the bases as a springboard for attack on any country.' The British were to take little notice of his objections and nuclear weapons were placed at RAF Akrotiri.

Not far from Noel Baker sat an old man in traditional Greek Cypriot costume, a wide smile on his weather-beaten face. He was Archbishop Makarios's father, Christodoulos Mouskos. 'Christodoulos and his wife, Eleni, lived in a one-storey house near the centre of Panayia village,' wrote Stanley Mayes in his biography, *Makarios*. 'The single large room was partly divided by a stone-wall, which left the smaller rear part for the yoke of oxen, or sick animals that needed attention. As a young boy, their son, the new president, herded sheep in the forest above the village before spending his adolescence as a novice at Kykko Monastery in the nearby mountains.'

Eventually Sir Hugh Foot, dressed in white tie and tails, announced the end of British rule – the shortest domination of Cyprus by any foreign power in its history. 'For the first time in its long and varied history, Cyprus undertook a government of the people, by the people and for the people,' reported Robert

The independence documents are signed by the new President, Archbishop Makarios, Sir Hugh Foot, and Vice-President Kutchuk.

Egby, the Forces Broadcasting Service news-reader, who had heard the first EOKA bombs explode in Nicosia on 1 April 1955. 'No longer will the Island be subjected to remote rule from a distant capital, as has been the case for countless centuries. Now Cyprus is free and its own master.'

The new flag of the Cyprus Republic now fluttered only a few hundred yards from the spot where, on 12 July 1878, at exactly 17.00, Cypriots had gathered near the Paphos Gate to witness 53 men of the Royal Marine Artillery presenting arms as a Captain Rawson lowered the Turkish Ottoman flag and raised in its place the Union flag, watched by Vice Admiral Lord John Hay on behalf of Queen Victoria.

DURING BRITISH rule there had been riots, mutinies, rebellions, near civil war between the two communities and eventually the EOKA conflict. It had lasted from 1 April 1955 and now it was finally ended. More than 400 British troops, policemen and civilians had lost their lives, while deaths amongst Turks and Greeks were more than three times that number. NATO's Eastern Wing had come near to collapsing as Greece and Turkey threatened each other. Realizing they could have gone to war over the Island – and under discreet but persistent prodding from the US – both Greece and Turkey had agreed to pull in their horns. Prime Minister Adan Menderes abandoned his unrealistic demand that Britain partition Cyprus between its 400,000 Greek and 100,000 Turkish inhabitants, while Prime Minister Constantine Karamanlis sacrificed his dream of *enosis* – union of Cyprus with Greece.

Under continued pressure from the United States and the United Kingdom, mainland Greece and Turkey had agreed on 11 February at a meeting in Zurich that Cyprus should become a co-partnership Republic, with a Greek Cypriot President and a Turkish Cypriot Vice-President. For its part, the United Kingdom promised to grant independence to all but 99 square miles of the Island, which would remain Sovereign property, until London decided otherwise. Here the UK would establish two military bases from which the Middle East and parts of the Communist bloc countries could be monitored. The bases would be home for a large rapid reaction force ready to deal with any contingency.

Time magazine observed: 'Of all those place names around the world which came to mean not a landscape but a problem, few seemed more bound up in hatreds and hopeless intricacies than Cyprus.' But now, for a brief moment, there was a chance for Cypriots to grasp the nettle and work together for a united, independent state, with guarantees for their protection.

On 15 February, Makarios, pushed by the Greek Prime Minister Constantine Karamanlis, had arrived in London for the conference, which opened on the 17th, chaired by the British Foreign Secretary, to moderate the haggling that would determine the Island's immediate future. At a press conference at the airport, Makarios, in the glare of arc lights, told waiting reporters and officials: 'I go to the conference with an open mind and with the utmost good will and friendliness toward all, and particularly toward those with whom good relations have been temporarily disturbed. I look forward to a sincere cooperation in the interests of the entire population of Cyprus, so that with the help of God happier days will come to the Island.' With the Archbishop were no less than 35 'advisers', most of whom he had not seen since his exile three years earlier.

Five hours later, Dr Kutchuk, the leader of the Turkish Cypriot delegation, landed at Heathrow. Like his Greek Cypriot opposite number, he said, he, too, had come with an 'open mind'. He stressed: 'It is a good, constructive plan and we are optimistic.' Asked by a reporter if the Turks would object to Makarios becoming president of an independent new republic, he replied: 'If the Greeks want him, they can have him. We shall have our Vice-President.'

As soon as the conference opened, however, the artful Archbishop began to complain. He protested that the Greek Cypriot President of the new Republic of Cyprus would have the trappings of power but not the authority, since the Turkish Cypriot Vice-President would have effective veto powers. Greek diplomat Angelos Vlachos noted: 'A five-day delirium began, a kind of nightmarish dance around the maypole that was Makarios, with all of us walking around him, each with a ribbon in hand trying to wrap him, and him in the centre, unwrapping.'

Mr Karamanlis, the Greek Prime Minister, displeased by the Archbishop's behaviour, took him aside and told him bluntly: 'I give you Cyprus on a plate, and you refuse to take it. It's monstrous.' He added that Makarios would have to accept the agreement or bear the blame for wrecking the conference. 'If Makarios wants to carry on the struggle he will have to look elsewhere for support,' Karamanlis said. He added that he would sign the agreements to protect the name of Greece and Makarios could continue the struggle alone, if he wished.

Prime Minister Karamanlis, suffering a bad cold and running a high temperature, was in no mood to allow the primate to continue like some trader in a Middle East bazaar. But there were more difficulties to come: that same day, the Viscount aircraft flying Turkish Prime Minister Menderes was diverted from London Heathrow because of fog and advised to land at Gatwick instead. Three miles from touch-down, it crashed in Jordan's Wood, on the Rusper-Newdigate road, at 17.00. Twelve of the occupants died. There were 10 survivors, including Mr Menderes, who suffered minor injuries, but was well enough to be able to be driven to the London Clinic for treatment.

The next day, the Conference at Lancaster House met briefly in the afternoon and then adjourned until the evening for delegates, apart from the Greek and Turkish Prime Ministers, to smooth any differences so that the final deal could be initialled in the morning. The Cypriots, led by Makarios and Kutchuk, went off together to talk away from the main gathering. Hopes for a successful conclusion were fading fast. The Archbishop was raising objection after objection. Asked by Selwyn Lloyd if he would sign the agreements as they stood, Makarios replied: 'If that is now, it is no.'

For the British Government, Lloyd extended the conference for an extra day. During the evening Makarios took a phone call from Queen Frederika in Athens who is said to have urged him to accept the agreements for the sake of Greece. More importantly, perhaps, others say, MI6 officers visited him at his suite in the Dorchester hotel and warned that if he refused to sign the deal, their dossier on his 'rather unusual homosexual proclivities' and 'penchant for young boys' would be given to the international press corps and their reports would not go down well in Cyprus.

'His fear of the damaging impact to his reputation in the eyes of his Cypriot followers by the disclosure of the material relating to his private life was too much for him,' intelligence expert Nigel West said. 'He was fully aware that any revelation about his homosexuality would have finished him.' He added that the compromising material had been collected by the intelligence service from an agent in the Archbishop's entourage and other means. The agent had been recruited by Sir Stephen Hastings, a founding member of the SAS, who had transferred to the intelligence at the end of the Second World War. By the time he reached Cyprus in 1958, he was highly experienced in the 'black arts'.

According to Doros Alastos, the Greek Cypriot historian, 'alone in a luxurious room of a Park Lane hotel, the Archbishop knelt in prayer. On one of the walls hung an icon of the Virgin to which occasionally, he lifted his eyes in an appeal for help. For Makarios this was the moment of choice. He told me later that it was the hardest one of his life. What was it to be? Peace or more violence in Cyprus? The dilemma had become intensely personal. Only he and the God he believed in could now decide.'

Next day – 19 February 1959 – at 08.00, Makarios summoned his advisers and announced he had decided to accept the agreement. At about half past nine he telephoned the Foreign Office to notify them of his decision. This time he did not consult Grivas. Asked why he had kept delegates in suspense, he replied enigmatically: 'I had my reasons.'

At 15.00 Prime Ministers Macmillan and Karamanlis put their signatures to the agreements and drove to the London Clinic to have Menderes add his. At 19.00 Macmillan went before the House of Commons, interrupted a foreign affairs debate and declared that a 'victory for reason and cooperation ... a victory for all' had been achieved. He said: 'Archbishop Makarios, as the representative of the Greek Cypriot community, and Dr Kutchuk, as the representative of the Turkish Cypriot community, have also accepted the declaration and the Zurich documents on the same basis. Our requirements have thus been fully met ... I believe that we have closed a chapter of bitterness and strife in the history of Cyprus and that we are now embarking, with our Greek and Turkish allies and the people of Cyprus themselves, on a new approach where partnership and cooperation take the place of strife and dissension ... Valuable lives have been lost by the services and by civilians. These can never be replaced, but I hope that all who mourn their loss will realize that they have not died in vain. For their sacrifice has prevented the widening of conflict and strife with all its attendant dangers.'

The British press gave the agreement a mixed reaction. 'Scuttle,' roared Lord Beaverbrook's *Daily Express*. 'The Ministers are ready to cast away another jewel of the empire.' 'Too good to be true,' suggested the London *Daily Mail*. 'Accept,' demanded the *News Chronicle*. 'Thank God,' exclaimed the *Daily Sketch*. 'Act of courage,' said *The Times*, while the tabloid *Daily Mirror* urged Macmillan to 'GRAB THIS CHANCE!' Which he did in a run-up to a General Election later in the year, hoping to prevent the deaths of more British soldiers, renew the UK's traditional friendship with Greece and re-establish NATO unity.

In Washington, President Eisenhower endorsed the agreement as 'a victory for common sense', an 'imaginative act of statesmanship' and 'a splendid achievement'.

At a celebration dinner at Claridge's hotel, Makarios turned to Greek Prime Minister Karamanlis and said: 'Prime Minister, did you imagine at any point that I would actually not sign?'

'Then why did you do all that to us?' Karamanlis replied.

'I had my reasons.' Makarios smiled like a cat that had finished a bowl of cream.

Historian Makarios Droushiotis believed that the Archbishop acted as he did 'not because he expected he could in any way alter the agreements, but for the sake of appearances. He had wanted to be seen not as the one who accepted the compromise solution, which fell far short of the aim of *Enosis* ... but as the one who was pressurized by everyone around him into signing it.' Karamanlis never forgave Makarios. 'We assented together in Zurich, but he exited London's Lancaster House an Ethnarch, and I was left looking like a sell-out,' he would say later.

In broad terms, the London Conference had agreed the following: a basic structure for the new Cyprus Republic, a treaty guaranteeing the independence, territorial integrity and constitution between the Republic of Cyprus, Greece, the United Kingdom and Turkey, and a treaty of alliance between Cyprus, Greece and Turkey. These treaties ruled out *enosis* and *taksim* – partition of the Island – allowed Turkey and Greece to base limited numbers of troops in Cyprus to protect the interests of the two communities, gave Britain, Turkey and Greece the right to intervene in the event they saw a breakdown in the republic's basic structure and the UK sovereignty over its base areas and facilities elsewhere for military use.

While many terms had to be defined and fleshed out by negotiations in the months ahead, for the moment they formed the best and only deal good enough to satisfy the three major powers. Cypriots, including Makarios, were left with no other option but to accept them in full.

The Bishop of Kyrenia back in his diocese rejected the treaties, refused to support Makarios and ignored the dangers of Greece and Turkey going to war over Cyprus. Instead he vigorously preached the *enosis* cause to his several thousand enthusiastic followers. H. D. Purcell wrote: 'A Greek shepherd whom the author met while climbing in the nearby mountains informed him that eight million Greeks would have no difficulty in defeating 30 million Turks.'

SERVING IN the RAF Military Police in Cyprus, Lance Corporal Martin Bailey told his men that a ceasefire was about to be announced. 'We'll believe it when we see it,' they chorused back. Pleased that they would no more risk bullets in their backs, they knew they could have trouble arresting miscreant soldiers. Bailey explained: 'It was instilled into us that if one charged somebody, whatever the charge – you always prefaced your words with: "Whilst on active service", which doubled the offence!'

Holed up in his 'safe house' in Limassol, Grivas was furious. He felt betrayed. Unaware that by early February 1959, British intelligence had discovered his hideout and was running a round-the-clock surveillance operation, his fate was no longer in his hands. Makarios had not invited any of the Colonel's supporters to the London Conference. Only Tassos Papadopoulos, the young Nicosia leader of PEKA, was present, but on his own initiative.

In 1958 MI6, the UK's overseas intelligence agency, had set up Operation *Sunshine*, bypassing the local Special Branch because many of its officers could not be trusted completely. Colonel Philip Kirby-Green was put in charge. Two agents, Peter Wright of MI5 and Bill Magan of E Branch (Colonial Affairs), were brought to the Island and told to use all their technical expertise to destroy EOKA and assassinate Grivas 'as a last resort'.

In January 1959 Wright and Magan found the radio transmitters by which Grivas communicated with his gangs. They were disguised as lightning rods on church roofs in Limassol. Earlier, the duo had 'persuaded' a Greek smuggler to sell Grivas a consignment of radio receivers with secret homing beacons that gave them the means to monitor EOKA communications. They also 'bugged' the telephone lines at Makarios's palace in Nicosia and collected the information that he was shown during the London peace talks.

The *Sunshine* team on 16 February told General Kenneth Darling, Director of Operations that they had homed in on Grivas's lair and asked permission to take him out. Darling decided to fly to London immediately to personally pass the news to Prime Minister Macmillan and seek advice on what action to take. Feigning a hypothetical situation, Macmillan asked the Greek delegation to the Lancaster House Conference what would be the reaction if Grivas were found and killed. The answer was simple: the talks would collapse and violence would resume.

Greek sources said that Foreign Minister Averoff immediately cabled the Greek Consulate in Nicosia to advise staff that the

British were hinting that Grivas's arrest was imminent. Whether the consulate notified Grivas is not known, but it appears MI5 had monitored Averoff's message. Its gist was that no drastic actions should be taken, leaving diplomacy to run its course. For several months, the security services had tapped the Greek Embassy's communications and now the latest telegram was passed to Macmillan for consideration.

Although Sir John Prendergast, the Island's Special Branch chief, was eager to send in a 'snatch squad' or simply kill 'The Leader' on the spot, the British Government refused him permission. It feared Grivas would become a martyr to the EOKA cause and so Special Branch was ordered to 'let Grivas stew in his own juice'. Much later, Grivas, in his *Memoirs*, said he believed Averoff had been led astray by a British ploy to get him out of his current hiding place so that Special Branch could then eliminate him, with or without permission from London.

Nevertheless Grivas was clearly shaken by the events taking place over which he had no control. He began firing a barrage of new orders to his still-active EOKA gang leaders. 'I advise you to remain in your positions and maintain an invincible front for the Organization. No one should have faith in what is written in the press or announced on the radio regarding decisions of the Organization. Only EOKA makes known the attitude its members should take, and they should pay attention only to these decisions and not to the words of third parties.'

He continued: 'As regards the public, EOKA has always expressed its views through pamphlets, and consequently since none have circulated on the Organization's attitude to the agreement, any views attributed to EOKA are unfounded and not the Organization's. Total obedience by members of the Organization is essential if we are to show everyone that we are not only united in battle but also

in our decisions on the political front and that the Organization is as one man. Tomorrow this will be history and part of all the other things the Organization has to its credit. I repeat: Do not give credence to what is broadcast and written, and carry out orders only from the Organization.' The written orders were signed 'Zappas', another code-name Grivas favoured.

In another order Grivas said: 'Whatever the terms of the amnesty to be made public by the Governor, everyone must remain in position until orders are given by the Organization. Security measures must not be relaxed for any reason. I particularly draw the attention of the guerrillas and fugitives to this.'

More hysterical orders followed: 'I have informed you in the past and I hereby inform you again that everyone must remain in position even after the terms of the amnesty are made known. You will receive orders from the Leader only. Newspaper reports claiming that the Leader has visited the Bishop of Kitium and held discussions with him on the question of an amnesty are unfounded as are so many other stories which are purposely circulated.'

Meanwhile, according to the historian H. D. Purcell, Makarios had written Grivas a conciliatory letter after the Conference, informing him, apparently in misleading terms, of what had been agreed, and mentioning nothing about the bases granted to the British. The Bishop of Kitium, in putting the case to Grivas, gave it as his 'personal opinion' that Britain would soon vacate the bases 'and even suggested that under international law Cyprus might be able to denounce the very treaty which made her independent and thus get the British out!' Averoff, the Greek Foreign Minister, also failed to send data on the base areas when he wrote Grivas his letter of explanation. 'Most Cypriots were by now heartily sick of the struggle, but a large minority joined the short-lived EDMA (United Democratic

Renascence Front), still willing to fight for *Enosis*,' wrote Purcell.

With the London Agreements in the bag, Sir Hugh Foot, the Governor, approved an amnesty for all wanted terrorists in Cyprus and those held in detention. *Time* magazine reported 'no one was quite sure how to react. In one town Greek Church bells pealed for 20 minutes after the agreement was announced, then stopped. When Governor Foot opened the gates for all 900 Greek Cypriot political prisoners held without trial in detention camps to leave, thousands thronged Nicosia's streets to welcome them. Officially EOKA and the TMT were no longer – or so it was said. On an Island ringed with barbed wire and stalked by terror for four years, it was not easy to forget overnight.' In Kyrenia, Purcell saw a teenage soldier lean out of a British Army lorry and pull down a string of small Greek flags. 'In a flash, a gesticulating crowd surrounded the lorry and its sheepish looking occupants, spitting, barring their way, tripping them up, and following them down the street with jeers and insults.'

The released prisoners suddenly donned freshly made uniforms and strutted the streets to the adoration of young Greek Cypriots. Few had shown much heroism in their attacks on the British. 'The whole effect was rather ludicrous, with a great many youths, who had been hiding in holes in the ground for the past three years, swaggering around in uniforms which they would never have dared to wear in the Emergency, and which were all too obviously brand new,' noted the Royal Horse Guards' diarist. The EOKA combatants, convinced that they had outfought the British Army, now mingled with British troops and offered them hospitality in the many coffee shops near Ledra Street. But not before a series of parades and celebration church services had been held.

'In Larnaca crowds went to the St George tou Kontou Monastery to await the arrival of the coaches bringing the prisoners. When they were sighted the whole crowd began shouting and cheering while Greek flags were raised high in the air,' remembered Elenitsa Seraphim-Loizou, the only female EOKA Area Commander. 'Mothers hugged their children with tears in their eyes, they stroked their hair, looking at them again and again almost voraciously. Young women threw themselves

EOKA guerrillas, suddenly in uniform, come out of hiding.

Uniformed EOKA guerrillas in Nicosia applauded by admiring Greek Cypriot schoolgirls.

passionately into their husbands' arms whilst more restrained fathers and brothers tried to restrict their joy to an enigmatic smile. When the first welcomes and the emotion were over an endless procession formed with Greek flags at the head, which then advanced to St Lazarus Church where a thanksgiving service was held and speeches were made. Many prisoners did not feel the need to celebrate and they preferred to return to their villages calmly and quietly.'

While there was an immediate amnesty for the EOKA prisoners held in Cyprus, it did not apply to those confined in UK prisons. They would be released, brought to the Island and immediately deported to Greece where they would have to stay until Cyprus became a fully independent republic, which was still many months away on a date yet to be agreed.

'I was on duty the night all the terrorists that were being kept in the UK were flown in to Akrotiri in a Comet. There were 16 of them, each handcuffed to a British Prison Officer,' said Allan Gilfillan, a 19-year-old

EOKA members invite British troops to join them in a street party.

RAF Police Corporal at the time. 'For about five nights in a row, all of us had to report to the guardroom at midnight and were never told why and then stood down at about two in the morning. All rest days had been cancelled and we were pissed off. Only on the night that the plane was on its way were we told what was happening. Security was beefed up round the camp and a squadron of Ferret armoured cars came through the main gate and parked along the airfield's perimeter fence.

'The Comet landed and eventually stopped on 6 Squadron Dispersal area. The whole place was bathed in mercury vapour light. They had put up extra lighting and everyone was coloured a yellowy orange. Sir Hugh Foot had arrived earlier by car, escorted by armed bodyguards. He boarded the aircraft and served deportation orders to each of the EOKA men. They then stepped down from the Comet in single file and were marched to a parked Dakota of the Royal Hellenic Air Force, where their handcuffs were removed.

Nicos Sampson on, the Ledra Street killer, returns to Nicosia to a hero's welcome on Independence Day.

All 16 terrorists, including Nicos Sampson, kissed the ground before they were boarded. No military personnel took part in the proceedings apart from securing the immediate area to prevent anyone running off.

'I had a front seat view of the whole proceedings. I was in a Land Rover on the port side of the aircraft. Corporal Cockburn drove it. In the passenger seat was Cpl Newsome and I sat in the back, armed with a .38 pistol and Mk 8 Sten – the one with a wooden butt, pistol grip and a bayonet boss.

'We followed the Dakota in two Land Rovers – one on each side of the aircraft – as it taxied to the runway, with searchlights playing on its doors. We had orders to shoot if anyone tried to get off. We chased the plane until it was airborne. A pair of Hawker Hunters, flying overhead, accompanied the Dakota out of the Cyprus air space, as it headed for Rhodes.'

MAKARIOS RETURNED to Cyprus from exile on 1 March 1959 and entered Nicosia triumphantly. Starting before dawn, groups of Greek Cypriots set out for Nicosia from their home villages across the Island to welcome their spiritual leader home. By the time they reached the capital they had become a crowd of thousands. Although the Archbishop had not achieved *enosis* – union with Greece – they still came with Greek standards raised. There was only one minor hitch: when his two cars and luggage arrived at Limassol there was a contretemps because Customs officials demanded £800 duty for a brand new Cadillac which Greek Cypriots in America had given him as a gift. At first, the Archbishopric authorities protested, but finally agreed to pay.

Seated in his open Cadillac, Makarios, escorted by former EOKA detainees, began the six-mile journey from the airport. It took over an hour as frenzied crowds clambered on his vehicle, chanting 'Makarios', 'Dighenis' and 'EOKA'. His first stop was at the Cathedral Church of St John the Evangelist for a service of celebration. In an impassioned address, relayed by loudspeakers, he declared: 'Centuries-long darkness already yields to the sweet light of day. And from the depths of distant history rises the immortal spirit of our ancestors, to spread everywhere the great message, "We are victorious". Cyprus is today free. Brothers, rejoice!'

He praised Grivas as 'a man whose name is written on the most glorious pages of the history of Cyprus ... To this great man, and to the gallant fighters of EOKA, we pay at this solemn hour our tribute of supreme gratitude and honour. Let us reflect that without their struggles this day of victory would not have been achieved.'

But on the outskirts of the capital, EOKA remained active. On the night of Makarios's arrival, a young National Serviceman, John Wilson, was escorting Colonel Pragnell, his CO, and Lieutenant-Colonel Gommershall to Famagusta from Nicosia, where they had attended a meeting at the Ledra Palace Hotel. Wilson was driving a Champ, with three others on board, ahead of the officers' staff car.

Before his death, he told the author: 'We had just passed the old Tymbou airfield, when a village bus blocked our path. As we came closer, there was a burst of small arms fire from the bus. I pulled across the road in front of the staff car and the four of us let fly with our Sterlings and advanced towards the bus. Four Greek Cypriots tumbled out of their vehicle, threw their weapons to the ground and raised their arms in surrender. We found an injured man inside the bullet-riddled bus. We radioed for assistance and a bunch of Cypriot policemen arrived from the nearby nick and took the shooters away. The injured man, we were told, was one of Grivas's relatives.'

Eventually Grivas decided to reject Sir Hugh Foot's amnesty offer. He informed his subordinates: 'As they stand, the terms are unacceptable to us. If they are not amended I shall take further decisions. No areas should worry because in time I shall speak on all matters such as the agreement, the amnesty, etc. I wish to recommend to all to show cohesion and solidarity. On the question of the amnesty the call should be: "All or no-one."'

Finally, Grivas demanded his area commanders inform him of the real names, professions, ages and correct addresses of their terrorist teams. He added: 'Please fill in and return the following forms – 1. Wanted men. 2. Those with a price on their heads. For each please give place of birth, profession and age. Please take care to fill in the forms correctly according to the above. They should be sent as soon as possible.'

On 5 March, Greek Foreign Minister Averoff invited the American Ambassador in Athens to a briefing on the London Conference Agreements and the Island's immediate future.

A US State Department memorandum of their conversation stated: 'It [success] would depend upon Grivas. He knew Grivas and had recently received communications from him. Grivas was not at all pleased with the settlement. However, in Grivas' last letter he had said that while he was dissatisfied he was, above all, a soldier, and he would remain silent. Mr. Averoff said: "That is the best we can expect at the moment, and perhaps it will be possible to bring Grivas around. We plan to give him very high honors, and the British have proved understanding." Grivas refuses to come out of his hiding place until after all the men who fought with him have been released. The British were very understanding in the matter, and he hoped that all this would be accomplished very soon and that Grivas would be coming to Greece.'

Averoff also told the Ambassador that he had suggested to Prime Minister Harold Macmillan 'that the wisest thing the British could do when Grivas left Cyprus was to send him out with a Guard of Honor at the airport.' He said Macmillan was at first taken aback, but when he – Averoff – explained that this single gesture would do a great deal to 'warm the hearts of the Greek Cypriots and the people of Greece, and restore goodwill toward the British', he saw the point, but said it was impossible to take such a dramatic step because of British public opinion. Averoff, however, claimed: 'The British gave indications that they would do something to indicate the respect in which they hold Grivas.'

Behind the scenes in Cyprus, Makarios and Sir Hugh Foot wracked their brains about how to deal with the Colonel. The London *Times* commented: 'Distasteful as it will seem to many Britons, there are many Greek Cypriots who undoubtedly desire strongly to give him a hero's welcome when he emerges.' The Government, however, was adamant that he would not be allowed to appear in public anywhere on the Island, but his departure would be conducted in 'a dignified manner'.

Eventually, convinced that he would receive safe conduct out of the Island, and take any other 'wanted men' with him, Grivas agreed to return to Greece and call an end to the EOKA conflict, knowing he had failed to achieve his primary goal: *enosis*. Soon afterwards, persuaded by Makarios, he ordered EOKA members to hand over their weapons and explosives to Greek Cypriot Police officers at eight selected points on the Island. Much of the explosive was in a dangerous condition through deterioration – one EOKA youth delivered a can dripping nitroglycerine. At one dump alone, outside Nicosia, military bomb disposal experts detonated several hundred home-made bombs and grenades. At the Kykko monastery. only a few hundred yards from Government House, a Cypriot crowd watched the weapons arrive on trucks with their number plates covered. One machine-gun was etched with the words 'Made by EOKA in Cyprus'. An American rifle was identified as coming from a lot sold by the United States to the Philippines in 1917.

On 9 March Grivas sent a long and meandering letter to all his EOKA fighters. In it, he tried to put the best spin on why the time had come for a permanent ceasefire and an end to terrorist operations. 'It is recognized throughout the Greek world that EOKA has performed a great task and has given Greek diplomacy a number of trump cards, so that the settlement which has been reached is, in large measure, due to the heroic resistance of the Organization,' he wrote. 'The task which you have performed in these four years is great and your glory shines throughout the world. The whole Greek world has recognized your sacrifices and your struggle: this must be your greatest satisfaction and your greatest badge of honour.

'An agreement has been signed which determines the future of Cyprus. It does not fully satisfy our desires, but it is a step forward, breaking the bonds of slavery. It is the agreement that diplomacy, as it claims, was able to achieve in current international conditions. Arms alone, especially in a small island which faces an all-powerful empire, cannot, as you will understand for yourselves, obtain a final solution; and our politicians say that they have done everything they can, and that it is impossible to achieve more.

'I confess that from the day the Zurich Agreement was announced I have passed through moments of anxiety and I have carefully considered my responsibilities to you, to Cyprus and to all Greece. I have asked myself whether we should accept an agreement, which does not completely fulfil our desires, and whether I should reject it and continue the struggle. On the criterion of national interest alone, unmoved by prejudice or obligation or pressure, I have reached the conclusion that the continuation of the fight would have disastrous results. It would not have the unanimous support of the whole nation or the whole Cypriot people, since the agreement has been approved by the Greek Government and the Ethnarch and it would divide Cyprus and perhaps the whole Greek people ...

'I shudder to think of the results of national division such as the conflict between King Constantine X and Eleftherios Venizelos, a division through which I lived and which not only destroyed the dreams of a greater Greece, but was a burden on the whole nation for decades after 1915, with tragic consequences which culminated in the Asia Minor disaster. Greece today has still not entirely recovered from this ...

'My single-minded patriotism, my love for Cyprus, my duty not to destroy what we have fought for, my responsibility to prevent the tragic consequences of civil strife have led me to take this decision ... The Organization, as a military body, must obey the orders of the leader. I therefore call on you all to obey your leader's order to cease-fire ... We must maintain the unity and iron discipline, which aroused the admiration of even our enemies. We must not, at the last, lose what we have won by discipline, in four hard years of struggle.'

In the final lines of his letter, Grivas hinted that EOKA would play a major role in the Republic – and so the organization did from the very start. 'In an independent Cyprus the future of EOKA fighters is wide open,' Grivas said. 'It is they who tomorrow will be its supports. I shall watch and help you ... Each of you will always be able to look to me as his leader, always ready with concern and affection.'

Grivas let it be known, through Archbishop Makarios, that he would come out of hiding and stay in the Ayio Omoloyitadhes' house of Loukia Gavrielides, a rich Nicosia business-

man, until arrangements were completed for his departure from the Island. He also invited key members to visit him so that he could express his thanks and farewells. Ankara and Athens suggested he leave on 17 March. With the aid of Special Branch, a plan was agreed to move him quietly from Gavrielides' house to Nicosia Airport. Meanwhile, there would be no efforts to stop those who came to visit Grivas.

Colonel 'Mad Mitch' Mitchell of the Argyll and Sutherland Highlanders was typical of many British soldiers who eagerly waited for Grivas to come out of hiding. 'Great mystery surrounded him,' said the Colonel. 'Was he on the Island and, if so, where had he been hiding? Did he, indeed, exist at all? Perhaps he had died and his name been assumed by another terrorist leader?'

There were rumours in Larnaca that he would appear there for the first time since the start of the conflict and large crowds gathered to see him. 'It so happened that one of our company commanders, bore a remarkable resemblance to Grivas, stocky and fiercely moustached,' Colonel Mitchell recounted. 'He therefore dressed up like Grivas in boots, breeches, battledress top and EOKA beret. Then with the Drum Major's mace, he took his place at the head of our pipes and drums and, twirling his mace, led them through Larnaca to the stirring music of Scotland. The Cypriots had had many bewildering experiences during the past few years but none matched the sight of Grivas making his triumphal appearance at the head of the Argyll and Sutherland Highlanders.'

LATE IN the evening of 15 March, 'the final dramatic act of EOKA was played out as I saw and lived it,' wrote Elenitsa Seraphim-Loizou, one of those present. 'The curtain was about to fall, marking the end of a titanic epic ... It was full of majesty on that night of 15 March, when Dighenis met with his Area Commanders, the leaders of the guerilla groups, some of EOKA Youth and PEKA leaders and other fighters. Among all these brave men there stood a white-haired old man. It was Pieris Afxentiou, Grigoris' father, whose presence at that historic meeting was a symbolic one. In him were represented all the fathers and mothers of EOKA's heroic dead.'

The time had come for the 'fighters' to be paid for their loyalty. Antonis Georgiades and Tassos Papadopoulos, two of Grivas's most trusted aides, sat at a low table piled with crisp British pounds from which they handed EOKA Area Commanders various amounts. A payment of £100 was granted every terrorist 'so as to be able to meet initial expenses now that they were returning home'. Elenitsa Seraphim-Loizou received £2,100 for the 21 men in her area. Like the others, she signed an obligatory receipt for the amount. During the EOKA campaign, the Orthodox Church had paid £200 a month – a small fortune in those days – to any young Greek Cypriot willing to learn bomb-making from Colonel Grivas. British intelligence estimated that more than 4,500 bombs were successfully produced.

The financial business completed, now 'The Leader' could make his grand entrance. He paused for a theatrical moment at the top of the marble staircase of the Omoloyitadhes house of the rich Nicosia businessman, Gabriel Gabrielides, and then walked slowly and majestically down to meet his followers. He was dressed in a new olive-green knitted jersey, riding breeches, bandolier and beret – all made in the past few days by his female devotees – with a pistol strapped to his hip. As he stepped onto the ground floor, several men kissed his hand and others burst into tears.

In the kitchen of the house, Neophytos Sophocleous, the former valet who had planted the bomb in Field Marshal Harding's bed, was preparing a buffet, watched by the house owner.

When all had eaten, Grivas circulated among the guests. There he was, 'the living legend' Dighenis, aged 60, barely five feet two inches tall, with a grey moustache, his face slightly emaciated and yellowed from his time in the darkness, gaunt, but very much alive. His devotees saw him differently. To them he was 'agile-looking, with large, expressive and clever eyes'. He was 'the man who took a nation which was quiet and inexperienced in war and turned it into a fighting force like a sculptor working a piece of marble'.

'Dighenis gave us advice and ideas,' Elenitsa Seraphim-Loizou said. 'It is a pity that no one thought to immortalize that historical meeting between Dighenis and his men, but none of us had thought of bringing a tape recorder although fortunately someone had a camera and we took a few souvenir photographs. But everything comes to an end and the end of that unforgettable meeting arrived too. The moment when Dighenis had to leave was here. Deeply moved, almost in tears, he kissed us all, asked us to maintain the love and harmony we had, and left in the company of Antonis Georgiades. When the door had closed behind him, the man who for four years had guided us and led us with wonderful clear sightedness, we felt as if we had suddenly become orphaned. We had lost our leader, our father, our teacher, the one who until that moment had kept us in constant contact with him through his orders, his handwritten letters and instructions.'

Grivas concluded his address to his comrades with the words: 'I am sorry for not being allowed to visit the graves of our dead people and to kneel in front of the greatness of their sacrifice. Cyprus owes, for respect to them and also for teaching the coming generations, to set up a tall monument equal to their glory, somewhere at a high mountain, very high, so that they embrace with their look all Cyprus and Cyprus embraces them back, and at a place where they left their blood, because the heroes must have such a place for bed and shroud.'

Earlier in the day, Fidel Castro, a dedicated Communist, had sent the extreme right-wing Grivas a congratulatory telegram for his rebel activities.

EARLY IN the morning of 17 March, Charles Foley, editor of the *Times of Cyprus*, and a group of Greek Cypriot journalists were summoned to meet Grivas at the house in Ayios Omoloyitadhes. There to greet the press was the Colonel, accompanied by Archbishop Makarios, the Bishop of Kitium, several prominent supporters of EOKA and Greek Consul Frydas. They readily answered the journalists' questions. Looking straight at a reporter from a left-wing newspaper, Grivas berated him: 'You said once that I came to Cyprus to fight Communism. I did not come for that at all. I made it clear from the start that I brought a liberation crusade to the whole of Cyprus.'

'And Christianity,' interrupted Makarios.

'Certainly,' said Grivas. 'Unity and Christianity.'

'The Leader' was in a jocular mood. He claimed that while the Security Forces had tried to capture him, he 'often walked about, unrecognized' and he added: 'I always hid amongst the British.' Foley smiled.

After the independence of Cyprus, a former terrorist told a Greek-speaking reporter that Grivas had hidden for two months in a British house in Nicosia. He refused to name the owner, but hinted that he held a senior position on an English language newspaper on the Island. Foley was the only non-Cypriot present. He had been invited because his newspaper had expressed sympathy for 'the cause' and frequently angered the authorities with its coverage of the conflict. He later helped Grivas write his *Memoirs* and edited the English-language edition.

The Greek Consul nudged Grivas and said

it was time to leave. The Colonel waved the paper that guaranteed his safe conduct from the Island and stepped outside and blinked in the morning sunshine. Someone shouted a final 'Dighenis!' There was a ripple of applause. 'A soldier cycling past nearly ran into the pavement,' Foley reported.

An unmarked, highly polished sky-blue Mercedes was parked outside, waiting to collect the Colonel and the Bishop of Kitium for their drive to Nicosia Airport. Until this moment, no local people knew he was leaving, not even Foley. British troops had been ordered to line the route, without being told the reason why. They were there to quietly disperse any crowds that might gather along the way, but, more importantly, they were to keep their backs turned to the road, a calculated insult to the Colonel.

Waiting for Grivas at the airport were two DC-3 Dakotas of the Royal Hellenic Air Force that had landed at 09.45. Four high-ranking Greek officers, all of whom had served under him, were on board to welcome 'The Leader' and accompany him back to Athens or, as EOKA put it later, 'Cyprus' most valuable treasure, the incarnation of the heroes of 1821, the unconquerable George Grivas who, at dawn on 1 April, had resurrected the legend of Dighenis and brought him back to life in Cyprus'.

Grivas is taken under escort to the Royal Hellenic Air Force DC-3 for his flight back to Greece. Lieutenant Colonel 'Bill' Gore-Langton of the Coldstream Guards stands behind the departing party.

There was only a small party of British officials to watch Grivas arrive. He was in jaunty form, dressed in his army clothes and boots, with a gun and a pair of cased binoculars slung around his neck. Nobody seemed to remember that he had left his original set behind, with other personal possessions, when he fled from British Paras in the Troodos Mountains, during Operation *Lucky Alphonse* in mid-June 1956. London's *Daily Express* was not impressed. It jeered he was wearing 'the incongruous clothing of some old-fashioned music hall turn'.

General Darling had assigned Lt Colonel 'Bill' Gore-Langton of the Coldstream Guards to greet Grivas and hand him over to General Nicolas Paparodu of the Greek Army to board one of the waiting Dakotas. Darling's choice was another masterful insult: Gore-Langton, at a height of six feet three inches, towered above Grivas and could look down on him. In addition the British officer, nicknamed the 'one-armed bandit' would not be embarrassed by having to observe customary military formalities by having to salute as his right arm had been amputated without anaesthetic at the Battle of Salerno in the Second World War.

Two RAF Javelin jet fighters roared into the sky 10 minutes before the Greek Dakotas took off at 10.00 to make sure they stuck to the agreed flight plan out of Cyprus. Grivas had been in Cyprus for 1,590 days as the leader of EOKA. Until his death, he believed the RAF had provided a formal escort to mark his achievements.

A few hours later, thousands of Athenians turned out to give their hero a tumultuous welcome, headed by the Greek Prime Minister and a host of dignitaries. He descended the gangway from the Dakota and strode briskly into the arms of his wife Kikki, whom he had not seen for almost five years. Then followed the formalities of inspecting a guard of honour, listening to speeches and accepting gifts.

Prime Minister Karamanlis of Greece welcomes Grivas. His wife, Kikki, stands on the colonel's right.

'Your name is a Doric column in the pantheon of the great heroes of our glorious nation,' said Archbishop Theoklitos, Greek Orthodox Primate of Greece, presenting him with the ancient Greek symbol of victory, a silvered laurel wreath. Grivas began to weep. 'Small Cyprus fought Goliath,' he said. 'It did not succumb.' He handed the Mayor of Athens a small bag of earth taken from his mountain lair, and said emotionally, 'This bit of soil, soaked with the blood of Cypriot fighters, will be the link between Cyprus and Greece.'

Security officers parted the crowds and led him to a Cadillac convertible, its roof down to allow him to be seen and cheered by a quarter of a million people lining the flag-decked streets. As he was driven to an audience with King Paul to receive the nation's highest award – the Medal of Bravery – and promotion from Colonel to Lieutenant General, he stood erect, giving a military salute. As a further reward, the Greek Parliament voted him a monthly salary of $300 for the rest of his life.

Despite the outward show of praise for the new general, he and the Government disagreed on the terms for Cyprus independence.

Grivas insisted he had no desire to enter politics again, but, in the months ahead, his actions contradicted his words.

'If the fatherland calls me, I shall once again obey the call,' he often repeated to friends, hoping the populace would take the hint. Time and time again, he pointed out that he had not been consulted about the future of the Island, disassociated himself from the peace deal 'in view of the unpardonable tendency to retreat before British and Turkish demands' and said he would not be held responsible for what happened next. Certainly the leaders of several opposition parties feted him, believing his popularity with the Greek masses would win them votes if he were to join them. *Eleftheria*, an opposition newspaper, editorialized sternly that 'the agreements constituted a conspiracy against the Cypriot people ... [and] were the fruits of the weakness of the present [Karamanlis] government'.

The General's critics, however, were just as convinced that his criticism of the London Agreements would do him no good in the long run. They believed the Greeks of the mainland were fed up and tired of the strife in Cyprus and did not want to see it revived at their expense.

But on the day of his arrival in Athens, before he, the non-smoker and non-drinker, did anything else, he needed medical treatment for his haemorrhoids and an injured finger, a dentist to have three teeth pulled and a lot of rest in his Athens apartment.

SIR HUGH Foot, Archbishop Makarios and Turkish leader Dr Kutchuk now had the task of creating a process for the transfer of power. Two committees and a commission were set up for this purpose. The commission's role was to draft a constitution satisfactory to all the parties involved. Called the Joint Council, this transitional committee planned the ways and means to adapt and reorganize governmental machinery. Its membership was composed of the Governor, Makarios and seven Greek interim ministers, and Dr Kutchuk and his Turkish ministers.

Makarios created a stir by including six young EOKA members in his team. They were Pascahi Pascahlides, 30, secretary to the Ethnarchy for the past four years; Mr Glafcos Clerides, 38, and Tassos Papadopoulos, 25, both barristers; Mr Andonis Georghiades, 26, formerly Grivas's second-in-command; Mr Polycarpos Georghadjis, 30, who escaped three times after capture; and Andreas Azinas, who arranged arms supplies from Greece. Dr Kutchuk's choices were more conservative and expected: Osman Orek, 38, a barrister to handle defence matters; Dr Nazim Maniera, 50, a general medical practitioner to deal with health; Fazil Plumer, 44, a magistrate; and Mehmet Nazim, 62, Larnaca's mayor-elect.

Sir Hugh Foot approved both lists. In the months ahead, British officials would be working with men they had been hunting until recently.

The second joint committee met in London composed of representatives of Britain, Greece, Turkey and the two Cypriot communities. Its purpose was to prepare the final treaties giving effect to the conclusions of the London Conference. The aim was for Cyprus to become independent on 19 February 1960, but the parties ran into obstacle after obstacle and so the date was changed to 19 March. Again this target could not be met. 'For six months more we wrestled with wearisome and infuriating negotiations about the bases,' noted Sir Hugh Foot.

Sitting in Athens, General Grivas tried to influence the negotiations by giving interviews to Greek language newspapers in which he warned the Nicosia and London committees 'to stop making concessions to the English and the Turks'. As a military expert, he said he would decide the size of the bases the British needed. His arrogance was growing daily from the adulation Athenians were heaping on him. In Cyprus, his supporters conducted a purge of Greek Cypriots suspected of being 'informers' and 'traitors'.

In the small village of Ayios Amvrosios, once an EOKA stronghold, Zacharias Karaphotias was set on fire and burnt to death in front of his wife who had been bound and gagged. The villagers who perpetrated the attack almost certainly included close friends of EOKA men rounded up in 1956 by British troops after Karaphotias was interrogated. Archbishop Makarios declined to condemn the outrage. Sir Hugh Foot, however, warned Cypriots that he still had full responsibility for public security on the Island in the transitional period and promised to arrest wrongdoers and bring them to court to face justice.

Nevertheless, the colonial authorities still found time on 12 April to hold memorial services to 'all those who lost their lives during the Cyprus Emergency in the service of the Crown' at military and civil Anglican churches throughout Cyprus. At St Paul's Church, Nicosia, the Governor was among the worshippers and read one of the lessons, while the Director of Operations, Major General Kenneth Darling, attended the service at Wolseley Barracks.

In May, Sir Hugh Foot lost one of his personal bodyguards, Sergeant William Gillett. He was on board a Cyprus Airways Viscount aircraft bound for London where he was to receive medical treatment for leukaemia, when he suddenly collapsed. By chance Mr Dennis Browne, an eminent surgeon, was a passenger and tried hard to revive him, but when the aircraft returned to Nicosia, Gillett was dead.

For Sir Hugh, these were bleak times. 'Every day I feared that the settlement made in the London Agreement would slip away from us, that the island would sink back into the enmities and bloodshed of the past,' Sir Hugh recorded. 'Nothing could be worse than to come out of the wood, and then to spend months following tortuous paths which seemed to lead back into the wood again. I can still feel the anguish of those months. At one stage the negotiations were dead-locked without even a meeting for forty-five days on end.'

Suha Faiz, whose police inspector father had helped Sir Ronald Storrs escape from Government House during the 1931 rebellion, was present as a British civil servant during many of the meetings of the 'Council of Ministers' with Archbishop Makarios and Dr Kutchuk attending. Sharing his memories with the author, he said: 'There was a complete absence of even the slightest evidence from Makarios and little enough from his colleagues in word or demeanour, to suggest an intention sincerely to work in true co-operation, much less in partnership, with the Turkish side.' He found the Archbishop's presence 'baleful, baneful and utterly noxious' and added: 'Inside that chamber I felt the sinister air of an intolerable malevolence.' Others spoke about how the Archbishop's answers to questions, delivered with a bland smile, always had double meanings. Eight months before formal independence, Faiz requested a transfer from Cyprus, convinced that the Republic was 'doomed by the curse of Makarios'.

Oriana Fallaci, an Italian journalist, perhaps judged Makarios better. 'His character cannot be judged by the yardstick we use in the West,' she wrote. 'He does not belong to the West. He belongs to something that is no longer the West, but is not yet the East, something that sinks its roots into a culture that is sophisticated and archaic at the same time, and which has mastered the art of survival. His gift of survival was gained and regained through fast stepping, contortions, cleverness, lucidity and cynicism.'

Only when Sir Hugh Foot felt the negotiations had stalled completely did the British

Archbishop Makarios inspects British troops, who once chased his 'freedom fighters'.

Government decide to send Julian Amery, Under-Secretary for the Colonies, to Cyprus to try to settle all remaining questions. He came for a week and stayed for six months. 'It was like a long drawn-out game of chess, with Archbishop Makarios on one side and Julian Amery on the other,' said Sir Hugh Foot. 'Their skill and their patience and their persistence were well-matched. Makarios took us right up to the last minute ...'

After several more deadlocks, walkouts and strong words, lasting nearly five months, agreement on all outstanding issues was finally reached on 1 July. A week later the documents were initialed and 16 August 1960 was scheduled as Independence Day.

The Greek Cypriots had elected Archbishop Makarios as their first president of the future Republic. Dr Kutchuk, leader of the Turkish Cypriots, was the first to offer his congratulations. The soon-to-be Vice-President said: '[Makarios], who has acted as leader of the Greek community for so many years, has achieved the success which, beyond doubt, he deserves'. In his first public statement as pres-ident-elect Makarios called on Greeks and Turks to co-operate 'in a spirit of sincerity,

absolute respect for each other's rights and real understanding of communal interests and deserts'. The omens were favourable for the future of the co-partnership Republic – until the Cabinet's Greek members began to belittle Kutchuk and destroy the trust between the two leaders.

None of this concerned Lionel Bruce Binnie, an RAF pilot based at Akrotiri. 'Those days, there was the stress of conflict still present, but it was also a more innocent time in a way,' he said, reflecting on whether his duties would allow him to marry on the date planned by his fiancée. 'She had sent me a telegram to say she would be waiting for me at London Heathrow on 10 July. If I wasn't there, she would go on to take a holiday in France. Luckily my Squadron Commander helped out by sending me home for a few days. We flew back to Cyprus together on 14 July, passing over Paris at the time of the big Bastille Day big parade. I told her to have a good look down, as it was as close as we were going to get for our honeymoon! We married on 3 August at RAF Akrotiri.'

For the British service personnel in summer 1959, life was returning to normal, but there were military jobs to be done. 'One of our more peculiar duties was guarding a lump of rock that was ringed with barbed wire, somewhere between Famagusta and Cape Greco. Within its perimeter, there were two small caravans. The Air Ministry owned the site, but why and for what, we never found out. Nevertheless, two station guards and a policeman were posted there for 48-hour spells, some of which they spent in the caravans. They took their own food with them and did their own cooking. The first time I was posted as a guard, I put on my big boots and I examined every inch of the ground and found nothing. Later that night, one of my fellow guards came to me and said "Ere, Corp, there's a lot of lights out there,"' RAF Military Policeman Martin Bailey told the author before his death.

Bailey continued after a tension-building pause: 'It was pitch dark and miles from anywhere, but far across the heathland, sure enough, there was a series of lights moving about and coming nearer. We watched curiously and waited with our weapons ready to fire. Eventually, a man with a torch appeared. In perfect English, he said: "We're collecting edible snails, they're very good snails and the best ones around here are on your lump of rock. Would it be possible for some of us to collect them?"

'As a goodwill gesture, I agreed. "But you'll have a guard with you and I'll only allow four villagers at a time, while you stay here with me. Right?"

'"Okay," the man agreed. The rest of his party was happy as sand boys to hear my decision and set about their task with glee. The English-speaking villager now fired off a set of instructions in Greek and one of his friends disappeared into the blackness to return later with several bottles of red wine, which he insisted were for us, an expression of their gratitude to be allowed to complete their snail hunt. We all sat down and the villagers prepared us a feast, using our small oil-fired stove. The snails were washed, salted, cooked in their own juices and sprinkled with chopped flat parsley. They were nutty and delicious – the best I've ever tasted.'

AT 10.00 on 16 August 1960, the first Parliament in the 3,000-year history of the Island met for the formal investiture of President Makarios and his Vice-President Kutchuk. New ministers were sworn in and the Cyprus flag rose above the building, replacing the flags of Britain, Turkey and Greece. The new flag, designed by a Turkish Cypriot, had a white background with a gold silhouette of the island and a pair of crossed green olive branches underneath to 'symbolize peace and unity between Greek and Turkish Cypriots'.

Thousands cheered, cars honked their horns and church bells rang out. Outside the Council of Ministers, President Makarios took up his first official public duties by inspecting a parade of the Police Force he had just inherited from the British. Many of these officers had faced death from EOKA terrorists for performing their duties for the Colonial administration.

The President and his advisers were quick to announce their new appointments. Several prominent EOKA gunmen received posts in the administration. Among them were Polycarpos Georghadjis and Onissiforos Andoni, who became Senior Superintendent of Prisons. Andoni played a leading role in EOKA and had been held in detention by the British. Georghadjis, the new Minister of the Interior, too, had been a major player who was caught by the Security forces in Andoni's house after one of his many escapes from captivity.

Adoni's first act was to order the tiny steel door in the walls of Nicosia's Central Prison to be swung open to allow 106 convicts to walk free to celebrate independence. Several had their belongings wrapped in old newspapers and shook hands with the guards as they left. One of the prisoners was a barrel-chested murderer saved from the gallows at the eleventh hour.

Georghadjis, whose code-names in EOKA were *Klimis* and *Cicero*, had been working as a clerk in the Cyprus Chamber of Commerce in 1955, when Grivas recruited him to gather intelligence on police officers and sign them up. Within three months he had 20 on his payroll. Although he had no formal education, Georghadjis was meticulous in filing the information he gathered and was wily as a fox. He became known as EOKA's Houdini for escaping from captivity.

Initially Makarios saw Georghadjis as a valuable asset he could use to control any Greek Cypriot opposition and further his aims by any means, including blackmail, using his young minister's files. In December 1963, he sanctioned Georghadjis, with Sampson and others, to lead their personal militias to implement the Akritas Plan, which he had authored. Its purpose was to rid Cyprus of the island's Turkish population.

Very soon Georgadjis was plotting to overthrow his mentor, having joined the Grivas clique who still dreamed of *enosis*. With the help of Colonel Papastolou of the Greek Army, he sabotaged the Archbishop's helicopter in 1970 as part of a planned coup – Operation *Hermes* – backed by the National Guard. Makarios survived, but the other conspirators could not risk Georghadjis being captured by the Archbishop's supporters, so they invited him to a secret meeting outside Mia Milia village. Just as he arrived, his car was machine-gunned and he was seriously injured. One of the ambushers then walked up to him and delivered a *coup de grace*. The evidence pointed to Papastolou and Poulitsas, another Greek officer, as the assassins, but both returned to Athens without facing any charges.

But all this was in the future. On Independence Day Makarios saw only his way open to becoming a world leader from his base in Cyprus. There was no other who was the head of a church and president of a country. And the Church in Cyprus was extremely rich, powerful and dictated the lives of most ordinary Greek Cypriots.

At Government House, Sir Hugh and Lady Foot had 'held a farewell dress reception for diplomats and a garden leave-taking for 200 personal friends' reported *Time* magazine. Among those who said goodbye were Archbishop Makarios and Dr Kutchuk. Government House became the Presidential Palace. Within hours the first ambassadors to the new Republic entered to present their credentials.

'Sylvia and I and our three sons drove to Famagusta and said goodbye to General Ken Darling and the Royal Horse Guards and the Black Watch,' Sir Hugh wrote. The port had been given a 'spit and polish' by British troops before the Governor's party arrived to board HMS *Chichester* at the dockside. Bryan Chinn worked at 20 Movements Unit RAF based there. He said: 'I was on the parade at the docks when Sir Hugh Foot left, resplendent in plumed hat and gold braid. I remember HMS *Chichester* coming into port and several days of bullshit time spent on her, as the area was washed clean.'

The Foots' departure was planned with military precision to the minute:

10.00:	Sir Hugh Foot arrives at Famagusta.
10.10–10.25:	Inspection of Guard of Honour, mounted by the 1st Battalion Black Watch and two troops of the Royal Horse Guards.
10.25:	Sir Hugh embarks on HMS *Chichester*.

Sir Hugh Foot leaves Cyprus
in style.

10.30:	HMS *Chichester* casts off, accompanied by music played by the pipers of the 1st Battalion Black Watch.
10.32:	17-gun salute by a battery of 42nd Field Regiment Royal artillery.
10.40:	Fly past by 653 Light A/C Squadron ACC and 25 Sqn RAF.
10.40:	HMS *Chichester* steams past the troopship *Dilwara*, which will be dressed over-all for the occasion.

As the Royal Navy frigate sailed out of harbour, she was accompanied by an especially composed bagpipe lament entitled *Sir Hugh's Farewell to Cyprus*, played by the Black Watch, the same regiment that had landed in Cyprus in 1878. From the ancient walls of old Famagusta, the Foots heard a salute of guns.

WITH HMS *Chichester* over the horizon,

1,600 Greek and Turkish soldiers began debarking in Cyprus to stand guard over the infant republic. Every possible step had been taken to prevent any obstructions on the roads to their bases. The Turkish troops travelled via Lefkoniko to the capital, while the Greeks went via Lysi. Both routes were closed to other traffic from 14.30 until the soldiers passed. Similar restrictions applied to civilian traffic through Nicosia. A Turkish Cypriot centenarian was seen falling on a startled Turkish infantryman's neck, blubbering that he had not set eyes on a Turkish uniform since the last Ottoman garrison sailed away 82 years earlier.

But for Greek Cypriots, the day was made when a plane from Athens landed bearing 21 EOKA terrorists whom the British had exiled 17 months earlier. President Makarios met them, accompanied by hundreds of screaming women and teenagers wanting to kiss their returning heroes and pelt them with garlands of laurel. He looked at the frenzied scene and commented that the best thing EOKA men could do now was to lay down their Sten guns and get to work. Some did, but most did not, and joined Greek Cypriot militia groups. For their part, the TMT kept their powder dry.

Within three years both sides would be at each other's throats, Grivas would return and the partition of the Island would begin.

CHAPTER TWENTY-SIX

13 reasons:
the breakdown of the Republic

'Prudence consists in the power to recognize the nature of disadvantages and to take the less disagreeable as good.'

Niccolo Machiavelli

WHEN THE UK granted Cyprus independence in August 1960, the new republic was established under a set of complicated rules and treaties, which did not completely satisfy the aspirations of either Greek or Turk. The Constitution guaranteed the two communities co-founder status, while Britain retained sovereignty over 99 square miles that would become its main military bases in the Middle East. Britain also retained control of sites on Mount Olympus, Cape Greco, RAF Nicosia and Famagusta harbour. The Turkish Cypriots, for their part, had won a large measure of self-government in their areas, certain key ministries, and the right to veto any decisions involving defence, internal security and foreign affairs with which they might disagree over their Greek Cypriot colleagues.

Although both Greek and Turkish Cypriots had largely co-existed under British colonial rule until the start of the EOKA conflict and retained their separate religions, languages and cultures, their political ambitions were starting to move poles apart.

Neither side had achieved its aims: Greek Cypriots were denied *enosis* and the Cypriot Turks stopped from partitioning the Island. In addition, the Greeks felt strongly that the Turks were given too much power for their numbers and claimed their rights made it impossible to govern effectively. President Makarios disapproved of the Treaty of Guarantee signed by the UK, Turkey and Greece. Vice-President Kutchuk believed it prevented the majority community from over-running his Turkish minority, outnumbered five to one.

This contentious treaty allowed the signatories individually or collectively to intervene in Cyprus if the integrity of the Republic were threatened from any quarter or if hostile acts were committed by either community against the other. The third treaty – the Treaty of Alliance – signed by Cyprus, Greece and Turkey to ensure 'peace', allowed small contingents of Greek and Turkish armed forces to base themselves on the Island.

President Makarios knew he would have to change the Constitution and neutralize the Cypriot Turkish community one way or another if *enosis* were to be pursued. On 4 September 1962, he preached: 'Unless this small Turkish community, forming part of the Turkish race, which has been the terrible enemy of Hellenism is expelled, the duty of the heroes of EOKA can never be considered terminated.' Even so, quite surprisingly, for the first three years of the Republic, there was little trouble between the two sides. But many former EOKA leaders held senior appointments in the administration and were vigorously preventing the full implementation of those sections of the Constitution that granted Cypriot Turks self-government in their scattered, but well-defined areas.

In April 1963, the Turks took their case to the independent Supreme Constitutional Court, which ruled in their favour. The Government's Greek Cypriot members, including Makarios, however, refused to accept the Court's judgment. As a direct consequence, the Court's neutral President, Ernest Forsthoff, Professor of Public Law at Heidelberg, resigned in anger.

A belligerent statement followed from Minister of Interior Polycarpos Georghadjis, known to his EOKA comrades as *Klimis* and *Cicero*. He declared: 'There is no place in Cyprus for anyone who is not Greek.' With his official command of the Republic's security forces, he had the means to turn his words into deeds – or so the Cypriot Turks believed. Unknown to them at this stage, Georghadjis was planning a 'final solution' with Nicos Sampson and Dr Vassos Lyssarides, Makarios's personal physician. Their so-called Akritas Plan was designed to launch coordinated, simultaneous military attacks in massive force against the Turkish Cypriots before mainland Turkey could intervene. Makarios was reluctant to put the plan into action until he had exhausted all other means, which might not provoke the United Nations.

In Washington, President John Kennedy was unhappy about the situation on the Island. On 17 October, McGeorge Bundy issued Memorandum 266, addressed to the Secretary of Defense and the Director of the CIA. It said: 'The President is concerned over reports that we may be headed for trouble in Cyprus. He feels we should do all we can in cooperation with the Guarantor Powers to prevent a showdown between the Greek and Turkish communities. He would like the Department of State to provide him by 28 October with its recommendations on what

measures might be taken to this end.' But there was no stopping the Greek Cypriots in government from putting the finishing touches to their plan to limit the powers of their Turkish partners.

Equally concerned was Greek Foreign Minister Averoff, who had warned Makarios not to introduce the constitutional changes: 'It is not permissible for Greece in any circumstances to accept the creation of a precedent by which one of the contracting parties can unilaterally abrogate or ignore provisions that are irksome to it in international acts which this same party has undertaken to respect.' The Archbishop binned Averoff's letter. Kennedy took his eyes off Cyprus and turned them on Cuba, where the Soviet Union was preparing to plant missiles, just 90 miles from the United States.

Challenged later by the Italian journalist Oriana Fallaci on the question of changes, Makarios reacted sharply: 'I simply complained about those privileges because they only served to hamper the functioning of the state. The Constitution provides that they [the Turks] be represented in the government at the ratio of 30 per cent. And very often the Turkish Cypriots didn't have people capable of filling that 30 per cent. There was, for example, a post that I could have filled by an intelligent Greek and it had to be given to an illiterate Turk just because he was a Turk.'

IN NOVEMBER 1963, Makarios summoned Kutchuk, his Vice-President, and told him that he would introduce 13 amendments to the Constitution. These would take away all the guarantees of the original. No debate or argument would be tolerated. Makarios pointed out that his ministers had been preparing for this moment since the creation of the Republic and had organized an underground military force to ensure the new arrangements. The Makarios proposals closed the debate on whether the Greek Cypriots had implemented the original Constitution or the Cypriot Turks were willing to negotiate any changes.

(Makarios was fixated on the number 13. He was born on 13 August 1913, was sent to be educated at the Kykko monastery on his 13th birthday and was ordained priest and archimandrite at St Irene's Church in Athens on 13 January 1946. Two years later he became a bishop on 13 June 1948. The first weapons and arms destined for EOKA were placed aboard the *Ayios Yeoryios* on 13 January 1955. During his peace talks with Lennox-Boyd on 29 February 1956, he ordered Grivas to explode 13 bombs in Nicosia. While in exile in the Seychelles, he completed his discussions with two British representatives on 13 January 1957.

After Britain negotiated independence for Cyprus in 1959, he withheld telling Grivas he was travelling to London to discuss the peace agreement until 13 February. Even his later intention to change the Republic's Constitution contained not 10 or 12 amendments, but 13. Then, on 13 December 1967, Makarios gave his backing to King Constantine's counter-coup to overthrow the 'Colonels' in Greece. A month later, on 13 January 1968, he announced a 'Charter of Rights' for Turkish Cypriots.)

Vice-President Kutchuk considered President Makarios deserved a reasoned response against his 13 amendments to the Constitution and asked Rauf Denktas to set up a committee to present the case against them. Just three days later, the Greek militia leaders blew up the statue of EOKA hero Markos Drakos near the capital's Paphos Gate and blamed the Turks for the incident.

By this action and his non-negotiable stance, Makarios brought into the open all the differences that existed between the two communities. He knew, too, that the world's attention was not on Cyprus, but on Washington, where Lyndon Johnson had

become President after John Kennedy's assassination and was grappling with more pressing problems.

For the breakdown of the 1960 Republic, the *Cyprus Mail* on 5 October 2008 put the blame squarely on Greece. The newspaper explained: 'When the 1960 Agreements were made, we had the belief that this Cypriot Partnership would be a bridge of friendship and cooperation between the two motherlands. This was a holy objective. What destroyed it was not reliance on motherlands and being Greeks and Turks of Cyprus, but the attempt by Guarantor Greece, again using the Church, to destroy the Greco-Turkish balance by acquiring the Island at the expense of the Turks of Cyprus (who do not exist as far as (our) history books are concerned) at the expense of Turkey.'

Known only to Makarios's inner cabinet there was a Greek military plan to secure *enosis*. Signed by the Chief of Staff Ioannis Pipiles, it said that, firstly, the President should 'attack the negative points of the Constitution'; second, denounce the Treaty of Guarantee; third, declare self-determination; and fourthly, apply to the 'Greek Government to accept unification of Cyprus with the Greek core'. Known as the *Akritas Plan*, it had been co-authored by Tassos Papadopoulos, who would become president in the early years of the twenty-first century. The first part of the plan had taken place. The rest waited for a moment decided by the Archbishop.

The atmosphere became heavy with fear and mistrust. Forgotten were the hopes that had existed in 1960 that there could be a unified Cyprus nation one day. Now it only needed a spark to ignite a violent explosion. Yet, on 20 December, Makarios reassured Sir Arthur Clark, the British High Commissioner, that he should go back to London and enjoy his Christmas vacation as calm would prevail until the Turks had given their answer to the Constitutional changes in January. Clark passed the Archbishop's view to the American Ambassador, Fraser Wilkins, that there would be 'no new developments in the immediate future, unless there should be some bombing incident'. And so Sir Arthur and his wife left Nicosia.

It was not a bombing incident that took place in the early hours of 21 December 1963. It was something more serious. A group of Cypriot Turks travelling back from the coastal port of Kyrenia to their homes in Nicosia was stopped on the road by a group of Greek Cypriots dressed in police uniforms. The latter, who belonged to a militia under the command of Minister of the Interior Georghadjis, claimed they were conducting a search for illegal weapons. A few moments later there was a burst of automatic gunfire and the driver and his passengers, one a pregnant woman, were riddled with bullets. However, the woman lived long enough to recount what had happened to some Cypriot Turks who came to her aid. Her story was immediately believed by their community.

Next morning Turkish Cypriots in their hundreds gathered in the streets of North Nicosia to protest. Immediately EOKA activists, many in uniform, began disarming Turkish police officers and accused them of defying the laws of the Republic. With scant regard for the civilian population, battle commenced. Wherever there were Turkish communities in Cyprus, the barricades went up.

Matters were made worse when EOKA strongman Nicos Sampson went on state radio and ordered his supporters to storm Turkish Cypriot enclaves. On 23 December, stopped from broadcasting by the official service, the Cypriot Turks set up a radio station of their own to keep their people informed. A call went out for engineers and technicians to come together in North Nicosia. In less than 48 hours they managed to build a small transmitter. Some of these workers had quit their jobs at the Cyprus Broadcasting Corporation (CyBC), while others, the future programme makers, were former producers and newsreaders with the BBC's Turkish Service. They had retired and returned to Cyprus after the formation of the independent Republic. They now saw their role as raising morale among their people at home and making their cause known abroad.

BY CHRISTMAS Eve, all the carefully crafted treaties giving Cyprus independence exploded in flames and civil war broke out. Vicious fighting developed wherever the two sides came into contact. The co-partnership government rapidly disintegrated. Makarios declared that he recognized no Turkish Cypriot Vice-President, refused him entry to his office, now occupied by former EOKA members, and cut off even telephone contacts with Dr Kutchuk. At the same time Cypriot Turks were expelled by force from all government offices and ministerial posts and virtually dumped in the streets. They now believed they were in mortal danger, despite Dr Kutchuk's call for calm.

The Greeks insist the Turks walked out, determined to overthrow the Island's legitimate authorities by using the TMT. Rauf Denktas responds with a different opinion: 'A few Turkish Cypriots who had taken the risk and returned to their jobs were not seen again until recently, when their bones were recovered in different places. Murder was afoot for any Turk who dared to enter the areas patrolled by the *enosis* patriots.' Whatever Denktas says, there is no doubt the TMT became involved at a very early stage. It may have mothballed its weapons in 1960, but its members had stayed in touch, ready to form up again as a defence force.

On Christmas Day 1963, Bayrak, 'the voice of the Turkish Cypriot people', was heard for the first time by a handful of listeners. With only a 10-watt transmitter, the range of the new station could be measured in metres, not kilometres, but it was able to keep people in its vicinity informed about where the Greek militias were operating and what the Cypriot Turks should do during the Emergency.

In the days ahead, Bayrak became the only official source of Cypriot Turkish news. In so doing, many fewer lives were lost. Because the TMT used the station to broadcast instructions on how enclaves should combine for their safety, Greek Cypriot critics said it was 'the voice of the Turkish Cypriot "terrorists"'. The Cypriot Turkish response was direct: 'We are all fighters.'

Within three months, Bayrak's engineers had raised their transmitter's power to 300 watts, still well below the strength of the CBC, which, by now, was 'the voice of the Greek Cypriot people'.

With the Turkish Cypriot enclaves blockaded, Bayrak became as vital to their survival as the TMT who defended them and organized their food supplies. Bayrak reporters, in grave danger to themselves, travelled clandestinely between the enclaves, where they recorded interviews with new arrivals and messages for missing relatives and friends as the numbers of refugees increased and people lost touch with each other. Through the radio station, their leaders could tell them what they were doing, knowing that they would get their words across.

Although widespread massacres of Cypriot Turks began throughout the Island, they were fighting back and inflicting serious casualties on their attackers. Several years later, the Greeks admitted that they had tried to implement their Akritas Plan. It failed because the Cypriot Turks had planned for such an eventuality. The TMT began moving 35,000 people, a quarter of the Cypriot Turkish population, to form a secure enclave in the Hilarion area. On 18 January 1964, five Turkish Cypriot teenagers took control of the castle from where any Greek movements in any direction could be seen from the battlements.

On 25 December, the 950 troops of the Greek Army stationed in Cyprus had joined Sampson and his mob, equipped with mortars, artillery and heavy machine guns. The Turkish contingent of 650 soldiers countered by taking up strategic positions on the Nicosia–Kyrenia road. *Enosis*, anathema to Turkey, would never be allowed to let Greece control its southern seaways. In the early afternoon, three Turkish F-84G fighter aircraft screamed across the capital as a warning to the Greeks to stop.

Andrew Bache, a recently recruited junior Foreign Office official, had just arrived in Cyprus and was on early duty at the British High Commission on Christmas Day. 'Duncan Sandys, Secretary of State, was at his country house and Sir Arthur Snelling, the Under-Secretary was also at home. We all began having a three-way conversation at seven o'clock in the morning,' he says. 'We discussed the present position: the Turkish Cypriots and the Greek Cypriots were killing each other at a tremendous rate. We wanted to intervene with our troops in Dhekelia, who were under General Young's command, ready to move, but they couldn't without the agreement of the Cyprus government. We couldn't make contact with Dr Kutchuk from the Turkish sector and Archbishop Makarios was also out of contact. Meanwhile the Turkish Navy had set sail from Iskenderun and was heading for Cyprus. At that point I was left, sitting in front of a desk, with telegrams coming through every other minute. To cut a long story short, during the course of the day we made contact with Archbishop Makarios, and with Dr Kutchuk. They both agreed that we should issue a communiqué, which allowed General Young to march from Dhekelia. When this happened the Turkish Navy put back to Iskenderun. When Sir Arthur Snelling came to have breakfast, he commented that he thought we had actually stopped a NATO war.'

Paul Marion, a member of the US Navy

The Turkish jets that crossed Nicosia on Christmas Day 1963.

electronics intelligence-gathering facility north of Nicosia, which had been set up in 1957, told the author: 'I was having a fine lunch at my house, when I heard the planes. They buzzed our neighbourhood so low that they had to climb to clear the slight hill on which we lived. I dashed up to the roof and saw my Greek neighbours watching the sky. They pleaded for assurances that the aircraft were American. "Sorry," I replied, "Turkish planes, Turkish insignia and Turkish pilots." Then we heard booms in the downtown area, which many of us thought were exploding bombs. In fact, they were the noise of the jets' afterburners. This was easily the most memorable Christmas of my 71 years.'

Bob Casale, a member of a United States Navy team at the American Embassy, adds his description of events: 'Battles were fought in all areas of Cyprus, day and night, but the most significant battles took place at night when bands of men roamed the streets. Most of the fighting in Nicosia was confined to the walled city, where small arms firing could be heard for miles. At our hotel, we kept the drapes drawn and lights off so as not to attract the attention of a wayward sniper looking for a target. Travel was significantly restricted and it had a dramatic effect on our work schedule.'

Britain called for an immediate ceasefire on Christmas Day. At this time, few people knew that it was the British High Commissioner who had given Makarios the 'green light' to demand his Constitutional amendments.

CLEARLY NO longer in control, Makarios and his team, terrified by what they had unleashed, called for urgent talks with the Cypriot Turkish leadership, as well as drawing into the discussions the diplomatic representatives of Britain and the United States. At no time, however, did they order their underground forces to stop their attacks. In Ormophita, a Nicosia suburb, Nicos Sampson, the EOKA gunman who murdered British servicemen in Ledra Street, waved a captured Turkish flag in front of the press and cowed Turkish Cypriot residents. A Greek newspaper reported 'what is taken after bloodshed is not given back'. The Turks responded in kind. Fighting raged in Nicosia and other towns over the Christmas holiday.

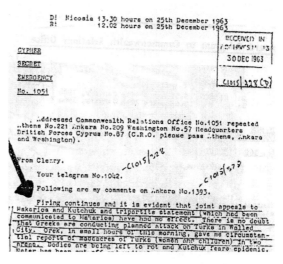

An urgent message from the British High Commission on Christmas Day 1963.

Nicos Sampson with a captured Turkish flag taken from Omorphita.

During Makarios's heated discussions with British officials on Christmas Day, he is reported to have told them: 'You can have Cyprus back.' There is no record of what was said in reply. At his request, Britain now provided a 'peace force' from its Sovereign Bases and British troops were back on the streets of Nicosia. 'Who are we fighting this time?' a soldier quipped.

Major-General Peter Young was placed in command of what was euphemistically called a Tripartite Truce Force, but he received no more than lip service from the Greek and Turkish military contingents. They were far too busy supporting the 'children' of their 'motherlands'. His force, created from Sovereign Base resources as only a temporary measure, became exclusively British, little trusted by either side. Young's first act was to look at a map of Nicosia, then with a green chinagraph pencil draw a line: Cypriot Turks were to stay north and the Greek Cypriots south. This has become known as the 'Green Line'. The term is often misused to indicate the division of Cyprus today, but actually only relates to Nicosia.

The partition of Cyprus had begun. Professor Ernst Forsthoff, who had been the

There was no mistaking British Army armoured cars of the Tripartite Force on patrol.

neutral President of the Supreme Constitutional Court of Cyprus, told the German newspaper *Die Welt*: 'Makarios bears on his shoulders the sole responsibility of the recent tragic events. All this happened because he wanted to remove all constitutional rights from the Turkish Cypriots.'

At Nicosia Airport, 3 Platoon, A Company of the 1st Battalion the Gloucestershire Regiment were already in place on 25 December. A Greek 'Security Force' fired a bazooka at the soldiers, who returned fire with a .30 caliber Browning. To allow British High Commission officials to move 'freely',

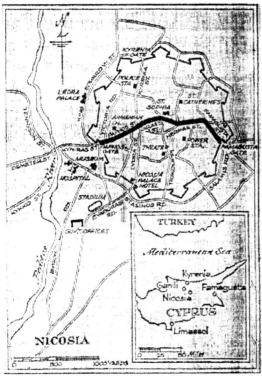

Nicosia's 'Green Line'.

the Glosters put two of their vehicles at their disposal with armed guards. The remainder of the company arrived the next day. The whole

Battalion had been ordered on Christmas Day to be ready to move off at 08.00.

'The first unit to enter Nicosia on Boxing Day was 34 (LAA) Squadron of the RAF Regiment,' John Kerr told the author. A member of the regiment, he and the others had arrived by air from Akrotiri the previous night. '27 (LAA) Squadron joined us by road the following day. We moved between the warring factions in the city, collected the dead from the streets and evacuated British service families. We escorted the Glosters into the capital.'

'It was a fine sight, the long column of vehicles moving at best speed with Union Jacks fluttering in the air,' an officer remembers. 'Both Greeks and Turks were pathetically glad to see us, and how we were clapped and cheered as we drove through Nicosia.' The Glosters moved on to the RAF station at the airport and established 'Alexandria Camp'.

'Mac' McElligott was a Flight Lieutenant with the RAF Regiment and tasked with setting up an intelligence unit in a mobile caravan that was parked in a Nicosia street. 'One incident I recall with amusement from

British troops of the Gloucestershire Regiment on patrol to keep the peace.

those days was when a Greek manager of the Ledra Palace Hotel, where we had moved our Ops, came and handed me a wad of bills for our accommodation. They totaled £8,000,' he laughs. 'I returned them to him and said: "We were brought into this conflict at the request of Makarios to aid the civil power – give the bills to him with my compliments." That was the last I heard.'

Troops of the Glosters, meanwhile, set up sandbag positions overlooking the Green Line. 'Several potential flash-points were calmed by the application of common sense and hours of talking,' an officer says. 'Private Abdullah – who had served with the Cyprus Police and spoke both Greek and Turkish – was a great asset to the Company in these matters.' One incident involved negotiating the release of three busloads of Greek hostages taken by the Turks.

On 27 December men of the RAF Regiment and the Glosters began round-the-clock patrolling of the capital's suburbs. 'Both Greeks and Turks were shut up in their houses or else standing armed guard outside. There were many casualties and gaunt unshaven faces everywhere. Everyone was glad to see us and relaxed when we came by. There were occasional shots to be heard but no real fighting.' A few days later the Company moved to Ormophita to assist the Rifle Brigade. After fierce fighting in this district, the Turkish residents had fled and their homes were looted and burnt by the Greeks.

At the Ledra Palace a small number of EOKA fighters rapidly vacated the hotel when the Glosters moved in. EOKA had been using the roof to fire at the Turkish Embassy. Support Platoon and Company HQ manned the hotel roof, set up roadblocks and patrolled the area. The situation was calmed down by their presence.

By now the hotel was also home to a vast contingent of the international press corps. It became their unofficial headquarters from which they began to report events. For 'leads', they relied on Savvas, the hotel's grasping night porter. He had served the British – for a price – as far back as anyone could remember. Because of his nocturnal role and long service, he had contacts everywhere, some seedier than others. At any given moment, he knew what was what, where, and who might be involved. His black book was crammed with names, addresses and phone numbers.

In return for a large fist of cash bunged in his direction by a journalist, Savvas was always ready, willing and able to give a good story. Or provide anything else that was required. He was a 'fixer' par excellence. Stelios, the Greek barman, was another member of the hotel staff whom the press cultivated. It was an open secret that he had direct links to the highest echelons of the capital's various Greek Cypriot militia. According to author H. Scott Gibbons, he had an agreement with the gang leaders not to interfere with the Fourth Estate's representatives while they were on his premises and settled their bar bills on time.

After the Turkish jets over flew Nicosia, the Swiss manager of the Ledra Palace had threatened to close the premises, but now said they would remain open, provided British soldiers were on guard. He told Scott Gibbons he wanted two armoured cars to be parked on either side of the front gate, guns pointing outwards. To the manager's delight and satisfaction, Major General Peter Young, the British commander, soon afterwards made the hotel his headquarters and stationed his armoured cars outside.

Sent by Rene McColl and Daniel McGeachie from the hotel, London's *Daily Express* carried their graphic report on its front page on the 28th: 'We went tonight into the sealed off Turkish quarter of Nicosia in which 200 to 300 people have been slaughtered in the last five days. Silence hung over the street (Irfan Bey Sok), and apart from a few dogs, the only living things were two or three unshaven scowling Turkish policemen carrying rifles ... We were the first Western reporters there, and we have seen sights too frightful to be described in print and horrors so extreme that people seemed stunned beyond tears and reduced to an hysterical and mirthless giggle that is more terrible than tears.'

By New Year's Day 1964 General Young had positioned his troops between the two sides in the Cyprus capital and tried to impose a ceasefire. Island-wide, in the space of just four days, 30,000 Cypriot Turks were forced to flee 103 villages, according to UN reports. McElligott remembers: 'On one occasion, at the request of the Turkish Vice-President, we had to send eight vehicles, drivers and escorts to a remote Turkish village which had been levelled to the ground by Greek elements using tractors and other heavy, armour-plated vehicles,' he recalls. 'The bodies of those killed were brought back and handed over to the Vice-President in the Turkish part of the walled city.'

At the same time, Makarios, having agreed in February 1959 that the responsibility for bringing peace rested with the three Guarantor Powers, took the matter to the UN and demanded an emergency session of the Security Council. He accused Turkey of aggression and intervention in the affairs of an independent state. In the end, Britain's 'Tommys' were left holding the ring – as a temporary measure, they thought. Apart from their work in Nicosia, they were also sent to keep the peace in other 'sensitive' areas, although they were prevented from using force to protect either side. Willpower was the British soldiers' chief weapon as they could only use their guns in self-defence.

John Barstow, a 19-year-old United States Navy sailor attached to the American Embassy in Nicosia, has a lasting high regard for the British soldiers he saw. 'They just seemed to conduct themselves in a mature manner and acted as if their actions would reflect on their country and their values,' he says. 'They manned the machine gun positions along the "Green Line" and their military bearing never faltered. This, in spite of some confrontations with the local Greeks. The Brits' military bearing, their coolness and nerve in the face of threats impressed me.' Joe Moody, another USN sailor, remembers: 'I had diplomatic immunity and US personnel had freedom of movement, which I found ironic as the Greeks and Turks were unable to travel from city to city and areas in Nicosia.'

All the Americans dressed in sweat-shorts and jeans, had their hair in crew cuts and draped their cars in the US flag to avoid being mistaken for combatants. Moody continues: 'At that time in my life I drank excessively and the drive over the Kyrenia pass was very dangerous. Many times, the Turkish Cypriot guards would invite us out of the car for a couple of cups of coffee and sober me up before allowing me to continue my journey.

'Many times, we would stop and share lunch with them in the pass or other remote checkpoints. They would also give us small gifts, again, not to bribe us, simply because they wanted to. In return for their favours, I sometimes brought cans of gas for them as a gift. It wasn't that they couldn't afford gas, they just could not get it for any price. Their enclaves had become Turkish islands without a sea. The Turks were dependant on the whims of the Greeks for most supplies and the Greeks acted as total asses and withheld supplies for no reason.'

Barstow adds: 'My sentiments did favour the Turks during this time. I thought they were a vastly outnumbered minority, many of whom were literally butchered for no other reason than being Turkish. As my knowledge of the Greek language grew, I began to realize that insults were being directed my way when it was thought that I could not understand. I

Turkish Cypriot fighters at one of their strongholds.

who provoked the fighting and deliberately engaged in atrocities. They have recruited into their ranks as "special constables" gun-happy young thugs. They threaten to try and punish any Turkish Cypriot police who wish to return to Cyprus Government ... Makarios assured Sir Arthur Clark that there will be no attack. His assurance is as worthless as previous assurances have proved.'

In the days ahead, a rag, tag and bobtail army of fighters reinforced the TMT at St Hilarion Castle. What they achieved cannot be overestimated. Armed only with light, antiquated weapons, some rusting from having been buried under soil, they succeeded in repulsing assault after assault by Greek forces in the months ahead. Despite their comparatively small number, they protected nearby Turkish Cypriot enclaves by controlling the

never felt that this sort of thing came from the Turks. I always felt welcome in Kyrenia with the Turks and they often invited me to join in their family activities.'

Another US sailor, Ken Wise, the Embassy's Chief Storekeeper, adds: 'We lived right among the Turks and learned a lot of their culture, attending their weddings and sharing their holidays. We made a lot of friends.' (Before Moody left Cyprus, he met a WRAC Corporal, who was the PA for the Royal Engineers' CO at Dhekelia. 'I arrived on the "Island of Love" single and left three years later married and the proud father of a daughter.')

WITH NO end in sight to the intercommunal fighting, a frustrated official at the British High Commission telegrammed London: 'The Greek (Cypriot) police are led by extremists

Turkish Cypriots bury their dead.

Nicosia–Kyrenia road, preventing its use by Greek forces. (Later on, they permitted Greek Cypriot civilians to use the road, providing UN soldiers escorted their convoys.)

In an attempt to restore peace, the United States, concerned about its radio monitoring station, and the UK, worried about the impact on its Sovereign Bases, concocted a stabilization plan to bring NATO troops to the Island. As Greece and Turkey were part of NATO to defend Europe against Soviet aggression, it seemed a workable idea, provided this allied peacekeeping force was stationed in Cyprus for three months and that during this period neither Greece nor Turkey intervened, allowing a 'neutral' mediator (from a NATO partner) to negotiate a return to 'normality'.

The Greek Cypriot militants, however, showed what they thought of any US involvement by bombing the code room of the American Embassy. The Ambassador was the probable target because his apartment was above. The culprits were never found. Makarios came the next day 'to offer apologies'. The Americans immediately evacuated their families to Italy, Turkey and the Lebanon. All sensitive electronics equipment was also sent abroad.

Watching from the sidelines with great interest at the disarray of NATO allies over the Cyprus question, the Soviet leadership thought it was an opportune time to further muddy the stormy waters of the Eastern Mediterranean. Premier Khruschev contacted Prime Minister Alec Douglas-Home at 10 Downing Street in London on 7 February and warned him that there would be serious international complications if NATO boots and bayonets were used to drag a 'small neutral state' into the Western alliance. The strong words from the Kremlin resonated with Makarios and, in the guise of a pacifist, he rejected the Anglo-American proposition, prompting US Assistant Secretary of State George Ball to tell the President that the 'Red

Priest' and his supporters 'do not want peace-keepers; they just want to be left alone to kill Turkish Cypriots'.

As Makarios saw matters, any NATO involvement in Cyprus would affect his chance to become leader of the 'Third World' or non-aligned nations, including Egypt and Yugoslavia.

Meanwhile, 3 LAA RAF Regiment was removed from its duties in Nicosia and sent to prevent trouble in the villages neighbouring the Western Sovereign Base. They found Episkopi deserted, but Kandou was still occupied by Turks. 'We joined the Turks in their trenches and draped them with Union flags as a warning to the Greeks to keep away. We also cleaned their weapons and cannibalized our Bren mags to make sure they didn't go short. Alas, there were no UN medals for us, because we wore our own berets during the trouble,' says John Kerr.

Encouraged by Makarios, the UN watched the situation deteriorate. As a consequence, Secretary-General U Thant decided to station an official observer in Cyprus. He was Lieutenant-General Prem Singh Gyani from India. Soon afterwards the London *Daily Telegraph* caustically observed: 'In endeavouring single-handedly to keep the peace, we [Britain] have clearly assumed a task which is already beyond our powers ... Greek opinion on the island grows daily more inflamed against us. Already Greek Cypriot forces openly defy our attempts to restore order and will deal only with the United Nations' representative, General Gyani. This might be welcome enough in a way, if in fact General Gyani represented anything of substance.'

Fearing Turkey might launch a full-scale invasion in support of its Island cousins and cause the partition of Cyprus, intense diplomatic activity took place during the first six weeks of 1964, with the international community making every effort to find a solution that would satisfy Greek and Turkish aspirations and keep NATO out. But fighting continued despite the sterling efforts and good intentions of British troops. Stopped from taking preventive action, they found their mission increasingly frustrating. Greek Cypriots mocked their impotence and accused them of partisanship. Cypriot Turks, while grateful for their limited protection, thought it was insufficient and wished they were fully defended by men of the Turkish Army. Fed up with the thankless position in which it found itself, Britain eventually handed the 'Cyprus Problem' to the UN in February to solve.

FROM 18 FEBRUARY to 4 March 1964, the UN debated Cyprus, listening intently to the Greek Cypriot leadership that officially attended the debates. Turkish Cypriots were excluded, until America's Ambassador to the UN, Adlai Stevenson, insisted that Rauf Denktas, the Turkish Cypriot leader, should be allowed to put his side's case. Stevenson's demand was vigorously opposed by the delegates from Greece and the Soviet Union.

Yet when Denktas addressed the Security Council, he was allowed only to speak 'not as a representative of his community in Cyprus, but as a private individual,' says Professor Michael Moran. 'Thus came about the quite extraordinary and calamitous exclusion by the international community of the Turkish Cypriots from their rightful place among the official representatives of the Cyprus Republic in international fora, which exists to this day.'

On 28 February Denktas spoke passionately, pointing out that 'genocide of Turks is in full swing' and emphasized that 'the principles of justice, of the role of law, humanity and equality have all been denied'. He continued: 'The Constitution as well as the International Treaty, which brought about Cyprus, have been wilfully and wickedly ignored. It is the people who have done or condoned all these acts and have not hesitated to resort to genocide who are before the Security Council

today claiming to be the victims of the situation.'

This was the first time Denktas had ever addressed such an important international assembly. 'They [the Greeks] themselves have deliberately brought about the situation with a view to annihilating the Turks of Cyprus, while the world is invited to look on and do nothing because, as they put it, "this is an internal affair and anyone who tries to intervene and stop the massacres, albeit under a Treaty recognized by the United Nations, is guilty of aggression." The Greek Cypriot delegation pretends to agree to the necessity of an international peacekeeping force. The Treaty of Guarantee provides for such a force.'

Denktas asked: 'Why do they object to the increase in number of the Greek and Turkish contingents in Cyprus who could effectively secure peace in the Island jointly with the British? Why prolong the debate while innocent Turkish lives are lost?' He pointed out that in just two months, more than 800 Turks had been killed – mostly women, old men and children – and their properties 'ruthlessly' destroyed.

'The Greek Cypriot insistence on recognition of the integrity and their sovereignty of Cyprus by the Security Council is a trick for finding the untenable excuse to argue that the Treaty of Guarantee is non-effective with getting a free licence to continue the massacre of the Turks under the umbrella of the United Nations. Why do the Greeks want to get rid of the Treaty? The answer is clear. They want to take away our constitutional rights by brute force and violence. The Treaty obliges them to respect the rule of law, human dignity and equal treatment of their fellow men in equality and justice. This the Greeks have refused to do for the last three years. When they realized that they could not get their way by intrigue and subversive activities, they did not fail to use the mass killing of Turks as a means. With this object in view, Turks have been attacked and killed since 21 December 1963, under the war cry of *enosis*.'

Although Denktas spoke movingly to the Security Council and left the chamber in tears, Moran maintains he need not have bothered, because, on 4 March, the UN Security Council passed Resolution 186. It cast the Turkish Cypriots in 'the preposterous role of a rebellious minority – an image that the Greek Cypriot delegates had repeatedly presented,' Moran argues. 'This situation still prevails, at least in the minds of those susceptible to Greek propaganda.'

After the UN debate, Denktas tried to return to Cyprus, but Makarios and Minister of the Interior Georghadjis issued an 'order of the day', which declared him *persona non grata* and wanted him arrested for starting the Turkish 'uprising'. 'Being "arrested" in those days meant disappearing,' the Turkish Cypriot leader remarked later. 'Prime Minister Inönü believed that UNFICYP would help in my safe return, but his idea didn't work out. In the end I had to try and enter the Island once through Erenköy/Kokkina and a second time through Larnaca, when we were caught in November 1967 and sent back [to Turkey] without any charge of "responsibility for the so-called non-existent uprising or any other crime".'

The London *Daily Telegraph* editorialized: 'By now the intentions of the Greek Cypriots – if not Archbishop Makarios, then of the gunmen who appear to surround, defy and terrorize him – can hardly be mistaken. Are they not at best to reduce the Turkish minority to total subjection, stripped of all rights and protection? If it is the duty of our [British] troops to obstruct these plans, it will also be the duty of any UN Peace Force worthy of its name ... The gunmen want no peace force, because they want no peace. All they want from outside is the ring held against the threat of Turkish invasion while they finish the job.'

CHAPTER TWENTY-SEVEN

UNFICYP referees in Cyprus: Makarios warns the Colonels

*'Chaos umpire sits,
And by decision more embroils the fray
By which he reigns . . .'*

John Milton

WHEN THE first Finnish soldiers of the United Nations Force in Cyprus (UNFICYP) arrived at Nicosia International airport on 26 March 1964, they unloaded bicycles from their aircraft, formed up in battalion rank, and, led by their commanding officer, pedalled down George Grivas Dhigenis Avenue in the direction of the capital of Cyprus to join the Britons who were there already, wearing blue berets. People who lined the route that sunny spring day said that the sight of 700 soldiers in white helmets cycling purposefully to take up positions on the feuding island was 'most impressive'.

The Finns would be followed by volunteers from Australia, Austria, Canada, Denmark, Finland, Ireland and the UK, bringing the number up to 7,000 troops. Indian Army Lieutenant General Gyani commanded the force. He reported directly to the UN Secretary-General. Britain found itself making the largest contribution, both with personnel and logistical support. From that moment two classes of British soldier were created in Cyprus: those who were retained at the Sovereign Bases of Episkopi in the west and Dhekelia in the east, directly under British

British troops become UN Blue Berets.

The Finnish contingent of the UN Force go to work.

command, and those who wore the Blue Beret and whose orders came from the Secretary-General of the UN.

UN Resolution 186 laid out UNFICYP's mission. It was:

- To prevent a recurrence of fighting by assisting pragmatically in the maintenance of the ceasefire;
- To contribute to the maintenance and restoration of law and order, with particular reference to the security and well-being of the communities, as requested and agreed by them; and
- To contribute to the restoration of normal conditions.

But UNFICYP was given no military muscle to enforce its authority. It was a toothless tiger from the moment it was formed. That original mandate still applies.

Paragraph 7 of the Resolution, however, recommended that 'the UN Secretary-General should appoint a mediator in agreement with the Governments of Cyprus, Greece, Turkey and the United Kingdom and that this mediator should use his best endeavours with the representatives of the two Cypriot communities and also the aforesaid four Govern-ments for the purpose of promoting a peaceful solution and an agreed solution to the problem confronting Cyprus.'

No wonder the Greek Cypriot delegation cheered when Resolution 186 was passed, because it accepted that the Government of Cyprus belonged to the Greeks, and the Turks were no longer part of it. Even today, the Turkish Cypriot point of view can only be expressed in the UN by other governments, in this case, Turkey.

Moran says: 'The exclusion of Turkish Cypriots from international fora originates from this time.' Within 10 days of Resolution 186 being passed, the UN's General Gyani refused to intervene in one of the fiercest battles launched by Greek Cypriots, who used mortars, heavy machine-guns, bazookas and armoured bulldozers to assault the Turks in the small south-west town of Ktima.

A detachment of Royal Artillery, accompanied by Brigadier Donald Crane, was pinned down and trapped in a police station as they tried to negotiate a ceasefire. Later, the Greek Cypriots accused the British of protecting the Turkish community. British soldiers, despite the firing, tried to bring the fighting to an end. Greeks wearing steel helmets pointed their guns at them. One soldier was slightly injured

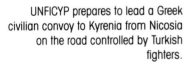

UNFICYP prepares to lead a Greek civilian convoy to Kyrenia from Nicosia on the road controlled by Turkish fighters.

when a bullet ricocheted off a wall. Captain William Bacon survived unscathed when a Greek bazooka rocket exploded near him as he was talking to a Turkish Cypriot civilian.

'Outgunned and outnumbered, 3,000 Turkish inhabitants of Ktima, ancient capital of the Paphos district, are fighting a desperate house-to-house battle for survival,' wrote Howard Johnson of the London *Daily Mirror* from the scene. 'Ninety-four British troops are helpless to do more than try to evacuate the wounded and dodge the bullets and mortar fire. Seventy of the men, of 18 Battery, Royal Artillery, are pinned down in a house in the market square. Twenty-four Royal Dragoons are isolated in the town in their Ferret armoured cars.

'The Greek Cypriot police chief said: "The forces of law and order will clear the town, disarm the Turks, and stop action only when the Turks completely surrender." In one incident, a Greek Cypriot armoured bulldozer threatened the house in which Royal Artillery troops were pinned down. Three times their officer shouted: "If you move any nearer, we will fire on you." Only when he gave the order for his men to aim their Browning machine guns did the Greeks pull back.'

A Canadian correspondent from the *Toronto Star* reported: 'Soon, weary British soldiers, armed only with persuasive tongues – and guns they aren't permitted to fire – will be there, wearing Blue Berets, trying to arrange a "peace". A UN resolution in far-off New York doesn't have much impact in Cyprus. The British Army is fighting a losing battle. And one wonders whether a United Nations force will do any better.'

A Greek Cypriot government spokesman said: 'Turkish insurgents continue to use minarets as machine posts. The forces of the state have no alternative but to consider such minarets as military targets in order to save the lives of innocent civilians. The Security Forces [Greek] are pounding the nests of the Turkish terrorists, forcing them to retreat from their original positions despite the protection afforded them by the intervention of British troops.'

When British General Richard Carver, who had replaced Major General Peter Young, arrived by helicopter in Paphos, the scene of another one-sided battle, 3,000 Greek Cypriots crowded him against a car. They shouted, 'English get out.' Only the intervention of a Greek police superintendent, Michael Papageorgiou, swinging a heavy cane at the demonstrators, saved Carver from harm. Later, British military observers confirmed that Greek Cypriots attacked the Turkish community without provocation. In hilly country in the north-west of the island, two British soldiers of the Life Guards died when their armoured car left the road and crashed. They were rushing to the scene of another Greek Cypriot attack.

On 5 March 1964, Templos/Zeytinlik and Kazaphani/Ozankoy, two villages in the Kyrenia district, were surrounded by Greek militia and threatened with destruction. Moving at night, down steep mountain paths, 12 TMT soldiers from Hilarion got through the Greek lines and entered the encircled area. Within hours, they broke the blockade and routed 200 Greeks, without assistance from British forces.

In 1964, however, the Security Council was so confident of the success of the UN Force, it set its mandate for six months only. UNFICYP continues to exist in 2009, 45 years later.

Of all the options which Makarios had reviewed, UNFICYP was the most acceptable, for it recognized him alone as the President, his authority as legal, Cyprus as independent and therefore, by implication, his right to change the Constitution and other laws as the Greek Cypriots saw fit. He and his supporters also believed now that Turkey would never dare attack.

With the establishment of UNFICYP, he

was convinced that the rights of intervention granted to the Guarantor Powers – Britain, Greece and Turkey – by the Treaty of Guarantee were no longer applicable. He considered UNFICYP his own military tool to prevent any violent responses from the Turkish Cypriots to his modifications of the Constitution and other laws he chose to reform. UNFICYP, he was sure, would stifle any opposition simply to keep the peace.

Makarios and his supporters believed that as long as UNFICYP fulfilled its very limited 'peace-keeping' mandate, Turkey would never again dare to exercise its rights under the Treaty of Guarantee. From now on 'the insurgents' – namely the Turkish Cypriots – could be controlled by a Cyprus government consisting exclusively of Greek Cypriots and backed by the United Nations.

Unfortunately for Makarios, all those assumptions were to prove incorrect during the next decade.

Nevertheless, the United States accepted UNFICYP as the least worst option to prevent Cyprus falling into the Eastern Block – providing Britain contributed the largest contingent and a British General was never less than second in command.

THE GREEK Cypriots now held all the reins of power and represented the Island in all foreign assemblies, especially the United Nations, where they could always count on the General Assembly. The Turkish Cypriots, confined largely to enclaves scattered throughout the Island, with no access to communications, had only one tiny port on the north coast through which they could acquire food and medical aid provided by Turkey, just 40 miles away across the water. They called the port Erenkoy (the Greeks knew it as Kokkina).

For the next 10 years UNFICYP soldiers were deployed Island-wide. They took up positions wherever there was 'a threatened minority', which usually meant the Cypriot Turks. There were other difficulties as well for the UN troops. Whose 'law and order' were they to 'maintain and restore'? Cypriot Turks, no longer part of the recognized Government, were managing their own affairs in their enclaves. What could UNFICYP do if the Greek Cypriot administration passed laws which Cypriot Turks deemed unconstitutional and refused to obey? After all, Cypriot Turks were never going to 'request' or 'agree to' anything of which they disapproved. As far as they were concerned the original 1960 Republic ceased to exist the moment they were no longer part of the state they had co-founded by international agreement. Equally difficult, therefore, for UNFICYP was how to implement the Security Council mandate which insisted the Force promote a return to 'normal conditions' and 'contribute to the security' of the communities in conflict.

Almost by definition, UNFICYP had its hands tied from the outset and could do little more than maintain the status quo. But as the Force could not act unilaterally, nor take preventive military action, it was unable to stop the Greek Cypriots from continuing their attacks and blockading the Cypriot Turks. Time and time again, UN soldiers who tried to prevent massacres by the Greeks were disarmed and marched away or left to watch and then to report the details of the incident. Blue Berets became known as 'umpires', and 'paid tourists'. It is a fact, however, that where there were British 'squaddies' and officers, hostile incidents were stopped and the instigators given 'short shrift'.

Leo Gordon Marchant of the Royal Signals, attached to UNFICYP, was posted to a small Turkish village (Anadhiou) between Polis and Paphos, which was surrounded by the Greeks. He was with a section of the 1st Battalion the Royal Green Jackets. 'While there I became very good friends with the Turks, found them to be a great people and I always tried to help them out – even if this meant bending a few rules,' he says.

Because there was no local electricity in the village, Marchant strung a power line from his small radio shack to the local café and plugged in some bulbs. These received electricity from his 1kw Onan battery-charging engine. He recalls: 'Everybody seemed pleased with the arrangement until this UN guy in charge of the area came up and told me it was "favouritism" because the Greeks in the adjoining village had no lights. I explained that I wasn't only a radio bod, but acted as "chief medic" as well and used the café for nightly "surgeries". I told him that I'd be delighted to treat the Greeks also, if they cared to visit. I got away without a reprimand and carried on.'

Meanwhile, at Kophinou, a small detachment of Royal Green Jackets was positioned twixt the Greek National Guard and a small Turkish village nearby. 'One evening the Greeks opened up, hitting the UN outpost with unerring accuracy,' Marchant remembers. 'When the CO of the RGJ at Polemedhia was informed, he instructed his men at Kophinou to remove their "blue" berets, replace them with the Light Infantry's green berets and return fire if they felt in danger! As soon as the Greeks saw the section taking off their blue berets and putting on green ones, all firing ceased!'

Cypriot Turks today acknowledge individual acts of bravery by the British members of UNFICYP. They also talk about soldiers who ignored the mandate, and provided humanitarian help to starving villages, against the wishes of senior non-British UN officers.

Peter Johnson, another signaller, has bitter memories of the British UN contingent's treatment by some senior officers and the UK government. While other nations' soldiers received a UN medal for their six-month tour of duty, 'we had to go begging for it, yes, begging for the bloody thing. We had actually gone there first in early '64, when it was our job to try keeping the peace, but then we were formed up as UNFICYP Signals Troop. Medals were handed out by the UN, but our Ministry of Defence at first said it was not a British campaign medal, later relenting.

'We were told to line up outside the Camp Commandant's office at 09.00, which everyone did – but in dribs and drabs, and put in position by an infantry sergeant major, a short, hairy arsed bugger, hard as nails. We lined up and eventually along came the CO. Trailing a boot step behind was a bombardier holding blue boxes piled high in his arms. Then we were told to hold out our hands. "Here, here," said the officer, giving us one each. Ceremony? It was a bloody disgrace. Still got the thing, up in the loft though.'

Did any British troops die in the early days of UNFICYP? Yes, claims Terry Devlin, a corporal from 7 Company RASC, who was based at the Eastern Sovereign Base, Dhekelia. 'When some riots started in Nicosia, our unit was dispatched at night to get there. We left as a convoy, but about five miles beyond Larnaca, near the old viaduct, we rounded a bend to see our lead vehicle burning in a clump of trees off the road,' he told the author. 'Somebody from one of the fighting Cypriot groups had poured oil on the road and our driver had skidded and crashed. He died in the fire. His parents came out to Cyprus and took his body home. I felt very bad as he had taken my place to drive the lead vehicle. He was 18 years old. Details of his death were kept hush-hush.'

On 24 April 1964, one of the TMT defenders at St Hilarion received a message from his father-in-law that Greek Cypriot irregulars had kidnapped his father, but UNFICYP was not in a position to help or prevent the attacks by 300 Greek Cypriot soldiers on nearby villages and the castle itself, which began next day at 03.00. The 25 *mucahit*, although outgunned and out-numbered, fought back until the 27th when the battle stopped. Six TMT members lay dead and six were wounded. UN Secretary-General U Thant immediately ordered UNFICYP to prevent similar events taking place again. His force set up permanent observation posts to provide early warning, but the UN soldiers never found the kidnapped Turkish Cypriot father and several others. It was a favourite ploy of the Greek militia to grab hostages. Sometimes they were released, but on this occasion, they were not.

FOR ITS apparent failures UNFICYP faced a barrage of criticism from all directions during the next 10 years. Its soldiers, dressed in the standard uniforms of their countries, except for their sleeve patches and distinctive blue berets, were seen as 'summertime soldiers'. When attacks took place, they could only put their heads down, wait for the shooting to stop, and then get up and count the casualties on both sides. Blaming the major powers for all the ills of this tiny Island had been a favourite Greek pastime, but now UNFICYP became the prime target for abuse. Very soon many of the UNFICYP soldiers began to think of their Cyprus tour as nothing more than 'our annual sunshine holiday'.

Cypriot academic Demetris Assos reflects: 'Grivas may have said that he was prepared to fight to the last man, but such self-consuming heroism would merely have accelerated the advance to partition, as there was no chance of an EOKA victory. It was [an error] to ignore Turkish objections. The Greek Cypriot leadership overlooked Turkish Cypriots' anxiety regarding their welfare in case Cyprus became part of Greece. The *enosists* thought the Turkish Cypriots would simply have to accept their fate as a minority. Not for a moment did they consider Turkey might concern itself with the Island's political future.'

Makarios believed that by creating UNFICYP, the UN Security Council had set aside the rights of intervention granted to

Turkey, Greece and the UK by the Treaty of Guarantee. The Greek Cypriots continued to contend that the Constitution and the provisions of other treaties were 'flexible and subject to change under changing conditions'; Turkish Cypriots argued the contrary. These diametrically opposed views illustrated the basic differences between the two sides.

Contrary to the Constitution of Cyprus, the Greek Cypriot House of Representatives now passed a bill in June 1964 establishing their own National Guard, in which all Greek males between the ages of 18 and 59 would be required to serve. General Grivas, who had returned to the Island uninvited, was given command of the new force by Makarios, with Greek mainland officers to assist.

As Commander of the National Guard, Grivas was back in his element, strutting in his customary uniform and proudly showing his supporters where he had hidden in the Spilia region during the 1955-59 EOKA conflict with the British. Spilia today is a 'freedom fighters' showcase for Greek Cypriots.

For the Turkish Cypriots to survive Greek attacks, the TMT had created a workable infrastructure to deliver supplies, relying on their needs to be met by Turkey. Vital to this operation was the tiny north coast port of Kokkina/Erenkoy, where the supplies arrived, after which they were smuggled through

At Kokkina, Turkish Cypriots are forced to live in caves.

Jimmy Keco Kutlay, one of the student volunteers, sits guard at Kokkina.

Greek lines to their surrounded enclaves by a network of back roads and country tracks. UNFICYP and the National Guard knew what was taking place, but could not stop it.

Celal Mahmudoglu, the owner of the *Eagle's Nest*, in Yeni Erenkoy in North Cyprus, talked eagerly with the author about Kokkina, the old Erenkoy. Almost every night he had taken his boat backwards and forwards across the strait to Turkey, nearly always alone, ferrying arms, food and medicines. 'In that summer – I can't remember the exact date – I was asked to carry a very special person from Turkey to Cyprus. He was Mr Denktas,' he said. 'He could not come here openly because the Greeks had warned he would be arrested. But he wanted to be with his people. The Government of Turkey, including the Prime Minister, Mr Inonu, advised him not to endanger himself, but he was very determined. That night, he came on my ship with only one other person, his bodyguard. They were both dressed in khaki uniforms, but Mr Denktas was wearing his favourite baseball cap.'

The three men began the 40-mile crossing in complete darkness, all ship lights switched off. They knew that it would be impossible to enter the blockaded port and another landing site nearby had been planned and notified to the party due to meet them onshore. If the Greeks intercepted them at sea, they had only two weapons with which to defend themselves. Denktas had a pistol in a holster strapped to his waist, while his bodyguard carried an old British Army Lee-Enfield .303 bolt-action rifle, loaded with a magazine holding five bullets. 'I don't think Mr Denktas was very well from being rocked in the boat,' Celal confided, 'but he tried not to vomit. He was very calm all the way.'

Navigating by the stars, they approached the coast. They had successfully eluded the Greek patrol craft and their radars. Celal anchored his boat in the coastal shallows and the three walked ashore, where they were met by a TMT group. Although Denktas was greeted with bear hugs, the young Turkish Cypriot officer in charge told the future president of the TRNC that he could not allow him to stay. It was far too dangerous and though Denktas would inspire the enclave, he would serve the cause better by returning to Turkey immediately, from where he would be able to keep the world informed about the Cyprus question. If the Greek Cypriots captured him, he would simply 'disappear', never to be seen or heard again.

Rauf Denktas confirmed Celal's tale in an interview with Johann Piliai of the *Journal of Cyprus Studies*. 'I tried to infiltrate in July 1964,' he said. 'I went to the Kokkina area by boat, but it was impossible for me to cross to Nicosia.'

Celal continued the story. 'Mr Denktas was very unhappy about the matter, but he agreed after a little time and so we sailed back for Turkey.' Three years later, on 31 October 1967, Denktas would make a second attempt to come home. This time he tried to land in the Karpas, but Greek Cypriot officers were there to grab him. Only after a great hue and cry by UNFICYP and the international community was he released from captivity. After several meetings with Glafkos Clerides, Makarios's friend and a former member of EOKA, the Turkish Cypriot leader was returned to Turkey to continue his exile. The following year Denktas was at last allowed back to the island to rejoin the Turkish community in North Nicosia. By then Grivas was no longer in command of the National Guard.

GENERAL GRIVAS had never had time for the UN Peace Force deployments. They were to be ignored at best and disarmed at worst if they interfered with his plans to attack the enclaves. The key to realizing his dream and establishing *enosis* was the elimination of Kokkina. The UNFICYP Force Commander, watching the build-up near the port, asked Makarios on 5 August what was being planned. Nothing, lied the Archbishop. Only the day before, 1,500 Greek soldiers had been assembled on their battle start line. They had six 251b cannons and two four-barrelled Oerlikon 20mm guns in support.

On 6 August 1964, after consultations in Athens, Grivas ordered his National Guard to take up positions on the high ridges above Kokkina/Erenkoy, supported by Greece's 12th Tactical Group, which included the 206th Infantry Battalion, 31st Raider Squadron and various artillery units. On 8 August, he launched his offensive using several thousand

General Grivas plans his next move against Turkish enclaves.

well-armed troops, believing the port was a potential bridgehead for a Turkish invasion.

Kutlay 'Jimmy' Keco, later the owner of *The Grapevine* in Kyrenia, was in Kokkina/Erenkoy when the Greek assault began. During the sixties, he attended Leeds University, where he studied textile engineering, but he admits that his university days were spent attending parties, watching *That Was The Week That Was* and participating in all the other activities that marked the rebellious youth of the 'flower power' generation that changed the face of Britain.

With 321 other student volunteers, he had returned to Cyprus on 29 April 1964 to defend the port. During the weeks ahead, they came ashore in groups of 12 from small fishing boats that had sailed from Turkey. None of the students had had more than one month's military training.

Standing behind the bar of *The Grapevine*, his outward appearance was still that of a bearded rebel. With his black hair falling to his shoulders, he belied his role as an amateur fighter. In near accentless English, 'Jimmy' spoke in short phrases, his words chosen carefully, but frankly. Without any bravado, he told the author: 'A legend was written at Erenkoy by a handful of Turkish Cypriots studying abroad. They rushed back to fight bravely side-by-side with the local community against an 18,000-strong enemy.' His face was a mask hardened by an unforgiving sun. The students did not beat the Greeks, but nor did the Greeks beat them.

'During the August attacks we were fighting night and day. We didn't have the heavy guns the Greeks had, the biggest of ours were 80mm mortars and there were only four of them. My team was placed on a hill looking down on the Greek soldiers. We held our position for days, but then we had to withdraw. It wasn't the Greeks who drove us back, it was because we had run out of ammunition and the forest was on fire. We had to escape.'

He paused and looked at the bar's surface, as if in deep thought, before continuing: 'How we survived, I don't know. Looking back I'm amazed what we fought with. Most of our weapons were very old, but we had some Bren guns that were good and also home-made machine guns that were effective. Whatever happened, we were never going to surrender. Each of us saved a grenade and would have blown ourselves up rather than be taken alive.'

In 2009, no longer the owner of *The Grapevine*, 'Jimmy', now 66, is a farmer near Alagardi beach. Still the president of the Erenkoy Fighters' Association, he arranged the annual pilgrimage of the former defenders to where they fought, but Erenkoy remained a Turkish enclave, only reached by sea or overland escorted by UNFICYP, when the veterans marked the 45th anniversary and visited the graveyard where their former comrades were buried.

The Turkish military authorities knew full well that Kokkina/Erenkoy was a vital stronghold that could not be allowed to fall in 1964. Noting the dire situation of the defenders, Ankara placed its armed forces on alert. By 17.00 on 8 August, battles were raging furiously, when two TAF F-100 Super Sabres made two low-level passes over the Greek lines. Just minutes later, more Super Sabres arrived and began to strafe the ground troops, wreaking havoc.

As the hour wore on, increased numbers of Turkish jet fighters criss-crossed the sky, making pass after pass, knocking out targets at will. A Russian-built patrol vessel was sunk near Kokkina's breakwater. Another raced for safety in Xeros harbour, but it was tracked and destroyed just as it got there.

American Angie Bowie, whose father, Lieutenant Colonel George Barnet, worked for the Cyprus Mining Corporation, says: 'I was out in our garden when the Turkish planes flew over. When they turned towards the jetty, I crouched next to a mint bush at the back gate. One of the jets chased and strafed a Cypriot boat. Then my mother screamed at me, "Get inside, if they see you, you'll be a target.' I didn't argue.'

Associated Press photographer Hal Mclure was on the scene and his pictures were flashed around the world. Fifty-five Greek Cypriots were killed and 125 wounded.

Meanwhile 12-year-old Angie was packing the family's passports, money and jewellery and hid them in a packet of cornflakes. 'Are you ready, Mom?' she shouted. 'Dad's going to be here in a minute, for us to leave. Remember he called about the evacuation?' Her mother Helena had lived with her husband in the same house for almost 20 years and was sad at leaving. 'The company – CMS – evacuated its overseas staff and their families to Skouriotissa. We fled in convoy to the mountains,' Angie recalls. 'For a week we knew nothing. There was no communication – except what we heard on the BBC's World Service. Then we went back to Xeros and life continued.'

The Greeks claimed there were more than 60 attacks by F-100Cs, F-100Ds and F-84Gs. Flying through smoke, the lead F-100D of one formation was hit by heavy AA fire, forcing its pilot to eject. The pilot, Captain Cengiz Topel, badly injured, was captured alive by Captain Kalenterides and Lieutenant Tsertos of the Greek forces. They said that he was rushed to hospital, but died during treatment. A Danish UN team collected and examined his body and accused the Greeks of burning him alive.

On 9 August, the Royal Hellenic Air Force ordered four F-84s from Souda Air Force Base to Cyprus to challenge the Turkish control of the Island's airspace. To increase the range of the fighters, technicians had to remove their rockets and launchers. Their journey went unnoticed, it appears, by both the RAF and TAF. Two flew towards Nicosia, and the other pair headed to Mansoura and made a couple of passes, only to find themselves encountering National Guard gunfire. The F-84 Thunderstreak crews considered their options and decided to return to their Souda base before their tanks ran out of fuel.

With the threat of an imminent invasion by Turkey, Makarios ordered Grivas to pull back. With Interior Minister Georghadjis Yorgadjis, he left the scene of battle by helicopter, narrowly escaping death when Turkish fighter pilots ignored their aircraft because they thought UN observers were flying it.

A member of his government, Tassos Papadopoulos, later President of the Cyprus Republic, shared the General's fury and advocated the immediate extermination of all Cypriot Turks should Turkey intervene. On 11 August, the combatants agreed a UN-supervised ceasefire. Four Turkish destroyers arrived off Erenkoy to evacuate casualties and replenish the defenders' food and medical supplies. How many Turks lost their lives has never been revealed, but the quiet cemetery there is filled with graves. The Greeks reported 52 National Guardsmen died.

The Manchester *Guardian* fumed: 'The President [Makarios] has no right to jeopardize the peace of the whole of the Levant merely in order to assert his hold over one mountain village. Nor has he done himself or the cause of peace a service by treating with disrespect the UN forces that came at his request to help him. The UN's good name matters to the whole world. If the President defies the United Nations he defies us all.'

UNKNOWN TO Makarios, however, Turkey had been bluffing about invading. Military analyst Tom Cooper argues that while 'the Turkish armed forces looked formidable on paper, they were ill prepared to deal with the troubles in Cyprus. The Turkish military was seriously overstretched and the Air Force and Navy were badly in need of modernization. With all the difficulties on the country's borders, any full-scale operation in Cyprus would have required resources the country did not have at the time. The Turkish Air Force had only three squadrons of fighters that could be considered modern and combatworthy. The air transport capability consisted of just three C-47 units, and a handful of helicopters.'

Despite the ceasefire, both Greek and Turkish warplanes continued to over fly the Island on reconnaissance missions, although one flight of Greek Thunderstreaks was intercepted by RAF Lightnings from Akrotiri and ordered to return whence they came. The Greek side immediately complained that the British were biased in favour of the Turks, whose aircraft were never warned off. Had they passed over British Sovereign territory, no doubt they would have been.

The London *Daily Mail* approved the Turkish air attacks: 'It has been half-forgotten that the Turkish raids were launched in defence of Turkish positions and under extreme provocation ... The eyes of the world seem at last to be opened to Makarios's real nature.' When the UN commander, General Thimayya, was eventually allowed into Kokkina, he found 800 starving civilian refugees. Horrified by the scene, he ordered immediate relief supplies.

From the United Nations, the British representative in the Security Council pleaded with Whitehall on 12 August for guidance. 'What is our policy and true feelings about the future of Cyprus and about Makarios? Judging from the English newspapers and many others, the feeling is very strong indeed against Makarios and his so-called government and nothing would please the British people more than to see him toppled and the Cyprus problem solved by the direct dealings between the Turks and the Greeks. We are of course supporting the latter course, but I have never seen any expression of the official disapproval in public against Makarios and his evil doings,' his cable said. 'Is there an official view about this, and what do we think we should do in the long run? Sometimes it seems that the obsession of some people with "the Commonwealth" blinds us to everything else and it would be high treason to take a more active line against Makarios and his henchmen. At other times the dominant feature seems to be concern lest active opposition against Makarios should lead to direct conflict with the Cypriots and end up with our losing our bases.

'I ask these questions, partly for background and partly because it really would be useful to know how far you feel we really are inhibited from taking up a more actively hostile attitude to the Greek Cypriots. Their representative here is, as you know, a horror, and even the Communists are thoroughly fed up with him, and it is therefore really not necessary for us to do anything more to weaken his position.

'But it is curious and sometimes very frustrating to sit in the Security Council and walk around the UN and have to listen to all the stuff about the wickedness of the Turks and their threats of invasion, when I and all my staff know very well what the real state of affairs is and how much Makarios and co. are to blame. One can say what one thinks of course to a few people, but one cannot produce the evidence or argue the case fully with the vast majority of my UN colleagues so long as the official public attitude seems to be not to say anything rude about Makarios and his gang.

'These, I realize, are not entirely easy questions and I suspect that the answers may well depend on differences of view and attitude at your end, revolving round such questions as the Commonwealth and the truth about our defence needs. Nevertheless I hope you can give us some of your real thoughts, if only for our private consumption. It would be a help to know what the thinking and the planning is and how far and for how long it is going to be

necessary to continue to behave in, what at times does appear an unrealistic way and contrary to the popular feeling in Britain.'

Soon afterwards the Swedish UN contingent was replaced by the Queen's Company of the British Grenadier Guards. Colonel Oliver Lindsay, CBE, was a young officer at the time. He told the author: 'The area looked and felt under siege, with Turkish Cypriots crammed into tents and makeshift shelters. A massacre was a real possibility.' Questioned about the UN Force's failure to stop the Greek Cypriot assaults, he replied: 'UNFICYP was not meant to fight. Fire could only be opened if attacked, and then only as a last resort. We were there to pacify, observe, report and act as a quick reaction force to prevent incidents developing into war.'

With the failure of Greek forces to capture Erenkoy, the Athens government decided to strengthen its capability in Cyprus and authorized an infantry division of 8,000 troops to move to the Island in secret, disguised as students and tourists, Turkey, meanwhile, instituted a programme to modernize its military resources from top to bottom.

Because of its limited mandate UNFICYP could never be an effective means to ensure peace. But British and Canadian contingents, the only full-time professional soldiers in the 'peace force', played an evenhanded game. An example of this occurred on 14 May 1966, when UNFICYP Command directed Major Bill Hamilton, the OC of the Canadians in Tjiklos, to supervise the dismantling of three newly constructed Turkish Cypriot bunkers dominating the Nicosia–Kyrenia road in the Kyrenia Pass. They contravened the ceasefire, UNFICYP said, and represented a potential provocation. Colonel Yaman, the local TMT commander, was ordered to destroy the bunkers within 24 hours. The fighters did not comply, so the Canadians rolled up their sleeves and did the job for them.

David Willard, a Canadian Blue Beret,

mused: 'Serving as a peacekeeper on this war-torn island was at times satisfying and enjoyable and at other times heartbreaking and full of frustration. Dealing with Greek and Turk came easily for the most part and many times I wondered how these great folks came to be at each other's throats and capable of such atrocities against each other.'

While the political situation stagnated in a morass of claims and counter-claims, UNFICYP did what it could to prevent incidents, small though they were, as an uneasy peace settled on the Island, but mainland Greece was passing through a politically unstable period, which culminated in a coup d'etat by the Army on 21 April 1967. Colonel George Papadopoulos became the country's dictator. Like Grivas, he wore his extreme right-wing credentials alongside his rows of medals. He had little time for Makarios's flirting with third world countries and relationships behind the Iron Curtain. By all accounts, he would have preferred to pray in a Mosque next to a Turk than bow and kiss the hand of the Archbishop.

General Grivas believed that with the military in charge in Athens he would have a green light to resume another full-scale assault on the Turkish Cypriot enclaves without having to consult Makarios or declare his hand to UNFICYP.

IN NOVEMBER 1967, Grivas decided to make one last major push for final victory – and *enosis*. Following a dispute over Greek Cypriot police patrols, he mounted a massive artillery attack against two Turkish villages Kophinou/Geçitkale and Bogaziçi, near Famagusta. He then sent in his National Guard. They surrounded several platoons of the Royal Green Jackets, part of UNFICYP, and ignored their protests.

One isolated Blue Beret platoon was ordered at gunpoint by the National Guard to hand over its weapons and vacate its position.

Some of the UN sections obeyed, but not Corporal Divine and his men. They sat obstinately in their trench and defied the Greeks to do their worst. Another section, commanded by Corporal Bradford did the same, but watched their personal clothing and equipment being stolen from their nearby tents. While the Greek soldiers were enjoying their robbing spree, the section's radio operator tried to get a message through to UNFICYP HQ, but was spotted by a Greek officer. The latter switched off the A41 radio set and slashed the cables to the headset with a knife. The operator, determined to protect his property, grappled with his Greek superior, according to Michael Dewar, despite his badly cut fingers in need of urgent medical attention. At this point the National Guard moved out.

Once again, the Turkish Air Force swooped and Ankara growled, for the second time threatening to invade and, if needs be, go to war with Greece. America stepped into the storm and helped defuse the situation by mediating an agreement. Grivas's attacks ceased immediately and Greek troops in excess of those permitted by the Treaty of Alliance were removed from the Island. By order of Colonel Papadopoulos, Grivas was recalled to Athens, taking 10,000 soldiers with him. A further demand that the Greek National Guard must be dismantled in exchange for immediate Turkish Cypriot demobilization fell on deaf ears.

Makarios no longer saw a future in pursuing *enosis* and welcomed the General's departure. Holding extreme right-wing opinions would run counter to his ambitions to be acknowledged as the grand political leader of the world's non-aligned nations. Grivas had dreams, too, and they did not include a place at the top table for Makarios, whom he considered was ungrateful and a traitor to the cause for which EOKA had fought in the Fifties. With the backing of the junta, he began plotting the prelate's over-throw.

Makarios antagonized Grivas even more by promising to compensate the Turkish villagers for deaths and damage – which he never did – and suggested Denktas and Clerides meet outside Cyprus in Beirut in an effort to settle the Island's differences. 'The result was a very close agreement on local autonomy,' Denktas remembers, 'but was rejected by Makarios because I had not accepted minority status for my people and he had not managed to get rid of the Treaty of Guarantee.'

In December that same year, Turkish Cypriot leaders announced a 'transitional administration' – *Geçici Kıbrıs Türk Yönetimi* – to govern their community's affairs, which included an elected legislative assembly composed of the Turkish Cypriot members – *in absentia* – of the original Republic's House of Representatives and their Communal Chamber. The TMT, established to counter EOKA before the Island gained independence, became their army and police force. By this stage, there was *de facto* partition of the island. While Makarios remained the 'official' President of Cyprus, his authority stopped at the Turkish enclaves. The violence continued in fits and starts and UNFICYP did its best to stamp it out.

Nevertheless tentative feelers continued to reach out to bring the Turkish Cypriots back into the fold and efforts were made to heal the wounds of the two Island communities. Then, on 13 December 1967, Makarios gave his backing to King Constantine's counter-coup to overthrow the 'Colonels' in Greece. Makarios, whose authority was being challenged by the Army in Athens, saw the king as a unifying element of Hellenism, alongside language and religion. To the surprise of many, a month later, on 13 January 1968, he said he wanted to build bridges with the Cypriot Turkish community and announced it would be given a 'Charter of Rights'. He also granted Cypriot

Turks freedom of movement throughout the Island.

President Makarios and Rauf Denktas talked, tried to find ways to settle their dispute and made concessions. However, Greek Cypriot extremists worked to turn the clock back. In his Athens apartment Grivas sulked and plotted to oust the Archbishop from the presidency and scupper any efforts to create unity.

ON 31 AUGUST 1971, Grivas returned secretly to lead his new organization – EOKA-B – to terrorize government supporters. Again, Grivas hid from security forces as he had done when the British were after him. Both times, he was never short of female companionship, despite his strictures on his gang members to avoid personal relationships with the opposite sex. His first mistress was Mrs Eli Christodoulides. The affair was conducted with the knowledge of her husband, who viewed the relationship as an honour as 'The Leader' was a guest in their house in Limassol. Diana Mavros, also of Limassol, was his second mistress. Her mother boasted to friends of their close 'friendship'.

While still in hiding, Grivas died, aged 75, of natural causes on 27 January 1974. At the exact moment of his death, like Elvis Presley, he was sitting on a lavatory in Mrs Christodoulides's home, while she was in the kitchen, preparing a dish of boiled beef and carrots for his dinner.

The deposed Bishop of Paphos – Yennadios – conducted the funeral. Among the 100,000 mourners was General George Denisis of the Greek Army who commanded the National Guard in Cyprus. Makarios was not represented. He was relieved by Grivas's death and gave an amnesty to all EOKA-B members, but terrorism did not cease. That 100,000 who turned out to mourn their hero showed that his *enosis* aims had not died with him.

Nicos Sampson, one of the mourners,

Greek Generals attend Grivas's funeral.

'bawled like a baby', one observer noted. He now saw himself as the natural successor to the EOKA-B leadership, but instead the leadership fell to Greek Army Major Assoils Karakas, a relative unknown to the Cypriot people.

An historian says Greeks today have 'fables about Grivas that will outshine even the heroic legends of ancient Hellas', but Nicos A. Pittas, writing in the *Cyprus Mail* on 4 April 2005, takes a different view: 'The EOKA fighters were engaged in a struggle for a goal that was strategically misguided and unachievable, using methods, including terrorizing civilians, that were extreme and unnecessary and in many ways counter-productive to achieving the realistic goal of an independent and democratic bicommunal republic.'

By the time of his death, Grivas's reputation had sunk so low that the Greek Cypriot House of Representatives was threatening to brand him 'a common criminal' unless his guerrilla activities ceased. As late as December 2008, Limassol Municipal Council rejected a request to build a museum dedicated to the EOKA leader, despite the plans having met the entire town's building requirements. 'We

cannot give our signature for a project that in any way glorifies Georgios Grivas Dighenis as that would be inconsistent and incompatible with our values and morals,' commented Tasos Tsaparellas, the Council spokesman for the majority AKEL party. 'The site cannot be disassociated from the entire work and role of Grivas in the ensuing period of illegality and terrorism.'

TWO MONTHS before Grivas's death, politics in the Greek mainland became increasingly divided between left and right. In November 1973, Brigadier Dimitrios Ioannides, the commander of the Military Police, overthrew the government of Colonel Papadopoulos and appointed General Phedon Gizikis as the new President and Brigadier Gregoris Bonanos as Commander-in-Chief of the Armed Forces. Ioannides, the real power in the new government, had served in Cyprus as part of the Greek Army contingent between 1963 and 1964, but had not become one of Makarios's fans. He saw him as devious and manipulative and so he chose to give his full backing to EOKA-B. While in Cyprus he and Nicos Sampson had become close friends and many believe that he encouraged the 'Murder Mile' killer to hone his skills as a psychopath against the Turks in Omorphita and elsewhere.

By Spring 1974, Makarios had survived three assassination attempts, one of which former High Commissioner Sir Peter Edward Ramsbotham recounts vividly: 'Makarios was very popular, of course, amongst the Greek Cypriots. On the great Byzantine Church feast days, there was his hieratic figure on a hot, hot day, with all his robes on, holding a sceptre. He was the last surviving priest-king. He believed, I think, that he was protected by providence, and in a sense he was.

'I remember an extraordinary, rather miraculous escape, from assassination in 1970 – 8 March was the date. Early that morning I woke up to the crackle of machine-gun fire. In the mornings, he was always the Archbishop and in the afternoons he was the President. He was just taking off in his small helicopter from the Palace to attend some ceremony in a monastery in the south somewhere. The would-be assassins, who probably came from Greece, had stationed themselves on the flat roof of a house nearby and opened fire at almost point blank range at the helicopter, not even grazing the Archbishop on their side, but riddling his Greek pilot, almost killing him, on the other side.

'Somehow, the pilot managed to land the helicopter in the street and Makarios commandeered a passing car and rushed to his house. The gunmen escaped. I immediately drove up to see him there. There was a weird atmosphere. You could see that a coup, in a sense, hadn't come off, and yet had, and there were weird, unknown figures moving around in the offices. It was one of those strange affairs. Makarios could escape from awkward situations like that.'

Colonel Dimitris Papoastolou of the National Guard and the former Interior Minister Polycarpos Georgadjis were believed

The wreckage of the helicopter shot down by EOKA-B in an attempt to kill Makarios.

Makarios survives a second assassination attempt by a roadside mine.

to be behind the attempt to murder the Archbishop-President.

Not wanting his luck to run out, Makarios eventually decided to act against the junta in Greece. It was a brave gamble with high stakes at risk. On 2 July, six months after Grivas's death, he wrote to Gizikis, accusing the junta of plotting against him and the government of Cyprus. He demanded the withdrawal of the 650 Greek officers who were commanding the Cyprus National Guard. He released his letter to the media to publicize and underline his message.

Makarios had always nimbly danced himself out of difficulties in the past, but now he had completely misjudged the political mood in Athens and Ankara. He underestimated the probability of a coup that could depose him and, expecting the Soviets and friendly Arab states' support, believed Turkey would not dare invade without America and the United Kingdom changing their red light to green, which would inevitably raise tensions in the Cold War, argues historian Vassilis Fouskas.

On instructions from his government, the Greek Ambassador in Nicosia went to see Makarios and told him that the decrease in the numerical strength of the National Guard or the withdrawal of the Greek officers would weaken the defence of Cyprus in case of danger from Turkey. Makarios listened, but concluded, as he explained later: 'This was an argument which, even though it appeared logical, was not convincing because I knew that behind this argument other interests were hidden. I replied that as things developed I considered the danger from Turkey of a lesser degree than the danger from them.'

Later, Makarios added: 'I never thought they'd be so stupid as to order a coup against me. In fact, to me it seemed impossible that they wouldn't consider its consequences. I mean Turkish intervention. At the most I thought they might do such a thing by making a deal with Turkey, that is, authorizing Turkey to intervene so that Greece could then respond, to be followed by partition and double *enosis*. It took some time for me to realize that Ioannides simply acted out of a lack of intelligence.'

Meanwhile, talks between Glafcos Clerides and Rauf Denktas had continued and settlement of their differences seemed close. On 9 July, they had parted on friendly terms with a promise to meet again soon.

On Saturday, 13 July, Greek President Phaedon Gizikis met his Chief of Staff, the Ambassador of Greece to Cyprus and the National Guard commander to review Makarios's demands. A few hours later, Athens told the Archbishop that another meeting would be held on Monday. But Brigadier Ioannides, the strongman behind Gizikis, had already told his supporters in Cyprus to stand by to act on his coded signal. 'The reference in the communiqué to a second conference was deceiving,' Makarios said later. 'For a while on Monday I was waiting for a reply to my letter. The reply came, and it was the coup.'

CHAPTER TWENTY-EIGHT

Greeks massacre Greeks: 'Makarios is dead'

'They change their sky, not their soul, who run across the sea.'
Horace

ALEXANDER HAS gone to hospital. The coded phrase was flashed to all senior National Guard commanders in Cyprus by the Greek junta in Athens. It signalled the start of its carefully rehearsed military coup against Archbishop Makarios. It was 08.00, Monday 15 July 1974 when 10 vintage Russian T-34 tanks began softening up the Presidential Palace with a bombardment of cannon fire. Behind the tanks, troops of the 31st and 32nd Mountain Commando Regiments, with Constantinos Kombokis in charge, waited in their Marmon armoured cars to rush the building, bringing an end to any remaining resistance. Because EOKA-B supporters and other soldiers encircled the palace grounds, Kombokis was sure nobody could escape. Simultaneously other government buildings were taken over, including the country's telecommunications' centre.

By 08.30 state radio and television was in the hands of the perpetrators of the coup. It went off the air for 10 minutes and then began telling listeners:'The National Guard has intervened in order to solve the problematical situation ... Makarios is dead ... In a short while there will be announcements by the National Guard to the Cypriot people.' The CyBC radio announcer was speaking literally with a pistol at his head. Martial music followed. From all visible signs it appeared the

President's body must lie buried somewhere in the palace ruins. By 09.30, the National Guard's were in charge of Nicosia Airport. The coup had succeeded without a hitch, except, except ...

Whether the Archbishop had got wind of the plot is hard to know, but he managed to escape from the west side of the palace, accompanied by his ADC Nicos Thrasyvoulou, another officer, Andreas Potamaris, and a third man. They moved quickly and reached the Pedios riverbed, where they caught up with Captain Takis Tsangaris, who, with loyal presidential guards, was holding off the National Guard. They stopped a passing car and demanded to be driven far from the palace, but the vehicle stalled and they had to halt another. In this, with the prelate lying on the floor, they drove first to Kykko Monastery in the Troodos Mountains, always just ahead of the roadblocks being put down by the National Guard. At Kykko, they heard Paphos was still in the hands of the Archbishop's supporters and decided they must head there to join them.

Like other Cypriots, Greek Cypriot Member of Parliament Rita Catselli had no idea if Makarios had survived. She wrote in her diary: 'Is Makarios alive? Is he dead? The Makarios supporters arrested, the EOKA-B supporters freed ... I do not shed a tear, why

The Presidential Palace after the coup. In the bottom right-hand corner, a BBC crew can be seen going about its business.

should I? Does the stupidity and fanaticism deserve a tear? There are some who beg Turkey to intervene. They prefer the intervention of Turkey. My God! Everyone is frozen with fear ... the old man who asked for the body of his son was shot on the spot ... the tortures and executions at the Central Prison. Nothing is sacred to these people, and they call themselves Greeks! We must not keep that name any longer.'

NICOS NICOLAIDES, a technician with CyBC, the state broadcaster, and an enthusiastic ham radio operator, was off duty in his Paphos home when he heard his employer's bulletins about the coup. They shocked and angered him. Despite the risk to his life, he supported his President and wanted to demonstrate his support. He decided to launch 'Free Radio Cyprus' from his home workshop, broadcasting material compiled by local journalists. Armed loyal volunteers stood guard outside the house in what today is known as Nicos Nicolaides Street.

When Makarios and his entourage reached Paphos, they sought safe haven in the Cathedral. News of the Archbishop's presence spread quickly. Nicolaides grabbed a portable tape-recorder and went to meet him. He suggested the deposed president broadcast that he was alive, contrary to whatever the coupists were telling the people. The Archbishop agreed and recorded a message in both English and Greek. Nicolaides left and began broadcasting the tape, again and again. *'I am Makarios, President and your leader, I am not dead. Rise against the traitors, against the junta and its collaborators.'*

The Western Sovereign Base of Episkopi/Akrotiri had heard about the coup at 08.15. Initially, Nicosia was placed 'out of bounds' to all British troops. As fighting spread, Limassol, Larnaca and Famagusta were added. In Limassol alone, there were some 4,000 service dependants and UK civilians living off base and there was great concern for their safety. Not that they were in general danger from direct attack, but rather as innocents caught in any spin-off action.

Group Captain K. J. Parfit, RAF, describes what happened at a British nursery school near the Polimedhia crossroads: 'An Episkopi officer's wife told her class of 70 children, all under the age of five, to sit quietly on the floor, while men were being killed outside. Later, with RAF Police help, she personally delivered every one of her charges safely home to their parents.'

The Coldstream Guards Battalion of UNFICYP saw the heavy fighting taking place in Limassol as the National Guard swooped on Greek Cypriot police stations and took them over. The Guards were powerless to intervene as the UN mandate prohibited action in purely Greek Cypriot internal matters, but they tried to persuade Turkish Cypriots not to get involved. They, however, began strengthening the fortifications in their section of the city.

Renata Frosdick was a pupil in Form 3A2 of St John's School, run for children of British service personnel living in Limassol. In her diary, she jotted down what happened to her on 15 July: 'I was sitting on the wall between my house and my neighbours', when a man with a machine-gun came dashing down the street firing. His first bullet just missed my brother's head and hit the veranda bars and rebounded onto the fence. My mum dragged Darren and our dog into the house. When the firing stopped I, being curious, opened the slats to see if the gunman had gone. For that I was told off and sent to my room!'

Meanwhile the Greek Colonels appointed 39-year-old Nicos Sampson, the 'Murder Mile killer' of EOKA days, president in place of the Archbishop. He was their only choice when, at 15.00, Bishop Gennadios of Paphos arrived to take the new man's oath of office. Other nominees had disappeared during the course of the morning. Various other EOKA-B favourites were given portfolios in the new administration and then began the systematic slaughter of those who had voiced any support for Makarios. They included fellow soldiers and police officers. Denktas declared Sampson's appointment 'as unacceptable as Adolf Hitler being made President of Israel'. The Athens junta bellowed that the Island was

Nicos Sampson takes over as President of Cyprus.

now 'Elliniki Kipriyaki Dimokratia' – the Hellenic Cyprus Republic.

Without official recognition, Sampson held the post for a mere eight days. At his press conference on 18 July, Sampson showed his emotional instability, lack of knowledge and, in a moment of recklessness, offered to show foreign newsmen a collection of Makarios's torture victims. All proved fake when the journalists investigated, He also stressed that 'the Turkish community is in no danger at all'. Recalling Sampson's actions in 1963 and 1964, Denktas was unconvinced and called on Turkey and Britain to oppose him. As it happened, Sampson's forces did not kill a single Turk during the period of the coup.

In Kyrenia, Rita Catselli noted: 'I saw the Greeks massacring their Greek brothers under the Greek flag ... They were not hesitating to crush anyone who was not supporting them ... An order was given to a Greek soldier with a machine gun to shoot at the Kyrenia Metropolit. He was killed by another Greek when he did not obey the order ... two children were killed by the Greek soldiers. The father asked for the bodies. They killed the father as well and buried all in the mass graves ... In the Nicosia General Hospital, the soldiers from Greece did not allow the doctors to treat the wounded people who supported Makarios ... If these people from Greece are Hellenes, we should stop calling ourselves Hellenes ... mass arrest of those not supporting them started.

'The roads of Kyrenia were full of armed persons sent by the Greek junta ... I have never thought that one day I would be arrested by brother Greeks and put in the Kyrenia Castle. I pray for justice and freedom to come back ...'

YUCEL ASAN, a Turkish Cypriot, was employed by the RAF as a head waiter in the in-flight catering section at Akrotiri. He had recently rented an apartment in the port city of Limassol in preparation for his marriage due to take place on 14 August. Because the Sovereign Base authorities considered the coup an internal matter for the Republic of Cyprus to handle, British subjects were ordered to give no assistance to their employees – Turk or Greek – to leave, but an RAF sergeant quietly disobeyed his superiors' instructions and agreed to take Yucel home. He told his friend to hide in the boot of his car and then drove out.

On the way, Greek Cypriot militia flagged down the sergeant. They demanded to see his identification papers and hear his reason for leaving British territory. The RAF NCO gave them plausible answers and volunteered to open the car's boot so that they could search for themselves and see he was not taking weapons to their enemies, 'the terrible Turks'. Stepping out of the car, he joked: 'You can't trust those buggers. That's why I'm going to sit with my family in our married quarters. You never know, the Turks might just try to take them and the others hostage to get us to intervene.'

'You support us?' a guard asked.

'Completely,' the sergeant replied, patting the soldier's back. 'Only yesterday I was telling my chaps that I couldn't understand why you fellows had waited so long to boot out Black Mak.'

'Very good, sir.'

'Hey, do you want to check the boot? I'll open it if you like so that you can see for yourself that I'm not carrying any weapons or stuff to aid your enemy.'

The Greek Cypriots moved closer, almost surrounding the sergeant, each staring deep into his eyes. Their leader chuckled. 'That will not be necessary, sir.'

The daring bluff worked. The guards smiled, shook the sergeant's hand and accepted him as one of their supporters, casting only a cursory glance at the car's rear seats before waving him on his way. For the next 30 minutes, the sergeant drove at a steady speed, raising a friendly hand at every Greek Cypriot he passed. In Limassol, he stopped the car in a quiet back street, some way from the Turkish quarter, separated by a barrel line of sand-filled oil drums since 1963. The town was eerily silent. He looked around to check nobody was watching before he opened the boot to allow Yucel to get out.

'From here, you're on your own, mate,' he told his friend. 'I'll catch you later. Good luck.' They embraced quickly and Yucel ran off. It was the last time they saw each other. Not far away, Greeks were fighting each other. Whether the sergeant would have been so helpful had he known his passenger was a member of the TMT, the Turkish Cypriot resistance movement, was something no one would ever know.

As the newly appointed British European Airways' operations control superintendent for the eastern Mediterranean, 'Taff' Lark found himself on the jump seat of the first Cyprus Airways BAC 111 from Athens to fly into Nicosia Airport after the coup. On arrival he found there were no Customs or immigration staff and only a minimal number of Air Traffic Controllers. The terminal, however, was rapidly filling up with passengers hoping to get off the Island. 'Our plan was to operate a shuttle service between Nicosia and Athens as aircraft and crews became available, to uplift as many passengers as possible in the shortest time,' he says.

Meanwhile a radio monitor in Israel had heard the Makarios broadcasts and notified the BBC in London to confirm whether the voice really belonged to him. Verification was swift in coming. News bulletins were re-written at stations around the world and the international community acted to save Makarios.

AT THE CyBC headquarters in Nicosia, the majority of staff were still sitting on the floor of a long corridor, hands on their heads. They had not been allowed water, food or the use of lavatories since the National Guard stormed the station. Several broadcasters had been kicked until they co-operated. Despite what international stations were saying about Makarios's survival, they were forced still to report his 'death'. With the arrival of a Colonel Athanasios Liasconis, interrogations began. Mr J. Hadjijoseph, the Deputy Managing Director, was told he would be in charge of the staff allowed to carry on working, but everything that went on air would have to be approved by the Colonel.

According to the acting Head of Television, Colonel Liasconis, 'surrounded by numerous armed officers and commandos, moved his headquarters into CyBC-Radio's continuity studio and imposed his rule on everything and anything broadcast and televised'. It was his responsibility to 'censor, check, reject, authorize every single word, every single lyric of a song, every breath going on the air, for our own good, of course'. He advised the staff to cooperate with him and carry out his instructions, otherwise 'other persuasive measures would be taken for safeguarding the general good'.

News bulletins were to be discontinued. Only when he decided that there was news would it be broadcast and then it would be written by his officers. For the time being, all scheduled programmes must be replaced by Greek military marches and patriotic music – nothing with 'revolutionary rhythms', he continued. A station executive asked how anybody could be expected to differentiate 'revolutionary' from 'patriotic' music. Liasconis replied that that was up to the staff to determine, but he would know if anyone tried to trick him. 'I am very intelligent, very observant and I have worked for YENED, the Greek Army Broadcasting Network,' he added. 'I have experience in this field and your future is in my hands.' The Colonel went about his business with zest, even checking tapes of classical Greek plays. Every so often a new bulletin would arrive, delivered by a high-ranking navy officer from the National Guard Headquarters.

IN LONDON, Foreign Secretary Callaghan watched the situation develop, but decided it was not in British interests to intervene, unless UK subjects were threatened. Although many had been taken to the safety of the Sovereign Bases, so far none of those left behind had been threatened.

Late in the afternoon of 15 July, Major MacFarlane of the Coldstream Guards attached to UNFICYP received a message from a Greek Cypriot that Makarios had survived. He was asked to transmit the news to UN HQ in New York. The British officer replied that his first priority would be to prevent Makarios from falling into the hands of the National Guard once it was *proved* the Archbishop was alive. His second priority would be to fly him in an unmarked Whirlwind helicopter of 84 Squadron RAF to the UN's St Patrick's Camp.

Makarios thanks UNFICYP Major Richard MacFarlane of the Coldstream Guards for giving him refuge.

Although still dubious as to the authenticity of the information, MacFarlane nevertheless transmitted the message and asked to meet Makarios, which he did that evening. At the meeting the Archbishop quizzed Major MacFarlane about events in Limassol. He believed that what happened there could decide the success or failure of the coup. He suggested he went to the city next day after holding talks with Mr Weckman-Munoz, the Secretary-General's Special Representative to Cyprus, and Indian General Dewan Prem Chand, UNFICYP Commander. Permission was refused.

Shortly afterwards the Archbishop arrived at St Patrick's Camp and spent the next few hours in the Officers' Mess while negotiations were held between HQ UNICYP, UN HQ and the British Foreign Office, where Callaghan did not know where to take Makarios. After consultations with US Secretary of State Kissinger in Washington, it was eventually agreed that an RAF Argosy aircraft from the Western Sovereign Base would rush him first to Malta and safety before deciding the next move.

Escorted by Wing Commander Hodgkinson, Makarios was airborne at 17.02 Cyprus time, believing he was bound for London. When he landed in Malta and was told he would be staying the night there, the prelate was not pleased. Next morning, Hodgkinson told him he would be taken to Britain where he could book an onward flight to New York to address the UN. To avoid crowds of his supporters causing any disturbances at London's Heathrow Airport, Makarios was landed at RAF Lyneham in Wiltshire and taken by car to Downing Street to meet Prime Minister Harold Wilson and then to the Foreign and Commonwealth Office for discussions with James Callaghan. Soon afterwards he was on his way to America.

THE FREE Radio Cyprus had increased its broadcasting range by hooking up with the official CyBC transmitter at Coral Bay, but it became an easier target to track and attack. On 16 July, the Hellenic Navy patrol vessel *Lesvos* blasted it off the air with shellfire.

Nicos Nicolaides, who arranged the clandestine Makarios broadcasts, died from a heart attack in 1995, but his son still stresses the historical significance of his father's radio station. 'The broadcasts were very important, as many governments had accepted the President was dead and were on the verge of recognizing the Sampson regime,' says Fotis Nicolaides. 'Because of my father and those who helped him, this didn't happen.'

ON THE second day, at 16.00, Captain Parfit says guards at the Episkopi Sovereign Base reported a heavy concentration of National Guardsmen with heavy field pieces on the main approach who had blocked the western end of the road – until it was cleared by unarmed RAF Police 'with faces as white as their hat covers'. The National Guardsmen then moved through the Sovereign Base Area towards Paphos, no doubt to engage the town. 'They moved very slowly and warily through the SBA and, when inside the confines of Episkopi, became models of military conduct; silent, helmets on, sitting erect and looking to the front as they passed the Station Commander who took some salutes and "inspected" them,' Parfit smiles.

At 22.15, the aircraft carrier HMS *Hermes*, accompanied by the guided missile destroyer HMS *Devonshire*, sailed for Cyprus at high speed. 41 Commando Group Royal Marines from Malta were embarked on *Hermes* and tasked to land at Dhekelia and strengthen the Sovereign Base defences. After the Marines disembarked the next afternoon, both vessels left Famagusta, heading towards Kyrenia.

On Wednesday afternoon BEA's marketing director Charles Stuart landed at Nicosia Airport from London. 'We were so short-handed that he was asked to lend a hand – and did, for 18 hours,' Taff Lark says. 'The following morning he and I went to the British High Commission to get an assessment of the situation. The advice given was that the new provisional president, Nicos Sampson appeared to have the situation under control and we should advise our passengers to carry on with their holidays and enjoy the sunshine.'

Stuart and Lark had barely returned to the airport when relief pilots and crew arrived from the Dome Hotel in Kyrenia, where they had been staying. One of them, a veteran of the Second World War, reported he had seen Turkish Cypriots clearing large areas of land north of Nicosia and was convinced they were preparing for a parachute drop.

While Makarios was on his way to America, Turkey's Prime Minister Bulent Ecevit had dashed to London for urgent consultations with British Prime Minister Harold Wilson and Foreign Minister James Callaghan. Ecevit feared Nicos Sampson would turn his threats into militarily actions against the Turks of the Island. He asked Britain to fight off the threat singularly or jointly with Turkey under the two countries' right to intervene under the 1960 Treaty of Guarantee. Britain, he pointed out, had sufficient troops at the Sovereign Bases to act. Prime Minister Harold Wilson and Foreign Secretary James Callaghan listened, but C. M. Woodhouse, an expert on Cypriot matters, concludes: 'The Labour Government behaved in a pusillanimous and evasive fashion.'

In Washington, the Nixon administration, fraught with the Watergate affair, established a Special Action Task Force to monitor the crisis and coordinate America's response. But, says Ellen B. Laipson, the author of 'A Quarter Century of US Diplomacy', 'One complicating factor in managing the crisis was that in the spring of 1974 the administrative decision was made to transfer the office covering Turkey, Greece and Cyprus from the Near East to the Western Europe bureau at the State Department. This meant that higher-level officials, at the Deputy Assistant Secretary level and above, were making key decisions although they may not have been well schooled in the complex history of Cyprus.

'US official statements failed to strongly condemn the coup. Instead, noncommittal statements that the political situation was unclear characterized the American response. Suspicions about possible American support for the coup were reinforced when the US Ambassador to Cyprus, Roger Davies, met with the Foreign Minister of the Sampson regime on 18 July, reportedly the only foreign emissary to grant him such recognition. On subsequent days, officials continued to equivocate on whether the United States still considered Makarios the legitimate President of the Republic, and whether the junta in Greece was responsible for the coup.'

From an American point of view, the worst-case scenario that could follow the coup was war between Greece and Turkey. Secretary of State Kissinger was cool: past tensions between Athens and Ankara had been defused easily whenever the US talked to the rival parties. Others in the State Department were more cautious. They felt Bulent Ecevit, the Turkish Prime Minister, was less pliant than his predecessors and might decide that the time for intervention in Cyprus had arrived.

Nevertheless Kissinger, who had little or no knowledge of Cypriot affairs, sent Joseph Sisco, a State Department official, as his emissary to persuade the leaders of the two countries to hold back from any use of force, by cajoling or threatening them. Dashing between the various capitals, Sisco found himself getting nowhere.

IN NICOSIA, Sampson, drunk with power, commanded local journalists: 'Support the respectable Greek officers. Be sure the day has come to unite us with our Motherland. Those who oppose Greece will find themselves before public courts.' True to his words, the new 'government' opened special courts, conducted swift trials of Makarios supporters, found them guilty of various crimes against the state and executed them within minutes by firing squads at the Central Prison.

At the CyBC, Colonel Liasconis suddenly resurrected Makarios without explanation. His latest news bulletin claimed the Archbishop was in London and had met Turkish Prime Minister Evecit over dinner with Foreign Minister James Callaghan where they plotted to overthrow the Greek Colonels in Athens, but their scheme would never succeed. To add a touch of journalistic colour, the 'news' said they had eaten lamb chops. Station announcers were also ordered to read postcards and telegrams, allegedly from the public at large with many others signed by prominent chairmen of societies, union leaders, star athletes and priests, all congratulating the new Sampson regime for freeing them from the 'vicious Archbishop'. All these messages had been written by EOKA-B members.

ON THURSDAY, 18 July, Nicosia Airport was allowed to re-open. A National Guard commando unit, wearing green berets and shorts, strolled around the entrance, as two Olympic Airlines aircraft from Athens brought more mainland troops. Dressed as civilians, they pushed their way through a crowd of desperate foreign tourists hoping to leave. Colin Smith of *The Observer* asked one of the uniformed commandoes what was happening. Smiling, he replied: 'Now everything is alright. Now Cyprus is a Greek island. Before it was very mixed up.'

In the Turkish quarter of Nicosia, Kubilay Ali saw a break in the internecine fighting and grabbed the opportunity to drive to Lapta/Lapithos, which had been a 'mixed' village until 1963, to collect a security guard from The Celebrity Hotel that was under construction. He had been trapped there alone since the coup and his safety could not be guaranteed. On the way there and back, Ali was stopped twice at checkpoints manned by the National Guard, with tanks in reserve. The soldiers allowed him through without difficulties. Nearer his destination, he was flagged down by some EOKA-B irregulars, who insisted on searching every nook and cranny of his car, while prodding him with their rifles. 'It was a most frightening experience,' he reflects.

'When I arrived at the hotel site,' he continues, 'I had time to have a quick coffee at the nearby seaside coffee restaurant. The owner, Mr Panayi, was crying. He told me his son was an officer responsible for guarding the Presidential Palace and had been wounded on the day of the coup. He had heard nothing since and was very worried. To this day, I wonder whether he and his son were reunited.'

With little time to argue with the British Government, the Turkish Prime Minister returned to Ankara from London to give the order to his Armed Forces to prepare to act alone. The Turkish General Staff replied that they could land in north Cyprus the following Saturday, 20 July.

Whether to build bridges or to threaten, Sampson sent his 'Foreign Minister' Dimis Dimitriou to meet Rauf Denktas, the notional Vice-President. He was admitted to an outer office in the Turkish Cypriot leader's sandbagged premises near the Green Line and told to wait. Denktas, surrounded by his close associates, continued to stroke his spaniel Banjo while he told his assembled company to expect a Turkish invasion shortly. 'The air force will drop leaflets and there will be all types of warning,' he predicted. There would be no 'massive blitz' and he was sure the first Turkish troops would go ashore somewhere on the north-western coast of Morphou Bay. He was wrong on all counts. The military command in Ankara had not shared the details of their invasion plans with the portly Turkish Cypriot lawyer. Some hours later Sampson's envoy Dimitriou was told to go away.

That same Friday afternoon, the 19th, a Cyprus Airways Trident was inbound from Rome with only crew on board. Lark and Stuart were listening to the air traffic control channel, awaiting the arrival of a VC-10 from Khartoum, diverted to pick up passengers. 'At approximately 16.00 the captain of the CYA Trident called up and urgently requested clearance to divert to Beirut,' Lark says. 'When questioned as to the reason, he said that he was descending through 12,000 feet and had just passed over a large fleet of warships and landing craft. He had made a circuit of these ships and seen that they were flying the Turkish flag. He was advised to break his transmission and land at Nicosia as planned … his was the last aircraft to land at the airport.'

When the airport closed for the night, after a long, exhausting day, Lark returned to his bedroom at the Hilton Hotel to catch up on sleep. At the Ledra Palace, about 200 journalists refreshed themselves at the hotel bars before trying to find bed space. Photographer Terry Fincher of the *Daily Express* volunteered to share his fourth floor room with *The Observer*'s Colin Smith. They were puzzled why Michael Nicholson and his TV camera crew were nowhere to be seen. That was because the ITN representatives had crawled into their room, where just after midnight, they had received a phone call from Peter Snow, ITN's diplomatic correspondent in London. In coded language, he alerted them to a possible invasion by Turkey in the morning. Just after 03.00, they tiptoed in their stockinged feet past the doors of the BBC correspondents, and in the car park they pushed their car out on to the road so no one, absolutely no one, should hear.

At about the same time, US Secretary of State Kissinger was warned by William Colby, the CIA Director, that Turkey was about to intervene militarily in Cyprus. He suggested Turkish forces would land near Famagusta and Kyrenia, with the aim of joining up and taking control of the north-west area of the Island. They would also try to capture the

Turkish Cypriot section of the capital and Nicosia's international airport. Later, Kissinger confided: 'We didn't think they'd act this fast.'

At the United Nations Security Council, meanwhile, Archbishop Makarios addressed delegates and indicted the Athens junta for instigating the coup. 'It is clearly an invasion from outside, in flagrant violation of the independence and sovereignty of the Republic of Cyprus. The so-called coup was the work of the Greek officers staffing and commanding the National Guard. I must also underline the fact that the Greek contingent, composed of 950 officers and men stationed in Cyprus by virtue of the Treaty of Alliance, played a predominant role in this aggressive affair against Cyprus. The coup of the Greek junta is an invasion, and from its consequences the whole people of Cyprus suffers, both Greeks and Turks.'

He also expressed his appreciation of the British Government, 'which made available a helicopter to pick me up from Paphos, transfer me to the British bases, and from there by plane to Malta and London. I am also grateful to the Special Representative of the Secretary-General and to the Commander of the Peace-Keeping Force in Cyprus for the interest which they have shown for my safety. My presence in this room of the Security Council was made possible thanks to the help given to me by the British Government and the representatives of the Secretary-General, Dr Waldheim.'

Kissinger listened to the Archbishop carefully. No fan of Makarios, he was happy to see him ousted for what he perceived as his left-wing opinions, which equalled anti-American. To have a right-wing Greek Cypriot administration suited him, as long as Turkey did not intervene, as Ankara was threatening. He was counting on Sisco to prevent Turkish action.

It was not until 02.00 on the morning of 20 July that Sisco was eventually granted a meeting with Turkey's Prime Minister Ecevit and Foreign Minister Turan Gunes. They talked and argued, but the American diplomat did not realize his hosts were stretching the conversation to buy time so that they could tell him at 04.30 that the Turkish military was already on its way to land in Cyprus. Nobody, not even the CIA, had predicted that the war would start before Sunday the 21st at the earliest.

IT WAS 05.30 on Saturday when Taff Lark was woken in his Hilton bedroom by the sounds of guests shouting and distant explosions. He pulled open the curtains of his window that faced north. 'The morning was a beautifully clear one,' he remembers. 'That moment I saw a Turkish Hercules, silhouetted against the mountains in the background, dropping parachutes. Still groggy from lack of sleep, I mouthed a suitable expletive, drew the heavy curtains, pulled the mattress into the bathroom – as explosions might shatter the window – and promptly went back to sleep.'

ITN's Michael Nicholson wrote later: 'On the outskirts of Nicosia, passing through the Turkish Cypriot suburbs, we saw families leaving their homes, hurrying for the shelters, carrying children and blankets and food. We did not need to stop and ask why. They had heard for themselves over the radio from Istanbul. The invasion had begun and we were

Stranded foreign tourists at the Ledra Palace Hotel.

a long way ahead of anyone else in covering it.'

CyBC went on air at its usual time of 06.00 with a short prayer, followed by Greek music. Twenty-five minutes later, Colonel Liasconis rushed into the announcer's studio, shoved a news bulletin into the nervous broadcaster's hands and told him to interrupt the transmission. Voice trembling, the announcer declared: 'Cyprus without any warning whatsoever has been invaded by the Turkish Army.'

CHAPTER TWENTY-NINE

Foreigners flee:
a very hot summer

'The deed is all, the glory nothing'
J. W. von Goethe

SUMMER SUN was slowly spreading over the deep purple mountains of the Kyrenia range and the burnt yellow plain below, when the first propeller-driven C-130 Hercules and C-47 Douglas transports began dropping their sticks of Turkish paratroopers from a cloudless sky at 06.07. As they floated towards the ground, north of Nicosia, crowds of vehicles, driven by eager Turkish Cypriots, waited to greet and drive them to their fighting positions. Even a bread van had been commandeered. As 29-year-old Sami unbuckled his parachute harness and adjusted the pack on his back, he smiled broadly at a British reporter. 'I am very happy,' he said in fractured English. 'We are here to look after our Turkish brothers in Cyprus.' The local welcoming committee cheered.

In the small hours, Rauf Denktas had slipped into a tiny Bayrak radio studio in North Nicosia and recorded a message that was to be broadcast as soon as Turkish forces landed. The station was about to assume a value beyond its size. It became a true public information service. Most Turkish Cypriots expected the invasion, but the question was when? Not even Denktas knew the exact time. He had been told only that the Turkish Army was on its way. His tape was laced into a player and his message was ready for broadcast at the push of a button.

Turkish paratroopers descend north of Nicosia.

Nicosia had been uncannily silent through the night. On the Turkish side of the Green Line, tension ran high as the population prepared for war. Every male adult collected arms, many made for use in the First World War, and joined 'The Fighters'. At first light irregulars from both sides began firing at each other half-heartedly. The Turkish Cypriots still had no idea where the mainland troops would land or when exactly.

At 03.30 Brigadier Frank Henn, the Chief of Staff at UNFICYP HQ, had notified the Canadian contingent in the Nicosia district to be prepared for any eventuality as 'visitors' from the North were expected. At 04.49 Turkish Air Force RF-84F reconnaissance took off from the Incirlik base.

At 06.00, a Bayrak Radio engineer pushed the button to start Denktas's taped announcement: 'Our century-old aspirations are bearing fruit and our day of salvation is at hand,' it told listeners. 'The Turkish Army has landed in Cyprus. This is a limited action against the Greek Junta and is not directed against the Greek Cypriot people, our fellow guardians of the independence of the Island. Stay peacefully at home and thank God for allowing us to witness this day.' His words were repeated many times on 20 July.

At the same time, Prime Minister Bulent Ecevit was on Turkish radio telling his people: 'The Turkish Armed Forces have started landing in Cyprus from the air and sea. Let this operation be auspicious to our nation and to all Cypriots. We believe that by acting in this manner we shall be rendering a great service to all mankind and to peace. I hope that our forces meet no resistance and that a bloody clash is avoided. We in fact are going to carry peace and not war to the island, and not only to the Turks but also to the Greeks. We have had to make this decision after we had exhausted all diplomatic and political methods. Meanwhile, I wish to express my gratitude to friends and allies, particularly the United States and Britain, which have displayed well-meaning efforts to have the dispute settled through diplomatic methods.'

Sixty minutes earlier, Turkish Air Force fighter jets and Turkish Navy ships had begun pounding Greek targets on the north coast.

Operation *Attila* was under way. Three hours later the first of 6,000 Turkish Marines and 40 tanks landed on Pentamili beach, five miles west of the port of Kyrenia/Girne, and gathered for their push inland.

Now the UNFICYP Observation Posts along the Green Line were reporting the build-up of light gunfire between the two sides. The UN troops were in a very vulnerable position caught in the middle. At 05.50, the first UN OP surrendered to Turkish Cypriot 'fighters'.

Turkish land forces storm ashore, east of Kyrenia.

Retired Turkish Marine Major Mesut Gunsev shows the author the beach where Turkish Forces landed.

At the offices of *Machi*, Nicos Sampson's newspaper, the presses were rolling off copies with a comforting message for readers: 'It is impossible for Turkey to intervene in Cyprus. Turkey's resources are limited.'

Nobody had told 'President' Sampson that the National Guard radar station at Apostolos Andreas began tracking a dozen Turkish warships steaming towards Cyprus territorial waters at 00.15. They had set sail from Mersin on the south coast of Turkey. As the craft came closer, they split into two groups, one steering north-west towards Kyrenia and the other towards Famagusta. By 04.00, the larger group was hovering 15 miles north of Kyrenia. However, at National Guard Headquarters in Nicosia, according to reliable sources, a duty major was still assuring his fellow officers: 'There is nothing to worry about. We have been told from above [Athens] that it's just another show of force by the Turks. We can relax.'

In Kyrenia, a Greek naval officer acted on his own initiative and ordered his two Greek patrol boats out of the port to investigate. Minutes later Turkish jet fighters swooped in attack formation. One of the boats limped back severely damaged and the other was sunk, leaving one survivor to swim back to the nearest beach.

The Turks planned to capture Kyrenia/ Girne, then move down the main road to the capital, linking on the way with Turkish Cypriot fighters who held St Hilarion Castle, and join up with the paratroopers. Overhead, Turkish F-84 fighter jets commanded the sky after striking Nicosia Airport and smashing two empty Cyprus Airways airliners, both Tridents. The shell of one of them remains there today.

'Early morning on 20 July – about 06.00 – I was on the roof of our flats overlooking Famagusta beach and I saw jets come screaming in towards the city from the sea. At first I thought it was the RAF on a training exercise,

The Turkish Cypriot fighters support the Turkish Army advance.

The rusting Cyprus Airways Trident from 1974 at Nicosia Airport.

until they started strafing the beach. They were shooting at Greek forces who were approaching the Turkish community who lived in the old part of town,' says Kelvin Nichols, whose parents were attached to the British Forces in Dhekelia. 'The following few days were fantastic ones for an impressionable young boy of 16. There was a lot of confusion and we weren't allowed to go to school, a journey of 12 miles. Instead we spent our days swimming and fishing as normal, but our catch consisted of shrapnel and bullets. I still have a large shell somewhere in my parents' house.'

IN SOUTH Nicosia, the sound of sirens at last began to scream across the city. CyBC broadcast orders that every able-bodied soldier must return to their unit. 'Greeks of Cyprus, the great hour has arrived,' the station railed. 'Our national dreams, our age-old aspiration will now be fulfilled.' At the General Hospital, Maroulla Siamisi prepared to receive war casualties. There would be too many arriving too fast to treat satisfactorily. Morgues would run out of space and many Greek Cypriot soldiers would have to be buried in mass graves, her husband among them. There was no time to keep proper records.

On the plain below St Hilarion Castle, Michael Nicholson and his ITN crew stood by their car and filmed the first Turkish para-troops floating slowly down from the cloudless sky. Their pictures would appear on the evening news bulletin from London.

At the Ledra Palace Hotel, from their east-facing window, Colin Smith and Terry Fincher, two of the 380 foreign occupants, watched 12 lumbering transport aircraft fly in sedate circles dropping paratroopers on the central plain. 'The Turks drifted towards the parched earth with impunity,' he reported. Most of the other 150 newsmen were still asleep – until a bazooka shell smashed into the hotel, killing two Greek soldiers. Seconds later the electric-ity was cut, killing the only telex machine the journalists could use to send their stories to their news organizations.

Michael Nicholson's ITN team, stranded on the plain between St Hilarion and Nicosia, because their car had run out of fuel, tried to catch a lift in camera vehicles driven by craggy-faced John Bierman and white-haired Michael Sullivan. Both BBC reporters, they were returning to the Ledra Palace. They responded by raising two fingers at their commercial rivals and drove on.

As the BBC men disappeared in a swirl of dust, they left Nicholson to get the only TV pictures of the Turkish paratroopers dropping from the clear blue sky. 'A thousand para-troopers were popping white into the sky, mushrooming on to Cyprus: by happy default we were witnessing an airborne invasion,' says Nicholson. 'We filmed them landing, we filmed them assembling, we filmed the red and gold Turkish flag hoisted triumphantly and then we followed as the brigade moved to Geunyeli within eyeshot of Nicosia, some few miles distant. Turkish Cypriots ran out of their bunkers and cellars to cheer them, and brought them food and water; children carried their packs, their ammunition, their rifles and machineguns; and, as luck would have it, the very first officer I pointed the microphone at spoke English back to me. It had become that sort of day.'

DEPENDING ON the radio station, Cypriots were either urged to defend themselves against 'the brutal and barbaric aggressors' or fight alongside 'our brothers from the mainland'. While CyBC's reports verged on the hysterical, adlibbed some of the time, the Bayrak men at the microphone were models of calm. They spoke in crisp, clipped English voices, controlled and modulated, reading from scripts. It was as if they had studied Lord Reith's handbook on broadcasting behaviour and had arrived on duty wearing dinner jackets with red roses in their buttonholes. However, the bulletins from both sides were confused and served only to spread fear and anger from one side of the Island to the other. 'Invasion' and 'intervention' became words that identified those who supported one side or the other.

Greek Cypriot civilians panicked as the Turkish, American-built C-130 Hercules continued to drop their loads every 90 minutes, but even more frightening were the low-flying Phantoms, the F4s of the Turkish Air Force. In flights of three, they spiralled away after releasing their rockets and bombs, which demolished targets in sheets of flame. The Turkish pilots were very confident of

Dropped by helicopters, Turkish troops prepare to counter Greek attacks.

success. They knew they were unlikely to encounter any enemy fighter aircraft, because the nearest Greek air base was on Rhodes, at the extreme limit of a fighter aircraft's range.

Turkish Forces were also using helicopters adventurously. Two days before the war began, 72 transport UH-1 helicopters had been assembled at a temporary base at Tasuçu, the southernmost point of mainland Turkey, under the command of the 2nd Army's Helicopter Regiment. During the night before the invasion men and material were loaded and, at exactly 07.07, the first squadron headed for Cyprus. Approaching in V-formation, 10 helicopters were damaged by ground fire as they neared North Nicosia. Later in the day, they changed tactics, coming in low at treetop level, and only two more helicopters received hits.

When TMT fighters first saw them, they thought they were carrying UN observers; nobody believed that fully loaded helicopters could fly from the mainland to Cyprus and then, without refuelling, return to their home bases.

Eighteen-year-old conscript Private Andreas Metaxas, on duty near Nicosia, saw what was happening, but was ordered by his commanders not to fire his Russian-made, 12.7mm DShKM anti-aircraft gun. Still unable to believe Turkey was invading, his commanders convinced themselves that the fighter aircraft and paratroopers were part of a NATO airborne exercise. Metaxas chose to disobey his superiors. For 10 minutes he followed a Turkish Air Force RF-84F swooping and strafing Greek positions ahead of the advancing paratroopers and it was time for him to respond. He fired his weapon and watched tracer rounds head towards the fighter plane. Its pilot, realizing he was being peppered with shrapnel, turned and took up an attack position against the young gunner. His aircraft screamed as he put it in a dive and aimed his missiles to eliminate the threat.

Pilot and gunner fired almost simultaneously. Metaxas survived the duel. Lieutenant Ilker Karter, the Turkish pilot, did not. The RF-84F hit the ground near Agyrta village and exploded. An orange fireball of burning jet fuel with metal shards rose upwards as if it were part of a slow-motion film.

THE GREEK forces, until now divided between the Tactical Reserve Force of 4,000 Makarios supporters and the 10,000 of the Greek Cypriot National Guard, loyal to the Colonels in Athens, tried to put aside their differences and wanted to fight, but they were ill-prepared and riven still with differences between themselves. At first, however, General Bonanas, Chief of the General Staff in Athens, ignored demands from ELDYEC (the Hellenic Forces in Cyprus) to counter-attack. He curtly replied: 'Turkey attacks Cyprus. But we are Greece.' Confusion reigned in the ranks of the junta.

Before General Grivas left Cyprus in 1967 he had drawn up plans for the Greek Army to defend the Island and counter any Turkish invasion. He had prioritized the defence of potential beachheads by key units, while others were to storm the Turkish Cypriot strongholds in and around St Hilarion Castle. At the same time, specially trained forces were to strike against the headquarters of TOURKDYK (the Turkish Forces in Cyprus) in Geunyeli.

Neither of the Grivas plans – codenamed *Aphrodite I* and *Aphrodite II* – was implemented, according to Greek historian Vassilis Fouskas. The Chief of the Cyprus National Guard Michael Georgitsis dithered for over two hours before ordering his troops into action at the Turkish landing beach, west of Kyrenia. Rather than advance on the Turkish Cypriot strong points in the Kyrenia Mountains, Major Constantine Kompokis, the officer commanding the forces assigned to that mission, kept his units in Nicosia to protect the puppet regime of Nicos Sampson from perceived threats by pro-Makarios forces. Only ELDYEC soldiers threw themselves at the Turkish Army contingent, but got no nearer than a mile from Geunyeli before they ran out of steam early on 21 July. Without air support and reinforcements from Nicosia, they became sitting targets for the screaming jets of the Turkish Air Force.

Due to the incompetence of their senior commanders, the first Greek Cypriot units – two companies of the 251st Infantry Battalion, supported by a platoon of five T-34 tanks seconded from the 23EMA Medium Tank Battalion – did not arrive in the area of the landing beach until 10.00 to engage the Turks, who had brought ashore a regiment, initially accompanied with only M-113 armoured personnel carriers. Although subjected to intense fire by the National Guard from positions overlooking the beach, the Turks were not to be dislodged.

'The initial stage of the landing was harder than we imagined it would be,' Mesut Gunsev, a retired Turkish Marine Corps major told the author. 'The Greeks recovered from their surprise quickly. They had been convinced any attack would not occur until Monday morning, but our Prime Minister, Bulent Ecevit, gave the order to intervene while he

was still flying back to Ankara from his unsuccessful talks in London with the British Prime Minister Harold Wilson and Foreign Secretary, Mr James Callaghan. As we were fighting our way to Girne, we came under heavy fire from Greek soldiers in the mountains. They were very clever fighters. When we brought out our aircraft to bomb their positions, they put their fluent Turkish-speaking officers on our radio net to confuse our pilots and misdirect the bombs. This caused us some difficulties. At one stage of the operation, our commanders had to order the planes to curtail their attacks. The Greeks were interrupting our communications and directing our fighters to attack our positions, not theirs. It was a very clever ruse, I must say.

'As soon as our commanders found out what the Greeks were doing, they told us, the officers on the ground, that the pilots would now question us on the radio to answer a specific question about a particular soldier in our group before doing anything we asked. As we knew all our men personally, only we could give the correct reply. That way the pilots could authenticate our messages and act on them.' At an especially tense moment at the height of the battle, Major Gunsev was asked a question to which he had forgotten the answer. 'I had to work hard to persuade my commander to ask me another to which I could give the right reply,' he laughed.

'A major difficulty for us in that first phase of the operation was telling who were real civilians and who were soldiers. Many Greeks stripped off their uniforms and put on civilian clothes and then began to operate as snipers from the roofs of schools and even churches. That is the wrong way to behave, because innocent people get killed. It was bad.'

During the conversation, Gunsev mentioned a Belgian woman, Nadia Brunton. She lived in Karmi/Karaman and later became known as the 'queen' of the village, which sat just below St Hilarion Castle, overlooking

Kyrenia. He said that soon after the Turkish forces came ashore at Yavuz Cikarma Plaji, now called Karaoglanoglu, they set up a military headquarters at Snake Island. It was there he met Nadia for the first time. She told the military commanders that hundreds of civilians were caught in the crossfire of the battle and she requested safe passage for the non-combatants, whom she wanted to bring down from the western villages of the Kyrenia range. 'She was a very brave woman. While all this was going on, Nadia managed to find her way down to meet us and ask to be allowed to perform her humanitarian work. Permission was granted and she brought out the civilians. We felt we could trust her. She was a very gutsy lady.'

He added: 'To the best of my knowledge, she was the only person to photograph our beach landing in the rush to come ashore; we did not have time to arrange for photographs to be taken. The ones you see today, I believe, are hers.'

The author asked how Greek prisoners were treated. 'All the enemy soldiers we captured were treated honourably,' Gunsev replied sharply, as if he were suggesting they were maltreated. He paused, took a deep breath and continued: 'During the first 24 hours of the operation, some may not have been given food and water. Until we became organized on shore, we were all short of supplies. What we had, we shared.'

As the Turkish forces gradually gained the high ground, many retreating Greek Cypriot soldiers were in disarray and seeking refuge wherever they could. In Lapta, Ephrosini Proestou first hid 12 of them in her house and later in a nearby cave. Panicos Paralimnitis, one of those soldiers, said later how 'grandmother Ephrosini' helped. 'We spent one night in an orchard, then she led us to a safer place, a cave not too far away from her house. She was scared but always willing to help us out,' he explained. 'She did her best to boost our

morale and keep our spirits up.' But, as Turkish troops rounded up Greek Cypriot soldiers, a tip-off led them to Mrs Proestou and the men she had sheltered. All were taken to Kyrenia Castle as Prisoners of War, where a Turkish Cypriot officer recognized her as the woman who helped his mother give birth to him. He organized her release and return to the Greek Cypriot-controlled areas. She died in 1993, aged 89.

Once the Turkish forces moved from their beachhead and headed to link up with their paratroopers north of Nicosia, they faced some of their severest opposition from Greek Army fortifications in the mountain villages. Both sides battered each other with all the arms and munitions at their disposal. How Karmi/Karaman had survived for Europeans to rebuild and renovate six years later amazed the author.

At the CyBC studios, Colonel Liasconis and his men were rushing out news bulletins to maintain the morale of their listeners, or so they thought, based on their experience of radio propaganda. Their bulletins, written at military headquarters and telephoned into the station, claimed 'the invaders are being defeated on all fronts ... the Turkish paratroopers who landed at Mia Milea have been eliminated by our heroic men ... the Turkish marines have been thrown back into the sea and their bodies lie scattered on the beach'. In addition, the newscasts included details of the locations to which Greek forces were headed. Turkish monitors listened and relayed the information to their raiding aircraft and they made sure their enemy's soldiers never made it.

ONCE NATIONAL Guard commanders recognized that the Turkish invasion had begun in earnest, a Greek commando unit, transported in old city buses driven by Greek Cypriot Military Police, was rushed to Nicosia Airport to mount a defence. The small RAF contingent based there had left earlier for

Dhekelia to escape the fierce air strikes of TAF F-100 combat aircraft that followed.

The Greek troops set up positions in and around the main terminal building, just as a convoy of Turkish soft-skin trucks arrived at the north end, 500 metres from them. Now they dared the Turks to advance so that they would be caught in a path of overlapping fire. Although the approaching infantry spotted the Greek positions, they moved forward regardless, only to have their advance rapidly blunted by heavy machine gun fire on three flanks. As their forward elements neared, shells, shot with pinpoint accuracy, pounded them. Hidden in a damaged civilian bus parked on a high bluff above the runways, Greek artillery spotters could see every move made by the Turks and were able to direct their fire without wasting shells. From the air the Greek vehicle appeared derelict and was therefore safe from counter-attack.

Taking heavy casualties, the Turks pulled back to re-group, while the Greeks considered a counter-attack. Mortar shells were fired from both sides and began hitting UN positions. During the lull in the fighting, National Guard soldiers were ordered to secretly remove debris from the airport runway and patch the holes caused by bombing so that reinforcements could land. As fighting intensified, UNFICYP requested UN HQ in New York to declare the airport a 'Protected Area' and waited for a reply.

TAFF LARK, the BEA manager, woke at 10.00 in his Hilton Hotel bedroom. 'I had a shower and decided to find out what was happening. In the breakfast room I met a BA engineer who had come to check out a Trident at the airport and was now stranded. A Cypriot National Guard base some 1,500 metres from the hotel was under attack from Turkish F-100 fighter-bombers,' Lark recalls.

'Together we tried to find out how many BA passengers were in the hotel – the hotel was a shambles with a lot of people milling around and news coming over the tannoy from the BBC Overseas Service every half hour. Several people had come to the hotel as a rallying point for some reason, including a large number of Americans who acted as if the Hilton was diplomatic territory.

'At 14.00 we were told that all American citizens were to assemble in the ballroom. It was announced that all US citizens would leave within the hour. The US Embassy officials in charge refused point blank to take any other nationals, not even women and children.'

Meanwhile, UNFICYP had declared the Ledra Palace Hotel on the Green Line a United Nations 'Protected Area' and placed UN flags on the roof of the building.

Back in Ankara, Prime Minister Ecevit gave the 635 members of the Turkish Parliament a 90-minute-long explanation of why he had ordered the invasion and asked for a declaration of war against Greece if one became necessary. Cheering legislators left no doubt they would grant it.

Forty-nine-year-old Ecevit's image had changed overnight from prim provincial schoolmaster, poet and former American university student lectured by Dr Henry Kissinger, to one of national hero, with the respect of Turkey's generals. 'Our main concern is the large Turkish community. It is our moral responsibility to help when needed,' he told *Time* magazine. 'The Greeks have been violating Cyprus agreements for a decade by illegally shipping in troops and military equipment. In the crises of 1964 and 1967, when Turkish Cypriots were being massacred, we wanted to go in and help, but our allies put obstacles in our way. Thus we hesitated. This time we knew we could not delay. If we did, then everything would have been lost for all Cypriots. The independent state of Cyprus would have ended, and *de facto enosis* would have occurred.

'It was our duty. So we took the initiative. We have limited our objectives to providing security and to restoring the constitutional status of Cyprus. We have now reached a position where we can ensure that any new solution to the Cyprus question does not conflict with the interests of Turkey or with the interests of the Turkish community on the island. It is a fact that the Turks on Cyprus can no longer live under Greek rule. This fact should be made part of the new constitutional solution for Cyprus. Separate governments for Greeks and Turks.'

On the Green Line, the National Guard, despite UN protestations, had made the flat roof of the Ledra Palace Hotel a Greek Cypriot stronghold, with firing points at each corner, two of them accommodating heavy 50mm Browning machine guns. They were countered by mortar fire from the Turkish fighters, killing one Greek and seriously injuring another, who was carried downstairs. 'As photographers and TV crews clustered around him, an hysterical young officer tried to pistol whip them aside and then rolled around the lobby floor with his drawn revolver in a paroxysm of rage,' said Colin Smith. 'Eventually, the press were redeemed by the *Daily Mirror*'s decorated World War II veteran Donald Wise who volunteered to make the dangerous drive to Nicosia General Hospital with the wounded man and then returned.'

New York businessman John Mazzarella, one of the trapped tourists, tells that the scenes were like a Hollywood movie. 'One second the waiters were doing their jobs, the next they disappeared to return wearing khaki uniforms,' he says. 'But at least we didn't have to pay them for our drinks.' With the lives of foreign tourists and journalists in danger, UNFICYP contacted the local Turkish and Greek commanders to tell them to stop firing. The battle continued.

'Reinforcements in the form of half a dozen EOKA-B fighters, Sampson's men, rushed into the hotel. One was immediately nicknamed Sergeant Pepper for his Adonis curls crushed firmly beneath a peaked service cap of airforce blue held firmly in place by its chin strap. Poor Pepper. He had not been with us long before he was shot through the wrist by a round that managed to penetrate the lobby and evacuated by a French Canadian UN patrol under a Sergeant-Major Rajotte, who carried a pace stick and a bullhorn and kept shouting, "Ceese fire! Ceese fire. UN patrol". Neither side took a blind bit of notice,' Colin Smith told *The Observer*.

Flown from Hong Kong by London's *Daily Mirror*, Donald Wise was not a man to let a good story stand in the way of his life. Among his peers, he was recognized as one of the twentieth century's great roving correspondents. Lean, tanned and urbane, his bearing was that of a military man, which he had been. A former member of Britain's elite Parachute Regiment, he feared nothing and nobody and was always perfectly dressed and groomed. During the Turkish advance on Nicosia, he watched events unfold from an open position on the Green Line. Bullets splattered surrounding buildings and mortar bombs exploded behind him, but he stood his ground, peering through binoculars. From time to time, biting on his cigarette holder and trailing tobacco smoke, he would stride back to the hotel, one hand in his trouser pocket, his other holding a notepad and pen.

From his quarters, he dictated copy to the *Mirror*'s newsdesk in London. His reports were composed of simple words and concise sentences that drove the Cyprus drama home to British breakfast tables. Sub-editors loved his work, because it never needed altering. A colleague once asked Wise why he never used long words and kept his sentences short. The veteran correspondent replied succinctly: 'I never forget my readers, old boy. They move their lips when they read.'

As the battle in Nicosia intensified, Wise spotted Jonathan Dimbleby and his television camera crew 'beating a hasty retreat' from a Greek Cypriot position that had come under Turkish fire. 'Stop!' ordered Wise, his voice heard above the bangs, thuds and clatter. 'We never run when the Greeks can see us.' Dimbleby and companions took note immediately and reacted by withdrawing as if they were walking to a cricket pavilion for afternoon tea.

In Room 268, a *Daily Telegraph* correspondent barely escaped with his life when a shell crashed through the wall, but failed to explode. Downstairs, the hack pack saw hotel staff run away and seized the chance to drink the main bar dry at the hotel management's expense. When they staggered out, they were ordered back by the Greek Cypriot National Guard who had surrounded the Ledra Palace and wanted to use the foreign journalists as hostages. The journalists were held captive for about 24 hours, released only when a British officer, supported by a Ferret armoured car of the 16/5 Lancers, threatened to attack the Greek Cypriot force, unless the press corps and tourists were freed immediately. For twins Amanda and Penny Mieras from Kent, it was their 16th birthday. Using a bed sheet, lipstick and blue eye makeup, they improvised a Union flag and draped it across their shoulders.

At 12.24 on the first day, three 60mm shells landed on Wolseley Barracks used by UNFICYP. The last caused the first five casualties among the Canadian Blue Berets. When the UN protested to National Guard officers, they replied that they could not distinguish between them and the Turkish airborne and commando forces as they were also uniformed in blue berets. Turkish Cypriot fighters, too, began wearing Canadian combat dress after capturing a UN laundry in North Nicosia.

Although some Greek units were fighting bravely, they stood little chance against the

Shells land near Wolseley Barracks used by UNFICYP.

overwhelming strength of their enemy's air and land attacks and fell back, but they left behind a field of dead Turkish paratroopers, said a British UN Major. Behind the Greek front lines, however, Turkish Cypriot 'fighters' were losing the battle.

SAILING OFF the coast, Lieutenant Commander Eleutherios Handrinos, the captain of the Hellenic Navy vessel LST *Lesvos*, heard the news of the invasion and the resistance of the TMT units in Paphos who were fighting from the castle by the sea. He immediately made for the port, disembarked the 450 troops he was carrying and turned his 40mm Bofors anti-aircraft guns on the Turkish militia, bringing about their surrender. It was the sole contribution to the war by the Greek ship. After the fall of Paphos, the National Guards boarded public transport buses and headed for Nicosia.

With the temperature hitting the 106°F mark and potential danger everywhere, the British in Limassol asked for refuge in the safety of Episkopi. They were advised to make their way there, bringing only their passports and barest essentials. Altogether, 3,000 vehicles entered the base, where the occupants were checked out. There were 14,000 British residents and another 1,000 foreign and British tourists who had been stranded in the town.

'A friend of ours went back to his house,' says one of the evacuees, 'and found his food gone and a crate of beer emptied! There was a note left behind which said "Sorry to use your home in this way. We hope the money will pay for the goods. From: The National Guard".'

Group Captain Parfit, the RAF station commander of the Episkopi Group, continues: 'During the afternoon, fighting broke out in the surrounding villages between Turks and Greeks and the immediate result was a third category of refugees: Cypriot Nationals seeking sanctuary within the SBA. The Greek problem was very small and, after a few days, the 100 or so accommodated on Curium Beach had left the area. The Turks presented a very different problem.

'Avoiding the main roads, they entered the SBA over the hills and, by early evening 1,200 of them were concentrated around "Dodge City". As there was no time to pitch a tented camp for them that evening, the Station Commander allowed them to shelter for the night in the Astra Cinema. Originally the plan had been to site the camp at Evdhimou Beach but its location in relation to the SBA boundary caused a switch of plan to set up the camp in Happy Valley.'

The Greek National Guard officers, with Nicos Sampson and others, had kept a telephone line open throughout the day between their command bunker near Nicosia and the Armed Forces Headquarters in Athens, but kept receiving contradictory instructions. It was only at 20.00 that they were finally ordered to wipe out the Turkish bridgehead as 'a priority at any cost'.

This was a bit late in the day as a Turkish Army officer's account reveals that 'the first organized attack on the landing beach occurred at around 14.00', with seven Russian T-34 tanks, three from the east Kyrenia road and four from the direction of Lapta. 'Our anti-tank platoon took up a position and opened fire, but our wire-guided missiles became entangled and missed their targets,' says an officer. 'Right at this moment, one of our 106mm recoilless rifle teams received a direct hit. General Suleyman Tuncer, our commander, who was standing in a citrus grove, turned to Lieutenant Colonel Ikiz and shouted: "We'll die, but we won't leave here."

'To the east of our position our battalion's 57mm recoilless team scored a direct hit on an enemy tank, but it had no effect. The tank's counter-fire killed the team instantly. Our infantry's anti-tank weapons hit two other tanks and both were destroyed. We were finally able to breath a sigh of relief as the tank assault diminished.

'I can't remember the exact time, but we began hearing the sound of tanks again. I ordered the recoilless rifle team to take cover and prepare to fire. The rifle officer reported, "We're out of shells, I'm going to go get more", but he was killed on the beach. On both sides of the road our teams took ambush positions. The enemy approached with five tanks. Our weapons' fire immediately destroyed three of them. The other two tank crews abandoned their tanks and fled. It was a great morale boost.'

At 21.15 on Saturday, the Turks ceased their air operations for the night. They had launched 117 ground attacks, 64 airborne assaults, 18 reconnaissance missions and eight air defence sorties during the day. They had made it possible for the land forces to secure their bridgehead in north Cyprus from where they could spread out. The Turkish Air Force could boast it had destroyed several columns of National Guard reinforcements, including half-tracks and several tanks moving towards Kyrenia, strafed Greek military positions in and around Nicosia and blasted targets on the north coast, but some pilots had missed and caused civilian casualties. Near Athalassa, rockets overshot a Greek military camp and destroyed a psychiatric hospital. Twenty patients were killed, terrifying the others. A nurse saw a small boy rolling on the ground in hysteria, chewing broken glass.

At the Kyrenia beachhead the Turkish Marines counted their dead. During the battle, they had lost one of their leading commanders, Colonel Karaoglanoglu, when a mortar bomb struck his position just as night started to fall.

Following their orders from Athens, the National Guard commanders somehow assembled a hotch-potch of various units under cover of darkness and free from air attack. It was a ragtag regiment with some soldiers dressed in EOKA-B camouflage uniforms and others in US Army fatigues, with American names still stencilled above their pockets. A few wore blue jeans and Second World War helmets and carried ancient bolt-action Lee Enfield .303 rifles. Brought together by 02.00 on 21 July, they gave defiant V-signs as they straggled off to the front to start the fight back against the better-trained and better-equipped Turkish Army – until TAF was back in the air at 05.50 and that was that. About the same time, Turkish Cypriot resistance in Limassol collapsed under the weight of a Greek Cypriot assault, and approximately 1,000 prisoners were taken and held in appalling conditions in the city's football stadium.

Turkish Cypriots held prisoner in the Limassol football stadium.

For the guests of the Hilton Hotel in Nicosia food supplies were down to bread and jam. Taff Lark says: 'The men agreed to let women and children eat first. While we were waiting our turn a group of National Guard soldiers turned up, demanding to be fed. We formed a barrier to stop them entering the dining room and the young lieutenant in charge was told he would have to wait. Two of the guards pointed their weapons at the barrier. At this a rather overweight Brit stepped forward and told the young guardsman that if he didn't put the weapon down he would suffer something rather nasty up his rear end … The guards left hastily.'

Soon afterwards, Air Chief Marshal Sir John Aiken, the British Commander of Near East Forces, used the services' radio stations to appeal to the combatants to allow foreign residents and tourists to reach Dhekelia and to give safe passage for a convoy to carry them. He said: 'The convoy's identity will be unmistakable. It will be clearly marked with the Union flag and escorted by military vehicles similarly marked. My orders are that my troops will not fire except in self-defence.'

At the start of the second day, British intelligence reported that the Turkish Army had landed 6,000 troops during the previous 24 hours, including the airborne soldiers. They had also brought ashore 40 tanks. Unexpectedly, the Turks were meeting heavy resistance and advancing only slowly.

Taff Lark continues: 'At lunchtime on Sunday we were advised that the British commander had negotiated a ceasefire with Turkish officers to allow evacuation of civilians from Nicosia to the safety of the Dhekelia Sovereign Base in the south of the Island. Promptly at 15.00 four armoured vehicles of the Finnish UN arrived with buses and lorries. Those wishing to leave were asked to board the vehicles or follow in their own cars. The convoy was so long that as I left on the last Finnish vehicle, the first was already arriving at the base. Along the way, the National Guard stopped us several times to check to see we weren't carrying any Turkish Cypriots.'

About the same time Private Metaxas's company, near St Hilarion Castle, was ordered to attack the hilltop opposite. Under cover of darkness Turkish paratroopers had captured it during the night. Now a local hand-to-hand battle began and the Greeks prevailed, but almost immediately their high command told them to withdraw. Convinced they could repulse any Turkish counter-offensive the soldiers pulled out, angry and bitter. They felt their sacrifices had been for nothing. A few hours later a Turkish air strike blew the hill apart.

At the American radio monitoring station at Karavas, euphemistically called the FBIS – United States Foreign Broadcast Information Service – staff kept their heads down as the area came under intense fire. They had spent the night there. Djev Basharan, a non-American, recalls: 'Shells from the warships and bombs and strafing from the planes came down thick and fast. Some exploded within the precincts of the FBIS, damaging doors and shattering windows. Some explosions were simply as deafening as they were horrifying. At times, death was not around the corner. It was inches away.

'Our morale was kept high due to our bureau Chief Mr Tom Weiss, but the highest credit goes to the US Marines in general and to their chief Ernesto Gutierrez in particular. I have never seen such a self-sacrificing young man in my life. He was on duty almost 24 hours a day. He was so efficient we soon felt and acted like disciplined soldiers under his command.'

Near Tjiklos, the UN Finnish contingent's small base had become a sanctuary for refugees from Kyrenia and its surroundings. An open-air dormitory had been created on either side of an old Roman road for them to spend the night. Among them was Allan Cavinder, a British mechanical services consultant from Kyrenia. He had driven to the UN camp in his Hillman Husky, followed by a bright orange Mini, which carried Len and Maureen Hudson, a honeymoon couple who had been camping at Snake Island.

Americans, Armenians and Syrians, who worked at the Karavas communications monitoring station, had attached themselves to what became a small convoy. Earlier the FBIS station staff had been gathered by the bureau chief who explained orders he had just received from Washington: he was to only evacuate Americans and 'third country' nationals. When asked what would happen to the locally-recruited monitors, who had borne the brunt of responsibility for keeping the station operational since the coup, tears filled his eyes when he said: 'I will try to make sure nobody is left behind me.' So far he had been true to his word.

As the Turkish troops punched their way forward, Greek Cypriot soldiers retreated into the UN camp, still shooting. 'Stop immediately. This is a United Nations Protected Area,' a Finnish officer bellowed over the noise of battle. 'We have women and children here.' The Turkish commander responded and ordered his troops to work their way round the camp. The Greeks continued their withdrawal in the opposite direction and, once they were out, began mortaring the UN position. A Finnish soldier, an American civilian and Peter Chiristodoulou, a Greek Cypriot restaurateur, were wounded. Forest fires caused by the battle began to race out of control.

Two Turkish soldiers attempted to escape the flames and ran into a hail of Greek bullets. They fell less than 50 yards from a house owned by British expatriates. Retired Majors Phyllis Heymann, MBE, and Betty Hunter Cowan, TD. 'Rather than be engulfed by the fire, the injured soldier put a rifle to his mouth and squeezed the trigger; the other was

The author (centre) with the 'Cave Ladies' – Major Betty Hunter Cowan, TD (left) and Major Phyllis Heymann, MBE (right) – who gave sanctuary to refugees near their Tjiklos home and witnessed the Turkish landings at close quarters.

already dead,' Heymann told the author. 'Later UN soldiers returned their bodies to the Turkish commander,' Cowan added.

Eventually the UN buildings at Tjiklos were destroyed by the fire started from sparks blown on the wind from the smouldering embers of the surrounding pine trees. The camp was abandoned and many of those there, including Cavinder and the Hudsons, the honeymooning couple, decided to return to Kyrenia, which was presumed safer. Forty minutes later their mini-convoy ran into Greek Cypriot sniper fire. The Hudsons' Mini was hit and crashed into the side of the mountain. Maureen Hudson took a bullet in her leg. Two UN soldiers in a Land Rover came to their rescue and all returned to Tjiklos to spend a second night in the open air.

At the Western Sovereign Base at Episkopi, more refugees poured in. Patrols from the Royal Scots and the RAF Police on the edge of the SBA collected Turks walking from outlying villages. Poorly clad, exhausted from a night spent in the difficult terrain, thirsty and afraid, they were disarmed, watered from urns of cold water carried in military vehicles and brought into the station.

An RAF policeman noted: 'At about 13.50 I saw a child about four years of age entering the SBA over the hills from the direction of Kandu, leading a blind old woman of 60 years or more. She had torn slippers on her feet; the child was barefoot, his feet bleeding. Both were exhausted and were immediately given medical treatment.'

Service families with accommodation on the Akrotiri-Episkopi base began taking in British evacuees. Carolyn Boyle, a young pupil at St John's School, remembers: 'We had a three bedroomed house and we put up 20 people, including ourselves. With my dad being away my mum became very nervous, as she wanted to do much more than she could manage. My brother and I babysat for all the children, so that mum and the other women could have a night out and enjoy themselves.'

IN GREECE, preparations were taking place for Operation *Niki*. It was a desperate last attempt to reinforce the National Guard with the 1st Paratroop Battalion. That night, carried in a squadron of 15 badly serviced Nord Atlas troop carriers, the paratroopers took off from Rhodes. Several of the aircraft were forced to return to their home base with technical problems, while others lost their way long before they came close to Cyprus. To avoid Turkish detection, the remainder flew almost at wave height over the Mediterranean and then climbed to soar through the Sovereign airspace of RAF Akrotiri. Furious British officers informed the Turkish Army that the Greek flights had not been authorized by them and were on a heading for Nicosia.

Wing Commander George Mitsenas, one of the Nord Atlas pilots, thought he was on a suicide mission from the start. 'After a four-hour flight in the dark, I breathed a sigh of relief when I spotted lights to the left. They were the lights of the British base in Akrotiri. At least I was sure I was on the right track. We climbed to 7,500 feet to clear the mountains

After the ill-fated Operation Niki, Squadron Leader Tzanakos points at the damage from anti-aircraft fire to the right wing of his Nord Atlas aircraft.

and then began to descend as we approached Nicosia Airport. We were advised to turn on our headlights just seconds before landing, as we made a fly-by north of the airport where Turkish forces had been deployed.

'I was nearing the runway at about 02.00 (22 July) when I noticed flares in the sky, very close to the aircraft. It became clear those red flashes were, in fact, anti-aircraft fire. I couldn't understand why Greek Cypriot soldiers would fire on us. To make matters worse, hundreds of armed citizens also opened fire against us, as they mistook the Hellenic aircraft for Turkish. It was like a firework display, albeit a very lethal one.

'Why did the Cypriot defenders open fire, even though they knew about the operation? Why did they disobey the orders of the senior officers who had specifically told them not to fire?' asks Wing Commander Mitsenas. 'I believe the answers lie in a combination of bad planning and blind panic. When you are at war – especially in the front line – even the simplest orders become confused. The situation in Cyprus was chaotic and the soldiers were mentally and physically drained.'

One after the other the Greek planes were hit. As a result, four commandos were killed and many others injured. Apart from two, the others landed, riddled with bullets. Paratrooper Anthanasios Zafiriou was aboard the third Nord Atlas when a large shell hit it. The explosion killed the flight crew and the aircraft spun out of control. The ammunition box under Zafiriou's feet caught light, setting him alight. He made for a door, pushed it open and jumped into the darkness without a second thought. He suffered severe wounds, but survived. The Nord Atlas smashed into a hill on the northern edge of the airport, burying the four-man crew and 28 other commandos.

Their mission a failure, the surviving aircraft limped home after depositing their loads. In total, Greek losses amounted to 33 dead and many more wounded. According to a Greek commentator, the disabled planes that remained behind were taken apart and removed to hide the fact that Greece had also intervened in the war.

The international community, meanwhile, was concerned for the safety of its citizens in the war zone. The Royal Navy aircraft carrier HMS *Hermes* had taken up station off Six and a Half Mile Beach, east of Kyrenia, with the Royal Fleet Auxiliary ship *Olma*, guarded by the frigates HMS *Devonshire* and HMS *Rhyl*.

AT DAWN on Monday, 22 July, an officer from HMS *Hermes* flew by helicopter to the UN landing site at Tjiklos. His purpose was to arrange a UN convoy to take civilians by road to a collection point on the beach. The evacuees consisted of 30 different nationalities.

While fighting continued on the ground and fires raged in the mountains, both Greece and Turkey told the British that the safety of RN vessels and aircraft could not be guaranteed. London replied that if either side in the conflict fired on UK service personnel, fire would be returned. In the event, nothing happened.

Foreign tourists and holidaymakers in the Kyrenia district were located quickly and their evacuation began. From Tjiklos, one convoy headed to the collection point on the beach, where 9,000 other refugees joined them. Many had been picked up from outside The Dome Hotel. Amongst them were several 'Ancient Brits' who had chosen to abandon their properties and possessions. Before leaving they had handed their car keys for safety to a local artist, William Dreghorn, who decided to remain.

'Come on, old man, this is the last trip,' an RN officer boomed. 'Aren't you coming with us?'

'No,' replied Dreghorn.

'If you stay, you'll be killed,' warned the officer.

The old-age pensioner pushed the car keys into the pockets of his khaki shorts and, wearing open-toed sandals, walked slowly home through the dusty streets of the town.

The second convoy left for Nicosia. UN personnel, flying large blue and white UN flags, accompanied both. The vehicle drivers moved with caution as both sides in the conflict had been generous in their laying of mines. On their way to Lapitos/Lapta, three cars filled with foreign reporters had been forced to stop when they ran into a minefield. 'There was an explosion, and the BBC sound recordist Ted Stoddard in the first car got out to warn the others behind,' writes Michael Nicholson. 'He stepped on a mine and, staggering, blinded by blood, he stepped on

another. Those behind watched and one cameraman, safely out of range, filmed his death.'

In Nicosia, the US Consul contacted the 6th Fleet to evacuate American citizens from Kingsfield in the Eastern Sovereign Base Area of Dhekelia. 'In a joint USN–Marines operation, 466 foreigners were put on board the USS *Inchon*, an amphibious assault ship, while the aircraft carrier USS *Forrestal* provided air cover using F-4 Phantoms. *Forrestal* took responsibility for the 500 American evacuees, sending CH-46 and CH-53 helicopters to collect them,' reminisces John Meyers of the USS *Little Rock*, which provided operational support. The American vessels stayed on station until 28 July.

From the beach in Kyrenia, British and foreign nationals were flown to *Hermes* in a relay of Sea King helicopters, aided by a Wessex HU-5 from HMS *Devonshire*. In a single day, 1,630 people were transferred to the Royal Navy ships, which then sailed to Dhekelia, where passengers were documented for repatriation to their home countries. Britons in the Famagusta district were also brought to ESBA, guarded by No. 3 Company of the Coldstream Guards, successfully evading a Turkish air strike. No. 2 Company, wearing UN blue berets, was sent to Nicosia Airport.

To the west of Kyrenia, RN helicopters

British subjects from Kyrenia board Royal Navy helicopters to escape the fighting.

Rescued British from Kyrenia arrive on board HMS *Hermes*.

UNFICYP digs in to defend Nicosia Airport from either side.

Guards remembers that not all the evacuated British tourists had behaved well. 'They had looted shops, taken fur coats, clothes, anything you can think of. They brought loaded suitcases of their loot to HMS *Hermes* where the matalots relieved them of their ill-gotten gains and tossed them into the sea. The sailors weren't too impressed by some of the Brits, to put it mildly.'

'A few had raided stores for alcohol and cigarettes on their way to Tjiklos,' Major Heymann told the author. 'Others had left Kyrenia wearing only their swimming costumes,' Major Betty Hunter Cowan interjected: 'It really wasn't quite the right thing at times like these and some were trembling a little too damned much.'

BY 13.00 MONDAY, the Turkish Army had completed its occupation of Kyrenia. Greek Cypriot resistance was over. Prisoners were interned at the Castle overlooking the port. Others were marched towards the Dome Hotel, where 300 foreign nationals were in residence. As soon as the invasion began, the British tourists took charge and formed a 12-man committee to organize food supplies, provide protection and give medical attention. The committee immediately closed the well-stocked bar in the lounge. 'Things were falling apart,' said one of the Brits, dressed in khaki shorts, knee-length white stockings and Jesus

helped the American Navy collect the FBIS staff, including locally recruited monitors, from Mare Monte beach. Bureau Chief Tom Weiss was the last to board, because he was struggling with an 'impossible radiotelephone' to get permission to take everybody, including the Greek Cypriots who had worked for him. Because he had turned a blind eye to those being picked up, he had probably saved several lives by knowingly defying bureaucratic rules and regulations. 'When we met on board HMS *Hermes* and the US warship *Trenton* off-shore, we all wept for joy,' says Djev Basharan. 'We were treated excellently on both ships. We were very proud of Mr Weiss and his loyalty.'

Alec Tonge of the 1st Battalion Coldstream

The Turkish Army occupies Kyrenia.

sandals. 'Too much alcohol, too little food, old boy, leads to a breakdown in good order, don't y'know.'

Near by at the Dudley Court Hotel, 21 British tourists huddled in the cellar after the building was raked with machine-gun fire, although they had draped a Union flag over the entrance. It, too, was ripped with bullet holes. Once the shooting was over and it was safe to emerge, one of the group, waving a blue British passport, marched towards the first Turkish officer he saw and complained about the desecration of the flag. The major listened patiently, grabbed a nearby lieutenant, ripped the badges of rank off his shoulders and presented them to the protester. 'A small token of our apologies,' he said and saluted.

At the Dhekelia Base, the authorities had prepared for the arrival of about 200 cars and around 800 evacuees. Instead, some 1,500 cars and well over 3,000 people came knocking at the entrance. Lark, because of his airline experience, was immediately put to work, drafting lists of outward passengers in co-operation with the military authorities. They were boarded 100 at time on C-130 Hercules which lumbered off Kingsfield airstrip for RAF Akrotiri. Here they were transferred to Transport Command Comets, VC-10s and Britannias for their flights back to the UK.

IN THE Mediterranean off Paphos, believing the LST *Lesvos* was part of a larger Greek fleet, the Turkish Navy ordered the ageing destroyers *Kocatepe*, *Adatepe* and *Tinaztepe*, which were in the area, to locate ships. A call also went out from Ankara to London and Washington to ask if they knew whether there was a Greek naval convoy carrying troops to Cyprus. Neither capital gave an answer to the Turks.

Suddenly, at about 14.30, the Turkish destroyers came under attack without warning from 28 TAF F-104Gs and F-100Ds, armed with 750lb bombs.

The Greeks, in a masterstroke of deception by the Greek Army Signals 2nd Directorate (Greek Army Intelligence), had broadcast that a Hellenic Navy Task Force was on its way to Paphos, conveniently providing the approximate position of the Turkish vessels – and then waited. As both the Greek and Turkish Navy had been supplied by the United States, their destroyers were very similar in appearance – especially from the air.

Unable to be contacted by the ships' malfunctioning Second World War radio equipment, the over-zealous Turkish pilots, not knowing they were blasting their own side, went out for a 'kill'. Furthermore, the Turkish Air Force and Navy had not agreed any identification signals in advance,

The destroyers suffered considerable damage, but *Kocatepe* was damaged beyond repair. A bomb hit the ship, smashed into the ammunition magazine and exploded, killing 80 sailors immediately. At 14.45, her captain gave the order to abandon ship. Surviving crew members dived overboard. A passing Israeli merchant ship rescued 42 and took them to Haifa.

The Royal Navy had monitored the Turkish disaster and moved a frigate, HMS *Andromeda*, into the 'war zone'. An RAF Nimrod aircraft spotted the survivors and directed the RN vessel to their location. *Andromeda* rescued 80 survivors in a ship-to-ship transfer by helicopter and took them to the RAF Hospital in Akrotiri for medical checks. 'They were suffering from sunburn and dehydration, having been in the sea for 24 hours,' one of the nurses recalls. 'They were soon evacuated back to Turkey with the assistance of the Turkish Red Cross.' Sixty of the destroyer's crew were never found.

For political reasons, the rescue was never publicized, but Captain Ian McKechnie was rewarded with the Turkish Distinguished Service Medal, the only foreign recipient in the history of the Republic. The Queen granted him permission to wear it.

Royal Navy crewmen of HMS *Andromeda* care for survivors of the Turkish destroyer *Kocatepe*.

During this turbulent period, in addition to caring for in-patients, medical and nursing staff at the Akrotiri hospital were also deployed to care for Turkish families from Limassol and the surrounding areas. The hospital, placed on a war footing, was stretched to breaking point.

While the *Kocatepe* was sinking, 54 British Army trucks, two minibuses and 10 civilians, all draped in Union flags, headed to the Ledra Palace Hotel to evacuate the trapped civilians. Most journalists had talked their own way out, without settling their bar bills. Eventually, after vigorous negotiations between UNFICYP and the agitated commander of the 40-man National Guard, the Greeks pulled out and the UN took over at 16.00.

AT THE start of the third day British observers claimed that the Turkish fatalities amounted to 6,000 soldiers, the largest number from among the paratroopers. By then, ITN's Michael Nicholson had reached Famagusta, after driving through the British military roadblocks that bordered the Dhekelia base. With his TV crew he had continued on through the Athna forest, 'which was already filling with Cypriot refugees, until we saw what until the previous weekend had been the southern Mediterranean's Mecca for British holidaymakers. It was said that business was bad in Famagusta if you could see sand between the bodies on the beaches,' he says in his memoir, *A Measure of Danger*. 'Famagusta had been only slightly less vulgar than the Spanish Costas: crowded and gaudy, a place of lotions and chips, lobster-pink bodies under parasols and Watney's Red Barrel on tap in pubs with names better suited to Oxford Street. Now the entire town was deserted and the lines of breezeblock hotels were empty, two already gutted by rocket attacks. The only visitors were the Turkish air force Phantoms. We filmed all there was to film and left, back along the same route to Dhekelia and Larnaca, to join the Nicosia road to Limassol and Akrotiri, another white pillowcase flying from our car radio aerial.'

At 11.00, Turkish soldiers eventually relieved the TMT irregulars at St Hilarion Castle. Ground and air battles continued apace. At 11.15, a further 300 paratroopers dropped from 15 C-47s near Geunyeli, a village on the south side of the Kyrenia Mountains, to add more punch to the forces moving towards Nicosia.

It had taken two and a half days for the Turks to break through the mountains and reach their airborne troops. Their other units moved towards the northern perimeter of Nicosia International Airport. Neither side paid much heed to UN soldiers in their way. In one battle in Nicosia, members of the Canadian contingent were given 20 minutes to clear their position before shelling began. They pulled out in a hurry and exactly 20 minutes later, the Turks flattened the buildings in which they had stayed.

On Monday afternoon, 17 F-104G ground attack aircraft swooped on the airport and dropped 750lb bombs. The Greek defenders took heavy casualties and lost their battle capabilities. Almost immediately, the UK Government warned Turkey not to advance any further. Turkey denies this, but there is no disputing the fact that Brigadier Frank Henn, the British Commander and General Prem Chand, the overall UNFICYP commander, ordered British troops to take up battle stations.

UN HQ in New York had given permission to UNFICYP to declare the airport area 'a UN Protected Area'. To achieve this, Canadian Blue Berets were given the task of negotiating the withdrawal of the Greek and Greek Cypriot troops who were there to prevent the Turkish advance. The Greek commandos, the

UNFICYP blocks runways at Nicosia Airport to prevent their use by either Greek or Turkish military aircraft.

survivors of Operation *Niki*, had covertly reinforced them and were inflicting heavy casualties among the Turks.

Late in the afternoon of the 23rd, the Greek forces at the airport were ordered to cease firing, much to their annoyance. 'UN soldiers started arriving outside the buildings,' a Greek commando sergeant recalls. 'There was almost a battalion of armed Canadians, with armoured personnel carriers. Their commander, a lieutenant colonel, ignored military protocol. He did not salute our officers and shouted: "What are you Greek commandos doing here?" One of our men, furious at his attitude, pointed his rifle from point blank range and squeezed the trigger. Miraculously his weapon jammed. Our comrades disarmed him quickly. If the UN commander had been killed, we would have been up to our necks in trouble.

'Negotiations between the Canadians and us started, but were interrupted as our sniper reported suspicious activity. Our lieutenant confirmed that Turkish tanks were advancing. He ordered me to radio them that we were observing a ceasefire. The Turks were playing games with us.

'The UN commander now demanded that we pull out and said his troops would take over as soon as the building was empty. His

UNFICYP occupies Nicosia Airport after it is declared 'a protected area'.

sympathy obviously lay with the Turks. If we left, we were sure he would allow them to take the airport. We had won the battle, the fire zone was full of Turkish corpses and yet the Turks would be the winners. We knew British soldiers openly collaborated with the Turks despite serving under the UN flag.

'"Commandos, listen up," our lieutenant shouted. "Load and prepare to move forward." A UN officer, with a radio operator, must come with us, he said. They must tell their HQ that if the Turks wouldn't retreat, we would break the ceasefire.

'A UN lieutenant, with a radio operator equipped with a US-made GRC radio, arrived on the roof. The two junior officers talked for a few minutes. Our lieutenant started shouting angrily, making gestures. The UN soldier begged him to calm down and said other UN personnel were talking to the Turks.

'Our lieutenant raised five fingers. "Five minutes. That's all. Then we'll resume fighting," he said. The radio operator relayed the warning to his superiors.

'Finally agreement was reached and the Turks returned to their original positions. The Canadians started their take-over of the airport. One of us left, one of them arrived to take our place. My officer and I were the last to quit. We went through a corridor and I noticed a vault. "We must take that with us and deliver it to the Cyprus command," I say.

'"Listen patriotaki," he replies. "Write this down inside your brain: we came to fight Turks; we won't pollute our hands with money."'

Eventually the Greek forces moved back to the airport's southern perimeter. Mervyn Lemon, a REME Major, was one of the Blue Berets caught between the Turkish and Greek front lines. He remembers: 'We were told to defend the site and my lads got ready. We dug trenches and took up defensive positions in the airport buildings. We had no anti-tank weapons until some were delivered out of

nowhere. I remember having to give orders to the lads as we sat under a snooker table, with blankets hanging down to hide the light. We were joined the next morning by an anti-tank 120mm Recoilless Gun and team from the Canadian 22nd – the infamous *Vingt Deux*.' Eventually they were reinforced by the British 16/5th Lancers equipped with Saladin and Vigilant Ferret armoured cars. Every available UN soldier – clerks, mechanics, drivers and cooks – collected weapons to do battle. A Canadian NCO says: 'It was obvious that the guys were ready to remain in position. They were ready to fight to the end if the airport perimeter was violated by the Turks.'

Foreign Minister Callaghan sent Turkish Prime Minister Ecevit a stern warning: the UK would not allow British forces at the airport to be endangered, without severe military retaliation. At RAF Akrotiri, four squadrons of F-4 Phantom jet bombers were on standby, together with two Companies of the Coldstream Guards. Even with these resources, military chiefs in Whitehall believed the UNFICYP defences could only hold out for a few more hours if the Turks decided on all-out assault.

From his dugout, Major Lemon saw 'four Turkish American-made tanks approaching our fence – made of triple rolls of barbed wire. The *Vingt Deux* "politely" threw them a 120mm round. The Turks withdrew, but their commander then approached under a white flag. Because he had been a *gast arbiter* in Germany and spoke German, we conversed in that language. He wanted confirmation that we were genuine UN troops and not Greek forces dressed in UN uniforms, a ploy Greeks had tried elsewhere. Having assured himself that we were genuine and my having made it clear that any further advance would be resisted by force, the officer returned to his tank. Subsequent to this, Brigadier Henn arrived and "ceasefire" negotiations began with the Turks and Greeks.'

Throughout the day National Guard officers remained in contact with General Georgios Bonanos, Head of the Greek Armed Forces. Send us air and sea support, they pleaded on their hotline to Athens. They are on the way, he promised. At one point, he assured Nicosia that Royal Hellenic Air Force Phantoms were airborne on their way from Crete, when, in fact, they were still on the ground because the Air Force Commander Papanicolaou refused them permission to leave. At sea, two Greek submarines were travelling at full speed and nearing Cyprus waters. Both were capable of causing serious damage to the Turkish vessels off Kyrenia. Just as they were in striking distance, Bonanos countermanded himself and ordered them to return.

At 16.00, the Turkish Army gave up its attempt to capture the airport. Everybody waited to see if Turkey would accept a United Nations' call for a ceasefire. Soon afterwards, with a quarter of the Island in its hands, the Turkish General Command agreed an armistice from 17.00 (local time), but in many parts of Cyprus fighting continued in bursts of sudden desperate activity. Neither side honoured the truce completely.

IN ATHENS, the junta contemplated its future and saw it was bleak. The economy was in ruins, the public was against the war and Turkey was massing troops on the border in Thrace. Lieutenant General Gizikis, the official president of Greece, decided it was time to throw in the towel. He summoned eight of the country's most illustrious civilian leaders and four of his highest-ranking generals to a meeting in his spacious office in the Parliamentary building, where, his voice cracking with emotion, he declared the country now had no government. The junta could no longer provide the leadership that was needed. It was, therefore, up to the men in the room to create a civilian administration of national unity that could extricate the nation with dignity from its present difficulties. The military officers nodded and promised to 'return to barracks' and no more get involved with politics. After six hours, it was decided that former Prime Minister Constantine Karamanlis should be brought back home from his exile in Paris to take charge. A diplomat in Athens sceptically quipped: 'The military made a mess of the Cyprus situation and the economy. Now they want the civilians to clean it up.'

Brigadier Dimitrios Ioannides, seeing his plans fall apart in Cyprus, surrendered the reins of government on 23 July. He had been the junta's strongman, but once Makarios was overthrown and Turkey intervened he became indecisive. He had considered declaring Cyprus part of the mainland, but held back. He had also thought of declaring war against Turkey. In fact, one of his officers sent Ankara a curt telegram via American officials: 'Either you halt all action in Cyprus and pull out invasion force by 14.00 local time (Sunday) or we proclaim *enosis* with Cyprus and we go to war.' Despite the threat and hours of debate, Ioannides and his officers could not make up their minds and so there was no attempt to implement either option.

As soon as the decision was made public to bring back Karamanlis, *Time* magazine reported, the capital's Constitution Square was transformed 'into a historic fiesta of joy' and, as if from nowhere, there was a crowd of 100,000 shouting, 'Victory to the people! Helas! Helas! The junta is dead. Democracy! Democracy!' Then it was off to Athens Airport to wait for Karamanlis, who arrived at 02.30 on a French Lear Jet made available to him by President Valéry Giscard d'Estaing, a close personal friend, and was sworn in as Prime Minister.

'The exultant Athenians welcomed him with what seemed a single voice exploding into a roar,' *Time* recorded. 'With a wave of

his Homburg hat, the tall, slender elder statesman climbed into a white Mercedes and drove
to the city center, the entire route lined by his
cheering countrymen, who showered his car
with blossoms. At 04.00, from the balcony of
the Parliament building he proclaimed: "I am
with you. Democracy is with you."' It was the
final stamp on the end of one of the world's
most reviled regimes. Karamanlis immediately
recognized Makarios as the only legitimate
President of Cyprus.

Prime Minister Ecevit observed: 'I think
that Karamanlis is the sort of man with whom
we can work. In the past, he has shown he
realizes the need for friendship with us and
contributed much to it. He may have to do
certain things that the Greek people may not
easily accept. Karamanlis has inherited an
accumulation of mistakes for which he is not
responsible. The military regime in Athens
made it impossible for us to have a dialogue
with the Greeks. But now we have a new
opportunity.'

Brigadier Ioannides was arrested, faced trial
and was sentenced to death, later commuted to
life in prison. Only 'future research may shed
light on why Greece did not supply any significant assistance to Cyprus or implement the
plans intended to defend the island,' says
Vassilis Fouskas, baffled by the errors made
by the commanders in Athens and Nicosia.

In 1999, President Clinton apologized to
Greece on behalf of the US Government for
supporting the gang of right-wing Colonels on
the excuse of preventing Soviet expansion
during the Cold War.

TWO HOURS before the ceasefire was
agreed, Nicos Sampson quit as President of
the Republic of Cyprus and scurried away to
the Troodos Mountains to hide with 50 armed
supporters. With his departure, Glafcos
Clerides, the Speaker of the House of
Representatives. became acting President of
the Republic, under the rules of the
Constitution. He immediately received an
urgent message from Makarios in New York,
via the Greek Ministry of Foreign Affairs, to
arrange a meeting with Rauf Denktas to tell
him that he wanted an immediate renewal of
the original London agreements 'and the
return to their posts of all Turkish Cypriot
officials, including the Vice-President,
Ministers, Members of the House of Representatives, members of the Police Force and
civil servants,' claims investigative journalist
Makarios Droushiotis.

Clerides, an RAF navigator in the Second
World War, was a London-trained and highly
skilled lawyer, and had acted as defence
attorney for terrorist suspects in court, while
Denktas acted as prosecutor in several EOKA
trials. Both were friends of long standing and
it was Clerides who persuaded Makarios to
allow Denktas to return to Cyprus from exile.
Both would become presidents of their respec-
tive states in divided Cyprus.

Denktas agreed to the meeting, which
would be held in the official residence of the
Vice-President of the Republic in the Turkish
quarter. At the appointed hour, Clerides
arrived, accompanied by Mr Weckman-
Munoz, the Special Representative of the
Secretary-General of the United Nations in
Cyprus and Commanding Officer of
UNFICYP General Prem Chand.

'Denktas, on hearing Clerides' request,
responded that that was a matter that required
consultation with the Turkish government,'
Droushiotis records. 'He told Clerides that he
would travel to Ankara by helicopter, and
would respond within four days. Denktas
eventually responded via the Special
Representative of the Secretary-General of the
United Nations, stating that the Turkish
government could not examine an issue of a
return to the London-Zurich agreements,
which "the Greek Cypriots refused to implement for ten years ... claiming that they were
not implementable any longer".'

Denktas expressed a different view of events: 'I saw the offer as a tactical move by Makarios in order to put a swift end to Turkish intervention. I did tell him [Clerides] that, though I saw no merit in it, I would discuss it with the Turkish Government. In order to do so, I had to be satisfied that he was really in charge of the situation. He was not. He had taken over the Sampson government and EOKA-B with some or all of the junta officers still active all over the country. Those who had staged the coup could not be arrested and tried. It was quite obvious that Makarios was up to his tricks again and the offer of going back to a situation, which had given us no protection for eleven years, could not be treated as a serious offer. By the time I replied, the three guarantors were already discussing the situation and at the first Geneva talks had agreed that two separate administrations existed in the island.'

By 16.30 on 23 July, the ships of Operation *Mercy* were sailing towards the British Sovereign Bases, carrying evacuees of 23 nationalities, including a group of Russian folk dancers.

On shore, Majors Phyllis Heymann and Betty Hunter Cowan, who had assisted the evacuation, were exhausted. As they pondered their next move, a Turkish Army colonel marched towards them as they stood by a water point. 'Can we go home now?' asked Phyllis. 'If you have a home to go to, of course, yes,' replied the officer, glancing at the smouldering remains of the forest fires and houses around them. 'You are quite safe now.'

Betty made a note of the Turk's remarks and looked at her watch. It was exactly five o'clock in the evening.

There was far less safety for Cypriot civilians caught behind the front lines. Extremists were swiftly meting out vengeance against their 'enemies'. International conventions were ignored and vigilante justice took their place in the days that followed. Hundreds of innocents were slaughtered and buried in mass graves. Acting President Glafcos Clerides suggested that Rauf Denktas, the leader of the Turkish Cypriot community, should tour the areas where their people were trapped and attempt to restore peace. The idea never became a reality.

TWO DAYS later, Alan Cavinder and his wife Jean drove to Varosha, the modern section of Famagusta, to find out how his fellow engineer and friend Len Raggett had fared during the three-day invasion. Together they toured a largely empty city. They found the Golden Sands Hotel deserted. All its guests had packed their bags and left after the coup, but remaining behind were their paperbacks. The two men collected as many as they could carry and continued their stroll. Several shops – Fred's Place, The Seashell and The Hideaway – lay open and looted. Other hotels were also empty, windows and doors broken, but none was in the state of the 10-storey Salaminia Tower. It had collapsed like a pack of cards from an air strike.

Soon after the attack, Raggett said he rushed to the hotel to photograph what remained. 'That's where his camera was smashed by a British press photographer,' Cavinder told the author. 'He had seen the man posing a dead boy's body upside down from a railing in the ruins of the Salaminia before taking pictures. Disgusted at what he saw, Len fired off a series of shots. The professional photographer – twice Len's size – reacted furiously, grabbed his expensive camera and smashed it to pieces, which he threw into the debris. That phony picture appeared unaccredited in the *Daily Express* issue of 24 July.'

CRITICS HAVE argued that UNFICYP should have fought the moment the Turks landed on Cyprus soil, but Major-General J. J. Quinn, a former UNFICYP Commander

A body carefully arranged for the press in the remains of the bombed Salaminia Tower hotel in Varosha.

Brendan O'Malley, who co-wrote *The Cyprus Conspiracy* with Ian Craig, claims Kissinger was 'responsible for US covert and overt diplomatic activity' and reminds readers that in 1969 former Acting Secretary of State George Ball said: 'That son of a bitch [Makarios] will have to be killed before anything happens.' Others point out that Tom Boyatt, the CIA desk officer at the US Embassy in Nicosia had warned the State Department months earlier that a coup was being plotted, but his report was ignored. They also add that on 17 July, Kissinger suggested to the *New York Times* that he was not averse to recognizing the legitimacy of the new Sampson regime. That alone would have green-lighted the Turkish invasion.

When O'Malley interviewed Kissinger, however, he 'strenuously denied that there was any grand design to get rid of Makarios and told me the idea that the US might have encouraged the coup and invasion was "absolute nonsense". He also justified US inaction on the grounds that his energies were taken up by the denouement of the Watergate debacle, though he stressed that once the crisis began, he was on top of it.'

If Kissinger and the CIA had plotted with the junta in Greece and the military establishment in Turkey, both had performed as desired and from now on pragmatism rather than loyalty would be the new order. Turkey had its army boots on Cyprus, something it had wanted since the British contemplated leaving and, with the promise of more US financial aid, would continue to be in thrall to the Americans. More importantly, cynics argue, both sides had respected US intelligence-gathering stations in Cyprus at Yerolakkos, Mia Milia, and Karavas. But the junta in Athens? It was expendable. It had never been popular with the mass of Greeks and so wasn't the time right for it to pack its bags and let the country return to democracy?

With the Greek Army no longer in power in

explained to the author: 'We were never intended to fend off a major attack by either side. However, our very presence in Cyprus resulted in peace being established at a very early stage. Had it not been for UNFICYP, I doubt you would have had a truce so very early on.'

Conspiracy theorists insist, however, that the coup and subsequent invasion of Cyprus were engineered by America's CIA, who saw Makarios as the Castro of the eastern Mediterranean and wanted a president who was more pro-West and would side with NATO. What the US policymakers did not want were leftists of any shade of red to hold power in either Athens or Nicosia. With the Watergate scandal nearing its climax in Washington and President Nixon on the eve of resigning, Secretary of State and National Security Henry Kissinger alone was overseeing the Cyprus crisis.

Athens and the presidency in Nicosia in the care of Glafcos Clerides, many in the West, not least the Americans, hoped he would make the post permanent, keeping Makarios far away from Aphrodite's Isle. For whatever reason, Clerides chose not to challenge the Archbishop, who returned in December, once some order was restored out of the chaos.

In 1976 Sampson was sentenced to 20 years' imprisonment for treason. He was released in 1990 and returned to his newspaper publishing business. 'Had Turkey not intervened,' Sampson told the Greek newspaper, *Eleftherotypia*, in 1981, 'I would not only have proclaimed *enosis* but I would have annihilated the Turks in Cyprus as well.'

Sampson met his maker on 9 May 2001, when he died from cancer in Nicosia. Among those he had gunned down during the EOKA conflict were Surgeon Captain Wilson of the Royal Horse Guards, as he returned home after attending a seriously ill Greek Cypriot woman; Sergeants H. B. Carter and C. J. Thorogood of the UK Police Unit; and Angus McDonald, a journalist who had recently joined Charles Foley at the *Times of Cyprus*. Grivas immediately ordered him never to kill again on his own initiative. McDonald was his last victim before the Island's independence.

During the Republic of Cyprus presidential election in 2008, Ioannis Kasoulides, one of the candidates, spoke glowingly about the EOKA killer and proud butcher of British troops and Turkish Cypriot civilians: 'Everyone has an obligation to recognize the man's faith and determination, his heroism and love of country, the self-denial of the fighter,' he railed. 'Nicos Sampson could not stay on the sidelines during the difficult years of the Turkish Cypriot mutiny and their armed uprising. Again he organized groups to protect the unarmed population which was at the mercy of the mob in Omorphita.'

With the Colonels out of office and Sampson without his title of president, CyBC returned to broadcasting real news. Colonel Liasconis listened quietly in the continuity studio to an address by acting President Clerides. 'Those American and Greek bastards, they betrayed us,' he shouted. 'We were holding the chicken and now we are left with a handful of feathers.' He marched out with his men, loaded with files containing every script that had been transmitted during his short reign. He was never seen again at the station.

Once CyBC employees were back in charge, they began to sort out their film and programme archives. The station's TV service had been broadcasting the BBC's 'Dr Who' series prior to the coup, but now was unable to complete the serial as several episodes had disappeared, never to be found again.

BEHIND THE ceasefire line, the Turkish Army consolidated its position and began mopping up operations of Greek soldiers still on the loose. By the time the Turks reached Bellapais, where once Lawrence Durrell had lived, they had found almost 1,000 Greek Cypriots: some were uniformed soldiers and others EOKA activists who had continued fighting in civilian clothes. George Lanitis, a well-known gourmand and wine drinker, was not one of them. Until the day of the coup, he had been Archbishop Makarios's personal photographer and a media specialist. When Nicos Sampson sat down in the presidency Lanitis switched sides in the blink of an eye. He organized Sampson's press conference.

Lanitis claimed later that he and his family would have been murdered if he had not cooperated with the short-lived Sampson regime. After its fall, he certainly had cause to fear the wrath of the Greeks of both sides as much as the Turks. For five days, he and his family lived in hiding, given sanctuary by a retired British couple who had moved to the village in 1968. Several years later, after her husband's death, the English lady, on the condition of anonymity, shared her undimmed memories with Gary Chapman of *Cyprus Today*.

In the days leading up to the Turkish invasion/intervention, she told him that Greek Cypriot youths in the village, 'all in flowered shirts and flared trousers', stood on every street corner, 'holding nice bright, shining guns' after the coup. She was positive they had been armed and trained by Greek Army officers. She recalled 20 July with absolute clarity. It was the day she and her husband, a former British Army soldier, had walked from their home in the morning to Dmitri's *Tree of Idleness* taverna to settle their account. 'All the Greek Cypriots were there talking,' she said.

'My husband went in and said, "Well, my goodness, you chaps have done it now." They replied, "What do you mean?" "You've brought the Turks here," he said. They just shrugged and said, "You're joking." I will never forget the contemptuous way they made funny gestures with their fingers and responded, "we will push them into the sea".' The old lady also remembered how Greek Cypriots looted British homes before they fled from the advancing Turkish Army. 'All the doors and windows of one home were open and there were two armed Greek National Guardsman sitting on the balcony, drinking the British resident's special malt whisky and smoking his cigars.' At another house, the owners found a man walking out with two suitcases full of plundered goods. The night before, the man had given a party for them, his British 'friends'. 'When people say the Turks did the looting, I like to remember that house,' the old lady said.

On 24 July, Taff Lark found an empty crew bunk in a noisy, cramped Hercules for his six-hour journey to RAF Lyneham and a routine job in the BEA London office.

UNDER THE changed conditions, peace negotiations began in Geneva on 25 July between representatives of the two Island communities and senior politicians from the Guarantor Powers – Britain, Greece and Turkey – and Cypriot representatives. Immediately Turkey's Prime Minister Ecevit thanked the British delegation for rescuing sailors after the *Kocatepe* disaster, but also protested the ongoing reconnaissance flights by the RAF over the Kyrenia area. Once the talks began properly, Denktas told Clerides he wanted the north to be declared a 'federated state', which would administer itself. Clerides said he needed time to consult Archbishop Makarios and others.

Behind the scenes, however, Washington had secured agreement from the new Greek Government to keep Makarios out of the Island until a peace deal for a federal solution of the 'Cyprus Problem' had been worked out in Geneva between Clerides and Denktas.

Makarios, however, had decided his own five conditions for a political settlement and these he handed to Robert J. McCloskey, a senior State Department official, who passed them to Henry Kissinger, his boss. The Archbishop wanted them to be forwarded to the Turkish Foreign Ministry in Ankara. He said that Cyprus should be governed by the terms that Britain, Turkey and Greece had agreed at the Zurich and London conferences in early 1959. These had established the eventual 1960 co-partnership Republic of Cyprus. It was a curious change of heart by the Ethnarch, as he had been responsible in 1963 for trying to change the rules on the grounds that they were impractical to implement.

Kissinger not only sent Turkey the Archbishop's conditions, but he added Greece to his mailing list as well as his Ambassador to Cyprus, Roger Davies, with instructions to share them with Clerides. Clerides read them and exclaimed: 'Makarios is dramatically out of touch with reality!'

Recently released documents by the US National Archive reveal details of a subsequent meeting on 29 July between Makarios and US Secretary of State Kissinger in Washington. It was held in the presence of the Greek Ambassador Dimitriou and Robert McCloskey.

The minutes show that Kissinger outclassed Makarios in playing word games. This is a transcript of part of their conversation:

Makarios: I have been telling that the Soviets are trying to exploit the situation and that their interest in this problem is not genuine. Yesterday they asked for a Security Council meeting and we were greatly disappointed at what proved to be a waste of time. But, as I said, to some extent the United States is giving ground to the Soviets.

Kissinger: We have three parties to consider and therefore our policy is more complex than for someone who backs only one of the parties.

Makarios: We don't want to do that.

Kissinger: We succeeded in bringing about the ceasefire. I don't see any reason now to take an anti-Turkish position publicly because it will only aggravate the situation.

Makarios: I am not asking that. I am interested in results, I believe only the United States can influence Turkey – and Greece – and Cyprus. Greece and Turkey are both members of NATO and both receive military aid from the United States. The Cyprus problem is only a small one for the United States and it is not proper to say that the United States must do this or that. We are not in a position to say anything to you about pressure.

Kissinger: We will not do anything under pressure, in no circumstance, and it is in our interest to make this clear. This is a fact of life, not a threat. You would do the same thing. I am not accusing you.

Makarios: We are not ...

Kissinger: You're an able person. What do you see as a solution?

Makarios: I am not satisfied with the position of the United States. It is in your interest to stop the Turkish invasion. I don't say you should exercise pressure and in the process develop anti-US attitudes. I don't know what you've conveyed to Turkey. But, despite this, Turkey is continuing its invasion without showing any respect for the Security Council Resolution.

Kissinger: Turkey is not advancing any further.

Makarios: They are now seeking to impose themselves in Cyprus. Greece is weakened. I don't know whether Karamanlis can survive. The Turkish demands are unreasonable.

Kissinger: What?

Makarios: One, they won't go back to the lines called for in the Security Council Resolution. Two, they are calling for federation. Three, Ecevit is saying 'our troops will stay'. This is blackmail! And the airport is under their control. Furthermore, they are demanding that the Vice-President should have veto power.

Kissinger: I thought you had agreed to the latter in the 1960 agreements.

Makarios: Yes, they want changes. We also want changes. Talks have been going on for years.

Kissinger: What concretely do you want us to do?

Makarios: Take a more decisive role. You are in a position to play this role. You can make certain proposals. Turkey will accept. When you sent Sisco to Athens and Ankara I have read that you used strong language. And now you are very cautious.

Kissinger: You don't know what we say privately. There was an improvement in the situation last week, as a result of what we did.

Makarios: The situation is worse now. People have been uprooted and a great number of refugees have been created.

Kissinger: While the UK is negotiating with Greece and Turkey it is not proper for the United States to attempt to take over the negotiations.

Makarios: But, behind the scenes ...

Kissinger: It depends on what you want. You have addressed the important problem of the long-term attitude of Turkey. From the point of view of the Geneva negotiations it is not necessarily decisive whether there are 20 or 23,000 troops there as far as this round of negotiations is concerned. It is important though whether agreement can be reached in a political context to reduce that number. Now, what we want is to settle this in terms of implementation of the ceasefire and thereby have that contribute to the further political negotiations.

Makarios: What disturbs me is that the Turks will not be in for settlement. As time passes they will be consolidating their position there. The talks will take months or years ...

Kissinger: I think they want a quick settlement, although it might have been their purpose to delay. Maybe we're wrong.

Makarios: Have they accepted a UN corridor?

Kissinger (after checking by telephone): Yes, they seem to have accepted that.

Makarios: I understand the Turks will not withdraw unless there is a final agreement.

Kissinger: Yes.

Makarios: If the talks are prolonged what will the situation be? Our people are suffering. They say they will accept the 1960 Constitution only with changes.

Kissinger: They haven't said this to me. My impression is they may want to keep troops there.

Makarios: Until a solution or forever?

Kissinger: Between a solution and forever. But I'm not here as their lawyer.

Makarios: They invaded they say to restore order and safeguard the Constitution.

Kissinger: During the first week we knew once they got there it would be difficult to get them out, but we didn't want to sanctify Turkish invasion.

Makarios: Suppose Greece and the UK do the same?

Kissinger: The result will be double *enosis*. I don't believe this should be the permanent solution. It is not being supported by the United States. There should be no Greek troops or that would lead to permanent partition.

Makarios: What are the prospects for settlement?

Kissinger: Right now there are too many cooks. Callaghan needs a quick success. The Soviets have their own motives. The Government in Greece has its problems. And, Ecevit ... We have been encouraging a settlement. We have not been all-out active. We can't be the only country to produce a settlement, but this may change. In this phase of the Geneva talks the prospects are good. In the next phase Turkey will have to change its position. There are still too many cooks.

Makarios: I prefer an American cook. Recently I read about military aid for Turkey announced in the *New York Times*.

Kissinger: We explained that if Greece and Turkey had gone to war neither could count on US military assistance continuing. Some thought was given to cutting aid to Greece under its military regime. This could be used against Sampson.

Makarios: What should I say my impressions are about our meeting today?

Kissinger: I wouldn't presume to tell you what to say.

Makarios: You will play a role?

Kissinger: Certainly, we will play a constructive role.

Makarios: You can play a decisive role.

Kissinger: It is a question of timing.

Ambassador Dimitriou: (Referring to conversations in the UN): All believe that if you were more active you could bring about a settlement. I have talked to members of the British and other European delegations. They all believe this and therefore the Geneva talks would be successful.

Kissinger: We can't conduct those negotiations. We have someone there and in each crucial development we have been asked our view and we have given it. We have been helpful in a quiet way. We have made major efforts in Geneva but it isn't our style to do it so vocally. Nobody has yet put all his cards on the table, either the Greeks or the Turks.

Makarios: We have no cards.

Kissinger: We know your views and have studied your six points. Unless you have others, we will send them to Turkey tonight ... You can say that I told you we will play an increasingly constructive role.

Makarios: Am I satisfied?

Ambassador Dimitriou: You'd be justified in saying that.

Kissinger: If I say you're not, I will be popular in Turkey. Frankly, it is better for me internationally if you're not satisfied.

Ambassador Dimitriou (to Makarios): Are you satisfied?

Makarios: I didn't get a clear answer.

Kissinger: Frankly, I can't say. I had to study your 1960 Constitution. I didn't know anything about it. Let me say we are in favor of independence. We are not in favor of partition. We are in favor of a solution agreeable to all three parties.

THE NEXT day, 30 July, the Foreign Ministers of Britain, Turkey and Greece noted the existence of two autonomous administrations in Cyprus and called on Greek forces to withdraw from Turkish Cypriot enclaves, while areas occupied by the Turkish Army were not to be expanded. They also wanted the two sides to arrange an immediate exchange of prisoners.

On the ground, nobody took any notice of what was aired in Geneva. Turkish troops moved forward and shelled Karavas and Lapithos, which they captured soon afterwards from the Greek National Guard.

The delegates at Geneva went away and resolved to meet for a second round, starting 10 August. That same day, Michael Nicholson received a letter from the manager of the Ledra Palace Hotel. It said: 'We hope that you had a pleasant journey home and that your stay at the hotel was an enjoyable one, up to the unfortunate moment when the Turkish invasion broke out, for which I am sure we will all have a memorable experience. I have invoiced your account up to the nineteenth of July. Thanking you in advance, we look forward to welcoming you back at the Ledra Palace on better conditions in due course.'

For two days in Geneva, where hotel bills were being paid, the delegations argued over their different solutions for peace. Then, the UK team sent a flash telegram to London: 'The Turkish Government has tabled ambitious proposals for a clearly defined Turkish Cypriot zone covering 34 per cent of the Island and has demanded a constructive reply by midnight. There is evidence, that, unless they receive such a reply, they will walk out and take military action in Cyprus early tomorrow morning. Slight prospect of a compromise and we are working on Clerides to table a counter draft which would at least concede the principle of geographical separation ...'

The next day, 13 August, Foreign Minister Callaghan cabled Prime Minister Wilson: 'This morning Clerides handed Denktas a counter-proposal which, while it conceded administrative autonomy and some grouping of Turkish villages, excluded the possibility of a geographical zone or of population movements. I told Clerides and Mavros (the Greek Minister) that this would not, in my judgement, satisfy the Turks.

'They [the Greek Cypriots] had to face the reality that there would be no United States military pressure, that UNFICYP would not oppose the Turkish forces and that, as a result, there was no prospect of external help against Turkish aggression. I urged them to produce a counter-proposal, which at least conceded the principle of geographical separation. Clerides said that he could not do so from Geneva: Greek Cypriot opinion was not ready and Makarios, with whom he spoke yesterday, would certainly disavow it. He agreed to fly to Athens and Nicosia to discuss the principle with their colleagues and to return tomorrow night with a clear answer ...'

The Turkish delegation thought Clerides was making another excuse to stall for time and held its negotiating ground, which Callaghan had clearly evaluated. Then the British Foreign Minister played his joker and expected to win the hand. He read Clerides and Mavros a draft agreement of his own, which he hoped Clerides and Denktas would initial.

It fundamentally revised the 1960 constitutional structure of the Republic of Cyprus, turning it into a federal government of a bicommunal nature operating as two autonomous administrations in defined geographical areas. But Denktas surprised everybody by producing his proposal for a clear bizonal bicommunal federation. It reflected the real Turkish objectives. By that time, the Turkish Army had 40,000 soldiers concentrated in the north.

Discussions went on without any progress until the late hours of the 13th, when Turkey suddenly gave an ultimatum to Foreign Secretary James Callaghan who was chairing the talks: stop the Greeks killing our people or we will move again. The Greeks did not stop. The Turks acted again. In protest, the new government in Greece withdrew from the military arm of NATO.

CHAPTER THIRTY

'The Turks are coming': an island divided

'August is a wicked month.'
Edna O'Brien

THE SECOND Turkish military operation began on Wednesday, 14 August.

At 00.20, HQ UNFICYP placed its troops on 'orange alert' and noted there were 60 Turkish Army vehicles, 38 of them tanks, gathering in Geunyeli. Their buildup continued through the dark hours. At 04.30, the opposing forces began occupying forward trenches along the ceasefire line. Twenty-five minutes later, Turkish artillery began shelling Karavas and Lapitos/Lapta on the north side of the Kyrenia Mountains. At 05.05, a formation of 10 Turkish F-100 Super Sabres bombed and strafed National Guard positions around Nicosia. Both sides ignored the safety of UN Observation Posts, despite knowing their every location.

Painted white overall to avoid confusion with any Turkish or Greek military transport, UNFICYP armoured personnel carriers and Lynx tracked reconnaissance vehicles were operational-ready at 06.00 to rescue any trapped UN soldiers.

Anticipating that Turkey's patience would run out, Greek Cypriot civilians had poured out of the Famagusta area for days prior to the Turks' second operation, their cars packed with relatives and goods, mattresses strapped to the roofs. As they rushed to escape, they shouted: 'The Turks are coming, the Turks are coming.' *The Times'* correspondent said:

'Every civilian I passed called the same warning. Most of the town's 20,000 Greek Cypriots had gone by the time it became obvious that the Turkish forces intended to save their people trapped in the old city. Shuttered and deserted, the once bustling town is now a war zone.'

Later he reported: 'War came early to Famagusta. Turkish jet fighters bombarded and strafed the near deserted town. Throughout the morning, fighter-bombers made bombing and strafing runs blocking the town and setting buildings on fire. Big plumes of black smoke rose over a wide area in the Greek Cypriot part of town.'

Warrant Officer John Kenwright, an RAOC butcher, was in the local abattoir supervising the killing of pigs for British Service consumption when the bombardment began. 'We had to leave quickly and it was three days before we could go back and bring the rest of the pigs out alive in trucks,' he recalled.

In the walled city, more than 10,000 Turkish Cypriots were under siege, many seeking refuge from outlying villages. Among them were Arif Gurbuz and Ali Ozel, both Turkish Cypriot 'Freedom Fighters' who were organizing the resistance. Arif, a robust Falstaffian character, was the Turkish Cypriot official responsible for the city's water. Because it was already one of the hottest summers on record, he found it impossible to calculate when the holding tanks would run dry. Yet confidence was high, food plentiful, and an underground hospital was dealing with casualties.

Famagusta had experienced sieges before in its turbulent history and was strongly defended by inhabitants determined to hold their ground until help arrived, but the surrounding villages were less protected. Arif's wife lived in one of them. She was pregnant and their baby was due within six weeks. Her vulnerability had strengthened his resolve to fight to the last bullet. A native of the city, he was not a stranger to death and violence. As a teenager he had witnessed several EOKA terrorist attacks against the British, including the murder of Mrs. Catherine Cutliffe. Now he never hid his contempt of Greeks. They only respected strength, he maintained. As a devout Muslim, he believed a place in heaven was assured for those who fought bravely in the defence of the weak.

Ali Ozel was a Muslim too, but he applied his faith in a more pragmatic fashion. Overweight from enjoying good food and drink, he fasted during Ramadan not only to observe the rules of the Qu'ran, but to slim as well. He was a former Customs officer from the port of Limassol and well versed in the tricks of both the gamekeeper and the poacher. He was enjoying to the full the role in which fate had cast him. He was an actor at heart and circumstances made him a star player in the place where Shakespeare had set his Othello. His uniform was scruffy and his face carried the stubble of several days' growth beneath a thick black moustache, but his appearance belied his true background. He spoke several languages fluently, including Greek; his knowledge of English literature and the history of Cyprus was extensive and objective. It was for these reasons that he acted as a liaison officer for the Turkish Cypriot 'Fighters' in their dealings with the Swedish

UN contingent stationed nearby. Like him, the other Turkish Cypriots were sure that the Swedes' sympathies lay with the Greek Cypriot administration.

Between 20 July and 14 August, both Ali and Arif had been tested many times under fire. For now they knew only that a second military operation was under way to lift their siege. The Turks were pushing forward on two fronts, west from Kyrenia towards Morphou/Guzelyurt and south-east to Famagusta. Greek forces were no match and fell back.

Two days later, the Turkish Cypriot defenders in the walled city saw trails of dust on the plain outside. As the dust clouds moved closer, armoured vehicles became visible. At first, they thought the Greeks were mounting a full-scale and final assault on their bastion and fired their rifles at the approaching columns. Suddenly, above their heads, Turkish fighter aircraft made low-level passes. The approaching tanks were identified as Turkish, the leading columns of the 39th Division under the command of General Suleyman Demirel. They were spearheading the Turkish advance. Rescue was at hand. The air attacks were concentrated on the sea front and the area where there were Greek Cypriot installations. Flights of six fighter-bombers made bombing and strafing runs, setting buildings on fire. Greek National Guardsmen fired volleys of machine gun fire at the attacking jets with no result.

At the sight of the closing Turkish armour and the overflying fighter aircraft, the Greeks began a rapid withdrawal from their sandbagged positions. The heavy bombardment of the old city stopped. Only limited and light mortar fire continued from a handful of Greek outposts. One of them was at the old Court House. Another was half a mile away, on the roof of the Palm Beach Hotel. A Jeep with two wounded National Guardsmen raced through the deserted town. They were shouting that they would defend Famagusta to the last. The siege of Famagusta ended on 15 August 1974, 403 years to the day since the Venetian domination of the city ended in the sixteenth century. On both occasions the Turks had come out the winners.

'The doors of the houses were wide open. People's belongings, food and clothing were abandoned inside. Baby food, unfinished meals and half-eaten fruit were in the kitchens,' a shocked Demirel noted as he passed through abandoned Greek properties. 'The bedrooms and living rooms were abandoned just as they were. It was impossible not to feel pain when faced with such events.'

'I was from a village called Davlos near Kantara Castle, which had a radio and television mast located on the mountain,' remembers Christopher Christofi, who was eight years old in 1974. 'I recall Turkish jets bombing the mountain, after which they flew past the burning forests and then down to the village. My father ordered me to dash across a hot and dusty wheat field to get away from the strafing, while he ran holding my newborn baby sister. I recall jumping into a five-foot crevice – an Olympian task for me. After the jets disappeared we popped our heads up over the edge and we saw a Turkish jet go spinning into a nearby mountain, its wing missing from the hit scored by the anti-aircraft guns on Kantara. The explosion was seen before it was heard and prompted a cheer from the villagers who had all tuned their radios in to hear the news and listen to incessant martial music.

'That evening the mountain had a red glow from the raging forest fires. My father went to Kantara to help the National Guardsmen. The next day he brought some "trophies" – bits of a Turkish jet shot down nearby. I held on to these as I saw the National Guard truck drive by containing the covered bodies of some Guardsmen who had been dining the night before in our village.'

Graeme Stanford was another eight-year-old. He still remembers clearly the day war came to Famagusta. 'My father was in the RAF at Ayios Nikaolas and we lived in a house with a Greek family,' he says. 'Being so young I had no idea what was happening at first, but I knew my parents were worried about something. I spent several days in my bedroom with my bed propped against the window. Then one day we were sitting on the veranda when a Turkish Phantom jet came streaking past and there was a loud explosion. Suddenly there was a gun battle ranging in the street outside. My father risked everything by driving out to his camp to get help.

'While he was gone my mother decided to bring the Greek Cypriot woman and her young daughter upstairs to join us, hopefully in safety. To get to her level in the house, my mum had to walk outside and risk being fired on. Eventually she got everyone upstairs and we waited to be evacuated. As there was no way to get away on our own, we went down to the beach for a break. I remember seeing a hotel on the beach that had been hit. Half was standing, the other half had collapsed. Soon afterwards, a British Army convoy arrived and we were taken to Pergamos for transfer to RAF Akrotiri. I don't know what happened to the Greek Cypriot woman. Her husband had gone to fight with the National Guard.'

Guardsman Tony Walker of the 2nd Battalion of the Coldstream Guards was a driver of one of 60 military trucks sent from

Greek Cypriots leave Famagusta to seek safety in the Eastern Sovereign Base.

the British Sovereign Base at Dhekelia to evacuate the Greek Cypriot holiday resort of foreign civilians caught in the crossfire. The military convoy was lined up outside the hotel waiting for a signal to board evacuees, when two Turkish Phantom fighter-bombers swooped. The British soldiers jumped from their trucks and ducked for cover. Walker found shelter behind a brick wall, just as the leading jet released its rockets and the other fired cannon shells. The side of the hotel took a direct hit and crumbled.

Shrapnel flew in all directions. A piece punctured the chest of Walker's colleague. A small medevac helicopter was rushed to where the wounded soldier lay. He was placed in a sling underneath the helicopter and taken out of the combat zone, coughing, not because his lung was damaged, but because he was breathing exhaust fumes from the aircraft's engines. In their hurry to get him away, the crew had placed him the wrong way round in his sling. Nevertheless the soldier survived.

Later Walker told the author that he believed the Turkish pilot probably thought his convoy was full of Greek reinforcements. With a laugh he added: 'Obviously I'm marked as a neutral and fair game for all sides. The Greeks also shot at me on the first day of the coup.' His wife was one of the British civilians evacuated by C-130 from the RAF base at Akrotiri after her husband was ordered to wear a blue beret and became part of the UN Force at Nicosia International Airport.

To protect themselves from air attack, three National Guard tanks parked on a small hill near the UN's Swedish Field hospital as a Turkish armoured column approached Famagusta. After a five-hour exchange of fire, the Greek Cypriots ran out of ammunition and surrendered to the Blue Berets. Another two wounded National Guardsmen escaped in a Jeep, complaining that they had expected reinforcements, which did not arrive, because all had been ordered to defend Nicosia at all

Swedish troops of UNFICYP protect surrendering Greek soldiers from angry Turkish Cypriots in Famagusta.

Famagusta falls to the Turkish Army.

costs. Had the capital fallen to the Turks, the Greek Cypriot government would have been occupied and the Republic might have collapsed and so Famagusta was abandoned.

Not one officer of a rank higher than lieutenant was left in charge, while the few remaining troops were scattered and disorganized. Once the Turkish tanks reached the city's main roundabout, every Greek retreated to Dherynia. UNFICYP searched in vain to find anyone with the authority who could transfer the city to the UN to make it a Protected Area as happened at Nicosia Airport. Famagusta's Mayor had left for Limassol several days before and the Town Hall had suffered extreme damage from

British Scorpion tanks arrive to reinforce Eastern Sovereign
Base defences.

rocket attacks, but after workers had removed title deeds for local properties to the basement of the Golden Sands Hotel, where they were found later by Turkish Cypriots.

As the advancing Turks neared Famagusta, there were fears that in the heat of the battle, their tanks might enter the British Eastern Sovereign Base area and UK forces would have to confront and remove them.

'At the northernmost perimeter of the British Sovereign Base Area, I watched as Turkish tanks half a mile away moved as they circled to the west of Famagusta,' an eyewitness told *Soldier* magazine. 'During this move, I heard only sporadic automatic fire as plumes of red dust marked the movement of the tanks.

'At 12.15 a Jeep with three Turkish officers drove up to our roadblock and asked for a conference with the senior British officer. A Turkish officer, the operations officer of the tank squadron, met Lieutenant Colonel Ian Cartwright, the Commanding Officer of the 3rd Battalion, the Royal Regiment of Fusiliers, and discussed the boundaries of the SBA.'

Two and a half hours later, there was another dangerous incident. 'A Ferret scout car of the 16th/5th Lancers and a press car close by were fired on by a Turkish tank while the scout car was within the SBA,' a soldier reported. 'There were no casualties and a strong protest was lodged. This area is protected by Scorpion and Ferret scout cars of the 16th/5th Lancers and men of the 3rd Battalion, the Royal Regiment of Fusiliers.'

Another recorded: 'At 17.00 I saw two squadrons of Turkish tanks with armoured personnel carriers drawn up in battle formation in a shallow valley. Colonel Cartwright drove his Land Rover 1,000 metres to the Turkish squadron and met the unit commander. After pointing out how close the tanks were to the British base, the battle tank formation turned and left. During the 15-minute conference an enormous pall of smoke rising from stricken Famagusta formed a backdrop to the proceedings.'

IN NICOSIA, UN Observation Posts were evacuated in a hurry, the last at 08.12 after 11 Turkish tanks moved to within 100 yards. The UN soldiers, unable to be rescued by armoured trucks, were ordered to get out by foot as best they could. Meanwhile, two APCs had managed to reach the Kennedy Hotel in the walled city to pull out civilian UN staff. A secretary hugged a UN soldier and said: 'Thank goodness, the United States Army has arrived.'

At 10.05, HQ UNFICYP was told that a Turkish tank flying a UN flag had been spotted near the RAF Nicosia Officers' Mess. When the tank moved off, it was discovered that the flag had been on a pole in front of where it had parked.

In Famagusta, foreign journalists grabbed the chance to move into a deserted five-star hotel 'with a well-stocked bar and a clear view of the city. The beds were neatly made; towels and soap were in the bathroom.' Peter Arnett, who later gained fame with his CNN reports from Iraq, filed his eyewitness account: 'The first half-dozen tanks reached the Greek

Cypriot suburbs before I drove through the deserted city to reach a telephone. As the tanks closed in on Famagusta the third air strike of the day crashed into the centre of the town, where Greek Cypriot troops were dug in.'

The Associated Press added: 'At dusk, even the oldest Greeks were heading south toward the sanctuary of the British base at Dhekelia. Famagusta tonight is silent and dark. The only glow of light comes from a smouldering fire left over from the day's fighting.' Quite surprisingly the telephone lines were still connected.

Eric Silver, a journalist on holiday with his family, was present in Cyprus throughout the period of the coup and the subsequent Turkish operations. 'On 20 July, the British Defence Attaché took me to the roof of the High Commission, on the Green Line between the Greek and Turkish sides of town, from where we watched the Turkish paratroopers dropping on the plain to the north,' he reflected in the London *Independent* recently.

'The Greek Cypriot National Guard, which was more a militia than an army, proved a poor match for them. It was a short, nasty war with atrocities and ethnic cleansing by both sides. I will always remember the stench of mass graves and the cowed faces of hostages sweating from the summer heat in requisitioned football stadiums.'

On 15 August, the Canadians and the British were still in charge of Nicosia International Airport. Their task force, commanded by a Major Harries, consisted of 1 AB Battery and 1 AB Field Squadron, supported by 106mm Recoilless Rifle detachments from 1 and 2 Commando. There was also a Swingfire missile troop, with a Forward Air Control Party that could summon 12 Phantom aircraft from RAF Akrotiri to provide additional protection.

Even so, the Turkish Army probed the airport perimeter as artillery shells from the

Lance Sergeant Mills checks the Observation Post on the roof of Nicosia Airport.

Greeks fell short near UN positions, due to the age of their ammunition. A British officer remarked: 'There were several occasions when we thought we'd have to practise what we preached to keep the opposing forces at bay. Fortunately, Turkish commanders were cooperative when we explained our intentions.'

On the third day, after a short lull, the Greek and Turkish forces began battling again for every square inch of ground in the Nicosia area, the Greeks slowly giving up their positions after intense pressure. Again, UNFICYP reminded both sides of the ground rules in the UN Protected Area. No armed military would be allowed to enter, although 'surrender would be accepted after soldiers gave up their weapons', another way of adding to the Canadians' Regimental Museum weapons collection.

Frequent local ceasefires were agreed. The shortest lasted three minutes. Then the Turks announced that their second operation would be complete at 18.00, when Morphou and Famagusta were in their hands, and the war would be over, as far as they were concerned.

By day's end of the 16th, the Turkish Army controlled 38 per cent of the Island's land area, more than Denktas had requested at the Geneva talks, including north Nicosia, Kyrenia/Girne, Lefke in the northern foothills of the Troodos,

Turkish tanks arrive in north Nicosia.

Rauf Denktas embraces senior Turkish Army officers when they reach north Nicosia.

Buffer Zone and began mapping the front lines of the two sides when the fighting stopped. Blue Beret patrols were warned to move with caution on roads given up by the National Guard. The warning was prompted by the deaths of two Danish UN soldiers whose vehicle hit a mine near Ambelikou.

At approximately 09.00 a UN patrol saw Turkish Cypriot soldiers had crossed the Pedios river in Nicosia for the first time in 10 years and were looting the residences of rich Cypriots. 'The hate that the factions had for each other and the minimal importance they attach to human life was evident in these incidents,' a UN official commented. The National Guard, meanwhile, had occupied the British High Commission. The Greeks were advised to leave and did, minus a stately Bentley parked in the grounds. It was the High Commissioner's official limousine in obvious danger of becoming either a war souvenir or a casualty of war. Not wanting this to happen, the commander of Canada's 2 Commando ordered that it be removed for safekeeping.

Master Corporal 'Boots' McDonald followed his orders to the letter. He gave up his Mercedes armoured car to make immediate use of the Bentley, driving it in style to various UN sites. At Blue Beret camp, Lt. Colonel

Morphou/Guzelyurt, Panhandle/Karpasia/Karpaz, Famagusta/G. Magusa and the Greek tourist resort of Varosha/Maras. The latter in 2008 was still off-limits to all except the Turkish Army and UN observers. The hotels, apartment blocks and shops are beyond practical repair, as far as the author could see when he visited.

The line along which the Turkish military stopped was exactly the one they had sought in 1965 in talks conducted with UN mediator Galo Plaza in response to his plan for a 'new' independent Cyprus in which Turkish Cypriots' safety would be guaranteed.

On 17 August, with a ceasefire established, UNFICYP started work on the creation of a

From left to right: Major F. Tsolakis (National Guard), UNFICYP Colonel C. Beattie, Colonel N. Cakar (Turkish Army) and Colonel G. Hunter (UK), back to camera, meet at UNFICYP Headquarters in Nicosia to discuss ceasefire lines.

Morris, the CO of the 16/5th Lancers, saw McDonald and requisitioned the car 'to impress some Turkish soldiers who had crossed the Morphou road and were too close to RAF Nicosia in breach of the ceasefire line'. With flags flying and in full dress uniform, Colonel Morris ordered the Turks to line up as if on parade, accepted their salutes and ordered them back. The soldiers left, very impressed.

On 18 August Turkish ground soldiers began trudging deep into the wilderness of the Karpas or Panhandle, where hundreds of Greek Cypriots had stayed in their villages. They passed through Boltasli (Lythragomi) on the south side of Karvella forest and began to 'liberate' the Turkish Cypriot enclaves. They met little resistance. Father Antonis Christopher told the BBC that Cypriot Turks emerged from their hiding places in the surrounding area and asked the soldiers not to harm his people and they did not. He said they only took prisoner those Greek Cypriots who were clearly identified as belonging to the National Guard. All the others were allowed to return to their homes and carry on as usual.

The situation was very different in several Greek villages in the Mesaoria plain. Here Turkish Cypriots looted deserted houses. If they found Greeks, they rounded them up and sprayed them with bullets. In Palekythro, 21 members of three families were stood by a ditch and shot, their bodies falling on top of each other. Four survived, including nine-year-old Costas Souppouris. Soon afterwards a Turkish patrol arrived. An officer gathered the wounded and arranged immediate medical assistance for them, after which they were handed to UN representatives for repatriation to the South. The dead he buried in an olive grove in a simple ceremony. Today Costas is employed by the Cyprus Police as a cryptographer.

Andreas Stylianouu was another Greek Cypriot who charged the Turks with atrocities. He told UNFICYP he had witnesses of the

UN officers watch the excavation of a mass burial site. It contains the bodies of Turkish Cypriots massacred by Greek militia withdrawing from Sandallaris.

cold-blooded shooting of 30 Prisoners of War by the Turkish Army on 14 August. But bloodletting was not a one-sided sport. Similar massacres took place in the Turkish Cypriot villages of Maratha and Sandallaris. Here a combined population of 139 men, women and children was mown down by Greek Cypriots and buried in mass graves. (Their bodies were uncovered in September in front of UNFICYP officers and the world's media.)

Munur Dilaver still talks about what happened to his close family relative of the same name: 'On 14 August 1974 at 12 noon he was taken from his home at Kitima Paphos by three EOKA gunmen and tortured in front of his two children, aged five and seven. All the pleas from his wife did not save him. He was hit with rifle butts repeatedly, kicked and dragged on the floor and taken away. His family immediately reported the abduction to the UN soldiers, only to be told they could do nothing to help. After two hours the EOKA men came back and dumped his body outside his door. A UN doctor examined the body. He reported death was caused by "42 bullets".' Dilaver alleges the killers have been identified as the Chelebos brothers, the dead man's neighbours.

For the next few weeks, UNFICYP worked

hard to establish a firm demarcation line between the belligerents. It was a difficult and dangerous job because of the many unmarked minefields and the aggressiveness of the Turkish Army's continuous attempts to creep forward.

A much greater a problem was the shortage of food in the South as most supplies had been stored in the area under Turkish control and the Turkish military commanders adamantly refused to open the warehouses to the International Red Cross and UNFICYP. 'We have personal pledges of cooperation from Turkish Premier Ecevit,' fumed one relief official. 'But the Turks on the Island just don't give a sweet goddam.' They also refused unarmed Greek farmers permission to pass through their lines to feed and water the live-stock they had left behind. As an uneasy calm settled on the Island, the two sides began PoW exchanges and lists of those who were missing. By 2008, these were issues that were still the subject of controversy.

AT DHEKELIA, the UK's Eastern Sovereign Base, the authorities rushed arrangements to accommodate another flood of Greek Cypriot refugees and tourists who had escaped from the holiday resort of Varosha during the second Turkish operation. They arrived in dribs and drabs, some with vehicles loaded

Greek Cypriot refugees at Anzio Camp at the Eastern Sovereign Base.

RAF aircraft bring aid for refugees.

with personal possessions, others with nothing except fear. They were deposited at Anzio Camp.

An eyewitness remembers: 'Throughout the night refugees poured into the SBA in lorries, cars and farm tractors, the line of vehicles stretching at one time to Famagusta, itself six miles away. Those with cars had plastered them with mud in the forlorn hope that the makeshift camouflage would protect them from air attack. I saw old women sitting on the ground near the sea rocking backwards, crying and wailing – a pitiful sight – they had lost everything and had nowhere to go. They had given up and their only immediate hope was with the British Army who began giving them cooking and toilet facilities and – above all – protection.'

The refugees were directed to Athna Forest, where they could find a little protection from the sun. Within hours the number swelled to an estimated 10,000 and the Army rushed to provide food and supplies. The camp was set up under the command of Lieutenant Colonel J. F. Bowman, of the Army Legal Service, who, with a very small staff, saw to the refugees' immediate needs. When an Army truck arrived with soup, there was nothing into which it could be put – except an old bucket, which one Greek found in the boot of his car.

The following day a tented hospital, under the command of Captain Tim Barber and staffed by a team from 19 Field Ambulance, was set up in the forest. As well as attending to medical needs, the medics also looked after feeding young babies in a special unit set up that supplied cans of strained baby food and baby milk.

Toilet facilities were arranged by men of the Royal Engineers and more than 500 latrines were constructed in the camp. Clothing was an immediate requirement for the very old and the very young and a volunteer team of teenagers from families living in the Dhekelia base made a house-to-house collection of clothing for distribution to the refugees, *Soldier* magazine reported.

Initial emergency rations supplied by the Army consisted of biscuits, tea and hot soup. The British Government and the Red Cross later reinforced these supplies. The refugees prepared meals under the supervision of cooks from the Army Catering Corps. Using Army field ovens, they baked 1,000 loaves of bread each day.

The population of the forest camp soon settled down to about 9,000 and command was taken over by Major John Long of the RCT, with a staff of 70 men from the Royal Regiment of Fusiliers.

During the EOKA conflict, political prisoners and suspected terrorists had been held in the area, which was nicknamed 'Pergamos prison'. Ironically, it was now a sanctuary for Greek Cypriot refugees, some of whom had been held there by the British between 1957 and 1959 as suspected terrorists.

'We escaped Famagusta at 16.00 on 15 August,' says 'Jim', who was 22 years old at the time. 'The city was virtually empty and we headed south to Ormidhia, where we stayed at the Romanzo on the coast for the night. I remember everyone listening to the news to see when we could get back to Famagusta and when there would be a "ceasefire". Very early next morning, we started off in our light blue 1969 Toyota Crown, with my dad driving.

'We reached Dherinia at 07.30. A National Guard soldier at the top of the road stopped us and said the Turks had reached Perchenes and it was chaos, with many Greek Cypriots being shot in cold blood and having their cars and other belongings stolen. I remember him telling my father "you can go down there at your own risk". My mum became very frightened for us – my sister was just 10. We remained at Dherinia for about half an hour and had some breakfast at the side of the road. My mother had brought some bread and a can of sardines from our house in Famagusta. After breakfast, we headed to Dasaki tis Achnas, but stayed there only a few hours until someone told us about Anzio Camp, where we arrived in the afternoon of the same day. I have the stamp in my passport dated 17 August 1974.'

Alexis Hadjisoteriou, too, was at Anzio camp. He lives in London today, unable to return to the family home at 73 Kennedy Avenue in Varosha. 'I have many memories including the fires at Pentadaktylos – that was very sad; the dust cloud from the Turkish tanks as they slowly made their way towards Famagusta; congregating around the family car's radio every hour, on the hour, to listen to the BBC World Service; the surprise of finding clean showers at Anzio Camp – a small of luxury; the entertainment from the Gurkhas; the joy I felt after volunteering to wash the camp's plates – about 1,500 if I remember correctly – with my brother Kleanthis and my cousin Patricia. The reward? A bottle of beer – a very special beer for me, as it was my first ever.'

Andreas Aristodemou adds: 'It seems most Famagustians went to Anzio Camp. I remember clearly the three nights we stayed there – the big fires all around us caused by the Turkish troops and the sadness when we believed the flames were burning down our beautiful Famagusta. Horrible thing, war.'

'Jim' continues: 'Most people took only the clothes they were wearing. There was a mad exodus, caused mainly by the absence of any official guidance or assistance from the police, fire-service or military forces who had already ordered a retreat to Alethriko in Larnaca district! Understandably, people panicked when they heard the second phase of the Turkish invasion starting. They fled, believing they would be able to return in a couple of days … The whole business is one of the biggest scandals of that period in the history of the Island and the Turkish Army walked into Varosha to find it empty. If everyone had stayed put, or returned *en-masse* by the weekend, we would have been there ever since!'

ON 14 August, with the start of the second phase of Turkish military operations, the authorities at the Western Sovereign Base had decided to evacuate all the families of military personnel who had been living in Cyprus – except those living in married quarters within the SBAs. A massive airlift was mounted and many harrowing scenes unfolded as service families were moved at less than an hour's notice – often with husbands and fathers remaining at their posts.

An immediate evacuation of 10,000 service dependants began, using 70 transport aircraft during the next four days. At any one time, there were 30 flights in the air between Cyprus and the UK. Their passengers were landed either at RAF Brize Norton or RAF Lyneham, 30 miles away.

'For some families arriving at Lyneham the flight had been a seven-and-a-half-hour ordeal in a Hercules freight-carrying aircraft,' *Soldier* magazine reported. 'A typical Hercules flight contained 60 children and 20 mothers, cooped up in a dimly lit aircraft, surrounded by luggage, with basic toilet facilities and forbid-

den to smoke. Yet the mothers emerged smiling into the English sunshine.'

Alan Cavinder had arrived in Dhekelia the night before the second military operation began and volunteered to help the over-stretched British troops. 'I went straight to see our military intelligence chaps but they were busy paying attention to their "mixed" netball match and there was nothing new or strange about that,' he mused. 'A short drive then to Alexander Barracks told us that these blocks had been taken over by Princess Mary's Own Gurkha Rifles who were, as I approached, vaguely practising *A Scottish Soldier* on bagpipes and drums. It all added to the weird-ness and you felt you'd stepped into a Salvador Dali painting. Then I spotted Squadron Leader Ron Lecky who took me to Camp Anzio.'

Working under Colonel Melly, he was 'lumbered', as he put it, 'with the vetting of passports held by these terrified refugees – alongside military and High Commission personnel – for qualification to be airlifted by the RAF to the UK. Refusal, which was more often than not, often provoked a wailing and a gnashing of teeth that was almost biblical.'

Those refugees who held British or dual nationality were given the opportunity to leave for the UK, flying out from Kingsfield by Hercules C-130 transport aircraft to RAF Lyneham in the UK. Each aircraft was loaded

British service families return to the UK.

Hercules aircraft leaves Kingsfield, Dhekelia, with service families repatriated to the UK.

with 82 evacuees consisting mainly of women and children. The youngest passenger was only five days old.

Group Captain Parfit estimated that 'approximately £400,000 worth of personal belongings were left behind, ranging from hi-fi stereos to framed paintings, washing machines, sewing machines and normal family possessions'. Hundreds of cars were found abandoned. They were rounded up and held in a compound in Dhekelia until they were reclaimed in the months ahead.

To prevent the base's thousands of new 'residents', from boredom, the authorities established an 'entertainments committee' who made sure everybody had 'something to do on a daily basis'. The spectrum of events ranged from donkey races for the children to a moonlit variety show presented by former Royal Artillery gunner Frankie Howerd, the first of several entertainers to give their time and energies to raise morale.

IN GREECE and Cyprus, anti-American feeling was running high. Athenians were sure the United States could have stopped the Turkish invasion if Washington had wanted. It

was an opinion held even more strongly by the Greek Cypriots – with some justification, as Washington had pursued a policy of 'constructive ambiguity' throughout the crisis. Although US officials pleaded innocent of any bias toward either Turkey or Greece, they did admit that they had blundered by not condemning Sampson's appointment as the junta's choice of president. Britain's former Prime Minister Sir Alec Douglas Home agreed. 'In the context of Sampson,' he said, 'the Turkish reaction was inevitable from the beginning.' He pointed to other State Department statements that could have been interpreted by Turkey as American approval to invade. Washington agreed that there should be have been less ambiguity and clearer warnings not to take military action. But Sir Alec concluded that once Ankara had decided to intervene, 'nothing short of total Greek capitulation would have stopped the Turks from going in'.

On 19 August, Greek Cypriots, angry, frustrated and demoralized, rioted in Nicosia and vented their wrath against all things American. The US Consulate was a clear target. Staff inside received word of the impending trouble in the morning and appealed several times to the Cypriot police for protection. Eventually 30 to 40 policemen appeared outside the three-storey building to stand fast against a stone-throwing mob outnumbering them more than 15 to 1. They waved banners that read 'KISSSINGER – HITLER – NATO, MURDERERS OF CYPRUS'. A breakaway group scrambled up and over the eight-foot spiked iron fence surrounding the building, tore down the Stars and Stripes and set the flag alight. They moved towards 10 official cars, doused them in petrol and added a match.

Eleven of the US Marines that guarded the consulate tried to disperse the rioters with tear gas, but to no avail. Roger Davies, 53, the US Consul who had presented Makarios with his credentials just five days before the coup, calmly moved his 38 non-security staff to a corridor on the second floor in an effort to prevent them being injured by flying debris if the cars exploded.

Now Greek National Guardsman arrived to reinforce the police. Suddenly, just before 13.00, armour-piercing 7.62 bullets from automatic rifles began striking the building. Fired from a partially constructed apartment house at the base of the hill 100 yards away, the marksmen were aiming at Davies's office on the south side and his bedroom on the north side.

A Marine told the Consul to take cover in his bathroom, the consulate's safest niche, but he refused, choosing to stay with his staff. The gunmen kept up their rapid fire and bullets ripped through windows, into offices and down the long hallway. For a brief moment, Davies raised his body from the floor. A single shot hit him in the chest. He gave a soft groan and fell back down, blood streaming from his body. Antoinette Varnava, the Consulate's Maronite receptionist, went to his aid. A second high-velocity bullet blew off her head.

The US Consul's body was flown by an RAF helicopter to Akrotiri, where it was put on board a USAF Boeing 707 for a flight to Washington DC.

Consulate staff telephoned the General Hospital 11 miles away for an ambulance. The driver said he dared not drive through the mob.

A block away, acting President Clerides, on hearing about the disturbance, broke off the press conference he was holding and raced to the Consulate and pushed his way through, ordering a police car to follow him. Davies was carried to a nearby clinic under police escort, but was pronounced dead on arrival. Clerides called his murder 'an abominable crime'. The killers, believed to belong to EOKA-B, were not found. The new Greek Cypriot administration never satisfactorily investigated the crime.

Newly appointed President Gerald Ford sent an Air Force 707 to bring home Davies's body and his son, John, 15, and daughter Anna Dana, 20. On arrival at Andrews Air Force Base outside Washington DC, they were met by Ford and Kissinger. Five howitzers fired a 19-gun salute. Posthumously the Consul was given the Secretary of State award, the department's highest honour.

The Greek lobby in Washington, however, pressed the US Government to look afresh at relations with Turkey and eventually Congress voted to suspend military assistance to its

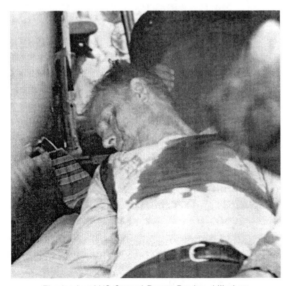

The body of US Consul Roger Davies, killed on 19 August 1974.

NATO ally. Turkish officials replied that they would have to reconsider their role in the alliance and all bilateral defence agreements. With Greece having already pulled out of NATO's military wing and now Turkey rumbling with discontent, the US military became very nervous.

If the Greeks in Cyprus were anti-American, so, too, were the Turks. When the US tried to assist the UN in the transfer of populations from one side to the other, their efforts were dismissed as a plot against both communities.

In Cyprus, the battles appeared over, but the political infighting was only beginning and continues to this day.

MEANWHILE, AT the new Happy Valley camp at Akrotiri, there were 5,698 Turkish Cypriot refugees. While the camp was equipped with showers, cooking facilities, field lavatories, a medical centre, tannoy system and a police control point, Group Captain Parfit says there was considerable suffering and another camp at Paramali, three miles away, had to be erected in a hurry and evacuees from specific villages taken there.

Although there was a shortage of medical teams to deal with their health issues, there was particular lack of sufficient teams of staff to handle ante- and post-natal care of pregnant women. Even so, 'there were 66 births – and not one child was lost, a tribute to hardworking, but seldom publicized British medical teams' and the two Turkish doctors who were also evacuees.

Pembe, a Turkish Cypriot seamstress, was one of the refugees in Happy Valley. She had lived in a house between the Greek and Turkish villages near Limassol until 20 July, a date she can never forget. 'When our *mujahits* – freedom fighters – took up positions in our house, I moved with my family to another near the Turkish hospital,' she explains. 'But in the first day one mortar bomb hit the roof of the house and we escaped from windows, because we couldn't find a door in the smoke and dust. A *mujahit* took us to the hospital, but after a two-hour fight with the *mujahits*, the hospital was captured by the Greeks and we were told to go home as prisoners. Some of them talked in Turkish and cursed us. We thought they would kill us.

'In the morning Greek soldiers with a Land

Happy Valley camp where 5,698 Turkish Cypriot refugees were held in the Western Sovereign Base.

Rover parked outside our house. My father knew some Greek and he translated what they said. "They were waiting for an order to kill us," he explained. After this, our Greek neighbour blocked off the street with barrels and he said to the soldiers that if they did anything to us he would kill them. After three days my husband came back and took me to Mutluyaka, his village. We lived 15 days there before we took shelter in the British base.'

Zehra, another Turkish Cypriot, was a 20-year-old mother, living in Evdim village near Limassol. Her husband was away, serving with the TMT, when she, with her baby, and 20 others decided to flee the Greek forces. 'Everyone was in fear and there was some panic,' she remembers. 'We began to walk to the British base. We passed very bad roads, streams, etc. I had slippers on my feet and they got damaged very quickly. So, I had no more shoes. Fortunately someone else gave me some other shoes and I could keep walking. Finally, we reached the base. People there gave us water, meals and tents. Seeing this kind of behaviour was good. Then, we were put in tents and we never came back to our homes. We lived in the tents for five months. We had to reorganize our whole life. I can say that I never want to live this kind of experience again.'

As autumn approached, the Turkish Cypriot leaders in the Happy Valley refugee camp were anxious to move before the onset of winter. Their agitation increased daily and there were short-lived demonstrations against the British base authorities. The Turks wanted to be given the status of 'international refugees'. The most serious demonstration took place when acting President Clerides attempted to visit the camp.

Eventually Turkey and Greece agreed for the Turks to leave under UN supervision either to the mainland or the North. They left without their tractors, buses, cars, and household goods. As part of Operation *Mayflower*, 8,000 Turks from their villages in the South were escorted to the North in large UN convoys.

The Cypriot Turks who had sought refuge in the British Sovereign Bases were flown from RAF Akrotiri by Turkish charter aircraft and then transferred from Ankara to northern Cyprus, as the Greek Cypriot authorities would not allow them to be moved by road. Pembe adds: 'Turkish planes took us from the base to Adana in Turkey. We were transferred to Iskenderun by bus. After 17 days we returned to the north side of the island on a ship. We were given a house in the same village with my husband's family, and we are here now.'

Hundreds of Greek Cypriots remained at Anzio Camp in Dhekelia in November. They included 'Jim' and his family, who had rented a house in Varosha close to a British service family. 'They found us and said they had been trying to locate us earlier, because they were given permission to enter Famagusta to pick up some of their goods, and, because we lived next door, they could get some things for us too,' he told the author.

'I remember saying to them that "I'm sure we'll be going home soon" and the wife saying to me, "No you will never go back – it's over." I was really shocked and couldn't believe her. They were urging my father to leave Cyprus or at least get out of the Camp and not to wait to return home. They most obviously had far more accurate information than us refugees who were fed hope by our Government that we would return "soon". Just like they've been feeding us this rubbish all these years that "all refugees will return to their homes".'

By the end of the evacuation, code-named Operation *Ablaut*, the UK's Air Mobile Movements Squadron (UKMAMS) had carried 5,255 people back home from both Akrotiri and Dhekelia. Several types of aircraft were involved at Akrotiri (Western SBA) including Swiss DC6s, Canadian 707s and USAF C-130s. Returning planes were loaded with supplies. A stretched DC-8 charter aircraft arrived with 22,000 blankets. Other aircraft from Britain, the US, Switzerland, Sweden, Holland and Germany brought 300 tons of tents, camp beds and medicine for use at the Sovereign Bases. In addition the Island's Red Cross received 125,000 blankets, 8,294 tents, 11,541 camp beds, 38,000 kilos of medicine and 105,000 kilos of food.

For their part in the Emergency, RAF Episkopi personnel were given the following awards:

The Queen's Commendation For Brave Conduct
Corporal J. Marshall
Corporal D. Cleaver

MBE
Warrant Officer R. Ensley

BEM
Corporal D. Millsop

Personal Commendation of Air Commander Cyprus
Warrant Officer C. Cotterill
Mrs S. Tempest
Chief Technician K. A. Johnson
Sergeant A. Erol (RAF Aux Police)

At Dhekelia, Greek Cypriot Petros Symeou, who had worked for the British Army for 30 years, stayed at his post throughout the Emergency, sleeping in his storeroom at night. He received a special commendation for his dedication to duty from the GOC Near East Land Forces.

WITH THE end of the short war, the British Sovereign Base at Dhekelia became a no-man's land between the opposing forces and a sanctuary for refugees. It was protected by the 3rd Battalion, the Royal Regiment of Fusiliers,

10th Battalion (Princess Mary's Own) Gurkha Rifles and the 1st Battalion of the Devonshire and Dorset Regiment. Its Commanding Officer, Lieutenant Colonel Colin Shortis, told *Soldier*: 'Not too long ago we were on the border in Ireland, then we were looking across the Belize border at the Guatemalans and now we are looking at the Turks.'

His regiment's role was to preserve the integrity of the British territory and protect the refugees, many of them concentrated in the Athna Forest, where enterprising Greek Cypriots soon constructed their own main street – John F. Kennedy Avenue (named after the main street in Famagusta) – containing shops, a church and a restaurant.

At Ayios Nikalaos, the Army recruited a team of craftsmen and women from among the refugees to sort and repair the furniture removed from the 400 married quarters in Varsoha after the ceasefire.

The task had fallen to 518 Company, Royal Pioneer Corps, who worked in five teams of seven men under the command of Major Chris Etherington, emptying houses and flats at a rate of four a day. The Pioneers had to contend not only with the tension of the front line situation and the oppressive silence of the deserted town but also with temperatures which often soared above 100 degrees Fahrenheit. Even so, the teams worked 13-hour days.

To reach their destinations, the Pioneers had to pass through a Turkish checkpoint, where passes were closely examined by guards with fixed bayonets whose only words were a curt 'good morning' as the daily six-vehicle convoy passed their unsmiling faces.

From then on the Pioneers saw nobody until they passed the Edelweiss restaurant in the centre of Varosha, where a Swedish UN detachment maintained a precarious foothold against all comers.

'It will take us months to sort this lot out,' Captain Harold Thomas said, pointing to the chairs, tables, beds and wardrobes. 'Anything

A UN vehicle drives through the deserted streets of Varosha.

which has potential future life will be made good to save money. Ragged armchairs will soon look nearly as new, carpets and curtains altered and remade, haversacks, tents, sleeping bags – all are undergoing the renewal process. Only what is definitely not useable again by the Army will be put up for auction.'

The Turkish Army and British front line positions were closest at Ayios Nikalaos, where tension was at its highest because of the frequent infringements of the agreed status quo. They were usually caused by Greek Cypriot orange pickers and shepherds who either accidentally or deliberately crossed 'the border' and were captured by the Turks.

After the British officers discovered that some local orange entrepreneurs were paying double rates to pickers to collect oranges from trees on the other side of the border, troops set up a barbed wire fence on their side of the entire 'orange grove frontier'. Said Lieutenant Colonel Colin Shortis: 'At least if they go across now we shall know it was not a mistake.'

More difficult to control were the flocks of sheep and goats that belonged to Greek Cypriot shepherds and were attracted to the literally greener pastures on the Turkish side. To limit the animals from crossing, the Devon and Dorsets borrowed two scout cars from the Royal Tank Regiment, based at nearby Pergamos, and used them in a herding role.

TWO YEARS after the conflict ended 750 displaced Greek Cypriots remained at Anzio camp in Dhekelia. Their free rations were stopped and they were told to fend for themselves.

Eight UN soldiers died during this short war, 60 were seriously injured and many others were put at risk trying to save Greek and Turkish Cypriot lives.

Greek Cypriots, some voluntarily, but most forced, left southwards as refugees, leaving behind their homes, possessions and properties. The Greeks claim there were 200,000 refugees who fled south. A similar flood of Turks flowed north under UNFICYP protection. These transfers of population were agreed between Glafcos Clerides and Rauf Denktas, now representing the Turkish Federated State of North Cyprus, as it was called.

On 15 November 1983, Denktas would declare it the TRNC – the Turkish Republic of North Cyprus – and Britain would convene a meeting of the UN Security Council to pass Resolution 541 (1983). It said that the 'attempt to create the Turkish Republic of Northern Cyprus is invalid, and will contribute to a worsening of the situation in Cyprus' and that it 'considers the declaration referred to above as legally invalid and calls for its withdrawal'. North Cyprus became an embargoed state. In Athens Prime Minister Andreas Papandreou, too, demanded that the proclamation be overturned. But Oktay Oksuzoglu, the North's Public Information Officer, reflecting the official line, told the author with a wide smile: 'We only changed our name from federation to republic to attract world attention.'

On 6 November 1974, acting President Clerides, however, had conceded in a speech in Nicosia that peace between Greek and Turk could only happen by accepting a two-state solution based on a geographically based federation. 'Any thought that it is now

Acting President Clerides and Turkish leader Rauf Denktas arrange details of a population exchange agreement.

possible for any solution to emerge on the basis of a unitary state is outside reality because Turkey would certainly not agree to discuss such a solution. If in the past there had been a possibility of finding a solution based on a unitary state/local autonomy for the Turks there is not such a possibility now. Since the state cannot be unitary, the only solution that can now emerge is that of a federal state. Such a solution can take various forms. It can be a cantonal solution through the creation of a number of cantons in which the Turks will be in the majority. This will be the best solution for us. The solution can also be a geographical federation, based on two regions corresponding to the population ratio.'

The Turks had achieved *taksim* or partition. The Greeks had failed with their ambitions for *enosis*.

In December 1974, Makarios returned to resume his role as President. With tears rolling down his face, he told a welcoming crowd of 200,000 in Nicosia: 'I was counted among the dead, but here I am among the living.' He declared his willingness for a settlement between the Turks and the Greeks. 'The people are with you,' the crowd shouted back.

Makarios returns to a divided Cyprus in December 1974.

'I am not just holding out an olive branch,' he proclaimed. 'I am holding out a whole olive tree.' But he ruled out partition of the Island.

Earlier he had told Kissinger in Washington that American and British involvement in peace-making was not wanted. He said: 'I cannot do anything about the settlement that is made on Cyprus by the superpowers, but it is well within my power to destroy what you decide.' Back in 1964, one of his Ministers had also told the United States: 'Of course we all realize Cyprus can never become a world power. All the same, we will certainly do our best to go on being a world problem.' On the other side of the fence, Rauf Denktas was insisting on the creation of separate states in Cyprus as the only way to lasting peace. Turks were Turks and Greeks were Greeks, each with their own cultures, religion and language. 'Do not dare to ask us if we are Cypriots! We would take this as an insult,' he bellowed like a belligerent hippopotamus. 'Why? Because in Cyprus the only thing that is Cypriot is the donkey.'

UNFICYP'S ROLE was now to maintain the peace between two defined areas. What had previously been 'green lines' became a 180-kilometre-long Buffer Zone.

It starts on the northern coast near Kokkina/Erenkoy and crosses the Troodos Mountains to reach Astromeritis. From there it continues through some of the Island's finest arable land and citrus producing areas until it reaches the eastern edge of Nicosia. Then it zigzags and divides the capital, emerging near Ormorphita, a place and name that stir violent passions. From Ormorphita the BZ cuts through the countryside until it stops on the perimeter of the Eastern Sovereign Base at Dhekelia. On the far side, near Dherinia, it resumes again until it reaches the coast just south of Famagusta. Parts of the BZ are several kilometres wide, others little more than a metre. In Nicosia, for example, the

distance may be less than the width of a narrow street. The total area between the two sides amounts to three per cent of the Island, in which there are two 'mixed' villages, where law and order is maintained by UN Civilian Police.

When ceasefire lines between the Turkish forces and the Greek Cypriot Army were established in August 1974, Pile/Pyla, one of the 'mixed' villages, found itself stranded in the UN Buffer Zone.

From the outskirts of the village, the modern Greek Cypriot freeway from Nicosia to Limassol is easily visible, as are the Turkish Army observation watchtowers that rise from a high ridge that runs along its western boundary. The Turks watching the Greeks are watched by UNICYP soldiers from their blue, corrugated iron observation posts: UN OP 129 stands in the town square.

A large Turkish coffee house faces a wall of Greek Cypriot restaurants and another coffee house, *Iy Makedhonia* is used exclusively by Greeks. Never the twain do meet in public, unless it is absolutely necessary.

Each community has its own schools and flies its own national flag. The Greek Cypriots take theirs from mainland Greece. The Cypriot Turks choose the red and white banner of the TRNC. Shop signs are in one language or the other, never both. There is an unspoken contest to see which side can be bigger or better. An Orthodox church is purposely grander and bigger than the old Turkish mosque. The Greeks ring their bells. The Turks call the faithful to prayer. 'God is great. I know and I let all know, there is only one God ... and Mohammed is His Prophet,' echoes through the village five times a day.

When it was first heard after the war, the Greek priest protested to UNFICYP, claiming there could be hidden messages for the TMT contained in the prayer delivered in Arabic. True, thought a junior officer and ordered the mosque to stop. Eventually he relented and allowed the calls to resume, providing a UN-sponsored Arabic speaker was present in the Observation Post to listen to every word from the muezzin spoken through the mosque's loudspeakers and report back immediately if any were added.

Ahmet Sakalli was a veteran TMT commander whom the author met in the village. He remembered when the British established two detention camps – Ryan and Anzio – in Pyla/Pile to hold terrorist suspects, amongst them troublemakers rounded up on 14 December 1955, after the Island's colonial authorities went on the offensive to stop labour difficulties caused by the Communists who controlled the Greek Cypriot trade unions. Those given lodgings in the camps included AKEL's General Secretary and the Greek Mayors of Limassol and Larnaca. It was ironic that the new left-wing captives now had to line up for their meals next to EOKA members from the extreme right, each group loathing the other's politics and desire for power outside the camp.

In 1956, at the height of the Suez crisis, a platoon of British soldiers from the Middlesex Regiment, known as the 'Diehards', led by a 2nd Lieutenant, was responsible for guarding the camps' perimeter fences, while civilian prison officers were in charge of those held inside. Sakalli said the perimeter patrols passed the kennels of the Army's guard dogs, Alsatians trained to attack and bring down escapees. The young officer had found his nightly inspections frightening. 'I knew, of course, that their area was totally secure and the dogs couldn't get out,' he said later, 'but I heard their low growls and thought they were discussing which part of my anatomy each of them was going to have for their dinner. I always unbuttoned my pistol holster as I went past.'

The Alsatians may have frightened the officer, but not, it appeared, the Greek Cypriot prisoners, because they rioted and civilian police officers were unable to restore order. It was left to the 'Diehards' to bring the situation under control. They did this with a mixture of good humour, patience and tolerance, qualities for which the British Army is noted, assisted considerably by the pickaxe handles each soldier carried. 'I saw one of my riflemen getting stuck into a large Greek Cypriot and putting in the boot with a vengeance,' an officer reported. 'The Greeks thereafter treated my soldiers with a lot more respect.'

Sonay 'Havva' Barutcu, a young civil servant in the Turkish Cypriot administration, invited the author to meet her parents who lived in an old house in the village. Their neighbours were Greeks. During his visit, a Greek Cypriot woman entered without knocking and spoke in her native language. Havva's mother replied in Greek. The woman had wanted something and it was provided.

'I'm surprised she didn't have the courtesy to say anything in Turkish, not even "thank you",' the author commented. 'I don't think any of them can speak Turkish. They never have. It's been left to us to learn their language,' Havva replied in a matter-of-fact voice. 'About 80 per cent of us can speak Greek.' Her maternal great-great grandfather had been the manager of an Ottoman estate in pre-colonial days. Her father had worked on the nearby British base. After years of service, he had retired without a pension due to complications which had arisen after the North had declared its independence.

During the Turkish 'peace operation' Havva had been studying at college in Southgate, near London, where her married sister lived. Her parents, however, remained in Pile/Pyla and remembered clearly what had taken place here. 'At first, the Greeks were crying and pleading for Turkey to come and save them from other Greeks, those that were supporting the new regime of Nicos Sampson and the Colonels in Greece,' her father said. 'They were very frightened, very frightened indeed. They were sure they would all be killed for having fraternized with Turks in a "mixed" village. There had always been a dialogue between us. Some parents said their sons would be shot because they had not joined EOKA-B. Many of these boys were taken away, never to be seen again.

'Many of the Turkish people were just as frightened over what might become of them, and so they sought refuge with the British on the base,' he recalled, while Havva's mother sat quietly in their small living room, filled with mementoes and photographs of a long married life. A stylized picture of them both on their wedding day was the centrepiece of a wall decorated with snaps of their sons and daughters. 'But for the Turks who remained, the elderly women, mainly Greek families, offered help. They baked bread together and guarded the empty Turkish houses. Then, when the Turkish Army arrived in Cyprus and we came back from the base, the Greek families fled. Then it was our turn to see their homes came to no harm and their chickens were fed.' Havva added: 'My mum used to take food to some very old Greek people who stayed throughout the war.'

SINCE 1974, there have been few violent incidents in the Buffer Zone. There was an occasion, however, when the calm of the BZ was disturbed and this caused different reactions from the administrators of the two sides. UNFICYP HQ was caught in the middle, as usual, where a spokesman discussed what happened with the author.

President Denktas, eager to reveal what took place in the BZ, assigned a television crew to report. The crew infiltrated the zone and moved gingerly towards a Greek military position. The Greek Cypriot soldiers spotted the media intruders, but were unsure how to react. They knew, of course, that to shoot would spark an international incident, but, at the same time, they wanted to demonstrate their disapproval and superiority. They decided the best way was to show their manhood and chant every insult listed in their anti-Turkish military training manuals. They rested their rifles on the ground and, almost in slow motion, unzipped the flies of their camouflage combat trousers. On a barked command, they flashed their organs while the Turkish video camera recorded their every gesture, its red light blinking above the lens in mock astonishment.

The video team's director was delighted by the Greek show. It gave him material better than anything he had ever seen on *Candid Camera* or in a fly-on-the-wall documentary, compiled from tapes taken by hidden cameras. 'Bloody hell,' he thought, 'this is great television.' And so it was, when Bayrak, the TRNC's TV service screened the tapes, close-ups and all. The programme made Cypriot Turks laugh more than any pirated *Benny Hill Show* ever had. Public reaction in the South was muted, but not among the Greek officer corps. Their reaction was far from stoic.

During his afternoon tea break, the Greek soldiers' Commanding Officer saw the broadcast and 'went ballistic' (according to a UN source), deciding to personally execute the offending troops at worst or castrate their pride and joys at best. Only a fistful of tranquillizers and some soothing words from his adjutant delivered him back within the boundaries of sanity. 'Sir,' said the junior officer, 'neither of those punitive options will be a good career move.'

'But those buggers have demeaned the honour of our army,' protested the Colonel.

'I know, sir, I know,' continued the adjutant. 'But one day I would like to tell my grandchildren that I had the privilege of serving under a brilliant general, whose actions were wise ...' His voice petered out.

'But I'm not a general,' the Colonel rasped.

'No, sir, but you will be.'

'Yes, very good. I hear what you say. What do you recommend?'

'Well, sir, in similar circumstances, we usually ask UNFICYP to sort things out ...'

'Fine. Then draft an appropriate protest. Mustn't let those Turks get away with this.'

That was how the author imagines the conversation between the two men, because, later in the day, UNFICYP received the Greeks' formal complaint. A British officer duly noted the Greek CO's ire, made copies for the Secretary-General's files in New York and sent a senior Blue Beret to carry the original protest document to North Nicosia or Lefkosa for President Denktas to consider, hoping that the genial leader of the TRNC would apologize for causing the incident.

At his Presidential Palace, Rauf Denktas invited the visiting UN envoy to relax on a cushioned sofa, accept some refreshment and then read the Greek side's complaint, while secretaries jotted every line spoken at the meeting. For as long as possible, the President and the UN representative maintained their aura of formality. 'At 09.45 yesterday, at grid reference etc. etc. ... in the BZ, Turkish Cypriots, believed to be official photographers, crossed the barrel line and proceeded in the direction of a Republic of Cyprus National Guard position, in breach of conditions laid down and agreed by both parties and United Nations representatives on etc. etc ... and on etc. etc. ...

'The Republic of Cyprus considers this action a most serious violation of those accords, demands an explanation of the occurrence and demands the appropriate apology from the offending party or parties to the offence, which could have caused the resumption of military operations that would have destroyed the peaceful status quo and diminished the chances of a satisfactory solution to the outstanding issues which hinder a unification of the island and its Cypriot peoples etc. etc. ...'

The tone of the UN officer's voice was solemn, but his eyes twinkled. The President, too, tried to keep a straight face. What happened after the formalities were completed was another matter. Without access to the official transcripts of the meeting, the author could only rely on hearsay. Apparently Denktas replied that he wanted Cypriots to be happy. He felt that the Turkish Broadcasting Service's transmission had contributed to this objective. Viewers had laughed. Laughter was a sign of happiness. If the Greek side wanted only misery, then that was just another difference between them and Turkish Cypriots.

He continued that he was a kindly man who looked forward to better times and, definitely, a resolution of the Cyprus question. He felt, however, that laughter was a cure for many ills. In this, he said, he had the support of leading authorities in the world of medicine. And so he had told the Turkish Broadcasting Service to give the Greeks a second opportunity to enjoy the programme, with their friends in the TRNC. The broadcast would be repeated the next evening.

Whether the Greek Colonel was promoted to general or the adjutant kept his job, the author never heard. His UN contacts merely told him that it was the last time the Greek National Guard was caught with its trousers down – by television.

IN 2009 UNFICYP numbers 860 troops and 69 UN Police officers to maintain the status quo, report breaches of the ceasefire conditions and liaise. There is still no peace agreement to prevent military action by either side. The budget for the Force between July 2008 and June 2009 was US$54.9 million, which included a one-third voluntary contribution from Cyprus and US$6.5 million from Greece. An UNFICYP spokesman justified the expense: 'We are still here to prevent the recurrence of conflict and to help bring about the right circumstances for a just and lasting settlement. The cost of the force is a small price to pay for maintaining harmony and giving the peace process a chance.'

Lieutenant Neil Dowdler, a troop commander from Britain's Territorial Army on six-month tour with UNFICYP, arrived on the Island in October 2008. Speaking to the *Cyprus Mail*, he explained some of the problems which confronted the British contingent at present: 'The main issue that we've had to deal with lately involves allegations of illegal immigrants trying to come into the Buffer Zone and staying in some of the abandoned property. This shows a move away from military issues in the BZ to more humanitarian topics.'

CHAPTER THIRTY-ONE

'Negotiation is not a football match': playing the end game

> 'Never ending, still beginning,
> Fighting still, and still destroying,
> If the world be worth thy winning,
> Think, oh think, it worth enjoying.'
> John Dryden

SINCE 1974, there have been talks aplenty and moments when the UN and other mediators thought they had solved the 'Cyprus Problem', only to find at the last minute that one side or the other raised an objection. Probably the nearest to a final settlement occurred in 1977, according to George Vassiliou, the President of the Republic of Cyprus from 1988 to 1993. Pressured by President Carter, he believes Denktas and Makarios agreed a form of non-aligned bizonal, bicommunal federation with political equality, but it was not implemented due to the latter's sudden death by heart attack on 3 August 1977.

The Archbishop's body lay in state for a week of mourning and more than a quarter of a million people filed past his coffin in the Archbishopric. 'Everyone cried and kissed his hand. Some Greek Cypriots were hysterical. I have never experienced or could have imagined such an outpouring of grief. I think three-quarters of Cyprus must have come and they kept coming,' recalls Toula Tryfon, a mother of two, who kept vigil for five days and nights until his funeral.

On the day of his funeral, there was a heavy rainstorm. 'When a good man is buried, even the heavens shed tears,' says a Greek proverb. A Turkish proverb's message is different:

Archbishop Makarios's tomb at Throni, high in the Troodos Mountains.

'When an evil man dies, the heavens try to wash away his misdeeds.' Spyros Kyprianou, who succeeded as president, and Tassos Papadopoulos, another future president, were present.

Archbishop Makarios III was buried at Throni, a site he chose himself, high in the Troodos Mountains, his coffin draped with the flag of Greece – but minus his heart. Until late 2006, it had been preserved in his bedroom in the Archbishopric after being removed by Dr Vassos Lyssarides so that it could be examined to ensure he had not been poisoned. Most Cypriots were astonished when they heard the news and expressed the hope that the heart would be buried in his tomb, which it was on 24 November 2006. The slogan 'Makarios Lives', painted in giant white letters, appears on the mountainside below.

The Turks, having unilaterally declared the Turkish Federated State of Cyprus (TFSC), new President Kyprianou and Denktas met almost as equals to sign a 10-point agreement for discussions to continue, providing the Turkish Army allowed Varosha to be resettled and the Greek Cypriot authorities lifted the economic blockade of the North. The boycott had deprived the Turkish Cypriots of normal communications and trading outlets, making them dependent on Turkey for their economic survival. The words on paper were not converted into actions.

On 15 November 1983, with his popularity running high, Rauf Denktas declared the Turkish Republic of Northern Cyprus with himself as President. Only his closest advisers knew about the announcement in advance. Denktas had chosen the date shrewdly because it was in the middle of the handover of Turkey by the military to civilian control.

More talks were scheduled and meetings held, and the UN believed in January 1985 that only agreements needed to be signed. Denktas and Kyprianou flew to New York and shook hands with each other in the spotlight of the international media. In public, everyone smiled. Behind closed UN doors, happy faces turned grim. Though both sides had told UN negotiators earlier that they had accepted everything written in the settlement papers as they stood, Kyprianou at the last moment demanded changes. The UN-supervised conference broke up and the two Cypriot leaders returned home to face domestic elections. The Cyprus merry-go-round kept turning.

THE YEARS passed, each blurring into the biased histories of the Island, as the stalemate between the two sides continued. British forces came and went, either fulfilling their tours of duty at the two Sovereign Bases or as part of UNFICYP's British contingent. For their families in Episkopi or Dhekelia, it was a long holiday in the sun, far from dangers elsewhere.

Then, on Sunday, 3 August 1986, the routine calm of the relaxed afternoon was broken when RAF Akrotiri came under mortar attack by a group of unknown terrorists. Miraculously no one was killed, although a service wife was injured in the leg from shrapnel after a bomb exploded outside her married quarter. Meanwhile a second group opened fire with machine guns and a rocket launcher from the Ladies Mile gate behind the Akrotiri Rowing and Board Sailing beach club. The gang also threw grenades into the car park. Families ran for cover into the club buildings and one sailor threw himself into the water as his dinghy came under fire.

Coincidentally, the children of Mrs Malpass, the injured woman, were in the club car park when the firing started, as they were about to get into a neighbour's car to be driven home. Eight-year-old Rebecca Malpass became the heroine of the day, when she bravely protected her two-year-old brother by throwing him onto the floor in the rear of the car and throwing her body over his. As soon as she thought the shooting was over, she picked up her brother and carried him to safety, returning minutes later with a first aider to help the neighbour, Mrs Edwards, whose foot was badly cut by a splinter from one of the rocket blasts.

The whole attack lasted barely five minutes. Taking their weapons with them, the terrorists ran down the packed beach, ignoring the thousands of sunbathing tourists and local holidaymakers, but firing bullets into the air to create confusion. They were never caught, but later a Beirut newspaper published a statement from an Islamic organization, which claimed responsibility:

'In the name of God, the merciful, the compassionate, the United Nasserite Organization announces that the three groups carried out their mission successfully and, according to plan, inflicted heavy damages at the British-US-Zionist bases situated on the coastal road between Limassol and Paphos. The three groups were able to destroy a number of helicopters, jetliners and transport planes ... The attack is a strong blow to Margaret Thatcher. The attack was never targeted against the Government of Cyprus or to the friendly Cypriot people. The group of the martyr Al Hilidi Ben Sarka suffered two wounded, who were slightly injured during the attack.'

The short attack suddenly produced exciting copy for the Island's newspapers, whose editors had been forced week after week to regurgitate what each side was saying about the other. Despite countless attempts to reconcile the demands of the leaders of the communities and create some form of single Cyprus Government, partition remained, one side known today as the Turkish Republic of North Cyprus (TRNC) – described as the 'occupied areas' by the South's media – and the other the Republic of Cyprus (RoC). Each was governing its part from Nicosia/Lefkosa, the divided capital. It took several years before any serious moves were made to break the deadlock, with the usual raising of hopes by the international community.

EARLY IN 2002, bilateral talks began again between Turkish Cypriot President Rauf Denktas and President Glafcos Clerides of the Republic of Cyprus in a conference room in the UN Protected Area. President Denktas initiated the meeting and President Clerides responded positively, but when the UN tried to act as negotiators, Denktas objected. The talks were prompted by the South's application to join the EU and the EU's willingness to accept South Cyprus as representing the whole island from 1 May 2004.

'Glafkos Clerides and Rauf Denktas were both "old friends" and long-standing antagonists,' writes Michael Jansen of the *Irish Times*. 'Amicable rather than inimical antagonists certainly, but men on opposite sides of a line. The two were said to have been schoolmates at the English School in Nicosia but, in fact, Clerides did not attend the English School, the elitist secondary educational institution of the British colonial administration. He went to the Pan-Cyprian Gymnasium where pupils raised the banner of freedom.

'According to Clerides, they did not get to know each other until 1950 when they were both back in Cyprus and in court, where Denktas was prosecuting and Clerides defending in a criminal case. The tendency of the two to be on opposite sides intensified during the Greek Cypriot struggle to unite the island with Greece, waged by EOKA from 1955 to 1959. While Clerides defended EOKA fighters in British courts, Denktas prosecuted until 1957, when he founded the Turkish Cypriot partitionist movement, TMT, his political power base and *raison d'être*.'

Despite all their differences, both understood each other and their personal relationship survived every crisis. In 1997, Clerides arranged the exhumation of the remains of Denktas's mother and sister from the Muslim cemetery in Paphos for re-burial in North Cyprus.

The talks, however, stalled as usual, but the UN pressed both sides to at least initial an outline agreement for a form of united Cyprus prior to EU membership. The UN drafted a comprehensive plan, which the Greek Cypriot authority broadly accepted with certain reservations. The Turkish Cypriot administration requested more time to study the proposals before giving its considered response in 2003.

While the UN waited to see what the two sides would decide, the South held presidential elections on 16 February 2003. To the surprise of many, Tassos Papadopoulos massively beat incumbent veteran politician Glafcos Clerides to become the fifth president of the Greek Cypriot Republic of Cyprus. Papadopoulos would now represent Greek Cypriots in the pivotal UN-sponsored negotiations with President Rauf Denktas of the TRNC. Because Papadopoulos had been committed to EOKA, he was not popular figure amongst Turkish Cypriots. However, he tried to assure the Turkish side that he was not hostile towards them and their rights would not be affected by changes he wanted in the 'reunification plan' presented by UN Secretary-General Kofi Annan.

On 10 March 2003, Annan summoned Papadopoulos and Denktas to The Hague to discuss the future, but the two Cypriot leaders would barely speak to each other. Following 20 hours of negotiations, the talks collapsed – yet again. Kofi Annan immediately issued a written statement: 'Regrettably these [peace] efforts were not a success. We have reached the end of the road.'

'This was not a plan we could ask the people to vote on,' said Denktas, adding that he was willing to continue talking to his opposite number to find a way of closing their differences outside the auspices of the UN. 'If there is a way out we'll find it,' he suggested. Papadopoulos expressed his 'sadness and disappointment' that the talks had ended in failure.

At UNFICYP headquarters in Nicosia Airport, where preliminary discussions had taken place for a year, a spokesman said: 'There is sadness but little surprise. Everyone feels sorry for the team and the Turkish Cypriots. We have seen the solution. No one ever said it would be palatable, but it was the most palatable that could be presented.'

The EU did not to wait for more and more talks and ... It immediately confirmed its intention to admit Greek Cyprus as a member state in 2004, acknowledging the administration as the government of the whole Island.

Asked whether the EU would then consider North Cyprus part of its territory and 'under occupation by Turkey', spokesman Jean-Christophe Filori replied: 'Yes, we can look at things in that way. The occupation has always been considered illegal by the international community, including the EU. Nothing changes that.'

Nevertheless all hope was not lost. Initiated as a gesture of goodwill, the Turkish Cypriot authorities opened their border to Greek Cypriots. The Greek administration followed with a reciprocal gesture. For the first time since the coup and Turkish invasion, Cypriots were able to see how the other half lived. Many old friendships were renewed. There were very few gestures of hostility. A lot of misconceptions about the two sides were cleared up.

AS WORLD attention concentrated on the situation in Iraq after the fall of Saddam, the Greek side in Cyprus prepared itself for full membership of the EU. Behind the scenes at the UN, the United States and Britain pushed the Secretary-General to devise a new settlement plan to avoid complications for the European nations and risk further instability in the Middle East.

Reluctantly the Greek and Turkish sides were brought back to discuss their differences. If they refused to agree, Annan warned, the UN would put its plan directly to the people of Cyprus in a simultaneous referendum. Meanwhile, Cypriot Turks elected a new prime minister – Mehmet Ali Talat – and demonstrated forcefully for a settlement. They saw the dangers ahead if the TRNC continued to be embargoed and excluded from membership of international bodies.

Despite world pressure, neither Denktas nor Papadopoulos believed the UN plan was in their interest. Both were assured that UNFICYP would be expanded and have power to ensure safety for the people, the smooth transfer of land, safe return for some refugees and compensation for lost properties. The UN, EU, US and UK warned the feuding parties that there would be no further talks or plans. This was their last chance to unite the Island before the internationally recognized Cyprus Republic became an EU member.

Annan urged the leaders of both sides to assess his document, which, he said, was a vast improvement on previous versions, to create a win-win situation. 'The process of negotiation is not a football match,' he said. 'It is not a question of keeping score of goals and own goals, of winners or losers.' In a dig at the leaders, Annan's Cyprus envoy Alvaro de Soto told the press later that the people in Cyprus had unfortunately become accustomed to the impression that a settlement meant something quite different than what it realistically could be. He said they now had a heavy responsibility in the run-up to the two referenda to explain the plan to the people. 'The plan is quite different than the one people have been trashing for the last year or so,' he said. 'It is improved in many ways, which is evident if you read it.'

'Let us be clear,' the UN Secretary-General warned, 'the choice is not between this settlement and some other magical mythical solution. In reality, the choice is between this settlement and no settlement.'

Papadopoulos was not willing to bend. He called on his people to reject the plan outright in the referendum on 24 April. 'After judging all the facts and with a full realization of the historic moment we live through and my heavy responsibility, I am sincerely sorry that I cannot sign acceptance of the Annan plan,' the Greek Cypriot said as he addressed his people on television. With tears in his eyes, he continued: 'I am asking you to defend what is right, your dignity and history.' He also said the plan effectively wrote off 'the 1974 Turkish invasion' and legitimized the presence of thousands of Turkish troops and settlers on the island.

Across the UN Buffer Zone, newly elected Prime Minister Talat pledged to vote 'Yes' for the UN plan. 'Let's say "yes" so that we can join the international community; let's say "yes' that we may bring an end to emigration and alienation. Let's say "yes" that the Turkish Cypriot community can grow in an atmosphere of political equality and EU membership,' he told mass crowds.

On the eve of the referendum, US State Department envoy Thomas Weston warned that if the Greek Cypriots failed to accept the Annan plan, Turkey should not be made to pay the price by means of obstacles to its EU path. 'The increasing consensus among the other EU member countries is that if Turkey fulfils its responsibilities and there is still no resolution because of the Cypriot Greek side's refusal, then under these circumstances a Turkey that has fulfilled the Copenhagen criteria should not be allowed to remain outside of the EU.'

Former President Clerides declared: 'I am the man who warned that there would be dramatic developments in the Cyprus problem in 2004 ... I am the man with 50 years of experience in negotiations ... and with my experience, I put my hand on the Holy Bible and swear: My assertions are not done for any other reason and let us be proven wrong, but they are serious and responsible assertions, that the dangers we face from a "No" would be the burial of the land of our fathers.'

US Secretary of State Colin Powell addressed the Greek Cypriot media: 'We have to act on this plan and not hope for something better, or that lightning will strike if we delay,' he said. 'We have made it clear, the United Nations has made it clear, the Secretary-General of the United Nations has made it clear and the European Union has made it clear that we expect both parties to abide by all elements of the plan. And I have been encouraged by the statements coming from Turkey, Prime Minister Erdogan and others in his government that they fully intend to meet their obligations under the plan.'

Eric Silver had returned to the Island to report the referendum. 'I should have known better,' he says. 'The Cypriots, as Israel's Abba Eban used to say in another conflict, never miss an opportunity to miss an opportunity. The shunned, impoverished 154,000 Turks, who won the war but lost the peace, were expected to vote "Yes". The prosperous 640,000 Greeks, who knew they were going into the European Union on 1 May regardless, appeared set to vote "No". The EU's decision to admit Cyprus without demanding that it first resolve its internal quarrels owed more to the politics of Western Europe, it seemed, than to those of the Eastern Mediterranean.'

ON 24 APRIL Cypriots went to the polls to decide the future of their island. Before sunset the world community knew the result:

OXI/No 76% on the Greek side.

EVET/Yes: 65% on the Turkish side.

'This overwhelming rejection of the UN-brokered plan by Greek Cypriots has sealed the permanent partition of the island,' Turkey's Foreign Minister Abdullah Gul immediately addressed reporters. 'With the Greek Cypriot "no", the partition of the island has been made permanent.'

The European Commission expressed deep regret that Greek Cypriots had not approved the Annan plan. 'A unique opportunity to bring about a solution to the long-lasting Cyprus issue has been missed.' It went on to 'warmly' congratulate the Turkish Cypriots for their 'Yes' vote. 'This signals a clear desire of the community to resolve the island's problem,' it said, adding that the Commission was ready to consider ways of further promoting economic development of the North.

The UN, which had spent extensive time and effort to complete the 9,000-page document, said a unique and historic chance had been lost. The statement continued: 'The Secretary-General applauds the Turkish Cypriots, who approved the plan notwithstanding the significant sacrifices it entailed for many of them.' He also regretted that the Turkish Cypriots would not equally enjoy the benefits of EU accession but he hoped that ways would be found to ease the plight they had found themselves in 'through no fault of their own'.

Britain and the US were no less disappointed. 'Failure of the referendum in the Greek Cypriot community is a setback to the hopes of those on the Island who voted for the settlement and to the international community,' said US State Department spokesman Richard Boucher. 'We commend all who voted to approve the plan – particularly a large majority of Turkish Cypriots – for their courage and their vote for peace and reconciliation.'

Charilaos Paikkos, a 55-year-old Greek Cypriot quality controller in the shoe trade, who grew up in London's Islington, represented the opinion of the voters in the South. He put it plainly: 'The Annan plan was a set-up from the start. It was blatantly pro-Turkish. It served the interests of Britain, America and Turkey more than Greek or Turkish Cypriots,' adding that he predicted, 'we'll get partition and the Turkish army stationed permanently in the North.'

Mrs Nafia Mehmet is in her seventies today. Meral, her daughter, was a babe in arms when Grivas led his onslaught on the Kokkina enclave in 1964 and the family left their home village of Mansoura to become refugees for the first time. During the following 12 years they lived a hand-to-mouth existence, often relying on aid from UNFICYP. 'Because our village had been destroyed by the Greeks, we lived in tents and haphazard dwellings and were starting to improve our livelihood when the Greeks toppled Makarios and started shedding blood and killing again in July 1974,' Mrs Mehmet says.

Two years after the 1974 coup and invasion, as part of a population exchange, the Mehmet family was settled in the North at Yialousa, known in the TRNC as Yeni Erenkoy. 'We were rehabilitated and started a new life,' Mrs Mehmet explains. Now she helps her married daughter Meral Sertsoy to run a restaurant called Mansoura. Mrs Sertsoy expresses no bitterness when she talks about her childhood. 'We remember the bitter and bloody days, but the past is gone. We have peace and they [Greek Cypriots] have peace. There is no need for bloodshed and fighting any more. Let us have peace,' she explains in measured tones. While she believes that Greeks and Turks 'must be free to go where they want', she is equally adamant that 'they cannot settle here again because we will have to be displaced again'.

Mrs. Sertsoy represents the opinions of most Turkish Cypriots when she declares: 'We are all peoples of Cyprus. Cyprus belongs to us. Our leaders must find a solution. Let them permanently settle the property issue and questions of territory. Let the people stay where they are. Do not force them to become refugees again, displaced and homeless. We are happy where we are. Let the Greek Cypriots be happy with what they have. After all, their leaders and fanatics started the bloodshed for *enosis*. Let the people of Cyprus live peacefully as close and good neighbours. Let us not have a repetition of those bad days. Give our leaders a chance to find a peaceful solution.'

BY 2008, Denktas had retired, Papadopoulos had lost the presidential election and there were two new leaders to represent their communities. Greek Cypriot Demetris Christofias was elected in the South and his Turkish Cypriot opposite number was Mehmet Ali Talat, both left-wingers, neither of whom had anything in common with EOKA, but who did share socialist ideals. Could they

President Demetris Christofias of the Republic of Cyprus.

President Mehmet Ali Talat of the Turkish Republic of Northern Cyprus in 2009.

finally reach a settlement on the future of the Island?

In an atmosphere of great hopes and supported by their constituents, they wasted no time in returning to the drawing board. They agreed that a solution would entail a bizonal and bicommunal federation, with a single international personality, consisting of a Greek Cypriot and a Turkish Cypriot constituent state enjoying equal status. Christofias and Talat also said they accepted in principle that a solution would entail a single sovereignty and citizenship on the Island. Always present at these talks was Australian diplomat Alexander Downer, the UN Secretary General's Special Adviser for Cyprus. His role was to observe, not negotiate, although the parties could raise questions with him about 'all the international precedents and approaches that have been taken to these types of issues . . .' Downer added: 'They have a way to go, of course. These are difficult issues and they are not going to be resolved in one meeting. Our role is not to write a settlement to the Cyprus problem. Our role is to be as helpful as we can and for the people of Cyprus in the end to make the decisions about any settlement that they may agree.'

Observers predicted agreement would be reached by the end of 2008. It did not happen. A survey conducted by the Centre for European Policy Studies (CEPS) in collaboration with Greek and Turkish Cypriots suggests why. The pollsters asked Cypriots what they thought of the current peace process, how it should be conducted and what kind of solution would be acceptable. They found important elements of mistrust and scepticism.

'Both communities tend to trust only their immediate surroundings including the family, people they know personally and their neighbourhood, while both are distrustful of strangers and people of other nationalities and faiths. Greek Cypriots in particular also appeared to be fomenting the potential for ethnic intolerance and xenophobia (probably not only towards Turkish Cypriots but also towards immigrants of other European countries), with only 8% of Greek Cypriots believing that ethnic diversity enriched life,' a survey found.

The Centre's reporters noted that, 'Greek Cypriots live in a comparatively multi-ethnic society whereas Turkish Cypriots live in a comparatively mono-ethnic society; at the same time, it is Turkish Cypriots who tend to espouse ethnic diversity and not the Greek Cypriots. Perhaps the responses of each community represent a form of over-compensation for their actual life experiences: the Greek Cypriots are becoming worried about the social consequences of an increasing influx of immigrants, while the Turkish Cypriots are becoming worried about their isolation from the other nations and nationalities of the world and acknowledge the need to achieve greater openness in society.'

The survey discovered that 'the Greek Cypriot notion that the Turkish Cypriots are mere puppets in the hands of Ankara is received by the Turkish Cypriots as hurtful and insulting, despite – or even because of – Greek Cypriot assurances that "our problem is not with you but with Ankara". At the same time, the perception among Turkish Cypriots that the Orthodox Church in the Greek Cypriot Community was somehow an equal partner of the President and the National Council in the formulation of Cyprus problem policy betrayed a narrative that is frozen in time since the early days of the conflict.'

Although both sides had taken confidence-building measures, such as opening their borders to visitors from both sides, particularly in Nicosia, where Ledra Street divided the two halves of the capital, Greek Cypriot media still referred to its side as 'the free area' and described the North as 'occupied' with a 'so-called' president and government. 'The absurdities of this situation become apparent when one realizes that the far-right, ultra-nationalist Greek Cypriot newspaper *Simerini* favours the far-left, ultra-radical Turkish Cypriot newspaper *Afrika* as its source of information about the North,' writes Rebecca Bryant of the *Middle East Review*.

Certainly the opening of the borders to

both sides generated excitement as Cypriots rushed to see how the other half lived. Long queues of Greek Cypriots extended more than three miles from the Ledra Palace checkpoint into the streets of South Nicosia as the clock ticked down to the opening of the border to the TRNC for the first time in 29 years on 23 April 2003. They all wanted to be the first to enter the North. Some had started queuing up in the middle of the night. Eventually their patience failed and they brushed their way past British UN peacekeepers in the Buffer Zone dividing the two Island states.

Nobody had expected such large crowds and there were delays in processing them, but as the week went on more entry points were opened and crossings became more orderly. North Nicosia's mayor Kutlay Erk admitted: 'We were caught off-guard.' He had been given only three days' notice by the TRNC's Deputy Prime Minister Serdar Denktas, the president's son, who had announced the landmark decision, aimed at building confidence between the two estranged communities. He said: 'This is a unilateral decision passed to promote peace. We hope the Greek Cypriots will follow suit.'

The people on both sides welcomed the move with enthusiasm, but none expected that the border crossings were the first steps towards re-uniting the Island under one administration. President Denktas observed: 'One should not be mistaken that the political reasons for the original conflict no longer exist.' He wanted the border to stay open, as long as there was no sign of inter-communal conflict starting again. The partial lifting of travel restrictions was not even a 'step' towards a Cyprus settlement, replied President Tassos Papadopoulos.

PERHAPS BOTH gentlemen should have remembered the unity that had occurred spontaneously in 2000, without any interference by a politician or outside agency.

After reading an appeal on the internet by Ayla Gurel, a lecturer at the Eastern Mediterranean University in Famagusta, hundreds of ordinary Turkish Cypriots crossed into the Buffer Zone and entered the Ledra Palace's disused ballroom to try to help Andreas Vassiliou, a six-year-old Greek Cypriot, who was critically ill in the South, suffering from leukaemia and urgently in need of a bone marrow transplant to save his life. 'Our goal was to gather as many people as possible to provide blood samples to help this boy,' Ayla said. Ignoring their political differences, they put aside years of enmity and responded. Nurses from the Greek Cypriot Karaiskakio hospital took their blood samples. Among the volunteers was Serdar Denktas.

Following his test, Denktas Jr. was introduced to the boy's businessman father, Vassos. The two men came together in a bear hug and both were close to tears. Serdar observed: 'This is a humanitarian issue and has nothing to do with politics.' Vassos agreed: 'This goes beyond politics, religions, nationalities and any hatred. When Turkish Cypriots see my Andreas, they just see an innocent child who desperately needs help. He could be one of theirs.' He continued: 'My son won't die. The people in Cyprus have shown they will not allow that to happen. It is just rather sad that it takes something like this to bring our two communities together. It's been compared to the earthquake diplomacy, which did so much for Greece and Turkey last year. Maybe here in Cyprus it will now be the same.'

The way Cypriot Turks went to the boy's assistance made the South aware, too, that there were similar cases in the North. Kemal Saracoglu, a Turkish 12-year-old, was waiting at London's Royal Free Hospital for a bone marrow transplant because such an operation could not be done at any of the Island's medical facilities. Greek Cypriots immediately said they would follow the example set by their traditional enemies. Following Ayla's lead in northern Cyprus, they publicized Kemal's case in the British media, calling on all 500,000 Cypriots, Turks and Greeks, in the UK to volunteer to be checked to see if any of them were suitable to give bone marrow.

Sitting at Kemal's bedside, Suha, the boy's father, said: 'There is a chance for Andreas on the Greek side and for Kemal on the Turkish side. This will be good for our sons, and good for the future.' Ayla Gurel remarked: 'This is bringing us together as human beings and building much-needed trust between the two communities. Our historical hostility contradicts the real nature of Turkish and Greek Cypriots who are generally very kindhearted people.'

A donor was found eventually for young Kemal and his transplant operation was scheduled for 27 July 2000, at London's Royal Free Hospital, but it was too late. His condition worsened a week before it could take place and was cancelled. The boy died on 30 August. His funeral took place a week later at the Selimiye Mosque in North Nicosia. Vassos Vassiliou, Andreas's father and Nikola Kyriacou, the dead boy's Greek Cypriot penpal, attended. Both had been given permission by the two sides to cross over at the Ledra Palace checkpoint.

In the mosque, the two fathers stood side by side in front of Kemal's flower-covered casket. Their eulogies were in Turkish, Greek and English. Vassos Vassiliou, whose son was in the United States awaiting a compatible donor, declared emotionally: 'Kemal and Andreas have become symbols of humanity. They have brought Turkish Cypriot and Greek Cypriot people together. Kemal became my son. I felt I had to come and say goodbye. I have to thank all of those who turned a blind eye to race and religion.'

Kemal's funeral service was conducted on the eve of the fourth round of UN sponsored 'proximity talks' in New York about the Island's future. They were to be attended by the presidents of the two parts of Cyprus. Neither expected to meet the other face-to-face. Despite the opinion of the 60,000 islanders who came forward in the search for suitable donors for both boys, the Greek Cypriot administration refused to accept President Denktas as the head of a legitimate, independent state.

THE CEPS report points out, too, that there was 'a significant distance and polarization between the two communities on other issues': questions of governance, property, residence, 'settlers' and security. On property, there was a wide divergence regarding whether a solution should primarily take the form of restitution or compensation. Many Turkish Cypriots visiting their former homes in the South report that the homes are now either rubble or have been flooded by dams or made into shopping malls, hotels and parking lots. 'Foreign residents in the North have borne the brunt of Greek Cypriot ire since the checkpoints opened, and Karmi, as a foreign enclave, has reportedly experienced more than most,' writes Rebecca Bryant. 'When a Greek Cypriot woman entered the garden of her father's former coffee shop to pick flowers, she was stopped by policemen called by the current resident. She and her companions were arrested for trespassing, detained overnight and released with a fine.'

On residence rights, there were clear differences in the interpretation of bizonality, with Greek Cypriots strongly opposing and Turkish Cypriots preferring that members of each community should live primarily within the boundaries of their own constituent state. Typical of many Greek Cypriots, Charalambos Pittas was a Morphou resident and says he dreams about his home town every night and is determined to return. The opposite view is taken by Havva Onbasioglulari, in her late 70s. She lives in a former Greek property in Morphou/Guzelyurt. She is a refugee from

Limassol. In July 1974, she and her family were removed from their property, held prisoner by Greek Cypriots and threatened with death in the grounds of a local hospital. With others they escaped and found sanctuary at RAF Akrotiri. She could not return to her original house even if she wanted to. It no longer exists, buried under a new motorway.

In Bellapais, Refet runs his modest café, the *Ulusogfu Kahvehanesi*, with its English phone kiosk, a reminder of the 82 years of British rule of this contested Island. Long out of use, the red booth now houses a fuse box and electricity meter. It stands in the shade of the mountain village's 'Tree of Idleness', which Lawrence Durrell described in his *Bitter Lemons*. Opposite, another larger restaurant's 'Tree of Repose' is a pretender to the title, but the original is an impoverished aristocrat by comparison. In true Cyprus tradition, however, there is yet another claimant, 'The Tree of Idleness' restaurant that squats on a hill outside South Nicosia.

Refet used to run a coffee shop in his home village of Tatlisu, where, in colonial times, many of the menfolk commuted to the RAF base at Akrotiri to work. Others were farmers. All used to gather at his place to exchange the news and gossip of the day. Life had been hard, but peaceful. In 1964, Tatlisu's tranquillity came to an end. Greek Cypriot militia laid siege to the village, confining all its inhabitants for two months, until British UN soldiers succeeded in relieving them. The people suffered even more harshly in 1967. Once again, they were surrounded, but now the Greek Cypriot forces shelled them, inflicting heavy casualties. Still the people refused to leave.

Seven years later, suddenly, on Sunday, 21 July 1974, the Greek National Guard struck again. They called for the villagers to lay down their simple weapons and surrender. They refused. They knew what would happen if they did. Earlier, 15 Cypriot Turks had given themselves up, only to be shot dead in cold blood. The Greek Cypriot response came the next day. The National Guard ringed the village with heavy artillery and, hour after hour, pounded the inhabitants with cannon fire.

The men of the village, their ammunition exhausted, had no alternative but to seek a truce to prevent the extermination of their families. Accompanied by UN soldiers, the Greek National guardsmen entered, removed all weapons and rounded up every male they could find. As soon as UN personnel withdrew, extremist members of EOKA-B began beating the unarmed civilians with rifle butts. The injured captives, one of whom was Refet, were then marched to the police station in Kalavasos.

At the police station, they were beaten again and held for three days, without food or water. The Turkish Cypriots were released eventually, only to be re-arrested a few hours later and beaten once more. Their beatings continued for a week. On one occasion, Refet was taken outside, told to walk towards a tree in the distance and not to look back. As he came closer to the tree, his captors started shooting in his direction. He turned and faced his attackers, walking slowly forward. The police stopped firing. They grabbed him and returned him to his cell. Several days later, with the others, he was returned to Tatlisu – what was left of it.

On 14 August EOKA-B attacked the village yet again. This time they took 89 males prisoner, including Refet, and transported them to Limassol. For the next 78 days they were held in a school building with another 1,100 Cypriot Turks, fed only bread and water. In October, after the Greek Cypriot and Turkish Cypriot administrations agreed an exchange of prisoners, Refet and the other males from Tatlisu were sent to Bellapais to make new homes. The Greeks there were moved to the South, with their families.

The newly arrived Cypriot Turks in

Bellapais were without their families. Nobody knew what had happened to them. When news came eventually, those whose relatives had survived had to 'purchase' their release from the Greek Cypriots. The South's government insisted that the Turkish families were not and never had been Prisoners of War and therefore were not subject to the exchange agreement. The release of these women and children had to be negotiated separately and informally. Seen from a Greek point of view, this was a reasonable demand, as otherwise, they would have been tacitly conceding the division of Cyprus into two parts, run by separate, independent Greek and Turkish administrations.

Back with her husband, the gutsy Mrs Refet began to organize their lives again. The Turkish Cypriot authorities made every effort to give these displaced people a business, home and land equivalent to that which they had lost. What the new arrivals received was what the Greeks had owned. Just as the restaurants had changed hands, so had the land near the magnificent Gothic Abbey that dominates the mountain.

'Both communities have had to make the best of their changed circumstances. To calculate the amounts owed to each other after so long a time would be an incredible challenge for any arbitrator,' comment neutral observers.

IN FEBRUARY 2009, the property issue caused Neoclis Sylikiotis, the Interior Minister of the RoC, to be sharply criticized by right-wing politicians when he announced that his government could not and would not stop Greek Cypriots from selling their properties in the North, as long as the transactions went through the South's Land Registry office and all taxes were paid. According to the Land Registry's records, there were 256 such transactions in 2007, but these fell to 150 in 2008, after the Interior Ministry imposed a temporary freeze to take advice from the Attorney General.

The opposition wanted a complete ban on the sales, because they said they were not in the national interest, Turks would exploit the Greek owners by not paying market prices and, finally, they might be sold on to foreigners. The *Cyprus Mail* was quick to quip: 'It is perfectly acceptable to sell land in Paphos and Larnaca to foreigners, but in the occupied [*sic*] North, we have a national duty not to sell to anyone – not even other Greek Cypriots. This perfectly illustrates the absurdity of the ultra-patriotic parties who, despite posing as champions of the rule of law and defenders of refugee rights, want to deprive refugees of their property rights by law.' Sylikiotis made it clear that such a law would be unconstitutional but, more importantly, it would penalize refugees – the few who could make some money out of selling their Turkish-held properties, he declared.

The CEPS report adds: 'Direct air links are also of fundamental importance to Turkish Cypriots, representing a critical asset for the development of the tourist industry. As in the case of direct trade, the absence of direct air links was a principal feature of the international isolation of the Turkish Cypriots. The Chicago Convention on International Civil Aviation acknowledges each state's "complete and exclusive sovereignty over airspace above its territory".

'The RoC government, recognized by the UN as the sole legitimate state on the Island, claims exclusive rights to designate which airports may be used. The simplest solution would be for the Greek Cypriots to allow direct flights to Ercan Airport in Northern Cyprus. However, there appeared to be little prospect for further movement on this front, despite its importance for the development of the North.'

'Everything must come to an end – even the Cyprus Problem, the never-ending saga of

Turkish and Greek Cypriots to find an acceptable formula of sovereignty sharing to live together in a united island,' wrote Dr Ozay Mehmet in the *Cyprus Mail*. The Professor Emeritus of International Affairs at Canada's Carleton University pointed out that 'the grassroots, both in the south and the north, are going nationalist and uncompromising'.

In North Cyprus, voters had ousted President Talat's party from Parliament and returned the 73-year-old veteran politician Dervis Eroglu to power as prime minister, just as the government in South Cyprus was cheering a landmark ruling by the European Court of Justice that gave Greek Cypriots the right to reclaim their pre-1974 properties. Put plainly, EU expats owning homes on Greek land in the TRNC would have to compensate the original owners for their loss. If they refused, their bank accounts could be seized as well as any property they owned in an EU state.

The two events, coupled together, left no incentive for the leaders of the two sides to negotiate, Dr Mehmet believed. 'The Christofias–Talat talks will simply vanish away,' he predicted. 'No one will walk away; they will simply melt away like spring snow. And with that the last hope for a united Cyprus will disappear.'

IN AUGUST 2009, another event occurred to hinder the peace negotiations. For several years a joint Greek and Turkish Cypriot Committee of Missing Persons had been making progress in exhuming the remains of many of those who had been killed during the Turkish invasion and the previous 10 years of communal strife. From the start of the CMP's work, both sides had agreed 'that no political exploitation should be made by either side of the problem of the missing persons', which would be treated as a 'purely humanitarian issue'.

The creation of the CMP was one of several

confidence-building measures aimed at giving closure to the relatives of 'the missing' and played an important role in the resumption of the peace process.

Then, whether by choice or ill-timing, the government of the Republic of Cyprus chose the 35th anniversary of the second phase of the Turkish military operations in Cyprus to release information about five Greek Cypriot soldiers still listed as 'missing in action'. The Greek side, in several propaganda campaigns, had used the photographs of them with their hands behind their heads, watched by Turkish troops.

A Greek Cypriot spokesman announced to the media that these soldiers' bodies now had been found at the bottom of a well, adding that it was clear that their Turkish captors had executed them after their surrender.

The five National Guardsmen were identified by DNA as Antonakis Korellis, 30, from Kythrea; Panicos Nikolaou, 26, from Achna; Christoforos Skordis, 25, from Dhali; Ioannis Papayiannis, 23, from Neo Horio, Kythrea; and Philipos Hatzikyriakos, 19, from Ammochostos.

There was an immediate outpouring of anger by Greek Cypriots. Their newspapers and politicians did nothing to calm the situation. Instead they called on the international community to charge Turkey with war crimes and take its leaders to The Hague for trial. *Phileleftheros*, a Greek Cypriot newspaper, claimed the government was gathering evidence to present to the Council of Europe.

Reaction from the Turkish Cypriots came from Hasan Ercakica, President Mehmet Talat's official spokesman. He stressed that 'the missing persons issue should not be politicised' and added: 'It is very concerning to see that the administration of Mr Christofias [the Greek Cypriot President] is tending to move away from the said agreement ... Our concern is that the works regarding determining the fate of the missing persons could be negatively affected by such efforts. The second reason is that the process to reach a comprehensive solution for the Cyprus problem could also be affected by such negative actions ... This will not only complicate the acceptance of a solution, but might render the efforts of the two leaders on the issue ineffective.'

It was left to the *Cyprus Mail* to editorialize: 'For close to two decades, no progress had been made on establishing the fate of a single missing person, because the issue was being used for political propaganda. Things changed with the election of Glafcos Clerides, but real progress was made with the opening of the checkpoints when it became easier to collect information.

'The fact that the representatives of both sides adopted a more constructive approach at CMP meetings also contributed to the progress. This was also helped by an understanding between the two sides not to exploit the Committee's findings politically. This understanding is now being threatened by the media reaction to the revelations about the killing of the five Greek Cypriot soldiers.

'What would the Cyprus government achieve by putting Turkey in the dock as newspapers have been demanding? The CMP's work would be halted, the settlement negotiations would be dealt a big blow and hostility between the two communities would be given a boost.

'This might be exactly what the newspapers want, but the government must not allow them to impose their negative agenda. If the peace drive is to be successful we need to accept that atrocities were committed by both sides and put the past behind us.'

In the midst of the furore, investigative journalist Makarios Droushiotis revealed the story behind the iconic photographs of the five soldiers. They had been taken by two Turkish photo-journalists, Ergin Konuksever and Adem Yavuz of the ANKA news agency, embedded with the Turkish Army. They were

The Greek soldiers captured by the Turkish Army and later shot in cold blood by Turkish Cypriots.

The Turkish press photographer who saw the Greek prisoners murdered.

travelling alongside a column of tanks commanded by Lieutenant Ersel Kayan.

Droushiotis reported: 'The National Guard's Infantry 398 Battalion was stationed in the area around the Turkish Cypriot village of Djiaos, situated in the plain of Mesaoria. A group of soldiers, headed by reserve Sergeant Antonis Korelis, received orders to open fire with their antiquated No. 4 rifles at an incoming column of tanks that was headed towards Famagusta.

'Having fired at the tanks, the soldiers themselves gave away their position and took fire from the Turkish forces. Three or perhaps four of the tanks broke from the column and headed for the hill where the Greek Cypriot soldiers had taken cover. Two of the soldiers managed to escape; the remaining five were surrounded by Turkish forces and forced to surrender.'

He pointed out that three weeks earlier, Greek forces and irregulars had captured a nearby Turkish village and attacked civilians. He quoted Yiannakis Christodoulou, one of those soldiers, as saying: 'We did so many [bad] things at Djiaos, it was only natural that whoever of us was caught was a goner.' Droushiotis added that a Greek officer had told him that on 22 July four Turkish Cypriots had been 'executed in a similar fashion by Greek Cypriot soldiers'.

Ergin Konuksever added: 'I want to talk about those soldiers now that their bodies have been found and identified. I remember that day like yesterday. Nobody expected them to be killed. Lieutenant Kayan even offered them cigarettes. Then Boratas Pasha arrived and took them to a nearby place, where prisoners were assembled and passed to the Mujahideen to guard.

'A few minutes later, we heard gunfire and ran towards it to find out what was happening. I saw one of the Turkish Cypriots shoot dead one of the prisoners. The others had been executed before we arrived. I asked the Turkish Cypriot why. He shouted back: "These men shot and killed my brother." He repeated himself several times. Another Turkish Cypriot also shouted: 'They killed my sister."

'Boratas Pasha was furious. He ordered the prisoners' documents to be handed to him. Then he and the tanks moved on. We left the area with our photographs, which we wanted to transmit to Turkey as soon as possible. We returned to our minibus and decided to drive to north Nicosia, where we hoped to board a military helicopter for Adana.

'Our driver thought he knew the way, but he took a wrong turning and Greek forces opened fire on us, because our bus was flying a Turkish flag. A bullet entered my back and came out of my shoulder. A very slim Greek officer, with blond hair, reached us. Adem Yavuz, my colleague, said: "We are journalists, not combatants. We are not fighting."

'The officer told his men to search us and bring me a towel so that Adem could wrap my wound. They confiscated our cameras, 11 lenses and all our films. We had used up 24 rolls. After waiting several hours, an armoured vehicle arrived and we were taken to their military headquarters. From there we were moved to a hospital. Carried on a stretcher, I was attacked by nurses as soon as the soldiers left and fell unconscious. The next thing I remember was being in a room with a doctor. He had operated and saved my life. He said, "I have taken the Hippocratic oath. My oath is more important for me than the war. Your security is my responsibility." Adem was lying in a bed next to mine.

'I was surprised to see him, because he had not been injured when I last saw him. But now . . .' Konuksever's voice trails away. 'Now Adem was lying with a bad wound in his abdomen. Although in great pain, he still managed to tell me what happened after the nurses started beating me.

'The soldiers had handcuffed us together, blind-folded and then shot him, before our doctor stopped further violence. During the next few hours, he only accepted local anaesthetic for the five operations he underwent. I still hear his screams in my ears. He apologized for not getting us back to Turkey with our photographs!

'Adem died before he could be repatriated. He must have know he would not survive, because he asked me to make sure he was buried in Sivas Cinarli, the place of his birth. "I want to be placed next to a stream, with a bottle of raki beside me," he said.

'Much later, when I was employed by *Milliyet*, I heard some of our pictures had been published in the foreign press, with a caption that said these prisoners were held in Turkey and forced to work in the mines. When the UN Commission on Missing Persons was created I was invited by President Denktas to tell them exactly what I had witnessed.

'I agreed and was interviewed by the members of the Commission, who had seen only some of our pictures, those given them by the Greeks. No one seemed to know where the others were. I wanted them to see everything we had shot. Later the chairman came to me and whispered: "I'm a citizen of a cold country. In Cyprus I live in a beautiful house, I have a luxury car and get paid a high salary. I do not want ever for our investigations to end. So say nothing more."'

Later two or three of their photographs appeared in *Machi*, the Greek Cypriot newspaper published by Nicos Sampson, the EOKA killer and short-lived president after the coup. The fate of the other pictures remains unknown, as does the reason why Greek authorities chose to reveal the fate of their soldiers at a time when the peace talks were reported to be making progress again.

In summer 2009, Ergin Konuksever went to Kyrenia to meet Greek Cypriot Dr Andreas Demetriades, whose surgery had kept him alive. 'I hope I saved many lives and I am sorry I could not prevent Adem's death, but our hospital was close to the front line, there were hundreds of injured and we were short of medical supplies. Today we hope for better times and no more fighting,' said the doctor. Then the two men hugged and shook hands.

Privately individuals were coming to terms with past and forming personal unions. On 5 September, Greek Cypriot Georgia Chappa and Turkish Cypriot Murat Kanatli married on the Greek island of Samos, near the Turkish mainland, reported the Associated Press. Chappa, 38, a clinical dietician, is involved with a women's group, *Hands Across the Divide*, while Kanatli, 36, leads the New Cyprus Party, a small leftist group that works towards rapprochement. As their relationship blossomed, the couple initially kept their families in the dark. When the secret was finally revealed, they had to face the objections of their families as well as the intimidation of nationalists on both sides.

FIFTY-FOUR years after Archbishop Makarios and Colonel George Grivas launched the EOKA conflict, however, the once united country was still divided due to their actions. They created the conditions for the eventual war between Greek and Turkish Cypriots and the partition of Aphrodite's Island, where the winter rains cannot wash away the pain and mistrust left behind.

Many claim that the division of Cyprus was plotted and achieved by politicians in Washington and London. Whichever theory is accepted, the fact remains that the total number of EOKA activists was probably no more than 600 individuals, even if today the EOKA Association's registry of members lists 20,633 names.

In 2005, the Association produced an eight-volume collection in Greek of 1,000 copies, sold only to former 'fighters' at a price of £75. A thousand entries cover 4,500 pages, giving details of where those named were born, were caught or killed and what they are alleged to have achieved. A resident Englishman who spoke fluent Greek saw that his gardener's name had been included and called him up. No, said the elderly Cypriot, he had never joined the 'Organization', but then his wife interrupted and said that someone had knocked on their door back in 1956 asking for food, telling them he represented EOKA. That, added the gardener, probably qualified him to be described as an honourable 'fighter'.

Such was the eagerness of old EOKA stalwarts to create legends that between 2005 and 2006, the late President Tassos Papadopoulos awarded medals and diplomas of service to 21,000 individuals for allegedly taking part in 'the struggle'. A cynical Greek Cypriot journalist rightly quipped: 'I would not be surprised if many of these people were honoured for doing nothing more heroic and dangerous than sacrificing their afternoon siesta to attend a meeting with the village priest.' One of the recipients of a bravery medal, he added, qualified only for being the son of Makarios's maid.

EOKA silver medals have been seen on sale on eBay, priced at $149.00 each.

The same Tassos Papadopoulos sent his condolences to British Prime Minister Blair as soon as the news broke on 7 July 2005 about the Islamist terrorist attacks on the London Underground. 'The Government and the people of Cyprus strongly condemn such horrendous acts of terror,' said the former EOKA member, 'and stand in full solidarity with the British people and the rest of the international community in the fight against terrorism of all kinds.'

On 20 June 2006, the media in Greek Cyprus reported that former Royal Signals soldier John Miller, 67, had given the EOKA Museum in Nicosia the flag that was lowered for the final time from the flagpole outside the Governor's Mansion on 15 August 1960 at 19.18, the evening before Britain gave up the Island. 'I love Cyprus and have made Finikaria village in Limassol my home. I believe the flag belongs here as part of the Island's history. I feel very proud and happy today in returning it,' said Miller. Thassos Sophocleos, the one-time gang leader in the Kyrenia district, accepted the flag on behalf of the EOKA Association.

Miller's action angered former British military personnel. Some servicemen believe he could not have been present at the formal standard-lowering ceremony to receive the flag from Sir Hugh Foot. They insist, too, that the flag would have been passed to British officers for safekeeping and returned to the United Kingdom. 'In my opinion that flag should have been given to a British Museum,'

said one. 'Miller has forgotten his countrymen who are buried in Wayne's Keep Cemetery.'

Another observed: 'He has insulted the memory of Mrs Cutliffe and all the good young men who died in Cyprus and are resting in Wayne's Keep Cemetery. I served there between 1957 and 1959, and am appalled at what he has done. I am positive all who served there feel the same.' A soldier who served at Kykko West with Cyprus District Signal Regiment best summed up the opinion of most. 'If this story is true, then the guy responsible wants shooting,' he declared bluntly.

Between March 1964 and May 2007, 172 UNFICYP soldiers lost their lives on duty. Michael Møller, the UNFICYP Chief of Mission, paid tribute to them when he unveiled a plaque at St Columba's Church in the United Nations Protected Area. Mr Møller said: 'We do well to remember that here in Cyprus, UNFICYP, a mission often overshadowed by the news from more embattled and less peaceful contemporary peacekeeping operations, has its own record of lives lost and sacrifices made in the name of peace and the healing of this divided island ... Some of our UNFICYP colleagues fell in the fire of conflict. Most died as the result of accidents or illness. Whatever the causes, all died in the service of peace – far from home and loved ones.'

During the EOKA conflict between 1 April 1955 and 31 March 1959, 371 British service personnel died on duty, of which the Royal Navy and Royal Marines lost 28, the RAF 69 and the Army 274. At the London Conference on 19 February 1959, Dr Kutchuk told their parents: 'Your sons have not died for nothing. Thanks to them we have come to today's understanding ... We will always remember them.' (*Halkin Sesi*, 2 February 1959)

To honour them, there is a permanent memorial in the old British Cemetery in Kyrenia. Established in 1878 when the British first arrived on the Island, it is the last resting place of Sergeant Samuel McGaw of the Black

Watch, the only VC laid to rest in Cyprus. Here, too, are the graves of two British Major Generals who served – Sir Courtenay Manifold (d. 1957) and Sir Charlton Spinks (d. 1959) – as well as that of a wartime governor and Commander-in-Chief, Sir William Battershill (1959). These were all distinguished servants of the Crown who died in the same years as those remembered on the memorial. Others with military connections share the cemetery with them. They include the holder of the Distinguished Service Order and another soldier awarded both a Military Cross and France's *Croix de Guerre*.

AS AUTUMN began and the swallows of Europe started their annual migration southwards for warmer climes in 2009, *Cyprus Mail* columnist Loucas Charalambous quoted Alexis Heraclides, a Greek Cypriot academician: 'The Cypriot Problem will be solved only when the Greek Cypriots admit and assume their responsibilities for its creation.'

Charalambous added: 'The above observation is probably the wisest view ever expressed in relation to the Cyprus problem. Its correctness is proved on a daily basis. Because Greek Cypriots, with their behaviour, show that not only have they not recognized our side's share of the blame, but also the denial of this gets worse with the passing of time. The obdurate refusal of the average Greek Cypriot to accept any blame for the mess we are in features triumphantly in the media every day ... For as long as Greek Cypriots carry on living with their illusions, based on official myths, they will never be able to accept their share of the blame and the Cyprus problem will never be solved.'

Suat Kiniklioglu, Deputy Chairman for External Affairs for Turkey's ruling Justice and Development Party and spokesman of the Foreign Affairs committee of the Turkish parliament, added his thoughts in a syndicated article.

'Contrary to many previous rounds of Cyprus negotiations, the issue this time is not confined to the Island alone,' he wrote, 'but embraces the wider region. The outcome of the ongoing talks will have a big impact on how Turkey assesses its relations with the EU. Should the talks fail, the side that behaves in an uncompromising manner will bear full responsibility for dividing the Island forever.'

As a gesture of goodwill, both sides cancelled their annual military exercises in October for the second year in a row. Hasan Ercakica, the Turkish Cypriot side's spokesman, said their decision had been taken in conjunction with the Turkish Armed Forces, while Stefanos Stefanou, the Greek Cypriot spokesman, replied that the Republic of Cyprus was responding in kind.

Yet, as 2010 approached, there were few certainties about the progress of the talks between the leaders of the two sides and the future of the Island. While those conducting the negotiations continued to express their commitment to forming a viable, bizonal, bicommunal federation, with political equality, represented as a single internationally recognized state, Turkish nationalist commentators stepped up their demands for two separate states. Quite surprisingly, their views were echoed by some Greek Cypriots.

One of them, Dr Takis Georgiou, took time out from his duties as a gynaecologist in Nicosia to write a book in which he also argued for partition. 'Taking all of the factors of the Cyprus problem into consideration, there is a very clear need for another strategy, one which is different to that of the federal "solution",' he says. 'We can maintain that a small, free homeland in the form of an independent Greek Cypriot state, which will be completely ours and will have the best chances of survival, is a thousand times better than a so-called "reunified" bizonal, bicommunal federal Cyprus that is doomed to failure.'

Georgiou insists that a 'federal' solution of

the type under discussion would 'cede the "occupied area" to the Turks. Even worse, with the retention rights of Turkey to intervene, sugar-coated or not, the whole of Cyprus will continue to be a Turkish protectorate, with the result that the road will remain open for the "Turkification" of the whole of Cyprus.' He foresees a situation where 80 per cent of the Cypriot [Greek] population will be governed by Turkey through the 20 per cent of Turkish Cypriots and settlers from the mainland, leading irrevocably to a 'racist' administration. His two-state solution, however, he maintains, would lead to peaceful co-existence and the 'survival of Hellenism in [South] Cyprus ... guaranteed to the largest possible degree'.

Dr Georgiou's views were considered heretical by the Greek Cypriot extremists, backed once again by the Church. Calling itself the Movement for Freedom and Justice in Cyprus, its members were among the most hysterical. 'Partition' was not a word to be imagined, let alone spoken aloud. For them, it was all or nothing. They demanded the removal of the Turkish Army in the North, the expulsion of all settlers since 1974 and reclamation of all Greek properties. They claimed that for 60 years the British and the Turks had been working to destroy the 1960 Republic and turn Cyprus into a Turkish state in the custody of the British. Ignoring realities, Archbishop Chrysostomos II declared: 'Our foreign policy should be aggressive and badger Turkey on a daily basis. Only in this way will Turkey understand our weight and give ground.' Until its demands were met, the Movement wanted the status quo to remain.

For the international community, however, the status quo could not be allowed to continue. The United Nations, the United States and the EU recognized that Turkey was now a major power in the region, with significant strategic alliances, and would not be pushed into surrendering what it considered

important to its national interests. While Ankara gave lip service to the ongoing talks, it was extremely unlikely that the Turkish Government would allow the Greek Cypriot side to drag them out for very much longer. Rather it might impose a 'solution', which could disrupt NATO, affect Europe economically and make the Middle East peace process more difficult for the West.

A leaked UN report, too, revealed that a strong body of opinion in the international organization no longer saw Turkey as an obstacle to a settlement, but were blaming the Greek Cypriot authorities for intransigency.

Loucas Charalambous, the *Cyprus Mail* columnist, put it pithily: 'I find it difficult to believe that despite all the experience foreigners have through dealing with us, they have still not understood what is blatantly obvious even to a 10-year-old. We have fully adjusted to partition; we are content with it and this is now a conscious choice ... No Cypriot is naive enough to think that a return to the pre-1974 state of affairs was remotely possible or to believe that a settlement better than the one offered in 2004 could be secured ... It is a historical truth that war always gives rise to new interests. The new interests created in the Greek Cypriot community in the last 35 years are now so powerful they would even reject *enosis* as a settlement if it were offered to us today.'

A more measured, yet no less accurate, assessment came from the International Crisis Group. It declared that unless the current talks produced a settlement by Spring 2010, the only option left was international recognition of *de facto* partition. With the passing of the years, the younger generations of Cypriots – Greeks and Turks – would have no recollection of a once united Island.

On the eve of the 60th anniversary of the creation of the original Republic of Cyprus, hardly anyone remembered the final broadcast of Sir Hugh Foot, the Island's last Governor, as he prepared to sail away. 'What of the future?' he asked. 'It is for you to answer that question. A few dismal commentators say that the people of Cyprus will destroy each other. They say that you will tear yourselves to bits – Greek against Turk and Left against Right. There are a few who say that the Island will go down in a sea of blood and hate. It could be – but I don't believe it. People who have been to the brink of hell don't want to go over the edge.'

With presidential elections due in North Cyprus in Spring 2010, the chances are that Mehmet Ali Talat will not be re-elected, unless he delivered something tangible that could benefit Turkish Cypriots. It was likely that a hardliner would be the peoples' choice and that would be the end of any future negotiations.

With Turkey bankrolling the North's economy, it was only time before the government in Ankara might have to ask how long this could be allowed to continue. Some wondered, would 'the motherland' simply declare the TRNC one of its provinces? And who would be able to stop it?

Reading the grounds in their coffee cups, optimists in the South, therefore, declared that the political leaders of the two sides were 'doomed' to succeed in devising a final answer to the Cyprus question. By contrast, optimists in the North hoped that President Talat and President Christofias would fail, that the UN Special envoy, Australian Alexander Downer, would give up and follow in the footsteps of his predecessors since 1964 and that the Security Council in New York would devise a 'Taiwan' solution: the acceptance of the TRNC as a legitimate state, the lifting of trade embargoes, and the granting of direct flights and communications, even if they did not have a seat in the United Nations.

If what was being called the 'Plan B' scenario were played out in 2010, the effect on the EU, South Cyprus and the UK could be profound. The EU had granted membership to the Republic of Cyprus as a single unitary state, while the British Sovereign Bases had been agreed under the original terms for the whole Island's independence in 1960. Would the EU and the new Greek Republic of South Cyprus now have to renegotiate its membership? What would be the status of the two British bases, both located in the South? And the UN Buffer Zone? In parts, up to three miles separate two armies that fought each other in 1974; in others, the distance is less than an arm's reach. Would the UN continue to control this Island-wide 'frontier', and, if not …?

At the end of 2009, questions still outnumbered answers, but as ordinary mortals struggled to make sense of an apparent intractable situation, Theodore M. Pizanis, Director of the Cyprus Association for the Advancement of Science of Creative Intelligence, brought his members to the Ledra Palace Hotel with the primary purpose of reunifying the Island – through transcendental meditation.

'Just 100 experts, trained in the Maharishi Technology of the Unified Field, are sufficient to create a strong harmonious and friendly atmosphere for the whole Island,' Pizanis proclaimed. 'They will promote peace, confidence and co-operation for all Cypriots so that the longtime separation of North and South will soon end.'

Said Mr Pizanis: 'With our programme we follow the UNESCO constitution, which states, "wars begin in the minds of men. It is in the minds of men that the defences of peace must be constructed". Our goal is to try to develop a programme for that purpose and present our knowledge and findings from various trouble zones, which are quite unprecedented.'

With the arrival of Spring 2010, waves still splashed Aphrodite's Rock, known in Greek as *Petra tou Romiou*, the mythical birthplace of the goddess of love. It was not eroding because of the sea, but it was slowly being destroyed by the graffiti carved into its stone. Said Bettina Hadjicharalambous, 'As it stands, it is a reflection of the Island's condition, a drifting Island in an undefined space, disassociated from the world and as attractive as a stained baby diaper.'

As this book went to press, there had been no sightings of Mr Pizanis's squadron of Yogic flyers.

'Nations and peoples are largely the stories they feed themselves. If they tell themselves stories that are lies, they will suffer the consequences of those lies. If they tell themselves stories that face their own truths, they will free their histories for future flowerings.'

BEN OKRI, Nigerian poet

Pictures from the Buffer Zone

Where farming is allowed in sections of the Buffer Zone, workers must be escorted by UNFICYP personnel.

Efforts continue to clear the Buffer Zone of mines laid in 1974.

A deserted school in the UN Buffer Zone, exactly as it was left in 1974.

Cars that were brand new in 1974 gather dust in a showroom in the narrow BZ in divided Nicosia.

The first British journalist to be allowed inside Varosha since the invasion, the author photographs a UN post in 1984.

A Turkish Cypriot official meets UNFICYP Major David Emmett and the author during one of his many visits to the Island.

The author discusses the Cyprus question with Rauf Denktas, the former president of the TRNC.

UNFICYP Captain Gamlin with the author, when members of the British contingent were at St David's Camp.

One of the author's many UNFICYP passes from his visits to Cyprus.

CHAPTER THIRTY-TWO

Last words

'ALTHOUGH ANDREAS and Ali may be natives and residents of Cyprus, and regard the Island as their common homeland, they do not normally regard themselves as compatriots, but rather as neighbours. The last sentence should not be misunderstood: Greeks and Turks have many things in common, including a love and pride for their Cypriot homeland ... The point remains, however, that Greekness and Turkishness, even when these characterize people born and bred in Cyprus, constitute different national identities. National consciousness among Cypriots has traditionally been either Greek or Turkish; and the assertion of national consciousness and pride, in other words nationalism, has traditionally been either Greece-orientated or Turkey-orientated. To see why this is so, we must first understand the character of Greek nationalism itself, as it has developed in Greece; and to gain this understanding it is necessary to acquire some minimal familiarity with Modern Greek history.'

Zenon Stavrinides

'Living during the EOKA conflict was never easy and many soldiers counted the days until they returned home. National Service taught me a lot and I'm glad I did it. I was 19 years old and I wanted a bit of action. I certainly found it in Cyprus.'

Private Eddie White, the Middlesex Regiment

'On arrival at RAF Nicosia we were initially billeted with 208 Squadron. The lavatories were awful: a seat under which was a 20 ft. pit. Apart from the smell, one had to put up with the rats in there. Several blokes had had to go to hospital with bites in a very embarrassing place.'

Graham Robinson, RAF

'When British forces were transferred from their bases in Egypt, there was insufficient accommodation in which to house them in Cyprus. Makeshift camps were prepared and the soldiers were placed in large tents. They had been made soon after the Indian Mutiny in India and were still going strong.'

Tom Glenister, Royal Military Police

'The actual equipment of 40 Coy was mainly a large fleet of Bedford QL three-tonners in sand beige, quite a few of which had come from World War II crates discovered in the evacuation of the base in Tel el Kebir in the Canal Zone of Egypt.'

Driver Stuart Beveridge, RASC

'After we had been attacked on Mobile Patrol, our Land Rovers were given some protection, Sandbags on the floor. Later we had a form of hook, put on the front, to stop our heads being whipped off by wire across the road. In

1957, we were given the first so-called bullet-proof jackets – no more than six between about 50 of us!'

Charles Bailey, Royal Military Police

'A few nights after we began foot-patrols, a masked terrorist fired at an Englishman, who was leaving a cinema with his Turkish wife and father-in-law. The terrorist fled, but ran straight towards us. The leading fusilier fired from the hip and shot him in the shoulder. The 2nd Battalion was thus credited with the first Cypriot to be caught in a terrorist act.'

Lieutenant Colonel John Filmer-Bennett, OBE, MC, Royal Innikilling Fusiliers

'We just received a telegram saying that he had been killed in an ambush and telling us he was being buried in Wayne's Keep Cemetery in Nicosia. We hadn't seen him since he went abroad.'

Mrs R. Morrison, mother of Private David Morrison, 22, of the Argyll and Sutherland Highlanders

'Sergeant Allan Frederick Pinner was the last Sergeant of the Guard in the Sudan before the Leicesters left for Cyprus. He was killed on 11 April 1956, a few days before his 30th birthday. Someone in the regiment was insensitive enough to send the gloves he was wearing when he was shot. My father opened the parcel to find them blood-stained. He was not impressed.'

Syd Pinner, brother of Sergeant Allan Pinner, Royal Leicestershire Regiment

'If someone wanted for questioning or a youngster was chased because of throwing stones, a protective ring of skirts would gather hastily around the culprit, helping him escape. The soldiers, faced by mobs of shouting and gesticulating women, were bewildered. They were not brought up to rain butt-blows on 'kerchiefed heads or to point bayonets at plump breasts. The foreign journalists, too, were watching like hawks. The officers would try to reason with them, to explain that it was their duty to restore order, but the pleas and excuses given in a foreign tongue acted more as a challenge than a soporific. I wonder if I am the only priest in the Church of England who was once spat upon by a Greek Orthodox priest. It was quite clear where their sympathies were.'

Canon David Staples, formerly Private Staples, Royal Warwickshire Regiment

'If we expected to get involved in a riot of hostile Greek Cypriots, we left Coke bottles in the backs of our trucks to "cook" in the hot sun. When a riot got under way, we grabbed a few of these bottles, gave the Coke a good shake and then threw them, so that they dropped just in front of the demonstrators. The bottles exploded like hand grenades and laid a carpet of thick glass across the street. Because many Cypriots wore shoes with very thin soles, the glass became a barrier they found painful to cross. We never had to hit or shoot any rioter, let alone release some tear gas and spoil a fine day.'

Private Bryan Hunter, the Parachute Regiment

'Largely we kept ourselves to ourselves, not really getting to know the local people, because it was hard to tell friend from foe in those days. Of course, there were Cypriots working in the camp and they were always ready to make a quick buck. Whether we wanted a lemonade or bottle of Keo beer, there was no shortage of volunteers ready to satisfy our needs – for a price. They laughed and joked with us, but what were they thinking?'

Private Eddie White, the Middlesex Regiment

'We never went out alone. Dance trips were arranged for us in Akrotiri and the various regimental camps around the area. Transport was laid on with two or three armed escorts. It's a memory one does not forget, going to a dance, all dressed-up and chaps sitting by you with loaded Sten guns. I am sure the soldiers disliked this detail. I was lucky in some ways that my work was interesting and with a great bunch of lads. They were mostly National Service conscripts, so when one completed their service, it was an excuse for a "party". We were young and tended not to worry too much about danger, even when a few small bombs went off in our cantonment.'

WRAC Ruth White (née Armstrong),
27 Independent Company, Episkopi

'In the woman's bedroom was an old Turk who couldn't speak English but he told me via her that he had fought at Gallipoli. Imagine that, meeting someone who had fought our Battalion 40 years earlier. He gave us a chorus of *It's a Long Way to Tiperary*.'

Fusilier Malcolm C. McDonald,
Lancashire Fusiliers

'Practically the only place in the whole of Nicosia which was air-conditioned was the long bar in the Ledra Palace Hotel, where drinks cost three or four times what they cost anywhere else, and sixty times what they cost in the officers' mess. A brother officer, visiting the toilets of this bar one evening, identified one of the lavatories as a crouching EOKA terrorist and shot it to pieces. Everybody in the bar drew his pistol and it was lucky there was not a massacre. Later everybody swore they had indeed seen some suspicious characters around the place, but I think the officer concerned was sent home.'

Cornet Auberon Waugh, the Royal Horse
Guards

'By summer '57, EOKA activity had eased and it was considered safe enough to go out-and-about unarmed. Local leave was allowed and I took advantage of the CO's UK holiday to have a short break at the Dome Hotel, Kyrenia. It was great. The only sour note happened when two of us were enjoying a relaxing walk along the rocky seashore west of the hotel. Ambling along, we were suddenly confronted by an ancient Brit female, who in a loud plummy voice informed us that we were trespassing on private property. Given all the circumstances, we were – to use a current phrase – absolutely "gobsmacked".'

Private Norman Goodwin, Ox and Bucks
Light Infantry

'Blighty 2,000 miles – death 100 yards.'
Sign at the Transit Camp, Nicosia

'One of the new responsibilities of the Regiment became the safety of 900 families living in Limassol. Husbands were organized to do Home Guard patrols each night, because no troops could be spared. Headquarter Company and the Band spent almost as much time patrolling the town by day as they did doing their own jobs. Somehow, the machine never quite broke down.'

Captain M. R. Pennell, Royal Norfolk
Regiment

'It was my privilege to have been Chaplain of the 1st Battalion of the Durham Light Infantry in Cyprus, and I feel that you would be interested to know that the troops maintained what was a regimental tradition – by building a Church. St Cuthbert's was erected in a most attractive setting under the trees in Pinefields Camp. A simple building of corrugated iron, lined inside with hardboard, it seats about 60. Every Sunday morning we prayed for our families and loved ones and said the Regimental Collect.'

Rev. W. Burns, CF

'The hate between Greek and Turk was really something in those days! I've seen trucks, buses and cars ram each other head on because they carried rival factions. The Greeks painted their vehicles blue and white. The Turks responded by colouring theirs red and white. Quite incredible!'

Fusilier John Niven, Royal Scots Fusiliers

'Two Fusiliers are etched in my memory from those far-off days: Norman Hurst, a National Serviceman, my batman and bodyguard. He was a body builder, Mr North West Great Britain, at one stage. He could lift a rioting Greek or Turk with one hand whilst holding his rifle in the other. Peter Bickerstaff was my driver. Regrettably, he was killed shortly after I left the Battalion. He really was a splendid, brave, cheerful young man and great company to have around no matter what the circumstances.'

2nd Lieutenant Maurice Taylor, Lancashire Fusiliers

'Our convoy was bombed as we drove through a village. We assembled beside the road and moved into the village to search the houses and round up all the men and take them to the village square. As we passed the lead truck I saw the body of a young man, a kid really, on the road. Apparently, the bomb had bounced off the front tyre of the truck, exploded and killed him.'

Private Jim Dunlop, Highland Light Infantry

'Because our patrols were kept secret and our boats did not carry any markings, we were spotted sometimes by larger Royal Navy ships and mistaken for potentially hostile vessels. In these circumstances, we had to use our radio call sign *Yankee Papa* for identification. Living conditions on board the patrol boats were very cramped. After four weeks at sea, we were in need of a good bath. Occasionally we met up with a frigate or destroyer and used their shower facilities. The crew of these ships looked at us as if we were some strange beings, because not only did we appear scruffy, we did not wear conventional RN uniforms. Worse still, our body odour was stronger than bad cheese.'

Seaman Colin Martin, RN

'On hearing footsteps the Lance Corporal in charge of the ambush told his men in a low whisper, "Right, lads, we have got them. On my count of three, open fire." At daylight they left their position to investigate. They found a donkey shot full of holes. While viewing their kill a very irate villager came up and started shouting at them. Only the arrival of the OC with his interpreter prevented more bloodshed.'

Company Sergeant Major L. W. Rusby, the Duke of Wellington's Regiment

'My friend Herbert Stubbs from Harrogate had his 21st birthday on 14 December 1958 and four of us celebrated the occasion with a trip to Kyrenia, followed by dinner at the Acropole Hotel. We didn't want to wear uniform, so we persuaded four subalterns to draw pistols from the armoury and loan them to us so we could go out in civvies.'

Gordon Cross, Army Catering Corps

'Our task was to find and capture small gangs of terrorists who were living in caves in the high Troodos. It involved patrolling and ambushing, mostly at night. It was early summer '57 and the mountains were outstandingly beautiful, covered in pines with ground cover of myrtle, thyme, myriad wild flowers and even scrumptious wild asparagus. We supplemented our tinned "compo" rations with pigeons. Our camp was by a clean fresh water stream. With the help of some plastic explosive, we enlarged a pool to make it large enough in which to swim. We lived in small bivouac tents – "bivvys" –

slept in sleeping bags, all of which we could carry on our backs.'

Lieutenant Anthony Paxford, the Gloucestershire Regiment

'With my background as a chemist, I was ordered to prepare a chemical mixture, concocted by a Mr Titt, a War Office boffin. It was put into 10-gallon containers and transported to remote locations, where the contents were transferred to special tanks fitted to helicopters. The helicopter then released the stuff over a designated location known to be a hiding place for an EOKA group. Anyone moving through that area, it was believed, would absorb some of this fine, colourless spray and become "scented", allowing tracker dogs to follow and capture them. For my work on this project, I was never told whether Mr Titt's perfume resulted in the apprehension of a single terrorist.'

Sergeant Harry Blackley, pharmacist, RAMC – 36 Field Ambulance

'One night we raided a brothel in Tanzimat Street in Nicosia and all the customers turned out to be senior army officers. We ordered the civilian police to guard all exits and sent for a covered truck. It backed to the front door and the officers were herded into it without charge. "Next time," I told each officer, "send for the women to come to you, sir."'

Lance Corporal Tom Glenister, Royal Military Police

'As I was being lifted into the military ambulance with more horrible gurgles, Corporal of Horse Chudleigh said: "I don't expect you will be needing your pistol any more," and removed it from my holster. It was a 9-millimeter Browning automatic, in short supply and much prized by those, like Chudleigh, who had been issued only with a .38 Smith and Wesson revolver.'

Cornet Auberon Waugh, Royal Horse Guards

'Women and children were generally safe in 1956 from EOKA gunmen, but adult males were not, and so we were forbidden in particular to walk down Ledra Street, which became known as "Murder Mile", so all our shopping was done by our wives.'

Anthony Windrum, junior officer in the Political Office, MELF

'The Greek Cypriot kids used to clamber aboard our vehicles. As we never knew what they would do next, we would give them chocolate from our compo rations to get them off. But, after learning from experience that they still threw stones at us on departing their villages, we treated them to *Exlax* chocolate the next time we visited.'

Danny Angus, 12 Royal Lancers

'To break the monotony of waiting, the troop had to line up on a patch of rough stony ground adjacent to the tents, pick up all the unemployed stones and put them at the edge of the area to try and make a small dry stone wall, which, when finished, was about three inches high. This was to keep the stones employed.'

Sapper Derek Horsfield, 3 Troop, 34 Field Squadron, Royal Engineers

'As musicians were non-combatants we had the choice of staying in camp behind barbed wire, practising to give concerts to the members of the Brigade which included our Regiment or volunteering to become combatants. It was always dangerous around Xeros travelling early in the morning, as EOKA would plant magnetic mines in the drains by the roads. Our platoon was responsible for checking them by using detectors.'

Bandsman Dave Bragg, Royal Welch Fusiliers

'A Labour MP, a woman [Barbara Castle], visits the island. She goes home protesting that the Security Forces are taking excessive and cruel measures against the civilian population. Her comments are widely reported. The troops are amazed and angry. Is the woman mad? The woman is not mad. She is a politician. By definition she is permitted to be an unfeeling fool.'

Walter Winward, Royal Marine

'At the end of the Karpas, there's Cape Andreas with a Greek Cypriot church and monastery, where – supposedly – virgins went to be blessed before marriage. Part of the ritual appeared to be leaving their knickers behind on the rocky shore. Whenever one of our patrols returned from that location, the radio aerials on our trucks were decorated with ladies' underwear fluttering in the breeze.'

Nigel Coplin, Royal Artillery

'We used to go on search operations outside the walls of Nicosia looking for lethal weapons. After one of these I remember seeing a whole bunch of foreign journalists, coming along at the end of the day and looking at our haul and saying to myself, "That would be a nice way to earn a living." This was the first time I'd ever really met the press in action.'

Sergeant Martin Bell, Royal Suffolk Regiment

'On the way to the Troodos Mountains, where a Welsh regiment was stationed, we saw the usual slogans of EOKA, ENOSIS and DEATH TO THE BRITISH. All of a sudden we came across a culvert painted with the slogan HOME RULE FOR WALES.'

Captain Dorothy Presswell, WRAC, GHQ MELF, 3 GHQ Signals Regiment

'Terrorist crimes during our period of stand-by were always aimed at defenceless people, whether out shopping, sitting in their homes, in restaurants, or even recuperating in hospitals. The time factor was always on the side of the assailant, who could easily commit his dastardly crime, and then have several minutes in hand before we could arrive on the scene. It was particularly easy to throw a bomb and then masquerade as an innocent bystander with no incriminating evidence even when searched.'

Letter home from a National Service Private, the Royal Norfolk Regiment

'The real problem in Cyprus was that you didn't know who your enemy was; whereas they would very often offer you drink, olives, fruit or something, but you were shot in the back when you left. I don't think there was hardly a soldier ever shot in his front.'

Private Geoffrey Saunders, Somerset Light Infantry, later the Green Jackets

'We cannot win our struggle if we fight you face-to-face. You have more men and guns. For us to fight you from the front, gives you victory, to fight you from behind, means I kill and you live in fear. I am like the camouflaged snake in the grass; you do not know I am there. You cannot see me until I bite you. If I bite you quickly and slide away to hide, I can bite someone else another day. This way, we, will win.'

Captured EOKA terrorist

'My father, Royston Sparrow, was a British Civil Servant. When the British Army pulled out of the Suez Canal area, in 1955, he was posted to Famagusta in Cyprus to work at the 625 Ordnance Depot RAOC. On 25 January 1957, at about 07.30 he said his goodbyes and told me he would walk to the main road – only a few metres from the house – and wait for any military vehicle that may be going his way to give him a lift. Ten minutes later I heard shots ring. I ran outside and I saw my father lying on the ground in the road. My mother had been asleep during the whole episode. I woke her and said father was unwell, to minimize the shock. My friends took me to the hospital, but father was DOA. Neither my mother nor I ever saw him again. When I asked the reason for his murder, I was told: "He was British, an unarmed civilian and he worked for the British Army".'

Elizabeth Harper, daughter

'No Police Force has been asked to perform a more difficult or a more dangerous task than that which has fallen to the Cyprus Police ... And out of our dangers and difficulties there has emerged one great lesson – the need for us to develop within our ranks a sense of loyalty to one another and to the Police Force to which we belong. We have to break down the barriers of race and creed and, no matter who we are, to work together as a team bound by a common bond of fellowship and trust.'

Chief Constable Lieutenant Colonel Geoffrey White, OBE, Cyprus Police Force

'When the political prisoners were released from the Central Prison, after the peace treaties were signed in February 1959, "C" Company had to watch them being greeted as heroes by the population. Wanted men, whom we had been seeking for months, openly wore EOKA uniform in the streets. These things were difficult for us to stomach. Even worse was the provocation by Cypriot youths of the troops when we were out in town. This sometimes led to fights.'

Anonymous private, the Queen's Own Royal West Kent Regiment

'Cyprus was a peaceful place at long last and we could go out and about again without guns. Steve and I got a couple of bikes one day and set off for Limassol, about nine miles away from

Epi. Before long we noticed that the policeman – on a bike – was riding with us. As "peace" had only been agreed about two weeks previously, the local Limassol Police Station had decided that it should provide us with an escort. Steve and I were the first "ex-enemy" to actually take advantage of the new freedoms!'

Private A. G. B. Lawrie, RASC

'My feelings towards the Greeks were simple: they were terrorists, our enemy and were to be shot and killed if possible. But, with hindsight, one man's terrorist is another man's patriot. Just depends which side of the fence you are on, but I wasn't into philosophy at that time.'

Private Bob Brenni, the Gloucestershire Regiment

'Ruthlessness became a habit on both sides. It was about this time that a photograph appeared in the world's leading newspapers. It came to symbolize the erosion of human values throughout the Island. The photograph showed a young woman, her face contorted with grief, kneeling beside her dead fiancé, killed in broad daylight in a Nicosia street.'

Sergeant Adrian Walker, Intelligence Corps

'Yes, many EOKA acts were despicable, but not all Greek Cypriots were cowardly villains. I was fortunate to know decent people from both sides and was saddened that the two communities became divided.'

Norman Goodwin, Ox and Bucks Light Infantry

'To many of the young men involved, their time in Cyprus was probably the adventure of a lifetime and a period in which they quickly changed from boys into men. They experienced fear, anxiety, fatigue and danger but also the joy of comradeship, hardship shared and the knowledge that their job was well done.'

Lieutenant Colonel Maurice Nicholls, RMP

'I do not think there is anyone who has served in Cyprus, as an administrator or as a member of the Security Forces, or anyone who has studied the problem seriously and objectively, who would deny that the answer to the problem of a permanent, lasting and peaceful solution to this dispute can be found only by a political settlement.'

Lord Harding of Petherton

'If we were truthful with ourselves, we would admit that for all their bravery and idealism, the EOKA fighters were engaged in a struggle for a goal that was strategically misguided and unachievable, using methods, including terrorizing civilians, that were extreme and unnecessary and in many ways counter-productive to achieving the realistic goal of an independent and democratic bicommunal republic.'

Nicos A. Pittas in the Cyprus Mail

'The real enemy of Cyprus is not a barbarian bloodthirsty Turkey, forever bent on the unbridled conquest of Cyprus; nor is it a secret conspiracy involving foreigners, who ensure Cyprus remains divided forever to secure their interests ... whatever they may be. The "enemies of Cyprus" have been created to cover up the real culprit. This true enemy has been lying right under our nose for hundreds of years. It has governed our lives and directed society. It has even gone so far as to select presidents and political parties. The only enemy with such influence, power and ability is none other than the Greek Orthodox Church of Cyprus, the so-called protector of Hellenism and the Greek identity. We have let it determine our fate for far too long ... For years it has advocated armed violence, a concept that all religions reject. The Church also ignores the principles of forgiveness and advocates revenge against Turkey and other claimed "enemies". My message to the people: the power to change the future is in your hands. Do not be a slave to the Church, which maintains its own agenda. I am not advocating abandoning your religious beliefs and traditions. On the contrary, I am asking you to enhance them, as it is clear that the Church does not hold true to its own religious doctrine.'

Part of a letter from an anonymous Greek Cypriot to the Cyprus Mail

'If you propose that a Cyprus solution may lie in NATO, then obviously you are an American spy! If you speak of the universality of human rights in Cyprus and refer not just to your own community's suffering but to another, then a conspiracy is thought up that you are paid by the Greeks! If you defend the human rights of all in Cyprus including Turkish/Kurdish settlers who have lived in Cyprus for decades then you must be an agent of the Turks!'

Alkan Chaglar, editor of the English pages of Toplum Postasi

Roll of Honour

The British military personnel who died in Cyprus between 1 April 1955 and 25 December 1959

Pte R. ADAMSON, Army Catering Corps (20.10.1959)

L/Cpl Alan ALDERSON, 19, Royal Engineers, from Brandon Colliery, Durham (9.11.1955)

Sgt Ernest John ALLEN, 28, 73rd Squadron RAF, from Clare, Suffolk (17.7.1956)

Able Seaman Peter John Keith ALLENGAME, 22, Royal Navy, from Folkestone (26.2.1958)

Major Edwin Alexander ANDREWS, 38, 188 RAD Battery, Royal Artillery, from Harrow, Middlesex (30.10.1958)

WO2 Leonard ARCHER, 43, attached to Headquarters Staff, from Wakefield, Yorkshire (11.8.1956)

Pte John Terence ARGYLE, 19, Royal Leicestershire Regiment (30.5.1956)

Marine Thomas ARMOUR, 23, HQ 3 Commando Brigade, from Gourock, Renfrewshire (7.3.1956)

Senior Aircraftman Percival Dunstan ARNOLDA, 28, RAF Regiment (25.10.1955)

Pte John ASHE, 19, King's Own Yorkshire Light Infantry (28.5.1956)

Pte William Henry ASPREY, 20, South Staffordshire Regiment, from Wolverhampton (9.4.1956)

Rifleman Karl George ATKINSON, 19, HQ Company, Royal Ulster Rifles (30.7.1958)

Pte John Thomas ATTENBOROUGH, 19, Royal Leicestershire Regiment (30.5.1956)

Chief Technician Cecil Edward AUSTIN, 35, RAF, from Somerset (9.11.1956)

Gunner Graham BALDRY, 22, 29 Field Regiment Royal Artillery, from Sutton, Surrey (10.8.1958)

Sgt David BALDWIN, 30, 45 Commando Royal Marines, from Watford (13.7.1958)

Pte Raymond BANKS, 20, South Staffordshire Regiment, from Bilston, Staffordshire (21.5.1956)

Flying Officer Kenneth Walter BANYARD, 24, 9 Squadron RAF Binbrook, from Ipswich (6.11.1956)

L/Bombardier Ernest Malcolm Douglas BARCLAY, 28, 25 Field Regiment Royal Artillery (8.10.1958)

Major V. M. BATESON, King's Regiment (Liverpool and Manchester), attached DAQMG, 51 Infantry Brigade Group, HQ Cyprus District, MELF (28.10.1959)

Pte Frederick George BAYLIS, 22, Royal Berkshire Regiment (3.11.1956)

Captain Michael Trevor BEAGLEY, 26, 3rd Battalion Parachute Regiment, from London (17.6.1956)

Pte John Lindop BEATTIE, 19, Highland Light Infantry, from Glasgow (24.10.1956)

Pte Robin BEAUMONT, 20, Royal Norfolk Regiment, from Stowmarket (17.6.1956)

L/Cpl William Rodger BELL, 20, Royal Military Police, from Bellshill, Lanarkshire (27.9.1958)

2nd Lt Andrew BELLAIRE, 20, Royal Fusiliers, attached to the Oxfordshire and Buckinghamshire Light Infantry (2.12.1957)

Fslr Peter BICKERSTAFFE, Lancashire Fusiliers (25.7.1959)

Ldg/Writer Philip Hugh BINGHAM, 23, Royal Navy, from Sheffield (14.1.1957)

Trooper Lawrence James BIRCH, 19, Royal Horse Guards, from Kidderminster (21.10.1958)

Cpl D. G. BLACKMAN, RAOC (22.8.1959)

Marine Benet Carr BLAKEWAY, 25, 45 Commando, from Kendal, Westmoreland (9.2.1956)

S/Sgt William Boardman BLOWER, RASC, from Leigh, Lancashire (6.10.1956)

Able Seaman Malcolm Charles BLUNDELL, 21, Royal Navy, from Pembury (2.7.1955)

Leading Aircraftman Thomas BOADEN, 19, RAF Ayios Nikolaos, from Newcastle-upon-Tyne (20.12.1958)

Driver Robert BODY, 23, 47 Air Despatch Company RASC, from Dover (18.6.1958)

Driver William BOOTMAN, 18, 65 Company RASC, from Edinburgh (14.1.1956)

Marine Harry Samuel BOSTOCK, 19, 40 Commando, from Lichfield, Staffordshire (15.7.1958)

Pte George Albert BOTT, 19, Royal Leicestershire Regiment, from Leicester (31.8.1956)

Pte Ronnie Newman BOWMAN, 21, Royal Leicestershire Regiment, from Burton on Trent (27.3.1956)

Pte James BOYLE, 23, 42 Company, RASC, from Glasgow (17.11.1958)

Senior Aircraftman Charles Jeffrey BRAY, 23, RAF, from Middlesbrough (8.11.1958)

L/Cpl James Stephen BREHENY, 19, RAOC, from Glasgow (9.7.1957)

Pte Alan BRITTON, 20, Durham Light Infantry, from Pontefract, Yorkshire (28.10.1958)

Sgt Hugh BRODIE, 24, Royal Army Educational Corps, from Glasgow (4.6.1957)

Pte Edward John BROOKS, 19, 1st Battalion Parachute Regiment, from Anfield, Liverpool (10.6.1956)

Sgt Alexander Mills BROWN, 44, RAF Abingdon, from Glasgow (1.6.1958)

Sapper John BROWN, 21, 9 Independent Parachute Field Squadron, Royal Engineers, from Liverpool (3.10.1956)

Flying Officer John Arthur Buckmaster BROWN, 24, 39 Squadron RAF, from London (6.12.1956)

Corporal of Horse Michael BROWN, 26, Governor General's Escort Troop, the Life Guards, from Banbury, Oxon (31.1.1956)

Cpl Peter BROWN, 23, Duke of Wellington's Regiment, from Leeds (3.3.1957)

Cpl Andrew BRYANS, Royal Ulster Rifles, from Belfast (13.9.1957)

Pte Derek BULLOCK, 23, Duke of Wellington's Regiment, from Sheffield (10.5.1957)

Signalman Robert Leslie BUNTON, 19, Royal Signals, from Barking, Essex (5.10.1958)

Pte Robert BURNETT, 19, Gordon Highlanders, from Raemoir, Aberdeenshire (17.6.1956)

Cpl Stephen Louis John BURROUGHS, 29, RAF Ayios Nikolaos, from Farnham, Surrey (19.1.1958)

L/Cpl Michael Islwyn BUTTON, 20, Welch Regiment, from Penygraig, Glamorgan (24.11.1958)

L/Cpl William Nicol CAMERON, 22, Royal Military Police, from Leven, Fife (4.5.1958)

Quartermaster Sergeant Graham Charles Nicol CASEY, 32, 45 Commando Royal Marines, from Dublin, Ireland (31.5.1957)

Cpl George CASSELLS, 21, 8 Infantry Workshops REME, from Windsor (11.6.1956)

WO1 Joseph Arthur CASTLE, 33, Royal Engineers, from Thame, Oxfordshire (20.9.1957)

Sapper George Ronald CAUNT, 21, Royal Engineers, from Sotby, Lincolnshire (13.10.1955)

Gunner Andrew Lawson CAVERS, 20, 40 Field Regiment, Royal Artillery, from Longholme, Dumfries (24.5.1955)

Cpl Richard John CHITTOCK, 22, Royal Norfolk Regiment, from Witnesham, Suffolk (4.11.1956)

L/Telegraphist Frank Julian CHIVERS, 22, 847 Squadron, Royal Navy, from Blackburn, Lancashire (20.2.1958)

L/PM Leonard CLARK, 36, Royal Navy, from Spennymoor, Durham (25.7.1958)

Pte James COCKIE, 18, Gordon Highlanders, from Banchory (17.6.1956)

Sgt Frederick COLEMAN, 40, Royal Warwickshire Regiment, from Stratford on Avon (13.5.1956)

Lt Col Frederick Lawrence COLLIER, 46, HQ staff officer, RASC, from Aldershot (3.8.1958)

Pte Ian Reginald COLLINS, 20, Royal Berkshire Regiment, from Reading (23.5.1957)

Flying Officer Leslie Ian COLLINS, 24, 9 Squadron RAF Binbrook, from Ulverston, Lancashire (6.11.1956)

Gunner Allen Rugely CONNELL, 19, 43 Light Anti-Aircraft Regiment, Royal Artillery, from Scunthorpe (25.5.1958)

Sgt James CONROY, 29, RAMC, from Lochgelly, Fife (13.10.1957)

Guardsman Patrick Joseph CONWAY, 18, Irish Guards, from Belfast (31.10.1958)

Pte Malcolm Alan COOK, 18, Royal Norfolk Regiment, from Great Yarmouth (4.11.1956)

Cpl Christopher John COOPER, 21, 3 GHQ Signals Regiment, Royal Signals from Poole, Dorset (22.5.1956)

Pte David COULTER, 37, RASC, from Belfast (18.11.1956)

Leading Aircraftman Roger Edward COX, 19, RAF, from Manor, Park, London (11.2.1956)

Staff Sgt Gilbert CRIPPS, 34, HQ Cyprus District, RASC, from Fulham, London (18.11.1955)

WO2 Ronald Archley CRISELL, 30, Royal Leicestershire Regiment, from Southampton (17.5.1956)

Staff Sgt Joseph Anthony CULKIN, 42, RAOC, from York (23.9.1956)

Pte George CULLEN, 18, Highland Light Infantry, from Glasgow (8.6.1956)

WO2 W. E. CUTHBURT, Royal Air Force (30.10.1959)

WO2 William Edwin CUTSFORTH, 30, 50 Medium Regiment, Royal Artillery, from Hull (3.11.1956)

Sgt William DARLOW, 23, REME, from Treochy, South Wales (1.1.1956)

Sgt Anthony Colin DAVIE, 20, 84 Squadron RAF, from Luton (1.10.1956)

Airman Anthony Douglas DAVIS, 19, RAF, from Greenwich, London (8.9.1956)

Driver Henry David DAY, 19, 42 Company RASC, from Islington, London (29.1.1956)

Guardsman Robert Michael DEAN, 19, Grenadier Guards, from Kingston on Thames, Surrey (30.11.1957)

Cpl Ronald DEBLEY, 21, Middlesex Regiment, from Willesden, London (19.4.1957)

Cpl Derek Arthur DELANEY, 20, RAOC, from Hammersmith, London (16.7.1957)

Lt Louis Timothy Mylius DICK, 26, 40 Commando Royal Marines, from Hampstead, London (9.5.1956)

Senior Aircraftman James Noel DINSMORE, 26, RAF, from Muff, Co. Donegal, Ireland (13.11.1955)

Aircraftman Melville Royston DIXON, 19, RAF Kormakiti, from York (26.2.1957)

Gunner William Robert DOE, 19, 50 Medium Regiment, Royal Artillery, from Cavendish, Suffolk (28.10.1956)

Pte Benjamin DOHERTY, 18, Highland Light Infantry, from Glasgow (23.10.1956)

Sgt Alexander Noel DOW, 28, Gordon Highlanders, from Perth (12.11.1956)

Pte Frederick John DOWNING, 19, Royal Warwickshire Regiment, from Birmingham (3.4.1956)

L/Cpl Roger John DOWNING, 19, Royal Military Police, from Edgware, Middlesex (23.11.1955)

Sgt John DUFFY, 26, Royal Engineers (16.1.1959)

Pte Alexander DUNBAR, 19, Gordon Highlanders, from Aberdeen (17.6.1956)

Gunner Graham EDWARDS, 27, 57 HAA Regiment, Royal Artillery (4.9.1956)

Driver Larry John EDWARDS, 19, RASC, from Cwmbran, Wales (24.10.1958)

Pte Norman Graham EGGLETON, 19, Royal Norfolk Regiment, from Thurning, Norfolk (14.9.1956)

L/Cpl Peter David ELLIOTT, 19, Royal Norfolk Regiment, from Diss, Norfolk (14.6.1956)

Driver Edward Richard ERRINGTON, 23, 40 Company RASC, from Northampton (3.5.1956)

Major John David EVANS, 44, Essex Regiment, from Ilford (20.1.1957)

Leading Aircraftman John FAITHFUL, 19, RAF Akrotiri, from London (18.5.1956)

Pte James Henry FALCONER, 19, Gordon Highlanders, from Aberdeen (13.4.1956)

Cpl Paul Greagson FARLEY, 21, RAOC, from Exeter (15.9.1956)

Cpl George FERGUSSON, 20, RAF Nicosia, from Govan, Glasgow (27.3.1959)

L/Cpl Roy David FERMOR, 20, Suffolk Regiment, from Dagenham, Essex (19.11.1957)

L/Cpl David Raymond FERRIE, 20, Gordon Highlanders, from Farnham, Surrey (17.6.1956)

Trooper R. A. FITZPATRICK, 12 Lancers (31.5.1959)

Sgt Norman Owen FOLKARD, 22, Royal Norfolk Regiment, from Norwich (1.9.1956)

Flight Lt William Charles FORD, 35, RAF Akrotiri, from Bexley Heath, Kent (8.7.1957)

L/Bombardier George Graham FOREMAN, 22, 43 LAA Royal Artillery, from Sale, Cheshire (25.5.1958)

WO2 James FORSTER, 34, 1st Battalion, Parachute Regiment, from Sunderland (10.6.1956)

Aircraftman Alan Michael FOSTER, 19, RAF Akrotiri, from West Marsh, Grimsby (28.7.1958)

Able Seaman Peter John FOWLER, 24, Royal Navy, from Toronto, Canada (18.3.1957)

2nd Lt The Hon. Charles Stephen FOX-STRANGWAYS, 20, Royal Horse Guards, from Evershot, Dorset (8.7.1958)

L/Cpl Bernard FOXTON, 20, Royal Horse Guards, from Malton, Yorkshire (15.4.1957)

Bombardier Emlyn FRANCIS, 32, 21 Medium Regiment, Royal Artillery, from Bedlinog, Glamorgan (17.11.1956)

Pte Stephen James FREEMAN, 19, Royal Berkshire Regiment, from Tipperary, Ireland (30.6.1958)

Pte Gerald Edward FRENCH, 21, Oxfordshire and Buckinghamshire Light Infantry, from Ratley, Warwickshire (28.10.1957)

Bombardier A. FROST, Royal Artillery (20.10.1959)

L/Cpl Ronald FRYER, 20, RAOC, from Birmingham (16.7.1957)

Leading Aircraftman Anastasio Giuseppe Sanzio FUSCO, 19, RAF Nicosia, from Margate, Kent (27.5.1956)

Sapper George GAHAGAN, 21, 18 Field Park Station, Royal Engineers, from Glasgow (14.2.1957)

Pte James GAYLER, 19, Argyll and Sutherland Highlanders, from Whiterich, Glasgow (9.2.1958)

Pte Harry Gall GERRARD, 18, Gordon Highlanders, from Tillyfourie, Aberdeenshire (17.6.1956)

Telegraphist Anthony Eric GIBBS, 30, Royal Navy, from Ashford, Kent (26.2.1958)

Sapper John Keith GIBSON, 19, Royal Engineers, from Hull (1.2.1957)

Rifleman Eric GILLETT, 19, Royal Ulster Rifles, from Colne, Lancashire (2.11.1957)

Pte Terence Arthur GILLOTT, 21, 1st Battalion Parachute Regiment, from Nottingham (28.8.1956)

Pte Derek Campbell GODDARD, 19, Royal Berkshire Regiment, from Lambourn, Berkshire (30.6.1958)

Pte Albert Frederick John GODSELL, 21, Wiltshire Regiment, from Cheltenham (13.3.1957)

Sub-Lt Michael Harry GOODWIN, 20, Royal Navy (19.5.1958)

Pte Clifford James GOSLING, 20, Royal Norfolk Regiment, from Kings Lynn, Norfolk (17.6.1956)

Pte James GOULD, 22, Welch Regiment, from Llannlleth (6.10.1958)

Pte Ronald GOULD, 23, Wiltshire Regiment, from Ilfracombe (18.3.1956)

L/Signalman Jack GRAHAM, 22, Royal Navy, from Felixstowe, Suffolk (23.7.1958)

L/Cpl Alexander GRAY, 20, 6 Army Guard Dog Unit, Royal Army Veterinary Corps, from Huntley, Leicestershire (30.3.1958)

Pte Ian GRAY, 21, Gordon Highlanders, from Cuminestown, Aberdeen (17.6.1956)

Pte William Albert GRAY, 20, Gordon Highlanders, from Birmingham (17.6.1956)

Marine Raymond Thomas GREENING, 18, 45 Commando, from Ongar, Essex (6.10.1958)

Lt Raymond James GREER, 29, 847 Squadron, Royal Navy, from Antrim, Belfast (20.2.1958)

Pte Ivan Frank GURR, 20, 1st Battalion Parachute Regiment, from Ipswich, Suffolk (10.6.1956)

Technician Alan Alfred GUTHRIE, 21, RAF Nicosia, from Dulwich, London (29.3.1958)

Sgt Arthur Llewellyn Bullin HAINES, 48, RAF Akrotiri, from Swansea, Glamorgan (13.3.1958)

Cpl Patrick Joseph HALE, 28, RAF Nicosia, from Kilglass, Sligo, Ireland (16.5.1956)

Sgt Reginald George HAMMOND, 23, RAOC, from London (2.8.1958)

Driver Arthur HAMPSON, 19, RASC, from Manchester (22.10.1955)

Craftsman D. HARDIE, REME (5.7.1959)

Gunner Ernest HARGREAVES, 19, 21 Medium Regiment, Royal Artillery, from Leeds (17.11.1956)

Pte Clarence HARKER, 19, Duke of Wellington's Regiment, from Bradford (12.5.1957)

Colonel Philip George HATCH, OBE, 45, HQ staff, Royal Engineers, from Tunbridge Wells, Kent (7.6.1955)

Cpl Charles HATFIELD, 49, RASC, from Birmingham (27.2.1956)

Pte Joseph Anthony HAWKER, 19, 3rd Battalion Parachute Regiment, from Brierley Hill, Staffordshire (17.6.1956)

Sgt Andrew HAY, 25, 50 Medium Regiment, Royal Artillery, from Kilbarchan, Renfrewshire (25.9.1956)

Leading Aircraftman Donald Thomas Frederick HAYES, 19, RAF, from Croydon, Surrey (7.10.1956)

Pte Harry Ralph HAYES, 21, Royal Army Veterinary Corps, from Newton-le-Willows, Lancashire (27.6.1958)

Cpl Keith Raymond HAYLOCK, 19, Royal Norfolk Regiment, from Steeple Bumpstead, Norfolk (17.6.1956)

Lt Peter Michael HAYNES, 20, 40 Commando, Royal Marines, from Birmingham (18.2.1957)

Trooper Leonard George HAYWARD, 19, Royal Horse Guards, from London (16.7.1956)

Cpl Jeremy George HEAD, 21, RAF, from Loddon, Norfolk (17.6.1957)

Major Gerard Patrick Joseph HEALY, 46, Royal Lincolnshire Regiment, from Dublin, Ireland (17.1.1957)

Pte Kenneth Michael HEBB, 20, Royal Leicestershire Regiment, from Nottingham (30.5.1956)

Capt Francis Ernest HELLIER, 31, RASC (16.9.1956)

SAC J. T. HENRY, Royal Air Force (3.7.1959)

Pte Cyril Keith HEWITT, 20, South Staffordshire Regiment, from Buxton, Derbyshire (1.4.1956)

Craftsman Kenneth HEYES, 22, REME, from Leeds (25.11.1955)

L/Cpl Alexander HICKEY, 20, Parachute Regiment, from Glasgow (7.10.1956)

Pte Roy HICKINSON, 20, Argyll and Sutherland Highlanders, from Sheffield (12.1.1959)

Flt Lt Ronald HIGGS, 25, RAF, from Woodley, Berkshire (10.2.1958)

Sgt Basil Leonard HILL, 34, Grenadier Guards, from Ledbury, Herefordshire (5.11.1958)

L/Cpl Harry Gordon HILL, 22, Royal Leicestershire Regiment, Langold, Worksop, Nottinghamshire (10.5.1956)

Senior Aircraftman T. Y. HILL, 103 Maintenance Unit, RAF Akrotiri (25.10.1959)

Pte Michael James HINDLE, 19, Gordon Highlanders, from Ilkley (17.6.1956)

WO2 George Leonard HOBBS, 39, Royal Engineers, from Bonwick, Cambridgeshire (28.5.1956

Craftsman Fred HOBSON, 21, REME, from Barnsley (30.6.1956)

Sapper Edward Fisher HODGSON, 20, 3 Field Squadron, Royal Engineers, from Blaydon, Co. Durham (11.5.1957)

Craftsman Noel HOGAN, 19, REME, from Calear, Dublin, Ireland (5.7.1956)

Sapper Vernon John Back HOLBROOK, 22, Royal Engineers, from Holbrook, Derbyshire (3.6.1955)

Cpl William Robert HOLDEN, 22, Royal Leicestershire Regiment, from Salthill, Galway, Ireland (13.6.1956)

Pte Brian Valentine HOLLANDS, 20, RAOC, from Muswell Hill, London (20.9.1957)

Sapper John David HOLLELY, 19, Royal Engineers, from Dagenham, Essex (12.6.1956)

Airman R. S. HOLLIDAY, RAF. (31.7.1959)

Sapper Edward HOLLIS, 19, Royal Engineers, from Preston, Lancashire (14.9.1955)

Pte Stephen Nicholas HOREMAN, 18, RAMC, from Bermondsey, London (25.8.1956)

L/Cpl R. G. HORLOCK, Devon and Dorset Regiment (20.5.1959)

Cpl Derek Joseph HUMPHREYS, MM, 23, Royal Welch Fusiliers from Mold, Flintshire (12.11.1958)

Sgt James Gordon HUNTER, 26, RAF Regiment, from Brighton, Sussex (7.9.1956)

L/Cpl Thomas HUTCHINSON, 20, RAOC, from Keighley, West Yorkshire (16.7.1957)

Pte Sidney Albert INGRAM, 22, South Staffordshire Regiment (21.10.1955)

Pte George ISBELL, 19, RAOC, from Carshalton, Surrey (3.6.1956)

Driver G. F. JACK, RASC, from the West Indies (2.5.1959)

Gunner Anthony John JASPER, 20, Royal Artillery, from Somerset (30.10.1958)

Pte Peter Gerard JENKINS, 20, RASC, from Manchester (25.10.1958)

Sgt Wilfred Henry JEPSON, 43, 14/20 King's Hussars, from St Helier, Jersey, Channel Islands (28.9.1956)

Lt John Alexander JOE, 24, Royal Artillery, from Hampstead, London (24.4.1956)

Gunner Adrian Robert JOHNSON, 20, Royal Artillery, from Hartlepool (5.11.1956)

Gunner Barry Baird JONES, 23, Royal Artillery, from Connahs Quay, Flintshire (18.8.1958)

Cpl Desmond Thomas JONES, 19, RAF, from Bedlinog, Glamorganshire (11.2.1956)

Sgt J. E. D. JONES, Royal Army Medical Corps (23.12.1959)

L/Cpl Colin Neville KEIGHTLEY, 19, Royal Military Police, from Leicester (13.5.1956)

Lt John Edward Theodore KELLY, 19, Royal Artillery, from Camberley, Surrey (17.12.1955)

L/Cpl David Warren KENNEDY, 19, RASC, from Stirling (18.6.1956)

Signalman John Joseph KENNEDY, 30, Royal Signals, from Wakefield (16.4.1958)

Pte Peter Gibb KETCHEN, 19, Royal Scots, from Edinburgh (9.12.1955)

Leading Aircraftman Leonard KINCHIN, 18, RAF, from Oldbury, Worcestershire (27.5.1956)

WO1 Victor Cuthbert KING, 35, Grenadier Guards, from Bristol (31.7.1957)

Rifleman Daniel Donald KINSELLA, 20, Royal Ulster Rifles, from Dublin, Ireland (2.9.1958)

Staff Sergeant Ronald KIRBY, 31, RAOC, from Huddersfield (31.7.1958)

Pte Robert Leslie KUNKEL, 18, Parachute Regiment from Londonderry, Ireland (13.4.1956)

2nd Lt Bruce Alan Gordon KYNOCH, 19, Gordon Highlanders, from Elgin (17.6.1956)

Marine Kenneth LAMB, 18, 45 Commando, Royal Marines (10.3.1956)

Craftsman Iain Buchanan LAMONT, 22, REME, from Rothesay (22.3.1959)

Staff Sgt James William LANE, 23, Royal Ulster Rifles, from Dublin, Ireland (3.10.1958)

Capt Joseph Peter LANE, 31, RAOC, from Horsham, Surrey (19.1.1956)

2nd Lt Clive Charles LAURENCE, 19, Duke of Wellington's Regiment, from Ilkley (25.11.1956)

Pte Douglas Henry LAVENTURE, 19, RASC, from Kenton, Middlesex (14.12.1955)

Flying Officer Terence Alfred George LEDGER, 24, 39 Squadron RAF, from London (6.12.1956)

L/Cpl Robert Brough LEITCH, 21, Royal Military Police, from Laurston, Stirling (15.12.1958)

Pte Robert Henry LIDDLE, 23, RAOC, from Sunderland (19.12.1955)

Trooper James Alfred LITTLE, 20, Royal Horse Guards, from Downham, Kent (6.6.1958)

Trooper Peter LIVINGSTONE, 21, Royal Horse Guards, from Tranent, East Lothian (31.12.1958)

L/Bombardier William LOFTHOUSE, 19, Royal Artillery, from Choppington, Northumberland (9.9.1958)

Sgt Arnold LONGFORD, BEM, 49, Royal Engineers, from Stockbridge, Yorkshire (4.8.1957)

Sapper William James LONGMAN, 20, Royal Engineers, from Barry, Glamorganshire (4.9.1957)

Marine Alexander MacDOUGALL, 20, 45 Commando, from Inverness (22.10.1958)

Major Patrick Joseph MACEY, 39, Royal Army Pay Corps, from Minehead, Somerset (23.10.1955)

Sapper Raymond Vincent MARCHANT, 19, Royal Engineers, from Buckhurst Hill, Essex (12.6.1956)

Gunner Paul William MARRIOTT, 19, 16 LAA Regiment Royal Artillery, from Chinley, Cheshire (23.2.1957)

WO2 Charles Francis MARTIN, 36, Royal Tank Regiment, from Wantage (4.11.1956)

Pte Ronald Stewart John MARTIN, 21, Royal West Kent Regiment, from Bexhill, Sussex (3.3.1957)

Cpl George MARTINDALE, 20, RASC, from Hornby, Lancashire (16.7.1955)

Sgt Walter MASON, 43, RASC, from Sandbach, Cheshire (16.1.1959)

Rifleman Michael Joseph McDONNELL, 20, Royal Ulster Rifles (17.12.1957)

Junior Technician Albert Edward McKINLEY, 22, RAF, from Birkenhead, Cheshire (3.11.1956)

Leading Aircraftman Joseph Michael Gerald McMANUS, 19, RAF Akrotiri, from Hamilton, Lanarkshire (18.5.1956)

Leading Aircraftman Kenneth John McNULTY, 19, RAF, from London (7.9.1956)

Sgt Arthur Matthew Paul McQUILLAN, 27, RAF Episkopi, from Down, Co. Down, Ireland (25.7.1956)

Pte George McRUVIE, 19, Gordon Highlanders, from Aberdeen (17.6.1956)

Sapper Robert Peter MELSON, 25, 37 Field Squadron, Royal Engineers, from Hinckley, Leicestershire (24.11.1955)

Petty Officer Thomas William MEYRICK, 26, Royal Navy, from Cheddleton, Staffordshire (26.2.1958)

Junior Technician Klaas MIENES, 21, RAF Akrotiri, from Northampton (10.5.1958)

Pte Alan Keith MILLINGTON, 18, 1st Battalion the Parachute Regiment, from Hawarden, Flintshire (10.6.1956)

L/Cpl Angus Robert Lindsay MILNE, 19, Royal Scots, from Bexley Heath, Kent (27.10.1955)

Pte Alan MOORHOUSE, 20, 1st Battalion the Parachute Regiment, from Chorley, Lancashire (2.8.1956)

L/Bombardier Edward Bruce MORGAN, 23, 50 Medium Regiment, Royal Artillery, from Mountain Ash, South Wales (28.10.1956)

Sapper Graham James MORGAN, 19, Royal Engineers, from Newport, Monmouthshire (12.6.1956)

Pte Derrick Arthur MORRIS, 20, Royal Leicestershire Regiment, from Knighton, Powys (13.10.1956)

Cpl Gordon MORRIS, 20, Royal Signals, from Cricklewood, London (20.1.1956)

Pte David Douglas MORRISON, 22, Argyll and Sutherland Highlanders, from Aberdeen (13.9.1958)

L/Cpl James Brian MORUM, 20, Royal Engineers, from Chiselhurst, Kent (15.12.1955)

Capt Terence Dominic George MULADY, 27, Queen's Regiment, serving with 653 Squadron Army Air Corps, from London (11.12.1958)

Tpr Brian NEALE, 12 Royal Lancers (24.9.1959)

Pte Matthew NEELY, 19, Highland Light Infantry, from Glasgow (23.10.1956)

Driver James Duncan NEIL, 19, RASC, from Glasgow (25.9.1956)

L/Cpl David Clark Bayne NEILL, 21, Oxfordshire and Buckinghamshire Light Infantry, from Renfrewshire (16.2.1957)

L/Cpl Roy NEWSOME, 21, RASC, from Doncaster (12.9.1956)

Cpl Aldo NICOLETTI, 20, RAF, from Glasgow (2.5.1956)

Gunner Peter John NOBLE, 21, 21 Medium Regiment, Royal Artillery, from St Agnes, Cornwall (22.9.1956)

Flt Lt William Frederick NUTHALL, 27, RAF, from London (10.2.1958)

Pte Michael O'CARROLL, 19, Oxfordshire and Buckinghamshire Light Infantry, from Banbury, Oxon (17.10.1956)

Cpl John Joseph O'GORMAN, 36, Royal West Kent Regiment, from Windsor, Berkshire (6.7.1957)

Leading Aircraftman Patrick Joseph O'REILLY, 25, RAF, from Cavan, Ireland (24.7.1958)

L/Cpl Percy OAKLEY, 20, Gordon Highlanders, from London (20.6.1956)

Flying Officer Robin Louis PARSONS, 25, 32 Squadron RAF, from London (8.7.1957)

Pte Peter PAYNE, 20, RE, RASC (28.10.1959)

Pte John PEGG, 20, Royal Leicestershire Regiment (19.4.1957)

Sapper Peter Harold PERCIVAL, 21, 37 Field Squadron, Royal Engineers, from Northampton (26.11.1955)

Pte William John PERKS, 19, 1st Battalion the Parachute Regiment, from Kidderminster (21.5.1956)

L/Cpl David William PERRY, 19, Royal Military Police, from London (17.7.1957)

Driver Dood Nauth PERSAUD, 24, RASC, from British Guiana (14.7.1956)

Cpl Bernard PETERS, 20, Welch Regiment, from Llanelli, Carmarthenshire (7.10.1958)

Cpl Murray Sinclair PETERSON, 20, 37 Field Engineer Regiment, Royal Engineers (5.6.1958)

Senior Aircraftman Michael Leslie PHILCOX, 20, RAF Akrotiri, from Horsham, Sussex (20.5.1958)

Flight Lt Peter John PHILLIPS, 25, 54 Squadron RAF, from Cwmparc, Rhondda (5.11.1957)

Sgt Thomas PHILLIPS, 28, Royal Leicestershire Regiment, from Chesterfield (24.10.1957)

Sgt Allan Frederick PINNER, 29, Royal Leicestershire Regiment, from Old Trafford, Manchester (10.4.1956)

Cpl Joseph Fern POLLOCK, 31, RAF, from Greenock, Renfrewshire (26.1.1959)

Sapper Geoffrey PONSONBY, 24, Royal Engineers, from Buxton, Derbyshire (16.10.1956)

Pte Roger Keith POULTNEY, 19, Royal Leicestershire Regiment (19.4.1958)

WO1 Joseph Edgar PRICE, 48, REME, from Wrexham (17.8.1956)

Trooper John Roy PROCTOR, 19, Royal Horse Guards, from Birmingham (8.7.1958)

2nd Lt Rodney Cragg PULFORD, 20, Royal Signals, from London (6.12.1956)

Sgt Leslie Clifford PULMAN, 26, Royal Engineers, from Southampton (20.7.1958)

Guardsman Christopher RATHBURN, 20, Grenadier Guards, from Salford, Lancashire (10.4.1957)

Leading Aircraftman Graham James RATTLE, 19, RAF, from Yeovil, Somerset (5.3.1956)

Pte Colin Vivian READ, 21, Wiltshire Regiment, from Weymouth, Dorset (28.9.1956)

Pte Kenneth James REYNOLDS, 20, Wiltshire Regiment, from Swindon (16.2.1956)

Flight Sgt Morris Allen RHODES, 32, 9 Squadron Binbrook, RAF, from Kirk Hammerton, Yorkshire (6.11.1956)

Leading Aircraftman James Reginald RICE, 23, 502 Squadron, RAF, from Weymouth, Dorset (19.9.1955)

Sgt George Edward RIPPINGALE, 39, RAF, from Croydon, Surrey (15.11.1956)

Lance Sgt George RISSBROOK, 25, Grenadier Guards, from Unstone, Derbyshire (2.11.1958)

Craftsman George Lloyd ROBERTS, 21, REME, from London (12.9.1956)

Bombardier George Ralph ROBERTS, 38, from Edinburgh (22.11.1956)

Marine Terence ROBERTS, 23, Royal Marines, from Caerphilly, Glamorgan (5.12.1955)

Pte John Robinson ROBERTSON, 19, Durham Light Infantry, from Edinburgh. (9.11.1958)

WO2 David ROBINSON, 43, RASC, from Salford, Lancashire (27.2.1959)

Cpl John ROCHFORD, 31, Lancashire Fusiliers, from Manchester (7.1.1959)

Senior Aircraftman Maurice George ROLLS, 20, RAF, from Earlswood, Surrey (3.7.1955)

Signalman John Norman ROONEY, 20, Royal Signals, from Liverpool (5.2.1956)

Fl Lt Douglas Newton ROTHWELL, 49, RAF, from South Africa (4.10.1958)

Sgt John Nixon ROUTLEDGE, 28, 40 Commando Royal Marines, from Haltwhistle, Northumberland (19.12.1955)

Pte Malcolm Thomas Henry ROWLEY, 19, Royal Leicestershire Regiment (9.3.1956)

Signalman Keith William RUSHIN, 20, Royal Signals, from Leicester (4.4.1959)

L/Cpl Charles Sidney RUSSELL, 20, King's Own Yorkshire Light Infantry, from Walsall (29.1.1956)

WO2 John Frederick Lawrence RUST, 33, Royal Engineers, from Shoeburyness (28.5.1956)

Senior Aircraftman John Albert SARGENT, 22, RAF, from Hackney, London (8.11.1958)

Sgt E, SAVORY, RAOC (23.5.1959)

Senior Aircraftman Alan SCAIFE, 27, RAF Ayios Nikolaos, from Kirkham, Lancashire (20.12.1958)

Cpl Duncan Fred SCHOLES, 19, Royal Engineers, from Luton, Bedfordshire (30.11.1957)

Gunner Graham David SCOTT, 19, 40 HAA Royal Artillery, from Glamorgan (29.9.1957)

L/Cpl Albert Robert SHAW, 19, Royal Military Police, from Dagenham, Essex (23.4.1956)

Craftsman Brian SHAW, 19, REME, from Huddersfield (18.7.1958)

Pte George William SHEFFIELD, 21, Royal Leicestershire Regiment (27.2.1956)

Sapper Daniel Victor SHEPPARD, 20, Royal Engineers, from Ashford, Middlesex (5.12.1956)

Pte Ronald SHILTON, 20, Royal Leicestershire Regiment, from Nottingham (10.5.1956)

Sgt James George Eustace SHIPMAN, 30, Royal Engineers, from London (24.11.1955)

Pte Ian Michael SIMPSON, 22, Gordon Highlanders, from Aberdeen (17.6.1956)

Flt Lt Peter Charles SKINNER, 28, 32 Squadron, RAF, from St Helier, Jersey, Channel Islands (13.9.1955)

WO Francis O'Hagan SLOANE, 44, RAF, from Gosforth, Northumberland (2.9.1958)

Craftsman Leslie Arthur SMALE, 19, REME, from London (30.9.1956)

Sgt Allan Thomson SMITH, 28, Gordon Highlanders, from Aberdeen (8.7.1956)

Cpl Edward Alfred SMITH, 26, 1st Battalion the Parachute Regiment, from Bolton, Lancashire (12.8.1956)

Sgt Edward Peter SMITH, 27, Royal Engineers, from Wisbech, Cambridgeshire (3.11.1956)

Gunner Harry Thomas SMITH, 34, Royal Artillery, from London (8.9.1955)

Pte James SMITH, 19, Gordon Highlanders, from Glasgow (17.6.1956)

L/Cpl John Barry SMITH, 19, Royal Signals, from Folkestone, Kent (27.1.1957)

L/Cpl Richard Geoffrey SMITH, 20, 35 Field Engineer Regiment, Royal Engineers, from Devizes, Wiltshire (26.5.1955

Cpl James SMITHERS, 27, RAF, from Barrow in Furness, Lancashire (6.11.1956)

Signalman Kenneth Henry SPRAGG, 20, Royal Signals, from Gosport, Hampshire (4.11.1956)

Lt David Neville SPURLING, 23, 45 Commando, Royal Marines, from Hazelbury Bryan, Dorset (3.11.1958)

Pte Kenneth Thomas SQUIRES, 19, Royal Norfolk Regiment, from Great Yarmouth, Norfolk (1.9.1956)

Craftsman Brian Frederick STEDMAN, 21, REME, from Sittingbourne, Kent (2.12.1956)

Sgt Andrew Dewar STEEL, 24, RASC, from Errol, Perthshire (21.11.1955)

2nd Lt Anthony Kemp STEPHENS, 20, Wiltshire Regiment, from London (17.11.1957)

Flying Officer William STEVENSON, 23, RAF, from Beadnell, Alnwick, Northumberland (20.8.1958)

Aircraftman Roy Albert John STONE, 19, RAF, from North Cadbury, Somerset (1.2.1956)

Gunner Edwin John STREFFORD, 20, Royal Artillery, from Shotton, County Durham (4.6.1958)

Sgt Alexander Stuart SUTTON, 39, RAF, from Kelvingrove, Lanarkshire (27.5.1956)

L/Bombardier John William SWEETZER, 21, 16 LAA Regiment, Royal Artillery, from Teignmouth, Devon (24.9.1956)

Sapper J. R. SWORD, Royal Engineers (10.11.1959)

Gunner Robert James TAYLOR, 20, 29 Field Regiment Royal Artillery, from Birmingham (14.11.1958)

Leading Aircraftman Donald Sidney THICKBROOM, 20, RAF Akrotiri, from Stratford, London (8.7.1957)

Technician Ian Francis THOMPSON, 26, RAF, from Thetford, Norfolk (18.9.1957)

Ft Lt Jack Walter THOMPSON, 34, 284 Squadron, RAF, from London (15.3.1957)

Pte Terence Romney THOMPSON, 19, Middlesex Regiment, from Manchester (8.11.1956)

Gunner Thomas Robert THOMPSON, 19, Royal Artillery, from London (9.9.1956)

Bombardier Derek THORNTON, 26, 43 LAA Regiment, Royal Artillery, from Blackburn, Lancashire (8.1.1959)

L/Cpl George Arnold TODD, 20, Royal Military Police, from Shipley, Yorkshire (9.6.1955)

Cpl P. TODD, 26, Royal Signals. (25.12.59)

Sgt Harry TOWNS, 35, Royal Signals, from Dundee (15.11.1955)

Staff Sgt Donald Benjamin Charles TROWBRIDGE, 25, Royal Signals, from Fareham, Hampshire (9.11.1956)

Driver Geoffrey John TUFFEE, 18, RASC, from West Thurrock, Essex (21.6.1957)

Pte Charles Leonard TULL, 19, Royal Berkshire Regiment, from Maidenhead, Berkshire (12.3.1957)

Leading Aircraftman David Blaylock TURNBULL, 19, RAF, from Carlisle (21.6.1957)

L/Cpl Brian Frank TURVEY, 20, Royal Military Police, from Dagenham, Essex (4.5.1958)

Fusilier Walter Vivian UPHILL, 20, Royal Welch Fusiliers (5.10.1958)

Cpl Roger Thomas VICKERS, 18, RAF (22.12.1958)

Sgt Leonard WADE, 28, King's Own Yorkshire Light Infantry (27.3.1956)

L/Cpl Dennis WAKELEY, 23, Grenadier Guards, from Workington, Cumbria (16.5.1958)

Lt Samuel James Gresham WALKER, 22, Royal Leicestershire Regiment, from Blandford, Dorset (27.3.1956)

Aircraftman Peter Walter WALSH, 19, RAF, from Darwen, Lancashire (25.9.1957)

Fusilier Brian Francis WALTERS, 19, Lancashire Fusiliers, from Manchester (13.9.1957)

Able Seaman Roy Joseph John WARBURTON, 23, Royal Navy, from London (17.6.1958)

Leading Aircraftman Stephen WARD, 21, RAF, from Rainford, Lancashire (2.3.1956)

Cpl Ernest WARREN, 23, REME, from London (3.2.1957)

Cpl Jack William WARREN, 25, Royal Warwickshire Regiment, from Nottingham (24.5.1956)

L/Cpl Bryan David George WELSH, 18, Royal Military Police, from Fleetwood, Lancashire (21.3.1956)

Quartermaster Sgt Alfred WHEELER, 31, from Elburton, Devon (9.2.1956)

Rifleman John WHITE, 20, Royal Ulster Rifles, from Liverpool (8.10.1958)

Marine David Glyn WHITHAM, 19, 45
Commando, from Bingley, Yorkshire
(13.7.1958)

Flying Officer Hugh Ivor WHITTLE, 24,
RAF Akrotiri, from Berwick on Tweed
(8.7.1957)

Cpl Mervyn Norman WHURR, 22, RAF,
from Plymouth, Devon (24.9.1956)

Signalman William WILCOCK, 20, Royal
Signals, from Newark, Nottinghamshire
(26.5.1956)

Cpl Leslie Richard WILKINS, 27, RAF, from
Portsmouth (31.12.1956)

Captain C. E. WILSON, 47, RAOC
(7.9.1959)

Surgeon-Captain Gordon Charles Edwyn
WILSON, 29, Royal Horse Guards, from
St Andrews, Fife (26.9.1956)

L/Cpl Charles Leonard WOOD, 20, Royal
Signals, from London (16.5.1955)

Gunner Frederick Nelson WOOD, 19, Royal
Artillery, from Barrow-in-Furness
(4.10.1956)

Flt Lt Stanley WOOD, 27, 72 Squadron,
RAF, from Stapleford, Nottinghamshire
(29.9.1958)

Pte William Ernest Victor WOODS, 20,
Royal Norfolk Regiment, from Norwich
(17.6.1956)

Lt Edward John WRIGHT, 29, 847
Squadron, Royal Navy, from Antrim,
Belfast (20.2.1958)

Pte William George WRIGHT, 20, Royal
Norfolk Regiment, from Tillingham, Essex
(17.6.1956)

Gunner Colin YATES, 19, Royal Artillery,
from Doncaster (17.3.1956)

Squadron Leader Kenneth Allen YOUNG,
DFC, 34, RAF, from London (6.4.1956)

UK POLICE UNIT OFFICERS
who died on active duty, listed in chronological order

Sgt G. T. ROONEY from the Kent
Constabulary (14.3.1956)

Sgt W. TIPPLE from the Metropolitan Police
(21.6.1956)

Sgt L. DEMMON from the Metropolitan
Police (31.8.1956)

Sgt C. J. THOROGOOD from Leicester and
Rutland Constabulary (28.9.1956)

Sgt J. P. CARTER from the Herefordshire
Constabulary (28.9.1956)

Sergeant M. EDEN, GM, of the
Metropolitan Police (17.12.1956)

Sergeant W. E. CRITCHLEY of the West
Riding Constabulary (8.6.1957)

Sergeant C. H. BROWN of the Cheshire
Constabulary (14.1.1958)

Sergeant A. J. COOTE of the Durham
Constabulary (9.6.1957)

Superintendent D. THOMPSON (1.9.1958)

Sgt S. WOODWARD from the Durham
Constabulary (13.10.1958)

Sgt W. S. GILLETT from the Bristol City
Police (17.5.59)

(During the Cyprus conflict, 45 officers of
the UK Police Unit were recognized for
bravery and distinguished service by being
awarded medals and honors.)

COLONIAL POLICE OFFICERS
Supt P. S. ATTFIELD (1.3.1956)
Inspector F. RAPER (8.3.1958)
Supt W. H. DEAR (17.4.1958)
Asst Supt D. T. M. THOMPSON (2.9.1958)

OTHER UK SUBJECTS KILLED ON DUTY

Special Constable C. G. T. KARBERRY (8.7.1956)

Special Constable J. C. MILES (21.11.1956)

Special Constable P. SHARP (8.11.1956)

Special Constable A. S. HALLAM (15.11.1956)

CYPRUS POLICE DEATHS in chronological order

Greek officers

Sgt Y. DEMOSTHENOUS (22.6.1955)

Sgt C. COSTAPOULOS (11.8.1955)

Constable H. POULLIS (28.8.1955)

Constable N. PANAYI (5.10.1955)

Constable P. CONSTANTINOU (5.12.1955)

Constable G. MORPHITIS (8.3.1956)

Inspector A. STAVROU (7.4.1956)

Superintendent K. ARISTOTELOUS (15.4.1956)

Auxiliary Constable A. ZANNETTOS (15.4.1956)

Sgt A. ANASTASIOU (5.11.1956)

Special Constable J. HJI IOANNOU (21.12.1956)

Constable A. GRIGORIOU (21.1.1957)

Constable S. KAZANAS (6.8.1958)

Constable I. MICHAEL (29.10.1958)

Constable T. MICHAELEROS (9.11.1958)

Turkish officers

Sgt A. ALI RIZA (11.1.1956)

Constable N. ASSAF (23.4.1956)

Constable L. AHMED (23.5.1956)

Constable A. HUSSEIN (27.5.1956)

Constable I. ALI (28.5.1956)

Constable A. SALIH (2.6.1956)

Special Constable S. AHMET (4.6.1956)

Constable D. ALI (19.1.1957)

Special Constable A. MEHMET (2.2.1957)

Inspector M. BEYAS (9.11.1957)

Constable A. HUSSEIN (9.6.1958)

Special Constable H. HJI ARIF (9.7.1958)

Special Constable H. MOUSTAFA (11.7.1958)

Auxiliary Constable S. TAHIR (18.7.1958)

Auxiliary Constable R. MOUSA (20.7.1958)

Sgt SULEIMAN (2.8.1958)

Auxiliary Constable A. HALIL (4.8.1958)

Auxiliary Constable K. ALI (4.8.1958)

Constable D. MEHMET (20.10.1956)

Auxiliary Constable R. MEHMET (20.10.1958)

Auxiliary Constable T. NIAZI (20.10.1958)

Special Constable M. HOUSSEIN (20.11.58)

Other nationalities

Special Constable B. MOMPALDA (25.7.1956)

Sgt. A. HADJIROUSSOU, Maronite (2.9.1956)

CIVILIAN DEATHS in chronological order

UK

Mr J. C. COOKE (1.4.1956)

Mr T. BOGDANOVITCH (20.4.1956)

Lt.Col. (Rtd) G. THOMPSON (14.5.1956)

Mr H. MOSELY (22.5.1956)

Mr T. MYLREA (6.6.1956)

Mrs K. KARBERRY (8.7.1956)

Mrs M. HOLTON (28.9.1956)

Assistant District Commissioner D. WILLIAMSON (6.11.1956)

Dr C. BEVAN (8.11.1956)

Mr A. GRICE (15.11.1956)

Mr A. MACDONALD (16.11.1956)

Mr P. FOX (8.12.1956)

Mr R. JAMES (4.1.1957)

Mr H. PRITCHARD (9.1.1957)

Mr C. P. COOK (11.1.1957)
Mr R. SPARROW (25.1.1957)
Mr J. SOUTH (2.10.1958)
Mrs C. CUTLIFFE (3.10.1958)
Mr J. BROOKES (12.10.1958)
Mr F. SHARMAN (24.10.1958)
Mr B. PREECE (31.10.1958)
Mr W. JAMIESON (1.11.1958)

Mr C. WOODS (3.11.1958)
Mr J. BRANDER (6.11.1958)
Mr A. BENSON (7.11.1958)

Other nationalities

Mr W. BOETELER, US Embassy official
    (16.6.1956)
Mr G. INJIRDJIAN, Armenian (11.7.1956)

Selected References

Alastos, Doros, *Cyprus Guerrilla*, Heinemann, London (1960)

Aldrich, Richard J., *The Hidden Hand – Britain, America and Cold War Secret Intelligence*, John Murray, London (2001)

Allen, Charles, *The Savage Wars of Peace*, Michael Joseph, London (1990)

Anderson, David M., *Policing and Decolonization*, Manchester University Press (1992)

Asmussen, Jan, *Cyprus At War*, I. B. Tauris, London (2008)

Azinas, Andreas, *Fifty Years of Silence*, Airwaves, Nicosia (2002)

Baker, Colin, *Sir Robert Armitage in Africa and Cyprus*, I. B. Tauris, London (1998)

Balmer, Albert, *A Cyprus Journey*, Published by the author (1998)

Barker, Dudley, *Grivas – Portrait of a Terrorist*, Cresset Press, London (1959)

Beadle, Major J. C., *The Light Blue Lanyard*, Square One, Worcester (1992)

Blair, John, *Conscript Doctors*, Edinburgh (2001)

Blaxland, Gregory, *The Regiments Depart*, Kimber, London (1971)

Borowiec, Andrew, *Cyprus – A Troubled Island*, Praeger, London (2000)

Boyer-Bell, J., *Strategies of National Liberation on Revolt*, Harvard University Press, Cambridge, Mass. (1976)

Byford-Jones, W., *Grivas and the Story of Eoka*, Robert Hale, London (1959)

Castle, Barbara, *Fighting All The Way*, Macmillan, London (1993)

Cavenagh, Sandy, *Airborne to Suez*, Gludy Publications (1996)

Cobham, Claude Deleval, *Excerpta Cyprus*, Cambridge University Press, Cambridge (1908)

Crawshaw, Nancy, *The Cyprus Revolt*, Allen & Unwin, London (1978)

Crook, Brigadier Paul, *Came The Dawn*, Hyperion Books, London (1991)

Crozier, Brian, *The Rebels*, Beacon Press, Boston, Mass. (1960)

Davidson, Michael, *The World, The Flesh and Myself*, David Bruce and Watson, London (1973)

Deeley, Peter, *Beyond Breaking Point,* Arthur Baker, London (1971)

Dewar, Michael, *Harding of Petherton*, Weidenfeld & Nicholson, London (1978)

Dewar, Michael, *Brush Fire Wars*, Robert Hale, London (1990)

Dixon, W. Hepworth, *British Cyprus*, Chapman & Hall, London (1879)

Dorril, Stephen, *MI6 – Fifty Years of Special Operations*, Fourth Estate, London (2000)

Droushiotis, Makarios, *Cyprus 1974*, Bibliopolis, Mannheim (2006)

Durrell, Lawrence, *Bitter Lemons of Cyprus*, Faber & Faber, London (1959)

Fallaci, Oriana, *Interview with History*, Houghton Mifflin, New York (1977)

Foley, Charles, *Island in Revolt*, Longmans Green, London (1962)

Foley, Charles, *Legacy of Strife*, Penguin, London (1964)

Foley, Charles, and Scobie, W. I., *The Struggle for Cyprus*, Hoover Institution Press, Stanford University, Stanford, California, (1975)

Foot, Sir Hugh, *A Start in Freedom*, Hodder & Stoughton, London (1964)

Foot, Sylvia, *Emergency Exit*, Chatto & Windus, London (1960)

Fraser, General Sir David, *War and Shadows*, Allen Lane-Penguin, London (2002)

Georghalides, George, *Cyprus and the Governorship of Sir Ronald Storrs*, Cyprus Research Centre, Nicosia (1985)

Greenhill Gardyne, A. D., *History of the Gordon Highlanders*, The Medici Society, London (1939)

Grivas, George, (ed. Charles Foley), *The Memoirs of General Grivas*, Longmans, London (1964)

Gup, Ted, *The Book of Honor*, Doubleday, New York (2007)

Hamilton Lang, R., *Cyprus: Its History, Its Present Resources and Future Prospects*, Macmillan, London (1878)

Herclerode, Peter, *Para*, Arms & Armour, London (1992)

Hill, George, *History of Cyprus*, Cambridge University Press, Cambridge (1952)

Holland, Robert, *Britain and the Revolt in Cyprus 1954–1959*, Clarendon Press, Oxford (1997)

Houssein, Altan, *The Cyprus Chronicles*, North Cyprus Property Consultants, Kyrenia (2007)

Hunt, Sir David, *Footprints in Cyprus*, Trigraph Ltd., London (1982)

Johnson, Malcolm, *Yield To None*, Propagator Press, Leeds (2005)

Laipson, Ellen, 'A Quarter Century of U.S. Diplomacy', in John T. A. Koumoulides (ed.), *Cyprus in Transition 1960–1985*, Trigraph, London (1986).

Laipson, Ellen, *Cyprus: A Regional Conflict and its Resolution*, St Martin's Press, London (1992)

Lapping, Brian, *End of Empire*, Granada, London (1990)

Le Geyt, Captain P. S., *Makarios in Exile*, Anagennisis Press, Nicosia (1961)

Lindsay, Oliver, *Once A Grenadier*, Leo Cooper, London (1996)

Macdonald, Peter, *Corners of My Mind*, Ulverscroft, UK (2002)

Matthews, David, *The Cyprus Tapes*, K. Rustem & Brother, London (1987)

Mayes, Stanley, *Cyprus and Makarios*, Putnam, London (1960)

Mayes, Stanley, *Makarios – A Biography*, Macmillan, London (1981)

Miller, Harry, *Service to the Services*, Newman & Neame, London (1971)

Mitchell, Lt.-Col. Colin, *Having Been a Soldier*, Hamish Hamilton, London (1969).

Mockaitis, Thomas, *British Counter-insurgency 1919–1960*, Palgrave-Macmillan, London (1990)

Neillands, Robin, *A Fighting Retreat*, Weidenfeld & Nicholson, London (1997)

Neillands, Robin, *By Land and By Sea*, Pen and Sword Books, Barnsley (2004)

Newsinger, John, *Counterinsurgency: From Palestine to Northern Ireland*, Palgrave, London (2002)

Nicolson, Michael, *A Measure of Danger*, HarperCollins, London (1991)

Noel-Baker, Philip, Private Memoirs, unpublished.

O'Malley, Brendan and CRAIG, Ian, *The Cyprus Conspiracy*, I. B. Tauris, London (1999)

Panteli, Stavros, *A History of Cyprus*, East-West Publications (UK) Ltd. (2000)

Paris, Peter, *The Impartial Knife*, McKay, New York (1962)

Parker, John, *The Paras*, Metro Publishing, London (2000)

Petley, Lawrence, *One Score Years and Two*, published by the author (1998)

Perkins, Anne, *Red Queen*, Pan, London (2004)

Purcell, H. D., *Cyprus*, Ernest Benn, London (1969)

Rathuone-Low, Charles, *General Lord Wolseley*, Naval and Military Press, London (1883)

Reddaway, John, *Burdened with Cyprus*, Weidenfeld & Nicholson, London (1986)

Redgrave, Major General Sir Roy, *Balkan Blue*, Pen & Sword Books, London (2001)

Scott-Stevenson, Esme, *Our Home in Cyprus*, Chapman & Hall, London (1880)

Seraphim-Loizou, Elenitsa, *The Cyprus Liberation Struggle*, Epiphaniou Publications, Nicosia (n.d.)

Stavrinides, Zenon, *The Cyprus Conflict: National Identity and Statehood*, Loris Stavrinides Press, Nicosia (1976)

Stefanides, Ioannis, *Isle of Discord*, C. Hurst & Co, London (1999)

Stephens, Robert, *A Place of Arms*, Praeger, London (1966)

Storrs, Sir Ronald, *Disturbances in Cyprus in October, 1931*, HMSO, London (1932)

Storrs, Sir Ronald, *Orientations*, Nicholson & Watson, London (1945)

Sutton, Brigadier D. J., *History of the RASC*, Leo Cooper, London (1983)

Taber, Robert, *The War of the Flea*, Brasseys, London (2002)

Taylor, Jack, *A Copper in Kypriou*, National Ex-Service Newspapers (2001)

Taylor, Lou, *The Study for Dress History*, Manchester University Press, Manchester (2002)

Thayer, Charles W., *Guerrilla*, Harper & Row, New York (1963)

Treymayne, Pamela, *Below The Tide*, Hutchinson, London (1958)

Varnavas, Andreas, *A History of the Liberation Struggle of Eoka*, The Foundation of the Eoka Liberation Struggle, Nicosia (2004)

Walker, Adrian, *Six Campaigns*, Pen & Sword, London (1993)

Watson, J. N. P., *The History of the Blues and Royals*, Pen & Sword, London (1993)

Waugh, Auberon, *Will This Do?* Carroll & Graf, New York (1998)

West, Nigel, *The Friends – Britain's Post-War Secret Intelligence Operations*, Weidenfeld & Nicholson, London (1998)

Wilson, Lt General Sir James, *Unusual Undertakings*, Pen & Sword, London (2002)

Woodhouse, C. M., *Apple of Discord*, William B Oneill, London (1985)

Wright, Peter, *Spy Catcher, The Candid Autobiography of a Senior Intelligence Officer*, Viking Penguin, New York (1987)

OTHER SOURCES

Kranidiotis, Nikos, *Cyprus in the Struggle for Freedom.*

Dimitrakis, Panagiotis, 'British Intelligence and the Cyprus Insurgency', International *Journal of Intelligence and Counter-intelligence* (Summer 2008)

Harding, Field Marshal Sir John, *Terrorism in Cyprus*, Daily Telegraph (January 1958)

Various, *Cyprus Handbook 1920*, HMSO, London (1920)

Why We Are In Cyprus – Background Notes for British Servicemen published by HMG May 1956 (revised)

Terrorism In Cyprus – The Captured Documents – Translated extracts issued by authority of The Secretary of State for the Colonies, HMSO, London (1956)

NEWSPAPERS
Cyprus Mail
Cyprus Observer
Cyprus Today
Daily Mirror
Daily Express
Daily Herald
Daily Telegraph
News Chronicle
The Independent
The Irish Times
Phos
Reveille
Sunday Dispatch
Sunday Express
The Globe
The New York Times
The Observer
The Times
The Times of Cyprus
Toronto Star

MAGAZINES AND JOURNALS
Army Quarterly
Combat
Falling Leaf
Hansard
Medal News
Soldier magazine
The Middle East Review
Time

REGIMENTAL MAGAZINES

Quis Separabit, the journal of the Royal Ulster Rifles
The Green Tiger, the journal of the Royal Leicestershire Regiment
The Gunner, the Royal Artillery magazine
The Iron Duke, the journal of the Duke of Wellington's Regiment
The Knot, the journal of the South Staffordshire Regiment
The Thin Red Line, the journal of the Argyll and Sutherland Highlanders

OTHER SOURCES
Center for European Policy Studies report
Research by Vasilis Fouskas
Hampshire and North-West Surrey Group of Newspapers
Research documents in the University of the Eastern Mediterranean, Famagusta
Research by James Meyer of the Woodrow Wilson School of Public & International Affairs
US Department of State Vol. X, Part 1, FRUS, 1958-60: E. Europe Region; Soviet Union; Cyprus